CompTIA
A+® Complete
Study Guide

CompTIA
A+® Complete
Study Guide

Quentin Docter
Emmett Dulaney
Toby Skandier

WILEY

Wiley Publishing, Inc.

Acquisitions Editor: Jeff Kellum
Development Editor: Sara Barry
Technical Editors: Steve Hyzny and Neil Hester
Production Editor: Rachel McConlogue
Copy Editors: Liz Welch and Linda Recktenwald
Editorial Manager: Pete Gaughan
Production Manager: Tim Tate
Vice President and Executive Group Publisher: Richard Swadley
Vice President and Publisher: Neil Edde
Media Associate Project Manager: Jenny Swisher
Media Associate Producer: Marilyn Hummel
Media Quality Assurance: Josh Frank
Book Designers: Judy Fung and Bill Gibson
Compositor: Craig Woods, Happenstance Type-O-Rama
Proofreader: Publication Services, Inc.
Indexer: Ted Laux
Project Coordinator, Cover: Lynsey Stanford
Cover Designer: Ryan Sneed

Copyright © 2009 by Wiley Publishing, Inc., Indianapolis, Indiana

Published simultaneously in Canada

ISBN: 978-0-470-48649-8

For general information on our other products and services or to obtain technical support, please contact our Customer Care Department within the U.S. at (877) 762-2974, outside the U.S. at (317) 572-3993 or fax (317) 572-4002.

Wiley also publishes its books in a variety of electronic formats. Some content that appears in print may not be available in electronic books.

Library of Congress Cataloging-in-Publication Data
Docter, Quentin.
CompTIA A+ complete study guide (exams 220-701/220-702) / Quentin Docter, Emmett Dulaney, Toby Skandier.
p. cm.

ISBN 978-0-470-48649-8 (pbk.)

1. Electronic data processing personnel—Certification. 2. Computer technicians—Certification—Study guides. 3. Micro-computers—Maintenance and repair—Examinations—Study guides. 4. Computing Technology Industry Association—Examinations—Study guides. I. Dulaney, Emmett A. II. Skandier, Toby. III. Title.

QA76.3.D598 2008

004.165—dc22

2009027780

10 9 8 7 6 5 4 3 2 1

The logo of the CompTIA Authorized Quality Curriculum (CAQC) program and the status of this or other training material as "Authorized" under the CompTIA Authorized Quality Curriculum program signifies that, in CompTIA's opinion, such training material covers the content of the CompTIA's related certification exam. CompTIA has not reviewed or approved the accuracy of the contents of this training material and specifically disclaims any warranties of merchantability or fitness for a particular purpose. CompTIA makes no guarantee concerning the success of persons using any such "Authorized" or other training material in order to prepare for any CompTIA certification exam.

The contents of this training material were created for the CompTIA A+ exams covering CompTIA certification objectives that were current as of 2009.

How to become CompTIA certified:

This training material can help you prepare for and pass a related CompTIA certification exam or exams. In order to achieve CompTIA certification, you must register for and pass a CompTIA certification exam or exams.

In order to become CompTIA certified, you must:

1. Select a certification exam provider. For more information please visit www.comptia .org/certifications/testprep/testingcenters.aspx.

2. Register for and schedule a time to take the CompTIA certification exam(s) at a convenient location.

3. Read and sign the Candidate Agreement, which will be presented at the time of the exam(s). The text of the Candidate Agreement can be found at www.comptia.org/ certifications/testprep/policies/agreement.aspx.

4. Take and pass the CompTIA certification exam(s).

For more information about CompTIA's certifications, such as its industry acceptance, benefits or program news, please visit http://www.comptia.org/certifications/.

CompTIA is a not-for-profit information technology (IT) trade association. CompTIA's certifications are designed by subject-matter experts from across the IT industry. Each CompTIA certification is vendor-neutral, covers multiple technologies and requires demonstration of skills and knowledge widely sought after by the IT industry.

To contact CompTIA with any questions or comments, please call 630-678-8300 or visit www.comptia.org/contactus.aspx.

Dear Reader,

Thank you for choosing *CompTIA A+ Complete Study Guide*. This book is part of a family of premium-quality Sybex books, all of which are written by outstanding authors who combine practical experience with a gift for teaching.

Sybex was founded in 1976. More than 30 years later, we're still committed to producing consistently exceptional books. With each of our titles, we're working hard to set a new standard for the industry. From the paper we print on, to the authors we work with, our goal is to bring you the best books available.

I hope you see all that reflected in these pages. I'd be very interested to hear your comments and get your feedback on how we're doing. Feel free to let me know what you think about this or any other Sybex book by sending me an email at nedde@wiley.com. If you think you've found a technical error in this book, please visit http://sybex.custhelp.com. Customer feedback is critical to our efforts at Sybex.

Best regards,

Neil Edde
Vice President and Publisher
Sybex, an Imprint of Wiley

To Kara, Abbie, Lauren, Reina, and Alina
—Quentin Docter

For Karen, Kristin, Evan, and Spencer
—Emmett Dulaney

To Karen, Toby, Tiffani, Trey, and Taylor
—Toby Skandier

Acknowledgments

It continues to amaze me how many people and how much time it takes to create a book of this scope and size. From beginning to end, there are scores of dedicated professionals focused on delivering the best book possible to you the readers.

First, I need to thank my coauthors Emmett Dulaney and Toby Skandier, as they did a tremendous job while being under a serious time crunch. Now, onto the rest of the team.

Jeff Kellum and Sara Barry kept us on track and moving forward, which was a challenge at times. Rachel McConlogue kept us organized, which is no small feat during writing. I owe special gratitude to tech editor Steve Hyzny, who kept me on my toes and made excellent suggestions. Copy editors Liz Welch and Linda Recktenwald provided clairvoyance and saved me from butchering the English language. Many thanks also go out to the proofreaders at Publication Services, our indexer Ted Laux, and Craig Woods, our compositor at Happenstance. Without their great contributions this book would not have made it to your hands.

—*Quentin Docter*

I would like to thank Jeff Kellum—an acquisitions editor who knows how to do a difficult job extremely well. I would also like to thank my coauthors, Quentin Docter and Toby Skandier, without whom this text would have never happened.

—*Emmett Dulaney*

I would like to thank our acquisitions editor, Jeff Kellum, who has a knack for matching me with the most interesting and challenging projects that enhance my knowledge and proficiency in my area of expertise and then keeping me on track with them. Thanks too to development editor Sara Barry, whose patience and level-headedness were much appreciated during the writing process.

I'm indebted to our technical editor, Steve Hyzny, for catching some of the most detailed technical issues. This book is vastly more solid for his vigilance. Our production editor, Rachel McConlogue, and copy editors, Liz Welch and Linda Recktenwald, have my deepest gratitude for repairing those things in which I am most certainly not an expert.

In addition, I'd like to thank our proofreaders at Publication Services, indexer Ted Laux, typesetter Craig Woods, and the CD developers: Jenny Swisher, Marilyn Hummel, and Josh Frank.

Thank you to my associates at Global Knowledge and Embarq Corporation for the support and challenges you continue to offer.

—*Toby Skandier*

About the Authors

Quentin Docter, A+, MCSE, CNE, CCNA, and SCSA   is an IT consultant with over 15 years of IT experience. He has written several books for Sybex, including books on A+, Server+, Windows, and Solaris 9 certifications, as well as coauthored *Mastering Windows XP Professional* and *The Complete PC Upgrade and Maintenance Guide.* Quentin can be reached at qdocter@yahoo.com.

Emmett Dulaney   is an assistant professor at Anderson University. The former director of training for Mercury Technical Solutions, he holds or has held 18 vendor certifications and is the author of over 30 books, including the *CompTIA Security+ Study Guide.* He specializes in certification and cross-platform integration, and is a columnist for CertCities. Emmett can be reached at eadulaney@comcast.net.

Toby Skandier, A+, Network +, i-Net+, Server+, MCSE, CCNP, CCDP, and CCSI   began his career in 1985 and is founder of Talskan Technologies, LLC, a technical-education provider based in North Carolina. He has coauthored numerous books for Sybex, including *Network Administrator Street Smarts* and the bestselling *Network+ Study Guide.* Toby can be reached at tskandier@talskan.com.

Contents at a Glance

Contents

Table of Exercises

Introduction

Welcome to the *CompTIA A+ Complete Study Guide*. This is the fifth edition of our best-selling study guide for the A+ certification sponsored by CompTIA (Computing Technology Industry Association).

This book was written at an intermediate technical level; we assume that you already know how to *use* a personal computer and its basic peripherals, such as USB devices and printers, but we also recognize that you may be learning how to *service* some of that computer equipment for the first time. The exams cover basic computer service topics as well as some more advanced issues, and they cover some topics that anyone already working as a technician, whether with computers or not, should be familiar with. The exams are designed to test you on these topics in order to certify that you have enough knowledge to fix and upgrade some of the most widely used types of personal desktop computers.

We've included review questions at the end of each chapter to give you a taste of what it's like to take the exams. If you're already working as a technical service or support technician, we recommend you check out these questions first to gauge your level of knowledge. (You can also take the Assessment Test at the end of this Introduction, which is designed to see how much you already know.)

Don't just study the questions and answers—the questions on the actual exams will be different from the practice ones included in this book and on the CD. The exams are designed to test your knowledge of a concept or objective, so use this book to learn the objective *behind* the question.

You can use the book mainly to fill in the gaps in your current computer service knowledge. You may find, as many PC technicians have, that being well versed in all the technical aspects of the equipment is not enough to provide a satisfactory level of support—you must also have customer-relations skills. We include helpful hints to get the customers to help you help them.

What Is A+ Certification?

The A+ certification program was developed by the Computer Technology Industry Association (CompTIA) to provide an industry-wide means of certifying the competency of computer service technicians. The A+ certification is granted to those who have attained the level of knowledge and troubleshooting skills that are needed to provide capable support in the field of personal computers. It is similar to other certifications in the computer industry, such the Cisco Certified Network Associate (CCNA) program and the Microsoft Certified Systems Engineer (MCSE) program. The theory behind these certifications is that if you need to have service performed on any of their products, you would sooner call a technician who has been certified in one of the appropriate certification programs than you would just call the first "expert" in the phone book.

The A+ certification program was created to offer a wide-ranging certification, in the sense that it is intended to certify competence with personal computers from many different makers/vendors. You must pass two tests to become A+ certified:

- The A+ Essentials (220-701) exam, which covers basic computer concepts, hardware troubleshooting, soft skills (such as customer service), and hardware upgrading, security, and safety

- The A+ Practical Application (220-702) exam, which covers repair and practical application of the concepts covered in the A+ Essentials exam

You don't have to take the Essentials and the Practical Application exams at the same time. The A+ certification is not awarded until you've passed both tests.

Why Become A+ Certified?

There are several good reasons to get your A+ certification. The CompTIA Candidate's Information packet lists five major benefits:

- It demonstrates proof of professional achievement.

- It increases your marketability.

- It provides greater opportunity for advancement in your field.

- It is increasingly a requirement for some types of advanced training.

- It raises customer confidence in you and your company's services.

Provides Proof of Professional Achievement

The A+ certification is quickly becoming a status symbol in the computer service industry. Organizations that include members of the computer service industry are recognizing the benefits of A+ certification and are pushing for their members to become certified. And more people every day are putting the "A+ Certified Technician" emblem on their business cards.

Increases Your Marketability

A+ certification makes individuals more marketable to potential employers. A+ certified employees also may receive a higher base salary because employers won't have to spend as much money on vendor-specific training.

What Is an ASC?

More service companies are becoming CompTIA A+ Authorized Service Centers (ASCs). This means that over 50 percent of the technicians employed by that service center are A+ certified. Customers and vendors alike recognize that ASCs employ the most qualified service technicians. As a result, an ASC gets more business than a nonauthorized service center. And, because more service centers want to reach the AASC level, they will give preference in hiring to a candidate who is A+ certified over one who is not.

Provides Opportunity for Advancement

Most raises and advancements are based on performance. A+ certified employees work faster and more efficiently and are thus more productive. The more productive employees are, the more money they make for their company. And, of course, the more money they make for the company, the more valuable they are to the company. So if an employee is A+ certified, their chances of being promoted are greater.

Fulfills Training Requirements

A+ certification is recognized by most major computer hardware vendors. Some of these vendors apply A+ certification toward prerequisites in their own respective certification programs, which has the side benefit of reducing training costs for employers.

Raises Customer Confidence

As the A+ Certified Technician moniker becomes better known among computer owners, more of them will realize that the A+ technician is more qualified to work on their computer equipment than a noncertified technician is.

How to Become A+ Certified

A+ certification is available to anyone who passes the tests. You don't have to work for any particular company. It's not a secret society. It is, however, an elite group. To become A+ certified, you must do two things:

- Pass the A+ Essentials exam
- Pass the A+ Practical Application exam

The exams can be taken at any Thompson Prometric or Pearson VUE testing center. If you pass both exams, you will get a certificate in the mail from CompTIA saying that you have passed, and you will also receive a lapel pin and business card.

To register for the tests, call Thompson Prometric at (800) 77-MICRO (776-4276) or register online at http://www.2test.com. For Pearson VUE, call (877) 551-PLUS (7587) or go to http://www.vue.com. You'll be asked for your name, Social Security Number (an optional number may be assigned if you don't wish to provide your Social Security Number), mailing address, phone number, employer, when and where you want to take the test, and your credit card number (arrangement for payment must be made at the time of registration).

Although you can save money by arranging to take more than one test at the same seating, there are no other discounts. If you have to repeat a test in order to get a passing grade, you must pay for each retake.

Who Should Buy This Book?

If you are one of the many people who want to pass the A+ exams, and pass them confidently, then you should buy this book and use it to study for the exams. The A+ Essentials exam is designed to measure essential competencies for an entry-level technician. The Practical Application exam is intended to certify that the exam candidate has the necessary skills to work on microcomputer hardware and typically has at least six months of on-the-job experience.

This book was written with one goal in mind: to prepare you for the challenges of the real IT world, not just to pass the A+ exams. This study guide will do that by describing in detail the concepts on which you'll be tested.

How to Use This Book and CD

We've included several testing features throughout the book and on the CD-ROM. At the beginning of the book (right after this Introduction) is an Assessment test that you can use to check your readiness for the actual exams. Take this exam before you begin reading the book. Doing so will help you determine the areas you may need to brush up on. The answers to the Assessment test appear on a separate page after the last question of the test. Each answer also includes an explanation and a note telling you the chapter in which this material appears.

To test your knowledge as you progress through the book, there are review questions at the end of each chapter. As you finish each chapter, answer the review questions and then check your answers—the correct answers appear on the page following the last review question. You can go back to reread the section that deals with each question you got wrong to ensure that you answer correctly the next time you are tested on the material. You'll also find flashcard questions on the CD. You can use these handy questions for on-the-go review. Download them right onto your handheld device for quick and convenient reviewing.

In addition to the Assessment test and the chapter review questions, you'll find sample exams for each of the A+ exams on the CD. Take these practice exams just as if you were actually taking the A+ exams (without any reference material).

Depending on what edition of the book you have, either the Standard or the Deluxe Edition, you will have either six exams (three each for the two A+ exams) or eight (four each). In the Deluxe Edition, we've also included a second CD, which contains a series of instructional videos with authors Emmett Dulaney and Toby Skandier. These videos show Emmett performing a number of hands-on tasks and processes you need to be familiar with as a CompTIA A+ technician.

If you are going to travel but still need to study for the A+ exams, and you have a laptop with a CD-ROM drive, you can take this entire book with you just by taking the CD. This book is in PDF (Adobe Acrobat) format so it can be easily read on any computer.

> ### Minimum System Requirements
>
> You should have a minimum of 45MB of disk space, as well as Windows 98 or higher, to use the Sybex Test Engine. You will also need Adobe Acrobat Reader (included).

The Exam Objectives

Behind every computer industry exam you can be sure to find exam objectives—the broad topics in which the exam developers want to ensure your competency.

As mentioned previously, two tests are required to become A+ certified: the A+ Essentials exam and the Practical Application exam. In the following sections, we have listed the official CompTIA exam objectives.

 Exam objectives are subject to change at any time without prior notice and at CompTIA's sole discretion. Please visit the A+ Certification page of CompTIA's website (http://www.comptia.org/certifications/listed/a.aspx) for the most current listing of exam objectives.

The A+ Essentials (220-701) Exam Objectives

The A+ Essentials exam is designed for candidates with at least 500 hours of hands-on experience. It expects you to understand how to install, build, upgrade, repair, configure, troubleshoot, optimize, diagnose, and perform preventive maintenance of basic personal computer hardware and operating systems.

The following are the areas (or *domains*, according to CompTIA) in which you must be proficient in order to pass the A+ Essentials:

Domain 1: Hardware	27%
Domain 2: Troubleshooting, Repair & Maintenance	20%
Domain 3: Operating System and Software	20%
Domain 4: Networking	15%
Domain 5: Security	8%
Domain 6: Operational Procedure	10%

Domain 1: Hardware

1.1 Categorize storage devices and backup media

- FDD
- HDD
    - Solid state vs. magnetic

- Optical drives
    - CD / DVD / RW / Blu-Ray
- Removable storage
    - Tape drive
    - Solid state (e.g. thumb drive, flash, SD cards, USB)
    - External CD-RW and hard drive
    - Hot swappable devices and non-hot swappable devices

1.2 Explain motherboard components, types and features

- Form Factor
    - ATX / BTX
    - micro ATX
    - NLX
- I/O interfaces
    - Sound
    - Video
    - USB 1.1 and 2.0
    - Serial
    - IEEE 1394 / Firewire
    - Parallel
    - NIC
    - Modem
    - PS/2
- Memory slots
    - RIMM
    - DIMM
    - SODIMM
    - SIMM
- Processor sockets
- Bus architecture
- Bus slots
    - PCI
    - AGP
    - PCIe
    - AMR

- - CNR
  - PCMCIA
- PATA
  - IDE
  - EIDE
- SATA, eSATA
- Contrast RAID (levels 0, 1, 5)
- Chipsets
- BIOS / CMOS / Firmware
  - POST
  - CMOS battery
- Riser card / daughter board

1.3 Classify power supplies types and characteristics

- AC adapter
- ATX proprietary
- Voltage, wattage and capacity
- Voltage selector switch
- Pins (20, 24)

1.4 Explain the purpose and characteristics of CPUs and their features

- Identify CPU types
  - AMD
  - Intel
- Hyper threading
- Multi core
  - Dual core
  - Triple core
  - Quad core
- Onchip cache
  - L1
  - L2
- Speed (real vs. actual)
- 32 bit vs. 64 bit

1.5 Explain cooling methods and devices

- Heat sinks
- CPU and case fans

- Liquid cooling systems
- Thermal compound

1.6 Compare and contrast memory types, characteristics and their purpose

- Types
    - DRAM
    - SRAM
    - SDRAM
    - DDR / DDR2 / DDR3
    - RAMBUS
- Parity vs. Non-parity
- ECC vs. non-ECC
- Single sided vs. double sided
- Single channel vs. dual channel
- Speed
    - PC100
    - PC133
    - PC2700
    - PC3200
    - DDR3-1600
    - DDR2-667

1.7 Distinguish between the different display devices and their characteristics

- Projectors, CRT and LCD
- LCD technologies
    - Resolution (e.g. XGA, SXGA+, UXGA, WUXGA)
    - Contrast ratio
    - Native resolution
- Connector types
    - VGA
    - HDMi
    - S-Video
    - Component / RGB
    - DVI pin compatibility
- Settings
    - Refresh rate
    - Resolution

- Multi-monitor
- Degauss

1.8 Install and configure peripherals and input devices

- Mouse
- Keyboard
- Bar code reader
- Multimedia (e.g. web and digital cameras, MIDI, microphones)
- Biometric devices
- Touch screen
- KVM switch

1.9 Summarize the function and types of adapter cards

- Video
  - PCI
  - PCIe
  - AGP
- Multimedia
  - Sound card
  - TV tuner cards
  - Capture cards
- I/O
  - SCSI
  - Serial
  - USB
  - Parallel
- Communications
  - NIC
  - Modem

1.10 Install, configure and optimize laptop components and features

- Expansion devices
  - PCMCIA cards
  - PCI Express cards
  - Docking station
- Communication connections
  - Bluetooth
  - Infrared

- Cellular WAN
- Ethernet
- Modem
- Power and electrical input devices
  - Auto-switching
  - Fixed input power supplies
  - Batteries
- Input devices
  - Stylus / digitizer
  - Function keys
  - Point devices (e.g. touch pad, point stick / track point)

1.11 Install and configure printers

- Differentiate between printer types
  - Laser
  - Inkjet
  - Thermal
  - Impact
- Local vs. network printers
- Printer drivers
- Consumables

Domain 2: Troubleshooting, Repair & Maintenance

2.1 Given a scenario, explain the troubleshooting theory

- Identify the problem
  - Question the user and identify user changes to computer and perform backups before making changes
- Establish a theory of probable cause (question the obvious)
- Test the theory to determine cause
  - Once theory is confirmed determine next steps to resolve problem
  - If theory is not confirmed re-establish new theory or escalate
- Establish a plan of action to resolve the problem and implement the solution
- Verify full system functionality and if applicable implement preventative measures
- Document findings, actions and outcomes

2.2 Given a scenario, explain and interpret common hardware and operating system symptoms and their causes

- OS related symptoms
    - Bluescreen
    - System lock-up
    - Input/output device
    - Application install
    - Start or load
    - Windows specific printing problems
        - Print spool stalled
        - Incorrect / incompatible driver
- Hardware related symptoms
    - Excessive heat
    - Noise
    - Odors
    - Status light indicators
    - Alerts
    - Visible damage (e.g. cable, plastic)
- Use documentation and resources
    - User / installation manuals
    - Internet / web based
    - Training materials

2.3 Given a scenario, determine the troubleshooting methods and tools for printers

- Manage print jobs
- Print spooler
- Printer properties and settings
- Print a test page

2.4 Given a scenario, explain and interpret common laptop issues and determine the appropriate basic troubleshooting method

- Issues
    - Power conditions
    - Video
    - Keyboard
    - Pointer

- Stylus
- Wireless card issues
- Methods
  - Verify power (e.g. LEDs, swap AC adapter)
  - Remove unneeded peripherals
  - Plug in external monitor
  - Toggle Fn keys or hardware switches
  - Check LCD cutoff switch
  - Verify backlight functionality and pixilation
  - Check switch for built-in WIFI antennas or external antennas

2.5 Given a scenario, integrate common preventative maintenance techniques

- Physical inspection
- Updates
  - Driver
  - Firmware
  - OS
  - Security
- Scheduling preventative maintenance
  - Defrag
  - Scandisk
  - Check disk
  - Startup programs
- Use of appropriate repair tools and cleaning materials
  - Compressed air
  - Lint free cloth
  - Computer vacuum and compressors
- Power devices
  - Appropriate source such as power strip, surge protector or UPS
- Ensuring proper environment
- Backup procedures

Domain 3: Operating Systems and Software

Unless otherwise noted, operating systems referred to within include Microsoft Windows 2000, Windows XP Professional, XP Home, XP MediaCenter, Windows Vista Home, Home Premium, Business and Ultimate.

3.1 Compare and contrast the different Windows Operating Systems and their features

- Windows 2000, Windows XP 32bit vs. 64bit, Windows Vista 32bit vs. 64bit
  - Side bar, Aero, UAC, minimum system requirements, system limits
  - Windows 2000 and newer – upgrade paths and requirements
  - Terminology (32bit vs. 64bit – x86 vs. x64)
  - Application compatibility, installed program locations (32bit vs. 64bit),
  - Windows compatibility mode
  - User interface, start bar layout

3.2 Given a scenario, demonstrate proper use of user interfaces

- Windows Explorer
- My Computer
- Control Panel
- Command prompt utilities
  - telnet
  - ping
  - ipconfig
- Run line utilities
  - msconfig
  - msinfo32
  - Dxdiag
  - Cmd
  - REGEDIT
- My Network Places
- Task bar / systray
- Administrative tools
  - Performance monitor, Event Viewer, Services, Computer Management
- MMC
- Task Manager
- Start Menu

3.3 Explain the process and steps to install and configure the Windows OS

- File systems
  - FAT32 vs. NTFS
- Directory structures
  - Create folders
  - Navigate directory structures

- Files
  - Creation
  - Extensions
  - Attributes
  - Permissions
- Verification of hardware compatibility and minimum requirements
- Installation methods
  - Boot media such as CD, floppy or USB
  - Network installation
  - Install from image
  - Recover CD
  - Factory recovery partition
- Operating system installation options
  - File system type
  - Network configuration
  - Repair install
- Disk preparation order
  - Format drive
  - Partition
  - Start installation
- Device Manager
  - Verify
  - Install and update devices drivers
  - Driver signing
- User data migration – User State Migration Tool (USMT)
- Virtual memory
- Configure power management
  - Suspend
  - Wake on LAN
  - Sleep timers
  - Hibernate
  - Standby
- Demonstrate safe removal of peripherals

3.4 Explain the basics of boot sequences, methods and startup utilities

- Disk boot order / device priority
  - Types of boot devices (disk, network, USB, other)
- Boot options
  - Safe mode
  - Boot to restore point
  - Recovery options
    - Automated System Recovery (ASR)
    - Emergency Repair Disk (ERD)
    - Recovery console

Domain 4: Networking

4.1 Summarize the basics of networking fundamentals, including technologies, devices and protocols

- Basics of configuring IP addressing and TCP/IP properties (DHCP, DNS)
- Bandwidth and latency
- Status indicators
- Protocols (TCP/IP, NETBIOS)
- Full-duplex, half-duplex
- Basics of workgroups and domains
- Common ports: HTTP, FTP, POP, SMTP, TELNET, HTTPS
- LAN / WAN
- Hub, switch and router
- Identify Virtual Private Networks (VPN)
- Basics class identification

4.2 Categorize network cables and connectors and their implementations

- Cables
  - Plenum / PVC
  - UTP (e.g. CAT3, CAT5 / 5e, CAT6)
  - STP
  - Fiber
  - Coaxial cable
- Connectors
  - RJ45
  - RJ11

4.3 Compare and contrast the different network types

- Broadband
    - DSL
    - Cable
    - Satellite
    - Fiber
- Dial-up
- Wireless
    - All 802.11 types
    - WEP
    - WPA
    - SSID
    - MAC filtering
    - DHCP settings
- Bluetooth
- Cellular

Domain 5: Security

5.1 Explain the basic principles of security concepts and technologies

- Encryption technologies
- Data wiping / hard drive destruction / hard drive recycling
- Software firewall
    - Port security
    - Exceptions
- Authentication technologies
    - User name
    - Password
    - Biometrics
    - Smart cards
- Basics of data sensitivity and data security
    - Compliance
    - Classifications
    - Social engineering

5.2 Summarize the following security features

- Wireless encryption
    - WEPx and WPAx
    - Client configuration (SSID)
- Malicious software protection
    - Viruses
    - Trojans
    - Worms
    - Spam
    - Spyware
    - Adware
    - Grayware
- BIOS Security
    - Drive lock
    - Passwords
    - Intrusion detection
    - TPM
- Password management / password complexity
- Locking workstation
    - Hardware
    - Operating system
    - Biometrics
        - Fingerprint scanner

Domain 6: Operational Procedure

6.1 Outline the purpose of appropriate safety and environmental procedures and given a scenario apply them

- ESD
- EMI
    - Network interference
    - Magnets
- RFI
    - Cordless phone interference
    - Microwaves

- Electrical safety
  - CRT
  - Power supply
  - Inverter
  - Laser printers
  - Matching power requirements of equipment with power distribution and UPSs
- Material Safety Data Sheets (MSDS)
- Cable management
  - Avoiding trip hazards
- Physical safety
  - Heavy devices
  - Hot components
- Environmental – consider proper disposal procedures

6.2 Given a scenario, demonstrate the appropriate use of communication skills and professionalism in the workplace

- Use proper language – avoid jargon, acronyms, slang
- Maintain a positive attitude
- Listen and do not interrupt a customer
- Be culturally sensitive
- Be on time
  - If late contact the customer
- Avoid distractions
  - Personal calls
  - Talking to co-workers while interacting with customers
  - Personal interruptions
- Dealing with a difficult customer or situation
  - Avoid arguing with customers and/or being defensive
  - Do not minimize customers' problems
  - Avoid being judgmental
  - Clarify customer statements
    - Ask open-ended questions to narrow the scope of the problem
    - Restate the issue or question to verify understanding
- Set and meet expectations / timeline and communicate status with the customer
  - Offer different repair / replacement options if applicable

- - Provide proper documentation on the services provided
  - Follow up with customer / user at a later date to verify satisfaction
- Deal appropriately with customers confidential materials
  - Located on computer, desktop, printer, etc.

The A+ Practical Application (220-702) Exam Objectives

The CompTIA A+ Practical Application exam is targeted at people who work in a remote or corporate technical environment with a high level of face-to-face client interaction. Ideally, they should have passed the CompTIA A+ Essentials exam. Typical job titles include enterprise technician, IT administrator, field service technician, and PC technician.

The following are the areas (or *domains*, according to CompTIA) in which you must be proficient in order to pass the A+ Practical Application exam:

Domain 1: Hardware   38%
Domain 2: Operating Systems 34%
Domain 3: Networking   15%
Domain 4: Security   13%

Domain 1: Hardware

1.1 Given a scenario, install, configure and maintain personal computer components

- Storage devices
  - HDD
    - SATA
    - PATA
    - Solid state
  - FDD
  - Optical drives
    - CD / DVD / RW / Blu-Ray
  - Removable
  - External
- Motherboards
  - Jumper settings
  - CMOS battery
  - Advanced BIOS settings
  - Bus speeds
  - Chipsets
  - Firmware updates

- Socket types
- Expansion slots
- Memory slots
- Front panel connectors
- I/O ports
  - Sound, video, USB 1.1, USB 2.0, serial, IEEE 1394 / Firewire, parallel, NIC, modem, PS/2
- Power supplies
  - Wattages and capacity
  - Connector types and quantity
  - Output voltage
- Processors
  - Socket types
  - Speed
  - Number of cores
  - Power consumption
  - Cache
  - Front side bus
  - 32bit vs. 64bit
- Memory
- Adapter cards
  - Graphics cards
  - Sound cards
  - Storage controllers
    - RAID cards (RAID array – levels 0, 1, 5)
    - eSATA cards
  - I/O cards
    - Firewire
    - USB
    - Parallel
    - Serial
  - Wired and wireless network cards
  - Capture cards (TV, video)
  - Media reader

- Cooling systems
  - Heat sinks
  - Thermal compound
  - CPU fans
  - Case fans

1.2 Given a scenario, detect problems, troubleshoot and repair/replace personal computer components

- Storage devices
  - HDD
    - SATA
    - PATA
    - Solid state
  - FDD
  - Optical drives
    - CD / DVD / RW / Blu-Ray
  - Removable
  - External
- Motherboards
  - Jumper settings
  - CMOS battery
  - Advanced BIOS settings
  - Bus speeds
  - Chipsets
  - Firmware updates
  - Socket types
  - Expansion slots
  - Memory slots
  - Front panel connectors
  - I/O ports
    - Sound, video, USB 1.1, USB 2.0, serial, IEEE 1394 / Firewire, parallel, NIC, modem, PS/2
- Power supplies
  - Wattages and capacity
  - Connector types and quantity
  - Output voltage

- Processors
  - Socket types
  - Speed
  - Number of cores
  - Power consumption
  - Cache
  - Front side bus
  - 32bit vs. 64bit
- Memory
- Adapter cards
  - Graphics cards - memory
  - Sound cards
  - Storage controllers
    - RAID cards
    - eSATA cards
  - I/O cards
    - Firewire
    - USB
    - Parallel
    - Serial
  - Wired and wireless network cards
  - Capture cards (TV, video)
  - Media reader
- Cooling systems
  - Heat sinks
  - Thermal compound
  - CPU fans
  - Case fans

1.3 Given a scenario, install, configure, detect problems, troubleshoot and repair/replace laptop components

- Components of the LCD including inverter, screen and video card
- Hard drive and memory
- Disassemble processes for proper re-assembly
  - Document and label cable and screw locations
  - Organize parts

- Refer to manufacturer documentation
- Use appropriate hand tools
- Recognize internal laptop expansion slot types
- Upgrade wireless cards and video card
- Replace keyboard, processor, plastics, pointer devices, heat sinks, fans, system board, CMOS battery, speakers

1.4 Given a scenario, select and use the following tools

- Multimeter
- Power supply tester
- Specialty hardware / tools
- Cable testers
- Loop back plugs
- Anti-static pad and wrist strap
- Extension magnet

1.5 Given a scenario, detect and resolve common printer issues

- Symptoms
  - Paper jams
  - Blank paper
  - Error codes
  - Out of memory error
  - Lines and smearing
  - Garbage printout
  - Ghosted image
  - No connectivity
- Issue resolution
  - Replace fuser
  - Replace drum
  - Clear paper jam
  - Power cycle
  - Install maintenance kit (reset page count)
  - Set IP on printer
  - Clean printer

Domain 2: Operating Systems

Unless otherwise noted, operating systems referred to within include Microsoft Windows 2000, Windows XP Professional, XP Home, XP MediaCenter, Windows Vista Home, Home Premium, Business and Ultimate.

2.1 Select the appropriate commands and options to troubleshoot and resolve problems

- MSCONFIG
- DIR
- CHKDSK (/f /r)
- EDIT
- COPY (/a /v /y)
- XCOPY
- FORMAT
- IPCONFIG (/all /release /renew)
- PING (-t –l)
- MD / CD / RD
- NET
- TRACERT
- NSLOOKUP
- [command name] /?
- SFC

2.2 Differentiate between Windows Operating System directory structures (Windows 2000, XP and Vista)

- User file locations
- System file locations
- Fonts
- Temporary files
- Program files
- Offline files and folders

2.3 Given a scenario, select and use system utilities / tools and evaluate the results

- Disk management tools
  - DEFRAG
  - NTBACKUP
  - Check Disk
- Disk Manager

2.4 Evaluate and resolve common issues

- Operational Problems
  - Windows specific printing problems
    - Print spool stalled
    - Incorrect / incompatible driver / form printing
  - Auto-restart errors
  - Bluescreen error
  - System lock-up
  - Devices drivers failure (input / output devices)
  - Application install, start or load failure
  - Service fails to start
- Error Messages and Conditions
  - Boot
    - Invalid boot disk
    - Inaccessible boot drive
    - Missing NTLDR
  - Startup
    - Device / service failed to start
    - Device / program in registry not found
  - Event viewer (errors in the event log)
  - System Performance and Optimization
    - Aero settings
    - Indexing settings
    - UAC
    - Side bar settings
    - Startup file maintenance
    - Background processes

Domain 3: Networking

3.1 Troubleshoot client-side connectivity issues using appropriate tools

- TCP/IP settings
  - Gateway

- Secure connection protocols
    - SSH
    - HTTPS
- Firewall settings
    - Open and closed ports
    - Program filters

3.2 Install and configure a small office home office (SOHO) network

- Connection types
    - Dial-up
    - Broadband
        - DSL
        - Cable
        - Satellite
        - ISDN
    - Wireless
        - All 802.11
        - WEP
        - WPA
        - SSID
        - MAC filtering
        - DHCP settings
    - Routers / Access Points
        - Disable DHCP
        - Use static IP
        - Change SSID from default
        - Disable SSID broadcast
        - MAC filtering
        - Change default username and password
        - Update firmware
        - Firewall
    - LAN (10/100/1000BaseT, Speeds)
    - Bluetooth (1.0 vs. 2.0)
    - Cellular
    - Basic VoIP (consumer applications)

- Basics of hardware and software firewall configuration
  - Port assignment / setting up rules (exceptions)
  - Port forwarding / port triggering
- Physical installation
  - Wireless router placement
  - Cable length

Domain 4: Security

4.1 Given a scenario, prevent, troubleshoot and remove viruses and malware

- Use antivirus software
- Identify malware symptoms
- Quarantine infected systems
- Research malware types, symptoms and solutions (virus encyclopedias)
- Remediate infected systems
- Update antivirus software
  - Signature and engine updates
  - Automatic vs. manual
- Schedule scans
- Repair boot blocks
- Scan and removal techniques
  - Safe mode
  - Boot environment
- Educate end user

4.2 Implement security and troubleshoot common issues

- Operating systems
  - Local users and groups: Administrator, Power Users, Guest, Users
  - Vista User Access Control (UAC)
  - NTFS vs. Share persmissions
    - Allow vs. deny
    - Difference between moving and copying folders and files
    - File attributes
  - Shared files and folders
    - Administrative shares vs. local shares
    - Permission propogation
    - Inheritance

- System files and folders
- Encryption (Bitlocker, EFS)
- User authentication
- System
  - BIOS security
    - Drive lock
    - Passwords
    - Intrusion detection
    - TPM

Assessment Test

1. Which of the following is not considered a system component that can be found inside a computer?
   A. CPU
   B. RAM
   C. PCIe graphics adapter
   D. Motherboard

2. Which of the following is *not* a physical memory format used in desktop computer systems?
   A. DRAM
   B. DIMM
   C. SIMM
   D. RIMM

3. Which of the following is a chip that is integrated into PATA drives, as opposed to being mounted on a daughter card?
   A. Controller
   B. CPU
   C. Host adapter
   D. IDE

4. What is the name of the power connector that is larger than the connector used for floppy diskette drives and that is commonly used with PATA drives?
   A. AT system connector
   B. Berg
   C. Molex
   D. ATX system connector

5. The _____ is the measurement of the number of pixels an LCD monitor can display without the image appearing distorted.
   A. Native resolution
   B. Contrast ratio
   C. Pixelation
   D. Base frequency

6. You are installing a new graphics adapter in a Windows Vista system. Which of the following expansion slots are designed for high-speed, 3D graphics adapters? (Choose two.)

   A. USB

   B. AGP

   C. PCI

   D. ISA

   E. PCIe

7. What is the legacy term for PC Card?

   A. CardBus

   B. PCMCIA

   C. Express Card

   D. CardBay

8. Which of the following sleep modes is also known as Standby?

   A. S1

   B. S2

   C. S3

   D. S4

9. What is the function of the laser in a laser printer?

   A. It heats up the toner so it adheres to the page.

   B. It charges the paper so it will attract toner.

   C. It creates an image of the page on the drum.

   D. It cleans the drum before a page is printed.

10. What is the component called that stores the material that ends up printed to the page in a laser printer?

    A. Toner cartridge

    B. Ink cartridge

    C. Laser module

    D. Laser cartridge

11. In Windows XP, how can you start a search for files and folders?

    A. Click Start ➤ All Programs ➤ Search.

    B. Run SEARCH.EXE at the command prompt.

    C. Left-click a directory and choose Find.

    D. Click Start ➤ Search.

12. Which of the following is not a hive in the Windows Registry?

   A. HKEY_CLASSES_ROOT

   B. HKEY_LOCAL_MACHINE

   C. HKEY_USERS

   D. HKEY_RESOURCES

13. Which of the following upgrade paths is *not* possible?

   A. Windows 95 to Windows XP

   B. Windows NT to Windows 2000

   C. Windows Me to Windows XP

   D. Windows 98 to Windows XP

14. The program that performs an upgrade from Windows NT to Windows XP is called _____.

   A. INSTALL.BAT

   B. SETUP.EXE

   C. WINNT.EXE

   D. WINNT32.EXE

15. You are troubleshooting a computer, and you have just established a theory of probable cause. What is your next step?

   A. Document findings

   B. Identify the problem

   C. Test the theory

   D. Verify functionality

16. You performed a normal backup on your Windows Vista computer two weeks ago and a differential backup one week ago. If you were to run an incremental backup today, which of the following is true about the files that it would back up?

   A. All files on your computer

   B. All files that have been modified in the last two weeks

   C. All files that have been modified in the last week

   D. All files that have been modified today

17. When a Windows-based application attempts to access memory another program is using, what is the error that will be generated?

   A. Windows protection error

   B. General protection fault

   C. Illegal operation

   D. System lock-up

18. You are sending print jobs to the printer, but nothing is printing. The printer is connected properly and online. What should you do?

   A. Delete and reinstall the printer.

   B. Delete and reinstall Windows.

   C. Open Printer Troubleshooting and have it diagnose the problem.

   D. Stop and restart the print spooler.

19. Which of the following topologies allows for network expansion with the least amount of disruption for the current network users?

   A. Star

   B. Bus

   C. Ring

   D. Mesh

20. Which layer of the OSI model has the important role of providing error checking?

   A. Session layer

   B. Presentation layer

   C. Application layer

   D. Transport layer

21. Which authentication protocol depends on a "secret" known only to the authenticator and that peer?

   A. PAP

   B. SLIP

   C. CHAP

   D. PPP

22. Which wireless protocol is an improvement on WEP?

   A. WAP

   B. WPA

   C. PAW

   D. PWA

23. Which of the following computer components can retain a lethal electrical charge even after the device is unplugged? (Choose all that apply.)

   A. Monitor

   B. Processor

   C. Power supply

   D. RAM

24. Roughly how much time spent communicating should be devoted to listening?

   A. 23 percent

   B. 40 percent

   C. 50 percent

   D. 80 percent

25. After SATA was introduced, what was the retroactive term used for the original ATA specification?

   A. EIDE

   B. IDE

   C. PATA

   D. SCSI

26. When retrieving small metallic parts dropped onto a motherboard, which of the following is the best tool to use?

   A. An extension magnet

   B. A magnetic screwdriver

   C. Gravity

   D. A parts grabber

27. What type of connector does a Mini PCI type IIIB card have?

   A. 52-pin card edge

   B. 100-pin card edge

   C. 124-pin card edge

   D. 144-pin card edge

28. Which LCD component is responsible for providing the right kind of power to the backlight?

   A. HVPS

   B. Inverter

   C. Power supply

   D. Power converter

29. Your laser printer has recently starting printing vertical white lines on documents it prints. What is the most likely cause of the problem?

   A. The print driver is faulty.

   B. The fuser is not heating properly.

   C. There is toner on the transfer corona wire.

   D. There is a scratch on the EP drum.

30. After upgrading to a new printer, you find that the text is coming out garbled and not readable. Which of the following might you suspect?

   A. Corrupt data input

   B. Incorrect print drivers

   C. Wrong DMA channel

   D. Unsupported printer

31. Which command-line utility enables you to verify entries on a DNS server?

   A. NET

   B. NSLOOKUP

   C. PING

   D. NETHELP

32. You are at a command prompt. A file called WORD1.DOC has been hidden by another user, and you want to unhide it. Which command should you use to accomplish this?

   A. ATTRIB +H WORD1.DOC

   B. ATTRIB -H WORD1.DOC

   C. ATTRIB -U WORD1.DOC

   D. ATTRIB +U WORD1.DOC

33. Which of the following Safe Mode options appears only with Windows Vista?

   A. Directory Services Restore Mode

   B. Repair Mode

   C. Repair Your Computer

   D. Enable Boot Logging

34. When you configure a task in Task Scheduler, a trigger must occur before the task is executed. An additional _____ can be configured that, along with the trigger, will determine if the task will run.

   A. Action

   B. Condition

   C. Charge

   D. Duty

35. Which of the following is a company that provides direct access to the Internet for home and business computer users?

   A. ASP

   B. ISP

   C. DNS

   D. DNP

36. Which of the following protocols can be used by a client to access email on a server?

    A. DNS

    B. FTP

    C. SMTP

    D. IMAP

37. What process involves making an application more difficult for unauthorized individuals to access, exploit, and so on?

    A. Application hardening

    B. Bulletproofing

    C. Pharprotecting

    D. EAL'ing

38. Which group should you make your mobile users a member of if they need to be able to install, delete, and modify their environment?

    A. Administrators

    B. Power Users

    C. Guests

    D. Travelers

Answers to Assessment Test

1. **C.** System components are essential for the basic functionality of a computer system. Many of the landmarks found on the motherboard can be considered system components, even expansion slots, to a degree. What you plug into those slots, however, must be considered peripheral to the basic operation of the system. For more information, see Chapter 1.

2. **A.** Although DRAM is a very common type of RAM essentially used in all computer systems today, it does not describe a physical memory format. SIMMs, DIMMs, and RIMMs are all technologies on which memory-module manufacturing is based. For more information, see Chapter 1.

3. **A.** A controller chip is responsible for encoding data to be stored on the disk platters as well as performing geometry translation for the BIOS. Translation is necessary because the true number of sectors per track of the hard disk drive system usually exceeds what is supported by the BIOS. For more information, see Chapter 2.

4. **C.** The standard peripheral power connector, or Molex connector, is commonly used on larger drives because it allows more current to flow to the drive than does the Berg connector, which is used with floppy diskette drives. For more information, see Chapter 2.

5. **A.** The native resolution refers to how many pixels an LCD screen can display (across and down) without distortion. The native resolution is based on the placement of the actual transistors that create the image by twisting the liquid crystals. The contrast ratio is the measurement between the darkest color and the lightest color that an LCD screen can display. For more information, see Chapter 3.

6. **B, E.** Although technically PCI and ISA could be used for graphics adapters, AGP was specifically designed for the use of high-speed, 3D graphic video cards. PCIe offers better performance than AGP for graphics adapters. For more information, see Chapter 3.

7. **B.** PCMCIA adapters are now called PC Card adapters. The other terms are newer than the PC Card name. For more information, see Chapter 4.

8. **C.** The S3 sleep mode is called Standby in Windows. Devices in this state consume less power than devices in S1 or S2 but more power than devices in S4. For more information, see Chapter 4.

9. **C.** The laser creates an image on the photosensitive drum that is then transferred to the paper by the transfer corona. The fuser heats up the toner so it adheres to the page. The transfer corona charges the page, and the eraser lamp cleans the drum before a page is printed. A rubber blade is also used to physically remove toner from the drum. See Chapter 5 for more information.

10. **A.** Laser printers use toner, which they melt to the page in the image of the text and graphics being printed. A toner cartridge holds the fine toner dust until it is used in the printing process. See Chapter 5 for more information.

11. **D.** In addition to using the Start menu to start a search, you can also right-click a file or folder and choose Search, or you can click the Search button in the Windows Explorer toolbar. For more information, see Chapter 6.

12. **D.** There are five basic hives in the Windows registry, and they are HKEY_CLASSES_ROOT, HKEY_CURRENT_USER, HKEY_LOCAL_MACHINE, HKEY_USERS, and HKEY_CURRENT_CONFIG. HKEY_RESOURCES does not exist. For more information, see Chapter 6.

13. **A.** Windows 95 cannot be directly upgraded to Windows XP. Instead, you must first upgrade to Windows 98 and then to Windows XP (or just do a fresh install of Windows XP). For more information, see Chapter 7.

14. **D.** To upgrade from a 32-bit OS such as Windows NT, you would use WINNT32.EXE. The program that performs an upgrade from Windows 9x to Windows 2000 is WINNT.EXE. For more information, see Chapter 7.

15. **C.** The first step is to identify the problem. Once you have done that, you should (in order) establish a theory of probable cause, test the theory, establish a plan of action to resolve the problem, verify full system functionality, and document your findings. See Chapter 8 for more information.

16. **B.** When you ran a normal backup, the archive bit was cleared for all backed up files. When you ran the differential backup, files that had been modified since the last normal backup were backed up, but the archive bit was not reset. Therefore, the incremental backup will back up all files that have changed since the last normal backup two weeks ago. See Chapter 8 for more information.

17. **B.** A general protection fault is a common error in Windows. It happens when a program accesses memory that another program is using or when a program accesses a memory address that doesn't exist. Generally, GPFs are the result of sloppy programming; they can often be fixed by clearing the memory with a reboot. For more information see Chapter 9.

18. **D.** If print jobs are seemingly getting "stuck" in the printer queue, you should stop and restart the print spooler service. There is no Printer Troubleshooting utility that will diagnose printer problems. Deleting and reinstalling is not necessary. For more information see Chapter 9.

19. **A.** The star topology is the easiest to modify. A physical star topology branches each network device off a central device called a hub, making it easy to add a new workstation. See Chapter 10 for more information.

20. **D.** A key role of the Transport layer is to provide error checking. The Transport layer also provides functions such as reliable end-to-end communications, segmentation and reassembly of larger messages, and combination of smaller messages into a single larger message. See Chapter 10 for more information.

21. **C.** CHAP depends on a "secret" known only to the authenticator and that peer. Part of configuring CHAP is setting the shared, predefined secret on both the client and server. For more information, see Chapter 11.

22. B. WPA is an improvement on WEP. For more information, see Chapter 11.

23. A, C. Monitors and power supplies can retain significant electrical charges, even after they're unplugged. Don't open the back of a monitor or the power supply unless you are specifically trained to do so. See Chapter 12 for more information.

24. C. Roughly half the time spent communicating should be devoted to listening. See Chapter 12 for more information.

25. C. IDE (ATA-1) and EIDE (ATA-2 and later) were specific nicknames for the ATA series of standards. Although ATA is technically accurate, it refers to both legacy IDE standards as well as newer SATA standards. Instead of using the term ATA to be synonymous with IDE and EIDE, as had been done in the past, the term PATA was coined, referring to the parallel nature of IDE communications. The term PATA differentiates the IDE and EIDE form of ATA from Serial ATA. SCSI is a related yet completely different type of technology. For more information, see Chapter 13.

26. D. Parts grabbers, also known as three-claw part holders (and sometimes four-claw part holders), are useful in situations within their reach and in which magnetic tools are not appropriate. Gravity, although often effective, can affect other components during construction of a computer system and should not be relied upon in many situations. For more information, see Chapter 13.

27. C. Mini PCI cards have either a 100-pin stacking connector or a 124-pin card edge connector. Type III cards have a 124-pin card edge connector. Mini PCIe cards have a 52-pin card edge connector.

28. B. The inverter provides power to the backlight. The backlight provides light to the LCD screen, and the screen displays the picture.

29. C. White streaks on printouts are most likely caused by toner on the transfer corona wire. Vertical black lines are caused by a scratch or a groove in the EP drum. If the fuser was not heating properly, toner would not bond to the paper, and you would have smearing. Faulty print drivers will cause garbage to print or there will be no printing at all. See Chapter 15 for more information.

30. B. If a printer is using out-of-date or incorrect printer drivers, then the printer may just produce pages of garbled text. The solution is to ensure that the most recent printer drivers are downloaded from the manufacturer's website. See Chapter 15 for more information.

31. B. NSLOOKUP is a command-line utility that enables you to verify entries on a DNS server. For more information, see Chapter 16.

32. B. The ATTRIB command is used to set file attributes. To add attributes, use the plus sign (+). To remove attributes, use the minus sign (−). The hidden attribute is designated by H. See chapter 16 for more information.

33. C. With the exception of Repair Your Computer, which appears only in Windows Vista, the other choices also appear in Windows 2000 and/or Windows XP. For more information, see Chapter 17.

34. B. An additional condition can be configured (such as how long the system needs to be idle, the type of power the system is running on, etc.) to allow the task to run only when it has been met. For more information, see Chapter 17.

35. B. An Internet Service Provider (ISP) provides direct access to the Internet. See Chapter 18 for more information.

36. D. The IMAP and POP3 protocols can be used to retrieve email from mail servers. See Chapter 18 for more information.

37. A. Application hardening involves making an application more difficult for non-authorized individuals to access, exploit, and so on. For more information, see Chapter 19.

38. B. If your mobile users need to be able to install, delete, and modify their environment, make them a member of the Power Users group. For more information, see Chapter 19.

CompTIA
A+® Complete
Study Guide

Chapter

1

Personal Computer System Components

THE FOLLOWING COMPTIA A+ ESSENTIALS EXAM OBJECTIVES ARE COVERED IN THIS CHAPTER:

✓ **1.2 Explain motherboard components, types and features**

- Form Factor
    - ATX / BTX,
    - micro ATX
    - NLX
- I/O interfaces
    - Sound
    - Video
    - USB 1.1 and 2.0
    - Serial
    - IEEE 1394 / FireWire
    - Parallel
    - NIC
    - Modem
    - PS/2
- Memory slots
    - RIMM
    - DIMM
    - SODIMM
    - SIMM
- Processor sockets
- Bus architecture

- Bus slots
  - PCI
  - AGP
  - PCIe
  - AMR
  - CNR
  - PCMCIA Chipsets
- BIOS / CMOS / Firmware
  - POST
  - CMOS battery
- Riser card / daughterboard
- [Additional subobjectives covered in chapter 2]

✓ **1.4 Explain the purpose and characteristics of CPUs and their features**

- Identify CPU types
  - AMD
  - Intel
- Hyper threading
- Multi core
  - Dual core
  - Triple core
  - Quad core
- Onchip cache
  - L1
  - L2
- Speed (real vs. actual)
- 32 bit vs. 64 bit

✓ **1.5 Explain cooling methods and devices**

- Heat sinks
- CPU and case fans

- Liquid cooling systems
- Thermal compound

✓ **1.6 Compare and contrast memory types, characteristics and their purpose**

- Types
  - DRAM
  - SRAM
  - SDRAM
  - DDR / DDR2 / DDR3
  - RAMBUS
- Parity vs. Non-parity
- ECC vs. non-ECC
- Single sided vs. double sided
- Single channel vs. dual channel
- Speed
  - PC100
  - PC133
  - PC2700
  - PC3200
  - DDR3-1600
  - DDR2-667

A personal computer (PC) is a computing device made up of many distinct electronic components that all function together in order to accomplish some useful task (such as adding up the numbers in a spreadsheet or helping you write a letter). Note that this definition describes a computer as having many distinct parts that work together. Most computers today are modular. That is, they have components that can be removed and replaced with a component of similar function in order to improve performance. Each component has a specific function. In this chapter, you will learn about the components that make up a typical PC, what their functions are, and how they work together inside the PC.

Unless specifically mentioned otherwise, throughout this book the terms *PC* and *computer* can be used interchangeably.

In this chapter, you will learn how to identify system components common to most personal computers, including the following:

- Motherboards
- Processors
- Memory
- Cooling systems

Identifying Components of Motherboards

The spine of the computer is the *motherboard*, otherwise known as the system board (and less commonly referred to as the planar board). This is the olive green or brown circuit board that lines the bottom of the computer. It is the most important component in the computer because it connects all the other components of a PC together. Figure 1.1 shows a typical PC system board, as seen from above. All other components are attached to this circuit board. On the system board, you will find the central processing unit (CPU), underlying circuitry, expansion slots, video components, random access memory (RAM) slots, and a variety of other chips.

FIGURE 1.1   A typical system board

Types of System Boards

There are two major types of system boards:

Nonintegrated system board   Each major assembly is installed in the computer as an expansion card. The major assemblies we're talking about are items like the video circuitry, disk controllers, and accessories. *Nonintegrated system boards* can be easily identified because each expansion slot is usually occupied by one of these components.

It is difficult to find nonintegrated motherboards these days. Many of what would normally be called nonintegrated system boards now incorporate the most commonly used circuitry (such as IDE and floppy controllers, serial controllers, and sound cards) onto the motherboard itself. In the early 1990s, these components had to be added to the motherboard using expansion slots.

Integrated system board   Most of the components that would otherwise be installed as expansion cards are integrated into the motherboard circuitry. *Integrated system boards* were designed for simplicity. Of course, there's a drawback to this simplicity: when one component breaks, you can't just replace the component that's broken; the whole motherboard must be replaced. Although these boards are cheaper to produce, they are more expensive to repair.

With integrated system boards, there is a way around having to replace the whole motherboard when a single component breaks. On some motherboards, you can disable the malfunctioning onboard component (for example, the sound circuitry) and simply add an expansion card to replace its functions.

System Board Form Factors

System boards are also classified by their form factor (design): ATX, micro ATX, BTX, or NLX (and variants of these). Exercise care and vigilance when acquiring a motherboard and case separately. Some cases are less flexible than others and might not accommodate the motherboard you choose.

Advanced Technology Extended (ATX)

The ATX motherboard has the processor and memory slots at right angles to the expansion cards. This arrangement puts the processor and memory in line with the fan output of the power supply, allowing the processor to run cooler. And because those components are not in line with the expansion cards, you can install full-length expansion cards in an ATX motherboard machine. ATX (and its derivatives) are the primary motherboards in use today.

Micro ATX

One form factor that is designed to work in standard ATX cases, as well as its own smaller cases, is known as micro ATX (also referred to as µATX). Micro ATX follows the same principle of component placement for enhanced cooling over pre-ATX designs but with a smaller footprint. With this smaller form come trade-offs. For the compact use of space, you must give up quantity: quantity of memory modules, quantity of motherboard headers, quantity of expansion slots, quantity of integrated components, even quantity of micro ATX chassis bays, although the same small-scale motherboard can fit into much larger cases, if your original peripherals are still a requirement.

Be aware, however, that micro ATX systems tend to be designed with power supplies of lower wattage, in order to help keep down power consumption and heat production, which is generally acceptable with the standard micro ATX suite of components. As more off-board USB ports are added and larger cases are used with additional in-case peripherals, larger power supplies might be required.

New Low-Profile Extended (NLX)

An alternative motherboard form factor, known as New Low-Profile Extended (NLX), is used in some low-profile case types. NLX continues the trend of the technology it succeeded, Low Profile Extended (LPX), placing the expansion slots (ISA, PCI, and so on) sideways on a special *riser card* to use the reduced vertical space optimally. Adapter cards, or daughterboards, that normally plug into expansion slots vertically in ATX motherboards, for example, plug in parallel to the motherboard, so their most demanding dimension does not affect case height. Figure 1.2 shows a low-profile motherboard with its riser card attached.

FIGURE 1.2   Both sides of a riser card with daughterboard

LPX, a technology that lacked formal standardization and whose riser card interfaces varied from vendor to vendor, enjoyed great success in the 1990s until the advent of the Pentium II processor and the Accelerated Graphics Port (AGP). These two technologies placed a spotlight on how inadequate LPX was at cooling and accommodating high pin counts. NLX, an official standard from Intel, IBM, and DEC, was designed to fix the variability and other shortcomings of LPX, but NLX never quite caught on the way LPX did. Newer technologies, such as micro ATX, and proprietary solutions have been more successful and have taken even more market share from NLX.

Balanced Technology Extended (BTX)

In 2003, Intel announced its design for a new motherboard, slated to hit the market mid- to late-2004. When that time came, the new BTX motherboard was met with mixed reactions. (Let's postpone accusations of acronym reverse-engineering until "CTX" is announced as the name of the next generation.) Intel and its consumers realized that the price for faster components that produced more heat would be a retooling of the now-classic (since mid-1990s) ATX design. The motherboard manufacturers saw research and development expense and potential profit loss simply to accommodate the next generation of hotter-running processors, processors manufactured by the same designers of the BTX technology. It was this resistance that caused the BTX form factor to gain very little ground over the next couple of years. Nevertheless, with the early support of Gateway, and later buy-in of Dell, the BTX design dug in and charted a path for future success.

Marketing aside, the BTX technology is well thought out and serves the purpose for which it was intended. By lining up all heat-producing components between air intake vents and the power supply's exhaust fan, Intel found that the CPU and other components could be cooled properly by passive heat sinks. A *heat sink* is a block of aluminum or other metal, with veins throughout, that sits on top of the CPU, drawing its heat away. Fewer fans and a more efficient airflow path create a quieter configuration overall. While the BTX design benefits any modern onboard implementation, Intel's recommitment to lower-power CPUs has at once lessened the need to rush to more expensive BTX systems and given the market a bit more time to assimilate this newer technology.

There are other motherboard designs, but these are the most popular and also the ones that are covered on the exam. Some manufacturers (such as Compaq and IBM) design and manufacture their own motherboards, which don't conform to the standards. This style of motherboard is known as a motherboard of proprietary design.

System Board Components

Now that you understand the basic types of motherboards and their form factors, it's time to look at the components found on the motherboard and their locations relative to each other. Figure 1.3 illustrates many of the following components found on a typical motherboard:

- Chipsets
- Expansion slots and buses
- Memory slots and external cache
- CPU and processor slots or sockets
- Power connectors
- Onboard disk drive connectors
- Keyboard connectors

- Peripheral ports and connectors
- BIOS
- CMOS battery
- Jumpers and DIP switches
- Firmware

In this subsection, you will learn about the most-used components of a motherboard, what they do, and where they are located on the motherboard. We'll show what each component looks like so you can identify it on most any motherboard you run across. Note, however, that this is just a brief introduction to the internal structures of a computer. The details of the various devices in the computer and their impact on computer service practices will be covered in later chapters.

FIGURE 1.3   Components on a motherboard

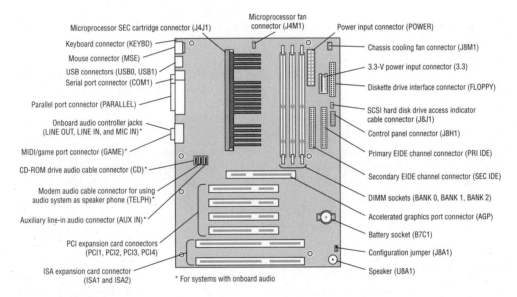

Bus Architecture

Many components of a computer system work on the basis of a bus. A *bus*, in this sense, is a common collection of signal pathways over which related devices communicate within the computer system. Expansion buses of various architectures, such as PCI and AGP, incorporate slots at certain points in the bus to allow insertion of external devices, or adapters, into the bus, usually with no regard to which adapters are inserted into which slots; insertion is generally arbitrary. Other buses exist within the system to allow communication between the CPU and other components with which data must be exchanged. Except for CPU slots and sockets and memory slots, there are no insertion points in such closed buses because no adapters exist for such an environment.

The term *bus* is also used in any parallel or bit-serial wiring implementation where multiple devices can be attached at the same time in parallel or in series (daisy-chained). Examples include Universal Serial Bus (USB), Small Computer System Interface (SCSI), and Ethernet.

Chipsets

A *chipset* is a collection of chips or circuits that perform interface and peripheral functions for the processor. This collection of chips is usually the circuitry that provides interfaces for memory, expansion cards, and onboard peripherals and generally dictates how a motherboard will communicate with the installed peripherals.

Chipsets are usually given a name and model number by the original manufacturer. For example, if you see that a motherboard has a VIA KT7 chipset, you would know that the circuitry for controlling peripherals was designed by VIA and was given the designation KT7. Typically, the manufacturer and model also tell you that your particular chipset has a certain set of features (for example, onboard video of a certain type/brand, onboard audio of a particular type, and so on).

Chipsets can be made up of one or several integrated circuit chips. Intel-based motherboards typically use two chips, whereas the SiS chipsets typically use one. To know for sure, you must check the manufacturer's documentation.

The functions of chipsets can be divided into two major functional groups, called Northbridge and Southbridge. Let's take a brief look at these groups and the functions they perform.

Northbridge

The *Northbridge* subset of a motherboard's chipset is the set of circuitry or chips that performs one very important function: management of high-speed peripheral communications. The Northbridge subset is responsible primarily for communications with integrated video using AGP and PCI Express, for instance, and processor-to-memory communications. Therefore, it can be said that much of the true performance of a PC relies on the specifications of the Northbridge component and its communications capability with the peripherals it controls.

When we use the term *Northbridge*, we are referring to the set of chips and circuits that make up a particular subset of a motherboard's chipset. There isn't actually a Northbridge brand of chipset.

The communications between the CPU and memory occur over what is known as the *frontside bus (FSB)*, which is just a set of signal pathways between the CPU and main memory. The clock signal that drives the FSB is used to drive communications by certain other devices, such as AGP and PCI Express slots, making them local-bus technologies. The *backside bus (BSB)*, if present, is a set of signal pathways between the CPU and Level 2 or 3 cache memory. The BSB uses the same clock signal that drives the FSB. If no backside bus exists, cache is placed on the frontside bus with the CPU and main memory.

The Northbridge is directly connected to the Southbridge (discussed next) and helps to manage the communications between the Southbridge and the rest of the computer.

Southbridge

The *Southbridge* subset of the chipset, as mentioned earlier, is responsible for providing support to the myriad onboard slower peripherals (PS/2, Parallel, IDE, and so on), managing their communications with the rest of the computer and the resources given to them. These components do not need to keep up with the external clock of the CPU and do not represent a bottleneck in the overall performance of the system. Any component that would impose such a restriction on the system should eventually be developed for FSB attachment.

Most motherboards today have integrated PS/2, USB, Parallel, and Serial. Some of the optional features handled by the Southbridge include LAN, audio, infrared, and FireWire (IEEE 1394). When first integrated, the quality of onboard audio was marginal at best, but the latest offerings rival external sound adapters in sound quality and number of features (including Dolby Digital Theater Surround technology, among others).

The Southbridge is also responsible for managing communications with the other expansion buses, such as PCI, USB, and legacy buses.

Figure 1.4 is a photo of the chipset of a motherboard, with the heat sink of the Northbridge, at the top left, connected to the cover of the Southbridge, at the bottom right.

FIGURE 1.4 A modern computer chipset

Figure 1.5 shows a schematic of a typical motherboard chipset (both Northbridge and Southbridge) and the components they interface with. Notice which components interface with which parts of the chipset.

FIGURE 1.5   A schematic of a typical motherboard chipset

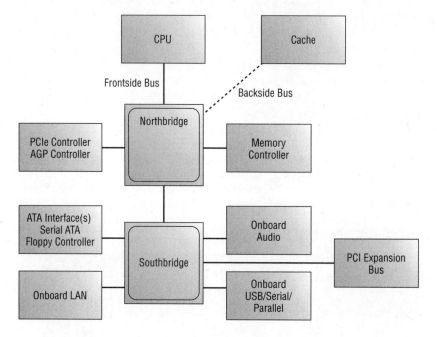

Expansion Slots

The most visible parts of any motherboard are the *expansion slots*. These look like small plastic slots, usually from 1 to 6 inches long and approximately ½ inch wide. As their name suggests, these slots are used to install various devices in the computer to expand its capabilities. Some expansion devices that might be installed in these slots include video, network, sound, and disk interface cards.

If you look at the motherboard in your computer, you will more than likely see one of the main types of expansion slots used in computers today:

- PCI
- AGP
- PCIe
- AMR
- CNR

Each type differs in appearance and function. In this section, we will cover how to visually identify the different expansion slots on the motherboard. Note that Industry Standard Architecture (ISA) expansion slots have been removed from the CompTIA A+ objectives, but you might wish to research these slots for your own edification and to be prepared, should you find yourself face to face with such a beast in the field. PC Card buses, such as PCMCIA, are related more to laptops than to desktop computers and are covered in Chapter 4.

PCI Expansion Slots

Many computers in force today contain 32-bit Peripheral Component Interconnect (PCI) slots. They are easily recognizable because they are short (around 3 inches long), compared to the classic ISA slot, and usually white. PCI slots can usually be found in any computer that has a Pentium-class processor or higher. PCI expansion buses operate at 33 or 66MHz over a 32-bit (4-byte) channel, resulting in data rates of 133 and 266MBps, respectively, with 133MBps the most common, server architectures excluded. Servers often feature 64-bit slots as well, which double the 32-bit data rates.

PCI slots and adapters are manufactured in 3.3 and 5V versions. Universal adapters are keyed to fit in slots based on either of the two voltages. The notch in the card edge of the common 5V slots and adapters is oriented toward the front of the motherboard, and the notch in the 3.3V adapters toward the rear. Figure 1.6 shows several PCI expansion slots. Note the 5V 32-bit slot in the foreground and the 3.3V 64-bit slots. Also notice that a universal 32-bit card fits fine in the 64-bit 3.3V slot.

FIGURE 1.6   PCI expansion slots

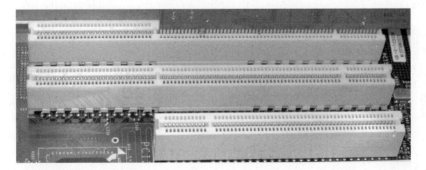

AGP Expansion Slots

Accelerated Graphics Port (AGP) slots are known mostly for video card use and are steadily being supplanted by PCI Express adapters. In the past, if you wanted to use a high-speed, accelerated 3D graphics video card, you had to install the card into an existing PCI or ISA slot. AGP slots were designed to be a direct connection between the video circuitry and the PC's memory. They are also easily recognizable because they are usually brown, are located right next to the PCI slots on the motherboard, and are slightly shorter than the PCI slots.

Another landmark to look for when identifying later AGP slots is the often alternate-colored shell surrounding the slot with an extension toward the front of the system that snaps into place at the "rear" of the adapter. It is necessary to pull the extension away from the adapter before removing it from the slot. Figure 1.7 shows an example of an AGP slot, along with a PCI slot for comparison. Notice the difference in length between the two.

FIGURE 1.7   An AGP slot compared to a PCI slot

AGP slot ⎯

⎯ PCI slot

AGP performance is based on the original specification, known as AGP 1x. It uses a 32-bit (4-byte) channel and a 66MHz clock, resulting in a data rate of 266.67MBps. AGP 2x, 4x, and 8x specifications multiply the 66MHz clock they receive to increase throughput linearly. For instance, AGP 8x uses the 66MHz clock to produce an effective clock frequency of 533MHz, resulting in throughput of 2133.33MBps over the 4-byte channel.

PCIe Expansion Slots

A newer expansion slot architecture that is being used by motherboards is PCI Express (PCIe). It was designed to be a replacement for AGP and PCI. It has the capability of being faster than AGP while maintaining the flexibility of PCI. And motherboards with PCIe might have regular PCI slots for backward compatibility with PCI.

PCIe is casually referred to as a bus architecture to simplify its comparison with other bus technologies. In fact, unlike true I/O buses, which share total bandwidth among all slots in a hub-like interconnectivity, PCIe uses a switching component with point-to-point connections to slots, giving each component full use of the corresponding bandwidth. Furthermore, true bus architectures are parallel in nature, while PCIe is a serial technology, striping data packets across multiple serial paths to achieve higher data rates.

PCIe uses the concept of *lanes*, which are the switched point-to-point signal paths between any two PCIe components. Each lane that the switch interconnects between any two intercommunicating devices comprises a separate pair of wires for both directions of traffic. Each PCIe pairing between cards requires a negotiation for the highest mutually supported number of lanes. The single lane or combined collection of lanes that the switch interconnects between devices is referred to as a *link*.

There are seven different link widths supported by PCIe, designated x1 (pronounced "by 1"), x2, x4, x8, x12, x16, and x32, with x1, x4, and x16 the most common. The x8 link width is less common than these but more common than the others. A slot that supports a particular link width is of a size related to that width because the width is based on the number of lanes supported, which requires a related number of wires. Therefore, a x8 slot is longer than a x1 slot but shorter than a x16 slot. Every PCIe slot has a 22-pin portion in common toward the rear of the motherboard, which you can see in Figure 1.8, which orients the rear of the motherboard to the left. These 22 pins comprise mostly voltage and ground leads.

There are three major versions of PCIe currently specified, 1.x, 2.0, and 3.0. For these three versions, a single lane, and hence a x1 slot, operates in each direction (or transmit and receive from either communicating device's perspective), at a data rate of 250MBps (almost twice the rate of the most common PCI slot), 500MBps, and 1GBps, respectively. Combining lanes results in a linear multiplication of these rates. For example, a PCIe 1.1 x16 slot is capable of 4GBps of throughput in each direction, 16 times the 250MBps x1 rate. As you can see, this fairly common slot doubles the throughput of an AGP 8x slot. Later PCIe specifications increase this data rate even more.

Up-plugging is defined in the PCIe specification as the ability to use a higher-capability slot for a lesser adapter. In other words, you can use a shorter (fewer-lane) card in a longer slot. For example, you can insert a x8 card into a x16 slot. The x8 card won't completely fill the slot, but it will work at x8 speeds if up-plugging is supported by the motherboard. Otherwise, the specification only requires up-plugged devices to operate at the x1 rate, something to be aware of and investigate in advance. Down-plugging is possible only on open-ended slots, although not specifically allowed in the official specification. Even if you find or make (by cutting a groove in the end) an open-ended slot that accepts a longer card edge, the inserted adapter cannot operate faster than the slot's maximum rated capability because the required physical wiring to the PCIe switch on the motherboard is not present.

Because of its high data rate, PCIe is the current choice of gaming aficionados. Additionally, technologies similar to NVIDIA's Scalable Link Interface (SLI) allow such users to combine preferably identical graphics adapters in neighboring PCIe x16 slots with a hardware bridge to form a single virtual graphics adapter. The job of the bridge is to provide non-chipset communication among the adapters. The bridge is not a requirement for SLI to work, but performance suffers without it. SLI-ready motherboards allow two, three, or four PCIe graphics adapters to pool their graphics processing units (GPUs) and memory to feed graphics output to a single monitor attached to the adapter acting as SLI master. SLI implementation results in increased graphics performance over single-PCIe and non-PCIe implementations.

Figure 1.8 is a photo of an SLI-ready motherboard with three PCIe x16 slots (every other slot, starting with the top one), one PCIe x1 slot (second slot from the top), and two PCI slots (first and third slots from the bottom). Notice the latch that secures the x16 adapters in place. Any movement of these high-performance devices can result in temporary failure or poor performance.

FIGURE 1.8   PCIe expansion slots

AMR Expansion Slots

As is always the case, Intel and other manufacturers are constantly looking for ways to improve the production process. One lengthy process that would often slow down the production of motherboards with integrated analog I/O functions was FCC certification. The manufacturers developed a way of separating the analog circuitry, for example, modem and analog audio, onto its own card. This allowed the analog circuitry to be separately certified (it was its own expansion card), thus reducing time for FCC certification.

This slot and riser card technology was known as the Audio Modem Riser (AMR). AMR's 46-pin slots were once fairly common on many Intel motherboards, but technologies including CNR and Advanced Communications Riser (ACR) are edging out AMR. In addition and despite FCC concerns, integrated components still appear to be enjoying the most success comparatively. Figure 1.9 shows an example of an AMR slot.

CNR Expansion Slots

The Communications and Networking Riser (CNR) slots that can be found on some Intel motherboards are a replacement for Intel's AMR slots. One portion of these slots is the same length as one of the portions of the AMR slot, but the other portion of the CNR slot is longer than that of the AMR slot. Essentially, these 60-pin slots allow a motherboard manufacturer to implement a motherboard chipset with certain integrated features. Then, if the built-in features of that chipset need to be enhanced (by adding Dolby Digital Surround to a standard sound chipset, for example), a CNR riser card could be added to enhance the onboard capabilities. Additional advantages of CNR over AMR include networking support, Plug and Play compatibility, support for hardware acceleration (as opposed to CPU control only), and the fact that there's no need to lose a competing PCI slot unless the CNR slot is in use. Figure 1.10 shows an example of a CNR slot (arrow).

FIGURE 1.9   An AMR slot

Memory Slots and Cache

Memory, or random access memory (RAM), slots are the next most prolific slots on a motherboard, and they contain the modules that hold memory chips that make up primary memory, the memory used to store currently used data and instructions for the CPU. Many and varied types of memory are available for PCs today. In this chapter, you will become familiar with the appearance and specifications of the slots on the motherboard, so you can identify them.

For the most part, PCs today use memory chips arranged on a small circuit board. Certain of these circuit boards are called *dual inline memory modules (DIMMs)*. Today's DIMMs differ in the number of conductors, or pins, that the particular physical specification uses. Some common examples include 168-, 184-, and 240-pin configurations. In addition, laptop memory comes in smaller form factors known as *small outline DIMMs (SODIMMs)* and MicroDIMMs. The *single inline memory module (SIMM)* is an older memory form factor that we'll discuss shortly. More detail on memory packaging and the technologies that use them can be found later in this chapter in the section "Identifying Purposes and Characteristics of Memory." Figure 1.11 shows the form factors for some popular memory modules. Notice how they basically look the same but the module sizes and keying notches are different.

FIGURE 1.10 A CNR slot

FIGURE 1.11 Different memory module form factors

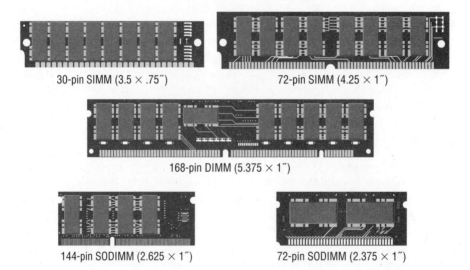

30-pin SIMM (3.5 × .75″)   72-pin SIMM (4.25 × 1″)

168-pin DIMM (5.375 × 1″)

144-pin SODIMM (2.625 × 1″)   72-pin SODIMM (2.375 × 1″)

Memory slots are easy to identify on a motherboard. DIMM slots are usually black and placed very close together. DIMM slots with pair-by-pair color coding can be observed these days, however. Generally, the pairs of slots must be filled together for best performance or to work at all, in some cases. Consult the motherboard's documentation to determine the specific modules allowed as well as their required orientation. The number of memory slots varies from motherboard to motherboard, but the structure of the different slots is similar. Metal pins in the bottom make contact with the metallic pins on each memory module. Small metal or plastic tabs on each side of the slot keep the memory module securely in its slot.

Sometimes the amount of primary memory installed is inadequate to service additional requests for memory resources from newly launched applications. When this condition occurs, the user receives an "out of memory" error, and the application fails to launch. One solution for this is to use the hard drive as additional RAM. This space on the hard drive is known as a swap file or a paging file. The technology in general is known as *virtual memory*. The swap file, `pagefile.sys` in modern Microsoft operating systems, is a contiguous, optimized space that can deliver information to RAM at the request of the memory controller faster than if it came from the general storage pool of the drive. Note that virtual memory cannot be used directly from the hard drive; it must be paged into RAM as the oldest contents of RAM are paged out to the hard drive to make room. The memory controller, by the way, is the chip that manages access to RAM, as well as adapters that have had a few hardware addresses reserved for their communication with the processor.

Nevertheless, relying too much on virtual memory (check your page fault statistics in the Reliability and Performance Monitor) results in the entire system slowing down noticeably. An inexpensive and highly effective solution is to add physical memory to the system, thus reducing its reliance on virtual memory. More information on virtual memory and its configuration can be found in Chapter 7, "Installing and Configuring Operating Systems."

When it's not the size of RAM that you need to enhance but its speed, you can add *cache memory* on the CPU side of RAM to take care of this. Cache is a very fast form of memory forged from static RAM, which is discussed in detail in the "Identifying Purposes and Characteristics of Memory" section later in this chapter. Cache improves system performance by predicting what the CPU will ask for next and prefetching this information before being asked. This paradigm allows the cache to be smaller in size than the RAM itself. Only the most recently used data and code or that which is expected to be used next is stored in cache. Cache on the motherboard is known as external cache because it is external to the processor, also referred to as *Level 2 (L2) cache*. *Level 1 (L1) cache*, by comparison, is internal cache because it is built into the processor's silicon wafer.

It is now common for chip makers to use extra space in the processor's packaging to bring the L2 cache from the motherboard closer to the CPU. When L2 cache is present in the processor's packaging, the cache on the motherboard is referred to as *Level 3 (L3) cache*. Unfortunately, due to the de facto naming of cache levels, the term L2 cache alone is not a definitive description of where the cache is located. The terms L1 cache and L3 cache do not vary in their meaning, however. The typical increasing order of capacity and distance from the processor die is L1 cache, L2 cache, L3 cache, RAM. This is also the typical decreasing order of speed.

Central Processing Unit (CPU) and Processor Socket or Slot

The "brain" of any computer is the *central processing unit (CPU)*. There's no computer without the CPU. There are many different types of processors for computers—so many, in fact, that you will learn about them later in this chapter in the section "Identifying Purposes and Characteristics of Processors."

Typically, in today's computers, the processor is the easiest component to identify on the motherboard. It is usually the component that has either a fan or a heat sink (usually both) attached to it (as shown in Figure 1.12). These devices are used to draw away and disperse the heat a processor generates. This is done because heat is the enemy of microelectronics. Theoretically, a Pentium (or higher) processor generates enough heat that without the heat sink it would permanently damage itself and the motherboard in a matter of hours or even minutes.

FIGURE 1.12   Two heat sinks, one with a fan

Sockets and slots on the motherboard are almost as plentiful and varied as processors. Sockets are basically flat and have several rows of holes or pins arranged in a square, as shown in Figure 1.13. The top socket is known as Socket A or Socket 462 and has holes to receive the pins on the CPU. The bottom socket is known as Socket T or Socket LGA 775 and has spring-loaded pins in the socket and a grid of lands on the CPU. The land grid array (LGA) is a newer technology that places the delicate pins on the cheaper motherboard, not the more expensive CPU, opposite to the way the aging pin grid array (PGA) does. The device with the pins has to be replaced if the pins become too damaged to function. PGA and LGA are mentioned again later in this chapter in the section "Identifying Purposes and Characteristics of Processors."

Modern CPU sockets have some sort of mechanism in place that reduces the need to apply the considerable force to the CPU that was necessary in the early days of personal computing to install a processor. Given the extra surface area on today's processors, excessive pressure applied in the wrong manner could damage the CPU packaging, its pins, or the motherboard itself. For CPUs based on the PGA concept, *zero insertion force (ZIF)* sockets are exceedingly popular. ZIF sockets use a plastic or metal lever on one edge to lock or release the mechanism that secures the CPU's pins in the socket. The CPU rides on the mobile top portion of the socket, and the socket's contacts that mate with the CPU's pins are in the fixed bottom portion of the socket. The Socket 462 image in Figure 1.13 shows the ZIF locking mechanism at the edge of the socket along the bottom of the photo.

For processors based on the LGA concept, a socket with a different locking mechanism is used. Because there are no receptacles in either the motherboard or the CPU, there is no opportunity for a locking mechanism that holds the component with the pins in place.

LGA-compatible sockets, as they're called despite the misnomer, have a lid of sorts that closes over the CPU and is locked in place by an L-shaped arm that borders two of the socket's edges. The nonlocking leg of the arm has a bend in the middle that latches the lid closed when the other leg of the arm is secured. The bottom image in Figure 1.13 shows an LGA socket with no CPU installed and the locking arm secured over the lid's tab (right-hand edge in the photo).

FIGURE 1.13   CPU socket examples

The processor slot is another method of connecting a processor to a motherboard, but one into which a processor (such as the AMD Athlon or the Intel Pentium II or Pentium III) on a special expansion card is inserted (the slot shown in Figure 1.14). Newer, more complex processors, such as the Intel Itanium, use a similar packaging, known as a Pin Array Cartridge (PAC), which uses a complex mechanism for inserting the large rectangular PAC CPU carrier. The connector that receives a PAC works on the Very Low Insertion Force (VLIF) principle. To see which socket type is used for which processors, examine Table 1.1.

FIGURE 1.14   A Slot 1 connection slot

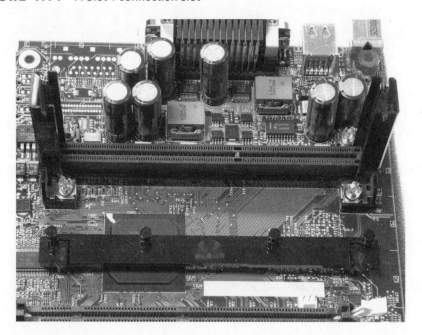

TABLE 1.1   Socket/Slot Types and the Processors They Support

Socket/Slot	Processors
Slot 1	Pentium II, Pentium III, Celeron, and all SECC and SECC2
Slot 2	Pentium II Xeon, Pentium III Xeon (server)—replaced by Socket 370
Slot A	Early AMD Athlon, physically the same as Slot 1, but not electrically—replaced by Socket A
Sockets 1, 2, 3, 6	486 and Pentium OverDrive

TABLE 1.1   Socket/Slot Types and the Processors They Support *(continued)*

Socket/Slot	Processors
Socket 4	Pentium 60/66, Pentium 60/66 OverDrive
Socket 5	Pentium 75-133, Pentium 75+ OverDrive, AMD K5
Socket 7	Pentium 75-200, Pentium 75+ OverDrive, Pentium MMX, AMD K6
Super Socket 7	AMD K6-2, K6-III
Socket 8	Oddly combined SPGA/PGA format for Pentium Pro—replaced by Slot 1 with the introduction of Pentium II
Socket 370	Plastic PGA (PPGA) processors, including Pentium III and Celeron
Socket 423	Early Pentium 4
Socket A (Socket 462)	AMD Athlon, Athlon XP, Athlon XP-M, Athlon MP, Thunderbird, Duron, Sempron
Socket 478	Pentium 4, Pentium 4 Extreme Edition, Celeron
Socket 479	Laptop Pentium M, Celeron M
Socket 563	AMD low-power mobile Athlon XP-M
Socket 603	Intel Xeon
Socket 604	Intel Xeon with Micro Flip-chip PGA (FCPGA) package
Socket 754	Athlon 64, Sempron, Turion 64
Socket P	For 478-pin Micro FCPGA mobile packages, such as Core 2 Duo, Celeron M, and Pentium Dual-Core
Socket T (LGA 775)	Desktop processors, such as Pentium 4, Pentium D, Celeron D, Pentium Extreme Edition, Core 2 Duo, Core 2 Extreme, Core 2 Quad
Socket J (LGA 771)	Server version of LGA 775, Dual-Core Xeon
Socket B (LGA 1366)	Intel Core i7
Socket 939	Athlon 64, Athlon 64 FX, Athlon 64 X2, Opteron 100-series
Socket 940	Intended for AMD servers, Athlon 64 FX (FX-51), Opteron

TABLE 1.1 Socket/Slot Types and the Processors They Support *(continued)*

Socket/Slot	Processors
Socket F (Socket 1207)	Replaces Socket 940 when used with Opteron multiprocessor systems—LGA packaging
Socket AM2	AMD single-processor systems, 940 pins (not same as server-based Socket 940), replaces Socket 754 and Socket 939
Socket AM3	DDR3 capable for Phenom series, Athlon X2, Sempron LE, Opteron (single-CPU servers)
Socket S1	AMD-based mobile platforms, replaces Socket 754 in the mobile sector
PAC418	Itanium (instead of proposed Slot 3/Slot M)
PAC611	Itanium 2

Power Connectors

In addition to these sockets and slots on the motherboard, a special connector (the 20-pin block connector shown in Figure 1.15) allows the motherboard to be connected to the power supply to receive power. This connector is where the ATX power connector (mentioned in Chapter 2 in the section "Identifying Purposes and Characteristics of Power Supplies") plugs in.

Onboard Floppy and Hard Disk Connectors

Almost every computer made today uses some type of disk drive to store data and programs until they are needed. All drives need some form of connection to the motherboard so the computer can "talk" to the disk drive. Regardless of whether the connection is built into the motherboard (*onboard*)—it could reside on an adapter card (*off-board*)—the standard for the attachment is based on the drive's requirements. These connections are known as *drive interfaces*, and there are two main types: floppy drive interfaces and hard disk drive interfaces. Floppy drive interfaces allow floppy disk drives (FDDs) to be connected to the motherboard, and similarly, hard disk drive interfaces do the same for hard disks and optical drives, among others. The interfaces consist of circuitry and a port, or header. Most motherboards produced today include both the floppy disk and non-SCSI hard disk interfaces on the motherboard. Server motherboards often include SCSI headers and circuitry instead.

FIGURE 1.15   An ATX power connector on a motherboard

Today, the headers you will find on most motherboards are for *Enhanced IDE (EIDE)*—also known retroactively as Parallel ATA (PATA)—or Serial ATA (SATA). Advanced Technology Attachment (ATA) is the standard term for what is more commonly referred to as Integrated Drive Electronics (IDE). The AT component of the name was borrowed from the IBM PC/AT, which was the standard of the day. However, because ATA is not the only technology that integrates the drive controller circuitry into the drive assembly (the antiquated Enhanced Small Device Interface [ESDI], for example, was another), IDE is somewhat of a misnomer and not the best term when referring only to ATA drives.

Nevertheless, the original ATA standard was referred to as IDE and had an upper limit of 528MB per logical drive. An enhanced version, EIDE (ATA-2 and higher), was developed to circumvent the obstacles to accessing more drive space per volume, increasing the limit to 8GB. Since then, the limit has been increased by the ATA-6 specification to 128PB (144.12e15). A petabyte (PB) is the number of bytes represented by 2 raised to the 50th power.

If your motherboard has PATA headers, they will normally be black or some other neutral color if they follow the classic ATA 40-wire standard. If your PATA headers are blue, they represent PATA interfaces that employ the ATA-5 or higher version of the Ultra DMA (UDMA) technology. These headers require 80-wire ribbon cables that allow increased transfer rates by reducing crosstalk in the parallel signal. These cables accomplish this by alternating among the other wires another 40 ground wires. The connectors and headers are still 40 pins, however. The color coding alerts you to the enhanced performance, which can be downward compatible with the 40-wire technology but at reduced performance.

The 40-pin ATA header transfers data between the drive and motherboard multiple bits in parallel, hence the name Parallel ATA. SATA, in comparison, which came out later and prompted the retroactive PATA moniker, transfers data in serial, allowing a higher data throughput because there is no need for more advanced parallel synchronization of data signals. The SATA headers are vastly different from the PATA headers. Figure 1.16 shows an example of the SATA data connector.

FIGURE 1.16   The Serial ATA connector

Keyboard Connectors

The most important input device for a PC is the keyboard. All PC motherboards contain a connector that allows a keyboard to be connected directly to the motherboard through the case. There are two main types of wired keyboard connectors. Once, these were the AT and PS/2 connectors. Today, the PS/2-style connector remains popular, but it is quickly being replaced by USB-attached keyboards. The all-but-extinct original AT connector is round, about ½ inch in diameter, in a 5-pin DIN configuration. Figure 1.17 shows an example of the AT-style keyboard connector.

The PS/2 connector (as shown in Figure 1.18) is a smaller 6-pin mini-DIN connector. Many new PCs you can purchase today contain a PS/2 keyboard connector as well as a PS/2 mouse connector right above it on the motherboard. Compare your PC's keyboard connector with Figures 1.17 and 1.18.

FIGURE 1.17   An AT connector on a motherboard

FIGURE 1.18   A PS/2-style keyboard connector on a motherboard

Wireless keyboard and mouse attachment is fairly popular today and is most often achieved with Bluetooth technology or a proprietary RF implementation.

Newer motherboards have color-coded the PS/2 mouse and keyboard connectors to make connection of keyboards and mice easier. PS/2 mouse connectors are green (to match the standard green connectors on some mice), and the keyboard connectors are purple.

Peripheral Ports and Connectors

In order for a computer to be useful and have the most functionality, there must be a way to get the data into and out of it. Many different ports are available for this purpose. We will discuss the different types of ports and how they work later in this chapter.

Briefly, the seven most common types of ports you will see on a computer are serial, parallel, Universal Serial Bus (USB), video (see Chapter 3), Ethernet, sound in/out, and game ports. Figure 1.19 shows some of these and others on a docking station or port replicator for a laptop. From left to right, the interfaces shown are as follows:

- DC power in
- Analog modem RJ-11
- Ethernet NIC RJ-45
- S-video out
- DVI-D (dual-link) out
- SVGA out
- Parallel (on top)
- Standard serial
- Mouse (on top)
- Keyboard
- S/PDIF (out)
- USB

FIGURE 1.19   Peripheral ports and connectors

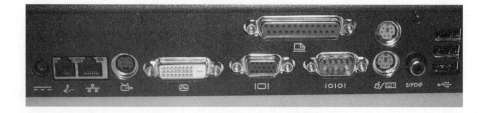

Figure 1.20 shows an example of a game port (also called a joystick port because that was the most common device that connected to it). As discussed later in this chapter, the game port can be used to connect to Musical Instrument Digital Interface (MIDI) devices

as well. Game ports connect such peripheral devices to the computer using a DA-15F 15-pin female *D-subminiature (D-sub)* connector. Devices that once connected to the game port have evolved, for the most part, into USB-attached devices.

FIGURE 1.20   A game port

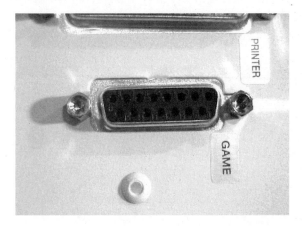

Figure 1.21 shows another set of interfaces not shown in Figure 1.19, the sound card jacks. These jacks are known as ⅛-inch (3.5mm) stereo minijacks, so called for their size and the fact that they make contact with both the left and right audio channels through their tip and ring. Shown in the diagram are an input, the microphone jack on the left, and an output, the speaker jack on the right. Software can use these interfaces to allow you to record and play back audio content in file or CD/DVD form.

FIGURE 1.21   Sound card jacks

Motherboard Attachment

There are two ways of connecting these ports to the motherboard (assuming the circuitry for providing these functions is integrated into the motherboard). The first, called a header connection, allows you to mount the ports into the computer's case, usually on the backplane, with a special cable connected to a *header*, or male connector that terminates the motherboard's traces for that function, as shown in Figure 1.22.

FIGURE 1.22   Connecting a port to the header on a motherboard

The second method of connecting a peripheral port is known as the direct-solder method. With this method, the individual ports are soldered directly to the motherboard. This method is used mostly in integrated motherboards. Figure 1.23 shows peripheral ports connected to a motherboard with the direct-solder method. Notice that there is no cable between the port and the motherboard and that the port is part of the motherboard. Some of these onboard ports can be disabled in the BIOS setup if necessary. You might need to disable an onboard port when an adapter with a more advanced version of the port or a replacement for a failed port is installed.

FIGURE 1.23   Peripheral ports directly soldered to a motherboard

BIOS and POST

Aside from the processor, the most important chip on the motherboard is the *Basic Input/ Output System (BIOS)* chip, also referred to as the ROM BIOS chip. This special memory chip contains the BIOS systems software that boots the system and allows the operating system to interact with certain hardware in the computer, in lieu of requiring a device driver to do so. The BIOS chip is easily identified: if you have a non-clone computer, this chip might have on it the name of the manufacturer and usually the word *BIOS*. For clones, the chip usually has a sticker or printing on it from one of the major BIOS manufacturers (AMI, Phoenix/Award, Winbond, and so on). On later motherboards, the BIOS might be difficult to identify, but the functionality remains, regardless of how it's implemented. Figure 1.24 gives you an idea of what a modern BIOS might look like. Despite the 1998 copyright on the label, this particular chip can be found on motherboards produced as late as 2009. Notice also the Reset CMOS jumper at lower left and its configuration silkscreen at upper left. You might use this jumper to clear the CMOS memory, discussed next, when an unknown password, for example, is keeping you out of the BIOS configuration utility. The jumper in the photo is in the clear position, not the normal operating position. System bootup is typically not possible in this state.

FIGURE 1.24   A BIOS chip on a motherboard

A major function of the BIOS is to perform a process known as *power-on self-test (POST)*. POST is a series of system checks performed by the system BIOS and other high-end components, such as the SCSI BIOS and the video BIOS. Among other things, the POST routine verifies the integrity of the BIOS itself. It also verifies and confirms the size of primary memory. During POST, the BIOS also analyzes and catalogs other forms of hardware, such as buses and boot devices, as well as manages the passing of control to the specialized BIOS routines mentioned earlier. The BIOS is responsible for offering the user a key sequence to enter the configuration routine as POST is beginning. Finally, once POST has completed successfully, the BIOS selects the boot device highest in the configured boot order and executes the master boot record (MBR) or similar construct on that device so that the MBR can call its associated operating system and continue booting up.

The POST process can end with a beep code or displayed code that indicates the issue discovered. Each BIOS publisher has its own series of codes that can be generated. Figure 1.25 shows a simplified POST display during the initial boot sequence of a computer.

FIGURE 1.25   An example of a BIOS boot screen

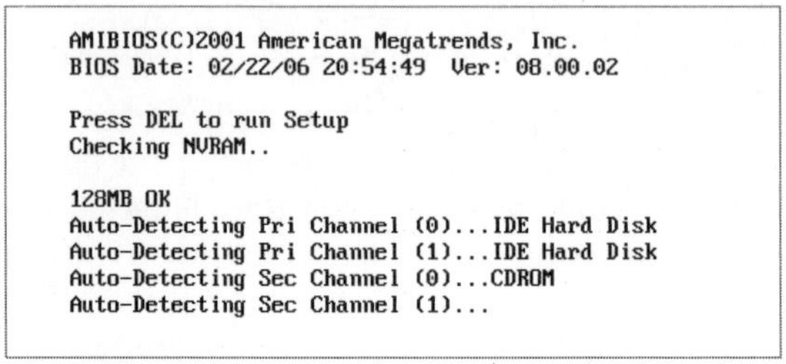

```
AMIBIOS(C)2001 American Megatrends, Inc.
BIOS Date: 02/22/06 20:54:49  Ver: 08.00.02

Press DEL to run Setup
Checking NVRAM..

128MB OK
Auto-Detecting Pri Channel (0)...IDE Hard Disk
Auto-Detecting Pri Channel (1)...IDE Hard Disk
Auto-Detecting Sec Channel (0)...CDROM
Auto-Detecting Sec Channel (1)...
```

CMOS and CMOS Battery

Your PC has to keep certain settings when it's turned off and its power cord is unplugged. These settings include the following:

- Date
- Time
- Hard drive configuration
- Memory
- Integrated ports
- Boot sequence
- Power management

Your PC keeps these settings in a special memory chip called the *complementary metal oxide semiconductor (CMOS) memory* chip. Actually, CMOS (usually pronounced *see-moss*) is a manufacturing technology for integrated circuits. The first commonly used chip made from CMOS technology was a type of memory chip, the memory for the BIOS. As a result, the term CMOS is the accepted name for this memory chip.

The BIOS starts with its own default information and then reads information from the CMOS, such as which hard drive types are configured for this computer to use, which drive(s) it should search for boot sectors, and so on. Any overlapping information read from the CMOS overrides the default information from the BIOS. A lack of corresponding information in the CMOS does not delete information that the BIOS knows natively. This process is a merge, not a write-over. CMOS memory is usually *not* upgradable in terms of its capacity and might be integrated into the BIOS chip or some other chip.

To keep its settings, integrated circuit-based memory must have power constantly. When you shut off a computer, anything that is left in this type of memory is lost forever. The CMOS manufacturing technology produces chips with very low power requirements. One ramification of this fact is that today's electronic circuitry is more susceptible to damage from electrostatic discharge (ESD). Another ramification is that it doesn't take much of a power source to keep CMOS chips from losing their contents.

To prevent CMOS from losing its rather important information, motherboard manufacturers include a small battery called the CMOS battery to power the CMOS memory. The batteries come in different shapes and sizes, but they all perform the same function. Most CMOS batteries look like large watch batteries or small, cylindrical batteries. Today's CMOS batteries are most often of a long-life, nonrechargeable lithium chemistry.

Jumpers and DIP Switches

The last components of the motherboard we will discuss in this section are jumpers and DIP switches. These two devices are used to configure various hardware options on the motherboard. For example, some motherboards support processors that use different core (internal) and I/O (external) voltages. You must set the motherboard to provide the correct voltage for the processor it is using. You do so by changing a setting on the motherboard with either a jumper or a DIP switch. Figure 1.26 shows both a jumper set and DIP switches. Motherboards often have either several jumpers or one bank of DIP switches. Individual jumpers are often labeled with the moniker JPx (where x is a unique number for the jumper).

FIGURE 1.26   Jumpers and DIP switches

Jumper   Rocker-type DIP switch   Slide-type DIP switch

Many of the motherboard settings that were set using jumpers and DIP switches are now either automatically detected or set manually in the BIOS setup program.

Firmware

Firmware is the name given to any software that is encoded in hardware, usually a read-only memory (ROM) chip, and can be run without extra instructions from the operating system. Most computers and large printers use firmware in some sense. The best example of firmware is a computer's BIOS routine, which is burned in to a chip. Also, some expansion cards, such as small computer system interface (SCSI) cards and graphics adapters, use their own firmware utilities for setting up peripherals.

Identifying Purposes and Characteristics of Processors

Now that you've learned the basics of the motherboard, you need to learn about the most important component on the motherboard: the CPU. The role of the CPU, or central processing unit, is to control and direct all the activities of the computer using both external and internal buses. It is a processor chip consisting of an array of *millions* of transistors. Intel and Advanced Micro Devices (AMD) are the two largest PC-compatible CPU manufacturers. Their chips were featured earlier in Table 1.1 during the discussion of the sockets and slots in which they fit.

The term *chip* has grown to describe the entire package that a technician might install in a socket. However, the word originally denoted the silicon wafer that is generally hidden within the carrier that you actually see. The external pins you see are structures that can withstand insertion into a socket and that are carefully threaded from the wafer's minuscule contacts. Just imagine how fragile the structures must be that you don't see.

Older CPUs are generally square, with contacts arranged in a pin grid array (PGA). Prior to 1981, chips were found in a rectangle with two rows of 20 pins known as a dual inline package (DIP); see Figure 1.27. There are still integrated circuits that use the DIP form factor. However, the DIP form factor is no longer used for PC CPUs. Most CPUs use either the PGA or the single edge contact cartridge (SECC) form factor. SECC is essentially a PGA-type socket on a special expansion card.

FIGURE 1.27   DIP and PGA

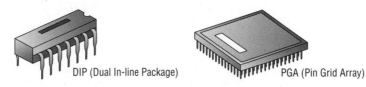

DIP (Dual In-line Package)   PGA (Pin Grid Array)

As processor technology grows and motherboard real estate stays the same, more must be done with the same amount of space. To this end, the staggered PGA (SPGA) layout was developed. An SPGA package arranges the pins in what appears to be a checkerboard pattern, but if you angle the chip diagonally, you'll notice straight rows, closer together than the right-angle rows and columns of a PGA. This feature allows a higher pin count per area. Intel and AMD are migrating toward the use of an inverted socket/processor combination of sorts. As mentioned earlier, the land grid array (LGA) packaging calls for the pins to be placed on the motherboard, while the mates for these pins are on the processor packaging. As with PGA, LGA is named for the landmarks on the processor, not the ones on the motherboard. As a result, the grid of metallic contact points, called lands, on the bottom of the CPU gives this format its name.

> This discussion only scratches the surface of the topic surrounding chip packaging and carriers. For more information on the various packaging for chips, start with en.wikipedia.org/wiki/Category:Chip_carriers.

You can easily identify which component inside the computer is the CPU because it is a large square lying flat on the motherboard with a very large heat sink and fan (as shown earlier in Figure 1.12). Or if the CPU is installed in a Slot 1 motherboard, it is a large ½-inch-thick expansion card with a large heat sink and fan integrated into the package. It is located away from the expansion cards. Figure 1.28 shows the location of the CPU in relation to the other components on a typical ATX motherboard. Notice how prominent the CPU is.

FIGURE 1.28 The location of a CPU inside a typical computer

Modern processors can feature the following:

Hyperthreading This term refers to Intel's Hyper-Threading Technology (HTT). HTT is a form of simultaneous multithreading (SMT). SMT takes advantage of a modern CPU's superscalar architecture. Superscalar processors are able to have multiple instructions operating on separate data in parallel.

HTT-capable processors appear to the operating system to be two processors. As a result, the operating system can schedule two processes at the same time, as in the case of symmetric multiprocessing (SMP), where two or more processors use the same system resources. In fact, the operating system must support SMP in order to take advantage of HTT. If the current process stalls because of missing data caused by, say, cache or branch prediction issues, the execution resources of the processor can be reallocated for a different process that is ready to go, reducing processor downtime.

Real World Scenario

Which CPU Do You Have?

The surest way to determine which CPU your computer is using is to open the case and view the numbers stamped on the CPU, which today requires removal of the active heat sink. However, you may be able to get an idea without opening the case and removing the heat sink and fan, because many manufacturers indicate the type of processor by placing a very obvious sticker somewhere on the case indicating the processor type. Failing this, you can always go to the manufacturer's website and look up the information on the model of computer you have.

If you have a no-name clone, there is always the System Properties pages, found by right-clicking My Computer (Computer in Windows Vista) and selecting Properties. The General tab, which is the default, contains such information. Even more detailed information can be found by running the System Information utility from Tools ➤ Advanced System Information in the Windows XP Help and Support Center or by entering `msinfo32.exe` in the Start ➤ Run dialog box for all modern Microsoft desktop operating systems.

Another way to determine a computer's CPU is to save your work, exit any open programs, and restart the computer. Watch closely as the computer returns to its normal state. You should see a notation that tells you what chip you are using.

Multicore   A processor that exhibits a *multicore* architecture has multiple completely separate processor dies in the same package. The operating system and applications see multiple processors in the same way that they see multiple processors in separate sockets. As with HTT, the operating system must support SMP to benefit from the separate processors. In addition, SMP is not an enhancement if the applications run on the SMP system are not written for parallel processing. Dual-core and quad-core processors are common specific cases for the multicore technology.

Don't be confused by Intel's Core 2 labeling. The numeric component does not imply there are two cores. There was a Core series of 32-bit mobile processors that featured one (Solo) or two (Duo) processing cores on a single die (silicon wafer). The same dual-core die was used for both classes of Core CPU. The second core was disabled for Core Solo processors.

The 64-bit Core 2 product line can be thought of as a second generation of the Core series. Core 2, by the way, reunited Intel mobile and desktop computing—the Pentium 4 family had a separate Pentium M for mobile computing. Intel describes and markets the microcode of certain processors as "Core microarchitecture." As confusing as it may sound, the Core 2 processors are based on the Core microarchitecture; the Core processors are not. Core 2 processors come in Solo (mobile only), Duo, and four-core (Quad) implementations. Solo and Duo processors have a single die; Quad processors have two Duo dies. A more capable Extreme version exists for the Duo and Quad models.

Processors, such as certain models of AMD's Phenom series, can contain an odd number of multiple cores as well. The triple-core processor, which obviously contains three cores, is the most common implementation of multiple odd cores.

Throttling   CPU throttling allows reducing the operating frequency of the CPU during times of less demand or during battery operation. CPU throttling is very common in processors for mobile devices, where heat generation and system-battery drain are key issues of full power usage. You might discover throttling in action when you use a utility that reports a lower CPU clock frequency than expected. If the load on the system does not require full-throttle operation, there is no need to push such a limit.

Microcode and multimedia extensions   Microcode is the set of instructions (known as an instruction set) that make up the various microprograms that the processor executes while carrying out its various duties. The Multimedia Extensions (MMX) microcode is a specialized example of a separate microprogram that carries out a particular set of functions. Microcode is at a much lower level than the code that makes up application programs. Each instruction in an application will end up being represented by many microinstructions, on average. The MMX instruction set is incorporated into most modern CPUs from Intel and others. MMX came about as a way to take much of the multimedia processing off the CPU's hands, leaving the processor to other tasks. Think of it as sort of a coprocessor for multimedia, much like the floating-point unit (FPU) is a math coprocessor.

Cache   As mentioned in the "Memory Slots and Cache" section earlier in this chapter, cache is a very fast chip memory that is used to hold data and instructions that are most likely to be requested next by the CPU. The cache located on the CPU die is known as L1 cache and is generally of a smaller capacity in comparison to L2 cache, which is located on the motherboard or off-die in the same CPU packaging. When the CPU requires outside information, it believes it requests that information from RAM. The cache controller, however, intercepts the request and consults its tag RAM to discover if the requested information is already cached, either at L1 or L2. If not, a cache miss is recorded and the information is brought back from the much slower RAM, but this new information sticks to the various levels of cache on its way to the CPU from RAM.

Speed   The speed of the processor is generally described in clock frequency (MHz or GHz). There can be a discrepancy between the advertised frequency and the frequency the CPU uses to latch data and instructions through the pipeline. This disagreement between the numbers comes from the fact that the CPU is capable of splitting the clock signal it receives from the external oscillator that drives the frontside bus into multiple regular signals for its own internal use. In fact, you might be able to purchase a number of processors rated for different (internal) speeds that are all compatible with a single motherboard that has a frontside bus rated, for instance, at 800MHz.

Matching System Components

In a world of clock doubling, tripling, quadrupling, and so forth, it becomes increasingly important to pay attention to what you are buying when you purchase CPUs, memory, and motherboards a la carte. The only weli-known relationship that exists among these components is the speed of the FSB (in MHz) and the throughput of the memory (in MBps). Because 8 bytes are transferred in parallel by a processor with a 64-bit (64 bits = 8 bytes) system data bus, you have to know the FSB rating before you choose the RAM for any particular modern motherboard. For example, a FSB of 800MHz requires memory rated at a throughput of 6400MBps (800 million cycles per second × 8 bytes per cycle).

Matching CPUs with motherboards or CPUs with memory requires consulting the documentation or packaging of the components. Generally, the CPU gets selected first. Once you know the CPU you want, the motherboard tends to come next. You must choose a motherboard that features a slot or socket compatible with your chosen CPU. The FSB used on the selected motherboard dictates the RAM you should purchase.

32- and 64-bit processors   The set of data lines between the CPU and the primary memory of the system can be 32 or 64 bits wide, among other widths. The wider the bus, the more data that can be processed per unit of time, and hence, the more work that can be performed. Internal registers in the CPU might be only 32 bits wide, but with a 64-bit system bus, two separate pipelines can receive information simultaneously. For true 64-bit CPUs, which have 64-bit internal registers and can run x64 versions of Microsoft operating systems, the external system data bus should be 64 bits wide or some larger multiple thereof.

Identifying Purposes and Characteristics of Memory

"More memory, more memory, I don't have enough memory!" Today, memory is one of the most popular, easy, and inexpensive ways to upgrade a computer. As the computer's CPU works, it stores data and instructions in the computer's memory. Contrary to what you might expect from an inexpensive solution, memory upgrades tend to afford the greatest performance increase as well, up to a point. Motherboards have memory limits; operating systems have memory limits; CPUs have memory limits.

To identify memory within a computer, look for several thin rows of small circuit boards sitting vertically, packed tightly together near the processor. In situations where only one memory stick is installed, it will be that stick and a few empty slots that are tightly packed together. Figure 1.29 shows where memory is located in a system.

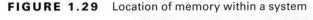

FIGURE 1.29   Location of memory within a system

Important Memory Terms

There are a few technical terms and phrases that you need to understand, with regard to memory and its function. These include:

- Parity checking
- Error checking and correcting (ECC)
- Single- and double-sided memory
- Single- and dual-channel memory

These terms are discussed in detail in the following sections.

Parity Checking and Memory Banks

Parity checking is a rudimentary error-checking scheme that offers no error correction. Parity checking works most often on a byte, or 8 bits, of data. A ninth bit is added at the transmitting end and removed at the receiving end so that it does not affect the actual data transmitted. The four most common parity schemes affecting this extra bit are known as even, odd, mark, and space. Even and odd parity are used in systems that actually compute parity. Mark (a term for a 1 bit) and space (a term for a 0 bit) parity are used in systems that do not compute parity, but expect to see a fixed bit value stored in the parity location. Systems that do not support or reserve the location required for the parity bit are said to implement *non-parity memory.*

The most basic model for implementing memory in a computer system uses eight memory chips to form a set. Each memory chip holds millions or billions of bits of information. For every byte in memory, one bit is stored in each of the eight chips. A ninth chip is added to the set to support the parity bit in systems that require it. One or more of these sets, implemented as individual chips or as chips mounted on a memory module, forms a *memory bank*. A bank of memory is required for the computer system to electrically recognize that memory or additional memory has been installed. The width of the system data bus, the external bus of the processor, dictates how many memory chips or modules are required to satisfy a bank. For example, one 32-bit, 72-pin SIMM satisfies a bank for a 32-bit CPU, such as a 386 or 486 processor. Two such modules are required to satisfy a bank for a 64-bit processor, a Pentium, for instance. However, only a single 64-bit, 168-pin DIMM is required to satisfy the same Pentium processor. For those modules that have fewer than eight or nine chips mounted on them, more than one bit for every byte is being handled by some of the chips. For example, if you see three chips mounted, the two larger chips probably handle 4 bits, a nybble, from each byte stored, and the third, smaller chip probably handles the single parity bit for each byte.

Even and odd parity schemes operate on each byte in the set of memory chips. In each case, the number of bits set to a value of 1 is counted up. If there are an even number of 1-bits in the byte (0, 2, 4, 6, or 8), even parity stores a 0 in the ninth bit, the parity bit; otherwise, it stores a 1 to even up the count. Odd parity does just the opposite, storing a 1 in the parity bit to make an even number of 1s odd and a 0 to keep an odd number of 1s odd. You can see that this is effective only for determining if there was a blatant error in the set of bits received, but there is no indication as to where the error is and how to fix it. Furthermore, the total 1-bit count is not important, only whether it's even or odd. Therefore, in either the even or odd scheme, if an even number of bits is altered in the same byte during transmission, the error goes undetected because flipping 2, 4, 6, or all 8 bits results in an even number of 1s remaining even and an odd number of 1s remaining odd.

Mark and space parity are used in systems that want to see 9 bits for every byte transmitted but don't compute the parity bit's value based on the bits in the byte. Mark parity always uses a 1 in the parity bit, and space parity always uses a 0. These schemes offer less error detection capability than the even and odd schemes because only changes in the parity bit can be detected. Again, parity checking is not error correction; it's error detection only, and not the best form of error detection at that. Nevertheless, finding an error can lock up the entire system and display a memory parity error. Enough of these errors and you need to replace the memory.

In the early days of personal computing, almost all memory was parity-based. Compaq was one of the first manufacturers to employ non-parity RAM in their mainstream systems. As quality has increased over the years, parity checking in the RAM subsystem has become rarer. As noted earlier, if parity checking is not supported, there will generally be fewer chips per module, usually one less per column of RAM.

Error Checking and Correction

The next step in the evolution of memory error detection is known as *error checking and correcting (ECC)*. If memory supports ECC, check bits are generated and stored with the data. An algorithm is performed on the data and its check bits whenever the memory is accessed. If the result of the algorithm is all zeros, then the data is deemed valid and processing continues. ECC can detect single- and double-bit errors and actually correct single-bit errors.

In this section, we'll outline the major types of computer memory as well as the methods of implementing, or packaging, such memory.

Single- and Double-Sided Memory

Ask just about anyone who doesn't manufacture memory for a living what the terms *single-sided memory* and *double-sided memory* mean, and you'll be treated to a blank stare or a short diatribe on how some memory modules have chips on one side, while others have chips on both sides. In fact, these terms have nothing to do with the physical attachment of chips to the modules. Either style can have chips on one or both sides of the module.

Double-sided memory is essentially treated by the system as two separate memory modules. Motherboards that support such memory have memory controllers that must switch between the two "sides" of the modules and, at any particular moment, can only access the side they have switched to. For the state-of-the-art memory at the time, double-sided memory allows more memory to be inserted into a computer using half the physical space of *single-sided memory*, which requires no switching by the memory controller.

Single- and Dual-Channel Memory

Standard memory controllers manage access to memory in chunks of the same size as the FSB's data width. This is considered communicating over a single channel. Most modern processors have a 64-bit system data bus. This means a standard memory controller can transfer exactly 64 bits of information at a time. Communicating over a single channel is a bottleneck in an environment where the CPU and memory can both operate faster than the conduit between them. Up to a point, every channel added in parallel between the CPU and RAM serves to ease this constriction.

Memory controllers that support or require dual-channel memory implementation were developed in an effort to alleviate the bottleneck between the CPU and RAM. *Dual-channel memory* is the memory controller's coordination of two memory banks to work as a synchronized set during communication with the CPU, doubling the specified system bus width, from the memory's perspective. Because today's processors largely have 64-bit external data buses, and because one stick of memory satisfies this bus width, there is a 1:1 ratio between banks and modules. This means that implementing dual-channel memory in today's most popular computer systems generally requires that pairs of memory modules be installed at a time. Note, however, that it's the motherboard, not the memory that implements dual-channel memory (more on this in a moment). *Single-channel memory*, in contrast, is the classic memory model that dictates only that a complete bank be satisfied whenever memory is initially installed or added. One bank supplies only half the width of the effective bus created by dual-channel support, which, by definition, pairs two banks at a time.

Because of the special tricks that are played with memory subsystems to improve overall system performance, care must be taken during the installation of disparate memory modules. In the worst case, the computer will cease to function when modules of different speeds, different capacities, or different numbers of sides are placed together in slots of the same channel. If all of these parameters are identical, there should be no problem with pairing modules. Nevertheless, problems could still occur when modules from two different manufacturers or certain unsupported manufacturers are installed, all other parameters being the same. Technical support or documentation from the manufacturer of your motherboard should be able to help with such issues.

Although it's not the make-up of the memory that leads to dual-channel support, but instead the technology on which the motherboard is based, some memory manufacturers still package and sell pairs of memory modules in an effort to give you peace of mind when you're buying memory for a system that implements dual-channel memory architecture. Keep in mind, the motherboard memory slots have the distinctive color coding, not the memory modules.

I Can't Fill All My Memory Slots

As a reminder, most motherboard manufacturers document the quantity and types of modules that their equipment supports. Consult your documentation, whether in print or online, when you have questions about supported memory. Most manufacturers require that slower or single-sided memory be inserted in lower-numbered memory slots than faster or double-sided memory. This is because such a system adapts to the first module it sees, looking at the lower-numbered slots first. Counterintuitively, however, it might be required that you install modules of larger capacity in lower-numbered slots than smaller modules.

Additionally, memory technology continues to advance after each generation of motherboard chipsets is announced. Don't be surprised when you attempt to install a single module of the highest available capacity in your motherboard, and the system doesn't recognize the module, either by itself or with others. That capacity of module might not have been in existence when the motherboard's chipset was released. Consult the motherboard's documentation!

One common point of confusion, not related to capacity, when installing memory includes lack of recognition of four modules, when two or three modules work fine, for example. In such a case, let's say your motherboard's memory controller supports a total of four modules. Recall that a double-sided module acts like two separate modules. If you are using double-sided memory, your motherboard might limit you to two such modules, comprising four sides (essentially four virtual modules), even though you have four slots on the board. If instead you start with three single-sided modules, when you attempt to install a double-sided module in the fourth slot, you are essentially asking the motherboard to accept five modules, which it cannot.

Types of Memory

Memory comes in many formats. Each one has a particular set of features and characteristics, making it best suited for a particular application. Some decisions about the application of the memory type are based on suitability; others are based on affordability to consumers or marketability to computer manufacturers. The following list gives you an idea of the vast array of memory types and subtypes:

- DRAM
  - Asynchronous DRAM
    - FPM DRAM
    - EDO DRAM
    - BEDO DRAM
  - Synchronous DRAM
    - SDR SDRAM
    - DDR SDRAM
    - DDR2 SDRAM
    - DDR3 SDRAM
    - DRDRAM
- SRAM
- ROM

Pay particular attention to all synchronous DRAM types. Note that the type of memory does not dictate the packaging of the memory. Conversely, however, you might notice one particular memory packaging holding the same type of memory every time you come across it. Nevertheless, there is no requirement to this end. Let's detail the intricacies of some of these memory types.

DRAM

DRAM is dynamic random access memory. (This is what most people are talking about when they mention RAM.) When you expand the memory in a computer, you are adding DRAM chips. You use DRAM to expand the memory in the computer because it's a cheaper type of memory. Dynamic RAM chips are cheaper to manufacture than most other types because they are less complex. *Dynamic* refers to the memory chips' need for a constant update signal (also called a *refresh* signal) in order to keep the information that is written there. If this signal is not received every so often, the information will bleed off and cease to exist. Currently, the most popular implementations of DRAM are based on synchronous DRAM and include SDR SDRAM, DDR, DDR2, DDR3, and DRDRAM. Before discussing these technologies, let's take a quick look at the all-but-defunct asynchronous memory types.

Asynchronous DRAM

Asynchronous DRAM is characterized by its independence from the CPU's external clock. Asynchronous DRAM chips have codes on them that end in a numerical value that is related to (often one tenth of the actual value) the access time of the memory. Access time is essentially the difference between the time when the information is requested from memory and the time when the data is returned. Common access times attributed to asynchronous DRAM were in the 40- to 120-nanosecond (ns) vicinity. A lower access time is obviously better for overall performance.

Because asynchronous DRAM is not synchronized to the frontside bus, you would often have to insert wait states through the BIOS setup for a faster CPU to be able to use such memory. These wait states represented intervals that the CPU had to mark time and do nothing while waiting for the memory subsystem to become ready again for subsequent access.

Common asynchronous DRAM technologies included Fast Page Mode (FPM), Extended Data Out (EDO), and Burst EDO (BEDO). Feel free to investigate the details of these particular technologies, but a thorough discussion of these memory types is not necessary here. The A+ technician should be concerned with synchronous forms of RAM, which are the only types of memory being installed in mainstream computer systems today.

Synchronous DRAM

Synchronous DRAM (SDRAM) shares a common clock signal with the computer's system-bus clock, which provides the common signal that all local-bus components use for each step that they perform. This characteristic ties SDRAM to the speed of the FSB and, hence, the processor, eliminating the need to configure the CPU to wait for the memory to catch up.

Originally, SDRAM was the term used to refer to the only form of synchronous DRAM on the market. As the technology progressed, and more was being done with each clock signal on the FSB, various forms of SDRAM were developed. What was once called simply SDRAM needed a new name retroactively. Today, we use the term single data rate SDRAM (SDR SDRAM) to refer to this original type of SDRAM.

SDR SDRAM

With SDR SDRAM, every time the system clock ticks, one bit of data can be transmitted per data pin, limiting the bit rate per pin of SDRAM to the corresponding numerical value of the clock's frequency. With today's processors interfacing with memory using a parallel data-bus width of 8 bytes (hence the term 64-bit processor), a 100MHz clock signal produces 800MBps. That's mega*bytes* per second, not mega*bits*. Such memory modules are referred to as *PC100*, named for the true FSB clock rate they rely on. PC100 was preceded by PC66 and succeeded by PC133, which used a 133MHz clock to produce 1067MBps of throughput.

Note that throughput in megabytes per second is easily computed as eight times the rating in the name. This trick works for the more advanced forms of SDRAM as well. The common thread is the 8-byte system data bus. Incidentally, you can double throughput results when implementing dual-channel memory.

DDR SDRAM

Double data rate (DDR) SDRAM earns its name by doubling the transfer rate of ordinary SDRAM by double-pumping the data, which means transferring it on both the rising and falling edges of the clock signal. This obtains twice the transfer rate at the same FSB clock frequency. It's the increasing clock frequency that generates heating issues with newer components, so keeping the clock the same is an advantage. The same 100MHz clock gives a DDR SDRAM system the impression of a 200MHz clock in comparison to an SDR SDRAM system. For marketing purposes and to aid in the comparison of disparate products (DDR vs. SDR, for example), the industry has settled on the practice of using this effective clock rate as the speed of the FSB.

Module Throughput Related to FSB Speed

There is always an 8:1 module-to-chip (or module-to-FSB speed) numbering ratio because of the 8 bytes that are transferred at a time with 64-bit processors. The following formula explains how this relationship works:

FSB in MHz	(~~cycles~~/second)
X 8 bytes	(bytes/~~cycle~~)
throughput	(bytes/second)

Because the actual clock speed is rarely mentioned in marketing literature, on packaging, or on store shelves for DDR and higher, you can use this advertised FSB frequency in your computations for DDR throughput. For example, with a 100MHz clock and two operations per cycle, motherboard makers will market their boards as having an FSB of 200MHz. Multiplying this effective rate by 8 bytes transferred per cycle, the data rate is 1600MBps. Now that throughput is becoming a bit trickier to compute, the industry uses this final throughput figure to name the memory modules instead of the actual frequency, which was used when naming SDR modules. This makes the result seem many times better (and much more marketable), while it's really only twice (or so) as good, or close to it.

In this example, the module is referred to as PC1600, based on a throughput of 1600MBps. The chips that go into making PC1600 modules are named DDR200 for the effective FSB frequency of 200MHz. Stated differently, the industry uses DDR200 memory chips to manufacture PC1600 memory modules.

Let's make sure you grasp the relationship between the speed of the FSB and the name for the related chips as well as the relationship between the name of the chips (or the speed of the FSB) and the name of the modules. Consider an FSB of 400MHz, meaning an actual clock signal of 200MHz, by the way—the FSB is double the actual clock for DDR, remember. It should be clear that this motherboard requires modules populated with DDR400 chips, and that you'll find such modules on the *PC3200* "rack."

Let's try another. What do you need for a motherboard that features a 333MHz FSB (actual clock is 166MHz)? Well, just using the 8:1 rule mentioned earlier, you might be on the lookout for a PC2667 module. However, note that sometimes the numbers have to be played with a bit to come up with the industry's marketing terms. You'll have an easier time finding *PC2700* modules that are designed specifically for a motherboard like yours, with an FSB of 333MHz. The label isn't always technically accurate, but round numbers sell better, perhaps. The important concept here is that if you find PC2700 modules and PC2667 modules, there's absolutely no difference; they both have a 2667MBps throughput rate. Go for the best deal; just make sure the memory manufacturer is reputable.

DDR2 SDRAM

Think of the *2* in *DDR2* as yet another multiplier of 2 in the SDRAM technology, using a lower peak voltage to keep power consumption down (1.8V vs. the 2.5V of DDR). Still double-pumping, DDR2, like DDR, uses both sweeps of the clock signal for data transfer. Internally, DDR2 further splits each clock pulse in two, doubling the number of operations it can perform per FSB clock cycle. Through enhancements in the electrical interface and buffers, as well as through adding off-chip drivers, DDR2 nominally produces four times the throughput that SDR is capable of producing.

Continuing the DDR example, DDR2, using a 100MHz actual clock, transfers data in four operations per cycle (effective 400MHz FSB) and still 8 bytes per operation, for a total of 3200MBps. Just like DDR, DDR2 names its chips based on the perceived frequency. In this case, you would be using DDR2-400 chips. DDR2 carries on the effective-FSB frequency method for naming modules but cannot simply call them PC3200 modules because those already exist in the DDR world. DDR2 calls these modules *PC2-3200* (note the dash to keep the numeric components separate).

As another example, it should make sense that PC2-5300 modules are populated with *DDR2-667* chips. Recall that you might have to play with the numbers a bit. If you multiply the well-known FSB speed of 667MHz by 8 to figure out what modules you need, you might go searching for PC2-5333 modules. You might find someone advertising such modules, but most compatible modules will be labeled PC2-5300 for the same marketability mentioned earlier. They both support 5333MBps of throughput.

DDR3 SDRAM

The next generation of memory devices was designed to roughly double the performance of DDR2 products. Based on the functionality and characteristics of DDR2's proposed successor, most informed consumers and some members of the industry surely assumed the forthcoming name would be DDR4. This was not to be, however, and DDR3 was born. This naming convention proved that the *2* in DDR2 was not meant to be a multiplier, but instead a revision mark of sorts. Well, if DDR2 was the second version of DDR, then DDR3 is the third. *DDR3* is a memory type that was designed to be twice as fast as the DDR2 memory that operates with the same FSB speed. Just as DDR2 was required to lower power consumption to make up for higher frequencies, DDR3 must do the same. In fact, the peak voltage for DDR3 is only 1.5V.

The most commonly found range of actual clock speeds for DDR3 tends to be from 133MHz at the low end to 250MHz. Because double-pumping continues with DDR3 and because four operations occur at each wave crest (8 operations per cycle), this frequency range translates to common FSB implementations from 1066MHz to 2000MHz in DDR3 systems. Naming these memory devices follows the conventions established earlier. Therefore, if you buy a motherboard with a 1600MHz FSB, you know immediately that you need a memory module populated with *DDR3-1600* chips because the chips are always named for the FSB speed. Using the 8:1 module-to-chip/FSB naming rule, the modules you need would be called PC3-12800, supporting a 12800MBps throughput.

The earliest DDR3 chips, however, were based on a 100MHz actual clock signal, so we can build on our earlier example, which was also based on an actual clock rate of 100MHz. With 8 operations per cycle, the FSB on DDR3 motherboards is rated at 800MHz, quite a lot of efficiency while still not needing to change the original clock our examples began with. Applying the 8:1 rule again, the resulting RAM modules for this motherboard are called PC3-6400 and support a throughput of 6400MBps, carrying chips called DDR3-800, again named for the FSB speed.

 Real World Scenario

Choosing the Right Memory for Your CPU

Let's say you head down to your local computer store, where motherboards, CPUs, memory, and other computer components are sold a la carte. You're interested in putting together your own system from scratch. Usually, you will have a CPU in mind that you would like to use in your new system. Assuming you choose, for example, an Intel Core 2 Quad Q8200 processor, you discover you need a motherboard that has an LGA 775 socket and supports a frontside bus of 1333MHz. You could assume you need DDR3 memory because DDR2 tops out around 1066MHz (PC2-8500). If you'd rather not assume, you can consult the chosen motherboard's documentation or display slick and confirm your suspicions. If you're right, you'll be buying at least one stick of your favorite capacity of PC3-10666 (multiplying 1333 by 8), two sticks if you need to feed a hungry dual-channel motherboard. In case you missed it, PC3-10666 modules are made using DDR3-1333 chips, so named for the speed of the FSB. Recall the 8:1 module-to-chip/FSB naming convention.

DRDRAM

Direct Rambus DRAM (DRDRAM), named for Rambus, the company that designed it, is a proprietary SDRAM technology, sometimes called RDRAM, dropping "direct." DRDRAM can be found in fewer new systems today than just a few years ago. This is because Intel once had a contractual agreement with Rambus to create chipsets for the motherboards of Intel and others that would primarily use DRDRAM in exchange for special licensing considerations and royalties from Rambus. The contract ran from 1996 until 2002. In 1999, Intel launched the first motherboards with DRDRAM support. Until then, Rambus could be found mainly in gaming consoles and home theater components. DRDRAM did not impact the market as Intel had hoped, and so motherboard manufacturers got around Intel's obligation by using chipsets from VIA Technologies, leading to the rise of that company.

Although other specifications preceded it, the first motherboard DRDRAM model was known as PC800. As with non-DRDRAM specifications that use this naming convention, PC800 specifies that, using a faster 400MHz actual clock signal and double-pumping like DDR SDRAM, an effective frequency and FSB speed of 800MHz is created. DRDRAM was originally named in a dissimilar fashion to other forms of SDRAM, instead based on the FSB speed. You might recall, for those memory types, that the FSB speed was used to name the actual chips on the modules, not the modules themselves. PC800 DRDRAM, then, features a double-pumped 800MHz FSB. Newer modules, such as the 32-bit RIMM 6400, are named for their actual throughput, 6400MBps, in this case. The section "RIMM" in this chapter details the physical details of the modules.

There are only 16 data pins per channel with DRDRAM, versus 64 bits per channel in other SDRAM implementations. This fact results in a 16-bit (2-byte) channel. A 2-byte packet, therefore, is exchanged during each read/write cycle, bringing the overall transfer rate of PC800 DRDRAM to 1600MBps per channel. DRDRAM chipsets require two 16-bit channels to communicate simultaneously for the same read/write request, creating a mandatory 32-bit dual-channel mode. Two PC800 DRDRAM modules in a dual-channel configuration produce transfer rates of 3200MBps. In motherboards that support 32-bit modules, you would use a single RIMM 3200 to achieve this 3200MBps of throughput, using the same actual 400MHz clock and 800MHz FSB and transferring 4 bytes at a time.

Despite DRDRAM's performance advantages, it has some drawbacks that keep it from taking over the market. Increased latency, heat output, complexity in the manufacturing process, and cost are the primary shortcomings. The additional heat that individual DRDRAM chips put out led to the requirement for heat sinks on all modules. High manufacturing costs and high licensing fees led to triple the cost to consumers over SDR, although today there is more parity between the prices.

In 2003, free from its contractual obligations to Rambus, Intel released the i875P chipset. This new chipset provides support for a dual-channel platform using standard PC3200 DDR modules. Dual-channel DDR transfers 16 bytes (128 bits) per read/write request, giving PC3200 a total throughput rate of 6400MBps. As a result, and because of the advent of DDR2 and DDR3, DRDRAM no longer holds any performance advantage.

To put each of the SDRAM types into perspective, consult Table 1.2, which summarizes how each technology in the SDRAM arena would achieve a transfer rate of 3200MBps, even if only theoretically. For example, PC400 doesn't exist in the SDR SDRAM world.

TABLE 1.2   How Some Memory Types Transfer 3200MBps per Channel

Memory Type	Actual/Effective (FSB) Clock Frequency (MHz)	Bytes per Transfer
SDR SDRAM PC400*	400/400	8
DDR SDRAM PC3200	200/400	8
DDR2 SDRAM PC2-3200	100/400	8
DDR3 SDRAM PC3-3200**	50/400	8
DRDRAM PC800	400/800	4***

* SDR SDRAM PC400 does not exist.

**PC3-3200 does not exist and is too slow for DDR3.

***Assuming requisite 32-bit dual-channel mode

SRAM

Static random access memory (SRAM) doesn't require a refresh signal like DRAM does. The chips are more complex and are thus more expensive. However, they are considerably faster. DRAM access times come in at 40 nanoseconds (ns) or more; SRAM has access times faster than 10ns. SRAM is often used for cache memory.

ROM

ROM stands for read-only memory. It is called read-only because the original form of this memory could not be written to. Once information had been etched on a silicon chip and manufactured into the ROM package, the information couldn't be changed. If you ran out of use for the information or code on the ROM, you added little eyes and some cute fuzzy extras and you had a bug that sat on your desk and looked back at you. Some form of ROM is normally used to store the computer's BIOS, because this information normally does not change very often.

The system ROM in the original IBM PC contained the power-on self-test (POST), Basic Input/Output System (BIOS), and cassette BASIC. Later IBM computers and compatibles include everything but the cassette BASIC. The system ROM enables the computer to "pull itself up by its bootstraps," or *boot* (find and start the operating system).

Through the years, different forms of ROM were developed that could be altered, later ones more easily than earlier ones. The first generation was the programmable ROM (PROM), which could be written to for the first time in the field using a special programming device, but then no more. You had a new bug to keep the ROM bug company. Liken this to the burning of a CD-R. Don't need it any longer? You've got a handy coaster. Following the PROM came erasable PROM (EPROM), which was able to be erased using ultraviolet light and subsequently reprogrammed using the original programming device. These days, our flash memory is a form of electrically erasable PROM (EEPROM), which does not require UV light to erase its contents, but rather a slightly higher than normal electrical pulse.

 Although the names of these memory devices are different, they all contain ROM. Therefore, regardless which of these technologies is used to manufacture a BIOS chip, it's never incorrect to say that the result is a ROM chip.

Memory Packaging

First of all, it should be noted that each motherboard supports memory based on the speed of the frontside bus and the memory's form factor. For example, if the motherboard's FSB is rated at a maximum speed of 533MHz, and you install memory that is rated at 300MHz, the memory will operate at only 300MHz, if it works at all, thus making the computer operate slower than what it could. In their documentation, most motherboard manufacturers list which type(s) of memory they support as well as its maximum speeds and required pairings.

The memory slots on a motherboard are designed for particular module form factors or styles. In case you run across the older terms, dual inline package (DIP), *single inline memory module (SIMM)*, and single inline pin package (SIPP) are obsolete memory packages. The most popular form factors for primary memory modules today are:

- DIMM
- RIMM
- SODIMM
- MicroDIMM

Note also that the various CPUs on the market tend to support only one form of physical memory packaging. For example, the Intel Pentium 4 class of processors is always going to be paired with DIMMs, while certain early Intel Xeon processors mated only with RIMMs. So, in addition to coordinating the speed of the components, their form factor is an issue that must be addressed as well.

DIMM

One type of memory package is known as a DIMM. As mentioned earlier in this chapter, DIMM stands for dual inline memory module. DIMMs are 64-bit memory modules that are used as a package for the SDRAM family: SDR, DDR, DDR2, and DDR3. The term *dual* refers to the fact that, unlike their SIMM predecessors, DIMMs differentiate the functionality of the pins on one side of the module from the corresponding pins on the other side.

With 84 pins per side, this makes 168 independent pins on each standard SDR module, as shown with its two keying notches as well as the last pin labeled 84 on the side shown in Figure 1.30.

FIGURE 1.30   An SDR dual inline memory module (DIMM)

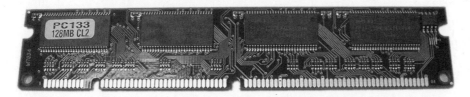

The DIMM used for DDR memory has a total of 184 pins and a single keying notch, while the DIMM used for DDR2 has a total of 240 pins, one keying notch, and possibly an aluminum cover for both sides, called a *heat spreader*, designed like a heat sink to dissipate heat away from the memory chips and prevent overheating. The DDR3 DIMM is similar to that of DDR2. It has 240 pins and a single keying notch, but the notch is in a different location to avoid cross-insertion. Not only is the DDR3 DIMM physically incompatible with DDR2 DIMM slots, it's also electrically incompatible.

Figure 1.31 is a photo of a DDR2 module. A matched pair of DDR3 modules with heat spreaders, suitable for dual-channel use in a high-end graphics adapter or motherboard, is shown in Figure 1.32.

FIGURE 1.31   A DDR2 SDRAM module

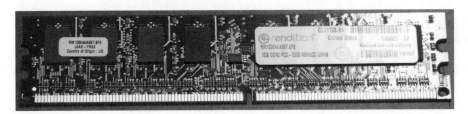

RIMM

Assumed to stand for Rambus inline memory module, but not really an acronym, RIMM is a trademark of Rambus, Inc. and perhaps a clever play on the acronym DIMM, a competing form factor. A RIMM is a custom memory module that carries DRDRAM and varies in physical specification, based on whether it is a 16-bit or 32-bit module. The 16-bit modules have 184 pins and two keying notches, while 32-bit modules have 232 pins and only one keying notch, reminiscent of the trend in SDRAM-to-DDR evolution. Figure 1.33 shows the two sides of a 16-bit RIMM module, including the aluminum heat spreaders.

FIGURE 1.32   A pair of DDR3 SDRAM modules

FIGURE 1.33   A Rambus RIMM module

As mentioned earlier, DRDRAM is based on a 16-bit channel. However, dual-channel implementation is required with DRDRAM; it's not an option. The dual-channel architecture can be implemented utilizing two separate 16-bit RIMMs (leading to the generally held view that RIMMs must always be installed in pairs) or the newer 32-bit single-module design (not doing much to dispel the "pair" view, despite the facts). Typically, motherboards with the 16-bit single- or dual-channel implementation provide four RIMM slots that must be filled in pairs, while the 32-bit versions provide two RIMM slots that can be filled one at a time. A 32-bit RIMM essentially has two 16-bit modules built in (possibly contributing to the persistence of the "pair" view) and requires only a single motherboard slot, albeit a physically different slot. So you must be sure of the module your motherboard accepts before upgrading.

Unique to the use of RIMM modules, a computer must have every RIMM slot occupied. Even one vacant slot will cause the computer not to boot. Any slot not populated with live memory requires an inexpensive blank of sorts called a continuity RIMM, or C-RIMM, for its role of keeping electrical continuity in the DRDRAM channel until the signal can terminate on the motherboard. Think of it like a fusible link in a string of holiday lights. It seems to do nothing, but no light works without it. However, 32-bit modules terminate themselves and do not rely on the motherboard circuitry for termination, so vacant 32-bit slots require a module known as a continuity and termination RIMM (CT-RIMM).

SODIMM

Notebook computers and other computers that require much smaller components don't use standard RAM packages, such as the SIMM or the DIMM. Instead, they call for a much smaller memory form factor, such as a small outline DIMM. SODIMMs are available in many physical implementations, including the older 32-bit (72- and 100-pin) configuration and newer 64-bit (144-pin SDR SDRAM, 200-pin DDR/DDR2, and 204-pin DDR3) configurations.

All 64-bit modules have a single keying notch. The 144-pin module's notch is slightly off-center. Note that although the 200-pin SODIMMs for DDR and DDR2 have slightly different keying, it's not so different that you don't need to pay close attention to differentiate the two. They are not, however, interchangeable. Figure 1.34 shows an example of a 144-pin, 64-bit module. Figure 1.35 is a photo of a 200-pin DDR2 SODIMM.

MicroDIMM

A newer, and smaller, RAM form factor is the MicroDIMM. The MicroDIMM is an extremely small RAM form factor. In fact, it is over 50 percent smaller than a SODIMM, only 45.5 millimeters (about 1.75 inches) long and 30 millimeters (about 1.2 inches—a bit bigger than a quarter) wide. It was designed for the ultralight and portable subnotebook style of computer. These modules have 144 pins or 172 pins and are similar to a DIMM in that they use a 64-bit data bus. Often employed in laptop computers, SODIMMs and MicroDIMMs are mentioned in Chapter 4 as well.

FIGURE 1.34   144-pin SODIMM

FIGURE 1.35   200-pin DDR2 SODIMM

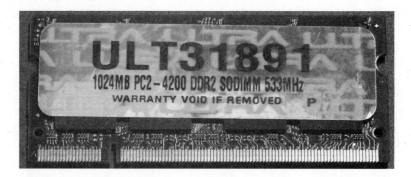

Identifying Characteristics
of Ports and Cables

Now that you've learned the various types of items found in a computer, let's discuss the various types of ports and cables used with computers. A *port* is a generic name for any connector on a computer into which a cable can be plugged. A cable is simply a way of connecting a peripheral or other device to a computer using multiple copper or fiber-optic conductors inside a common wrapping or sheath. Typically, cables connect two ports: one on the computer and one on some other device.

Let's take a quick look at some of the different styles of port connector types as well as peripheral port and cable types. We'll begin by looking at peripheral port connector types.

Peripheral Port Connector Types

Computer ports are interfaces that allow other devices to be connected to a computer. Their appearance varies widely, depending on their function. In this section we'll examine the following types of peripheral ports:

- D-subminiature
- RJ-series
- Other types

D-subminiature Connectors

D-sub connectors, for a number of years the most common style of connector found on computers, are typically designated with DXn, where the letter X is replaced by the letters A through E, which refer to the size of the connector, and the letter n is replaced by the number of pins or sockets in the connector. D-sub connectors are usually shaped like a trapezoid, as you can see in Figure 1.36. The nice part about these connectors is that only one orientation is possible. If you try to connect them upside down or try to connect a male connector to another male connector, they just won't go together, and the connection can't be made. Table 1.3 lists common D-sub ports and connectors as well as their most common uses. Be on the lookout for the casual use of "DB" to represent any D-sub connector. This is very common and is accepted as an unwritten de facto standard.

At the bottom left in Figure 1.36 is a DE15F 15-pin video port, in the center is a DB25F 25-pin female printer port, and on the right is a DE9M 9-pin male serial port.

TABLE 1.3   Common D-sub Connectors

Connector	Gender	Use
DE9	Male	Serial port
DE9	Female	Connector on a serial cable
DB25	Male	Serial port or connector on a parallel cable
DB25	Female	Parallel port, or connector on a serial cable
DA15	Female	Game port or MIDI port
DA15	Male	Connector on a game peripheral cable or MIDI cable
DE15	Female	Video port (has three rows of 5 pins as opposed to two rows)
DE15	Male	Connector on a monitor cable

FIGURE 1.36   D-sub ports and connectors

RJ-Series

Registered jack (RJ) connectors are most often used in telecommunications. The two most common examples of RJ ports are RJ-11 and RJ-45. RJ-11 connectors are used most often in telephone hookups; your home phone jack is probably an RJ-11 jack. The ports in your external and internal modems, assuming you still have one, are RJ-11.

RJ-45 connectors, on the other hand, are most commonly found on Ethernet networks that use twisted-pair cabling. Your Ethernet NIC likely has an RJ-45 socket on it. See Chapter 10, "Understanding Networking," for details on networking interfaces. Although RJ-45 is a widely accepted description for the larger connectors, it is not correct. Generically speaking, they are 8-pin modular connectors, or 8P8C connectors, meaning there are 8 pin positions, and all 8 of them are connected, or used. RJ-45 not only specifies the physical appearance of the connector, but also how the contacts are wired from one end to the other. That specification does not match the T568A and T568B wiring standards used in data communications.

Figure 1.37 shows an RJ-11 connector on the left and an RJ-45 connector on the right. Notice the size difference. As you can see, RJ connectors are typically square with multiple gold contacts on the flat side. A small locking tab on the other side prevents the connector and cable from falling or being pulled out of the jack accidentally.

Other Types of Ports

A few other ports are used with computers today. These ports include the following:

- Universal Serial Bus (USB)
- IEEE 1394 (FireWire)
- Infrared

- Audio jacks
- PS/2 (mini-DIN)
- Centronics

Let's look at each one and how it is used.

FIGURE 1.37   RJ ports

Universal Serial Bus (USB)

Most computers built after 1997 have one or more flat ports in place of one DE9M serial port. These ports are Universal Serial Bus (USB) ports, and they are used for connecting multiple (up to 127) peripherals to one computer through a single port (and the use of multiport peripheral *hubs*). USB version 1.1 supported data rates as high as 12Mbps (1.5MBps). USB 2.0 supports data rates as high as 480Mbps (60MBps), 40 times that of its predecessor. Figure 1.38 shows an example of a set of Type A USB ports. Port types are explained in the "Common Peripheral Interfaces and Cables" section later in this chapter.

USB 2.0 uses the same physical connection as the original USB, but it is much higher in transfer rates and requires a cable with more shielding that is less susceptible to noise. You can tell if a computer, hub, or cable supports USB 2.0 by looking for the red and blue "High Speed USB" graphic somewhere on the computer, device, or cable (or on its packaging).

FIGURE 1.38   USB ports

Because of USB's higher transfer rate, flexibility, and ease of use, most devices that in the past used serial interfaces now come with USB interfaces. It's rare to see a newly introduced PC accessory with a standard serial interface cable. For example, PC cameras used to come as standard serial-only interfaces. Now you can buy them only with USB interfaces.

IEEE 1394 (FireWire)

Recently, one port has been slowly creeping into the mainstream and is seen more and more often on desktop PCs. That port is the IEEE 1394 port (shown in Figure 1.39), more commonly known as a *FireWire* port. Its popularity is due to its ease of use and very high (400Mbps) transmission rates. Originally developed by Apple, it was standardized by IEEE in 1995 as IEEE 1394. It is most often used as a way to get digital video into a PC so it can be edited with digital video editing tools.

FIGURE 1.39   A FireWire port on a PC

Infrared

Increasing numbers of people are getting fed up with being tethered to their computers by cords. As a result, many computers (especially portable computing devices like laptops and PDAs) are now using infrared ports to send and receive data. An infrared (IR) port is a small port on the computer that allows data to be sent and received using electromagnetic radiation in the infrared band. The infrared port itself is a small, dark square of plastic (usually a very dark maroon) and can typically be found on the front of a PC or on the side of a laptop or portable. Figure 1.40 shows an example of an infrared port.

FIGURE 1.40   An infrared port

Infrared ports send and receive data at a very slow rate (the maximum speed on PC infrared ports is less than 4Mbps). Most infrared ports on PCs that have them support the Infrared Data Association (IrDA) standard, which outlines a standard way of transmitting and receiving information by infrared so that devices can communicate with one another.

 More information on the IrDA standard can be found at the organization's website: http://www.irda.org.

Note that although infrared is a wireless technology, most infrared communications (especially those that conform to the IrDA standards) are line-of-sight only and take place within a short distance (typically less than four meters). Infrared is generally used for point-to-point communications such as controlling the volume on a device with a handheld remote control.

Audio/Video Jacks

The RCA jack (shown in Figure 1.41) was developed by the RCA Victor Company in the late 1940s for use with its phonographs. You bought a phonograph, connected the RCA plug on the back of your phonograph to the RCA jack on the back of your radio or television, and used the speaker and amplifier in the radio or television to listen to records. It made phonographs cheaper to produce and had the added bonus of making sure everyone had an RCA Victor radio or television (or at the very least, one with the RCA jack on the back). Either way, RCA made money.

FIGURE 1.41   An RCA jack (female) and RCA plug (male)

Female

Male

Today, RCA jacks and connectors (or plugs) are used to transmit both audio and video information. Typically, when you see a yellow-coded RCA connector on a PC video card (next to a DE15F connector), it's for composite video output (output to a television or VCR). However, digital audio can be implemented with *S/PDIF*, which can be deployed with an RCA jack. Figure 1.19 showed an S/PDIF RCA jack. Other options for S/PDIF include BNC coaxial and TOSLINK fiber connectors. Toshiba's TOSLINK interface is a digital fiber-optic audio technology that is implemented with its own connector.

Although they aren't used for video, it bears mentioning that the ⅛-inch stereo mini-jack and mating miniplug are more commonly used on computers these days for analog audio. Your sound card, microphone, and speakers have them. Figure 1.42 is a photo of a TOSLINK optical interface with a flip-up cover and pictured to the left of a set of standard analog minijacks.

FIGURE 1.42   The TOSLINK interface

In the spirit of covering interfaces that support both audio and video, don't forget the HDMI interface, which carries both over the same interface. Only CATV coaxial connections to TV cards can boast that on the PC. An RCA jack and cable carry either audio or video, not both simultaneously.

PS/2 (Keyboard and Mouse)

Another common port, as mentioned earlier, is the PS/2 port. A *PS/2 port* (also known as a mini-DIN 6 connector) is a mouse and keyboard interface port first found on the IBM PS/2 (hence the name). It is smaller than previous interfaces (the DIN-5 keyboard port and serial mouse connector), and thus its popularity increased quickly. Figure 1.43 shows examples of both PS/2 keyboard and mouse ports. You can tell the difference because the keyboard port is usually purple and the mouse port is usually green. Also, typically there are small graphics of a keyboard and mouse, respectively, imprinted next to the ports.

FIGURE 1.43   PS/2 keyboard and mouse ports

Centronics

The last type of port connector is the Centronics connector, a micro ribbon connector named for the Wang subsidiary that created it. It has a unique shape, as shown in Figure 1.44. It consists of a central connection bar surrounding by an outer shielding ring. The Centronics connector was primarily used in parallel printer connections and SCSI interfaces. It is most often found on peripherals, not on computers themselves (except in the case of some older SCSI interface cards).

FIGURE 1.44   A Centronics connector

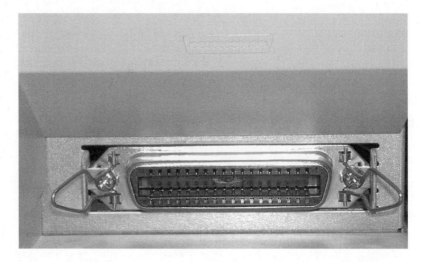

Common Peripheral Interfaces and Cables

An *interface* is a method of connecting two dissimilar items together. A peripheral interface is a method of connecting a peripheral or accessory to a computer, including the specification of cabling, connector and port type, speed, and method of communication used.

The most common interfaces used in PCs today include:

- Parallel
- Serial
- USB
- IEEE 1394 (FireWire)
- Infrared
- RCA
- PS/2

For each type, let's look at the cabling and connector used as well as the type(s) of peripherals that are connected.

Parallel

For many years, the most popular type of interface available on computers was the parallel interface. Parallel communications take the interstate approach to data communications. Normally, interstate travel is faster than driving on city roads. This is the case mainly because you can fit multiple cars going the same direction on the same highway by using multiple lanes. On the return trip, you take a similar path, but on a completely separate road. The *parallel interface* (an example is shown at the top of Figure 1.36) transfers data 8 bits at a time over eight separate transmit wires inside a parallel cable (one bit per wire). Normal parallel interfaces use a DB-25 female connector on the computer to transfer data to peripherals. Parallel was faster than the original serial technology, which was also once used for printers in electrically noisy environments or at greater distances from the computer, but the advent of USB has brought serial, fast serial, back to the limelight.

The most common use of the parallel interface is printer communication. There are three major types: standard, bidirectional, and enhanced parallel ports. Let's look at the differences between the three.

Standard Parallel Ports

The standard parallel port only transmits data *out* of the computer. It cannot receive data (except for a single wire carrying a Ready signal). This parallel port came with the original IBM PC, XT, and AT. It can transmit data at 150KBps and is commonly used to transmit data to printers. This technology also had a maximum transmission distance of 10 feet.

Bidirectional Parallel Ports

As its name suggests, the bidirectional parallel port has one important advantage over a standard parallel port: it can both transmit and receive data. These parallel ports are capable of interfacing with such devices as external CD-ROM drives and external parallel port backup drives (Zip, Jaz, and tape drives). Most computers made since 1994 have a bidirectional parallel port.

In order for bidirectional communication to occur properly, the cable must support bidirectional communication as well.

Enhanced Parallel Ports

As more people began using parallel ports to interface with devices other than printers, they started to notice that the available speed wasn't good enough. Double-speed CD-ROM drives had a transfer rate of 300KBps, but the parallel port could transfer data at only 150KBps, thus limiting the speed at which a computer could retrieve data from an external device. To solve that problem, the Institute of Electrical and Electronics Engineers (IEEE) came up with a standard for enhanced parallel ports called IEEE 1284. The IEEE 1284 standard provides for greater data transfer speeds and the ability to send memory addresses as well as data through a parallel port. This standard allows the parallel port to theoretically act as an extension to the main bus. In addition, these ports are backward compatible with the standard and bidirectional ports and support cable lengths of 4.5 meters, which is almost 15 feet.

There are two implementations of IEEE 1284: EPP parallel ports and ECP parallel ports. An enhanced parallel port (EPP) increases bidirectional throughput from 150KBps to anywhere from 600KBps to 1.5MBps. An enhanced capabilities port (ECP) is designed to transfer data at even higher speeds, around 2MBps. ECP uses direct memory access (DMA) and buffering to increase printing performance over EPP.

The cable must also have full support for IEEE 1284 in order for proper communications to occur in both directions and at rated speeds.

Parallel Interfaces and Cables

Most parallel interfaces use a DB-25 female connector, as shown earlier in this chapter. Most parallel cables use a DB-25 male connector on one end and either a DB-25 male connector or Centronics-36 connector on the other. The original printer cables typically used the DB-25M–to–Centronics-36 configuration. Inside a parallel cable, eight wires are used for transmitting data, so one byte can be transmitted at a time. Figure 1.45 shows an example of a typical parallel cable (in this case, a printer cable).

If a printer today uses a parallel port through which to connect to the computer, a possible interface on the printer is known as a mini-Centronics. Figure 1.46 shows the component end of a mini-Centronics cable. The mini-Centronics did not enjoy the success expected due to design issues regarding attachment reliability. Again, however, nothing is more popular today for printer connectivity than USB, so efforts to perpetuate the use of and improve the mini-Centronics were abandoned.

FIGURE 1.45   A typical parallel cable

FIGURE 1.46   The mini-Centronics connector

Serial

If standard parallel communications were similar to taking the interstate, then RS-232 serial communications were similar to taking a country road. In serial communications, bits of data are sent one after another (single file, if you will) down one wire, and they return on a different wire in the same cable. Three main types of serial interfaces are available today: standard serial, Universal Serial Bus (USB), and FireWire. USB and FireWire use increased signaling frequencies to overcome serial's stigma and join other serial technologies, such as PCIe and SATA, as frontrunners in data communications.

Standard Serial

Almost every computer made since the original IBM PC has at least one serial port. These computers are easily identified because they have either a DE-9 male or a DB-25 male port (shown in Figure 1.47). Standard serial ports have a maximum data transmission speed of 57Kbps and a maximum cable length of 50 feet.

Serial cables come in two common wiring configurations: standard serial cable and null modem serial cable. A standard serial cable is used to hook various peripherals such as modems and printers to a computer. A null modem serial cable is used to hook two computers together without a modem. The transmit wires on one end are wired to the receive pins on the other side, so it's as if a modem connection exists between the two computers but without the need for a modem. Figures 1.48 and 1.49 show the wiring differences (the *pinouts*) between a standard serial cable and a null modem cable. In the null modem diagram, notice how the transmit (tx) pins on one end are wired to the receive (rx) pins on the other.

FIGURE 1.47   Standard DE-9 and DB-25 male serial ports

FIGURE 1.48   A standard serial cable wiring diagram

```
                    Pin#              Pin#
                     2 ──────────────── 3
                     3 ──────────────── 2
      1      13       4 ──────────────── 7        5   1
     DB-25            5 ──────────────── 8      DB-9
     Male             6 ──────────────── 6      Female
                     7 ──────────────── 5
                     8 ──────────────── 1
                    20 ──────────────── 4
                    22 ──────────────── 9
```

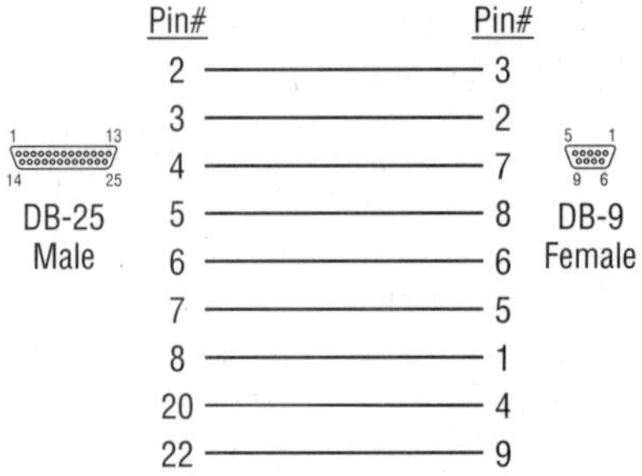

FIGURE 1.49   A null modem serial cable wiring diagram

```
                    Pin#              Pin#
                     5 ──────────────── 5
      5   1          2 ──────────────── 3        5   1
     DB-9            3 ──────────────── 2      DB-9
     Female          7 ──────────────── 8      Female
                     8 ──────────────── 7
                     6 ─┐           ┌── 4
                     1 ─┘           └── 6
                     4 ──────────────── 1
```

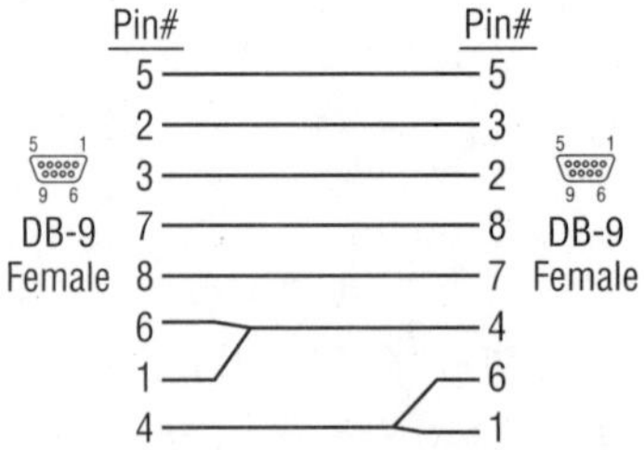

Finally, because of the two different device connectors (DE-9M and DB-25M), serial cables have a few different configurations. Table 1.4 shows the most common serial cable configurations.

TABLE 1.4   Common Serial Cable Configurations

1st Connector	2nd Connector	Description
DE-9 female	DB-25 male	Standard modem cable
DE-9 female	DE-9 male	Standard serial extension cable
DE-9 female	DE-9 female	Null modem cable
DB-25 female	DB-25 female	Null modem cable
DB-25 female	DB-25 male	Standard serial cable or standard serial extension cable

Universal Serial Bus (USB)

USB cables are used to connect a wide variety of peripherals to computers, including keyboards, mice, digital cameras, printers, and scanners. The latest version of USB, version 2.0, requires a cable with better shielding than did earlier versions. Not all USB cables work with USB 2.0 ports. The connectors are identical, so perhaps look for cables that are transparent with a view to the silver metallic shielding within.

USB's simplicity of use and ease of expansion make it an excellent interface for just about any kind of peripheral. This fact alone makes the USB interface one of the most popular on the modern computer, perhaps behind only the video, input, and network connectors.

The USB interface is fairly straightforward. Essentially, it was designed to be Plug and Play—just plug in the peripheral, and it should work (providing the software is installed to support it). The USB cable varies based on the USB male connector on each end. Because there can be quite a number of daisy-chained USB devices on a single system, it helps to have a scheme to clarify their connectivity. The USB standard specifies two broad types of connectors. They are designated Type A and Type B connectors. A standard USB cable has some form of Type A connector on one end and some form of Type B connector on the other end. Figure 1.50 shows four USB cable connectors. From left to right, they are:

- Type A
- Standard Mini-B
- Type B
- Alternate Mini-B

One part of the USB interface specification that makes it so appealing is the fact that if your computer runs out of USB ports, you can simply plug a device known as a *USB hub* into one of your computer's USB ports, which will give you several more USB ports from one USB port. Figure 1.51 shows an example of a USB hub.

Be aware of the limitations in the USB specification. The commonly quoted length limit for USB cables is 5 meters. If you use hubs, you should not use more than 5 hubs between any two components.

Through the use of a 7-bit identifier, overall, no more than 127 devices, including hubs, should be connected back to a single USB host controller in the computer, not that you would ever want to approach this number. The 128th identifier is used for broadcasting. No interconnection of host controllers is allowed with USB; each one and its connected devices are isolated from other controllers and their devices. As a result, USB ports are not considered networkable ports. Consult your system's documentation to find out if your USB ports operate on the same host controller.

From the perspective of the cable's plug, Type A is always oriented toward the system from the component. As a result, you might notice that the USB receptacle on the computer system that a component cables back to is the same as the receptacle on the USB hub that components cable back to. The USB hub is simply an extension of the system and becomes a component that cables back to the system.

FIGURE 1.50   USB cables and connectors

FIGURE 1.51   A USB hub

Type B plugs connect in the direction of the component. Therefore, you see a Type B interface on the hub as well as on the end devices to allow them to cable back to the system or another hub. Although they exist, USB cables with both ends of the same type, a sort of extension cable, are in violation of the USB specification. Collectively, these rules make cabling your USB subsystem quite straightforward.

Although the system receptacle, the Type A, remains somewhat of a constant, the component receptacle often differs, usually based on the size of the USB device. For example, a USB-attached printer is large enough for a Type B connector, but a compact digital camera might only be large enough to accommodate a Mini-B receptacle of some sort. While the standard calls for one Mini-B connector, others have been developed, some common, others a bit rarer. The four connectors shown in Figure 1.50 are the most common. You might also run across older, rare Mini-A connectors or newer small-form factor interfaces, called Micro-A and Micro-B, none of which are discussed further in this book.

USB connectors are keyed and will go into a USB port only one way. If the connector will not go into the port properly, try rotating it.

For more information on USB, check out http://www.usb.org.

IEEE 1394 (FireWire)

The IEEE 1394 interface is about one thing: speed. Its first iteration, now known as FireWire 400, has a maximum data throughput of 400Mbps in half duplex. The next iteration, FireWire 800 (specified under IEEE 1394b), has a maximum data throughput of 800Mbps and works in full duplex. FireWire 400 carries data over a maximum cable length of 4.5 meters with a maximum of 63 devices connected to each interface on the computer. Using new beta connectors and associated cabling, including a fiber-optic solution, FireWire 800 extends to 100 meters. IEEE 1394c proposes to run FireWire over the same Category 5e infrastructure that supports Ethernet, including the use of RJ-45 connectors.

FireWire (also known as i.LINK in Sony's parlance) uses a very special type of cable, as shown in Figure 1.52 for FireWire 400. Notice the difference in the system end on the left and the component end on the right. It is difficult to mistake this cable for anything but a FireWire cable. The beta connector of a FireWire 800 cable is equally distinctive.

Although most people think of FireWire as a tool for connecting their digital camcorders to their computers, it's much more than that. Because of its high data transfer rate, it is being used more and more as a universal, high-speed data interface for things like hard drives, optical drives, and digital video editing equipment.

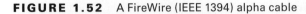

FIGURE 1.52   A FireWire (IEEE 1394) alpha cable

Because the FireWire specification was conceived to allow peripherals to be networked together in much the same fashion as intelligent hosts are networked together in LANs and WANs, a quick introduction to the concept of networking is in order; see Chapter 10 for more detail on networking concepts. A *topology* can be thought of as the layout of the nodes that make up the endpoints and connecting devices of the network. One of the most popular topologies today is the *star topology*, which uses a central concentrating device that is cabled directly to the endpoints. A *tree* structure is formed when these concentrating devices are interconnected to one another, each attached to their own set of endpoints. One or few concentrators appear at the first tier of the tree, sort of like the "root system" of the tree. These root devices are expected to carry more traffic than other concentrators because of their position in the hierarchy. In subsequent tiers, other concentrators branch off from the root and each other to complete the tree analogy.

The 1995 IEEE 1394 specification that is equivalent to FireWire 400 allows 1,023 buses, each supporting 63 devices, to be bridged together. This networkable architecture supports over 64,000 interconnected devices that can communicate directly with one another instead of communicating through a host computer the way USB is required to do. Star and tree topologies can be formed, as long as no two devices are separated by more than 16 hops. A *hop* can be thought of as a link between any two end devices, repeaters, or bridges, resulting in a total maximum distance between devices of 72 meters. Through an internal hub, a single end device can use two IEEE 1394 ports to connect to two different devices, creating a daisy-chained pathway that allows the other two devices to communicate with one another as well. The device in the middle affords a physical pathway between the other two devices but is not otherwise involved in their communication with one another.

RCA

The RCA cable is simple. There are two connectors, usually male, one on each end of the cable. The male connector connects to the female connector on the equipment. Figure 1.53 shows an example of an RCA cable. An RCA male-to-RCA female connector is also available; it's used to extend the reach of audio or video signals.

FIGURE 1.53   An RCA cable

The RCA male connectors on a connection cable are sometimes plated in gold to increase their corrosion resistance and to improve longevity.

PS/2 (Keyboard and Mouse)

The final interface we'll discuss is the PS/2 interface for mice and keyboards. Essentially, it is the same connector for the cables from both items: a male mini-DIN 6 connector. Most keyboards today still use the PS/2 interface, whereas most mice are gravitating toward the USB interface (especially optical mice). However, mice that have USB cables still may include a special USB-to-PS/2 adapter so they can be used with the PS/2 interface. Figure 1.54 shows an example of a PS/2 keyboard cable.

FIGURE 1.54   A PS/2 keyboard cable

Most often, PS/2 cables have only one connector, because the other end is connected directly to the device being plugged in. The only exception is PS/2 extension cables used to extend the length of a PS/2 device's cable.

Identifying Purposes and Characteristics of Cooling Systems

It's a basic concept of physics: electronic components turn electricity into work and heat. The heat must be dissipated or the excess heat will shorten the life of the components. In some cases (like the CPU), the component will produce so much heat that it can destroy itself in a matter of seconds if there is not some way to remove this extra heat.

Most PCs use air-cooling methods to cool their internal components. With air cooling, the movement of air removes the heat from the component. Sometimes, large blocks of metal called heat sinks are attached to a heat-producing component in order to dissipate the heat more rapidly.

Fans

When you turn on a computer, you will often hear lots of whirring. Contrary to popular opinion, the majority of the noise isn't coming from the hard disk (unless it's about to go bad). Most of this noise is coming from the various fans inside the computer. Fans provide airflow within the computer.

Most PCs have a combination of these six fans:

Front intake fan   This fan is used to bring fresh, cool air into the computer for cooling purposes.

Rear exhaust fan   This fan is used to take hot air out of the case.

Power supply exhaust fan   This fan is usually found at the back of the power supply and is used to cool the power supply. In addition, this fan draws air from inside the case into vents in the power supply. This pulls hot air through the power supply so that it can be blown out of the case. The front intake fan assists with this airflow. The rear exhaust fan supplements the power supply fan to achieve the same result outside of the power supply.

CPU fan   This fan is used to cool the processor. Typically, this fan is attached to a large heat sink, which is in turn attached directly to the processor.

Chipset fan   Some motherboard manufacturers replaced the heat sink on their onboard chipset with a heat sink and fan combination as the chipset became more advanced. This fan aids in the cooling of the onboard chipset (especially useful when overclocking).

Video card chipset fan   As video cards get more complex and have higher performance, more video cards have cooling fans directly attached. Despite their name, these fans don't attach to a chipset in the same sense as a chipset on a motherboard. The chipset here is the set of chips mounted on the adapter, including the graphics processing unit (GPU) and graphics memory.

Memory module fan   The more capable our memory becomes of keeping up with our CPU, the hotter it runs. As an extra measure of safety, regardless of the presence of heat spreaders on the modules, an optional fan setup for your memory might be in order. See the following section for more.

Ideally, the airflow inside a computer should resemble what is shown in Figure 1.55.

FIGURE 1.55   System-unit Airflow

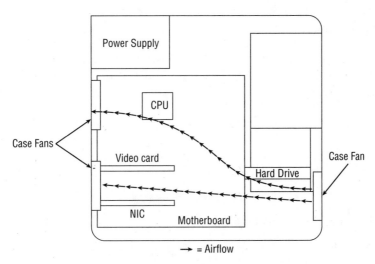

→ = Airflow

Note that you must pay attention to the orientation of the power supply's airflow. If the power supply fan is an exhaust fan, as assumed in this discussion, the front and rear fans will match their earlier descriptions: front, intake; rear, exhaust. If you run across a power supply that has an intake fan, the orientation of the supplemental chassis fans should be reversed as well. The rear chassis fan(s) should always be installed in the same orientation as the power supply fan runs to avoid creating a small airflow circuit that circumvents the cross-flow of air through the case. The front chassis fan should always be installed in the reverse orientation of the rear fans to avoid fighting against them and reducing the internal airflow. Reversing supplemental chassis fans is usually no harder than removing four screws and flipping the fan. Sometimes, the fan might just snap out, flip, and then snap back in, depending on the way it is rigged up.

Memory Cooling

If you are going to start overclocking your computer, you will want to do everything in your power to cool all the components in your computer, and that includes the memory.

There are two methods of cooling memory: passive and active. The passive memory cooling method just uses the ambient case airflow to cool the memory through the use of enhanced heat dissipation. For this, you can buy either heat sinks or, as mentioned earlier, special "for memory chips only" devices known as heat spreaders. These are special aluminum or copper housings that wrap around memory chips and conduct the heat away from the memory chips.

Active cooling, on the other hand, usually involves forcing some kind of cooling medium (air or water) around the RAM chips themselves or around their heat sinks. Most often, active cooling methods are just high-speed fans directing air right over a set of heat spreaders.

Hard Drive Cooling

You might be thinking, "Hey, my hard drive is working all the time. Is there anything I can do to cool it off as well?" There are both active and passive cooling devices for hard drives. Most common, however, is the active cooling bay. You install a hard drive in a special device that fits into a 5¼″ expansion bay. This device contains fans that draw in cool air over the hard drive, thus cooling it. Figure 1.56 shows an example of one of these active hard drive coolers. As you might suspect, you can also get heat sinks for hard drives.

FIGURE 1.56   An active hard disk cooler

Chipset Cooling

Every motherboard has a chip or chipset that controls how the computer operates. As with other chips in the computer, the chipset is normally cooled by the ambient air movement in the case. However, when you overclock a computer, the chipset may need to be cooled more as it is working harder than it normally would be. Therefore, it is often desirable to replace the onboard chipset cooler with a more efficient one. Refer back to Figure 1.4 for a look at a modern chipset cooling solution.

CPU Cooling

Probably the greatest challenge in cooling is the cooling of the computer's CPU. It is the component that generates the most heat in a computer. As a matter of fact, if a modern processor isn't actively cooled all the time, it will generate enough heat to burn itself up in an instant. That's why most motherboards have an internal CPU heat sensor and a CPU_FAN sensor. If no cooling fan is active, these devices will shut down the computer before damage occurs.

There are a few different types of CPU cooling methods, but the most important can be grouped into two broad categories: air cooling and advanced cooling methods.

Air Cooling

The parts inside most computers are cooled by air moving through the case. The CPU is no exception. However, because of the large amount of heat produced, the CPU must have (proportionately) the largest surface area exposed to the moving air in the case. Therefore, the heat sinks on the CPU are the largest of any inside the computer.

This fan often blows air down through the body of the heat sink to force the heat into the ambient internal air where it can join the airflow circuit for removal from the case. However, the latest trend, in support of high-end processors, is a redesign of the classic heat sink. The heat sink extends up farther, using radiator-type fins, and the fan is placed at a right angle and to the side of the heat sink. This design moves the heat away from the heat sink immediately, instead of pushing the air down through the heat sink. CPU fans can be purchased that have an adjustable rheostat to allow you to dial in as little airflow as you need, aiding in noise reduction but potentially leading to accidental overheating.

It should be noted that the highest-performing CPU coolers use copper plates in direct contact with the CPU. They also use high-speed and high-CFM cooling fans to dissipate the heat produced by the processor. CFM is short for cubic feet per minute, an airflow measurement of the volume of air that passes by a stationary object per minute.

Most new CPU heat sinks use tubing to transfer heat away from the CPU. With any cooling system, the more surface area exposed to the cooling method, the better the cooling. Plus, the heat pipes can be used to transfer heat to a location away from the heat source before cooling. This is especially useful in small-form factor cases and laptops, where open space is limited.

With advanced heat sinks and CPU cooling methods like this, it is important to improve the thermal transfer efficiency as much as possible. To that end, cooling engineers came up with a compound that helps to bridge the extremely small gaps between the CPU and the heat sink, which avoids superheated pockets of air that can lead to focal damage of the CPU. This product is known as thermal transfer compound or simply thermal compound (alternatively, thermal grease or thermal paste) and can be bought in small tubes. Single-use tubes alleviate the guessing involved with how much you should apply. Watch out, though; this stuff makes quite a mess and doesn't want to come off your fingers very easily.

Apply the compound by placing a bead in the center of the heat sink, not on the CPU because some heat sinks don't cover the entire CPU package. That might sound like an issue, but some CPUs don't have heat-producing components all the way out to the edges. Some CPUs even have a raised area directly over where the silicon die is within the packaging, resulting in a smaller contact area between the components. You should apply less than you think you need because the pressure of attaching the heat sink to the CPU will spread the compound across the entire surface in a very thin layer. It's advisable to use a clean, lint-free applicator of your choosing to spread the compound around a bit as well, just to get the spreading started. You don't need to concern yourself with spreading it too thoroughly or too neatly because the pressure applied during attachment will equalize the compound quite well. During attachment, watch for oozing compound around the edges, clean it off immediately, and use less next time.

Improving and Maintaining CPU Cooling

In addition to using thermal compound, you can enhance the cooling efficiency of a CPU heat sink by lapping the heat sink, which smoothes the mating surface using a very fine sanding element, about 1000-grit in the finishing stage. Some vendors of the more expensive heat sinks will offer this service as an add-on.

If your CPU has been in service for an extended period of time, perhaps three years or more, it is a smart idea to remove the heat sink and old thermal compound and then apply fresh thermal compound and reattach the heat sink. Be careful, though; if your thermal paste has already turned into thermal "glue," you can wrench the processor right out of the socket, even with the release mechanism locked in place. Invariably, this damages the pins on the chip.

Counterintuitively, perhaps, you can remove a released heat sink from the processor by gently rotating the heat sink to break the paste's seal. If the CPU has risen in the socket already, however, this would be an extremely bad idea. Sometimes, after you realize that the CPU has risen a bit and that you need to release the mechanism holding it in to reseat it, you find the release arm is not accessible with the heat sink in place. This is an unfortunate predicament that will present plenty of opportunity to learn.

If you've ever installed a brand-new heat sink onto a CPU, you've most likely used thermal compound or the thermal compound patch that was already applied to the heat sink for you. If your new heat sink has a patch of thermal compound preapplied, don't add more. If you ever remove the heat sink, don't try to reuse the patch or any other form of thermal compound. Clean it all off and start fresh.

Advanced CPU Cooling Methods

Advancements in air cooling have led to products like the Scythe Ninja 2, which is a stack of thin aluminum fins with copper tubing running up through them. Some of the hottest-running CPUs can be passively cooled with a device like this, using only the existing air-movement scheme from your computer's case. Adding a fan to the side, however, adds to the cooling efficiency, but also to the noise level.

In addition to standard and advanced air-cooling methods, there are other methods of cooling a CPU (and other chips as well). These methods might appear somewhat unorthodox but often deliver extreme results.

These methods can also result in permanent damage to your computer, so try them at your own risk.

Liquid Cooling

Liquid cooling is a technology whereby a special water block is used to conduct heat away from the processor (as well as from the chipset). Water is circulated through this block to a radiator, where it is cooled.

The theory is that you could achieve better cooling performance through the use of liquid cooling. For the most part, this is true. However, with traditional cooling methods (which use air and water), the lowest temperature you can achieve is room temperature. Plus, with liquid cooling, the pump is submerged in the coolant (generally speaking), so as it works, it produces heat, which adds to the overall liquid temperature.

The main benefit to liquid cooling is silence. There is only one fan needed: the fan on the radiator to cool the water. So a liquid-cooled system can run extremely quietly.

Liquid cooling, while more efficient than air cooling and much quieter, has its drawbacks. Most liquid-cooling systems are more expensive than supplemental fan sets, and require less familiar components, such as reservoir, pump, water block(s), hose, and radiator.

The relative complexity of installing liquid cooling systems, coupled with the perceived danger of liquids in close proximity to electronics, leads most computer owners to consider liquid cooling a novelty or a liability. The primary market for liquid cooling is the high-performance niche that engages in overclocking to some degree. However, developments in active air cooling, including extensive piping of heat away from the body of the heat sink, have kept advanced cooling methods out of the forefront.

Heat Pipes

Heat pipes are closed systems that employ some form of tubing filled with a liquid suitable for the applicable temperature range. Pure physics are used with this technology to achieve cooling to ambient temperatures; no outside mechanism is used. One end of the heat pipe is heated by the component being cooled. This causes the liquid at the heated end to evaporate and increase the relative pressure at that end of the heat pipe with respect to the cooler end. This pressure imbalance causes the heated vapor to equalize the pressure by migrating to the cooler end, where the vapor condenses and releases its heat, warming the nonheated end of the pipe. The cooler environment surrounding this end transfers the heat away from the pipe by convection. The condensed liquid drifts to the pipe's walls and is drawn back to the heated end of the heat pipe by gravity or by a wicking material or texture that lines the inside of the pipe. Once the liquid returns, the process repeats.

Peltier Cooling Devices

Water- and air-cooling devices are extremely effective by themselves, but they are more effective when used with a device known as a Peltier cooling element. These devices, also known as thermoelectric coolers (TECs), facilitate the transfer of heat from one side of the element, made of one material, to the other side, made of a different material. Thus, they have a hot side and a cold side. The cold side should always be against the CPU surface, and optimally, the hot side should be mated with a heat sink or water block for heat dissipation. Consequently, TECs are not meant to replace air-cooling mechanisms but to complement them.

One of the downsides to TECs is the likelihood of condensation because of the sub-ambient temperatures these devices produce. Closed-cell foams can be used to guard against damage from condensation.

Phase-Change Cooling

There is one new type of PC cooling that is just starting to be seen: phase-change cooling. With this type of cooling, the cooling effect from the change of a liquid to a gas is used to cool the inside of a PC. It is a very expensive method of cooling, but it does work. Most often, external air-conditioner-like pumps, coils, and evaporators cool the coolant, which is sent, ice cold, to the heat sink blocks on the processor and chipset. Think of it as a water-cooling system that chills the water below room temperature. It is possible to get CPU temps in the range of −4°F (−20°C). Normal CPU temperatures hover between 104°F and 122°F (40°C and 50°C).

The major drawback to this method is that in higher-humidity conditions, condensation can be a problem. The moisture from the air condenses on the heat sink and can run off onto and under the processor, thus shorting out the electronics. Designers of phase-change cooling systems offer solutions to help ensure this isn't a problem. Products in the form of foam; silicone adhesive; and greaseless, non-curing adhesives are available to seal the surface and perimeter of the processor. Additionally, manufacturers sell gaskets and shims that correspond to specific processors, all designed to protect your delicate and expensive components from damage.

Liquid Nitrogen and Helium Cooling

In the interest of completeness, there is a novel approach to super-cooling processors that is ill-advised under all but the most extreme circumstances. By filling a vessel placed over the component to be cooled with a liquid form of nitrogen or, for an even more intense effect, helium, temperatures from −100 to −240 degrees Celsius can be achieved. The results are short-lived and only useful in overclocking with a view to setting records. The processor is not likely to survive the incident, due to the internal stress from the extreme temperature changes.

Summary

In this chapter, we took a tour of the system components of a PC. You learned about some of the elements that make up a PC. You'll learn about others in the next two chapters. In addition, we discussed common peripheral ports and cables and their appearance. Finally, you learned about the various methods used for cooling a PC. You also saw what many of these items look like and how they function.

Exam Essentials

Know the types of system boards.   Know the characteristics of and differences between ATX, micro ATX, NLX, and BTX motherboards.

Know the components of a motherboard.   Be able to describe motherboard components, such as chipsets, expansion slots, memory slots, and external cache; CPU and processor slots or sockets; power connectors; onboard disk drive connectors; keyboard connectors; peripheral ports and connectors; BIOS (firmware) chips; CMOS batteries; jumpers; and DIP switches.

Understand the purposes and characteristics of processors.   Be able to discuss the different processor packaging, old and new, and know the meaning of the terms hyperthreading, multi-core, throttling, microcode, overclocking, cache, speed, and system bus width.

Understand the purposes and characteristics of memory.   Know about the characteristics that set the various types of memory apart from one another. This includes the actual types of memory, such as DRAM, which includes several varieties, SRAM, ROM, and CMOS, as well as memory packaging, such as SIMMs, DIMMs, RIMMs, SODIMMS, and MicroDIMMs. Also have a firm understanding of the different levels of cache memory as well as its purpose in general.

Understand the purposes and characteristics of adapter cards and their ports and cables.   Familiarize yourself with the variety of expansion cards and integrated components in today's computer systems, as well as the ports they use and any cables that connect to external devices.

Understand the purposes and characteristics of cooling systems.   Know the different ways that internal components can be cooled and how overheating can be prevented.

Review Questions

1. Which computer component contains all the circuitry necessary for other components or devices to communicate with one another?

    A. Motherboard

    B. Adapter card

    C. Hard drive

    D. Expansion bus

2. Which packaging is used for DDR SDRAM memory?

    A. 168-pin DIMM

    B. 72-pin SIMM

    C. 184-pin DIMM

    D. RIMM

3. What memory chips would you find on a stick of PC3-16000?

    A. DDR-2000

    B. DDR3-2000

    C. DDR3-16000

    D. PC3-2000

4. Which motherboard design style is most widely implemented?

    A. ATX

    B. AT

    C. Baby AT

    D. NLX

5. Which motherboard socket type is used on the Pentium 4 chip?

    A. Slot 1

    B. Socket A

    C. Socket 370

    D. Socket 478

6. Which of the following is a socket technology that is designed to ease insertion of modern CPUs?

    A. Socket 479

    B. ZIF

    C. LPGA

    D. SPGA

7. Which of the following is *not* controlled by the Northbridge?

  A. PCIe

  B. SATA

  C. AGP

  D. Cache memory

8. Which of the following is used to store data and programs for repeated use? Information can be added and deleted at will, and it does *not* lose its data when power is removed.

  A. Hard drive

  B. RAM

  C. Internal cache memory

  D. ROM

9. Which motherboard socket type is used with the AMD Athlon XP?

  A. Slot 1

  B. Socket A

  C. Socket 370

  D. Socket 478

10. You want to plug a keyboard into the back of a computer. You know that you need to plug the keyboard cable into a PS/2 port. Which style of port is the PS/2?

  A. RJ-11

  B. DE9

  C. DIN 5

  D. Mini-DIN 6

11. Which of the following are the numbers of pins that can be found on DIMM modules used in desktop motherboards? (Choose three.)

  A. 168

  B. 180

  C. 184

  D. 200

  E. 204

  F. 232

  G. 240

12. What is the maximum speed of USB 2.0 in Mbps?

  A. 1.5

  B. 12

  C. 60

  D. 480

13. Which of the following standards are specified by IEEE 1284? (Choose two.)

   A. SPP

   B. RS-232

   C. EPP

   D. ECP

   E. FireWire

   F. USB

14. What peripheral port type was originally developed by Apple and is currently the optimal interface for digital video transfers?

   A. DVD

   B. USB

   C. IEEE 1394

   D. IEEE 1284

15. What peripheral port type is expandable using a hub, operates at 1.5MBps, and is used to connect various devices (from printers to cameras) to PCs?

   A. DVD 1.0

   B. USB 1.1

   C. IEEE 1394

   D. IEEE 1284

16. Which peripheral port type was designed to transfer data at high speeds over a D-sub interface?

   A. DVD

   B. USB

   C. IEEE 1394

   D. IEEE 1284

17. Which motherboard form factor places expansion slots on a special riser card and is used in low-profile PCs?

   A. AT

   B. Baby AT

   C. ATX

   D. NLX

18. Which Intel processor type might be mounted on a SECC for motherboard installation?

   A. Athlon

   B. 486

   C. Pentium

   D. Pentium II

19. You have just purchased a motherboard that has an LGA775 socket for an Intel Pentium 4 processor. What type of memory modules will you need for this motherboard?

    A. DIP

    B. SIMM

    C. RIMM

    D. DIMM

20. What type of expansion slot is preferred today for high-performance graphics adapters?

    A. AGP

    B. PCIe

    C. PCI

    D. ISA

Answers to Review Questions

1. A. The spine of the computer is the system board, otherwise known as the motherboard. On the motherboard you will find the CPU, underlying circuitry, expansion slots, video components, RAM slots, and various other chips.

2. C. DDR SDRAM is manufactured on a 184-pin DIMM. DIMMs with 168 pins were used for SDR SDRAM. The SIMM is the predecessor to the DIMM, on which SDRAM was never deployed. RIMM is the Rambus proprietary competitor for the DIMM that carries DRDRAM instead of SDRAM.

3. B. Remember the 8:1 rule. Modules greater than, but not including, SDR SDRAM are named with a number 8 times larger than the number used to name the chips on the module. The initials *PC* are used to describe the module, the initials *DDR* for the chips, and a number to represent the level of DDR. The lack of a number represents DDR, as long as the associated number is greater than 133. Otherwise, you're dealing with SDR. This means that PC3-16000 modules are DDR3 modules and are populated with chips named DDR3 and a number that is ⅛ of the module's numeric code: 2000.

4. A. Although all the motherboard design styles listed are in use today, the ATX motherboard style (and its derivatives) is the most popular design.

5. D. Most Pentium 4 chips use the Socket 478 motherboard CPU socket, although not exclusively. Nevertheless, no other option listed is used for these processors.

6. B. ZIF sockets are designed with a locking mechanism that, when released, alleviates the resistance of the socket to receiving the pins of the chip being inserted. Make sure you know your socket types so that the appearance of a specific model, such as Socket 479, in a question like this does not distract you from the correct answer. Only LGA would be another acceptable answer to this question because, with a lack of pin receptacles, there is no insertion resistance. However, no other pin-layout format, such as SPGA, addresses issues with inserting chips. LPGA might have evoked an image of LGA, leading you to that answer, but that term means nothing outside of the golfing community.

7. B. The Northbridge is in control of the local-bus components that share the clock of the frontside bus. SATA and all other drive interfaces do not share this clock and are controlled by the Southbridge.

8. A. A hard drive stores data on a magnetic medium, which does not lose its information after the power is removed, and which can be repeatedly written to and erased.

9. B. The Socket A (remember *A* for AMD) motherboard socket is used primarily with AMD processors, including the Athlon XP.

10. D. A PS/2 port is also known as a mini-DIN 6 connector.

11. **A, C, G.** DIMMs used in desktop-motherboard applications have one of three possible pin counts. SDR SDRAM is implemented on 168-pin modules. DDR SDRAM and 16-bit RIMMs are implemented on 184-pin modules. DDR2 and DDR3 are implemented on 240-pin modules with different keying. Dual-channel RIMM modules have 232 pins. Modules with 200 and 204 pins are used in the SODIMM line, and there are no modules with 180 pins.

12. **D.** The USB 2.0 spec provides for a maximum speed of 480 megabits per second (Mbps— not megabytes per second, or MBps).

13. **C, D.** Bidirectional parallel ports can both transmit and receive data. EPP and ECP are IEEE-1284 standards that were designed to transfer data at high speeds in both directions so that devices could return status information to the system. The standard parallel port only transmits data out of the computer. It cannot receive data. FireWire is specified by IEEE 1394. IEEE 1284 does not specify serial protocols, such as RS-232 and USB.

14. **C.** The 1394 standard provides for greater data transfer speeds and the ability to send memory addresses as well as data through a serial port.

15. **B.** USBs are used to connect multiple peripherals to one computer through a single port. They support data transfer rates as high as 12Mbps, or 1.5MBps (for USB 1.1, which is the option listed here).

16. **D.** IEEE 1284 standard defines the ECP parallel port to use a DMA channel and the buffer to be able to transfer data at high speeds to printers.

17. **D.** The NLX form factor places expansion slots on a special riser card and is used in low-profile PCs.

18. **D.** The unique thing about the Pentium II is that it was attached to a single edge contact cartridge (SECC) for insertion into the motherboard, instead of the standard PGA package. Athlon is an AMD processor, the early version of which was slot-based, but not considered SECC, in any event.

19. **D.** Pentium 4 processors are always mated with memory mounted on DIMMs.

20. **B.** Although technically all slots listed could be used for video adapters, PCIe excels when compared to the other options and offers technologies, such as SLI, which only make PCIe's advantage more noticeable.

Chapter 2

Storage Devices, Power Supplies, and Adapters

THE FOLLOWING COMPTIA A+ ESSENTIALS EXAM OBJECTIVES ARE COVERED IN THIS CHAPTER:

✓ **1.1 Categorize storage devices and backup media**

- FDD
- HDD
    - Solid state vs. magnetic
- Optical drives
    - CD / DVD / RW / Blu-Ray
- Removable storage
    - Tape drive
    - Solid state (e.g. thumb drive, flash, SD cards, USB)
    - External CD-RW and hard drive
    - Hot swappable devices and non-hot swappable devices

✓ **1.2 Explain motherboard components, types and features**

- PATA
    - IDE
    - EIDE
- SATA, eSATA
- Contrast RAID (levels 0, 1, 5)

✓ **1.3 Classify power supplies types and characteristics**

- AC adapter
- ATX proprietary

- Voltage, wattage and capacity
- Voltage selector switch
- Pins (20, 24)

✓ 1.8 Install and configure peripherals and input devices

- Mouse
- Keyboard
- Bar code reader
- Multimedia (e.g. web and digital cameras, MIDI, micro-phones)
- Biometric devices
- Touch screen
- KVM switch

✓ 1.9 Summarize the function and types of adapter cards

- Video
  - PCI
  - PCIe
  - AGP
- Multimedia
  - Sound card
  - TV tuner cards
  - Capture cards
- I/O
  - SCSI
  - Serial
  - USB
  - Parallel
- Communications
  - NIC
  - Modem

As a PC technician, you need to know quite a bit about hardware. Given the importance and magnitude of this knowledge, the best way to approach it is in sections. The first chapter introduced the topic, and this chapter follows up where it left off. Specifically, this chapter focuses on storage devices, power supplies, and expansion adapters.

Identifying Purposes and Characteristics of Storage Devices

What good is a computer without a place to put everything? Storage media hold the data being accessed, as well as the files the system needs to operate and data that needs to be saved. The many different types of storage differ in terms of their capacity (how much they can store), access time (how fast the computer can access the information), and the physical type of media used.

Hard Disk Drive Systems

Hard disk drive (HDD) systems (hard disks or hard drives for short) are used for permanent storage and quick access. Hard disks typically reside inside the computer, where they are semipermanently mounted with no external access (although there are external and removable hard drives), and can hold more information than other forms of storage.

The hard disk drive system contains three critical components:

Controller This component controls the drive. The controller chip controls how the drive operates, sends signals to the various motors in the disk, and receives signals from the sensors inside the drive. Most of today's hard disk technologies incorporate the controller and drive into one enclosure. The most common and well-known of these are PATA and SATA. You can read more about these technologies later in this chapter as well as in Chapter 13, "Installing, Maintaining, and Troubleshooting Hardware."

Hard disk This is the physical storage medium. Hard disk drive systems store information on small discs (from under one inch to five inches in diameter), also called *platters*, stacked together and placed in an enclosure.

Host adapter This is the translator, converting signals from the hard drive and controller to signals the computer can understand. Most motherboards today incorporate the host adapter into the motherboard's circuitry, offering headers for drive-cable connection. Legacy host adapters and certain modern adapters house the hard drive controller circuitry.

Figure 2.1 shows a hard disk drive and host adapter. The hard drive controller is integrated into the drive in this case, but could be resident on the host adapter in other hard drive technologies.

FIGURE 2.1   A hard disk drive system

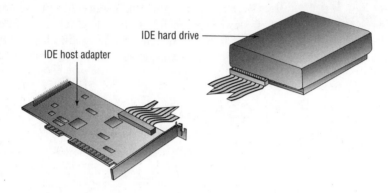

Anatomy of a Hard Drive

A hard drive is constructed in a cleanroom to avoid the introduction of contaminants into the hermetically sealed drive casing. Once it's sealed, most manufacturers seal one or more of the screws, thus sealing the casing with a warning sticker that removal of or damage to the seal will result in voiding the drive's warranty. Even some of the smallest contaminants can damage the precision components if allowed inside the hard drive's external shell.

Inside the sealed case of the hard drive lie one or more platters, where the actual data are stored by the read/write heads. The heads are mounted on a mechanism that moves them in tandem across both surfaces of all platters. Older drives used a stepper motor to position the heads at discrete points along the surface of the platters. Newer drives use voice coils for a more analog movement, resulting in reduced data loss because the circuitry can sense where the data is located through a servo scheme, even if the data shifts due to changes in physical disc geometry.

Factory preparation for newer drives or low-level formatting in the field for legacy drives map the inherent flaws of the platters so that the drive controllers know not to place data in these compromised locations. Additionally, this phase in drive preparation creates the magnetic domains that represent the smallest units of storage on the discs' platters, the *sector*. Magnetic-drive sectors commonly store only 512 bytes of data each. Sectors are created only after concentric rings, or *tracks*, are drawn magnetically around the surface of the platters. Sectors are then delineated within each of the tracks.

The capacity of a hard drive is a function of the number of sectors it contains. The controller for the hard drive knows exactly how the sectors are laid out within the disk assembly. It takes direction from the BIOS when writing information to and reading information from the drive. The BIOS, however, does not always understand the actual geometry of the drive. For example, the BIOS does not support more than 63 sectors per track. Nevertheless, many hard drives have tracks that contain many more than 63 sectors per track. As a result, a translation must occur from where the BIOS believes it is directing information to be written to where the information is actually written by the controller. When the BIOS detects the geometry of the drive, it is because the controller reports dimensions the BIOS can understand. The same sort of trickery occurs when the BIOS reports to the operating system a linear address space for the operating system to use when requesting data be written to or read from the drive through the BIOS.

The basic hard disk geometry consists of three components: the number of sectors that each track contains, the number of read/write heads in the disk assembly, and the number of cylinders in the assembly. This set of values is known as CHS (for cylinders/heads/sectors). A *cylinder* is the number of tracks that can be found on any single surface of any single platter. It is called a cylinder because the collection of all same-number tracks on all writable surfaces of the hard disk assembly looks like a geometric cylinder when connected together vertically. Therefore, cylinder 1, for instance, on an assembly that contains three platters comprises six tracks (one on each side of each platter), each labeled track 1 on its respective surface. Figure 2.2 illustrates the key terms presented in this discussion.

FIGURE 2.2   Anatomy of a hard drive

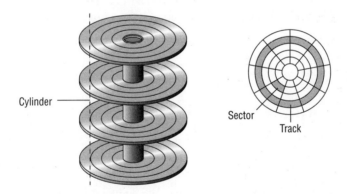

Because the number of cylinders indicates only the number of tracks on any one writable surface in the assembly, the number of writable surfaces must be factored into the equation to produce the total number of tracks in the entire assembly. This is where the number of heads comes in. There is a single head dedicated to each writable surface, two per platter. By multiplying the number of cylinders by the number of heads, you produce the total number of tracks throughout the disk assembly. By multiplying the number of sectors per track, you discover the total number of sectors throughout the disk assembly. Dividing the result by 2 provides the number of KB the hard drive can store. This works because each sector holds 512 bytes, which is equivalent to ½KB. Each time you divide the result by 1024, you obtain a smaller number, but the unit of measure increases from KB to MB, from MB to GB, and so on.

File systems laid down on the tracks and their sectors routinely group a configurable number of sectors into equal or larger sets called *clusters* or *allocation units*. This concept exists because operating system designers have to settle on a finite number of addressable units of storage and a fixed number of bits to address them uniquely. Because the units of storage can vary in size, however, the maximum amount of a drive's storage capacity can vary accordingly, but not unless drive capacities in excess of 2TB are implemented. Be aware that volumes created with RAID (see Chapter 13) can certainly exceed 2TB.

No two files are allowed to occupy the same sector, so the opportunity exists for a waste of space that defragmenting cannot correct. Clusters exacerbate the problem by having a similar foible: no two files are allowed by the operating system to occupy the same cluster. The larger the cluster size, then, the larger the potential waste. So, although you can increase the cluster size (generally to as large as 64KB, which corresponds to 128 sectors), you should keep in mind that unless you are storing a notable number of very large files, the waste will escalate astoundingly, perhaps negating or reversing your perceived storage-capacity increase. Nevertheless, if you have single files larger than 2TB, increased cluster sizes are for you. A 64KB cluster size results in a maximum volume size in Windows XP, for example, of 256TB.

Solid-State Drives

Conventional hard disk drive platters are still manufactured the same way they have always been. They are metal or glass discs with a magnetic coating on their surface. The read/write heads change the magnetic orientation of each bit location, storing either a binary one or a binary zero. The same head senses the magnetic orientation of each location as the data is read from the disc.

In contrast, *solid-state drives (SSD)* have no moving parts, but use the same solid-state memory technology found in the flash memory of recent years. All solid-state memory is limited to a finite number of write (including erase) operations. Algorithms have been developed to constantly spread the write operations over the entire device. Such "wear leveling" increases the life of the SSD, but lack of longevity remains a disadvantage of this technology.

SSDs are more reliable and less susceptible to damage from physical shock than their magnetic counterparts. However, the technology to build an SSD is still more expensive per byte, and SSDs are not yet available in capacities high enough to rival the upper limits of legacy hard disk drive technology.

Floppy Drives

A *floppy disk* (or floppy diskette) is a magnetic storage medium that uses a diskette made of thin, flexible plastic enclosed in a protective casing. The floppy disk once enabled information to be transported from one computer to another very easily. Today, floppies are a little too small in capacity to be efficient anymore. They were first replaced by writable CD-ROMs and DVD-ROMs. Today, solid-state storage is the closest analog to how floppies were originally used. The term *floppy disk* initially referred to the antiquated 8″ medium used with minicomputers and mainframes. The original PC floppy diskette, which used a platter that was

5¼ inches in diameter and known as a *minifloppy diskette*, is also obsolete; the *microfloppy diskette* is a diskette that is 3½ inches in diameter. Most computers today use microfloppy diskettes or no floppy at all.

> Generally speaking, throughout this book we will use the term *floppy drive* to refer to a 3½″ microfloppy diskette drive. Additionally, it is important to understand that the term "floppy" refers to the enclosed disk platter, and not to the external enclosure. A mistake made by many uninformed individuals during the transition from 5¼″ floppies to 3½″ floppies was to refer to the newer, smaller diskettes as "hard disks." The microfloppy diskettes are still considered floppy because of the internal platter. The rigidity of the newer enclosure, in contrast to the flexibility of the older diskettes, had nothing to do with the name of the technology.

A *floppy diskette drive (FDD)* (shown in Figure 2.3) is used to read and write information to and from these disks. The advantage of these drives is that they allow portability of data: you can transfer data from one computer to another on a diskette. The downside of a floppy disk drive is its limited storage capacity. Whereas a hard drive can store hundreds or thousands of gigabytes of information, floppy disks allow storage of only one or two megabytes, although much higher formats exist, using roughly the same physical form factor but largely incompatible technology.

FIGURE 2.3   A floppy disk drive

Table 2.1 shows five different floppy-diskette formats with their corresponding data capacities supported in PC systems over the years. The following abbreviations are used: DD means double density; HD means high density; ED means extended density. A sector

holds 512 bytes; call it ½KB to make the math easier. Just remember, all your computations result in KB. Unlike other storage capacities, which shift magnitudes by multiplying or dividing by 1024, floppy storage capacities move up one order of magnitude each time you divide by 1000, for example KB to MB, then MB to GB. For instance the 3½″ HD floppy has two sides to its single platter, yielding a total of 160 tracks. With 18 sectors per track, the total number of sectors on such a floppy diskette totals 2880. Because each sector represents ½KB, the resulting disk capacity totals 1440KB. Dividing by an even 1000 changes the magnitude from KB to MB and arrives at the 1.44MB capacity commonly associated with these diskettes.

TABLE 2.1 Floppy Diskette Capacities

Floppy Drive Size	Tracks per Side	Sectors per Track	Capacity
5¼″ DD	40	9	360KB
5¼″ HD	80	15	1.2MB
3½″ DD	80	9	720KB
3½″ HD	80	18	1.44MB
3½″ ED	80	36	2.88MB

Optical Storage Drives

Most computers today have an optical storage drive, such as a CD (compact disc) or DVD (digital versatile disc or digital video disc) drive. Such optical storage devices have replaced floppy diskette drives steadily since the late 1990s. Although these discs have greater data capacity and increased performance over floppies, they are not meant to replace hard disk drives. HDDs greatly exceed the capacity and performance of CD and DVD drives. The CDs and DVDs used for data storage are virtually the same as those used for permanent recorded audio and video. The recordable versions can be written with information that makes them virtually indistinguishable from such manufactured discs. Any differences arise from the format used to encode the digital information on the disc. The encoding method used to store data on such discs is incompatible with the method used to record audio and video to the same discs.

CD-ROMs, DVD-ROMs, and Capacities

The CD-ROM (read-only memory) is used for long-term storage of data. CD-ROMs are read-only, meaning that once information is written to a CD, it can't be erased or changed. CD-ROMs became so popular because they make a great software distribution medium.

Programs are always getting larger and have increasingly required more disks to install, version after version. Instead of installing a program using 100 floppy disks (a real possibility), you can use a single CD, which can hold approximately 650MB in its original, least-capable format. Although CDs capable of storing 700MB were and continue to be the most common, discs with 800MB and 900MB capacities have been standardized as well. See Table 2.2 for a complete list of optical discs and their capacities.

For even more storage capacity, many computers feature some form of DVD drive, such as the original DVD-ROM drive. The basic DVD-ROM disc is a single-sided disc that has a single layer of encoded information. These discs have a capacity of 4.7GB, many times the highest CD-ROM capacity. Simple multiplication can be used to arrive at the capacities of other DVD-ROM varieties. For example, by adding another media surface on the side of the disc where the label is often applied, a double-sided disc is created. Such double-sided discs have a capacity of 9.4GB, exactly twice that of a single-sided disc.

Roughly the same 9.4GB capacity (actually only 8.5GB) is realized by placing two media surfaces on the same side of the disc, one on top of the other, and using a more sophisticated burning mechanism that burns the inner layer without altering the outer layer and vice versa, all from the same side of the disc. This technology is known as DVD DL, *DL* for *double-layer.* The loss of capacity is due to the space between tracks on both layers being 10 percent wider than normal to facilitate burning one layer without affecting the other. This results in about 90 percent remaining capacity per layer. Add the DL technology to a double-sided disc, and you have a disc capable of holding 17GB of information, again twice the capacity of the single-sided version. Figure 2.4 shows an example of an early DVD-ROM drive, which also accepts CD-ROM discs.

Table 2.2 draws together the most popular optical-disc formats and lists their respective capacities. Some of these formats have already been introduced; others are mentioned in the following sections. Boldfaced capacities in the table are the commonly accepted values for their respective formats.

FIGURE 2.4 An early DVD-ROM drive

TABLE 2.2   Optical Discs and Their Capacities

Disc Format	Capacity
CD SS (includes recordable versions)	650MB, **700MB**, 800MB, 900MB
DVD-R/RW SS, SL	4.71GB (**4.7GB**)
DVD+R/RW SS, SL	4.70GB (**4.7GB**)
DVD-R, DVD+R DS, SL	**9.4GB**
DVD-R SS, DL	8.54GB
DVD+R SS, DL	8.55GB
DVD+R DS, DL	17.1GB

SS: single-sided; DS: double-sided; DL: double-layer

Optical Drive Data Rates

CD-ROM drives are rated in terms of their data transfer speed. The first CD-ROM drives transferred data at the same speed as home audio CD players, 150KBps. Soon after, CD drives rated as "2X" drives that would transfer data at 300KBps appeared (they just increased the spin speed in order to increase the data transfer rate). This system of ratings continued up until the 8X speed was reached. At that point, the CDs were spinning so fast that there was a danger of the CDs flying apart inside the drive. So, although future CD drives used the same rating (as in 16X, 32X, and so on), their rating was expressed in terms of theoretical maximum transfer rate. Therefore, the drive isn't necessarily spinning faster, but through electronic and buffering advances, the transfer rates have continued to increase.

The standard DVD-ROM "1X" transfer rate is 600KBps, already four times that of the comparably labeled CD-ROM. As a result, to match the transfer rate of a 64X CD-ROM drive, a DVD-ROM drive need only be rated 16X.

Recordable Discs and Burners

Years after the original factory-made CD-ROM discs and the drives that could read them were developed, the industry, strongly persuaded by consumer demand, developed discs that, through the use of associated drives, could be written to once and then used in the same fashion as the original CD-ROM discs. The firmware with which the drives were equipped could vary the power of the laser to achieve the desired result. At standard power, the laser in these drives allowed inserted discs to be read from. Increasing the power of the laser allowed the crystalline media surface to be melted and changed in such a way that light would reflect or refract from the surface in microscopic increments. This characteristic allowed mimicking of the way in which the original CD-ROM discs stored data.

Eventually, discs that could be written to, erased, and rewritten were developed. Drives that contained the firmware to recognize these discs and control the laser varied the laser's power in three levels. The original two levels closely matched those of the writable discs and drives. The third level, somewhere in between, could neutralize the crystalline material without writing new information to the disc. This medium level of power left the disc surface in a state similar to its original, unwritten state. Subsequent high-power laser usage could write new information to the neutralized locations.

The best algorithms for such drives, which are still available today, allow two types of disc erasure. The entire disc can be erased before new data is written (*erased* or *formatted*, in various application interfaces), or the data can be erased on the fly, just fractions of a second before new data is written to the same location. If not properly implemented in a slow, determined fashion, the latter method can result in write errors because the crystalline material does not adequately return to its neutral state before the write operation. The downside to slowing down the process is obvious, and methods exist to allow a small level of encoding error without data loss.

Recordable CD Formats

CD-recordable (CD-R) and *CD-rewritable (CD-RW)* drives (also known as CD *burners*) are essentially CD-ROM drives that allow users to create (or *burn*) their own CD-ROMs. They look very similar to CD-ROM drives, but feature a logo on the front panel that represents the drive's CD-R or CD-RW capability. Figure 2.5 shows the CD-R and CD-RW logos that you are likely to see on such drives.

The difference between these two types of drives is that CD-R drives can write to a CD-R disc only once. A CD-RW can erase information from a CD-RW disc and rewrite to it multiple times. Also, CD-RW drives are rated according to their write, rewrite, and read times. So instead of a single rating like 64X, in the case of CD-ROM drives, they have a compound rating, such as 52X-32X-52X, which means it writes at 52X, rewrites at 32X, and reads at 52X.

FIGURE 2.5   CD-R and CD-RW logos

Recordable DVD Formats

A DVD burner operates in a similar manner to a CD-R or CD-RW drive: it can store large amounts of data onto a special, writable DVD. Today, single-sided, double-layered (DL) discs can be burned right in your home computer, writing 8.5GB of information to one single-sided disc. Common names for the variations of DVD burning technologies include DVD+R, DVD+RW, DVD-R, DVD-RW, DVD-RAM, DVD-R DL, and DVD+R DL. The "plus" standards come from the DVD Alliance, while the "dash" counterparts are specifications of the DVD Forum. The number of sectors per disc varies between the "plus" and "dash" variants, so older drives might not support both types. The firmware in today's drives knows to check for all possible variations in encoding and capability.

A DVD-ROM or recordable drive looks very similar to a CD-ROM drive. The main difference is the presence of one of the various DVD logos on the front of the drive. CD-ROM and recordable CDs are usually able to be read and, if applicable, burned in DVD burners. Figure 2.6 shows the most popular data-oriented logos you are likely to see when dealing with DVD drives suited for computers.

FIGURE 2.6   DVD logos

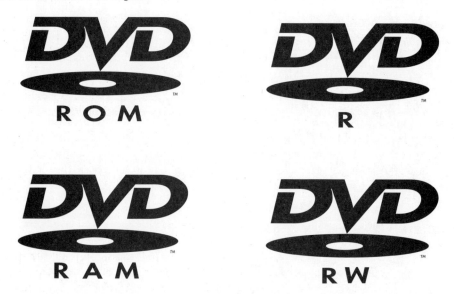

Table 2.3 lists the main DVD formats used for storing and accessing data in computer systems as well as their characteristics.

TABLE 2.3   DVD Formats and Characteristics

Format	Characteristics
DVD-ROM	Purchased with data encoded; not able to be changed

TABLE 2.3   DVD Formats and Characteristics *(continued)*

Format	Characteristics
DVD-R, DVD+R	Purchased blank; able to be written to once and then treated like a DVD-ROM
DVD-RW, DVD+RW	Purchased blank; able to be written to and erased multiple times; session usually must be closed for subsequent access to stored data
DVD-RAM	Purchased blank; able to be written to and erased just like a hard or floppy disk; no session to close before subsequent access to stored data

Blu-ray Disc

The next generation of optical storage technology was designed for modern high-definition video sources. The equipment used to read the resulting discs employs a violet laser, in contrast to the red laser used with standard DVD and CD technologies. Taking a bit of license with the color of the laser, the Blu-ray Disc Association names itself and the technology *Blu-ray Disc (BD)*, after this "visibly" different characteristic.

The Blu-ray laser is of a shorter wavelength (450nm) than that of DVD (650nm) and CD (780nm) technologies. As a result, and through the use of refined optics, the laser can be focused on a much smaller area of the disc. This leads to a higher density of information being stored in the same area. In fact, Blu-ray discs are the same size as conventional DVDs and CDs. The capacity, however, is astoundingly higher. A single-sided, single-layer Blu-ray disc is capable of holding 25GB of information. Thinning of the external covering of the disc further improves the ability to focus the laser on a smaller area. This thinning leads to a required hardening of the material. Most manufacturers add scratch resistance to the surface as well.

Burnable Blu-ray discs hit the market in 2006. Blu-ray disc players and burners are recommended by the association to be backward compatible with standard DVDs and CDs, increasing their overall acceptance in the marketplace. Compatibility with DVDs is more likely than compatibility with CDs, however. The "1X" transfer rate for Blu-ray is 4.5MBps, roughly 7.5 times that of the comparable DVD multiplier. An interesting point to note is that designers of the Blu-ray technology do not have to stop with the common double-layer solution to increasing capacity. Blu-ray discs with four and six layers on a side have been demonstrated, largely owing to the extremely accurate focus attainable with the Blu-ray laser.

In the interest of completeness, it should be mentioned that a high-definition technology directly related to DVD, because it comes from the same forum, and named HD DVD remains only as a footnote to the Blu-ray story. In February 2008, Toshiba, HD DVD's primary champion, gave up the fight, conceding Blu-ray disc as the winner in the high-definition optical-disc race. HD DVD featured red- and blue-laser compatibility and 15GB data storage capacity.

Other Storage Media

Many additional types of storage are available for PCs today. Among the other types of storage are tape backup devices, solid-state memory, and advanced optical drives. There are also external hard drives and optical drives as well as new storage media, such as USB thumb drives that can store many gigabytes (more all the time) on a single small plastic device that can be carried on a key chain.

Removable Storage

Removable storage once meant something vastly different from what it means today. Sequential tape backup is one of the only remnants of the old forms of removable storage that can be seen in the market today. The more modern solution is random-access, solid-state removable storage. This section presents details of tape backup and the newer removable storage solutions.

Tape Backup Devices

An older form of removable storage is the tape backup. Tape backup devices can be installed internally or externally and use either a digital or analog magnetic tape medium instead of disks for storage. They hold much more data than any other medium but are also much slower. They are primarily used for archival storage, not interactive storage.

With hard disks, it's not a matter of "if they fail"; it's "when they fail." So you must back up the information onto some other storage medium. Tape backup devices were once the most common choice in larger enterprises and networks because they were able to hold the most data and were the most reliable over the long term. Today, however, tape backup systems are seeing competition from writable and rewritable optical discs, which continue to advance in technology and size. Nevertheless, when an enterprise needs to back up large amounts of data on a regular basis, some form of tape media is the most popular choice. Table 2.4 lists the best-known tape formats in order of market release dates, oldest first.

TABLE 2.4   Sequential Tape Formats

Format Name
Quarter-inch Cartridge (QIC)
Digital Linear Tape (DLT)
Eight Millimeter (Exabyte)
Digital Audio Tape (DAT)/Digital Data Storage (DDS)
Linear Tape-Open (LTO)

Flash Memory

Once only for primary memory usage, the same components that sit on your motherboard as RAM can be found in various physical sizes and quantities in today's solid-state storage solutions. These include older removable and nonremovable flash memory mechanisms, Secure Digital (SD) cards and other memory cards, and USB thumb drives. Each of these technologies has the potential to reliably store a staggering amount of information in a minute form factor. Manufacturers are using innovative packaging for some of these products to provide convenient transport options, such as key-chain attachments, to users. Additionally, recall the SSD alternatives to magnetic hard drives mentioned earlier in this chapter.

For many years, modules and PC Cards known as *flash memory* have offered low- to mid-capacity storage for devices. The name comes from the concept of easily being able to use electricity to instantly alter the contents of the memory. The original flash memory is still used in devices, such as routers and switches, that require a nonvolatile means of storing critical data and code often used in booting the device.

For example, Cisco Systems uses flash memory in various forms to store their Internetwork Operating System (IOS), which is accessed from flash during boot-up and, in certain cases, throughout operation uptime and, therefore, during an administrator's configuration sessions. Lesser models store the IOS in compressed form on the flash and then decompress the IOS into RAM, where it is used during configuration and operation. In this case, the flash is not accessed again after the boot-up process is complete, unless its contents are being changed, as in an IOS upgrade. Certain devices use externally removable PC Card technology as flash for similar purposes.

The following sections explain a bit more about today's most popular forms of flash memory, memory cards, and thumb drives.

SD AND OTHER MEMORY CARDS

Today's smaller devices require some form of removable solid-state memory that can be used for temporary and permanent storage of digital information. Gone are the days of using microfloppies in your digital camera. Even the most popular video-camera media, such as mini-DVD and HDD, are giving way to solid-state multi-GB models. These more modern electronics, as well as most contemporary digital still cameras, already use some form of removable memory card to store still images permanently or until they can be copied off or printed out. Of these, the *Secure Digital (SD)* format has emerged as the preeminent leader of the pack, which includes the older *MultiMediaCard (MMC)* format on which SD is based. Both of these cards measure 32mm by 24mm, and slots that receive them are often marked for both. The SD card is slightly thicker than the MMC and has a write-protect notch (and often a switch to open and close the notch), unlike MMC. Figure 2.7 is a photo of an older SD card with size reference.

Even smaller devices, such as mobile phones, have an SD solution for them. One of these products, known as *miniSD*, is slightly thinner than SD and measures 21.5mm by 20mm. The other, *microSD*, is thinner yet and only 15mm by 11mm. Both of these reduced formats have adapters allowing them to be used in standard SD slots.

Table 1.4 lists additional memory card formats, some of which can be seen in the images that follow the table.

FIGURE 2.7 A typical SD card

TABLE 1.4 Additional Memory Card Formats

Format	Dimensions	Details	Year Introduced
Subscriber Identity Module (SIM)	25mm by 15mm	Used to store a subscriber's key on a telephone	1991
CompactFlash (CF)	36mm by 43mm	Type I and Type II variants; Type II used by IBM for Microdrives	1994
SmartMedia (SM)	45mm by 37mm	From Toshiba; intended to replace floppies; still sells well	1995
Memory Stick (MS)	50mm by 21.5mm	From Sony; standard, Pro, Duo, and Micro formats available	1998
xD-Picture Card	20mm by 25mm	Used primarily in digital cameras	2002

Figure 2.8 shows the memory-card slots of an HP PhotoSmart printer, which is capable of reading these devices and printing them directly or creating a drive letter for access to the contents over its USB connection to the computer. Clockwise from upper left, these slots accommodate CF/Microdrive, SmartMedia, Memory Stick (bottom right), and MMC/ SD. The industry provides almost any adapter or converter to allow the various formats to work together.

Many other devices exist for allowing access to memory cards. For example, a 3½″ form-factor device can be purchased—some of which have multiformat floppy drives embedded—and installed in a standard front-access drive bay. One such device is shown in Figure 2.9. External card readers, such as the USB-attached one shown in Figure 2.10 (front first, then back), are widely available in many different configurations.

FIGURE 2.8   Card slots in a printer

FIGURE 2.9   An internal card reader with floppy drive

Many of today's laptops have built-in memory-card slots, such as the ones shown in Figure 2.11.

THUMB DRIVES

Also known as USB flash drives, *thumb drives* are incredibly versatile and convenient devices that allow you to store large quantities of information in a very small form factor. Many such devices are merely extensions of the host's USB connector, extending out from the interface but adding little to its width, making them easy to transport, whether in a pocket or laptop bag. Figure 2.12 illustrates an example of one of these components and its relative size.

FIGURE 2.10 A USB card reader

FIGURE 2.11 Memory-card slots in a laptop

FIGURE 2.12   A USB thumb drive

Thumb drives capitalize on the versatility of the USB interface, taking advantage of the Plug and Play feature and the physical connector strength. Upon insertion, these devices announce themselves to Windows Explorer as removable drives and show up in the Explorer window with a drive letter. This software interface allows for drag-and-drop copying and most of the other Explorer functions performed on standard drives. Make a mental note, until the Disk Management utility is discussed later in this book, that you might have to use that utility to manually assign a drive letter to a thumb drive if it fails to acquire one itself. This can happen in certain cases, such as when the previous letter the drive was assigned has been taken by another device in the thumb drive's temporary absence.

USB thumb drives emerged as the de facto replacement for other, now legacy, removable storage devices, such as floppies, edging out Zip and Jaz offerings from Iomega as well as other proprietary solutions for the honor.

USB-Attached External Disk Drives

Before USB, an external drive used a proprietary adapter and interface/cable combination or the standard RS-232 serial or the parallel port usually built in to the computer. Since USB, there seems to be a sense that there is no other way to do it. The fact is, there are other ways, but why muddy the water with options when USB covers all the bases at high data rates and is so ubiquitous in today's systems?

Many external optical and hard disk drives today are manufactured into their own chassis and have detachable connectivity for USB (and/or FireWire). If the power requirement for the unit is high enough, there might also be a separate power connection for the device. Otherwise, the USB interface on the host provides all the power for the drive. Figure 2.13 is a photo of a small external hard disk drive with no separate power attachment.

FIGURE 2.13 A self-contained external hard disk drive

More flexibly, USB-attached external disk drives can use the same drives that you might install in a drive bay in your chassis; they simply employ a specialty chassis that houses only the drive and the supporting circuitry that converts the drive interface to USB. Almost always, the drive enclosure has a DC power input and a Type-B USB interface, as shown in Figure 2.14. This external chassis has its cover removed, and you can see the internal protective casing, inside of which the hard drive is mounted.

FIGURE 2.14 External drive enclosure

eSATA-Attached External Disk Drives

Having sung the praises of USB as the savior of the external drive market, let's dispense with the illusion. An external drive-attachment technology based on SATA, called *eSATA* for "external" SATA, promises to offer external attachment with no compromises. Where the very nature of USB can hinder the achievement of maximum SATA drive performance, eSATA, by its nature, pledges to represent SATA faithfully, because it is SATA. Many enhancements over the SATA physical interface and signal levels, however, were required with eSATA to accommodate the harsher external environment. A different interface, without the recognizable L-shaped key, had to be specified to avoid accidental or intentional insertion of inadequately shielded internal cables. The eSATA specification is likely to ride the coattails of internal SATA to appreciable success.

Hot-Swappable Devices

Many of the removable storage devices mentioned are *hot-swappable*. This means that you can insert and remove the device with the system powered on. Most USB-attached devices without a file system fall into this category. Non-hot-swappable devices, in contrast, either cannot have the system's power applied when inserting or removing them or they have some sort of additional conditions for their insertion or removal.

One subset is occasionally referred to as cold-swappable, the other as warm-swappable. Cold-swappable devices must have the system power off before you can insert or remove them. An example of a cold-swappable device is anything connected to the PS/2-style mini-DIN connector, such as a keyboard or mouse. Insertion with the power on generally results in lack of recognition for the device and might damage the motherboard. AT keyboards and the full-sized DIN connector have the same restriction.

Warm-swappable devices include USB thumb drives and external drives that have a file system. Windows and other operating systems tend to leave files open while accessing them and write cached changes to them at a later time, based on the algorithm in use by the software. Removing such a device without using the Safely Remove Hardware utility can result in data loss. However, after stopping the device with the utility, you can remove it without powering down the system, hence the "warm" component of the category's name.

Identifying Purposes and Characteristics of Power Supplies

The computer's components would not be able to operate without power. The device in the computer that provides this power is the *power supply* (Figure 2.15). A power supply converts 110V or 220V AC current into the DC voltages that a computer needs to operate. These are +3.3VDC, +5VDC, –5VDC, +12VDC, and –12VDC. The jacket on the leads carrying each type of voltage has a different industry-standard color coding for faster recognition. Black ground leads offer the reference that gives the voltage leads their respective magnitudes. The +3.3VDC voltage was first offered on ATX motherboards.

FIGURE 2.15   A power supply

    The abbreviation VDC stands for volts DC. DC is short for direct current. Unlike alternating current (AC), DC does not alter the direction in which the electrons flow. AC for standard power distribution does so 50 or 60 times per second (50 or 60Hz, respectively).

    Power supplies contain transformers and capacitors that can discharge *lethal* amounts of current even when disconnected from the wall outlet for long periods. They are not meant to be serviced, especially by untrained personnel. *Do not* attempt to open them or do any work on them. Simply replace and recycle them when they go bad.

Power supplies are rated in watts. A *watt* is a unit of power. The higher the number, the more power your computer can draw from the power supply. Think of this rating as the "capacity" of the device to supply power. Most computers require power supplies in the 250- to 500-watt range. Higher wattage power supplies might be required for more advanced systems that employ power-hungry graphics technologies or multiple disk drives, for instance. It is important to consider the draw that the various components and subcomponents of your computer place on the power supply before choosing one or its replacement.

Classic power supplies used only three types of connectors to power the various devices within the computer: floppy drive power connectors, AT system connectors, and standard peripheral power connectors. Each has a different appearance and way of connecting to the device. In addition, each type is used for a specific purpose. Newer systems have a variety of similar, replacement, and additional connectors, such as dedicated power connectors for fans, integrated ports, and PCIe adapters.

Most power supplies have a recessed, two-position slider switch, often a red one, on the rear that is exposed through the case. Selections read 110 and 220; 115 and 230; or 120 and 240. This *voltage selector switch* is used to select the voltage level used in the country where the computer is in service. For example, in the United States, the power grid supplies anywhere from 110 to 120VAC. However, in Europe, for instance, the voltage supplied is double, ranging from 220 to 240VAC.

Although the voltage is the same, the amperage is much lower than what is used in the United States to power high-voltage appliances, such as electric ranges and clothes driers. The point is, the switch is not there to match the type of outlet used in the same country. If the wrong voltage is chosen in the US, the power supply expects more voltage than it receives and might not power up at all. If the wrong voltage is selected in Europe, however, the power supply receives more voltage than it is set for. The result could be disastrous for the entire computer. Sparks could also ignite a fire that could destroy nearby property and endanger lives. Always check the switch before powering up a new or recently relocated computer. In the US and other countries that use the same voltage, check the setting of this switch if the computer fails to power up.

Floppy Drive Power Connectors

Floppy drive power connectors are most commonly used to power floppy disk drives and other small form-factor devices. This type of connector is smaller and flatter (as shown in Figure 2.16) than any of the other types of power connectors. These connectors are also called *Berg connectors*. Notice that there are four wires going into this connector. These wires carry the two voltages used by the motors and logic circuits: +5VDC (carried on the red wire) and +12VDC (carried on the yellow wire); the two black wires are ground wires.

FIGURE 2.16   Floppy drive power connector

AT System Connectors

The next type of power connector is called the *AT system connector*. There are two six-wire connectors, labeled P8 and P9 (as shown in Figure 2.17). They connect to an AT-style motherboard and deliver the power that feeds the electronic components on it. These connectors have small tabs on them that interlock with tabs on the motherboard's receptacle.

The P8 and P9 connectors must be installed correctly, or you will damage the motherboard and possibly other components. To do this (on standard systems), place the connectors side by side with their black wires together, and then push the connectors together or separately onto the 12-pin receptacle on the motherboard. Although there is keying on these connectors, they both use the exact same keying structure. In other words, they can still be swapped with one another and inserted. By placing the black ground leads together when the connectors are side by side, it is not possible to flip the pair 180 degrees and still insert the two connectors without physically defeating the keying. Most technicians would give up and figure out their mistake before any damage occurs if they always place the grounds together in the middle.

FIGURE 2.17 AT power supply system board connectors

 Although it's easy to remove this type of connector from the motherboard, the tabs on the connector make it difficult to reinstall it. Here's a hint: place the connector at an almost right angle to the motherboard's connector, interlocking the tabs in their correct positions. Then tilt the connector to the vertical position. The connector will slide into place more easily.

It is important to note that only computers with AT and baby AT motherboards use this type of power connector.

 Most computers today use some form of ATX power connector to provide power to the motherboard.

Standard Peripheral Power Connector

The standard peripheral power connector is generally used to power different types of internal disk drives. This type of connector is also called a *Molex connector*. Figure 2.18 shows an example of a standard peripheral power connector. This power connector, though larger than the floppy drive power connector, uses the same wiring color code scheme as the floppy drive connector. You might notice that the gauge of wire is heavier than that of the Berg connector. The added copper is for the additional current drawn by most devices that call for the Molex interface.

FIGURE 2.18   A standard peripheral power connector

Modern Power Connectors

Modern components have exceeded the capabilities of some of the original power supply connectors. The Molex and Berg peripheral connectors remain, but the P8/P9 motherboard connectors have been consolidated, and additional connectors have sprung up.

ATX, ATX12V, and EPS12V Connectors

With ATX motherboards came a new, single connector from the power supply. PCI Express has power requirements that even this connector could not satisfy. Additional 4- and 8-pin connectors supply power to components of the motherboard, such as network interfaces, specialty server components, and the CPU itself, that require a +12V supply in addition to the +12V of the standard ATX connector. These additional connectors follow the ATX12V and EPS12V standards. The ATX connector was further expanded by an additional four pins in later specifications.

The *ATX system connector* (also known as the ATX motherboard power connector) feeds an ATX motherboard. It provides the six voltages required, plus it delivers them all through one connector: a single 20-pin connector. This connector is much easier to work with than the dual connectors of the AT power supply. Figure 2.19 shows an example of an ATX system connector.

FIGURE 2.19   ATX power connector

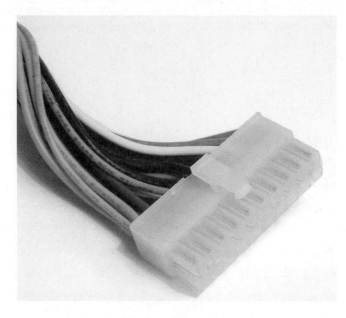

When the Pentium 4 processor was introduced, motherboard and power supply manufacturers needed to get more power to the system. The solution was the ATXV12 standard, which added two supplemental connectors. One was a six-pin auxiliary connector similar to the P8/P9 AT connectors that supplied additional +3.3V and +5V leads and their grounds. The other was a four-pin square mini-version of the ATX connector, referred to as a P4 connector, that supplied two +12V leads and their grounds. EPS12V uses an eight-pin version, called the processor power connector, that doubles the P4's function with four +12V leads and four grounds. Figure 2.20 illustrates the P4 connector. The eight-pin processor power connector is similar but has two rows of four.

FIGURE 2.20   ATX12V P4 power connector

For servers and more advanced ATX motherboards that include PCIe slots, the 20-pin system connector proved inadequate. This led to the ATX12V 2.0 standard and the even higher-end EPS12V standard for servers. These specifications call for a 24-pin connector that adds additional positive voltage leads directly to the system connector. The 24-pin connector looks like a larger version of the 20-pin connector. Adapters are available if you find yourself with the wrong combination of motherboard and power supply. The six-pin auxiliary connector disappeared with the ATX12V 2.0 specification and was never part of the EPS12V standard.

Proprietary Power Connectors

Although the internal peripheral devices have standard power connectors, manufacturers of computer systems sometimes take liberties with the power interface between the motherboard and power supply of their systems. In some cases, the same voltages required by a standard ATX power connector are supplied using one or more proprietary connectors. This makes it virtually impossible to replace power supplies and motherboards with other units "off the shelf." Manufacturers might do this to solve a design issue or simply to ensure repeat business.

SATA Power Connectors

SATA drives arrived on the market with their own power requirements, in addition to their new data interfaces. Refer back to Figure 1.16 and imagine a larger but similar connector for power. You get the 15-pin SATA power connector, shown in Figure 2.21. This connector is made up of three each of +3.3V, +5V, and +12V leads, as well as five ground leads.

FIGURE 2.21   SATA power connector

AC Adapters as Power Supplies

Just as the power supply in a desktop computer converts AC voltages to DC for the internal components to run on, so does the AC adapter of a laptop computer for the laptop's internal components. Just as power supplies are rated in watts and selected for use with a specific voltage, so are AC adapters. One difference is that AC adapters are also rated in terms of DC volts out to the laptop or other device, such as certain brands and models of printer.

Because both power supplies and AC adapters go bad on occasion, you should replace them both and not attempt to repair them yourself. When replacing an AC adapter, be sure to match the size, shape, and polarity of the tip with the adapter you are replacing. However, because the output DC voltage is specified for the AC adapter, be sure to replace it with one of equal output voltage, an issue not seen when replacing AT or ATX power supplies, which have standard outputs. Additionally, and as with power supplies, you can replace an AC adapter with a model that supplies more watts to the component because the component only uses what it needs.

Identifying Input Devices

An *input device* is one that transfers information outside the computer system to an internal storage location, such as system RAM, video RAM, flash memory, or disk storage. Without input devices, computers would be unable to change from their default boot-up state. This section details six different classes of input devices and a hub, of sorts, used for switching between the most common of these devices. This section also demonstrates the similarities shared by devices that provide input to computer systems as well as their differences. Installation considerations will be presented where appropriate. The input devices covered in the following sections are

- Mouse
- Keyboard
- Barcode reader
- Multimedia devices
- Biometric devices
- Touchscreen
- KVM switch

Mouse

Although the computer mouse was born in the 1970s at Xerox's Palo Alto Research Center (PARC), it was Apple in 1984 that made the mouse an integral part of the personal computer image with the introduction of the Macintosh. In its most basic form, the mouse is a hand-fitting device that uses some form of motion-detection mechanism to translate its own physical two-dimensional movement into onscreen cursor motion. Many variations of the mouse exist, including trackballs, tablets, touchpads, and pointing sticks. Figure 2.22 illustrates the most recognizable form of the mouse.

The motion-detection mechanism of the original Apple mouse was a simple ball that protruded from the bottom of the device so that when the bottom was placed against a flat surface that offered a slight amount of friction, the mouse would glide over the surface, but the ball would roll, actuating two rollers that mapped the linear movement to a Cartesian plane and transmitted the results to the software interface. This method of motion detection remains available today.

FIGURE 2.22 A computer mouse

Later technologies used optical receptors to catch LED light reflected from specially made surfaces purchased with the devices and used like a *mouse pad*. A mouse pad is a special surface to improve mechanical mouse traction while offering very little resistance to the mouse itself. As optical science advanced for the mouse, lasers were used to allow a sharper image to be captured by the mouse and more sensitivity in motion detection. The mouse today can be wired to the computer system or connected wirelessly. Wireless versions use batteries to power them, and the optical varieties deplete these batteries more quickly than their mechanical counterparts.

The final topic is one that is relevant for any mouse: buttons. The number of buttons you need for your mouse to have is dependent on the software interfaces you use. For the Macintosh, one button has always been sufficient, but for a Windows-based computer, at least two are recommended, hence the term *right-click*. Today, the mouse is commonly found to have a wheel on top to aid in scrolling. The wheel has even developed a click in many models, sort of an additional button underneath the wheel. Buttons on the side of the mouse that can be programmed for whatever the user desires are more common today as well.

Touchpads and pointing sticks are found mainly on laptops and are discussed in more detail in Chapter 4, "Understanding Laptops and Portable Devices." A trackball, however, is more like an inverted mouse, so let's look at how they compare to each other. Both devices place the buttons on the top, which is where your fingers will be. A mouse places its tracking mechanism on the bottom, requiring that you move the entire assembly as an analog for how you want the cursor on the screen to move. In contrast, a trackball places the tracking mechanism, usually a ball that is larger than that of a mouse, on the top with the buttons. In doing so, you have a device that need not be moved around on the desktop and can work in tight spaces and on surfaces that would be incompatible with the use of a mouse. The better trackballs place the ball and buttons in such a configuration that your hand rests ergonomically on the device, allowing effortless control of the onscreen cursor.

Keyboard

More ubiquitous than the mouse, the keyboard is easily the most popular input device, so much so that its popularity is more of a necessity. Very few users would even think of beginning a computing session without a working keyboard. Few would even know how. The US English keyboard places keys in the same orientation as the QWERTY typewriter keyboards, which were developed in the 1860s.

In addition to the standard QWERTY layout, modern computer keyboards often have separate cursor-movement and numerical keypads. The numerical keys in a row above the alphabet keys send different scan codes to the computer from those sent by the numerical keypad.

Keyboards have also added function keys (not to be confused with the common laptop key labeled Fn), which are often placed in a row across the top of the keyboard above the numerical row. Key functionality can be modified by using one or more combinations of the Ctrl, Alt, Shift, and laptop Fn keys along with the normal QWERTY keys.

Technically speaking, the keys on a keyboard complete individual circuits when each one is pressed. The completion of each circuit leads to a unique scan code that is sent to the keyboard connector on the computer system. The computer uses a keyboard controller chip to interpret the code as the corresponding key sequence. The computer then decides what action to take based on the key sequence and what it means to the computer and the active application, including simply displaying the character printed on the key.

In addition to the layout a standard keyboard is known for, other keyboard layouts exist, some not nearly as popular, however. For example, without changing the order of the keys, an ergonomic keyboard is designed to feel more comfortable to users as they type. To accomplish that goal, manufacturers split the keyboard down the middle, angling keys on each side downward from the center. Additionally, the Dvorak Simplified Keyboard, patented in 1936, was designed to reduce fatigue in the hands of typists by placing characters that are more commonly used in the home row, among other physiologic enhancements. The QWERTY layout was designed to keep the hammers of a typewriter from becoming entangled. Although the Dvorak keyboard makes logical sense, especially with the decline in manufacturing and sales of the classic typewriter, the QWERTY keyboard remains dominant. One reason the Dvorak keyboard has failed to take over might be the loss of productivity to a touch-typist as they retrain on the new format.

Installing Your Mouse and Keyboard

In the early days of the mouse for the PC, the original AT keyboard was still in use. The nine-pin D-sub RS-232 serial ports the mouse used looked nothing like the five-pin DIN to which the keyboard attached. Not long thereafter, the PS/2 product line blurred the distinction; indeed, it removed it. With both interfaces being matching six-pin mini-DIN connectors, care was paramount during installation. Standard industry color coding has simplified the installation process, but the ports are still easily interchanged during blind insertion. If you have visibility of the ports, remembering that the keyboard interface is coded purple and the mouse green takes much of the guesswork out of analyzing icons stamped into or printed on the case. Of course, graduation to USB-attached devices alleviates the hassle. Consult the accompanying documentation for the installation of all types of wireless input devices.

Barcode Reader

A *barcode reader* (or *barcode scanner*) is a specialized input device commonly used in retail and other industrial sectors that manage inventory. The systems that the reader connects to can be so specialized that they have no other input device. Barcode readers can use LEDs or lasers as light sources and can scan one- or two-dimensional barcodes.

Barcode readers can connect to the host system in a number of ways, but serial connections, such as RS-232 and USB, are fairly common. If the system uses proprietary software to receive the reader's input, the connection between the two might be proprietary as well. The simplest software interfaces call for the reader to be plugged into the keyboard's PS/2 connector using a splitter, or "wedge," that allows the keyboard to remain connected. The scanner converts all output to keyboard scans so that the system treats the input as if it came from a keyboard. For certain readers, wireless communication with the host is also possible, using IR, RF, Bluetooth, Wi-Fi, and more.

Multimedia Devices

Multimedia input devices vary in functionality based on the type of input being gathered. Two broad categories of multimedia input are audio and video. Digital motion and still cameras are incredibly popular as a replacement for similar video products that do not transfer information to a computer, making sharing and collaboration so much easier than before. Years ago, owing to the continued growth in the Internet's popularity, video camera-only devices, known as *webcams*, started their climb in esteem. Today, anyone who does a fair amount of instant messaging, whether professional or personal, has likely used or at least been introduced to webcams, often used in conjunction with messaging user interfaces.

Webcams make great security devices as well. Users can keep an eye on loved ones or property from anywhere that Internet access is offered. Care must be taken, however, because the security that the webcam is intended to provide can backfire on the user if the webcam is not set up properly. Anyone who happens upon the web interface for the device can control its actions if there is no authentication enabled. Some webcams provide an activity light when someone is using the camera to watch whatever it's pointed at. Nevertheless, it is possible to decouple the camera's operation and that of its light.

A webcam connects directly to the computer through an I/O interface, such as USB, and does not have any self-contained recording mechanism. Its sole purpose is to transfer its captured video directly to the host computer, usually for further transfer over the Internet. Webcams that have built-in wired and wireless NIC interfaces for direct network attachment are prevalent as well. The newest evolution of the webcam for laptops, however, is for manufacturers to build the device into the bezel of the display. Connectivity is generally through an internal USB or FireWire interface.

Microphones, audio playback, and audio synthesizing devices are common input components connected to a sound card or serial port so that audio from these devices can be collected and processed. As an example, consider *Musical Instrument Digital Interface (MIDI)* devices, called controllers, which create messages describing, and thus synthesizing, the user's intended musical performance. These devices do not make sound that is recorded directly; they are merely designed to somewhat realistically fabricate the music the instruments they represent might produce. MIDI files, therefore, are much smaller than files that contain digitized audio waveforms.

Modern MIDI controllers use 5-pin DIN connectors that look like the original AT keyboard connector. Controllers can be interconnected in one of two ways. The original method is to provide devices with two ports, an input and an output port, and daisy-chain them in a ring. This arrangement introduces a delay caused by devices processing and retransmitting messages that were not destined for them, but instead for devices downstream from them. One solution is to replace the output port with one that merely replicates the input signal. If the receiving device is the intended destination, then the unnecessarily repeated message is ignored by downstream recipients. Otherwise, the actual recipient receives its message with far less delay. The second method of connection is another solution that reduces delay. A device with one input and multiple outputs interconnects many devices directly.

Regardless of the controller interconnection method, computers can receive MIDI controllers directly, such as through a sound card with a built-in MIDI interface, or through the use of an external MIDI interface that originally connected to the computer's game port. Today, USB and FireWire ports are more commonly used. Ethernet-attached interfaces also exist and require very little processing power to convert the MIDI messages into Ethernet frames.

Biometric Devices

Any device that measures one or more physical or behavioral features of an organism is considered a *biometric device*. When the same device forwards this biometric information to the computer, it becomes an input device. The list includes fingerprint scanners, retinal scanners, voice recognition, and facial recognition, to name a few. A computer can use this input to authenticate the user based on preestablished information regarding this biometric information. Even cipher locks that authenticate personnel before allowing entry to secure environments can be replaced with biometric devices.

Because there are many manufacturers of biometric devices, the installation of any particular model is best performed while consulting that company's documentation. If the device is not built into the computer, at a minimum some form of interface, such as USB, must be used to attach the device, and software must be installed to lock the system until authentication occurs. Many offerings allow multiple forms of authentication to be required in sequence. An example of a highly secure approach to authentication would be a biometric scan, followed by a challenge that requires a code from a token card, followed finally by the opportunity to enter a password. This "something you are, something you have, and something you know" technique works to secure some of the world's most sensitive installations.

Touchscreens

Touchscreen technology converts stimuli of some sort, which are generated by actually touching the screen, to electrical impulses that travel over serial connections to the computer system. These input signals allow for the replacement of the mouse, simultaneously in movement and in click. With onscreen keyboards, the external keyboard can be retired as well. However, standard computer systems are not the only application for touchscreen enhancement. This technology can also be seen in PDAs, point-of-sale venues for such things as PIN entry and signature capture, handheld and bar-mounted games, ATMs, remote controls, appliances, and vehicles. The list continues to grow as technology advances.

For touchscreens, a handful of solutions exist for converting a touch to a signal. Some less-successful ones rely on warm hands, sound waves, or dust-free screens. The more successful screens have optical or electrical sensors that are quite a bit less fastidious. In any event, the sensory system is added onto a standard monitor at some point, whether in the field by the user or in a more seamless fashion by the manufacturer.

Installing monitors with touch capability on standard computers entails not only attachment to the graphics adapter, but also attachment to a serial interface. The most popular of these has become the USB port, much as it has for the mouse and keyboard.

KVM Switch

A KVM switch isn't an input device, but it allows you to switch between sets of input devices. The *KVM switch* is named after the devices it allows you to switch between or among sets of. The initials stand for *keyboard*, *video*, and *mouse*. KVM switches come in a variety of models. You can select the switch that accommodates the type of interfaces your components require. For example, your keyboard and mouse might attach with mini-DIN connectors or with USB connectors; your monitor might attach with a VGA or DVI connector.

The purpose of the switch is to allow you to have multiple systems attached to the same keyboard, monitor, and mouse. You can use these three devices with only one system at a time. Some switches have a dial that you turn to select which system attaches to the components, while others feature buttons for each system connected. Common uses of KVM switches include using the same components alternately for a desktop computer and a laptop docking station or having a server room with multiple servers but no need to interface with them simultaneously.

Identifying Purposes and Characteristics of Adapter Cards

An *adapter card* (also known as an *expansion card*) is simply a circuit board you install into a computer to increase the capabilities of that computer. Adapter cards come in varying formats for different uses, but the important thing to note is that no matter what function a card has, the card being installed must match the bus type of the motherboard you are installing it into. For example, you can only install a PCI network card into a PCI expansion slot.

For today's integrated components, you might not need an adapter to achieve the related services, but you will still need to install drivers to make the integrated devices function with the operating system. As this trend was maturing, many installers found most of the integrated components to be nonfunctional. A quick check in Device Manager showed a small collection of devices to be without their device drivers. Most motherboard manufacturers supply CD-ROM discs with their motherboards that contain all the device drivers needed to get the built-in electronics recognized by the operating system. Execution of the disc's setup program generally results in all components working and Device Manager clearing its warnings.

The following are the four most common categories of expansion card installed today:

- Video
- Multimedia
- I/O
- Communications

Let's take a quick look at each of these card types, their functions, and what some of them look like.

Video

A video adapter (more commonly called a video card) is the expansion card you put into a computer in order to allow the computer to display information on some kind of monitor or LCD display. A video card is also responsible for converting the data sent to it by the CPU into the pixels, addresses, and other items required for display. Sometimes, video cards can include dedicated chips to perform certain of these functions, thus accelerating the speed of display.

At a basic level, video adapters that have a PCI interface operate sufficiently. However, because AGP and PCIe slots offer more resources to the adapter, most manufacturers and computer owners prefer not to use PCI slots for video adapters. Today's motherboards might still offer an AGP slot of some sort, but increasingly, PCIe is becoming the preferred slot for video card attachment. The technology on which PCIe was designed performs better for video than those on which AGP and PCI are based. Figure 2.23 shows an example of a PCIe-based video card.

FIGURE 2.23   A video expansion card

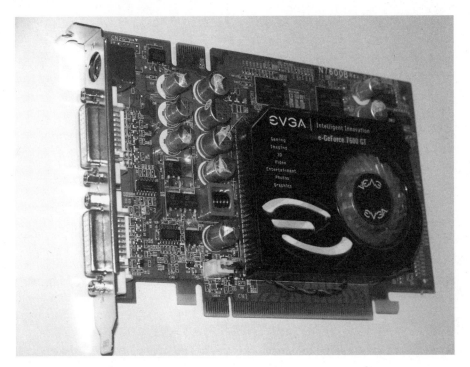

Multimedia

The most basic and prolific multimedia adapter is the sound card. TV tuner cards and video capture cards are newer multimedia adapters that continue to gain in popularity due to decreasing cost and the rise of the Internet as a forum for creative sharing.

Sound Card

Just as there are devices to convert computer signals into printouts and video information, there are devices to convert those signals into sound. These devices are known as *sound cards*. Although sound cards started out as pluggable adapters, this functionality is one of the most common integrated technologies found on motherboards today. A sound card typically has small, round, ⅛-inch jacks on the back of it for connecting to microphones, headphones, and speakers as well as other sound equipment. Many sound cards used to have a DA15 game port, which can be used for either joysticks or MIDI controllers. Figure 2.24 shows an example of a legacy sound card with a DA15 game port.

FIGURE 2.24   A typical sound card

Sound cards today might come with an RCA jack (see the section "Audio/Video Jacks" in Chapter 1). This is decidedly not for composite video. Instead, there is a digital audio specification known as the *Sony/Philips Digital Interface (S/PDIF)*. Not only does this format allow you to transmit audio in digital clarity, but in addition to the RCA jack and coaxial copper cabling, it specifies optical fiber connectors (TOSLINK) and cabling for electrically noisy environments, further increasing transmission quality of the digital signal.

TV Tuner Cards and Video Capture Cards

The *TV tuner card* is a class of internal and external devices that allows you to connect a broadcast signal, such as home cable television, to your computer and display it. TV tuner cards come in analog, digital, and hybrid varieties. Most TV tuner cards act as video capture cards as well. A *video capture card* can also be a stand-alone device and is often used to save a video stream to the computer for later manipulation or sharing. Video-sharing sites on the Internet make video capture cards quite popular with enterprises and Internet social-ites alike. TV tuner cards and video capture cards need and often come with software to aid in the processing of multimedia input.

I/O

I/O card is often a catchall phrase for any adapter card that expands the system to interface with devices that offer input to the system, output from the system, or both. Common examples of I/O are the classic serial and parallel ports of the system and drive interface connections. A popular expansion card of the 1980s and early 1990s was known as the Super I/O card. This one adapter had the circuitry for two standard serial ports, one parallel port, two IDE (PATA) controllers, and one floppy controller. Some versions included other components, such as a game port.

For many years, if you wanted to use a SCSI hard drive in your system or a SCSI-attached printer or scanner, you had to install an adapter card that expanded the motherboard's capabilities to allow the use of SCSI hard drives. The drives would then cable to the adapter, and the adapter would perform the requisite conversion of the drive signals to those that the motherboard and the circuits installed on it could use. Today, many server motherboards have SCSI controllers built in for such internal hard drives, and everything else tends to use integrated USB and FireWire interfaces.

Communications

Communications adapters give a computer the ability to transmit information to other devices that might be too distant to cable up to directly. Network adapters and modems are the two most popular types of communications adapter. Network adapters are generally used within the administrative domain of a home or enterprise and rely on other devices to relay their transmissions around the world. In contrast, modems allow direct domestic or international communication between two devices across the Public Switched Telephone Network (PSTN).

Network Interface Card (NIC)

A *network interface card (NIC)* is an expansion card that connects a computer to a network so that it can communicate with other computers on that network. NIC can also stand for network interface controller. It translates the data from the parallel data stream used inside the computer into the serial data stream that makes up the frames used on the network. It has a connector for the type of expansion bus on the motherboard (PCIe, PCI, ISA, and so on) as well as a connector for the type of network (such as RJ-45 for UTP, antenna for wireless, or BNC for coax). In addition to the NIC, you need to install drivers for the NIC in order for the computer to use the adapter to access the network. Figure 2.25 shows an example of a NIC.

Some computers have NIC circuitry integrated into their motherboards. Therefore, a computer with an integrated NIC wouldn't need to have a NIC expansion card installed, unless you were using the second NIC for load balancing, security, or fault-tolerance applications.

Modem

Any computer that connects to the Internet using a dial-up connection needs a modem, or *modulator/demodulator*. A *modem* is a device that converts digital signals from a computer into analog signals that can be transmitted over phone lines and back again. These expansion card devices have one connector for the expansion bus being used (PCIe, PCI, ISA, and so on) and another for connection to the telephone line. Actually, as you can see in Figure 2.26, which shows an old ISA modem, there might be two RJ-11 ports: one for connection to the telephone line and the other for connection to a telephone. This is the case primarily so that putting a computer online still lets someone hook a phone to that wall jack (although they won't be able to use the phone while the computer is connected to the Internet).

FIGURE 2.25   A network interface card

FIGURE 2.26   A modem

Summary

In this chapter, you learned about personal computer components, specifically storage devices, power supplies, input devices, and adapter cards. We covered storage devices, such as hard drives, both conventional and solid state; floppy drives; optical drives; tape drives; and flash memory. We discussed power supply safety, as well as the various connectors and formats, and investigated the similarity between power supplies and AC adapters. Well-known input devices, such as the mouse and keyboard, and less conventional, yet popular, input devices were also examined in this chapter. You also learned about the KVM switch, a device that allows you to share input devices among computers. The adapter cards highlighted in this chapter fall into four broad categories: video, multimedia, I/O, and communications.

Exam Essentials

Be familiar with the components of a conventional hard drive system and the anatomy of a hard drive.   Most of today's hard drive systems consist of an integrated controller and disc assembly that communicates to the rest of the system through an external host adapter. The hard disk drives consist of many components that work together, some in a physical sense and other in a magnetic sense, to store data on the disc surfaces for later retrieval.

Get to know the newer solid-state drives.   SSDs are growing in popularity and will replace conventional drives as they become more reliable and less expensive.

Know the technology of floppy drives.   Become familiar with the various floppy diskette capacities and the technology behind these drives.

Understand the details surrounding optical storage.   From capacities to speeds, you should know what the varieties of optical storage offer as well as the specifics of the technologies that comprise this storage category.

Be able to differentiate among removable-storage options.   There are numerous tape and solid-state storage formats. Know the names of the options in each category.

Know about power supplies and their connectors.   Power supplies are made in AT, ATX, and proprietary form factors. Regardless, they must offer connectors for motherboards and internal devices. Know the differences among the connectors and how power supplies are rated. Also understand why AC adapters are related to power supplies.

Compare and contrast input devices.   Although input devices vary widely in their functionality, they all provide external input to the computer. Familiarize yourself with the specifics of the devices mentioned in this chapter.

Review Questions

1. What is the physical component where data are stored in a HDD?
   A. Read/write head
   B. Platter
   C. Sector
   D. Cluster

2. Which of the following is not one of the three major components of a hard disk drive system?
   A. Drive interface
   B. Controller
   C. Hard disk
   D. Host adapter

3. What is the largest NTFS volume size supported by Windows XP?
   A. 256GB
   B. 2TB
   C. 128TB
   D. 256TB

4. Which technology is based on flash memory and is intended to eventually replace conventional hard disk drives that have moving discs and other mechanisms?
   A. Thumb drives
   B. Memory cards
   C. Solid-state drives
   D. Optical drives

5. High-density 3½″ floppy diskettes have a formatted capacity of:
   A. 360KB
   B. 720KB
   C. 1.44MB
   D. 2.88MB

6. Which optical disc format supports a data capacity of 25GB?
   A. Double-sided, double-layer DVD+R
   B. Single-sided, single-layer Blu-ray disc
   C. Double-sided, single-layer DVD-R
   D. Double-sided, single-layer DVD+R

7. Which of the following best describes the concept of hot-swappable devices?

   A. Power does not need turned off before the device is inserted or removed.

   B. The device can be removed with power applied after the device is properly stopped in the operating system.

   C. Care must be taken when swapping the device because it can be hot to the touch.

   D. The device can be swapped while still hot, immediately after powering down the system.

8. Of the following voltage pairings, which one accurately represents the input and output, respectively, of power supplies and AC adapters?

   A. AC in, AC out

   B. DC in, DC out

   C. AC in, DC out

   D. DC in, AC out

9. What are the five output voltages produced by a common PC power supply? (Choose five.)

   A. +3.3VDC

   B. −3.3VDC

   C. +5VDC

   D. −5VDC

   E. +12VDC

   F. −12VDC

   G. +110VAC

   H. −110VAC

10. Which of the following statements about power supplies is true?

    A. You must make sure the voltage selector switch on the back of the power supply is switched to the lower setting if the computer is going to be used in Europe.

    B. SATA hard drives most often use the same type of power connector as PATA hard drives.

    C. Power supplies supply power to ATX-based motherboards with connectors known commonly as P8 and P9.

    D. Molex connectors are used with PATA hard drives, while Berg connectors are used with floppy drives.

11. What kind of device uses unique physical traits of the user to authenticate their access to a secure system or location?

    A. Barcode reader

    B. Biometric device

    C. Keyboard

    D. Touch screen

12. What kind of media is most commonly used when large amounts of data need to be archived on a regular basis?

   A. Tape

   B. Optical disc

   C. External hard drive

   D. Floppy diskette

13. Which type of input device employs roughly the same connector as the original AT keyboard?

   A. Barcode reader

   B. PS/2 keyboard

   C. MIDI

   D. Touch screen

14. What can you use to convert video to a format that can be uploaded to the Internet, among other things?

   A. A barcode reader

   B. A video capture card

   C. A TV tuner card

   D. A MIDI device

15. Why might you use a KVM switch?

   A. You have multiple Ethernet devices that need to communicate with one another.

   B. You need to be able to switch the voltage supplied to a particular device.

   C. You do not have a non-network-attached printer but want multiple computers to be able to print to it.

   D. You have more than one server and don't want to buy certain external peripherals separately for each.

16. Which category of adapters includes NICs?

   A. Multimedia

   B. I/O

   C. Communications

   D. Video

17. What category of adapter would you need to install to equip a system with one or more USB ports?

   A. Multimedia

   B. I/O

   C. Communications

   D. Video

18. What type of adapter has an RJ-11 jack built in?

    A. Modem

    B. Video

    C. Sound

    D. NIC

19. What type of pointing device features a ball and buttons on the top and a flat, steady surface on the bottom?

    A. Mouse

    B. Touchpad

    C. Trackball

    D. Trackpad

20. When replacing a power supply, which of the following tends to vary among power supplies and must be chosen properly to support all connected devices?

    A. Wattage

    B. Voltage

    C. Amperage

    D. Resistance

Answers to Review Questions

1.   B. A conventional HDD contains discs called platters, on which data are stored magnetically through read/write heads by way of a magnetic coating.

2.   A. A conventional hard disk drive system consists of the hard disk and its often-integrated controller as well as a host adapter to gain access to the rest of the computer system. The drive interface is a common component of the controller and host adapter.

3.   D. A fixed number of clusters is supported by each operating system, leading to a corresponding maximum volume size. If the maximum NTFS cluster size of 64KB is used, Windows XP can support a single-volume size of 256TB. When a cluster size of one sector, or 512 bytes (½KB), is used, the maximum volume size reduces to 2TB.

4.   C. Solid-state disks (SSDs) are capable of replacing conventional HDDs, contingent upon cheaper components and higher capacities.

5.   C. High-density 3½″ floppy diskettes have a formatted capacity of 1.44MB. Double-density 5¼″ floppies can be formatted to a capacity of 360KB, while double-density floppies support 720KB. The extended-density 3½″ floppy diskettes can be formatted to 2.88MB.

6.   B. Blu-ray discs have a single-sided, single-layer capacity of 25GB. The best of the other options achieve no more than roughly 17GB.

7.   A. Hot-swappable devices can be removed while the power to the system is still on. Warm-swappable devices need to be stopped in the operating system before being removed. The term has nothing to do with the heat level of the device.

8.   C. Power supplies and AC adapters use standard wall outlets for an input of AC voltage, which they convert to the DC voltages required by the components they supply power to.

9.   A, C, D, E, F. A PC's power supply produces +3.3VDC, +5VDC, −5VDC, +12VDC, and −12VDC from a 110VAC input.

10. D. Molex power connectors have been used with larger internal devices since the original PCs hit the market. When the 3½″ floppy diskette drives were launched, they used the newer Berg connectors. Europe requires the voltage selector switch be set at the higher setting. SATA drives most often use a specific power connector that is not compatible with the Molex connector used by PATA drives. AT-based motherboards call for P8 and P9 connectors; ATX motherboards have a newer 20- or 24-pin single power connector.

11. B. Biometric input devices scan a physical trait of the user, such as voice, fingerprint, and retina, for authentication purposes during attempts to access computer systems and other property.

12. A. Although inefficient as an interactive medium, sequential tape-based storage continues to be developed in increasing capacities. Tape remains the best choice for frequently backing up large amounts of data for redundancy and archival purposes.

13. C. MIDI devices use a 5-pin DIN connector similar to the one used with the original AT keyboard.

14. B. A video capture card is used to convert raw video input to a format that can be shared electronically. Although many TV tuner cards provide this functionality, it is their video-capture component that gives them this capability. Any adapter that is strictly a TV tuner cannot capture video.

15. D. KVM switches are ideal when you have multiple computers situated near one another and do not want to commit the extra desk space to each computer having its own keyboard, mouse, and monitor.

16. C. Network interface cards are considered to be a form of communications adapter.

17. B. Interfaces, such as USB ports, are considered input/output ports. If you have to add USB capability to a computer, an I/O adapter with USB ports on it would meet the need.

18. A. Modems have RJ-11 jacks for interface to the Public Switched Telephone Network (PSTN). The modular jacks that Ethernet NICs have are known as RJ-45 jacks.

19. C. A trackball is a sort of stationary mouse that has the ball for movement detection on the top of the device along with the keys. The ball is actuated by the thumb or fingers, not by moving the device along a flat surface or mouse pad. Trackballs are ideal where desk space is limited. There is no such thing as a trackpad.

20. A. Power supplies are rated in watts. When you purchase a power supply, you should make sure that the devices inside the computer do not require more wattage than the chosen power supply can offer. The voltage is fairly standard among power supplies and has nothing to do with the devices connected to the power supply. Amperage and resistance are not selling points for power supplies.

Chapter
3

Understanding Display Devices

THE FOLLOWING COMPTIA A+ ESSENTIALS EXAM OBJECTIVES ARE COVERED IN THIS CHAPTER:

✓ **1.7 Distinguish between the different display devices and their characteristics**

- Projectors, CRT and LCD
- LCD technologies
  - Resolution (e.g. XGA, SXGA+, UXGA, WUXGA)
  - Contrast ratio
  - Native resolution
- Connector types
  - VGA
  - HDMI
  - S-Video
  - Component / RGB
  - DVI pin compatibility
- Settings
  - Refresh rate
  - Resolution
  - Multi-monitor
  - Degauss

The primary method of getting information out of a computer is to use a computer *video display unit (VDU)*. Display systems convert computer signals into text and pictures and display them on a TV-like screen. As a matter of fact, the first personal computers used television screens because it was simpler to use an existing display technology rather than to develop a new one. Various types of computer displays are in use today, including the TV. Most all of them, projection systems as well, use the same *cathode ray tube (CRT)* technology found in conventional television sets or the *liquid crystal display (LCD)* technology found on nearly all laptop, notebook, and palmtop computers. In fact, more LCDs than CRTs are sold with computers today. Only the cheapest display units or high-end specialized units (used for enhanced clarity and video performance) are CRT-based.

This chapter introduces you to concepts surrounding displays and the adapters to which they connect. Other topics covered in this chapter include display standards, such as VGA, the interfaces used between monitors and adapters, and settings common to most display devices.

Understanding Display Types and Settings

Most display systems work the same way. First, the computer sends a signal to a device called the video adapter—an expansion board installed in an expansion bus slot or the equivalent circuitry integrated into the motherboard—telling it to display a particular graphic or character. The adapter then renders the character for the display—that is, it converts the single instruction into several instructions that tell the display device how to draw the graphic—and sends the instructions to the display device. The primary differences after that are in the type of video adapter you are using (digital or analog) and the type of display (CRT, LCD, projector, etc.). We'll talk about some of these differences now.

Video Display Types

To truly understand the video-display arena, you must be introduced to a few terms and concepts that you may not be familiar with. The legacy digital transistor-transistor logic (TTL) and the analog technologies that began with video graphics array (VGA) are the two broad categories of video technologies. These categories have nothing to do with the makeup of the VDU, but instead how the graphics adapter communicates with the VDU. You will read about many of the TTL and VGA technologies in coming sections of this chapter. First, however, let's explore three different VDU types:

- CRT displays
- LCD displays
- Projection systems

CRT Displays

As already mentioned, conventional computer monitors contain a CRT. In a CRT, a device called an electron gun shoots a beam of electrons toward the back side of the monitor screen (see Figure 3.1). Color CRTs often use three guns, one each for red, green, and blue image components. The back of the screen is coated with special chemical dots called phosphors (often zinc sulfide combined with other elements for color variation, but no phosphorus, ironically) that glow when electrons strike them.

FIGURE 3.1   Cutaway of a CRT monitor

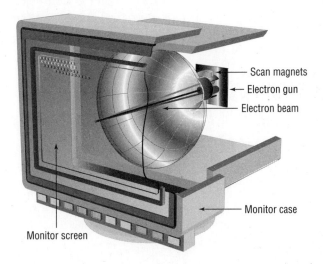

The beam of electrons scans across the monitor from left to right and top to bottom in a raster pattern to create the image. A special metallic screen called a shadow mask (in most implementations) has holes spaced and angled in an extremely precise manner. For color CRTs that employ shadow masks, a trio of dot phosphors is often grouped in a triangle for each hardware picture element. The separate electron beams that control red, green, and blue only strike their own phosphors at the correct angle to cause them to glow. The glow of the phosphors decays very quickly, requiring the electron beam's regular return to each phosphor to sustain the glow. The more dot phosphors that are placed in a given area, the better the image quality at higher resolutions.

There are two ways to measure a CRT monitor's image quality: dot pitch and resolution. Dot pitch is a physical characteristic of the monitor hardware, but resolution is configurable through software.

Dot pitch   *Dot pitch* is the measurement between the same spot in two vertically adjacent dot trios. In other words, it's the height of the trio added to the distance between the next trio above or below it. Expressed in millimeters or dots per inch, the dot pitch tells how "sharp" the picture is. The lower the measurement in millimeters or the higher the number of dots per inch, the closer together the phosphors are, and as a result, the sharper the image. An average dot pitch is 0.28mm to 0.32mm. Anything closer than 0.28mm is considered exceptional. Dot pitch in the LCD arena translates to the LCD's native resolution, discussed later in the "LCD-Specific Concepts" section. Essentially, software-pixel placement is limited to the hardware's transistor placement, leading to one optimal resolution for each LCD. The transistors that make up the hardware's picture elements are discussed later in the section "Liquid Crystal Displays (LCDs)."

Resolution   *Resolution* is defined by how many software picture elements (*pixels*) are used to draw the screen. An advantage of higher resolutions is that more information can be displayed in the same screen area. A disadvantage is that the same objects and text displayed at a higher resolution appear smaller and might be harder to see. The resolution is described in terms of the visible image's dimensions, which indicate how many rows and columns of pixels are used to draw the screen. For example, a resolution of 1,024×768 means 1,024 pixels across (columns) and 768 pixels down (rows) were used to draw the pixel matrix. The video technology in this example would use $1,024 \times 768 = 786,432$ pixels to draw the screen. Resolution is a software setting that is common among CRTs, LCDs, and projection systems as well as other display devices.

Resolution's Memory Requirement

Video memory is used to store rendered screen images. The memory required for a screen image varies directly as the color depth, which is defined as the number of colors in which each pixel can be displayed. A palette with a 24-bit color depth is capable of displaying each pixel in one of $2^{24} = 16,777,216$ distinct colors.

In the preceding example, if you were using 24-bit graphics, meaning each pixel requires 24 bits of memory to store that one screen element, 786,432 pixels would require 18,874,368 bits, or 2,359,296 bytes. Because this boils down to 2.25MB, an early (bordering on ancient) video adapter with only 2MB of RAM would not be capable of such resolution at 24 bits per pixel. Today's adapters have absolutely no trouble displaying such a resolution with a 24- or 32-bit color depth.

Liquid Crystal Displays (LCDs)

Portable computers were originally designed to be compact versions of their bigger brothers. They crammed all the components of the big desktop computers into a small, suitcase-like box called (laughably) a *portable computer*. No matter what the designers did to reduce the size of the computer, the display remained as large as the desktop version's—that is, until an inventor found that when he passed an electric current through a semi-crystalline liquid, the crystals aligned themselves with the current. It was found that by combining transistors with these liquid crystals, patterns could be formed. These patterns could represent numbers or letters. The first application of these *liquid crystal displays (LCDs)* was the LCD watch. It was rather bulky, but it was cool.

As LCD elements got smaller, the detail of the patterns became greater, until one day someone thought to make a computer screen out of several of these elements. This screen was very light compared to computer monitors of the day, and it consumed relatively little power. It could easily be added to a portable computer to reduce the weight by as much as 30 pounds. As the components got smaller, so did the computer, and the laptop computer was born.

LCDs are not just limited to laptops; desktop versions of LCD displays are available as well. Additionally, the home television market has been enjoying the LCD as a competitor of plasma for years. LCDs used with desktop computer systems use the same technology as their laptop counterparts but potentially on a much larger scale.

These external LCDs are available in either analog or digital interfaces. The analog interface is exactly the same as the interface used for analog CRT monitors. Internal digital signals from the computer are rendered and output as analog signals by the video card and are then sent along the same 15-pin connector as used with analog CRT monitors. Digital LCDs with a digital interface, on the other hand, require no analog modulation by the graphics adapter. They require the video card to support digital output using a different interface, such as DVI, for instance. The advantage is that because the video signal never changes from digital to analog, there is less chance of interference and no conversion-related quality loss. Digital displays are generally sharper than their analog counterparts.

Two major types of LCD displays have been implemented over the years: active-matrix screens and passive-matrix screens. Another type, dual scan, is a passive-matrix variant. The main differences lie in the quality of the image. However, when used with computers, each type uses lighting behind the LCD panel (backlighting) to make the screen easier to view.

Active matrix   An active-matrix screen works in a similar manner to the LCD watch. The screen is made up of several individual LCD pixels. A transistor behind each pixel, when switched on, activates two electrodes that align the crystals and alter the passage of light at that location. This type of display is very crisp and easy to look at and does not require constant refreshing to maintain an image. The major disadvantage of an active-matrix screen is that it requires large amounts of power to operate all the transistors. Even with the backlight turned off, the screen can still consume battery power at an alarming rate. Most laptops with active-matrix screens can't operate on a battery for more than two hours. The vast majority of LCDs manufactured today are based on active-matrix technology.

Passive matrix   Within the passive-matrix screen are two rows of transistors: one at the top, another at the side. In simplified terms for a single pixel, when the display is instructed to change the crystalline alignment of a particular pixel, it sends a signal to the x- and y-coordinate transistors for that pixel, thus turning them on. This then causes voltage lines from each axis to intersect at the desired coordinates, turning the desired pixel black. Figure 3.2 illustrates this concept. More realistically, transistors controlling the rows fire in series to refresh or newly activate pixels on each row in succession. The transistors controlling the columns are synchronized to fire when that row's transistor is active and only for the pixels that should be affected on that row. Although the passive-matrix concept fell out of favor for a number of years as active-matrix displays became more affordable, advances in passive-matrix technology could lead to resurgence in the future.

FIGURE 3.2   A passive-matrix display

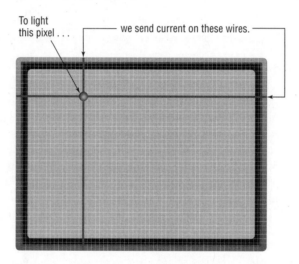

Dual scan   Dual scan is a variation of the passive-matrix display. The classic passive-matrix screen is split in half to implement a dual-scan display. Each half of the display is refreshed separately, leading to increased quality. Although dual scan improves on the quality of conventional passive-matrix displays, it has not historically rivaled the quality produced by active matrix.

The main differences between active matrix and typical passive matrix are image quality and viewing angle. Because the computer takes a millisecond or two to light the coordinates for a pixel in passive-matrix displays, the response of the screen to rapid changes is poor, causing, for example, an effect known as *submarining*: On a computer with a passive-matrix display, if you move the mouse pointer rapidly from one location to another, it will disappear from the first location and reappear in the new location without appearing anywhere in between. If you move toward the side of a passive-matrix LCD, you eventually notice the display turning dark. In contrast, active-matrix LCDs have a viewing angle wider than 179 degrees.

We'll discuss some LCD-specific concepts later in this chapter.

Projection Systems

The third major category of display device is the video projection system. Portable *projectors* can be thought of as condensed video display units with a lighting system that projects the VDU's image onto a screen or other flat surface for group viewing. Interactive white boards have become popular over the past decade to allow presenters to project an image onto the board as they use virtual markers to electronically draw on the displayed image. Remote participants can see the slide on their terminal as well as the markups made by the presenter. The presenter can see the same markups because the board transmits them to the computer to which the projector is attached, causing them to be displayed in real time.

Another popular implementation of projection systems has been the rear-projection television, in which a projector is built into a cabinet behind a screen onto which the image is projected in reverse so that an observer in front of the TV can view the image correctly. Early rear-projection TVs as well as ceiling-mounted home-theater units used CRT technology to drive three filtered light sources that work together to create an RGB image.

Later rear-projection systems, including most modern portable projectors, implement LCD gates. These units shine a bright light through three LCD panels that adjust pixels in the same manner as an LCD monitor, except the projected image is formed as with the CRT projector by synchronizing the projection of the red, green, and blue images onto the same surface.

Digital light processing (DLP) is another popular technology that keeps rear-projection TVs on the market and benefits portable projectors as well, allowing some projectors to be extremely small. Special DLP chips, referred to as optical semiconductors, have roughly as many rotatable mirrors on their surface as pixels in the display resolution. A light source and colored filter wheel or colored light sources are used to rapidly switch among primary, and sometimes secondary, colors in synchronization with the chip's mirror positions, thousands of times per second.

To accommodate using portable units at variable distances from the projection surface, a focusing mechanism is included on the lens. Other adjustments, such as Keystone and Pincushion, are provided through a menu system on many models as well as a way to rotate the image 180° for ceiling-mount applications.

Although it doesn't take long for the fan to stop running on its own, this is a phase that should never be skipped to save time. With projector bulbs one of the priciest consumables in the world of technology, doing so may cost you more than a change in your travel arrangements.

Adjusting Display Settings

Let's start by defining a few important terms:

- Refresh rate
- Resolution
- Multimonitor
- Degauss

Real World Scenario

Factor In Some Time

A fellow instructor had his own portable projector that he carried with him on the road. At the end of a week's class, he would power down the projector and get his laptop and other goodies packed away. Just before running out the door, he would unplug the projector and pack it up. As with many instructors, this gentleman's presentations increased in density and length as he became more and more comfortable with the material.

I ran into him at a training center some time after this trend had begun. His presentation had been running later and later each Friday afternoon, edging him ever closer to his airline departure time. He admitted he had gotten into the habit of yanking the power plug for his projector from the wall and quickly stuffing the unit into the carrying case before darting out the door. Not long after our meeting, I heard that his projector failed catastrophically. Replacing the bulb was not the solution.

One caveat with projectors is that you must never pull the electrical plug from the outlet until you hear the internal fan cut off. There is enough residual heat generated by the projector bulb that damage to the electronics or the bulb itself can occur if the fan is not allowed to remove enough heat before it stops running. Without a connection to an electrical outlet, the fan stops immediately. The electronics have enough heat shielding that the fan removes enough heat during normal operation to avoid damage to the shielded components.

Each of these terms relates to settings available through the operating system by way of display-option settings or through the monitor's control panel (degauss).

Refresh Rate

The *refresh rate* is technically the vertical scan frequency and specifies how many times in one second the scanning beam of electrons redraws the screen in CRTs. The phosphors stay bright for only a fraction of a second, so they must constantly be hit with electrons to appear to stay lit to the human eye. Given in draws per second, or Hertz, the refresh rate is directly proportional to how much effort is being put into keeping the screen lit. The refresh rate on smaller monitors, say 14 to 16 inches, does fine in the range 60 to 72Hz. However, the larger a monitor gets, the higher the refresh rate needs to be to reduce eyestrain from perceivable flicker. It is not uncommon to see refresh rates of 85Hz and higher.

Refresh rates apply to LCDs as well. For televisions, the refresh rate is a characteristic of the LCD, generally not an adjustment to be made. LCD televisions that support 120Hz refresh rates are common. For computer monitors, you might be able to select among multiple refresh rates. However, because LCDs do not illuminate phosphors, there is no concern of pixel decay (for which refreshing the pixel is necessary). Instead, higher refresh rates translate to more fluid video motion. If a pixel changes before the next refresh, the monitor is unable to display the change in that pixel. Therefore, for gaming systems, higher refresh rates are an advantage.

> CRT monitors manufactured today are not susceptible to damage caused by setting the video adapter's refresh rate too high, unlike older monitors. They simply refuse to operate at a rate higher than they are capable of. Refresh rates are set on the video card through the operating system or special utility software. In order for you to see a proper image, however, the monitor must support the rate you select.

The refresh rate is selected for the monitor. Nevertheless, the refresh rate you select must be supported by both your graphics adapter and your monitor. If a monitor only supports one refresh rate, it does not matter how many different rates your adapter supports—without overriding the defaults, you will only be able to choose the one common refresh rate. It is important to note that as the resolution you select increases, the higher supported refresh rates begin to disappear from the selection menu. If you want a higher refresh rate, you might have to compromise by choosing a lower resolution. Exercise 3.1 steps you through the process of changing the refresh rate in Windows Vista.

EXERCISE 3.1

Changing the Refresh Rate in Windows Vista

1. Right-click a blank portion of the Desktop.

2. Click Personalize.

EXERCISE 3.1 *(continued)*

3. Click the Display Settings link.

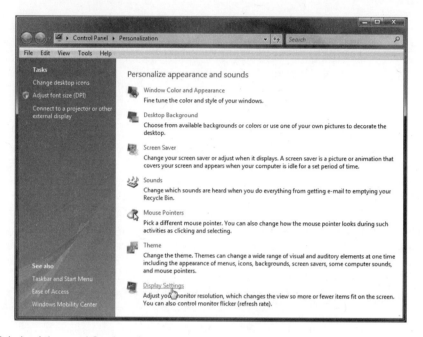

4. Click the Advanced Settings button.

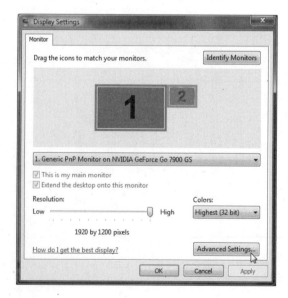

5. Click the Monitor tab.

6. Select the desired screen refresh rate from the drop-down menu.

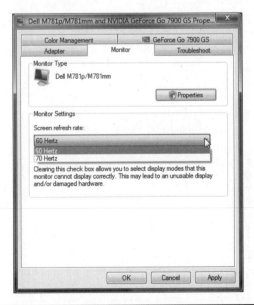

Just because refresh rates appear in this dialog box does not mean that the associated monitor will be able to handle that rate. Figure 3.3 shows a CRT when a refresh rate that is out of range has been selected. Without changing anything, if possible, clear the Hide Modes That This Monitor Cannot Display check box to possibly see other refresh rates not supported by your hardware. Figure 3.4 shows the same monitor with additional refresh rates after clearing the check box. If you unchecked the box, place a check in the box before leaving this dialog box.

FIGURE 3.3   An internal monitor error for an unsupported refresh rate

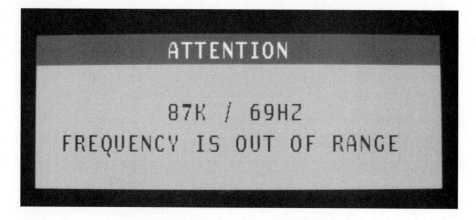

FIGURE 3.4   Unsupported refresh rates for a CRT monitor

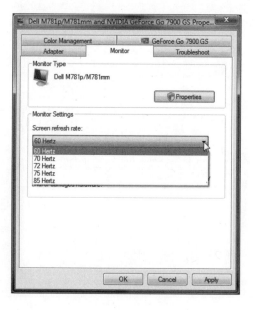

Resolution

Setting the resolution for your monitor is fairly straightforward. If you are using an LCD, you should use the native resolution of that monitor for best results. (See "LCD-Specific Concepts" later in this chapter.) Some systems will scale the image to avoid distortion, but others will try to fill the screen with the image, resulting in distortion. On occasion, you might find that increasing the resolution beyond the native resolution results in the need to scroll the Desktop in order to view other portions of it. In such instances, you cannot see the entire Desktop all at the same time. The monitor has the last word in how the signal it receives from the adapter is displayed. Adjusting your display settings to those that are recommended for your monitor can alleviate this scrolling effect.

In Windows Vista, follow Exercise 3.1 up to step 3. Click the monitor for which you want to alter the resolution, and then move the resolution slider to the right for higher resolutions, as shown in Figure 3.5, or to the left for lower resolutions.

FIGURE 3.5　Adjusting the resolution in Windows Vista

Some adapters come with their own utilities for changing settings, such as the refresh rate and resolution. For example, Figure 3.6 shows two windows from the NVIDIA Control Panel. The first window has resolution, color depth, and refresh rate, all in the same spot. The second window shows you the native resolution of the LCD and the current resolution selected. If they are different, you can have the utility immediately make the current resolution match the native resolution.

FIGURE 3.6   The NVIDIA Control Panel

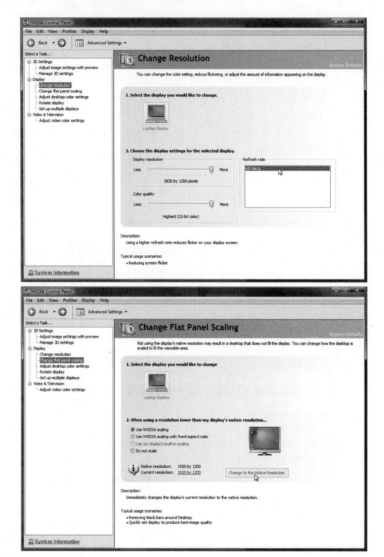

Multimonitor

Whether regularly or just on occasion, you may find yourself in a position where you need to use two monitors on the same computer simultaneously. For example, if you are giving a presentation and would like to have a presenter's view on your laptop's LCD but need to project a slideshow onto a screen, you might need to connect an external projector to the laptop.

Simply connecting an external display device does not guarantee it will be recognized and automatically work. You might need to change settings for the external device, such as the resolution or the device's virtual orientation with respect to the built-in display, which affects how you drag objects between the screens. Exercise 3.2 guides you through this process.

Microsoft calls its multimonitor feature Dual View. You have the option to extend your Desktop onto a second monitor or to clone your Desktop on the second monitor. You can use one graphics adapter with multiple monitor interfaces or multiple adapters. However, as of Vista, the newly introduced Windows Display Driver Model (WDDM) version 1.0 requires the same driver be used for all adapters. This doesn't mean that you cannot use two adapters that fit into different expansion slot types, such as PCIe and AGP. It just means that both cards have to use the same driver. Incidentally, laptops that support external monitors use the same driver for the external interface as for the internal LCD attachment. Version 1.1, introduced with Windows 7, relaxes this requirement. WDDM is a graphics-driver architecture that provides enhanced graphics functionality that was not available before Windows Vista, such as virtualized video memory, preemptive task scheduling, and sharing of Direct3D surfaces among processes.

To change the settings for multiple monitors in Windows Vista, again perform Exercise 3.1 up to step 3, and then follow the steps in Exercise 3.2.

EXERCISE 3.2

Changing the Settings for Multiple Monitors

1. Click on the picture of the monitor with the number 2 on it.

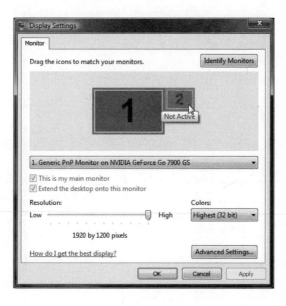

2. Check the Extend The Desktop Onto This Monitor box.

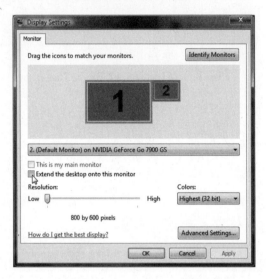

3. Click and drag the second monitor to the desired virtual position around the primary monitor.

4. While the second monitor is still selected, change its refresh rate and resolution, if necessary, as outlined in the previous sections.

Degauss

Degaussing is the reduction of the magnetic field of an object. It is generally impossible to completely neutralize an object's magnetic field, so reducing it is the objective. One application of degaussing is to randomize the magnetic domains on the surface of a magnetic storage medium, such as a hard disk drive. Degaussing the drive makes previously saved information all but unrecoverable. This, however, is a discussion of display devices and, as such, degaussing has a related but different implication.

Because CRTs use magnetic fields to guide the electron beams to their intended targets, and LCDs do not, degaussing a monitor is strictly a CRT-related practice. Due to the fact that you cannot completely eradicate the magnetic field of an object, repeated degaussing of a CRT monitor is not advised. In fact, the monitor can be damaged by degaussing it more than once in a short period of time.

The constant bombardment of the metallic shadow mask of a CRT monitor by the electron beams can cause magnetic fields to build up on the mask that result in distortions that manifest themselves as image discoloration and rainbow effects. Many later-generation CRTs have an internal degaussing coil wrapped around the front portion of the unit near the shadow mask. Newer CRTs activate the coil each time the unit is turned on with the power button, resulting in a sometimes dramatic, humming noise of extremely short duration whenever power is applied. These monitors rarely require intentional manual degaussing by the user or technician, as a result.

When these internal degaussing coils are activated manually by a button on the monitor or through the monitor's internal menu system, the same noise can be heard. Additionally, because the monitor is already powered up and displaying an image, you will notice the image shaking at the same time. Unadvised, repeated coil activation results in increasingly less dramatic results with each iteration.

External degaussing devices exist that reduce the magnetic field in the shadow mask. Because these tools can be made considerably stronger than the space-restricted internal coils, they can at once be more effective and more damaging to the sensitive magnetic yokes that guide the electron beams. Excessive electromagnetic energy has been known to permanently damage CRTs. You should take great care when using external degaussing devices on CRTs.

Some monitors have a degaussing button right on the front panel. The CRT used in the following exercise requires that you degauss from an onscreen menu system that is independent of the operating system. Nevertheless, if this monitor does not detect an attached system, it will not let you into the menu. Exercise 3.3 guides you through using the built-in degaussing feature of a Dell M781 monitor.

EXERCISE 3.3

Degaussing a CRT Monitor

1. Attach the CRT to a working computer system and power on the monitor.

2. Press the Menu button on the front panel of the CRT cabinet (the button on the far right in the following photo).

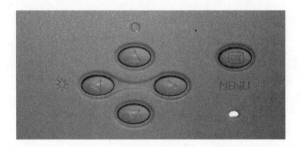

The following screen shot shows the resulting menu. Notice that the monitor detects the signal it is receiving from the graphics adapter. In this case, a resolution of 1600×1200 (UXGA—see Table 3.1 later in this chapter) and a refresh rate of 60Hz are detected. This monitor even offers advice on the recommended resolution for best results. In this case, 1024×768 is recommended. By following the recommendation, a better fit to the dot phosphors and a wider selection of refresh rates are likely.

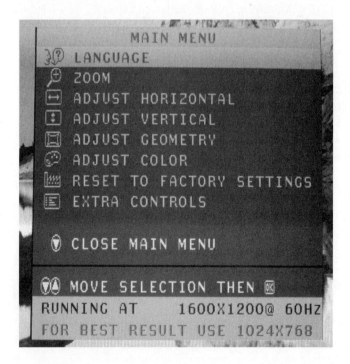

3. Use the up- and down-arrow keys on the front panel of the CRT to select the Extra Controls menu item.

4. Press the Menu button on the front panel to select the Extra Controls submenu, shown here.

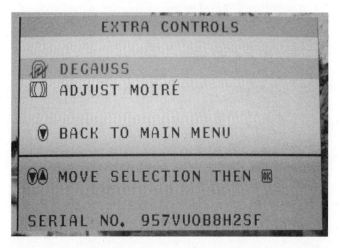

5. Press the Menu button on the front panel of the CRT because the Degauss menu item is already selected. If degaussing was required, you should hear the distinctive degaussing noise and notice the image distorting as shown here.

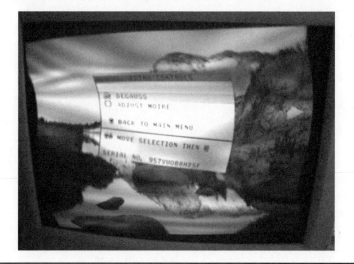

Understanding Video Standards and Technologies

This section introduces the various video standards, from the earlier digital standards, to the later analog standards, to the most current digital high-definition standards. You will also learn about LCD-specific terms and ideas.

Video Standards

The early video standards differ in two major areas: the highest resolution supported and the maximum number of colors in their palette. The supported resolution and palette size are directly related to the amount of memory on the adapter, which is used to hold the rendered images to be displayed. Display adapters through the years can be divided into four primary groups:

- Monochrome
- CGA
- EGA
- VGA

Because the amount of memory used to implement these early adapters was fixed, the resolution and number of colors supported by these cards was fixed as well. Newer standards, based on VGA analog technology and connectivity, were eventually developed using adapters with expandable memory. Adapters featuring variable amounts of memory resulted in selectable resolutions and color palettes. In time, 24-bit color palettes known as Truecolor and made up of almost 17 million colors, which exceed the number of colors the human eye can distinguish, were implemented. As a result, in keeping with growing screen sizes, the latest commercial video standards continue to grow in resolution, their distinguishing trait, but not in palette size. These post-VGA resolutions are discussed later in this chapter in the section, "Advanced Video Resolutions."

Monochrome

The first video technology for PCs was *monochrome* (from the Latin *mono*, meaning one, and *chroma*, meaning color). This black-and-white video (actually, it was green or amber text on a black background) was fine for the main operating system of the day, DOS. DOS didn't have any need for color. Thus, the video adapter was very basic. The first adapter, developed by IBM, was known as the Monochrome Display Adapter (MDA). It could display text but not graphics and used a resolution of 720×350 pixels.

The Hercules Graphics Card (HGC), introduced by Hercules Computer Technology, had a resolution of 720×350 and could display graphics as well as text. It did this by using two separate modes: a *text mode* that allowed the adapter to optimize its resources for displaying pre-drawn characters from its onboard library, *and* a *graphics mode* that optimized the adapter for drawing individual pixels for on-screen graphics. It could switch between these modes on the fly. These modes of operation have been included in all graphics adapters since the introduction of the HGC.

CGA

The next logical step for displays was to add a splash of color. IBM was the first with color, with the introduction of the Color Graphics Adapter (CGA). CGA displays 16-color text in resolutions of 320×200 (40 columns) and 640×200 (80 columns), but it displays 320×200 graphics with only four colors per mode. Each of the six possible modes has three fixed colors and a selectable fourth; each of the four colors comes from the 16 used for text. CGA's 640×200 graphics resolution has only two colors—black and one other color from the same palette of 16.

EGA

After a time, people wanted more colors and higher resolution, so IBM responded with the Enhanced Graphics Adapter (EGA). EGA could display 16 colors out of a palette of 64 with CGA resolutions as well as a high-resolution 640×350 mode. EGA marks the end of classic digital-video technology. The digital data pins on the nine-pin D-subminiature connector accounted for six of the nine pins. As a solution, analog technologies, starting with VGA, would all but stand alone in the market until the advent of DVI and HDMI, discussed later in this chapter.

VGA

With the PS/2 line of computers, IBM wanted to answer the cry for "more resolution, more colors" by introducing its best video adapter to date: the Video Graphics Array (VGA). This video technology had a whopping 256KB of video memory on board and could display 16 colors at 640×480, 640×350, and 320×200 pixels or, using mode 13h of the VGA BIOS, 256 colors at 320×200 pixels. It became widely used and has since become the base standard for color PC video. For many years, it was the starting point for computers, as far as video is concerned. Today, however, your computer likely only defaults to this video technology's resolution and color palette when there is an issue with the driver for your graphics adapter or when you enter Safe Mode.

One unique feature of VGA is that it's an analog technology, unlike the preceding standards. Technically, all CRT monitors produce an analog signal from the information received over the data cable attached to the computer. The difference in VGA-based technologies is that monitors receive an analog signal over the cable, whereas MDA, CGA, and EGA signals arrive at the monitor as digital pulse streams and have to be modulated to analog by the monitor before being displayed.

VGA builds a dynamic palette of 256 colors, which are chosen from various shades and hues of an 18-bit palette of 262,114 colors. When only 16 colors are displayed, they are chosen from the 256 selected colors. VGA sold well mainly because users could choose from almost any color they wanted (or at least one that was close). The reason for moving away from the original digital signal is because for every power of 2 that the number of colors in the palette increases, you need at least one more pin on the connector. A minimum of four pins for 16 colors is not a big deal, but a minimum of 32 pins for 32-bit graphics become a bit unwieldy. The cable has to grow with the connector, as well, affecting transmission quality and cable length. VGA, on the other hand, requires only three pins, one each for red, green, and blue modulated analog color levels, not including the necessary complement of ground and control signals. Twelve to 14 of the 15 pins of a VGA connector are adequate for this application.

One note about monitors that may seem rather obvious: you must use a video card that supports the type of monitor you are using. For example, you can't use a CGA monitor on a VGA adapter.

Advanced Video Resolutions

The following sections detail what might, at first, appear to be technologies based on new graphics adapters. However, advancements after the VGA adapter occurred only in the memory and firmware of the adapter, not the connector or its fundamental functionality. As a result, the following technologies are distinguished early on by supported resolutions and color palettes and later by resolutions alone.

Super VGA

Up until the late 1980s, IBM set most personal-computer video standards. IBM made the adapters, everyone bought them, and they became a standard. Some manufacturers didn't like this monopoly and set up the Video Electronics Standards Association (VESA) to try to enhance IBM's video technology and make the enhanced technology a public standard. The result of this work was Super VGA (SVGA). This new standard was indeed an enhancement because it could support 16 colors at a resolution of 800×600 (the VESA standard), but it soon expanded to support 1,024×768 pixels with 256 colors.

Since that time, SVGA has been a term used loosely for any resolution and color palette to exceed that of standard VGA. This even includes the resolution presented next, XGA. New names still continue to be introduced, mainly as a marketing tool to tout the new resolution du jour. While display devices must be manufactured to support a certain display resolution, one of the benefits of analog video technology is that modern VGA monitors can advance along with the graphics adapter, in terms of the color palette. The analog signal is what dictates the color palette, and the standard for the signal has not changed since its VGA origin. This makes a discussion of a VGA monitor's color limitations a non-issue. Such a topic makes sense only in reference to graphics adapters.

XGA

IBM introduced a new technology in 1990 known as the Extended Graphics Array (XGA). This technology was available only as a Micro Channel Architecture (MCA) expansion board and not as an ISA or EISA board. XGA could support 256 colors at 1,024×768 pixels or 65,536 colors at 800×600 pixels. It was a different design, optimized for GUIs like Windows or OS/2. It was also an *interlaced* technology at 1024×768, meaning that rather than scan every line one at a time to create the image, it scanned every other line on each pass, using the phenomenon known as *persistence of vision* to produce what appears to our eyes as a continuous image.

The advertised refresh rate specifies the frequency with which all odd or all even rows are scanned. The drawback to interlacing is that the refresh rate used on a CRT has to be twice the minimum comfort level for refreshing an entire screen. Otherwise, the human eye will interpret the uncomfortably noticeable decay of the pixels as flicker. Therefore, a refresh rate of 120Hz would result in a comfortable effective refresh rate of 60Hz. Unfortunately, 84Hz was a popular refresh rate for interlaced display signals, resulting in an entire screen being redrawn only 42 times per second, a rate below the minimum comfort level.

More Recent Video Standards

Any standard other than the ones already mentioned are probably extensions of SVGA or XGA. It is becoming easier and easier to predict the approximate resolution of a video specification based on its name. Whenever a known technology is preceded by the letter *W*, you can assume roughly the same vertical resolution but a wider horizontal resolution to accommodate 16:10 wide-screen formats (16:9 for LCD televisions). Preceding the technology with the letter *Q* indicates that the horizontal and vertical resolutions were each doubled, making a final resolution four times (quadruple) the original. To imply four times each, for a final resolution enhancement of 16 times, the letter *H* for hexadecatuple is used.

Therefore, if XGA has a resolution of 1024×768, then QXGA will have a resolution of 2048×1536. If Ultra XGA (UXGA) has a resolution of 1600×1200 and an aspect ratio of 4:3, then WUXGA has a resolution of 1920×1200 and a 16:10 aspect ratio. Clearly, there have been a large number of seemingly minute increases in resolution column and row sizes. However, consider that at 1024×768, for instance, the screen will display a total of 786,432 *pixels*. At 1280×1024, comparatively, the number of pixels increases to 1,310,720—nearly double the pixels for what doesn't sound like much of a difference. As mentioned, you need better technology and more video memory to display even slightly higher resolutions.

The term *aspect ratio* refers to the relationship between the horizontal and vertical pixel counts that a monitor can display. For example, for a display that supports 4:3 ratios, such as 1024×768, if you divide the first number by 4 and multiply the result by 3, the product is equal to the second number. Additionally, if you divide the first number by the second number, the result is approximately 1.3, the same as 4 ÷ 3. Displays with a 16:10 aspect ratio have measurements that result in a dividend of 16 ÷ 10 = 1.6.

Table 3.1 lists the various video technologies, their resolutions, and the maximum color palette they support, if specified as part of the standard. All resolutions, VGA and higher, have a 4:3 aspect ratio, unless otherwise noted.

TABLE 3.1 Video Display Technology Comparison

Name	Resolutions	Colors
Monochrome Display Adapter (MDA)	720×350	Mono (text only)
Hercules Graphics Card (HGC)	720×350	Mono (text and graphics)
Color Graphics Adapter (CGA)	320×200	4
	640×200	2
Enhanced Graphics Adapter (EGA)	Up to	
	640×350	16
Video Graphics Array (VGA)	640×480	16
	320×200	256
Super VGA (SVGA)	800×600	16
Extended Graphics Array (XGA)	800×600	65,536
	1024×768	256
Widescreen XGA (WXGA), 16:10	1280×800	Not specified
Super XGA (SXGA), 5:4	1280×1024	Not specified
SXGA+	1400×1050	Not specified
WSXGA+, 16:10	1680×1050	Not specified
Ultra XGA (UXGA)	1600×1200	Not specified
WUXGA, 16:10	1920×1200	Not specified
Quad XGA (QXGA)	2048×1536	Not specified
WQXGA, 16:10	2560×1600	Not specified
WQUXGA, 16:10	3840×2400	Not specified
WHUXGA, 16:10	7680×4800	Not specified

Starting with SXGA, the more advanced resolutions can be paired with 32-bit graphics, which specifies the 24-bit Truecolor palette of 16,777,216 colors and uses the other 8 bits for enhanced non-color features, if at all. In some cases, using 32 bits to store 24 bits of color information per pixel increases performance because the bit boundaries are divisible by a power of 2; 32 is a power of two, but 24 is not. That being said, however, unlike with the older standards, the color palette is not officially part of the newer specifications.

LCD-Specific Concepts

Some LCD topics are unique to LCDs; others simply have a decidedly LCD twist. In the following sections, we will discuss these concepts as they relate to LCDs:

- Native resolution
- LCD resolutions
- Contrast ratio

Native resolution is limited to flat-panel technologies, such as LCDs. Contrast ratio is discussed most often in reference to the same devices, but can apply to any domain of the visible. Resolution, in general, is not an LCD-specific concept, but LCDs have their own slant on resolution, native resolution notwithstanding.

Native Resolution

One of the peculiarities of desktop LCD displays is that they have a single fixed resolution, known as the *native resolution*. Unlike CRT monitors, which can display a crisp image at many resolutions within a supported range, LCD monitors have trouble displaying most resolutions other than their native resolution. Not to confuse the issue, but laptop LCDs tend not to have an apparent native resolution that they are bound to, possibly because the adapter and display are factory-mated in laptops. The result is that you have a large range of resolutions to choose from on laptops without the drawback of distortion.

The native resolution comes from the placement of the transistors in the hardware display matrix of the monitor. For a native resolution of 1680×1050, for example, there are 1,764,000 transistors arranged in a grid of 1680 columns and 1050 rows. Trying to display a resolution other than 1680×1050 through the operating system tends to result in the monitor or, as in the case of DVI, the graphics adapter interpolating the resolution to fit the differing number of software pixels to the 1,764,000 transistors, often resulting in a distortion of the image on the screen.

The distortion can take various forms, such as blurred text, elliptical circles, and so forth. SXGA (1280×1024) was once one of the most popular native resolutions for larger LCD computer monitors before use of widescreen monitors became pervasive. For widescreen aspects, especially for widescreen LCD displays of 15.4″ and larger, WSXGA+ (1680×1050) has proven the most popular native resolution in recent years.

LCD Resolutions

The concept of resolution on an LCD screen is similar to the concept on a standard CRT monitor. Resolution is still measured by the number of pixels used to draw the screen. If you use more pixels, you can display a higher level of detail.

There are over 20 different video standards that various LCD monitors support, often starting with SVGA. One primary difference, however, is that although LCDs support low resolutions that correspond to legacy video standards, they normally support 32-bit graphics, unlike the earlier standards, which are adapter-based.

The non-widescreen resolutions in Table 3.1, starting with SVGA and continuing through UXGA, can be found in some CRT and most LCD monitors. Widescreen resolutions and resolutions higher than UXGA are found almost exclusively in LCD monitors. Nevertheless, if someone in a specialty market will pay for a CRT capable of displaying higher resolutions, someone else will produce one.

Contrast Ratio

The *contrast ratio* is the measure of the ratio of the luminance of the brightest color to that of the darkest color the screen is capable of producing. One of the original problems with LCD displays, and a continuing problem with cheaper versions, is that they have low contrast ratios. A display with a low contrast ratio won't show a "true black" very well, and the other colors will look washed out when you have a light source nearby. Try to use the device in full sunshine, and you're not going to see much of anything. Also, lower contrast ratios mean that you'll have a harder time viewing images from the side as compared with being directly in front of the display.

Ratios for smaller LCD monitors and televisions typically start out around 500:1. Common ratios for larger units range from 20,000:1 to 100,000:1. Extreme specifications on commercial high-end televisions and monitors using LEDs as backlights have reached 1,000,000:1, as in the case of Sony's 55″ BRAVIA® XBR8. Other vendors, such as Sharp, Samsung, and LG, have produced displays with similar characteristics.

One caveat to contrast ratios is that there is no vendor-neutral measurement. The contrast ratio claimed by one manufacturer can take into account variables that another manufacturer does not. A manufacturer can boost the ratio simply by increasing how bright the monitor can go. This doesn't do anything to help the display of darker colors, though. All it will do is wash out the lighter colors and make white seem like it's glowing, which is hardly useful to the user.

Another caveat is that most manufacturers market their LCDs based on a dynamic contrast ratio. A dynamic ratio is realized by reducing power to the backlight for darker images. The downside is that the signal to the LCD panel is amplified to compensate, occasionally resulting in overcompensation manifested as areas of extreme brightness. So, although the contrast ratio is certainly a selling point, don't just take it at face value. Always compare displays in person to see which one works better for the situation in which you use it.

Additional Video Technologies

While the VGA-spawned standards might keep the computing industry satisfied for quite some time to come, there is a sector in the market driving development of non-VGA specifications. These high-resolution, high-performance junkies approach video from the broadcast angle. They are interested in the increased quality of digital transmission. For them, the industry responded with technologies like DVI and HDMI. The computing market benefits from these technologies as well. Recent years have seen DVI interfaces on graphics adapters and laptops becoming commonplace.

Other consumers desire specialized methods to connect analog display devices by splitting out colors from the component to improve quality or simply to provide video output to displays not meant for computers. For this group, a few older standards remain viable: component video, S-video, and composite video. The following sections present the details of these five specifications.

DVI

In an effort to return to digital video, which can typically be transmitted farther and at higher quality than analog, a series of connectors known collectively as the *Digital Visual (or Video) Interface (DVI)* was developed for the technology of the same name. At first glance, the DVI connector might look like a standard D-sub connector, but on closer inspection, it begins to look somewhat different. For one thing, it has quite a few pins, and for another, the pins it has are asymmetrical in their placement on the connector. Figure 3.7 illustrates the five types of connector that the DVI standard specifies.

FIGURE 3.7   Types of DVI connector

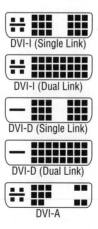

The three main categories of DVI cable connector are

DVI-A   A cable and device analog-only connector

DVI-D   A cable and device digital-only connector

DVI-I   A cable connector that is a combination analog/digital connector

The DVI-D and DVI-I connectors come in two varieties: single link and dual link. The dual-link options have more conductors—taking into account the six center conductors—than their single-link counterparts, which accommodate higher speed and signal quality. The additional link can be used to increase resolution from 1920×1080 to 2048×1536 for devices with a 16:9 aspect ratio or from WUXGA to WQXGA for devices with a 16:10 aspect ratio. Of course, all components, as well as the cable, must support the dual-link feature.

DVI-A and DVI-I analog quality is superior to that of VGA, but it's still analog, meaning it is more susceptible to noise. However, the DVI analog signal will travel farther than the VGA signal before degrading beyond usability. The analog portion of the connector, if it exists, comprises the four separate pins and the horizontal blade that they surround, which happens to be the analog ground lead.

It's important to note that DVI-I connectors are found on cables, not on devices. DVI-I cables are designed to interconnect two analog or two digital devices; they cannot convert between analog and digital. DVI cables must support a signal of at least 5 meters, but stronger transmitters result in signals extending over longer distances.

HDMI

High-Definition Multimedia Interface (HDMI) is an all-digital technology that advances the work of DVI to include the same dual-link resolutions using a standard HDMI cable, but with higher motion-picture frame rates and digital audio right on the same connector. HDMI cabling also supports an optional Consumer Electronics Control (CEC) feature that allows transmission of signals from a remote control unit to control multiple devices without separate cabling to carry infrared signals. The HDMI connector is not the same as the one used for DVI. Nevertheless, the two technologies are electrically compatible. In June 2006, revision 1.3 of the HDMI specification was released to support the bit rates necessary for HD DVD and Blu-ray disc. Since that time, version 1.3 has been refined, resulting in version 1.3c, released in late 2008.

HDMI is compatible with DVI-D and DVI-I cables through proper adapters, but only single-link is supported, and HDMI's audio and remote-control pass-through features are lost. Figure 3.8 shows a DVI-to-HDMI adapter for single-link DVI-D and the Type-A 19-pin HDMI cable. There is also a Type-B connector that has 29 pins and is intended to support higher resolution for the components that use it. As of version 1.3, a newer 19-pin Type C connector exists for portable devices. The Type C connector is compatible with the Type A connector but still requires an adapter due to its smaller size.

FIGURE 3.8 HDMI-to-DVI adapter

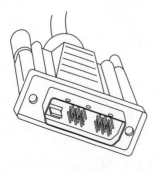

HDMI cables should meet the signal requirements of the latest specification. As a result, and as with DVI, the maximum cable length is somewhat variable. For HDMI, cable length depends heavily on the materials used to construct the cable. Passive cables tend to extend no farther than 15 meters, while adding electronics within the cable to create an active version results in lengths as long as 30 meters. Twisted-pair and fiber cabling options can extend cabling to 50 meters and 100 meters, respectively.

Component Video

When analog technologies outside the VGA realm are used for broadcast video, you are generally able to get better-quality video by splitting the red, green, and blue components in the signal into different streams right at the source. The technology known as *component video* performs a signal-splitting function similar to RGB separation. However, unlike RGB separation, which requires full-bandwidth red, green, and blue signals, the most popular implementation of component video uses one uncompressed signal and two compressed signals, reducing the overall bandwidth needed.

The uncompressed signal is called *luma* (Y), which is essentially the colorless version of the original signal that represents the "brightness" of the source feed as a grayscale image. The component-video source also creates two compressed color-difference signals known as Pb and Pr. These two *chrominance* (chroma, for short) signals are also known as B – Y and R – Y, respectively, because they are created by subtracting out the luma from the blue and red source signals. It might make sense, then, that the analog technology presented here is most often referred to and labeled as YPbPr. A digital version of this technology, usually found on high-end devices, replaces analog's Pb and Pr with Cb and Cr, respectively, and is most often labeled YCbCr. Figure 3.9 shows the three RCA connectors of a component video cable.

FIGURE 3.9   A component video cable

> As a slightly technical aside, luma is a gamma-correcting, nonlinear display concept related to but not equivalent to luminance, which is a linear, non-gamma-corrected measure of light intensity. Display devices perform nonlinear gamma decompression, which means a complementary nonlinear gamma compression (correction) must have been performed by the transmitter for the resulting image to be displayed properly. Thus, luma, not luminance, is the appropriate term when discussing component video. Furthermore, although Y is commonly used to represent luma, it actually stands for luminance. As a result, if you ever see a reference to Y′PbPr or Y′CbCr, the Y-prime refers correctly to luma. The more common, yet less correct, "Y" is used here to refer to luma.

Note that in the foregoing discussion, there is no mention of a green component-video signal. In fact, the often green-colored lead in the component-video cable carries the luma. There is no need for a separate green color-difference signal. Essentially, the luma signal is used as a colorless map for the detail of the image. The receiving display device adds the luma signal from the Y lead back to the blue and red color-difference signals that were received on the Pb and Pr leads, re-creating compressed versions of the full blue and red source signals. Whatever details in the luma version of the image have weak representation in the blue and red versions of the image are inferred to be green.

Therefore, you can conclude that by providing one full signal (Y) and two compressed signals (Pb and Pr) that are related to the full signal (Pb = B − Y and Pr = R − Y), you can transmit roughly the same information as three full signals (R, G, and B), but with less bandwidth. Incidentally, component video is capable of transmitting HD video at full 1080p (1920×1080, progressive-scan) resolution.

S-video

S-video is a component video technology that, in its basic form, combines the two chroma signals into one, resulting in video quality not quite as high as that of YPbPr. This is because the R, G, and B signals are harder to approximate after the Pb and Pr signals have been combined. One example of an S-video connector, shown in Figure 3.10, is a 7-pin mini-DIN, mini-DIN of various pin counts being the most common connector type. The most basic connector is a 4-pin mini-DIN that has, quite simply, one luma and one chroma (C) output lead and a ground for each. A 4-pin male connector is compatible with a 7-pin female connector, both in fit and pin functionality. The converse is not also true, however. These are the only two standard S-video connectors.

The 6-pin and 7-pin versions are also output only, but they add composite video leads, which are discussed next, as well. Some 7-pin ports use the extra pins to provide full Y, Pb, and Pr leads with four ground leads, making those implementations of S-video equivalent to component video. ATI has used 8-, 9-, and 10-pin versions of the connector that include such added features as S-video input in addition to output, or even bidirectional pin functionality, and audio input/output.

FIGURE 3.10   A 7-pin S-video port

Composite Video

When the preceding component video technologies are not feasible, the last related standard, *composite video*, combines all luma and chroma leads into one. Composite video is truly the bottom of the analog-video barrel. However, the National Television System Committee (NTSC) signal received by over-the-air antennas or by cable-TV feeds is composite video, making it a very common video signal. Unfortunately, once the four signals are combined into one, the display equipment has no way of faithfully splitting them back out, leading to less than optimal quality but great cost efficiency.

A single yellow RCA jack, the composite video jack is rather common on computers and home and industrial video components. While still fairly decent in video quality, composite video is more susceptible to undesirable video phenomena and artifacts, such as aliasing, cross coloration, and dot crawl. If you have a three-connector cable on your home video equipment, such as a DVD player connected to a TV, odds are the tips will be yellow, red, and white. The red and white leads are for left and right stereo audio; the yellow lead is your composite video.

Summary

In this chapter, you read about various display technologies and settings. Three primary categories of video display unit were mentioned and explained: CRT, LCD, and projector. Concepts unique to each of these categories were explored. Additionally, the similarities among them were highlighted. We identified names and characteristics of display resolutions and explained the process of configuring settings, such as resolution, refresh rate, and multimonitor support, in Windows Vista.

You also learned about the variety of connection mechanisms for attaching display devices to sources of video information.

Exam Essentials

Be able to compare and contrast the three main categories of display technology.   Although video display units all have roughly the same purpose—to display images created by the computer and rendered by the graphics adapter—CRTs, LCDs, and projectors go about the task in slightly different ways.

Understand key concepts behind LCD technology.   You need to be familiar with active and passive matrix; resolution standards, such as XGA and UXGA; and terms such as *contrast ratio* and *native resolution*.

Know the various video connectors and the technologies behind them.   You should be able to recognize the various connectors used when interfacing VDUs with computers, home-entertainment systems, and the like. You should also be conversational in the peculiarities of each of the technologies they represent.

Familiarize yourself with the steps that must be taken to configure display settings in Windows.   Most of the operating system–based settings are found in roughly the same place. However, nuances found in the details of configuring these settings make it important for you to familiarize yourself with the specific configuration procedures.

Review Questions

1. Which of the following would be the best choice as a personal display technology if a user wants to save desk space and not have to deal with interference from nearby speakers?

   A. CRT

   B. HDMI

   C. LCD

   D. Projector

2. An associate is trying to explain why a particular model of CRT monitor displays images in such high quality but is unable to recall a specific term. The associate mentions that each phosphor is on average only 0.25mm away from the nearest phosphor of the same color. What is the associate trying to describe?

   A. Resolution

   B. Dot pitch

   C. Refresh rate

   D. The number of dots per inch

3. Which of the following is true regarding a monitor's refresh rate?

   A. As long as the graphics adapter can refresh the image at a particular rate, the attached monitor can accommodate that refresh rate.

   B. The refresh rate is normally expressed in MHz.

   C. The refresh rate is normally selected by using the controls on the front panel of the monitor.

   D. As you lower the resolution, the maximum refresh rate allowed tends to increase.

4. Which statement about LCDs is most accurate?

   A. The concept of refresh rate has no meaning, with regard to LCDs.

   B. LCDs are preferred to CRTs because they can display a larger range of resolutions.

   C. LCDs tend not to be as clear as CRTs.

   D. LCDs require more power than CRTs.

5. If you are unable to display a given resolution on a monitor, which of the following might explain why?

   A. The graphics adapter does not have enough memory installed.

   B. The video display unit does not have enough memory installed.

   C. You are using a CRT with a single fixed resolution.

   D. You have the refresh rate set too high.

6. Which video technology has a resolution of 1280×1024?

    A. SVGA

    B. SXGA

    C. WSXGA

    D. UXGA

7. What does a Q in video resolution names, such as QXGA, refer to?

    A. Both the horizontal and vertical components of the resolution have been quadrupled.

    B. The resolution is cut to one fourth.

    C. The technology is faster.

    D. Both the horizontal and vertical components of the resolution have been doubled.

8. What is contrast ratio?

    A. The ratio of luminance between the darkest and lightest colors that can be displayed

    B. A term that was used with CRTs but has no meaning with LCDs

    C. The ratio of luminance between two adjacent pixels

    D. Something that can be corrected through degaussing

9. Which of the following interfaces allows audio to be sent out over the same cabling infrastructure as video?

    A. VGA

    B. DVI

    C. HDMI

    D. Composite

10. How do you connect a DVI-A interface on a peripheral to a DVI-D interface on the computer?

    A. With a DVI-I cable

    B. With a cable that is terminated on one end with a DVI-A connector and on the other end with a DVI-D connector

    C. You wouldn't interconnect those two interfaces.

    D. With a standard DVI cable

11. On which properties tab do you select the refresh rate to use between the graphics adapter and monitor in Windows Vista?

    A. Adapter

    B. Monitor

    C. Advanced

    D. Display Settings

12. After a presentation using a video projector, when in a hurry to pack everything up and head to the airport, which of the following should you avoid doing immediately?

A. Unplugging the projector's power cable

B. Unplugging the projector's video cable from your laptop

C. Turning off the power to the projector

D. Turning off your laptop

13. What might cause your display to appear in a resolution of 640×480?

A. You have your resolution set to SVGA.

B. You added memory to your graphics adapter but have not informed the BIOS of the new memory.

C. You have your resolution set to XGA.

D. You have booted into Safe Mode.

14. Which of the following results can occur with improper display settings?

A. The computer spontaneously reboots.

B. The graphics adapter automatically chooses to use the highest supported resolution.

C. You might have to scroll to see parts of the Desktop.

D. The mouse cursor changes or permanently disappears.

15. What is the single, fixed resolution of an LCD called?

A. Native resolution

B. Default resolution

C. Refresh rate

D. Burned-in resolution

16. Which of the following is it possible to do with multimonitor settings?

A. Connect multiple monitors to your computer only by using a graphics adapter with two video interfaces

B. Cause two different Desktops to merge onto the same monitor

C. Connect two laptops together so they display the same Desktop

D. Display different parts of your Desktop on different monitors

17. Which of the following types of LCD has the best performance characteristics?

A. Active matrix

B. Passive matrix

C. Dual matrix

D. Dual scan

18. Which of the following resolutions is an example of a 16:10 aspect ratio?

    A. 1280×1024

    B. 1920×1200

    C. 800×600

    D. 2048×1536

19. Where can you find the best degaussing tool for modern CRT monitors?

    A. At a computer specialty shop

    B. At a consumer electronics store

    C. Built into the monitor

    D. As a freeware download

20. VGA-based video technologies use what type of signal between the adapter and monitor?

    A. Digital

    B. Analog

    C. Compressed

    D. Composite

Answers to Review Questions

1. C. LCDs do not have electron guns that are aimed by magnets like CRTs do. This difference makes LCDs more compatible with nearby speaker magnets. Additionally, the cathode ray tube for which such monitors are named is a rather bulky component, requiring more desk space to accommodate the CRT's cabinet. Projectors are not common personal display devices; they are used more in group environments. HDMI is a standard for connecting display devices, not a type of display device.

2. B. The associate is trying to think of the term *dot pitch*. Essentially, dot pitch is the height of a dot-phosphor trio added to the distance between the next dot trio in the same direction. It works out to be the distance from any point on one dot to the same point on the next dot of the same color. The smaller this number is, the better the display quality is. The number of dots per inch is a similar concept but inversely proportional and not measured in fractions of a millimeter. Resolution is a software concept; dot phosphors are hardware-related. The refresh rate has nothing to do with how close the chemical dots are to one another.

3. D. The maximum allowable refresh rate does tend to be affected by the resolution you choose in the operating system. The refresh rate is most often expressed in cycles per second (Hz), not millions of cycles per second (MHz). You must usually select the refresh rate you want from the display settings dialog pages, not through the monitor's built-in menu system, although the monitor can often tell you which refresh rate you're using. Finally, both the monitor and adapter must agree on the refresh rate you select. If either device does not support a particular refresh rate, such a rate cannot be used.

4. C. At the same resolution, CRTs are more likely to display a clearer image than LCDs. LCDs are normally limited to a fixed, native resolution but require less power than CRT monitors. Although LCD screens are not regularly and systematically refreshed the way CRTs are, the LCD refresh rate dictates how often any one pixel is allowed to change.

5. A. The amount of memory installed on a graphics adapter is directly related to how many pixels can be displayed at one time and how many colors the pixels can be set to. Monitors don't have memory installed in them. LCDs, not CRTs, have a single, fixed resolution called the native resolution. You might be limited to a particular refresh rate because the resolution is too high, but the refresh rate is automatically adjusted down, if necessary, when you select a resolution.

6. B. SXGA has a resolution of 1280×1024. Consult Table 3.1 for the resolutions that characterize other technologies.

7. D. Although the Q stands for *quad*, the pixel count for each axis is only doubled, resulting in four times as many total pixels.

8. A. Contrast ratio is a selling point for LCDs. Higher contrast ratios mean darker blacks and brighter whites. The measure of luminance between adjacent pixels is known as contrast, not contrast ratio.

9. C. HDMI is a digital interface and cabling specification that allows digital audio to be carried over the same cable as video.

10. C. Such a connection should not be made. DVI-I cables act like universal cables; they can connect two DVI-A interfaces or two DVI-D interfaces. They are unable to convert the analog signal to a digital one, however. Analog and digital DVI interfaces are too disparate to interconnect.

11. B. Although it's true that you must start with the Display Settings dialog box, which ironically shows a single tab labeled Monitor, and that you subsequently click the Advanced Settings button, it's on the Monitor properties tab thereafter that you select the refresh rate. The Adapter tab in those same properties pages has no selection for refresh rate.

12. A. Unplugging the power to the projector before the projector's fan has had the opportunity to cool the unit and stop running on its own can lead to expensive repairs on the projector or to the cost of replacing the projector outright.

13. D. Safe Mode disables as many nonessential drivers and services as possible. One of the nonessential drivers it disables is the driver for the graphics adapter. Windows uses its standard VGA driver to control the graphics adapter while you are in Safe Mode. Another reason for defaulting back to standard VGA is that you might have a corrupt or incorrect driver for your adapter.

14. C. If your monitor allows you to change the resolution, it might not actually allow you to change the resolution. As confusing as that sounds, your monitor might maintain its optimal hardware resolution, such as an LCD's native resolution, and force you to scroll to see any pixels created by the chosen software resolution that it cannot fit on the hardware screen at that particular moment.

15. A. An LCD's native resolution is the single, fixed resolution that provides optimal clarity.

16. D. The multimonitor feature allows two monitors to display exactly the same thing (clone) or to extend your desktop onto the second monitor. There is no need to use one adapter to achieve this result. In fact, the two adapters don't even have to use the same expansion-bus architecture. The two cards must, however, use the same graphics-adapter driver.

17. A. Active matrix is a superior technology to passive matrix. Dual scan is merely an enhanced form of passive matrix but is not on par with active matrix. Dual matrix isn't an LCD type.

18. B. Dividing 16 by 10 produces a value of 1.6. Dividing the first number of a 16:10 resolution by the second number always results in 1.6. Resolutions with a 4:3 aspect ratio produce the value 1.333, while 5:4 resolutions such as 1280×1024 produce the value 1.25.

19. C. The built-in degaussing tool of the latest CRT monitors is designed to work with the monitor in which it is found. External degaussing tools, while effective, can be a little hard on the delicate inner workings of the CRT. Software alone cannot degauss a CRT monitor.

20. B. VGA signals are analog, uncompressed, component signals that carry all the video information for all three components of the original RGB signal.

Chapter 4

Understanding Laptops and Portable Devices

THE FOLLOWING COMPTIA A+ ESSENTIALS EXAM OBJECTIVES ARE COVERED IN THIS CHAPTER:

✓ **1.10 Install, configure and optimize laptop components and features**

- Expansion devices
- PCMCIA cards
- Express bus
- Docking station
- Communication connections
- Bluetooth
- Infrared
- Cellular WAN
- Ethernet
- Modem
- Power and electrical input devices
- Auto-switching
- Fixed input power supplies
- Batteries
- Input devices
- Stylus / digitizer
- Function keys
- Point devices (e.g. touch pad, point stick / track point)

As recently as the early 1990s, portable computers were luxuries that were affordable to only the wealthy or to the select few businesspeople who traveled extensively. As with all other technologies, though, portable systems have gotten smaller, lighter (more portable), more powerful, and less expensive. Because the technology and price disparity between the two platforms has decreased significantly, more laptops than desktops are now sold every year.

Every indication is that the movement toward mobile computing will continue, so you definitely need to be well versed in portable technologies, which contain both nifty features and frustrating quirks. For this discussion, assume that a *portable computer* is any computer that contains all the functionality of a desktop computer system but is portable. Most people define *portable* in terms of weight and size. So we can discuss things on the same level, let's define *portable* as less than 20 pounds and smaller than an average desktop computer.

Most portable computers fall into one of three categories: luggable, laptop, or PDA.

The original portable computers were hardly portable, hence the unofficial term "luggable." They were the size of a small suitcase and could weigh 50 pounds. Not only were they greatly inferior to desktops in technology, they were also outrageously expensive. It's no wonder few people purchased them. Compaq, Kaypro, and Osborne made some of the first luggable computers.

Laptops were the next type of portable computer. They contain a built-in keyboard, pointing device, and LCD screen in a clamshell design. They are also called *notebook* computers because they resemble large notebooks. Most portable computers in use today are laptop computers.

The final type of portable computer, which is still popular despite the influx of cell phones with similar functionality, is the palmtop computer, also known as a personal digital assistant (PDA). These computers are designed to keep the information you need close by so you can access it whenever you need it. There are two different approaches to the PDA. Some, such as the Palm series of PDAs and HP iPAQ, are basically small digital notepads. Others, such as the RIM BlackBerry, are known as a handheld PC (HPC). These are basically shrunken laptops. HPCs run an operating system known as Windows Mobile (the most popular previous mobile version was Windows CE). Windows Mobile is basically Windows XP, shrunk to fit into the limited RAM of the HPC.

Many high-end cellular phones run a version of Windows Mobile. In fact, many portable computers also incorporate cell phone features as well. The line between mobile computing and mobile communication has definitely blurred, and we'll likely see a continuation of this technology consolidation for years to come.

In this chapter, you will learn about laptop computer architecture and how it differs from desktop computer architecture, as well as about managing power on laptops.

Understanding Laptop Architecture

Laptops are similar to desktop computers in architecture in that they contain many parts that perform similar functions. However, the parts that make up a laptop are completely different from those in desktop computers. The obvious major difference is size; laptops are space-challenged. Another primary concern is heat. Restricted space means less airflow, meaning parts can heat up and overheat faster.

To overcome space limitations, laptop parts are physically much smaller and lighter, and they must fit into the compact space of a laptop's case. It might not sound like much, but there really is a major difference between a 4.5 pound laptop and a 5.5 pound laptop if you're hauling it around in its carrying case with a shoulder strap all day. Also, laptop parts are designed to consume less power and to shut themselves off when not being used, although many desktops also have components that go into a low-power state when not active, such as video circuitry. Finally, most laptop components, especially the motherboard, are proprietary—the LCD screen from one laptop will not necessarily fit on another.

A recent development in the laptop arena has been the netbook computer. A *netbook* is an extremely small laptop computer that is lighter in weight and more scaled-down in features than a standard laptop. Users are attracted to netbooks because of their enhanced portability and affordability. The features that remain are ideal for Internet access and e-mailing. However, many users would find netbooks insufficient for mainstream usage.

In this section, you will learn about the various components that make up laptops and how they differ from desktop computer components. If you don't remember exactly what each component does, it may help you to refer back to Chapter 1, "Personal Computer System Components," occasionally as you read this chapter.

Laptops vs. Desktops

If you've ever shopped for a laptop, you have no doubt noticed that the prices of desktop PCs are often quite a bit lower than those for notebook computers, yet the desktops are faster and more powerful. If you've ever wondered what makes a laptop so much different than a PC, here are the primary differences between laptops and desktops:

Portability   This is probably the most obvious difference. Laptops are designed to be portable. They run on batteries, so you aren't tied to one spot at home or at the office. Networking options are available that allow you to connect to a network wirelessly and do work from just about anywhere, including malls, airports, coffee shops, and so on. As anyone who's tried to bring their full-tower PC to a LAN party can tell you, desktops just aren't that portable.

Cost   Laptops tend to cost more than desktop computers with similar features. The primary reason is that portability requires small components and unique proprietary designs so that those components fit into the small size necessary. Miniature versions of components cost more money than standard-sized (desktop) versions.

Performance   By and large, laptops are always going to lose out somewhere in the performance department. Compromises must often be made between performance and portability, and considering that portability is the major feature of a laptop, performance is what usually suffers. While it is possible to have a laptop with comparable performance to a desktop, the amount of money one would have to spend for a "desktop replacement" laptop is considerable. This is not to say that a laptop can't outperform a desktop, it's just that the "bang for the buck" factor is higher in a desktop.

Expandability   Because desktop computers were designed to be modular, their capabilities can be upgraded quite easily. It is next to impossible to upgrade the processor or motherboard on most laptops. Other than memory and hard drives, most laptop upgrades consist of adding an external device through one of the laptop's ports, such as a USB port.

Quality of construction   Considering how much abuse laptops get, it is much more important that the materials used to construct the laptop case and other components be extremely durable. Durability is important in a desktop too, but it won't be tested as much as in a laptop.

Building Your Own

During an A+ course, I gave the class the assignment to go out on the Web and put together the most powerful and complete computer they could for under a thousand dollars. The class was for non-degree-seeking adults, so nothing was graded; it was simply to provide experience with speccing out and pricing the parts that go into making a complete system.

One of the students had her eye on a new laptop for personal use. Because she noticed the trend toward being able to build a desktop computer for less than she could buy one, the student assumed the same about laptops. Unfortunately, I had not specifically mentioned the fact that there are no standards for building complete laptop clones, unlike with desktops.

You can't reliably build your own laptop. Because laptop components are designed to exacting specifications to fit properly inside one manufacturer's notebook, there generally are no universal motherboards, video boards, and so on for laptops. Memory and hard drives are the exception. You can get different brands of memory and hard drives for laptops, but you can't buy a motherboard from one company and the video circuitry from another. Even things as mundane as floppy drives are usually designed to work only with a specific brand or model.

Now that we've illustrated the primary differences between laptops and desktops, let's examine the parts of the laptop and what they do.

Laptop Case

A typical laptop case is made up of three main parts:

- The display—usually an LCD display
- The case frame, which is the metal reinforcing structure inside the laptop that provides rigidity and strength and that most components mount to
- The case, or the plastic cover that surrounds the components and provides protection from the elements

The cases are typically made of some type of plastic (usually ABS plastic or ABS composite) to provide for light weight as well as strength.

A few notebooks have cases made of a strong, lightweight metal, such as aluminum or titanium. However, the majority of laptop cases are made of plastic.

Laptop cases are made in what is known as a clamshell design. In a clamshell design, the laptop has two halves, hinged together at the back. Usually, the display is the top half and everything else is in the bottom half.

Occasionally, part of the laptop's case will crack and need to be replaced. However, you usually can't just replace the cracked section. Most often, you must remove every component from inside the laptop's case and swap the components over to the new case. This is a labor-intensive process, because the screws in laptops are often very small and hard to reach. Often, repairing a cracked case may cost several hundred dollars in labor alone. Most times, people who have cracked laptop cases wait until something else needs to be repaired before having the case fixed.

Motherboards and Processors

As with desktop computers, the motherboard of a laptop is the backbone structure to which all internal components connect. However, with a laptop, almost all components must be integrated onto the motherboard, including onboard circuitry for the serial, parallel, USB, IEEE 1394, video, expansion, and network ports of the laptop. With desktop systems, the option remains to not integrate such components. Because of the similarities between laptop and desktop components, some material in the next few sections will be familiar to you if you have read Chapters 1 and 2.

Laptop Motherboards

The primary differences between a laptop motherboard and a desktop motherboard are the lack of standards and the much smaller form factor. As mentioned earlier, most motherboards are designed along with the laptop case so that all the components will fit inside. Therefore, the motherboard is mostly proprietary. Figure 4.1 shows an example of a laptop motherboard.

FIGURE 4.1   A laptop motherboard

To save space, components of the video circuitry (and possibly other circuits as well) are placed on a thin circuit board that connects directly to the motherboard. This circuit board is often known as a *daughterboard*.

Having components performing different functions (such as video, audio, and networking) integrated on the same board is a mixed bag. On one hand, it saves a lot of space. On the other hand, if one part goes bad, you have to replace the entire board, which is more expensive than just replacing one expansion card.

Laptop Processors

Just like in desktop computers, the processor is the brain of the computer. And just like everything else, compared to desktop hardware, laptop hardware means a smaller device that isn't quite as powerful. The spread between the speed of a laptop CPU and that of a desktop motherboard can be a gigahertz or more.

Laptops have less space, and thus, heat is a major concern. Add to that the fact that processors are the hottest-running component, and you can see where cooling can be an issue. To help combat this heat problem, laptop processors are engineered with the following features:

Streamlined connection to the motherboard   Nearly all desktop processors mount using pin connectors, whether on the CPU or on the motherboard (as is the case with LGA sockets). Pins and sockets are big and bulky, meaning they're not a laptop's friends. Laptop processors are generally either soldered directly to the motherboard or attached using the Micro-FCBGA (Flip Chip Ball Grid Array) standard, which uses balls instead of pins. In most cases, this means that the processor cannot be removed, meaning no processor upgrades are possible.

Lower voltages and clock speeds   Two ways to combat heat are to slow the processor down (run it at a lower speed) or give it less juice (run it at a lower voltage). Again, performance will suffer compared to a desktop processor, but lowering heat is the goal here.

Active sleep and slowdown modes   Most laptops will run in a lower power state when on battery power, in an effort to extend the life of the battery. This is known as processor throttling. The motherboard works closely with the operating system to determine if the processor really needs to run at full speed. If it doesn't, it's slowed down to save energy and to reduce heat. When more processing power is needed, the CPU is throttled back up.

One of the best features of many laptop processors is that they include built-in wireless networking. By far the most common laptop processor is the Pentium M chip made by Intel. The Pentium M consists of three separate components:

- The Mobile Intel Express chipset (such as the Mobile Intel 915GM Express or the Mobile Intel 910GML), which is the graphics memory controller hub

- The Intel/PRO Wireless Network Connection, providing an integrated wireless LAN connection

- The Intel Centrino chipset, which is the "brain" of the chipset, designed to run on lower power than the desktop processor

Some portable computers will simply use stripped-down versions of desktop processors such as the Pentium 4. While there's nothing wrong with this, it makes sense that components specifically designed for notebooks fit the application better than components that have been retrofitted for notebook use. Consider an analogy to the automobile industry: it's better to design a convertible from the ground up than to simply cut the top off an existing coupe or sedan.

Memory

Notebooks don't use standard desktop computer memory chips, because they're too big. In fact, for most of the history of laptops there were no standard types of memory chips. If you wanted to add memory to your laptop, you had to order it from the laptop manufacturer. Of course, because you could get memory from only one supplier, you got the privilege of paying a premium over and above a similar-sized desktop memory chip.

However, there are now two common types of laptop memory package: SODIMM and MicroDIMM. Nevertheless, modern laptop manufacturers may still opt to go the proprietary route due to design considerations that favor a custom solution. To see what kind of memory your laptop uses, check either the manual or the manufacturer's website. You can also check third-party memory producers' websites (such as `www.crucial.com`).

SODIMM

As introduced in Chapter 1, the most common memory form factor for laptops is called a Small Outline DIMM (SODIMM). They're much smaller than standard DIMMs, measuring about 67 millimeters (2.6 inches) long and 32 millimeters (1.25 inches) tall. SODIMMs are available in a variety of configurations, including 32-bit (72-pin) and 64-bit (144-pin SDRAM, 200-pin DDR, 200-pin DDR2, and 204-pin DDR3) options. Figure 4.2 shows an example of the classic 144-pin variety.

Just like with desktop computers, make sure the SODIMM you want to put into the laptop is compatible with the motherboard. The same standards that apply to desktop memory compatibility apply to laptops. This means you can find DDR, DDR2, and DDR3 SODIMMs for laptops. DDR has all but topped out at 1GB per module, while DDR2 and DDR3 SODIMM modules can be purchased in 4GB capacities, which is on par with desktop DIMMs.

FIGURE 4.2   144-pin SODIMM

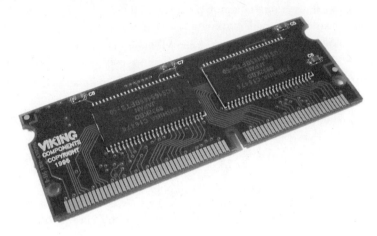

MicroDIMM

Although no longer new, the MicroDIMM is the most recent form factor for laptop memory modules. The MicroDIMM is an extremely small RAM form factor. In fact, it is over 50 percent smaller than a SODIMM—only about 45.5mm (about 1.75 inches) long and 30mm (about 1.2 inches, a bit bigger than a US quarter-dollar wide. Another major difference is that the MicroDIMM does not have any notches on the bottom. Figure 4.3 shows a 172-pin MicroDIMM. It was designed for the ultralight and portable subnotebook style of computer. Popular MicroDIMM form factors include 64-bit modules with 172 pins for DDR and 214 pins for DDR2.

FIGURE 4.3   172-pin MicroDIMM

Storage

Nearly all laptops have a hard drive, but not all laptops have both a floppy drive and an optical drive. Many times there just isn't room for both, and considering floppy drives are practically obsolete, why have one anyway? Often there is a multipurpose bay that can be used to hold either drive. If this drive bay exists, users generally keep the optical drive installed most of the time and leave out the floppy drive. In some cases, the floppy drive is an external device that you connect with a special cable to a proprietary connector. Figure 4.4 shows an example of one of these connectors, and Figure 4.5 shows an example of a laptop floppy drive with a proprietary connector. Notice how thin the floppy drive is and how compact the electronics are. When used at all, floppy drives that attach to the laptop through a USB port are more common today.

FIGURE 4.4   A proprietary floppy connector

FIGURE 4.5   A laptop floppy drive

Laptops don't have the room for the full-sized 3½″ hard drives that desktop computers use. Instead, they use a hard drive with a 2½″ form factor that is less than ½″ thick. These drives share the same controller technologies as desktop computers; however, they use smaller connectors. Figure 4.6 shows an example of a standard hard drive compared to a laptop hard drive.

Optical drives on laptops are necessarily smaller than their desktop counterparts as well. Figure 4.7 shows an example of a desktop CD-ROM drive compared to a laptop CD-ROM drive. Note that the laptop drive is very small, but it has all the functionality of a desktop unit. The drive mechanism and circuits have all been miniaturized to save space. As a result, the functionality is basically the same, but the cost is usually higher. Any time a component's functionality remains the same while its size decreases, you will notice an increase in price over the standard-sized item.

FIGURE 4.6 A desktop hard drive compared to a laptop hard drive

FIGURE 4.7 A desktop CD-ROM drive compared to a laptop CD-ROM drive

CD, DVD, or Blu-ray burners are great to have on laptops as backup devices. Simply copy the contents of the hard drive (or just important files) to the optical discs and store them in a safe location.

Input Devices

Because of laptops' small size, getting data into them presents unique challenges to designers. They must design a keyboard that fits within the case of the laptop. They must also design some sort of pointing device that users can use in graphical interfaces like Windows. The primary challenge in both cases is to design these peripherals so they fit within the design constraints of the laptop (low power and small form factor) while remaining usable.

Keyboards

A standard-sized desktop keyboard wasn't designed to be portable. It wouldn't fit well with the portable nature of a laptop. That usually means laptop keys are not normal size; they must be smaller and packed together more tightly. People who learned to type on a typewriter or regular computer often have a difficult time adjusting to a laptop keyboard because the keys are smaller and closer together.

Laptop keyboards are built into the lower portion of the clamshell. Sometimes, they can be removed easily to access peripherals below them (like memory and hard drives, as in the IBM, now known as Lenovo, ThinkPad series).

Because of the much smaller space available for keys, some laptop keys (like the number pad, Home, Insert, PgUp, and PgDn keys) are consolidated into special multifunction keys. These keys are accessed through the standard keys by using a special function key (usually labeled Fn in lettering of an alternate color that matches the lettering of the labels for alternate functions on other keys). To use a multifunction key, you press and hold the Fn key (as you would the Shift, Ctrl, and Alt keys) and then tap the key labeled with the function you want, finally releasing the Fn key.

Mice and Pointing Devices

In addition to the keyboard, you must have a method of controlling the onscreen pointer in the Windows interface. There are many methods of doing this, but the most common are

- Trackball
- Touchpad
- Point stick
- Touchscreen

 Some laptops use multiple pointing devices to appeal to a wider variety of people who have different pointing-device preferences.

Most laptops today include a mouse/keyboard port, a USB port, or both. Either of these ports can be used to add an input device like a mouse or a standard-sized keyboard.

Trackball

Many early laptops used trackballs as pointing devices. A *trackball* is essentially the same as a mouse turned upside down. When you move the ball with your thumb or fingers, the onscreen pointer moves in the same direction and at the same speed you move the trackball.

Trackballs are cheap to produce. However, the primary problem with trackballs is that they do not last as long as other types of pointing devices; a trackball picks up dirt and oil from operators' fingers, and those substances clog the rollers on the trackball and prevent it from functioning properly.

Touchpad

To overcome the problems of trackballs, a new technology that has become known as the touchpad was developed. Touchpad is actually the trade name of a product. However, the trade name is now used to describe an entire genre of products that are similar in function.

A touchpad is a device that has a pad of touch-sensitive material. The user draws with their finger on the touchpad, and the onscreen pointer follows the finger motions. Included with the touchpad are two buttons for left- or right-clicking (although with some touchpads, you can perform the functions of the left-click by tapping on the touchpad).

Point Stick

With the introduction of the ThinkPad series of laptops, IBM introduced a new feature known as the Touchpoint or, generically, as a *point stick*. The point stick is a pointing device that uses a small rubber-tipped stick. When you push the point stick in a particular direction, the onscreen pointer goes in the same direction. The harder you push, the faster the onscreen pointer moves. The point allows fingertip control of the onscreen pointer, without the reliability problems associated with trackballs.

Point sticks have their own problems, however. Often, the stick does not return to center properly, causing the pointer to drift when not in use. You might also notice the rubber cover for the stick becoming a bit gummy with extended use. Most manufacturers supply replacement covers of varying textures with new systems. Some later systems employ a concave version of the cover and updated workings that tend to minimize a lot of these concerns.

Touchscreen

The last type of pointing device we'll discuss can be found in use at many department stores: the informational *kiosks* with screens that respond to your touch and give you information about product specials or bridal registries. Instead of a keyboard and mouse, these computer screens have a film over them that is sensitive to touch. This technology is known as a *touchscreen* (see Figure 4.8). With most of the interfaces in use on touchscreens, touching a box drawn on the monitor does the same thing as double-clicking that box with a mouse. These screens are most commonly found on monitors; however, with the advent of the *tablet* PC (a laptop designed to be held like a pad of paper), the touchscreen is becoming more popular as an input device for a laptop.

Cleaning a touchscreen is usually just as easy as cleaning a regular monitor. With optical touch screens, the monitor *is* a regular monitor, so it can be cleaned with glass cleaner. However, if the screen has a capacitive coating, glass cleaner may damage it. Instead, use a cloth dampened with water to clean the dirt, dust, and fingerprints from the screen.

FIGURE 4.8 A typical touchscreen

Styluses and Digitizers

A *stylus* is an input device that works on the principle of a *digitizer*, which is an input device that converts pen or mouse-like analog movements by the user into digital input to the computer. Some PDAs use a stylus and handwriting-interpretation software to perform operations.

Instead of using a mouse to point to the icons and menus in Windows Mobile, you use a stylus on the HPC's touch-sensitive screen or a thumbwheel on the side of the device.

Expansion Buses and Ports

Although laptop computers are less expandable than their desktop counterparts, they can be expanded to some extent. Laptops have expansion ports similar to those found on desktop computers, as well as a couple that are found only on laptops.

PCMCIA (PC Card) Expansion Bus

The tongue-twister *PCMCIA* stands for Personal Computer Memory Card International Association. The PCMCIA was organized to provide a standard way of expanding portable computers. The PCMCIA bus was originally designed to provide a way of expanding the memory in a small, handheld computer, referred to generically as a PCMCIA host. The PCMCIA bus has been renamed *PC Card* to make it easier to pronounce. PC Card uses a small expansion card (about the size of a credit card). The interface is a thin, 68-pin connector that has remained relatively unchanged from the original specification. Although this form factor is primarily used in portable computers, PC Card adapters (converters) are available for desktop PCs. The PC Card bus now serves as a universal expansion bus that can accommodate nearly any device.

In addition to the card, the PC Card architecture includes two other components:

Socket Services software is a BIOS-level interface to the PCMCIA bus slot. When loaded, it hides the details of the PC Card hardware from the computer. This software can detect when a card has been inserted and what type of card it is.

Card Services software is the interface between the application and Socket Services. It tells the applications which interrupts and I/O ports the card is using. Applications that need to access the PC Card don't access the hardware directly; instead, they tell Card Services that they need access to a particular feature, and Card Services gets the appropriate feature from the PC Card.

This dual-component architecture allows the PCMCIA architecture to be used in different types of computer systems (that is, not just Intel's). For example, Apple laptop computers based on Motorola processors currently use PC Cards for modems and LAN interface cards.

The first release of the PCMCIA standard (PCMCIA 1.0, circa 1990) defined a 16-bit ISA-like bus to be used for memory expansion only. PCMCIA 1.0 supported 5V memory cards. The second major release (PCMCIA 2.*x*) introduced 3.3V cards and host slots. PCMCIA 2.*x* was designed to be backward compatible with version 1, so 5V memory cards can be used in version 2 host slots. Cards that are only capable of 3.3V operation are keyed to prevent damage from insertion into older 5V-only host slots. PCMCIA Version 2.01 was released in 1992 to specify the use of Card and Socket Services as a standard driver platform.

PCMCIA 5.0 increased the bus width to 32 bits and the bus speed from 8MHz to a maximum of 33MHz. In addition, the new CardBus PC Card adapters used PCI-like access methods, and the throughput speeds increased dramatically, up to a maximum of 133MBps (1.06Gbps). These cards are differentiated from the 16-bit cards by a metal grounding strip, often gold in color, along the insertion edge of the card. You can insert 16-bit PC Cards in a CardBus slot, but the converse is not also true.

PCMCIA standards jumped from PCMCIA 2.1 to PC Card 5.0 as PCMCIA and JEIDA standards were merged. At the same time, the name CardBus was introduced to differentiate the new 32-bit cards from their 16-bit ancestors.

The bus width of these cards and slots is either 16 or 32 bits, as previously discussed. Also, the original PCMCIA specification supported only one interrupt request (IRQ) (a problem if you needed to install two devices that both need interrupts in the same PC Card bus). Card and Socket Services took care of this deficiency. PC Cards also support bus mastering and Direct Memory Access (DMA), but only as of PC Card 5.0. DMA support was eventually removed in version 7.2. PC Card 8.0, released in 2001, specifies a newer CardBay standard designed to integrate USB functionality into the PC Card format. The benefit would be for devices that have PC Card slots but no USB ports. The reverse is more common, however.

Three major types of PC Cards (and slots) have been specified. Each has different uses and physical characteristics, although each one measures 54mm in width and 85.6mm in length. They are called Type I, Type II, and Type III:

- Type I cards are 3.3mm thick and are most commonly used for memory cards.

- Type II cards are 5mm thick and are mostly used for modems and LAN adapters, but for sound cards, SCSI controllers, and other devices as well. This is the most common PC Card type found today, and most systems have at least two Type II slots (or one Type III slot).

- The Type III slot is 10.5mm thick. Its most common application is PC Card hard disks. These slots are all but extinct.

ExpressCard

ExpressCard was launched by PCMCIA as a way to support USB 2.0 and PCI Express (hence the term *Express*Card) connectivity for portable computers. In fact, with support for transfer rates 2.5 times that of CardBus, ExpressCard is capable of transferring data at 2.5Gbps, approximately the rate of a single lane of PCIe. Cards can be created that support either specification or both. The manufacturer chooses the option that matches the application. ExpressCard 1.0 was published in 2003 and updated in 2006 to Release 1.1. Version 2 of the ExpressCard specification is designed to support USB 3.0 and PCIe 2.0.

With ExpressCard technology, portable computers can be adapted to support faster versions of legacy technologies. Standards not supported by CardBus, such as Gigabit Ethernet, IEEE 1394b, and eSATA, are accessible through the use of ExpressCard. Whereas CardBus required additional hardware and software to support non-native hot swapping thorough the ISA and PCI buses, ExpressCard takes advantage of hot swapping natively through the USB and PCIe buses. As an added bonus, the ExpressCard adapters are smaller than their CardBus cousins. The smaller size can be attributed to the PCIe-based serial technology on which ExpressCard is based. The PCI-based parallel communications used by CardBus require the larger 68-pin and -socket interface, while ExpressCard is implemented on a 26-contact blade interface.

ExpressCard adapters are 75mm in length. The standard ExpressCard, known as ExpressCard/34, is only 34mm wide. A 54mm-wide version, known appropriately as ExpressCard/54, is still only 34mm at its insertion point, but 22mm from that end, it expands to 54mm to accommodate more internal electronics. The additional space allows for better heat dissipation and the support of applications such as 1.8″ disk drives, card readers, and CompactFlash readers. While a Universal ExpressCard host slot appears to be able to accept a CardBus adapter, the card inserts not even an inch before stopping on the internal guide that assures correct ExpressCard/34 insertion. ExpressCard shares with CardBus the use of 3.3V to power some cards but swaps the 5V versions for a new, lower 1.5V offering.

> You may see the term ExpressBus used in reference to this technology. Despite the source, it's not a valid term.

Mini PCI and Mini PCIe

Mini PCI is an adaptation of the Peripheral Component Interconnect (PCI) standard used in desktop computers. As its name implies, it's just a smaller version (about ¼ the size of PCI cards) designed primarily for laptops.

These cards reside internally in the laptop, with their connection ports generally lining up with the edge of the outside of the case.

Mini PCI is functionally identical to the PCI version 2.2, meaning it's a 32-bit, 33MHz bus with a 3.3V-powered connection. It also supports bus mastering and DMA. There are three different Mini PCI form factors: Type I, Type II, and Type III. The size and connector types are listed in Table 4.1.

TABLE 4.1   Mini PCI Form Factors

Type	Connector	Size
IA	100-pin, stacking	7.5 × 70 × 45 millimeters
IB	100-pin, stacking	5.5 × 70 × 45 millimeters

TABLE 4.1   Mini PCI Form Factors *(continued)*

Type	Connector	Size
IIA	100-pin, stacking	7.5 × 70 × 45 millimeters
IIB	100-pin, stacking	17.44 × 78 × 45 millimeters
IIIA	124-pin, card edge	2.4 × 59.6 × 50.95 millimeters
IIIB	124-pin, card edge	2.4 × 59.6 × 44.6 millimeters

The extra 24 pins on Type III connectors allow for routing information back to the system, which is required for audio, phone line, or network connections.

Common Mini PCI devices include sound cards, modems, networking cards, and SCSI, ATA, and SATA controllers. Adapters are available that allow you to use a Mini PCI adapter in a standard PCI slot.

Mini PCIe cards are essentially ExpressCard devices without the external cover, measuring a few millimeters less in length and width as a result. In reality, however, they have a completely different, 52-pin edge connector. Nevertheless, like ExpressCard, Mini PCIe cards support USB 2.0 and PCIe x1 functionality. Additionally, Mini PCIe cards have the 1.5V and 3.3V power options in common with ExpressCard.

USB Ports

Like desktops, laptops use USB ports for expansion. However, because of the lack of internal expansion in laptops, most peripherals for laptops are found either as PC Cards or USB expansion devices.

For more information about USB ports and their function, refer to Chapter 1.

Mouse/Keyboard Port

Just in case you don't like using your laptop's built-in keyboard or pointing device, most laptops come with a combination *keyboard/mouse port* that allows you to connect either an external keyboard or an external mouse to the laptop. On laptops that don't have USB ports, this port is most often used for a standard PS/2 mouse. On those laptops that do have USB ports, this port is used for an external keypad or keyboard (because the USB port can accommodate an external mouse).

Communications Ports

Laptops are built to make computing mobile. And in this world where it seems like you always need to be in touch with others while you're mobile, it makes sense that laptops have a variety of methods to communicate while you're on the go. Several communication methods are available, and all new laptops have at least one of the following connections: analog dial-up modem, infrared, cellular, Bluetooth, 802.11, or Ethernet. Each of these can also be added to laptops through USB or PC Card connection. Refer to Chapter 10 for detailed discussions on each of these communications ports.

Docking Stations

Some laptops are designed to be desktop replacement laptops. That is, they will replace a standard desktop computer for day-to-day use and are thus more full-featured than other laptops. These laptops often have a proprietary docking port. A docking port (as shown in Figure 4.9) is used to connect the laptop to a special laptop-only peripheral known as a *docking station*. A docking station is basically an extension of the motherboard of a laptop. Because a docking station is designed to stay behind when the laptop is removed, it can contain things like a full-sized drive bay and expansion bus slots. Also, the docking station can function as a port replicator.

FIGURE 4.9   A docking port

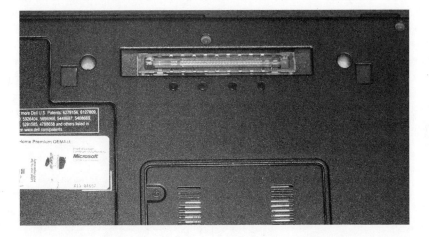

A port replicator reproduces the functions of the ports on the back of a laptop so that peripherals such as monitors, keyboards, printers, and so on that don't travel with the laptop can remain connected to the dock and don't have to all be physically unplugged each time the laptop is taken away. Figure 4.10 is a photo of the back of a docking station, showing the replicated ports, some of which are only available on the docking station and not on the laptop. Finally, there are accessory bays (also called media bays). These external bays allow you to plug your full-sized devices into them and take your laptop with you (for example, a full-sized hard drive that connects to an external USB or FireWire port). As a point of clarification (or perhaps confusion), media bays and accessory bays are sometimes used to refer to laptop drive bays.

FIGURE 4.10   Ports on a docking station

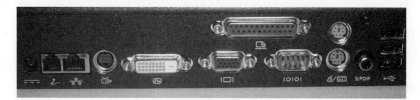

These docking ports and docking stations are *proprietary*. That is, the port works only with docking stations designed by the laptop's manufacturer, and vice versa.

Power Systems

Because portable computers have unique characteristics as a result of their portability, they have unique power systems as well. Portable computers can use either of two power sources: batteries or adapted power from an AC or DC source. Regardless the source of their power, laptops utilize DC power to energize their internal components. Therefore, any AC power source needs to be rectified (converted to DC). Most laptop backlights, on the other hand, require high-voltage, low-amperage AC power. To avoid a separate external AC input, an inverter is used to convert the DC power that is supplied for the rest of the system to AC for the backlight. In case it's not obvious, rectifiers and inverters perform opposite functions, more or less.

Batteries

There are many different battery chemistries that come in various sizes and shapes. Nickel cadmium (NiCd), lithium-ion (Li-Ion), and nickel-metal hydride (NiMH) have been the most popular chemistries for laptops. A newer battery chemistry, lithium-polymer (Li-poly), has been gaining in prominence over recent years for limited categories of devices, mostly the smaller ones. Li-poly still has issues that need to be worked out before mainstream acceptance for a wider range of applications is seen. Figure 4.11 is a photo of a Li-Ion battery for a Dell laptop. Notice the meter on the left side in the bottom view.

Battery chemistries can be compared by energy density and power density. Energy density measures how much energy a battery can hold. Power density measures how quickly the stored energy can be accessed, focusing on access in bursts, not prolonged runtime. An analogy to the storage and distribution of liquids might help solidify these concepts. A gallon bucket has a higher "energy density" and "power density" than a pint bottle; the bucket holds more and can pour its contents more quickly. Another common metric for battery comparison is rate of self-discharge, or how fast an unused battery reduces its stored charge.

FIGURE 4.11   A laptop Li-Ion battery

Nickel Cadmium

NiCd batteries are known for relatively low energy density, compared to batteries of other chemical makeup. NiMH batteries, for example, exhibit densities as much as 40 percent higher. Li-Ion's energy density is higher yet, doubling that of NiCd. It's the appreciable power density of NiCd batteries, however, that makes them, along with their NiMH cousins, the preferred power source for portable power tools and other applications that rely on ready bursts of power. Laptops and other portable electronics require a battery that will sustain longer than the nickel family of chemistries and do not benefit from such power density.

Nickel-based batteries tend to develop a chemical memory that causes them to discharge very quickly once they reach a certain point. The memory forms more quickly when the battery is left in the charger for long periods of time or recharged frequently and not fully discharged on a regular basis. Unlike NiMH batteries, NiCd batteries have two metals to contend with: nickel and cadmium. The active cadmium plate in a new battery has a fine crystalline surface, kept separate from the nickel plate by a separator. As the battery is used, cadmium hydroxide crystals increase in size, obscuring the active cadmium from the electrolyte that has to contact the cadmium to transfer the charge. A freshly charged battery operates normally, but eventually the charge reduces to the memory point where access to the cadmium plate is insufficient for operation, making the battery appear prematurely dead.

To reduce the size of the crystals and rejuvenate the active cadmium plate, a complete discharge is recommended for every 30 recharge cycles, or about once a month. This is known as exercising the battery and results in an 80 percent discharge, to about 1V per cell. A battery comprises one or more cells. You might be able to run the battery down in the device it operates. Some such devices will not discharge a NiCd battery to the proper voltage, and a separate deep-discharging unit for the specific battery might be necessary. If the battery cannot be exercised for three months or more, it becomes much harder to reduce the size of the crystals. In that case, a process known as reconditioning must be performed to save the battery. A special device is required for reconditioning. Many recyclers can perform this process and sell the NiCd batteries as reconditioned. However, after about a year of neglect, there is little hope of saving the battery. Even before this point, the cadmium crystals have likely breached the separator between the plates, resulting in electrical shorts or, at a minimum, increased self-discharge.

Batteries of nickel chemistry have a characteristically high self-discharge rate. NiCd batteries can be expected to lose 10 percent of their capacity shortly after charging and another 10 percent for each month they are left unused. You should expect even worse results from NiMH batteries. NiCd batteries exhibit some of the highest lifetime recharge cycles of any of the battery chemistries. You can recharge these batteries over 1,000 times with proper maintenance. If you can deal with the progressive increase in self-discharge, another 1,000 cycles can be attained in some cases. One caveat about nickel-based—especially NiCd—cells: new batteries and those not used for some time might require priming, a slow charge followed by repeated discharge/recharge cycling to redistribute the electrolyte evenly along the separator between the plates.

Nickel-Metal Hydride

NiMH batteries don't develop as much of a memory as NiCd batteries and have a higher energy density. However, in addition to a roughly 50 percent higher rate of self-discharge over NiCd, NiMH batteries are not rated for the number of charge cycles that NiCd batteries are rated for. Nevertheless, the average NiMH battery should be good for no fewer than 300 charging cycles. To control the chemical memory NiMH batteries do develop, it is recommended that they be exercised once every three months, less frequently than NiCd batteries. Otherwise, NiMH batteries are useful in most of the same applications for which NiCd batteries excel.

Lithium-Ion

Li-Ion batteries don't really suffer from a performance-affecting chemical memory. Their affliction comes from the so-called digital memory that plagues the built-in gauges that monitor the charge left in the battery. This effect can also be observed in software gauges that read the battery's charge level. The digital memory effect manifests itself as a sudden loss of power when the gauges register, say, 30 percent remaining capacity. The fix, much like the fix for chemical memory in NiCd batteries, is to allow a full discharge once a month or so. This is called *battery calibration* and can be performed right in the device being powered by the battery. Other than this occasional full discharge, Li-Ion batteries last longer when you partially discharge them and then recharge them, making them ideal for laptops and personal handheld devices, such as cell phones, that tend to get used sporadically on battery power before being plugged back in to charge.

The life of these batteries is affected mostly by age and only to a small degree by wear. Nevertheless, exposure to heat and frequent full discharges may accelerate the aging process. By using a Li-Ion battery in a normal fashion and not necessarily observing the best care recommended, these batteries can still last 2 or 3 years and accept 500 charge cycles at the high end. However, laptop Li-Ion batteries left installed and kept mostly at maximum charge tend to last about half as long due to the excessive heat to which they are exposed. Fully charged batteries are affected most by such heat.

Li-Ion batteries are a bit more expensive to manufacture because their chemistry requires that an internal safety circuit be built in. Without such a circuit, the battery would continue to charge after reaching full capacity. Although Li-Ion batteries do not contain metallic lithium, the heat generated from such an event would lead to metallic lithium plating from the ions and, consequently, probable ignition. For the same reason, Li-Ion batteries are not manufactured in standard formats, such as AAA, AA, C, and D. Doing so would lead to inappropriate insertion into chargers designed for nickel-based rechargeable batteries.

The protective cut-off circuitry monitors the charge level as well as the heat of the charging battery. As a result, full charge cycles are difficult to attain when performed in a hot car or similar environment. Despite the fact that these batteries should be stored in a cool place with roughly 40 percent charge while not being used, it is best not to keep spares on hand for too long. Allowing the battery to discharge too much can cause the safety circuitry to prohibit recharging of the battery due to the expected heat that could be generated.

Although, the high energy density of Li-Ion batteries is one of its selling points, you should not expect them to be able to power portable tools in the same way that nickel-based batteries do. This is because the power density of Li-Ion batteries leaves a bit to be desired. Such energy density, does, however, allow better efficiencies when compared with nickel-based cells. Typical cells are rated for about 3.6V, three times that of NiCd and NiMH cells. As a result, two-thirds fewer cells need to be used in the same applications.

In summary, because of its energy density, Li-Ion is the preferred chemistry for batteries designed to power laptops and other portable computing devices.

Lithium-Polymer

Lithium-polymer is a newer form of lithium-ion chemistry. As a result, you may notice the use of other terms, such as lithium-ion polymer and polymer lithium-ion, as well as a host of abbreviations derived from these names. Li-poly cells are rated for voltages similar to those mentioned earlier for Li-Ion. The dry chemical makeup of the Li-poly cell allows the metal casing of the Li-Ion cell to be replaced with a flexible casing without fear of leakage. A film-like polymer separator between extremely thin plates makes cells of only a millimeter in thickness a possibility.

Besides making the cell more lightweight than a comparable Li-Ion cell, these characteristics allow the Li-poly battery to be formed in whatever shape lends itself best to the application at hand. The result is smaller and lighter electronic components. Ultra-light notebooks and super-slim cellular phones and MP3 players have already benefited from Li-poly technology.

Li-poly doesn't quite match the energy density of Li-Ion, but the advantages mentioned make Li-poly the obvious choice over Li-Ion in certain applications. Nevertheless, Li-poly cells are still relatively expensive to manufacture because they need the same type of protection circuitry as Li-Ion cells and because there are no standard sizes for Li-poly. Manufacturers of

Li-poly cells cater to equipment makers who need a large volume of batteries for a particular application, thus reducing the apparent expense somewhat.

Alkaline and Lithium Primary Batteries

Nonrechargeable alkaline batteries have an extremely high energy density. However, when used in power-hungry applications, such as digital cameras, alkaline batteries cannot keep up with the draw on their power and quickly lose the ability to provide the energy requested. As a result, alkaline use in laptop applications is out of the question. Besides, the relative cost of a one-use battery compared to that of a rechargeable battery is prohibitive in such devices. If a primary battery is to be used in a smaller device with high power requirements, such as a digital camera, nonrechargeable lithium cells outperform even the secondary batteries, such as Li-Ion.

Primary batteries are not rechargeable; secondary batteries are.

Power Adapters

Most notebook computers can also use AC power with a special adapter (called an *AC adapter*) that converts AC-power input to DC output. The adapter is either integrated into the notebook or is more often a separate "brick" with two cords, one that plugs into the back of the laptop and another that plugs into a wall outlet. Figure 4.12 is a photo of the latter.

FIGURE 4.12 A laptop AC adapter

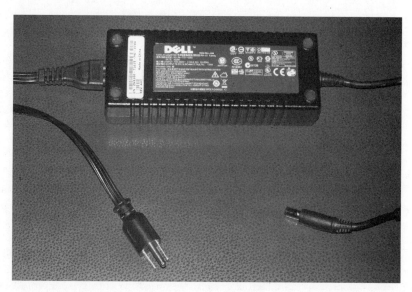

Another power accessory that is often used is a *DC adapter*, which allows a user to plug the laptop into the power source (usually a cigarette lighter) inside a car or on an airplane. These adapters allow people who travel frequently to use their laptops while on the road (literally).

Use caution when selecting a replacement AC adapter for your laptop. You should choose one rated for the same or higher wattage than the original. You must also pay special attention to the polarity of the plug that interfaces with the laptop. If the laptop requires the positive lead to be the center conductor, for instance, then you must take care not to reverse the polarity.

Regarding the input voltage of the adapter, care must also be taken to match the adapter to the power grid of the surrounding region. Some adapters have a fixed AC input requirement. Purchasing the wrong unit can result in lack of functionality or damage to the laptop. Other adapters are autoswitching, meaning they are able to automatically switch the input voltage they expect based on the voltage supplied by the wall outlet. These units are often labeled with voltage-input ranges, such as 100–240V, and frequency ranges, such as 50–60Hz, and are able to accommodate deployment in practically any country around the world. Nevertheless, you should still ascertain whether some sort of converter is required, even for autoswitching adapters.

Laptop Power Management

Being free to roam with your laptop wherever you want is a great thing. Unplugging from the wall and running on battery power means you can leap through a field of spring daisies holding your laptop instead of being chained to your gray desk and low cubicle walls. It also presents an opportunity to manage devices and how much power they consume, as batteries don't last forever. Finding a way to manage power efficiently gives batteries longer lives and you more time with your daisies.

In addition, as we've mentioned before, laptops were not designed with internal expandability in mind. Most add-on devices are external. Some peripherals can just be plugged in and unplugged, whereas with others you must follow a specific sequence to safely remove the device.

This section focuses on power management as well as the safe removal of hardware devices on laptops.

Understanding Laptop Power Management

As you learned in Chapter 1, the Basic Input/Output System (BIOS) is run when the computer is first powered up. It checks the hardware to make sure there are no major problems, bootstraps the computer, and then hands control over to the operating system. One of the features of most modern BIOS systems is support for *Advanced Configuration and Power Interface (ACPI)*. First released as an open standard in 1996, ACPI defines common interfaces for hardware recognition and configuration and, more important, power management. ACPI replaced Advanced Power Management (APM), which was excluded by Microsoft in their Windows Vista line of operating systems.

ACPI has two important power management features. First, it gives control of power management to the operating system. With older versions of power management, control was BIOS-related, and the user had little control through the operating system. Today, the BIOS handles power management communication between the operating system and the device. Second, ACPI allows power management features that were once only found on laptops to be available on desktops as well.

For ACPI to work, the motherboard, CPU, and operating system all need to support the standard. The first Windows operating system to support ACPI was Windows 98.

The ACPI standard defines four power level states, called *global states*. The global states are computer-wide, and there are other device, processor, and performance states as well.

Global States

There are four global states, ranging from G0 (normal working state) to G3 (mechanical off). Within G1, there are four substates, or sleep modes:

G0 Working   The normal working state of a computer is called G0 Working. It's assumed that all devices are running at full power. However, while in G0 state, various devices can be put into lower power modes (C and D states, discussed in the next two sections), as the computer sees fit. Most laptops will power down individual devices when they're not being used, to save battery life.

G1 Sleeping   The first power-saving mode is called G1 Sleeping. G1 is divided into four sub-modes, or sleep modes, called S1–S4. Higher S state numbers indicate more power savings but also longer latency before the device can be powered back up to G0.

- S1 is the most power-hungry sleep mode. The CPU stops executing instructions and the processor cache is flushed, but power is still provided to the CPU and memory. All devices not being used are powered down.

- S2 uses less power than S1 because in this state the processor is powered down. S2 is not typically utilized.

- S3 is also called *Standby* in Windows. When put into S3, the computer maintains power only to the RAM. Because of this, and because all running application information is stored in RAM, when the user brings the computer back from S3, the user can start right where he or she left off. However, if you lose power while in S3, all of the information being held in RAM is gone. This level is also called Suspend to RAM.

- S4 is called *Hibernation* in Windows. In S4, the information in RAM is written to the hard disk, and the RAM is powered off as well. This means that a user can take the computer from S4 back to G0 and still work from where he or she left off, but it will take longer for the applications to be available. The other good news is, because the information in RAM is written to the hard disk, if a power loss occurs, the user's information will not be lost. This level is also called Suspend to Disk.

G2 Soft Off   The G2 power state is called *soft off.* You execute a soft off by clicking the Turn Off Computer or Shutdown buttons in Windows or by otherwise letting the operating system shut the computer down, without a physical power outage. To boot back up from G2, the entire boot process must be run.

G3 Mechanical Off   If a complete power loss occurs (such as by unplugging the cord), the system enters into G3 *mechanical off.* In this state, the computer can be safely disassembled. To bring the computer from G3 to G0, the complete boot process must be run.

Processor States

The processor is one of the most critical components inside a computer, and as such it's often one of the last components to get powered down. There are four processor states:

- C0 is the operational state; no power is being saved.

- C1, or Halt, is a powered-down state, but the processor can return to action nearly instantaneously.

- C2, sometimes called Stop-Clock, uses less power than C1. The processor is still visible to software applications but takes longer to wake up if a request is made.

- C3 is Sleep mode. In this state, the processor cache is flushed, and it will take a few seconds for the processor to be available.

Device States

As with processor states, there are four device states. These apply only to peripheral devices within the computer.

- D0 Fully On is the full operating state.

- D1 and D2 are intermediate power states. Neither uses full power, and each device specifically defines its own D1 and D2 states.

- In D3 Off, the device is completely powered down and not responsive.

Performance States

Think of performance states as sublevels to processor and device states. Processors or devices in normal running modes (C0 or D0 state) can be in a lower power-level using a performance state. Performance states are designated P0-Pn, where n can be 1–16. As with all other states, bigger numbers indicate greater power savings, as well as more latency to become fully operational.

Some manufacturers have tried to brand their performance states. Intel calls its implementation SpeedStep, and AMD labels its version as Cool'n'Quiet.

Managing Power in Windows

As stated in the last section, Windows 98 and newer can handle all aspects of hardware power management. This means you don't need to configure anything in the BIOS other than to ensure that the power management setting (if it has one) is enabled, which it is by default.

To get to the power management features of Windows XP, open Control Panel, and in the Performance and Maintenance category (Mobile PC category in Windows Vista), choose Power Options. The Power Options applet has its own icon in the Classic view of Control Panel. Alternatively, you can right-click an empty area on the Desktop, click Properties, select the Screen Saver tab, and click the Power button. You will get a screen like the one shown in Figure 4.13.

FIGURE 4.13 Windows power management

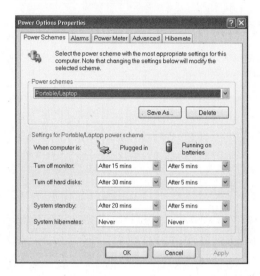

You can see that there are five tabs. You can do this on a desktop computer, too, but desktops don't typically have the Alarms and Power Meter tabs and may add a UPS tab for an uninterruptible power supply. Looking at Figure 4.13, you can see that it's set on the Portable/Laptop scheme, which allows you to define separate settings for when the laptop is plugged in versus running on the battery. Clicking the down arrow for Power Schemes, you have the option to choose from multiple schemes, if they exist. If you want to make your own scheme, configure the settings to your liking, and then click Save As.

The Alarms tab allows you to configure how your system will respond when battery power gets low. The Power Meter tab shows you the current battery life, as shown in Figure 4.14.

You can also get to the same information by clicking the battery icon in your system tray, as shown in Figure 4.15. It's good to keep an eye out for a low-battery warning when you're on battery power, so you don't run out.

The Advanced tab, shown in Figure 4.16, lets you configure the function of the power buttons.

Finally, the Hibernate tab allows you to turn off or turn on whether your computer can enter Hibernation mode.

The default power management settings are pretty relaxed. It's a good idea to be much more conservative, especially if you are on battery power a lot and want to maximize battery life.

FIGURE 4.14   Power Meter tab

FIGURE 4.15   Battery icon

FIGURE 4.16   Advanced Power Options

Summary

In this chapter, you learned about the various laptop issues that face the A+ technician. We discussed differences between laptops and desktops, including the various components that make up a laptop and how they differ in appearance and function from those on a desktop.

Input devices, expansion buses, and interfaces found in laptops were presented in detail. You also learned about power systems and how to configure power management in laptops.

Exam Essentials

Know the differences between laptop processors and desktop processors.   Laptops have less room in them, so it makes sense that laptop processors are smaller than their desktop brethren. They also operate at lower voltages, have more advanced power-down or sleep modes, and are often soldered directly to the motherboard. Finally, chipsets such as the Intel Pentium M chipset also include built-in video processing and networking capabilities.

Understand the differences between laptop memory standards and desktop memory standards.   Continuing a main theme of this chapter, memory in laptops needs to be smaller than in desktops, and so it is. The two main standards for laptop memory are SODIMM and MicroDIMM.

Understand the various power sources for laptops.   You should know that the Li-Ion battery is the preferred rechargeable power source for laptops and that active power supplies that plug into AC and DC power sources are available. Additionally, knowing the difference between autoswitching and fixed power supplies is essential.

Know how laptops handle power management.   Laptops should power down devices much quicker than desktops do, in an effort to save battery life. This is all set up by the Advanced Configuration and Power Interface (ACPI) feature of the BIOS and the operating system.

Know the various input devices and expansion buses and ports found on laptop computers.   Although many of these technologies are available in desktop computers as well, the science behind outfitting laptops with similar functionality presents unique details the A+ technician should know. PC Card-based expansion buses have their own specific traits, which you should be familiar with.

Review Questions

1. Which of the following battery chemistries has the longest life when used with portable computing devices?

   A. NiCd

   B. NiMH

   C. Alkaline

   D. Li-Ion

2. Which of the following is *not* a benefit of laptop design?

   A. Portability

   B. Increased performance

   C. Desktop replacement

   D. Higher-quality construction

3. Which of the following is *not* a requirement for ACPI to function?

   A. The BIOS must support ACPI.

   B. You must be running Windows 95 or later.

   C. The motherboard must support ACPI.

   D. The processor must support ACPI.

4. Which laptop input device was released with the IBM ThinkPad series of laptops?

   A. Touchpad

   B. Mouse

   C. Point stick

   D. Trackball

5. Which laptop accessory allows you to power your laptop from a car or airplane?

   A. AC adapter

   B. DC adapter

   C. Battery converter

   D. Automotive Wizard

6. Which of the following rechargeable battery types is least desirable due to its minimal power duration when used with laptops?

   A. NiCd

   B. NiMH

   C. Li-poly

   D. Li-Ion

7. _____ is the fastest and most modern interface used as an expansion method for external peripherals, such as mice, web cams, scanners, and printers, and is popular on laptops and desktops alike.

    A. Parallel

    B. PS/2

    C. USB

    D. ATA

8. Which kind of laptop was designed to look and function like a paper notebook?

    A. Luggable

    B. Tablet

    C. Netbook

    D. Notebook

9. Which of the following power states consumes the least amount of power?

    A. G0

    B. S1

    C. S2

    D. S4

10. Which type of PC Card is used most often for expansion devices like NICs, sound cards, and so on?

    A. Type I

    B. Type II

    C. Type III

    D. Type IV

11. Which of the following expansion buses uses serial communications and is capable of operating in USB and PCIe modes?

    A. ExpressCard

    B. CardBus

    C. Mini PCI

    D. FireWire

12. Which tab of the Display Properties dialog box in Windows XP has a button that launches Power Options Properties, allowing you to enable hibernation and set power schemes, among other things?

    A. Settings

    B. Desktop

    C. Screen Saver

    D. Themes

13. PC Cards rely on which type of software in order to operate? (Choose two.)

    A. Cardmember Services

    B. Card Services

    C. Modem Services

    D. Socket Services

14. What component allows you to keep desktop devices, such as keyboard, monitor, and mouse, permanently connected so they can be used by an attached laptop?

    A. Docking station

    B. Keyboard, video, mouse (KVM) switch

    C. Print server

    D. USB hub

15. The process by which the processor slows down to conserve power is officially called _____.

    A. Underclocking

    B. Cooling

    C. Disengaging

    D. Throttling

16. When replacing your laptop's AC adapter, which of the following purchase is acceptable to obtain the same or better results?

    A. An AC adapter with a higher voltage rating than the original

    B. An AC adapter with a higher wattage rating than the original

    C. A DC adapter with the same voltage rating than the original

    D. An AC adapter with a lower voltage and wattage rating than the original

17. What should you do for a Li-Ion battery that appears to charge fully, but does not last as long as the battery's meter indicates it will last?

    A. Replace the battery.

    B. Exercise the battery.

    C. Calibrate the battery.

    D. Short the terminals to discharge the battery.

18. How do laptop hard drives differ from desktop hard drives?

    A. Laptop hard drives use completely different standards from those used by desktop hard drives for communication with the host.

    B. Laptop hard drives are solid state; desktop hard drives have spinning platters.

    C. Laptop hard drives require a separate power connection; desktop hard drives are powered through the drive interface.

    D. The most common form factor of a laptop hard drive is about an inch smaller than that of a desktop hard drive.

19. Which laptop input device is a flat surface that you can slide across with your finger to control the cursor?

   A. Touchpad

   B. Trackball

   C. Point stick

   D. Mouse

20. Which of the following memory types has the smallest form factor?

   A. RIMM

   B. DIMM

   C. MicroDIMM

   D. SODIMM

Answers to Review Questions

1. D. Because of its high energy density, Li-Ion is the preferred battery chemistry for portable computing devices.

2. B. By and large, compromises always must be made when comparing laptops to desktops. Although laptops can be used as desktop replacements, their performance is almost always lower than comparably priced desktops.

3. B. For ACPI power management to work, it first must be a feature of the BIOS. In addition, the motherboard and processor must support the standard. Finally, you need Windows 98 or newer.

4. C. The Touchpoint point stick was released with the IBM ThinkPad series of laptops.

5. B. A DC adapter converts the DC output from a car or airplane accessory power plug into the DC voltages required by your laptop.

6. A. Nickel cadmium batteries have a very low energy density compared to the lithium chemistries and NiMH batteries. Battery packs have to be made larger to provide the same voltages and still discharge faster than their lithium counterparts.

7. C. USB is used most often in laptops as an expansion bus for external peripherals. Although parallel and PS/2 allow for connection of external peripherals, they are not as flexible or widely used for expansion as USB.

8. B. The tablet PC is a notebook with a flip-around screen that allows a user to hold it like a large notebook and write notes directly on the screen with a special stylus.

9. D. The S4 hardware state is also called Hibernation mode, and it consumes very little power. G0 is the fully powered operational state. S1 and S2 consume less power than full power but more than S4.

10. B. A Type II PC Card is the type used most often for expansion devices like NICs, sound cards, SCSI controllers, modems, and so on.

11. A. The ExpressCard bus brings USB 2.0 and PCIe to the small-form factor computing industry. CardBus supports USB 1.1 and PCI only. Mini PCI *is* PCI, not PCIe.

12. C. The Screen Saver tab of Display Options has a Power button in its Monitor Power section that launches the Power Options Properties applet.

13. B, D. The PC Card architecture has two components. The first is the Socket Services software, and the second is the Card Services software.

14. A. A docking station made specifically for its associated brand and model of laptop can host desktop components permanently, regardless of whether the laptop is attached to the docking station. When the laptop's portability is not required, but instead use of the desktop components is the priority, attaching the laptop to the docking station makes such components available to the laptop without separately attaching each component.

15. D. The processor can reduce how fast it's working, which is called throttling, to help conserve battery life.

16. B. Think of wattage as a "bucket" of power that the attached device can draw on. A bigger bucket simply holds more power but does not force the power on the device. Less wattage is not advised, however. Voltage can be thought of as the pressure behind the power to the device. Anything but the proper voltage is dangerous for the device. When you replace a laptop's AC adapter, you should match the voltage ratings of the original adapter. This also means you should use an adapter with a fixed voltage if that matches the characteristics of the original; otherwise, obtain one that automatically switches voltages at the levels needed.

17. C. Battery calibration for Li-Ion batteries allows the powered device to drain the battery's power before recharging. Battery exercising is the initial charging and discharging of nickel-based batteries so that they will function as expected. You should never short a battery's terminals, and replacement is a last resort when any battery has reached the end of its life.

18. D. Laptop hard drives commonly have a 2½″ form factor. The most common form factor for desktop hard drives is 3½″. Laptop hard drives use the same drive technologies as their desktop counterparts, such as serial and parallel ATA. As with desktop hard drives, laptop hard drives are available in both solid-state and conventional varieties. Unlike desktop hard drives, laptop hard drives do not have separate power connectors.

19. A. The touchpad is an input device usually built into the laptop. It allows you to control the mouse pointer by dragging your finger across the surface.

20. C. The SODIMM and MicroDIMM are the common laptop small-form factor memory standards. Of the two, MicroDIMM is smaller.

Chapter

5

Installing and Configuring Printers

**THE FOLLOWING COMPTIA A+ ESSENTIALS
EXAM OBJECTIVES ARE COVERED IN THIS
CHAPTER:**

✓ **1.11 Install and configure printers**

- Differentiate between printer types
  - Laser
  - Inkjet
  - Thermal
  - Impact
- Local vs. network printers
- Printer drivers (compatibility)
- Consumables

Let's face it. Our society is dependent on paper. When we conduct business, we use different types of paper documents. Contracts, letters, and, of course, money are all used to conduct business. And as most of those documents are created on computers, printers are inherently important. Even in today's age where electronic business is becoming the norm, you still have daily situations that require an old-fashioned hard copy of something.

Printers are electromechanical output devices that are used to put information from the computer onto paper. They have been around since the introduction of the computer. Other than the display monitor, the printer is the most popular peripheral purchased for a computer, because a lot of people want to have paper copies of the documents they create.

In this chapter, we will discuss the details of each major type of printer, including impact printers, inkjet printers, laser (page) printers, and thermal printers. Once we cover the different types, we'll talk about installing printers, printer interfaces, and the supplies used for printers.

Take special note of the section on laser and page printers. The A+ exams test these subjects in detail, so we'll cover them in depth.

Printer troubleshooting is an objective of the elective exams, and consequently is covered in Chapter 15, "Resolving Printer Problems."

Understanding Printer Types and Processes

Several types of printers are available on the market today. As with all other computer components, there have been significant advancements in printer technology over the years. Most of the time when faced with the decision of purchasing a printer, you're going to be weighing performance versus cost. Some of the higher-quality technologies, such as color laser printing, are rather expensive for the home user. Other technologies are less expensive but might not provide the same level of quality.

In this section, you will learn about the various types of printers that you will see as a technician, their basic components, and how they function. Specifically, we are going to look at impact printers, bubble-jet (inkjet) printers, laser (page) printers, and several other less common printer types, including thermal printers.

Impact Printers

The most basic type of printer is the category known as *impact printers*. Impact printers, as their name suggests, use some form of impact and an inked ribbon to make an imprint on the paper. In a manner of speaking, typewriters are like impact printers. Both use an inked ribbon and an impact head to make letters on the paper. The major difference is that the printer can accept input from a computer.

There are two major types of impact printers: daisy wheel and dot matrix. Each type has its own service and maintenance issues.

Daisy-Wheel Printers

The first type of impact printer we're going to discuss is the *daisy-wheel printer*. This is one of the oldest printing technologies in use. These impact printers contain a wheel (called the daisy wheel because it looks like a daisy) with raised letters and symbols on each "petal" (see Figure 5.1). When the printer needs to print a character, it sends a signal to the mechanism that contains the wheel. This mechanism is called the printhead. The printhead rotates the daisy wheel until the required character is in place. An electromechanical hammer (called a *solenoid*) then strikes the back of the petal containing the character. The character pushes up against an inked ribbon that ultimately strikes the paper, making the impression of the requested character.

FIGURE 5.1   A daisy-wheel printer mechanism

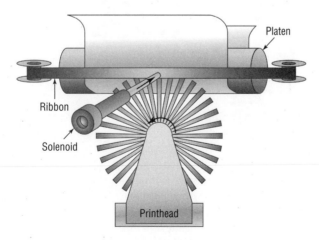

Daisy-wheel printers were one of the first types of impact printer developed. Their speed is rated by the number of *characters per second (cps)* they can print. The early printers could only print between two and four characters per second. Aside from their poor speed, the main disadvantage to this type of printer is that it makes a lot of noise when printing—so much, in fact, that special enclosures were developed to contain the noise.

The daisy-wheel printer has a few advantages, of course. First, because it is an impact printer, you can print on multipart forms (like carbonless receipts), assuming they can be fed into the printer properly. Second, it is relatively inexpensive compared to the price of a laser printer of the same vintage. Finally, the print quality is comparable to that of a typewriter because it uses a very similar technology. This typewriter level of quality was given a name: *letter quality (LQ)*.

Dot-Matrix Printers

The other type of impact printer we'll discuss is the *dot-matrix printer*. These printers work in a manner similar to daisy-wheel printers, but instead of a spinning, character-imprinted wheel, the printhead contains a row of pins (short, sturdy stalks of hard wire). These pins are triggered in patterns that form letters and numbers as the printhead moves across the paper (see Figure 5.2).

FIGURE 5.2   Formation of images in a dot-matrix printer

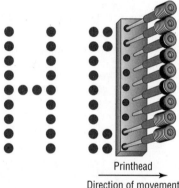

Printhead
→
Direction of movement

The pins in the printhead are wrapped with coils of wire to create a solenoid and are held in the rest position by a combination of a small magnet and a spring. To trigger a particular pin, the printer controller sends a signal to the printhead, which energizes the wires around the appropriate print wire. This turns the print wire into an electromagnet, which repels the print pin, forcing it against the ink ribbon and making a dot on the paper. The arrangement of the dots in columns and rows creates the letters and numbers you see on the page. Figure 5.2 shows this process.

The main disadvantage of dot-matrix printers is their image quality, which can be quite poor compared to the quality produced with a daisy wheel. Dot-matrix printers use patterns of dots to make letters and images, and the early dot-matrix printers used only nine pins to make those patterns. The output quality of such printers is referred to as *draft quality*— good mainly for providing your initial text to a correspondent or reviser. Each letter looked fuzzy because the dots were spaced as far as they could be and still be perceived as a letter or image. As more pins were crammed into the printhead (17-pin and 24-pin models were eventually developed), the quality increased because the dots were closer together. Dot-matrix technology ultimately improved to the point that a letter printed on a dot-matrix printer was *almost* indistinguishable from typewriter output. This level of quality is known as *near letter quality (NLQ)*.

Dot-matrix printers are noisy, but the print wires and printhead are covered by a plastic dust cover, making them quieter than daisy-wheel printers. They also use a more efficient printing technology, so the print speed is faster (typically in the range of 36 to 72cps). Some dot-matrix printers (like the Epson DFX series) can print at close to a page per second! Finally, because dot-matrix printers are also impact printers, they can use multipart forms. Because of these advantages, dot-matrix printers quickly made daisy-wheel printers obsolete.

Most impact printers have an option to adjust how close the printhead rests from the ribbon. So if your printing is too light, you may be able to adjust the printhead closer to the ribbon. If it's too dark or you get smeared printing, you may be able to move the printhead back.

Bubble-Jet Printers

The next category of printer technology is one of the most popular in use today. This category is an advanced form of an older technology known as *inkjet printers*. Both types of printers spray ink on the page, but inkjet printers used a reservoir of ink, a pump, and an ink nozzle to accomplish this. They were messy, noisy, and inefficient. Bubble-jet printers work much more efficiently and are much cheaper.

In a *bubble-jet printer*, bubbles of ink are sprayed onto a page and form patterns that resemble the items being printed. In this section, you will learn the parts of a bubble-jet printer, as well as how bubble-jet printers work.

Parts of a Typical Bubble-Jet Printer

Bubble-jet printers are simple devices. They contain very few parts (even fewer than dot-matrix printers) and, as such, are inexpensive to manufacture. It's common today to have a $40–$50 bubble-jet printer with print quality that rivals that of basic laser printers.

In this section, you will learn the parts of a typical bubble-jet printer and what they do. The printer parts can be divided into the following categories:

- Printhead/ink cartridge
- Head carriage, belt, and stepper motor
- Paper-feed mechanism
- Control, interface, and power circuitry

Printhead/Ink Cartridge

The first part of a bubble-jet printer is the one people see the most: the *printhead*. This part of a printer contains many small nozzles (usually 100–200) that spray the ink in small dots onto the page. Many times the printhead is part of the *ink cartridge*, which contains a reservoir of ink and the printhead in a removable package. Color bubble-jet printers include multiple printheads, one for each of the *CMYK (cyan, magenta, yellow, and black)* print inks.

Every bubble-jet printer works in a similar fashion. As we just mentioned, each bubble-jet printer contains a special part called an ink cartridge that contains the printhead and ink supply (although some printers separate them so they can be replaced separately). The print cartridge must be replaced as the ink supply runs out.

Inside the ink cartridge are several small chambers. At the top of each chamber are a metal plate and a tube leading to the ink supply. At the bottom of each chamber is a small pinhole. These pinholes are used to spray ink on the page to form characters and images as patterns of dots (similar to the way a dot-matrix printer works but with much higher resolution).

There are two methods of spraying the ink out of the cartridge. The first was developed by Hewlett-Packard (HP): when a particular chamber needs to spray ink, an electric signal is sent to the heating element, energizing it. The elements heat up quickly, causing the ink to vaporize. Because of the expanding ink vapor, the ink is pushed out the pinhole and forms a bubble. As the vapor expands, the bubble eventually gets large enough to break off into a droplet. The rest of the ink is pulled back into the chamber by the surface tension of the ink. When another drop needs to be sprayed, the process begins again. The second method, developed by Epson, uses a piezoelectric element that flexes when energized. The outward flex pushes the ink from the nozzle; on the return, it sucks more ink from the reservoir.

When the printer is done printing, the printhead moves back to its maintenance station. The *maintenance station* contains a small suction pump and ink-absorbing pad. To keep the ink flowing freely, before each print cycle the maintenance station pulls ink through the ink nozzles using vacuum suction. This expelled ink is absorbed by the pad. The station serves two functions: to provide a place for the printhead to rest when the printer isn't printing and to keep the printhead in working order.

Head Carriage, Belt, and Stepper Motor

Another major component of the bubble-jet printer is the head carriage and the associated parts that make it move. The *printhead carriage* is the component of a bubble-jet printer that moves back and forth during printing. It contains the physical as well as electronic connections for the printhead and (in some cases) the ink reservoir. Figure 5.3 shows an example of a head carriage. Note the clips that keep the ink cartridge in place and the electronic connections for the ink cartridge. These connections cause the nozzles to fire, and if they aren't kept clean, you may have printing problems.

The stepper motor and belt make the printhead carriage move. A *stepper motor* is a precisely made electric motor that can move in the same very small increments each time it is activated. That way, it can move to the same position(s) time after time. The motor that makes the printhead carriage move is most often called the *carriage motor* or *carriage stepper motor*. Figure 5.4 shows an example of a stepper motor.

FIGURE 5.3   A printhead carriage in a bubble-jet printer

FIGURE 5.4   A carriage stepper motor

In addition to the motor, a belt is placed around two small wheels or pulleys and attached to the printhead carriage. This belt, called the *carriage belt*, is driven by the carriage motor and moves the printhead back and forth across the page while it prints. To keep the printhead carriage aligned and stable while it traverses the page, the carriage rests on a small metal *stabilizer bar*. Figure 5.5 shows the stabilizer bar, carriage belt, and pulleys.

Paper-Feed Mechanism

In addition to getting the ink onto the paper, the printer must have a way to get the paper into the printer. That's where the paper-feed mechanism comes in. The *paper-feed mechanism* picks up paper from the paper drawer and feeds it into the printer. This assembly consists of several smaller assemblies. First are the *pickup rollers* (Figure 5.6), which are several rubber rollers with a slightly flat spot; they rub against the paper as they rotate, and feed the paper into the printer. They work against small cork or rubber patches known as *separator pads* (Figure 5.7), which help keep the rest of the paper in place (so only one sheet goes into the printer). The pickup rollers are turned on a shaft by the *pickup stepper motor*.

FIGURE 5.5   Stabilizer bar, carriage belt, and pulleys in a bubble-jet printer

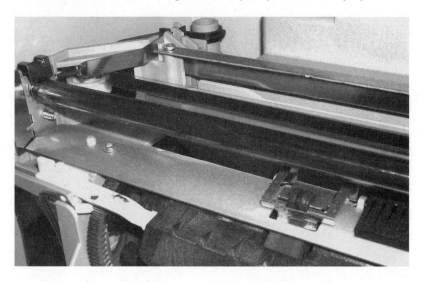

   Clean pickup rollers (and other rubber rollers) with mild soap and water and not alcohol. Alcohol can dry out the rollers, making them ineffective.

FIGURE 5.6   Bubble-jet pickup rollers

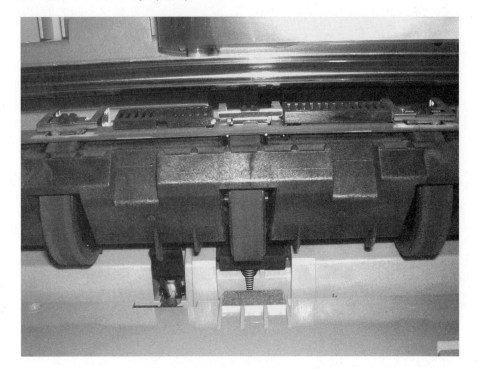

FIGURE 5.7   Bubble-jet separator pads

Sometimes the paper that is fed into a bubble-jet printer is placed into a *paper tray*, which is simply a small plastic tray in the front of the printer that holds the paper until it is fed into the printer by the paper-feed mechanism. On smaller printers, the paper is placed vertically into a *paper feeder* at the back of the printer; it uses gravity, in combination with feed rollers and separator pads, to get the paper into the printer. No real rhyme or reason dictates which manufacturers use these different parts; some models use them, and some don't. Generally, more expensive printers use paper trays, because they hold more paper. Figure 5.8 shows an example of a paper tray on a bubble-jet printer.

FIGURE 5.8 A paper tray on a bubble-jet printer

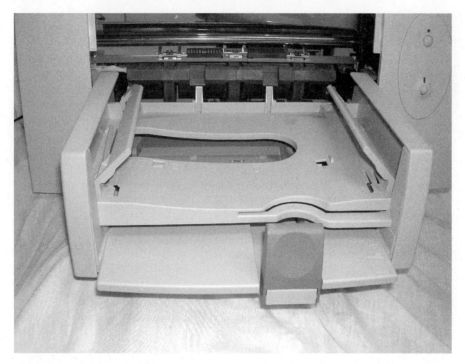

The final part of the paper-feed mechanism is the *paper-feed sensors*. These components tell the printer when it is out of paper, as well as when a paper jam has occurred during the paper-feed process. Figure 5.9 shows an example of a paper-feed sensor.

EXERCISE 5.1

Identifying the Parts of a Bubble-jet Printer

Being able to identify the parts of a bubble-jet printer is an important skill for an A+ candidate. For this exercise, you'll need a bubble-jet printer.

1. Unplug the bubble-jet printer from the power source and the computer.

2. Open the top cover to expose the inner print mechanism.

3. Locate and identify the paper tray.

4. Locate and identify the paper-feed sensor.

5. Locate and identify the pickup roller(s).

6. Locate and identify the separator pad(s).

7. Locate and identify the printhead and carriage assembly.

FIGURE 5.9   A paper-feed sensor on a bubble-jet printer

Control, Interface, and Power Circuitry

The final component group is the electronic circuitry for printer control, printer interfaces, and printer power. The *printer control circuits* are usually on a small circuit board that contains all the circuitry to run the stepper motors the way the printer needs them to work (back and forth, load paper and then stop, and so on). These circuits are also responsible for monitoring the health of the printer and reporting that information back to the PC.

The second power component, the interface circuitry (commonly called a port), makes the physical connection to whatever signal is coming from the computer (parallel, serial, SCSI, network, infrared, and so on) and also connects the physical interface to the control circuitry. The interface circuitry converts the signals from the interface into the datastream that the printer uses.

The last set of circuits the printer uses is the *power circuits*. Essentially, these conductive pathways convert 110V or 220V house current into the voltages the bubble-jet printer uses (usually 12V and 5V) and distribute those voltages to the other printer circuits and devices that need it. This is accomplished through the use of a *transformer*. A transformer, in this case, takes the 110V AC current and changes it to 12V DC (among others). This transformer can be either internal (incorporated into the body of the printer) or external. Today's bubble-jets can use either design, although the integrated design is preferred because it is simpler and doesn't show the bulky transformer.

The Bubble-Jet Printing Process

Just as with other types of printing, the bubble-jet printing process consists of a set of steps the printer must follow in order to put the data onto the page being printed. The following steps take place whenever you click the Print button in your favorite software (like Microsoft Word or Internet Explorer):

1. You click the Print button (or similar) that initiates the printing process.

2. The software you are printing from sends the data to be printed to the printer driver you have selected.

 The function and use of the printer driver are discussed later in this chapter.

3. The printer driver uses a page-description language to convert the data being printed into the proper format that the printer can understand. The driver also ensures that the printer is ready to print.

4. The printer driver sends the information to the printer via whatever connection method is being used (USB, network, parallel, and so on).

5. The printer stores the received data in its onboard *print buffer* memory. A print buffer is a small amount of memory (typically 512KB to 16MB) used to store print jobs as they are received from the printing computer. This buffer allows several jobs to be printed at once and helps printing to be completed quickly.

6. If the printer has not printed in a while, the printer's control circuits activate a cleaning cycle. A *cleaning cycle* is a set of steps the bubble-jet printer goes through in order to purge the printheads of any dried ink. It uses a special suction cup and sucking action to pull ink through the printhead, dislodging any dried ink or clearing stuck passageways.

7. Once the printer is ready to print, the control circuitry activates the paper-feed motor. This causes a sheet of paper to be fed into the printer until the paper activates the paper-feed sensor, which stops the feed until the printhead is in the right position and the leading edge of the paper is under the printhead. If the paper doesn't reach the paper-feed sensor in a specified amount of time after the stepper motor has been activated, the Out of Paper light is turned on and a message is sent to the computer.

8. Once the paper is positioned properly, the printhead stepper motor uses the printhead belt and carriage to move the printhead across the page, little by little. The motor is moved one small step, and the printhead sprays the dots of ink on the paper in the pattern dictated by the control circuitry. Typically, this is either a pattern of black dots or a pattern of CMYK inks that are mixed to make colors. Then the stepper motor moves the printhead another small step; the process repeats all the way across the page. This process is so quick, however, that the entire motion of starts and stops across the page looks like one smooth motion.

9. At the end of a pass across the page, the paper-feed stepper motor advances the page a small amount. Then the printhead repeats step 8. Depending on the model, the printhead either returns to the beginning of the line and prints again in the same direction only, or it moves backward across the page so that printing occurs in both directions. This process continues until the page is finished.

10. Once the page is finished, the feed-stepper motor is actuated and ejects the page from the printer into the output tray. If more pages need to print, printing the next page begins again at step 7.

11. Once printing is complete and the final page has been ejected from the printer, the printhead is *parked* (locked into rest position) and the print process is finished.

Laser Printers

Laser printers and inkjet printers are referred to as *page printers* because they receive their print job instructions one page at a time (rather than receiving instructions one line at a time). There are two major types of page printers: those that use the electrophotographic (EP) print process and those that use the light-emitting diode (LED) print process. Each works in basically the same way, with slight differences.

Electrophotographic (EP) Laser Printers

Xerox, Hewlett-Packard, and Canon were pioneers in developing the laser printer technology we use today. Scientists at Xerox developed the electrophotographic (EP) process in 1971. The first successful desktop laser printer was introduced by HP in 1984 using Canon hardware that used the EP process. This technology uses a combination of static electric charges, laser light, and a black powdery substance called *toner*. Printers that use this technology are called EP process laser printers, or just *laser printers*. Every laser printer technology has its foundations in the EP printer process.

Let's discuss the basic components of the EP laser printer and how they operate so you can understand the way an EP laser printer works.

Basic Components

Most printers that use the EP process contain nine standard assemblies: the toner cartridge, laser scanner, high-voltage power supply, DC power supply, paper transport assembly (including paper-pickup rollers and paper-registration rollers), transfer corona, fusing assembly, printer controller circuitry, and ozone filter. Let's discuss each of the components individually before we examine how they all work together to make the printer function.

THE TONER CARTRIDGE

The EP toner cartridge (Figure 5.10), as its name suggests, holds the toner. Toner is a black carbon substance mixed with polyester resins (to make it flow better) and iron oxide particles (to make the toner sensitive to electrical charges). These two components make the toner capable of being attracted to the photosensitive drum and of melting into the paper. In addition to these components, toner contains a medium called the *developer* (also called the *carrier*), which carries the toner until it is used by the EP process. The toner cartridge also contains the EP print drum. This drum is coated with a photosensitive material that can hold a static charge when not exposed to light (but *cannot* hold a charge when it *is* exposed to light—a curious phenomenon and one that EP printers exploit for the purpose of making images). Finally, the drum contains a cleaning blade that continuously scrapes the used toner off the photosensitive drum to keep it clean.

FIGURE 5.10   An EP toner cartridge

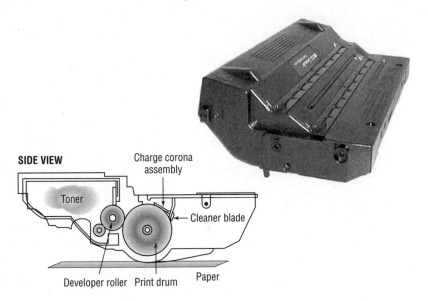

SIDE VIEW · Charge corona assembly · Toner · Cleaner blade · Developer roller · Print drum · Paper

 In most laser printers, *toner cartridge* means an EP toner cartridge that contains toner and a photosensitive drum in one plastic case. In some laser printers, however, the toner and photosensitive drum can be replaced separately instead of as a single unit. If you ask for a toner cartridge for one of these printers, all you will receive is a cylinder full of toner. Consult the printer's manual to find out which kind of toner cartridge your laser printer uses.

THE LASER SCANNING ASSEMBLY

As we mentioned earlier, the EP photosensitive drum can hold a charge if it's not exposed to light. It is dark inside an EP printer, except when the laser scanning assembly shines on particular areas of the photosensitive drum. When it does that, the drum discharges, but only in that area. As the drum rotates, the laser scanning assembly scans the laser across the photosensitive drum. Figure 5.11 shows the laser scanning assembly.

FIGURE 5.11   The EP laser scanning assembly (side view and simplified top view)

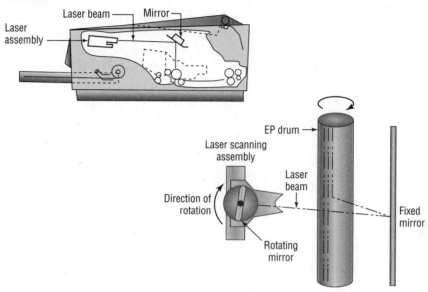

Laser light is damaging to human eyes. Therefore, the laser is kept in an enclosure and will operate only when the laser printer's cover is closed.

HIGH-VOLTAGE POWER SUPPLY (HVPS)

The EP process requires high-voltage electricity. The high-voltage power supply (HVPS) provides the high voltages used during the EP process. This component converts house AC current (120V, and 60Hz) into higher voltages that the printer can use. This high voltage is used to energize both the charging corona and the transfer corona.

Anything with the words "high voltage" in it should make you pause before getting into it. The HVPS can hurt or kill you if you're inside a laser printer and don't know what you're doing.

DC POWER SUPPLY (DCPS)

The high voltages used in the EP process can't power the other components in the printer (the logic circuitry and motors). These components require low voltages, between +5 and +24VDC. The DC power supply (DCPS) converts house current into three voltages: +5VDC and −5VDC for the logic circuitry and +24VDC for the paper-transport motors. This component also runs the fan that cools the internal components of the printer.

PAPER-TRANSPORT ASSEMBLY

The paper-transport assembly is responsible for moving the paper through the printer. It consists of a motor and several rubberized rollers that each performs a different function.

The first type of roller found in most laser printers is the *feed roller*, or *paper-pickup roller* (Figure 5.12). This D-shaped roller, when activated, rotates against the paper and pushes one sheet into the printer. This roller works in conjunction with a special rubber separator pad to prevent more than one sheet from being fed into the printer at a time.

FIGURE 5.12   Paper-transport rollers

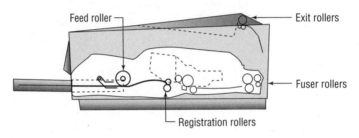

Another type of roller that is used in the printer is the *registration roller* (also shown in Figure 5.12). There are actually two registration rollers, which work together. These rollers synchronize the paper movement with the image-formation process in the EP cartridge. The rollers don't feed the paper past the EP cartridge until the cartridge is ready for it.

Both of these rollers are operated with a special electric motor known as an *electronic stepper motor*. This type of motor can accurately move in very small increments. It powers all the paper-transport rollers as well as the fuser rollers.

THE TRANSFER CORONA ASSEMBLY

When the laser writes the images on the photosensitive drum, the toner then sticks to the exposed areas; we'll cover this in the next section, "Electrophotographic (EP) Print Process." How does the toner get from the photosensitive drum onto the paper? The *transfer corona assembly* (Figure 5.13) is given a high-voltage charge, which is transferred to the paper, which pulls the toner from the photosensitive drum.

Included in the transfer corona assembly is a *static-charge eliminator strip* that drains away the charge imparted to the paper by the corona. If you didn't drain away the charge, the paper would stick to the EP cartridge and jam the printer.

There are two types of transfer corona assemblies: those that contain a transfer *corona wire* and those that contain a transfer *corona roller*. The transfer corona wire is a small-diameter wire that is charged by the HVPS. The wire is located in a special notch in the floor of the laser printer (under the EP print cartridge). The transfer corona roller performs the same function as the transfer corona wire, but it's a roller rather than a wire. Because the transfer corona roller is directly in contact with the paper, it supports higher speeds. For this reason, the transfer corona wire is no longer used much in laser printers.

FIGURE 5.13   The transfer corona assembly

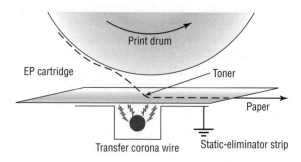

Print drum

EP cartridge

Toner

Paper

Transfer corona wire   Static-eliminator strip

FUSING ASSEMBLY

The toner in the EP toner cartridge will stick to just about anything, including paper. This is true because the toner has a negative static charge and most objects have a net positive charge. However, these toner particles can be removed by brushing any object across the page. This could be a problem if you want the images and letters to stay on the paper permanently!

To solve this problem, EP laser printers incorporate a device known as a *fuser* (Figure 5.14), which uses two rollers that apply pressure and heat to fuse the plastic toner particles to the paper. You may have noticed that pages from either a laser printer or a copier (which uses a similar device) come out warm. This is because of the fuser.

FIGURE 5.14   The fuser

Fusing roller

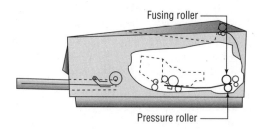

Pressure roller

The fuser is made up of three main parts: a halogen heating lamp, a Teflon-coated aluminum fusing roller, and a rubberized pressure roller. The fuser uses the halogen lamp to heat the fusing roller to between 329° F (165° C) and 356° F (180° C). As the paper passes between the two rollers, the pressure roller pushes the paper against the fusing roller, which melts the toner into the paper.

WARNING   The fuser can cause severe burns! Be careful when working with it.

PRINTER CONTROLLER CIRCUITRY

Another component in the laser printer we need to discuss is the *printer controller assembly*. This large circuit board converts signals from the computer into signals for the various assemblies in the laser printer, using a process known as *rasterizing*. This circuit board is usually mounted under the printer. The board has connectors for each type of interface and cables to each assembly.

When a computer prints to a laser printer, it sends a signal through a cable to the printer controller assembly. The controller assembly formats the information into a page's worth of line-by-line commands for the laser scanner. The controller sends commands to each of the components, telling them to wake up and begin the EP print process.

OZONE FILTER

Your laser printer uses various high-voltage biases inside the case. As anyone who has been outside during a lightning storm can tell you, high voltages create ozone. Ozone is a chemically reactive gas that is created by the high-voltage coronas (charging and transfer) inside the printer. Because ozone is chemically reactive and can severely reduce the life of laser printer components, most laser printers contain a filter to remove ozone gas from inside the printer as it is produced. This filter must be removed and cleaned with compressed air periodically (cleaning it whenever the toner cartridge is replaced is usually sufficient). Most newer laser printers don't have ozone filters. This is because these printers don't use transfer corona wires but instead use transfer corona rollers, which dramatically reduce ozone emissions.

Electrophotographic (EP) Print Process

The *EP print process* is the process by which an EP laser printer forms images on paper. It consists of six major steps, each for a specific goal. Although many different manufacturers call these steps different things or place them in a different order, the basic process is still the same. Here are the steps in the order you will see them on the exam:

1. Cleaning
2. Charging
3. Writing
4. Developing
5. Transferring
6. Fusing

To help you remember the steps of the EP print process in order, learn the first letter of each step: CCWDTF. The most often used mnemonic sentence for this combination of letters is "Charlie Can Walk, Dance, and Talk French."

Before any of these steps can begin, however, the controller must sense that the printer is ready to start printing (toner cartridge installed, fuser warmed to temperature, and all covers in place). Printing cannot take place until the printer is in its ready state, usually indicated by an illuminated Ready LED light or a display that says something like 00 READY (on HP printers).

STEP 1: CLEANING

In the first part of the laser print process, a rubber blade inside the EP cartridge scrapes any toner left on the drum into a used toner receptacle inside the EP cartridge, and a fluorescent lamp discharges any remaining charge on the photosensitive drum (remember that the drum, being photosensitive, loses its charge when exposed to light). This step is called the *cleaning step* (Figure 5.15).

FIGURE 5.15   The cleaning step of the EP process

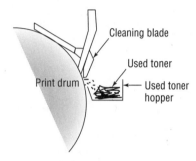

The EP cartridge is constantly cleaning the drum. It may take more than one rotation of the photosensitive drum to make an image on the paper. The cleaning step keeps the drum fresh for each use. If you didn't clean the drum, you would see ghosts of previous pages printed along with your image.

The amount of toner removed in the cleaning process is quite small. The cartridge will run out of toner before the used toner receptacle fills up.

STEP 2: CHARGING

The next step in the EP process is the *charging step* (Figure 5.16). In this step, a special wire or roller (called a *charging corona*) within the EP toner cartridge (above the photosensitive drum) gets a high voltage from the HVPS. It uses this high voltage to apply a strong, uniform negative charge (around −600VDC) to the surface of the photosensitive drum.

STEP 3: WRITING

Next is the *writing step*. In this step, the laser is turned on and scans the drum from side to side, flashing on and off according to the bits of information the printer controller sends it as it communicates the individual bits of the image. Wherever the laser beam touches, the photosensitive drum's charge is severely reduced from −600VDC to a slight negative charge (around −100VDC). As the drum rotates, a pattern of exposed areas is formed, representing the image to be printed. Figure 5.17 shows this process.

FIGURE 5.16   The charging step of the EP process

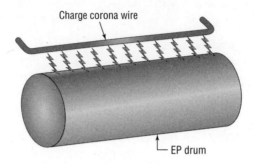

FIGURE 5.17   The writing step of the EP process

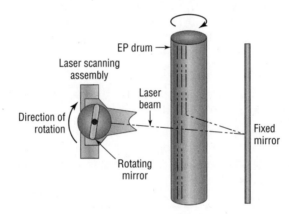

At this point, the controller sends a signal to the pickup roller to feed a piece of paper into the printer, where it stops at the registration rollers.

STEP 4: DEVELOPING

Now that the surface of the drum holds an electrical representation of the image being printed, its discrete electrical charges need to be converted into something that can be transferred to a piece of paper. The EP process step that accomplishes this is the *developing step* (Figure 5.18). In this step, toner is transferred to the areas that were exposed in the writing step.

A metallic roller called the *developing roller* inside an EP cartridge acquires a –600VDC charge (called a *bias voltage*) from the HVPS. The toner sticks to this roller because there is a magnet located inside the roller and because of the electrostatic charges between the toner and the developing roller. While the developing roller rotates toward the photo-sensitive drum, the toner acquires the charge of the roller (–600VDC). When the toner comes between the developing roller and the photosensitive drum, the toner is attracted to the areas that have been exposed by the laser (because these areas have a lesser charge, –100VDC). The toner also is repelled from the unexposed areas (because they are at the same –600VDC charge, and like charges repel). This toner transfer creates a fog of toner between the EP drum and the developing roller.

FIGURE 5.18   The developing step of the EP process

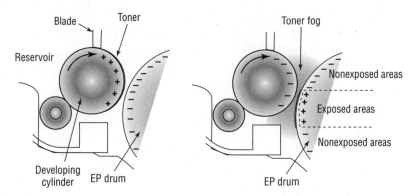

The photosensitive drum now has toner stuck to it where the laser has written. The photosensitive drum continues to rotate until the developed image is ready to be transferred to paper in the next step.

STEP 5: TRANSFERRING

At this point in the EP process, the developed image is rotating into position. The controller notifies the registration rollers that the paper should be fed through. The registration rollers move the paper underneath the photosensitive drum, and the process of transferring the image can begin, with the *transferring step.*

The controller sends a signal to the charging corona wire or roller (depending on which one the printer has) and tells it to turn on. The corona wire/roller then acquires a strong *positive* charge (+600VDC) and applies that charge to the paper. The paper, thus charged, pulls the toner from the photosensitive drum at the line of contact between the roller and the paper, because the paper and toner have opposite charges. Once the registration rollers move the paper past the corona wire, the static-eliminator strip removes all charge from that line of the paper. Figure 5.19 details this step. If the strip didn't bleed this charge away, the paper would attract itself to the toner cartridge and cause a paper jam.

The toner is now held in place by weak electrostatic charges and gravity. It will not stay there, however, unless it is made permanent, which is the reason for the fusing step.

FIGURE 5.19   The transferring step of the EP process

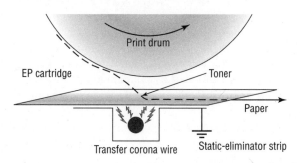

STEP 6: FUSING

In the final step, the *fusing step*, the toner image is made permanent. The registration rollers push the paper toward the fuser rollers. Once the fuser grabs the paper, the registration rollers push for only a short time more. The fuser is now in control of moving the paper.

As the paper passes through the fuser, the 350° F fuser roller melts the polyester resin of the toner, and the rubberized pressure roller presses it permanently into the paper (Figure 5.20). The paper continues through the fuser and eventually exits the printer.

FIGURE 5.20   The fusing step of the EP process

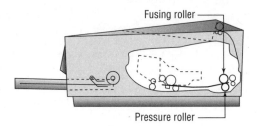

Fusing roller

Pressure roller

Once the paper completely exits the fuser, it trips a sensor that tells the printer to finish the EP process with the cleaning step. At this point, the printer can print another page, and the EP process can begin again.

SUMMARY OF THE EP PRINT PROCESS

Figure 5.21 summarizes all the EP process printing steps. First, the printer uses a rubber scraper to clean the photosensitive drum. Then the printer places a uniform –600VDC charge on the photosensitive drum by means of a charging corona. The laser "paints" an image onto the photosensitive drum, discharging the image areas to a much lower voltage (–100VDC). The developing roller in the toner cartridge has charged (–600VDC) toner stuck to it. As it rolls the toner toward the photosensitive drum, the toner is attracted to (and sticks to) the areas of the photosensitive drum that the laser has discharged. The image is then transferred from the drum to the paper at its line of contact by means of the transfer corona wire (or corona roller) with a +600VDC charge. The static-eliminator strip removes the high, positive charge from the paper, and the paper, now holding the image, moves on. The paper then enters the fuser, where a fuser roller and the pressure roller make the image permanent. The paper exits the printer, and the printer begins printing the next page or returns to its ready state.

LED Page Printers

Now we'll discuss another laser printer: the light-emitting diode (LED) page printer. This technology is primarily developed and used by Okidata and Panasonic. Because the A+ exam does not currently cover LED page printers, we will discuss only the differences between them and laser printers.

The two main differences between a LED page printer and a laser printer are the toner cartridges and the print process.

FIGURE 5.21   The EP print process

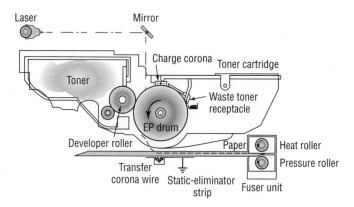

LED Page Printer Toner Cartridges

One problem with laser printers is that the toner usually runs out before the photosensitive drum needs to be replaced. But because they're usually both housed in the same replaceable unit, every time you replace the toner, you're also replacing the drum, whether or not it needs replacing. So the designers of LED page printers made the photosensitive drum and toner separate, replaceable items.

> The main parts of the LED page printer toner assembly are integrated into the printer. The charging corona (or roller) and erasing lamps are also integrated into the printer. The average user cannot replace these items; an authorized service technician must replace them.

When replacing the photosensitive drum, you swing the photosensitive drum/toner cartridge out of the printer first. Then you remove the drum from its carrier and install the new one (this also replaces the waste toner receptacle).

Filling the toner hopper is fairly easy. On most LED page printers, you place the new toner cartridge over the toner hopper and lock it in place. Between the new toner cartridge and the toner hopper are a lever and door. When you slide the lever over, it opens the door and allows the toner to fall through the opening. Once all the toner is out of the cartridge and hopper, you slide the lever back, closing the door. You can then remove the cartridge and throw it away.

The LED Page Printer Process

The LED page printer uses the same process as a laser printer, with one major exception. It uses a row of small light-emitting diodes held very close to the photosensitive drum to expose it. Each LED is about the same size as the diameter of the laser beam used in laser printers. These printers are basically the same as EP process printers, except that in the writing step, they use LEDs instead of a laser.

LED page printers offer several benefits over laser printers. First, because they use LEDs instead of lasers, LED page printers are much cheaper than similar laser printers—they're about half the cost. Also, because the LEDs are close to the drum, the whole printer is smaller—about two-thirds the size of a comparable laser printer. Finally, LEDs aren't as dangerous to the eye as lasers (you could probably damage your eyes if you stared at one long enough, but it's unlikely you'd do such a thing).

If they have so many advantages, why isn't everyone using them? Mainly because LED technology isn't as advanced as laser technology. The resolutions of LED page printers have yet to break the 800 dots per inch (dpi) mark. Another reason is that the toner system in an LED printer, although more efficient, is also messier. Because of its slight static charge, toner isn't easy to remove from surfaces.

> **WARNING** Never ship a printer anywhere with a toner cartridge installed! If the printer is a laser printer, remove the toner cartridge first. If it's an LED page printer, there is a method to remove the photosensitive drum and toner hopper (check your manual for details).

Other Types of Printers

The types of printers you have learned about so far in this chapter account for 90 percent of all printers used with home or office computers and that you will see as a repair technician. The other 10 percent consist of other types of printers that primarily differ by the method they use to put colored material on the paper to represent what is being printed.

The three other major types of printers in use today are as follows:

- Solid ink
- Thermal
- Dye sublimation

Keep in mind throughout this section that for the most part, these printers operate like other printers in many ways: they all have a paper-feed mechanism (sheet-fed or roll); they all require consumables; they all use the same interfaces, for the most part, as other types of printers; and they are usually about the same size.

Solid-Ink Printers

Solid-ink printers work much like bubble-jet printers. However, in a solid-ink printer, the ink is in a waxy solid form rather than in liquid form, which allows it to stay fresh and not cause problems like spillage. In addition, solid-ink printers usually print an entire line at one time, which makes them faster than bubble-jet printers. Because of the type of ink used, solid-ink printers are better for graphics companies that need true color at a price lower than a color laser printer.

Thermal Printers

You almost surely have seen a direct thermal printer. They can be found in many older fax machines (most newer ones use either inkjet or laser printing). They print on a kind of special, waxy paper that comes on a roll; the paper turns black when heat passes over it. *Thermal printers* work by using a printhead the width of the paper. When it needs to print, the printhead heats and cools spots on the printhead. The paper below the heated printhead turns black in those spots. As the paper moves through the printer, the pattern of blackened spots forms an image on the page of what is being printed. Another type of thermal printer uses a heat-sensitive ribbon instead of heat-sensitive paper. A thermal printhead melts wax-based ink from the ribbon onto the paper. These are called thermal transfer or thermal wax-transfer printers.

Thermal direct printers typically have long lives because they have few moving parts. However, the paper is somewhat expensive, doesn't last long (especially if it is left in a very warm place, like a closed car in summer), and produces poorer-quality images than most of the other printing technologies.

Dye-Sublimation Printers

The last type of printer you will learn about in this chapter is the *dye-sublimation printer*. These printers use sheets of solid ink that *sublimate*, or go from the solid phase directly to gas. During printing, a printhead passes over these sheets (one each of cyan, magenta, yellow, and gray for tonal change) inside the printer. As it passes over the page, spots on the printhead heat up, causing the ink under those spots to sublimate into gas. This gas then passes through the paper being printed, where the ink turns back into a solid, embedded into the paper. The printhead in most printers makes four passes, one for each color.

Dye-sublimation printers are used most often in the graphics or printing industries, because they really do only one thing well: photo-quality images. They take time to produce their images, but those images are of extremely high quality. It would be expensive and impractical to use a dye-sublimation printer for word processing.

Printer Interfaces and Supplies

Besides understanding the printer's operation, for the A+ exam you need to know how the printer talks to a computer and all the items involved in that process. You must also understand how the different types of print media affect the print process.

Interface Components

A printer's *interface* is the collection of hardware and software that allows the printer to communicate with a computer. The hardware interface is commonly called a port. Each printer has at least one interface, but some printers have several, in order to make them more flexible in a multiplatform environment. If a printer has several interfaces, it can usually switch between them on the fly so that several computers can print at the same time.

An interface incorporates several components, including its communication type and the *interface software*. Each aspect must be matched on both the printer and the computer. For example, if you have an older HP LaserJet 4L, it only has a parallel port. Therefore, you must use a parallel cable as well as the correct software for the platform being used (for example, a Macintosh HP LaserJet 4L driver if you connect it to a Macintosh computer).

Communication Types

When we say *communication types*, we're talking about the ports used in getting the printed information from the computer to the printer. There are eight major types: serial, parallel, SCSI, Universal Serial Bus (USB), network, IEEE 1394b, infrared, and wireless. You've learned about these connections in earlier chapters, but now you will learn how they apply to printers.

SERIAL

When computers send data serially, they send it one bit at a time, one after another. The bits stand in line like people at a movie theater, waiting to get in. Just as with modems, you must set the communication parameters (baud, parity, start and stop bits) on both entities—in this case, the computer and its printer(s)—before communication can take place.

 It's very rare to find a serial printer in use today due to slow data transmission speed.

PARALLEL

When a printer uses parallel communication, it is receiving data 8 bits at a time over eight separate wires (one for each bit). Parallel communication was the most popular way of communicating from computer to printer for many years, mainly because it's faster than serial.

A parallel cable consists of a male DB-25 connector that connects to the computer and a male 36-pin Centronics connector that connects to the printer. Most of the cables are less than 10′ long. Parallel cables should be IEEE 1284 compliant.

 Keep printer cable lengths to less than 10′. Some people try to run printer cables more than 50′. If the length is greater than 10′, communications can become unreliable due to crosstalk.

SCSI

Only a few types of printers use SCSI interfaces to the PC, and most of them are laser printers, dye-sublimation printers, or typesetters. When these printers were introduced, they all came with an option for a SCSI interface. The benefits in these situations were as follows:

- There could be more than one device on a single SCSI connection through daisy chaining.
- It was fairly simple to implement.
- It had relatively large throughput compared to other interfaces of the time.

Because of the advent of higher-speed peripheral connection methods, such as IEEE 1394b/FireWire and USB, SCSI interfaces for printers are all but obsolete.

UNIVERSAL SERIAL BUS (USB)

The most popular type of printer interface as this book is being written is the Universal Serial Bus (USB). In fact, it is the most popular interface for just about every peripheral.

The convenience for printers is that it has a higher transfer rate than either serial or parallel and it automatically recognizes new devices.

NETWORK

Many newer printers (primarily laser and LED printers) have a special interface that allows them to be hooked directly to a network. These printers have a network interface card (NIC) and ROM-based software that allow them to communicate with networks, servers, and workstations.

The type of network interface used on the printer depends on the type of network to which the printer is being attached. For example, if you're using a token ring network, the printer should have a token ring interface. The most common interface you'll see is RJ-45 for an Ethernet connection.

IEEE 1394B FIREWIRE

The IEEE 1394b interface (also known as *FireWire*—an Apple trademark) had an explosion of popularity in the early to mid-2000s. This interface currently supports devices with a maximum throughput of 800MBps and is capable of speeds up to 3.2Gbps, so more and more devices that need to send a lot of data in a short period of time will use this interface. Printers used for tasks such as graphics and typesetting that need to receive hundreds of megabytes of camera-ready art and graphics have IEEE 1394b ports. Not many home printers use IEEE 1394b, however, because it is an extra feature most people wouldn't use and thus don't want to pay for.

INFRARED

With the explosion of personal digital assistants (PDAs), the need grew for printing under the constraints they provide. The biggest hurdle faced by PDA owners who need to print is the lack of any kind of universal interface. Most interfaces are too big and bulky to be used on handheld computers such as PDAs. The solution was to incorporate the standardized technology used on some remote controls: infrared transmissions. *Infrared transmissions* are simply wireless transmissions that use radiation in the infrared range of the electromagnetic spectrum. Many laser printers (and some computers) come with infrared transmitter/receivers (transceivers) so that they can communicate with the infrared ports on many handhelds. This allows the user of a PDA, handheld, or laptop to print to that printer by pointing the device at the printer and initiating the print process.

As far as configuring the interface is concerned, very little needs to be done. The infrared interfaces are enabled by default on most computers, handhelds, and printers equipped with them. The only additional item that must be configured is the print driver on the PDA, handheld, or computer. The driver must be the correct one for the printer to which you are printing.

WIRELESS

The latest boom in printer interface technology is wireless (of many different kinds). With the advent of IEEE 802.11 wireless networking, it is possible for people to roam around an office and still remain connected to one another and to their corporate network. So someone had the idea that it would be nice if printers could be that mobile as well (after all, many are on carts with wheels). Some printers either have built-in 802.11 interfaces or are hooked to 802.11 bridges with their built-in network cards.

Another wireless technology that has wide acceptance, especially among peripheral manufacturers, is *Bluetooth*. Bluetooth is a wireless technology that is used to replace the myriad of interface cables that run between your computer and all its peripherals. It's not meant to work over long distances; its absolute maximum range is 100 meters (330 feet), and most devices are specified to work within 10 meters (33 feet). Printers such as the HP DeskJet 450wbt mobile printer have Bluetooth capability.

When printing with a Bluetooth-enabled device (like a PDA or cell phone) and a Bluetooth-enabled printer, all you need to do is get within range of the device (that is, move closer), select the print driver from the device, and choose Print. The information is transmitted wirelessly through the air using radio waves and is received by the device.

 For more information about the Bluetooth specification and its details, visit www.bluetooth.org. We also cover Bluetooth more extensively in Chapter 10, "Networking."

Interface Software

Computers and printers can't talk to each other by themselves. They need interface software to translate software commands into commands the printer can understand.

There are two factors to consider with interface software: the page-description language and the driver software. The page-description language determines how efficient the printer is at converting the information to be printed into signals the printer can understand. The driver software understands and controls the printer. It is very important that you use the correct interface software for your printer. If you use either the wrong page-description language or the wrong driver software, the printer will print garbage—or possibly nothing at all.

PAGE-DESCRIPTION LANGUAGES

A *page-description language* works just as its name says it does: it describes the whole page being printed by sending commands that describe the text as well as the margins and other settings. The controller in the printer interprets these commands and turns them into laser pulses (or pin strikes).

The first page-description language was PostScript. Developed by Adobe, it was first used in the Apple LaserWriter printer. It made printing graphics fast and simple. Here's how PostScript works: The PostScript printer driver describes the page in terms of "draw" and "position" commands. The page is divided into a very fine grid (as fine as the resolution of the printer). When you want to print a square, a communication like the following takes place:

```
POSITION 1,42%DRAW 10%POSITION 1,64%DRAW10D% . . .
```

Real World Scenario

Life without a Page-Description Language

The most basic page-description language is no page-description language. The computer sends all the instructions the printer needs in a serial stream, like so: Position 1, print nothing; Position 2, strike pins 1 and 3; Position 3, print nothing. This type of description language works great for dot-matrix printers, but it can be inefficient for laser printers. For example, if you wanted to print a page using a standard page-description language and there was only one character on the page, there would be a lot of wasted signal for the "print nothing" commands.

With graphics, the commands to draw a shape on the page are relatively complex. For example, to draw a square, the computer (or printer) has to calculate the size of the square and convert that into lots of "strike pin x" (or "turn on laser") and "print nothing" commands. This is where the other types of page-description languages come into the picture.

These commands tell the printer to draw a line on the page from line 42 to line 64 (vertically). In other words, a page-description language tells the printer to draw a line on the page, gives it the starting and ending points, and that's that. Rather than send the printer the location of each and every dot in the line and an instruction at each and every location to print that location's individual dot, PostScript can get the line drawn with fewer than five instructions. As you can see, PostScript uses commands that are more or less in English. The commands are interpreted by the processor on the printer's controller and converted into the print-control signals.

Another page-description language is the Printer Control Language (PCL). Currently in revision 6 (PCL 6), it was developed by Hewlett-Packard for its LaserJet series of printers as a competitor to PostScript. PCL works in much the same manner as PostScript, but it's found mainly in HP printers (including the DeskJet bubble-jet printers). Other manufacturers use PCL, however. In fact, some printers support both page-description languages and will automatically switch between them.

The main advantage of page-description languages is that they move some of the processing from the computer to the printer. With text-only documents, they offer little benefit. However, with documents that have large amounts of graphics or that use numerous fonts, page-description languages make the processing of those print jobs happen much faster. This makes them an ideal choice for laser printers. However, other printers can use them as well (the aforementioned DeskJets, as well as some dot-matrix printers).

DRIVER SOFTWARE

The *driver* software controls how the printer processes the print job. When you install a printer driver for the printer you are using, it allows the computer to print to that printer correctly (assuming you have the correct interface configured between the computer and printer).

Installation and configuration of printer drivers will be covered in the "Installing and Configuring Printers" section later in this chapter.

When you need to print, you select the printer driver for your printer from a preconfigured list. The driver you select has been configured for the type, brand, and model of printer as well as the computer port to which it is connected. You can also select which paper tray the printer should use, as well as any other features the printer has (if applicable). Also, each printer driver is configured to use a particular page-description language.

If the wrong printer driver is selected, the computer will send commands in the wrong language. If that occurs, the printer will print several pages full of garbage (even if only one page of information was sent). This "garbage" isn't garbage at all but the printer page-description language commands printed literally as text instead of being interpreted as control commands.

Printer Supplies

Just as it is important to use the correct printer interface and printer software, you must use the correct printer supplies. These supplies include the print media (what you print on) and the consumables (what you print with). The quality of the final print job has a great deal to do with the print supplies.

Print Media

The *print media* is what you put through the printer to print on. There are two major types of print media: paper and transparencies. Of the two types, paper is by far the most commonly used.

PAPER

Most people don't give much thought to the kind of paper they use in their printers. It's a factor that can have tremendous effect on the quality of the hard-copy printout, however, and the topic is more complex than people think. For example, if the wrong paper is used, it can cause the paper to jam frequently and possibly even damage components.

Several aspects of paper can be measured; each gives an indication as to the paper's quality. The first factor is *composition*. Paper is made from a variety of substances. Paper used to be made from cotton and was called rag stock. It can also be made from wood pulp, which is cheaper. Most paper today is made from the latter or a combination of the two.

Another aspect of paper is the property known as *basis weight* (or simply *weight* for short). The weight of a particular type of paper is the actual weight, in pounds (lb.), of 500 sheets of the standard (basic) size of that paper made of that material. For regular bond paper, that size is 17×22. The most common paper used in printers is 20 lb. bond paper. Manufacturers divide the standard size into four sheets, resulting in the 8.5×11 size we are all familiar with. So a ream of 500 sheets of 20 lb. bond paper weighs 5 pounds.

The final paper property we'll discuss is the *caliper* (or thickness) of an individual sheet of paper. If the paper is too thick, it may jam in feed mechanisms that have several curves in the paper path. (On the other hand, a paper that's too thin may not feed at all.)

These are just three of the categories we use to judge the quality of paper. Because there are so many different types and brands of printers as well as paper, it would be impossible to give the specifications for the "perfect" paper. However, the documentation for any printer will give specifications for the paper that should be used in that printer.

> For best results, store paper in an area where it will not get wet or be exposed to excessive humidity.

> For best results with any printer, buy the paper that has been designated specifically for that printer by the manufacturer. It will be more expensive, but you'll have fewer problems related to having the wrong type of paper for the printer. The print quality will also be the best it can possibly be.

LABELS

From the printer's perspective, labels are just another type of paper. But because of their thickness and occasional tendency to peel off before you want them to, they can cause problems.

Always make sure that the labels you are using are meant to be put into the type of printer you are using. In addition, if you notice any peeling labels, discard the sheet to avoid a likely jam in your printer.

> Manufacturers that specialize in making labels, such as Avery, have templates you can download from their website (www.avery.com). These templates are used in word processing programs such as Microsoft Word and correspond to the different styles of labels they produce. Using these templates makes it easy to set up and print labels of any size.

TRANSPARENCIES

Transparencies are still used for presentations made with overhead projectors, even with the explosion of programs like Microsoft's PowerPoint and peripherals like LCD computer displays, both of which let you show a whole roomful of people exactly what's on your computer screen. PowerPoint has an option to print slides, and you can also use any program to print to a transparent sheet of plastic or vinyl for use with an overhead projector. The problem is these "papers" are *exceedingly* difficult for printers to work with. That's why special transparencies were developed for use with laser and bubble-jet printers.

Each type of transparency was designed for a particular brand and model of printer. Again, check the printer's documentation to find out which type of transparency works in that printer. Don't use any other type of transparency!

Never run transparencies through a laser printer without first checking to see if it's the type recommended by the printer manufacturer. The heat from the fuser will melt most other transparencies, and they will wrap themselves around it. It is impossible to clean a fuser after this has happened. The fuser will have to be replaced. *Use only the transparencies that are recommended by the printer manufacturer.*

Print Consumables

Besides print media, other things in the printer run out and need to be replenished. These items are the *print consumables*. Most consumables are used to form the images on the print media. There are two main types of consumables in printers today: ink and toner. Toner is used primarily in laser printers; most other printers use ink.

INK

Ink is a liquid that is used to stain the paper. Printers use several different colors of ink, but the majority use some shade of black or blue. Both dot-matrix printers and bubble-jet printers use ink, but with different methods.

Dot-matrix printers use a cloth or polyester ribbon soaked in ink and coiled up inside a plastic case. This assembly is called a *printer ribbon* (or *ribbon cartridge*). It's very similar to a typewriter ribbon, but instead of being coiled into the two rolls you'd see on a typewriter, the ribbon is continuously coiled inside the plastic case. Once the ribbon has run out of ink, it must be discarded and replaced. Ribbon cartridges are developed closely with their respective printers. For this reason, ribbons should be purchased from the same manufacturer as the printer. The wrong ribbon could jam in the printer as well as cause quality problems.

It is possible to re-ink a ribbon. Some vendors sell a bottle of ink solution that can be poured into the plastic casing, where the cloth ribbon will soak up the solution.

Bubble-jet cartridges have a liquid ink reservoir. The ink in these cartridges is sealed inside. Once the ink runs out, the cartridge must be removed and discarded. A new, full one is installed in its place. Because the ink cartridge contains the printing mechanism as well as ink, it's like getting a new printer every time you replace the ink cartridge.

In some bubble-jet printers, the ink cartridge and the printhead are in separate assemblies. This way, the ink can be replaced when it runs out, and the printhead can be used several times. This works fine if the printer is designed to work this way. However, some people think they can do this on their integrated cartridge/printhead system, using special ink cartridge refill kits. These kits consist of a syringe filled with ink and a long needle. The needle is used to puncture the top of an empty ink cartridge, and the syringe is then used to refill the reservoir. Don't use these kits! See the warning about using them for more information.

Do not use ink cartridge refill kits! These kits (the ones you see advertised with a syringe and a needle) have several problems. First, the kits don't use the same kind of ink that was originally in the ink cartridges. The new ink may be thinner, causing the ink to run out or not print properly. Also, the printhead is supposed to be replaced around this same time. Refilling the cartridge doesn't replace the printhead, so you'll have print-quality problems. Finally, the hole the syringe leaves cannot be plugged and may allow ink to leak out. These problems can happen with do-it-yourself kits, as well as from cartridges refilled by office supply stores or private printer supply sellers. Here's the bottom line: *buy new ink cartridges from the printer manufacturer.* Yes, they are a bit more expensive, but in the long run you will save money because you won't have any of the problems described here.

TONER

The final type of consumable is toner. Each model of laser printer uses a specific toner cartridge. We covered the types of toner cartridges when we talked about the different types of printers. You should check the printer's manual to see which toner cartridge it needs.

 Real World Scenario

Think Before You Refill

Just as with ink cartridges, you should always buy the exact model recommended by the manufacturer. The toner cartridges have been designed specifically for a particular model. Additionally, *never* refill toner cartridges, for most of the same reasons we don't recommend refilling ink cartridges. The printout quality will be poor, and the fact that you're just refilling the toner means you're *not* replacing the photosensitive drum (which is usually inside the cartridge), and the drum might *need* to be replaced. Simply replacing refilled toner cartridges with proper, name-brand toner cartridges has solved most laser printer quality problems we have run across. We keep recommending the right ones, but clients keep coming back with the refilled ones. The result is that we take our clients' money to solve their print-quality problems when all it involves is a toner cartridge, our (usually repeat) advice to buy the proper cartridge next time, and the obligatory minimum charge for a half hour of labor (even though the job of replacing the cartridge takes all of five minutes!).

Always recycle your used ink and toner cartridges! Just don't buy recycled cartridges.

Options/Upgrades

Most printers (especially laser printers) can be upgraded with different capabilities. This is done to add functions or to increase the printing capacity of a printer. As the complexity of laser printers increases, they are often becoming what are known as *mopiers* (short for multiple original copiers). Rather than your having to print one copy of a document and then copy it with double-sided and stapling or hole-punch options, the laser printer manufacturer has included those functions in the printer, so each printed "copy" is essentially an original.

Each manufacturer, with the documentation for each printer, includes a list of all the accessories, options, and upgrades available for that printer. These options include the following:

- Memory
- Hard drives
- Print server with a network card interface
- Trays and feeders
- Finishers
- Scanners, fax modems, and copiers

MEMORY

One of the most common options for a printer is to add memory to it to increase its buffer size. The larger the buffer, the larger a print job it can handle. So, by adding memory, you can increase the performance of a printer.

For the most part, printer memory is specific to the make and model of printer being upgraded. You can check with the manufacturer of your printer to see what kind of memory it takes and how best to upgrade it. The procedures are slightly different for each make and model of printer.

HARD DRIVES

In order to print properly, the type style or *font* being printed must be downloaded to the printer along with the job being printed. Desktop-publishing and graphic-design businesses that print color pages on slower color printers are always looking for ways to speed up their print jobs. So they install multiple fonts into the onboard memory of the printer to make them *printer-resident fonts*.

But there's a problem: most printers have a limited amount of storage space for these fonts. To solve this problem, printer manufacturers made it possible for hard drives to be added to many printers. These hard drives can be used to store many fonts used during the print process and are also used to store the large document file while it is being processed for printing.

PRINT SERVER WITH A NETWORK INTERFACE CARD

Networks are everywhere. Almost every business has one, as do many homes. They are used to share information and resources between computers. In the past, you could share your printer with your neighbor over the network through software installed on your computer. But doing so had two drawbacks: it was slow, because your computer does other things in addition to sharing the printer, and it was cumbersome, because your computer had to be on in order for someone to print to your printer. Thus, the network print server (with a network interface card [NIC]) option for a printer became popular as more and more people needed their printers to be on the network without the need for a host computer.

The NIC in a printer is similar to the NIC in a computer, with a couple of important differences. First, the NIC in a printer has a small processor on it to perform the management of the NIC interface (functions that the software on a host computer would do). Second, the NIC in a printer is proprietary, for the most part. It is made by the same manufacturer as the printer.

When a person on the network prints to a printer with a NIC, they are printing right to the printer and not going through any third-party device (although in some situations, that is desirable and possible with NICs). Because of its dedicated nature, the NIC option installed in a printer makes printing to that printer faster and more efficient—that NIC is dedicated to receiving print jobs and sending printer status to clients.

 Most printer NICs come with management software installed that allows clients to check their print jobs' status as well as toner levels from any computer on the network.

TRAYS AND FEEDERS

One option that is popular in office environments is the addition of paper trays. Most laser and bubble-jet printers come with at least one paper tray (usually 500 sheets or less). The addition of a paper tray allows a printer to print more sheets between paper refills, thus reducing its operating cost. In addition, some printers can accommodate multiple paper trays, which can be loaded with different types of paper, stationery, and envelopes. The benefit is that you can print a letter and an envelope from the same printer without having to leave your desk or change the paper in the printer.

Related to trays is the option of *feeders*. Some types of paper products need to be watched as they are printed, to make sure the printing happens properly. One example is envelopes: you usually can't put a stack of envelopes in a printer, because they won't line up straight or may get jammed. An accessory that you might add for this purpose is the *envelope feeder*. An envelope feeder typically attaches to the front of a laser printer and feeds in envelopes, one at a time. It can hold usually between 100 and 200 envelopes.

 If you're curious about the procedure for installing an envelope feeder, go to www.hp.com and search for "Envelope Feeder Install."

FINISHERS

A printer's *finisher* does just what it says: it finishes the document being printed. It does this by folding, stapling, hole punching, sorting, or collating the sets of documents being printed into their final form. So rather than your printing out a bunch of paper sheets and then having to collate and staple them, the finisher can do the same thing for you.

This particular option, while not cheap, is becoming more popular on laser printers in order to turn them into the aforementioned mopiers. As a matter of fact, many copiers are now digital and can do all the same things a laser printer can, but much faster and for a much cheaper cost per page.

SCANNERS, FAX MODEMS, AND COPIERS

The last few options are a bit of a stretch for laser printers, but they do somewhat fit. First, it is possible to add a scanner to a laser printer. A *scanner* is an accessory that takes a document and puts it into digital form. From there it can be edited or printed. If you use the scanner and print directly from the scanned-in image, you have just made a copy and turned the laser printer into a digital version of a copier. You can also add a device known as a fax modem to a printer configured with a scanner to turn the printer into a fax machine. A *fax modem* is a device you install into a computer or other device that takes the signals from that device and turns them into signals a fax machine can understand over a phone line.

By adding these two accessories, you can turn your simple printer into a home office copier capable of sending faxes as well. In this age of home offices, such devices are becoming commonplace. Several printer companies manufacture *multifunction printers*. These peripherals are essentially a printer, copier, scanner, and fax machine all in one. They're perfect for the home office without a lot of desk space.

Installing and Configuring Printers

Odds are that if someone owns a computer they own a printer as well. If they don't, they have easy access to a printer at a library, work, or some other place. Many retailers and computer manufacturers make it incredibly easy to buy a printer, since they often bundle a printer with a computer system as an incentive to get you to buy.

The A+ Essentials exam will test your knowledge of the procedures to install printers. In this section, you will learn the proper procedures for installing and initially configuring printers.

Printer Installation Procedures

Although every device is different, there are certain accepted methods used for installing any device. The following procedure works for installing many kinds of devices:

1. Attach the device using a local or network port and connect the power.

2. Install and update the device driver and calibrate the device.

3. Configure options and default settings.

4. Print a test page.

5. Verify compatibility with the operating system and applications.

6. Educate users about basic functionality.

Before installing any device, read your device's installation instructions. There are exceptions to every rule.

Step 1: Attach the Device Using a Local or Network Port and Connect Power

When installing a printer, you must first take the device out of its packaging and set it up on a flat, stable surface. Then connect the device to either the host computer with its power off (if it is a stand-alone device) or to the network (if it is a network device).

Once you have connected the device, connect power to it using whatever supplied power adapter comes with it. Some devices have their own built-in power supply and just need an AC power cord connecting the device to the wall outlet, while others rely on an external transformer and power supply. Finally, turn on the device.

Step 2: Install and Update the Device Driver and Calibrate the Device

Once you have connected and powered up the device, boot up the computer and wait for Windows to recognize the device. It will pop up a screen similar to the one shown in Figure 5.22. This wizard will allow you to configure the driver for the printer (depending on the device). You can insert the driver CD or DVD that comes with the device, and the wizard will guide you through the device driver installation. If Windows fails to recognize the device, you can use the Add Hardware Wizard to troubleshoot the installation and to install the device drivers.

FIGURE 5.22   The Windows Add Hardware Wizard

Once the driver is installed, the device will function. But some devices, such as ink-jet printers, require that you calibrate the device. *Calibration* is the process by which a device is brought within functional specifications. For example, inkjet printers need their printheads aligned so they print evenly and don't print funny-looking letters and unevenly spaced lines. The process is part of the installation of all inkjet printers.

When working with print media, it is especially important to calibrate all your hardware, including your monitor, scanner, printer, and digital camera, to ensure color matching.

Each manufacturer's process is different, but a typical alignment/calibration works like this:

1. During software installation, the installation wizard asks you if you would like to calibrate now, to which you respond Yes or OK.

2. The printer prints out a sheet with multiple sets of numbered lines. Each set of lines represents an alignment instance.

3. The software will ask you which set(s) looks the best. Enter the number and click OK or Continue.

4. Some alignment routines end at this point. Others will reprint the alignment page and see if the alignment "took." If not, you can reenter the number of which one looks the best.

5. Click Finish to end the alignment routine.

Understanding and Installing PCL, PostScript, and GDI Drivers

For your printer to work properly, you need to install the right driver for the device. In addition, you need to make sure you're talking to the device in the language that it speaks.

There are several printer communication languages in existence, but the three most common ones are Printer Command Language (PCL), PostScript, and Graphics Device Interface (GDI).

PCL was developed by Hewlett-Packard in 1984 and originally intended for use with inkjet printers. Since then, its role has been expanded to virtually every printer type, and it's a de facto industry standard.

PostScript (PS) is a page description language that allows computers to communicate with printers. One of the early advantages of PS was that it allowed any font to be scaled to any size and printed properly. This might not sound like an earth-shattering feature, but at the time it was revolutionary for home and business printers. (Previously, these types of features were only found on high-end image plotters.)

GDI is actually a Windows component and is not specific to printers. Instead, it's a series of components that govern how graphics images are presented to both monitors and printers. GDI printers work by using computer processing power instead of their own. The printed image is rendered to a bitmap on the computer, and then sent to the printer. This means that the printer hardware doesn't need to be as powerful, which results in a less expensive printer. Generally speaking, the least expensive laser printers on the market are GDI printers.

When you install your printer driver, you will often have to make the choice between PCL and PS or PCL, PS, and GDI drivers. Figure 5.23 shows the Add Printer Wizard to illustrate an example of this.

You're installing a LaserJet 8150. Do you select PS or PCL? It depends on if your printer is set for PS or PCL mode. This can be configured through your printer's menu system. If you're not sure how to do this, check your printer's manual. If the driver and printer setting do not match, the printer will only print garbage.

Many newer printers can handle both PS and PCL (and GDI), and will automatically translate for you. Therefore, it's less likely that you'll install the "wrong" print driver than it was several years ago.

Step 3: Configure Options and Default Settings

Once you have installed the software and calibrated the device, you can configure any options you would like for the printer. All of the settings and how to change them can be found online or in your user manual.

FIGURE 5.23   PS and PCL print drivers

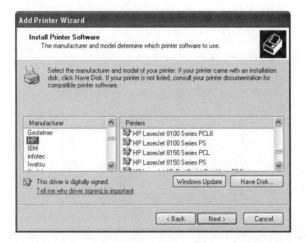

Where you configure specific printer properties depends a lot on the printer itself. Figure 5.24 shows the Printers and Faxes window in Windows XP. On the left-hand side under Printer Tasks, you can see that there's an option to select printing preferences and another option to set printer properties (in addition, both options can be executed by right-clicking on the printer and choosing Printing Preferences or Properties, respectively).

If you don't see these options under Printer Tasks, highlight the printer first.

FIGURE 5.24   Printers and Faxes

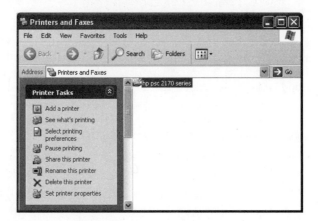

Various configuration features can be set from each menu option. The Printing Preferences window of this printer is shown in Figure 5.25.

FIGURE 5.25   Printing Preferences

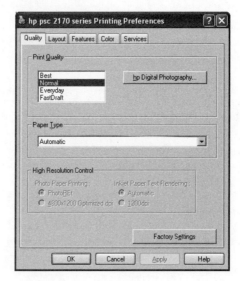

Under Printing Preferences (for this printer) you can select the quality of the print job, layout (portrait vs. landscape), paper size, two-sided printing, and use of color. By contrast, Figure 5.26 shows the printer Properties screen.

FIGURE 5.26   Printer Properties

Here the options are different. The printer Properties is less about how the printer does its job and more about how people can access the printer. From the printer Properties, you can share the printer, set up the port that it's on, and configure when the printer will be available throughout the day (and to which specific users). Figure 5.27 shows the important Advanced tab of the printer Properties.

FIGURE 5.27   Printer Properties Advanced tab

On this tab, you can configure the printer to be available only during certain hours of the day. This might be useful if you're trying to curtail after-hours printing of non-work-related documents, for example. You can also configure the spool settings. For faster printing, you should always spool the jobs instead of printing directly to the printer. However, if the printer is printing garbage, you can try printing directly to it to see if the spooler is causing the problem.

Regarding the check boxes at the bottom, you will want to always print spooled documents first, as it speeds up the printing process. If you need to maintain an electronic copy of all printed files, check the Keep Printed Documents check box. Keep in mind that this will eat up a lot of hard disk space.

Finally, the Printing Defaults button takes you to the Printing Preferences (see Figure 5.25), Print Processor lets you select alternate methods of processing print jobs (not usually needed), and Separator Page lets you specify a file to use as a separator page (a document that prints out at the beginning of each separate print job, usually with the user's name on it), which can be useful if you have several (or several dozen) users sharing one printer.

Step 4: Print a Test Page

Once you have done all of these steps, you are finished and can print a test page to test the output of the printer. Windows has a built-in function for doing just that. To print a test page, right-click on the printer you installed from within the Printer control panel and click Properties. On the General tab of the printer Properties (as shown in Figure 5.26), there will be a Print Test Page button. Click that button, and Windows will send a test page to the printer. If the page prints, your printer is working. If not, double-check all of your connections. If they appear to be in order, then read ahead to Chapter 15 for troubleshooting tips.

Step 5: Validate Compatibility with Operating System and Applications

Once your printer is installed and you have tried out a test page, everything else should work well, right? That's usually true, but it's good practice to verify compatibility with applications before you consider the device fully installed.

With printers, this process is rather straightforward. Open the application you wonder about and print something. For example, open up Microsoft Word, type in some gibberish (or open a real document if you want), and print it out. If you are running non-Microsoft applications (such as a computer-aided drafting program or accounting software) and have questions about their compatibility with the printer, try printing from those programs as well.

Step 6: Educate Users about Basic Functionality

Most users today know how to print, but not everyone knows how to install the right printer or print efficiently. This can be a significant issue in work environments.

Say that your workplace has 10 different printers, and you just installed number 11. First, your company should use a naming process to identify the printers in a way that makes sense. Calling a printer HPLJ4 on a network does little to help users understand where that printer is in the building. After installing the printer, offer installation assistance to those who might want to use the device. Show users how to install the printer in Windows (or if printer installation is automated, let them know they have a new printer and where it is). Also let the users know the various options available on that printer. Can it print double-sided? If so, you can save a lot of paper. Show users how to configure that. Is it a color printer? Do users really need color for rough drafts of documents or presentations? Show users how to print in black-and-white on a color printer to save the expensive color ink or toner cartridges.

In Exercise 5.2 we'll step through the process of installing a USB printer in Windows XP or Vista.

EXERCISE 5.2

Installing a USB printer in Windows XP or Vista

In this exercise, you will install a printer. You will need the following:

- A USB printer

- A USB printer cable

- The software driver CD or DVD that came with the printer

- A computer with a free USB port and a CD-ROM drive

1. Turn on the computer.

2. Plug in the printer and turn it on.

3. Insert the CD into the computer's CD-ROM drive. The driver CD's auto-run should automatically start the installation program. If not, click Start ➤ Run and type in **D:\setup** or **D:\install** (if your CD-ROM drive letter is different, substitute that letter for *D*).

4. Follow the prompts in the installation program to install the driver.

5. Once the software has been installed, plug one end of the USB cable into the printer and the other end into the free USB port. Some installation programs will prompt you for this step.

6. Windows will automatically detect the new printer, install the driver, and configure it automatically. Windows will display a balloon in the lower-right corner of the screen saying "Your hardware is now installed and is ready to use."

7. Print a test page to see if the printer can communicate and print properly.

Real World Scenario

Which Printer Did That Go To?

I used to work at a satellite office for a company whose headquarters were in Houston. Because of recent printer problems, we just had a new network printer installed, and it had a different network name from the previous printer.

At the end of the month, one of our accountants printed off her monthly reconciliation report, which typically ran about 400 pages. Puzzled when it didn't come out on the printer, she printed it again. And again. And again. After the fourth time (and a few hours later), she decided to ask someone in IT what the problem was.

It turns out that she had mapped (installed) the new network printer but had gotten a few letters wrong in the printer name. Instead of being at our office, all of her print jobs were sent to a printer in the Houston office. And of course, there were people in Houston trying to print similar reports and who just kept refilling the printer with paper because they didn't want to cut someone else's report off in the middle.

While this wasn't a catastrophic failure, it was annoying. She had unintentionally wasted three reams of paper, the associated toner, and hours of printer life. It wasn't a malicious act and she was a literate computer user, but it's illustrative of the need to educate and help users with installing and configuring devices. Had the printer been mapped correctly the first time, the waste could have been avoided.

Summary

In this chapter, we discussed how different types of printers work, as well as the most common methods of connecting them to computers. You learned how computers use page-description languages to format data before they send it to printers. You also learned about the various types of consumable supplies and how they relate to each type of printer.

The most basic category of printer currently in use is the impact printer. Impact printers form images by striking something against a ribbon, which in turn makes a mark on the paper. You learned how these printers work and the service concepts associated with them.

One of the most popular types of printer today is the bubble-jet printer, so named because of the mechanism used to put ink on the paper.

The most complex type of printer is the laser printer. The A+ Essentials exam covers this type of printer more than any other. You learned about the steps in the electrophotographic (EP) process, the process that explains how laser printers print. We also explained the various components that make up this printer and how they work together.

You then learned about the interfaces used to connect printers to PCs and the consumable supplies printers use. We discussed various interfaces and how they are used and how printer supplies can affect print output quality.

Finally, you learned about installing a printer. Proper steps include connecting the device, installing the driver, configuring options, validating application and operating system compatibility, and educating users on how to use the device. Installing the device is the first step, but you're not done until you ensure that it works properly and that users know how to access it.

Exam Essentials

Know the differences between types of printer technologies (e.g., laser, inkjet, thermal, impact).   Laser printers use a laser and toner to create the page. Inkjet printers spray ink onto the page. Thermal printers use heat to form the characters on the page. Impact printers use a mechanical device to strike a ribbon, thus forming an image on the page.

Know the names, purposes, and characteristics of printer components (e.g., memory, driver, firmware) and consumables (e.g., toner, ink cartridge, paper).   Each printer contains different components that allow the printer to do its job. The components work together to form the image on the page. Each printer has a print mechanism, power supply, and interface. But each printer differs in how those components work.

Know the names, purposes, and characteristics of interfaces used by printers, including port and cable types.   Most printers today use the same interfaces, no matter what their type. Printers use parallel, USB, serial, IEEE 1394b (FireWire), wireless, Bluetooth, or network interfaces to connect to their host computers. By far the most common is USB.

Know how to install and configure printers.   The basic procedure is as follows:

1. Attach the device using a local or network port and connect the power.
2. Install and update the device driver and calibrate the device.
3. Configure options and default settings.
4. Print a test page.
5. Verify compatibility with the operating system and applications.
6. Educate users about basic functionality.

Know the six steps in the laser printing print sequence.   The six steps are cleaning, conditioning, writing, developing, transferring, and fusing.

Review Questions

1. Which voltage is applied to the paper to transfer the toner to the paper in an EP process laser printer?

    A. +600VDC

    B. –600VDC

    C. +6000VDC

    D. –6000VDC

2. Which types of printers are referred to as page printers, because they receive their print job instructions one page at a time? (Select all that apply.)

    A. Daisy wheel

    B. Dot matrix

    C. Bubble-jet

    D. Laser

3. Which of the following is *not* an advantage of a Universal Serial Bus (USB) printer interface?

    A. It has a higher transfer rate than a serial connection.

    B. It has a higher transfer rate than a parallel connection.

    C. It automatically recognizes new devices.

    D. It allows the printer to communicate with networks, servers, and workstations.

4. Which type of printers can be used with multipart forms?

    A. Bubble-jet printers

    B. Laser printers

    C. Thermal printers

    D. Dot-matrix printers

5. Which step in the EP print process uses a laser to discharge selected areas of the photosensitive drum, thus forming an image on the drum?

    A. Writing

    B. Transferring

    C. Developing

    D. Cleaning

6. Which of the following are page-description languages? (Select all that apply.)

   A. Page Description Language (PDL)

   B. PostScript

   C. PageScript

   D. Printer Control Language (PCL)

7. What voltage does the corona wire or corona roller hold?

   A. +600VDC

   B. −600VDC

   C. 0VDC

   D. −100VDC

8. Which device in a bubble-jet printer contains the printhead?

   A. Ink cartridge

   B. Toner cartridge

   C. Daisy wheel

   D. Paper tray

9. What is the correct order of the steps in the EP print process?

   A. Developing, writing, transferring, fusing, charging, cleaning

   B. Charging, writing, developing, transferring, fusing, cleaning

   C. Transferring, writing, developing, charging, cleaning, fusing

   D. Cleaning, charging, writing, developing, transferring, fusing

10. Any printer that uses the electrophotographic process contains how many standard assemblies?

    A. Five

    B. Six

    C. Four

    D. Nine

11. What is included in the EP laser printer toner cartridge? (Choose all that apply.)

    A. Toner

    B. Print drum

    C. Laser

    D. Cleaning blade

12. What happens during the developing stage of laser printing?

   A. An electrostatic charge is applied to the drum to attract toner particles.

   B. Heat is applied to the paper to melt the toner.

   C. The laser creates an image of the page on the drum.

   D. An electrostatic charge is applied to the paper to attract toner particles.

13. Which of the following are possible interfaces for printers? (Select all that apply.)

   A. Parallel

   B. Mouse port

   C. Serial

   D. Network

14. The basis weight is the weight in pounds of 500 sheets of bond paper for what size of paper?

   A. 8½×11 inch

   B. 11×17 inch

   C. 17×22 inch

   D. 8½×17 inch

15. Which printer contains a wheel that looks like a flower with raised letters and symbols on each petal?

   A. Bubble-jet printers

   B. Daisy-wheel printer

   C. Dot-matrix printer

   D. Laser printer

16. What part of a laser printer supplies the voltages for the charging and transfer corona assemblies?

   A. High-voltage power supply (HVPS)

   B. DC power supply (DCPS)

   C. Controller circuitry

   D. Transfer corona

17. Which printer part gets the toner from the photosensitive drum onto the paper?

   A. Laser-scanning assembly

   B. Fusing assembly

   C. Corona assembly

   D. Drum

18. LED page printers differ from EP process laser printers in which step?

    A. Writing

    B. Charging

    C. Fusing

    D. Cleaning

    E. Developing

    F. Transferring

19. Which step in the laser printer printing process occurs immediately after the writing phase?

    A. Charging

    B. Fusing

    C. Transferring

    D. Developing

20. Which assembly permanently presses the toner into the paper?

    A. Transfer corona

    B. Fuser

    C. Printer controller circuitry

    D. Paper transport assembly

Answers to Review Questions

1. A. Because the toner on the drum has a slight negative charge (–100VDC), it requires a positive charge to transfer it to the paper; +600VDC is the voltage used in an EP process laser printer.

2. C, D. A page printer is a type of computer printer that prints a page at a time. Common types of page printers are the laser printer and the inkjet (or bubble-jet) printer.

3. D. The rate of transfer and the ability to automatically recognize new devices are two of the major advantages that make USB the current most popular type of printer interface. However, it is the network printer interface that allows the printer to communicate with networks, servers, and workstations.

4. D. Of the choices listed, only dot-matrix printers are impact printers and therefore can be used with multipart forms.

5. A. The writing step uses a laser to discharge selected areas of the photosensitive drum, thus forming an image on the drum.

6. B, D. Of those listed, only PostScript and PCL are page-description languages. There is no PDL or PageScript.

7. A. For the toner (which has a charge of –100VDC) to be transferred from the print drum (which has a charge of –600VDC) to the paper, there must be a positive, or opposite, charge of greater difference to break the –100VDC charge from the drum.

8. A. In a bubble-jet printer, the ink cartridge is the actual printhead. This is where the ink is expelled to form letters or graphics. Toner cartridges are used by laser printers to store toner. A daisy wheel is the device that impacts the letters on the paper in a daisy-wheel printer. Paper trays are the storage bins in laser printers and bubble-jet printers that allow the pickup rollers to feed the paper into the printer.

9. D. The correct sequence in the EP print process is cleaning, charging, writing, developing, transferring, and fusing.

10. D. There are nine standard assemblies in an electrophotographic process printer. Early laser printers using the electrographic process contained nine standard assemblies. Newer laser printers do not require an ozone filter and contain only eight standard assemblies.

11. A, B, D. In an electrophotographic (EP) laser printer toner cartridge, the toner, print drum, and cleaning blade are all contained in the toner cartridge. The laser is contained within the printer, not within the toner cartridge.

12. A. After a laser has created an image of the page, the developing roller uses a magnet and electrostatic charges to attract toner to itself and then transfers the toner to the areas on the drum that have been exposed to the laser. The toner is melted during the fusing stage. The laser creates an image of the page on the drum in the writing stage. An electrostatic charge is applied to the paper to attract toner in the transferring stage, which happens immediately after the developing stage.

13. A, C, D. Printers can communicate via parallel, serial, USB, infrared, SCSI, 1394b, wireless, and network connections.

14. C. The basis weight is the weight in pounds of 500 sheets of bond 17×22 inch paper.

15. B. The daisy-wheel printer gets its name because it contains a wheel with raised letters and symbols on each "petal."

16. A. The high-voltage power supply is the part of the laser printer that supplies the voltages for the charging and transfer corona assemblies.

17. C. The transfer corona assembly gets the toner from the photosensitive drum onto the paper. For some printers, this is a transfer corona wire, and for others, it is a transfer corona roller.

18. A. LED page printers differ from EP process laser printers in the writing step. They use a different process to write the image on the EP drum.

19. D. Developing happens after writing. The correct order is cleaning, charging, writing, developing, transferring, and fusing.

20. B. The fuser assembly presses and melts the toner into the paper. The transfer corona transfers the toner from the drum to the paper. The printer controller circuitry converts signals from the PC into signals for the various printer assemblies. The paper transport assembly controls the movement of the paper through the printer.

Chapter 6

Operating System Features and Interfaces

THE FOLLOWING COMPTIA A+ ESSENTIALS EXAM OBJECTIVES ARE COVERED IN THIS CHAPTER:

✓ **3.1 Compare and contrast the different Windows Operating Systems and their features**

- Windows 2000, Windows XP 32bit vs. 64bit, Windows Vista 32bit vs. 64bit

    - Side bar, Aero, UAC, minimum system requirements, system limits

    - Windows 2000 and newer – upgrade paths and requirements

    - Terminology (32bit vs. 64bit – x86 vs. x64)

    - Application compatibility, installed program locations (32bit vs. 64bit), Windows compatibility mode

    - User interface, start bar layout

✓ **3.2 Given a scenario, demonstrate proper use of user interfaces**

- Windows Explorer

- My Computer

- Control Panel

- Command prompt utilities

    - telnet

    - ping

    - ipconfig

- Run line utilities
  - msconfig
  - msinfo32
  - Dxdiag
  - Cmd
  - REGEDIT
- My Network Places
- Task bar / systray
- Administrative tools
  - Performance monitor, Event Viewer, Services, Computer Management
- MMC
- Task Manager
- Start Menu

In the previous chapters, we looked at the hardware that comprises a personal computer's and laptop's physical components. Hardware is only half the story, though. When Thomas Watson, chairman of IBM, said in 1943, "I think there is a world market for maybe five computers," he was looking at a very different machine from the ones we have today. At that time computers were bulky—as in room sized—slow, and difficult to use. As recently as the 1970s, most machines were still using punch cards as a primary data input tool, and anyone wanting to use a computer had to navigate a complex, uninviting interface with only a keyboard to help them. In such an environment, Watson probably was correct to believe that few people would go through the time, effort, and expense to use computers.

As computer technology has evolved toward smaller, more powerful machines, the personal computer has made significant strides toward Microsoft's grandiose stated goal of "a computer in every home." The incredible global computer revolution is not due just to hardware, though. In many ways, the acceleration of computer usage over the last decade has had more to do with the ever-improving operating systems that humans use to interact with these machines. Computers require programmed code (called *software*) to run, and they require an input-output mechanism to allow users to give the machine instructions and to view the results of those commands. The operating system (OS) is the primary software used to achieve these ends, and the evolution of more powerful and user-friendly operating systems has made computers less difficult to use and more enjoyable.

To understand the emergence of modern personal computer OSs, you should know about the technologies that led to our present systems and about the critical relationship between hardware and software over the course of the PC's development. Graphics, speed, GUI interfaces, and multiple programs running concurrently are all made possible because software designers take full advantage of the hardware for which they are designing their software. As a result, you will see that as computer hardware has improved, software has improved with it. Because the OS is the platform on which all other software builds, it is generally the development of a new OS that drives the development of other software.

This chapter is therefore the story of that very special, and crucial, type of software—the personal computer OS. Although there are several commonly used operating systems in the market today, no one operating system family has garnered more market share and attention than Microsoft's Windows operating systems. Therefore, the focus of this chapter—as is the focus on the A+ exam— will be on Windows. We'll dive specifically into three of the most common end-user operating systems of today's computing world: Windows Vista, Windows XP, and Windows 2000.

There are some differences between Windows XP Home and Windows XP Professional. Throughout this chapter and book we'll refer to them collectively as Windows XP (for brevity's sake), unless specific differences exist, in which case we'll point them out. Likewise, there are some differences between the various versions of Windows Vista (Home, Home Premium, Business, and Ultimate). Throughout this chapter and book we'll refer to them collectively as Windows Vista (for brevity's sake), unless specific differences exist, in which case we'll point them out.

Understanding Operating Systems

Computers are pretty much useless without software. A piece of hardware makes a good paperweight or doorstop, unless you have an easy way to interface with it. Software is that interface. While there are many types of software, or programs, the most important application you'll ever deal with is the operating system. Operating systems have many different, complex functions, but two of them jump out as being critical: interfacing with the hardware and providing a platform on which other applications can run.

Here are three major distinctions of software you should be aware of:

Operating system (OS)   Provides a consistent environment for other software to execute commands. The OS gives users an interface with the computer so they can send commands (input) and receive feedback or results (output). To do this, the OS must communicate with the computer hardware to perform the following tasks, as illustrated in Figure 6.1:

- Disk and file management
- Device access
- Memory management
- Output format

Once the OS has organized these basic resources, users can give the computer instructions through input devices (such as a keyboard or a mouse). Some of these commands are built into the OS, whereas others are issued through the use of applications. The OS becomes the center through which the system hardware, other software, and the user communicate; the rest of the components of the system work together through the OS, which coordinates their communication.

Application   Used to accomplish a particular task, an application is software that is written to supplement the commands available to a particular OS. Each application is specifically compiled (configured) for the OS on which it will run. For this reason, the application relies on the OS to do many of its basic tasks. Examples of applications include complex programs, such as Microsoft Word and Internet Explorer, as well as simple programs, such as a command-line FTP program. Either way, when accessing devices and memory, the programs can simply request that the OS do it for them. This arrangement saves substantially on programming overhead, because much of the executable code is *shared*—it is written into the operating system and can therefore be used by multiple applications running on that OS.

FIGURE 6.1   The operating system interacts with resources.

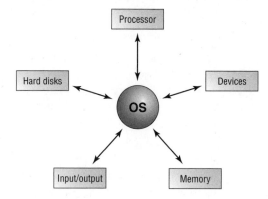

Driver   Extremely specific software written for the purpose of instructing a particular OS on how to access a piece of hardware. Each modem or printer has unique features and configuration settings, and the driver allows the OS to properly understand how the hardware works and what it is able to do.

In the following sections, we'll look at some terms and concepts central to all operating systems. Then we'll move into specific discussions on Windows operating systems.

Operating System Terms and Concepts

Before we get too far into our discussion of PC operating systems, it will be useful to define a few key terms. The following are some terms you will come across as you study this chapter and visit with people in the computer industry:

Version   A particular revision of a piece of software, normally described by a number, which tells you how new the product is in relation to other versions of the product.

Source   The actual code that defines how a piece of software works. Computer operating systems can be *open source*, meaning the OS can be examined and modified by users, or they can be *closed source*, meaning users cannot modify or examine the code.

A word often used interchangeably with closed source is *proprietary*.

Shell   A program that runs on top of the OS and allows the user to issue commands through a set of menus or some other graphical interface. Shells make an OS easier to use by changing the user interface.

Graphical user interface (GUI)   A method by which a person communicates with a computer. GUIs use a mouse, touchpad, or another mechanism (in addition to the keyboard) to interact with the computer to issue commands.

Network   Any group of computers that have a communication link between them. Networks allow computers to share information and resources quickly and securely.

Cooperative multitasking   A multitasking method that depends on the application itself to be responsible for using and then freeing access to the processor. This is the way very early versions of Windows managed multiple applications. If any application locked up while using the processor, the application was unable to properly free the processor to do other tasks, and the entire system locked, usually forcing a reboot.

Preemptive multitasking   A multitasking method in which the OS allots each application a certain amount of processor time and then forcibly takes back control and gives another application or task access to the processor. This means that if an application crashes, the OS takes control of the processor away from the locked application and passes it on to the next application, which should be unaffected. Although unstable programs still lock, only the locked application will stall—not the entire system.

Multithreading   The ability of a single application to have multiple requests in to the processor at one time. This results in faster application performance, because it allows a program to do many things at once.

32-bit   An operating system that is 32-bit is one that can not only run on 32-bit processors but can utilize the capabilities of the processor fully. While this may sound simple, the truth of the matter is that it took many years after the 32-bit processor became available before operating systems (which were 16-bit at the time) were able to utilize their features.

64-bit   A 64-bit operating system is one that is written to utilize the instructions possible with 64-bit processors. Originally, these were more common with servers than desktops, but with prices dropping, 64-bit processors have become more common on the desktop, as have operating systems that will run on them.

x86   The phrase *x86* is commonly used to refer to operating systems intended to run on the Intel processor since Intel initially numbered their processors with numbers ending in 86 prior to switching to the Pentium line.

x64   The phrase *x64* is commonly used to denote operating systems that can run on 64-bit processors.

Microsoft Windows

Microsoft Windows was born out of the Microsoft Disk Operating System (MS-DOS) world. It was a dark place with no graphical interface. If you wanted something accomplished, you had to know the command and type it in. Although it doesn't sound user friendly, it was pretty advanced for its time.

Any real understanding of the success of DOS after 1987 requires knowledge of Windows. In the early years of its existence, Microsoft's DOS gained great acceptance and became a standard as a PC OS. Even so, as computers became more powerful and programs more complex, the limitations of the DOS command-line interface became apparent.

The solution to the problem was to make the OS easier to navigate, more uniform, and generally friendlier to the user. IBM understood that the average user did not want to receive their computer in pieces but preferred to have it ready to go out of the box. Oddly, the company did not understand that the same user who wanted their hardware to be ready to go also wanted their software to be the same way. They also did not want to edit batch files or hunt through directories using CD or DIR commands. As a result, when Microsoft came to IBM with a GUI based on groundbreaking work done by Xerox labs, IBM was not interested, preferring to go onward with the development of OS/2 (a project it had already started with Microsoft).

Early Work on Windows

The Xerox Corporation maintains a think tank of computer designers in Palo Alto, California, called the Palo Alto Research Center (PARC). One of the results of its work was the Alto workstation, which is generally thought to be the forerunner of all modern graphical OSs. The Alto had a mouse and a GUI interface, and it communicated with other workstations via Ethernet. Oh, and it was finished in 1974! Although it was never promoted commercially, both Microsoft and Apple viewed the Alto and incorporated its technology into their own systems. The accomplishments of the PARC lab in laying the groundwork for modern graphical computing systems cannot be overstated. Check out http://www.parc.xerox.com for more information on PARC past and present.

Regardless of IBM's interest, Microsoft continued on its own with development of the GUI—which it named *Windows* after its rectangular work areas—and released the first version to the market in 1985. Apple filed a lawsuit soon after, claiming that the Microsoft GUI had been built using Apple technology, but the suit was dismissed. Both Apple's Macintosh and Microsoft's DOS-with-Windows combo have continued to evolve, but until a recent deal between Apple and Microsoft, tensions have always been high. Mac and PC users, of course, remain adamantly opinionated about their respective platforms.

The original Windows interface to MS-DOS was just a shell program that allowed users to issue DOS commands through a graphical interface—a prettier version of Microsoft's earlier DOS Shell work. The integration of a mouse for nearly all tasks—a legacy of the Xerox Alto computer on which both the Macintosh and Windows GUIs are based—further freed users from DOS by allowing them to issue common commands without using the keyboard. Word processors, spreadsheets, and especially games were revolutionized as software manufacturers happily took advantage of the ease of use and flexibility that Windows added to DOS.

When the NT kernel was released, it signaled the end of real DOS. As opposed to the DOS-based kernel, the NT kernel integrated the GUI in the operating system. The NT kernel is the one used in Windows 2000, Windows XP, and Windows Vista.

Windows Versions

After the development of Windows, many of the enhancements made to subsequent versions of DOS were designed to help free up and reallocate resources to better run Windows and Windows-based applications. Similarly, PC hardware continued to evolve far past the limits of DOS's ability to effectively use the power available to it, and later versions of Windows were designed to hide and overcome the limitations of the OS. The combination of MS-DOS and its Windows shell made Microsoft the industry leader and spurred the PC movement to new heights in the early 1990s. Next is a brief examination of the development of the Windows shell and a look at its different versions.

Windows 1

Version 1 of Windows featured the tiling windows, mouse support, and menu systems that still drive next-generation OSs such as Windows Vista, Windows XP, and Windows 2000. It also offered *cooperative multitasking*, meaning that more than one Windows application could run concurrently. This was something that MS-DOS, up to this point, could not do.

Windows 1 was far from a finished product. For one thing, it didn't use icons, and it had few of the programs we have come to expect as Windows standards. Windows 1 was basically just an updated, more graphical version of the DOSSHELL.EXE program.

Windows 2

Version 2, released in 1987, added icons and allowed application windows to overlap each other, as well as tile. Support was also added for PIFs (program information files), which allowed the user to configure Windows to run their DOS applications more efficiently.

Windows 3.*x*

Windows 3.0 featured a far more flexible memory model, allowing it to access more memory than the 640KB limit normally imposed by DOS. It also featured the addition of the File Manager and Program Manager, allowed for network support, and could operate in *386 Enhanced mode*. This mode used parts of the hard drive as *virtual memory* and was therefore able to use disk memory to supplement the RAM in the machine. Windows today is still quite similar to the Windows of version 3.0.

In 1992, a revision of Windows 3, known as Windows 3.1, provided for better graphical display capability and multimedia support. It also improved the Windows error-protection system and let applications work together more easily through the use of object linking and embedding (OLE).

After the introduction of version 3.1, Windows took a marked turn for the better, because Microsoft started making a serious effort to change to a full 32-bit application environment. With version 3.11, also known as Windows for Workgroups, Windows offered support for both 16-bit and 32-bit applications. (Windows 3.1 could support only

16-bit applications.) Significant progress on the 32-bit front was not made until very late in 1995, however, when Microsoft introduced Windows 95. Since that time, the venerable DOS/Windows team has been largely replaced by newer, more advanced systems.

With the introduction of Windows for Workgroups, people speaking generically about the two flavors of Windows—3.1 and 3.11—started referring to them collectively as Windows 3.*x*, as in the heading of this section.

Windows 95

Although it dominated the market with its DOS operating system and its add-on Windows interface, Microsoft found that the constraints of DOS were rapidly making it difficult to take full advantage of rapidly improving hardware and software developments. The future of computing was clearly a 32-bit, preemptively multitasked system such as IBM's OS/2; but many current users had DOS-based software or older hardware that was specifically designed for DOS and would not operate outside of its cooperatively multitasked Windows 3.1 environment.

Because of this problem, in the fall of 1995 Microsoft released a major upgrade to the DOS/Windows environment. Called Windows 95, the new product integrated the OS and the shell. Where previous versions of Windows simply provided a graphical interface to the existing DOS OS, the Windows 95 graphical interface is *part* of the OS. Moreover, Windows 95 was designed to be a hybrid of the features of previous DOS versions and newer 32-bit systems. It also supports both 32-bit and 16-bit drivers as well as DOS drivers, although the 32-bit drivers are strongly recommended over the DOS ones because they are far faster and more stable.

Among the most important of the other enhancements debuted by Microsoft with Windows 95 was support for the *Plug and Play* (PnP) standard. This meant that if a device was designed to be Plug and Play, a technician could install the device into the computer, start the machine, and have the device automatically recognized and configured by Windows 95. This was a major advance; but unfortunately, in order for PnP to work properly, three things had to be true:

- The OS had to be PnP compatible.
- The computer motherboard had to support PnP.
- All devices in the machine had to be PnP compatible.

At the time Windows 95 came out, many manufacturers were creating their hardware for use in DOS/Windows machines, and DOS did not support PnP, so most pre-1995 computer components (sound cards, modems, NICs, and so on) were not PnP compliant. As a result, these components—generally referred to as *legacy* devices—often interfered with the PnP environment. Such devices are not able to dynamically interact with newer systems. They therefore require manual configuration or must be replaced by newer devices, which don't usually need manual configuration. Because of problems managing legacy hardware under Windows 95, many people soured on PnP technology. Worse, they blamed Windows 95 for their problems, not the old hardware. "It worked fine in DOS" was the standard logic!

The foibles of PnP aside, to say that the new system was a success would be a major understatement. Within just a few years of its release, the Windows 95–style GUI had won over nearly all Windows users, and the more resilient architecture of Windows 95 had won over network administrators and computer technicians. Although it was far from perfect, Windows 95 was a tremendous advance out of the DOS age. Perhaps the only ones not thrilled were the folks at Apple, who continued to make a cottage industry out of starting lawsuits against Microsoft. This time, Apple contended that the Windows 95 interface itself was stolen from the Macintosh. It is undeniable that the Windows 95 interface is nearly a twin of the Mac interface; it turned out that Apple itself got its GUI from Palo Alto Research Center (PARC)! Xerox not only designed the first computer GUI but had created an interface that would not be significantly improved upon in over 20 years of OS development—and both Apple and Microsoft settled on it as the basis for their GUIs. All subsequent versions of Windows (Vista, XP, and 2000) use an interface essentially identical to the Windows 95 GUI.

Windows 98/Me/NT/2000/XP

After Windows 95, Windows 98 was introduced as its successor, followed by Windows Me (Millennium Edition). Finding Windows 98 in use today is a true rarity, as Windows XP has replaced it on the user's desktop. One of the earlier options that offered more power than Windows 95 is the Windows NT OS. NT (which unofficially stands for New Technology) is an OS that was designed to be far more powerful than any previous Windows version. It uses an architecture based entirely on 32-bit code and is capable of accessing up to 4GB (4,000MB) of RAM.

After Windows 98 and NT, Windows 2000 was released. It used the same interface as Windows 98 (with a few important enhancements). It came in many versions, but the most popular were Windows 2000 Professional (workstation OS) and Windows 2000 Server (server OS).

Then came the introduction of Windows XP. XP comes in three versions: XP Home, XP Professional, and Media Center. They are all nearly the same. However, XP Professional contains more corporate and networking features, and Media Center is designed to exploit multimedia connectivity by allowing you to set up your TV through your computer.

Windows Vista

Microsoft then released Windows Vista in 2007. Like Windows XP, Vista comes in several flavors: Windows Vista Home, Vista Home Premium, Business, and Ultimate. All Windows Vista versions have the same core technology, but the different versions are designed to work around the role your PC (or handheld PC) plays, not the hardware that it uses.

Among the prominent features included with Vista are a new user interface named Windows Aero, Internet Explorer 7, speech and handwriting recognition, and easy-access pop-up sidebars and gadgets. UAC (User Account Control) was added to increase security as well—something it accomplishes by routinely asking you (through pop-ups) if you are sure you want to perform an action that could have negative consequences or if you want to keep an action that just occurred. UAC can be turned off by choosing Start ➢ Control Panel ➢ Security ➢ Security Center ➢ Other Security Settings.

Though it was released to replace Windows XP, many users—and businesses—have been slow to adopt it, and Windows XP installations remain common.

> We will mostly talk about Windows Vista, Windows XP, and Windows 2000 in depth throughout the rest of this book, because they are the OSs you need to know for the A+ exam.

Windows 7

As of this writing, Microsoft has not announced an official release date for Windows 7, but it is expected for the fall of 2009. When released, it will be the newest major edition of the Microsoft platform. Key goals of Windows 7 include overcoming the sluggishness in Vista as well as the incompatibilities with applications written for previous versions.

Minimum System Requirements

Chapter 7 explores the installation and upgrading of operating systems, but one of the things that can prevent you from even considering these options is the hardware requirements of the operating system you are contemplating. Before you can begin to install an OS, there are several items you must consider in order to have a flawless installation. You must perform these tasks before you even put the OS installation disc into your computer's CD-ROM drive. These items essentially set the stage for the procedure you are about to perform:

- Determining hardware compatibility and minimum requirements
- Determining installation options
- Determining the installation method
- Preparing the computer for installation

Let's begin our discussion by talking about hardware compatibility issues and requirements for installing the various versions of Windows.

Determining Hardware Compatibility and Minimum Requirements

Before you can begin to install any version of Windows, it is important that you determine whether the hardware you will be using is supported by the Windows version you will be running. That is, will the version of Windows have problems running any drivers for the hardware you have?

To answer this question, Microsoft has come up with several versions of its *Hardware Compatibility List (HCL)*. This is a list of all the hardware that works with Windows and which versions of Windows it works with. You can find this list at http://www.microsoft.com/whdc/hcl/search.mspx. With the release of Windows XP, Microsoft expanded the idea of the HCL to include software as well—and a list that includes both hardware and software can hardly be called a Hardware Compatibility List. The new term is the *Windows Catalog*, and eventually the Windows Catalog will completely replace HCLs.

NOTE   Another name for the Windows Catalog is the Windows Marketplace, available at http://www.windowsmarketplace.com.

The point is, before you install Windows, you should check all your computer's components against this list and make sure each item is compatible with the version of Windows you plan to install.

In addition to general compatibility, it is important that your computer have enough "oomph" to run the version of Windows you plan to install. For that matter, it is important for your computer to have enough resources to run any software you plan to use. Toward that end, Microsoft (as well as other software publishers) publishes a list of both minimum and recommended hardware specifications that you should follow when installing Windows.

Minimum specifications are the absolute minimum requirements for hardware you should have in your system in order to install and run the OS you have chosen. *Recommended* hardware specifications are what you should have in your system to realize usable performance. Always try to have the recommended hardware (or better) in your system. If you don't, you may have to upgrade your hardware before you upgrade your OS. Table 6.1 lists the minimum and recommended hardware specifications for Windows 2000 and Windows XP. Note that in addition to these minimums, the hardware must be compatible with Windows. Also, additional hardware may be required if certain features are installed (for example, a NIC is required for networking support).

TABLE 6.1   Windows 2000 and XP Minimum and Recommended Hardware

Hardware	2000 Professional Requirement	2000 Professional Recommendation	XP Professional Requirement	XP Professional Recommendation
Processor	Pentium 133	Pentium II or higher	233MHz Pentium/ Celeron or AMD K6/Athlon/Duron	300 MHz or higher Intel-compatible processor
Memory	64MB	128MB or more	64MB	128MB
Free Hard Disk Space	650MB	2GB, plus what is needed for applications and storage	1.5GB	1.5GB
Floppy Disk	Required only if installing from boot disks	Yes	Not required	Not required
CD-ROM or DVD	Required	Yes	Required	Required
Video	VGA	SuperVGA	SuperVGA or better	SuperVGA or better

TABLE 6.1   Windows 2000 and XP Minimum and Recommended Hardware *(continued)*

Hardware	2000 Professional Requirement	2000 Professional Recommendation	XP Professional Requirement	XP Professional Recommendation
Mouse	Required (but not listed as a requirement)	Required (but not listed as a requirement)	Required	Required
Keyboard	Required	Required	Required	Required

Table 6.2 lists the minimum system requirements for the various versions of Windows Vista.

TABLE 6.2   Windows Vista Minimum Hardware

Hardware	Minimum Supported for All Versions	Home Basic Recommendation	Home Premium/ Business/ Ultimate Recommendation
Processor	800 MHz	1 GHz 32-bit (x86) or 64-bit (x64) processor	1 GHz 32-bit (x86) or 64-bit (x64) processor
Memory	512MB	512MB	1GB
Free Hard Disk Space	15GB free on a 20GB drive	15GB free on a 20GB drive	15GB free on a 40GB drive
CD-ROM or DVD	CD-ROM	DVD-ROM	DVD-ROM
Video	SVGA	Support for DirectX 9 graphics and 32MG graphics memory	Support for DirectX 9 with: WDDM Driver 128MB of graphics memory Pixel Shader 2.0 in hardware 32 bits per pixel
Mouse	Required (but not listed as a requirement)	Required (but not listed as a requirement)	Required (but not listed as a requirement)
Keyboard	Required (but not listed as a requirement)	Required (but not listed as a requirement)	Required (but not listed as a requirement)
Internet Access	Not listed as a requirement	Required	Required

If there is one thing to be learned from Tables 6.1 and 6.2, it is that Microsoft is nothing if not optimistic. For your own sanity, though, we strongly suggest that you always take the minimum requirements with a grain of salt. They are *minimums*. Even the recommended requirements should be considered minimums. Bottom line: Make sure you have a good margin between your system's performance and the minimum requirements listed. Always run Windows on more hardware, rather than less!

Other hardware—sound cards, network cards, modems, video cards, and so on—may or may not work with Windows. If the device is fairly recent, you can be relatively certain that it was built to work with the newest version of Windows. But if it is older, you may need to find out who made the hardware and check their website to see if they have drivers for the version of Windows you are installing.

 The easiest way to see if your current hardware can run Windows Vista is to download and run the Windows Vista Upgrade Advisor available at `http://www.microsoft.com/windows/windows-vista/get/upgrade-advisor.aspx`.

There's one more thing to consider when evaluating installation methods. Some methods only work if you're performing a clean installation, and not an upgrade. We'll discuss this in greater detail in the next chapter.

Using Operating Systems

In this section, we will look at the Microsoft GUI from the ground up, beginning with a detailed look at its key components and ending with an exploration of basic tasks common across Windows Vista, XP, and 2000. The following general topics will be covered:

- Windows GUI components
- My Computer
- My Network Places
- Control Panel
- The command prompt
- The Windows Registry
- Virtual memory
- System files
- Windows Explorer
- File and disk management

The Windows GUI has been incredibly successful since its debut. All Microsoft operating system GUIs share features, but they also have differences.

For the A+ Essentials exam, you'll need to know various aspects of the GUI interface for the Windows Vista, Windows XP, and Windows 2000. operating systems.

The Windows Interface

The interface of a machine running Windows 2000 looks very similar to that of a machine running Windows 95/98/Me/NT; it can be difficult to tell them apart. If you look closely, you will notice that the names of some of the icons are different, but for the most part they're identical and look very much like the screen in Figure 6.2. If you look at the monitor of a machine running Windows XP (shown in Figure 6.3), you'll notice that it looks a bit different than the older interfaces. However, things still basically work the same way.

FIGURE 6.2   The Windows 2000 interface

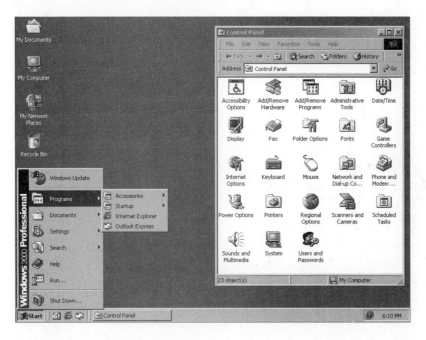

As a technician, you will quickly realize that this overall standardization of Microsoft's graphical interface for all of its OSs is good for you. Most basic tasks are accomplished in almost identical fashion on everything from a Windows 95 workstation computer to a Windows 2008 Server computer to a Windows XP Professional computer. Also, although the tools that are used often vary between the different OSs, the way you use those tools remains remarkably consistent across *platforms*. This has changed a bit with Windows Vista and the Aero interface, as Figure 6.4 shows, but not as dramatically as many in the media have made it out to be.

FIGURE 6.3   The Windows XP interface

FIGURE 6.4   The Windows Vista interface

We will begin with an overview of the common elements of the Windows GUI. We will then look at some tasks that are similar across Windows operating systems. If you have a copy of Windows Vista, Windows XP, or Windows 2000 available, you may want to follow along by exploring each of the elements as they are discussed.

If you are able to follow along, you may notice that there are numerous icons and options we do not mention. Quite honestly, there are too many to cover, and they're out of the scope of this chapter. For now, simply ignore them, or browse through them on your own and then return to the text.

The Desktop

The Desktop is the virtual desk on which all of your other programs and utilities run. By default it contains the *Start menu*, the *Taskbar*, and a number of *icons*. The Desktop can also contain additional elements, such as web page content, through the use of the Active Desktop feature. Because it is the base on which everything else sits, the way the Desktop is configured can have a major effect on how the GUI looks and how convenient it is for users.

You can change the Desktop's background patterns, screensaver, color scheme, and size by right-clicking any area of the Desktop that doesn't contain an icon. The menu that appears allows you to do several things, such as creating new Desktop items, changing how your icons are arranged, or selecting a special command called Properties, similar to the one shown in Figure 6.5.

FIGURE 6.5   The Desktop context menu

The Three Clicks in Windows

When it comes to interacting with a mouse in Windows, there are three possibilities:

- *Primary mouse click*—A single click used to select an object or place a cursor.

- *Double-click*—Two primary mouse clicks in quick succession. Used to open a program through an icon or for other application-specific functions.

- *Secondary mouse click (or alternate click)*—Most mice have two buttons. Clicking once on the secondary button (usually the one on the right, although that can be modified) is interpreted differently from a left mouse click. Generally in Windows this click displays a context-sensitive menu from which you can perform tasks or view object properties.

When you right-click the Desktop and choose Properties, you will see the Display Properties screen shown in Figure 6.6.

FIGURE 6.6   The Display Properties screen

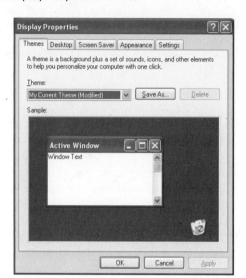

On this screen, you can click the various tabs at the top to move to the different screens of information about the way Windows looks. Tabs are similar to index cards, in that they are staggered across the top so you can see and access large amounts of data within a single small window. Each Properties window has a different set of tabs. The tabs will differ based on the operating system, but among the tabs in the Display Properties window of most are the following:

Themes   Used to select a theme that enables you to quickly customize the look and feel of your machine. Selecting a theme sets several items at once, such as a picture to display on the Desktop, the look of icons, sounds to use, and so on. All of these options can also be selected individually through the other Desktop Properties tabs. For example, if you're more comfortable with the look and feel of previous versions of Windows, you can select the Windows Classic theme.

Background or Desktop   The Background tab in Windows 2000 is used to select an HTML document or a picture to display on the Desktop. In addition to letting you perform this same function, the Desktop tab in Windows XP lets you configure other items through the Customize Desktop button. Examples include changing which default icons to display on the Desktop and configuring web content for the Desktop.

Screen Saver   Sets up an automatic screensaver to cover your screen if you have not been active for a certain period of time. Originally used to prevent burned-in monitors, screensavers are now generally used for entertainment or to password-protect users' Desktops. The Screen Saver tab also gives you access to other power settings.

Appearance   Used to select a color scheme for the Desktop or to change the color or size of other Desktop elements.

Effects (Windows 2000 only) Contains numerous assorted visual options. In other operating systems, some of these visual options are available via the Customize Desktop button on the Desktop tab.

Web (Windows 2000 only) Lets you configure Active Desktop settings. In other operating systems, you can access this tab via the Customize Desktop button on the Desktop tab.

Settings Used to set the color depth or screen size. Also contains the Advanced button, which leads to graphics driver and monitor configuration settings.

You can also access the Display Properties settings by using the Display icon under Control Panel.

In Exercise 6.1, you will see how to change a screensaver.

EXERCISE 6.1

Changing a Screensaver

To change the screensaver, perform the following steps:

1. Right-click the Desktop.

2. Choose Properties from the context menu.

3. Click the Screen Saver tab.

4. Choose 3D Flower Box. Click Preview to see the new screensaver. Move the mouse to cancel the screensaver and return to the Display Properties dialog box.

5. Click the OK button or the Apply button. (OK performs two tasks—Apply and Exit Window—whereas Apply leaves the window open.)

The Taskbar

The Taskbar (see Figure 6.7) is another standard component of the Windows interface. Note that although the colors and feel of the Desktop components, including the Taskbar, have changed throughout the operating systems, the components themselves are the same. The Taskbar contains two major items: the Start menu and the *System Tray* (systray). The Start menu is on the left side of the Taskbar and is easily identifiable: it is a button that has the word *Start* on it or—in the case of Windows Vista—is the large Windows icon. The *System Tray* is located on the right side of the Taskbar and contains only a clock by default, but other Windows utilities (for example, screensavers or virus-protection utilities) may put their icons here to indicate that they are running and to provide the user with a quick way to access their features.

FIGURE 6.7   The Taskbar

Windows also uses the middle area of the Taskbar. When you open a new window or program, it gets a button on the Taskbar with an icon that represents the window or program as well as the name of the window or program. To bring that window or program to the front (or to maximize it if it was minimized), click its button on the Taskbar. As the middle area of the Taskbar fills with buttons, the buttons become smaller so they can all be displayed.

You can increase the size of the Taskbar by moving the mouse pointer to the top of the Taskbar and pausing until the pointer turns into a double-headed arrow. Once this happens, click the mouse and move it up to make the Taskbar bigger. Or move it down to make the Taskbar smaller. You can also move the Taskbar to the top or side of the screen by clicking the Taskbar and dragging it to the new location.

In Windows XP, once you've configured the Taskbar position and layout to your liking, you can configure it so that it can't be changed accidentally. To do so, right-click the Taskbar and select Lock The Taskbar. To unlock the Taskbar and make changes, right-click the Taskbar and select Lock The Taskbar again.

In Exercise 6.2, we will show you how to auto-hide the Taskbar.

EXERCISE 6.2

Auto-Hiding the Taskbar

You can make the Taskbar automatically hide itself when it isn't being used (thus freeing that space for use by the Desktop or other windows):

1. Right-click the Taskbar.

2. Choose Properties, which will bring up the Taskbar And Start Menu Properties screen.

3. In Windows 2000, check the Auto Hide option on the General tab. In other operating systems, check the Auto-Hide The Taskbar option on the Taskbar tab of the Taskbar and Start Menu Properties dialog box.

4. Click OK.

5. In Windows 2000, move your mouse to the top of the Desktop or click on the Desktop. The Taskbar will retract off the screen. In other operating systems, the Taskbar retracts as soon as you click OK.

6. Move the mouse pointer to the bottom of the screen, and the Taskbar will pop up and be available for normal use.

In addition to the Taskbar, Windows Vista also includes the Sidebar, shown in Figure 6.8. This provides a quick interface allowing you to access common utilities such as the headlines.

FIGURE 6.8   The Windows Vista Sidebar

The Start Menu

Back when Microsoft officially introduced Windows 95, it bought the rights to use the Rolling Stones' song "Start Me Up" in its advertisements and at the introduction party. Microsoft chose that particular song because the Start menu was the central point of focus in the new Windows interface, as it has been in all subsequent versions.

To display the Start menu, click the Start button in the Taskbar. You'll see a Start menu similar to that shown in Figure 6.9 for Windows XP and Figure 6.10 for Windows Vista. You'll notice that in Windows XP the look of the Start menu is slightly different than that in earlier versions of Windows or Windows Vista, but they all behave the same. Regardless of the operating system, the Start menu always serves the same function: providing quick access to important features and programs.

From the Start menu, you can select any of the various options the menu presents. An arrow pointing to the right indicates that a submenu is available. To select a submenu, move the mouse pointer over the submenu title and pause. The submenu will appear; you don't even have to click. (You have to click to choose an option on the submenu, though.) We'll discuss each of the default Start menu's submenu options and how to use them.

FIGURE 6.9   The Windows XP Start menu

FIGURE 6.10   The Windows Vista Start menu

One handy feature of the Start menu in pre–Windows XP versions of Windows is that it usually displays the name of the OS type along its side when you activate it. This provides an excellent way to quickly see whether you are on Windows 9*x*, NT, or 2000. In Windows XP and Vista you don't see the name of the OS; however, the Start menu looks so different that you should be able to identify which operating system you are using.

You can also check which OS you are using by right-clicking the My Computer check box on the Desktop and selecting Properties. The OS type and version are displayed on the first tab. Note that the My Computer check box may not display on the Desktop by default. You can add the check box to the Desktop by using the Display Properties (click Customize Desktop on the Desktop tab, select My Computer on the General tab, and apply your changes), or you can click Start and then right-click the My Computer option and select Properties.

If you are running Windows XP and are attached to the look and feel of the pre–Windows XP Start menu, you can configure XP to use the old Start menu layout. To do so, right-click on the Taskbar and select Properties. Click the Start Menu tab, select Classic Start Menu, and click OK.

Programs (Windows 2000)/All Programs (Windows XP and Vista) Submenu

The Programs/All Programs submenu holds the program groups and program icons you can use. When you select this submenu, you will be shown another submenu, with a submenu for each program group. In Windows XP and Vista, the look is again a little different, but the functionality is the same. You can navigate through this menu and its submenus and click the program you wish to start.

The most common way to add programs to this submenu is by using an application's installation program. In Windows 2000 (and Windows XP if you're using the Classic Start Menu), you can also add programs to this submenu by using the Taskbar Properties screen (right-click on the Taskbar and choose Properties).

Documents (2000)/My Recent Documents (Windows XP)/Recent Items (Windows Vista) Submenu

The Documents/My Recent Documents/Recent Items submenu has only one function: to keep track of the last data files you opened. Whenever you open a file, a shortcut to it is automatically made in this menu. To open the document again, click the document in the Documents menu to open it in its associated application.

In some versions of Windows XP, this feature is not enabled by default. To enable it, in the Taskbar And Start Menu Properties screen, click the Start Menu tab and then click Customize next to Start Menu. Click the Advanced tab, select the List My Most Recently Opened Documents option, and then click OK. An option called My Recent Documents is added to the Start menu; it lists the 15 most recently opened data files.

To clear the list of documents shown in the Documents/My Recent Documents/Recent Items submenu, go to the Taskbar And Start Menu Properties screen. Then use the Clear button on the Advanced tab. (Remember that you access the Advanced tab in Windows XP via the Customize button on the Start Menu tab.)

Settings Submenu (Windows 2000)

The Settings submenu provides easy access to the configuration of Windows. This menu has numerous submenus, including Control Panel, Printers, and Taskbar & Start Menu. Additional menus are available, depending on which version of Windows you are using. These submenus give you access to the Control Panel, printer driver, and Taskbar configuration areas. You can also access the first two areas from the My Computer icon; they are placed together here to provide a common area to access Windows settings.

In Windows XP and Windows Vista, you'll find Control Panel as an option directly off the Start menu (not below a submenu). You can add other options (such as Printers And Faxes) to the Start menu by using the options on the Advanced tab of the Taskbar And Start Menu Properties screen (via the Customize button).

Search (Find) Submenu/Option

The name of this submenu (Windows 2000) or Start menu option (Windows XP and Vista) differs between Search and Find in the various versions of Windows, but its purpose doesn't. In all cases, it's used to locate information on your computer or on a network.

In Windows 2000, to find a file or directory, select the Find or Search submenu and then select Files Or Folders. In the Named field in this dialog box, type in the name of the file or directory you are looking for and click Find Now. Windows will search whatever is specified in the Look In parameter for the file or directory. Matches are listed in a window under the Find window. You can use wildcards (* and ?) to look for multiple files and directories. You can also click the Advanced tab to further refine your search.

In Windows XP or Vista, to find a file or directory click the Search option in the Start menu. Doing so opens the Search Results dialog box. In the left pane, click All Files And Folders, and then enter the appropriate information in the text fields. Expand the down-pointing double arrows to access advanced search options. To start the search, click Search. The search results display in the right pane.

Windows Search 4.0, which is an automatic update, can change this behavior in Windows XP and Windows Vista. For more information, see http://support.microsoft.com/kb/940157.

Help Command (Windows 2000)/Help And Support Command (Windows XP and Vista)

Windows has always included a very good Help system. In addition, the Help system was updated with a new interface and new tools in Windows XP and Vista. Because of its usefulness and power, it was placed in the Start menu for easy access.

In Windows 2000, when you select the Help command, it brings up the Windows Help window. In the newer operating systems, when you click Help And Support, the Help And Support Center home page opens. This screen may have been slightly customized by a hardware vendor if the operating system was preinstalled on your machine. However, all the options and available tools will still be present.

A quick way to access Help is to press the F1 key.

Run Command (Windows 2000 and Windows XP)

You can use the Run command to start programs if they don't have a shortcut on the Desktop or in the Programs submenu. When you choose Run from the Start menu, a pop-up window appears. To execute a particular program, type its name in the Open field. If you don't know the exact path, you can browse to find the file by clicking the Browse button. Once you have typed in the executable name, click OK to run the program.

In Exercise 6.3, you will see how to start a program from the Run window.

EXERCISE 6.3

Starting a Program from the Run Window

Applications can easily be started from the Run window; often you will find it faster to open programs this way than search for their icons in the Start menu maze.

1. Click Start ➢ Run.

2. In the Open field, type **notepad**.

3. Click OK. Notepad will open in a new window.

If the program you want to run has been run from the Run window before, you can find it on the Open field's drop-down list. Click the down arrow to display the list, and then select the program you want by clicking its name and clicking OK.

While this functionality has not disappeared from Windows Vista, it is a bit different. A blank dialog box appears at the bottom of the Start menu with the default phrase "Start Search" within. Type the name of the command you want to run in here, and press Enter. Vista will look for the executable and run it.

Shut Down Command (Windows 2000)/Turn Off Computer Command (Windows XP and Vista)

Windows operating systems are very complex. At any one time, many files are open in memory. If you accidentally hit the power switch and turn off the computer while these files are open, there is a good chance they will be corrupted. For this reason, Microsoft has added the

Shut Down (pre–Windows XP) or Turn Off Computer (Windows XP and Vista) command under the Start menu (in Vista, it appears as an icon of an on/off button and does not have a label). Note that with a configuration called Fast User Switching, Windows XP also displays Shut Down rather than Turn Off Computer. When you select this option, Windows presents you with several choices. Exactly which options are available depends on the Windows version you are running.

The possible choices are as follows:

Shut Down (Windows 2000)/Turn Off (Windows XP and Vista)   This option writes any unsaved data to disk, closes any open applications, makes a copy of the Registry, and gets the computer ready to be powered off. Depending on the OS, the computer is then powered down automatically, or you'll see a black screen with the message *It's now safe to turn off your computer.* In this case, you can power off the computer or press Ctrl+Alt+Del to reboot the computer.

Restart   This option works the same as the first option, but instead of shutting down completely, it automatically reboots the computer with a warm reboot.

Stand By (Windows XP only)   This option places the computer into a low-power state. The monitor and hard disks are turned off, and the computer uses less power. To resume working, press a key on the keyboard; the computer is returned to its original state. In this state, information in memory is not saved to hard disk, so if a power loss occurs, any data in memory will be lost.

If you enable Hibernation on a Windows XP machine, you can place the computer into hibernation by holding down the Shift key while clicking Stand By in the Turn Off Computer screen. Using the Hibernation feature, any information in memory is saved to disk before the computer is put into a low power state. Thus, if power is lost while the machine is in hibernation, your data is not lost. However, going into and coming out of hibernation takes more time than going into and coming out of stand-by mode.

Icons

Icons are not nearly as complex in structure, but they are very important nonetheless. Icons are shortcuts that allow a user to open a program or a utility without knowing where that program is located or how it needs to be configured. Icons consist of several major elements:

- Icon label
- Icon graphic
- Program location

The label and graphic simply tell the user the name of the program and give a visual hint about what that program does. The icon for the Solitaire program, for instance, is labeled *Solitaire*, and its icon graphic is a deck of cards. By right-clicking an icon once, you make that icon the active icon, and a drop-down menu appears. One of the selections is Properties. Clicking Properties brings up the icon's attributes (see Figure 6.11) and is the only way to see exactly which program an icon is configured to start and where the program's executable is located. You can also specify whether to run the program in a normal window or maximized or minimized.

FIGURE 6.11   The Properties window of an application with its icon above it

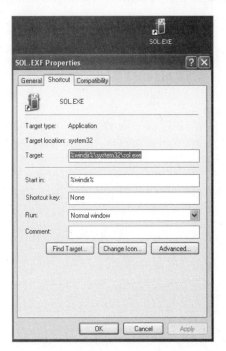

In operating systems newer than Windows 2000, additional functionality has been added to an icon's properties to allow for backward compatibility with older versions of Windows. To configure this, click the Compatibility tab and specify the version of Windows for which you want to configure compatibility. This feature is helpful if you own programs that used to work in older versions of Windows but no longer run under the current Windows version. In addition, you can specify different display settings that might be required by older programs.

Standard Desktop Icons

In addition to the options in your Start menu, a number of icons are placed directly on the Desktop in Windows 2000 and Windows XP and Vista. Three of the most important icons are My Computer, Network Neighborhood/My Network Places, and the Recycle Bin. While these three are important, the My Computer and My Network Places icons no longer display by default on the Desktop; however, you might want to add them. Instructions on how to add My Computer were given earlier in the section "The Start Menu"; you can select My Network Places in the same place you select My Computer to display that icon on the Desktop.

THE MY COMPUTER ICON

If you double-click the My Computer icon, it displays a list of all the disk drives installed in your computer. In pre–Windows XP versions of Windows, it also displays an icon for the Control Panel and Printers folders, which can be used to configure the system.

In Windows XP, My Computer does not by default display an icon for Control Panel (although you can configure it to do so by choosing Tools ➢ Folder Options and specifying to show Control Panel in My Computer on the View tab) or for printers; however, in addition to displaying disk drives, it also displays a list of other devices attached to the computer, such as scanners, cameras, mobile devices, and so on. In Windows XP, all the disk devices are sorted into categories such as Hard Disk Drives, Devices With Removable Storage, Scanners And Cameras, and so on. If you double-click a disk drive or device, you will see the contents of that disk drive or device.

You can delve deeper into each disk drive or device by double-clicking it. The contents are displayed in the same window. You can select Tools ➢ Folder to configure each folder to open in a new window. Having multiple windows open makes it easy to copy and move files between drives and between directories using these windows.

In addition to allowing you access to your computer's files, the My Computer icon lets you view your machine's configuration and hardware, also called the System Properties.

With Vista and XP, right-clicking on Computer in the Start menu allows you to choose Properties and see the same information (choosing Manage, instead of Properties, brings up the Computer Management interface, in which you can make a plethora of changes).

MY NETWORK PLACES

Another icon in Windows relates to accessing other computers to which the local computer is connected, and it's called My Network Places (Network Neighborhood pre–Windows 2000).

In Windows XP, the My Network Places icon may not display on the Desktop by default. You can add the icon to the Desktop through the Display Properties (in the same manner you can add the My Computer icon to the Desktop if it isn't there), or you can reach My Network Places by clicking Start ➢ My Network Places.

Opening My Network Places enables you to browse for and access other computers and shared resources to which your computer is connected. This might be another computer in a workgroup, domain, or other network environment (such as a Novell NetWare network). You can also use My Network Places to establish new connections to shared resources.

Through the properties of My Network Places, you can configure your network connections, including LAN and dial-up connections. You will learn about networking in detail in Chapter 10.

In Windows Vista, the wording of this option has been changed to simply Network. You can choose it from the Start menu or you can add it—and other common icons—to the Desktop by choosing Start ➢ Control Panel, clicking Appearance And Personalization, and then clicking Personalization. Choose Change Desktop Icons from the choices on the left to open the dialog box shown in Figure 6.12.

THE RECYCLE BIN

All files, directories, and programs in Windows are represented by icons and are generally referred to as *objects*. When you want to remove an object from Windows, you do so by deleting it. Deleting doesn't just remove the object, though; it also removes the ability of the system to access the information or application the object represents. For this reason, Windows includes a special directory where all deleted files are placed: the Recycle Bin. The Recycle Bin holds the files until it is emptied or you fill the bin, and it gives users the opportunity to recover files that they delete accidentally. By right-clicking, you can see how much disk space is allocated, and some larger files that cannot fit in the bin will be erased after a warning.

FIGURE 6.12   Common icons can easily be added to the Vista desktop.

You can retrieve a file you have deleted by opening the Recycle Bin icon and then dragging the file from the Recycle Bin to where you want to restore it. Alternatively, you can right-click a file and select Restore, and the file will be restored to the location it was deleted from.

 If you have antivirus software installed, option names in the Recycle Bin might change. For example, if you have Norton Antivirus installed and you right-click on a file, you'll see that the Restore option has been renamed to Recover.

To permanently erase files, you need to empty the Recycle Bin, thereby deleting any items in it and freeing the hard drive space they took up. If you want to delete only specific, but not all, files, you can select those file(s) in the Recycle Bin, right-click, and choose

Delete. You can also permanently erase files (bypassing the Recycle Bin) by holding down the Shift key as you delete the file (either by dragging the file and dropping it in the Recycle Bin, pressing the Del key, or clicking Delete on the file's context menu). If the Recycle Bin has files in it, its icon looks like a full trash can; when there are no files in it, it looks like an empty trash can.

What's in a Window?

We have now looked at the nature of the Desktop, the Taskbar, the Start menu, and icons. Each of these items was created for the primary purpose of making access to user applications easier, and these applications are in turn used and managed through the use of *windows*, the rectangular application environments for which the Windows family of operating systems is named. We will now examine how windows work and what they are made of.

A program window is a rectangular area created on the screen when an application is opened within Windows. This window can have a number of different forms, but most windows include at least a few basic elements.

Elements of a Window

Several basic elements are present in a standard window. Figure 6.13 shows the control box, title bar, Minimize button, Restore button, Close button, and resizable border in a text editor called Notepad (NOTEPAD.EXE) that has all the basic window elements—and little else.

FIGURE 6.13 The basic elements of a window

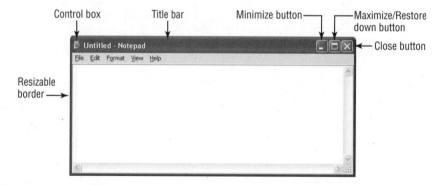

The basic window elements are as follows:

Control box   Located in the upper-left corner of the window, the control box is used to control the state of the application. It can be used to maximize, minimize, and close the application. Clicking it once brings into view a selection menu. Double-clicking it closes the window and shuts down the application.

Minimize and Maximize/Restore buttons   Used to change the state of the window on the Desktop. They are discussed in the "States of a Window" section later in this chapter.

Close button   Used to easily end a program and return any resources it was using to the system. It essentially does the same thing as double-clicking the control box, but with one less click.

Title Bar   The area between the control box and the Minimize button. It states the name of the program and in some cases gives information about the particular document being accessed by that program. The color of the title bar indicates whether a particular window is the active window. Clicking on it is an easy way to move the window on the screen.

Menu bar   Used to present useful commands in an easily accessible format. Clicking one of the menu choices displays a list of related options you may choose from.

Active window   The window that is currently being used. It has two attributes. First, any keystrokes that are entered are directed there by default. Second, any other windows that overlap the active window are pushed behind it.

Border   A thin line that surrounds the window in its restored down state and allows it to be resized.

Not every element is found on every window, because programmers can choose to eliminate or modify them. Still, in most cases they will be constant, with the rest of the window filled in with menus, toolbars, a workspace, or other application-specific elements. For instance, Microsoft Word, the program with which this book was written, adds an additional control box and Minimize and Maximize buttons for each document. It also has a menu bar, a number of optional toolbars, scroll bars at the right and bottom of the window, and a status bar at the very bottom. Application windows can become quite cluttered.

Notepad is a very simple Windows program. It has only a single menu bar and the basic elements seen previously in Figure 6.13. Figure 6.14 shows a Microsoft Word window. Both Word and Notepad are used to create and edit documents, but Word is far more configurable and powerful and therefore has many more optional components available within its window.

States of a Window

There is more to the Windows interface than the specific parts of a window. Windows also are movable, stackable, and resizable, and they can be hidden behind other windows (often unintentionally!).

When an application window has been launched, it exists in one of three states:

Maximized   A maximized window takes up all available space on the screen. When it is in front of other programs, it is the only thing visible—even the Desktop is hidden. It takes up the entire space of the Desktop, and the middle button in the upper-right corner displays two rectangles rather than one. The sides of the window no longer have borders. The window is flush with the edges of the screen. Maximizing a window provides the maximum workspace possible for that window's application, and the window can be accessed actively by the user. In general, maximized mode is the preferred window size for most word processing, graphics-creation, and other user applications.

FIGURE 6.14   A window with more components

Restored   A restored window can be used interactively and is identical in function to a maximized window, with the simple difference that it does not necessarily take up the entire screen. Restored windows can be very small, or they can take up almost as much space as maximized windows. Generally, how large the restored window becomes is the user's choice. Restored windows display a Maximize button (the middle button in the upper-right corner) with a single rectangle in it; this is used to maximize the window. Restored windows have a border.

Minimized   Minimized program windows are represented by nothing but an icon and title on the Taskbar, and they are not usable until they have been either maximized or restored. The only difference between a minimized program and a closed program is that a minimized program is out of the way but is still taking up resources and is therefore ready to use if you need it. It also leaves the content of the window in the same place when you return to it as when you minimized it.

When a program is open and you need to open another program (or maybe you need to stop playing a game because your boss has entered the room), you have two choices. First, you can close the program and reopen it later. If you do this, however, your current game will be lost and you will have to start over. Minimizing the game window, on the other hand, removes the open window from the screen and leaves the program open but displays nothing more than an icon and title on the Taskbar. Later, you can restore the window to its previous size and finish the game in progress.

Keep in mind that applications in the background are still running. There-fore, if you minimize your game, you might return to find that you've been eaten by whatever monster you were running from in the game. Running while minimized can be a good thing, however, if you're running a useful utility such as a long search or a disk defrag.

Control Panel

Although for the most part the Windows system is functional from the time it is installed, Microsoft realized that if someone were going to use computers regularly, they would probably want to be able to customize their environment so it would be better suited to their needs—or at least more fun to use. As a result, the Windows environment has a large number of utilities that are intended to give you control over the look and feel of the Desktop.

This is, of course, an excellent idea. It is also a bit more freedom than some less-than-cautious users seem to be capable of handling, and you will undoubtedly serve a number of customers who call you in to restore their configuration after botched attempts at changing one setting or another.

More than likely, you will also have to reinstall Windows yourself a few times because of accidents that occur while you are studying or testing the system's limits. This is actually a good thing, because no competent computer technician can say that they have never had to reinstall because of an error. You can't really know how to fix Windows until you are experienced at breaking it. So it is extremely important to experiment and find out what can be changed in the Windows environment, what results from those changes, and how to undo any unwanted results. To this end, we will examine the most common configuration utility in Windows: Control Panel. The names of some panels are different in various versions of Windows; different names are indicated in parentheses. And not all panels are available in all versions. You'll see some of the more popular panels described in Table 6.3.

TABLE 6.3   Selected Windows Control Panel Programs (Windows 2000 Names and Other Variations in Parentheses)

Program Name	Function
Add Hardware (Add/Remove Hardware in Windows 2000)	Adds and configures new hardware.
Add Or Remove Programs (Add/Remove Programs)	Changes, adds, or deletes software.
Administrative Tools	Performs administrative tasks on the computer.
Date And Time (Date/Time)	Sets the system time and configures options such as time zone.

TABLE 6.3   Selected Windows Control Panel Programs (Windows 2000 Names and Other Variations in Parentheses) *(continued)*

Program Name	Function
Display	Configures screensavers, colors, display options, and monitor drivers.
Folder Options	Configures the look and feel of how folders are displayed in Windows Explorer.
Fonts	Adds and removes fonts.
Internet Options	Sets a number of Internet connectivity options.
Sounds And Multimedia; Sounds And Audio Devices; also Scanners And Cameras (Multimedia)	Configures audio, video, or audio and video options.
Network And Dial-Up Connections; Network Connections (Network)	Sets options for connecting to other computers.
Phone And Modem Options (Modems)	Sets options for using phone lines to dial out to a network or the Internet.
Power Options	Configures different power schemes to adjust power consumption.
Printers And Faxes (Printers)	Configures printer settings and print defaults.
System	Allows you to view and configure various system elements. We'll look at this in more detail later in this chapter.

In Windows XP, when you first open Control Panel, it displays in Category view. This view provides you with different categories to choose from, into which Control Panel programs have been organized. Once you choose a category, you can pick a task and the appropriate Control Panel program is opened for you; or you can select one of the Control Panel programs that is part of the category. However, you can change this view to Classic View, which displays all the Control Panel programs in a list, as in older versions of Windows. We suggest that administrators of Windows XP and Vista computers change to this view. To do so, click Switch To Classic View in the left pane. Throughout this chapter, when we refer to accessing Control Panel programs, we will assume that you have changed the view to Classic View.

For a quick look at how the Control Panel programs work, the following exercise examines some of the settings in the Date/Time program. The Date/Time program is used to configure the system time, date, and time-zone settings, which can be important for files that require accurate timestamps or to users who don't have a watch. Because it is a simple program, it's a perfect example to use. In pre–Windows XP versions of Windows, the Date/Time program includes only two sets of *tabs* (Date & Time and Time Zone) and one option (whether to use Daylight Savings). Windows XP and Vista also have an Internet Time tab, which enables you to synchronize time on the computer with an Internet time server (the options in Vista are shown in Figure 6.15).

FIGURE 6.15   System time can be configured to be retrieved from an Internet time server.

In Exercise 6.4, you will see how to change the time zone.

EXERCISE 6.4

Changing the Time Zone

Did you recently move from one time zone to the other? Keep up with the time(s)!

1. In pre–Windows XP versions of Windows, click Start ➢ Settings ➢ Control Panel. In Windows XP, click Start ➢ Control Panel.

2. From Control Panel, double-click the Date/Time (Date And Time) icon (by default, the programs are listed alphabetically).

3. Click the Time Zone tab and use the drop-down menu to select (GMT –03:30) Newfoundland.

4. Hop a plane to Newfoundland, secure in the knowledge that you will know what time it is once you get there.

5. If you skipped step 4, change the time zone back to where it should be before closing the window.

The System Control Panel

The System control panel (see Figure 6.16 for the Windows XP System control panel) is one of the most important control panels, and it's nearly all business. From within this one relatively innocuous panel, you can make a large number of configuration changes to a Windows machine. The different versions of Windows have different options available in this panel; as a general rule, the newer the OS, the more options you'll find. The System Properties panel is divided into tabs. They can include some of the following: General, Network Identification, Device Manager, Hardware, Hardware Profiles, User Profiles, Environment, Startup/Shutdown, Performance, System Restore, Automatic Updates, Remote, Computer Name, and Advanced. The General tab gives you an overview of the system, such as OS version, registration information, basic hardware levels (Processor and RAM), and the Service Pack level that's installed, if any. For the rest of the tabs, we will look a bit more closely at their functionality. For each tab, we identify which versions of Windows contain the tab.

FIGURE 6.16   The System Properties control panel on a Windows XP computer with the Advanced tab selected

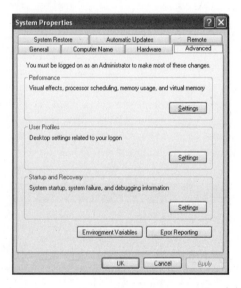

Computer Name (Windows XP and Vista)/Network Identification (Windows 2000)

This tab is used to define whether the machine is in a workgroup or a domain environment. We will talk more about networking in Chapter 10, but in general terms, here's the difference between a workgroup and a domain:

Workgroup   Loosely associated computers, each of which is its own security authority.

Domain   A group of computers that is tightly connected or associated. Has a single authority (called a *domain controller*) that manages security for all the computers.

Hardware

This tab includes a number of tools, all of which allow you to change how the hardware on your machine is used:

(Add) Hardware Wizard   The Hardware Wizard in Windows 2000 is used, as it says, to "install, uninstall, repair, unplug, eject, and configure" hardware in the system. Essentially, this means that if you want to add a new device to the system or uninstall drivers that are already there, this is the place to go. You can also use this tool to temporarily eject *PC Card* devices or other removable components.

WARNING   Even in a Plug and Play system, it is important to properly unplug a device if you wish to remove it while the system is running. If you don't do this, nothing may go wrong, but you can sometimes damage the device or cause the system to become unstable.

In Vista, you can add and configure devices from this interface (now called Hardware And Sound).

Driver Signing   This is an option first introduced in Windows 2000. To minimize the risks involved with adding third-party software to your Windows 2000 Professional machine, Microsoft came up with a technique called *driver signing*. Installing new hardware drivers onto the system is a situation in which both viruses and badly written software can threaten your system's health. To minimize the risks, you can choose to only use drivers that have been signed. The signing process is meant to ensure that you are getting drivers that have been checked with Windows Vista/XP/2000 and that those drivers have not been modified maliciously.

Device Manager

Although you can make many hardware changes through the Hardware Wizard, it is often easier to use the Device Manager. We'll discuss the Device Manager in more detail later in this chapter.

Hardware Profiles

A hardware profile lets you start the computer with different hardware configurations. This ability is most useful on laptops, which often have docking stations, or at the very least are moved from place to place. You might have one profile that loads a network card driver and another profile that loads your laptop's modem driver, for example.

User Profiles (Windows 2000; on the Advanced Tab in Windows XP and Vista)

Unlike Windows *9x*, where *user profiles* are an optional setting, in Windows Vista, XP, and 2000 every user automatically is given a user profile when they log on to the workstation. This profile contains information about the user's settings and preferences. Although it does not happen often, occasionally a user profile becomes corrupted or needs to be destroyed.

Alternatively, if a particular profile is set up exceptionally well, you can copy it so that it is available for other users. To do either of these tasks, use the User Profiles box to select the user profile you want to work with. At that point, you will be given three options:

Delete Removes the user's profile entirely. When that user logs on again, they will be given a fresh profile taken from the system default. Any settings they have added will be lost, as will any profile-related problems they have caused.

Change Type Configures a profile as local (the default) or roaming. If a user works at two machines, each machine will use a different profile. Updates to one machine will not be reflected on the other. If you have a network, roaming profiles can be configured to allow a user to have a single profile anywhere on the network. Further discussion of this topic is beyond the scope of this book.

Copy To Copies a profile from one user to another. Often the source profile is a template set up to provide a standard configuration.

Advanced

The Advanced tab has three subheadings, each of which can be configured separately. They're not identical in Windows Vista/XP/2000, however. (This could also be called the Etc. tab rather than the Advanced tab.) Among its options are the following:

- Performance
- Environment Variables
- User Profiles
- Startup And Recovery

We discussed User Profiles earlier, so we won't cover it again here.

Performance (Windows Vista/XP/2000) Although it is hidden in the backwaters of Windows Vista/XP/2000's system configuration settings, the Performance option holds some important settings you may need to configure on a system. To access it in Windows 2000, on the Advanced tab click Performance Options. In Windows XP and Vista, on the Advanced tab click Settings in the Performance area.

Among the settings in the Performance window are the size of your virtual memory and how the system handles the allocation of processor time. In addition, in Windows 2000 this is the place to specify the maximum Registry size (through the Virtual Memory options). In Windows XP/Vista, you also use Performance to configure visual effects for the XP GUI.

WARNING Letting the Registry fill up is a serious problem. Although the default level is usually fine, if you think this may happen you should change this option. An extra 10MB today could save you a lot of pain tomorrow.

How resources are allocated to the processor is normally not something you will need to modify. It is set by default to optimize the system for foreground applications, making the system most responsive to the user who is running programs. This is generally best, but it means that any applications (databases, network services, and so on) that are run by the system are given less time by the system.

If the Windows machine will be working primarily as a network server, you may want to change this option to Background Services. Otherwise, leave it as is.

Environment Variables   There are two types of *environment variables*, and you can access either one by clicking the Environment Variables button:

User Variables   Specify settings that are specific to an individual user and do not affect others who log on to the machine.

System Variables   Set for all users on the machine. System variables are used to provide information needed by the system when running applications or performing system tasks.

System and user variables were extremely important in DOS and Windows 3.1. Their importance has been more subdued since, but this is the location where TEMP variables, the location of the OS, and other important settings for Windows reside.

Startup And Recovery   The Windows Vista/XP/2000 Startup And Recovery options are relatively straightforward. They involve two areas: what to do during system startup and what to do in case of unexpected system shutdown:

System Startup   The System Startup option defaults to the Windows OS you installed, but you can change this default behavior if you like. Unless you are *dual-booting*, only one option is available; but if you have another OS installed, you can change the Windows boot manager to load that as the default. You can also reduce the time the menu is displayed or remove the menu entirely. In Windows XP, you can also click Edit to edit the BOOT.INI.

If you choose to completely disable the menu on a dual-boot system, you will find that doing so may cause you annoyance in the future when you want to boot into a different OS but no longer have a choice to do so. Thus, you should always let the boot menu appear for at least two to five seconds if you are dual-booting.

System Failure   A number of options are available in the Startup And Recovery screen for use in case of problems. These include writing an event about the problem, sending out an alert to the network, and saving information about the problem to disk. These options come into play only in case of a major system problem, though.

Your options for handling system failures will be covered along with the troubleshooting information later in this chapter.

System Restore (Windows XP and Vista)

The System Restore tab lets you disable/enable and configure the new System Restore feature in Windows XP and Vista. When it's enabled on one or more drives, the operating system monitors the changes you make on your drives. From time to time it creates what is called a *restore point*. Then, if you have a system crash, it can restore your data back to the restore point. You can turn on System Restore for all drives on your system or for individual drives. Note that turning off System Restore on the system drive (the drive on which the OS is installed) automatically turns it off on all drives.

Automatic Updates (Windows XP and Vista)

The Automatic Updates tab in Windows lets you configure how you want to handle updating the OS. You can specify that you want to automatically download updates, notify the user when updates are available (but not automatically install them), or turn off the feature. You can also specify that you want the operating system to notify you again of updates you declined to download at an earlier point in time.

Remote (Windows XP)

The Remote tab in Windows XP lets you enable or disable Remote Assistance. Remote Assistance allows the local workstation to be used from a remote computer. This can help an administrator or other support person troubleshoot problems with the machine from a remote location.

Remote Assistance is enabled by default. It is handled at two levels. Just having Remote Assistance turned on allows the person connecting only to view the computer's screen. To let that person take over the computer and be able to control the keyboard and mouse, click Advanced, and then in the Remote Control section, click Allow This Computer To Be Controlled Remotely. We can also configure Remote Desktop here.

The Command Prompt

Although the exam is on the Windows operating systems, it tests a great deal of concepts that carry over from the Microsoft Disk Operating System (MS-DOS), which was discussed previously. MS-DOS was never meant to be extremely friendly. Its roots are in CP/M, which, in turn, has its roots in Unix. Both of these older OSs are command line–based, and so is MS-DOS. In other words, they all use long strings of commands typed in at the computer keyboard to perform operations. Some people prefer this type of interaction with the computer, including many folks with technical backgrounds (such as yours truly). Although Windows has left the full command-line interface behind, it still contains a bit of DOS, and you get to it through the command prompt.

Although you can't tell from looking at it, the Windows command prompt is actually a 16- or 32-bit Windows program that is intentionally *designed* to have the look and feel of a DOS command line. Because it is, despite its appearance, a Windows program, the command prompt provides all the stability and configurability you expect from Windows. You can access a command prompt by running the 32-bit CMD.EXE.

Three diagnostic utilities are often run at the command prompt: Telnet, ping, and ipconfig. All three are TCP/IP utilities (TCP/IP is the protocol that allows networked computers to use the Internet and is something you will probably see a lot of. It's discussed in detail in a later chapter.)

Telnet

Telnet is a protocol that functions at the Application layer of the OSI model, providing terminal-emulation capabilities. Telnet uses the connection-oriented services of the TCP/IP protocol for communications at port 23. With Telnet, the command to initiate the session is TELNET itself, or TELNET followed by an IP address or hostname to connect to a specific remote host.

The remote host system must be running a Telnet daemon or service, and after a connection is established, you must log on to the server by using a valid username and password (plain text) as if you were sitting at the server. If you connect to a remote host by using the Connect/Remote system option, you may be prompted for the information required for a Telnet session.

 Telnet shouldn't be used if possible. Telnet sends user ID and password information to the Telnet server unencrypted. This creates a potential security problem in an Internet environment. SSH provides a more secure alternative to Telnet.

Ping

Another useful connectivity troubleshooting tool is ping, which stands for packet Internet groper. The PING command sends out four 32-byte packets to a destination and waits for a reply. If you cannot make a connection to the remote host, you will get back the following:

```
Request timed out.
Request timed out.
Request timed out.
Request timed out.
```

Keep in mind that some Internet sites block pings as a precautionary security measure, so be sure to use a site that you know accepts them if you're using ping as a troubleshooting tool. Generally, you don't use any switches with the PING command. Just type in **PING *IPaddress*** or **PING *hostname*** and see if it works. However, switches are available to persistently ping (until we press Ctrl+C to stop pinging), change the packet size, change the number of packets sent, and various other things.

Along with IPCONFIG and PING, another handy connectivity troubleshooting command is TRACERT, or trace route. It traces the route between your computer and the destination computer and can help determine where the breakdown is if you're having connectivity problems.

Ipconfig

The ipconfig utility allows you to check on the TCP/IP settings of the machine. In a world where it seems every computer is connected to a network, you'll do a lot of network connection troubleshooting. The IPCONFIG command is one of the first ones you should use when troubleshooting why someone can't get on the network. In fact, it's often the first one I do use. The IPCONFIG command checks your computer's IP configuration. Table 6.4 lists useful switches for IPCONFIG.

TABLE 6.4 IPCONFIG Switches

Switch	Purpose
/ALL	Shows full configuration information
/RELEASE	Releases the IP address, if you are getting addresses from a Dynamic Host Configuration Protocol (DHCP) server
/RENEW	Obtains a new IP address from a DHCP server
/FLUSHDNS	Flushes the domain name server (DNS) name resolver cache

Running IPCONFIG can tell you a lot. For example, if the network cable is disconnected, it will tell you. Also, if your IP address is 0.0.0.0, you're not going to connect to any network resources. An address starting with 169.254 is an address that Microsoft automatically assigns if a DHCP server cannot be found; while this can allow you to continue to network, it will not allow Internet access. This is what is referred to as Automatic Private IP Addressing (APIPA).

If you get an IP address from a DHCP server but are having connectivity problems, a common troubleshooting method is to release the IP address with IPCONFIG /RELEASE, and get a new one with IPCONFIG /RENEW.

More often than not, when you release and renew an IP address, you'll get the same one you had before. This in itself isn't a problem. The idea is that you basically "reset" your network card to try to get it working again.

Administrative Tools

Microsoft has included a number of tools with each iteration of Windows to simplify system administration. While some tools have very specific purposes and are only used on rare occasions, you will come to rely on a number of them and access them on a regular basis. It is this latter set that we will examine in this section. These tools include the Task Manager, MMC, Event Viewer, Computer Management, Services, and Performance Monitor.

Task Manager

This tool lets you shut down nonresponsive applications selectively in all Windows versions. Ever since Windows 2000, it has also been able to do so much more: allowing you to see which processes and applications are using the most system resources, view network usage, see connected users, and so on. To display Task Manager, press Ctrl+Alt+Delete and click the Task Manager button to display it (in earlier Windows versions, you needed only press Ctrl+Alt+Delete). In Windows 2000, you then have to click Task Manager on the Windows Security screen. In Windows XP, whether the Security screen displays depends on whether you're using the Windows XP Welcome screen (you can change this setting on the Screen Saver tab of the computer's Display Properties). By default, in Windows XP and Vista, the Windows Security screen does not display if you press Ctrl+Alt+Del; instead, Task Manager opens right away or you are given a set of tasks, among them Start Task Manager.

You can also right-click on an empty spot in the Taskbar and choose it from the pop-up menu that appears.

To get to the Task Manager directly in any of the Windows versions that include it, you can press Ctrl+Shift+Esc.

In Windows 2000, the Task Manager has three tabs: Applications, Processes, and Performance. In versions since then, the Task Manager can include two additional tabs: Networking and Users. The Networking tab is only shown if your system has a network card installed (it is rare to find one that doesn't). The Users tab is displayed only if the computer you are working on has Fast User Switching enabled and is a member of a workgroup or is a stand-alone computer. The Users tab is unavailable on computers that are members of a network domain. Let's look at these tabs in more detail:

Applications   The Applications tab lets you see which tasks are open on the machine. You also see the status of each task, which can be either Running or Not Responding. If a task/application has stopped responding (that is, it's hung), you can select the task in the list and click End Task. Doing so closes the program, and you can try to open it again. Often, although certainly not always, if an application hangs you have to reboot the computer to prevent the same thing from happening again shortly after you restart the application. You can also use the Applications tab to switch to a different task or create new tasks.

Processes   The Processes tab lets you see the names of all the processes running on the machine. You also see the user account that's running the process, as well as how much CPU and RAM resources that each process is using. To end a process, select it in the list and click End Process. Be careful with this choice since ending some processes can cause Windows to shut down. If you don't know what a particular process does, you can look for it in any search engine and find a number of sites that will explain it.

Performance   The Performance tab contains a variety of information, including overall CPU usage percentage, a graphical display of CPU usage history, page-file usage in MB, and a graphical display of page-file usage. This tab also provides you with additional memory-related information such as physical and kernel memory usage, as well as the total number of handles, threads, and processes. Total, limit, and peak commit-charge information also displays. Some of the items are beyond the scope of this book, but it's good to know that you can use the Performance tab to keep track of system performance. Note that the number of processes, CPU usage percentage, and commit charge always display at the bottom of the Task Manager window, regardless of which tab you have currently selected.

Networking   The Networking tab provides you with a graphical display of the performance of your network connection. It also tells you the network adapter name, link speed, and state. If you have more than one network adapter installed in the machine, you can select the appropriate adapter to see graphical usage data for that adapter.

Users   The Users tab provides you with information about the users connected to the local machine. You'll see the username, ID, status, client name, and session type. You can right-click on any connected user to perform a variety of functions, including sending the user a message, disconnecting the user, logging off the user, and initiating a remote-control session to the user's machine.

Use Task Manager whenever the system seems bogged down by an unresponsive application.

MMC

Microsoft created the Microsoft Management Console (MMC) interface as a front-end that you can run administrative tools in. Many administrators don't even know that applications they use regularly run within an MMC. In Exercise 6.5, you will see how to use an MMC to interact with security templates.

EXERCISE 6.5

Changing the Minimum Password Age

Security templates can give you access to system setting and allow you to make policy changes. The Minimum Password Age setting defines how long a user must have a password before they can change it. The default is usually two days, but there can be little reason for a user to change their password every two days. This exercise walks through the steps of changing the minimum age to 10 days. To make this change, you must be logged in as a member of the Administrators group (or as Administrator) to be able to make this change.

1. Choose Start ≻ Run

2. Type **mmc** and press Enter. This opens a console window.

EXERCISE 6.5 *(continued)*

3. Choose File, then Add/Remove Snap-in. Beneath Add/Remove Snap-in, click Add and a list of available add-ins will appear.

4. Choose Security Templates and click Add.

5. Click Close.

6. Click OK.

7. Expand Security Templates.

8. Expand hisecws (high security workstation).

9. Click Password Policy, and the available policies/settings will appear on the right.

10. Double-click on Minimum Password Age and increase the value from 2 to 10.

11. Click OK.

12. Click File ➢ Save.

13. Close the console. A prompt will appear asking if you want to save your change to the hisecws.inf file. Click Yes.

Event Viewer

Windows Vista/XP/2000 employs comprehensive error and informational logging routines. Every program and process theoretically could have its own logging utility, but Microsoft has come up with a rather slick utility, Event Viewer, which, through log files, tracks all events on a particular Windows computer. Normally, though, you must be an administrator or a member of the Administrators group to have access to Event Viewer.

To start Event Viewer, log in as an administrator (or equivalent) and choose Start ➢ Programs ➢ Administrative Tools ➢ Event Viewer. From here, you can view the System, Application, and Security log files:

- The System log file displays alerts that pertain to the general operation of Windows.

- The Application log file logs application errors.

- The Security log file logs security events such as login successes and failures.

These log files can give a general indication of a Windows computer's health.

One situation that does occur with the Event Viewer is that the Event Viewer log files get full. Although this isn't really a problem, it can make viewing log files confusing because there are many entries. Even though each event is time- and date-stamped, you should clear the Event Viewer every so often. To do this, open the Event Viewer and choose Clear All Events from the Log menu. Doing so erases all events in the current log file, allowing you to see new events more easily when they occur.

You can save the log files before erasing them. The saved files can be burned to a CD or DVD for future reference.

Computer Management

Windows Vista/XP/2000 includes a piece of software to manage computer settings: the Computer Management Console. The Computer Management Console can manage more than just the installed hardware devices; in addition to a Device Manager that functions almost identically to the one that has existed since Windows 9x, the Computer Management Console can also manage all the services running on that computer. It contains an Event Viewer to show any system errors and events, as well as methods to configure the software components of all the computer's hardware.

To access the Computer Management Console in Windows 2000, choose Start ➤ Settings ➤ Control Panel ➤ Administrative Tools ➤ Computer Management. In Windows XP/Vista, you can access Control Panel through the Start button directly. In both operating systems, you can also access Computer Management by right-clicking the My Computer icon and choosing Manage.

After you are in Computer Management, you will see all of the tools available. This is one power-packed interface, which includes the following system tools:

Device Manager   Lets you manage hardware devices.

Event Viewer   A link to the previously discussed tool that allows you to view application error logs, security audit records, and system errors.

Shared Folders   Allows you to manage all of your computer's shared folders.

Local Users and Groups   Allows you to create and manage user and group accounts.

Performance Logs and Alerts   Shows you how your system hardware is performing, and alerts you if system performance goes under a threshold you set.

Computer Management also has the Storage area, which lets you manage removable media, defragment your hard drives, or manage partitions through the Disk Management utility. Finally, you can manage system services and applications through Computer Management as well.

Services

This tool is an MMC snap-in that allows you to interact with the services running on the computer. Select Start ➤ Settings ➤ Control Panel ➤ Administrative Tools and choose Services, and you will see those configured on the system. The status of the services will typically either be started or stopped, and you can right-click and make a choice from the context menu: Start, Stop, Pause, Resume, Restart. Services can be started automatically or manually, or be disabled. If you right-click on the service and choose Properties from the menu, you can choose the startup type as well as see the path to the executable and any dependencies.

Performance Monitor

The Performance Monitor differs a bit in versions, but has the same purpose throughout: to display performance counters. While lumped under one heading, two tools are available— System Monitor and Performance Logs And Alerts. The System Monitor will show the performance counters in graphical format. The Performance Logs And Alerts utility will collect the counter information and then send that information to a console or event log.

In Exercise 6.6, you will see how to work with Performance Monitor.

EXERCISE 6.6

Working with Performance Monitor

Performance Monitor's objects and counters are very specific; you can use Performance Monitor as a general troubleshooting tool as well as a security troubleshooting tool. For instance, you can see where resources are being utilized and where the activity is coming from. In this exercise, you'll use the Performance Monitor tool to become more familiar with its functionality.

1. Select Start ➢ Settings ➢ Control Panel ➢ Administrative Tools, and choose Performance.

2. Click the Add Counters button, and choose to add the Processor Performance object.

3. Add the %Processor Time counter, and then click Close.

4. Choose Start ➢ Search ➢ For Files And Folders and click the Search Now button without specifying any particular files to look for. Quickly change to Performance Monitor and watch the impact of this search on the processor. This action is time consuming and therefore will help you notice the changes that take place in Performance Monitor.

5. Run the same operation again, but this time change your view within Performance Monitor to histogram (click the two buttons to the left of the plus sign [+]).

6. Run the same operation again, and change your view within Performance Monitor to report (click the button directly to the left of the plus sign [+]).

7. Exit Performance Monitor.

The Registry

Windows configuration information is stored in a special configuration database known as the *Registry*. This centralized database contains environmental settings for various Windows programs. It also contains registration information that details which types of file extensions are associated with which applications. So, when you double-click a file in Windows Explorer, the associated application runs and opens the file you double-clicked.

The Registry was introduced with Windows 95. Most OSs up until Windows 95 were configured through text files, which can be edited with almost any text editor. However, the Registry database is contained in a special binary file that can be edited only with the special Registry Editor provided with Windows.

Windows Vista, XP, and 2000 have two applications that can be used to edit the Registry, REGEDIT and REGEDT32 (with no *I*). In Windows XP, regedt32 opens regedit. They work similarly, but each has slightly different options for navigation and browsing. In addition, REGEDT32 allows you to configure security-related settings for Registry keys, such as assigning permissions.

The Registry is broken down into a series of separate areas called hives. These keys are divided into two basic sections—user settings and computer settings. In Windows, a number of files are created corresponding to each of the different hives. Most of these files do not have extensions, and their names are system, software, security, sam, and default. One additional file that does have an extension is NTUSER.DAT.

The basic hives of the Registry are as follows:

HKEY_CLASSES_ROOT   Includes information about which file extensions map to particular applications.

HKEY_CURRENT_USER   Holds all configuration information specific to a particular user, such as their Desktop settings and history information.

HKEY_LOCAL_MACHINE   Includes nearly all configuration information about the actual computer hardware and software.

HKEY_USERS   Includes information about all users who have logged on to the system. The HKEY_CURRENT_USER hive is actually a subkey of this hive.

HKEY_CURRENT_CONFIG   Provides quick access to a number of commonly needed keys that are otherwise buried deep in the HKEY_LOCAL_MACHINE structure.

Modifying a Registry Entry

If you need to modify the Registry, you can modify the values in the database or create new entries or keys. You will find the options for adding a new element to the Registry under the Edit menu. To edit an existing value, double-click the entry and modify it as needed. You need administrative-level access to modify the Registry.

WARNING

Windows uses the Registry extensively to store all kinds of information. Indeed, the Registry holds most, if not all, of the configuration information for Windows. Modifying the Registry in Windows is a potentially dangerous task. Control Panel and other configuration tools are provided so you have graphical tools for modifying system settings. Directly modifying the Registry can have unforeseen—and unpleasant—results. You should only modify the Registry when told to do so by an extremely trustworthy source or if you are absolutely certain you have the knowledge to do so without causing havoc in the Registry.

Real World Scenario

Beware Editing the Registry

Just in case it hasn't sunk in yet, be careful editing the Registry. There is no Undo button, nor do you have the safety net of choosing not to save your edits before you close. Once you make the change, it's made, for better or for worse.

There have been countless examples throughout my career of people going in to edit the Registry without really knowing what they were doing. In many cases, making small changes to the Registry, without having a viable backup, means having to reinstall Windows. At the very least, this is inconvenient.

Windows can help in this regard if you are in a networked environment with Windows-based servers. You can create system policies that prevent users from performing certain tasks, and the most important task to restrict is running Registry editors.

Restoring the Registry

Windows Vista, XP, and 2000 store Registry information in files on the hard drive. You can restore this information using the *Last Known Good Configuration* option, which restores the Registry from a backup of its last functional state. To use this option:

- Press F8 during startup and then select Last Known Good Configuration from the menu that appears. You can also back up the Registry files to the `systemroot\repair` directory by using the Windows Backup program, or you can save them to tape during a normal *backup*. To repair the Registry from a backup, overwrite the Registry files in `systemroot\system32\config`.

- In Windows 2000, creating an *Emergency Repair Disk* (ERD) also backs up the Registry files (to floppy disk, in this case). To create an ERD, in Windows 2000, use the Backup utility.

- In Windows XP and Vista, the ERD has been replaced with *Automated System Recovery* (ASR), which is accessible through the Backup utility.

   Note that ERD and ASR are considered last-resort options for system recovery.

Virtual Memory

Another thing you may need to configure is *virtual memory*. Virtual memory uses what's called a swap file, or paging file. A swap file is actually hard drive space into which idle pieces of programs are placed, while other active parts of programs are kept in or swapped into main memory. The programs running in Windows believe that their information is still in RAM, but Windows has moved the data into near-line storage on the hard drive. When the application needs the information again, it is swapped back into RAM so that it can be used by the processor.

Random access memory (RAM) is the computer's physical memory. The more RAM you put into the machine, the more items it can remember without looking anything up. And the larger the swap file, the fewer times the machine has to do intensive drive searches. The maximum possible size of your swap file depends on the amount of disk space you have available on the drive where the swap file is placed:

- Windows XP and Vista configure the minimum and maximum swap file size automatically, but if you want Windows to handle the size of the swap file dynamically, you have to change the default setting by selecting System Managed Size in the Virtual Memory dialog box. We'll show you how to get there in a moment.

- In Windows 2000, Windows sets the minimum and maximum swap file size for you, and you can adjust these settings. Windows 2000 handles the swap file much the same as Windows XP. In Windows 2000 if you set a minimum and maximum size and the OS dynamically manages the swap file size within those parameters, 2000 automatically creates a virtual-memory swap file during installation that is approximately 1.5 times the size of installed RAM.

In Windows, the swap file is called PAGEFILE.SYS, and it's located in the root directory of the drive on which you installed the OS files. The swap file is a hidden file, so to see the file in Windows Explorer you must have the folder options configured to show hidden files. Typically, there's no reason to view the swap file in the file system, because you'll use Control Panel to configure it. However, you may want to check its size, and in that case you'd use Windows Explorer.

The moral of the story: As with most things virtual, a swap file is not nearly as good as actual RAM, but it is better than nothing!

To modify the default Virtual Memory settings, follow these steps:

- In Windows 2000, click Start ➤ Settings ➤ Control Panel. Double-click the System icon and select the Advanced tab. Then click Performance Options and, in the Virtual Memory area, click Change.

- In Windows XP and Vista, click Start ➤ Control Panel. Double-click the System icon, and select the Advanced tab. In the Performance area, click Settings. Next, click the Advanced tab (yes, another Advanced tab), and then, in the Virtual Memory area, click Change.

Note that in addition to changing the swap file's size and how Windows handles it, you can also specify the drive on which you want to place the file.

You should place the swap file on a drive with plenty of empty space. As a general rule, try to keep 20 percent of your drive space free for the overhead of various elements of the OS, like the swap file.

Do not set the swap file to an extremely small size. If you make the swap file too small, the system can become unbootable, or at least unstable. In general, the swap file should be at least as big as the amount of RAM in the machine.

Windows System Files

Among the things you must be familiar with in preparation for the A+ exam are the startup and system files used by Windows Vista, Windows XP, and Windows 2000. We will look at each of them individually, but Windows makes nosing around in the startup environment difficult, and so there is a change you need to make first.

To protect Windows system files from accidental deletion, and to get them out of the way of the average user, they are hidden from the user by default. Because of this, many of the files we are about to talk about will not be visible to you.

To make them visible, you need to change the display properties of Windows Explorer. We will show you how to do this in Exercise 6.7.

EXERCISE 6.7

Showing Hidden Files and Folders

Some of the more important files you will need to work on are hidden by default as a security precaution. Let's throw caution to the wind.

1. Open Windows Explorer.

2. Browse to the root of the C: drive. Look for the IO.SYS system file. It should be hidden and will not appear in the file list.

3. Choose Tools ➤ Folder Options. The Folder Options window opens.

4. Select the View tab, and scroll until you find the Hidden Files option.

5. Select Show All Files.

6. Deselect Hide Protected Operating System Files (Recommended).

7. Uncheck Hide File Extensions For Known File Types.

8. Click OK. You will now be able to see the Windows system files discussed in the following sections. For security reasons, you should set these attributes back to the defaults after you've read this chapter.

Windows Vista, Windows XP, and Windows 2000 are all based on Windows NT, and as such each of their boot processes uses the same key boot files as Windows NT did. In this section, we will discuss these files.

Key Boot Files

Windows Vista/XP/2000 require only a few files, each of which performs specific tasks. We will discuss them in the order in which they load:

NTLDR   Bootstraps the system. In other words, this file starts the loading of an OS on the computer.

BOOT.INI   Holds information about which OSs are installed on the computer.

BOOTSECT.DOS   In a dual-boot configuration, keeps a copy of the DOS or Windows 9x boot sector so that the Windows 9x environment can be restored and loaded as needed.

NTDETECT.COM   Parses the system for hardware information each time Windows 2000/XP is loaded. This information is then used to create dynamic hardware information in the Registry.

NTBOOTDD.SYS   On a system with a SCSI boot device, used to recognize and load the SCSI interface. On EIDE systems, this file is not needed and is not even installed.

NTOSKRNL.EXE   The Windows OS kernel.

System Files   In addition to the previously listed files, all of which except NTOSKRNL.EXE are located in the root of the C: partition on the computer, Windows Vista/XP/2000 needs a number of files from its system directories (e.g., system and system32), such as the hardware abstraction layer (HAL.DLL).

Numerous other DLL (dynamic link library) files are also required, but usually the lack or corruption of one of them produces a noncritical error, whereas the absence of HAL.DLL causes the system to be nonfunctional.

System Files Configuration Tools

The Msconfig system configuration tool that was available in Windows 9x doesn't exist in Windows 2000. It is, however, included with Windows XP and Vista. Some tabs in the Windows XP/Vista version of Msconfig are the same as those available in the Windows 9x version, such as General and Startup Tools. New tabs in the Windows XP version include Boot.ini and Services. The Boot.ini tab lets you modify the BOOT.INI file and also specify other boot options. On the Services tab, you can view the services installed on the system and their current status (running or stopped). You can also enable and disable services as necessary.

If you want to use the Msconfig configuration tool on a Windows computer system lacking it, you can do so by copying MSCONFIG.EXE from a Windows XP/Vista computer to the Windows 2000 computer.

The Msinfo32 tool, shown in Figure 6.17, displays a fairly thorough list of settings on the machine. You cannot change any values from here, but you can search, export, save, and run a number of utilities (accessed through the Tools menu option). There are a number of command-line options that can be used when starting Msinfo32, and Table 6.5 summarizes them.

FIGURE 6.17   The Msinfo32 interface shows configuration values for the system.

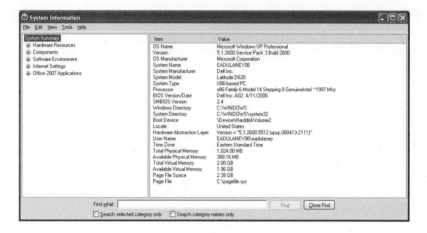

TABLE 6.5   Msinfo32 Command-Line Options for Windows XP and Vista

Option	Function
/category (only available in Windows XP)	Specify a category to be selected when the utility starts
/computer	Allows you to specify a remote computer to run the utility on
/nfo	Creates a file and saves it in .nfo format
/pch (only available in Windows XP)	Displays the history view
/report	Creates a file and saves it in .txt format
/showcategories (only available in Windows XP)	Shows category IDs instead of friendly names
/? (only available in Windows XP)	Shows the command-line options available for use with the utility

Another utility to know is the DxDiag (DirectX Diagnostic) tool, shown in Figure 6.18. This tool (which can be summoned alone, or from the Tools menu of Msinfo32) allows you to test DirectX functionality. When you start it, you can also verify that your drivers have been signed by Microsoft, as shown in Figure 6.19. DirectX is a collection of APIs (application programming interfaces) related to multimedia.

FIGURE 6.18 The DxDiag tool lets you test functionality with DirectX components

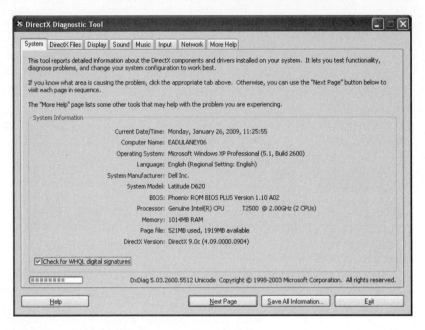

FIGURE 6.19 Verification that drivers have been signed

Disk Management

Where there are files, there are disks. That is to say, all the files and programs we've talked about so far reside on disks. Disks are physical storage devices, and these disks also need to be managed. There are several aspects to disk management. One is concerned with getting disks ready to be able to store files and programs; another deals with backing up your data. Yet another involves checking the health of disks and optimizing their performance. We'll look at these aspects in more detail.

Getting Disks Ready to Store Files and Programs

For a hard disk to be able to hold files and programs, it has to be partitioned and formatted. Partitioning is the process of creating logical divisions on a hard drive. A hard drive can have one or more partitions. Formatting is the process of creating and configuring a file allocation table (FAT) and creating the root directory. Several file system types are supported by the various versions of Windows, such as FAT16, FAT32, and NTFS. Windows 9*x*/Me and newer use FAT32, but they recognize and support FAT16. Windows Vista/XP/2000/NT also support a more robust file system type called NTFS (New Technology Filesystem) and recognize and support FAT16 and FAT32. The file table for the NTFS is called the Master File Table (MFT).

The following is a list of the major file systems that are used with Windows and the differences among them:

File Allocation Table (FAT) An acronym for the file on this file system used to keep track of where files are. It's also the name given to this type of file system, introduced in 1981. Many OSs have built their file system on the design of FAT, but without its limitations. A FAT file system uses the *8.3 naming convention* (eight letters for the name, a period, and then a three-letter file identifier). This later became known as *FAT16* (to differentiate it from FAT32) because it used a 16-bit binary number to hold cluster-numbering information. Because of that number, the largest FAT disk partition that could be created was approximately 2GB.

Virtual FAT (VFAT) An extension of the FAT file system that was introduced with Windows 95. It augmented the 8.3 file-naming convention and allowed filenames with up to 255 characters. It created two names for each file: a long name and an 8.3-compatible name so that older programs could still access files. When VFAT was incorporated into Windows 95, it used 32-bit code for improved disk access while keeping the 16-bit naming system for backward compatibility with FAT. It also had the 2GB disk partition limitation.

FAT32 Introduced along with Windows 95 OEM Service Release 2. As disk sizes grew, so did the need to be able to format a partition larger than 2GB. FAT32 was based more on VFAT than on FAT16. It allowed for 32-bit cluster addressing, which in turn provided for a maximum partition size of 2 terabytes (2048GB). It also included smaller cluster sizes to avoid wasted space (discussed later). FAT32 support is included in Windows 98/Me/2000/XP.

Older versions of Windows (Windows 3.*x* and Windows 95 original release) as well as all versions of DOS cannot read FAT32 partitions.

NT File System (NTFS) Introduced along with Windows NT (and available on Vista/XP/2000). NTFS is a much more advanced file system in almost every way than all versions of the FAT file system. It includes such features as individual file security and *compression*, RAID support, as well as support for extremely large file and partition sizes and disk transaction monitoring. It is the file system of choice for higher-performance computing.

When you're installing any Windows OS, you will be asked first to format the drive using one of these disk technologies. Choose the disk technology based on what the computer will be doing and which OS you are installing.

To create a FAT16 or FAT32 partition, you can use the FDISK command. To format a partition, you can use the FORMAT command. FDISK.EXE is available only with Windows 9*x*/Me (not Vista/XP/2000), and you can run it from a command prompt. FORMAT.EXE is available with all versions of Windows. You can run FORMAT from a command prompt or by right-clicking a drive in Windows Explorer and selecting Format. However, when you install Windows it performs the process of partitioning and formatting for you if a partitioned and formatted drive does not already exist.

WARNING   Be extremely careful with the FORMAT command! When you format a drive, all data on the drive is erased.

In Windows Vista/XP/2000, you can manage your hard drives through the Disk Management component. To access Disk Management, open Control Panel and double-click Administrative Tools. Then, double-click Computer Management. Finally, double-click Disk Management.

The Disk Management screen lets you view a host of information regarding all the drives installed in your system, including CD-ROM and DVD drives. The list of devices in the top portion of the screen shows you additional information for each partition on each drive, such as the file system used, status, free space, and so on. If you right-click a partition in either area, you can perform a variety of functions, such as formatting the partition and changing the name and drive-letter assignment. For additional options and information, you can also access the properties of a partition by right-clicking it and selecting Properties.

Windows Vista, XP Professional, and Vista support both basic and dynamic storage. Basic can have a primary and an extended partition, while dynamic can be simple, spanned, or striped. The partition that the operating system boots from must be designated as *active*. Only one partition on a disk may be marked active. With basic storage, Windows Vista, XP Professional, and Vista drives can be partitioned with *primary* or *extended* partitions. The difference is that extended partitions can be divided into one or more logical drives and primary partitions cannot be further subdivided. Each Vista/XP Professional/2000 hard disk can be divided into a total of four partitions, either four primary partitions or three primary and one extended partition.

NOTE   Basic partitions are a fixed size and are always on a single physical disk. Dynamic partitions can increase in size (without reformatting) and can span multiple physical disks.

Finally, there is the concept of a *logical partition*. In reality, all partitions are logical in the sense that they don't necessarily correspond to one physical disk. One disk can have several logical divisions (partitions). A logical partition is any partition that has a drive letter.

NOTE   Sometimes, you will also hear of a logical partition as one that spans multiple physical disks. For example, a network drive that you know as drive H: might actually be located on several physical disks on a server. To the user, all that is seen is one drive, or H:.

Backing Up the Data on Your Drives

Another very important aspect of disk management is backing up the data on your drives. Sooner or later, you can count on running into a situation where a hard drive fails or data becomes corrupted. Without a backup copy of your data, you're facing a world of trouble trying to re-create the data, if that's even possible or economically feasible. You also shouldn't rely on the Recycle Bin. Although it is a good utility to restore an occasional file or directory that a user has accidentally deleted, it will not help you if your drives and the data on them become unusable.

Toward that end, Windows has a built-in backup feature called, you guessed it, Backup. To access Backup, click Start ➤ Programs (All Programs) ➤ Accessories ➤ System Tools ➤ Backup. This will open the Backup Wizard. To move on to the Backup utility, click Advanced Mode.

The Backup utility in each of the different versions of Windows has different capabilities, with newer versions having greater capabilities. In general, you can either run a wizard to create a backup job or manually specify the files to back up. You can also run backup jobs or schedule them to run at specific time at a specific interval. Refer to the Windows Help system for in-depth information on how to use Backup.

Checking the Health of Hard Disks and Optimizing Their Performance

As time goes on, it's important to check the health of Windows computers' hard disks and optimize their performance. Windows provides you with several tools to do so, some of which we've already mentioned in this chapter. One important tool is Disk Defragmenter, which has existed in all versions of Windows except Windows NT.

When files are written to a hard drive, they're not always written contiguously, or with all the data located in a single location. Files are stored in numbered blocks on the disk similar to PO boxes—when they are written, they are written to free blocks. As a result, file data is spread out over the disk, and the time it takes to retrieve files from the disk increases. Defragmenting a disk involves analyzing the disk and then consolidating fragmented files and folders so they occupy a contiguous space (consecutive blocks), thus increasing performance during file retrieval.

To access Disk Defragmenter, click Start ➤ Programs (All Programs) ➤ Accessories ➤ System Tools ➤ Disk Defragmenter. In the list of drives, select the drive you want to defragment, and then click Analyze. When the analysis is finished, Disk Defragmenter tells you how much the drive is fragmented and whether defragmentation is recommended. If it is, click Defragment. Be aware that for large disks with a lot of fragmented files, this process can take quite some time to finish.

In Windows Vista/XP/2000, you can also access Disk Defragmenter through the properties of any partition listed in Disk Management. Click the Tools tab and then click Defragment.

File Management

File management is the process by which a computer stores data and retrieves it from storage. Although some of the file-management interfaces across Windows interfaces may have a different look and feel, the process of managing files is similar across the board.

Files and Folders

For a program to run, it must be able to read information off the disk and write information back to the disk. To be able to organize and access information—especially in larger new systems that may have thousands of files—it is necessary to have a structure and an ordering process.

Windows provides this process by allowing you to create *directories*, also known as *folders*, in which to organize files. Windows also regulates the way that files are named and the properties of files. Each file created in Windows has to follow certain rules, and any program that accesses files through Windows also must comply with these rules. Files created on a Windows system must follow these rules:

- Each file has a filename of up to 255 characters.

- Certain characters, such as a period (.) and slash (\ or /), are reserved for other uses and cannot be used in the filename. Periods are used to separate the filename from the extension, and the backslash is used to separate the directories in a filename.

- An extension (generally three or four characters) can be added to identify the file's type.

- Filenames are not case sensitive. (You can create files with names that use both upper- and lowercase letters, but to identify the file within the file system, it is not necessary to adhere to the capitalization in the filename.) Thus, you cannot have a file named working.txt and another called WORKING.TXT in the same directory. To Windows, these filenames are identical, and you can't have two files with the same filename in the same directory. We'll get into more detail on this topic a little later.

- In Windows 3.x and DOS, filenames were limited to eight characters and a three-character extension, separated by a period. This is also called the 8.3 file-naming convention. With Windows 95, long filenames were introduced, which allowed the 255-character filename convention.

The Windows file system is arranged like a filing cabinet. In a filing cabinet, paper is placed into folders, which are inside dividers, which are in a drawer of the filing cabinet. In the Windows file system, individual files are placed in subdirectories that are inside directories, which are stored on different disks or different partitions.

Windows also protects against duplicate filenames, so no two files on the system can have exactly the same name and *path*. A path indicates the location of the file on the disk; it is composed of the logical drive letter the file is on and, if the file is located in a directory or subdirectory, the names of those directories. For instance, if a file named AUTOEXEC.BAT is located in the root of the C: drive—meaning it is not within a directory—the path to the file is C:\AUTOEXEC.BAT. If, as another example, a file called FDISK.EXE is located in the Command directory under Windows under the root of C:, then the path to this file is C:\WINDOWS\COMMAND\FDISK.EXE.

The *root directory* of any drive is the place where the hierarchy of folders for that drive begins. On a C: drive, for instance, C:\ is the root directory of the drive.

Common file extensions you may encounter are .EXE for executable files (applications), .DLL for dynamic linked library (DLL) files, .SYS for system files, .LOG for log files, .DRV for driver files, .TXT for text files, and others. Note that DLL files contain additional functions and commands applications can use and share. In addition, most applications use specific file extensions for the documents created with each application. For example, documents created in Microsoft Word have a .DOC or .DOCX extension. You'll also encounter extensions such as .MPG for video files, .MP3 for music files, .TIF and .JPG for graphics files, .HTM or .HTML for web pages, and so on. Being familiar with different filename extensions is helpful in working with the Windows file system.

Capabilities of Windows Explorer

Although it is technically possible to use the command-line utilities provided within the command prompt to manage your files, this generally is not the most efficient way to accomplish most tasks. The ability to use drag-and-drop techniques and other graphical tools to manage the file system makes the process far simpler, and Windows Explorer is a utility that allows you to accomplish a number of important file-related tasks from a single graphical interface.

Some of the tasks you can accomplish using Windows Explorer include the following:

- Viewing files and directories
- Opening programs or data files
- Creating directories and files
- Copying objects (files or directories) to other locations
- Moving objects (files or directories) to other locations
- Deleting or renaming objects (files or directories)
- Searching for a particular file or type of file
- Changing file attributes
- Formatting new disks

You can access many of these functions by right-clicking a file or folder and selecting the appropriate option, such as Copy or Delete, from the context menu.

Navigating and Using Windows Explorer

Using Windows Explorer is simple. A few basic instructions are all you need to start working with it. First, the Windows Explorer interface has a number of parts, each of which serves a specific purpose. The top area of Windows Explorer is dominated by a set of menus and toolbars that give you easy access to common commands. The main section of the window is divided into two panes: the left pane displays the drives and folders available, and the right pane displays the contents of the currently selected folder. By default, in pre-Windows XP versions, along the bottom of the window, the status bar displays information about the used and free space on the current directory. Some common actions in Explorer include the following:

Expanding a folder   You can double-click a folder in the left pane to expand the folder (show its subfolders in the left pane) and display the contents of the folder in the right pane. Clicking the plus sign (+) to the left of a folder expands the folder without changing the display in the right pane.

The status bar is available in XP (Click View, then Status Bar). The Vista Details pane has similar information.

Collapsing a folder   Clicking the minus sign (–) next to a folder collapses it.

Selecting a file   If you click the file in the right pane, Windows highlights the file by marking it with a darker color.

Selecting multiple files   The Ctrl and Shift keys allow you to select multiple files at once. Holding down Ctrl while clicking individual files selects each new file while leaving the currently selected file(s) selected as well. Holding down Shift while selecting two files selects both of them and all files in between.

Opening a file   Double-clicking a file in the right pane opens the program if the file is an application; if it is a data file, it will open using whichever application the file extension is configured for it.

Changing the view type   Windows 2000 has five different view types: Large Icons, Small Icons, List, Details, and Thumbnail. In Windows XP, the Tiles view was added. In XP, you can still choose to view objects with icons, but you can no longer choose between large and small icons. The choices in Windows Vista are: Extra Large Icons, Large Icons, Medium Icons, Small Icons, List, Details, and Tile. You can move between these views by clicking the View menu and selecting the view you prefer.

Finding specific files   You access this option by using the Search button. You can search for files based on their name, file size, file type, and other attributes.

When you're searching, you can also use wildcards. *Wildcards* are characters that act as placeholders for a character or set of characters, allowing, for instance, a search for all files with a text (.TXT) extension. To perform such a search, you'd type an asterisk (*) as a stand-in for the filename: *.TXT. An asterisk takes the place of any number of characters in a search. A question mark (?) takes the place of a single number or letter. For example, AUTOEX??.BAT would return the file AUTOEXEC.BAT as part of its results.

Creating new objects   To create a new file, folder, or other object, navigate to the location where you want to create the object, and then right-click in the right pane (without selecting a file or directory). In the menu that appears, select New and then choose the object you want to create.

Deleting objects   Select the object and press the Del key on the keyboard, or right-click the object and select Delete from the menu that appears.

The simplicity of deleting in Windows makes it likely that you or one of the people you support will delete or misplace a file or a number of files that are still needed. In such a case, the Recycle Bin (mentioned earlier) is a lifesaver.

Besides simplifying most file-management commands as shown here, Windows Explorer allows you to easily complete a number of disk-management tasks. You can format and label floppy disks and, in some cases, copy the Windows system files to a floppy so that you can use a disk to boot a machine if you are running an old operating system such as Windows 2000. Windows 2000 requires a total of four floppy disks to boot.

Changing File Attributes

File attributes determine what specific users can do to files or directories. For example, if a file or directory is flagged with the Read Only attribute, then users can read the file or directory but not make changes to it or delete it. Attributes include Read Only, Hidden, System, and Archive, as well as Compression, Indexing, and Encryption. Not all attributes are available with all versions of Windows. We'll look at this subject in more detail in a moment.

Some attributes date back to DOS—such are Read Only, Hidden, System, and Archive. All others, such as Compression, Indexing, and Encryption, are a part of NTFS.

You can view and change file attributes either by entering **ATTRIB** at the command prompt or by changing the properties of a file or directory. To access the properties of a file or directory in the Windows GUI, right-click the file or directory and select Properties. Figure 6.20 shows the Properties screen of a file in Windows XP. In Windows XP, you can view and configure the Read Only and Hidden file attributes on the General tab. To view and configure additional attributes, click Advanced.

System files are usually flagged with the Hidden attribute, meaning they don't appear when a user displays a directory listing. You should not change this attribute on a system file unless absolutely necessary. System files are required for the OS to function. If they are visible, users might delete them (perhaps thinking they can clear some disk space by deleting files they don't recognize). Needless to say, that would be a bad thing!

File System Advanced Attributes

Windows Vista, XP, and 2000 use the NT File System (NTFS), which gives you a number of options that are not available on earlier file systems such as FAT or FAT32. A number of these options are implemented through the use of the Advanced Attributes window, shown in Figure 6.21. To reach these options in Windows 2000/XP/Vista, right-click the folder or file you wish to modify and select Properties from the menu. On the main Properties page of the folder or file, click the Advanced button in the lower-right corner.

FIGURE 6.20 The General tab of a file's Properties screen

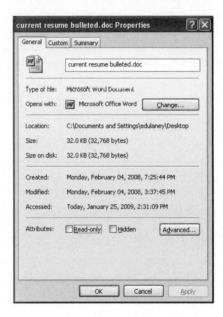

FIGURE 6.21 The Advanced Attributes window

On the Advanced Attributes screen, you have access to the following settings:

Archiving   This option tells the system whether the file has changed since the last time it was backed up. Technically it is known as the Archive Needed attribute; if this box is selected, the file should be backed up. If it is not selected, a current version of the file is already backed up.

Indexing   Windows Vista/XP/2000 implement a feature called the Index Service to catalog and improve the search capabilities of your drive. Once files are indexed, you can search them more quickly by name, date, or other attributes. Setting the index option on a folder causes a prompt to appear, asking whether you want the existing files in the folder to be indexed as well. If you choose to do this, Windows Vista, XP, and 2000 automatically reset this attribute on subfolders and files. If not, only new files created in the directory are indexed.

Compression   Windows Vista/XP/2000 support advanced *compression* options, which were first introduced in Windows NT. NTFS files and folders can be dynamically compressed and uncompressed, often saving a great deal of space on the drive. As with indexing, when you turn on Compression for a folder, you'll be prompted as to whether you want the existing files in the folder to be compressed. If you choose to do this, Windows automatically compresses the subfolders and files. If not, only new files created in the directory are compressed.

Compression works best on such files as word processing documents and uncompressed images. Word files and Microsoft Paint bitmaps can be compressed up to 80 percent. Files that are already packed well do not compress as effectively; EXE and zip files generally compress only about 2 percent. Similarly GIF and JPEG images are already compressed (which is why they are used in Internet web pages), so they compress a little or not at all.

Encryption   First introduced in Windows 2000 and also available in Windows XP and Vista, *encryption* lets you secure files against anyone else's being able to view them, by encoding the files with a key that only you have access to. This can be useful if you're worried about extremely sensitive information, but in general, encryption is not necessary on the network. NTFS local file security is usually enough to provide users with access to what they need and prevent others from getting to what they shouldn't. If you want to encrypt a file, go through the same process you would for indexing or compression.

Encryption and Compression are mutually exclusive—you can set one but not both features on a file or folder. Neither feature is available in XP Home edition.

If a user forgets their password or is unable to access the network to authenticate their account, they will not be able to open encrypted files. By default, if the user's account is lost or deleted, the only other user who can decrypt the file is the Administrator account.

File Permissions

Windows Vista, XP, and 2000 also support the use of *file permissions*, because these OSs use NTFS, which includes file-level file system security (along with share-level security).

Permissions serve the purpose of controlling who has access and what type of access to what files or folders. Several permissions are available, such as Read, Write, Execute, Delete, Change Permissions, Take Ownership, Full Control, and so on. The list is quite extensive. For a complete list, consult the Windows Help files. These are called *special permissions*.

Assigning special permissions individually could be a tedious task. To make it easier for administrators to assign multiple permissions at once, Windows incorporates *standard permissions*. Standard permissions are collections of special permissions, including Full Control, Modify, Read & Execute, Read, and Write. As we said, each of these standard permissions automatically assigns multiple special permissions at once. To see which special permissions are assigned by the different standard permissions, enter **File Permissions (List)** in the Help system's index keyword area.

Note that you can assign permissions to individual users or to groups. You assign standard permissions on the Security tab of a file or folder, which you access through the file or folder's properties.

In Exercise 6.8, we will show you how to examine file permissions.

EXERCISE 6.8

Examining File Permissions

Being able to set file permissions is a great reason to use NTFS. Here's how to examine file permissions:

1. Open Windows Explorer.

2. Right-click a file or folder and choose Properties.

3. Select and then examine the Security tab. The Security tab will not appear if Simple File Sharing is selected. If this is the case, you can turn off Simple File Sharing by selecting Tools ➢ Folder Options and clicking the View tab in the resulting dialog box. Then scroll down to the Advanced Settings area and deselect Use Simple File Sharing.

4. You'll see the users and/or groups to which permissions have been assigned. Select a user or group in the list and examine the list of standard permissions. (To add a new user or group, click Add and follow the prompts.) Any standard permissions that are checked in the Allow column are applied. If a check box is grayed out, this means the permission was inherited. To revoke a set of standard permissions, click the appropriate check box in the Deny column. If you click the check box in the Deny column for the Full Control permission, all other standard permissions are denied also.

5. Click Advanced to examine advanced options.

6. Click Cancel twice to close the file or folder's properties.

WARNING Be sure you don't accidentally make any changes you didn't intend to make. Changing permissions without understanding the ramifications can have negative consequences, such as losing access to files or folders. It is a best practice to limit Denied permissions. Unchecking Permit is better (you may need to turn off inheritance).

Summary

In this chapter, you learned about Windows, where it came from, the basics of Windows structure, critical boot files, and window management. Because Windows is a graphical system, the key to success in learning to use it is to click every option and examine every window. By exploring the system to find out what it can do, you will be better prepared to later decipher what a user has done.

First, we covered a brief history of Windows and operating system concepts. To understand why we are where we are today with operating systems, you need to know where they came from and how their features sprang from necessity.

Next, we covered the Windows interface. Among other things, we looked at the layout and components of the Desktop, the Taskbar, and the Start menu, as well as at basic icons present in default Windows installations. Next, we covered what the component that gives Windows its name (the window) actually is and how windows are used.

We then went over how Windows Vista, Windows XP, and Windows 2000 boot up, including critical files involved in the boot process.

Finally, we covered basic Windows management concepts. Concepts included managing disks, using file systems and managing files, and understanding directory structure.

With the basic knowledge gained in this chapter, you are now ready to learn how to install, upgrade, configure, and optimize the most popular operating systems in use today. These topics are covered in the next chapter.

Exam Essentials

Understand the fundamental reasons for choosing one operating system over another. The most important factor when choosing an operating system is to ensure that your hardware and software will be compatible with the operating system. If you have older hardware or mission-critical applications that will not run with the current version of Windows, for example, then it might make sense to run an older operating system.

Know what the critical Windows interfaces are and how to use them.   This list includes the Desktop, Taskbar, Start menu, icons, windows, Control Panel, the command prompt, My Computer, My Network Places, the system tray, and the Registry editor.

Know what the boot files are and the order in which they load.   The order is NTLDR, BOOT.INI, BOOTSECT.DOS (for systems booting into an older operating system, such as Windows 9x or DOS), NTDETECT.COM, NTBOOTDD.SYS (for systems using a SCSI boot device), and NTOSKRNL.EXE.

Know what file systems are available in Windows and what the differences between them are.   The two most commonly used file systems used on Windows Vista, XP, and 2000 hard drives are FAT32 and NTFS. (FAT16, often referred to as FAT, is also available but is much less efficient than FAT32.) FAT32 is older and perhaps a bit quicker for smaller hard drives. NTFS adds a bunch of important features, including security and auditing.

Understand how to manage files in Windows.   Nearly all file management is accomplished through Windows Explorer, including moving, copying, renaming, and deleting files and changing file attributes, advanced attributes, and permissions.

Review Questions

1. What is the Desktop?
   A. The top of the desk where the computer sits
   B. A tool that keeps track of all the data on disk
   C. Where all of a computer's memory is stored
   D. The virtual desk on which all of your other programs and utilities run

2. The screensaver can be changed in the _____ dialog box.
   A. Display Properties
   B. Taskbar
   C. Menu Bar
   D. Shortcut Menu

3. The Taskbar can be increased in size by _____.
   A. Right-clicking the mouse and dragging the Taskbar to make it bigger
   B. Left-clicking the mouse and double-clicking the Taskbar
   C. Moving the mouse pointer to the top of the Taskbar, pausing until the pointer turns into a double-headed arrow, and then clicking and dragging
   D. Highlighting the Taskbar and double-clicking in the center

4. Which of the following file attributes are available to files on a FAT32 partition?
   A. Hidden, Read Only, Archive, System
   B. Compression, Hidden, Archive, Encryption, Read Only
   C. Read Only, Hidden, System, Encryption
   D. Indexing, Read Only, Hidden, System, Compression

5. The Windows Explorer program can be used to do which of the following? (Choose all that apply.)
   A. Browse the Internet
   B. Copy and move files
   C. Change file attributes
   D. Create backup jobs

6. Standard permissions are _____.
   A. The same as special permissions
   B. Only the Read, Write, and Execute permissions
   C. Permissions assigned to users but not to groups
   D. Permissions grouped together for easy assignment

7. Virtual memory is configured through which system tool?

    A. Taskbar

    B. System control panel

    C. Memory Manager

    D. Virtual Configuration

8. If a program doesn't have a shortcut on the Desktop or in the Programs submenu, you can start it by _____.

    A. Using the Shut Down command

    B. Typing **cmd** in the Start Run box

    C. Using the Run command and typing in the name of the program

    D. Typing **cmd** in the Start box followed by the program name

9. What can you do if a program is not responding to any commands and appears to be locked up?

    A. Open the System control panel and choose Performance to see what process is causing the problem.

    B. Add more memory.

    C. Press Ctrl+Alt+Del to reboot the computer.

    D. Open Task Manager, select the appropriate task, and click End Task.

10. In Windows, a deleted file can be retrieved using which of the following?

    A. My Computer icon

    B. Recycle Bin

    C. Control Panel

    D. Settings panel

11. To turn off a Windows 2000 machine, you should _____.

    A. Run the Shut Down (Turn Off) command at a command prompt.

    B. Turn off the switch and unplug the machine.

    C. Press Ctrl+Alt+Del.

    D. Select Start ➤ Shut Down, choose Shut Down, and turn off the computer.

12. Which type of resource do you configure in Device Manager?

    A. Hardware

    B. Files and folders

    C. Applications

    D. Memory

13. To back up the files on your disks in Windows, which Windows program can you use?

    A. Disk Management

    B. Backup

    C. My Computer

    D. Windows doesn't come with a backup program.

14. Which of the following files bootstraps Windows XP?

    A. NTLDR

    B. BOOT.INI

    C. BOOTSTRAP.EXE

    D. NTBOOTDD.SYS

15. Which of the following partitions is specifically the partition from which the operating system boots?

    A. Primary partition

    B. Extended partition

    C. Active partition

    D. Logical partition

16. Which of the following Registry hives contains information about the computer's hardware?

    A. HKEY_CURRENT_MACHINE

    B. HKEY_LOCAL_MACHINE

    C. HKEY_MACHINE

    D. HKEY_RESOURCES

17. Within Windows 2000, what is the maximum length of a filename?

    A. 8 characters plus a 3-character extension

    B. 64 characters

    C. 255 characters

    D. Unlimited

18. Which of the following utilities will rearrange the files on your hard disk to occupy contiguous chunks of space?

    A. Disk Defragmenter

    B. Windows Explorer

    C. Scandisk

    D. Windows Backup

19. Which of the following is the name of the graphical interface included with Windows Vista?

    A. Start

    B. Aero

    C. KDE

    D. GNOME

20. Which of the following tools allows you to test DirectX functionality?

    A. Msinfo32

    B. Ping

    C. Telnet

    D. DxDiag

Answers to Review Questions

1. D. By default, the Desktop contains the Start menu, the Taskbar, and a number of icons. Because it is the base on which everything else sits, how the Desktop is configured can have a major effect on how the GUI looks and how convenient it is for users.

2. A. The screensaver can be changed in the Display Properties dialog box. To access this dialog box, you can either right-click anywhere on the Desktop and choose Properties from the context menu or open Control Panel and click the Display applet.

3. C. You can increase the Taskbar's size by moving the mouse pointer to the top of the Taskbar, pausing until the pointer turns into a double-headed arrow, and then clicking and dragging. Keep in mind that in Windows XP, you have to unlock the Taskbar first by right-clicking on it and deselecting Lock The Taskbar.

4. A. FAT32 does not have as many options as NTFS, such as Encryption and Compression. These attributes are available only on NTFS partitions.

5. B, C. The Windows Explorer program can be used to copy and move files and to change file attributes.

6. D. Standard permissions, unlike special permissions, have been grouped together to make it easier for administrators to assign permissions.

7. B. Virtual memory settings are accessed through the Performance tab or area of the System control panel.

8. C. To run any program, select Start ➢ Run and type the name of the program in the Open field. If you don't know the exact name of the program, you can find the file by clicking the Browse button. Once you have typed in the executable name, click OK to run the program.

9. D. You can use Task Manager to deal with applications that have stopped responding.

10. B. All deleted files are placed in the Recycle Bin. Deleted files are held there until the Recycle Bin is emptied. Users can easily recover accidentally deleted files from the Recycle Bin.

11. D. To turn off a Windows 2000 machine, select Start ➢ Shut Down, choose Shut Down, and turn off the computer.

12. A. Device Manager is used in Windows to configure all hardware resources that Windows knows about.

13. B. The Backup utility is provided with all versions of Windows, but it has different levels of functionality in the different versions.

14. A. The NTLDR file bootstraps the system (is the initial file that starts the operating system) and in turn loads the BOOT.INI. There is no file called BOOTSTRAP.EXE, and NTBOOTDD.SYS is called only if you're using a SCSI boot device.

15. C. The operating system boots from the active partition. Active partitions must be primary partitions, but a primary partition does not have to be active (as there can be up to four primary partitions per hard drive).

16. B. There are five basic hives in the Windows Registry: HKEY_CLASSES_ROOT, HKEY_CURRENT_USER, HKEY_LOCAL_MACHINE, HKEY_USERS, and HKEY_CURRENT_CONFIG. HKEY_LOCAL_MACHINE stores information about the computer's hardware. HKEY_CURRENT_MACHINE, HKEY_MACHINE, and HKEY_RESOURCES do not exist.

17. C. In Windows 2000 (and XP/Vista), filenames can be no longer than 255 characters. Under DOS, files were limited by the 8.3 standard of 8 characters plus a 3-character file extension.

18. A. Windows Disk Defragmenter rearranges files on your hard disk so they occupy contiguous spaces (as much as possible). Windows Explorer lets you view and manage files but not manage their location on the physical hard disk. Scandisk will check the hard drive for errors, and Windows Backup backs up files but does not manage their physical location.

19. B. The interface included with Windows Vista is called Aero.

20. D. The DxDiag utility (DirectX Diagnostics) is used to test DirectX functionality. Telnet is used to establish a remote connection, Msinfo32 shows configuration settings, and ping can let you know if a remote host can be reached.

Chapter

7

Installing and Configuring Operating Systems

THE FOLLOWING COMPTIA A+ ESSENTIALS EXAM OBJECTIVES ARE COVERED IN THIS CHAPTER:

✓ **3.3 Explain the process and steps to install and configure the Windows OS**

- File systems
  - FAT32 vs. NTFS
- Directory structures
  - Create folders
  - Navigate directory structures
- Files
  - Creation
  - Extensions
  - Attributes
  - Permissions
- Verification of hardware compatibility and minimum requirements
- Installation methods
  - Boot methods such as CD, floppy or USB
  - Network installation
  - Install from image
  - Recover CD
  - Factory recovery partition

- Operating system installation options
  - File system type
  - Network configuration
  - Repair install
- Disk preparation order
  - Format drive
  - Partition
  - Start installation
- Device manager
  - Verify
  - Install and update device drivers
  - Driver signing
- User data migration – User State Migration Tool (USMT)
- Virtual memory
- Configure power management
  - Suspend
  - Wake on LAN
  - Sleep timers
  - Hibernate
  - Standby
- Demonstrate safe removal of peripherals

✓ **3.4 Explain the basics of boot sequences, methods and startup utilities**

- Disk boot order / device priority
  - Type of boot devices (disk, network, USB, other)
- Boot options
  - Safe mode
  - Boot to restore point
    - Recovery options
    - Automated System Recovery (ASR)
    - Emergency Repair Disk (ERD)
    - Recovery Console

This chapter picks up from the previous one and rounds out the discussion of operating systems that you need to know for the A+ Essentials exam. As with the previous chapter, CompTIA wants you to know three operating systems for this exam: Windows Vista, Windows XP, and Windows 2000.

At some point, an operating system—one of these, or another—must be installed, reinstalled, or upgraded. Often, this is the case because you have built a new computer and need to install the OS to get the computer up and operating. Or you may have an older OS and want to upgrade it to the newest version. In either case, the ability to install an OS and configure it properly is an important skill to have.

In the previous chapter, Tables 6.1 and 6.2 listed the minimum system requirements for these operating systems. This chapter focuses more on installation methods and options. Before performing any installation or upgrade, you must back up your existing files to removable media. Doing so provides you with an insurance policy in the event of an unforeseen disaster and therefore is highly recommended.

Aside from installing operating systems, technicians are frequently asked to install new hardware devices. Along with installing the physical hardware, you must install the proper software to make the device work. This chapter looks at device driver installation, to help devices work problem-free the first time.

Finally, we'll look at a problem that really doesn't need to be a problem. It's when your perfectly wonderful computer starts showing performance issues and running slower, and slower, and slower. This problem can often be fixed by optimizing your Windows installation, and we'll end the chapter looking at how to do that.

Given the pending release of Windows 7, you may question the need to know information about these older versions of Windows. Nevertheless, it's tested on by CompTIA, and you should know the information given here in order to pass this exam.

File Systems and Directories

Before you can understand installation of an operating system, you need to know a bit about file systems and directory structures.

File Systems: FAT32 vs. NTFS

As explained in Chapter 6, "Operating System Features and Interfaces," a hard drive must be partitioned and formatted before it can hold files or programs. The basic building block of storage is the disk. Disks are partitioned (primary, logical, extended) and then formatted for use. With the Windows operating systems this exam focuses on, you can choose to use either FAT32 or NTFS.

Here's a quick review of these file systems:

FAT32   Introduced with Windows 95 Release 2, FAT32 is similar to FAT but has a number of advantages. It supports larger drives and smaller allocation units. As a comparison of how the new system saves you space, a 2GB drive with FAT16 has clusters of 32KB; with FAT32, the clusters sizes are 4KB. If you save a 15KB file, FAT needs to allocate an entire 32KB cluster; FAT32 uses four 4KB clusters, for a total of 16KB. FAT32 wastes an unused 1KB, but FAT wastes 15 times as much!

The disadvantage of FAT32 is that it isn't compatible with older DOS, Windows 3.*x*, and Windows 95 OSs. This means that when you boot a Windows 95 Rev B. or Windows 98 FAT32-formatted partition with a DOS boot floppy, you can't read the partition.

NTFS   This is Windows NT's file system. NTFS4 includes enhanced attributes for compressing files or for setting file security. Updating a FAT drive to NTFS is relatively easy and can be done through a command called CONVERT. This conversion doesn't destroy any information but updates the file system. NTFS4 was used only with Windows NT 4.0.

WARNING   Once a drive is converted to NTFS, it cannot be undone.

The NTFS system updated with Windows 2000 and is used with that OS as well as Windows XP and Vista. It includes enhancements such as file encryption. NTFS5 also includes support for larger drive sizes and a new feature called Dynamic Disks.

NOTE   Technically, the use of volumes changes partitioning to require one partition per disk that is then configured into volumes based on need. Therefore, partitioning is not gone—just modified.

When you're installing any Windows OS, you will be asked first to define the drive using one of these disk technologies. Choose the disk technology based on what the computer will be doing and which OS you are installing. Remember that NTFS offers security and many other features that FAT32 can't handle.

TIP   If you're using FAT32 and want to change to NTFS, the convert utility will allow you to do so. For example, to change the E: drive to NTFS, the command is convert e: /FS:NTFS.

When you install Windows, it partitions and formats the drive for you if a partitioned and formatted drive does not exist. See Chapter 6 to review how to create and format partitions yourself.

Once the disk is formatted, the next building block is the directory structure, in which you divide the partition into logical locations for storing data. Whether these storage units are called directories or folders is a matter of semantics—they tend to be called *folders* when viewed in the graphical user interface (GUI) and *directories* when viewed from the command line.

Files and Folders

Windows organizes files into *directories*, or *folders*. Chapter 6 describes the rules and organization for using and naming directories. Here we'll look at creating and working with directories and files.

Creating Directories

You can create directories from the command line using the MD command and from within the GUI by right-clicking in a Windows Explorer window and choosing New ➢ Folder. Once the folder exists, you can view or change its properties, as shown in Figure 7.1, by right-clicking the icon of its folder and choosing Properties.

FIGURE 7.1   Changing the attributes associated with a directory

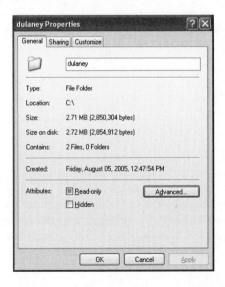

In the Attributes section, you can choose to make the directory read-only or hidden. By clicking the Advanced button, you can configure indexing, archiving, encryption, and compression settings.

Even though encryption and compression settings appear in the same frame on the dialog box, the two features are mutually exclusive.

Creating Files

The building blocks of directories are files. You can create a file either from within an application or by right-clicking, choosing New, and then selecting the type of item you want to create, as shown in Figure 7.2.

FIGURE 7.2 You can create files of various types with a right-click.

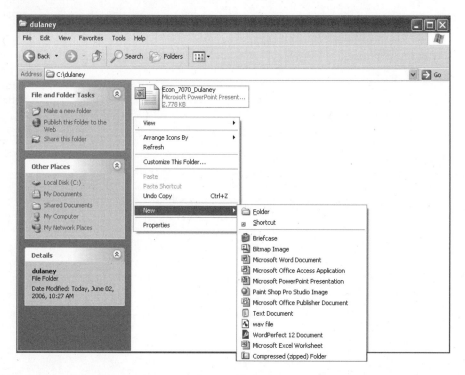

Once the file has been created, you can right-click the file's icon and change properties and permissions associated with the file by choosing Properties from the context menu.

Let's review how to change file attributes and permissions. If you remember this from Chapter 6, feel free to skip ahead to the section "Installing Operating Systems."

Changing File Attributes

File attributes determine what specific users can do to files or directories. For example, if a file or directory is flagged with the Read Only attribute, then users can read the file or directory but not make changes to it or delete it. Attributes include Read Only, Hidden, System, and Archive, as well as Compression, Indexing, and Encryption. Not all attributes are available with all versions of Windows. We'll look at this subject in more detail in a moment.

 Some attributes date back to DOS—such as Read Only, Hidden, System, and Archive. All others—such as Compression, Indexing, and Encryption—are a part of NTFS.

You can view and change file attributes either with the ATTRIB command-prompt command or through the properties of a file or directory. To access the properties of a file or directory in the Windows GUI, right-click the file or directory and select Properties. In Windows XP, you can view and configure the Read Only and Hidden file attributes on the General tab. To view and configure additional attributes, click Advanced.

System files are usually flagged with the Hidden attribute, meaning they don't appear when a user displays a directory listing. You should not change this attribute on a system file unless absolutely necessary. System files are required for the OS to function. If they are visible, users might delete them (perhaps thinking they can clear some disk space by deleting files they don't recognize). Needless to say, that would be a bad thing!

File System Advanced Attributes

Windows Vista, XP, and 2000 use NTFS, which gives you a number of options that are not available on earlier file systems such as FAT or FAT32. A number of these options are implemented through the use of the Advanced Attributes window. To reach these options in Windows Vista, XP, or 2000, right-click the folder or file you wish to modify, and select Properties from the context menu. On the main Properties page of the folder or file, click the Advanced button in the lower-right corner.

On the Advanced Attributes screen, you have access to the following settings:

Archiving   This option tells the system whether the file has changed since the last time it was backed up. Technically it is known as the Archive Needed attribute; if this option is selected, the file should be backed up. If it is not selected, a current version of the file is already backed up.

Indexing   Windows Vista, XP, and 2000 implement an Index Service to catalog and improve the search capabilities of your drive. Once files are indexed, you can search them more quickly by name, date, or other attributes. Setting the index option on a folder causes a prompt to appear, asking whether you want the existing files in the folder to be indexed as well. If you choose to do this, Windows Vista, XP, and 2000 automatically reset this attribute on subfolders and files. If not, only new files created in the directory are indexed.

Compression   Windows Vista, XP, and 2000 support advanced compression options, which were first introduced in Windows NT. NTFS files and folders can be dynamically compressed and uncompressed, often saving a great deal of space on the drive. As with Indexing, turning on Compression for a folder results in your being prompted as to whether you want the existing files in the folder to be compressed. If you choose to do this, Windows automatically compresses the subfolders and files. If not, only new files created in the directory are compressed.

Compression works best on such files as word processing documents and uncompressed images. Word files and Microsoft Paint bitmaps can be compressed up to 80 percent. Files that are already packed well do not compress as effectively; .exe and Zip files generally compress only about 2 percent. Similarly GIF and JPEG images are already compressed (which is why they are used in Internet web pages), so they compress a little or not at all.

Encryption   Encryption lets you secure files against anyone else's being able to view them, by encoding the files with a key that only you have access to. This can be useful if you're worried about extremely sensitive information, but in general, encryption is not necessary on the network. NTFS local file security is usually enough to provide users with access to what they need and prevent others from getting to what they shouldn't. If you want to encrypt a file, go through the same process you would for indexing or compression.

Encryption and Compression are mutually exclusive—you can set one but not both features on a file or folder. Neither feature is available in XP Home Edition.

If a user forgets their password or is unable to access the network to authenticate their account, they will not be able to open encrypted files. By default, if the user's account is lost or deleted, the only other user who can decrypt the file is the Administrator account.

File Permissions

Windows Vista, XP, and 2000 also support the use of file permissions because these OSs use NTFS, which includes file-level file system security (along with share-level security). Permissions serve the purpose of controlling who has access and what type of access to what files or folders. Several permissions are available, such as Read, Write, Execute, Delete, Change Permissions, Take Ownership, Full Control, and so on. The list is quite extensive. For a complete list, consult the Windows Help files. These permissions are called special permissions.

Assigning special permissions individually could be a tedious task. To make it easier for administrators to assign multiple permissions at once, Windows incorporates standard permissions. Standard permissions are collections of special permissions, including Full Control, Modify, Read & Execute, Read, and Write. As we said, each of these standard permissions automatically assigns multiple special permissions at once. To see which special permissions are assigned by the different standard permissions, enter **File Permissions (List)** into the Help system's index keyword area.

Note that you can assign permissions to individual users or to groups. You assign standard permissions on the Security tab of a file or folder, which you access through the file or folder's Properties.

> Be sure you don't accidentally make any changes you're not intending to make. Changing permissions without understanding the ramifications can have negative consequences, such as losing access to files or folders.

Installing Operating Systems

Operating systems can be installed in two generic ways: attended or unattended. During an attended installation, you walk through the installation and answer the questions as prompted. Questions typically ask for the product key, the directory in which you want to install the OS, and relevant network settings.

As simple as attended installations may be, they're time-consuming and administrator-intensive in that they require someone to fill in a fair number of fields to move through the process. Unattended installations allow you to configure the OS with little or no human intervention.

> Working in the computing field, you know that Windows 2000 is a decade old and that you would *never* install it on a system today, let alone "upgrade" another operating system to it. Sadly, that reality can cost you valuable points on this exam if you don't take the time to study properly. CompTIA specifically wants you to know about Windows 2000 and the intricacies of it. The domain, and corresponding objectives, list Windows 2000, then XP, then Vista. Take the time to read the Windows 2000 material carefully since you are unlikely to ever find it in the workplace, or have it at your disposal, and you are likely less familiar with it than you are with Windows XP or Windows Vista. The time you spend doing this will be rewarded when you pass this exam.

Windows 2000 Professional offers three main methods for performing unattended installations: Remote Installation Service (RIS), System Preparation Tool, and Setup Manager.

The RIS is a service that runs on a Windows 2000 Server. Client machines to be converted to Windows 2000 Professional access the server service and run the installation across the network.

The System Preparation Tool takes a completely different approach. Sysprep.exe is used to prepare an ideal Windows 2000 Professional workstation so that an image can be made of it (this requires a third-party utility). That image, which lacks user/computer-specific information and SIDs (Security IDs), can then be loaded on other computers.

Setup Manager is used to create answer files (known as uniqueness database files [UDFs]) for automatically providing computer or user information during setup. Setup Manager, like Sysprep, isn't installed on the system by default but is stored within the Deploy cabinet file on the CD beneath Support\Tools.

Windows XP offers similar installation options as well. For the exam, you should be familiar with the attended installation and know that the other methods exist.

Two methods that CompTIA lists in the objectives as installation methods— Recover CD and Factory Recovery Partition—are not so much installation options as they are reinstallation options that allow you to reinstall the operating system in the event of a system crash. Some manufacturers include a recover/recovery CD with their systems that are licensed to be used only for the purpose of recovering the system, while others include a fresh copy of the OS on a hard drive partition for this same purpose.

Determining OS Installation Options

One of the first steps in preparing to install an OS is to make sure you have enough and the right kind of hardware (see Chapter 6 for information on compatibility and minimum system requirements). In addition, you must make decisions about a few of the Windows installation options. These options control how Windows will be installed, as well as which Windows components will be installed. These options include:

- Installation type
- Network configuration
- File system type
- Dual-boot support

Installation Type

When you install applications, OSs, or any software, you almost always have options as to how that software is installed. Especially with OSs, there are usually many packages that make up the software. You can choose how to install the many different components; these options are usually called something like Typical, Full, Minimal, and Custom:

- A typical installation installs the most commonly used components of the software, but not all of the components.
- A full installation installs every last component, even those that may not be required or used frequently.
- A minimal installation (also known as a compact installation) installs only those components needed to get the software functional.
- A custom installation usually allows you to choose exactly which components are installed.

Some Windows Setup programs include a *portable installation* type as well, which installs components needed for portable system installations on laptops. It includes such features as power management and LCD display software.

All Windows versions use these, or derivations of these installation types, and you should decide ahead of time which method you are going to use (which may be dictated by the amount of disk space you have available).

Network Configuration

With many versions of Windows, you can choose whether to install networking options. If you do install networking, you can also choose (with some versions of Windows) which networking components you want installed. With Windows Vista, XP, and 2000, you also must know which workgroup or domain you are going to install.

File System Type

As Windows has evolved, a number of changes have been made to the basic architecture, as you might expect. One of the architecture items that had changed the most is the disk system structure. When you're installing any Windows OS, you will be asked first to format the drive using one of the available file systems (options are discussed earlier in the chapter). Choose based on what the computer will be doing and which OS you are installing. NTFS is generally used (and strongly recommended) unless you will be creating a dual-boot machine.

Dual-Boot Support

Occasionally, a mission-critical program (one you or your business can't function without) doesn't support the OS to which you are upgrading. There may be a newer release in the future, but as of this writing it isn't supported. In that case, you may have to install the new OS in a dual-boot configuration.

It is also possible, in some situations, to have a multiboot configuration where you can choose from a list of OSs. However, this setup makes it more difficult to choose compatible disk formats and often requires multiple disks to accomplish properly.

In a *dual-boot configuration*, you install two OSs on the computer (Windows XP and Windows 2000, for example). At boot time, you have the option of selecting which OS you want to use.

It is possible to multiple-boot to all Microsoft OSs, including DOS and all versions of Windows. Microsoft recommends that each installation be done to a separate disk (or partition) in order to avoid conflicts with built-in programs like Internet Explorer. In addition, you should install the oldest OS first and then proceed in chronological order to the newest.

For more information on dual-boot and multiboot configurations, visit the Microsoft support website at http://support.microsoft.com.

Thanks to the ability to create virtual machines (VMs), it is becoming far less common to need dual-boot machines today than in the past. Using VMs, you can run multiple operating systems (or multiple instances of the same operating system) on the same hardware at the same time and not need to reboot the system each time you want a different OS.

Determining the Installation Method

Another decision you must make is which method you are going to use to install Windows. Most versions of Windows come on a CD or DVD. CDs, because of their large storage capacity, are an excellent medium to distribute software, and DVDs have even greater capacity.

Windows 2000 and Windows XP each come on a single CD (not together, of course, but each on its own CD). Windows Vista is available on DVD or CDs. It is possible to boot to this disc and begin the installation process. However, your system must have a system BIOS and be capable of supporting bootable media.

If you don't have a bootable CD or DVD, you must first boot the computer using some other bootable media, which then loads the disk driver so that you can access the installation program on the CD or DVD. With Windows 2000, these bootable disks usually come with the packaged operating system or they can be created with the makeboot command.

There's one more thing to consider when evaluating installation methods. Some methods only work if you're performing a clean installation and not an upgrade. Table 7.1 shows you four common unattended installation methods and when they can be used. In the following sections, we'll look at each of these methods in a bit more detail.

TABLE 7.1   Windows Unattended Installation Methods

Method	Clean Installation	Upgrade
Unattended Install	Yes	Yes
Bootable Media	Yes	No
Sysprep	Yes	No
Remote Install	Yes	No

Unattended Installation

Answering the myriad of questions posed by Windows Setup doesn't qualify as exciting work for most people. Fortunately, there is a way to answer the questions automatically: through an unattended installation. In this type of installation, an *answer file* is supplied with all of the correct parameters (time zone, regional settings, administrator user name, and so on), so no one needs to be there to tell the computer what to choose or to hit Next 500 times.

Unattended installations are great because they can be used to upgrade operating systems to Windows Vista, XP, or 2000. The first step is to create an answer file. Generally speaking, you'll want to run a test installation using that answer file first before deploying it on a large scale, because you'll probably need to make some tweaks to it. After you create your answer file, place it on a network share that will be accessible from the target computer. (Most people put it in the same place as the Windows Vista, XP, or 2000 installation files for convenience.)

Boot the computer that you want to install on using a boot disk or CD, and establish the network connection. Once you start the setup process, everything should run automatically.

Sysprep

Another common unattended installation tool is the system preparation tool, or *Sysprep*. The Sysprep utility works by making an exact image or replica of a computer (called the *master computer*), to be installed on other computers. Sysprep removes the master computer's Security ID and will generate new IDs for each computer the image is used to install.

 All Sysprep does is create the system image. You still need a third-party cloning utility to copy the image to other computers.

Perhaps the biggest caveat to using Sysprep is that because you are making an exact image of an installed computer (including drivers and settings), all of the computers that you will be installing the image on need to be identical (or very close) to the configuration of the master computer. Otherwise, you could have to go through and fix driver problems on every installed computer. Sysprep images can be installed across a network or copied to a CD for local installation. Sysprep cannot be used to upgrade a system; plan on all data on the system (if there is any) being lost after a format.

There are several third-party vendors that provide similar services, and you'll often hear the process referred to as *disk imaging* or *drive imaging*. The process works the same way as Sysprep, except that the third-party utility makes the image as well. Then the image file is transferred to the computer without an OS. You boot the new system with the imaging software and start the image download. The new system's disk drive is made into an exact sector-by-sector copy of the original system.

Imaging has major upsides. The biggest one is speed. In larger networks with multiple new computers, you can configure tens to hundreds of computers by using imaging in just hours, rather than the days it would take to individually install the OS, applications, and drivers.

Bootable Media

For computers not connected to a network, images can be copied to a CD or DVD for local installation with an answer file you create. This is a quick way to perform a clean installation of an operating system without consuming all of your network bandwidth.

Remote Install

Windows 2000 Server and newer Windows Server operating systems have a feature called Remote Installation Service (RIS), which allows you to perform several network installations at one time. A *network installation* is handy when you have many installs to do and installing by CD is too much work.

 Beginning with Windows Server 2003, RIS was replaced by Windows Deployment Service (WDS). This utility offers the same functionality as RIS and is available for use with Windows Vista.

In a network installation, the installation CD is copied to a shared location on the network. Then individual workstations boot and access the network share. The workstations can boot either through a boot disk or through a built-in network boot device known as a *boot ROM*. Boot ROMs essentially download a small file that contains an OS and network drivers and has enough information to boot the computer in a limited fashion. At the very least, it can boot the computer so it can access the network share and begin the installation.

Preparing the Computer for Installation

Once you have verified that the machine on which you are planning to install Windows is capable of running it properly, you're sure all hardware is supported, and you have chosen your installation options, you need to make certain that the system is ready for the install. The primary question is whether you are planning to perform a fresh install of Windows or whether you are going to upgrade an existing system. We'll deal with upgrading later in the chapter; for now, we'll focus on new installations.

Preparing the Hard Drive

If you are installing Windows onto a system that does not already have a functioning OS, you have a bit of work to do before you get to the installation itself. New disk drives need two critical functions performed on them before they can be used:

- *Partitioning* is the process of assigning part or all of the drive for use by the computer.
- *Formatting* is the process of preparing the partition to store data in a particular fashion.

With older operating systems, you dealt with these two procedures by using the FDISK .EXE and FORMAT.COM commands. Running any sort of command on a machine that has no OS is impossible, though. You need a way to boot the computer—usually with a disk that is bootable.

For Windows Vista, XP, and 2000 the process is to boot up (which starts the installation process), partition the drive, and then format the drive.

Partitioning the Hard Drive

Partitioning refers to establishing large allocations of hard drive space. A partition is a continuous section of sectors that are next to each other. In DOS and Windows, a partition is referred to by a drive letter, such as C: or D:. Partitioning a drive into two or more parts gives it the appearance of being two or more physical hard drives. At the beginning of each hard drive is a special file called the *master boot record* (MBR). The MBR contains the partition information about the beginning and end of each partition.

> The size of a partition determines certain aspects of a file pointer table called the File Allocation Table (FAT). The larger the drive partition, the more space will be wasted on the drive. NTFS partitions are less wasteful of space than FAT partitions are, because of limitations in FAT cluster sizes.

Formatting the Hard Drive

The next step in management of a hard drive is formatting, initiated by the FORMAT command (or automatically by the installation program). When formatting is performed, the surface of the hard drive platter is briefly scanned to find any possible bad spots, and the areas surrounding a bad spot are marked as bad sectors. Then magnetic tracks are laid down in concentric circles. These tracks are where information is eventually encoded. These tracks, in turn, are split into pieces of 512 bytes called *sectors*. Some space is reserved in between the sectors for error-correction information, referred to as cyclic redundancy check (CRC) information. The OS may use CRC information to re-create data that has been partially lost from a sector. An operating system boot record is created along with the root directory. Finally, the File Allocation Table (FAT) or Master File Table (MFT) is created. This table contains information about the location of files as they are placed onto the hard drive.

Starting the Installation

The installation processes for operating systems has arguably gotten easier over time. Being able to boot to a CD and automatically begin the installation is an example. Although modern operating systems have more options for you to choose from, care has also been taken to minimize the stress involved in the process. In the next sections, we will look at the installation of Windows Vista, XP, and 2000.

Installing Windows 2000

While a bit more complex than installing Vista or XP, installing Windows 2000 is much easier than the Windows *9x* Setup. Make sure you have at least the minimum required hardware before you begin—but really, go for at least the recommended level of hardware. (See Chapter 6 to review minimum and recommended levels of hardware.)

Accessing the Setup Files

To start the install process, place the Windows 2000 Professional CD into the CD-ROM drive and restart the computer. After the POST routine for the computer has completed, a message appears that says *Press any key to boot from CD*. Hit a key, any key, and the Windows 2000 Setup program will start.

That is a "perfect world" situation, and sometimes reality intrudes. If the *Press any key* message does not appear, that generally means your PC is not configured to boot from CD-ROM or does not have that capability. In such a case, you need to do one of two things:

- Go into the BIOS to set the machine to boot to its CD drive. Consult your computer's user guide for more information about examining and making changes to the BIOS.

- Create and use Windows 2000 boot disks to start the setup.

Starting a Windows 2000 Installation

The startup options we've listed all eventually lead you to the same point: executing the Setup routine for Windows 2000 Professional. Professional has two different executables used to start Setup, depending on the OS you are using to start the install. These executables are WINNT (a 16-bit command used when running the command from a system using DOS or Windows 3.*x*), and WINNT32 (a 32-bit command for 9*x*/NT/2000). These commands have various options associated with them, as shown in Table 7.2.

TABLE 7.2 Common WINNT.EXE Options

Option	Function
/s:*sourcepath*	Allows you to specify the location of the Windows 2000 source files.
/t:*tempdrive*	Allows you to specify the drive that Setup uses to store temporary installation files.
/u:*answer file*	Used in an unattended installation to provide responses to questions the user would normally be prompted for.
/udf:*id* [,UDB_file]	If you are installing numerous machines, each must have a unique computer name. This setting lets you specify a file with unique values for these settings.
/e:*command*	Allows you to add a command (such as a batch script) to execute at the end of Setup.
/a	Tells Setup to enable accessibility options.
/s:*sourcepath*	Allows you to specify the location of the Windows 2000 source files.

TABLE 7.2   Common WINNT.EXE Options *(continued)*

Option	Function
/tempdrive:*drive_letter*	Allows you to specify the drive Setup uses to store temporary installation files.
/unattend	Used to run the install without user intervention.
/unattend[*num*]:[*answer_file*]	Allows you to specify custom settings for machines during an unattended installation.
/cmd:*command_line*	Executes a command (such as a batch file at the end of Setup).
/debug[*level*]:[*filename*]	Used to troubleshoot problems during an upgrade.
/udf:*id*[,*UDB_file*]	Allows certain values that need to be unique to be set separately for each machine installed.
/checkupgradeonly	Performs all the steps of an upgrade, but only as a test. The results are saved to an UPGRADE.TXT file that can be examined for potential problems.
/makelocalsource	Specifies that the i386 installation directory from the CD should be copied to the hard drive, allowing for easier updates later.

If you start the install from CD-ROM or create the Windows 2000 boot disks, WINNT. EXE starts the install by loading a number of files and then presents you with a screen that says *Welcome to Setup*.

Partitioning the Drive in Windows 2000

To start Setup, click Enter at the welcome screen, and you will be shown a list of the partitions currently configured on the machine. If one of them is acceptable, select that partition and click Enter. If you wish to create a new partition, you can do so using the Setup program itself, which replaces Fdisk as a way to set up the system's hard drive(s).

To delete an existing partition, highlight the partition and press D. You will be asked to confirm your choice and will be reminded that all information on the partition will be lost. If the disk is new or if the old information is no longer needed, this is fine.

If you are not sure what is on the drive, find out before you repartition it!

WARNING

To create a new partition, highlight some free space and press C. You will be asked how big you want the partition to be. Remember that Windows 2000 Professional wants you to have about 2GB as a minimum, but the partition can be as large as the entire drive.

Formatting the Partition in Windows 2000

Once you have created or decided on a partition to use, you are asked to format that partition. In doing so, you need to choose between NTFS and the FAT filesystem. FAT is the file system of DOS, and its advantages include the following:

- Compatible with DOS and Windows 9x dual-boot configurations
- Excellent speed on small drives
- Accessible and modifiable with many standard DOS disk utilities

NTFS, as you might expect, comes from Windows NT and is a more sophisticated file system that has a number of enhancements that set it apart from FAT:

- Supports larger partition sizes than FAT
- Allows for file-level security to protect system resources
- Supports compression, encryption, disk quotas, and file ownership

 In most cases, you will find that it is better to go with NTFS.

When you choose one of the format options, the machine formats the installation partition. This generally takes a few minutes, even on a fast PC.

Installing Windows 2000

After the installation partition is formatted, the system checks the new partition for errors and then begins to copy files. While the files are being copied, a progress indicator displays on the screen showing you how far along the process is. Windows installs files into temporary installation folders on the drive and asks you to reboot once the copy is complete. If you do not reboot within 15 seconds of the end of the file copy, the system automatically reboots for you.

 If Setup detects any problems during the partition check, it attempts to fix them and immediately asks you to reboot. At that point the install will need to start over. If problems are found, this often indicates problems with the hard drive, and you may want to run a full ScanDisk before returning to the install.

When Windows 2000 Professional reboots, it automatically brings you into a graphical setup that resembles a massive Windows wizard (see Figure 7.3). This is generally referred to as the graphical phase of Windows 2000 Setup, due to the contrast between this phase and the earlier blue-background-and-text text phase where you configured partitions and copied temporary files.

FIGURE 7.3   The Windows 2000 Setup Wizard

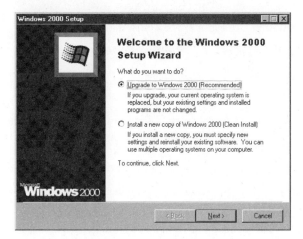

During this phase, Windows attempts to identify and configure the hardware in the computer, which may take a few minutes. One of the more unsettling parts of Setup occurs during this time, because the screen flickers—and often goes completely black—while monitor detection occurs.

Windows 2000 came packaged with drivers that allowed it to identify and load most hardware. Still, not all devices have compatible drivers on the Windows 2000 CD. If your hardware is not detected during startup, you can install additional device drivers after Setup completes, as shown later in the chapter.

After hardware detection is completed, the ever-polite Windows 2000 Setup Wizard welcomes you once again. To move through the wizard, click the Next and Back buttons along the bottom of the window. The screens of the setup process are as follows:

Regional Settings   The first screen rarely needs to be modified if you are configuring the machine for use in the United States, but users in other countries will find that this is where they can change keyboard and language settings.

Personalize Your Software   Enter the name (required) and organization (optional) of the person to whom the software is registered. Both fields are just text boxes. Enter any values that apply.

Personalize Your Software   If you're using a retail version of the OS, you will be prompted for the 25-character product key. You must enter it to proceed.

Computer Name and Administrator Password   The *computer name* is the name by which a machine will be known if it participates on a network. This name is generally 15 characters or fewer. The administrator password is used to protect access to the powerful Administrator account. Unlike Windows 9*x*, where usernames and password security are optional, all users must log on with a username and password to use a Windows 2000 Professional Desktop.

Modem Dialing Information   If a modem has been detected, you are asked for country, area code, and dialing preference information. If you do not have a modem, this screen is skipped.

Date and Time Settings   The Date and Time dialog box also has time zone and daylight savings time information. Any data on this screen can easily be changed later.

Networking Settings/Installing Components   After you enter the date and time, you will wait a minute or two as Windows 2000 installs any networking components it has found and prepares to walk you through the network configuration. As you are waiting, the Status area shows you which components are being installed.

Performing Final Tasks   The Final Tasks page reports on Setup's progress while it does the following:

> **Installs Start Menu Items**   Shortcuts are created to the applications and options installed during Setup.
>
> **Registers Components**   The Registry is updated with Setup information.
>
> **Saves Settings**   Configuration information is saved to disk, and other defaults and user selections are applied (such as area code and time zone).
>
> **Removes Any Temporary Files Used**   The temporary files saved to the hard drive at the start of Setup and used to install Windows are removed to free drive space.

Eventually, the wizard completes, and you are asked to reboot by clicking the Finish button. When the system restarts, Windows 2000 Professional Setup is complete, and the standard Windows 2000 boot process initiates.

Windows XP Installation

As of this writing, Windows XP is the most common end-user operating system in the Microsoft OS family as Vista has failed to catch on. Installing it is a breeze compared to previous editions of Windows. As a matter of fact, you can install it with a minimum of user interaction. Microsoft has designed Windows XP to be incredibly simple to install.

As with other versions of Windows, you will go through various phases of the installation:

- Starting the installation
- Text-based installation phase
- Graphical installation phase

Notice, however, that Windows XP does almost everything for you. It is a very quick OS installation.

This installation process assumes that there is no OS on the computer already. If there is, check out "Upgrading to Windows XP" later in this chapter.

Starting the Installation

During this phase, you begin the installation of Windows XP, configure the disk system to accept Windows XP, and start the graphical phase of Windows XP Setup.

To start a Windows XP installation, as with the other Windows OSs, you must first check your prerequisites (hardware support, available disk space, and so on). Plus, you must ensure that your computer supports booting to a CD-ROM (most do these days, especially those that are able to support Windows XP).

Once you do, to start the installation power up the computer and quickly insert the Windows XP CD. If you don't do this quickly enough, you may get an *Operating system not found* message because the CD-ROM wasn't ready as a boot device (it hadn't spun up yet). If this happens, leave the CD in the drive and reboot the computer.

You may have to press a key on some systems. A phrase like *Press any key to boot from CD-ROM* may appear. If it does, press a key to do just that so you can begin the installation.

If the CD is inserted successfully, the screen clears, and the words *Setup is inspecting your computer's configuration* appear. After that, you'll see the Windows XP Setup main screen. Then the Windows XP main Setup screen appears, as shown in Figure 7.4.

FIGURE 7.4   Windows XP main Setup screen

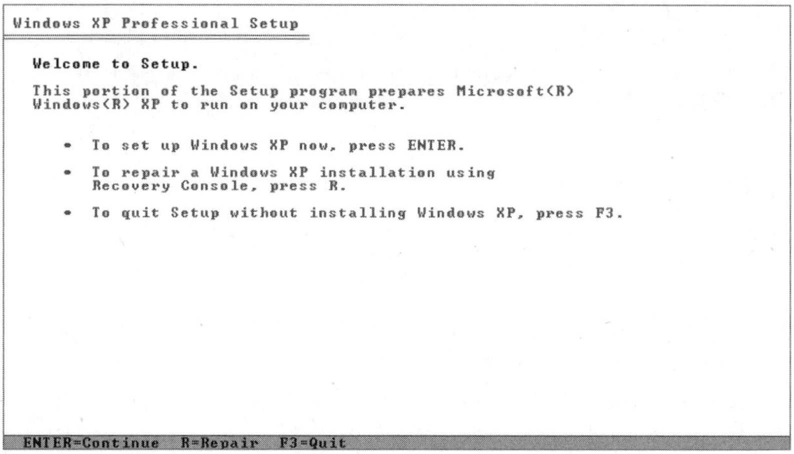

```
Windows XP Professional Setup
═══════════════════════════════════════════════

  Welcome to Setup.

  This portion of the Setup program prepares Microsoft(R)
  Windows(R) XP to run on your computer.

     •  To set up Windows XP now, press ENTER.

     •  To repair a Windows XP installation using
        Recovery Console, press R.

     •  To quit Setup without installing Windows XP, press F3.














  ENTER=Continue   R=Repair   F3=Quit
```

If your computer was produced after the release of Windows XP and you need to install a third-party SCSI, IDE, or RAID driver in order to recognize the disk drives, press F6 as soon as the screen turns from black to blue (Setup will prompt you at the bottom of the screen).

Text-Based Installation Phase

When the Setup screen appears, you can press Enter to begin the installation. The End User License Agreement (EULA) screen appears, which you must accept (otherwise you can't install Windows XP—as with other versions of Windows). Windows Setup then presents you with a series of screens similar to those in previous versions, where you can set up the disk to accept Windows XP with either FAT or NTFS. It is best to choose NTFS for performance reasons.

Windows Setup now formats the partition as you specified and copies the files needed to start the graphical portion of Setup. When it's finished copying and unpacking the files, Setup reboots the computer and starts the graphical portion of Windows XP Setup. If all is successful, you will see a screen similar to that in Figure 7.5.

FIGURE 7.5   Windows XP Setup

Graphical Installation Phase

During the graphical installation phase, Windows XP Setup performs almost all of the actions necessary to bring Windows XP to a functional level. The first thing it does is copy files to the hard disk and begin installing devices (as shown in Figure 7.6). This process takes several minutes and should not be interrupted.

Now, follow these steps:

1. Setup asks you for regional and language settings. The defaults are English (United States) for the language, United States for the location, and US Keyboard Layout for the default text-input method. If you are in a different location or prefer a different input method, you can change either item by clicking the button next to that item (Customize for language and location, Details for text-input method). If you accept the displayed options, click Next to continue the installation.

2. Identify yourself to Windows XP Setup by entering your name and company.

FIGURE 7.6   Installing devices in Windows XP Setup

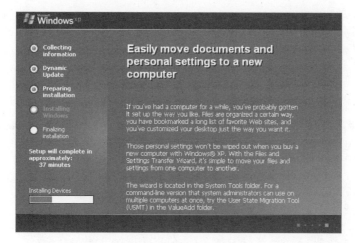

3. Windows asks you for the product key. You must enter the product key that comes with your version of Windows XP. This product key can be used only on this computer. To prevent product key theft, Microsoft requires that you go through product activation after the installation is complete.

4. Enter a computer name to identify this computer. Use something that will be completely unique on the entire network. Windows XP Setup suggests a name automatically, but you can overwrite it and choose your own. You also must enter a password for the Administrator user account (just as with Windows 2000).

5. Set the time, date, and time zone, as well as whether to adjust for daylight saving time. Click Next.

6. Setup prompts you for the network setup information. You can either have Setup install the network for you or choose the settings yourself. My personal preference is to accept the Typical Settings option and to go back and configure them later if they don't work. The typical settings include TCP/IP set to get its IP address automatically via DHCP (most networks are configured this way).

7. Setup asks you if you want to use a workgroup or a domain, similar to the installation of Windows 2000. Select either choice and continue.

8. Windows finishes the installation by copying all the remaining necessary files, puts items on the Start menu, builds the Registry, and cleans up after itself. This last step should take several minutes to complete. When it's finished, Setup reboots the computer.

Upon reboot, Windows automatically adjusts the screen size for optimum use. You are presented with a screen welcoming you to Windows XP. It walks you through connecting your computer to the Internet and registering and activating your copy of Windows XP, asks you for the names of people who are going to use this computer, and then presents you with the login screen (Figure 7.7). Click on a username you want to log in as, and Windows XP will present you with a Desktop (Figure 7.8).

FIGURE 7.7 A Windows XP login screen

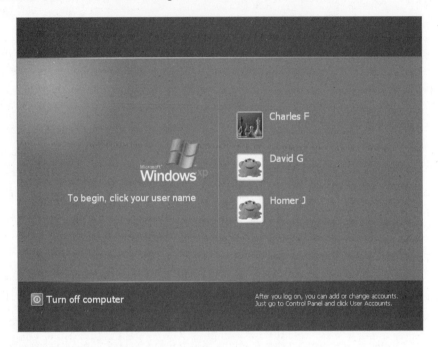

FIGURE 7.8 A Windows XP Desktop

Windows Vista Installation

As of this writing, Windows Vista is the most current Windows version available, but Windows 7 is slated for release. You can install Windows Vista on a machine as a clean install (discussed here) or upgrade the existing operating system to Vista (discussed later in this chapter).

There are two methods of running a clean installation (which deletes all data currently on your computer). The first is to start the computer with the bootable Windows Vista DVD (CDs are available if you need them) and run begin the installation.

The second method—the one Microsoft recommends—is that you run Setup from the DVD within your current Windows version. Once the DVD is inserted, the Setup program should automatically begin (if it does not, run `setup.exe` from the root folder) and a menu appears. On the menu, choose Install Now and then select Custom (advanced) when the Which Type Of Installation Do You Want? screen appears. Answer the prompts to walk through the installation.

If booting from the DVD, you will get a message upon startup that tells you to Press Any Key To Boot From CD, and at this point you simply press a key (don't worry that it is a DVD and not a CD) and walk through the installation.

Windows Activation

Windows Vista and XP require a process known as product activation. To curb software piracy, Microsoft requires that each copy of Windows now be *activated* (either by phone or Internet) after installation. Without activation, you can run the operating system, but use it for only a limited number of days. During that period of time, Windows will constantly remind you to activate your product.

In addition, the activation records what kind(s) of hardware are in your system, and if three or more pieces change, it requires you to activate again. It's somewhat of a hassle on the part of a system owner if they are constantly upgrading systems. However, some types of Windows distributions don't require activation (like those under volume license agreements with Microsoft).

The activation process is simple. After installation is complete, a wizard pops up, asking if you want to activate Windows. You can choose either the Internet or Phone option. If you have a connection to the Internet, the Activation Wizard asks you only which country you live in. No other personal information is required. You can then click Activate, and the Activation Wizard will send a unique identifier built from the different types of hardware in your system across the Internet to Microsoft's activation servers. These servers will send back a code to the Activation Wizard that activates your copy of Windows. The phone process is similar, but you must enter the code manually after calling Microsoft and receiving it.

Postinstallation Routines

Even though you have installed your OS, you are not quite finished. There are a few items you must do in order to be truly finished. These items include the following:

- Updating drivers
- Restoring user data files
- Verifying installation

If you don't perform these tasks, you will find using the newly installed OS less than enjoyable.

Updating Drivers

After you have gotten the OS up and running, you may find that a few items aren't configured or working properly. That is somewhat typical. The drivers for some hardware aren't found on the Windows installation disc. Or, more commonly, the drivers on the installation disc are horribly out of date. It's a good idea, then, to go back after an installation and update the drivers for your hardware.

You should check the version of drivers for the following hardware against their manufacturer's website and ensure you have the most current driver for that item:

- Motherboard and chipset
- Video card
- Network card
- Sound card
- Disk controller

To update a driver, download the appropriate driver file package from the hardware manufacturer's website, extract it, and either run the setup utility that is included or use the Add Hardware Wizard that comes Windows Vista, XP, and 2000.

Adding the /sos option to the operating system option in the BOOT.INI file will show the drivers as they're loaded in Windows XP and 2000.

The easiest way to see or change drivers in Windows Vista, XP, and 2000 is to click the Driver tab in the properties for the device. For example, to see the driver associated with the hard drive in Windows XP, double-click the hard drive in Device Manager (Start ➢ Control Panel ➢ System, and then click the Hardware tab and the Device Manager button), and choose the Driver tab. Among other things, this shows the driver provider, date, version, and signer. You can choose to view details about it, update it, roll it back to a previous driver, or uninstall it. We'll talk more drivers later in this chapter.

Restoring User Data Files

After you have installed an OS, you will want to use the computer. This involves installing applications and (if applicable) restoring data from either an older computer or this computer if you are reinstalling the OS.

Most often, restoring data files simply involves copying them from a different medium (such as a floppy disk, removable hard disk, magnetic tape, or other removable media). However, it can also involve copying the older data files from another computer. Windows Vista includes the *Windows Easy Transfer* tool (beneath System Tools on the Accessories menu), while Windows XP includes a utility known as the *Files and Settings Transfer Wizard* that will transfer most of your files and individual application settings from an old computer to a new one. You connect the two computers (either by LAN or by null modem serial cable) and run the wizard on both computers. The files and settings are transferred to the new computer without much trouble.

Verifying Installation

The last thing you should do after installing any operating system is perform a verification. It sounds easy enough, but many people forget to do it, and not doing it can come back to haunt you later. Simply reboot, again (not that the installation didn't reboot a few dozen times already), and log in as a user. Make sure all of the appropriate programs are there and all of the devices (such as the network card and video card) are working properly.

Upgrading Operating Systems

If you add an OS to a machine that doesn't currently have one (recently formatted, built from scratch, and so on), that is *installing*. If you add an OS so that you can dual-boot (choose which one to run at start), that is *installing*. If you replace one OS with another and attempt to keep the same data/application files, that is *upgrading*.

Whereas installation can typically be done over any existing OS, upgrading can only be done from OSs that are generally compatible with the one you're adding. For example, with Windows Vista you can upgrade to various versions based on the operating system that you are coming from. Table 7.3 lists the upgrade paths for each Windows Vista version based on the operating system you are coming from. Those listed as No must be clean installations.

TABLE 7.3   Windows Vista Upgrade Options

Existing Operating System	Vista Home Basic	Vista Home Premium	Vista Business	Vista Ultimate
Windows XP Home	Yes	Yes	Yes	Yes
Windows XP Professional	No	No	Yes	Yes

TABLE 7.3   Windows Vista Upgrade Options *(continued)*

Existing Operating System	Vista Home Basic	Vista Home Premium	Vista Business	Vista Ultimate
Windows XP Professional x64	No	No	No	No
Windows XP Media Center	No	Yes	No	Yes
Windows XP Tablet PC	No	No	Yes	Yes
Windows 2000	No	No	No	No

With Windows XP, you can upgrade to the Home version only from Windows 98 or Windows Me. You can upgrade to the Professional version from Windows 98, Windows Me, Windows NT Workstation 4.0, Windows 2000 Professional, or even from Windows XP Home.

Step-by-step upgrade information for Windows XP can be found at http://www.microsoft.com/windowsxp/using/setup/getstarted/default.mspx.

With Windows 2000, upgrades can only be done from the following programs:

- Windows 95
- Windows 98
- Windows NT Workstation 3.51
- Windows NT Workstation 4.0

WINNT32.EXE is the utility to use to initiate the upgrade. The Setup Wizard automatically creates a report of devices that can't be upgraded. Keep in mind that you must uncompress any DoubleSpace or DriveSpace volumes before you start an upgrade.

Upgrading to Windows Vista

Your ability to upgrade from Windows Vista is based on the operating system you are coming from (see Table 7.3). To begin an upgrade, download, install, and run the Windows Vista Upgrade Advisor from the Microsoft site: http://www.microsoft.com/windows/windows-vista/get/upgrade-advisor.aspx. This will check your system, verify that it can run Windows Vista, and give you a report of any identified compatibility issues.

To begin the upgrade, insert the DVD, and the Setup program should automatically begin (if it does not, run `setup.exe` from the root folder) and a menu appears. On the menu, choose Install Now and then select Upgrade when the Which Type Of Installation Do You Want? screen appears. Answer the prompts to walk through the upgrade.

 If you need CDs instead of the Windows Vista DVD, you can obtain them from `http://www.microsoft.com/windows/windows-vista/get/order-cds.aspx`.

Booting from the DVD is also possible, but recommended only if the method just described does not work. When you boot, you will get a message upon startup that tells you to Press Any Key To Boot From CD, and at this point you simply press a key (don't worry that it is a DVD and not a CD) and walk through the upgrade.

Upgrading to Windows XP

Upgrading to XP is quite simple:

1. Insert the CD and choose Install Windows XP from the menu that appears.

2. The Setup program detects that you already have an OS installed and presents you with a menu that says Upgrade (Recommended). Click Next to begin the upgrade.

3. Setup asks you to agree to the EULA, enter the product key, and download an updated version of the Setup program (if necessary).

4. Setup copies several files over, reboots a couple of times, and continues like a standard Windows XP installation.

Once you have finished the installation, you must activate it (like a standard installation of Windows XP), but that's about it. Windows XP Setup makes most of the decisions about the upgrade for you, so only a minimal amount of interaction is necessary.

Finalizing Your Upgrade

Now that you've completed your upgrade, you need to think about making this computer functional, like you would have if you had just installed a new operating system. The first step after a reboot should always be to make sure that the newest service patches and updates are applied. Fortunately, Windows 2000, Windows XP, and Windows Vista participate in the automatic *Windows Update* program, which will automatically download new patches if you allow it to. Still, when you've just performed an upgrade (or new installation), it's best to force this action by manually initiating Windows Update in the Start menu.

After your updates and patches are applied, verify that the user's data transferred properly, including checking to ensure that critical programs work. Finally, install any additional services that might be necessary—the computer is ready to go!

Migrating User Data

Installing an operating system would be simple if it weren't for users and the data that they want to bring with them. To simplify this task, Microsoft has offered a free tool for a number of years: Microsoft Windows User State Migration Tool (USMT). It allows you to migrate user files settings related to the applications, desktop configuration, and accounts.

Version 3.0 works with Windows Vista and XP, while previous versions—such as 2.6—also worked with Windows 2000. You can download this tool from http://technet .microsoft.com/en-us/library/cc722032.aspx. If all you are doing is a simple migration from one OS to another, you do not need this tool, but it is invaluable during large deployments.

Performing a Repair Install

There are occasions where a system will become unstable, and the operating system is suspected as a likely culprit. When this happens, you can attempt what is known as a *repair install*. The concept behind a repair install is simple: you want to fix the operating system but keep all of your user and data files. This is accomplished by running an upgrade of the operating system to the same operating system already running.

Both Windows XP and Windows 2000 include an option to press R during installation to repair the operating system. You would see this option soon as you booted from the installation media. This choice is not present with Windows Vista, but a repair install can still be done.

For example, assume that a workstation running Windows Vista becomes suspect. As always, run a full backup and hope that you don't need it. Next, insert the Windows Vista DVD in the DVD drive. It should automatically start. Click on Install Now and a few cursory screens will appear (asking for the product key, and so forth). You will come to the Install Windows dialog box; it will ask what version of Windows Vista to install and has an option at the bottom that you need to check: I Have Selected The Edition Of Windows That I Purchased.

Following this, choose Upgrade from the options, and the operating system files will be copied over with all user data and files maintained. The repair install will be complete.

Common Installation Problems

For the most part, the days of having to suffer through installation issues are a thing of the past. The wizards available in the Microsoft OSs tend to make installation errors much less common than they were with earlier operating systems. Several categories of errors and fixes that still crop up from time to time are as follows:

Installation disk errors   Retry the installation once more. If the errors persist, change to a new installation DVD or CD.

Inadequate disk space   Take corrective action to proceed with the installation, such as deleting temporary files and archiving old data.

Disk configuration errors   Make sure you're using hardware compatible with the operating system. Do this by checking for the presence of the Windows certified logos for each operating system you are using.

Can't connect to a domain controller   Verify that you're entering the correct username and password and that the Caps Lock key isn't on.

Domain name error   Reselect or retype the correct domain name.

Installing Device Drivers

Hardware devices come in all shapes and sizes, adding a variety of capabilities to your computer system. In this section, you will learn the specifics of installing device drivers for various types of peripherals. You will learn the methods of connecting a peripheral as well as the steps required to install a driver on Windows Vista, Windows XP, and Windows 2000.

As a technician, one task you will constantly be asked to perform is to install a device driver. A *device driver* (or just *driver* for short) is a small piece of software that allows the OS to communicate directly with a specific piece of hardware. Without the driver, the OS wouldn't know the special commands to send to the device to make it do what you want.

Most often, you will be adding a device or component to your computer in order to expand the computer's capabilities. Regardless of function, devices that you can install can be divided into two primary groups:

Plug and Play   *Plug and Play (PnP)* is a standard set of specifications that was developed by Intel to enable a computer to detect a new device automatically and install the appropriate driver. PnP makes a technician's job easier because the system already knows what hardware settings are in use, and it sets the new device's hardware settings (IRQ, I/O address, and so on) to appropriate, nonconflicting settings. Almost every new device introduced since 1995 is a PnP device.

Non–Plug and Play   If you have to configure a device's hardware settings manually in order to install it, the device can be considered a non-PnP device. These devices are nearly obsolete (but you'll still see them out there, hanging on) as manufacturers embrace PnP methods.

The basic process for installing these devices is the same for all versions of Windows. There are simply some minor differences in procedures and the appearance of the dialog boxes.

Rights and Security Issues

Whenever you are installing a new device, Windows Vista, XP, or 2000 may consider that process a security threat. After all, you might be installing some kind of snooping or monitoring device. Therefore, you must have certain permissions to be able to install a new piece of hardware in Windows.

The primary requirement is that in most cases, in order to install a device, you must be logged in either as an administrator or as a user who is a member of the Administrators group. However, if the device driver has a digital signature, Windows may consider it okay to install without the administrator's permission. A *digitally signed driver* is a driver that has been digitally "signed" by Microsoft with a special value that only Windows can read. This signature tells the Windows installer that the driver being installed has been tested for security and stability on the chosen Windows platform and that the driver is from a reputable source. Using digitally signed drivers increases the stability and reliability of your system.

WARNING   Although more and more companies are signing their drivers, many still do not. Microsoft's official stance on unsigned drivers is "Use them at your own risk!"

Another requirement to installing hardware without the administrator's permission is if the device can be installed without user interaction. That is, a window does not have to be displayed that requires the user to make a choice of some kind.

Basic Procedure for Device Installation

The basic procedure for installing any device into a Windows computer is the same no matter what version of Windows you are using or whether the device is PnP compliant. The process is as follows:

1. Locate drivers for the device.

2. Connect the device to your computer (either internally or externally).

3. Load or install the proper drivers.

4. Configure the device.

The last two steps will not require your intervention if the device you are installing is PnP compliant.

Keep in mind that these are general steps. Whenever possible, it is advisable to follow the manufacturer's exact instructions when installing any piece of hardware. Failure to do so may possibly damage the device and void the device's warranty.

Locating Drivers for the Device

Device drivers are software, and they are distributed much like any other software. Usually, a CD comes with whatever hardware you are installing. On that CD is the device driver for the OS version you have. Most driver CDs contain drivers for all possible compatible OSs (usually the version for each different OS is in its own directory). However, the drivers on these CDs aren't always the most up-to-date ones.

To find more up-to-date drivers, there are many places you can go. Often, if the OS you have installed is newer than the hardware in your computer, a more current driver may be on the operating system CD. The most current driver can often be found on the device manufacturer's support website. Go to that company's main website. Usually, the main page has a link to Support, Product Support, Download Drivers, or something similar.

Once on the support website, you download an archive file that contains all the driver files needed for your device (including any setup program and supporting utilities). Download it to a directory on your computer, and then double-click on the archive to open it and extract all the files (this may also start the installation program).

Connecting the Device

Connecting devices to your computer can be accomplished in many ways. There are several different ports and interfaces to your computer. Each one of them may be used to add a new device to your computer (or to upgrade an existing device).

Generally speaking, when you are connecting a device to the inside of your computer (either in an expansion slot or connecting to an existing expansion bus), you should power down the computer, unplug it, and wait at least 30 seconds before attempting to install or remove any device. This is necessary because power in the newer ATX-style motherboards remains supplied to the motherboard for at least that long until the capacitors in the power supply drain completely. Some motherboards have a small LED that indicates whether the board has power (even if the power switch is off). If your motherboard has one of these LEDs, wait until it goes out (usually 20 to 30 seconds) before attempting to add or remove a device.

 The procedure for USB devices is contrary to this rule. Generally, you install the driver and software for the USB device first and then plug in the device *while the computer is on*. Doing so allows the computer to recognize the new component and configure it properly.

To connect the device, follow the manufacturer's instructions and insert the card, plug in the cable, or connect the device in whatever method it uses. Make sure it is firmly secured before you attempt to power up the computer.

Loading or Installing the Proper Drivers

There are two main methods of installing device drivers. You can either use the setup program that comes with the hardware driver CD (or downloaded file) or use the Windows hardware installation wizard. Either method will get the software installed. However, if the driver is for a device that requires a monitoring utility (like a webcam utility for a webcam), you *must* use the setup utility that comes with the driver software. Often, if you try to install hardware that requires such a utility with the Windows Add/Remove Hardware Wizard, the wizard will tell you exactly that and halt the installation.

Often, after installing a device, you must reboot the computer so that Windows will recognize and load the driver properly.

 For devices that are not hot swappable (or pluggable), rebooting is a must. However, for many external devices, such as USB devices, rebooting is not necessary. Just plug in the device, let Windows detect it, and use the device.

Configuring the Device

Once the device has been installed, you must configure its various options so that it functions the way you want it to. In the case of a video card, you must ensure that it is set to the right resolution for the monitor you are using, so you get the highest possible performance out of the system.

Often, this step is overlooked. Some people install the driver, and if the device works, that's the key. However, you can often obtain the best performance with only a few more minutes of adjustment.

Usually, in order to configure the device, you must either open the System control panel in Windows and view the properties of the device you are concerned with, or use the utility that comes with the device. The latter method is more common with many peripherals and complex expansion cards.

Safely Removing Peripherals

PC Card devices are designed to be easily removed and installed. They're approximately the size and shape of a thick credit card, and they fit into PC Card (PCMCIA) slots in the side of the notebook PC. PC Card devices can include modems, network interface cards (NICs), SCSI adapters, USB adapters, FireWire adapters, and wireless Ethernet cards.

To prevent potential problems or loss of data, follow the PC Card manufacturer's removal procedure. To eject a PC Card device, press the eject button next to its slot. To insert a PC Card device, press the device into the slot. You can do this while the computer is running. (That's called *hot-plugging* or *hot-swapping*.) However, in Windows it's a good idea to stop the PC Card device before ejecting it, to ensure that all operations involving it complete normally. To do so, double-click the Safely Remove Hardware icon in the system tray, click the device, and then click Stop.

Windows Version-Specific Installation Items

For the most part, installing a new device is similar in the different versions of Windows. However, there are a few areas where installation differs. In this section, you will learn the differences between adding hardware on Windows Vista and XP and Windows 2000.

Adding Hardware in Windows Vista and Windows XP

As with previous versions of Windows, to install hardware you can:

- Let Windows recognize new hardware on boot-up and install drivers then.
- Use the manufacturer's installation program.
- Manually install hardware using the Add Hardware Wizard.

When you install some hardware under Windows Vista and XP, the operating system will warn you to install software before installing the device. You will notice this requirement mainly on USB devices and some other PnP devices.

To begin installing a driver for a new piece of hardware, follow these steps:

1. Install the hardware (either insert the expansion card or plug in the device).

2. Boot the computer and wait for Windows to recognize the new hardware. If Windows recognizes the new hardware, it displays a screen similar to the one shown in Figure 7.9, which asks if you want Windows to install the driver automatically or if you want to pick the driver from a list. If you go with the default choice of having Windows install the driver automatically, Windows locates the driver in its database of drivers that come with the operating system or that have already been installed. It then proceeds to install the driver and activate the new hardware.

FIGURE 7.9   XP detecting new hardware

You may see a warning telling you that if your hardware came with an installation CD, you should insert it now. That way, Windows can find the driver automatically.

3. Once Windows has found the driver, it determines whether the driver is properly signed (and gives you the chance to stop the installation if it's not).

4. Windows tells you that the device has been installed.

If Windows Vista or XP can't find the right driver for the device, it will start a troubleshooting wizard to help you along the installation. Clearly, Microsoft has streamlined the hardware installation process for Windows Vista and XP.

Always check Device Manager to make sure that the device is recognized by the system and the driver is working properly! Device Manager shows a list of all installed hardware and lets you add items, remove items, update drivers, and more. This is a Windows-only utility. In Windows Vista, right-click My Computer, choose Manage, and then click on Device Manager. With Windows XP and 2000, when you display the System Properties, click the Hardware tab, and then click the Device Manager button to display it.

Adding Hardware in Windows 2000

Windows 2000 relies heavily on PnP. Installing a piece of hardware in a Windows 2000 computer basically involves physically installing the device, booting the computer, and letting Windows 2000 automatically install the driver for that device. If it can't find the driver, it will ask you for the location. In addition, the screens have the Windows 2000 look and feel. Finally, you can use the Add/Remove Hardware Wizard to both add new hardware and update drivers for existing hardware.

Follow these steps:

1. Begin the process by double-clicking the Add/Remove Hardware icon (found in Start ➤ Settings ➤ Control Panel). Doing so starts the Add/Remove Hardware Wizard.

2. After clicking Next to move past the first screen, you are asked if you want to add/ troubleshoot a device or uninstall/unplug a device. The latter choice allows you to pre- pare Windows to completely remove a device or temporarily disable a device. To con- tinue adding a hardware device, choose Add/Troubleshoot A Device and click Next.

3. Windows 2000 searches for any uninstalled PnP devices. It also searches for a list of currently installed devices that may or may not need new drivers. The wizard then presents you with a list of devices so you can choose the device for which you want to install a new driver (either a new device or an existing one), as shown in Figure 7.10. If you are installing a new device, choose Add A New Device. If you are updating a driver for an existing device, choose the device whose driver you want to update. When you've made your choice, click Next.

FIGURE 7.10   Choosing a device for which to install a driver

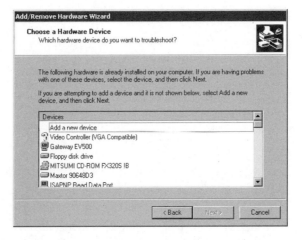

4. At this point, the Add/Remove Hardware Wizard asks you whether you want Win- dows to search for the hardware or whether you'll select it from a list. The wizard then installs the hardware driver or asks you for the appropriate driver, and the installation finishes.

One nice feature of adding hardware is that if the device driver can't be found or won't install correctly, Windows 2000 starts a troubleshooting wizard to help you finish installing the new hardware.

Optimizing Windows

Let's face it. Windows is a resource hog. The more hardware a computer has (memory, hard disk space, and so on), the more resources Windows will use. You can never have enough memory. Toward that end, Microsoft developed for Windows its own virtual memory technology. *Virtual memory* is the general term for a type of computer technology where hard disk space is used as a kind of backup memory.

 Real World Scenario

Why Do We Have Virtual Memory?

People wonder this all the time: "My computer has two gigs of RAM. Why would I need more?"

Like many other things in the computer industry, virtual memory was born out of necessity. Fairly early on in personal computer evolution, it was decided that a computer would never need more than 640KB (yes, *kilo*bytes) of memory. Oops. For DOS it was fine, mostly, but once graphical operating systems came into the world, the required resources jumped significantly.

Flash back to the late 1980s/early 1990s. If you had 4MB of RAM in your system, you were doing well. Very well, in fact, because RAM cost over $100 *per megabyte*. If you wanted more memory for Windows to use, then you had two choices. One was to mortgage your house, and the other was to use another source: virtual memory.

Hard disk space was and probably always will be cheaper per megabyte than RAM, simply because of the technology involved. So while hard disks might be slower than RAM, they are bigger and cheaper. Using space on them for virtual memory made a ton of economic sense then and still does today.

Chapter 6 explains the *swap file*, which is used to provide virtual memory to the Windows system. Here we'll look at how to set the swap file size and location in Windows Vista, XP, and 2000.

 Throughout this section, you will see the terms *swap file*, *page file*, and *paging file*. They are all synonyms.

Virtual Memory in Windows Vista

Setting the swap-file size and location in Windows Vista is similar to doing so in Windows XP, but it's worth walking through the process. To begin, open the System control panel, as shown in Figure 7.11. Click Advanced System Settings on the left. You will be prompted by User Access Control (UAC) if you want to follow through on this action. Click Continue.

FIGURE 7.11 The System Control Panel applet in Windows Vista

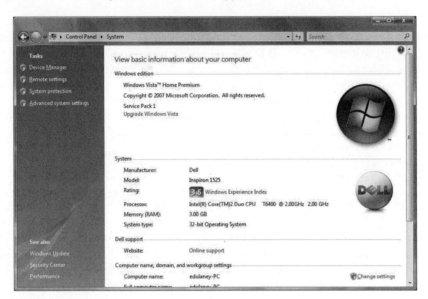

The System Properties will appear; click the Advanced tab if it is not already the active tab and choose Settings under Performance. Here is where the difference between Vista and the previous operating systems comes in, as Figure 7.12 illustrates. Do not be fooled by the plethora of options here—these only change the look and feel of Windows on this computer and do not control behind the scenes operations.

Click the Advanced tab, and Virtual Memory appears in the second section. Choose Change, and you can override the default setting of allowing Windows Vista to automatically manage paging file size for all drives (Figure 7.13).

Virtual Memory in Windows XP

Setting the swap-file size and location in Windows XP is almost identical to the process in Windows 2000. The major differences are how you get to the controls and what the screen looks like.

As in Windows 2000, you must be logged on as an administrator. However, the screen that allows you to change your virtual memory settings is buried a bit deeper. To begin, open the System control panel, as shown in Figure 7.14. Click the Advanced tab. On this tab, click the button labeled Settings in the Performance section to access the Performance Options window. Click the Advanced tab.

FIGURE 7.12   The Visual Effects Performance options in Windows Vista

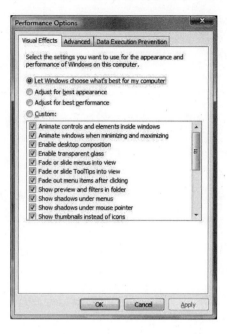

FIGURE 7.13   The Virtual Memory Performance options in Windows Vista

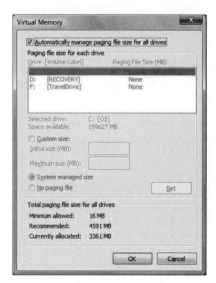

FIGURE 7.14 Windows XP System control panel

On this tab are various performance-tuning options. At the bottom of the displayed tab are the virtual memory settings (see Figure 7.15). This area tells you the total paging-file size for all drives. If you have multiple swap files on multiple drives, the number listed tells the total size for all swap files.

FIGURE 7.15 Advanced performance settings

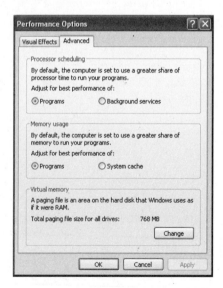

To change the size of your swap files, click the Change button. In the Drive [Volume Label] section, select the drive that contains the swap file you want to change. Then, in the paging section change the minimum and maximum numbers as in Windows 2000. Click Set to make the changes, and click OK in each open window. Windows may ask you to reboot to complete the changes, but (as in Windows 2000) only if you've reduced the swap-file size.

> To let Windows manage the swap-file size, choose the System Managed Size option on the screen shown in Figure 7.16.

FIGURE 7.16   Changing the Windows XP paging-file size

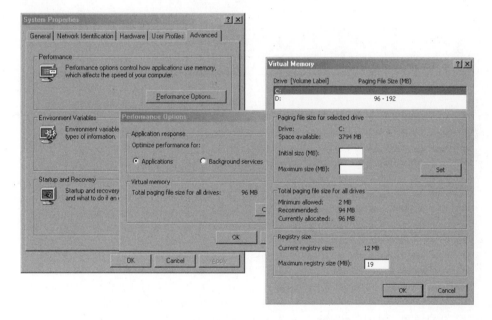

Virtual Memory in Windows 2000

The virtual memory settings in Windows 2000 (see Figure 7.17) tell you how much hard drive space is allocated to the system as a swap file. Windows 2000 recommends a particular virtual memory level, but you can add to or subtract from this value as necessary. Often, certain applications (SQL Server, for instance) need you to raise Windows 2000 Professional's virtual memory limit in order to work properly. Graphics and CAD applications also require you to raise the virtual memory level, but if this is the case, the setup instructions for the application will generally tell you what modifications need to be made.

FIGURE 7.17   The Virtual Memory window in Windows 2000

Adding to the swap-file size is not always helpful and can sometimes slow down the system. Modify this setting only if you have been instructed to or if you are testing to see whether the change speeds up or slows down the computer. Reducing the swap-file size is generally not recommended and can have serious consequences on performance.

To access the virtual memory settings, open the System control panel, click the Advanced tab, and then click the Performance Options button. Doing so will bring up the Performance Options window, where you can view the current virtual memory settings.

To change the size of the paging file, you must be logged on as Administrator. If you're not an administrator, the options will be grayed out. To begin, click Change under the size of the current page file. Type in values for the maximum and minimum sizes of the page file (Microsoft recommends a value at least 1.5 times the amount of RAM as in your system), click Set, and then click OK.

If you reduce the minimum or maximum size of the page file, you will have to reboot your computer. However, in Windows 2000 increases don't require a restart.

If you need to delete a paging file, set both the minimum and maximum sizes to zero.

Keeping the System Current

Upgrades to Windows (all versions) come in the form of *service packs*. Each service pack contains patches and fixes to OS components, as well as additional features. A service pack is a self-running program that modifies your OS. It isn't uncommon within the lifetime of an OS to have two or three service packs.

Successive service packs include all files that have been in previous ones. Therefore, if you perform a new installation, and the latest service pack is Service Pack 4, you don't need to install Service Packs 1, 2, and 3. You need install only Service Pack 4 after the installation to bring the OS up to the current feature set.

As they're released, service packs are shipped monthly for all Microsoft OSs with TechNet. TechNet is a subscription CD service available through Microsoft.

 As of this writing, Service Pack 2 is the latest available for Windows Vista and Service Pack 3 is the latest available for Windows XP.

Power Management

The Advanced Configuration Power Interface (ACPI) must be supported by the system BIOS in order to work properly. With ACPI, it is the BIOS that provides the operating system with the necessary methods for controlling the hardware. This is in contrast to APM (Advanced Power Management), which only gave a limited amount of power to the operating system and let the BIOS do all the real work. Because of this, it is not uncommon to find legacy systems that can support APM but not ACPI.

There are three main states of power management common in most operating systems:

Hibernate   This state saves all the contents of memory to the hard drive and preserves all data and applications exactly where they are. When the system comes out of hibernation, it returns to its previous state.

Standby   This state leaves memory active but saves everything else to disk.

Suspend   In most operating systems, this term is used interchangeably with Hibernate. In Windows XP, Hibernate is used instead of Suspend.

If you are interested in saving power with a system that is not accessed often, one option is to employ Wake on LAN (WoL). Wake on LAN is an Ethernet standard implemented via a card that allows a "sleeping" machine to awaken when it receives a wakeup signal. Wake on LAN cards have more problems than standard network cards. In our opinion, this is because they're always on. In some cases, you'll be unable to get the card working again unless you unplug the PC's power supply and reset the card.

Windows offers quite a range of choices from the Shut Down (pre–Windows XP) or Turn Off Computer (Windows XP and Vista) command under the Start menu (in Vista, it appears as an icon of an on/off button and does not have a label). Note that with a configuration called Fast User Switching, Windows XP also displays Shut Down rather than Turn Off Computer.

When you select this option, Windows presents you with several choices. Exactly which options are available depends on the Windows version you are running.

Whether you see Shut Down or Turn Off Computer has a lot to do with the way your user interface is configured (Classic View, for example). Regardless of the name of the choice, it performs the same function.

The possible choices are as follows:

Shut Down (Windows 2000)/Turn Off (Windows XP and Vista)   This option writes any unsaved data to disk, closes any open applications, makes a copy of the Registry, and gets the computer ready to be powered off. Depending on the OS, the computer is then powered down automatically, or you'll see a black screen with the message *It's now safe to turn off your computer.* In this case, you can power off the computer or press Ctrl+Alt+Del to reboot the computer.

Restart   This option works the same as the first option, but instead of shutting down completely, it automatically reboots the computer with a warm reboot.

Stand By (Windows XP and 2000 only)   This option places the computer into a low-power state. The monitor and hard disks are turned off, and the computer uses less power. To resume working, press a key on the keyboard; the computer is returned to its original state. In this state, information in memory is not saved to hard disk, so if a power loss occurs, any data in memory will be lost.

Switch User (Windows Vista and XP only)   This option allows you to switch users on a machine without closing programs. This is generally not recommended in a work environment for the security reasons associated with leaving programs running.

Log Off   This option is recommended over Switch User as it closes all open programs and then logs off—allowing another user to then log on.

Lock   This option leaves programs running, but locks the computer and requires the user's password to be entered again before the session can continue.

Hibernate   This option saves the session and turns off the computer. When powered back up, the session resumes.

Sleep   This option keeps the session in memory and puts the computer in a low-power state that you can quickly resume from. This is like Hibernate, but without fully powering down the computer.

If you enable Hibernation on a Windows XP machine, you can place the computer into hibernation by holding down the Shift key while clicking Stand By on the Turn Off Computer screen. Using the Hibernation feature, any information in memory is saved to disk before the computer is put into a low-power state. Thus, if power is lost while the machine is in hibernation, your data is not lost. However, going into and coming out of hibernation takes more time than going into and coming out of stand-by mode.

Sleep timers allow you to configure a system to sleep for certain periods of time in order to conserve power. While not included with the operating system, a number of downloadable programs can be found that will turn the machine off at a certain time or after some specified condition is met.

Identifying Boot Sequences

Both for the test and for real life, you should know how to recognize common problems with operating systems and make certain they're booting correctly. The sections that follow look at a number of topics related to keeping your OSs booting and running properly.

Key Boot Files

Windows Vista, XP, and 2000 require only a few files, each of which performs specific tasks. These are discussed next in the order in which they load:

NTLDR/BOOTMGR   Bootstraps the system. In other words, this file starts the loading of an OS on the computer. While Windows Vista uses BOOTMGR, both Windows XP and 2000 use NTLDR. Whichever of the two files the operating system uses, that file is responsible for switching from real to protected mode during the boot process.

BOOT.INI   Holds information about which OSs are installed on the computer. This file also contains the location of the OS files with Windows XP and 2000. Windows Vista uses Boot Configuration Data (BCD) in place of the BOOT.INI file and is configured with BCDEDIT.EXE.

BOOTSECT.DOS   In a dual-boot configuration, keeps a copy of the DOS or Windows 9x boot sector so that the Windows 9x environment can be restored and loaded as needed.

NTDETECT.COM   Parses the system for hardware information each time Windows Vista, XP, or 2000 is loaded. This information is then used to create dynamic hardware information in the Registry.

NTBOOTDD.SYS   On a system with a SCSI boot device, this file is used to recognize and load the SCSI interface. On EIDE systems, this file is not needed and is not even installed.

NTOSKRNL.EXE   The Windows OS kernel. The solution to a corrupted NTOSKRNL.EXE file is to boot from a startup disk and replace the file from the setup disks or CD.

NTBTLOG.TXT   While not an executable file, this log file is very important; it holds the information collected if you choose to boot using the Boot Logging startup option.

System Files   In addition to the previously listed files, all of which except NTOSKRNL.EXE are located in the root of the C: partition on the computer, Windows Vista, XP, or 2000 needs a number of files from its system directories (e.g., system and system32), such as the hardware abstraction layer (HAL.DLL).

Numerous other DLL (dynamic link library) files are also required, but usually the lack or corruption of one of them produces a noncritical error, whereas the absence of HAL.DLL causes the system to be nonfunctional.

We'll now look at the Windows XP/2000 boot process. It's a pretty long and complicated process, but keep in mind that these are complex operating systems, providing you with a lot more functionality than older versions of Windows could offer:

1. The system self-checks and enumerates hardware resources. Each machine has a different startup routine, called the POST (power-on self-test), which is executed by the commands written to the motherboard of the computer. Newer PnP boards not only check memory and processors, but also poll the systems for other devices and peripherals.

2. The Master Boot Record (MBR) loads and finds the boot sector. Once the system has finished with its housekeeping, the MBR is located on the first hard drive and loaded into memory. The MBR finds the bootable partition and searches it for the boot sector of that partition.

3. The MBR determines the file system and loads NTLDR. Information in the boot sector allows the system to locate the system partition and to find and load into memory the NTLDR.EXE file located there.

4. NTLDR switches the system from real mode to protected mode and enables paging. Protected mode enables the system to address all of the available physical memory. It's also referred to as *32-bit flat mode*. At this point, the file system is also started.

5. NTLDR processes BOOT.INI. BOOT.INI is a text file that resides in the root directory. It specifies what OSs are installed on the computer and where the OS resides on the disk. During this step of the boot process, you may be presented with a list of the installed OSs (depending on how your startup options are configured and whether you have multiple OSs installed). If you're presented with the list, you can choose an OS, or if you don't take any action, the default selection is chosen automatically. If you have multiple OSs installed and you choose a DOS-based OS from the list (such as Windows *9x*), NTLDR processes BOOTSECT.DOS and does a warm boot. The MBR code contained in BOOTSECT.DOS is run after the computer goes through the POST, and IO.SYS is loaded, starting the DOS-based OS's boot process. We will, however, continue with the Vista, XP, and 2000 boot process.

6. NTLDR loads and runs NTDETECT.COM. NTDETECT.COM checks the system for installed devices and device configurations and initializes the devices it finds. It passes the information to NTLDR, which collects this information and passes it to NTOSKRNL.EXE after that file is loaded.

7. NTLDR loads NTOSKRNL.EXE and HAL.DLL. NTOSKRNL.EXE holds the OS kernel and also what's known as the *executive subsystems*. Executive subsystems are software components that parse the Registry for configuration information and start needed services and drivers. HAL.DLL enables communication between the OS and the installed hardware.

8. NTLDR loads the HKEY_LOCAL_MACHINE\SYSTEM Registry hive and loads device drivers. The drivers that load at this time serve as boot drivers, using an initial value called a *start value*.

9. NTLDR transfers control to NTOSKRNL.EXE. NTOSKRNL.EXE initializes loaded drivers and completes the boot process.

10. Winlogon loads. At this point, you are presented with the Logon screen. After you enter a username and password, you're taken to the Windows Desktop.

Working with the Boot Sequence

Under a normal boot, these files are accessed as needed, and the system is brought to its ready state. If problems are occurring, however, you may need to alter the boot method used. Windows offers a number of choices of altered boot sequences:

Safe Mode   To access Safe Mode, you must press F8 when the OS menu is displayed during the boot process. A menu of Safe Mode choices appears, and you can select the mode you want to boot into. This is the mode to boot into if you suspect driver problems and want to load with a minimal set while you diagnose the problem.

Recovery Console   This is a command-line utility used for troubleshooting. From it, you can format drives, stop and start services, and interact with files stored on FAT, FAT32, or NTFS. The Recovery Console isn't installed on a system by default, but you can add it as a menu choice at the bottom of the startup menu.

Restore points   System Restore is arguably the most powerful tool in Windows Vista and XP. It allows you to restore the system to a previous point in time. This feature is accessed from Start ➤ All Programs ➤ Accessories ➤ System Tools ➤ System Restore and can be used to roll back as well as to create a restore point. Restore points are created automatically in Windows Vista and XP by default. If you ever need to create them manually, you can also use the System Restore utility to do this.

Automated System Recovery (ASR)   It's possible to automate the process of creating a system recovery set by choosing the ASR Wizard on the Tools menu of the Backup utility (Start ➤ All Programs ➤ Accessories ➤ System Tools ➤ Backup). This wizard walks you through the process of creating a disk that can be used to restore parts of the system in the event of a major system failure.

Emergency repair disk (ERD)   The Windows Backup and Recovery Tool/Wizard also allows you to create an ERD. As the name implies, this is a disk you can use to repair a portion of the system in the event of a failure. ERD is only in Windows 2000; ASR is the replacement in Vista and XP.

In Chapter 6 we looked at the startup and system files used by Windows Vista, XP, and 2000. Here we'll review the files and look more closely at the process.

Remember that the system files are hidden from the user by default. To make them visible, you need to change the display properties of Windows Explorer as you did previously. Exercise 7.1 walks you through the steps.

EXERCISE 7.1

Showing Hidden Files and Folders

1. Open Windows Explorer.

2. Browse to the root of the C: drive. Look for the IO.SYS system file. It should be hidden and will not appear in the file list.

3. Choose Tools ➤ Folder Options. The Folder Options window opens.

4. Select the View tab, and scroll until you find the Hidden Files option.

5. Select Show All Files.

6. Deselect Hide Protected Operating System Files (Recommended).

7. Uncheck Hide File Extensions For Known File Types.

8. Click OK. You will now be able to see the Windows system files discussed in the following sections. For security reasons, you should set these attributes back to the defaults after you've read this chapter.

Advanced Startup Options

In addition to performing a regular boot into the OS of your choice, you can make additional selections for advanced startup options. In Windows, you access the options by pressing the F8 key when you're presented with the list of OSs installed on the computer. If you don't have the system configured to display the list of OSs (for example, if you have only one OS installed), press F8 when a message on the screen tells you that you can do so.

In most cases you will be able to just boot into your OS without worrying about the advanced options. Occasionally, though, problems may arise. If you have a problem that makes it difficult to get Windows up and running, the advanced options offer a number of useful tools. The options are not identical on the various versions of Windows. Here are the advanced startup options available in Windows Vista, XP, and 2000:

Repair Your Computer (Windows Vista only)   Offers a list of system recovery tools that you can run to fix problems, run diagnostics, or restore the system.

Safe Mode   Starts Windows Vista, XP, or 2000 using only basic files and drivers (mouse, except serial mice; monitor; keyboard; mass storage; base video; default system services; and no network connections). Once in Safe Mode, you can restore files that are missing or fix a configuration error.

Safe Mode With Networking   Same as Safe Mode but tries to load networking components as well.

Safe Mode With Command Prompt   Similar to Safe Mode but doesn't load the Windows GUI. Presents the user with a Windows Vista, XP, or 2000 command-prompt interface.

Enable Boot Logging   Logs all boot information to a file called NTBTLOG.TXT. This file can be found in the \WINNT directory. You can then check the log for assistance in diagnosing system startup problems.

Enable VGA Mode (Windows XP and Windows 2000)   Starts Windows 2000/XP using the basic VGA driver but loads the rest of the system as normal. If you happen to install an incorrect video driver or a video driver becomes corrupted, this allows you to get into the system to fix the problem.

Enable Low-Resolution Video (640×480) (Windows Vista only)   Starts Windows Vista using the basic VGA driver but loads the rest of the system as normal. If you happen to install an incorrect video driver or a video driver becomes corrupted, this allows you to get into the system to fix the problem.

Last Known Good Configuration (advanced)   Useful if you have changed a configuration setting in the Registry, which then causes the system to have serious problems and you're not able to log in. Use Last Known Good Configuration restores the system to a prior, functional state, which will allow you to log in again. It will not save you from a corrupted file or a deleted file error.

Directory Services Restore Mode   Used only with domain controllers. If you choose this option, Windows boots into a mode that doesn't load directory services. This enables you to restore directory services, such as Active Directory, to the machine. (You can't restore directory services if directory services are running.)

Debugging Mode   A sort of advanced boot logging. Requires that another machine be hooked up to the computer through a serial port. The debug information is then passed to that machine during the boot process. This option is rarely used and should not be bothered with in most cases. If it comes to this, reinstalling is far faster!

Disable Automatic Restart On System Failure (Windows Vista only)   Toggling this stops Windows from automatically rebooting when it encounters a crash.

Disable Driver Signature Enforcement (Windows Vista only)   Toggling this allows Windows to load drivers containing improper signatures.

Boot Normally (Windows 2000 only)   Continues the boot normally. It's equivalent to the Normal option in Windows 9*x*.

Start Windows Normally (Windows Vista and XP only)   Continues the boot normally. It's equivalent to the Normal option in Windows 9*x* and the Boot Normally option in Windows 2000.

Reboot (Windows XP only)   As the name implies, reboots the computer (warm boot).

Return To OS Choices Menu (Windows XP only)   Self-explanatory; returns you to the choice of installed OSs.

Boot Order and Boot Devices

Within the BIOS of each machine, you can configure which devices are bootable and in what order they will be tried. Depending on your machine and the BIOS version, the list of devices possible may range from floppy disks all the way up to USB devices and include everything in between. For example, assume you want to be able to boot from a flash drive. To configure this, reboot the workstation and press the corresponding key to take you into the BIOS configuration. (F12 works often, as does Delete. If it is not one of these two, it is usually F1 or F2.)

Within the BIOS configuration options, access the Boot menu and enable Boot USB Devices First or a setting with similar wording. If the option to boot from USB is simply

Enable/Disable, choose Enable and then go to the order of boot devices and move USB above the hard drive.

Save the changes and exit the BIOS configuration. This will continue with the reboot and—if your USB drive is plugged in—should boot whatever operating system files are there.

If you get the single line entry "Boot Error" and nothing else happens, update the BIOS, and all should work as intended.

Common Error Messages

Unfortunately, there are times when systems do fail. Fortunately, when they do, they now try to explain why. Depending on the OS and settings, it's possible that the user will be asked if they want a report sent to Microsoft, dump logs will be created, log files will be written to, and so on. All of this makes your job as a troubleshooting administrator much easier than it was in the days when the solution to every problem was Ctrl+Alt+Del.

Boot problems can occur with corruption of the boot files or missing components (such as the NTLDR file being "accidentally" deleted by an overzealous user). Luckily, during the installation of the OS, log files are created in the %SystemRoot% or %SystemRoot%\Debug folder (C:\WINNT and C:\WINNT\DEBUG, by default). If you have a puzzling problem, look at these logs and see if you can find error entries there.

During startup, problems with devices that fail to be recognized properly, services that fail to start, and so on are written to the System log and can be viewed with the Event Viewer. This utility provides information about what's been going on system-wise, to help you troubleshoot problems. The Event Viewer shows warnings, error messages, and records of things happening successfully. You can access it through Computer Management or directly from the Administrative Tools in Control Panel.

Configuration information for Windows is stored in a special configuration database known as the Registry. This centralized database contains environmental settings for various Windows programs. It also contains what is known as *registration* information, which details the types of file extensions associated with applications. So, when you double-click a file in Windows Explorer, the associated application runs and opens the file you double-clicked.

The Registry Editor enables you to make changes to the large hierarchical database that contains all of Windows' settings. These changes can potentially disable the entire system, so they should not be made lightly.

Changes made in the Registry Editor are implemented immediately; you don't have the opportunity to save or reject your changes.

There is no menu command for the Registry Editor. You must run it with the Run command (type **REGEDIT**).

Windows 2000 includes a second Registry Editor program called Regedt32. This alternative program accesses the same Registry, but it does so in a slightly different way; it shows each of the major key areas in a separate window. One nice thing is that Regedt32 provides a Read Only mode that allows you to read the Registry without any fear of making unintended changes.

In Windows Vista and XP, the command REGEDT32 is still present, but running it launches Regedit; they have been rolled into a single utility.

You can configure problems with system failure to write *dump files* (debugging information) for later analysis when they occur by opening the System applet in Control Panel, choosing the Advanced tab, and clicking Settings under Startup And Recovery. Here, in addition to choosing the default OS, you can configure whether events should be written to the system log, whether an alert should be sent to the administrator, and the type of memory dump to be written.

Recovering Operating Systems

Windows includes a number of tools to simplify recovering an operating system after a serious problem has occurred. System Restore is one such tool, as discussed previously. Three others we'll look at here are the Recovery Console, Automated System Recovery (ASR), and emergency repair disks (ERDs).

Recovery Console

The Recovery Console is a command-line utility used for troubleshooting that exists in Windows 2000 and Windows XP. From it, you can format drives, stop and start services, and interact with files. The latter is extremely important because many boot and command-line utilities bring you into a position where you can interact with files stored on FAT or FAT32 but not NTFS. The Recovery Console can work with files stored on all three file systems.

The Recovery Console isn't installed on a system by default. To install it, use the following steps:

1. Place the Windows CD in the system.

2. From a command prompt, change to the i386 directory of the CD.

3. Type winnt32 /cmdcons.

4. A prompt appears, alerting you to the fact that 7MB of hard drive space is required and asking if you want to continue. Click Yes.

Upon successful completion of the installation, the Recovery Console (Microsoft Windows 2000 Recovery Console, for example) is added as a menu choice at the bottom of the startup menu. To access it, you must choose it from the list at startup. If more than one installation exists on the system, another boot menu will appear, asking which you want to boot into, and you must make a selection to continue.

To perform this task, you must give the administrator password. You'll then arrive at a command prompt. You can give a number of commands from this prompt, two of which are worth special attention: EXIT restarts the computer, and HELP lists the commands you can give. Table 7.4 lists the other commands available, most of which will be familiar to administrators who have worked with MS-DOS.

TABLE 7.4   Recovery Console Commands

Command	Purpose
ATTRIB	Shows the current attributes of a file or folder, and lets you change them.
BATCH	Runs the commands within an ASCII text file.
CD	Used without parameters, it shows the current directory. Used with parameters, it changes to the directory specified.
CHDIR	Works the same as CD.
CHKDSK	Checks the disk for errors.
CLS	Clears the screen.
COPY	Allows you to copy a file (or files, if used with wildcards) from one location to another.
DEL	Deletes a file.
DELTREE	Recursively deletes files and directories.
DIR	Shows the contents of the current directory.
DISABLE	Allows you to stop a service/driver.
DISKPART	Shows the partitions on the drive, and lets you manage them.
EXPAND	Extracts compressed files.
ENABLE	Allows you to start a service/driver.
FIXBOOT	Writes a new boot sector.
FIXMBR	Checks and fixes (if possible) the master boot record.
FORMAT	Allows you to format a floppy or partition.
LISTSVC	Shows the services/drivers on the system.
LOGON	Lets you log on to Windows 2000.
MAP	Shows the maps currently created.
MD	Makes a new folder/directory.

TABLE 7.4   Recovery Console Commands *(continued)*

Command	Purpose
MKDIR	Works the same as MD.
MORE	Shows only one screen of a text file at a time.
RD	Removes a directory or folder.
REN	Renames a file or folder.
RENAME	Works the same as REN.
RMDIR	Works the same as RD.
SYSTEMROOT	Works like CD but takes you to the system root of whichever OS installation you're logged on to.
TYPE	Displays the contents of an ASCII text file.

During the installation of the Recovery Console, a folder named Cmdcons is created in the root directory to hold the executable files and drivers it needs. A file named Cmldr, with attributes of System, Hidden, and Read-Only, is also placed in the root directory.

If you want to delete the Recovery Console (to prevent users from playing around, for example), you can do so by deleting the Cmldr file and the Cmdcons folder, and removing the entry from the Boot.ini file.

Automated System Recovery

It's possible to automate the process of creating a system recovery set by choosing the ASR Wizard on the Tools menu of the Backup utility (Start ≻ All Programs ≻ Accessories ≻ System Tools ≻ Backup). This wizard walks you through the process of creating a disk that can be used to restore parts of the system in the event of a major system failure.

The default name of this file is BACKUP.BKF; it requires a floppy disk. The backup set contains all the files necessary for starting the system, whereas the floppy becomes a bootable pointer to that backup set and can access or decompress it.

A weakness of this tool is its reliance on a bootable floppy in a day when many new systems no longer include a 3.5-inch drive.

Emergency Repair Disk

The Windows Backup and Recovery Tool/Wizard allows you to create an emergency repair disk (ERD). As the name implies, this is a disk you can use to repair a portion of the system in the event of a failure.

When you choose this option, the tab changes to the Backup tab, and a prompt tells you to install a blank, formatted floppy disk. Click the check box if you want to save the Registry as well. (The default is no.) If you don't choose to save the Registry, the following files are placed on the floppy disk:

- SETUP.LOG
- CONFIG.NT
- AUTOEXEC.NT

This doesn't leave you much to work with. The disk isn't bootable and contains only three minor configuration utilities.

If you check the box to include the Registry in the backup, the floppy disk contains the preceding files plus the following:

- SECURITY._
- SOFTWARE._
- SYSTEM._
- DEFAULT._
- SAM._
- NTUSER.DAT
- USRCLASS.DAT

The user profile (NTUSER.DAT) is for the default user; the files with the ._ extension are compressed files from the Registry. The compression utility used is EXPAND.EXE, which offers you the flexibility of restoring any or all files from any Microsoft operating system, including this utility (Windows Vista, XP, 2000, and so on). Because this floppy contains key Registry files, it's important that you label it appropriately and store it in a safe location, away from users who should not have access to it.

 During the process of creating the floppy, the Registry files are also backed up (in uncompressed state) to %systemroot%\repair\RegBack.

As before, the floppy isn't bootable, and you must bring the system up to a point (booted) where the floppy can be accessed before it's of any use.

Summary

In this chapter, you learned the different methods of installing and upgrading Windows Vista, XP, and 2000. For each type of OS installation, you learned the installation prerequisites and how to install that OS.

You also learned the methods used to upgrade from one OS to another. We looked at the steps necessary to upgrade as well as how an upgrade differs from a standard installation.

We discussed methods used to optimize system performance on the various Windows platforms. For the most part, Windows manages virtual memory on its own, but sometimes you can tweak performance by increasing the size of the page file.

Finally, we discussed the Windows boot sequence along with many of the boot options. Some of the recovery options available include Automated System Recovery (ASR), Emergency Repair Disk (ERD), and the Recovery Console.

Exam Essentials

Know how to install Windows.   You should know the steps for installing Windows Vista, XP, and 2000.

Understand upgrading.   You should know that an installation overwrites any existing files, whereas an upgrade keeps the same data and application files.

Be able to define hot-swappable.   PC Card devices are hot-swappable, meaning you can remove and insert them while the computer is running. So are USB and FireWire devices. However, if you need to remove a drive, add or remove RAM, or connect or disconnect a monitor or a parallel or serial device, you must shut down the computer.

Know how to boot into Safe Mode.   To access Safe Mode, you must press F8 when the operating system menu is displayed during the boot process.

Know the file systems.   Make sure you can explain the differences between FAT32 and NTFS and tell which OSs they're compatible with.

Understand the Windows boot process, in order.   The NTLDR utility bootstraps Windows and calls the BOOT.INI file. Then, NTLDR loads NTDETECT.COM, ntoskrnl.exe, and hal.dll. After the registry loading begins, control is handed over to ntoskrnl.exe, and the WINLOGON process starts.

Know the advanced boot options.   Advanced boot options available in Windows include Repair Your Computer, Safe Mode, Safe Mode With Networking, Safe Mode With Command Prompt, Enable Boot Logging, Enable VGA Mode, Enable Low-Resolution Video, Last Known Good Configuration, Directory Services Restore Mode, Debugging Mode, Disable Automatic Restart On System Failure, Disable Driver Signature Enforcement, Boot Normally, and Start Windows Normally.

Review Questions

1. What do you use in Windows XP to create a recovery disk?

   A. Automated System Recovery (ASR)

   B. RDISK.EXE

   C. Enhanced Startup Disk (ESD)

   D. Emergency Recovery System (ERS)

2. What is the first file used in the boot-up of Windows XP?

   A. NTOSKRNL.EXE

   B. CONFIG.SYS

   C. AUTOEXEC.BAT

   D. NTLDR

   E. NTBOOTDD.SYS

3. What does Safe Mode allow you to do?

   A. Run Windows without processing AUTOEXEC.BAT and CONFIG.SYS.

   B. Boot the system without scanning drives.

   C. Start Windows using only basic files and drivers.

   D. Skip loading the Registry.

4. Which of the following is an Ethernet standard implemented via a card that allows a "sleeping" machine to awaken when it receives a wakeup signal?

   A. Sleep timer

   B. WEP

   C. Wake on LAN

   D. WPA

5. What is the quickest solution to fixing a corrupted NTOSKRNL.EXE file?

   A. Reinstall Windows.

   B. Replace the corrupted file with a new one.

   C. Modify the BOOT.INI file to point to the backup NTOSKRNL.EXE file.

   D. Boot from a startup disk and replace the file from the setup disks or CD.

6. During what type of installation must a user be present to choose all options as they appear?

   A. Attended

   B. Existing

   C. Bootstrap

   D. Denote

7. In Windows Vista and XP, how do you access advanced startup options?

- **A.** By pressing the spacebar when prompted to do so
- **B.** By holding down Ctrl+Alt+Del after the Windows logo displays for the first time
- **C.** By pressing Esc after the OS menu displays
- **D.** By pressing F8 during the first phase of the boot process

8. Which advanced startup option in Windows 2000 would you use to be able to return to a previously functioning environment?

- **A.** Command Prompt Only
- **B.** Safe Mode
- **C.** Step-By-Step Configuration
- **D.** Debugging Mode
- **E.** Last Known Good Configuration

9. In Windows 2000 and XP, which of the following files is specifically responsible for enabling communication between the system hardware and the operating system?

- **A.** NTDETECT.COM
- **B.** NTOSKRNL.EXE
- **C.** NTBOOTDD.SYS
- **D.** HAL.DLL
- **E.** NTLDR

10. Which of the following is a replacement for RIS?

- **A.** STIR
- **B.** UAC
- **C.** WDS
- **D.** SIR

11. What is the first step when installing Windows onto a system that doesn't already have a functioning operating system?

- **A.** Formatting
- **B.** Partitioning
- **C.** Redirecting
- **D.** Installing the OS

12. Which of the following is/are performed by formatting the hard drive? (Choose all that apply.)

- **A.** Formatting scans the surface of the hard drive platter to find bad spots and marks the areas surrounding a bad spot as bad sectors.
- **B.** Formatting lays down magnetic tracks in concentric circles.
- **C.** The tracks are split into pieces of 512 bytes called sectors.
- **D.** Formatting creates a File Allocation Table that contains information about the location of files.

13. After installation of the operating system, what do the newer versions of Windows require in order to curb software piracy?

    A. Certification

    B. Confirmation

    C. Activation

    D. Substantiation

14. You've successfully completed an upgrade to Windows 2000 Professional. Several days later, you add your old printer, using the driver that originally came with it. Now the printer, which has never had a problem, won't print. What do you need to do to fix the problem?

    A. Older printers are often not compatible with Windows 2000. You may need to replace the printer.

    B. Your printer driver is out-of-date. Contact the vendor or visit its website for an updated driver.

    C. Uninstall, and then reinstall the printer using the original driver.

    D. None of the above.

15. Which of the following methods correctly adds new hardware to a Windows 2000 system if Plug and Play does not work? (Select all that apply.)

    A. Exit to a command prompt and use the software that came with the device to run the installation.

    B. Choose Start ➢ Settings ➢ Control Panel and then double-click the Add/Remove Hardware icon.

    C. If Plug and Play does not work, there is no way to get the hardware working in the Windows 2000 environment.

    D. On the Desktop, double-click the My Computer icon, double-click the Control Panel icon, and then double-click the Add/Remove Hardware icon.

16. If Plug and Play does not work with a particular device on a Windows Vista machine, what Control Panel utility can you use?

    A. Update

    B. System

    C. Add/Remove Hardware

    D. Add Hardware

17. Which utility that comes with Windows 2000 Professional is used to create an image of an existing computer for network installation?

    A. Ghost

    B. Sysprep

    C. Sysimage

    D. RIS

18. The name of the swap file is _____ in Windows Vista.

    A. SWAPFILE.SYS

    B. PAGEFILE.SYS

    C. SWAPPINGFILE.SYS

    D. PAGINGFILE.SYS

19. If you have 256MB of RAM in a Windows 2000 machine, what is the minimum recommended size for the swap file?

    A. 128MB

    B. 256MB

    C. 384MB

    D. 512MB

20. Where would you configure a workstation to boot from the USB drive first and hard drive only if there is not a bootable USB device attached?

    A. NTLDR

    B. C:\WINDOWS\TEMP\1st.txt

    C. Boot.ini

    D. None of the above

Answers to Review Questions

1. A. Windows XP uses Automated System Recovery (ASR). It makes a backup of your system partition and creates a recovery disk.

2. D. The first file used in the Windows Vista (as well as 2000) boot process is NTLDR. Both the NTOSKRNL.EXE and NTBOOTDD.SYS files are used in the boot process, but neither is the first file run. Neither AUTOEXEC.BAT nor CONFIG.SYS is involved in the Windows Vista/XP/2000 boot process.

3. C. Safe Mode is a good option to choose to restore files that are missing or to fix a configuration error. With only basic files and drivers loaded, you can more easily identify the source of the problem.

4. C. Wake on LAN is an Ethernet standard implemented via a card that allows a "sleeping" machine to awaken when it receives a wakeup signal

5. D. The solution to a corrupted NTOSKRNL.EXE file is to boot from a startup disk and replace the file from the setup disks or CD.

6. A. In an attended installation, a user must be present to choose all of the options when the installation program gets to that point.

7. D. Pressing F8 during the first phase of the boot process brings up the Advanced Startup Options menu in Windows.

8. E. Last Known Good Configuration enables you to restore the system to a prior, functional state if a change was made to the Registry that turned out to be problematic.

9. D. HAL, or the Hardware Abstraction Layer, is the translator between the hardware and the operating system.

10. C. Beginning with Windows Server 2003, RIS was replaced by Windows Deployment Service (WDS). This utility offers the same functionality as RIS.

11. B. New disk drives or PCs with no OS need to have two critical functions performed on them before they can be used: partitioning and formatting. These two functions are performed by two commands, FDISK.EXE and FORMAT.COM, or by the Windows installation program itself.

12. A, B, C, D. Formatting does all of the listed processes.

13. C. Windows Vista and XP require the installation to be followed by a process known as product activation to curb software piracy.

14. B. When installing a printer, or any hardware device for that matter, you must always be sure to have an updated driver. Many device problems originate with out-of-date hardware drivers.

15. B, D. Plug and Play will automatically detect new hardware and install the proper software. If it is not successful, you can use the Add/Remove Hardware Wizard.

16. D. When Plug and Play does not work, the Add New Hardware applet in the Control Panel can be used in Windows Vista. In some earlier versions of Windows, this same functionality was provided by the Add/Remove Hardware Wizard.

17. B. The Sysprep utility comes with Windows 2000 Professional and is used to make an image of a computer. Ghost is a third-party utility made by Norton. Sysimage is not a known Windows utility, and RIS only comes with Windows Server operating systems.

18. B. The name of the virtual memory swap file is `PAGEFILE.SYS`.

19. C. The minimum recommended swap-file size under Windows 2000 is 1.5 times the amount of physical RAM: $1.5 \times 256MB = 384MB$.

20. D. Boot order is configured in the BIOS of the workstation and not in a Windows-related file.

Chapter 8

Troubleshooting Theory and Preventive Maintenance

THE FOLLOWING COMPTIA A+ ESSENTIALS EXAM OBJECTIVES ARE COVERED IN THIS CHAPTER:

✓ **2.1 Given a scenario, explain the troubleshooting theory**

- Identify the problem
    - Question user and identify user changes to computer and perform backups before making changes
- Establish a theory of probable cause (question the obvious)
- Test the theory to determine cause
    - Once theory is confirmed determine next steps to resolve problem
    - If theory is not confirmed re-establish new theory or escalate
- Establish a plan of action to resolve the problem and implement the solution
- Verify full system functionality and if applicable implement preventative measures
- Document findings, actions and outcomes

✓ **2.5 Given a scenario, integrate common preventative maintenance techniques**

- Physical inspection
- Updates
    - Driver
    - Firmware
    - OS
    - Security

- Scheduling preventative maintenance
  - Defrag
  - Scandisk
  - Check disk
  - Startup programs
- Use of appropriate repair tools and cleaning materials
  - Compressed air
  - Lint free cloth
  - Computer vacuum and compressors
- Power devices
  - Appropriate source such as power strip, surge protector, or UPS
- Ensuring proper environment
- Backup procedures

Mentioning the words *troubleshooting theory* to many technicians can cause their eyes to roll back in their heads. It doesn't sound glamorous or sexy, and a lot of techs believe the only way to solve a problem is to just dive right in and start working on it. Theories are for academics. In a way they're right; you do need to dive in to solve problems as they don't just solve themselves. But to be successful at troubleshooting, you must take a systematic approach.

You may hear people say, "Troubleshooting is as much of an art as it is a science," and my personal favorite, "You just need to get more experience to be good at it." While there is an art to fixing problems, you can't ignore science. And if you need experience to be any good, why are some less experienced folks incredibly good at solving problems while their more seasoned counterparts seem to take forever to fix anything? More experience is good, but it's not a prerequisite to being a good troubleshooter. It's all about a systematic approach.

Applying a systematic approach to troubleshooting is key; systematic solutions also work well in preventing problems in the first place. Many of the computer problems you stress over can be prevented.

Preventive maintenance tends to get neglected at many companies because technicians are too busy fixing problems. Spending some time on keeping those problems from occurring in the first place is a good investment of resources.

In this chapter, we'll look at the two systematic methods I've just talked about. First, we'll cover troubleshooting theory and the steps you need to take to successfully solve problems. Then, we'll look at some ways to help keep your systems running in top shape.

Understanding Troubleshooting Theory

When troubleshooting, you should assess every problem systematically and try to isolate the root cause. Yes, there is a lot of art to troubleshooting, and experience plays a part too. But regardless of how "artful" or experienced you are, haphazard troubleshooting is doomed to fail. Conversely, even technicians with limited experience can be effective troubleshooters if they stick to the principles. The major key is to start with the issue and whittle away at it until you can get down to the point where you can pinpoint the problem—this often means eliminating, or verifying, the obvious.

Although everyone approaches troubleshooting from a different perspective, a few things should remain constant. First, always back up your data before making any changes to a system. Hardware components can be replaced but data often can't be. For that reason, always be vigilant about making data backups.

Second, establish priorities—one user being unable to print to the printer of her choice isn't as important as a floor full of accountants unable to run payroll. Prioritize every job and escalate it (or de-escalate it) as you need to.

Third, but perhaps most important, document everything—not just that there was a problem but also the solution you found, the actions you tried, and the outcomes of each. In the next few sections I'll take you through each step of the troubleshooting process.

Identifying the Problem

While this may seem obvious, it can't be overlooked: if you can't define the problem, you can't begin to solve it. Sometimes problems are relatively straightforward, but other times they're just a symptom of a bigger issue. For example, if a user isn't able to connect to the Internet from her computer, it could indeed be an issue with her system. But if other users are having similar problems, then her difficulties might just be one example of the real problem.

Ask yourself, "Is there a problem?" Perhaps "the problem" is as simple as a customer expecting too much from the computer.

Problems in computer systems generally occur in one (or more) of four areas, each of which is in turn made up of many pieces:

- A collection of hardware pieces integrated into a working system. As you know, the hardware can be quite complex, what with motherboards, hard drives, video cards, and so on. Software can be equally perplexing.

- An operating system, which in turn is dependent on the hardware.

- An application or software program that is supposed to do something. Programs such as Microsoft Word and Excel are bundled with a great many features.

- A computer user, ready to take the computer system to its limits (and beyond). A technician can often forget that the user is a very complex and important part of the puzzle.

Talking to the Customer

Many times you can define the problem by asking questions of the user. One of the keys to working with your users or customers is to ensure, much like a medical professional, that you have good bedside manner. Most people are not as technically hip as you, and when something goes wrong they become confused or even fearful that they'll take the blame. Assure them that you're just trying to fix the problem, but that they can probably help because they know what went on before you got there. It's important to instill trust with your customer. Believe what they are saying, but also believe that they might not tell you everything right away. It's not that they're necessarily lying; they just might not know what's important to tell.

⊕ **Real World Scenario**

Is the Power On?

It's a classic IT story that almost sounds like a joke, but it's happened. A customer calls technical support because his computer won't turn on. After 20 minutes of troubleshooting, the technician is becoming frustrated...maybe it's a bad power supply? The technician asks the user to read some numbers off of the back of his computer, and the user tells him, "Hold on, I need to get a flashlight. It's dark in here with the power out."

Help clarify things by having the customer show you what the problem is. The best method I've seen of doing this is to say to him, "Show me what 'not working' looks like." That way, you see the conditions and methods under which the problem occurs. The problem may be a simple matter of an improper method. The user may be performing an operation incorrectly or performing the operation in the wrong order. During this step, you have the opportunity to observe how the problem occurs, so pay attention.

Here are a few questions to ask the user to aid in determining what the problem is:

Can you show me the problem?   This question is one of the best. It allows the user to show you exactly where and when he experiences the problem.

How often does this happen?   This question establishes whether this problem is a onetime occurrence that can be solved with a reboot or whether a specific sequence of events causes the problem to happen. The latter usually indicates a more serious problem that may require software installation or hardware replacement.

Has any new hardware or software been installed recently?   New hardware or software can mean compatibility problems with existing devices or applications. For example, a newly installed device may want to use the same resource settings as an existing device. This can cause both devices to become disabled. When you install a new application, that application is likely to install several support files. If those support files are also used by an existing application, then there could be a conflict.

Has the computer recently been moved?   Moving a computer can cause things to become loose and then fail to work. Perhaps all of the peripherals of the computer didn't complete the move, meaning there's less functionality than the user expects.

Has someone who normally doesn't use the computer recently used it?   That person could have mistakenly (or intentionally) done something to make the computer the way it is.

Have any other changes been made to the computer recently?   If the answer is yes, ask if the user can remember approximately when the change was made. Then ask her approximately when the problem started. If the two dates seem related, then there's a good chance that the problem is related to the change. If it's a new hardware component, check to see that the hardware component was installed correctly.

Be careful of how you ask questions as to not appear accusatory. You can't assume that the user did something to mess up the computer. Then again, you also can't assume that they don't know anything about why it's not working.

 Real World Scenario

The Social Side of Troubleshooting

When you're looking for clues as to the nature of a problem, no one can give you more information than the person who was there when it happened. She can tell you what led up to the problem, what software was running, and the exact nature of the problem ("It happened when I tried to print"), and she can help you re-create the problem, if possible.

Use questioning techniques that are neutral in nature. Instead of saying, "What were you doing when it broke?" be more compassionate and say, "What was going on when the computer decided not to work?" Frame the question in a way that makes it sound like the computer did something wrong, and not the person. It might sound silly, but these types of changes can make your job a lot easier!

While it's sometimes frustrating dealing with end users and computer problems, such as the user who calls you up and gives you the "My computer's not working" line (okay, and what *exactly* is that supposed to mean?), even more frustrating is when no one was around to see what happened. In cases like this, do your best to find out where the problem is by establishing what works and what doesn't work.

Gathering Information

Let's say that you get to a computer and the power light is on and you can hear the hard drive spinning, but there is no video and the system seems to be unresponsive. At least you know that the system has power and you can start investigating where things start to break down. (I sense a reboot in your future!)

The whole key to this step is to identify, as specifically as possible, what the problem is. The more specific you can be in identifying what's not working, the easier it will be for you to understand why it's not working and fix it. If you have users available who were there when the thing stopped working, you can try to gather information from them. If not, you're on your own to gather clues. It's like *CSI* but not as gory.

 If a computer seems to have multiple problems that appear to be unrelated, identify what they are one at a time and fix them one at a time. For example, if the sound is not working and you can't get on the Internet, deal with those separately. If they seem related, such as not being able to get on the Internet and you can't access a network file server, then one solution might solve both problems.

So now instead of having users to ask questions of, you need to use your own investigative services to determine what's wrong. The questions you would have otherwise asked the user are still a good starting point. Does anything appear amiss or seem to have been changed recently? What is working and what's not? Was there a storm recently? Can I reboot? If I reboot, does the problem seem to go away?

The key is to find out everything you can that might be related to the problem. Document exactly what works and what doesn't, and if you can, why. If the power is out in the house, like in the story I related earlier, then there's no sense in trying the power plug in another outlet.

Determining if the Problem Is Hardware or Software Related

This step is important because it determines what part of the computer you should focus your troubleshooting skills on. Each part requires different skills and different tools.

To determine whether a problem is hardware or software related, you can do a few things to narrow down the issue. For instance, does the problem manifest itself when the user uses a particular piece of hardware (a DVD-ROM or USB hard drive, for example)? If it does, the problem is more than likely hardware related.

This step relies on personal experience more than any of the other steps do. You'll without a doubt run into strange software problems. Each one has a particular solution. Some may even require reinstallation of the software or the entire operating system. If that doesn't work, you may need to resort to restoring the entire system from a data backup when the computer was working properly.

Determining Which Component Is Failing (for Hardware Problems)

Hardware problems are usually pretty easy to figure out. Let's say the sound card doesn't work, you've tried new speakers that you know do work, and you've reinstalled the driver. All of the settings look right but it just won't respond. The sound card is probably the piece of hardware that needs to be replaced.

With many newer computers, several components such as sound, video, and networking cards are integrated into the motherboard. If you troubleshoot the computer and find a hardware component to be bad, there's a good chance that the bad component is integrated into the motherboard and the whole motherboard must be replaced—an expensive proposition, to be sure.

Laptops and a lot of desktops have components (network card, sound card, video adapter) integrated into the motherboard. If an integrated component fails, you may be able to use an expansion device (such as a USB or PC Card network adapter) to give the system full functionality without a costly repair.

Establishing a Theory

Way back when, probably in your middle school or junior high school years, you learned about the scientific method. In a nutshell, scientists develop a hypothesis, test it, and then figure out if their hypothesis is still valid. Troubleshooting involves much the same process.

Once you have determined what the problem is, you need to develop a theory as to why the problem is happening. No video? It could be something to do with the monitor or the video card. Can't get to your favorite website? Is it that site? Is it your network card, the cable, your IP address, DNS server settings, or something else? Once you have defined the problem, establishing a theory about the cause of the problem, what is wrong, helps you develop possible solutions to the problem.

Eliminating Possibilities

Theories can either state what can be true or what can't be true. However you choose to approach your theory generation, it's usually helpful to take a mental inventory to see what is possible and what's not. Start eliminating possibilities and eventually the only thing that can be wrong is what's left. This type of approach works well when it's an ambiguous problem; start broad and narrow your scope. For example, if the hard drive won't read, there is likely one of three culprits: the drive itself, the cable it's on, or the connector on the motherboard. Try plugging the drive into the other connector or using a different cable. Narrow down the options.

A common troubleshooting technique is to strip the system down to the bare bones. In a hardware situation, this could mean removing all interface cards except those absolutely required for the system to operate. In a software situation, this usually means booting up in Safe Mode so most of the drivers do not load.

Once you have isolated the problem, slowly rebuild the system to see if the problem comes back (or goes away). This helps you identify what is really causing the problem, and determine if there are other factors affecting the situation. For example, I have seen memory problems that are fixed by switching the slot that the memory chips are in.

Using External Resources

Sometimes you can figure out what's not working, but you have no idea why or what you can do to fix it. That's okay. In situations like those, it may be best to fall back on an old trick called reading the manual. As they say, "When all else fails, read the instructions." The service manuals are your instructions for troubleshooting and service information. Virtually every computer and peripheral made today has service documentation on the company's website, or on a DVD or even in a paper manual. Don't be afraid to use them!

Before starting to eliminate possibilities, check the vendor's website for any information that might help you. For example, typing in a specific error message on a vendor's website might get you directly to specific steps to fix the problem.

If you're lucky enough to have experienced, knowledgeable, and friendly co-workers, be open to asking for help if you get stuck on a problem.

Testing Solutions

You've eliminated possibilities and developed a theory as to what the problem is. Your theory may be pretty specific, such as "The power cable is fried," or it may be a bit more general, like "The hard drive isn't working" or "There's a connectivity problem." No matter your theory, now is the time to start testing solutions. Again, if you're not sure where to begin to find a solution, the manufacturer's website is a good place to start!

Check the Simple Stuff First

This step is the one that even experienced technicians overlook. Often, computer problems are the result of something simple. Technicians overlook these problems because they're so simple that the technicians assume they *couldn't* be the problem. Here are some examples of simple problems:

Is it plugged in?   And plugged in at both ends? Cables must be plugged in at *both ends* in order to function correctly. Cables can easily be tripped over and inadvertently pulled from their sockets.

 Real World Scenario

"Is It Plugged In?" and Other Insulting Questions

Think about how you feel if someone asks you this question. Your likely response is "Of course it is!" After all, you're not an idiot, right? The same reaction often happens to similar questions about the device being turned on. The problem is, making sure it's plugged in and turned on are the first things you should always do when investigating a problem.

When asking these types of questions, it's not what you say but how you say it. For example, instead of asking if it's plugged in, you could say something like, "Can you do me a favor and check to see what color the end of the keyboard plug is? Is that the same color of the port where it's plugged into on the computer?" That generally gets the user to at least look at it without making them feel dumb. For power, something like, "What color are the lights on the front of the router? Are any of them blinking?" can work well.

Ask neutral and nonthreatening questions. Make it sound like the computer is at fault, not the user. These types of things will help you build rapport and be able to get more information so you can solve problems faster.

Is it turned on?   This one seems the most obvious, but we've all fallen victim to it at one point or another. Computers and their peripherals must be turned on in order to function. Most have power switches with LEDs that glow when the power is turned on.

Is the system ready? Computers must be ready before they can be used. *Ready* means the system is ready to accept commands from the user. An indication that a computer is ready is when the operating system screens come up and the computer presents you with a menu or a command prompt. If that computer uses a graphical interface, the computer is ready when the mouse pointer appears. Printers are ready when the Online or Ready light on the front panel is lit.

Do the chips and cables need to be reseated? You can solve some of the strangest problems (random hang-ups or errors) by opening the case and pressing down on each socketed chip. This remedies the chip-creep problem discussed later in this chapter. In addition, you should reseat any cables to make sure that they're making good contact.

 Always be sure you're grounded before operating inside the case! If you're not, you could create a static charge (ESD) that could damage components.

Check to See If It's User Error

User error is common but preventable. If a user says he can't perform some very common computer task, such as printing or saving a file, the problem is likely due to user error. As soon as you hear a problem like this, you should begin asking questions to determine if the solution is as simple as teaching the user the correct procedure. A good question to ask is, "Were you *ever* able to perform that task?" If he answers no to this question, it means he's probably doing the procedure wrong. If he answers yes, you must ask additional questions to get at the root of the problem.

If you suspect user error, tread carefully in regard to your line of questioning, to avoid making the user defensive. User errors are an opportunity to teach the users the right way to do things. Again, what you say matters. Offer a "different" or "another" way of doing things instead of the "right" way.

Restart the Computer

It's amazing how often a simple computer restart can solve a problem. Restarting the computer clears the memory and starts the computer with a clean slate. Whenever we perform phone support, we always ask the customer to restart the computer and try again. If restarting doesn't work, try powering down the system completely and then powering it up again (rebooting). More often than not, that will solve the problem.

Establishing a Plan of Action

If your fix worked, then you're brilliant! If not, then you need to reevaluate and look for the next option. After testing solutions, your plan of action may take one of three paths:

- If the first fix didn't work, try something else.
- If needed, implement the fix on other computers.
- If everything is working, document the solution.

Try, Try Again

So you tried the hard drive with a new (verified) cable and it still doesn't work. Now what? Your sound card won't play and you've just deleted and reinstalled the driver. Next steps? Move on and try the next logical thing in line.

> When trying solutions to fix a problem, only make one change to the computer at a time. If the change doesn't fix the problem, revert the system back to the way it was and then make your next change. Making more than one change at a time has two problems. One, you are never sure which change actually worked. Two, by making multiple changes at once, you might actually cause more problems than what you started with.

When evaluating your results and looking for that golden "next step," don't forget other resources you might have available. Use the Internet to look at the manufacturer's website. Read the manual. Talk to your friend who knows everything about obscure hardware (or arcane versions of Windows). When fixing problems, two heads can be better than one.

Spread the Solution

If the problem was isolated to one computer, this step doesn't apply. But some problems you deal with may affect an entire group of computers. For example, perhaps some configuration information was entered incorrectly into the DHCP server, giving everyone the wrong DNS server address. The DHCP server is now fixed, but all of the clients need to renew their IP addresses.

Document the Solution

Once everything is working, you'll need to document what happened and how you fixed it. If the problem looks to be long and complex, I suggest taking notes as you're trying to fix it. It will help you remember what you've already tried and what didn't work. We'll discuss documenting in more depth in a separate step later in this chapter.

Verifying Functionality

After fixing the system, or all of the systems affected by the problem, go back and verify full functionality. For example, if the users couldn't get to any network resources, check to make sure they can get to the Internet as well as internal resources.

Some solutions may actually cause another problem on the system. For example, if you update software or drivers, you may inadvertently cause another application to have problems. There's obviously no way you can or should test all applications on a computer after applying a fix, but know that these types of problems can occur. Just make sure that what you've fixed works, and that there aren't any obvious signs of something else not working all of a sudden.

Another important thing to do at this time is to implement preventive measures, if possible. If it was a user error, ensure that the user understands ways to accomplish the task that don't cause the error. If a cable melted because it was too close to someone's space heater under her desk, resolve the issue. If the computer overheated because there was an inch of dust clogging the fan...you get the idea.

Documenting the Work

Lots of people can fix problems. But can you remember what you did when you fixed a problem a month ago? Maybe. Can one of your co-workers remember something you did to fix the same problem on that machine a month ago? Unlikely. Always document your work so that you or someone else can learn from that experience. Good documentation of past troubleshooting can save hours of stress in the future.

Documentation can take a few different forms, but the two most common are personal and system-based.

One thing I always recommend to technicians is to carry a personal notebook to take notes in. The type of notebook doesn't matter—use whatever works best for you. The notebook can be a lifesaver, especially when you're new to a job. Write down the problem, what you tried, and the solution. The next time you run across the same or a similar problem, you'll have a better idea of what to try. Eventually you'll find yourself less and less reliant on it, but it's incredibly handy to have!

System-based documentation is useful to both you and your co-workers. Many facilities have server logs of one type or another, conveniently located close to the machine. If someone makes a fix or a change, it gets noted in the log. If there's a problem, it's noted in the log. They're critical to have for a few reasons. One, if you weren't there the first time it was fixed, you might not have an idea of what to try and it could take you a long time using trial and error. Two, if you begin to see a repeated pattern of problems, you can make a permanent intervention before the system completely dies.

I've seen several different forms of system-based documentation. Again, the type doesn't matter as long as you do it! Often it's a notebook or a binder next to the system or on a nearby shelf. If you have a rack, you can mount something on the side to hold a binder or notebook. For client computers, one way is to tape an index card to the top or side of the power supply (don't cover any vents!) so if a tech has to go inside the case, she can see if anyone else has been in there to fix something too.

When doctors take the Hippocratic Oath, they promise to not make their patients any sicker than they already were. Technicians should take a similar oath. It all boils down to "If it ain't broke, don't fix it." When you troubleshoot, make one change at a time. If the change doesn't solve the problem, revert the computer to its previous state before making a different change. Otherwise, you could cause more problems than you started with. There's no sense in making things more difficult than they need to be!

Understanding Preventive Maintenance

We get the oil changed in our cars so the engine doesn't blow up. We go to the dentist to make sure our teeth don't fall out. We buy life insurance, just in case. We do a lot of preventive maintenance in our lives, but these types of activities don't typically fall on our "fun things to do" list. We do them because we know what the consequences could be if we didn't.

The same principles hold true for our computers. Preventive maintenance is one of the most overlooked ways to reduce the cost of ownership in any environment. It can make our machines run longer and faster, which is good for everyone involved. This section outlines some preventive maintenance ideas, tools, and procedures.

Managing the Physical Environment

Some of our computers sit in the same dark, dusty corner for their entire lives. Other computers are lucky enough to be carried around, thrown into bags, and occasionally dropped. Either way, the physical environment in which our computers exist can have a major effect on how long those computers last. It's smart to periodically inspect the physical environment to ensure that there are no working hazards. Routinely cleaning components will also extend their useful life, and so will ensuring that the power supplying them is maintained as well.

Inspecting the Environment

Sometimes we can't help how clean—or unclean—our environments are. A computer in an auto body shop is going to face dangers that one in a receptionist's office won't. Still, there are things you can do to help keep your systems clean and working well.

We're going to cover the physical environment a lot more in Chapter 12, "Understanding Operational Procedures," as CompTIA A+ Objective 6.1 requires you to know more detail about the environment than Objective 2.5 does. In a nutshell, though, water and other liquids, dirt, dust, rogue power sources, and heat aren't good for electronic components.

Inspect your environment to eliminate as many of these risks as possible. Leaving your laptop running outside in a rainstorm? Not such a good idea. (Been there, done that.)

Cleaning Computers

Cleaning a computer system is the most important part of maintaining it. Computer components get dirty. Dirt reduces their operating efficiency and, ultimately, their life. Cleaning them is definitely important. But cleaning them with the right cleaning compounds is equally important. Using the wrong compounds can leave residue behind that is more harmful than the dirt you're trying to remove!

Most computer cases and monitor cases can be cleaned using mild soap and water on a clean, lint-free cloth. Make sure the power is off before you put anything wet near a computer. Dampen (don't soak) a cloth with a mild soap solution, and wipe the dirt and dust from the case. Then wipe the moisture from the case with a dry, lint-free cloth. Anything with a plastic or metal case can be cleaned in this manner.

Don't drip liquid into any vent holes on equipment. Monitors in particular have vent holes in the top.

To clean a monitor screen, use glass cleaner designed specifically for monitors and a soft cloth. Don't use commercial window cleaner, because the chemicals in it can ruin the anti-glare coating on some monitors.

To clean a keyboard, use canned air to blow debris out from under keys, and use towelettes designed for use with computers to keep the key tops clean. If you spill anything on a keyboard, you can clean it by soaking it in distilled, *demineralized water*. The minerals and impurities have been removed from this type of water, so it won't leave any traces of residue that might interfere with the proper operation of the keyboard after cleaning. Make sure you let the keyboard dry for at least 48 hours before using it.

The electronic connectors of computer equipment, on the other hand, should never touch water. Instead, use a swab moistened in distilled, *denatured isopropyl alcohol* (also known as electronics cleaner and found in electronics stores) to clean contacts. Doing so will take the oxidation off the copper contacts.

A good way to remove dust and dirt from the inside of the computer is to use compressed air. Blow the dust from inside the computer using a stream of compressed air. However, be sure you do this outdoors, so you don't blow dust all over your work area or yourself. You can also use a vacuum, but it must be designed specifically for electronics—such models don't generate *electrostatic discharge (ESD)* and have a finer filter than normal.

To prevent a computer from becoming dirty in the first place, control its environment. Make sure there is adequate ventilation in the work area and that the dust level isn't excessive. To avoid ESD, you should maintain 50 to 80 percent humidity in the room where the computer is operating.

You should visually inspect the computer for signs of distress within it. Discolored areas on the board are often caused by overheating. The overheating can be caused by power surges or overclocking and is an indication that all is not right.

One unique challenge when cleaning printers is spilled toner. It sticks to everything and should not be inhaled. Use an electronics vacuum that is designed specifically to pick up toner. A normal vacuum's filter isn't fine enough to catch all the particles, so the toner may be circulated into the air. Normal electronics vacuums may melt the toner instead of picking it up.

 If you get toner on your clothes, use a magnet to get it out (toner is half iron).

Removable media devices such as floppy and CD and DVD drives don't usually need to be cleaned during preventive maintenance. Clean one only if you're experiencing problems with it. Cleaning kits sold in computer stores provide the needed supplies. Usually, cleaning a floppy drive involves using a dummy disk made of semi-abrasive material. When you insert the disk in the drive, the drive spins it, and the abrasive action on the read-write head removes any debris.

Maintaining Power

As electronics, computers need a power source. Laptops can free you from your power cord leash for a while, but only temporarily. Power is something we often take for granted until we lose it, then we twiddle our thumbs and wonder what people did before the Internet. Most people realize that having too much power is a bad thing because it can fry electronic components. Having too little power can also wreak havoc on electrical circuits.

Power strips come in all shapes and sizes and are convenient for plugging multiple devices into one wall outlet. Most of them even have an on/off switch so you can turn all of the devices on or off at the same time.

Don't make the mistake of thinking that power strips will protect you from electrical surges, though. If you get a strong power surge through one of these $10 devices, the strip and everything plugged into it can be fried. Some people like to call power strips "surge protectors" or "surge suppressors," but power strips do nothing to protect or suppress.

Devices that actually attempt to keep power surges at bay are called *surge protectors*. They often look just like a power strip so it's easy to mistake them for each other, but protectors are more expensive, usually starting in the $25 range. They have a fuse inside them that is designed to blow if it receives too much current and not transfer the current to the devices plugged into it. Surge protectors may also have plug-ins for RJ-11 (phone), RJ-45 (Ethernet), and BNC (coaxial cable) connectors as well. Figure 8.1 shows a surge protector.

FIGURE 8.1   Surge protector

The best device for power protection is called an *uninterruptible power supply (UPS)*. These devices can be as small as a brick, like the one in Figure 8.2, or as large as an entire server rack. Some just have a few indicator lights, while others have LCD displays that show status and menus and come with their own management software.

FIGURE 8.2   An uninterruptible power supply

Inside the UPS is one or more batteries and fuses. Much like a surge suppressor, a UPS is designed to protect everything that's plugged into it from power surges. UPSs are also designed to protect against power sags and even power outages. Energy is stored in the batteries, and if the power fails, the batteries can power the computer for a period of time so the administrator can then safely power it down. Many UPSs and operating systems will also work together to automatically (and safely) power down a system that gets switched to UPS power. These types of devices may be overkill for Uncle Bob's machine at home, but they're critically important fixtures in server rooms.

The UPS should be checked periodically as part of the preventive maintenance routine to make sure that its battery is operational. Most UPSs have a test button you can press to simulate a power outage. You will find that batteries wear out over time, and you should replace the battery in the UPS every couple of years in order to keep the UPS dependable.

The motherboard contains a battery as well, which is used to maintain internal settings when power is not provided to the unit. Resembling large watch batteries, these entities tend to have a considerable life, on average, but can lose their charge over time. If you boot a system and find that the date and time and other variables have not been maintained, you will want to change the internal battery.

Using the Right Repair Tools and Cleaning Materials

It's a little-known fact, but dust bunnies actually multiply just like real-life bunnies. (It's true!) So when you open the computer case and see a whole family of these little critters, it may be tempting to break out the old Hoover and suck them all up. While getting rid of the dust is a good idea, using a standard vacuum isn't because it generates ESD. When performing preventive maintenance, using the right tools is as important as the procedure itself.

Dust is bad for computers for a few reasons. One, it carries a slight electric charge, which is why it collects on electronics in the first place. That charge can build up to levels that are dangerous to circuits. Two, dust acts as an insulator, trapping heat inside components instead of letting the heat dissipate. Overheated electronic components are likely to have short life spans.

A few of the tools useful in preventive maintenance have already been covered in this chapter, but now is a good time to review them. A *computer vacuum* is a small handheld device perfect for sucking up dust and other little particles without causing ESD problems. One is pictured in Figure 8.3. This model plugs into your USB port, making it handy for laptops too. Many vacuums come with a brush attachment, but depending on who you talk to the brushes have limited usefulness.

FIGURE 8.3   A computer vacuum

Table 8.1 lists the more common preventive maintenance tools and their uses.

TABLE 8.1   Preventive Maintenance Tools

Tool	Purpose
Computer vacuum	Sucking up dust and small particles.
Mild soap and water	Cleaning external computer and monitor cases.
Demineralized water	Cleaning keyboards or other devices that have contact points that are not metal.
Denatured isopropyl alcohol	Cleaning metal contacts, such as those on expansion cards.
Monitor wipes	Cleaning monitor screens. Do *not* use window cleaner!
Lint-free cloth	Wiping down anything. Don't use a cloth that will leave lint or other residue behind.
Compressed air	Blowing dust or other particles out of hard to reach areas.

The tools listed in Table 8.1 should cover most of your preventive maintenance needs from a physical standpoint. Other types of tools to help you troubleshoot will be covered in Chapter 13, "Installing, Maintaining, and Troubleshooting Hardware."

Preventive maintenance isn't just about controlling the physical environment around your computer. There are many tasks you can perform within your operating system or software to keep your system running well.

Running Updates

You may have heard the old adage that "Once you drive a car off of the dealer's lot, it's lost half of its value." A similar saying applies to computers in that "Once you get it home from the store, it's already obsolete." While the second saying isn't entirely true, it does speak to the whirlwind pace of innovation in personal computing.

When developers release software, it might not be perfect. They do their best, but when you consider that Windows Vista has an estimated 50 million lines of code (and more than 50 dependency layers, or processes that depend on other processes), you can imagine that mistakes are bound to happen. And hackers are bound to find those mistakes. So once those mistakes are uncovered, the developer needs to issue a fix, typically released as an update, as soon as possible.

Operating systems are arguably the most complex software programs written, but there are other applications and areas that need to be updated periodically as well. In this section we will focus on four areas: the operating system (specifically Windows), drivers, firmware, and security.

Updating Windows

Windows Vista, XP, and 2000 include *Windows Update*, a feature designed to keep Windows current by automatically downloading updates such as patches and security fixes and installing these fixes automatically.

Windows Update is configured to run automatically when any administrator user is logged in. However, if you want to run it manually, you can do so by clicking Start ➤ All Programs ➤ Windows Update in Windows Vista or XP, or by clicking Start ➤ Programs ➤ Windows Update in Windows 2000. You can also go to `http://update.microsoft.com` to start the process.

 Often, bundles of major updates to Windows are released as *service packs*. Microsoft typically releases major patches and Windows updates on the second Tuesday of every month; this is a good time to go hunting for a fix if you know that you need one!

Here is an overview of how Windows Update works:

1. Windows Update starts (either by itself or manually).

2. Windows Update goes online to check to see what updates are available. It compares the update list to the updates that have already been applied to the computer or have been refused by the administrator.

3. If updates are available, they are downloaded automatically in the background.

4. Once the updates are downloaded, Windows Update notifies you that the download is complete and asks you if you want to install them.

If you choose not to install the updates right away, Windows will do so for you when you shut off the computer. Instead of shutting off right away, Windows Update will install the updates first and then perform a proper shutdown.

Windows Update comes enabled by default, and it's a good idea to leave it running. But there might be times you want to configure it. Exercise 8.1 steps through the process of configuring Windows Update in Windows Vista, and Exercise 8.2 steps you through the process for Windows XP.

EXERCISE 8.1

Configuring Windows Update in Windows Vista

To configure Windows Update in Windows Vista, follow these steps:

1. Open the System Properties box (right-click Computer and choose Properties, or double-click the System icon in Control Panel).

2. Click on Windows Update under See Also in the lower-left corner.

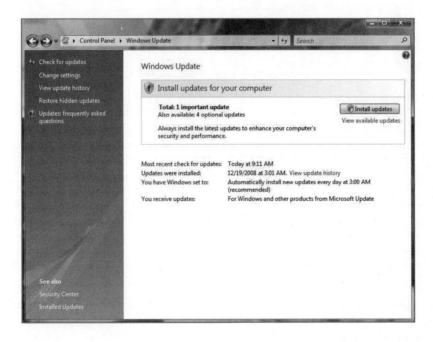

3.   Click Change Settings to open this screen:

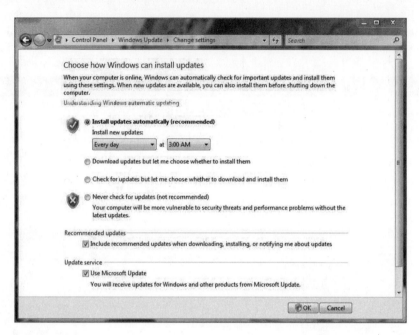

4.   Choose the option that best suits your needs. You have four choices:

   ▪   Install Updates Automatically (Recommended)

   ▪   Download Updates but Let Me Choose Whether to Install Them

   ▪   Check for Updates but Let Me Choose Whether to Download and Install Them

   ▪   Never Check for Updates (Not Recommended)

5.   Click OK to apply changes or Cancel to exit.

It's not a problem if you want to choose to have control over which updates get installed and when. However, it is in your best interest to have Windows Update enabled to ensure that you have the most current patches available.

You will notice at the bottom of the Change Settings page that there's an option called Use Microsoft Update. This is the same as Windows Update, except that by selecting this, your computer will also look for updates to other Microsoft products installed on your system, such as Microsoft Office.

EXERCISE 8.2

Configuring Windows Update in Windows XP

To configure Windows Update in Windows XP, follow these steps:

1. Open the System Properties box (right-click My Computer and choose Properties, or double-click the System icon in Control Panel).

2. Click the Automatic Updates tab.

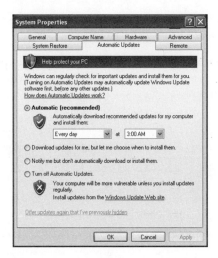

3. Choose the option that best suits your needs. You have four choices:

   - Automatically Download Recommended Updates for My Computer and Install Them

   - Download Updates for Me, but Let Me Choose When to Install Them

   - Notify Me but Don't Automatically Download or Install Them

   - Turn Off Automatic Updates

4. Click OK to apply changes or Cancel to exit.

Updating Drivers

Device drivers are software programs that tell the operating system how to work with the hardware. When you purchase a hardware device, odds are it's been in that box for a while. By the time it gets made, packaged, stored, delivered to the store, stored again at the retailer, and then purchased by you, it's entirely likely that the company that made the device has updated the driver—even possibly a few times if there have been a lot of reported problems.

When you install a device, always go to the manufacturer's website to see if a newer driver is available. You should also periodically check the website to see if new drivers are available. The old driver might work fine, but the newest driver is the one most likely to be bug-free and have all of the most current bells and whistles for your device. Exercise 8.3 shows you one way to update a driver in Windows Vista, and Exercise 8.4 shows you how to update a driver in Windows XP.

EXERCISE 8.3

Updating a Driver in Windows Vista

To update a device driver in Windows Vista, follow these steps:

1. Open the Computer Management box (right-click Computer and choose Manage) and go to Device Manager, or double-click the System icon in Control Panel and then choose Device Manager.

2. Click on the plus sign next to the device category you want to update.

3. Right-click on the device and choose Update Driver Software, or right-click on the device and choose Properties, then select the Driver tab.

4. Click the Update Driver button.

5. Follow the prompts to search for a driver on the Internet or specify the location of the driver on your computer.

EXERCISE 8.4

Updating a Driver in Windows XP

To update a device driver in Windows XP, follow these steps:

1. Open the Computer Management box (right-click My Computer and choose Manage) and go to Device Manager, or double-click the System icon in Control Panel and then choose Device Manager.

2. Click on the plus sign next to the device category you want to update.

3. Right-click on the device and choose Update Driver, or right-click on the device and choose Properties, then select the Driver tab.

4. Click the Update Driver button.

5. Choose whether or not to connect to Windows Update to search for a driver.

6. Follow the prompts to search for a driver on the Internet or specify the location of the driver on your computer.

If your device driver is not digitally signed by Microsoft—that is, it hasn't been tested for compatibility with Windows—then you will get a warning message when attempting to install the driver. You can tell Windows to continue the installation, and most of the time this doesn't cause any problems. Be aware, though, that if the driver isn't signed, that means that there could be problems with it after you complete the installation. I've installed dozens of unsigned drivers without problems, but I've also run across a few that didn't work as advertised.

Driver signing is part of Objective 3.3, and is covered in more depth in Chapter 7, "Installing and Configuring Operating Systems."

In Windows XP and 2000, you can change how Windows responds to unsigned device drivers. By default, Windows is set to warn you if the driver is unsigned, but you can also tell Windows to ignore unsigned drivers or block their installation. To do so, open System Management (right-click My Computer and choose Properties, or open the System applet in Control Panel) and select the Hardware tab. On that tab, you will see a Driver Signing button. Click that and you will get a screen similar to the one shown in Figure 8.4.

FIGURE 8.4 Windows XP Driver Signing Options

Windows Vista will always warn you about unsigned drivers. If you're using a 64-bit version of Windows Vista, then you are only allowed to install signed drivers.

Updating Firmware

Any software that is encoded into a read-only memory (ROM) chip is called *firmware*. Most computers have some amount of firmware, whether it's the CMOS program stored on the BIOS chip or firmware for configuring expansion cards such as SCSI controllers.

In the old days (pre-mid-1990s) updating firmware meant taking the old chip out and replacing it with a newer chip. Today, most firmware is actually on a flash ROM chip, meaning that it can be updated through a software program much like any device driver can. As is the case with drivers, firmware can be updated to fix any bugs or add new features.

Updating Security

Security is at the forefront of nearly every network administrator's mind these days. Most networks are connected to the Internet, and it seems as if hackers are waiting in every dark corner of cyberspace, eager to ruin your life.

Keeping your security up to date isn't a simple task. It's not like you can download one program or flip one switch and make all of your security headaches disappear. Good security measures are complex—so complex, in fact, that there are entire certifications just for security, such as the CompTIA Security+ exam and the Cisco Certified Security Professional (CCSP), among others.

The A+ exam will test your knowledge of security as well but not on as deep of a level as the other exams. For more on security in this book, see Chapters 11 and 19. In this chapter, we'll look at two preventive maintenance security measures: identifying potential problem areas and guarding against viruses.

Identifying Security Problem Areas

Keeping your systems up to date is the best way to ensure you don't have security problems. You can't always be proactive and stay ahead of hackers, but there are a few areas that you can concentrate on to eliminate most problems. The following list briefly summarizes the areas you must be concerned about:

Operating system updates   Make sure all scheduled maintenance is performed and updates and service packs are installed on all the systems in your environment.

Application updates   Make sure all applications are kept to the most current levels. One of the biggest exploitations that occur today involves application programs such as e-mail clients and word processing software. The manufacturers of these products regularly release updates to attempt to make them more secure.

Network device updates   Most network devices can provide high levels of security, or they can be configured to block certain types of traffic and IP addresses. Make sure logs are reviewed and, where necessary, access control lists (ACLs) updated to prevent attackers from disrupting your systems.

 ACL, like many other acronyms in computing, can stand for more than one thing. Access control lists are used with both permissions for files/folders and network access.

Policies and procedures   A policy that is out of date may be worse than no policy. Be aware of any changes in your organization and in the industry that make existing policies out of date. Periodically review your documentation to verify that your policies are effective and current.

In addition to focusing on these areas, you should stay current on security trends, threats, and tools available to help you provide security. The volume of threats is increasing, as are the measures, methods, and procedures used to counter them.

You should also make it a priority to train and educate users about malicious software. The more they know about the threats that are present—and the harm they can inflict—the more likely they are to act accordingly when they encounter a possible threat.

Guarding Against Viruses

This type of preventive maintenance is absolutely critical these days if you have a connection to the Internet. A *computer virus* is a small, deviously ingenious program that replicates itself to other computers, generally causing those computers to behave abnormally. Generally speaking, a virus's main function is to reproduce. A virus attaches itself to files on a hard disk and modifies those files. When the files are accessed by a program, the virus can infect the program with its own code. The program may then, in turn, replicate the virus code to other files and other programs. In this manner, a virus may infect an entire computer.

When an infected file is transferred to another computer (via disk or download), the process begins on the other computer. Because of the frequency of downloads from the Internet, viruses can run rampant if left unchecked. For this reason, antivirus programs were developed. They check files and programs for any program code that shouldn't be there and either eradicate it or prevent the virus from replicating. An antivirus program is generally run in the background on a computer, and it examines all the file activity on that computer. When it detects a suspicious activity, it notifies the user of a potential problem and asks the user what to do about it. Some antivirus programs can also make intelligent decisions about what to do. The process of running an antivirus program on a computer is known as *inoculating* the computer against a virus.

For a listing of most of the viruses that are currently out there, refer to Symantec's Anti-Virus Research Center (SARC) at `http://www.symantec.com/avcenter/index.html`.

You may notice that a lot of the language surrounding computer viruses sounds like language we use to discuss human illness. The moniker *virus* was given to these programs because a computer virus functions much like a human virus, and the term helped to anthropomorphize the computer a bit. Somehow, if people can think of a computer as getting sick, it breaks down the computer phobia that many people have.

There are two categories of viruses: benign and malicious. Benign viruses don't do much besides replicate themselves and exist. They may cause the occasional problem, but it is usually an unintentional side effect. Malicious viruses, on the other hand, are designed to destroy things. Once a malicious virus (for example, the Michelangelo virus) infects your machine, you can usually kiss the contents of your hard drive good-bye.

To prevent virus-related problems, you can install one of any number of antivirus programs (Norton AntiVirus or McAfee VirusScan, for example). These programs will periodically scan your computer for viruses, monitor regular use of the computer, and note any suspicious activity that might indicate a virus. In addition, these programs have a database of known viruses and the symptoms each one causes.

Antivirus databases should be updated frequently (about once a week, although more often is better) to keep your antivirus program up to date with all the possible virus definitions. Most antivirus programs will automatically update themselves (if configured properly) just like Windows Update will update Windows, provided that the computer has a live Internet connection. It's a good idea to let them automatically update, just in case you forget to do it yourself.

Using Disk Management Tools

For the most part, Windows runs pretty well considering how massive and complex it is. But over time its performance can degrade just through use. It's not really Windows' fault—it's just what happens when people use it every day, opening and closing dozens or hundreds of files and accessing scores more on other computers. These actions take their toll on the file storage system.

Preventive maintenance encompasses running software utilities on a regular basis to keep the file system fit. Often you can schedule these activities to run automatically, which is a good idea. Disk management utilities that are bundled with Windows include Disk Defragmenter, ScanDisk and Checkdisk, and Disk Cleanup.

There are more disk management tools than what I have covered here, but they are tested under another objective. For more Windows utilities, please refer to Chapters 6 and 7.

Task Scheduler, which can be used to schedule many services, is discussed in detail in Chapter 17, "Operating System Utilities and Troubleshooting Issues."

Disk Defragmenter

When you save files to a hard drive, Windows will generally write the file into the first available space on the disk. So let's say you create an Excel spreadsheet and save it. It will be written to the disk. Next, you create a dozen new Word documents and save them as well. Then, you go back and add a ton of data to your spreadsheet. Now the Excel file is much bigger. Instead of moving it all to a space on the hard drive big enough to handle the file, Windows will keep part of the file in its original location and write the rest of the data to another available space on the hard drive. When a file is in several places on a disk, it's called a *fragmented* file. Excessive fragmentation of your files can slow down your computer's performance.

Defragmenting a disk involves analyzing the disk and then consolidating fragmented files and folders so they occupy a contiguous space, thus increasing performance during file retrieval. In Windows there are a few different ways you can get to the Disk Defragmenter :

- In Windows Vista, click Start and type **defrag** into the Start Search box. Choose Disk Defragmenter from the Programs list.

- In Windows Vista or XP, open Computer or My Computer, right-click on a hard drive, choose Properties, select the Tools tab, and choose Defragment Now as shown in Figure 8.5.

- In Windows XP, open Computer Management (right-click My Computer and choose Manage) and select Disk Defragmenter from the Storage section.

FIGURE 8.5   Choose Defragment Now.

When you open Disk Defragmenter in Windows Vista, the first page gives you options for scheduling defragmentation, as shown in Figure 8.6.

FIGURE 8.6   Disk Defragmenter in Vista

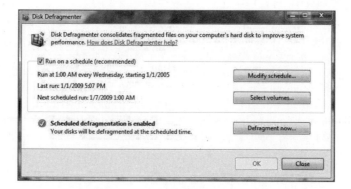

Microsoft recommends that you enable scheduled defragmentation. If you want to defragment immediately, click the Defragment Now button.

Windows XP does not give you the option to schedule defragmentation through Disk Defragmenter. To run a defrag in XP, highlight the appropriate drive, as shown in Figure 8.7, and click the Defragment button. If you're not sure whether the drive needs to be defragmented, you can choose to Analyze instead, which will provide you with a report on how fragmented your drive is, as shown in Figure 8.8.

FIGURE 8.7   Disk Defragmenter in Windows XP

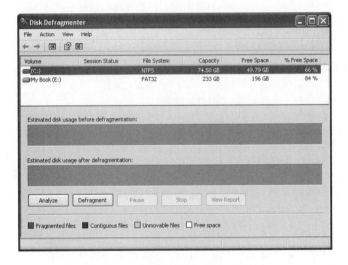

FIGURE 8.8   Defrag analysis report in Windows XP

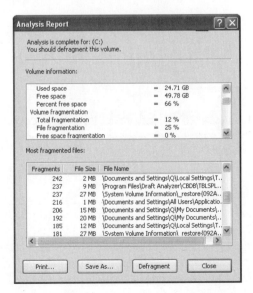

ScanDisk and Chkdsk

Depending on the version of Windows you're running, or if you're really old school and still like to run DOS, ScanDisk and Chkdsk may be one and the same or they may be different utilities.

The Chkdsk utility was the first of the two to be released. It was a command-prompt utility that looked at file system integrity and could fix logical disk errors, such as file pointers that pointed to nothing or cross-linked files. Later versions of Chkdsk were also able to scan for physical disk errors.

A newer disk-checking utility called ScanDisk was introduced with DOS 6.2. It had a so-called graphical interface and was able to scan the physical disk for errors in addition to fixing everything that Chkdsk could.

Then things got a bit fuzzy. Microsoft continued to provide disk-checking utilities in Windows, but you often had the choice of Chkdsk or ScanDisk. Once Windows NT hit the market, it included Chkdsk but it wasn't the same as the old DOS version. In fact, it looked and acted a lot like ScanDisk. Confusion reigned.

Today, Microsoft has made it all easier again by calling the disk-checking utility "Error checking," and it is found on the Tools tab of the hard disk properties, as shown in Figure 8.5. You start it by clicking the Check Now button.

 Perhaps as a salute to the tweed-wearing techies of the 1980s, Microsoft still does include Chkdsk in its operating systems, including Vista.

Once you click Check Now, a window like the one in Figure 8.9 will appear. Choose the options you want, and click Start.

FIGURE 8.9 Disk error checking

Disk Cleanup

Disk Cleanup is a relatively new Windows utility that allows you to free up hard disk space by removing temporary and downloaded files, emptying the Recycle Bin, and performing several other services to clean out unneeded files.

You get to Disk Cleanup by right-clicking on your hard drive, clicking Properties, and choosing Disk Cleanup from the General tab. After asking you a few simple questions, Windows will give you a screen like the one in Figure 8.10.

All you need to do is check the types of files you want Disk Cleanup to remove and click OK. Windows takes care of the rest for you. The More Options tab allows you to free up more disk space by removing programs you don't use and deleting old restore points.

FIGURE 8.10   Disk Cleanup

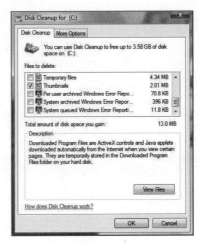

Backing Up Data and Creating Restore Points

Simply put, data is probably the most important resource your company has. Hardware can be replaced, and in most cases people can be too. But if a company loses its data, prospects for success are bleak.

An organization's *backup policy* dictates what information should be backed up and how it should be backed up. Backup policies also need to set guidelines for information archiving. Many managers and users don't understand the difference between a backup and an archive. A *backup* is a restorable copy of any set of data that is needed on the system; an *archive* is any collection of data that is removed from the system because it's no longer needed on a regular basis.

Along with making the backup, you also need to consider who can get to the backup. If data is valuable enough to spend the resources required to back it up, it is clearly important enough to protect carefully. As a backup, all of your company's data is in an easily transported form and should be protected from access by those who should not see it.

Scheduling Backups

This is one of the areas most users, and even most companies, fail to manage properly. At the same time, it's one of the most important. Backups serve several key purposes, such as protecting against hard drive failure, protecting against accidental deletion, protecting against malicious deletion or attacks, and making an archive of important files for later use. Any time you make major changes to your system, including installing new software, you should perform a backup of important files before making those changes.

All Windows versions since Windows 2000 allow you to schedule backups, which is a great feature that not all versions of Windows have had.

Now that you know you can schedule backups to make your life easy, and of course you want to make backups because it's the right thing to do, the question becomes: How often do you need to back up your files?

The answer depends on what the computer does and what you do on the computer. How often does your data change? Every day? Every week or every month? How important are your files? Can you afford to lose them? How much time or money will it cost to replace lost files? Can they be replaced? By answering these questions, you can get an idea of how often you want to run scheduled backups. As a rule of thumb, the more important the data is and the more often it changes, the more often you want to back up. If you don't care about losing the data, then there's no need for backups—but most of us do care about losing our stuff. Exercise 8.5 demonstrates how to enable scheduled backups in Windows Vista.

EXERCISE 8.5

Scheduling Backups in Windows Vista

To schedule a backup in Windows Vista, follow these steps:

1. Open Windows Backup by choosing Start ➢ All Programs ➢ Accessories ➢ System Tools ➢ Backup Status and Configuration.

2. For this exercise, we assume you do not have automatic file backup configured, so choose Set Up Automatic File Backup. (If Backup has been previously configured, you won't see this option. If this is the case for you, go to Step 6.)

3. After selecting Set Up Automatic File Backup, you will be asked where you want to save your backup to. Options include hard drives, CD, DVD, and network locations. Note that you can't back up data on a hard drive to the same hard drive. Click Next.

4. Choose what types of files you want to back up (as shown in the graphic), and click Next.

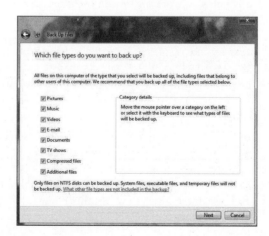

5. Confirm the backup schedule you want, and click Save Settings And Exit, then Back Up Now. If this is your first backup, Vista will create a full backup.

6. If Backup has been previously configured, or if you want to change backup options, you can either close and reopen Backup or navigate to the main screen as shown here:

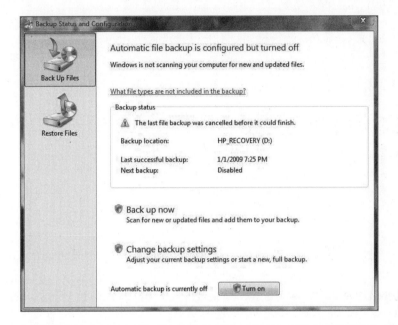

7. As you can see in the graphic, there is information on when the last backup was performed. If you want to run a manual backup, choose Back Up Now. To change any settings, select Change Backup Settings. Finally, the button at the bottom lets you turn automatic backups on and off.

One key thing to remember is that for the backups to run properly as scheduled, the computer needs to be on when the scheduled backup is supposed to take place.

If you do have automatic backup enabled, your screen will look a little different when you open up Backup Status And Configuration. It will show the last time a backup was completed and the next time a backup is scheduled for, as shown in Figure 8.11. If you want to run another backup immediately, choose the Back Up Now option. Vista will scan for files that have been changed since your last backup and add them to the backup file.

If you do have backup enabled but want to change settings, choose Change Backup Settings. Selecting this option will give you the same screens as you saw in steps 3, 4, and 5 in Exercise 8.5, letting you change the backup location, types of files, and schedule. If you want to turn automatic backups off, click the Turn Off button at the bottom of the screen. Notice that if you want to restore files, that option is one of the selections on the left. We'll look at how to restore files in Chapter 17, "Operating System Utilities and Troubleshooting Issues."

FIGURE 8.11 Backup status

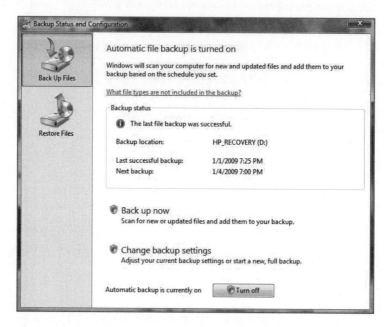

Scheduling backups in Windows XP is similar to doing it in Vista, but there are more steps involved. Exercise 8.6 walks you through setting up backups in Windows XP.

EXERCISE 8.6

Scheduling Backups in Windows XP

To schedule a backup in Windows XP, follow these steps:

1. Open Windows Backup by selecting Start ➤ All Programs ➤ Accessories ➤ System Tools ➤ Backup. This will open the Backup Or Restore Wizard. The wizard will walk you through all of the options you can use, or you can click the Advanced Mode link to set up things manually.

2. On the Backup Or Restore Wizard screen, click Next to continue.

3. Choose Back Up Files And Settings, and click Next.

4. Choose what you want to back up (as shown in the graphic), and click Next.

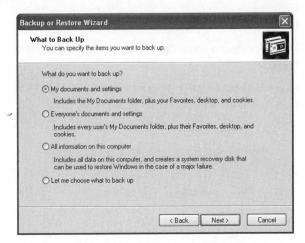

5. Confirm the backup type and the destination, and give the backup file a name (it will have a .BKF extension). For the destination, you can click the Browse button to select the right location, which might be a floppy drive, a CD or DVD burner, a USB hard drive, or a network drive. Click Next.

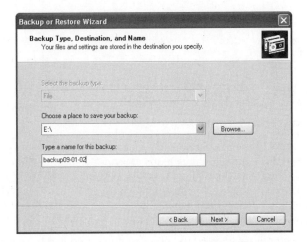

6. Depending on the type of backup you chose, you might have different options here. If you see the Completing The Backup Or Restore Wizard summary page, click the Advanced button and then to go to step 7. If you are asked to specify the type of backup, choose the type you want. If you're not sure, choose Normal. Click Next.

EXERCISE 8.6 *(continued)*

7. Choose your backup options: Verify Data, Hardware Compression, and Disable Volume Shadow Copy. It's a good idea to verify data, but it does take extra time. Click Next.

8. Choose to replace the current backup file (if one exists) or append the data to the end of the backup. Click Next.

9. Here is where you can schedule the backup. Choose Later, and then click the Set Schedule button. (If you don't want to schedule but want to back up the files now, click Now.)

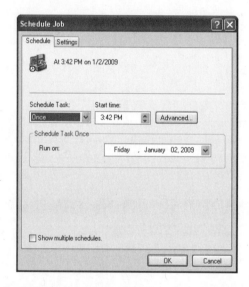

10. In the Schedule Job window, choose how often and at what time you would like to run backups, and click OK. Then click Next.

11. You will be prompted for a username and password to run the backup. This is because only certain user accounts (such as the Administrator account) have the ability to run backups. When the process starts, Windows will log itself in as the user account you specify to perform the backup. Click Next.

12. Review the information on the confirmation page, and click Finish.

Don't forget that the computer needs to be on when the scheduled backup is supposed to take place for it to work!

> ## 🌐 Real World Scenario
>
> ### Learning Lessons about Backups
>
> People don't back up data enough, plain and simple. Scheduling regular backups is a good protective measure, but just because you are backing up your data doesn't mean you're completely saved if something goes wrong.
>
> Several years ago, one of my former students related a story to me about a server crash at his company. A server had mysteriously died over the weekend, and the technicians were greeted with the problem first thing Monday morning. Not to worry, they thought, because they made regular backups.
>
> After several attempts to restore the backup tape, a second, more serious problem was readily apparent. The backup didn't work. They couldn't read the data from the tape, and it was the only backup tape they had. It wasn't going to be a very good Monday. Ultimately, they ended up losing extensive data from the server because their backup didn't work.
>
> How do you prevent tragedies like this from happening? Test your backups. After you make a backup, ensure that you can read from it. If you've just backed up a small amount of data, restore it to an alternate location and make sure you can read it. If you are backing up entire computers, a good idea is to run a test restore on a separate computer. No matter what your method, test your backup, especially when it's the first one you've made after setting up backups or you have made backup configuration changes. It isn't necessary to fully test each single backup after that, but it is a good idea to spot-check backups on occasion.
>
> Here are two more ideas that will help too. One, rotate backup tapes (or CDs/DVDs). Alternate tapes every other backup period, or use a separate tape for each day of the week. This lessens the risk of having a bad tape bring you down. Two, store your backups offsite. If your backup is sitting on top of the server, and you have a fire that destroys the building, then your backup didn't do you any good. There are data archiving firms that will, for a small fee, come and pick up your backup tapes and store them in their secure location.
>
> Be vigilant about backing up your data, and in the event of a failure, you'll be back up and running in short order.

Understanding Backup Types

The Windows Backup utility has several different options when it comes to backing up your files. The choices that Backup provides when asking you what you want to back up include:

- My Documents And Settings
- Everyone's Documents And Settings

- All Information On This Computer

- Let Me Choose What To Back Up

The first three are common options, and of course you can always select specific files you want to back up by telling Backup to let you choose the files yourself.

 For security purposes, you must have administrative rights to be able to back up files belonging to people other than yourself.

Windows Backup works by looking at an attribute of the file known as an *archive bit*. When a file is created or modified, the archive bit is set to 1, indicating that the file has not been backed up in its current state. When a backup is made, that archive bit may be cleared—that is, set back to 0—to indicate that the file has been backed up. Some backup types do not clear the archive bit.

There are a couple of quick and easy ways you can see if the archive bit for a file is or is not set. The first is in Windows Explorer. Navigate to a file, such as a Word document, right-click on it, and choose Properties. At the bottom of the General tab, you will see an Attributes section and an Advanced button. Click the Advanced button to display a window like the one in Figure 8.12.

FIGURE 8.12   Advanced file attributes

If the File Is Ready For Archiving box is checked, that means that the archive bit is set. If you uncheck the box, then the archive bit is set back to 0.

The second way is from a command prompt. In a directory, type **attrib** and press Enter. You will see a directory listing. If off to the left of the filename you see the letter A, that means that the archive bit is set. The attrib command can be used to clear and set this bit. For help with this, type **attrib /?** at the command prompt.

Windows Backup gives you several choices for the type of backup you can make. They are as follows:

Normal   Backs up selected files and clears the archive bit.

Copy   Backs up selected files but does not clear the archive bit.

Incremental   Backs up selected files only if they were created or modified since the previous backup.

Differential   Backs up selected files only if they were created or modified since the previous backup, but does not clear the archive bit.

Daily   Backs up files that were created or modified today. It doesn't look at the archive bit, but only the date when the file was modified.

The most thorough backup is Normal, as it will back up everything you've selected. But since this backs up everything, it can take the longest amount of time. At one company where I used to consult, it took over 16 hours to make a full backup of one of their file servers! This is obviously something they couldn't do every night, nor did they need to as not all files changed every day. Their solution was to start a full (Normal) backup on Saturday evening and to make incremental backups every night during the week.

Creating Restore Points

There are times when bad things happen to good computers. No matter how hard you've tried to keep a system running flawlessly, karma is against you, and your computer crashes. There are several ways to get your computer back up and running, but many of them (such as reinstalling the operating system) take a lot of time. A new feature called System Restore was introduced with Windows XP, and it allows you to create restore points to make recovery of the operating system easier.

A *restore point* is a copy of your system configuration at a given point in time. It's like a backup of your configuration, but not necessarily your data. Restore points are created one of three ways. One, Windows creates them automatically by default. Two, you can manually create them yourself. Three, during the installation of some programs, a restore point is created before the installation (that way, if the install fails, you can "roll back" the system to a preinstallation configuration). Restore points are useful for when Windows fails to boot but the computer appears to be fine otherwise, or if Windows doesn't seem to be acting right and you think it was because of a recent configuration change.

To open System Restore, click Start ➤ All Programs ➤ Accessories ➤ System Tools ➤ System Restore. It will open a screen like the one in Figure 8.13.

By clicking Next, you can choose a restore point to restore your computer back to. An example of this is shown in Figure 8.14.

You'll notice that checkpoints are included in this list along with backups that you have performed.

> If you need to use a restore point and Windows won't boot, you can reboot into Safe Mode. After Safe Mode loads, you will have the option to work in Safe Mode or to use System Restore. Choose System Restore and you'll be presented with restore points (if any) you can use.

Creating a restore point manually is easy to do using the System Restore utility. In Exercise 8.7, we'll walk through the process of creating a restore point in Windows Vista.

FIGURE 8.13 System Restore

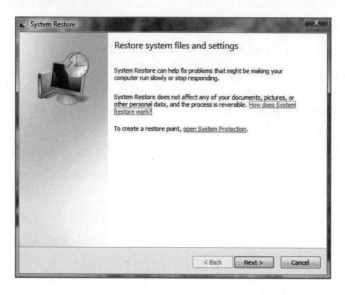

FIGURE 8.14 Restore points

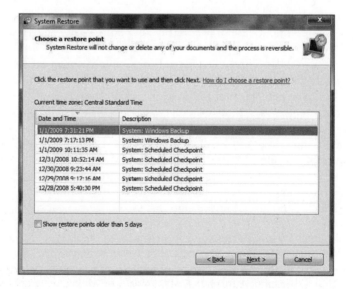

EXERCISE 8.7

Creating a Restore Point in Windows Vista

To create a restore point, follow these steps:

1. Open System Restore by clicking Start ➢ All Programs ➢ Accessories ➢ System Tools ➢ System Restore.

2. Click the Open System Protection link. (You can also get to System Protection by right-clicking on My Computer, choosing Properties, and then selecting the System Protection tab.)

3. Choose the disk or disks you want to create restore points for, and then click Create.

4. Type a description to help you identify the restore point, and then click Create.

5. Within a minute, you will be presented with a confirmation screen with the time, date, and name of your restore point.

Exercise 8.8 shows you how to create restore points in Windows XP.

EXERCISE 8.8

Creating a Restore Point in Windows XP

To create a restore point in Windows XP, follow these steps:

1. Open System Restore by clicking Start ➢ All Programs ➢ Accessories ➢ System Tools ➢ System Restore.

EXERCISE 8.8 *(continued)*

2. Choose Create A Restore Point, and click Next.

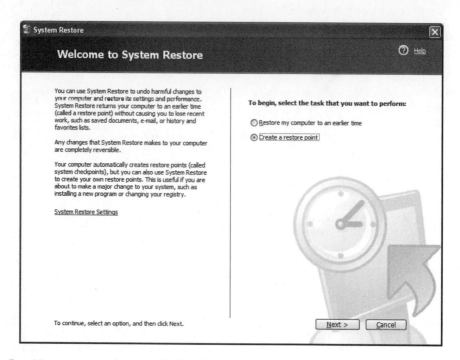

3. Provide a restore point description. Click Create.

4. Within a minute, you will be presented with a confirmation screen with the time, date, and name of your restore point.

We'll look at how to restore a system using restore points in Chapter 17.

Summary

This chapter was about systematic approaches to working with computers. The first topic was troubleshooting theory, and the second was preventive maintenance.

In our discussion of troubleshooting theory, you learned that you need to take a systematic approach to problem solving. There is both art and science involved, and experience in troubleshooting is helpful but not a prerequisite to being a good troubleshooter. You learned that in troubleshooting, the first objective is to identify the problem. Many times this can be the most time-consuming task!

Once you've identified the problem, you need to establish a theory of why the problem is happening, test your theories, establish a plan of action, verify full functionality, and then document your work. Documentation is frequently the most overlooked aspect of working with computers, but it's an absolutely critical step!

Next we discussed preventive maintenance. Again, this is something that is often overlooked but should be a key component of your administrative duties. Preventive maintenance has both physical and logical components. On the physical side, you need to make sure the environment is suitable for computers, the computers are getting the right power protection, and the right tools are used to prevent problems.

On the logical side, keeping your programs up to date is key. Install operating system patches regularly, and ensure that your antivirus software is up to date. You can also help keep your system running smoothly by telling the software to routinely clean up the hard drive. Finally, we talked about the importance of backing up your data and ways to accomplish that task.

Exam Essentials

Know the steps to take in troubleshooting computers. First identify the problem. Then establish a theory of probable cause, test your theory, establish a plan of action to resolve the problem, verify full system functionality, and finally document your findings.

Understand how to talk to the customer. Questions should be nonaccusatory and neutral in tone. Seek to understand what happened, but be careful to not blame the users, as they may become defensive and not give you the information you need to solve the problem.

Know what tools to use when cleaning the outside of computers and monitors. For cases, mild soap and water on a damp (not dripping wet) cloth is fine. For monitor screens, use wipes or sprays specifically designed for computer monitors. Never use glass cleaner!

Know what tools to use for cleaning computer parts. For parts such as the keyboard, which don't have exposed copper connectors, use demineralized water. For copper contacts, denatured alcohol (isopropyl alcohol) is appropriate.

Understand how to properly remove dust and debris from computers. If you need to blow dust or debris out of the way, use compressed air. To suck up stuff, use a computer vacuum, not a regular vacuum. For other cleaning, use a lint-free cloth.

Know what a UPS can do for you. A UPS can help prevent computers from being fried if there is a power spike. UPSs can also keep computers running for a short time in the event of a power outage or sag.

Understand how to update Windows. Windows Vista, XP, and 2000 are automatically updated (by default) through the Windows Update utility.

Know what disk management tools can help you keep your hard drives running optimally.   Windows comes with Disk Defragmenter, Error Checking (also called Checkdisk, chkdsk, and ScanDisk), and Disk Cleanup.

Know how to schedule backups.   Backups in Windows Vista, XP, and 2000 are scheduled through the Windows Backup utility.

Know how to create restore points.   Restore points in Windows Vista and XP are created through the System Restore utility. Windows 2000 does not use restore points.

Review Questions

1. In Windows XP, which utility is responsible for finding, downloading, and installing Windows service packs?

   A. Update Manager

   B. Service Pack Manager

   C. Download Manager

   D. Windows Update

2. What should you use to clean electronic connectors on expansion cards?

   A. Demineralized water

   B. Soap and water

   C. Denatured alcohol

   D. Acetone

3. What type of backup will back up all selected files and then clear the archive bit?

   A. Complete

   B. Normal

   C. Incremental

   D. Copy

4. What is the first step in the troubleshooting process?

   A. Document findings

   B. Identify the problem

   C. Establish a theory

   D. Verify functionality

5. Which tool do you use to create a restore point in Windows XP?

   A. Backup

   B. System Restore

   C. Restore Point

   D. Emergency Repair

6. What type of device can help keep your computers running for a short period of time in the event of a power outage?

   A. Uninterruptable power supply (UPS)

   B. Solar panels

   C. Surge protector

   D. Power strip

7. On Sunday you ran a normal backup, and on Monday and Tuesday you ran incremental backups. When you run an incremental backup on Wednesday, which files are backed up?

   A. All files that have changed since Sunday

   B. All files that have changed since Monday

   C. All files that have changed since Tuesday

   D. All files on your computer

8. Windows Vista includes a feature called a _____, which is a copy of your system configuration that can be used to roll back the system to a previous state if a configuration error occurs.

   A. Restore point

   B. Repair point

   C. Rollback point

   D. Registry point

9. When you make a normal backup of your files, what does Windows clear to show that the file was backed up?

   A. Backup bit

   B. Archive bit

   C. System bit

   D. Nothing

10. In general, how often should you update your antivirus definitions?

    A. Once a week

    B. Once a month

    C. Once a year

    D. Antivirus definitions do not need to be updated.

11. One of your users claims that his hard drive seems to be running slowly. What tool can you use to check to see how fragmented the hard drive is?

    A. Disk Analyzer

    B. Disk Cleanup

    C. Disk Defragmenter

    D. Chkdsk

12. You want to ensure that your computer receives automatic updates to Windows and Microsoft Office. Which tool will take care of this for you?

    A. Windows Update

    B. Microsoft Update

    C. System Update

    D. None of the above

13. You open a computer case and discover an excessive amount of dust inside. What should you do?

   A. Use a computer vacuum to remove the dust.

   B. Use a regular vacuum cleaner to remove the dust.

   C. Take a deep breath and blow as much of the dust out as you can.

   D. Nothing, dust does not harm computers.

14. Which tool do you use to create a copy of all of the data on your Windows XP computer?

   A. Backup

   B. System Restore

   C. Restore Point

   D. Emergency Repair

15. Which of the following can you do to help eliminate security problems? (Choose all that apply.)

   A. Establish security policies and procedures.

   B. Update your operating systems.

   C. Update your applications.

   D. Update your network devices.

16. Last night after you went home, your Windows XP computer ran a normal backup of your My Documents folder. Today you want to back up only the files that you've made changes to since then. Which options can you choose to do this? (Choose all that apply.)

   A. Incremental

   B. Normal

   C. Daily

   D. Copy

17. Which of the following tools can you use to delete temporary Internet files and other unneeded files to free up disk space?

   A. Disk Analyzer

   B. Disk Cleanup

   C. Disk Defragmenter

   D. Chkdsk

18. Which of the following utilities can scan the hard drive for physical errors?

   A. Disk Analyzer

   B. Disk Cleanup

   C. Disk Defragmenter

   D. Chkdsk

19. Your backup routine is to make a normal backup at the beginning of the month and incremental backups of your My Documents folder every Friday evening. On Wednesday, you decide you want to back up three subfolders in your My Documents folder but you do not want it to affect your usual backup routine. Which option should you choose?

   A. Normal

   B. Incremental

   C. Daily

   D. Copy

20. Which of the following types of backups mark the files as being backed up? (Choose all that apply.)

   A. Normal

   B. Copy

   C. Incremental

   D. Differential

Answers to Review Questions

1. D. Windows Update automatically (by default) finds, downloads, and installs service packs and other Windows updates. None of the other options are real utilities.

2. C. To clean electronic connectors, use denatured isopropyl alcohol. Water will corrode the connectors. Acetone is a solvent, but it's too powerful for circuit boards as it will eat plastic.

3. B. A normal backup will back up all selected files and then clear the archive bit, letting the system know that the file was backed up. There is no Complete backup option. Incremental will only back up files that have changed since the last backup, and it does clear the archive bit. Copy backs up all files but does not clear the archive bit.

4. B. The first step is to identify the problem. Once you have done that, you should (in order) establish a theory of probable cause, test the theory, establish a plan of action to resolve the problem, verify full system functionality, and document your findings.

5. B. The System Restore tool is used to create restore points. Backup creates backups of your hard drive. You can use Backup to create copies of your configuration (like a restore point) along with other data, but to specifically create a restore point, use System Restore. There are no Restore Point or Emergency Repair tools (although there is an emergency repair disk).

6. A. A UPS contains batteries that can keep your system running for a short period of time in case of a power outage. Solar panels may work but it depends on how you have them set up, and that is outside the scope of this book. Surge protectors and power strips are not able to provide power in a power outage.

7. C. A normal backup will back up all selected files. When you run an incremental backup, it backs up only the files that have changed since the last backup, and then it clears the archive bit. Since your last backup was Tuesday, the incremental backup on Wednesday will back up all files modified since the Tuesday backup was made.

8. A. Windows Vista (and XP) can use restore points to roll back the system configuration to a previous state. None of the other options exist.

9. B. When you make a normal or incremental backup, the archive bit gets cleared, indicating that the file was backed up.

10. A. It's critical to keep your antivirus software up to date, so you should update your definitions at least once per week.

11. C. Disk Defragmenter will analyze the hard drive to determine how fragmented it is and will allow you to defragment the hard drive. There is no Disk Analyzer tool. Disk Cleanup can help you free up space by deleting unneeded files. Checkdisk (Chkdsk) can help you find problems on the hard drive, but it does not look for fragmentation.

12. B. Windows Update downloads patches for the Windows operating system. Microsoft Update downloads patches for Windows and other Microsoft applications.

13. A. A computer vacuum should be used to suck up dust and other small particles. A regular vacuum generates electrostatic discharge (ESD) and should never be used. Blowing into a computer case isn't recommended; if needed, you can use compressed air to blow small bits of dust or debris out of a computer. Dust can harm computer components.

14. A. The Backup utility is used to create copies of data on your computer. The System Restore tool is used to create restore points. There are no Restore Point or Emergency Repair tools (although there is an emergency repair disk).

15. A, B, C, D. Establishing security policies and procedures, updating your operating systems, updating your applications, and updating your network devices are all good measures to take to help eliminate potential security problems.

16. A, C. Both Normal and Copy will back up all files, not just those that have changed. Incremental will back up all files that have changed since your last backup. Daily will back up all files that have changed during that day.

17. B. Disk Cleanup can help you free up space by deleting unneeded files. Disk Defragmenter will analyze the hard drive to determine how fragmented it is, and will allow you to defragment the hard drive. There is no Disk Analyzer tool. Checkdisk (Chkdsk) can help you find problems on the hard drive, but it does not delete files.

18. D. Chkdsk, which is now called Error Checking, will scan the hard drive for physical errors. There is no Disk Analyzer tool. Disk Cleanup deletes unneeded files, and Disk Defragmenter can defragment files on a hard drive.

19. D. A copy will back up the files you select without clearing the archive bit. This will keep your routine intact. A normal backup will back up all files and clear the archive bit, which could affect your incremental backup. A daily backup will only back up files you modified that day, which may not be true of all files in those folders.

20. A, C. Normal and incremental backups clear the archive bit. Copy and differential backups do not.

Chapter

9

Troubleshooting Operating Systems, Hardware, Printers, and Laptops

THE FOLLOWING COMPTIA A+ ESSENTIALS EXAM OBJECTIVES ARE COVERED IN THIS CHAPTER:

✓ **2.2 Given a scenario, explain and interpret common hardware and operating system symptoms and their causes**

- OS related symptoms
  - Bluescreen
  - System lock-up
  - Input/output device
  - Application install
  - Start or load
  - Windows specific printing problems
    - Print spool stalled
    - Incorrect/incompatible driver
- Hardware related symptoms
  - Excessive heat
  - Noise
  - Odors
  - Status light indicators
  - Alerts
  - Visible damage (e.g. cable, plastic)

- Use documentation and resources
  - User/installation manuals
  - Internet/web based
  - Training materials

✓ **2.3 Given a scenario, determine the troubleshooting methods and tools for printers**

- Manage print jobs
- Print spooler
- Printer properties and settings
- Print a test page

✓ **2.4 Given a scenario, explain and interpret common laptop issues and determine the appropriate basic troubleshooting method**

- Issues
  - Power conditions
  - Video
  - Keyboard
  - Pointer
  - Stylus
  - Wireless card issues
- Methods
  - Verify power (e.g. LEDs, swap AC adapter)
  - Remove unneeded peripherals
  - Plug in external monitor
  - Toggle Fn keys or hardware switches
  - Check LCD cutoff switch
  - Verify backlight functionality and pixilation
  - Check switch for built-in WiFi antennas or external antennas

In the previous chapter, we looked at ways to keep your systems running in good shape and talked a lot about troubleshooting theory. While theory is great to know (just ask economists or weather forecasters), your true worth as a technician depends on how good you are at actually fixing the problems that do happen. You can memorize all of the theories and specifications in the world, but if you don't know how to apply them, your usefulness is limited.

In this chapter we'll focus on more practical applications of troubleshooting. Before we get into too many details, though, remember that in order to troubleshoot anything you need to have a base level of knowledge. For example, if you've never opened the hood of a car, it will be a bit challenging for you to figure out why your car won't start in the morning. If you're not a medical professional, you might not know why that body part hurts or how to make it feel better. In the same vein, if you don't know how data is stored and accessed on a computer, it's unlikely you'll be able to fix related computer problems. So, before you get too heavy into troubleshooting, make sure you understand how the systems you are working on are supposed to function in the first place!

The first part of this chapter will cover the use of documentation and other resources. From there, we'll move into a discussion of general operating system issues and hardware problems, including printer problems. We'll finish up by looking at some topics specific to troubleshooting laptops.

Identifying Troubleshooting Resources

Most of us are naturally curious and like to solve problems, which is why we work with computers. Because of our nature, we tend to like to dive right in and solve problems. As well intentioned as we are, that approach isn't always the most efficient.

You have lots of hardware and software tools available to help you resolve problems. In addition, there are some important resources you should use to make troubleshooting easier. These resources, like hardware and software tools, can definitely aid in the troubleshooting process. These resources include the following:

- Manuals
- Internet resources
- Training materials

User/Installation Manuals

Technicians are usually guilty of not using this readily available resource when troubleshooting a system. In fact, most often, a technician will rely on his own experience and try to install a new component without reading the manual. Then, when the installation doesn't work, he might go back and look at the manual after spending time looking for the solution to a problem that might have been avoided in the first place.

Typically, in addition to the steps needed to install software or a device, a manual includes a section on the most common problems and the solutions to those problems. This area of the manual would be especially useful for the technician we just described.

It used to be that all products came with paper manuals. Now manuals are often found on manufacturer's websites. Some products include them on a bundled CD, but due to printing and shipping costs, paper manuals are all but extinct.

> If you have electronic copies of several different manuals that you need to access, copy them all to a hard drive and then burn your own CD or DVD with the manuals on it. Then you only have to carry around one disc with all of the information you need on it.

Internet/Web Resources

Possibly the most useful resource to the technician is the Internet. As mentioned throughout this book, a manufacturer's website is the best place to get the most current drivers, fixes, and technical information. Often, you can search a hardware or software vendor's website for a problem you might be having with that hardware or software, and find the fix for it.

In addition, you can use Microsoft's support website (http://support.microsoft.com), shown in Figure 9.1, which describes a wide variety of known problems and issues with Windows and its interaction with other software. Sometimes a solution that can't be found at the software vendor's website can be found by viewing the Microsoft support website because Microsoft has a larger staff and has been able to document a larger variety of problems. As you can see in Figure 9.1, Microsoft has links to many common categories in which technicians have questions. There's also a search bar near the top. This is very handy if you have a specific error message you're working on.

The support website for HP (www.hp.com/#support) is shown in Figure 9.2. A lot of hardware vendors will try to help get you to the right place or guide you through the troubleshooting process much like the HP site does. Once you tell the site whether you need to download something or look for information, you input the product number. If you have the hardware attached to your computer, you can tell the site to scan your system.

If you can't find an answer at the manufacturer's or Microsoft's website, you might try entering your problem into one of the many search engines, such as Yahoo! (www.yahoo.com) or Google (www.google.com). There are websites dedicated to communities of technical individuals (such as yourself) that can be a great source of information. Chances are, if you're having a computer or technical problem, someone else, somewhere in the world, has the solution—and the Internet can bring you together. You can post your problem to any number of website forums and newsgroups and receive a response, possibly within minutes.

FIGURE 9.1   Microsoft's support website

FIGURE 9.2   HP's Support & Drivers website

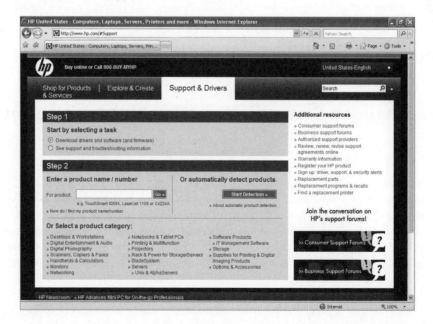

Training Materials

The final resource is one that most people overlook. Individuals do not acquire knowledge magically—they either learn it by themselves with self-study materials or are taught by an experienced instructor. In either case, books and other training materials (like the one you are reading right now) are excellent sources of information. Although training materials don't often contain patches or updates, they can and do teach concepts you can apply to help you with troubleshooting. After all, if you had not read this book, you might not have gotten the information you needed to pass the A+ exam.

Understanding Operating System and Hardware Symptoms

Operating systems and hardware are so intertwined that it can sometimes be difficult to tell where a problem truly is. Printing is a great example. If you send something to print, what went wrong? Well, there could be a number of things wrong with the printer itself or with the cable connecting the printer to your computer or the network. But it could also be the software that the operating system is using to communicate with the hardware—the driver. It could also be a problem with the print spooler, which is integrated into the operating system. Without more information it's hard to tell what the problem could be.

Software problems tend to be harder to isolate. It might seem like a software problem if Windows keeps crashing on you, but it may actually be a misbehaving hardware device causing the problems.

Some problems are pretty easy, though. Windows telling you that it can't find a specific file is most likely software-related. If you have smoke billowing up from the back of your PC, you're probably right if you suspect a hardware failure.

In this section we'll look at some common operating system issues as well as hardware symptoms and some specific printer troubleshooting methods.

Troubleshooting Common Operating System Problems

Windows is mind-bogglingly complex. Other operating systems are too, but the mere fact that Windows Vista has nearly 50 million lines of code (and over 2,000 developers worked on it!) makes you pause and shake your head.

Other operating systems can have issues that are not covered in this chapter. The CompTIA A+ exam only asks questions on Windows operating systems so that's all we'll cover here. There are several good books on the market on other operating systems such as UNIX, Linux, or MAC OS X that are handy references to have if you work on those operating systems.

Windows-based issues can be grouped into several categories based on their cause, such as boot problems, missing files (such as system files), configuration files, and virtual memory. If you're troubleshooting a boot problem, it's imperative that you understand the Windows boot process as described in Chapter 7.

The A+ exam divides Windows troubleshooting objectives between the Essentials exam and the Practical Application exam. Many Windows issues, such as boot-related problems, are covered in the Practical Application exam. For coverage of this material, please see Chapter 17, "Operating System Utilities and Troubleshooting Issues."

Some common Windows problems don't fall into any category other than "common Windows problems." We cover those in the following sections.

General Protection Faults (GPFs)

A *general protection fault (GPF)* happens in Windows when a program accesses memory that another program is using or when a program accesses a memory address that doesn't exist. Generally, GPFs are the result of sloppy programming. To fix this type of problem, a simple reboot will usually clear memory. If GPFs keep occurring, check to see which software is causing the error. Then find out if the manufacturer of the software has a patch to prevent GPFs. A sample GPF from Windows 2000 is shown in Figure 9.3.

FIGURE 9.3   A general protection fault

With Windows XP, Microsoft changed the format of the GPF error dialog box to the one shown in Figure 9.4. If you choose to, you can send Microsoft an error report detailing the problem.

FIGURE 9.4   A Windows XP GPF

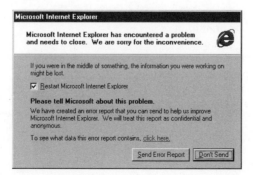

GPFs can occasionally be caused by failing or damaged memory modules. If you are seeing the same memory address appear time and time again, the physical memory could be at fault. If you have multiple memory modules, you can try switching the slots they're in. If that doesn't resolve it, or if you only have one module, then you might need to replace it.

Illegal Operation

Occasionally a program will quit, apparently for no reason, and present you with a window that reads "This program has performed an illegal operation and will be shut down. If the problem persists, contact the program vendor." An *illegal operation error* usually means that a program was forced to quit because it did something Windows didn't like. Windows then displays this error window. The name of the program that quit appears at the top of the window, along with three buttons: OK, Cancel, and Details. The OK and Cancel buttons do the same thing: dismiss the window. The Details button opens the window a little further and shows the details of the error, including which module experienced the problem, the memory location being accessed at the time, and the registers and flags of the processor at the time of the error.

System Lock-Up

It is obvious when a system lock-up occurs. The system simply stops responding to commands and stops processing completely. System lock-ups can occur when a computer is asked to process too many instructions at once with too little memory. Usually, the cure for a system lock-up is to reboot. If the lock-ups are persistent, it may be a hardware-related problem instead of a software problem.

Remember that there are two universal solutions to Windows problems: rebooting and obtaining an update from the software manufacturer. If neither of these solutions work, it could be hardware causing the problem.

Dr. Watson

Windows 2000 and Windows XP include a special utility known as Dr. Watson. This utility intercepts all error conditions and, instead of presenting the user with a cryptic Windows error, displays a slew of information that can be used to troubleshoot the problem. This is probably most useful if you have programming skills and want to debug the program that caused the error.

Windows Vista does not include Dr. Watson for debugging. Instead, the program is called Problem Reports And Solutions.

Failure to Start GUI

Occasionally, the Windows graphical user interface (GUI) won't appear. The system will hang just before the GUI appears. Or, sometimes, the *Blue Screen of Death (BSOD)*—not a technical term, by the way—appears. The BSOD is another way of describing the blue-screen error condition that occurs when Windows Vista/XP/2000 fails to boot properly or quits unexpectedly. Because it is at this stage that the device drivers for the various pieces of hardware are installed, if your Windows GUI fails to start properly, more than likely the problem is related to a misconfigured driver or misconfigured hardware.

There are a few things you can try if you believe that a driver is causing the problem. One is to try booting Windows in Safe Mode. Safe Mode only loads basic drivers, such as a standard VGA video driver and the keyboard and mouse. Once in Safe Mode you can uninstall the driver you think is causing the problem. Another option is to boot into the Last Known Good Configuration. Doing this will revert the system drivers back to the state they were in when the last login was successfully completed.

Device Will Not Function

When you are using Windows, you are constantly interacting with pieces of hardware. Each piece of hardware has a Windows driver that must be loaded in order for Windows to be able to use it. In addition, the hardware must be installed and functioning properly. If the device driver is not installed properly or the hardware is misconfigured, the device won't function properly.

If you have just updated a driver and the device isn't functioning, rolling back the driver installation can sometimes solve the problem. To roll back a driver, right-click on the device in Device Manager and choose Properties. On the Drivers tab, click the Roll Back Driver button.

Cannot Log On to the Network

If your computer is hooked up to a network (and more and more computers today are), you need to know when your computer is not functioning on the network properly and what to do about it. In most cases, the problem can be attributed to either a malfunctioning network interface card (NIC) or improperly installed network software. The biggest indicator in Windows that some component of the network software is nonfunctional is that you can't log on to the network or access any network service. To fix this problem, you must first fix the underlying hardware problem (if one exists) and then properly install or configure the network software.

Application Will Not Install

We've all experienced this frustration. You are trying to install the coolest new program, and, for whatever reason, it just won't install properly. It may give you one of the previously mentioned errors or a cryptic installation error. If a software program won't install and it gives you any of the errors we've mentioned (such as a GPF or illegal operation), use the solutions for those errors first. If the error that occurs during install is unique to the application being installed, check the application manufacturer's website for an explanation or update. These errors generally occur when you're trying to install over an application that already exists or when you're trying to replace a file that already exists but that another application is using. When you're installing an application, it is extremely important that you first quit all running programs so the installer can replace any files it needs to.

Application Will Not Start

Once you have an application successfully installed, you may run into a problem getting it to start properly. This problem can come from any number of sources, including an improper installation, a software conflict, or system instability. If your application was installed incorrectly, the files required to properly run the program may not be present, and the program can't function without them. If a shared file that's used by other programs is installed, installation of the wrong (usually older) version can cause conflicts with other already-installed programs. Finally, if one program causes a GPF, it can result in memory problems that can destabilize the system and cause other programs to crash. The solution to these problems is to uninstall and reinstall the offending application, first making sure that all programs are closed.

Real World Scenario

Did You Reboot Your Computer?

Quick quiz: You just got an error in Windows, and it appears that you are on the verge of a crash (of your application or the whole system). What do you do?

The first thing is to write down any error messages that appear. Then, save your work (if possible) and reboot your computer.

Anyone who has called tech support, or who has been a tech support person, knows how demeaning the question "Did you restart your computer?" can seem. Most people respond with an indignant, "Of course!" when the reality is they might or might not have actually done it.

Whenever there's a software problem, always, always reboot the computer before trying to troubleshoot. Often, the problem will disappear, and you'll have just saved yourself half an hour of frustration. If the same problem reappears, then you know you have work to do.

Why does rebooting help? When an application is running, it creates one or more temporary files that it uses to store information, and it also stores information in memory (RAM). If a temporary file or information in RAM becomes corrupted (such as by application A writing its information into application B's memory space), the application can have problems. Rebooting will clear the memory registers and most often remove problematic temporary files, thus eliminating the issue.

It might sound trite, but the first axiom in troubleshooting software really is to reboot. Even if the user says she did it, ask her to reboot again. (Tell her you want to see the opening screen for any possible error messages, or make up another good excuse.) If the problem doesn't come back, it's not a problem. If it does, then you can use your software skills to fix it.

Invalid Working Directory

Some Windows programs are extremely processor intensive. These programs require an area on the hard disk to store their temporary files while they work. This area is commonly known as a *working directory*, and its location is usually specified during that program's installation. However, if that directory changes after installation and the program still thinks its working directory is in the old location, the program will issue an error that says something like *Invalid working directory*. The solution is to reinstall the program with the correct parameters for the working directory.

> For this reason, many programs use the Windows TEMP directory as their working directory. You will see this error if the programmer chose to use a user-settable working directory, or if the application references a non-existent TEMP directory.

Troubleshooting Hardware Symptoms

As you continue to learn and increase your troubleshooting experience, your value will increase as well. This is because, if nothing else, it will take you less time to accomplish common repairs. Your ability to troubleshoot by past experiences and gut feelings will make you more efficient and more valuable, which in turn will allow you to advance and earn a better income. This section will give you some guidelines you can use to evaluate common hardware issues that you're sure to face.

POST Routines

Every computer has a diagnostic program built into its BIOS called the *power-on self-test (POST)*. When you turn on the computer, it executes this set of diagnostics. Many steps are involved in the POST, but they happen very quickly, they're invisible to the user, and they vary among BIOS versions. The steps include checking the CPU, checking the RAM, checking for the presence of a video card, and verifying basic hardware functionality. The main reason to be aware of the POST's existence is that if it encounters a problem, the boot process stops. Being able to determine at what point the problem occurred can help you troubleshoot.

If the computer doesn't POST like it should, one way to determine the source of a problem is to listen for a *beep code*. This is a series of beeps from the computer's speaker. The number, duration, and pattern of the beeps can sometimes tell you what component is causing the problem. However, the beeps differ depending on the BIOS manufacturer and version, so you must look up the beep code in a chart for your particular BIOS. Different BIOS manufacturers use the beeping differently. AMI BIOS, for example, relies on a raw number of beeps and uses patterns of short and long beeps.

Another way to determine a problem during the POST routine is to use a *POST card*. This is a circuit board that fits into an ISA or PCI expansion slot in the motherboard and reports numeric codes as the boot process progresses. Each of those codes corresponds to a particular component being checked. If the POST card stops at a certain number, you can look up that number in the manual that came with the card to determine the problem.

Motherboard manufacturers tend to use different beep codes to indicate different error messages. If you're getting a beep code during POST, check the motherboard manufacturer's website for information on what the beep code means.

Identifying Hardware Symptoms and Causes

As I mentioned in the introduction to this chapter, some hardware issues are pretty easy to identify. If there are flames shooting out of the back of your computer, then it's probably the power supply. (I've never actually seen flames shoot out of the back of a computer, but it is possible!) Other hardware symptoms are a bit more ambiguous. In this section, we'll look at some hardware-related symptoms and their possible causes.

The CompTIA A+ Essentials exam objectives cover the symptoms we'll discuss here. Specific hardware device problems (such as hard drive failures, video card problems, and motherboard issues) are covered in the Practical Application exam. Most system issues will be covered in Chapter 13. Laptop troubleshooting is in Chapter 14, and printer troubleshooting is covered in Chapter 15.

Excessive Heat

Electronic components produce heat; it's a fact of life. While they're designed to withstand a certain amount of the heat that's produced, excessive heat can drastically shorten the life of components. There are two common ways to reduce heat-related problems in computers: heat sinks and case fans.

Any component with its own processor will have a heat sink. Typically these look like big, finned hunks of aluminum or other metal attached to the processor. Their job is to dissipate heat from the component so it doesn't become too hot. Never run a processor without a heat sink!

One way to ensure your processor dies quickly is to overclock it. Overclocking is a process where you run the processor faster than it was designed to run. While it may work in the short run, it's never a good idea to do this!

Case fans are designed to take hot air from inside the case and blow it out of the case. There are many different designs, from simple motors to high tech liquid-cooled models. Put your hand up to the back of your computer at the case fan and you should feel warm air. If there's nothing coming out, you either need to clean your fan or replace your power supply. Some cases also come with additional cooling fans to help dissipate heat.

Computers are like human beings: they have similar tolerances to heat and cold. In general, anything comfortable to us is comfortable to computers. They need lots of clean, moving air to keep them functioning.

We've mentioned dust before and now is a good time to bring it up again. Dust, dirt, grime, paint, smoke, and other airborne particles can become caked on the inside of the components. This is most common in automotive and manufacturing environments. The contaminants create a film that coats the components, causing them to overheat and/or conduct electricity on their surface. Blowing out these exposed systems with a can of condensed air from time to time can prevent damage to the components. While you're cleaning the components, be sure to clean any cooling fans in the power supply or on the heat sink.

To clean the power supply fan, blow the air from the inside of the case. When you do this, the fan will blow the contaminants out the cooling vents. If you spray from the vents toward the inside of the box, you'll be blowing the dust and grime inside the case or back into the fan motor.

One way to ensure that dust and grime don't find their ways into your computer is to always leave the *blanks* in the empty slots on the back of your box. Blanks are the pieces of metal or plastic that come with the case and cover the expansion slot openings. They are designed to keep dirt, dust, and other foreign matter from the inside of the computer. They also maintain proper airflow within the case to ensure that the computer doesn't overheat.

Real World Scenario

Creeping Chips

The inside of a computer is a harsh environment. The temperature inside the case of many computers is well over 100° F! When you turn on your computer, it heats up. Turn it off, and it cools down. After several hundred such cycles, some components can't handle the stress and begin to move out of their sockets. This phenomenon is known as *chip creep*, and it can be really frustrating.

Chip creep can affect any socketed device, including ICs, RAM chips, and expansion cards. The solution to chip creep is simple: open the case, and reseat the devices. It's surprising how often this is the solution to phantom problems of all sorts.

Noise

Have you ever been working on a computer and heard a noise that resembles fingernails on a chalkboard? If so you will always remember that sound, along with the impending feeling of doom as the computer stopped working.

Some noises on a computer are normal. The POST beep is a good sound. The whirring of your hard drive and power supply fan almost give you a feeling of familiarity with your system. Many techs I know get so used to their "normal" system noises that if anything is slightly off pitch, they go digging for problems even if none are readily apparent.

For the most part the components that can produce noise problems are those that move. Hard drives have motors that spin the platters. Power supply fans spin. CD and DVD (and floppy, if you still have one) drives spin the disks. If you're hearing excessive noise, these are the likely culprits.

If you hear a whining sound and it seems to be fairly constant, it's more than likely a fan. Either it needs to be cleaned (desperately) or replaced. Power supplies that are failing can also sound louder and quieter intermittently as a fan will run at alternating speeds.

The "fingernails on a chalkboard" squealing could be an indicator that the hard drive heads have crashed into the platter. This thankfully doesn't seem to be as common today as it used to be, but it still happens. Note that this type of sound can also be caused by a power supply fan's motor binding up. A rhythmic ticking sound is also likely to be the hard drive.

Problems with the CD-ROM or DVD-ROM drive tend to be the easiest to diagnose. Those drives aren't constantly spinning unless you put some media in them. If you put a disc in and the drive makes a terrible noise, you have a good idea what the problem is.

So what do you do if you hear a terrible noise from the computer? If it's still responsive, shut it down normally as soon as possible. If it's not responsive, then shut off the power as quickly as you can. Examine the power supply to see if there are any obvious problems such as excessive dust, and clean as needed. Power the system back on. If the noise was caused by the hard drive, odds are that the drive has failed and the system won't boot normally. You may need to replace some parts.

If the noise is mildly annoying but doesn't sound drastic, boot up the computer with the case off and listen. By getting up close and personal with the system you can often tell where the noise is coming from and then troubleshoot or fix the appropriate part.

Never touch internal components when the case is off and the power is on! Doing so could result in a severe electrical shock to you and/or your components.

Odors

Bad smells coming from your computer are never a good thing. While it normally gets pretty warm inside a computer case, it should never be hot enough inside there to melt plastic components, but it does happen from time to time.

If you smell an odd odor coming from a computer, shut it down immediately. Open the case and start looking for visible signs of damage. Things to look for include melted plastic components and burn marks on circuit boards. If components appear to be damaged, it's best to replace them before returning the computer to service.

If you have scorch marks on a component, say a video card or a motherboard, it could be that the specific component went bad. It could also be a sign of a problem with the power supply. If you replace the component and a similar problem occurs, definitely replace the power supply.

Status Light Indicators

Most hardware devices have status light indicators that can help you identify when there is a problem. Obviously, when you power on a system you expect the power light to come on. If it doesn't you have a problem. The same holds true for other external devices such as wireless routers, external hard drives, and printers. In situations where the power light doesn't come on and the device has no power, always obey the first rule of troubleshooting: check your connections first!

Beyond power indicators, several types of devices have additional lights that can help you troubleshoot. If you have a hub, switch, or other connectivity device, you should have an indicator for each port that lights up when there is a connection. Some devices will give you a green light for a good connection, and a yellow or red light if it detects a problem. A lot of connectivity devices will also have an indicator that blinks or flashes when traffic is going through the port. Sometimes it's the same light that indicates a connection, but other times it's a separate indicator.

If you have a device with lights and you're not sure what they mean, it's best to check the manual or the manufacturer's website to learn.

Alerts

An alert is a message generated by a hardware device. In some cases, the device has a display panel that will tell you what the alert is. Many office printers are great examples of this, as they have an LCD display that can tell you if something is wrong.

Other alerts will pop up on the computer screen. If the device is attached to a specific computer, the alert will generally pop up on that computer's screen. Some devices can be configured to send an alert to a specific user account or system administrator, so the admin will get the alert regardless of which computer she is logged in to.

Visible Damage

The good news about visible damage is that you can usually figure out which component is damaged pretty quickly. The bad news is it often means you need to replace parts.

Visible damage to the outside of the case or the monitor casing might not matter much as long as the device still works. But if you're looking inside a case and see burn marks or melted components, that's a sure sign of a problem. Replace damaged circuit boards or melted plastic components immediately.

Troubleshooting Printers

Even as our society becomes ever more e-based, printers still play a critical role on most networks. Printer troubleshooting can take many forms depending on the issue you're having. In this section we'll look at printer configuration and management from the software side of things.

Printer installation and configuration is covered in Chapter 5. Troubleshooting printing issues and resolving other printer problems are addressed in Chapter 15.

Real World Scenario

Hot, Hot, Hot

Several years ago the company I was working for got in a batch of hardware we had purchased from another company. Another tech and I were building Frankensteins out of the plethora of parts we had.

We put RAM into one of the systems and powered it on. Immediately there was an electrical arc from the RAM to the motherboard, so I shut it back off. The arc was present for maybe half a second, and I had the box powered down within a second or two after that.

The RAM module had a pretty obvious burn mark on it, so I went to take it out, and promptly scorched my fingers when I touched it. It was searing hot! We let it cool down for about 20 minutes before going back to take it out. The moral of the story: be careful not to burn yourself on fried components.

Incidentally, we put a new motherboard and new RAM into the same case and powered it up only to see the exact same thing happen. Fried. (Fortunately I was smart enough not to burn myself a second time!) The verdict? Bad power supply. After replacing the power supply and trying a third motherboard and RAM combination, we had a functioning system.

If you'll recall from Chapter 5, there are six steps to installing and configuring a printer:

1. Attach the printer using a local or network port and connect the power.
2. Install and update the device driver.
3. Configure options and default settings.
4. Print a test page.
5. Validate compatibility with the operating system and applications.
6. Educate users about basic functionality.

The purpose of this section isn't to reiterate those steps; we assume here that you have installed and configured your printer and it's working or has worked in the past. In this section we'll talk about managing print jobs and working with the print spooler, and also look at managing printer properties and settings.

Managing Print Jobs

Most people know how to send a job to the printer. Clicking File, then Print, or pressing Ctrl+P on your keyboard generally does the trick. But once the job gets sent to the printer, what do you do if it doesn't print?

When you send a job to the printer, that print job ends up in a line with all other documents sent to that printer. The line of all print jobs is called the *print queue*. In most cases, the printer will print jobs on a first-come, first-serve basis. (There are exceptions, but we'll cover those in the "Configuring Printer Properties and Settings" section.) Once you send the job to the printer, a small printer icon will appear in the system tray in the lower-right corner of your desktop, near the clock. By double-clicking on it (or by right-clicking on it and selecting the printer name), you will end up looking at the jobs in the print queue, like the one shown in Figure 9.5.

FIGURE 9.5   Print jobs in the print queue

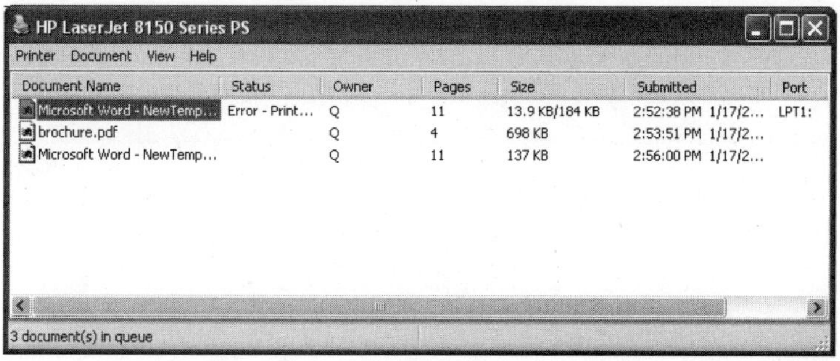

In Figure 9.5 you can see that the first document submitted has an error, which may explain why it hasn't printed. All of the other documents in the queue are blocked until the job with the error is cleared. You can clear it one of two ways. Either right-click on the document and choose Cancel, or select Document ➢ Cancel, as shown in Figure 9.6.

FIGURE 9.6   Printer documents menu

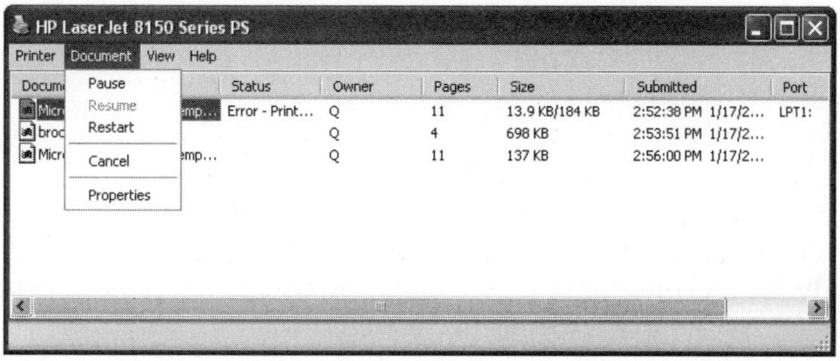

Note that from the menu you see in Figure 9.6, you can pause, resume, restart, and cancel print jobs, as well as see properties of the selected print job. If you wanted to pause or cancel all jobs going to a printer, you would do that from the Printer menu, as shown in Figure 9.7.

Once you have cleared the print job causing the problem, the next job will move to the top of the queue. It should show its status as Printing, like the one shown in Figure 9.8. But what if it shows it's printing but it still isn't working? (We're assuming the printer is powered on, connected properly, and online.) It could be a problem with the print spooler.

FIGURE 9.7   Printer menu

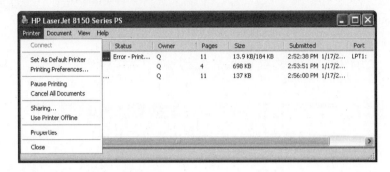

FIGURE 9.8   Print job printing correctly

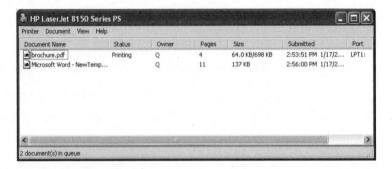

Managing the Print Spooler

The *print spooler* is a service that formats print jobs in the language that the printer needs. Think of it as a holding area where the print jobs are prepared for the printer. In Windows the spooler is a service that's started automatically when Windows loads.

If jobs aren't printing and there's no apparent reason why, it could be that the print spooler has stalled. To fix the problem, you need to stop and restart the print spooler. Exercise 9.1 walks you through stopping and restarting the spooler in Windows XP.

EXERCISE 9.1

Stopping and Restarting the Print Spooler in Windows XP

To stop and restart the print spooler in Windows XP, follow these steps:

1. Open Computer Management and navigate to Services (right-click on My Computer and choose Manage; if necessary, click on the plus sign next to Services And Applications to expand the list).

EXERCISE 9.1 *(continued)*

2. Find the Print Spooler service, shown in the right-hand pane.

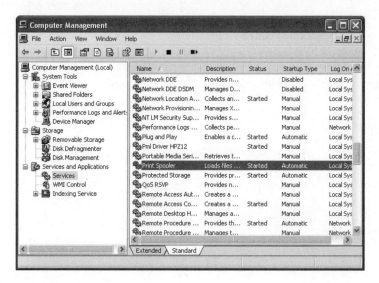

3. Stop the spooler by right-clicking on the service and choosing Stop, or by clicking on the Stop square above the list of services.

4. Restart the spooler by right-clicking on the service and choosing Start, or by clicking the Start arrow above the list of services. After it's restarted, the service's Status column should display Started.

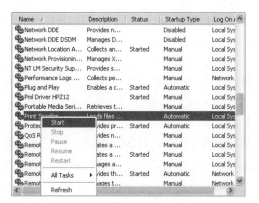

5. Close Computer Management.

If you have Windows Vista, the steps to stop and restart the spooler are the same as in Exercise 9.1; the only difference is that in Step 1 you right-click on Computer and then choose Manage.

Configuring Printer Properties and Settings

Where you configure specific printer properties depends a lot on the printer itself. Figure 9.9 shows the Printers And Faxes window in Windows XP. On the left-hand side under Printer Tasks, you can see that there's an option to select printing preferences and another option to set printer properties (in addition, both options can be executed by right-clicking on the printer and choosing Printing Preferences or Properties, respectively).

FIGURE 9.9   Printers And Faxes

 If you don't see these options under Printer Tasks, highlight the printer first.

Various configuration features can be set from each menu option. The Printing Preferences window of this printer is shown in Figure 9.10.

Under Printing Preferences (for this printer) you can select the quality of the print job, layout (portrait versus landscape), paper size, two-sided printing, and use of color. By contrast, Figure 9.11 shows the printer's Properties window.

Here the options are different. The printer's Properties window is less about how the printer does its job and more about how people can access the printer. You can use these options to share the printer, set up the port that it's on, and configure when the printer will be available throughout the day (and to which specific users). Figure 9.12 shows the important Advanced tab of the Properties window.

FIGURE 9.10   Printing Preferences

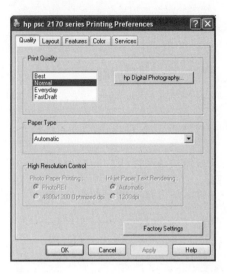

FIGURE 9.11   Printer's Properties window

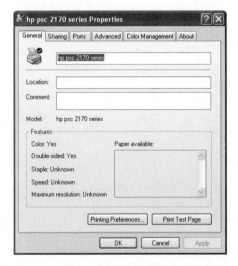

On the Advanced tab, you can configure the printer to be available only during certain hours of the day. This might be useful if you're trying to curtail after-hours printing of non-work-related documents, for example. Configuring a printer priority lets you insert higher-priority jobs in front of lower-priority ones, based on the logical printer it's sent to. You can also configure the spool settings. We recommend always spooling the jobs instead of printing directly to the printer. However, if the printer is printing garbage, you can try printing directly to it to see if the spooler is causing the problem.

FIGURE 9.12   The Advanced tab of the printer's Properties window

Regarding the check boxes at the bottom, you will want to always print spooled documents first, as it speeds up the printing process. If you need to maintain an electronic copy of all printed files, select the Keep Printed Documents check box. Keep in mind that this will eat up a lot of hard disk space on the print server.

Finally, the Printing Defaults button takes you to the Printing Preferences (see Figure 9.10). Print Processor lets you select alternate methods of processing print jobs (not usually needed), and Separator Page lets you specify a file to use as a separator page (a document that prints out at the beginning of each separate print job, usually with the user's name on it), which can be useful if you have several (or several dozen) users sharing one printer.

Printing a Test Page

If your printer isn't spitting out print jobs, it may be a good idea to print a test page and see if that works. The test page information is stored in the printer's memory, so there's no formatting or translating of jobs required. It's simply a test to make sure your printer hears your computer.

When you install a printer, one of the last questions it asks you is if you want to print a test page. If there's any question, go ahead and do it. If the printer is already installed, you can print a test page from the printer's Properties window, as shown in Figure 9.11. Just click the Print Test Page button and it should work. If nothing happens, double-check your connections and stop and restart the print spooler. If garbage prints, there is likely a problem with the printer or the print driver.

Giving Important People Print Priority

By using the printer's Properties window's Advanced tab, you can give certain people priority access to the printer. It's almost like being a celebrity A-lister and getting to cut in front of the long line to get right into the swanky club.

At one company where I worked, the director's administrator always needed to print things in an "emergency." Often these emergencies were that the director was running late for a meeting and he needed her to print off some papers for the meeting ASAP. (Of course, he could have told her well before the meeting, but that didn't happen.)

There were two choices. One would be to give her an individual printer, but that was against company policy and didn't fit the tight budget. The second was to give her priority.

When I installed her printer, I selected the Advanced tab and set her priority to 99. Then, I went to the computers of the other administrators who shared the printer and set all of their priorities to 1. (I could have set them to anything as long as it was lower than 99.) So when she printed, if there were documents in the queue, hers would cut to the top of the line.

This solution wouldn't abort a job that was already printing to print her job, but it did ensure that her job would be the next one to begin printing. It made the director happy, and saved the company some money.

Troubleshooting Common Laptop Issues

Laptops use essentially the same types of devices as desktops, but troubleshooting the two can feel very different. While the general troubleshooting philosophies never change—steps such as gathering information, isolating the problem, and then testing one fix at a time—the space and configuration limitations can make laptop troubleshooting more frustrating.

Preventive maintenance is critical to the long-term well-being of any computer system. But because laptops are moved around so much, they're often exposed to many environmental hazards that desktops aren't. For example, how many people worry about accidentally sitting on their desktop computer?

This section looks at troubleshooting techniques for some common laptop-specific issues as well as preventive maintenance measures to keep your laptop running well into its old age.

Diagnosing Laptop Problems

Before getting into specific laptop-type issues, remember that good troubleshooting means acting in a methodical manner. You need to find out if the device or software ever worked, what happened before the problem occurred, and what changes were made (if any). Then you must try to isolate the problem and test one fix at a time.

There are four typical areas where laptops could have different problems than their desktop counterparts: power, video, input, and wireless networking.

Power Issues

Is it plugged in? Everyone hates getting asked that question if their computer doesn't work. But it's the critical first question to ask. After all, if it's not plugged in, who knows whether or not it will work? You can't assume that the battery is working (or is attached) like it's supposed to. Always check power and connections first!

> If the laptop works while it's plugged in but not while on battery power, the battery itself may be the culprit. As batteries get older, they are not able to hold as much of a charge, and in some cases, they are not able to hold a charge at all.

Most laptop power adapters have a light on them indicating they're plugged in. If there's no light, check to make sure the outlet is working, or switch outlets. Also, most laptops have a power-ready indicator light when plugged into a wall outlet as well. Check to see if it's lit. If the outlet is fine, try another power adapter. They do fail on occasion.

If you're working on a DC adapter, the same thing applies. Check for lights, try changing plugs if possible (many newer cars have secondary power sources, such as ones in the console between the seats), or try another adapter if you have one.

Another thing to remember when troubleshooting power problems is to remove all external peripherals. Strip your laptop down to the base computer, so there isn't a short or other power drain coming from an external device.

> Windows has built-in power management features to help conserve laptop battery life. In Windows, open the Power Options applet in Control Panel. Once there you can configure different power-saving settings to maximize the battery life of your laptop.

Video Difficulties

Video problems are usually caused by the video card (built into the motherboard on most laptops) or the display unit. Video problems on laptops can also occur if the connection between the motherboard and the LCD screen becomes damaged. This connection typically passes through the hinges of the case, which is the weakest part.

The video section follows the power section for a reason: make sure the computer is on before diagnosing the issue as a video problem!

Here are a few things to try:

- Plug in an external monitor that you know works. On most laptops, you need to press the function key and another key known as the LCD cutoff switch (often F8 or F4) to direct the video output to an external monitor. This is called *toggling* the display. You might need to do this a few times. Figure 9.13 shows a laptop keyboard where F4 is the appropriate toggle key. Look for the box with the vertical lines next to it.

FIGURE 9.13   Video adjustment keys F4 (LCD toggle), F7 (dim), and F8 (brighten)

- Check the *LCD cutoff switch*. Remember the function+F8 idea? Try toggling it a few times, waiting a few seconds between each press of the toggle key to let the display power up. Most laptops have three display states: LCD only, external only, and both.

- Raise or lower the brightness level. This is usually done with a function key combination as well, such as function+F7 or function+F8, as shown in Figure 9.13, or F9 and F10, as shown in Figure 9.14. Check your keyboard for function keys that have a sun on them.

- If you have a handheld computer, try turning the backlight feature on or off. For specifics on how to do this, check your manual.

If the display is not working, you can order a new one from the laptop manufacturer—although it may be cheaper to just buy a new laptop. If the computer won't output a display to an external monitor as well, you likely need a new motherboard.

Input Problems

Laptop keyboards aren't as easy to switch out as desktop keyboards. You can, however, very easily attach an external keyboard to your laptop if the keys on your laptop don't appear to work. If you have the wrong type of connector, most electronics stores will have USB-to-PS/2 or PS/2-to-USB converters.

FIGURE 9.14   Video and other function keys

Another problem unique to laptop keyboards is the *Fn key*. (It can be your friend or your enemy.) You can identify it on your laptop keyboard as it's in the lower-left corner and has the letters Fn on it (often in blue), as shown in Figure 9.15. If the Fn key is "stuck" on, the only keys that will work are those with functions on them. If you look at other keys on your laptop, several of them will have blue lettering too. Those are the functions the keys may perform if you press and hold the Fn key before pressing the function key you want. If the Fn key is stuck on, try toggling it just as you would a Caps Lock key.

FIGURE 9.15   Fn key

One of the conveniences that users often take advantage of in laptops is built-in pointing devices. They're nice because you don't need to carry an external mouse around with you. A lot of laptops now have touchpads like the one shown in Figure 9.16. Touchpads are touch-sensitive, flat, rectangular spaces located below the keyboard. While they're usually considered very handy (I love mine), some people find that they're annoying. For example, if your laptop also has a touchpoint, which would be located right in the middle of your keyboard between your *g*, *h*, *t*, and *y* keys, and you are trying to use that, your palm might rest on the touchpad, causing erratic pointer behavior. You can turn the touchpad off through Control Panel. While understanding that you can turn it off on purpose, remember that it can be turned off accidentally as well. Check to make sure it's enabled. Some laptops allow you to disable or change the sensitivity of the touchpoint as well, just as you can adjust the sensitivity of your mouse.

FIGURE 9.16   Laptop touchpad

On handhelds or other touch screen devices (including devices that use a stylus), the screen input can occasionally fail. This indicates a problem with the digitizer, and it generally means you need a repair or a replacement.

Networking Troubles

Nearly all modern laptops are equipped with wireless networking built into the computer. In many cases, the wireless antenna is run into the LCD panel. This allows the antenna to stand up higher and pick up a better signal.

If your wireless isn't working, check to make sure that the LEDs on your network card are functioning. If there are no lights, it could indicate a problem with the card itself, or on some cards, that there is no connection or signal. First, make sure that the wireless card is enabled through Windows. You generally do this in Windows by right-clicking on My Network Places, selecting Properties, right-clicking the wireless network connection, and selecting Properties in order to look at the network card properties. However, some network cards have their own proprietary configuration software. You can also often check here by clicking a tab (often called Wireless Networks) to see if you're getting a signal and the strength of that signal.

A lot of laptops now also come with an external switch on the front, side, or above the keyboard that can toggle the network card on and off. Be sure that this is set to the on position! Figure 9.17 shows a toggle switch on the front of a computer. Figure 9.18 shows a toggle on the strip above the keyboard. It looks like an indicator light only, but the strip is touch-sensitive.

FIGURE 9.17   Front of computer network card toggle switch

FIGURE 9.18   Network card toggle switch above the keyboard

If you have a USB network adapter, try unplugging it and plugging it back in. Make sure that Windows recognizes the card properly.

When wireless fails but the network card appears to be working, try plugging it in. Most laptops with wireless cards also have wired RJ-45 network ports. Plug the card in and see if you get lights, and see if the network works.

 Real World Scenario

Potential Wireless and Wired Conflicts

A short time ago, a friend of mine was frustrated because he couldn't get to the network in his office with his laptop plugged into his docking station. He had used the laptop at home the night before and gotten on his wireless network without a problem. But this day, his wired connection would not work. He checked his cables (always your first step!) and saw that there were lights (a good sign). He had tried to access both the Internet and intranet sites but to no avail.

We opened a command prompt and ran `ipconfig`. He didn't have an IP address, but I noticed that his built-in wireless card was listed and active.

What he needed to do was to disable his built-in wireless card. He had enabled the wireless to work at home, and it was still enabled. Because it was enabled, the wireless card was trying to obtain an IP address, and it refused to let the wired "portion" of the card pick up an address from the company DHCP server (there was no wireless in the building). After disabling his wireless card, his wired connection picked up an IP address, and all was well.

Most laptop network cards have a wired connection in addition to their wireless capabilities. For many (but not all) of them, the wired connection will not work if the wireless is enabled. It's an attempt to prevent conflicts if both connection types are active.

Preventive Maintenance on Laptops

As we discussed in Chapter 8, many problems people have with their computers can be prevented. By taking good care of your equipment, you can dramatically extend the life of your hardware, and laptops are no exception. Two ways to look at preventive maintenance include being careful of what the computer is exposed to (the environment) and taking steps to proactively protect your computer (tools and techniques).

The Environment

Environmental issues are where laptops usually take a severe beating. Desktops don't have to worry about being constantly moved around, shaken, opened and closed, and occasionally dropped. Laptops live in fear of users who forget to zip their carrying case or those who leave it closed and sitting on the couch.

I'm going to use the term "environment" here to refer to all of those external things that can affect a computer. At the top of the list is transportation. Laptops get moved around all the time, and if you're going to carry one around, always put it in a carrying case designed for such a purpose. Too many people just stuff them into a backpack or briefcase and then wonder why things like broken screens happen.

Another issue unique to laptops is due to their clamshell design. When the laptop is closed, the screen is basically face to face with the keyboard. Any pressure or squeezing together of the sides causes the keys to press into the screen. Over time, the keys will mar the coating of the LCD screen, and you'll be left with permanent marks in your display. One way to prevent this problem is to place a screen-sized piece of foam (they usually come between the keyboard and screen when the laptop is shipped) or heavy cloth between the keyboard and screen when you close your laptop. It will keep the display nicer for a longer time.

Computer components get very hot, and that's especially true of laptops because of their confined space. Don't operate your laptop for long periods of time in the sun or in very hot conditions. Laptops have cooling fans, but the fans are small and can only do so much.

Speaking of fans, dust and dirt can get into them, rendering them useless for cooling your computer. Make sure the area you're working in doesn't have a lot of dust flying around—a construction site isn't a good place for a laptop, for example. The air vents on a laptop are typically on the bottom of the case. Setting your laptop on your lap or another soft surface such as a blanket or a bed can prohibit airflow and cause your system to overheat.

Tools and Techniques

We know that heat always has been and probably always will be an enemy of computers, and small computers have even bigger heat problems. Cramming all of those electronic components into a small space just begs for overheating. All laptops have fans to keep the processor and memory cool, and laptop components are designed to run cooler than their desktop counterparts, but overheating is still a problem.

You can purchase external cooling devices for your laptop, which promise to keep it cooler and extend the life of your system. The most common version is a cooling pad. It sits on your desk (most are about 1 inch high), and the laptop sits on the cooling pad. Inside the pad are fans that circulate hot air away from the bottom of your laptop, the part that usually gets the hottest. There are dozens of varieties of cooling pads, starting off around $15 and going up to several hundred dollars for exotic cooling fan/docking station combos.

One of the most common "mistakes" people make is when cleaning their laptop display. They figure it's just like cleaning the TV, so they get out the glass cleaner and a paper towel and clean away. Two mistakes there. First, don't use abrasive cloths to clean the screen. The coating on LCD screens will scratch easily, and you'll be left staring at scratch marks until you decide to upgrade. Second, don't use commercial glass cleaners. They often contain chemicals that will damage the LCD screen. To do the job right, there are two ways you can go. One, use a slightly damp (and soft!) cloth. Two, buy a cleaner designed for LCD screens. You can find them at most any office supply store. There are even premoistened towelette versions that are handy to carry with you in your laptop case.

Summary

In this chapter, we went from discussing troubleshooting theory to actual applications of troubleshooting. The first aspect of that is knowing where to look for information on problems, and we talked about using manuals, the Internet, and training materials to help out.

Our first troubleshooting section centered on operating system issues, such as the Blue Screen of Death, system lockups, failed input/output devices, and problematic applications.

Next, we looked at general hardware troubleshooting. We investigated the causes for hardware problems, such as excessive heat, and signs of problems, such as noise, odors, and visible damage. We also discussed alerts and status lights.

After general hardware we talked about troubleshooting and configuring printers in Windows. Specifically, we discussed managing print jobs, the print spooler, configuring your printer properties, and printing a test page.

Finally, we ended the chapter with a section on troubleshooting issues that are specific to laptop computers. Because of their compact nature, they have unique issues relating to heat, power, and input and output. Laptops also typically have built-in wireless networking, which is a blessing but occasionally needs to be fixed.

Exam Essentials

Know what causes Windows problems such as general protection faults and the Blue Screen of Death. General protection faults are caused when a program accesses an area of memory that it shouldn't. The Blue Screen of Death is a fatal Windows error (you need to reboot) that can be caused by various things, including both hardware and software problems.

Know what to do if a device fails to work properly in Windows. First, make sure the device is connected and has appropriate power. Then, you may want to uninstall and reinstall the device driver.

Know what can cause an application to fail to install or start. An application may fail to install if a file that the installation needs to modify is being used by another program. Applications may fail to start due to file version conflicts or corrupted files.

Know what to do when confronted with a software error. Write down the error message if there is one, and reboot! If rebooting doesn't work, you may want to search the vendor's website or the Internet for a solution.

Understand what happens during the POST routine.   During the power-on self-test (POST), the BIOS checks to ensure that the base hardware is installed and working. Generally, one POST beep is good. Any more than that and you might have an error.

Know where to find information to help you troubleshoot.   Available resources include installation manuals, the Internet, and training materials. Don't forget co-workers too!

Understand the types of symptoms that misbehaving hardware can cause.   Hardware symptoms include excessive heat, noise, odors, and visible damage. Some devices can also warn of problems with status light indicators or alerts.

Know how to stop and restart the print spooler.   Open the Services applet of Computer Management. Find Print Spooler on the right side. Right-click on it and click Stop, or highlight it and click the stop square above the list of services. To restart it, right-click and select Start or click the start triangle above the list of services.

Understand what to do for laptop video issues.   If you have no video, you can try an external monitor or try toggling the LCD cutoff switch. For screens that are too dim or too bright, you can raise and lower the brightness by using the Fn key plus the appropriate function key on your keyboard.

Know what to check if your wireless networking card isn't working.   Make sure the card has lights indicating it's working. You might also have an external toggle switch to turn the card on and off. Finally, if your computer has an external RJ-45 connection, you can plug it in and see if it works when wired.

Review Questions

1. If the video on your laptop is not working, what should you do to troubleshoot it? (Choose all that apply.)

    A. Toggle the video function key.

    B. Try using an external monitor.

    C. Remove the display unit and reattach it.

    D. Power the system off and back on.

2. While inspecting a motherboard, you notice a discolored area. What is usually a cause of this?

    A. Spilled liquid

    B. Improper manufacture

    C. Power surge

    D. Underclocking

3. All of the following are common problems faced in troubleshooting Windows and applications except _____.

    A. General protection faults

    B. Valid working directory

    C. System lockup

    D. Application will not start or load

4. Every computer has a diagnostic program built into its BIOS called the _____.

    A. CMOS

    B. BIOS

    C. POST

    D. DNS

5. Which of the following is an error in Windows that happens when a program accesses memory another program is using or when a program accesses a memory address that doesn't exist?

    A. General protection fault

    B. Windows protection error

    C. Illegal operation

    D. System lock-up

6. What would be the best thing to use to clean a laptop display?

    A. A dry cloth

    B. Glass cleaner

    C. Abrasive cleaning powder

    D. LCD cleaner

7. What two devices are commonly used to cool components within a PC? (Choose two.)

    A. Fans

    B. Compressed air

    C. Freon

    D. Heat sinks

8. You are having problems with the video card in one of your computers. Where could you check for troubleshooting information? (Choose all that apply.)

    A. Another computer with the same video card

    B. The video card manufacturer's website

    C. The manual that came with the card

    D. The server log

9. Which Windows error message is displayed when a program is forced to quit because it did something Windows didn't like?

    A. General protection fault

    B. Windows protection error

    C. Illegal operation

    D. System lock-up

10. The display on your laptop appears warped and fuzzy. You plug in an external monitor, and the image on it is fine. What is the most likely cause of the problem?

    A. The video card

    B. The LCD display

    C. The motherboard

    D. The video driver

11. Windows XP comes with a utility called _____ for troubleshooting error conditions.

    A. Windows Debugger

    B. Problem Reports And Solutions

    C. Windows Solutions

    D. Dr. Watson

12. Which laptop input device is a flat surface that you can draw on with your finger to control the mouse pointer?

    A. Touchpad

    B. Touchball

    C. Touchpoint

    D. Touchway

13. Before installing a new application on a computer, which of the following should you do?

    A. Format the hard drive.

    B. Reinstall Windows.

    C. Close all running applications.

    D. Open Install Shield.

14. You turn a computer on, but nothing shows up on the monitor. Instead of one beep, you hear one long beep followed by three short beeps. What is the problem?

    A. The video card is dead.

    B. The motherboard is dead.

    C. The BIOS is not functioning.

    D. Not enough information; you need to look up the beep code to determine the problem.

15. A user has an application that is constantly crashing. The user has rebooted, and the application is still failing. What should you do?

    A. Reinstall Windows.

    B. Reinstall the application.

    C. Use System Debugger to troubleshoot the problem.

    D. Restore a previous version of the application from a backup.

16. You turn a computer on and it doesn't boot up properly. From inside the case you hear a rhythmic ticking sound. What is most likely the problem?

    A. The motherboard

    B. The power supply fan

    C. The hard drive

    D. The video card

17. Users are complaining that their print jobs are not printing. You open the print queue and see 50 jobs lined up. The printer is connected properly and online. What should you do?

    A. Open Printer Troubleshooting and have it diagnose the problem.

    B. Stop and restart the print spooler.

    C. Delete and reinstall the printer.

    D. Delete and reinstall Windows.

18. A user calls saying his laptop won't power on. He charged it all night so he knows the battery is fine. What should you have him do first?

    A. Plug the laptop in using an AC adapter and try to power it on.

    B. Replace the battery with a spare and try to power it on.

    C. Toggle the battery power switch on the front of the laptop, then try to power it on.

    D. Send the laptop in for service.

19. You have a user who needs to ensure that her print jobs are always first in the print queue. How can you accomplish this?

    A. You can't; she has to wait in line like everyone else.

    B. By setting the priority to 1 in the printer's properties

    C. By setting her priority to 99 and everyone else's priority to 1 in the printer's properties.

    D. By deleting everyone's printers and reinstalling. Be sure to reinstall this user's printer first.

20. Which of the following options in a printer's properties will speed up printing for your users?

    A. Print Spooled Documents First

    B. Keep Printed Documents

    C. Separator Page

    D. Print Directly To The Printer

Answers to Review Questions

1. **A, B.** Two helpful things to try are toggling the video output function key (usually Fn+F8) and plugging an external monitor into the laptop. Removing the display is possible but not recommended. Powering the system off and back on isn't likely to correct the problem.

2. **C.** Discolored areas on the board are often caused by overheating. This can be the result of power surges.

3. **B.** A valid working directory is not a common problem faced in troubleshooting Windows and applications. An invalid working directory is a common problem.

4. **C.** Every computer has a diagnostic program built into its BIOS called the power-on self-test (POST). The BIOS is the software stored on the CMOS chip. DNS is Domain Name Service, which in networking resolves hostnames to IP addresses.

5. **A.** A general protection fault (GPF) is a common error in Windows. It happens when a program accesses memory that another program is using or when a program accesses a memory address that doesn't exist. Typically, GPFs are the result of sloppy programming; they can often be fixed by clearing the memory with a reboot.

6. **D.** Laptop LCD video displays can scratch easily. To clean them, it's best to use a cleaner designed specifically for LCD screens. They can be found at any office supply store.

7. **A, D.** Heat sinks and fans are commonly used to cool components within a PC. Compressed air can be used to blow out small particles or dust. Freon is a coolant used in some air conditioners but is not typically used for personal computers.

8. **B, C.** Good sources of troubleshooting information are manufacturer's websites, product manuals, and training materials.

9. **C.** *Illegal operation* is the Windows error message displayed when a program is forced to quit because it did something Windows didn't like. The error's details include which module experienced the problem, the memory location being accessed at the time, and the registers and flags of the processor at the time of the error.

10. **B.** It has to be a problem with the LCD display. If it were the video card, then the display would appear warped and fuzzy on the external monitor as well. While many motherboards contain video circuitry, this answer is not specific enough. If the video driver were corrupted, you would have the same problem on all displays.

11. **D.** Windows 2000 and XP come with Dr. Watson, which is a debugger that can help troubleshoot error conditions. Windows Vista replaced Dr. Watson with Problem Reports And Solutions.

12. **A.** The touchpad is a mousing surface built into the laptop. It allows you to use your finger to control the mouse pointer by drawing on the surface.

13. C. Before installing an application, it's best to close all open applications first. If an open application is using a file that the installation process needs to access, the installation could fail. Formatting the hard drive and reinstalling Windows are unnecessary. Install Shield is a wizard that Windows-based applications typically use to aid in the installation, but it's not something you open manually.

14. D. It may well be that the video card is dead. Different BIOS manufacturers use different beep codes, though, so you'll want to look it up to be sure. If the motherboard were dead or the BIOS weren't functioning, you wouldn't get to the POST routine, so you wouldn't get a beep code.

15. B. If an application is crashing, it's likely that there is a missing or corrupted file. The easiest way to fix this is to reinstall the application. Reinstalling Windows isn't necessary. There is no System Debugger tool that will help this situation. Restoring from a backup may or may not fix the problem, depending on if the backup has a corrupted file or the correct one. In any case, it's a more drastic step than what is necessary.

16. C. The only components that typically make noise are the ones that have moving parts, such as fans and hard drives. In most cases, a rhythmic ticking sound will be something that's generated by the hard drive.

17. B. If print jobs are seemingly getting "stuck" in the printer queue, you should stop and restart the print spooler service. There is no Printer Troubleshooting utility that will diagnose printer problems. Deleting and reinstalling is not necessary.

18. A. If a laptop won't power up on battery, always try to use AC power. You never know when a battery could have failed. If he had a spare and didn't have an AC power cord, trying a spare might work, but trying AC power is the best bet. There is no battery power switch on laptops.

19. C. Printer priorities can ensure a user (or users) have priority access to a printer. Giving users a higher priority (a higher number) means their jobs will print first.

20. A. Printing Spooled Documents First will enable faster printing. Printing directly to the printer uses physical memory on the printer to spool instead of using server memory, which can slow down the process greatly. Keeping printed documents does not affect printing speed. Separator pages don't slow down printing much, except that each job essentially has a cover sheet.

Chapter 10

Understanding Networking

THE FOLLOWING COMPTIA A+ ESSENTIALS EXAM OBJECTIVES ARE COVERED IN THIS CHAPTER:

✓ **4.1 Summarize the basics of networking fundamentals, including technologies, devices and protocols**

- Basics of configuring IP addressing and TCP/IP properties (DHCP, DNS)

- Bandwidth and latency

- Status indicators

- Protocols (TCP/IP, NetBIOS)

- Full-duplex, half-duplex

- Basics of workgroups and domains

- Common ports: HTTP, FTP, POP, SMTP, TELNET, HTTPS

- LAN / WAN

- Hub, switch and router

- Identify Virtual Private Networks (VPN)

- Basics class identification

✓ **4.2 Categorize network cables and connectors and their implementations**

- Cables

  - Plenum / PVC

  - UTP (e.g. CAT3, CAT5 / 5e, CAT6)

  - STP

  - Fiber

  - Coaxial Cable

- Connectors
  - RJ45
  - RJ11

✓ **4.3 Compare and contrast the different network types**

- Broadband
  - DSL
  - Cable
  - Satellite
  - Fiber
- Dial-up
- Wireless
  - All 802.11 types
  - WEP
  - WPA
  - SSID
  - MAC filtering
  - DHCP settings
- Bluetooth
- Cellular

Imagine working in an office 20 years ago with little or no computer equipment. It's hard to envision now, isn't it? We take for granted a lot of what we have gained in technology the past few decades. Now, imagine having to send a memo to everyone in the company. Back then we used interoffice mail; today we use e-mail. It used to take days to get a document to someone in a remote office, and now it may just take a few seconds. E-mail is an example of one form of communication that only became available due to the introduction and growth of networks.

This chapter focuses on the basic concepts of how a network works, including the way it sends information, the hardware used, and common types of networks that you might encounter. It used to be that in order to be a PC technician you only needed to focus on one individual computer at a time. In today's environment, though, you will in all likelihood be asked to troubleshoot both hardware and software problems on existing networks.

If the material in this chapter interests you, you might consider studying for, and eventually taking, CompTIA's Network+ exam. It is a non-company-specific networking certification similar to A+, but for network-related topics. You can study for it using Sybex's *CompTIA Network+ Study Guide* materials, available at www.sybex.com.

Understanding Networking Principles

Stand-alone personal computers, first introduced in the late 1970s, gave users the ability to create documents, spreadsheets, and other types of data and save them for future use. For the small-business user or home-computer enthusiast, this was great. For larger companies, however, it was not enough. Larger companies had greater needs to share information between offices and sometimes over great distances. Stand-alone computers were insufficient for the following reasons:

- Their small hard-drive capacities were insufficient.

- To print, each computer required a printer attached locally.

- Sharing documents was cumbersome. People grew tired of having to save to a floppy and then take that disk to the recipient. (This procedure was called *sneakernet*.)

- There was no e-mail. Instead, there was interoffice mail, which was slow and unreliable.

To address these problems, networks were born. A *network* links two or more computers together to communicate and share resources. Their success was a revelation to the computer industry as well as businesses. Now, departments could be linked internally to offer better performance and increase efficiency.

You have probably heard the term *networking* in the business context, where people come together and exchange names for future contact and to give them access to more resources. The same is true with a computer network. A computer network allows computers to link to each other's resources. For example, in a network, every computer does not need a printer connected locally in order to print. Instead, you can connect a printer to one computer or directly to the network and allow all of the other computers to access this resource. Because they allow users to share resources, networks can increase productivity as well as decrease cash outlay for new hardware and software.

In the following sections, we will discuss the fundamentals of networking, as well as the specifics of networking media and components.

Understanding Networking Fundamentals

In many cases, networking today has become a relatively simple plug-and-play process. Wireless network cards can automatically detect and join networks, and you're seconds away from surfing the Web or sending e-mail. Of course, not all networks are that simple. Getting your network running may require a lot of configuration, and one messed up setting can cause the whole thing to fail.

Just as there is a lot of information to know about how to configure your network, there is a lot of background information you should understand about *how* networks work. This section covers the fundamental knowledge, and armed with this information, you can then move on to how to make it work *right*. The basics covered here include:

- LANs vs. WANs
- Primary network components
- Network operating systems (NOSs)
- Network resource access
- Network topologies
- Network architectures
- Transmitting data on a network

LANs vs. WANs

Local area networks (LANs) were introduced to connect computers in a single office. *Wide area networks (WANs)* expanded the LANs to include networks outside the local environment and also to distribute resources across long distances. Generally, it's safe to think of a WAN as multiple, disbursed LANs connected together. Today, LANs exist in many homes (wireless networks) and nearly all businesses. WANs are becoming more common as businesses become more mobile and as more of them span greater distances. WANs were historically only used by larger corporations, but many smaller companies with remote locations now use them as well. It is important to understand LANs and WANs as a service professional, because when you're repairing computers you are likely to come in contact with problems that are associated with the computer's connection to a network.

Local Area Networks (LANs)

The 1970s brought us the minicomputer, which was a smaller version of the mainframe. Whereas the mainframe used *centralized processing* (all programs ran on the same computer), the minicomputer used *distributed processing* to access programs across other computers. As depicted in Figure 10.1, distributed processing allows a user at one computer to use a program on another computer as a *back end* to process and store information. The user's computer is the *front end*, where data entry and minor processing functions are performed. This arrangement allowed programs to be distributed across computers rather than centralized. This was also the first time computers used network cables to connect rather than phone lines.

FIGURE 10.1   Distributed processing

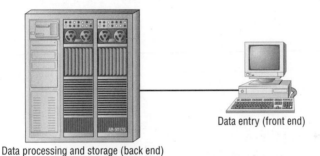

Data entry (front end)

Data processing and storage (back end)

By the 1980s, offices were beginning to buy PCs in large numbers. Portables were also introduced, allowing computing to become mobile. Neither PCs nor portables, however, were efficient in sharing information. As timeliness and security became more important, floppy disks were just not cutting it. Offices needed to find a way to implement a better means to share and access resources. This led to the introduction of the first type of PC LAN: ShareNet by Novell. LANs are simply the linking of computers to share resources within a closed environment. The first simple LANs were constructed a lot like Figure 10.2.

FIGURE 10.2   A simple LAN

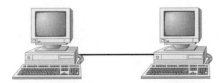

After the introduction of ShareNet, more LANs sprouted. The earliest LANs could not cover large distances. Most of them could only stretch across a single floor of the office and could support no more than 30 users. Further, they were still very rudimentary and only a few software programs supported them. The first software programs that ran on a LAN were not capable of permitting more than one user at a time to use a program (this constraint was known as *file locking*). Nowadays, we can see multiple users accessing a program at one time, limited only by restrictions at the record level.

Wide Area Networks (WANs)

By the late 1980s, networks were expanding to cover ranges considered geographical in size and were supporting thousands of users. WANs, first implemented with mainframes at massive government expense, started attracting PC users as networks went to this new level. Businesses with offices across the country communicated as if they were only desks apart. Soon the whole world saw a change in its way of doing business, across not only a few miles but across countries. Whereas LANs are limited to single buildings, WANs can span buildings, states, countries, and even continental boundaries. Figure 10.3 gives an example of a simple WAN.

FIGURE 10.3   A simple WAN

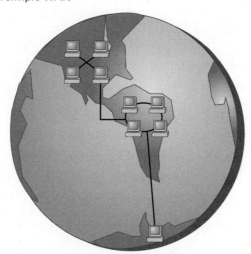

Networks of today and tomorrow are no longer limited by the inability of LANs to cover distance and handle mobility. WANs play an important role in the future development of corporate networks worldwide.

Primary Network Components

Technically speaking, two or more computers connected together make up a network. But networks are rarely that simple. When looking at the devices or resources available on a network, there are three types of components to be aware of:

- Servers
- Clients or workstations
- Resources

Blurring the Lines

In the 1980s and 90s, LANs and WANs were often differentiated by their connection speeds. For example, if you had a 10Mbps connection or faster to other computers, you were often considered to be on a LAN. WANs were often connected to each other by very expensive T1 connections, which have a maximum bandwidth of 1.544Mbps.

As with all other technologies, networking capacity has exploded. In today's office network, anything slower than 100Mbps is considered archaic. Connections of 1Gbps are fairly common. WAN connectivity, although still slower than LAN connectivity, can easily be several times faster than the T1. Because of the speed increases in WAN connectivity, the old practice of categorizing your network based on connection speed is outdated.

Today, the most common way to classify a network is based on geographical distance. If your network is in one central location, whether that is one office, one floor of an office building, or maybe even one entire building, it's usually considered a LAN. If your network is spread out among multiple distant locations, it's a WAN.

 Every network requires two more items to tie these three components together: a network operating system (NOS) and some kind of shared medium. These components are covered later in their own sections.

Servers

Servers come in many shapes and sizes. They are a core component of the network, providing a link to the resources necessary to perform any task. The link the server provides could be to a resource existing on the server itself or a resource on a client computer. The server is the "leader of the pack," offering directions to the client computers regarding where to go to get what they need.

Servers offer networks the capability of centralizing the control of resources and security thereby reducing administrative difficulties. They can be used to distribute processes for balancing the load on computers and can thus increase speed and performance. They can also compartmentalize files for improved reliability. That way, if one server goes down, not all of the files are lost.

Servers can perform several different critical tasks. For example, servers that provide files to the users on the network are called *file servers*. Likewise, servers that host printing services for users are called *print servers*. (There are other tasks as well, such as authentication, remote access services, administration, mail, and so on.) Servers can be *multipurpose* or *single-purpose*. If they are multipurpose, they can be, for example, both a file server and a print server at the same time. If the server is a single-purpose server, it is a file server only or a print server only. Another distinction we use in categorizing servers is whether they are *dedicated* or *nondedicated*:

Dedicated servers   A dedicated server is assigned to provide specific applications or services for the network and nothing else. Because a *dedicated server* specializes in only a few tasks, it requires fewer resources from the computer that is hosting it than a nondedicated server might require. This savings in overhead may translate to a certain efficiency and can thus be considered as having a beneficial impact on network performance. A web server is an example of a dedicated server: it is dedicated to the task of serving up web pages.

Nondedicated servers   Nondedicated servers are assigned to provide one or more network services *and* local access. A *nondedicated server* is expected to be slightly more flexible in its day-to-day use than a dedicated server. Nondedicated servers can be used not only to direct network traffic and perform administrative actions but also often to serve as a front-end for the administrator to work with other applications or services or perform services for more than one network. For example, a nondedicated web server might serve out more than one website, where a dedicated web server serves out just one website. The nondedicated server is not what some would consider a true server, because it can act as a workstation as well as a server. The workgroup server at your office is an example of a nondedicated server. It might be a combination file, print, and e-mail server. Plus, because of its nature, a nondedicated server could also function well in a peer-to-peer environment. It could be used as a workstation, in addition to being a file, print, and e-mail server.

Many networks use both dedicated and nondedicated servers in order to incorporate the best of both worlds, offering improved network performance with the dedicated servers and flexibility with the nondedicated servers.

Workstations

Workstations are the computers on which the network users do their work, performing activities such as word processing, database design, graphic design, e-mail, and other office or personal tasks. Workstations are basically everyday computers, except for the fact that they are connected to a network that offers additional resources. Workstations can range from diskless computer systems to desktop systems. In network terms, workstations are also known as *client computers*. As clients, they are allowed to communicate with the servers in the network in order to use the network's resources.

It takes several items to make a workstation into a network client. You must install a *network interface card (NIC)*, a special expansion card that allows the PC to talk on a network. You must connect it to a cabling system that connects to another computer (or several other computers). And you must install special software, called *client software*, which allows the computer to talk to the servers and request resources from them. Once all this has been accomplished, the computer is "on the network."

Network client software comes with all operating systems today. When you configure your computer to participate in the network, the operating system activates this software.

To the client, the server may be nothing more than just another drive letter. However, because it is in a network environment, the client can use the server as a doorway to more storage or more applications, or through which it may communicate with other computers or other networks. To users, being on a network changes a few things:

- They can store more information, because they can store data on other computers on the network.

- They can share and receive information from other users, perhaps even collaborating on the same document.

- They can use programs that would be too large or complex for their computer to use by itself.

- They can use hardware not attached directly to their computer, such as a printer.

 Real World Scenario

Is That a Server or a Workstation?

This is one of the things I do when teaching novice technicians. In the room will be a typical mini-tower desktop computer. I point to it and ask, "Is that a server or a workstation?" A lot of techs will look at it and say it's a workstation because it is a desktop computer. The real answer is, "It depends."

Although many people have a perception that servers are an ultra-fancy, rack-mounted device, that isn't necessarily true. It's true that servers typically need more powerful hardware than workstations do because of their role on the network, but that isn't a law. What really differentiates a workstation from a server is what operating system it has installed and what role it plays on the network.

For example, if that system has Windows Server 2008 installed on it, you can be pretty sure it's a server. If it has Windows Vista or XP, it's more than likely going to be a client, but not always. Computers with operating systems such as Vista or XP can be both clients on the network and nondedicated servers, as would be the case if you share your local printer with others on the network.

The moral of the story? Don't assume a computer's role simply by looking at it. You need to understand what is on it and what its role on the network is to make that determination.

Network Resources

We now have the server to share the resources and the workstation to use them, but what about the resources themselves? A *resource* (as far as the network is concerned) is any item that can be used on a network. Resources can include a broad range of items, but the most important ones include the following:

- Printers and other peripherals
- Disk storage and file access
- Applications

When an office only has to purchase a few printers (and all of the associated consumables) for the entire office, the costs are dramatically lower than the costs for supplying printers at every workstation.

Networks also give users more storage space to store their files. Client computers can't always handle the overhead involved in storing large files (for example, database files) because they are already heavily involved in users' day-to-day work activities. Because servers in a network can be dedicated to only certain functions, a server can be allocated to store all the larger files that are worked with every day, freeing up disk space on client computers. In addition, if users store their files on a server, the administrator can back up the server periodically to ensure that if something happens to the user's files, those files can be recovered.

Files that all users need to access (such as emergency contact lists and company policies) can also be stored on a server. Having one copy of these files in a central location saves disk space as opposed to storing the files locally on everyone's system.

Applications (programs) no longer need to be on every computer in the office. If the server is capable of handling the overhead an application requires, the application can reside on the server and be used by workstations through a network connection.

The sharing of applications over a network requires a special arrangement with the application vendor, which may wish to set the price of the application according to the number of users who will be using it. The arrangement allowing multiple users to use a single installation of an application is called a *site license*.

Being on a Network Brings Responsibilities

You are part of a community when you are on a network, which means you need to take responsibility for your actions. First, a network is only as secure as the users who use it. You cannot randomly delete files or move documents from server to server. You do not own your e-mail, so anyone in your company's management can choose to read it. In addition, printing does not mean that if you send something to print it will print immediately—your document may not be the first in line to be printed at the shared printer. Plus, if your workstation has also been set up as a nondedicated server, you cannot turn it off.

Network Operating Systems (NOSs)

PCs use a disk operating system that controls the file system and how the applications communicate with the hard disk. Networks use a network operating system (NOS) to control the communication with resources and the flow of data across the network. The NOS runs on the server. Some of the more popular NOSs at this time include Unix, Linux, and Microsoft's

Windows Server 2008, Windows Server 2003, and Windows 2000 Server. Several other companies offer network operating systems as well.

Back in the early days of mainframes, it took a full staff of people working around the clock to keep the machines going. With today's NOSs, servers are able to monitor memory, CPU time, disk space, and peripherals without a babysitter. Each of these operating systems allows processes to respond in a certain way with the processor.

With the functionality of LANs and WANs, you can be sitting in your office in Milwaukee and carry on a real-time electronic chat with a coworker in France, or maybe print an invoice at the home office in California, or manage someone else's computer from your own while they are on vacation. Gone are the days of passing around floppy disks, leaving phone messages that aren't received, or having to wait a month to receive a letter from someone in Hong Kong. NOSs provide this functionality on a network.

Network Resource Access

Now that we have discussed the makeup of a typical network, let's examine the way resources are accessed on a network. There are generally two resource access models: peer-to-peer and client-server. It is important to choose the appropriate model. How do you decide what type of resource model is needed? You must first think about the following questions:

- What is the size of the organization?
- How much security does the company require?
- What software or hardware does the resource require?
- How much administration does it need?
- How much will it cost?
- Will this resource meet the needs of the organization today and in the future?
- Will additional training be needed?

Networks cannot just be put together at the drop of a hat. A lot of planning is required before implementation of a network to ensure that whatever design is chosen will be effective and efficient, and not just for today but for the future as well. The forethought of the designer will lead to the best network with the least amount of administrative overhead. In each network, it is important that a plan be developed to answer the previous questions. The answers will help the designer choose the type of resource model to use.

Peer-to-Peer Networks

In a peer-to-peer network, the computers act as both service providers and service requestors. An example of a peer-to-peer resource model is shown in Figure 10.4.

FIGURE 10.4   The peer-to-peer resource model

Peer-to-peer networks are great for small, simple, inexpensive networks. This model can be set up almost immediately, with little extra hardware required. Windows 2000, Windows XP, and Windows Vista, Linux, and Mac OS are popular operating system environments that support a peer-to-peer resource model. Peer-to-peer networks are also referred to as *workgroups.*

Generally speaking, there is no centralized administration or control in the peer-to-peer resource model. Every station has unique control over the resources the computer owns, and each station must be administrated separately. However, this very lack of centralized control can make it difficult to administer the network; for the same reason, the network isn't very secure. Moreover, because each computer is acting as both a workstation and server, it may not be easy to locate resources. The person who is in charge of a file may have moved it without anyone's knowledge. Also, the users who work under this arrangement need more training, because they are not only users but also administrators.

Will this type of network meet the needs of the organization today and in the future? Peer-to-peer resource models are generally considered the right choice for small companies that don't expect future growth. For example, the business might be small, possibly an independent subsidiary of a specialty company, and has no plans to increase its market size or number of employees. Small companies that expect growth, on the other hand, should not choose this type of model. Although it could very well meet the company's needs today, the growth of the company will necessitate making major changes over time. Choosing to set up a peer-to-peer resource model simply because it is cheap and easy to install could be a costly mistake. A company's management may find that it costs them more in the long run than if they had chosen a server-based resource model.

A rule of thumb is that if you have 10 computers or less and centralized security is not a key priority, then a workgroup may be a good choice for you.

Client-Server Resource Model

The client-server (also known as server-based) model is better than the peer-to-peer model for large networks (say, more than 10 computers) that need a more secure environment and centralized control. Server-based networks use one or more dedicated, centralized servers. All administrative functions and resource sharing are performed from this point. This makes it easier to share resources, perform backups, and support an almost unlimited number of users. This model also offers better security. However, the server needs more hardware than a typical workstation/server computer in a peer-to-peer resource model. In addition, it requires specialized software (the NOS) to manage the server's role in the environment. With the addition of a server and the NOS, server-based networks can easily cost more than peer-to-peer resource models. However, for large networks, it's the only choice. An example of a client-server resource model is shown in Figure 10.5.

Server-based networks are also known as *domains.* The key characteristic of a domain is that security is centrally administered. When you log in to the network, the login request is passed to the server responsible for security, sometimes known as a *domain controller.*

(Microsoft uses the term domain controller, whereas other vendor's server products do not.) This is different from the peer-to-peer model, where each individual workstation validates users. In a peer-to-peer model, if the user jsmith wants to be able to log in to different workstations, she needs to have a user account set up on each machine. This can quickly become an administrative nightmare! In a domain, all user accounts are stored on the server. User jsmith needs only one account and can log on to any of the workstations in the domain.

FIGURE 10.5 The client-server resource model

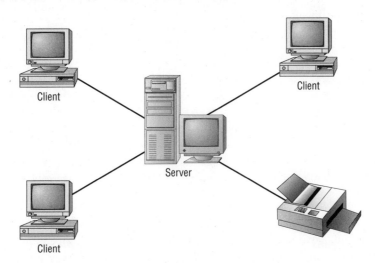

Will this type of network meet the needs of the organization today and in the future? Client-server resource models are the desired models for companies that are continually growing or that need to initially support a large environment. Server-based networks offer the flexibility to add more resources and clients almost indefinitely into the future. Hardware costs may be more, but, with the centralized administration, managing resources becomes less time consuming. Also, only a few administrators need to be trained, and users are responsible for only their own work environment.

If you are looking for an inexpensive, simple network with little setup required, and there is no need for the company to grow in the future, then the peer-to-peer network is the way to go. If you are looking for a network to support many users (more than 10 computers), strong security, and centralized administration, consider the server-based network your only choice.

Whatever you decide, always take the time to plan your network before installing it. A network is not something you can just throw together. You don't want to find out a few months down the road that the type of network you chose does not meet the needs of the company—this could be a time-consuming and costly mistake.

Network Topologies

A *topology* is a way of laying out the network. Topologies can be either physical or logical. *Physical topologies* describe how the cables are run. *Logical topologies* describe how the network messages travel. Deciding which type of topology to use is the next step when designing your network.

You must choose the appropriate topology in which to arrange your network. Each type differs by its cost, ease of installation, fault tolerance (how the topology handles problems such as cable breaks), and ease of reconfiguration (like adding a new workstation to the existing network).

There are five primary topologies (some of which can be both logical and physical):

- Bus (can be both logical and physical)
- Star (physical only)
- Ring (can be both logical and physical)
- Mesh (can be both logical and physical)
- Hybrid (usually physical)

Each topology has advantages and disadvantages. At the end of this section, check out Table 10.1, which summarizes the advantages and disadvantages of each topology.

Bus Topology

A bus is the simplest physical topology. It consists of a single cable that runs to every workstation, as shown in Figure 10.6. This topology uses the least amount of cabling. Each computer shares the same data and address path. With a logical bus topology, messages pass through the trunk, and each workstation checks to see if the message is addressed to itself. If the address of the message matches the workstation's address, the network adapter copies the message to the card's onboard memory.

FIGURE 10.6   The bus topology

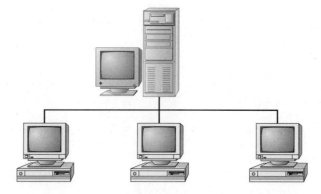

Cable systems that use the bus topology are easy to install. You run a cable from the first computer to the last computer. All the remaining computers attach to the cable somewhere in between. Because of the simplicity of installation, and because of the low cost of the cable, bus topology cabling systems (such as Ethernet) are the cheapest to install.

Although the bus topology uses the least amount of cabling, it is difficult to add a workstation. If you want to add another workstation, you have to completely reroute the cable and possibly run two additional lengths of it. Also, if any one of the cables breaks, the entire network is disrupted. Therefore, such a system is expensive to maintain.

Star Topology

A physical star topology branches each network device off a central device called a *hub*, making it easy to add a new workstation. Also, if any workstation goes down, it does not affect the entire network. (But, as you might expect, if the central device goes down, the entire network goes down.) Some types of Ethernet, ARCNet, and Token Ring use a physical star topology. Figure 10.7 shows an example of the organization of the star network.

FIGURE 10.7   The star topology

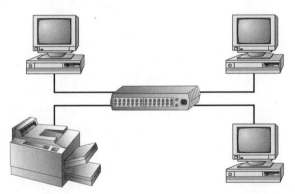

Star topologies are easy to install. A cable is run from each workstation to the hub. The hub is placed in a central location in the office (for example, a utility closet). Star topologies are more expensive to install than bus networks, because several more cables need to be installed, plus the hubs. But the ease of reconfiguration and fault tolerance (one cable failing does not bring down the entire network) far outweigh the drawbacks.

Although the hub is the central portion of a star topology, many networks use a device known as a switch instead of a hub. The primary difference between them is that the switch makes a virtual connection between sender and receiver instead of simply sending each message to every port. Thus, a switch provides better performance over a hub for only a small price increase.

Ring Topology

A physical ring topology is a unique topology. Each computer connects to two other computers, joining them in a circle and creating a unidirectional path where messages move from workstation to workstation. Each entity participating in the ring reads a message and then regenerates it and hands it to its neighbor on a different network cable. See Figure 10.8 for an example of a ring topology.

FIGURE 10.8 The ring topology

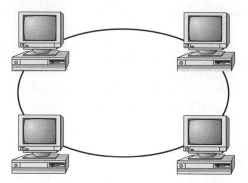

The ring makes it difficult to add new computers. Unlike a star topology network, the ring topology network will go down if one entity is removed from the ring. Physical ring topology systems rarely exist anymore, mainly because the hardware involved was fairly expensive and the fault tolerance was very low. However, one type of logical ring still exists: IBM's Token Ring technology. We'll discuss this technology later in the "Network Architectures" section.

Token Ring does *not* use a physical ring. It actually uses a physical star topology. Remember that physical topologies describe how the cables are connected, and logical topologies describe information flow.

Mesh Topology

The *mesh topology* is the most complex in terms of physical design. In this physical topology, each device is connected to every other device (Figure 10.9). This topology is rarely found in LANs, mainly because of the complexity of the cabling. If there are x computers, there will be $(x \times (x-1)) \div 2$ cables in the network. For example, if you have five computers in a mesh network, it will use $5 \times (5 - 1) \div 2 = 10$ cables. This complexity is compounded when you add another workstation. For example, your 5-computer, 10-cable network will jump to 15 cables if you add just one more computer. Imagine how the person doing the cabling would feel if you told them they had to cable 50 computers in a mesh network—they'd have to come up with $50 \times (50 - 1) \div 2 = 1225$ cables!

Because of its design, the physical mesh topology is expensive to install and maintain. Cables must be run from each device to every other device. The advantage you gain is high fault tolerance. With a logical mesh topology, there will always be a way to get the data from source to destination. The data may not be able to take the direct route, but it can take an alternate, indirect route. For this reason, the mesh topology is found in WANs to connect multiple sites across WAN links. It uses devices called *routers* to search multiple routes through the mesh and determine the best path. However, the mesh topology does become inefficient with five or more entities because of the number of connections that need to be maintained.

FIGURE 10.9 The mesh topology

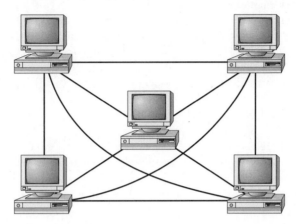

Hybrid Topology

The hybrid topology is simply a mix of the other topologies. It would be impossible to illustrate it, because there are many combinations. In fact, most networks today are not only hybrid but heterogeneous (they include a mix of components of different types and brands). The hybrid network may be more expensive than some types of network topologies, but it takes the best features of all the other topologies and exploits them.

Table 10.1 summarizes the advantages and disadvantages of each type of network topology.

TABLE 10.1 Topologies—Advantages and Disadvantages

Topology	Advantages	Disadvantages
Bus	Cheap. Easy to install.	Difficult to reconfigure. A break in the bus disables the entire network.
Star	Cheap. Easy to install. Easy to reconfigure. Fault tolerant.	More expensive than bus.
Ring	Efficient. Easy to install.	Reconfiguration is difficult. Very expensive.
Mesh	Simplest for data flow. Most fault tolerant.	Reconfiguration is extremely difficult, extremely expensive, and very complex.
Hybrid	Gives a combination of the best features of each topology used.	Complex (less so than mesh, however).

Network Architectures

Network architectures define the structure of the network, including hardware, software, and physical layout. We differentiate each architecture by the hardware and software required to maintain optimum performance levels. A network architecture's performance is usually discussed in terms of *bandwidth*, or how much data a particular network technology can handle in a period of time. The major architectures in use today are Ethernet and Token Ring.

Ethernet

The original definition of the IEEE 802.3 model (discussed in the "IEEE 802.3 CSMA/CD (Ethernet)" section later in this chapter) included a bus topology using coaxial cable and baseband signaling. From this model came the first Ethernet architecture. *Ethernet* was originally codeveloped by Digital, Intel, and Xerox and was known as DIX Ethernet.

Ethernet has several specifications, each one specifying the speed, communication method, and cable. The original Ethernet was given a designation of 10Base5. The *10* in Ethernet 10Base5 stands for the 10Mbps transmission rate, *Base* stands for the baseband communications used, and *5* stands for the maximum distance of 500 meters to carry transmissions. This method of identification soon caught on, and as vendors changed the specifications of the Ethernet architecture, they followed the same pattern in the way they identified these specifications.

You may see the terms *baseband* and *broadband* used in networking. When discussing networking technologies, baseband means that only one signal can be passed along a cable at one time, whereas broadband means that multiple signals can be transmitted on the medium at one time.

After 10Base5 came 10Base2 and 10BaseT. These quickly became standards in Ethernet technology. Many other standards have developed since then. Table 10.2 gives you a snapshot of some of them.

TABLE 10.2 Ethernet Standards

Types	Cables Used	Speed	Distance
10Base2	Coaxial copper	10Mbps	185m
10BaseT	Twisted-pair copper	10Mbps	100m
100BaseTX	Twisted-pair copper	100Mbps	100m
100BaseFX	Multimode fiber	100Mbps	400m
1000BaseT	Multimode fiber	1Gbps	100m
1000BaseX	Fiber or copper	1Gbps	(Overall standard for 1Gbps on fiber and copper)

TABLE 10.2 Ethernet Standards *(continued)*

Types	Cables Used	Speed	Distance
10GBaseSR	Multimode fiber	10Gbps	26m
10GBaseLR	Single-mode fiber	10Gbps	25km (~16 miles)
10GBaseER	Single-mode fiber	10Gbps	40km (~25 miles)
10GBaseSW	Multimode fiber	10Gbps	26m
10GBaseLW	Single-mode fiber	10Gbps	10km
10GBaseEW	Single-mode fiber	10Gbps	40km
10GBaseT	Twisted-pair cable	10Gbps	100m

You may hear terms like "Fast Ethernet" and "Gigabit Ethernet" thrown around. Fast Ethernet refers to Ethernet running at 100Mbps or faster, whereas Gigabit Ethernet means Ethernet running at 1Gbps or faster. They are both technological extensions of the original Ethernet standard.

Token Ring

Ethernet is by far the most widely implemented network architecture today. But there are literally hundreds of other standards. One such standard, for a point of comparison, is Token Ring. *Token Ring* networks are exactly like the IEEE 802.5 specification because the specification is based on IBM's Token Ring technology. Token Ring uses a physical star, logical ring topology. All workstations are cabled to a central device called a *multistation access unit (MAU)*. The ring is created within the MAU by connecting every port together with special circuitry in the MAU. Token Ring can use shielded or unshielded cable and can transmit data at either 4Mbps or 16Mbps.

Transmitting Data on a Network

Regardless of the type of network you choose to implement, the computers on that network need to know how to talk to each other. To facilitate communication across a network, computers use a common language called a protocol. We'll cover protocols in the next section, but essentially they are a language much like English is. Within that language, there are rules that need to be followed so that both computers understand the right communication behavior. To use a human example, within English there are grammar rules. If you put a bunch of English words together in a way that doesn't make sense, no one will understand you. If you just decide to omit verbs from your language, you're going to be challenged to get your point across. And if everyone talks at the same time, the conversation can be hard to follow.

Computers need standards to follow to keep their communication clear. Different standards are used to describe the rules that computers need to follow to communicate with each other. We will discuss two of the most common: the OSI model and the IEEE 802 standards.

OSI Model

The International Organization for Standardization (ISO) introduced the *Open Systems Interconnection (OSI)* model to provide a common way of describing network protocols. The ISO put together a seven-layer model providing a relationship between the stages of communication, with each layer adding to the layer above or below it.

 This OSI model is a theoretical model governing computer communication. Even though at one point an "OSI protocol" was developed, it never gained wide acceptance. You will never find a network that is running the "OSI protocol."

The theory behind the OSI model is that as transmission takes place, the higher layers pass data through the lower layers. As the data passes through a layer, the layer tacks its information (also called a *header*) onto the beginning of the information being transmitted until it reaches the bottom layer. A layer may also add a trailer to the end of the data. At this point, the bottom layer sends the information out on the wire.

At the receiving end, the bottom layer receives the information, reads its information from its header, removes its header and any associated trailer from the information, and then passes the remainder to the next highest layer. This procedure continues until the top-most layer receives the data that the sending computer sent.

The OSI model layers from top to bottom are listed here, as well as descriptions for what each of the layers is responsible for. After the descriptions, we'll summarize the entire model:

7. Application layer

6. Presentation layer

5. Session layer

4. Transport layer

3. Network layer

2. Data Link layer

1. Physical layer

Application layer   Allows access to network services. This is the layer at which file services and print services operate.

Presentation layer   Determines the "look," or format, of the data. This layer performs protocol conversion and manages data compression, data translation, and encryption. The character set information also is determined at this level. (The character set determines which numbers represent which alphanumeric characters.)

Session layer   Allows applications on different computers to establish, maintain, and end a session. A session is one virtual conversation. For example, all the procedures needed to transfer a single file make up one session. Once the session is over, a new process begins. This layer enables network procedures, such as identifying passwords, logons, and network monitoring.

Transport layer   Verifies that all packets were received by the destination host on a TCP/IP network. This layer also controls the data flow and troubleshoots any problems with transmitting or receiving datagrams. This layer's most important job is to provide error checking and reliable, end-to-end communications. It also takes large messages and segments them into smaller ones, and takes smaller segments and combines them into a single, larger message, depending on which way the traffic is flowing.

Network layer   Responsible for logical addressing of messages. At this layer, the data is organized into chunks called *packets*. The Network layer is something like the traffic cop. It is able to judge the best network path for the data based on network conditions, priority, and other variables. This layer manages traffic through packet switching, routing, and controlling congestion of data.

Data Link layer   Arranges data into chunks called *frames*. Included in these chunks is control information indicating the beginning and end of the datastream. This layer is very important because it makes transmission easier and more manageable and allows for error checking within the data frames. The Data Link layer also describes the unique physical address (also known as the *MAC address*) for each NIC. The Data Link layer is actually subdivided into two sections: Media Access Control (MAC) and Logical Link Control (LLC).

Physical layer   Describes how the data gets transmitted over a physical medium. This layer defines how long each piece of data is and the translation of each into the electrical pulses that are sent over the wires. It decides whether data travels unidirectionally or bidirectionally across the hardware. It also relates electrical, optical, mechanical, and functional interfaces to the cable.

Figure 10.10 shows the complete OSI model. Note the relation of each layer to the others and the function of each layer.

A helpful mnemonic device to remember the OSI layers in order is, "All People Seem To Need Data Processing."

IEEE 802 Standards

The Institute of Electrical and Electronics Engineers (IEEE) formed a subcommittee to create standards for network types. These standards specify certain types of networks, although not every network protocol is covered by the IEEE 802 committee specifications. This model breaks down into several categories, but the following are the most popularly referenced:

- 802.1 Internetworking
- 802.2 Logic Link Control

- 802.3 CSMA/CD (Ethernet) LAN

- 802.4 Token Bus LAN

- 802.5 Token Ring LAN

- 802.6 Metropolitan Area Network

- 802.7 Broadband Technical Advisory Group

- 802.8 Fiber Optic Technical Advisory Group

- 802.9 Integrated Voice/Data Networks

- 802.10 Network Security

- 802.11 Wireless Networks

- 802.12 Demand Priority Access LAN

FIGURE 10.10   OSI model and characteristics

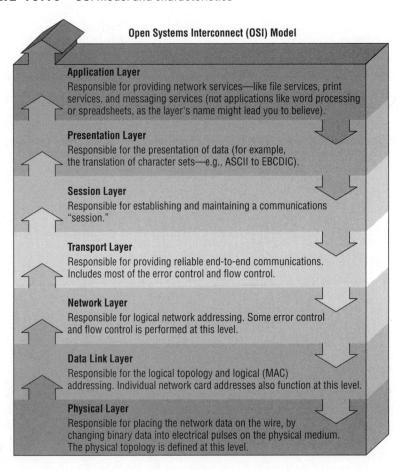

Open Systems Interconnect (OSI) Model

Application Layer
Responsible for providing network services—like file services, print services, and messaging services (not applications like word processing or spreadsheets, as the layer's name might lead you to believe).

Presentation Layer
Responsible for the presentation of data (for example, the translation of character sets—e.g., ASCII to EBCDIC).

Session Layer
Responsible for establishing and maintaining a communications "session."

Transport Layer
Responsible for providing reliable end-to-end communications. Includes most of the error control and flow control.

Network Layer
Responsible for logical network addressing. Some error control and flow control is performed at this level.

Data Link Layer
Responsible for the logical topology and logical (MAC) addressing. Individual network card addresses also function at this level.

Physical Layer
Responsible for placing the network data on the wire, by changing binary data into electrical pulses on the physical medium. The physical topology is defined at this level.

The IEEE 802 standards were designed primarily for enhancements to the bottom three layers of the OSI model. The IEEE 802 standard breaks the Data Link layer into two sublayers: a Logical Link Control (LLC) sublayer and a Media Access Control (MAC) sublayer. In the Logical Link Control sublayer, data link communications are managed. The Media Access Control sublayer watches out for data collisions, as well as assigning physical addresses.

We will focus on the two predominant 802 standards on which existing network architectures have been based: 802.3 CSMA/CD (Ethernet) and 802.5 Token Ring.

IEEE 802.3 CSMA/CD (ETHERNET)

Ethernet is the most well-known example of a protocol based on the IEEE 802.3 CSMA/CD standard. The original *802.3* CSMA/CD standard defines a bus topology network that uses a 50 ohm coaxial baseband cable and carries transmissions at 10Mbps. This standard groups data bits into frames and uses the Carrier Sense Multiple Access with Collision Detection (CSMA/CD) cable access method to put data on the cable. Currently, the 802.3 standard has been amended to include speeds up to 10Gbps.

Breaking the CSMA/CD acronym apart may help illustrate how it works. First, there is the Carrier Sense (CS) part, which means that computers on the network are listening to the wire at all times. Multiple Access (MA) means that multiple computers have access to the line at the same time. This is analogous to having five people on a conference call. Everyone is listening, and everyone in theory can try to talk at the same time. Of course, when more than one person talks at once, there is a communication error. In CSMA/CD, when two machines transmit at the same time, a data *collision* takes place, and none of the data is received by the intended recipients. This is where the Collision Detection (CD) portion of the acronym comes in; the collision is detected and each sender knows they need to send again. Each sender then waits for a short random period of time and tries to transmit again. This process repeats until transmission takes place successfully. The CSMA/CD technology is considered a *contention-based* access method.

The only major downside to 802.3 is that with large networks (more than 100 computers on the same cable), the number of collisions increases to the point where more collisions than transmissions are taking place.

IEEE 802.5 TOKEN RING

The IEEE *802.5* standard specifies a physical star, logical ring topology that uses a token-passing technology to put the data on the cable. IBM developed this technology for its mainframe and minicomputer networks. IBM's name for it was Token Ring. The name stuck, and any network using this type of technology is called a Token Ring network.

In *token passing*, a special chunk of data called a *token* circulates through the ring from computer to computer. Any computer that has data to transmit must wait for the token. A transmitting computer that has data to transmit waits for a free token and takes it off the ring. Once it has the token, this computer modifies it in a way that tells the computers which one has the token. The transmitting computer then places the token (along with the data it needs to transmit) on the ring, and the token travels around the ring until it gets to the destination computer. The destination computer takes the token and data off the wire, modifies the token (indicating it has received the data), and places the token back on the wire. When the original sender receives the token back and sees that the destination computer has received the data, the sender modifies the token to make it free for use again. It then sends the token back on the ring and waits until it has more data to transmit.

The main advantage of the token-passing access method, which is a deterministic method, over contention (the 802.3 model) is that it eliminates collisions. Only workstations that have the token can transmit. It would seem that this technology has a lot of overhead and would be slow. But remember that this whole procedure takes place in a few milliseconds.

This technology scales very well. It is not uncommon for Token Ring networks based on the IEEE 802.5 standard to reach hundreds of workstations on a single ring.

IEEE 802.5

The story of the IEEE 802.5 standard is rather interesting. It's a story of the tail wagging the dog. With all the other IEEE 802 standards, the committee either saw a need for a new protocol on its own or got a request for one. They would then sit down and hammer out the new standard. A standard created by this process is known as a *de jure* ("by law") standard. With the IEEE 802.5, however, everyone was already using this technology, so the IEEE 802 committee got involved and simply declared it a standard. This type of standard is known as a *de facto* ("from the fact") standard—a standard that was being followed without having been formally recognized.

Understanding Networking Protocols

As we mentioned in the previous section, computers use a protocol as a common language for communication. A *protocol* is a set of rules that govern communications. Protocols detail what "language" the computers are speaking when they talk over a network. If two computers are going to communicate, they both must be using the same protocol. This is similar to languages that humans use. If I address you in English and you speak English, you will respond. If I address you in Japanese but you don't speak Japanese, then we are not going to be able to communicate. Some people can speak multiple languages, and computers are capable of speaking multiple languages as well.

While there are literally hundreds of different network protocols, the A+ exam objectives list two common ones: TCP/IP and NetBIOS. The most common protocol in use today by far is TCP/IP. It's the language of the Internet and one of the more complex protocols as well. In this section, we'll spend the most time looking at TCP/IP, but we will also look at a few other common protocols you might run across, such as NetBIOS, IPX/SPX, and AppleTalk.

TCP/IP

The *Transmission Control Protocol/Internet Protocol (TCP/IP) suite* is the most popular network protocol in use today, thanks mostly to the rise of the Internet. While the protocol suite is named after two of its hardest-working protocols, *Transmission Control Protocol (TCP)* and *Internet Protocol (IP)*, TCP/IP actually contains dozens of protocols working together to help computers communicate with one another.

TCP/IP is the protocol of the Internet.

TCP/IP is robust and flexible. For example, if you want to ensure that the packets are delivered from one computer to another, TCP/IP can do that. If guaranteed delivery isn't as important as speed, TCP/IP can ensure that, too. The protocol can work on disparate operating systems such as Unix, Linux, and Windows. It can also support a variety of programs, applications, and required network functions. Much of its flexibility comes from its modular nature.

You're familiar with the seven-layer OSI model we discussed earlier in this chapter. The structure of TCP/IP is based on a similar model created by the United States Department of Defense: the *Department of Defense (DOD) model*. The DOD model has four layers that map to the seven OSI layers, as shown in Figure 10.11.

FIGURE 10.11   The DOD and OSI models

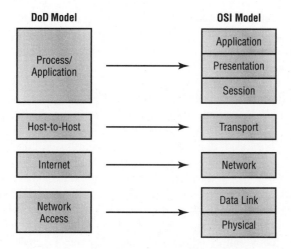

Keep in mind that the overall functionality between these two models is virtually identical; they just call the layers different things. For example, the Process/Application layer of the DOD model is designed to combine the functionality of the top three layers of the OSI model. Therefore, any protocol designed against the Process/Application layer would need to be able to perform all functions associated with the Application, Presentation, and Session layers in the OSI model.

TCP/IP's modular nature and common protocols are shown in Figure 10.12.

FIGURE 10.12 TCP/IP protocol suite

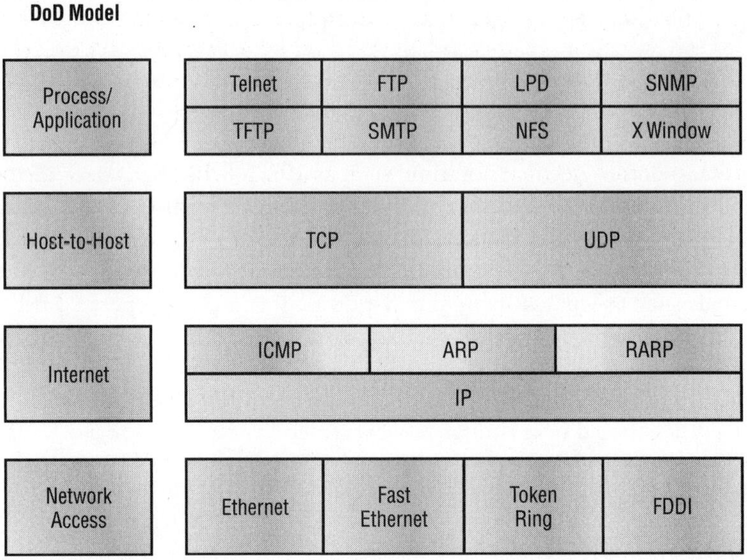

DoD Model

Process/ Application	Telnet	FTP	LPD	SNMP
	TFTP	SMTP	NFS	X Window

Host-to-Host	TCP	UDP

Internet	ICMP	ARP	RARP
	IP		

Network Access	Ethernet	Fast Ethernet	Token Ring	FDDI

The majority of TCP/IP protocols are located at the Process/Application layer. These include protocols you are probably pretty familiar with, such as *Hypertext Transfer Protocol (HTTP)*, *File Transfer Protocol (FTP)*, *Simple Mail Transfer Protocol (SMTP)*, *Post Office Protocol (POP)*, and others.

At the Host-to-Host layer, there are only two protocols: TCP and *User Datagram Protocol (UDP)*. Applications will use one or the other to transmit data. The major difference between the two is that TCP guarantees packet delivery whereas UDP does not. Because of this, TCP is often referred to as *connection oriented*, whereas UDP is *connectionless*. Because UDP is connectionless, it does tend to be somewhat faster, but then again we're talking about milliseconds here.

The most important protocol at the Internet layer is IP. This is the backbone of TCP/IP. Other protocols at this layer work in conjunction with IP, such as *Internet Control Message Protocol (ICMP)* and *Address Resolution Protocol (ARP)*. ICMP is responsible for delivering error messages. If you're familiar with the ping utility, it uses ICMP as well. (If you're not familiar with ping, we talk about it and other utilities in Chapter 18.) ARP resolves logical IP addresses to physical *Media Access Control (MAC)* addresses built in to network cards.

You'll notice that the Network Access layer doesn't have any protocols per se. This layer describes the type of network access method you are using, such as Ethernet, Token Ring, or others.

IP Addresses

To communicate on a TCP/IP network, each device needs to have a unique IP address. Any device with an IP address is referred to as a *host*.

You either enter the host's configuration information manually or you can have it automatically receive an address and other IP configuration information from a *Dynamic Host Configuration Protocol (DHCP)* server. We'll cover how to configure your computer's IP address in Chapter 18.

An IP address is a 32-bit hierarchical address that identifies a host on the network. It's typically written in dotted-decimal notation, such as 192.168.10.55. Each of the numbers in this example represents eight bits (or one byte) of the address, also known as an *octet*. The same address written in binary (how the computer thinks about it) would be 11000000 10101000 00001010 00110111. As you can see, the dotted-decimal version is a much more convenient way to write these numbers!

When working with IP addressing, all numbers will be between 0 and 255.

The addresses are said to be hierarchical, as opposed to "flat," because the numbers at the beginning of the address identify groups of computers that belong to the same network. This has the very important practical application of being able to route the protocol through routers. If we couldn't do this, there would be no Internet.

Another example of a hierarchical addressing scheme is telephone numbers. The first three digits, the area code, groups all other telephone numbers into one logical network. The second grouping of three numbers defines a local calling area, and the last grouping of numbers is the unique identifier within that local calling area.

PARTS OF THE IP ADDRESS

Each IP address is made up of two components: the *network ID* and the *host ID*. The network portion of the address always comes before the host portion. Because of the way IP is structured, the network portion does not have to be a specific fixed length. In other words, some computers will use 8 of the 32 bits for the network portion and the other 24 for the host portion, while other computers might use 24 bits for the network portion and the remaining 8 bits for the host portion.

Computers are able to differentiate where the network address ends and the host address begins through the use of a *subnet mask*. This is a value written just like an IP address and may look something like 255.255.255.0. Any bit that is set to a 1 in the subnet mask makes the corresponding bit in the IP address part of the network address. The rest will be the host address. The number 255 is the highest number you will ever see in IP addressing, and it means that all bits in the octet are set to 1.

Here's an example based on two numbers we have used in this chapter. The subnet mask of 255.255.255.0 indicates that the first three octets are the network portion of the address, and the last octet is the host portion. So if we look at the IP address of 192.168.10.55, the network portion is 192.168.10, and the host portion is 55.

To communicate using TCP/IP, each computer is *required* to have an IP address and correct subnet mask. A third component, called a *default gateway* (which is the IP address of the device that will take you outside of your network), is required if you want to communicate with computers outside of your local network. We'll talk about default gateways more in Chapter 18.

IP ADDRESS CLASSES

The designers of TCP/IP created classes of networks based on their size. For huge companies with thousands of computers there are Class A addresses. For companies with few computers, there are Class C addresses. For medium-sized companies, there are Class B addresses. There are also class D and E, but those are reserved and you'll never use those for your computers. The class of address can be identified by the first octet of the IP address.

Here are some characteristics of the three classes of addresses you will commonly deal with:

Class A Class A was designed for very large networks only. The default network portion for Class A networks is the first 8 bits, leaving 24 bits for host identification. Because the network portion is only 8 bits long (and 0 and 127 are reserved), there are only 126 Class A network addresses available. The remaining 24 bits of the address allow each Class A network to hold as many as 16,777,214 hosts. Examples of Class A networks include telecommunications giants such as Sprint and AT&T, and organizations such as General Electric, IBM, Hewlett-Packard, Apple, Xerox, Compaq, Columbia University, and MIT. All possible Class A networks are in use; no more are available.

Class B Class B was designed for medium-sized networks. The default network portion for Class B networks is the first 16 bits, leaving 16 bits for host identification. This allows for 16,384 networks, each with as many as 65,534 hosts attached. Examples of Class B networks include Microsoft, ExxonMobil, and Purdue University. Class B networks are generally regarded as unavailable, but address-conservation techniques have made some of these addresses available from time to time over the years.

Class C Class C was designed for smaller networks. The default network portion for Class C networks is the first 24 bits, leaving 8 bits for host identification. This allows for 2,097,152 networks, but each network can have a maximum of only 254 hosts. Most companies have Class C network addresses. Class C networks are still available.

The addresses and examples in this chapter refer to addresses that are live on the Internet. For example, MIT has the network address of 18.0.0.0. No one else on the Internet can use addresses in that network's range. But if you are using IP addresses on an internal network that never connects to the Internet, you are free to use whatever addresses you would like. More on that in Chapter 18.

Table 10.3 shows the IP classes, their ranges, and their default subnet masks.

TABLE 10.3 IP Address Classes

Class	First Octet	Default Subnet Mask	Comments
A	1–126	255.0.0.0	For very large networks
B	128–191	255.255.0.0	For medium-sized networks
C	192–223	255.255.255.0	For smaller networks with fewer hosts
D	224–239	N/A	Reserved for multicasts (sending messages to multiple systems)
E	240–255	N/A	Reserved for testing

The network addresses 0 and 127 are reserved and not available for use. Specifically, the address 127.0.0.1 is called the *loopback address*, which is used for troubleshooting network adapters. We'll talk more about this in Chapter 18.

Common Ports

Each protocol in the TCP/IP suite that operates at the Process/Application layer uses a *port number* to identify information it sends or receives. The port number, when combined with the host's IP address, is called a *socket*.

A good analogy for understanding port numbers is to think of cable or satellite television. In this analogy, the IP address is your house. The cable company needs to know where to send the data. But once the data is in your house, which channel are you going to receive? If you want sports, that might be on one channel, but weather is on a different channel, and the cooking show is on yet another. Those channels are analogous to ports.

There are 65,536 ports numbered from 0 to 65535. Ports 0 through 1023 are called the *well-known ports*, and 1024 through 49151 are called the *registered ports*. Anything from 49152 to 65535 is free to be used by application vendors. Fortunately you don't need to memorize them all.

Table 10.4 shows the ports you should know for the A+ exam.

TABLE 10.4 Common Port Numbers

Service	Port	Description
File Transfer Protocol (FTP)	20, 21	Optimized for file downloads
Telnet	23	Terminal emulation–logging in remotely to a terminal server

TABLE 10.4   Common Port Numbers *(continued)*

Service	Port	Description
Simple Mail Transfer Protocol (SMTP)	25	Sending e-mail
Hypertext Transfer Protocol (HTTP)	80	Web (Internet) traffic
Domain Name Service (DNS)	53	Resolves hostnames to IP addresses
Dynamic Host Configuration Protocol (DHCP)	67	Automatically assigns IP configuration information to clients
Post Office Protocol 3 (POP3)	110	Receiving e-mail
Hypertext Transfer Protocol Secure (HTTPS)	443	Secure Internet traffic

A complete list of registered port numbers can be found at `www.iana.org/assignments/port-numbers`.

DHCP and DNS

Two critical TCP/IP services you need to be aware of are Dynamic Host Configuration Protocol (DHCP) and Domain Name System (DNS). Both are run off a server and provide key services to network clients.

A DHCP server can be configured to automatically provide IP configuration information to clients. Configuration information provided typically includes:

- IP address
- Subnet mask
- Default gateway (the "door" to the outside world)
- DNS server address

DHCP servers can provide a lot more than this list, but those are the most common items. When a DHCP-configured client boots up, it sends out a broadcast on the network (called a *DHCP DISCOVER*) requesting a DHCP server. The DHCP server then returns configuration information to the client.

DNS has one function on the network, and that is to resolve hostnames to IP addresses. This sounds simple enough, but it has profound implications.

Think about using the Internet. You open your browser, and in the address bar type the name of your favorite website, something like **www.google.com**, and press Enter. The first question your computer asks is, "Who is that?" The DNS server provides the answer, "That is 72.14.205.104." Now that your computer knows the address of the website you want, it's able to traverse the Internet to find it.

Each DNS server has a database where it stores hostname-to-IP address pairs. If the DNS server does not know the address of the host you are looking for, it has the ability to query other DNS servers to help answer the request.

Think about the implications of that for just a minute. I know that I use Google several times a day, but in all honesty in order to write the previous paragraph I had to go out and find its IP address. It's certainly not something I have memorized. Much less, how could you possibly memorize the IP addresses of all of the websites you visit? Because of DNS, it's easy to find resources. Whether you want to find Coca Cola, Toyota, Amazon, or thousands of other companies, it's usually pretty easy to figure out how. Type in the name with a .com on the end of it and you're usually right.

DNS works the same way on an intranet (a local network not attached to the Internet) as it does on the Internet. The only difference is that instead of helping you find google.com, it may help you find Jenny's print server or Joe's file server.

The Future of TCP/IP

The present incarnation of TCP/IP that is used on the Internet was originally developed in 1973. Considering how fast technology evolves, it's pretty amazing to think that the protocol still enjoys immense popularity nearly 40 years later. This version is known as IPv4.

There are a few problems with IPv4, though. One is that we're quickly running out of available network addresses, and the other is that TCP/IP can be somewhat tricky to configure.

You may nod your head at the configuration part, but you might be wondering how we can run out of addresses. After all, IPv4 has 32 bits of addressing space, which allows for nearly 4.3 billion addresses! With the way it's structured, only about 250 million of those addresses are actually usable, and at the time of this writing, all of those are pretty much spoken for.

A new version of TCP/IP has been developed and it's called IPv6. Instead of a 32-bit address, it provides for 128-bit addresses. That will give us 3.4×10^{38} addresses, which should be more than enough. Its address structure looks something like this:

```
2001:0db8:3c4d:0012:0000:0000:1234:56ab
_____|___|_____
Global prefix  Subnet    Interface ID
```

IPv6 also has many features standard that are optional (but useful) in IPv4. While the addresses may be more difficult to remember, the automatic configuration and enhanced flexibility make the new version sparkle compared to the old one. Best of all, it's backward-compatible with IPv4, so networks can migrate to it without a complete restructure.

Over the next few years, expect to see more and more implementations of IPv6, and watch IPv4 be phased into the annals of history.

Other Protocols

Because of TCP/IP's ubiquity and flexibility, there probably aren't any reasons why you would want to use a different protocol. The only knock on TCP/IP is that it can be more difficult to configure than other protocols. The only other protocol called out on the A+ Essentials exam objectives is NetBIOS. We will cover that one, as well as a few others you may run into.

NetBEUI/NetBIOS

NetBIOS (pronounced "net-bye-os") is an acronym formed from *network basic input/ output system.* It's a Session layer network protocol originally developed by IBM and Sytek to manage data exchange and network access. NetBIOS provides an interface with a consistent set of commands for requesting lower-level network services to transmit information from node to node, thus separating the applications from the underlying NOS. Many vendors provide either their own version of NetBIOS or an emulation of its communications services in their products.

NetBIOS, in essence, helps you give your computer a name and easily find and talk to other computers on the local network.

NetBEUI (pronounced "net-boo-ee") is an acronym formed from NetBIOS Extended User Interface. It's an implementation and extension of IBM's NetBIOS transport protocol from Microsoft. NetBEUI communicates with the network through Microsoft's Network Driver Interface Specification (NDIS). NetBEUI is shipped with all versions of Microsoft's operating systems and is generally considered to have a lot of overhead. NetBEUI also has no networking layer and therefore no routing capability, which means it is suitable only for small networks; you cannot build internetworks with NetBEUI, so it is often replaced with TCP/IP.

Together, these protocols make up a very fast protocol suite that most people call NetBEUI/ NetBIOS. It is a good protocol for small LANs because it's simple and requires little or no setup, apart from giving each workstation a name. It allows users to find and use the network services they need easily, by simply browsing for them. However, because it contains no Network layer protocol, it cannot be routed and thus cannot be used on a WAN. It also would make a poor choice for a WAN protocol because of the protocol overhead involved.

NetBIOS can be used over other protocols in addition to NetBEUI. Many Windows computers use NetBIOS over TCP/IP. This allows them to have NetBIOS functionality over a routed network.

IPX/SPX

The *Internetwork Packet Exchange/Sequenced Packet Exchange (IPX/SPX)* is the default communication protocol for versions of the Novell NetWare operating system before NetWare 5. It was often used with Windows networks as well, but in Windows networks, the implementation of the IPX/SPX protocol is known as *NWLINK.*

IPX/SPX is a communication protocol similar to TCP/IP, but it's used primarily in LANs. It has features for use in WAN environments as well; before the mid-1990s, most corporate networks ran IPX/SPX because it was easy to configure and could be routed across WANs.

The two main protocols in IPX/SPX are IPX and SPX. SPX provides similar functions to TCP, and IPX provides functions similar to the TCP/IP suite protocols IP and UDP.

IPX addresses use an eight-digit hexadecimal number for the network portion. This number, called the *IPX network address*, can be assigned randomly by the installation program or manually by the network administrator. The node portion is the 12-digit hexadecimal MAC address assigned to the network card by the manufacturer. A colon separates the two portions. The first six digits identify the hardware manufacturer and are assigned to the manufacturer by the IEEE. The last six digits are a unique number given to that card by the manufacturer. Figure 10.13 shows a sample IPX address.

FIGURE 10.13 An IPX address

NOTE

For information about IPX/SPX, search Novell's knowledgebase by using the Search link at http://support.novell.com.

AppleTalk

AppleTalk is not just a protocol; it is a proprietary network architecture for Macintosh computers. It uses a bus and typically either shielded or unshielded cable.

AppleTalk uses a Carrier Sense Multiple Access with Collision Avoidance (CSMA/CA) technology to put data on the cable. Unlike Ethernet, which uses a CSMA/CD method (where the CD stands for *Collision Detection*), this technology uses smart interface cards to detect traffic *before* it tries to send data. A CSMA/CA card listens to the wire. If there is no traffic, it sends a small amount of data. If no collisions occur, it follows that amount of data with the data it wants to transmit. In either case, if a collision happens, it backs off for a random amount of time and tries to transmit again.

A common analogy is used to describe the difference between CSMA/CD and CSMA/CA. Sending data is like walking across the street. With CSMA/CD, you just cross the street. If you get run over, you go back and try again. With CSMA/CA, you look both ways and send your little brother across the street. If he makes it, you can follow him. If either of you get run over, you both go back and try again.

The big selling point of AppleTalk was that it was simple and cheap. It came installed on Macintosh computers, and it assigned itself an address. The problems were that it was slow, limited in capacity (it allowed a maximum of 32 devices on a network), and developers had to license it from Apple. Today, TCP/IP is the default networking protocol on Macs, and AppleTalk is only available for backward-compatibility.

Identifying Common Network Hardware

We have looked at the types of networks, network architectures, and the way a network communicates. To get a network to work also requires hardware. Every computer on the network needs to have a network adapter of some type. In many cases, you also need some sort of cable to hook them together. (Wireless networking is the exception, but at the back end of wireless network there are still components wired together.) And finally, you might also need connectivity devices to attach several computers or network to each other.

Network Interface Cards (NICs)

The *network interface card (NIC)* provides the physical interface between computer and cabling. It prepares data, sends data, and controls the flow of data. It can also receive and translate data into bytes for the CPU to understand. NICs come in many shapes and sizes.

Different NICs are distinguished by the PC bus type and the network for which they are used. This section describes the role of the NIC and how to choose the appropriate one. The following factors should be taken into consideration when choosing a NIC:

- Preparing data
- Sending and controlling data
- Configuration
- Drivers
- Compatibility
- Performance

Preparing Data

In the computer, data moves along buses in parallel, as on a four-lane interstate highway. But on a network cable, data travels in a single stream, as on a one-lane highway. This difference can cause problems when you're transmitting and receiving data, because the paths traveled are not the same. It is the NIC's job to translate the data from the computer into signals that can flow easily along the cable. It does this by translating digital signals into electrical signals (and in the case of fiber-optic NICs, to optical signals).

Sending and Controlling Data

For two computers to send and receive data, the cards must agree on several things. These include the following:

- The maximum size of the data frames
- The amount of data sent before giving confirmation
- The time needed between transmissions

- The amount of time to wait before sending confirmation
- The amount of data a card can hold
- The speed at which data transmits

If the cards can agree, then the sending of the data is successful. If the cards cannot agree, the sending of data does not occur.

To successfully send data on the network, all NICs need to use the same media access method (such as Ethernet and Token Ring) and they are connected to the same piece of cable. This usually isn't a problem today, because the vast majority of network cards sold today are Ethernet. If you were to try to use cards of different types (for example, one Ethernet and one Token Ring), neither of them would be able to communicate with the other unless you had a separate hardware device between them that could translate.

In addition, NICs can send data using either full-duplex or half-duplex mode. *Half-duplex communication* means that between the sender and receiver, only one of them can transmit at any one time. In *full-duplex communication*, a computer can send and receive data simultaneously. The main advantage of full-duplex over half-duplex communication is performance. NICs (specifically Fast Ethernet NICs) can operate twice as fast (200Mbps) in full-duplex mode as they do normally in half-duplex mode (100Mbps).

NIC Configuration

The NIC's configuration may include such things as a manufacturer's hardware address, IRQ address, base I/O port address, and base memory address. Before the emergence of Plug-and-Play, you might have had to configure some or all of these settings yourself and ensure that there were no conflicts with other devices. Now all of the required settings are configured for you.

Each card must have a unique hardware address, called a *MAC address*. If two cards on the same network have the same hardware address, neither one will be able to communicate. For this reason, the IEEE has established a standard for hardware addresses and assigns blocks of these addresses to NIC manufacturers, which then hard-wire the addresses into the cards.

Although it is possible for NIC manufacturers to produce multiple NICs with the same MAC address, it happens very rarely. If you do encounter this type of problem, contact the hardware manufacturer.

NIC Drivers

For the computer to use the NIC, it is very important to install the proper device drivers. These drivers communicate directly with the network redirector and adapter. They operate in the Media Access Control sublayer of the Data Link layer of the OSI model.

PC Bus Type

When you're choosing a NIC, use one that fits the bus type of your PC. If you have more than one type of bus in your PC (for example, a combination PCI/PCI Express), use a NIC that fits into the fastest type (the PCI Express, in this case). This is especially important in servers, because the NIC can quickly become a bottleneck if this guideline isn't followed.

More and more computers are using network cards that have either PC Card or USB interfaces. For laptop computers that don't otherwise have a network card built in to them, these small portable cards are very handy.

A USB network card can also be handy for troubleshooting. If a laptop isn't connecting to the network properly with its built-in card, you may be able to use the USB network card to see if it's an issue with the card or perhaps a software problem.

Network Interface Card Performance

The most important goal of the network adapter card is to optimize network performance and minimize the amount of time needed to transfer data packets across the network. The key is to ensure you get the fastest card you can for the type of network you're on. For example, if your wireless network supports 802.11b/g, make sure to get an 802.11g card as it's faster.

Cabling and Connectors

When the data is passing through the OSI model and reaches the Physical layer, it must find its way onto the medium that is used to physically transfer data from computer to computer. This medium is *cable* (or in the case of wireless networks, the air). It is the NIC's role to prepare the data for transmission, but it is the cable's role to properly move the data to its intended destination. It is not as simple as just plugging it into the computer. The cabling you choose must support both the network architecture and topology. There are four main types of cabling methods: coaxial cable, twisted-pair cable, fiber-optic cable, and wireless. We'll summarize all four cabling methods after the brief descriptions that follow.

Coaxial

Coaxial cable (or coax) contains a center conductor made of copper, surrounded by a plastic jacket, with a braided shield over the jacket (as shown in Figure 10.14). Either Teflon or a plastic such as PVC covers this metal shield. The Teflon-type covering is frequently referred to as a plenum-rated coating. That simply means that the coating does not produce toxic gas when burned (as PVC does) and is rated for use in ventilation plenums that carry breathable air. This type of cable is more expensive but may be mandated by electrical code whenever cable is hidden in walls or ceilings. Plenum rating applies to all types of cabling.

Other types of cabling (namely, twisted pair) can be rated for plenum use.

FIGURE 10.14   Coaxial cable

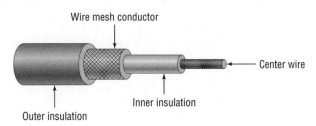

Coaxial cable is available in various specifications that are rated according to the *RG* Type system. Different cables have different specifications and, therefore, different RG grading designations (according to the U.S. military specification MIL-C-17). Distance and cost are considerations when selecting coax cable. The thicker the copper, the farther a signal can travel—and with that comes a higher cost and a less-flexible cable.

Coaxial cable comes in many thicknesses and types. The most common use for this type of cable is Ethernet 10Base2 cabling. It is known as thinnet or cheapernet. Table 10.5 shows the different types of RG cabling and their uses.

TABLE 10.5   Coax RG Types

RG #	Popular Name	Ethernet Implementation	Type of Cable
RG-6	Satellite/cable TV, cable modems	N/A	Solid copper
RG-8	Thicknet	10Base5	Solid copper
RG-58 U	N/A	None	Solid copper
RG-58 AU	Thinnet	10Base2	Stranded copper
RG-59	Cable television	N/A	Solid copper
RG-62	ARCNet (obsolete)	N/A	Solid/stranded copper

Coax Connector Types

With coax cable used in networking, generally you use *BNC connectors* (see Figure 10.15) to attach stations to a thinnet network. It is beyond our scope to settle the long-standing argument over the meaning of the abbreviation BNC. We have heard Bayonet Connector, Bayonet Nut Connector, and British Naval Connector. What is relevant is that the BNC connector locks securely with a quarter-twist motion.

FIGURE 10.15   Male and female BNC connectors

Male

Female

With Thick Ethernet, a station attaches to the main cable via a vampire tap, which clamps onto the cable. A *vampire tap* is so named because a metal tooth sinks into the cable, thus making the connection with the inner conductor. The tap is connected to an external transceiver that in turn has a 15-pin AUI connector (also called *DIX* or *DB-15* connector) to which you attach a cable that connects to the station (shown in Figure 10.16). DIX got its name from the companies that worked on this format—Digital, Intel, and Xerox.

FIGURE 10.16   Thicknet and vampire taps

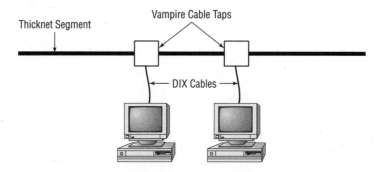

Twisted Pair

Twisted pair is the most popular type of cabling to use because of its flexibility and low cost. It consists of several pairs of wire twisted around each other within an insulated jacket, as shown in Figure 10.17. Twisted pair is most often found in 100BaseT Ethernet networks, although other systems can use it.

FIGURE 10.17   Twisted-pair cable

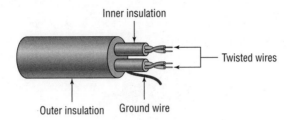

There are two different types of twisted-pair: *shielded twisted-pair (STP)* and *unshielded twisted-pair (UTP)*. Both types of cable have two or four pairs of twisted wires going through them. The difference is that STP has an extra layer of braided foil shielding surrounding the wires to decrease electrical interference. UTP has a PVC or plenum coating, but no foil shield.

UTP comes in seven grades to offer different levels of protection against electrical interference:

- Category 1 is for voice-only transmissions and is in most phone systems today. It contains two twisted pairs.

- Category 2 is able to transmit data at speeds up to 4Mbps. It contains four twisted pairs of wires.

- Category 3 is able to transmit data at speeds up to 10Mbps. It contains four twisted pairs of wires.

- Category 4 is able to transmit data at speeds up to 16Mbps. It contains four twisted pairs of wires.

- Category 5 is able to transmit data at speeds up to 100Mbps. It contains four twisted pairs of copper wire to give the most protection.

- Category 5e is able to transmit data at speeds up to 1Gbps. It also contains four twisted pairs of copper wire, but they are physically separated and contain more twists per foot than Category 5 to provide maximum interference protection.

- Category 6 is able to transmit data at speeds up to 1Gbps and beyond. It also contains four twisted pairs of copper wire, and they are oriented differently than in Category 5 or 5e. You can use it as a backbone to connect different parts of your network together, such as those on different floors of a building. If you're going to install a new network, there's no reason to use anything but CAT-6 unless you choose to use fiber.

Each of these levels has a maximum transmission distance of 100 meters.

CompTIA (and many others) usually shorten the word *category* to "CAT" and use the form CAT-5 to refer to Category 5, for example. This is a common way to refer to these categories, and you can feel free to use these terms interchangeably. If you are buying cable today, you shouldn't buy anything older than CAT-5e.

Twisted-Pair Connector Types

A BNC connector won't fit easily on UTP cable, so you need to use an *RJ (registered jack)* connector. You are probably familiar with RJ connectors. Most telephones connect with an RJ-11 connector. The connector used with UTP cable is called RJ-45. The RJ-11 has four wires, or two pairs, and the network connector RJ-45 has four pairs, or eight wires.

In almost every case, UTP uses RJ connectors; a crimper is used to attach an RJ connector to a cable. Higher-quality crimping tools have interchangeable dies for both types of connectors. Figure 10.18 shows an RJ-11 and an RJ-45 connector.

FIGURE 10.18   RJ-11 and RJ-45 connectors

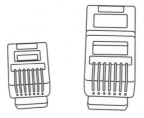

In addition to the RJ series used on UTP, STP (when used with Token Ring) often uses a special connector known as the *IBM data connector (IDC)*, *universal data connector (UDC)*, or *hermaphroditic data connector.* An example of this type of connector is shown in Figure 10.19. The IDC is unique in many ways. First, it isn't as universal as the other types of network connectors. Second, there aren't male and female versions, as with the others—the IDC is both male and female, so any two data connectors can connect. This connector was most commonly used with IBM's Token Ring technology and Type 1 or 2 STP cable.

The IDC also uses a tab to hold the connectors together, but this tab is a little more rigid than the tab on the RJ series connectors and doesn't move as much. Therefore, breakage is not much of an issue.

FIGURE 10.19   An IDC/UDC

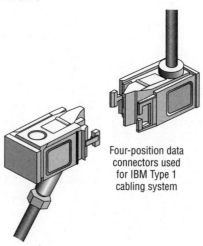

Four-position data
connectors used
for IBM Type 1
cabling system

Fiber-Optic

Fiber-optic cabling has been called one of the best advances in cabling. It consists of a thin, flexible glass or plastic fiber surrounded by a rubberized outer coating (see Figure 10.20). It provides transmission speeds from 100Mbps to 10Gbps and a maximum distance of several miles. Because it uses pulses of light instead of electric voltages to transmit data, it is immune to electrical interference and to wiretapping.

FIGURE 10.20   Fiber-optic cable

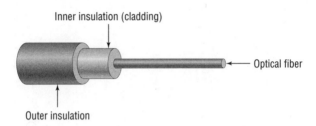

Inner insulation (cladding)

Optical fiber

Outer insulation

Fiber-optic cable has not been widely adopted for local area networks, however, because of its high cost of installation. Networks that need extremely fast transmission rates, transmissions over long distances, or have had problems with electrical interference in the past often use fiber-optic cabling.

Fiber-optic cable is referred to as either single-mode or multimode fiber. The term *mode* refers to the bundles of light that enter the fiber-optic cable. Single-mode fiber-optic cable uses only a single mode of light to propagate through the fiber cable, whereas multimode fiber allows multiple modes of light to propagate. In multimode fiber-optic cable, the light bounces off the cable walls as it travels through the cable, which causes the signal to weaken more quickly.

Multimode fiber-optic is most often used as horizontal cable. It permits multiple modes of light to propagate through the cable, which shortens cable distances and delivers a less available bandwidth. Devices that use multimode fiber-optic cable typically use light-emitting diodes (LEDs) to generate the light that travels through the cable; however, higher bandwidth network devices such as Gigabit Ethernet are now using lasers with multimode fiber-optic cable. ANSI/TIA/EIA-568-B recognizes two-fiber (duplex) 62.5/125 micron multimode fiber; ANSI/TIA/EIA-568-B also recognizes 50/125 micron multimode fiber-optic cable.

Single-mode optical fiber cable is commonly used as backbone cabling; it is also usually the cable type used in phone systems. Light travels through single-mode fiber-optic cable using only a single mode, meaning it travels straight down the fiber and does not bounce off the cable walls. Because only a single mode of light travels through the cable, single-mode fiber-optic cable supports higher bandwidth and longer distances than multimode fiber-optic cable. Devices that use single-mode fiber-optic cable typically use lasers to generate the light that travels through the cable.

ANSI/TIA/EIA-568-B recognizes 62.5/125 micron, 50/125 micron, and 8.3/125 micron single-mode optical fiber cables. ANSI/TIA/EIA-568-B states that the maximum backbone distance using single-mode fiber-optic cable is 3,000 meters (9,840 feet), and the maximum backbone distance using multimode fiber is 2,000 meters (6,560 feet).

Fiber-Optic Connector Types

The *subscriber connector (SC)*, also sometimes known as a square connector, is a type of fiber-optic connector, as shown in Figure 10.21. As you can see, SCs are latched connectors. This makes it impossible for you to pull out the connector without releasing the connector's latch, usually by pressing a button or release.

FIGURE 10.21   A sample SC

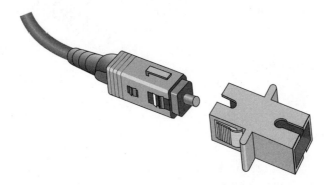

SCs work with either single- or multimode optical fibers. They aren't as popular as ST connectors for LAN connections.

The *straight tip (ST)* fiber-optic connector, developed by AT&T, is probably the most widely used fiber-optic connector. It uses a BNC attachment mechanism, similar to the Thinnet Ethernet connection mechanism, which makes connections and disconnections fairly easy. The ease of use of the ST is one of the attributes that makes this connector so popular. Figure 10.22 shows some examples of ST connectors. Notice the BNC attachment mechanism.

Wireless Networks

One of the most fascinating cabling technologies today—actually, it doesn't really *use* cable—is wireless. Wireless networks offer the ability to extend a LAN without the use of traditional cabling methods. Wireless transmissions are made through the air by infrared light, laser light, narrow-band radio, microwave, or spread-spectrum radio.

Wireless LANs are becoming increasingly popular as businesses become more mobile and less centralized. You can see them most often in environments where standard cabling methods are not possible or wanted. However, they are still not as fast or efficient as standard cabling methods. They are also more susceptible to eavesdropping and interference than standard cabling methods.

Summary of Cabling Types

Each type of cabling has its own benefits and drawbacks. Table 10.6 details the most common types of cabling in use today. As you look at this table, pay particular attention to the cost, length, and maximum transmission rates of each cabling type.

FIGURE 10.22   Examples of ST connectors

TABLE 10.6   Cable Types and Characteristics

Characteristics	Twisted-Pair	Coaxial	Fiber-Optic	Wireless
Cost	Least expensive	More than twisted-pair	Expensive	N/A
Maximum length	100 meters (328 feet)	185 meters (607 feet) to 500 meters (1640 feet)	>10 miles	Up to 2 miles
Transmission rate	10Mbps to 100Mbps	10Mbps	100Mbps or more	2Mbps to 54Mbps
Flexibility	Most flexible	Fair	Fair	Limited
Ease of installation	Very easy	Easy	Difficult	Depends on the implementation

TABLE 10.6   Cable Types and Characteristics *(continued)*

Characteristics	Twisted-Pair	Coaxial	Fiber-Optic	Wireless
Interference	Susceptible	Better than UTP; more susceptible than STP	Not susceptible	Susceptible
Special features	Often pre-installed; similar to the wiring used in tele-phone systems	Easiest installation	Supports voice, data, and video at the highest transmission speeds	Very flexible
Preferred uses	Networks	Medium-sized networks with high security needs	Networks of any size requiring high speed and data security	WANs and radio/TV communications
Connector	RJ-45	BNC-T and AUI	Special (SC, ST, and others)	Dish, transceiver, or access point
Physical topology	Star	Bus	Star (typically)	Bus or star

Networking Components

The cabling links computer to computer. Most cabling allows networks to be hundreds of feet long. But what if your network needs to be bigger than that? What if you need to connect your LANs to other LANs to make a WAN? What if the architecture you've picked for your network is limiting the growth of your network along with the growth of your company? The answer to these questions is found in a special class of networking devices known as *connectivity devices*. These devices allow communications to break the boundaries of local networks and let your computers talk to other computers in the next building, the next city, or the next country.

There are several categories of connectivity devices, but we are going to discuss the most important and frequently used:

- Repeaters
- Hubs
- Switches
- Bridges
- Routers

These connectivity devices have made it possible to lengthen networks to almost unlimited distances.

Repeaters

Repeaters are simple devices. They allow a cabling system to extend beyond its maximum allowed length by amplifying the network voltages so they travel farther. Repeaters are nothing more than amplifiers and, as such, are very inexpensive.

Repeaters operate at the Physical layer of the OSI model. Because of this, repeaters can only be used to regenerate signals between similar network segments. For example, you can extend an Ethernet 10Base2 network to 400 meters with a repeater. But you can't connect an Ethernet network and a Token Ring network together with one.

The main disadvantage of repeaters is that they just amplify signals. These signals include not only the network signals but any noise on the wire as well. Eventually, if you use enough repeaters, you could possibly drown out the signal with the amplified noise. For this reason, repeaters are used only as a temporary fix.

Hubs

Hubs are devices used to link several computers together. They are most often used on Ethernet networks. They are also simple devices. In fact, they are just multiport repeaters and work at Layer 1 of the OSI model just as repeaters do. They repeat any signal that comes in on one port and copy it to the other ports (a process that is also called *broadcasting*).

There are two types of hubs: active and passive. *Passive hubs* connect all ports together electrically but do not have their own power source. *Active hubs* use electronics to amplify and clean up the signal before it is broadcast to the other ports. In the category of active hubs, there is also a class called *intelligent hubs*, which are hubs that can be remotely managed on the network.

Switches

Switches provide centralized connectivity just as hubs do (usually on twisted-pair Ethernet networks), and they often look similar, so it's easy to confuse them. However, switches don't pass along everything they receive on one port to every other port as hubs do. Rather, switches examine the Layer 2 header of the incoming packet and forward it properly to the right port and only that port. This greatly reduces overhead and thus performance as there is essentially a virtual connection between sender and receiver.

If it helps you to remember their functions, a hub is essentially a multiport repeater, whereas a switch functions like a multiport bridge and in some cases, a multiport router.

Nearly every hub or switch you will see has one or more status indicator lights on it. If there is a connection to that port of the switch, a light either above the connector or on an LED panel elsewhere on the device will light up. If traffic is crossing the port, the light may flash, or there may be a secondary light that will light up. Many devices can also detect a problem in the connection. If a normal connection produces a green light, a bad connection might produce an amber one. Bridges and routers will also have similar status lights on them, as do network cards.

Bridges

Bridges operate in the Data Link layer of the OSI model. They join similar topologies and are used to divide network segments. Bridges keep traffic on one side from crossing to the other. For this reason, they are often used to increase performance on a high-traffic segment.

For example, with 200 people on one Ethernet segment, performance will be mediocre, because of the design of Ethernet and the number of workstations that are fighting to transmit. If you divide the segment into two segments of 100 workstations each, the traffic will be much lower on either side and performance will increase.

Bridges are not able to distinguish one protocol from another, because higher levels of the OSI model are not available to them. If a bridge is aware of the destination MAC address, it can forward packets; otherwise, it forwards the packets to all segments.

Because bridges work at the Data Link layer, they are only aware of hardware (MAC) addresses. They are not aware of and do not deal with IP addresses.

Bridges are more intelligent than repeaters but are unable to move data across multiple networks simultaneously.

The main disadvantage of bridges is that they forward broadcast packets. Broadcasts are addressed to all computers, so the bridge just does its job and forwards the packets. Bridges also cannot perform intelligent path selection, meaning that the path from the sender to the destination will always be the same regardless of network conditions. To stop broadcasts or perform intelligent path selection, you need a router.

Routers

Routers are highly intelligent devices that connect multiple network types and determine the best path for sending data. They can route packets across multiple networks and use *routing tables* to store network addresses to determine the best destination. Routers operate at the Network layer of the OSI model. Because of this, they make their decisions on what to do with traffic based on logical addresses, such as an IP address.

The advantage of using a router over a bridge is that routers can determine the best path for data to take to get to its destination. Like bridges, they can segment large networks. However, they are slower than bridges because they are more intelligent devices; as such, they analyze every packet, causing packet-forwarding delays. Because of this intelligence, they are also more expensive.

Routers are normally used to connect one LAN to another. Typically, when a WAN is set up, at least two routers are used.

In the last few years, wireless routers have become all the rage for small and home networks. They possess all of the functionality of routers historically associated with networking, but they are relatively inexpensive.

Comparing Network Types

So far throughout this chapter we have talked a lot about different parts of the networking puzzle. You need the hardware to let computers talk to each other, the protocols to help them communicate, and the various other parts such as OSI models and topologies to make sure the developers are on the same page.

Now we'll turn to a more practical subject: types of networks you should be familiar with. You may be setting up or troubleshooting a network in a small or home office, and these are the most common types you'll see. Some of the network types are geared more toward getting online, while others are suited perfectly for the small office looking to collaborate. In this section, we'll break the network types into two different groups: wired and wireless.

Wired Networks

As the name implies, a wired network is a network where you are using a cable to plug into a socket in the wall or a connectivity device on your table. For most of computer history, using wires was the only way to connect several machines together. Today, though, wired options are becoming few and far between. Sure, in most of your corporate networks you're still plugged in somewhere, but the reality is that the most common wired options these days are for home users or small businesses to access the Internet. Here we'll look at two broad categories of choices to get online: dial-up and broadband.

Dial-up

One of the oldest ways of communicating with *Internet service providers (ISPs)* and remote networks is through dial-up connections. Although this is still possible, dial-up is not used much anymore due to limitations on modem speed, which top out at 56Kbps. Dial-up modems operate over regular phone lines—that is, the *plain old telephone service (POTS)*, and cannot compare to speeds possible with DSL and cable modems. Reputable sources claim that dial-up Internet connections dropped from 74 percent of all U.S. residential Internet connections in 2000 to 15 percent in 2008. Most of the people who still use dial-up do it because it's cheaper than broadband or high-speed isn't available where they live.

The biggest advantage to dial-up is that it's cheap and relatively easy to configure. The only hardware you need is a modem and a phone cable. You dial in to a server (such as an ISP), provide a username and a password, and you're on the Internet.

Companies also have the option to grant users dial-up access to their networks. As with Internet connections, this option used to be a lot more popular than it is today. Microsoft offered a server-side product to facilitate this called *Remote Access Service (RAS)*, as did many other companies. ISPs and RAS servers would use the Data Link layer *Point-to-Point Protocol (PPP)* to establish and maintain the connection.

Broadband

In data communications, *broadband* is a term that describes a connection that is capable of transmitting multiple pieces of data simultaneously in order to achieve higher data rates.

The opposite of broadband is baseband, which allows only one signal at a time to be transmitted. You will often hear the term broadband used to mean "high-speed Internet connection." While there's nothing wrong with this usage, know that broadband can actually mean more than just that.

Several different types of broadband Internet access are available, including DSL, Cable, fiber-optic, and satellite.

 Remember that broadband can also refer to multimode fiber-optic cables, which are capable of transmitting multiple signals at one time.

DSL

One of the two most popular broadband choices for home use is *Digital Subscriber Line (DSL).* It utilizes existing phone lines and provides fairly reliable high-speed access. To use DSL you need a DSL modem, provided by your phone company, and a network card in your computer. You use an Ethernet cable with an RJ-45 connector to plug your network card into the DSL modem, and the phone cord to plug the DSL modem into the phone outlet. Typically, you will plug the phone cord into a DSL splitter (such as the one shown in Figure 10.23) and plug the splitter into the wall. The splitter does two things for you. One, it allows you to still plug your phone into the same connection. Two, it filters the "noise" from the DSL modem so you don't hear it when you are on the phone. Your phone line will still work when you have DSL even if you don't use the splitter, but you will hear a lot of static (try it sometime!).

FIGURE 10.23   A DSL splitter

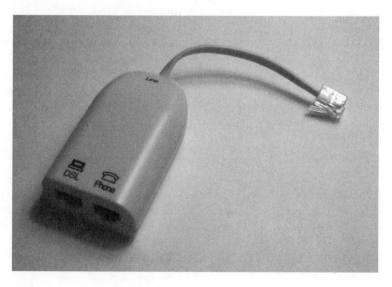

Instead of plugging your computer directly into the DSL modem, you can plug your computer into a router (such as a wireless router) and then plug the router into the DSL modem. Most phone companies will tell you that you can't (or shouldn't) do this, but if you want to connect multiple computers to the Internet and don't mind sharing the bandwidth, there is no reason not to.

There are actually several different forms of DSL, including *high bit-rate DSL (HDSL)*, *symmetric DSL (SDSL)*, *very high bit-rate DSL (VDSL)*, *rate-adaptive DSL (RADSL)*, and *asymmetric DSL (ADSL)*. The most popular in home use is ADSL. It's asymmetrical because it supports faster download speeds than upload speeds. Dividing up the total available bandwidth this way makes sense, because most Internet traffic is downloaded, not uploaded. Imagine a 10-lane highway. If you knew that 8 out of 10 cars that drove the highway went south, wouldn't you make eight lanes southbound and only two lanes northbound? That is essentially what ADSL does.

ADSL can work at the same time with your voice communications over the phone line because they use different frequencies on the same wire. Regular phone communications use frequencies from 0 to 4kHz, whereas ADSL uses frequencies in the 25.875–138kHz range for upstream traffic and frequencies in the 138–1104KHz range for downstream traffic. Figure 10.24 illustrates this.

FIGURE 10.24   Voice telephone and ADSL frequencies used

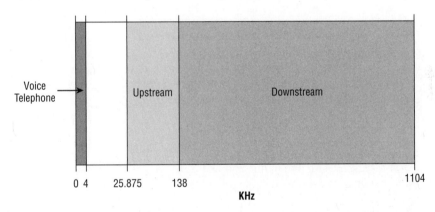

The first ADSL standard was approved in 1998 and offered maximum download speeds of 8Mbps and upload speeds of 1Mbps. The newest standard supports speeds up to 24Mbps download and 3.5Mbps upload. In practice, the best rate plans typically offered by service providers max out at about 10–12Mbps download and 1Mbps upload. Most ADSL communications are full-duplex.

One major advantage that ADSL providers tout is that with DSL you do not share bandwidth with other customers, whereas that may not be true with cable modems.

Cable Modem

The other half of the popular home-broadband duet is the *cable modem*. These provide high-speed Internet access through your cable service, much like DSL does over phone lines. You plug your computer into the cable modem using a standard Ethernet cable, just like you would plug into a DSL modem.

In theory, cable Internet connections are faster than DSL connections. Some cable companies offer packages with download speeds up to 30Mbps or 50Mbps and uploads of 5Mbps. (For business customers, download speeds can be 400Mbps.) If it's that fast, why wouldn't everyone choose it? A caveat to these speeds is that they are not guaranteed and they can vary.

One of the reasons that speeds may vary is that you are sharing available bandwidth within your distribution network. The size of the network varies, but is usually between 100 and 2,000 customers. Some of them may have cable modems too, and access can be slower during peak usage times. Another reason is that cable companies make liberal use of bandwidth throttling. If you read the fine print on some of their packages that promise the fast speeds, one of the technical details of that is that they boost your download speed for the first 10MB or 20MB of a file transfer, and then they throttle your speed back down to your normal rate.

To see how this could affect everyone's speed on the shared bandwidth, let's think about a simplified example. Let's say that two users (Sally and John) are sharing a connection that has a maximum capacity of 40Mbps. For the sake of argument, let's assume that they are the only two users and that they share the bandwidth equally. That would mean normally each person gets 20Mbps of bandwidth. If Sally gets a boost that allows her to download 30Mbps, for however long, that only leaves John with 10Mbps of available bandwidth. If John is used to having 20Mbps, that 10Mbps is going to seem awfully slow.

While it may seem as though we are down on cable modems, you just need to understand exactly what you and your customers are getting. In practice, the speeds of a cable modem are pretty comparable to those of DSL. Both have pros and cons when it comes to reliability and speed of service, but a lot of that varies by service provider and isn't necessarily reflective of the technology. When it comes right down to it, the choice you make between DSL and cable (if both are available in your area) may depend on which company you get the best package deal from: phone and DSL through your telephone company or cable TV and cable modem from your cable provider.

Fiber-Optic Cable

We discussed fiber-optic cable earlier in this chapter, and if you're anything like us you're pretty impressed with the speed and bandwidth it delivers. For nearly all of fiber-optic cable's existence, it's been used mostly for high-speed telecommunications and network backbones. This is because it is much more expensive than copper to install and operate. The cables themselves are pricier, and so is the hardware at the end of the cables.

Technology follows this inevitable path of getting cheaper the longer it exists, and fiber is starting to embrace its destiny. Some phone and media companies are now offering fiber-optic Internet connections for home subscribers.

An example of one such option is FiOS, offered by Verizon. They offer *Fiber-to-the-Home (FTTH)* service, which means that the cables are 100 percent fiber from their data centers to your home. As of the time of this writing, the fastest speeds offered are 50Mbps download and 20Mbps upload. That means you could download a 6GB movie in about 16 minutes. FTTH is capable of reaching speeds of 100Mbps, and 400Mbps implementations are being planned.

Other companies may offer a service called *Fiber-to-the-Node (FTTN)*, sometimes called "Fiber to the Curb." This runs fiber to the phone or cable company's utility box near the street and then runs copper from there to your house. Maximum speeds for this type of service are around 25Mbps. These options are probably best suited for small businesses or home offices with significant data requirements, unless online gaming is *really* important to you.

> Some cable companies promise a high-speed, fiber-optic connection for your TV cable as well as cable Internet service. In the vast majority of cases, the fiber is FTTN, and the fiber only runs from their network to the junction box at the entrance to your neighborhood or possibly to your curb. From there, the cable is coaxial copper. If you're paying for a fiber connection, be sure you're actually *getting* a fiber connection.

Satellite

Okay, so we will be the first to admit that satellite is *not* a wired type of Internet connection. But it is a way to get broadband Internet access, so since we're talking about broadband now is a good time to talk about satellite.

As its name implies, satellite broadband transmits signals through the air to you as opposed to using a cable. The service provider beams a microwave signal from a dish on the ground to an orbiting satellite, which in turn sends the signal back down to your receiver. Receivers are typically small satellite dishes (like the ones used for DirecTV or DishNetwork) but can also be portable satellite modems (modems the size of a briefcase) or portable satellite phones.

This type of communication is called *point-to-multipoint* because one satellite can provide a signal to a number of receivers. Satellite technology is invaluable when you are in an area where it's difficult or impossible to run a cable, and handy if the location where you need Internet access is mobile. It's used in a variety of applications from telecommunications to handheld GPSs to television and radio broadcasts to a host of others.

Here are a few considerations to keep in mind regarding satellite:

Installation can be tricky.   When installing a satellite system, you need to ensure that the satellite dish on the ground is pointed at precisely the right spot in the sky. This can be tricky to do if you're not trained, but some have a utility that helps you see how close you are to being right on (you're getting warmer... warmer...).

Line of sight is required.   Satellite communications also require line of sight. A tree between you and your orbiting partner will cause problems. Rain and other atmospheric conditions can cause problems as well.

Latency can be a problem. Because of the long distance the message must travel, satellites can be subject to long *latency* times. Latency is the delay between requesting data and getting a response. It happens with wired connections too, but it disproportionately affects satellite transmissions. Have you ever watched a national news channel when a reporter is reporting from some location halfway across the world? The anchor behind the desk will ask a question, and the reporter will nod, and nod, and finally about five to ten excruciating seconds after the anchor is done the reporter will start to answer. That's latency.

Most satellite connections are also pretty slow compared to the other broadband methods. Average speed for downloads is often 256Kbps–1.5Mbps, and uploads are in the 128–256Kbps range. In addition, many providers set thresholds on the amount of data you can download per month. Going over that amount can result in extra charges.

 Real World Scenario

Sometimes, the Choices Are Limited...

Before you decide which broadband connection sounds the most appealing to you, you should also factor in something very important: what is available in your area. DSL is available at different rates of connectivity based on distance from a central station. If you live far enough from a central station, or near a central station that has not been updated lately (such as in the middle of rural America), DSL may not be an option.

Similarly, not all cable providers are willing to take the steps necessary to run a connection in all situations. One of the authors once had a small business in a section of an old industrial building. The cable provider said the office where the modem was desired was too far from their nearest pole and there was nothing that could be done about it. He offered to pay the expense to have an additional pole placed closer to the location, but they would not discuss it further.

Make certain you know the available options—not just the technological options—before you spend too much time determining what is best for you.

Wireless Networks

Perhaps no area of networking has seen as rapid an ascent as wireless networking has over the last few years. What used to be slow and unreliable is now fast and pretty stable, not to mention convenient. It seems like everywhere you go these days there are Internet cafés with wireless hotspots. No matter where you go, you can be just seconds away from getting "online oxygen."

As a technician, it often falls to you to provide the oxygen that users need. You must make sure that their computers can connect and they can get their e-mail, and that downtime is something that resides only in history books. To be able to make that a reality, you must understand as much as you can about networking and the topics discussed in this section.

In this section, we'll look at four methods of wireless communication: 802.11x, Bluetooth, cellular, and infrared. We'll look at some wireless security features as well.

802.11x

In the United States, wireless LAN (WLAN) standards are created and managed by the Institute of Electrical and Electronics Engineers (IEEE). The most commonly used WLAN standards used today are in the IEEE 802.11x family. Eventually, 802.11 will likely be made obsolete by newer standards such as 802.16 or 802.20, but that is some time off.

IEEE 802.11 was ratified in 1997, and was the first standardized WLAN implementation. There are over twenty 802.11 standards defined, but you will only see a few in common operation: 802.11a, b, and g. Among all of the wireless technologies covered in this chapter, 802.11 is the one best suited for WLANs.

802.11x Networks

An 802.11 network is just like an Ethernet network, only wireless. At the center of the network is a connectivity device such as a hub or a router, and all computers connect to it. In order to connect to the wireless hub or router, the client needs to know the *service-set identifier (SSID)* of the device. Wireless access points may connect to other wireless access points, but eventually they connect back to a wired connection with the rest of the network.

802.11x Technical Specifications

802.11x networks use the CSMA/CA access method, which is similar to that of shared Ethernet. Packet collisions are generally avoided, but when they do happen, the sender will need to wait a random period of time (called a *back-off time*) before transmitting again.

Since the original 802.11 standard was published in 1997, there have been several upgrades and extensions of the standard released. The most common ones are as follows:

802.11   The original *802.11* standard defines WLANs transmitting at 1Mbps or 2Mbps bandwidths using the 2.4GHz frequency spectrum and using either frequency-hopping spread spectrum (FHSS) or direct-sequence spread spectrum (DSSS) for data encoding.

802.11a   The *802.11a* standard provides WLAN bandwidth of up to 54Mbps in the 5GHz frequency spectrum. The 802.11a standard also uses a more efficient encoding system, orthogonal frequency division multiplexing (OFDM), rather than FHSS or DSSS.

This standard never gained widespread popularity. The biggest reason is that 802.11b devices beat it to market and were significantly cheaper. 802.11a devices are also highly susceptible to external interference. Even so, you will still see it out in the wild.

802.11b   The *802.11b* standard provides for bandwidths of up to 11Mbps (with fallback rates of 5.5, 2, and 1Mbps) in the 2.4GHz frequency spectrum. This standard is also called *WiFi* or *802.11 high rate*. The 802.11b standard uses only DSSS for data encoding. Because 802.11b operates in the 2.4GHz frequency, it is incompatible with 802.11a, which runs at 5Ghz. Between the two, 802.11b was (and is) far more popular.

802.11g   The *802.11g* standard provides for bandwidths of 54Mbps+ in the 2.4GHz frequency spectrum using OFDM encoding. One of the advantages of this standard is that it is backward compatible with 802.11b; you can think of it as its faster big brother.

Because the two standards are compatible, you will see devices marked as 802.11b/g. They can run on either network, and b and g devices can be commingled on the same network.

While backward compatibility with legacy 802.11b devices has been a big selling point for 802.11g hardware, there are some interoperability concerns to be aware of. 802.11b devices are not capable of understanding OFDM transmissions; therefore, they are not able to tell when the 802.11g access point is free or busy. To counteract this problem, when an 802.11b device is associated with an 802.11g access point, the access point uses an additional signaling mechanism called Request to Send/Clear to Send (RTS/CTS) to provide backward compatibility.

With RTS/CTS, the client must first send an RTS signal to the access point, and then wait. Once the access point sends a CTS back to the client, the client can transmit. When the other clients on the network receive the CTS signal, they interpret it as a "do not send" message, and need to wait for an all-clear to send.

Finally, 802.11g operating in native mode uses a back-off timing similar to that of 802.11a, which is more efficient than the back-off timing of 802.11b. When operating in mixed mode, 802.11g will use the less-efficient 802.11b back-off timing.

The additional layer of communication required to support legacy 802.11b devices, combined with the use of less-efficient back-off timing, slows down the throughput of the 802.11g access point. Even with all of this taken into consideration, the pros of 802.11g/b backward compatibility still far outweigh the cons.

802.11n   At the time of this writing, the *802.11n* standard is still in development and is expected to be ratified in early 2010. The standard claims to provide for bandwidths from 54Mbps to 600Mbps. With current technology it's more realistic to expect maximum throughput in the 300Mbps range, which is still pretty fast.

802.11n achieves faster throughput a couple of ways. Some of the enhancements include the use of multiple-input multiple-output (MIMO), channel bonding, and Spatial Division Multiplexing (SDM) technologies. MIMO uses multiple antennas to communicate information rather than a single antenna. Channel bonding allows the device to use two separate non-overlapping channels to transmit data at the same time which increases throughput. SDM is capable of spatially dividing the multiple data streams that MIMO supports.

One advantage to 802.11n is that it is backward compatible with 802.11a/b/g. This is because 802.11n is capable of simultaneously servicing 802.11b/g/n clients operating in the 2.4GHz range as well as 802.11a/n clients operating in the 5GHz range. There is 802.11n hardware on the market today, but as the standard is still not official these devices are called "pre-N" devices. While you shouldn't run into any problems using them, you may have compatibility issues between different vendors' pre-N products.

Table 10.7 summarizes the 802.11*x* standards we discussed here.

TABLE 10.7 802.11x Standards

Type	Frequency	Maximum Data Rate	Modulation	Indoor Range	Outdoor Range
	2.4GHz	2Mbps	FHSS/DSSS	20m	100m
a	5GHz	54Mbps	OFDM	35m	120m
b	2.4GHz	11Mbps	DSSS	40m	140m
g	2.4GHz	54Mbps	OFDM	40m	140m
n	2.4/5GHz	300 Mbps	SDM	70m	250m

The ranges provided in Table 10.7 are approximate and may differ based on your environment. For example, thick walls and steel beams will dramatically reduce your range.

We have mentioned four signal modulation techniques used in the 802.11 standards. Here is how the three in common use today work:

Direct-Sequence Spread Spectrum (DSSS)   DSSS accomplishes communication by adding the data that is to be transmitted to a higher-speed transmission. The higher-speed transmission contains redundant information to ensure data accuracy. Each packet can then be reconstructed in the event of a disruption.

Frequency-Hopping Spread Spectrum (FHSS)   FHSS accomplishes communication by hopping the transmission over a range of predefined frequencies. The changing or hopping is synchronized between both ends and appears to be a single transmission channel to both ends.

Orthogonal Frequency Division Multiplexing (OFDM)   OFDM accomplishes communication by breaking the data into subsignals and transmitting them simultaneously. These transmissions occur on different frequencies or subbands.

The mathematics and theories of these transmission technologies are beyond the scope of this book and far beyond the scope of this exam.

There are many other commercial devices that transmit frequencies at the same ones that 802.11 operates at. When this happens there can be a lot of interference. Bluetooth devices, cordless phones, cell phones, other WLANs, and microwave ovens can all create interference problems for 802.11 networks.

802.11x Devices

If you think about a standard wired network and the devices required on such a network, you can easily determine what types of devices are available for 802.11 networks. Network cards come in a variety of shapes and sizes, including USB and PCMCIA Type II models and wireless print servers for your printers. As for connectivity devices, the most common are wireless routers (as shown in Figure 10.25) and a type of hub called a *wireless access point (WAP)*. They look nearly identical to wireless routers and provide central connectivity like wireless routers, but they don't have nearly as many features. The main one most people worry about is Internet connection sharing. You can share an Internet connection using a wireless router, but not with a WAP.

FIGURE 10.25   Wireless router

Most wireless routers and WAPs also have wired ports for RJ-45 connectors. The router shown in Figure 10.25 has four wired connections, but they are on the back side of the device (meaning you can't see them in the figure). Your wireless router can act as a DHCP server to wireless clients, providing them with IP configuration information when they join the network.

802.11x Security

The growth of wireless systems has created several opportunities for attackers. These systems are relatively new, they use well-established communications mechanisms, and they're easily intercepted. Wireless controllers such as 802.11x routers use *service-set identifiers (SSIDs)* to allow communications with a specific access point. By default, most wireless controllers will broadcast their SSID, so a wireless client just needs to search for an available signal. You can also configure the client manually with the SSID of the device. Using SSID configurations doesn't necessarily prevent wireless networks from being compromised.

We'll discuss more on SSIDs and configuring your wireless routers to be more secure than their default settings in Chapter 18.

Other than the use of SSIDs, there are a few additional security protocols and features that you can utilize to help protect your network. Examples of these are WEP, EPA, and MAC filtering, which we discuss next.

WEP

Wired Equivalency Protocol (WEP) is a security standard for wireless devices. WEP encrypts data to provide data security. The protocol has always been under scrutiny for not being as secure as initially intended.

 You may see the use of the notation WEP.*x*, which refers to the key size; 64-bit, 128-bit, and 256-bit keys are commonly supported (WEP.64, WEP.128, and WEP.256).

WEP is vulnerable due to weaknesses in the encryption algorithms. These weaknesses allow the algorithm to potentially be cracked in a very short amount of time—no more than two or three minutes. This makes WEP one of the more vulnerable protocols available for security.

WPA

WiFi Protected Access (WPA) is an improvement on WEP that was developed in 2003. It implements some of the standards defined in the IEEE 802.11i specification. An improvement over WPA is WPA2, which implements the full 802.11i standard.

MAC FILTERING

MAC filtering can be used on a wireless network to prevent certain clients from accessing the network. In essence, you can tell your wireless router to only allow access to certain MAC addresses. Your router will allow you to deny service to a set list of MAC addresses (and allow all others) or allow service only to a set of MAC addresses (and deny all others).

Bluetooth

In 1998, a consortium of companies formed the *Bluetooth Special Interest Group (SIG)*, and formally adopted the name *Bluetooth* for its technology. The name comes from a 10th-century Danish king named Harald Blåtand, known as Harold Bluetooth in English. (One can only imagine how he got that name.) King Blåtand had successfully unified warring factions in the areas of Norway, Sweden, and Denmark. The makers of Bluetooth were trying to unite disparate technology industries, namely computing, mobile communications, and the auto industry.

Current membership in the Bluetooth SIG includes Microsoft, Intel, Apple, IBM, Toshiba, and several cell phone manufacturers. The technical specification IEEE 802.15.1 describes a *wireless personal area network (WPAN)* based on Bluetooth version 1.1.

The first Bluetooth device on the market was an Ericsson headset and cell phone adapter, which arrived on the scene in 2000. By 2002, there were over 500 Bluetooth certified products, and as of 2005 over 5 million Bluetooth chipsets shipped each week. The current Bluetooth specification is Version 2.1+ Enhanced Data Rate.

Bluetooth Networks

According to the Bluetooth SIG, "Bluetooth wireless technology is a short-range communications technology intended to replace the cables connecting portable and/or fixed devices while maintaining high levels of security." Bluetooth also operates at low power and low cost and can handle simultaneous voice and data transmissions.

One of the unusual features of Bluetooth networks is their temporary nature. With other popular wireless standards, you need a central communication point, such as a hub or router. Bluetooth networks are formed on an ad hoc basis, meaning that whenever two Bluetooth devices get close enough to each other, they can communicate directly with each other. This dynamically created network is called a *piconet*. A Bluetooth-enabled device can communicate with up to seven other devices in one piconet.

Within the piconet, one device is the master and the other seven devices are slaves. Technically, communication can occur only between the master and a slave. While this might sound like a problem, the role of master rotates quickly among the devices in a round-robin fashion. In this way, all devices in a piconet can communicate with each other directly. Current Bluetooth specifications allow for connecting two or more piconets together in a *scatternet*. In a scatternet, one or more devices would serve as a bridge between the piconets.

Bluetooth Technical Specifications

There are three different supported versions of Bluetooth. Version 1.2 was adopted in November 2003, and it supports data transmissions of up to 1Mbps. Version 2.0+ Enhanced Data Rate (EDR), adopted in November 2004, and Version 2.1+EDR, adopted in July 2007, can support data rates up to 3Mbps. All standards transmit in the 2.4–2.485GHz range.

> The 2.4GHz range is unlicensed, meaning that any wireless technology can use it. Indeed, many cell phone technologies as well as wireless networking technologies do use it. To avoid interference, Bluetooth can "signal hop" at different frequencies to avoid conflicts with devices using other technologies in the area.

Bluetooth is a short-range technology. There are three different device classes, and each one is detailed in Table 10.8.

TABLE 10.8   Bluetooth Classes

Class	Range	Use	Power
1	100 meters (300 feet)	Industrial usage	100 milliwatts
2	10 meters (30 feet)	Mobile devices	2.5 milliwatts
3	1 meter (3 feet)	Rarely used	1 milliwatt

Class 2 is the most common Bluetooth class, and it operates at 2.5 milliwatts (mW) of power.

For security, Bluetooth uses the *Secure and Fast Encryption Routine (SAFER+)* encryption routine, a 128-bit algorithm developed in 1998. There have been questions surrounding how secure Bluetooth really is, and the best advice is to not leave powered-on devices unattended.

Bluetooth Devices

As mentioned earlier, the first device was a wireless headset for a cell phone, and Bluetooth continues to excel in this field, considering its low power consumption and ample bandwidth for voice communications.

Bluetooth-enabled computer peripherals include keyboards and mice, printers, digital cameras, and MP3 players. The technology is also prevalent in PDAs and handheld computers as well as in several cars, including those made by BMW and Toyota (and Lexus).

Cards for laptops come in USB and PCMCIA Type II varieties. Figure 10.26 shows a USB model by Linksys.

FIGURE 10.26   Bluetooth USB adapter

Figure 10.27 shows a card made for printers—quite handy to have if you're on the road with a mobile printer!

FIGURE 10.27   Bluetooth print server

All in all, Bluetooth is a solid technology that should be around for a while. It doesn't have the range of cellular or the capacity of WiFi, but it fills a nice niche, uses low power, and has developed a critical mass of devices that support it.

Infrared

Infrared waves have been around since the beginning of time. Infrared waves are longer than light waves but shorter than microwaves. The most common use of infrared technology is the television remote control, although infrared is also used in night-vision goggles and medical and scientific imaging.

In 1994, the *Infrared Data Association (IrDA)* was formed as a technical consortium to support "interoperable, low-cost infrared data interconnection standards that support a walk-up, point-to-point user model." The key terms here are "walk-up" and "point-to-point," meaning that you need to be at very close range to use infrared, and it's designed for one-to-one communication. Infrared requires line of sight, and generally speaking the two devices need to be pointed at each other to work. If you point your remote away from the television, how well does it work?

> More information on the IrDA standard can be found at the organization's website: http://www.irda.org.

Most laptops have a built-in infrared port, which is a small, dark square of plastic, usually black or dark maroon. For easy access, infrared ports are located on the front or sides of devices that have them. Figure 10.28 shows an example of an infrared port.

FIGURE 10.28 Infrared port

Infrared Networks

An infrared network is a point-to-point network between two devices. There is no master or slave or hub-type device required. Simply point one infrared-enabled device at another and transmit.

Infrared Technical Specifications

Current IrDA specifications allow transmission of data up to 16Mbps, and IrDA claims that 100Mbps and 500Mbps standards are on the horizon. Because it does not use radio waves, there are no concerns of interference or signal conflicts. Atmospheric conditions can play a role in disrupting infrared waves, but considering that the maximum functional range of an IrDA device is about one meter, weather is not likely to cause you any problems.

Security is not an issue with infrared. Considering that the maximum range is about one meter with an angle of about 30 degrees and the signal does not go through walls, hacking prospects are limited. If someone is going to intercept an infrared signal, you will know that the person is there and trying to intercept the signal. The data is directional, and you choose when and where to send it.

Infrared Devices

Infrared mice were all the rage a few years ago and are still popular today. Also readily available are infrared keyboards and printers. Perhaps some of the most useful infrared devices are keyboards for PDAs. They're smaller than standard laptop keyboards (but not by much), and they generally fold up to a convenient travel size. Speaking of PDAs, many of them are infrared-enabled, as are many cell phones. Finally, don't forget the almighty remote control. Although not necessarily computer related, it's hard to imagine society without that ubiquitous device of convenience.

Cellular (Cellular WAN)

The cell phone, once a clunky brick-like status symbol of the well-to-do, is now pervasive in our society. It seems that everyone—from kindergarteners to 80-year-old grandmothers—has a cell. The industry has revolutionized the way we communicate and, some say, contributed to the furthering of an attention deficit disorder–like, instant-gratification-hungry society.

Regardless of your feelings about cell phones, whether you text-message like a maniac or long for the good old days when you could escape your phone, because it had a functional radius as long as your cord, you need to understand the basics of cell technology. It's primarily been developing in the realm of small handheld communications devices (phones and the BlackBerrys), but technologies converge, and that's definitely what's happening between cell phones and computers.

Cellular Networks

Cellular networks are very complex behind the scenes, but unless you are working at a major cell provider, learning a ton of information won't give you a lot of practical help. What you do need to know is that cell communications require the use of a central access point, generally a cell tower, which is connected to a main hub. Cellular networks are very large mesh networks with extensive range. The term *cell* refers to a cell phone network.

Cellular Technical Specifications

There are two major cell standards in the United States. The *Global System for Mobile Communications (GSM)* is the most popular, boasting over 1.5 billion users in 210 countries. The other standard is *Code Division Multiple Access (CDMA)*, which was developed by Qualcomm and is available only in the United States. GSM and CDMA are not compatible with each other.

GSM uses a variety of bands to transmit. The most popular are 900MHz and 1800MHz, but 400, 450, and 850MHz are also used. Because of this, one phone cannot work at full capacity on all the GSM networks in the world. GSM splits up its channels by time division, in a process called Time Division Multiple Access (TDMA).

The maximum rate for GSM is about 270 kilobits per second (Kbps). While this is incredibly low based on current networking standards, it's ample for voice communications. The maximum functional distance of GSM is about 22 miles (35 kilometers). For security, GSM uses the A5/1 and A5/2 stream ciphers.

A newer enhancement to GSM is called General Packet Radio Service (GPRS). It's designed to provide data transmissions over a GSM network at up to 171Kbps.

CDMA is considered a superior technology to GSM because it doesn't break up its channels by time but rather by a code inserted into the communicated message. This allows for multiple transmissions to occur at the same time without interference. CDMA was first used by the English in World War II, and today it is used in global positioning systems (GPSs) as well.

Current CDMA-based technologies support download rates of over 3Mbps, with upload speeds of nearly 2Mbps. Not only does CDMA have better transmission speeds than GSM, but it works in ranges up to 100 kilometers.

Newer takeoffs of the CDMA technology include Wideband Code Division Multiple Access (W-CDMA), CDMA2000, and Evolution Data Optimized (EVDO).

Cellular Devices

Cellular communication is still much further developed in the phone industry than the computer industry. Cell phones and BlackBerrys are the most common cellular-equipped devices you'll find. However, cellular modems are widely available for laptops, most of them with a PC Card interface.

Virtual Private Networks (VPNs)

A *virtual private network (VPN)* isn't necessarily wired or wireless, so it gets its own section here. It's also not a LAN or a WAN, but rather something in between. The easiest way to think of a VPN is that it makes computers that are on opposite sides of a WAN link think they are on the same safe and secure LAN with each other. The key word for VPNs really is *security*.

Let's use an example. Imagine that you have your corporate headquarters in Chicago, but a remote sales office in Miami. Your network is configured so that using a WAN link, computers in Miami can talk to the ones in Chicago. The problem with this setup is that WAN links are inherently unsecure. You don't want to open up your network to hackers, so you create a VPN.

What the VPN will do is create a secure point-to-point connection between two connectivity devices at the remote locations. For this example we'll assume you have a router at each location that gets users on the intranet out to the Internet. After you create a VPN between the two routers, the link is secure.

After creating the VPN link, the network administrator can use more restrictive policies on the servers in Chicago, only allowing access to clients on the LAN. Since the computers in Miami now appear to be on the LAN, they can still access the Chicago servers.

VPNs can also be created for network users who need to access the network through remote access, such as a traveling salesperson.

Although some routers come with the capability built-in, the device that provides VPN service is called a *VPN concentrator.* VPN concentrators can create virtual private networks for users logging in using remote access or for a large site-to-site VPN. As opposed to typical remote access connections, remote access VPNs provide higher data throughput and authentication and encryption options. Cisco produces VPN concentrators that support anywhere from 100 users up to 10,000 simultaneous remote access connections!

Summary

In this chapter, you learned about a broad variety of networking topics. This chapter has everything you need to get you ready for the networking questions on the A+ Essentials exam. At the same time, the A+ exam (and consequently this chapter) barely scratches the surface of the things you can learn about networking. If making computers talk to each other effectively is an area of interest to you, we suggest you consider studying for the CompTIA Network+ exam after you pass your A+ tests.

First, we started with networking fundamentals. A lot of the fundamentals section was about understanding the concepts behind networking so you know how to set them up later. Topics included LANs versus WANs; clients, servers, and resources; network operating systems; peer-to-peer and server-based resource models; network topologies such as bus, star, and ring; network architectures, such as Ethernet; and theoretical networking models and standards, such as the OSI model and IEEE standards.

Next, you learned about networking protocols. They are the communication language computers use to talk to each other. The most important protocol in use today is TCP/IP. TCP/IP is a fairly complex protocol to set up and manage. We talked about IP addressing and address classes, TCP/IP ports, and the ever-important DHCP and DNS servers. Other protocols we touched on were NetBEUI/NetBIOS, IPX/SPX, and AppleTalk.

After protocols we looked at various hardware devices used in networking. Each computer needs a network adapter (NIC) of some sort to connect to the network. On a wired network, cables are required and there are several different types, including coaxial, STP, UTP, and fiber optic. Each cable type has its own specific connector. All wired computers will plug into a connectivity device such as a hub or a switch, which in turn is connected to another connectivity device, which may be a bridge or a router.

Finally, we discussed various types of networks and how they are utilized. For wired networks, we specifically looked at ways to get on the Internet, which included dial-up and several types of broadband: DSL, cable modems, fiber, and (wireless) satellite. Wireless technologies we talked about were 802.11, Bluetooth, infrared, and cellular. We ended the chapter with virtual private networks.

Exam Essentials

Understand how IP addressing works.   IP addresses are 32-bit addresses written as four octets in dotted-decimal notation, such as 192.168.5.18. To communicate on an IP network, a host also needs a subnet mask, which may look something like 255.255.255.0.

Know what DHCP and DNS do.   On TCP/IP networks, the DHCP server can provide IP configuration information to hosts. A DNS server resolves hostnames to IP addresses.

Understand what bandwidth and latency are.   Bandwidth is the amount of data that can go through a device or cable. For example, Category 3 UTP has a maximum bandwidth of 10Mbps whereas the wireless standard 802.11g supports bandwidth of up to 54Mbps. Latency is how much delay there is between sending a data request and receiving a response.

Know what status indicators are.   Most network adapters and connectivity devices will have LED lights on them that are status indicators. If there is an active connection, the light will turn on. Many status indicators will blink if traffic is going through that port.

Understand what protocols do and be able to name some common protocols.   Protocols are the language of communication for computers. The most common protocol is TCP/IP. Other protocols you might see are NetBEUI/NetBIOS, IPX/SPX, and AppleTalk.

Know the difference between full-duplex and half-duplex.   In a full-duplex environment, the devices can talk to each other in both directions at the same time. In half-duplex, only one side can talk at one time and the other side has to wait until the first one is done to send information.

Know the difference between workgroups and domains.   A workgroup is often referred to as a peer-to-peer network, and there is no centralized administration. A domain is a server-based network, where the server (often called a domain controller) manages user accounts and security for the network. Workgroups are best suited for networks with 10 or fewer computers and low security requirements.

Know common TCP/IP ports.   Some common protocol and port parings you should know are HTTP (80), FTP (20 and 21), POP3 (110), SMTP (25), Telnet (23), and HTTPS (443).

Know the difference between a LAN and a WAN.   A LAN is a local area network, which typically means a network in one centralized location. A WAN is a wide area network, which means several LANs in remote locations connected to each other.

Know what hubs, switches, and routers are.   These are all network connectivity devices. Hubs and switches are used to connect several computers or groups of computers to each other. Routers are more complex devices that are often used to connect network segments or networks to each other.

Know what a VPN is.   A virtual private network is a network where computers are connected via a WAN connection, but the connection is secured and appears to be a LAN connection.

Be able to identify IP address classes.   Know how to identify Class A, B, and C IP addresses. Class A addresses will have a *first octet* in the 1–126 range. B is from 128 to 191, and C is from 192 to 223.

Know what types of cables are used in networking and the connectors for each.   Common network cables include coaxial, STP, UTP (Category 5/5e and Category 6), and fiber optic. Coax cables use BNC connectors, STP and UTP use RJ-45 connectors, and fiber optic uses SC and ST connectors. (You may also be tested on phone connectors, which are called RJ-11.)

Know the different types of available broadband connections.   Broadband connections include DSL, cable, satellite, and fiber optic.

Know what is required to access the Internet through a dial-up connection.   To use dial-up, you need a modem in your computer, a phone cord, a phone line, and an account with an Internet service provider (ISP).

Know the different 802.11 standards.   Standards you should be familiar with are 802.11a, 802.11b, 802.11g, and 802.11n.

Understand security mechanisms used for wireless networking.   Security mechanisms include WEP, WPA, SSID management, and MAC filtering.

Know other wireless technologies that are available for data transmissions.   Other common wireless technologies are Bluetooth, infrared, and cellular.

Review Questions

1. You have just set up a network that will use the TCP/IP protocol, and you want client computers to automatically obtain IP configuration information. Which type of server do you need for this?

   A. DNS

   B. DHCP

   C. Domain controller

   D. IP configuration server

2. You have a computer with the IP address 171.226.18.1. What class is this address?

   A. Class A

   B. Class B

   C. Class C

   D. This is not a valid IP address

3. _____ is immune to electromagnetic or radio-frequency interference.

   A. Twisted-pair cabling

   B. CSMA/CD

   C. Broadband coaxial cabling

   D. Fiber-optic cabling

4. Which IEEE 802 standard defines a bus topology using coaxial baseband cable and is able to transmit at 10Mbps?

   A. 802.1

   B. 802.2

   C. 802.3

   D. 802.4

5. Which of the following wireless IEEE standards operate on the 2.4GHz radio frequency and are directly compatible with each other? (Choose all that apply.)

   A. 802.11a

   B. 802.11b

   C. 802.11d

   D. 802.11g

6. Which OSI layer signals "all clear" by making sure the data segments are error free?

   A. Application layer

   B. Session layer

   C. Transport layer

   D. Network layer

7. Which TCP/IP protocol uses port 80?

    A. HTTP

    B. HTTPS

    C. Telnet

    D. POP3

8. _____ is the type of media access method used by NICs that listen to or sense the cable to check for traffic and send only when they hear that no one else is transmitting.

    A. Token passing

    B. CSMA/CD

    C. CSMA/CA

    D. Demand priority

9. What model is used to provide a common way to describe network protocols?

    A. OSI

    B. ISO

    C. CSMA/CA

    D. CSMA/CD

10. What is the primary function of the SSID?

    A. Secure communication between a web server and browser

    B. Secure communication between a server and remote host

    C. A type of password used to help secure a wireless connection

    D. A type of password used to secure an Ethernet 802.3 connection

11. A physical star topology consists of several workstations that branch off a central device called a _____ .

    A. NIC

    B. Bridge

    C. Router

    D. Hub

12. Of all network cabling options, _____ offers the longest possible segment length.

    A. Unshielded twisted-pair

    B. Coaxial

    C. Fiber-optic

    D. Shielded twisted-pair

13. What devices transfer packets across multiple networks and use tables to store network addresses to determine the best destination?

   A. Routers

   B. Bridges

   C. Hubs

   D. Switches

14. In which network design do users access resources from other workstations rather than from a central location?

   A. Client-server

   B. Star

   C. Ring

   D. Peer-to-peer

15. Which of the following wireless communication standards is often described in terms of a wireless personal area network?

   A. Bluetooth

   B. Infrared

   C. Cellular

   D. Ethernet

16. Which two of the following are standards for cellular communications?

   A. GSM

   B. SIG

   C. CDMA

   D. CCFL

17. Which of the following statements are *not* associated with a star network? (Choose all that apply.)

   A. A single cable break can cause complete network disruption.

   B. All devices connect to a central device.

   C. It uses a single backbone computer to connect all network devices.

   D. It uses a dual-ring configuration.

18. A _____ is a type of network where all of the computers appear to be on the local network even if they are physically located in a remote location.

   A. VPN

   B. WAN

   C. LAN

   D. Domain

19. What is the most secure wireless encryption standard for 802.11*x* networks?

    A. WEP

    B. WPA

    C. WPA2

    D. SAFER+

20. If you are going to run a network cable in the space above the drop ceiling in your office, which type of cable should you use?

    A. Plenum

    B. PVC

    C. Coaxial

    D. Fiber optic

Answers to Review Questions

1. B. A Dynamic Host Configuration Protocol (DHCP) server provides IP configuration information to hosts when they join the network. A Domain Name System (DNS) server resolves hostnames to IP addresses. A domain controller may provide login authentication, but it does not provide IP configuration information. There is no IP configuration server.

2. B. Class A addresses have a first octet between 1 and 126, Class B between 128 and 191, and class C between 192 and 223. With a first octet of 171, this is a Class B address.

3. D. Companies that want to ensure the safety and integrity of their data should use fiber-optic cable, because it cannot be affected by electromagnetic or radio-frequency interference. Even though some copper cables have shielding, they are not immune to EMI or RFI. This eliminates twisted-pair and coaxial. CSMA/CD is an access method, not a cable type.

4. C. The IEEE 802.3 standard specifies the use of a bus topology, typically using coaxial baseband cable, and can transmit data up to 10Mbps.

5. B, D. Both 802.11b and 802.11g operate in the 2.4GHz range and use similar transmission standards. Many devices on the market are listed as 802.11b/g, meaning they will work with either system. Alternatively, 802.11a operates in the 5GHz range. Finally, 802.11d is not a commonly implemented standard.

6. C. It is the responsibility of the Transport layer to signal an "all clear" by making sure the data segments are error free. It also controls the data flow and troubleshoots any problems with transmitting or receiving data frames.

7. A. HTTP uses port 80. HTTPS uses 443, Telnet 23, and POP3 110.

8. B. CSMA/CD (Carrier Sense Multiple Access with Collision Detection) specifies that the NIC pause before transmitting a packet to ensure that the line is not being used. If no activity is detected, then it transmits the packet. If activity is detected, it waits until it is clear. In the case of two NICs transmitting at the same time (a collision), both NICs pause to detect and then retransmit the data.

9. A. The Open Systems Interconnection (OSI) model is used to describe how network protocols should function. The OSI model was designed by the International Organization for Standardization (ISO).

10. C. A service-set identifier (SSID) is the unique name given to the wireless network. All hardware that is to participate on the network must be configured to use the same SSID. Essentially, it is the network name. When you are using Windows to connect to a wireless network, all available wireless networks will be listed by their SSID.

11. D. At the center of a star topology is a hub or a switch. A NIC is a network card, which each computer must have to be on the network. Bridges and routers are higher-level connectivity devices that connect network segments or networks together.

12. C. Fiber-optic cable can span distances of several kilometers, because it has much lower crosstalk and interference in comparison to copper cables.

13. A. Routers are designed to route (transfer) packets across networks. They are able to do this routing, and determine the best path to take, based on internal routing tables they maintain.

14. D. A peer-to-peer network has no servers, so all of the resources are shared from the various workstations on which they reside. This is the opposite of a client-server network, in which the majority of resources are located on servers that are dedicated to responding to client requests.

15. A. Bluetooth networks are often called wireless personal area networks (WPANs).

16. A, C. The Global System for Mobile Communications (GSM) and Code Division Multiple Access (CDMA) are cellular standards. A SIG is a Special Interest Group, and cold cathode fluorescent lamp (CCFL) is a backlight on a laptop.

17. A, C, D. In a star network, all systems are connected using a central device such as a hub or a switch. The network is not disrupted for other users when more systems are added or removed. The star network design is used with today's UTP-based networks.

18. A. A virtual private network (VPN) is one where all computers appear to be on the local LAN even if they are not. VPNs are useful for remote access as well as if you have networks in multiple locations.

19. C. WEP was the original encryption standard developed for WiFi networks, but it is easily hacked. WPA is an upgrade, but WPA2 is more secure and incorporates the entire 802.11i standard. SAFER+ is used to encrypt Bluetooth communications.

20. A. For areas where a cable must be fire retardant, such as in a drop ceiling, you must run plenum-grade cable. Plenum refers to the coating on the sleeve of the cable, not the media (copper or fiber) within the cable itself. PVC is the other type of coating typically found on network cables, but it produces poisonous gas when burned.

Chapter

11

Understanding Network Security Fundamentals

THE FOLLOWING COMPTIA A+ ESSENTIALS EXAM OBJECTIVES ARE COVERED IN THIS CHAPTER:

✓ **5.1 Explain the basic principles of security concepts and technologies**

- Encryption technologies

- Data wiping / hard drive destruction / hard drive recycling

- Software firewall

  - Port security

  - Exceptions

- Authentication technologies

  - User name

  - Password

  - Biometrics

  - Smart cards

- Basics of data sensitivity and data security

  - Compliance

  - Classifications

  - Social Engineering

✓ **5.2 Summarize the following security features**

- Wireless encryption

  - WEPx and WPAx

  - Client configuration (SSID)

- Malicious software protection
  - Viruses
  - Trojans
  - Worms
  - Spam
  - Spyware
  - Adware
  - Grayware
- BIOS Security
  - Drive lock
  - Passwords
  - Intrusion detection
  - TPM
- Password management / password complexity
- Locking workstation
  - Hardware
  - Operating system
- Biometrics
  - Fingerprint scanner

Think of how much simpler an administrator's life was in the days before every user had to be able to access the Internet.

Think of how much simpler it must have been when you only had to maintain a number of dumb terminals connected to a minitower. Much of what has created headaches for an administrator since then is the inherent security risk that comes about as the network expands. As our world—and our networks—have become more connected, the need to secure data and keep it away from the eyes of those who can do harm has increased exponentially.

Realizing this, CompTIA added the security domain to the A+ exams a few years back. Security is now a topic that every administrator and technician must not only be aware of and care about, but also be actively involved in. In the world of production, quality may be job one, but in the IT world, it is security.

The SANS (SysAdmin, Audit, Network Security) Institute is a leading source for information on security-related issues and training. According to the Internet Storm Center (http://isc.sans.org), which they maintain, a computer connected to the Internet has an average of 5 minutes before it falls under some form of attack.

This chapter looks at security primarily from the standpoint of the network. All of the topics relevant to the Essentials exam are covered, and a thorough overview of the topic is provided.

Understanding Security

Security is unlike any other topic in computing. The word *security* is so broad that it's impossible to know exactly what you mean when you say it. When you talk about security, do you mean physically protecting servers and workstations from those who might try to steal them or from damage that may occur if the side of the building collapses? Or do you mean the security of data from viruses and worms and the means by which you keep those threats from entering the network? Or do you mean security of data from hackers and miscreants who have targeted you and have no other purpose in life than to keep you up at night? Or is security the comfort that comes from knowing you can restore files if a user accidentally deletes them?

The first problem with security is that it's next to impossible to have everyone agree on what it means, because it can include all these items. The next problem is that we don't *really* want things to be completely secured. For example, if you wanted your customer-list file to be truly secure, you wouldn't put it on the server and make it available. It's on the server because you need to access it, and so do 30 other people. In this sense, security means that only 30 select people can get to the data.

The next problem is that although everyone wants security, no one wants to be inconvenienced by it. To use an analogy, few travelers don't feel safer by watching airport personnel pat down everyone who heads to the terminal—they just don't want it to happen to them. This is true in computing as well; we all want to make sure data is accessed only by those who truly should be working with it, but we don't want to have to enter 12-digit passwords and submit to retinal scans.

As a computer professional, you have to understand all these concerns. You have to know that a great deal is expected of you, but few people want to be hassled or inconvenienced by the measures you must put in place. You have a primary responsibility to protect and safeguard the information your organization uses. Many times, that means educating your users and making certain they understand the "why" behind what is being implemented. When discussing computer security, you must be able to identify the names, purposes, and characteristics of three key areas: hardware/software security, wireless security, and physical/data security. We'll discuss these topics following an overview of authentication technologies.

Authentication Technologies

Authentication proves that a user or system is actually who they say they are. This is one of the most critical parts of a security system. It's part of a process that is also referred to as *identification and authentication (I&A)*. The identification process starts when a user ID or logon name is typed into a sign-on screen. Authentication is accomplished by challenging the claim about who is accessing the resource. Without authentication, anybody can claim to be anybody.

Authentication systems or methods are based on one or more of these three factors:

- Something you know, such as a password or PIN
- Something you have, such as a smart card or an identification device
- Something physically unique to you, such as your fingerprints or retinal pattern

Systems authenticate each other using similar methods. Frequently, systems pass private information between each other to establish identity. Once authentication has occurred, the two systems can communicate in the manner specified in the design.

Several common methods are used for authentication. Each has advantages and disadvantages that must be considered when you're evaluating authentication schemes.

Username/Password

A username and password are unique identifiers for a logon process. When users sit down in front of a computer system, the first thing a security system requires is that they establish who they are. Identification is typically confirmed through a logon process. Most operating systems use a user ID and password to accomplish this. These values can be sent across the connection as plain text or can be encrypted.

The logon process identifies to the operating system, and possibly the network, that you are who you say you are. Figure 11.1 illustrates this logon and password process. The operating system compares this information to the stored information from the security processor and either accepts or denies the logon attempt. The operating system may establish privileges or permissions based on stored data about that particular ID.

FIGURE 11.1 A logon process occurring on a workstation

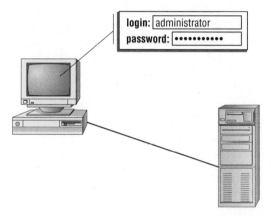

Logon or Security Server

Password Authentication Protocol (PAP)

Password Authentication Protocol (PAP) offers no true security, but it's one of the simplest forms of authentication. The username and password values are both sent to the server as clear text and checked for a match; the trouble with clear text is that it can be intercepted by someone monitoring the network, and this makes PAP unsecure. If the values match, the user is granted access; if they don't match, the user is denied access. In most modern implementations, PAP is shunned in favor of other, more secure, authentication methods.

Challenge Handshake Authentication Protocol (CHAP)

Challenge Handshake Authentication Protocol (CHAP) challenges a system to verify identity. CHAP doesn't use a user ID/password mechanism. Instead, the initiator sends a logon request from the client to the server. The server sends a challenge back to the client. The challenge is encrypted and then sent back to the server. The server compares the value from the client and, if the information matches, grants authorization. If the response fails, the session fails, and the request phase starts over. Figure 11.2 illustrates the CHAP procedure. This handshake method involves a number of steps and is usually automatic between systems after it's configured.

FIGURE 11.2   CHAP authentication

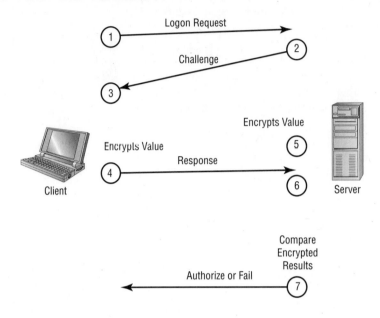

CHAP depends on a "secret" known only to the authenticator and that peer. Part of configuring CHAP is setting the shared, predefined secret on both the client and server. For more information, see the current edition of the *CompTIA Network+ Study Guide* (Sybex, 2009).

Certificates

Certificates are another common form of authentication. A server or *certificate authority (CA)* can issue a certificate that will be accepted by the challenging system. Certificates can be stored on physical access devices such as smart cards or stored on the user's computer as a digital signature used as part of the logon process. A *Certificate Practice Statement (CPS)* outlines the rules used for issuing and managing certificates. A *Certificate Revocation List (CRL)* lists the revocations that must be addressed (often due to expiration) in order to stay current.

A simple way to think of certificates is like hall passes at school. Figure 11.3 illustrates a certificate being handed from the server to the client once authentication has been established. If you have a hall pass, you can wander the halls of your school. If your pass is invalid, the hallway monitor can send you to the principal's office. Similarly, if you have a certificate, you can prove to the system that you are who you say you are and are authenticated to work with the resources.

FIGURE 11.3   A certificate being issued once identification has been verified

Security Tokens

Security tokens are similar to certificates. They contain the rights and access privileges of the token bearer as part of the token. Think of a token as a small piece of data that holds a sliver of information about the user. Both software and hardware tokens exist.

Many operating systems generate a token that is applied to every action taken on the computer system. If your token doesn't grant you access to certain information, then either that information won't be displayed or your access will be denied. The authentication system creates a token every time a user connects or a session begins. At the completion of a session, the token is destroyed. Figure 11.4 shows the security token process.

FIGURE 11.4   Security token authentication

Kerberos

Kerberos is an authentication protocol named after the mythical three-headed dog that stood at the gates of Hades. Originally designed by MIT, Kerberos is becoming very popular as an authentication method. It allows for a single sign-on to a distributed network.

Kerberos authentication uses a *key distribution center (KDC)* to orchestrate the process. The KDC authenticates the *principal* (which can be a user, a program, or a system) and provides it with a ticket. Once this ticket is issued, it can be used to authenticate against other principals. This occurs automatically when a request or service is performed by another principal.

Kerberos is quickly becoming a common standard in network environments. Its only significant weakness is that the KDC can be a single point of failure. If the KDC goes down, the authentication process will stop. Figure 11.5 shows the Kerberos authentication process and the ticket being presented to systems that are authorized by the KDC.

FIGURE 11.5   Kerberos authentication process

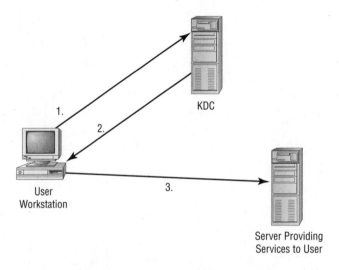

1. User requests access to service running on a different server.
2. KDC authenticates user and sends a ticket to be used between the user and the service on the server.
3. User's workstation sends a ticket to the service.

Multifactor Authentication

When two or more access methods are included as part of the authentication process, you're implementing a *multifactor* system. A system that uses smart cards and passwords is referred to as a *two-factor authentication* system. Two-factor authentication is shown in Figure 11.6. This example requires both a smart card and a logon password process.

FIGURE 11.6   Two-factor authentication

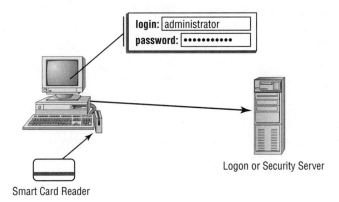

Smart Card Reader

Logon or Security Server

Both factors must be valid:
• User ID and Password
• Smart Card

Working with Hardware and Software Security

When it comes to hardware, it's important to understand that although the user interacts with software, the hardware actually stores the data. The hardware in question can be a hard disk, a backup tape, or some other storage device. This overly simplistic concept is important when it comes to choosing how to dispose of hardware.

If it's possible to verify beyond a reasonable doubt that a piece of hardware that's no longer being used doesn't contain any data of a sensitive or proprietary nature, then that hardware can be recycled (sold to employees, sold to a third party, donated to a school, and so on). That level of assurance can come from wiping a hard drive, reformatting it with a low-level format (normal formatting will not ensure the data cannot be restored), or using specialized utilities. When computer systems are retired, the disk drives should be zeroed out, and all magnetic media should be degaussed. Degaussing involves applying a strong magnetic field to initialize the media (this is also referred to as *disk wiping*). Erasing files on a computer system doesn't guarantee that the information isn't still on the disk; a low-level format (typically only accomplished in the factory) can be performed on the system, or a utility can be used to completely wipe the disk clean. This process helps ensure that information doesn't fall into the wrong hands.

Degaussing hard drives is difficult and may render the drive unusable. Degaussing works better for floppy drives while utilities are often used for hard drives.

If you can't be assured that the hardware in question doesn't contain important data, then the hardware should be destroyed. You cannot, and should not, take a risk that the data your company depends on could fall into the wrong hands.

In the following sections, we'll discuss a number of the elements you need to know as you study for the exam.

Smart Cards

A *smart card* is a type of badge or card that gives you access to resources including buildings, parking lots, and computers. It contains information about your identity and access privileges. Each area or computer has a card scanner or a reader in which you insert your card.

The reader is connected to the workstation and validates against the security system. This increases the security of the authentication process, because you must be in physical possession of the smart card to use the resources. Of course, if the card is lost or stolen, the person who finds the card can access the resources it allows. Smart cards are difficult to counterfeit, but they're easy to steal. Once a thief has a smart card, she has all the access the card allows. To prevent this, many organizations don't put any identifying marks on their smart cards, making it harder for someone to utilize them.

> Most smart cards also require the use of a PIN, just in case the card is lost or stolen.

Many European countries are beginning to use smart cards instead of magnetic-strip credit cards because they offer additional security and can contain more information.

Biometrics

Biometric devices use physical characteristics to identify the user. Such devices are becoming more common in the business environment. Biometric systems include hand scanners, retinal scanners, and soon, possibly, DNA scanners. To gain access to resources, you must pass a physical screening process. In the case of a hand scanner, this may include identifying fingerprints, scars, and markings on your hand. Retinal scanners compare your eye's retinal pattern to a stored retinal pattern to verify your identity. DNA scanners will examine a unique portion of your DNA structure in order to verify that you are who you say you are.

Many laptop manufacturers are including fingerprint scanners on the current model of their machines. If you are working with computers that do not have these scanners, you can purchase a USB-based scanner for under $100 (some manufacturers have built this into their mouse). The scanner takes an image of your fingerprint and compares it to the image on file. While far from infallible, they do provide another layer of security and work well when coupled with another form of authentication.

Key Fobs

Key fobs are named after the chains that used to be used to hold pocket watches to clothes. They are security devices that you carry with you that display a randomly generated code that you can then use for authentication. This code usually changes very quickly (every 60 seconds is probably the average), and you combine this code with your PIN for authentication.

> The term *key fob* is used to describe a great many things. While something dangling from your key chain that can be used for keyless entry can constitute a key fob as well, when it comes to computer security, there usually needs to be some challenge/authentication process involved for it to be of any great value.

Authentication Issues to Consider

You can set up many different parameters and standards to force the people in your organization to conform. In establishing these parameters, it's important that you consider the capabilities of the people who will be working with these policies. If you're working in an environment where people aren't computer savvy, you may spend a lot of time helping them remember and recover passwords. Many organizations have had to reevaluate their security guidelines after they've invested great time and expense to implement high-security systems.

Setting authentication security, especially in supporting users, can become a high-maintenance activity for network administrators. On one hand, you want people to be able to authenticate themselves easily; on the other hand, you want to establish security that protects your company's resources.

 Real World Scenario

Check the Movie Listings

Be wary of popular names or current trends that make certain passwords predictable. For example, during the first release of *Star Wars*, two of the most popular passwords used on college campuses were C3PO and R2D2. This created a security problem for campus computer centers.

A few years back, characters from the *Matrix* trilogy became popular passwords as those working in offices tried to live out their lives in fantasy. While you may truly like a movie or character that is popular at the moment, you need to understand that those names will be tried as password possibilities very quickly.

Understanding Software Exploitation

The term *software exploitation* refers to attacks launched against applications and higher-level services. They include gaining access to data using weaknesses in the data-access objects of a database or a flaw in a service. This section briefly outlines some common exploitations that have been successful in the past. The following exploitations can be introduced using viruses, as in the case of the Klez32 virus, or by using access attacks described later in this chapter:

 Viruses can be stored/transported through any media. They can enter your system on thumb drives, CDs, e-mail, or just about any way imaginable.

Database exploitation   Many database products allow sophisticated access queries to be made in the client-server environment. If a client session can be hijacked or spoofed, the attacker can formulate queries against the database that disclose unauthorized information. For this attack to be successful, the attacker must first gain access to the environment through one of the attacks outlined later.

Application exploitation   The macro virus is another example of software exploitation. A macro virus is a set of programming instructions in a language such as VBScript that commands an application to perform illicit instructions. Users want more powerful tools, and manufacturers want to sell users what they want. The macro virus takes advantage of the power offered by word processors, spreadsheets, or other applications. This exploitation is inherent in the product, and all users are susceptible to it unless they disable all macros.

E-mail exploitation   Hardly a day goes by without another e-mail virus being reported. This is a result of a weakness in many common e-mail clients. Modern e-mail clients offer many shortcuts, lists, and other capabilities to meet user demands. A popular exploitation of e-mail clients involves accessing the client address book and propagating viruses. There is virtually nothing a client user can do about these exploitations, although antivirus software that integrates with your e-mail client does offer some protection. To be truly successful, the software manufacturer must fix the weaknesses—an example is Microsoft Outlook's option to protect against access to the address book. This type of weakness isn't a bug, in many cases, but a feature that users wanted.

 Some viruses won't damage a system in an attempt to spread into all the other systems in a network. These viruses use that system as the carrier of the virus.

One of the most important measures you can take to proactively combat software attacks is to know common file extensions and the applications they're associated with. For example, .SCR files are screensavers, and viruses are often distributed through the use of these files. No legitimate user should be sending screensavers via e-mail to your users, and all .SCR attachments should be banned from entering the network.

Table 11.1, although not comprehensive, contains the most common file extensions that should or should not, as a general rule, be allowed into the network as e-mail attachments. This chart simply lists file extensions that would (or would not) commonly be expected as e-mail attachments. It does not mean that viruses and other malware won't be propagated using the allowed file extensions.

As a general rule, never open an attachment in e-mail from any unknown sender or from a sender you are not expecting an attachment from.

TABLE 11.1   Common File Extensions for E-mail Attachments

Should Be Allowed	Should *Not* Be Allowed
.DOC/.DOCX	.BAT
.PDF	.COM
.TXT	.EXE
.XLS/.XLSX	.HLP
.ZIP	.PIF
	.SCR

Spyware   *Spyware* differs from other malware in that it works—often actively—on behalf of a third party. Rather than self-replicating, like viruses and worms, spyware is spread to machines by users who inadvertently ask for it. The users often don't know they have asked for it but have done so by downloading other programs, visiting infected sites, and so on.

The spyware program monitors the user's activity and responds by offering unsolicited pop-up advertisements (sometimes known as *adware*), gathers information about the user to pass on to marketers, or intercepts personal data such as credit-card numbers. One thing separating spyware from most other malware is that it almost always exists to provide commercial gain. The operating systems from Microsoft are the ones most affected by spyware, and Microsoft has released Windows Defender to combat the problem.

 All OSs are susceptible to spyware. Microsoft gets the most attention because of its wide use.

Rootkits   Recently, *rootkits* have become the software exploitation program du jour. Rootkits are software programs that have the ability to hide certain things from the operating system. With a rootkit, there may be a number of processes running on a system that don't show up in Task Manager, or connections may be established/available that don't appear in a Netstat display—the rootkit masks the presence of these items. The rootkit does this by manipulating function calls to the operating system and filtering out information that would normally appear.

Unfortunately, many rootkits are written to get around antivirus and antispyware programs that aren't kept up to date. The best defense you have is to monitor what your system is doing and catch the rootkit in the process of installation.

Viruses   A *virus* is a piece of software designed to infect a computer system. The virus may do nothing more than reside on the computer. A virus may also damage the data on your hard disk, destroy your operating system, and possibly spread to other systems. Viruses get into your computer in one of three ways: on a contaminated floppy, DVD, memory card, or CD; through e-mail; or as part of another program.

> Important distinguishing elements of viruses are that they attach them-
> selves to a program or file (a host) and that they cannot spread without
> human interaction (such as running an infected program).

Viruses can be classified as several types: polymorphic, stealth, retroviruses, multipartite, armored, companion, phage, and macro viruses. Each type of virus has a different attack strategy and different consequences.

> A symptom of many viruses is unusual activity on the system disk.

Trojan horses   *Trojan horses* are programs that enter a system or network under the guise of another program. A Trojan horse may be included as an attachment or as part of an installation program. The Trojan horse can create a back door (an opening into the system that someone can take advantage of) or replace a valid program during installation. It then accomplishes its mission under the guise of another program. Trojan horses can be used to compromise the security of your system, and they can exist on a system for years before they're detected.

The best preventive measure for Trojan horses is to not allow them entry into your system. Immediately before and after you install a new software program or operating system, back that system up! If you suspect a Trojan horse, you can reinstall the original programs, which should delete the Trojan horse. A port scan may also reveal a Trojan horse on your system. If an application opens a TCP or UDP port that isn't supported in your network, you can track it down and determine which port is being used.

Worms   A *worm* is different from a virus in that it can reproduce itself, it is self-contained, and it doesn't need a host application to be transported. Many of the so-called viruses that have made the papers and media were actually worms. However, it's possible for a worm to contain or deliver a virus to a target system.

By their nature and origin, worms are supposed to propagate, and they use whatever services they're capable of to do that. Early worms filled up memory and bred inside the RAM of the target computer. Worms can use TCP/IP, e-mail, Internet services, or any number of possibilities to reach their target.

Spam   *Spam* is defined as any unwanted, unsolicited e-mail. Not only can the sheer volume of it be irritating, but it can often provide the door to larger problems. Some of the sites advertised in spam may be infected with viruses, worms, and other unwanted programs. If users begin to respond to spam by visiting those sites, then your problems will only multiply.

Just as you can, and must, install good antivirus software programs, you should also consider similar measures for spam. Filtering messages and preventing them from ever entering the network is the most effective method of dealing with the problem.

Grayware   *Grayware* is a term used to describe any application that is annoying or negatively affecting the performance of your computer. If an application doesn't fall into the virus or Trojan category, it can get lumped under grayware. Spyware and adware are often considered types of grayware, as are programs that log user keystrokes and certain hacking programs.

Firewalls

Firewalls are one of the first lines of defense in a network. There are different types of firewalls, and they can be either stand-alone systems or included in other devices such as routers or servers. You can find firewall solutions that are marketed as hardware-only and others that are software-only. Many firewalls, however, consist of add-in software that is available for servers or workstations.

 Although solutions are sold as hardware-only, the hardware still runs some sort of software. It may be hardened and in ROM to prevent tampering, and it may be customized—but software is present, nonetheless.

The basic purpose of a firewall is to isolate one network from another. Firewalls are becoming available as appliances, meaning they're installed into the network between two networks. *Appliances* are freestanding devices that operate in a largely self-contained manner, requiring less maintenance and support than a server-based product.

Firewalls function as one or more of the following:

- Packet filter
- Proxy firewall
- Stateful inspection

A firewall operating as a *packet filter* passes or blocks traffic to specific addresses based on the IP address, protocol, type of application being addressed (identified by a port number), or many other attributes. The packet filter doesn't analyze the contents of a packet; it decides whether to pass it based on the packet's addressing information. For instance, a packet filter may allow web traffic on port 80 and block Telnet traffic on port 23. This type of filtering is included in many routers. If a received packet request asks for a port that isn't authorized, the filter may reject the request or ignore it. Many packet filters can also specify which IP addresses can request which ports and allow or deny them based on the security settings of the firewall.

Telnet shouldn't be used if possible. Telnet sends user ID and password information to the Telnet server unencrypted. This creates a potential security problem in an Internet environment. A much better solution is to use SSH in place of Telnet.

You can think of a *proxy firewall* as an intermediary between your network and any other network. Proxy firewalls are used to process requests from an outside network; the proxy firewall examines the data and makes rules-based decisions about whether the request should be forwarded or refused. The proxy intercepts all the packages and reprocesses them for use internally. This process includes hiding IP addresses.

Stateful inspection is also referred to as *stateful packet filtering*. Most of the devices used in networks don't keep track of how information is routed or used. Once a packet is passed, the packet and path are forgotten. In stateful inspection (or stateful packet filtering), records are kept using a state table that tracks every communications channel. When you have a table, only communication specifically mentioned in that table will be allowed. Stateful inspections occur at all levels of the network and provide additional security.

File System Security

Microsoft's earliest file system was referred to as File Allocation Table (FAT). FAT was designed for relatively small disk drives. It was upgraded first to FAT16 and finally to FAT32. FAT32 (also written as FAT-32) allows large disk systems to be used on Windows systems.

FAT allows only two types of protection: share-level and user-level access privileges. Share-level security is security that applies to the folder as it is shared, while user-level security bases access on the login of the user. If a user has write or change access to a drive or directory, he has access to any file in that directory. This is very unsecure in an Internet environment.

The New Technology File System (NTFS) was introduced with Windows NT to address security problems. Before Windows NT was released, it had become apparent to Microsoft that a new file system was needed to handle growing disk sizes, security concerns, and the need for more stability. NTFS was created to address those issues.

With NTFS, files, directories, and volumes can each have their own security. NTFS's security is flexible and built in. Not only does NTFS track security in access control lists (ACLs), which can hold permissions for local users and groups, but each entry in the ACL can also specify what type of access is given—which is not possible with FAT. This allows a great deal of flexibility in setting up a network. In addition, special file-encryption programs were developed to encrypt data while it was stored on the hard disk.

Microsoft strongly recommends that all network shares be established using NTFS.

One of the newest security features that is available only in the Enterprise and Ultimate versions of Windows Vista is BitLocker. BitLocker is a drive encryption feature that can encrypt an entire volume with 128-bit encryption. By encrypting the entire volume, the data is not accessible to someone who may boot another operating system in an attempt to bypass the computer's security.

BitLocker requires two partitions—one for the operating system volume and another for the system volume. It also requires that the system partition be set to active and have at least 1.5GB.

Prior to Windows Vista's Service Pack 1, BitLocker could only encrypt the Windows partition. SP1 expanded this capability to all local drives.

Understanding Wireless Security

Wireless systems are those that don't use wires to send information but rather transmit data through the air. The growth of wireless systems creates several opportunities for attackers. These systems are relatively new, they use well-established communications mechanisms, and they're easily intercepted. Wireless controllers use service-set identifiers (SSIDs) that must be configured in the network cards to allow communications with a specific access point. However, using SSID configurations doesn't necessarily prevent wireless networks from being monitored.

This section discusses the various types of wireless systems that you'll encounter, and it mentions some of the security issues associated with this technology. Specifically, this section deals with Wireless Transport Layer Security (WTLS), the IEEE 802 wireless standards, Wired Equivalent Privacy (WEP)/Wireless Applications Protocol (WAP) applications, and the vulnerabilities that each presents.

Wireless Transport Layer Security

Wireless Transport Layer Security (WTLS) is the security layer of WAP, discussed in the section "WAP/WEP/WPA." WTLS provides authentication, encryption, and data integrity for wireless devices. It's designed to utilize the relatively narrow bandwidth of these types of devices, and it's moderately secure. WTLS provides reasonable security for mobile devices (such as mobile phones), and it's being widely implemented.

WTLS is part of the WAP environment: WAP provides the functional equivalent of TCP/IP for wireless devices. Many devices, including newer cell phones and PDAs, include support for WTLS as part of their networking protocol capabilities.

IEEE 802.11x Wireless Protocols

The IEEE 802.11x family of protocols provides for wireless communications using radio frequency transmissions. The frequencies in use for 802.11 standards are the 2.4GHz and the 5GHz frequency spectrum. Several standards and bandwidths have been defined for use in wireless environments, and they aren't extremely compatible with each other:

802.11 The *802.11* standard defines wireless LANs transmitting at 1Mbps or 2Mbps bandwidths using the 2.4GHz frequency spectrum and using either frequency-hopping spread spectrum (FHSS) or direct-sequence spread spectrum (DSSS) for data encoding.

802.11a The *802.11a* standard provides wireless LAN bandwidth of up to 54Mbps in the 5GHz frequency spectrum. The 802.11a standard also uses orthogonal frequency division multiplexing (OFDM) for encoding rather than FHSS or DSSS.

802.11b The *802.11b* standard provides for bandwidths of up to 11Mbps (with fallback rates of 5.5, 2, and 1Mbps) in the 2.4GHz frequency spectrum. This standard is also called *WiFi* or *802.11 high rate*. The 802.11b standard uses only DSSS for data encoding.

802.11g The *802.11g* standard provides for bandwidths of 54Mbps+ in the 2.4GHz frequency spectrum.

We have mentioned three signal modulation techniques used in the 802.11 standards. You do not need to know these for the A+ certification exam, but knowledge of them is useful when dealing with security in the real world:

Direct-sequence spread spectrum (DSSS) DSSS accomplishes communication by adding the data that is to be transmitted to a higher-speed transmission. The higher-speed transmission contains redundant information to ensure data accuracy. Each packet can then be reconstructed in the event of a disruption.

Frequency-hopping spread spectrum (FHSS) FHSS accomplishes communication by hopping the transmission over a range of predefined frequencies. The changing or hopping is synchronized between both ends and appears to be a single transmission channel to both ends.

Orthogonal frequency division multiplexing (OFDM) OFDM accomplishes communication by breaking the data into subsignals and transmitting them simultaneously. These transmissions occur on different frequencies or subbands.

The mathematics and theories of these transmission technologies are beyond the scope of this book and far beyond the scope of this exam.

WAP/WEP/WPA

Wireless systems frequently use WAP for network communications. WEP is intended to provide the equivalent security of a wired network protocol. WPA is an improvement on WEP. This section briefly discusses these three terms and provides you with an understanding of their relative capabilities.

WAP

The *Wireless Access Protocol (WAP)* is the technology designed for use with wireless devices. Many manufacturers, including Motorola, Nokia, and others, have adopted WAP as a standard.WAP functions are equivalent to TCP/IP functions in that they're trying to serve the same purpose for wireless devices. WAP uses a smaller version of HTML called *Wireless Markup Language (WML)*, which is used for Internet displays. WAP-enabled devices can also respond to scripts using an environment called *WMLScript*. This scripting language is similar to JavaScript, which is a programming language.

The ability to accept web pages and scripts produces the opportunity for malicious code and viruses to be transported to WAP-enabled devices. This creates a new set of problems, and antivirus software must be able to deal with them.

WAP systems communicate using a WAP gateway system. The gateway converts information back and forth between HTTP and WAP, and it also encodes and decodes the security protocols. This structure provides a reasonable assurance that WAP-enabled devices can be secured. If the interconnection between the WAP server and the Internet isn't encrypted, packets between the devices may be intercepted, creating a potential vulnerability. This vulnerability is called a *gap in the WAP*.

WEP

Wired Equivalent Privacy (WEP) is a security standard for wireless devices. WEP encrypts data to provide data security. The protocol has always been under scrutiny for not being as secure as initially intended.

> The CompTIA objectives use the notation WEP.x, which refers to the key size. Keys that are commonly supported include 64-bit, 128-bit, and 256-bit (WEP 64, WEP 128, and WEP 256).

WEP is vulnerable due to weaknesses in the encryption algorithms. These weaknesses allow the algorithm to potentially be cracked in a short period of time using available PC software. This makes WEP one of the more vulnerable protocols available for security.

> MAC address filtering can be used on a wireless network to prevent certain clients from accessing the Internet. You can choose to deny service to a set list of MAC addresses (and allow all others) or allow service only to a set of MAC addresses (and deny all others).

WPA

WiFi Protected Access (WPA) is an improvement on WEP that implements some of the 802.11i standards. An improvement over WPA is WPA2, which implements the full 802.11i standard.

Wireless Vulnerabilities to Know

Wireless systems are vulnerable to all the different attacks that wired networks are vulnerable to. However, because these protocols use radio frequency signals, they have an additional weakness: all radio frequency signals can be easily intercepted. To intercept 802.11*x* traffic, all you need is a PC with an appropriate 802.11*x* card installed. Simple software on the PC can capture the link traffic in the WAP and then process this data in order to decrypt account and password information.

An additional issue with wireless systems is the *site survey*. The term initially meant determining whether a proposed location was free from interference. The term now also refers to listening in on an existing wireless network using commercially available technologies. Doing so allows intelligence, and possibly data capture, to be performed on systems in your wireless network.

When used by an attacker, a site survey can determine what types of systems are in use, the protocols used, and other critical information about your network. It's the primary method used to gather data about wireless networks. Virtually all wireless networks are vulnerable to site surveys.

In reality, wardriving is probably a more current threat that emphasizes the need for paying attention to wireless security. Make sure you are limiting your network to those who need access to it and not those sitting in the parking lot.

Understanding Physical and Data Security

Physical security, as the name implies, involves protecting your assets and information from physical access by unauthorized personnel. In other words, you're trying to protect those items that can be seen, touched, and stolen. These threats often present themselves as service technicians, janitors, customers, vendors, or even employees. They can steal your equipment, damage it, or take documents from offices, garbage cans, or filing cabinets. Their motivation may be retribution for some perceived misgiving, a desire to steal your trade secrets to sell to a competitor as an act of vengeance, or just greed. They might steal $1,000 worth of hardware that they can sell to a friend for a fraction of that and have no concept of the value of the data stored on the hardware.

Physical security is relatively easy to accomplish. You can secure facilities by controlling access to the office, shredding unneeded documents, installing security systems, and limiting access to sensitive areas of the business. Most office buildings provide perimeter and corridor security during unoccupied hours, and it isn't difficult to implement commonsense measures during occupied hours as well. Sometimes just having a person present can be all the deterrent needed to prevent petty thefts.

The first layer of access control is always perimeter security. Perimeter security is intended to delay or deter entrance into a facility.

Many office complexes also offer roving security patrols, multiple-lock access control methods, and electronic or password access. Typically, the facility managers handle these arrangements. They won't generally deal with internal security as it relates to your records, computer systems, and papers; that is your responsibility in most situations.

The first component of physical security involves making a physical location less tempting as a target. If the office or building you're in is open all the time, gaining entry into a business in the building is easy. You must prevent people from seeing your organization as a tempting target. Locking doors and installing surveillance or alarm systems can make a physical location a less-desirable target. You can also add controls to elevators requiring keys or badges in order to reach upper floors. Plenty of wide-open targets are available, involving less risk on the part of the people involved. Try to make your office not worth the trouble.

The second component of physical security involves detecting a *penetration* or theft. You want to know what was broken into, what is missing, and how the loss occurred. Passive videotape systems are one good way to obtain this information. Most retail environments routinely tape key areas of the business to identify how thefts occur and who was involved. These tapes are admissible as evidence in most courts. Law enforcement should be involved as soon as a penetration or theft occurs. More important from a deterrent standpoint, you should make it well known that you'll prosecute anyone caught in the act of theft to the fullest extent of the law. Making the video cameras as conspicuous as possible will deter many would-be criminals.

The third component of physical security involves recovering from a theft or loss of critical information or systems. How will the organization recover from the loss and get on with normal business? If a vandal destroyed your server room with a fire or flood, how long would it take your organization to get back into operation and return to full productivity?

Recovery involves a great deal of planning, thought, and testing. What would happen if the files containing all your bank accounts, purchase orders, and customer information became a pile of ashes in the middle of the smoldering ruins that used to be your office? Ideally, critical copies of records and inventories should be stored off site in a secure facility.

Encryption Technologies

Cryptographic algorithms are used to encode a message from its unencrypted or clear-text state into an encrypted message. The three primary methods are hashing, symmetric, and asymmetric.

Hashing is the process of converting a message, or data, into a numeric value. The numeric value that a hashing process creates is referred to as a *hash total* or *value*. Hashing functions are considered either one-way or two-way. A one-way hash doesn't allow a message to be decoded back to its original value (we match the hashes instead of the original documentation). A two-way hash allows a message to be reconstructed from the hash. Most hashing functions are one-way hashing. Two primary standards exist that use the hashing process for encryption:

Secure Hash Algorithm (SHA)   The *Secure Hash Algorithm (SHA)* was designed to ensure the integrity of a message. The SHA is a one-way hash that provides a hash value that can be used with an encryption protocol. This algorithm produces a 160-bit hash value. SHA has been updated; four new standards, collectively called SHA-2, have been developed.

Message Digest Algorithm (MDA)   The *Message Digest Algorithm (MDA)* also creates a hash value and uses a one-way hash. The hash value is used to help maintain integrity. There are several versions of MD; the most common are MD5, MD4, and MD2.

Symmetric algorithms require both ends of an encrypted message to have the same key and processing algorithms. Symmetric algorithms generate a secret key that must be protected. A secret key—sometimes referred to as a *private key*—is a key that isn't disclosed to people who aren't authorized to use the encryption system. The disclosure of a private key breaches the security of the encryption system. If a key is lost or stolen, the entire process is breached. These types of systems are common, and examples include AES and IDEA.

Asymmetric algorithms use two keys to encrypt and decrypt data. These keys are referred to as the *public key* and the *private key*. The public key can be used by the sender to encrypt a message, and the private key can be used by the receiver to decrypt the message. Symmetrical systems require the key to be private between the two parties, but with asymmetric systems, each circuit has one key. Examples include Diffie-Hellman and RSA.

The public key may be truly public or it may be a secret between the two parties. The private key is kept private and is known only by the owner (receiver). If someone wants to send you an encrypted message, he can use your public key to encrypt the message and then send you the message. You can use your private key to decrypt the message. One of the keys is always kept private. If both keys become available to a third party, the encryption system won't protect the privacy of the message.

Perhaps the best way to think about this system is that it's similar to a safe-deposit box. Two keys are needed: the box owner keeps the public key, and the bank retains the second or private key. In order to open the box, both keys must be used simultaneously.

Incidence Reporting

Incident response policies define how an organization will respond to an incident. These policies may involve third parties, and they need to be comprehensive. The term *incident* is somewhat nebulous in scope; for our purposes, an incident is any attempt to violate a security policy, a successful penetration, a compromise of a system, or any unauthorized access to information. This term includes system failures and disruption of services in the organization.

It's important that an incident response policy minimally establish the following items:

- Outside agencies that should be contacted or notified in case of an incident

- Resources used to deal with an incident

- Procedures to gather and secure evidence

- List of information that should be collected about the incident

- Outside experts who can be used to address issues if needed

- Policies and guidelines regarding how to handle the incident

According to the Computer Emergency Response Team (more commonly known as CERT), a Computer Security Incident Response Team (CSIRT) can be a formalized team or ad hoc. You can toss a team together to respond to an incident after it arises, but investing time in the development process can make an incident more manageable, because many decisions about dealing with an incident will have been considered earlier. Incidents are high-stress situations; therefore, it's better to simplify the process by considering important aspects in advance. If civil or criminal actions are part of the process, evidence must be gathered and safeguarded properly.

Assume you've discovered a situation where a fraud has been perpetrated internally using a corporate computer. You're part of the investigating team. Your incident response policy lists the specialists you need to contact for an investigation. Ideally, you've already met the investigator or investigating firm, you've developed an understanding of how to protect the scene, and you know how to properly deal with the media (if they become involved).

While a response policy is important to have, don't let it stop there. You must make certain the policy is followed when an incident occurs. The importance of responding to, and acting upon an incident—including correctly reporting it—is imperative.

Social Engineering

Social engineering is a process in which an attacker attempts to acquire information about your network and system by social means, such as talking to people in the organization. A social-engineering attack may occur over the phone, by e-mail, or by a visit. The intent is to acquire access information, such as user IDs and passwords.

These types of attacks are relatively low-tech and are more akin to con jobs. Take the following example. Your help desk gets a call at 4:00 a.m. from someone purporting to be the vice president of your company. She tells the help desk personnel that she is out of town to attend a meeting, her computer just failed, and she is sitting in a Kinko's trying to get a file from her desktop computer back at the office. She can't seem to remember her password and user ID. She tells the help desk representative that she needs access to the information right away or the company could lose millions of dollars. Your help desk rep knows how important this meeting is and gives the vice president her user ID and password over the phone, or allows it to be reset to whatever value the caller specifies.

Another common approach is initiated by a phone call or e-mail from your software vendor, telling you that they have a critical fix that must be installed on your computer system. If this patch isn't installed right away, your system will crash and you'll lose all your data. For some reason, you've changed your maintenance account password and they can't log on. Your systems operator gives the password to the person. You've been hit again.

In Exercise 11.1, you'll test your users to determine the likelihood of a social-engineering attack.

EXERCISE 11.1

Testing Social Engineering

The following are suggestions for tests; you may need to modify them slightly to be appropriate at your workplace. Before doing any of them, make certain your manager knows that you're conducting such an exam and approves of it:

1. Call the receptionist from an outside line when the sales manager is at lunch. Tell her that you're a new salesperson, that you didn't write down the username and password the sales manager gave you last week, and that you need to get a file from the e-mail system for a presentation tomorrow. Does she direct you to the appropriate person or attempt to help you receive the file?

2. Call the human resources department from an outside line. Don't give your real name, but instead say that you're a vendor who has been working with this company for years. You'd like a copy of the employee phone list to be e-mailed to you, if possible. Do they agree to send you the list, which would contain information that could be used to try to guess usernames and passwords?

3. Pick a user at random. Call them and identify yourself as someone who does work with the company. Tell them that you're supposed to have some new software ready for them by next week and that you need to know their password in order to finish configuring it. Do they do the right thing?

The best defense against any social-engineering attack is education. Make certain the employees of your company would know how to react to the requests presented here.

Security Solutions

There are a number of security solutions that can be implemented to help make your systems and networks more secure—remember that the network is only as secure as the weakest host connected to it.

BIOS Security

The system Basic Input/Output System (BIOS) is used to power up the system and can also allow you to assign a password. Once enabled/activated, that password is stored in CMOS and must be given before the system will fully boot. Most BIOS implementations allow for two different passwords—one for the user and one for the supervisor. The difference between the two is whether or not the ability to access the BIOS setup program is granted.

This provides a simple security solution for a workstation/laptop as the user must give the user password (sometimes also called the system password) in order to be able to access the system; if they cannot give the correct value, the drives are essentially locked. The supervisor password (sometimes also called the setup password) is only needed when the user attempts to access the setup program.

Passwords used for BIOS-level security should follow the same rules as passwords for any account. One other feature to be aware of in the BIOS setup from most vendors is the ability to toggle chassis intrusion detection. If enabled, this will notify you (via a pop-up) if someone has opened the case.

The casual hacker's most common way of working around the password requirement is to remove the battery (thus erasing the CMOS). You should be aware, however, that many BIOS manufacturers include a backdoor password that can be given to bypass the one set by the user. Many of these values can be found on the Internet and are known by more professional hackers.

Another method for getting around the password is to change the jumper for resetting CMOS settings to defaults. To protect against this, you want to add as much physical security, in the form of case locks and similar measures, as possible.

Within the advanced configuration settings on some BIOS configuration menus, you can choose to enable or disable TPM. A *Trusted Platform Module (TPM)* can be used to assist with hash key generation. TPM is the name assigned to a chip that can store cryptographic keys, passwords, or certificates. TPM can be used to protect cell phones and devices other than PCs as well. The TPM can be used to generate values used with whole disk encryption such as Windows Vista's BitLocker. The TPM chip may be installed on the motherboard; when it is, in many cases it is set to off in the BIOS by default.

    BitLocker can be used with or without TPM. It is much more secure when coupled with TPM (and is preferable), but does not require it.

In Exercises 11.2 and 11.3, you'll test your system to see if a TPM chip is installed.

EXERCISE 11.2

Verifying the Presence of a TPM Chip in Windows XP

The following steps will allow you to verify whether or not a TPM chip is installed on your computer:

1. In Windows XP, go to Control Panel and choose System.

2. Click the Hardware tab and then choose Device Manager.

3. Expand the System Devices category. If a TPM chip is installed, it should appear here (common listings include NSC Integrated Platform Module, NSC TPM Device, or Winbond Trusted Platform Module). If you don't see the listing but are certain that you computer has such a chip, you may need to boot into your BIOS Setup menu and enable TPM before trying this again.

EXERCISE 11.3

Verifying the Presence of a TPM Chip in Windows Vista

The following steps will allow you to verify whether or not a TPM chip is installed on your computer:

1. In Windows Vista, go to Control Panel and choose Security.

2. Beneath Security, choose BitLocker Drive Encryption.

3. A dialog box will appear. The contents of the box do not matter, but what does matter is a link in the lower-left corner that will read TPM Administration. If this link is there, TPM is installed and active. If you don't see the link but are certain that your computer has such a chip, you may need to boot into your BIOS Setup menu and enable TPM before trying this again.

More information on TPM can be found at the Trusted Computing Group's website: `https://www.trustedcomputinggroup.org/home`.

Malicious Software Protection

Computer *viruses*—applications that carry out malicious actions—are one of the most annoying trends happening today: they are but one form of threat. Malicious software—also called malware—also includes worms, Trojan horses, spyware, and adware. It seems that almost every day someone invents a new virus. Some of these viruses do nothing more than give you a big "gotcha"; others destroy systems, contaminate networks, and wreak havoc on computer systems. A virus may act on your data or your operating system, but it's intent on doing harm and doing so without your consent. Viruses often include replication as a primary objective and try to infect as many machines as they can, as quickly as possible.

The business of providing software to computer users to protect them from viruses has become a huge industry. Several very good and well-established suppliers of antivirus software exist, and new virus-protection methods come on the scene almost as fast as new viruses. Antivirus software scans the computer's memory, disk files, and incoming and outgoing e-mail. The software typically uses a virus-definition file that is updated regularly by the manufacturer. If these files are kept up to date, the computer system will be relatively secure. Unfortunately, most people don't keep their virus definitions up to date. Users will exclaim that a new virus has come out, because they just got it. Upon examination, you'll often discover that their virus-definition file is months out of date. As you can see, the software part of the system will break down if the definition files aren't updated on a regular basis.

Data Access

Access control defines the methods used to ensure that users of your network can access only what they're authorized to access. The process of access control should be spelled out in the organization's security policies and standards. Several models exist to accomplish this. This section will briefly explain the following models:

- Bell-La Padula model
- Biba model
- Clark-Wilson model
- Information Flow model
- Noninterference model

Bell-La Padula Model

The *Bell-La Padula model* was designed for the military to address the storage and protection of classified information. The model is specifically designed to prevent unauthorized access to classified information. The model prevents the user from accessing information that has a higher security rating than she is authorized to access. The model also prevents information from being written to a lower level of security.

For example, if you're authorized to access Secret information, you aren't allowed to access Top Secret information, nor are you allowed to write to the system at a level lower than the Secret level. This creates upper and lower bounds for information storage; you can't *read up* or *write down*. This means that a user can't read information at a higher level than she's authorized to access. A person writing a file can't write down to a lower level than the security level she's authorized to access.

The process of preventing a write down keeps a user from accidentally breaching security by writing Secret information to the next lower level, Confidential. In our example, you can read Confidential information, but because you're approved at the Secret level, you can't write to the Confidential level. This model doesn't deal with integrity, only confidentiality. A user of Secret information can potentially modify other documents at the same level she possesses.

To see how this model works, think about corporate financial information. The chief financial officer (CFO) may have financial information about the company that he needs to protect. The Bell-La Padula model keeps him from inadvertently posting information at an access level lower than his access level (writing down), thus preventing unauthorized or accidental disclosure of sensitive information. Lower-level employees can't access this information because they can't read up to the level of the CFO.

The Biba Model

The *Biba model* was designed after the Bell-La Padula model. It's similar in concept to the Bell-La Padula model, but it's more concerned with information integrity, an area that the Bell-La Padula model doesn't address. In this model, there is no write up or read down. In short, if you're assigned access to Top Secret information, you can't read Secret information or write to any level higher than the level to which you're authorized. This keeps higher-level information pure by preventing less-reliable information from being intermixed with it. The Biba model was developed primarily for industrial uses, where confidentiality is usually less important than integrity.

Think about the data that is generated by a researcher for a scientific project. The researcher is responsible for managing the results of research from a lower-level project and incorporating it into her research data. If bad data were to get into her research, the whole research project would be ruined. With the Biba model, this accident can't happen. The researcher doesn't have access to the information from lower levels: that information must be promoted to the level of the researcher. This system keeps the researcher's data intact and prevents accidental contamination.

The Clark-Wilson Model

The *Clark-Wilson model* was developed after the Biba model. The approach is a little different from either the Biba or the Bell-La Padula method. In this model, data can't be accessed directly: it must be accessed through applications that have predefined capabilities. This process prevents unauthorized modification, errors, and fraud from occurring. If a user needs access to information at a certain level of security, a specific program is used. This program may allow only read access to the information. If a user needs to modify data, another application must be used. This allows a separation of duties in that individuals are granted access only to the tools they need. All transactions have associated audit files and mechanisms to report modifications. Access to information is gained by using a program that specializes in access management; this can be either a single program that controls all access or a set of programs that controls access. Many software-management programs work using this method of security.

Let's say you're working on a software product as part of a team. You may need to access certain code to include in your programs. You aren't authorized to modify this code; you're merely authorized to use it. You use a checkout program to get the code from the source library. Any attempt to put modified code back is prevented. The developers of the code in the source library are authorized to make changes. This process ensures that only people authorized to change the code can accomplish the task.

Information Flow Model

The *Information Flow model* is concerned with the properties of information flow, not only the direction of the flow. Both the Bell-La Padula and Biba models are concerned with information flow in predefined manners; they're considered information-flow models. However, this particular Information Flow model is concerned with all information flow, not just up or down. This model requires that each piece of information have unique properties, including operation capabilities. If an attempt is made to write lower-level information to a higher level, the model evaluates the properties of the information and determines whether the operation is legal. If the operation is illegal, the model prevents it from occurring.

Let's use the previous software project as an example. A developer may be working with a version of the software to improve functionality. When the programmer makes improvements to the code, he wants to put that code back into the library. If the attempt to write the code is successful, the code replaces the existing code. If a subsequent bug is found in the new code, the old code has been changed. The solution is to create a new version of the code that incorporates both the new code and the old code. Each subsequent change to the code requires a new version to be created. This process may consume more disk space, but it prevents things from getting lost, and it provides a mechanism to use or evaluate an older version of the code.

Noninterference Model

The *Noninterference model* is intended to ensure that higher-level security functions don't interfere with lower-level functions. In essence, if a higher-level user changes information, the lower-level user doesn't know about and isn't affected by the changes. This approach prevents the lower-level user from being able to deduce what changes are being made to the system; the lower-level user isn't aware that any changes have occurred above him.

Let's take one last look at the software project example with which we've been working. If a systems developer is making changes to the library that's being used by a lower-level programmer, changes may be made to the library without the lower-level programmer being aware of them. This lets the higher-level developer work on prototypes without affecting the development effort of the lower-level programmer. When the developer finishes the code, she publishes it to lower-level programmers. At this point, all users have access to the changes, and they can use them in their programs.

Data Remnant Removal

Data remnant removal is typically the name given to removing all usable data from media (usually hard drives, but any media can be included). Earlier in this chapter, we discussed the topic of wiping a hard drive, reformatting it, or using specialized utilities. Remember that when computer systems are retired, the disk drives should be zeroed out, and all magnetic media should be degaussed.

On a related topic, when data ages, it must often be archived and removed from live systems—it must often be archived and able to be retrieved at a later point in time if needed. Policies should be in place to dictate who has access to the archives, how and where the archives are stored, and how they're cataloged. The latter is of key importance because you want to be able to find data as expeditiously as possible, even when it has been removed from the system.

Password Management

One of the strongest ways to keep a system safe is to employ strong passwords and educate your users. To be strong, passwords should include upper- and lowercase letters, numbers, and other characters as allowed (which characters are allowed may differ based upon the operating system).

Users should be educated to understand how valuable data is and why it is important to keep their password strong, secret, and regularly changed.

Locking Workstations

Just as you would not park your car in a public garage and leave its doors wide open with the key in the ignition, you should educate users to not leave a workstation that they are logged in to when they attend meetings, go to lunch, and so forth. They should log out of the workstation or lock it. Locking the workstation should require a password (usually the same as their user password) in order to resume working at the workstation.

Identifying Security Problem Areas

The landscape of security is changing at a very fast pace. You, as a security professional, are primarily responsible for keeping current on the threats and changes that are occurring. You're also responsible for ensuring that systems are kept up-to-date. The following list briefly summarizes the areas you must be concerned about:

Operating system updates Make sure all scheduled maintenance is performed and updates and service packs are installed on all the systems in your environment. Many manufacturers are releasing security updates on their products to deal with newly discovered vulnerabilities. For example, Novell, Microsoft, and Linux manufacturers offer updates on their websites. In some cases, you can have the OS automatically notify you when an update becomes available; this notification helps busy administrators remember to keep their systems current.

As a security administrator, you understand the importance of applying all patches and updates to keep systems current and to close found weaknesses.

Always test updates on nonproduction machines before applying them to all computers and servers.

Application updates   Make sure all applications are kept to the most current levels. Older software may contain vulnerabilities that weren't detected until after the software was released. New software may have recently discovered vulnerabilities as well as yet-to-be-discovered ones. Apply updates to your application software when they're released to help minimize the impact of attacks on your systems.

One of the biggest exploitations that occur today involves application programs such as e-mail clients and word processing software. The manufacturers of these products regularly release updates to attempt to make them more secure. Like operating system updates, these should be checked regularly and applied.

Network device updates   Most newer network devices can provide high levels of security, or they can be configured to block certain types of traffic and IP addresses. Make sure logs are reviewed and, where necessary, ACLs updated to prevent attackers from disrupting your systems. These network devices are also frequently updated to counter new vulnerabilities and threats. Network devices should have their BIOS updated when the updates become available; doing so allows for an ever-increasing level of security in your environment.

ACL, like many other acronyms in computing, can stand for more than one thing. Access control lists are used with both permissions for files/folders and network access.

Cisco, 3Com, and other network manufacturers regularly offer network updates. These can frequently be applied online or by web-enabled systems. These devices are your front line of defense: you want to make sure they're kept up-to-date.

Policies and procedures   A policy that is out-of-date may be worse than no policy. Be aware of any changes in your organization and in the industry that make existing policies out-of-date. Many organizations set a review date as part of their policy-creation procedures. Periodically review your documentation to verify that your policies are effective and current.

In addition to focusing on these areas, you must stay current on security trends, threats, and tools available to help you provide security. The volume of threats is increasing, as are the measures, methods, and procedures used to counter them.

You must keep abreast of what is happening in the field, as well as the current best practices of the systems and applications you support. You're basically going to be functioning as a clearinghouse and data repository for your company's security. Make it a point to become a walking encyclopedia on security issues: doing so will improve your credibility and demonstrate your expertise. Both of these aspects enhance your career opportunities and equip you to be a leader in the field.

You should also make it a priority to train and educate users about malicious software. The more they know about the threats that are present—and the harm they can inflict—the more likely they are to act accordingly when they encounter a possible threat.

Table 11.2 summarizes the items where problems may occur and ways to identify that a problem exists.

TABLE 11.2   Identifying Problem Issues

Area	Identifying Symptoms
BIOS	Problems/compromises involving the BIOS typically prevent the system from starting properly. You may be asked to enter a password you don't know, or control of the system is never handed to the OS after POST.
Smart cards	Problems with smart cards become apparent when users are unable to access data or logs show that they accessed data they never truly did.
Biometrics	If there is a problem with biometrics, the user is unable to authenticate and unable to access resources.
Malicious software	Malicious software should be first detected by an antivirus program or other routine operation. If not, it will begin to show itself in the actions taking place on the system (deletion of executables, mass mailing, and so on).
File system	File system problems can fall into the category of users not being able to access data as they need to or everyone being granted access to data that they should not see.
Data access	Data access problems, as with file system issues, are usually those where users legitimately needing access to data can't access it, or too much permission is granted to users who don't need such access.

Exercises 11.4 and 11.5 walk you through one of the most basic tools included with Windows—Performance Monitor—and show how to use it effectively. Performance Monitor's objects and counters are very specific; you can use Performance Monitor as a general troubleshooting tool as well as a security-troubleshooting tool. For instance, you can see where resources are being utilized and where the activity is coming from. In this exercise, you'll use the Performance Monitor tool to become more familiar with its functionality.

EXERCISE 11.4

Working with Performance Monitor in Windows 2000 and Windows XP

1. Select Start ➢ Settings ➢ Control Panel ➢ Administrative Tools, and choose Performance. In XP, select Start ➢ Control Panel ➢ Administrative Tools ➢ Performance.

2. Click the Add Counters button, and choose to add the Processor Performance object.

3. Add the %Processor Time counter, and then click Close.

4. Choose Start ➢ Search ➢ For Files And Folders and click the Search Now button without specifying any particular files to look for. Quickly change to Performance Monitor and watch the impact of this search on the processor. This action is time consuming and therefore will help you notice the changes that take place in Performance Monitor. In XP, select Start ➢ Search ➢ Click here to use Search Companion ➢ All Files and Folders ➢ Search button.

5. Run the same operation again, but this time change your view within Performance Monitor to histogram (click the two buttons to the left of the plus sign [+]).

6. Run the same operation again, and change your view within Performance Monitor to report (click the button directly to the left of the plus sign).

7. Exit Performance Monitor.

EXERCISE 11.5

Working with Performance Monitor in Windows Vista

1. Select Start ➢ Control Panel ➢ Performance Information And Tools, and choose Advanced Tools.

2. Choose Open Reliability and Performance Monitor. You will be prompted to continue since the program must run with elevated privileges. Click Continue.

3. Click on Performance Monitor. A screen similar to the one shown here will appear.

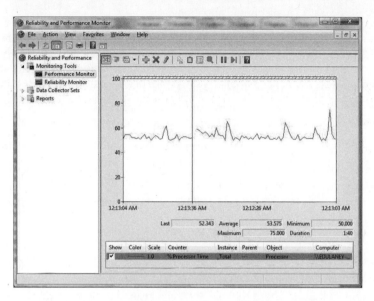

4. Click the Add Counters button (it looks like a large "+"), and a screen similar to this one will appear. Choose to add the Processor Performance object.

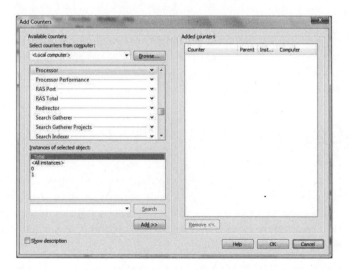

5. Add the %Processor Time counter, and then click Close.

6. Click the Start button, and then place your cursor in the Start Search box on the main menu. Enter ***.*** and click to start the search. Quickly change to Performance Monitor and watch the impact of this search on the processor. This action is time consuming and therefore will help you notice the changes that take place in Performance Monitor.

7. Run the same operation again, but this time change your view within Performance Monitor to histogram (click the two buttons to the left of the plus sign [+]).

8. Run the same operation again, and change your view within Performance Monitor to report (click the button directly to the left of the plus sign).

9. Exit Performance Monitor.

Summary

In this chapter, you learned about the various issues related to security that appear on the A+ Essentials exam. Security is a popular topic in computing and the ways in which a miscreant can cause harm increase regularly. Because of this, CompTIA expects everyone who is A+ certified to understand the basic principles of security and be familiar with solutions that exist.

In this chapter, you learned of security problem areas and issues that can be easily identified. Problem areas include viruses, Trojans, worms, and spyware. Security solutions include implementing encryption technology, using authentication, implementing firewalls, and incorporating security at the BIOS level.

Exam Essentials

Know the names, purpose, and characteristics of hardware and software security. Many types of hardware and software are used to provide security to an organization. These can range from firewalls (which can be software or hardware based) to smart cards. It's important to also know the different types of authentication technologies available and the various types of malicious software that exist.

Know the names, purpose, and characteristics of wireless security. Wireless networks can be encrypted through WEP and WPA technologies. Wireless controllers use SSIDs that must be configured in the network cards to allow communication with a specific access point. However, using SSIDs doesn't necessarily prevent wireless networks from being monitored, and there are vulnerabilities specific to wireless devices.

Know the names, purpose, and characteristics of data and physical security.   Know the basics of encryption. You should also be aware of social-engineering concerns and the need for a useful incident response policy.

Implement software security preventive maintenance techniques.   Know the importance of keeping the systems current, applying patches as they're released/needed, and keeping your knowledge/skills up-to-date.

Install, configure, upgrade, and optimize hardware, software, and data security.   Know the basics of the following items: BIOS, smart cards, authentication technologies, malicious software protection, data access, and data remnant removal.

Diagnose and troubleshoot procedures and troubleshooting techniques for security.   It's important to know the symptoms that may arise in the problem areas and to be able to quickly identify them. This allows you to then hone in on the source of the problem and begin troubleshooting in earnest.

Review Questions

1. Which component of physical security addresses outer-level access control?

   A. Perimeter security

   B. Mantraps

   C. Security zones

   D. Strong passwords

2. Which technology uses a physical characteristic to establish identity?

   A. Biometrics

   B. Surveillance

   C. Smart card

   D. CHAP authenticator

3. As part of your training program, you're trying to educate users on the importance of security. You explain to them that not every attack depends on implementing advanced technological methods. Some attacks, you explain, take advantage of human shortcoming to gain access that should otherwise be denied. What term do you use to describe attacks of this type?

   A. Social engineering

   B. IDS system

   C. Perimeter security

   D. Biometrics

4. You've recently been hired by ACME to do a security audit. The managers of this company feel that their current security measures are inadequate. Which information access control prevents users from writing information down to a lower level of security and prevents users from reading above their level of security?

   A. Bell-La Padula model

   B. Biba model

   C. Clark-Wilson model

   D. Noninterference model

5. What tool is used in Windows Vista to encrypt an entire volume?

   A. BitLocker

   B. Syslock

   C. Drive Defender

   D. NLock

6. Which of the following is a chip that can store cryptographic keys, passwords, or certificates and can be used to generate values used with whole disk encryption?

   A. CHAP

   B. MAC

   C. TPM

   D. BAP

7. What biometric reader are many laptop manufacturers now including on their systems?

   A. Voice recognition

   B. Retinal scanner

   C. Fingerprint scanner

   D. Face recognition

8. You've been assigned to mentor a junior administrator and bring him up to speed quickly. The topic you're currently explaining is authentication. Which method uses a KDC to accomplish authentication for users, programs, or systems?

   A. CHAP

   B. Kerberos

   C. Biometrics

   D. Smart cards

9. Which authentication method sends a challenge to the client that is encrypted and then sent back to the server?

   A. Kerberos

   B. PAP

   C. DAC

   D. CHAP

10. After a careful risk analysis, the value of your company's data has been increased. Accordingly, you're expected to implement authentication solutions that reflect the increased value of the data. Which of the following authentication methods uses more than one authentication process for a logon?

    A. Multifactor

    B. Biometrics

    C. Smart card

    D. Kerberos

11. Which of the following services or protocols should be avoided in a network if possible in order to increase security?

    A. E-mail

    B. Telnet

    C. WWW

    D. ICMP

12. Of the following services, which one would be most likely to utilize a retinal scan?

    A. Auditing

    B. Authentication

    C. Access control

    D. Data confidentiality

13. One of the vice presidents of the company calls a meeting with information technology after a recent trip to competitors' sites. She reports that many of the companies she visited granted access to their buildings only after fingerprint scans, and she wants similar technology employed at this company. Of the following, which technology relies on a physical attribute of the user for authentication?

    A. Smart card

    B. Biometrics

    C. Mutual authentication

    D. Tokens

14. Your company provides medical data to doctors from a worldwide database. Because of the sensitive nature of the data you work with, it's imperative that authentication be established on each session and be valid only for that session. Which of the following authentication methods provides credentials that are valid only during a single session?

    A. Tokens

    B. Certificate

    C. Smart card

    D. Kerberos

15. Your help desk has informed you that they received an urgent call from the vice president last night requesting his logon ID and password. What type of attack is this?

    A. Spoofing

    B. Replay attack

    C. Social engineering

    D. Trojan horse

16. Internal users are reporting repeated attempts to infect their systems as reported to them by pop-up messages from their virus-scanning software. According to the pop-up messages, the virus seems to be the same in every case. What is the most likely culprit?

    A. A server is acting as a carrier for a virus.

    B. You have a caterpillar virus.

    C. Your antivirus software has malfunctioned.

    D. A DoS attack is under way.

17. You're working late one night, and you notice that the hard disk on your new computer is very active even though you aren't doing anything on the computer and it isn't connected to the Internet. What is the most likely suspect?

    A. A disk failure is imminent.

    B. A virus is spreading in your system.

    C. Your system is under a DoS attack.

    D. TCP/IP hijacking is being attempted.

18. You're the administrator for a large bottling company. At the end of each month, you routinely view all logs and look for discrepancies. This month, your e-mail system error log reports a large number of unsuccessful attempts to log on. It's apparent that the e-mail server is being targeted. Which type of attack is most likely occurring?

    A. Software exploitation attack

    B. Backdoor attack

    C. Worm

    D. TCP/IP hijacking

19. Upper management has decreed that a firewall must be put in place immediately, before your site suffers an attack similar to one that struck a sister company. Responding to this order, your boss instructs you to implement a packet filter by the end of the week. A packet filter performs which function?

    A. Prevents unauthorized packets from entering the network

    B. Allows all packets to leave the network

    C. Allows all packets to enter the network

    D. Eliminates collisions in the network

20. Which media is susceptible to viruses?

    A. Tape

    B. Memory stick

    C. CD-R

    D. All of the above

Answers to Review Questions

1. **A.** The first layer of access control is perimeter security. Perimeter security is intended to delay or deter entrance into a facility.

2. **A.** Biometrics is a technology that uses personal characteristics, such as a retinal pattern or fingerprint, to establish identity.

3. **A.** Social engineering uses the inherent trust in the human species, as opposed to technology, to gain access to your environment.

4. **A.** The Bell-La Padula model is intended to protect confidentiality of information. This is accomplished by prohibiting users from reading above their security level and preventing them from writing below their security level.

5. **A.** BitLocker provides drive encryption and is available with Windows Vista.

6. **C.** TPM is the name assigned to a chip that can store cryptographic keys, passwords, or certificates. The TPM can be used to generate values used with whole disk encryption.

7. **C.** Many laptop manufacturers now including fingerprint scanners on their systems.

8. **B.** Kerberos uses a key distribution center to authenticate a principle. The KDC provides a credential that can be used by all Kerberos-enabled servers and applications.

9. **D.** Challenge Handshake Authentication Protocol (CHAP) sends a challenge to the originating client. This challenge is sent back to the server, and the encryption results are compared. If the challenge is successful, the client is logged on.

10. **A.** A multifactor-authentication process uses two or more processes for logon. A two-factor method might use smart cards and biometrics for logon.

11. **B.** Telnet shouldn't be used if possible. Telnet sends user ID and password information to the Telnet server unencrypted. This creates a potential security problem in an Internet environment.

12. **B.** Authentication is a service that requests the principal user to provide proof of his identity. A retinal scan is a very secure form of evidence used in high-security companies and government agencies.

13. **B.** Biometric technologies rely on a physical characteristic of the user to verify identity. Biometric devices typically use either a hand pattern or a retinal scan to accomplish this.

14. **A.** Tokens are created when a user or system successfully authenticates. The token is destroyed when the session is over.

15. **C.** Someone trying to con your organization into revealing account and password information is launching a social engineering attack.

16. A. Some viruses won't damage a system in an attempt to spread into all the other systems in a network. These viruses use that system as the carrier of the virus.

17. B. A symptom of many viruses is unusual activity on the system disk. This is caused by the virus spreading to other files on your system.

18. A. A software exploitation attack attempts to exploit weaknesses in software. A common attack attempts to communicate with an established port to gain unauthorized access.

19. A. Packet filters prevent unauthorized packets from entering or leaving a network. Packet filters are a type of firewall that block specified traffic based on IP address, protocol, and many other attributes.

20. D. All of these devices can store and pass viruses to uninfected systems. Make sure that all files are scanned for viruses before they're copied to these media.

Chapter

12

Understanding Operational Procedures

THE FOLLOWING COMPTIA A+ ESSENTIALS EXAM OBJECTIVES ARE COVERED IN THIS CHAPTER:

- ✓ **6.1 Outline the purpose of appropriate safety and environmental procedures and given a scenario apply them**

  - ▪ ESD
  - ▪ EMI
    - ▪ Network interference
    - ▪ Magnets
  - ▪ RFI
    - ▪ Cordless phone interference
    - ▪ Microwaves
  - ▪ Electrical safety
    - ▪ CRT
    - ▪ Power supply
    - ▪ Inverter
    - ▪ Laser printers
    - ▪ Matching power requirements of equipment with power distribution and UPSs
  - ▪ Material Safety Data Sheets (MSDS)
  - ▪ Cable management
    - ▪ Avoiding trip hazards

- Physical safety
  - Heavy devices
  - Hot components
- Environmental—consider proper disposal procedures

✓ **6.2 Given a scenario, demonstrate the appropriate use of communication skills and professionalism in the workplace**

- Use proper language—avoid jargon, acronyms, slang
- Maintain a positive attitude
- Listen and do not interrupt a customer
- Be culturally sensitive
- Be on time
  - If late contact the customer
- Avoid distractions
  - Personal calls
  - Talking to co-workers while interacting with customers
  - Personal interruptions
- Dealing with a difficult customer or situation
  - Avoid arguing with customers and/or being defensive
  - Do not minimize customers' problems
  - Avoid being judgmental
  - Clarify customer statements
    - Ask open-ended questions to narrow the scope of the problem
    - Restate the issue of question to verify understanding
- Set and meet expectations/timeline and communicate status with the customer
  - Offer different repair/replacement options of applicable
  - Provide proper documentation on the services provided
  - Follow up with customers/users at a later date to verify satisfaction
- Deal appropriately with customers confidential materials
  - Located on computer, desktop, printer, etc.

If you talk to anyone who has been in the computer industry for several years, they will tell you about the remarkable number of changes that have transformed and keep transforming their work environment. If you talk to someone who was working on computers back in the 1980s or even further back in the 1970s about those times, you'll quickly realize that the computer world was only for those with technical savvy and, in many cases, a soldering iron.

Today's computing world is obviously very different. We live in a world where computers are a ubiquitous part of home offices, schools, and workplaces. Most people born in the 1990s or later probably can't remember a life without computers or the Internet. There's little doubt that computers have revolutionized the way we live and work. Computers allow us to be more productive, stay in touch with friends and family, and learn about any topic under the sun with just a few clicks of the mouse.

The proliferation of computers in today's society has created numerous jobs for technicians. Presumably that's why you're reading this book: you want to get your CompTIA A+ certification. Many others who don't fix computers professionally do like tinkering with them as a hobby. Regardless of your reason, if you're going to be inside a computer, you always need to be aware of safety issues. There's no sense in getting yourself hurt or killed—literally.

Think of the number of people today who own computers. You probably know people—maybe yourself—who own several. Because computers have become easier to use, more people are using them. More people using them means more people who don't understand technology (or who are even scared of the technology) are using them. Your job as a technician (or tech-savvy friend) is to help those with less knowledge solve their computer problems. To do that you need to have a good bedside manner.

As a technician and a professional you need to know how to interact with others, whether they're customers, vendors, fellow employees, managers, or your grandma. CompTIA recognizes the importance of this ability and has added it to the A+ Essentials exam.

This chapter looks at the foundations of two key operational procedures you should follow: safety and communication and professionalism. While these two topics might not be top-of-mind for you every day (hopefully you don't go to work every day thinking, "Okay, don't get killed by a monitor" or, "Let's see if I can be nice to someone today"), they should be integrated into your work processes.

In this chapter we will start off talking about safety and the environment. Observing proper safety procedures can help prevent injury or death. The environment is a two-sided discussion. The environment affects computers (via things like dust, sunlight, and water), but computers can also potentially harm the environment. We'll consider both sides as we move through this chapter.

In the second part of this chapter, we'll switch to discussing professionalism and communication, and focus on topics you need to know for your exam study. While many will argue that soft skills are beyond the scope of an IT book, they are tested in the A+ exam. The coverage here will help you in your exam preparation.

Understanding Safety and Environmental Issues

As a provider of a hands-on service (repairing, maintaining, or upgrading someone's computer), you need to be aware of some general safety tips, because if you are not careful, you could harm yourself or the equipment. You also need to be aware of the environment, considering that it plays a role in how the computer can perform and for how long. In the following sections, we'll talk about identifying hazards and environmental concerns, understanding safety documentation, using the right tools for the job, and handling accidents.

Identifying Potential Safety Hazards

Anything can be a potential safety hazard, right? Okay, maybe that statement is a bit too paranoid, but there *are* many things, both human-created and environmental, that can cause safety problems when working with and around computers.

Perhaps the most important aspect of computers that you should be aware of is that they not only *use* electricity, they also *store* electrical charge after they're turned off. This makes the power supply and the monitor pretty much off-limits to anyone but a repair person trained specifically for those devices. In addition, the computer's processor and various parts of the printer run at extremely high temperatures, and you can get burned if you try to handle them immediately after they've been in operation.

Those are just two general safety measures that should concern you. There are plenty more. When discussing safety issues with regard to PCs, let's break them down into three general areas:

- Computer components
- Natural elements
- Work environment

Computer Components

As mentioned earlier, computers use electricity. And as you're probably aware, electricity can hurt or kill you. The first rule when working inside a computer is to always make sure it's powered off. So if you have to open the computer to inspect or replace parts (as you will with most repairs), be sure to turn off the machine before you begin. Leaving it plugged in is fine in most cases (we'll talk about that more in the section titled "Preventing Electrostatic Discharge," later in this chapter).

There's one exception to the power-off rule: you don't have to power off the computer when working with hot-swappable parts, which are designed to be unplugged and plugged back in when the computer is on. Most of these components have an externally accessible interface (such as USB devices or hot-swappable hard drives), so you don't need to crack the computer case.

 Real World Scenario

Don't Forget the Case

One aspect people frequently overlook is the case. Cases are generally made of metal, and some computer cases have very sharp edges inside, so be careful when handling them. You can, for example, cut yourself by jamming your fingers between the case and the frame when you try to force the case back on. Also of particular interest are drive bays. Countless technicians have scraped or cut their hands on drive bays when trying in vain to plug a drive cable into the motherboard. Particularly sharp edges can be covered with duct tape—just make sure you're covering only metal, and nothing with electrical components on it.

The Power Supply

Do not take the issue of safety and electricity lightly. Removing the power supply from its internal casing can be dangerous. The current flowing through the power supply normally follows a complete circuit; when your body breaks the circuit, your body becomes part of that circuit.

The two biggest dangers with power supplies are burning yourself and electrocuting yourself. These risks usually go hand in hand. If you touch a bare wire that is carrying current, you could get electrocuted. A large-enough current passing through the wire (and you) can cause severe burns. (It can also cause your heart to stop, your muscles to seize, and your brain to stop functioning. In short, it can kill you.) Electricity always finds the best path to ground. And because people are basically bags of saltwater (an excellent conductor of electricity), electricity will use us as a conductor if we are grounded.

Although it is possible to open a power supply to work on it, doing so is *not* recommended. Power supplies contain several capacitors that can hold *lethal* charges *long after they have been unplugged!* It is extremely dangerous to open the case of a power supply. Besides, power supplies are pretty cheap. It would probably cost less to replace one than to try to fix it, and this approach would be much safer.

In the late 1990s, a few mass computer manufacturers experimented with using open power supplies in their computers to save money. I don't know if any deaths occurred because of such incompetence, but it was definitely a very bad idea.

Real World Scenario

Fire Safety

Repairing a computer isn't often the cause of an electrical fire. However, you should know how to extinguish such a fire properly. Four major classes of fire extinguishers are available, one for each type of flammable substance: A for wood and paper fires, B for flammable liquids, C for electrical fires, and D (metal powder or NaCl [salt]) for flammable metals such as phosphorus and sodium.

The most popular type of fire extinguisher today is the multipurpose, or ABC-rated, extinguisher. It contains a dry chemical powder (e.g., sodium bicarbonate, monoammonium phosphate) that smothers the fire and cools it at the same time. For electrical fires (which may be related to a shorted-out wire in a power supply), make sure the fire extinguisher will work for class C fires. If you don't have an extinguisher that is specifically rated for electrical fires (type C), you can use an ABC-rated extinguisher.

Unless you have been specifically trained to do so, *never* open a power supply.

Current vs. Voltage—Which Is More Dangerous?

When talking about power and safety, you will almost always hear the saying, "It's not the volts that kill you, it's the amps." That's mostly true. However, an explanation is in order.

The number of volts in a power source represents its potential to do work. But volts don't do anything by themselves. Current (amperage, or amps) is the force behind the work done by electricity. Here's an analogy to help explain this concept. Say you have two boulders; one weighs 10 pounds, the other 100 pounds, and each is 100' off the ground. If you drop them, which one will do more work? The obvious answer is the 100 pound boulder. They both have the same potential to do work (100' of travel), but the 100 pound boulder has more mass and thus more force. Voltage is analogous to the distance the boulder is from the ground, and amperage is analogous to the mass of the boulder.

This is why you can produce static electricity on the order of 50,000 volts and not electrocute yourself. Even though this electricity has a great *potential* for work, it does very little work because the amperage is so low. This also explains why you can weld metal with 110 volts. Welders use only 110 (sometimes 220) volts, but they also use anywhere from 50 to 200 amps!

If you ever have to work on a power supply, for safety's sake you should discharge all capacitors within it. To do this, connect a resistor across the leads of the capacitor with a rating of 3 watts or more and a resistance of 100 ohms (Ω) per volt. For example, to discharge a 225-volt capacitor, you would use a 22.5kΩ resistor (225 volts times 100Ω = 22,500Ω, or 22.5kΩ).

The Printer

If you've ever attempted to repair a printer, you might have sometimes thought there was a little monster in there hiding all the screws from you. Besides missing screws, here are some things to watch out for when repairing printers:

Using an egg carton (or other container with small compartments) is a great way to store and keep track of screws you take out of a device when you're working on it.

- When handling a toner cartridge from a laser printer or page printer, do not turn it upside down. You will find yourself spending more time cleaning the printer and the surrounding area than fixing the printer.

- Do not put any objects into the feeding system (in an attempt to clear the path) when the printer is running.

- Laser printers generate a laser that is hazardous to your eyes. Do not look directly into the source of the laser.

- If it's an inkjet printer, do not try to blow in the ink cartridge to clear a clogged opening— that is, unless you like the taste of ink.

- Some parts of a laser printer (such as the EP cartridge) will be damaged if you touch them. Your skin produces oils and has a small surface layer of dead skin cells. These substances can collect on the delicate surface of the EP cartridge and cause malfunctions. Bottom line: Keep your fingers out of places they don't belong!

- Laser printers can get extremely hot. Don't burn yourself on internal components.

When working with printers, we follow some pretty simple guidelines. If there's a messed-up setting, paper jam, or ink or toner problem, we will fix it. If it's something other than that, we call a certified printer repair person. The inner workings of printers can get pretty complex, and it's best to call someone trained to make those types of repairs.

The Monitor

Other than the power supply, the most dangerous component to try to repair is the monitor, or cathode-ray tube (CRT). In fact, we recommend that you *do not* try to repair monitors of any kind.

To avoid the extremely hazardous environment contained inside the monitor—it can retain a high-voltage charge for hours after it's been turned off—take it to a certified monitor technician or television repair shop. The repair shop or certified technician will know the proper procedures for discharging the monitor, which involve attaching a resistor to the flyback transformer's charging capacitor to release the high-voltage electrical charge that builds up during use. They will also be able to determine whether the monitor can be repaired or needs to be replaced. Remember, the monitor works in its own extremely protected environment (the monitor case) and may not respond well to your desire to try to open it.

WARNING   The CRT is vacuum sealed. Be extremely careful when handling the CRT. If you break the glass, it will implode, which can send glass in any direction.

Even though we recommend not repairing monitors, the A+ exam tests your knowledge of the safety practices to use when you need to do so. If you have to open a monitor, you must first discharge the high-voltage charge on it by using a *high-voltage probe*. This probe has a very large needle, a gauge that indicates volts, and a wire with an alligator clip. Attach the alligator clip to a ground (usually the round pin on the power cord). Slip the probe needle underneath the high-voltage cup on the monitor. You will see the gauge spike to around 15,000 volts and slowly reduce to zero. When it reaches zero, you may remove the high-voltage probe and service the high-voltage components of the monitor.

WARNING   Do *not* use an ESD strap when discharging the monitor; doing so can lead to a fatal electric shock.

Working with LCD monitors or any device with a fluorescent or LCD backlight presents a unique safety challenge. These types of devices require an *inverter*, which provides the high-voltage, high-frequency energy needed to power the backlight.

The inverter is a small circuit board installed behind the LCD panel that takes AC power and converts (inverts) it for the backlight. If you've ever seen a laptop or handheld device with a flickering screen or perpetual dimness, it was likely an inverter problem. Inverters store energy even when their power source is cut off, so they have the potential to discharge that energy if you mess with them. Be careful!

The Keyboard and Mouse

Okay, we know you're thinking, "What danger could a keyboard or mouse cause?" We admit that not much danger is associated with these components, but there are a couple of safety concerns you should always keep in mind.

First, if your mouse has a cord, you can trip over it so make sure it's safely out of the way. Second, you could short-circuit your keyboard if you accidentally spill liquid on it. Keyboards don't function well with half a can of cola in their innards!

Natural Elements

Computers should always be operated in cool environments away from direct sunlight and water sources. This is also true when you're working on computers. We know that heat is an enemy of electrical components. Dirt and dust act as great insulators, trapping heat inside components. When components run hotter than they should, they have a greater chance of breaking down faster.

 Real World Scenario

Play It Safe with Common Sense

When you're repairing a PC, do not leave it unattended. Someone could walk into the room and inadvertently bump the machine, causing failure. Worse, they could step on pieces that may be lying around and get hurt. It is also not a good idea to work on the PC alone. If you're injured, someone should be around to help if you need it. Finally, if you're fatigued, you may find it difficult to concentrate and focus on what you are doing. There are real safety measures related to repairing PCs, so the most important thing to remember is to pay close attention to what you are doing.

It pretty much should go without saying, but I'll say it anyway: water and electricity don't mix. Keep liquids away from computers. If you need your morning coffee while fixing a PC, make sure the coffee has a tight and secure lid.

Water and Servers Don't Mix

This situation happened at one of the companies one of the authors used to work for. The building needed some roof repairs. Repairs went on for several days, and then the weekend came. It just so happened that the area they were working on was over the server room. That weekend was a particularly rainy one, and of course over the weekend no one was in the office.

Monday morning came, and the IT staff arrived to find that the server room was partially flooded. Rain had come in through weaknesses in the roof, caused by the maintenance, and had flooded through the drop ceiling and into the server room. Nearly half a million dollars of equipment was ruined.

Although this is an extreme example, it illustrates an important point: always be aware of the environment you're working in, and be alert to potential sources of problems for your computer equipment.

Work Environment

We've already talked about some work environment issues to be aware of. For example, don't put a computer next to the break room sink, and keep computers out of direct sunlight (even if the desk location is great).

A couple of other things to watch out for include trip hazards, atmospheric conditions, and high-voltage areas.

Cables are a common cause of tripping. If at all possible, run cables through drop ceilings or through conduits to keep them out of the way. If you need to lay a cable through a trafficked area, use a cable floor guard to keep the cables in place and safe from crushing. Floor guards come in a variety of lengths and sizes (for just a few cables or for a lot of cables). Figure 12.1 shows a cable guard.

FIGURE 12.1 Floor cable guard

Another useful tool to keep cables under control is a cable tie, like the one shown in Figure 12.2. It's simply a plastic tie that holds two or more cables together. They come in different sizes and colors so you're bound to find one that suits your needs.

FIGURE 12.2 Cable tie

In a pinch, and without a floor cable guard, you can use tape such as duct tape to secure your cables to the floor. This is recommended only as a temporary fix for two reasons. First, it's not much less of a trip hazard than just having the cables run across the floor. Second, duct tape doesn't protect the cables from being crushed if people step on them or heavy objects are moved over them.

Exercise 12.1 can help increase your awareness of trip hazards.

EXERCISE 12.1

Finding Trip Hazards

This is a simple exercise that you can modify and use as needed. Its purpose is to illustrate the hazards that are around your office that you may have not realized were there.

1. Walk around the server room and count how many cables are lying on the floor.

2. Walk around the client areas and see how many cables are lying on the floor, or are exposed underneath cubicles.

Maybe you're fortunate and don't find any, but odds are you found at least one area that has exposed cables that should not be exposed. You can reapply this exercise for other dangerous items such as exposed wires and exposed sharp edges.

Atmospheric conditions that you need to be aware of include areas with high static electricity or excessive humidity.

We'll talk more about atmospheric conditions in the section "Preventing Electrostatic Discharge," later in this chapter.

Finally, be aware of high-voltage areas. Computers do need electricity to run but only in measured amounts. Running or fixing computers in high-voltage areas can cause problems for the electrical components and can cause problems for you if something should go wrong.

Identifying Environmental Concerns

It is estimated that more than 25 percent of all the lead (a poisonous substance) in landfills today is a result of consumer electronics components. Because consumer electronics (televisions, VCRs, stereos) contain hazardous substances, many states require that they be disposed of as hazardous waste. Computers are no exception. Monitors contain several carcinogens and phosphors, as well as mercury and lead. The computer itself may contain several lubricants and chemicals as well as lead. Printers contain plastics and chemicals such as toners and inks that are also hazardous. All of these items should be disposed of properly.

Remember all those 386 and 486 computers that came out in the late 1980s and are now considered antiques? Where did they all go? Is there an Old Computers Home somewhere that is using these computer systems for good purposes, or are they lying in a junkyard somewhere? Or could it be that some folks just cannot let go, and have a stash of old computer systems and computer parts in the dark depths of their basements?

Although it is relatively easy to put old machines away, thinking you might be able to put them to good use again someday, doing so is not realistic. Most computers are obsolete as soon as you buy them. And if you have not used them recently, your old computer components will more than likely never be used again.

We recycle cans, plastic, and newspaper, so why not recycle computer equipment? The problem, as we mentioned, is that most computers contain small amounts of hazardous substances. Some countries are exploring the option of recycling electrical machines, but most have still not enacted appropriate measures to enforce their proper disposal. However, we can do a few things as consumers and caretakers of our environment to promote the proper disposal of computer equipment:

- Check with the manufacturer. Some manufacturers will take back outdated equipment for parts (and may even pay you for them).

- Properly dispose of solvents or cleaners used with computers, as well as their containers, at a local hazardous waste disposal facility.

- Disassemble the machine and reuse the parts that are good.

- Check out businesses that can melt down the components for the lead or gold plating.

- Contact the Environmental Protection Agency (EPA) for a list of local or regional waste disposal sites that accept used computer equipment. The EPA's web address is http://www.epa.gov.

- Check with the EPA to see if what you are disposing of has a Material Safety Data Sheet (MSDS). These sheets contain information about the toxicity of a product and whether it can be disposed of in the trash. They also contain lethal-dose information.

- Check with local nonprofit or education organizations that may be interested in using the equipment.

- Check out the Internet for possible waste disposal sites. Table 12.1 lists a few websites we came across that deal with disposal of used computer equipment.

TABLE 12.1 Computer Recycling Websites

Site Name	Web Address
Computer Recycle Center	http://www.recycles.com
Computer Recycling Center	http://www.crc.org
RE-PC	http://www.repc.com

In addition to recycling hardware, you can recycle consumables. In particular, you should make a special effort to recycle batteries. Batteries contain several chemicals that are harmful to the environment and won't degrade safely. Batteries should not be thrown away; they should be recycled according to your local laws. Check with your local authorities to find out how batteries should be recycled.

There are businesses that offer to recycle consumables, such as ink cartridges or printer ribbons. However, although these businesses are doing us a favor in our quest to recycle, it might not be the best way to keep up with the recycling agenda. Why? Well, we don't recommend the use of recycled ink cartridges; they may clog, the ink quality is not as good, and the small circuit board on the cartridge may be damaged. Similarly, recycled printer ribbons will lose their ability to hold ink after a while and don't last as long as new ribbons. And recycled toner cartridges don't operate properly after refilling. However, when you are through with the old cartridges, give them to organizations that do recycle so they can have some fresh cores. That way, you can safely dispose of your cartridge and benefit the environment at the same time.

Remember that recycling is a way to keep our environment clean and our landfills empty. If we can take one step to recycle or redistribute outdated computer equipment, we are one step closer to having a healthier environment. However, we should not have to sacrifice quality in the process.

 We will discuss the proper disposal of display devices and batteries later in this chapter.

Cleaning Systems

The cleanliness of a computer is extremely important. Buildup of dust, dirt, and oils can prevent various mechanical parts of a computer from operating. Because this topic is important, the A+ exam will test your knowledge of the proper way to use various cleaning products on computer systems.

Computer components get dirty. Dirt reduces their operating efficiency and, ultimately, their life. Cleaning them is definitely important. But cleaning them with the right cleaning compounds is equally important. Using the wrong compounds can leave residue behind that is more harmful than the dirt you are trying to remove.

Most computer cases and monitor cases can be cleaned by using mild soapy water on a clean, lint-free cloth. Do *not* use any kind of solvent-based cleaner on either monitor or LCD screens, because doing so can cause discoloration and damage to the screen surface. Most often, a simple dusting with a damp cloth (moistened with water) will suffice. Make sure the power is off before you put anything wet near a computer. Dampen (don't soak) a cloth in mild soap solution and wipe the dirt and dust from the case. Then wipe the moisture from the case with a dry, lint-free cloth. Anything with a plastic or metal case can be cleaned in this manner.

Additionally, if you spill anything on a keyboard, you can clean it by soaking it in distilled, demineralized water and drying it off. The extra minerals and impurities have been removed from this type of water, so it will not leave any traces of residue that might interfere with the proper operation of the keyboard after cleaning. The same holds true for the keyboard's cable and its connector.

The electronic connectors of computer equipment, on the other hand, should never touch water. Instead, use a swab moistened in distilled, denatured isopropyl alcohol (also known as electronics or contact cleaner and found in electronics stores) to clean contacts. Doing so will take oxidation off the copper contacts.

Some technicians say you can use a pencil eraser to clean the oxidation from contacts. You should *never* do this, because erasers contain trace amounts of acids from their manufacturing process that can damage the contacts after cleaning.

Finally, the best way to remove dust and dirt from the inside of the computer is to use compressed air instead of vacuuming. Compressed air can be more easily directed and doesn't easily produce electrostatic discharge (ESD) damage (as vacuuming could). Simply blow the dust from inside the computer by using a stream of compressed air. However, make sure to do this outside, so you don't blow dust all over your work area or yourself. Nonstatic vacuum cleaners are available that are specially made for cleaning computer components (such as keyboards and case fans). Their nozzles are grounded to prevent ESD from damaging the components of the computer. However, compressed air is usually a better method, as long as it's done outside.

One unique challenge when cleaning printers is spilled toner. It sticks to everything. There are two methods to deal with this. First, blow all the loose toner out of the printer by using compressed air, being careful not to blow the toner into any of the printing mechanisms. Then, using a cool, damp cloth, wipe any remaining particles out of the printer.

Environmental Problems

Computers in manufacturing plants are particularly susceptible to environmental hazards. One technician reported a situation with a computer that had been used on the manufacturing floor of a large equipment manufacturer. The computer and keyboard were covered with a black substance that would not come off. (It was later revealed to be a combination of paint mist and molybdenum grease.) There was so much diesel fume residue in the power supply fan that it would barely turn. The insides and components were covered with a thin, greasy layer of muck. To top it all off, the computer *smelled terrible*!

Despite all this, the computer still functioned. However, it was prone to reboot itself every now and again. The solution was (as you may have guessed) to clean every component thoroughly and replace the power supply. The muck on the components was able to conduct a small current. Sometimes that current would go where it wasn't wanted, and zap!—a reboot. In addition, the power supply fan is supposed to partially cool the inside of the computer. In this computer, the fan was detrimental to the computer because it got its cooling air from the shop floor, which contained diesel fumes, paint fumes, and other chemical fumes. Needless to say, those fumes aren't good for computer components.

Computers are like human beings. They have similar tolerances to heat and cold (although computers like the cold better than we do). In general, anything comfortable to us is comfortable to a computer. Computers need lots of clean, moving air to keep them functioning. They don't, however, require food or drink (except maybe a few RAM chips now and again)—keep those away from the computer.

It's bad practice to eat, drink, or smoke around your computer. Smoke particles contain tar that can get inside the computer and cause problems similar to those described earlier.

One way to ensure that the environment has the least possible effect on your computer is to always leave the blanks in the empty slots on the back of your box. These pieces of metal are designed to keep dirt, dust, and other foreign matter out of the inside of the computer. They also maintain proper airflow within the case to ensure that the computer does not overheat.

Using Safety Documentation

Each piece of computer equipment you purchase comes with a manual. In the manual are detailed instructions on the proper handling and use of that component. In addition, many manuals give information on how to open the device for maintenance, or on whether you should even open the device at all.

Don't throw manuals away. Keep a drawer of a file cabinet specifically for hardware manuals (and keep it organized!). You can always look up information on the Internet as well, but having paper manuals on hand is useful for two reasons. One, you may need to fix something when Internet access isn't readily available (router problems, anyone?). Two, some companies are required to keep hardware documentation in case of an audit (such as for ISO 9000–compliant organizations).

Another place to find safety information is in *Material Safety Data Sheets (MSDSs)*. MSDSs include information such as physical product data (boiling point, melting point, flash point, and so forth), potential health risks, storage and disposal recommendations, and spill/leak procedures. With this information, technicians and emergency personnel know how to handle the product as well as respond in the event of an emergency.

MSDSs are typically associated with hazardous chemicals. Indeed, chemicals do not ship without them. MSDSs are not intended for consumer use; rather, they're made for employees or emergency workers who are consistently exposed to the risks of the particular product.

The United States *Occupational Safety and Health Administration (OSHA)* mandates MSDSs only for products that

- Meet OSHA's definition of *hazardous* (it poses a physical or health hazard)

  and

- Are "known to be present in the workplace in such a manner that employees may be exposed under normal conditions of use or in a foreseeable emergency"

We will look at OSHA more closely in the section "Working in a Safe Environment" later in this chapter.

One of the interesting things about MSDSs is that OSHA does not require companies to distribute them to consumers. Most companies will be happy to distribute one for their products, but again, they are under no obligation to do so.

If employees are working with materials that have MSDSs, those employees are required by OSHA to have "ready access" to MSDS sheets. This means that employees need to be able to get to the sheets without having to fetch a key, contact a supervisor, or submit a procedure request. Remember the file cabinet drawer you have for the hardware manuals? MSDSs should also be kept readily accessible. Exercise 12.2 helps you find your MSDS sheets and get familiar with them.

EXERCISE 12.2

Finding MSDS Sheets

This exercise has you locate your MSDS sheets and find critical information on them.

1. Locate the MSDS sheets in your workplace. You might have to ask a manager. (Do you even have them?)

2. Find one for a product you're interested in.

3. Are there any potential health effects listed for this item? What are they?

4. What is the proper disposal procedure for this item?

It's not likely that you're going to memorize or need to memorize everything on an MSDS sheet. The key is knowing where to find them and knowing how to quickly find information on them. If you have a spill of a potentially dangerous chemical, the last thing you need to spend time on is figuring out how to handle the spill without causing injury to yourself or others.

At this point, you might stop to think for a second. Do computers really come with hazardous chemicals? Do I really need an MSDS? Consider this as an example: oxygen. Hardly a dangerous chemical, considering we need to breathe it to live, right? In the atmosphere, oxygen is at 21 percent concentration. At 100 percent concentration, oxygen is highly flammable and can even spontaneously ignite some organic materials. In that sense, and in the eyes of OSHA, nearly everything can be a dangerous chemical.

If you are interested in searching for free MSDSs, two free websites are http://www.msds.com and http://www.msdssearch.com. Many manufacturers of components will also provide MSDSs on their websites.

Here is a sample MSDS for ammonium hydrogen sulfate:

**** MATERIAL SAFETY DATA SHEET ****

Ammonium Hydrogen Sulfate
90009

**** SECTION 1--CHEMICAL PRODUCT AND COMPANY IDENTIFICATION ****

MSDS Name: Ammonium Hydrogen Sulfate
Catalog Numbers:
    A/5400
Synonyms:
    Sulfuric acid, monoammonium salt; Acid ammonium sulfate; Ammonium
    acid sulfate.
Company Identification:
For information, call:
For emergencies, call:

**** SECTION 2--COMPOSITION, INFORMATION ON INGREDIENTS ****

CAS#	Chemical Name	%	EINECS#
7803-63-6	Ammonium hydrogen sulfate	100 %	232-265-5
	Hazard Symbols: C		
	Risk Phrases: 34		

**** SECTION 3--HAZARDS IDENTIFICATION ****

EMERGENCY OVERVIEW
Causes burns. Corrosive. Hygroscopic (absorbs moisture from the air).

Potential Health Effects
    Eye:
        Causes eye burns.
    Skin:
        Causes skin burns.
    Ingestion:
 May cause severe gastrointestinal tract irritation with nausea, vomiting,
and possible burns.
    Inhalation:
 Causes severe irritation of upper respiratory tract with coughing, burns,

breathing difficulty, and possible coma.
Chronic:
No information found.

**** SECTION 4--FIRST-AID MEASURES ****

Eyes:
Immediately flush eyes with plenty of water for at least 15 minutes, occasionally lifting the upper and lower eyelids. Get medical aid immediately.
Skin:
Get medical aid immediately. Immediately flush skin with plenty of water for at least 15 minutes while removing contaminated clothing and shoes.
Ingestion:
Do not induce vomiting. If victim is conscious and alert, give 2-4 cupfuls of milk or water. Never give anything by mouth to an unconscious person. Get medical aid immediately.
Inhalation:
Get medical aid immediately. Remove from exposure and move to fresh air immediately.
If not breathing, give artificial respiration. If breathing is difficult, give oxygen.
Notes to Physician:

**** SECTION 5--FIREFIGHTING MEASURES ****

General Information:
As in any fire, wear a self-contained breathing apparatus in pressure-demand, MSHA/NIOSH (approved or equivalent), and full protective gear. During a fire, irritating and highly toxic gases may be generated by thermal decomposition or combustion.
Extinguishing Media:
Substance is noncombustible; use agent most appropriate to extinguish surrounding fire.

**** SECTION 6--ACCIDENTAL RELEASE MEASURES ****

General Information: Use proper personal protective equipment as indicated in Section 8.

Spills/Leaks:
Vacuum or sweep up material and place into a suitable disposal container.

Reduce airborne dust and prevent scattering by moistening with water. Clean up spills immediately, observing precautions in the Protective Equipment section.

**** SECTION 7--HANDLING and STORAGE ****

Handling:

Wash thoroughly after handling. Wash hands before eating. Use only in a well-ventilated area. Do not get in eyes, on skin, or on clothing. Do not ingest or inhale.

Storage:

Store in a cool, dry place. Keep container closed when not in use.

**** SECTION 8--EXPOSURE CONTROLS, PERSONAL PROTECTION ****

Engineering Controls:

Use adequate general or local exhaust ventilation to keep airborne concentrations below the permissible exposure limits.

Personal Protective Equipment

Eyes:

Not available.

Skin:

Wear appropriate protective gloves to prevent skin exposure.

Clothing:

Wear appropriate protective clothing to prevent skin exposure.

Respirators:

Follow the OSHA respirator regulations found in 29 CFR 1910.134 or European Standard

EN 149. Always use a NIOSH or European Standard EN 149 approved respirator when necessary.

**** SECTION 9--PHYSICAL AND CHEMICAL PROPERTIES ****

Physical State:	Solid
Color:	White
Odor:	Not available
pH:	Not available
Vapor Pressure:	Not available
Viscosity:	Not available
Boiling Point:	Not available
Freezing/Melting Point:	147 deg C
Autoignition Temperature:	Not applicable
Flash Point:	Not applicable

```
Explosion Limits, lower:     Not available
Explosion Limits, upper:     Not available
Decomposition Temperature:   Not available
Solubility in Water:         Soluble in water
Specific Gravity/Density:    Not available
Molecular Formula:           NH4HSO4
Molecular Weight:            115.0993
```

**** SECTION 10--STABILITY AND REACTIVITY ****

Chemical Stability:
    Stable under normal temperatures and pressures.
Conditions to Avoid:
 Incompatible materials, dust generation, exposure to moist air or water.
Incompatibilities with Other Materials:
    Strong oxidizing agents and moist air.
Hazardous Decomposition Products:
    Oxides of nitrogen, oxides of sulfur.
Hazardous Polymerization: Has not been reported.

**** SECTION 11--TOXICOLOGICAL INFORMATION ****

RTECS#:
    CAS# 7803-63-6: BS4400500
LD50/LC50:
    Not available.
Carcinogenicity:
  Ammonium hydrogen sulfate -
    Not listed by ACGIH, IARC, NIOSH, NTP, or OSHA.
    See actual entry in RTECS for complete information.

**** SECTION 12--ECOLOGICAL INFORMATION ****

**** SECTION 13--DISPOSAL CONSIDERATIONS ****

Products which are considered hazardous for supply are classified as Special
Waste, and the disposal of such chemicals is covered by regulations which may
vary according to location. Contact a specialist disposal company or the local
waste regulator for advice. Empty containers must be decontaminated before
returning for recycling.

**** SECTION 14--TRANSPORT INFORMATION ****

IATA
>   Shipping Name: AMMONIUM HYDROGEN SULPHATE
>   Hazard Class: 8
>   UN Number: 2506
>   Packing Group: II

IMO
>   Shipping Name: AMMONIUM HYDROGEN SULPHATE
>   Hazard Class: 8
>   UN Number: 2506
>   Packing Group: II

RID/ADR
>   Shipping Name: AMMONIUM HYDROGEN SULPHATE
>   Hazard Class: 8
>   UN Number: 2506
>   Packing group: II

**** SECTION 15--REGULATORY INFORMATION ****

European/International Regulations
>   European Labeling in Accordance with EC Directives
>   Hazard Symbols: C
>   Risk Phrases:
>   R 34   Causes burns.
>   Safety Phrases:
 S 26 In case of contact with eyes, rinse immediately with plenty of water and
seek medical advice. S 28 After contact with skin, wash immediately
                    with...
>   WGK (Water Danger/Protection)
>   CAS# 7803-63-6: 1
United Kingdom Occupational Exposure Limits

United Kingdom Maximum Exposure Limits

Canada
>   CAS# 7803-63-6 is listed on Canada's DSL List.
>   CAS# 7803-63-6 is not listed on Canada's Ingredient Disclosure List.
>   Exposure Limits
US FEDERAL
>   TSCA
>   CAS# 7803-63-6 is listed on the TSCA inventory.

```
**** SECTION 16--ADDITIONAL INFORMATION ****
```

MSDS Creation Date: 6/23/2004 Revision #0 Date: Original.

The information above is believed to be accurate and represents the best
information currently available to us. However, we make no warranty of
merchantability or any other warranty, express or implied, with respect to such
information, and we assume no liability resulting from its use. Users should
make their own investigations to determine the suitability of the information
for their particular purposes. In no way shall the company be liable for any
claims, losses, or damages of any third party or for lost profits or any special,
indirect, incidental, consequential or exemplary damages, howsoever arising,
even if the company has been advised of the possibility of such damages.

Using Appropriate Repair Tools

Whether building a shed, fixing a car, or troubleshooting a computer, you need the right
tools for the job at hand. Most of the time, computers can be opened and devices removed
with nothing more than a simple screwdriver. But if you do a lot of work on PCs, you'll
definitely want to have additional tools on hand.

Computer toolkits are readily available on the Internet or at any electronics store. They
come in versions from inexpensive (under $10) kits that have around 10 pieces, to several-
hundred-dollar kits that have more tools than you will probably ever need. Figure 12.3
shows an example of a basic 11-piece PC toolkit. All of these tools come in a handy zip-
pered case so it's hard to lose them.

Looking at Figure 12.3, from left to right you have two nut drivers (1/4" and 3/16"), a
1/8" flat screwdriver, a #0 Phillips screwdriver, a T-15 Torx driver, a screw tube, an integrated circuit (IC) extractor, tweezers, a three-claw retriever, a #1 Phillips screwdriver, and
a 3/16" flat screwdriver. Most of these tools are incredibly useful, but the IC extractor probably won't be. In today's environment, it's rare to find an IC that you can extract, much less
find a reason to extract one.

This section looks at some of the tools of the PC troubleshooting trade.

FIGURE 12.3   PC toolkit

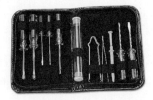

Screwdrivers

Every PC technician worth his or her weight in pocket protectors needs to have a screwdriver. At least one. There are three major categories of screwdrivers: flat-blade, Phillips, and Torx. In addition, there are devices that look like screwdrivers, except they have a hex-shaped indented head on them. They're called hex drivers and belong in the screwdriver family.

Whenever picking a screwdriver, always keep in mind that you want to match the size of the screwdriver head to the size of the screw. Using a screwdriver that's too small will cause it to spin inside the head of the screw, stripping the screw and making it useless. And if the screwdriver is too large, you won't be able to get the head in far enough to generate any torque to loosen the screw. Of course, if the screwdriver is way too big, it won't even fit inside the screw head at all. Common sizes for Phillips-head screws are 000, 00, 0, 1, 2, and 3. When dealing with Torx screws, the two most common sizes are T-10 and T-15.

When tightening screws, you don't need to make them so tight that they could survive the vibrations of an atmospheric reentry. Snug is fine. Making them too tight can cause problems loosening them, which could cause you (or someone else not so strong) to strip the head.

Using an electric screwdriver is fine if you have one. The only problem with them is that they tend to be larger than manual screwdrivers and can be difficult to get inside a case.

Using magnetic-tipped screwdrivers is not recommended. Many computer disks contain magnetically coded information, and the magnetic tip of a screwdriver could cause a problem. Keep a retrieving tool handy, instead, just in case you drop a screw.

Antistatic Wrist Straps

Essential to any PC technician's arsenal is an antistatic wrist strap. These don't typically come with smaller PC toolkits, but you should always have one or two handy.

We'll talk more about these straps in the "Preventing Electrostatic Discharge" section later in this chapter.

Other Useful Tools

Some other things that PC techs commonly carry include the following:

Pliers   Pliers are useful for a variety of tasks, especially gripping something. Long-nose or needle-nose pliers extend your reach.

Wire cutters   Wire cutters come in a variety of forms but are primarily used for cutting cables. It's not likely you'll need any sort of heavy-duty metal cutters.

Strippers   If you are making your own network cables or fixing them, having a cable stripper (and crimper) is essential.

Mirrors   Mirrors are handy inside tight spaces. Many techs like to use a dentist-style mirror because of its compact size and good reach.

Flashlight   Never underestimate the utility of a good flashlight. You never know what your lighting situation will be like when you're at a repair site. Smaller flashlights with good output are great to have, because they can fit into tight spaces.

Compressed air   For as much as computers and dust don't get along, it sure seems like they are attracted to each other. In all seriousness, computer components are powered by electricity, which causes the components to have a slight electrical charge. Dust is also electrically charged, so it's attracted to computer components. Compressed air can help you clean off components, especially in hard-to-reach places.

Be judicious about your use of compressed air. Often, you will find yourself just blowing the dust from one part of a computer to another.

Multimeter   If you're having power issues, a multimeter can be an invaluable tool. (You'll also hear of voltmeters, and while the two have somewhat different functions, both of them can be used to troubleshoot power problems.) Using a voltmeter, you can see if a computer power supply is producing the right amount of current for the devices that depend on it.

Some of these tools, such as compressed air, are also discussed in Chapter 8. Multimeters are also discussed in Chapter 16.

Handling Accidents

Accidents happen. Hopefully, they don't happen too often, but we know that they do. So what do you do when one happens? First, handle the situation. Second, report the incident. Two major classifications of accidents are environmental and human.

Environmental Accidents

When related to computers, environmental accidents typically come in one of two forms: electricity or water. Too much electricity is bad for computer components. If lightning is striking in your area, you run a major risk of frying computer parts. Even if you have a surge protector, you could still be at risk.

The best bet in a lightning storm is to power off your equipment and unplug it from outlets. Make the lightning have to come inside a window and hit your computer directly in order to fry it.

Those cheap $10 surge suppressors will fry right along with your computer. And don't be fooled—most power strips do *not* protect against power surges.

Modems are particularly susceptible to surges in electricity. If you're still using modems, be sure to unplug them from the wall outlet during an electrical storm, just as you would a power cord.

Water is obviously also bad for computer components. If there is water in the area, and you believe it will contact your computers, it's best to get the machines powered off as quickly as possible. If components are not powered on but get wet, they may still work after thoroughly drying out. But if they're on when they get wet, they're likely cooked. Water + electronic components = bad. Water + electronic components + electricity = *really* bad.

Many server rooms have raised floors. Although this serves several purposes, one is that equipment stored on the floor is less susceptible to water damage if flooding occurs.

Human Accidents

Human nature dictates that we are not infallible, so of course we're going to make mistakes and have accidents. The key is to minimize the damage caused when an accident happens.

If a chemical spill occurs, make sure that the area gets cordoned off as soon as possible. Then clean up the spill. The specific procedure on how to do that depends on the chemical, and that information can be found on an MSDS. Depending on the severity of the spill or the chemical released, you may also need to contact the local authorities. Again, the MSDS should have related information.

Physical accidents are more worrisome. People can trip on wires and fall, cut or burn themselves repairing computers, and incur a variety of other injuries as well. Computer components can be replaced, but that's not always true of human parts (or lives). The first thing to keep in mind is to always be careful and use common sense. If you're trying to work inside a computer case and you see sharp metal edges inside the case, see whether the metal (or component you are working on) can be moved to another location until you finish. Before you stick your hand into an area, make sure nothing is hot or is going to grab and cut you.

When an accident does happen (or almost happens), be sure to report it. Many companies pay for workers' compensation insurance. If you're injured on the job, you're required to report the incident, and you might also get temporary payments if you are unable to work because of the accident. Also, if the accident was anything but minor, seek medical attention. Just as victims in auto accidents might not feel pain for a day or two, victims in other physical accidents might be in the same position. If you never reported the accident, the insurance companies may find it less plausible that your suffering was work related.

Applying Proper Safety and Disposal Procedures

Safety is usually something that's talked about only during company-mandated training or after someone has an accident. Instead, proper safety procedures should be ingrained into the culture of an organization. It will take a while to change some people's behaviors, but constantly reinforcing the benefits of safe operations will eventually become second nature.

One of the ways to implement safety in the IT workplace is to educate technicians and users on the dangers of electrostatic discharge. Relatively simple steps can keep your equipment running longer by avoiding this dangerous phenomenon. In addition, management and all employees must work together to promote a safe work environment, which includes handling and moving equipment the right way. Finally, we owe it to ourselves and others to minimize the possible damage to our environment by disposing of used parts and chemicals in the right way.

This section specifically looks at preventing electrostatic discharge, preventing electromagnetic interference and radio frequency interference, promoting a safe work environment, properly handling equipment, and following recommended disposal procedures.

Preventing Electrostatic Discharge

Electrostatic discharge (ESD) can cause problems such as making a computer hang or reboot. ESD happens when two objects of dissimilar charge come in contact with one another. The two objects exchange electrons in order to standardize the electrostatic charge between them. This charge can, and often does, damage electronic components.

CPU chips and memory chips are particularly sensitive to ESD. Be extremely cautious when handling these chips.

When you shuffle your feet across the floor and shock your best friend on the ear, you are discharging static electricity into the ear of your friend. The lowest static voltage transfer you can feel is around 3,000 volts (it doesn't electrocute you because there is extremely little current). A static transfer that you can *see* is at least 10,000 volts! Just by sitting in a chair, you can generate around 100 volts of static electricity. Walking around wearing synthetic materials can generate around 1,000 volts. You can easily generate around 20,000 volts simply by dragging your smooth-soled shoes across a shag carpet in the winter. (Actually, it doesn't have to be winter to run this danger. This voltage can occur in any room with very low humidity—like a heated room in wintertime.)

Relative humidity has a significant impact on the electricity you generate. Walking around can generate 1,500 volts at 65–90 percent relative humidity, but it can produce 35,000 volts if the relative humidity is in the 10–25 percent range.

It makes sense that these thousands of volts can damage computer components. However, a component can be damaged with under 100 volts! That means if a small charge is built up in your body, you could damage a component without realizing it.

Real World Scenario

ESD Symptoms

Symptoms of ESD damage may be subtle, but they can be detected. One of the authors relates this experience:

"When I think of ESD, I always think of the same instance. A few years ago, I was working on an Apple Macintosh. This computer seemed to have a mind of its own. I would troubleshoot it, find the defective component, and replace it. The problem was that as soon as I replaced the component, it failed. I thought maybe the power supply was frying the boards, so I replaced both at the same time, but to no avail.

"I was about to send the computer off to Apple when I realized that it was winter. Normally this would not be a factor, but winters where I live are extremely dry. Dry air promotes static electricity. At first I thought my problem couldn't be that simple, but I was at the end of my rope. So, when I received my next set of new parts, I grounded myself with an antistatic strap for the time it took to install the components, and prayed while I turned on the power. Success! The components worked as they should, and a new advocate of ESD prevention was born."

Do you have long hair or (gasp!) have to wear a tie when fixing computers? Tie it back. Long hair or dangling cloth inside an open computer case is asking for trouble, as both are notorious for carrying and conducting static electricity.

The good news is that there are measures you can implement to help contain the effects of ESD. The first and easiest item to implement is the antistatic wrist strap, also referred to as an ESD strap. We will look at the antistatic wrist strap, as well as other ESD prevention tools, in the following sections.

Antistatic Wrist Straps

To use the ESD strap, you attach one end to an earth ground (typically, the ground pin on an extension cord) or the computer case and wrap the other end around your wrist. This strap grounds your body and keeps it at a zero charge. Figure 12.4 shows the proper way to attach an antistatic strap. There are several varieties of wrist straps available. The one in Figure 12.4 uses a banana clip, while others use alligator clips and are attached to the computer case itself.

FIGURE 12.4 Proper ESD strap connection

Pin connects to ground pin (small round hole) or earth ground

ESD strap

Outlet

For an antistatic wrist strap to work properly, the computer must be plugged in but turned off. When the computer is plugged in, it is grounded through the power cord. When you attach yourself to it with the wrist strap, you are grounded through the power cord as well. If the computer is not plugged in, there is no ground, and any excess electricity on you will just discharge into the case, which is not good.

An ESD strap is a specially designed device to bleed electrical charges away *safely*. It uses a 1 megohm resistor to bleed the charge away slowly. A simple wire wrapped around your wrist will not work correctly and could electrocute you!

Never wear an ESD strap if you're working inside a monitor or inside a power supply. If you wear one while working on the inside of these components, you increase the chance of getting a lethal shock.

ESD Antistatic Mats

It is possible to damage a device by simply laying it on a bench top. For this reason, you should have an ESD mat in addition to an ESD strap. This mat drains excess charge away from any item coming in contact with it (see Figure 12.5). ESD mats are also sold as mouse/keyboard pads to prevent ESD charges from interfering with the operation of the computer. Many wrist straps can be connected to the mat, thus causing the technician and any equipment in contact with the mat to be at the same electrical potential and eliminating ESD. There are even ESD bootstraps and ESD floor mats, which are used to keep the technician's entire body at the same potential.

FIGURE 12.5   Proper use of an ESD antistatic mat

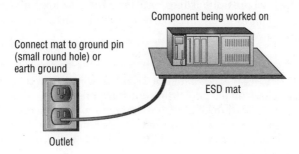

Antistatic Bags for Parts

Antistatic bags are important tools to have at your disposal when servicing electronic components because they protect the sensitive electronic devices from stray static charges. These silver or pink bags are designed so that the static charges collect on the outside of the bags rather than on the electronic components.

 WARNING   Unlike antistatic mats, antistatic bags do not "drain" the charges away, and they should never be used in place of an antistatic mat.

You can obtain the bags from several sources. The most direct way to acquire antistatic bags is to go to an electronics supply store and purchase them in bulk. Most supply stores have several sizes available. Perhaps the easiest way to obtain them, however, is simply to hold on to the ones that come your way. That is, when you purchase any new component, it usually comes in an antistatic bag. After you have installed the component, keep the bag. It may take you a while to gather a collection of bags if you take this approach, but eventually you will have a fairly large assortment.

Other Protection Methods

Another preventive measure you can take is to maintain the relative humidity at around 50 percent. Be careful not to increase the humidity too far—to the point where moisture begins to condense on the equipment. Also, use antistatic spray, which is available commercially, to reduce static buildup on clothing and carpets.

 TIP   If you don't have any antistatic spray, you can always use the "Downy solution." In a spray bottle, combine one part water with one part liquid fabric softener. Mist areas such as carpet and clothing that cause problems. If used regularly, it will keep static away and keep your office smelling nice too!

Vendors have methods of protecting components in transit from manufacture to installation. They press the pins of ICs into antistatic foam to keep all the pins at the same potential. In addition, most circuit boards are shipped in antistatic bags, as discussed earlier.

> Antistatic foam looks a lot like Styrofoam. However, there are huge differences between the two. While antistatic foam helps reduce the transfer of electricity, Styrofoam does not. Styrofoam holds a charge on its surface quite easily. Have you ever tried to get some of those small packing "peanuts" off your hands?) Be careful to not mix the two up, lest you fry your components.

At the very least, you can be mindful of the dangers of ESD and take steps to reduce its effects. Beyond that, you should educate yourself about those effects so you know when ESD is becoming a major problem.

> If an ESD strap or mat is not available, you can discharge excess static voltage by touching the metal case of the power supply. However, the power supply *must be plugged into a properly grounded outlet* for this technique to work as intended. Also, for this to work you need to maintain contact to continuously drain excess charge away. As you can see, it's easier to have an antistatic wrist strap.

Preventing Electromagnetic Interference

When compared to the other dangers we've discussed in this chapter, *electromagnetic interference (EMI)*, also known as *radio frequency interference (RFI)*, is by far the least dangerous. EMI really poses no threats to you in terms of bodily harm. What it can do is make your equipment or network malfunction.

EMI is an unwanted disturbance caused by electromagnetic radiation generated by another source. In other words, some of your electrical equipment may interfere with other equipment. Here are some common sources of interference:

Network devices   The popularity of wireless networking devices has introduced the possibility of interference. The most popular wireless networking standard, 802.11b/g, uses the 2.4GHz range for transmissions. Bluetooth devices happen to use the same frequency. In theory, they won't interfere with each other because they use different modulation techniques. In practice, interference between the two types of devices can happen.

Magnets   Magnets work by generating an electromagnetic field. It might make sense, then, that this field could cause electromagnetic interference. For the most part, you don't need to worry about this unless you have huge magnets at work. Do note, however, that many motors use magnets, which can cause interference. For example, one of our friends used to have his computer on the opposite side of a wall from his refrigerator. Whenever the compressor kicked in, his monitor display would become wavy and unreadable. It was time to move his home office. Another common culprit is desk fans. Put a desk fan next to a CRT and turn the fan on. What happens to the display? It will become wavy. This is another example of EMI.

Cordless phones   Cordless phones can operate at a variety of frequencies. Some of the more common ones are 900MHz, 1.9GHz, 2.4GHz, and 5.8GHz. Many of these are common ranges for computer equipment to operate in as well. The newest cordless phone standard is DECT 6.0, which uses the 1.9GHz range. This range is reserved for voice communication, so these devices should not interfere with your networking equipment.

Microwave ovens   Microwave ovens are convenient devices to heat food and beverages. The radiation they generate is typically in the 2.45GHz range, although it can vary slightly. If a microwave is being used near your computer, you'll often see a distorted display just as if a fan or motor were being run next to your computer. You may also experience interference with wireless network communications.

Copper wires are susceptible to EMI. Fiber-optic cables, which use light to transmit data, are not susceptible to EMI.

Working in a Safe Environment

The Occupational Safety and Health Act states that every working American has the right to a safe and healthy work environment. To enforce the act, the Occupational Safety and Health Administration (OSHA) was formed. OSHA covers all private sector employees and post office workers. Public sector employees are covered by state programs, and federal employees are covered under a presidential executive order. In a nutshell, OSHA requires employers to "provide a workplace that is free of recognized dangers and hazards."

There are three overarching criteria to a safe work environment:

- The company and its employees have identified all significant hazards in the work setting.

- Preventive measures have been taken to address each significant hazard.

- The company and its employees understand how to respond to accidents or near-miss accidents if or when they occur.

The following sections explore specific responsibilities and how to create a safe work environment plan.

Employer and Employee Responsibilities

Maintaining workplace safety is the responsibility of employers as well as employees. Here are some of the important responsibilities of employers:

- Provide properly maintained tools and equipment.

- Provide a warning system, such as codes or labels, to warn employees of potential hazards or dangerous chemicals.

- Post the OSHA poster in a prominent location.
- Keep records of workplace injuries or illnesses.
- Continuously examine workplace conditions to ensure OSHA compliance.

It's also the responsibility of the employee to help maintain a safe work environment. Specifically, employees are charged with the following tasks:

- Read and understand OSHA posters.
- Follow all employer-implemented health and safety rules and safe work practices.
- Use all required protective gear and equipment.
- Report hazardous conditions to the employer.
- Report hazardous conditions that the employer does not correct to OSHA.

As you can see, both employers and employees need to work together to keep the workplace safe. It is illegal for an employee to be punished in any way for exercising their rights under the Occupational Safety and Health Act.

Safety Plans

We recommend that your company create and follow a workplace safety plan. Having a safety plan can help avoid accidents that result in lost productivity, equipment damage, and employee injury or death.

A good safety plan should include the following elements:

- A written plan of the program, including who is responsible for implementing and managing the program
- Systematic periodic inspections to identify workplace hazards
- Procedures for eliminating hazards once identified
- Processes for investigating the cause of accidents, injuries, or illnesses
- A safety and health training program specific to the job duties performed
- A system for employees to communicate safety or health concerns, without fears of reprisal
- A system to ensure that employees comply with safety and health rules
- A system to maintain safety and health records, including steps taken to implement accident prevention initiatives

It might seem like a laundry list of items to consider, but a good safety program needs to be holistic in nature for it to be effective.

Many companies are also incorporating rules against drug or alcohol use in their safety and health plans. Specifically, employees are not allowed to come to work if under the influence of alcohol or illegal drugs. Employees who do come to work under the influence may be subject to disciplinary action up to and including termination of employment.

After your safety plan has been created, you need to ensure that all employees receive necessary training. Have each employee sign a form at the end of training to signify that they attended, and keep the forms in a central location (such as with or near the official safety policy). In addition to the training record, you should make available and keep records of the following:

- Safety improvement suggestion form
- Accident and near-accident reporting form
- Injury and illness log
- Safety inspection checklist
- Hazard removal form
- MSDSs

Safety rules and regulations will work only if they have the broad support of management from the top down. Everyone in the organization needs to buy into the plan or it won't be a success. Make sure that everyone understands the importance of a safe work environment, and make sure that the culture of the company supports safety in the workplace.

Handling Equipment

One of the ways IT employees get hurt is by moving equipment in an improper way. Changing the location of computers is a task often completed by IT personnel, and ensuring that you move things the right way can avoid injury.

Here are some safe lifting techniques to always keep in mind:

- Lift with your legs, not your back (bend at the knees when picking something up, not at the waist).
- Do not twist when lifting.
- Maintain the natural curves of the back and spine when lifting.
- Keep objects close to your body and at waist level.
- Push rather than pull if possible.

The muscles in the lower back aren't nearly as strong as those in the legs or other parts of the body. Whenever lifting, you want to reduce the strain on those lower back muscles as much as possible. If you want, use a back belt or brace to help you maintain the proper position while lifting.

Monitors can be heavy. (Thank goodness for flat screens!) When lifting and carrying a monitor, always keep the glass face toward your body. The front of the monitor is the heaviest part, and you want the heavy part closest to your body to reduce strain on your muscles.

If you believe the load is too much for you to carry, don't try to pick it up! Get assistance from a coworker. Another great idea is to use a cart. It will save you trips if you have multiple items to move, and it saves you the stress of carrying components.

When moving loads, always be aware of your surrounding environment. Before you move, scout out the path to see whether there are any trip hazards or other safety concerns such as spills, stairs, uneven floors (or ripped carpet), tight turns, or narrow doorways.

Following Disposal Procedures

After electronic devices reach the end of their useful life and it's time for them to fade away into the sunset, what do we do with them? With the proliferation of electronic devices over the last few decades, this has become an increasingly important question. As we discussed earlier, throwing them in landfills is a bad idea because these devices often contain hazardous materials. On the other hand, standards for proper disposal are not always clear. So again, what do we do with them? This section takes a look at three classifications of computer-related components and proper disposal procedures for each.

Batteries

The EPA estimates that there are over 350 million batteries purchased annually in the United States. One can only imagine what the worldwide figure is. Batteries contain several heavy metals and other toxic ingredients, including alkaline, mercury, lead acid, nickel cadmium, and nickel metal hydride.

Never burn a battery to destroy it. That will cause the battery to explode, which could result in serious injury.

When these batteries are thrown away and deposited into landfills, the heavy metals inside them will find their way into the ground. From there, they can pollute water sources and eventually find their way into the supply of drinking water. In 1996, the United States passed the Battery Act to address two issues: to phase out the use of mercury in disposable batteries and to provide collection methods and recycling procedures for batteries.

There are several countries around the world with battery recycling programs. Information on battery recycling in the United States can be found at http://www.ibm.com/ibm/environment/products/battery_us.shtml.

There are five types of batteries most commonly associated with computers and handheld electronic devices: alkaline, nickel cadmium (NiCd), nickel metal hydride (NiMH), lithium ion, and button cell.

Alkaline batteries   Alkaline batteries have been incredibly popular portable batteries for several decades now. Before 1984, one of the major ingredients in this type of battery was mercury, which is highly toxic to the environment. In 1984, battery companies began reduction of mercury levels, and in 1996 mercury was outlawed in alkaline batteries in the United States. Still, it's strongly recommended that you recycle these batteries at a recycling center. Although newer alkaline batteries contain less mercury than their predecessors, they are still made of metals and other toxins that contaminate the air and soil.

Nickel cadmium (NiCd)   Nickel cadmium is a popular format for rechargeable batteries. As their name indicates, they contain high levels of nickel and cadmium. Although nickel is only semi-toxic, cadmium is highly toxic. These types of batteries are categorized by the EPA as hazardous waste and should be recycled.

Nickel metal hydride (NiMH) and lithium ion   Laptop batteries are commonly made with NiMH and lithium ion. Unlike the previous types of batteries we have discussed, these are not considered hazardous waste, and there are no regulations on recycling them. However, these batteries do contain elements that can be recycled, so it's still a good idea to go that route.

Button cell   These batteries are named because they look like a button. They're commonly used in calculators and watches as well as portable computers. They often contain mercury and silver (and are environmental hazards due to the mercury), and need to be recycled.

You may have noticed a theme regarding disposal of batteries: recycling. Many people just throw batteries in the trash and don't think twice about it. However, there are several laws in the United States requiring the recycling of many types of batteries. Not only that, but recycling does indeed help keep the environment clean. For a list of recycling centers in your area, use your local yellow pages (under Recycling Centers) or do an Internet search.

If you're ever exposed to the electrolyte (the inside "juice") of the battery, immediately flush the exposed area with water. If exposed to the eye, wash the eye for 15 minutes and immediately contact a physician.

Display Devices

Computer monitors (CRT monitors, not LCD ones) are big and bulky, so what do you do when it's time to get rid of them? As we mentioned earlier in this chapter, monitors have capacitors in them that are capable of retaining a lethal electric charge after they've been unplugged. You wouldn't want anyone to accidentally set off the charge and die. But the thing we didn't mention earlier, which is important now, is that most CRT monitors contain high amounts of lead. Most monitors contain several pounds of lead, in fact. Lead is very dangerous to humans and the environment, and must be dealt with carefully. Other harmful elements found in CRTs include arsenic, beryllium, cadmium, chromium, mercury, nickel, and zinc.

If you have a monitor to dispose of, contact a computer recycling firm. It's best to let professional recyclers handle the monitor for you.

Real World Scenario

How *Not* to Dispose of Your Monitors

This story comes from the technical support division of a now-defunct major computer manufacturer, who used a lot of computers at their own facility. At one time, they had as many as 500 technicians working the phones. So you can imagine that they burned out a lot of equipment.

Here's how dead monitors would be disposed of. An IT staff member would take the monitor out to the dumpster and bring along a sledgehammer. Setting the monitor on its back, he would take one good swing at the glass panel with the hammer to shatter the screen. (This was done, by policy, to ensure that no one would want to go out to the dumpster and try to salvage the dead monitor.) After glass went everywhere, he picked up the monitor and threw it in the dumpster.

One employee made an observation that it probably wasn't good for us to be spreading glass all over the parking lot by shattering monitors. That advice was taken, and the sledge-hammer was done away with. Instead, an IT staff member would use a permanent black marker and draw all over the screen (again, so no one would want to try to salvage it), and again, it was thrown in the dumpster.

In our enlightened state today, we can see how this was not a good plan for disposing of broken monitors. In fact, many states today have laws prohibiting the disposal of computer monitors in trash bins. This is a good law, because with the amount of harmful elements in monitors, they're every bit the environmental hazard that batteries are.

Chemical Solvents and Cans

Nearly every chemical solvent you encounter will have a corresponding MSDS. On the MSDS you will find a section detailing the proper methods for disposing of that chemical. These chemicals were not designed to be released into nature, because they could cause significant harm to living organisms if they're ingested. If in doubt, contact a local hazardous materials handler to find out the best way to dispose of the chemical solvent.

Cans are generally made from aluminum or other metals, which are not biodegradable. It's best to always recycle these materials. If the cans were used to hold a chemical solvent or otherwise hazardous material, contact a hazardous materials disposal center instead of a recycling center.

Demonstrating Communication Skills and Professionalism

Good communication includes listening to what the user or manager or developer is telling you and making certain that you understand completely what he is trying to say: approximately half of all communication should be listening. Just because a user or customer does not understand the terminology or syntax or concepts that you use or understand does not mean he does not have a real problem that needs addressing. You must, therefore, be skilled not only at listening but also at translating.

Professional conduct encompasses politeness, guidance, punctuality, and accountability. Always treat the customer with the same respect and empathy you would expect if the situation were reversed. Likewise, guide the customer through the problem and the explanation. Tell him what has caused the problem he is currently experiencing and the best solution for preventing it from reoccurring in the future.

 Real World Scenario

Communication Is Key

Marriages disintegrate when couples do not communicate effectively, or so many experts proclaim. Communication is ranked as one of the most important skills needed in order to make a marriage, or any similar partnership, work. The same can be said for business partnerships—it is important to make certain you are listening to your customers, whether they are truly customers in the traditional sense of the word or internal users that you support. The same is true of managers and vendors—you need to listen to their concerns and their information and then make sure you understand them before beginning a project.

Similarly, you need to make certain that the parties in question understand what you are saying to them. It isn't acceptable to resort to the "But I told you ..." excuse when customers or partners aren't pleased with the results. Making certain they understand what you are telling them is equally important as making certain you understand what they are telling you.

Customer satisfaction goes a long way toward generating repeat business. If you can *meet* the customer's expectations, you will almost assuredly hear from him again when another problem arises. However, if you can *exceed* the customer's expectations, you can almost guarantee that he will call you the next time a problem arises.

Customer satisfaction is important in all communication media—whether you are on-site, providing phone support, or communicating through e-mail or other correspondence. If you are on-site, follow these rules:

- When you arrive, immediately look for the person (user, manager, administrator, and so on) who is affected by the problem. Announce that you are there and assure that person that you will do all you can to remedy the problem.

- Listen intently to what your customer is saying. Make it obvious to her that you are listening and respecting what she is telling you. If there is a problem with understanding the client, go to whatever lengths you need to in order to remedy the situation. Look for verbal and nonverbal cues that can help you isolate the problem.

- Share the customer's sense of urgency. What may seem like a small problem to you can appear as if the whole world were collapsing around your customer.

- Be honest and fair with the customer and try to establish a personal rapport. Explain what the problem is, what you believe is the cause of it, and what can be done in the future to prevent it from recurring.

- Handle complaints as professionally as possible. Accept responsibility for errors that may have occurred on your part, and never try to pass the blame elsewhere. Avoid arguing with a customer, as it serves no purpose; resolve her anger with as little conflict as possible. Remember: The goal is to keep her as a customer and not to win an argument.

- When you finish a job, notify the user that you have finished. Make every attempt to find the user and inform her of the resolution. If it is impossible to find her, leave a note explaining the resolution to find when she returns. You should also leave a means by which she can contact you should she have a question about the resolution or a related problem. In most cases, the number you should leave would be that of your business during working hours and that of your pager, where applicable, after hours. Notification should also be given to both managers—yours and the user's—that the job has been completed.

If you are providing phone support, keep these guidelines in mind:

- Always answer the telephone in a professional manner, announcing the name of the company and yourself.

- Using the customer's name can help build rapport. Using it in every sentence can sound condescending, but using it once in a while can make you seem more personable.

- Make a concentrated effort to ascertain the customer's technical level and communicate at that level, not above or below it.

- The most important skill you can have is the ability to listen. You have to rely on the customer to tell you the problem and describe it accurately. She cannot do that if you are second-guessing or jumping to conclusions before the whole story is told. Ask broad questions to begin, and then narrow them down to help isolate the problem. It is your job to help guide the description of the problem from the user. For example, you might ask:

- Is the printer plugged in?
- Is it online?
- Are there any lights flashing on it?

- Complaints should be handled in the same manner as if you were on-site. Make your best effort to resolve the problem and not argue its points. Again, you want to keep the customer more than you want to accomplish any other goal.

- Close the incident only when the customer is satisfied that the solution you have given her is the correct one and the problem has gone away.

- End the telephone call in a courteous manner—thanking the customer for the opportunity to serve her is often the best way.

Talking to the user is an important first step in the troubleshooting process. Your first contact with a computer that has a problem is usually through the customer, either directly or by way of a work order that contains the user's complaint. Often, the complaint is something straightforward, such as "There's smoke coming from the back of my flat panel monitor." At other times, the problem is complex, and the customer does not mention everything that has been going wrong.

 Real World Scenario

Communication Is Everywhere

Communication, and problems that can occur with it, are not isolated to the IT world. Almost every profession stresses the importance of good communication. As an example of this, Jamie Walters, founder and chief vision and strategy officer for Ivy Sea, Inc., and Sarah Fenson, Ivy Sea's guide to client services, wrote an article for Inc.com on steps to smooth conversations (http://www.inc.com/articles/2000/08/20000.html) that included this advice:

- Don't take things personally. If someone acts inappropriately toward you, just react in a calm manner. They are likely responding that way because of outside factors.

- Admit when you don't know the answer to something. It's okay to defer to somebody else, or tell the user or customer that you'll have to look into their complaint and will get back with them as soon as possible.

- It is better to validate someone's feeling or respond to the information they have given you than reacting to them. For instance, if somebody complains that a help ticket has not been responded to in a timely manner, tell them you understand how they feel and will look into it versus reacting in a defensive manner.

- Don't let your personal opinions or feelings get in the way of what the real complaint is. Try to put yourself in the user's or customer's shoes.

- Be sympathetic. If you need a user to leave his or her laptop with you overnight, tell them you realize it's frustrating and apologize.

- Try to provide a solution that you both can benefit from. Look for commonalities between you and the client, and work to find a solution that is agreeable to both of you.

- Try to be as informative as possible when discussing a solution to their problem. Most people are uncomfortable with change, so explaining the benefits of a particular solution might help ease this discomfort.

- Try to keep a positive attitude and be optimistic.

- Always work on your listening skills!

Communicating with Customers

The act of diagnosis starts with the art of customer relations. Go to the customer with an attitude of trust: believe what the customer is saying. At the same time, retain an attitude of hidden skepticism; *don't* believe that the customer has told you everything. This attitude of hidden skepticism is not the same as distrust, but just remember that what you hear isn't always the whole story, and customers may inadvertently forget to give some crucial detail.

One of the best ways to become proficient in this is to put yourself in the shoes of the novice user. None of us are experts in every field, so think of an area where you are weak—auto repair, home repair, etc.—and imagine how you would want a professional in that area to discourse with you.

For example, a customer may complain that his CD-ROM drive doesn't work. What he fails to mention is that it has never worked and that he installed it himself. On examining the machine, you realize that he mounted it with screws that are too long and that these prevent the tray from ejecting properly.

Here are a few suggestions for making your communication with the customer easier:

Have the customer reproduce the error   The most important part of this step is to have the customer show you what the problem is. The best method I've seen of doing this is to ask him, "Show me what 'not working' looks like." That way, you see the conditions and methods under which the problem occurs. The problem may be a simple matter of an improper method. The user may be doing an operation incorrectly or performing the operation in the wrong order. During this step, you have the opportunity to observe how the problem occurs, so pay attention.

Identify recent changes   The user can give you vital information. The most important question is, "What changed?" Problems don't usually come out of nowhere. Was a new piece of hardware or software added? Did the user drop some equipment? Was there a power outage or a storm? These are the types of questions you can ask a user in trying to find out what is different.

If nothing changed, at least outwardly, then what was going on at the time of failure? Can the problem be reproduced? Can the problem be worked around? The point here is to ask as many questions as you need to in order to pinpoint the source of the trouble.

Use the collected information   Once the problem or problems have been clearly identified, your next step is to isolate possible causes. If the problem cannot be clearly identified, then further tests will be necessary. A common technique for hardware and software problems alike is to strip the system down to bare-bones basics. In a hardware situation, this could mean removing all interface cards except those absolutely required for the system to operate. In a software situation, this may mean disabling elements within Device Manager.

Generally, then, you can gradually rebuild the system toward the point where the trouble started. When you reintroduce a component and the problem reappears, you know that component is the one causing the problem.

Using Appropriate Behavior

Critical to appropriate behavior is to treat the customer, or user, the way you want to be treated. Much has been made of the Golden Rule—treating others the way you would have them treat you. Six key elements to this, from a business perspective, are punctuality, accountability, flexibility, confidentiality, respect, and privacy. The following sections discuss these elements in detail.

Punctuality

Punctuality is important and should be a part of your planning process before you ever arrive at the site: if you tell the customer you will be there at 10:30 a.m., you need to make every attempt to be there at that time. If you arrive late, you have given her false hope that the problem will be solved by a set time. That false hope can lead to anger when you arrive late and appear not to be taking her problem seriously. Punctuality continues to be important throughout the service call and does not end with your arrival. If you need to leave to get parts and return, tell the customer when you will be back, and be there at that time. If, for some reason, you cannot return at the expected time, alert the customer and inform her of your new time.

In conjunction with time and punctuality, if a user asks how much longer the server will be down and you respond that it will up in 5 minutes, only to have it down for 5 more hours, you are creating resentment and possibly anger. When estimating downtime, always allow for more time than you think you will need just in case other problems occur. If you greatly underestimate the time, always inform the affected parties and give them a new time estimate. To use an analogy that will put it in perspective, if you take your car to get an oil change and the counter clerk tells you it will be "about 15 minutes," the last thing you want is to be still sitting there four hours later.

Exercise 12.3 tests the importance of punctuality.

EXERCISE 12.3

Understanding Punctuality

This Is a simple exercise that you can modify and use as needed. Its purpose is to illustrate the importance of punctuality as it relates to situations with which you can associate.

1. Call someone important in your life—your spouse, a parent, an in-law, or a close friend—and tell him or her you have something very important you need to discuss. Give that person no other details, but ask him or her to meet you in exactly 1 hour at a location familiar to both of you.

2. Wait 2 hours before showing up.

3. Notice the person's reaction. How did that person feel about having to wait for you? Even though your lateness was not that great, what kind of an impact did it have on the person's mood and behavior?

This is an interaction with someone who matters in your life—imagine a customer who does not know you waiting for you when he perceives his system problem to be the most serious thing in his life at the moment. Punctuality can go a long way toward keeping dialogue pleasant between any two parties.

Accountability

Accountability is a trait every technician should possess. When problems occur, you need to be accountable for them and not attempt to pass the buck to someone else. For example, you are called to a site to put a larger hard drive into a server. While performing this operation, you inadvertently scrape your feet across the carpeted floor, build up energy, and zap the memory in the server. Some technicians would pretend the electrostatic discharge (ESD) never happened, put the new hard drive in, and then act completely baffled by the fact that problems unrelated to the hard drive are occurring. An accountable technician would explain to the customer exactly what happened and suggest ways of proceeding from that point—addressing and solving the problem as quickly and efficiently as possible.

Accountability also means you do what you say you're going to do and ensure that expectations are set and met. For example, you should:

- Offer different repair or replacement options if they're available.

- Provide documentation on the services you provided.

- Follow up with the customer at a later date to ensure satisfaction.

The last one is the most overlooked, yet can be the most important. Some technicians fix a problem and then develop an "I hope that worked and I never hear from them again" attitude. Calling your customer back (or dropping by their desk) to ensure that everything is still working right is an amazing way to quickly build credibility and rapport.

Flexibility

Flexibility is another equally important trait for a service technician. While it is important that you respond to service calls promptly and close them (solve them) as quickly as you can, you must also be flexible. If a customer cannot have you on-site until the afternoon, you must make your best effort to work them into your schedule around the time most convenient for them. Likewise, if you are called to a site to solve a problem, and the customer brings another problem to your attention while you are there, you should make every attempt to address that problem as well. Under no circumstances should you ever give a customer the cold shoulder or not respond to additional problems because they were not on an initial incident report.

You should always follow the express guidelines of the company for which you work as they relate to flexibility, empowerment, and other issues.

Another way that flexibility is important is that you have personal flexibility to deal with challenging or difficult situations. When someone's computer has failed, they likely aren't going to be in a good mood and that can make them a "difficult customer" to deal with. In situations like these, keep in mind the following principles:

Avoid arguing   Arguing with the customer—about anything—is only going to make the situation worse. The customer may be mad and may be yelling at you, but don't argue back or take their comments personally. Try to diffuse the situation by calmly reminding them that you're here to help, and you want to understand what's going on so you can do that. They may need to vent for a bit, so let them to do that. Just keep your focus on doing what you need to in order to resolve the problem.

Don't minimize their problems   While the customer's problem might seem trivial to you, it isn't to them. Treat the problem as seriously as they're treating it. Keep in mind that facial expressions and body language is also important here. If someone tells you their problem and you look at them like they're delusional, they're probably going to pick up on that, which can make the situation worse.

Avoid being judgmental   Don't blame or criticize. As stated before, just focus on what needs to happen to fix the problem. Accusing the user of messing it up does not build rapport.

Focus on your communication skills   If you have a difficult customer, treat it as an opportunity to see how good a communicator you really are. (Maybe your next job will be a foreign ambassador!) Ask nonconfrontational, open-ended questions. "When was the last time it worked?" is more helpful then "Did it work yesterday" or "Did you break it this morning?"

Another good tactic here is to restate the issue or question to verify you understand. Starting with "I understand that the problem is…" and repeating it back can show empathy and proves you were listening. If you have it wrong, it's also a good opportunity to let your customer correct you so you're on track to solve the right problem.

Confidentiality

The goal of *confidentiality* is to prevent or minimize unauthorized access to files and folders and disclosure of data and information. In many instances, laws and regulations require confidentiality for specific information. For example, Social Security records, payroll and employee records, medical records, and corporate information are high-value assets. This information could create liability issues or embarrassment if it fell into the wrong hands. Over the last few years, there have been a number of cases in which bank account and credit card numbers were published on the Internet. The costs of these types of breaches of confidentiality far exceed the actual losses from the misuse of this information.

Confidentiality entails ensuring that data expected to remain private is seen only by those who should see it. Confidentiality is implemented through authentication and access controls.

Just as confidentiality issues are addressed early in the design phase of a project, you—as a computer professional—are expected to uphold a high level of confidentiality. Should a user approach you with a sensitive issue—telling you his password, asking for assistance obtaining access to medical forms, and so on—it is your obligation as a part of your job to make certain that information passes no further.

Confidential materials on workspaces and printers should always be protected.

Respect

Much of the discussion in this chapter is focused on respecting the customer as an individual. However, you must also respect the tangibles that are important to the customer. While you may look at a monitor they are using as an outdated piece of equipment that should be scrapped, the business owners may see it as a gift from their children when they first started their business.

Treat the customers' property as if it had value, and you will win their respect. Their property includes the system you are working on (laptop/desktop computer, monitor, peripherals, and the like) as well as other items associated with their business. Do not use their telephone to make personal calls or call other customers while you are at this site. Do not use their printers or other equipment, unless it is in a role associated with the problem you've been summoned to fix.

The Customer Respect Group, http://www.customerrespect.com, measures the behavior of corporations and the respect they give to customers through their websites. Such items as privacy, responsiveness, attitude, simplicity, transparency, and business principles are combined to create a Customer Respect Index (CRI) ranking. The items they rank in the online world are just as important in the offline world and mirror those presented here.

Respecting the customer is not rocket science. All you need to do—for this exam and in the real world—is think of how you would want someone to treat you. Exercise 12.4 explores this topic further.

EXERCISE 12.4

Surprise Someone

This exercise, like Exercise 12.3, can be modified to fit your purpose or constraints. Its goal is to illustrate the positive power of the unexpected:

1. Pick a random, toll-free number used for business solicitation and call it.

2. Chat with the operator for a few moments about the company's product or service, and then ask to speak to the supervisor.

3. When the supervisor comes on, tell her about the operator you have been speaking with and commend him for the job that he has done.

It is likely the operator became confused when you asked to speak to his supervisor; this almost always occurs only in a negative situation. How did the operator handle the request? Did it change the tone of the communication that was taking place? Did he fulfill your request even though he feared he could lose from it? How did the supervisor respond when she came to the phone—was she expecting negative comments? How did she accept the positive information you offered?

Ideally, this illustrated the importance of staying professional and keeping the channel of communication open even in a tough situation. You should be able to adapt this to the workplace when a customer asks to speak to your superior or has another request that is difficult for you to fulfill.

One last area to consider that directly relates to this topic is that of ethics. Ethics is the application of morality to situations. While there are different schools of thought, one of the most popular areas of study is known as normative ethics, focusing on what is normal or practical (right versus wrong and so on). Regardless of religion, culture, and other influences, there are generally accepted beliefs that some things are wrong (stealing, murder, and the like) and some things are right (for example, the Golden Rule). You should always attempt to be ethical in everything you do because it reflects not only on your character but also on the company for which you work.

Real World Scenario

A Little Goes a Long Way

The following examples of respecting and disrespecting the customer come from one of the authors' own experiences:

"My wife and I were in an unfamiliar part of Chicago without ready access to a vehicle when we started to get hungry. I am a meat-and-potatoes man and rarely take a chance on anything else. There were no restaurants of that type around, however, and we wound up in an Asian grill. Expecting not to like the buffet, we ordered a side of lettuce wraps and then two buffets and drinks. As it turned out, I liked the buffet a great deal and went back through the line many times. We also liked the drinks and got several of those. Everything was great, except the waiter forgot to bring the lettuce wraps. I dismissed it and made a mental note to inform the waiter when he brought the bill and have him deduct them from our tab. Instead, the manager brought the bill over when we were finished eating, and he had scribbled on it "no charge." When I asked him why, he apologized that no one brought the wraps and said he hoped we would come back another time. I was beside myself with disbelief and thanked him profusely, and since then I have told many people about the best place in Chicago I know of to eat.

In a very different situation, while driving home one night, a dashboard light came on reading "Low tire pressure." Upon inspection, I could hear the right-rear tire hissing. I drove to a tire store and explained the situation. I had used this same tire store over the past 14 years for tires, oil changes, exhaust, maintenance, and a number of other things on the vehicles I've owned. The manager came out and said they found a nail in the tire. They removed the nail, patched the tire, and charged me $13. I was delighted, expecting it to cost much more, and so I paid the bill and went on my way. The next morning, I woke up to find the right-rear tire completely flat. I canceled the morning's appointment, filled the tire with an air compressor, and drove back to the tire store. Shortly, the manager came out and told me that they found another nail in that tire; they were going to eat the $13 on this one, but it had better not happen again. I could not believe the insinuation—that I was driving about looking for nails to hit with that one tire just so I could spend my morning taking them for $13! Instead of offering the possibility that they had overlooked a nail the previous night, apologizing for the inconvenience, or anything of that sort, he shifted the responsibility to me. Needless to say, I have not been back since, and all of my repair business is now done elsewhere.

These two examples illustrate two different approaches to treating the customer. In the first example, the customer is well respected and treated better than expected. In the second example, the customer is disrespected and is treated as an inconvenience. Given the lifetime value of customers, it is always better to respect them—and retain them—than to offhandedly dismiss them."

Privacy

While there is some overlap between confidentiality and privacy, privacy is an area of computing that is becoming considerably more regulated. As a computing professional, you must stay current with applicable laws, because you're often one of the primary agents expected to ensure compliance.

In addition to the federal laws about computer crime, there are similar laws in most states. Check `http://www.nsi.org/Library/Compsec/computerlaw/statelaws.html` for information on your state's regulations.

Although the laws provide a minimal level of privacy, you should go out of your way to respect the privacy of your users beyond what the law establishes. If you discover information about a user that you should not be privy to, you should not share it with anyone, and you should alert the customers that their data is accessible and encourage them—if applicable—to remedy the situation.

Putting It All in Perspective

Whether you are dealing with customers in person or on the phone, there are rules to which you should adhere. These were implied and discussed in the previous sections, but you must understand them and remember them for the exam:

- Use proper language and avoid using jargon, abbreviations, and acronyms. Every field has its own language, and outsiders feel lost when they start hearing it. Put yourself in the position of someone not in the field and explain what is going on by using words they can relate to.

- Maintain a positive attitude and tone of voice. The customer is counting on you to fix their problem. The last thing they want is for you to sound defeated when you hear the problem.

- Listen to your customers. Allow them to complete their statements and avoid interrupting them. People like to know they are being heard, and, as simple an act as it is, this can make all the difference in making them feel at ease with your work. Everyone has been in a situation where they have not been able to fully explain their problem without being interrupted or ignored. It is not enjoyable in a social setting, and it is intolerable in a business setting.

- Be culturally sensitive. Some people may have a language barrier that makes it difficult to explain their problem. (Think about how much computer language you learned in your high school language courses!) Others may have different habits or practices in their workplace. Be respectful of their world.

- Be on time. If you're going to be late, be sure to contact your customer. Not doing so indicates that you think their problem isn't important.

- Avoid distraction and/or interruptions when talking with customers. You need to make them feel like their problem is important and that it has your full attention.

- Exercise patience with difficult customers and situations, including:

  - Avoid arguing with customers and/or becoming defensive.

  - Do not minimize customers' problems. While it may be a situation you see every day, it is a crisis to them.

  - Avoid being judgmental and/or insulting or calling the customer names.

  - Clarify customer statements and ask pertinent questions. The questions you ask should help guide you toward isolating the problem and identifying possible solutions. Don't be afraid to nod, ask questions, and repeat to the customer what you think they are saying to make sure you are understanding it correctly.

- Set and meet—or exceed—expectations and communicate timelines and status. Customers want to know what is going on. They want to know that you understand the problem and can deal with it. Being honest and direct is almost always appreciated.

- Deal appropriately with confidential materials. Don't look at files or printouts that you have no business looking at. Make sure the customer's confidential materials stay that way.

Summary

This chapter covered two key areas of operational procedures that you should integrate into your work: safety and environmental procedures and communication and professionalism.

First, we looked at the importance of safety and environmental issues. We identified potential safety hazards and examined preventive actions. Then we talked about Material Safety Data Sheets (MSDSs) and their importance. Next, we discussed the importance of using the right tool for the right job, and which tools to avoid using. That was followed by a section on handling accidents, including incident reporting.

Next, we outlined some methods to apply safe working environment policies and procedures. Included were preventing electrostatic discharge (ESD) and electromagnetic interference (EMI), creating a safe work environment, and handling computer equipment properly. Then, we looked at proper disposal procedures for batteries, display devices, and chemical solvents and cans. These items need to be kept out of the environment because of the damage they can cause.

Finally, we moved on to professionalism and communication. You should treat your customers as you would want to be treated and let them know that you respect them and their business through your actions and behavior.

Exam Essentials

Know which computer components are particularly dangerous to technicians.   The most dangerous are the power supply and the monitor. Both are capable of storing lethal charges of electricity, even when unplugged. You also need to be aware of parts that get incredibly hot, such as the processor, which can cause severe burns if touched.

Understand where to find safety information regarding chemicals.   You can find this information on a Material Safety Data Sheet (MSDS). An MSDS might not have come with your purchase, but most suppliers will gladly supply one if requested.

Know which tool to use for which job.   The majority of computer repair jobs can be handled with nothing more than a Phillips-head screwdriver. However, you might need cutters, extra light, or a mirror for some jobs. Never use magnetically tipped tools.

Understand methods to help prevent ESD.   One of the biggest and most common dangers to electronic components is electrostatic discharge (ESD). There are several methods you can employ to help avoid ESD problems, such as grounding yourself; using an antistatic wrist strap, bag, or mat; and controlling the humidity levels.

Know proper disposal procedures for used computer parts, batteries, and chemical solvents.   The specific disposal procedure depends on what you are trying to dispose of. However, the safe answer is to always recycle the component and not throw it in the trash bin.

Use good communication skills.   Listen to your customers. Let them tell you what they understand the problem to be, and then interpret the problem and see if you can get them to agree to what you are hearing them say. Treat your customers, whether they be end users or colleagues, with respect, and take their issues and problems seriously.

Use job-related professional behavior.   The Golden Rule should govern your professional behavior. Five key elements to this, from a business perspective, are punctuality, accountability, flexibility, confidentiality, and privacy.

Review Questions

1. A computer is experiencing random reboots and phantom problems that disappear after reboot. What should you do?

    A. Tell the customer that it's normal for the computer to do that.

    B. Replace the motherboard.

    C. Boot clean.

    D. Replace the power supply.

    E. Open the cover, clean the inside of the computer, and reseat all cards and chips.

2. Which of the following is used to properly discharge voltage from an unplugged computer monitor?

    A. Antistatic wrist strap

    B. Screwdriver

    C. High-voltage probe

    D. Power cord

3. Which of the following must contain information about a chemical solvent's emergency cleanup procedures?

    A. OSHA

    B. MSDS

    C. Product label

    D. CRT

4. You are purchasing, for home use, an inkjet printer cartridge that you know has an MSDS. How do you obtain the MSDS for this product?

    A. The store is required to give you one at the time of purchase.

    B. It's contained in the packaging of the printer cartridge.

    C. You are not legally allowed to have an MSDS for this product.

    D. Visit the website of the printer cartridge manufacturer.

5. In the interest of a safe work environment, which of the following should you report? (Choose all that apply.)

    A. An accident

    B. A near-accident

    C. Dirt on the floor inside a building

    D. Water puddles in a hallway

6. What is the approximate minimum level of static charge for humans to feel a shock?

  A. 300 volts

  B. 3,000 volts

  C. 30,000 volts

  D. 300,000 volts

7. Which of the following measures can be implemented to reduce the risk of ESD? (Choose all that apply.)

  A. Antistatic wrist strap

  B. Antistatic bag

  C. Antistatic floor mat

  D. Antistatic hair net

8. Which of the following are OSHA requirements for a safe work environment that must be followed by employers? (Choose all that apply.)

  A. Attend yearly OSHA safe work environment seminars.

  B. Provide properly maintained tools and equipment.

  C. Keep records of accident reports.

  D. Display an OSHA poster in a prominent location.

9. What is the proper way to dispose of a broken CRT monitor?

  A. Take it to a computer recycling center.

  B. Discharge the monitor with a high-volt probe and throw it away.

  C. Throw it away.

  D. None of the above.

10. When moving computer equipment, which of the following are good procedures to follow? (Choose all that apply.)

  A. Lift by bending over at the waist.

  B. Carry monitors with the glass face away from your body.

  C. Use a cart for heavy objects.

  D. Ensure that there are no safety hazards in your path.

11. You have four AA alkaline batteries that you just removed from a remote-control device. What is the recommended way to dispose of these batteries?

  A. Throw them in the trash.

  B. Incinerate them.

  C. Take them to a recycling center.

  D. Flush them in the sewer.

12. Which of the following are good ways to show you are listening to someone explaining a problem?

    A. Nodding

    B. Repeating what she is saying

    C. Asking questions

    D. All of the above

13. While working on a user's system, you discover a sticky note attached to the bottom of the keyboard that has their username and password written on it. The user is not around, and you need to verify that the network connection is working. What should you do?

    A. Log in, verify access, and log out.

    B. Log in and stay logged in when you are finished.

    C. Page the user.

    D. Log in and change the user's password.

14. You promised a customer that you would be out to service his problem before the end of the day but have been tied up at another site. As it now becomes apparent that you will not be able to make it to his location, what should you do?

    A. Arrive first thing in the morning.

    B. Wait until after hours and then leave a message that you were there.

    C. Call the customer and inform him of the situation.

    D. Send off an e-mail letting him know you will be late.

15. A customer is trying to explain to you a problem with his system. Unfortunately, he has such a thick accent that you are unable to understand what he is saying. What should you do?

    A. Just start working on the system and looking for obvious errors.

    B. Call your supervisor.

    C. Ask that another technician be sent in your place.

    D. Apologize and find another user or manager who can help you translate.

16. You have been trying to troubleshoot a user's system all day when it suddenly becomes clear that the data is irretrievably lost. Upon informing the customer of this, he becomes so angry that he shoves you against a wall. What should you do?

    A. Shove the user back, only a little harder than he shoved you.

    B. Shove the user back, only a little easier than he shoved you.

    C. Try to calm the user down, and leave the site if you cannot.

    D. Yell for everyone in the area to come quickly.

17. A customer tells you that the last technician who was there spent three hours on the phone making personal calls. What should you do with this information?

A. Nothing.

B. Inform your manager.

C. Talk to the technician personally.

D. Ask the customer to prove it.

18. You arrive at the site of a failed server to find the vice president nervously pacing and worrying about lost data. What should you do?

A. Offer a joke to lighten things up.

B. Downplay the situation and tell him that customers lose data every day.

C. Keep your head down and keep looking at manuals to let him know you are serious.

D. Inform him that you've dealt with similar situations and will let him know what needs to be done as soon as possible.

19. You're temporarily filling in on phone support when a caller tells you that they are sick and tired of being bounced from one hold queue to another. He wants his problem fixed, and he wants it fixed now. What should you do?

A. Inform him up front that you are only filling in temporarily and won't be of much help.

B. Transfer him to another technician who handles phone calls more often.

C. Try to solve his problem without putting him on hold or transferring him elsewhere

D. Suggest that he call back at another time when you are not there.

20. At the end of the day, you finish a job only to find the user you were doing it for had to leave. What should you do?

A. Notify your manager that the user has gone.

B. Leave a note for the user detailing what was done and how to contact you.

C. Notify the user's manager and your own that you have finished.

D. All of the above.

Answers to Review Questions

1. E. When a computer is experiencing random reboots and phantom problems that disappear after reboot, you should open the cover, clean everything (if it's dirty), and reseat all cards and chips. Some components could have gunk on them that carries an electrical charge, or could have experienced "chip creep," where they slowly work themselves out of their sockets.

2. C. A high-voltage probe is designed to release the electricity from high-voltage components, which are found in the back of CRT computer monitors. Wearing an antistatic wrist strap when working on a computer monitor can cause the stored up electric current to be released through your body, which could result in serious injury or death!

3. B. The Material Safety Data Sheet (MSDS) contains information about chemical properties, including what to do if an accident occurs.

4. D. Companies are not legally required to provide MSDSs to consumers. However, most will if you ask. The best place to look is the manufacturer's website.

5. A, B, D. Accidents and near-accidents should always be reported. Dirt isn't usually a safety issue, but water in a hallway could cause people to slip and fall.

6. B. Most people can feel an electric shock at about 3,000 volts. However, computer equipment can be damaged with as little as 100 volts.

7. A, B, C. Antistatic wrist straps, bags (for parts), and floor mats can all help reduce the risk of ESD. There are no antistatic hair nets (but if you have long hair, it's best to tie it back so it doesn't contact the computer parts).

8. B, C, D. Private sector employers are required by OSHA to maintain a safe work environment. This includes maintaining tools and equipment, keeping records of accidents, and displaying a safety information poster.

9. A. Monitors should be recycled after the end of their useful life. They contain many harmful elements, including lead, that can cause environmental problems.

10. C, D. You should always lift with your legs, not your back. This means bending at the knees and not the waist. Monitors should be carried with the glass face toward your body. Using carts for heavy objects is a good idea, as is ensuring that your path is free of safety hazards, such as trip hazards.

11. C. Alkaline batteries should always be recycled. Throwing them in the trash means they'll end up in a landfill where they can contaminate the environment. Burning batteries is always a bad idea, because they will explode.

12. D. All of these actions can indicate to the speaker that you are listening to what she is saying.

13. C. You should page the user and let her know she needs to verify access. You also should tell her that you saw the sticky note and highly recommend that she change her password to a new value and not write it down. Logging in to the system using the information you found would be violating the privacy of that user and should not be done. Further, logging in with someone else's information makes you a potential scapegoat for any data that is corrupted or missing until the user changes the password.

14. C. While calling and sending e-mail are both solutions to this situation, calling the customer provides an immediate means of communication that you know will get there. Inform the customer of the situation and offer to be out the first opportunity you can— which will hopefully be first thing in the morning.

15. D. While there is no perfect solution to problems of this type, the best solution is to find someone else who can mediate and help you understand the problem.

16. C. Physical abuse violates respect and should be avoided at all costs. You should try to calm the user down. If you cannot do this, you should leave the site immediately and not return until it is safe to do so. You may also want to report the incident to your management so that they're aware of the situation.

17. B. The customer is expressing a concern that she was not shown respect by a technician from your company. You should apologize and make your manager aware of the situation or concern. Unless you are a supervisor, which is not implied in the question, you should not personally talk to the technician about the issue.

18. D. You should always act with confidence and in a way similar to how you would want to be treated if you were in the customer's situation. Ignoring, downplaying, or joking about the vice president's obvious concern are very poor choices.

19. C. The best solution is to meet the customer's needs and solve his problem. If that means you have to summon additional help or resources, you should do so.

20. D. You should perform all of these operations to sign off on the job and leave the user with a sense that his problem has been taken care of.

Chapter 13

Installing, Maintaining, and Troubleshooting Hardware

THE FOLLOWING COMPTIA A+ PRACTICAL APPLICATION EXAM OBJECTIVES ARE COVERED IN THIS CHAPTER:

✓ **1.1 Given a scenario, install, configure and maintain personal computer components**

- Storage devices
    - HDD
    - SATA
        - PATA
        - Solid state
    - FDD
    - Optical drives
        - CD / DVD / RW / Blu-Ray
    - Removable
    - External
- Motherboards
    - Jumper settings
    - CMOS battery
    - Advanced BIOS settings
    - Bus speeds
    - Chipsets
    - Firmware updates

- Socket types
- Expansion slots
- Memory slots
- Front panel connectors
- I/O ports
    - Sound, video, USB 1.1, USB 2.0, serial, IEEE 1394 / Firewire, parallel, NIC, modem, PS/2)
- Power supplies
  - Wattages and capacity
  - Connector types and quantity
  - Output voltage
- Processors
  - Socket types
  - Speed
  - Number of cores
  - Power consumption
  - Cache
  - Front side bus
  - 32bit vs. 64bit
- Memory
- Adapter cards
  - Graphics cards
  - Sound cards
  - Storage controllers
    - RAID cards (RAID array – levels 0,1,5)
    - eSATA cards
  - I/O cards
    - Firewire
    - USB
    - Parallel
    - Serial

- Wired and wireless network cards
- Capture cards (TV, video)
- Media reader
- Cooling systems
  - Heat sinks
  - Thermal compound
  - CPU fans
  - Case fans

✓ **1.2 Given a scenario, detect problems, troubleshoot and repair/replace personal computer components**

- Storage devices
  - HDD
    - SATA
    - PATA
    - Solid state
  - FDD
  - Optical drives
    - CD / DVD / RW / Blu-Ray
  - Removable
  - External
- Motherboards
  - Jumper settings
  - CMOS battery
  - Advanced BIOS settings
  - Bus speeds
  - Chipsets
  - Firmware updates
  - Socket types
  - Expansion slots
  - Memory slots
  - Front panel connectors

- I/O ports
  - Sound, video, USB 1.1, USB 2.0, serial, IEEE 1394 / Firewire, parallel, NIC, modem, PS/2)
- Power supplies
  - Wattages and capacity
  - Connector types and quantity
  - Output voltage
- Processors
  - Socket types
  - Speed
  - Number of cores
  - Power consumption
  - Cache
  - Front side bus
  - 32bit vs. 64bit
- Memory
- Adapter cards
  - Graphics cards—memory
  - Sound cards
  - Storage controllers
    - RAID cards
    - eSATA cards
  - I/O cards
    - Firewire
    - USB
    - Parallel
    - Serial
  - Wired and wireless network cards
  - Capture cards (TV, video)
  - Media reader

- Cooling systems
  - Heat sinks
  - Thermal compound
  - CPU fans
  - Case fans

✓ **1.4 Given a scenario, select and use the following tools**

- Multimeter
- Power supply tester
- Specialty hardware / tools
- Cable testers
- Loop back plugs
- Anti-static pad and wrist strap
- Extension magnet

You cannot become A+ certified without knowing personal computers inside and out. To that end, this chapter guides you through the installation, removal, and configuration of some of the most common devices found in modern computer systems. First, though, we provide tips on selecting components. Then you will dive right into removal and installation of components. Finally, we reveal troubleshooting techniques that you can use in case removing or installing components goes awry.

Installing, Configuring, and Maintaining PC Components

While being able to identify the various components of a personal computer is important, knowing how to install, configure, and maintain them is equally, if not more, important. The components in question are storage devices (internal and external), motherboards and related components, power supplies, processors, memory, adapter cards, and cooling systems.

Working with Storage Devices

Storage devices come in many shapes and sizes. In addition to IDE/EIDE and SCSI, two of the older standards, there are now Serial ATA (SATA) and Parallel ATA (PATA—a newer term for IDE), and you can differentiate between internally and externally attached drives. This section looks at storage devices from a number of those perspectives.

Parallel ATA (PATA) is the name retroactively given to the ATA/IDE standards when SATA became available. PATA uses the classic 40-pin connector for parallel data communications, whereas SATA uses a more modern 7-pin connector for serial data transfer.

Drive Preparation

Regardless of the type of technology used, drives or discs (where the disc is separate from the drive) need to be formatted prior to use, sometimes at a hardware level (low-level) and always at an operating system level (high-level). Every operating system includes a utility for high-level formatting. With Windows-based operating systems, you can use the FORMAT command from the command line and the Disk Management graphical utility with Windows 2000 and newer operating systems.

Except for floppy diskettes, optical discs, and very few others, before you can format a drive for the first time, you have to partition it. Drive partitioning segregates a physical part of the drive from the rest so that the operating system can lay out the data structures required for the formatted volume to be recognizable by the operating system as one or more drive letters. A partition can span an entire physical drive as well. Each partition is routinely given its own drive letter by a Microsoft operating system and is referred to synonymously as a volume. Multiple partitions on the same drive or among many drives can be grouped into a complex volume as well. In such an array, one drive letter refers to the entire group of partitions.

 Many other chapters of this book look at the operating systems and contain more information on these and other utilities.

Working with IDE

Traditionally, integrated drive electronics (IDE) drives have been the most common type of hard drive found in computers. Though so often thought of in relation to hard drives, IDE is much more than a hard drive interface; it's also a popular interface for many other drive types, including optical drives and tape drives.

The design of IDE is simple: put the controller chip and its related electronics right on the drive, and use a relatively short ribbon cable to connect the drive and controller to an interface on the system. This offers the benefits of decreasing signal loss (thus increasing reliability), eliminating the need for low-level formatting in the field, and making the drive easier to install. The IDE interface can be an expansion board (often referred to as a paddle card because it does little more than transfer pins from the drive to pins on the expansion bus; it has no real intelligence onboard), or it can be built into the motherboard, as is the case on almost all new systems today and for quite a few generations past, especially non-server, desktop systems.

IDE generically refers to any drive that has a built-in controller. Enhanced Small Device Interface (ESDI—an all-but-dead technology) and, to a certain degree, SCSI drives have drive electronics integrated into them. The IDE we know today is more properly called *AT Attachment (ATA)*; the terms *SATA* and *PATA* were derived from ATA.

There have been many revisions of the IDE standard over the years, and each one is designated with a certain AT Attachment number—ATA-1 through ATA-8, so far. Drives that support ATA-2 and higher are generically referred to as *Enhanced IDE (EIDE)*.

With ATA-3, a technology called ATA Packet Interface (ATAPI) was introduced to help deal with IDE devices other than hard disks. ATAPI enables the BIOS to recognize an IDE CD-ROM drive, for example, or a tape backup or Zip drive. ATA-3 also introduced the Self-Monitoring and Reporting Technology (SMART). SMART allows a hard drive to monitor itself and warn the user during bootup of any impending failure. When heeded, these warnings allow you time to salvage data before it is lost. Generally, backing up the potentially ailing drive, before replacing it and restoring your data, is the best route. Note, however, that drives can still fail, and data loss can still occur, even without a warning from SMART.

Starting with ATA-4, a new technology was introduced called UltraDMA, supporting transfer modes capable of rates of up to 33MBps.

ATA-5 supports UltraDMA/66, with transfer modes having rates of up to 66MBps. To achieve this high rate, the drive must have a special ribbon cable (still with only 40 pins, however), and the motherboard or IDE controller card must support ATA-5.

ATA-6 supports UltraDMA/100, with transfer modes capable of up to 100MBps.

If an ATA-5 or ATA-6 drive is used with a normal 40-wire cable or is used on a system that doesn't support the higher-speed modes, it reverts to the ATA-4 performance level.

ATA-7 supports UltraDMA/133, with transfer modes of 133MBps and up to 150MBps for serial ATA.

ATA-8 made only minor revisions to ATA-7 and also supports UltraDMA/133 and 150MBps SATA as well as the potential for the next generation of SATA, with throughput in excess of 500MBps.

IDE Pros and Cons

The primary benefit of IDE is that it's nearly universally supported. Almost every motherboard has IDE connectors. A typical motherboard has two IDE connectors, and each connector can support a single channel of up to two drives on the same cable. That means you're limited to four IDE devices per system, unless you add an expansion board containing another IDE interface. In contrast, with SCSI you can have up to seven devices (including drives) per interface, roughly double or quadruple that on some types of SCSI.

Performance also may suffer when certain IDE devices share an interface. It is recommended that you pair like devices on a channel. Otherwise, the slower device can have a negative impact on the faster one. SCSI drives are much more efficient with this type of transfer.

IDE Installation and Configuration

To install an IDE drive, do the following:

1. Set the master/slave jumper on the drive.

2. Install the drive in the drive bay.

3. Connect the power-supply cable.

4. Connect the ribbon cable to the drive and to the motherboard or IDE expansion board. There is a colored (usually red) stripe down one edge of the ribbon cable that is used to correctly orient the cable both where it connects to the drive and to the motherboard. If there is no marking for pin 1, you'll usually orient the red stripe toward the drive's power connector. Don't rely on that too much, though. Floppy drives are notorious for placing pin 1 away from their power connector.

5. Configure the drive in BIOS Setup if it isn't automatically detected.

6. Partition and format the drive using the operating system.

Each IDE channel can have only one *master* drive on it. If there are two drives on a single cable, one of them must be the *slave* drive. This setting is accomplished via a jumper on the drive. Some drives have a separate setting for Single (that is, master with no slave) and Master (that is, master with a slave); others use the Master setting generically to configure either case. Figure 13.1 shows a typical master/slave jumper scenario, but different drives may have different jumper positions to represent each state.

FIGURE 13.1 Master/slave jumpers

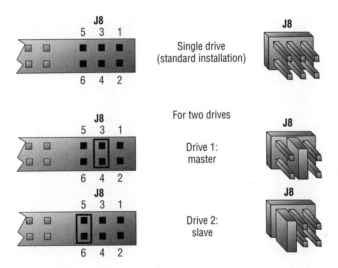

Another option is to use the Cable Select setting for master/slave selection. Most cables support Cable Select, but it won't work if the cable is not wired properly. Another caveat is that you must never mix Cable Select with Master and Slave settings. If one drive is set manually as Master, the other on the same cable must be set as Slave. If you set one drive to be configured as master or slave automatically with Cable Select, the other must be set for Cable Select as well. The wiring of the cable will result in the drive at the end of the cable being selected as master.

Most BIOS Setup programs today support Plug and Play, so they detect the new drive automatically at startup. If this doesn't work, the drive may not be installed correctly, the jumper settings may be wrong, or the BIOS Setup may have the IDE interface set to None or Disable rather than Auto. Enter BIOS Setup and find out. Setting the IDE interface to Auto and then allowing the BIOS to detect the drive is usually all that is required.

In BIOS Setup for the drive, you might have the option of selecting a DMA or programmed input/output (PIO) setting for the drive. Both are methods for improving drive performance by allowing the drive to write directly to RAM, bypassing the CPU when possible. For modern drives that support UltraDMA, neither of these settings is necessary or desirable.

Now that your drive is installed, you can proceed to partition and format it for the operating system you've chosen. Then, finally, you can install your operating system of choice.

For a Windows 2000 or later system, including XP and Vista, allow the Windows Setup program to partition and format the drive, or use the Disk Management utility in Windows to perform those tasks. To access Disk Management from Control Panel, choose Administrative Tools and then choose Computer Management.

Working with SCSI

Small Computer System Interface (SCSI) devices can be either internal or external to the computer. Eight-bit SCSI-1 and SCSI-2 internal devices use a SCSI A cable, a 50-pin ribbon cable similar to that of an IDE drive. Sixteen-bit SCSI uses a SCSI P cable, with 68 wires and a 68-pin DB-style connector. There is also an 80-pin internal connector called SCA used for some high-end SCSI devices. Like IDE and floppy-drive cables, 50-pin SCSI ribbon cables have a colored stripe (usually blue or red, but it depends on the color of the rest of the cable) down one side to indicate the orientation of pin 1. The 68-wire ribbon requires no indicator because the connector is keyed. External SCSI connectors depend on the type. SCSI-1 uses a 50-pin Centronics connector, as for a parallel printer. SCSI-2 uses a 25-, 50-, or 68-pin connector. SCSI-3 uses a 68- or 80-pin connector.

To configure SCSI, you must assign a unique device number (often called a SCSI address, SCSI ID, or SCSI device ID) to each device on the SCSI bus. These numbers are configured through jumpers, DIP switches, up/down pushbuttons with the selected ID displayed through a hole on a wheel, among other ways. When the SCSI controller needs to send data to the device, it activates the wire dedicated to signaling that address.

A device called a *terminator* (technically a *terminating resistor pack*) must be installed at both ends of the bus to keep the signals "on the bus." The device then responds with a signal that contains the number of the device that sent the information and the data itself. The terminator can be built into the device and activated/deactivated with a jumper, or it can be a separate block or connector hooked onto the device when termination is required.

Termination can be either active or passive. A passive terminator works with resistors driven by the small amount of electricity that travels through the SCSI bus. Active termination uses voltage regulators inside the terminator. Active termination is much better, and you should use it whenever you have fast, wide, or Ultra SCSI devices on the chain and/or more than two SCSI devices on the chain. It may not be obvious from looking at a terminator whether it's active or passive.

SCSI Device Installation and Configuration

Installing SCSI devices is more complex than installing an IDE drive. The main issues with installing SCSI devices are cabling, termination, and addressing.

We'll discuss termination and cabling together because they're closely tied. There are two types of cabling:

- Internal cabling uses a 50-wire ribbon cable with several keyed connectors. These connectors are attached to the devices in the computer (the order is unimportant), with one connector connecting to the adapter.

- External cabling uses thick, shielded cables that run from adapter to device to device in a fashion known as *daisy-chaining*. Each device has two ports on it (most of the time). When hooking up external SCSI devices, you run a cable from the adapter to the first device. Then you run a cable from the first device to the second device, from the second to the third, and so on.

Because there are two types of cabling devices, you have three ways to connect them. The methods differ by where the devices are located and whether the adapter has the terminator installed. The guide to remember here is that *both ends* of the bus must be terminated. Let's look briefly at the three connection methods:

Internal devices only   When you have only internal SCSI devices, you connect the cable to the adapter and to every SCSI device in the computer. You then install the terminating resistors on the adapter and terminate the last drive in the chain. All other devices are unterminated. This is demonstrated in Figure 13.2.

FIGURE 13.2   Cabling internal SCSI devices only

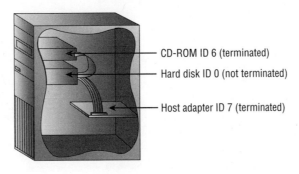

- CD-ROM ID 6 (terminated)
- Hard disk ID 0 (not terminated)
- Host adapter ID 7 (terminated)

Some devices and adapters don't use terminating resistor packs; instead, you use a jumper or DIP switch to activate or deactivate SCSI termination on such devices. Check the documentation to find out what type your device uses.

External devices only   In the next situation, you have external devices only, as shown in Figure 13.3. By external devices, we mean that each has its own power supply. You connect the devices in the same manner in which you connected internal devices, but in this method you use several very short (less than 0.5 meters) *stub* cables to run between the devices in a daisy chain (rather than one long cable with several connectors). The effect is the same. The adapter and the last device in the chain (which has only one stub cable attached to it) must be terminated.

Both internal and external devices   Finally, there's the hybrid situation in which you have both internal and external devices (Figure 13.4). Most adapters have connectors for both internal and external SCSI devices—if yours doesn't have both, you'll need to see if anybody makes one that will work with your devices. For adapters that do have both types of connectors, you connect your internal devices to the ribbon cable and attach the cable to the adapter. Then you daisy-chain your external devices off the external port. You terminate the last device on each chain, leaving the adapter unterminated.

FIGURE 13.3 Cabling external SCSI devices only

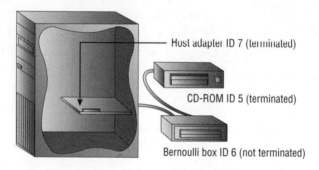

Host adapter ID 7 (terminated)

CD-ROM ID 5 (terminated)

Bernoulli box ID 6 (not terminated)

FIGURE 13.4 Cabling internal and external SCSI devices together

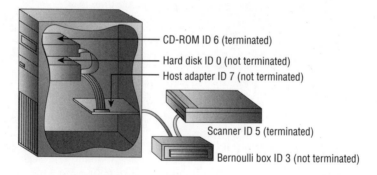

CD-ROM ID 6 (terminated)

Hard disk ID 0 (not terminated)

Host adapter ID 7 (not terminated)

Scanner ID 5 (terminated)

Bernoulli box ID 3 (not terminated)

Even though the third technique described is the technically correct way to install termination for the hybrid situation (in which you have both internal and external devices), some adapter cards still need to have terminators installed. Both ends of a SCSI chain must be terminated.

Each device must also have a unique SCSI ID number. This number can be assigned by the jumper (with internal devices) or with a rotary switch (on external devices). You start by assigning your adapter an address. This can be any number from 0 to 7 on an 8-bit bus, 0 to 15 on a 16-bit bus, and 0 to 31 on a 32-bit bus, as long as no other device is using that ID. This ID has the highest priority for arbitration and therefore the Host adapter will always take priority.

Here are some recommendations that are commonly accepted by the PC community. Remember that these are guidelines, not rules:

- Generally speaking, give slower devices higher priority so they can access the bus whenever they need it. Higher numbers are higher priority.
- Set the bootable (or first) hard disk to ID 0.
- Set the CD-ROM to ID 3.

After setting the IDs and the devices are cabled and terminated, you have to get the PC to recognize the SCSI adapter and its devices. The SCSI adapter manages all SCSI device resource allocation, so generally all that is required is to make sure the operating system is able to see the SCSI adapter. This involves installing a Windows driver for the adapter in Windows, for example, or a real-mode driver in CONFIG.SYS for MS-DOS.

However, if you want to boot from a SCSI drive, the system must be able to read from that drive in order to load the operating system; you must enable the SCSI adapter's own BIOS extension so that the PC can read from it at startup without a driver. Check the documentation for the adapter; sometimes the BIOS Setup program for the SCSI adapter is activated via a function key at startup.

Once the drive is installed and talking to the computer, you can high-level format the media and install the operating system.

If there are problems, double-check the termination and ID numbers. Termination will most likely be the problem, but you might need to make sure no two devices are set to the same ID.

RAID

RAID stands for Redundant Array of Independent Disks. It's a way of combining the storage power of more than one hard disk for a special purpose, such as increased performance or fault tolerance. RAID is more commonly done with SCSI drives, but it can be done with IDE drives.

There are several types of RAID. The following are the most commonly used RAID levels:

RAID 0   Also known as *disk striping* or a simple *volume set*. This is technically not RAID, because it doesn't provide the fault tolerance implied by the *redundant* component of the name. Data is written across multiple drives, so one drive can be reading or writing while the next drive's read-write head is moving. This makes for faster data access. However, if any one of the drives fails, all content is lost.

RAID 1   Also known as *disk mirroring*. This is a method of producing fault tolerance by writing all data simultaneously to two separate drives. If one drive fails, the other contains all the data and can be switched to. However, disk mirroring doesn't help access speed, and the cost is double that of a single drive. If a separate host adapter is used for the second drive, the term *duplexing* is attributed to RAID 1.

RAID 5 Combines the benefits of both RAID 0 and RAID 1, creating a redundant volume set. Unlike RAID 1, however, RAID 5 does not employ mirroring for redundancy. It uses a parity block interleaved across all the drives in the array, in addition to striping the data across the same drives. That way, if one drive fails, the parity information can be used with the remaining data from the working drive or drives to recover what was on the failed drive and rebuild the set. A minimum of three drives is required for RAID 5.

To summarize, although there are other implementations of RAID, such as RAID 3, RAID 4, and RAID 6, as well as composite implementations, such as RAID 10, which is a combination of RAID 0 and RAID 1 (also known as RAID 1+0 and RAID 0+1), the three detailed here are by far the most prolific.

External Storage Drives

As prices decrease and capacities increase, the number of external storage drives in use continues to climb. In addition to the SCSI variety, you can find drives with USB connections as well as ones that connect directly to the network. USB drives are recognized by the operating system upon connection, and if the external drive is to be used as a backup location, you simply install any additional software you want to use. Windows Vista's built-in backup utility is a form of drive imaging software that works well with external drives. Symantec offers personal and enterprise lines of Ghost software for the same purpose as well as to create drive images for mass installations of a reference system onto clones.

If the external drive connects directly to the network, simply connect it as outlined in the included instructions and install the optional software on any clients that will be maintaining it. The benefit of connecting directly to the network is that the drive(s) can be easily accessed by all clients.

Installing, Removing, and Configuring Storage Devices

The removal and installation of storage devices, such as hard drives, floppy drives, CD/DVD drives, and tape drives, is pretty straightforward. There really isn't any deviation in the process of installing or exchanging the hardware. Fortunately, with today's operating systems, little to no configuration is required for such devices. The *Plug and Play BIOS* and operating system work together to recognize such components. However, you still have to *partition* and *format* out-of-the-box hard drives before they will allow the installation of the operating system. Nevertheless, today's operating systems allow for a pain-free partition/format/install experience by handling the entire process if you let them.

Removing Storage Devices

Removing any component is frequently easier than installing the same part. Consider the fact that most people could destroy a house, perhaps not safely enough to ensure their well-being, but they don't have to know the intricacies of construction to start smashing away. Building a house, on the other hand, is an art of which very few people are capable. Similarly, many could figure out how to remove a storage device, as long as they can get into the case to begin with, but only a few could start from scratch and successfully install one without tutelage.

In Exercise 13.1, you remove an internal storage device.

 This section details the removal of internal storage devices, and the section "Installing Storage Devices" details their installation. Be aware that external storage devices exist, but today's external storage devices are USB- and FireWire-attached, making them completely Plug and Play. Only the software preparation of external hard drives is a consideration, but the same procedure outlined for internal devices works for external devices as well.

EXERCISE 13.1

Removing an Internal Storage Device

1. With the power source removed from the system, ground yourself and the computer to the same source of ground.

2. Remove the cover from the system, exposing the internal components.

3. Targeting the storage device you wish to remove, unplug all connections from the device. These include data and power connections as well as any other connections, such as audio connections to the sound card or motherboard. The beveled Molex power connectors can be difficult to remove, but they fit very tightly, so don't worry about how hard they seem to be to remove. There is no clip to release. Do, however, be sure to grip the connector, not the wires.

4. Gather the appropriate antistatic packaging to plan ahead for all static-sensitive components that will be reused in the future, including any adapter cards that the storage device plugs into.

5. Remove any obstructions that might hinder device removal, such as component cables attached to adapter cards or adapter cards themselves, storing those to be reused in antistatic packaging.

6. Remove related adapter cards from the motherboard, storing those to be reused in antistatic packaging.

7. Remove the machine screws holding the storage device to the chassis. These could be on the side of the device or on the bottom.

8. Some devices, especially hard drives because they have no front access from the case, pull out of the chassis toward the rear of the case, while others, such as CD/DVD and floppy drives, generally pull out from the front. A gentle nudge from the rear of the device starts it on its way out the front. Go ahead and remove the device from the case. If you discover other components that obstruct the storage device's removal, repeat step 5.

Installing Storage Devices

An obvious difference among storage devices is their form factor. This is the term used to describe the physical dimensions of a storage device. Common form-factor characteristics include:

- 3.5 inches wide vs. 5.25 inches wide
- Half height vs. full height vs. 1 inch high and more
- Any of the laptop specialty form factors

You will need to figure out whether you have an open bay in the chassis to accommodate the form factor of the storage device you want to install. Adapters exist that allow a device of small size to fit into a larger bay. For obvious reasons, the converse is not also true.

In Exercise 13.2, you install an internal storage device.

EXERCISE 13.2

Installing an Internal Storage Device

1. With the power source removed from the system, ground yourself and the computer to the same source of ground.

2. Remove the cover from the system, exposing the internal components.

3. Locate an available bay for your component, paying attention to your device's need for front access. If you do not see one, look around; some cases provide fastening points near the power supply or other open areas of the case. If you still do not see one, investigate the possibility of sacrificing a rarely or never used device to make room.

4. Remove any obstructions that might hinder device installation, such as component cables attached to adapter cards or adapter cards themselves, storing those to be reused in antistatic packaging.

5. Insert the storage device into the bay, keeping in mind that some insert from the rear of the bay and some from the front.

6. Line up the screw holes in the device with the holes in the bay. Note that many devices rarely insert as far as they can before lining up with the chassis's holes. So don't be surprised when pushing the device all the way into the bay results in misalignment. Other devices that require front access stop themselves flush with the front of the case, and still others require you to secure them while holding them flush.

7. Use at least two screws on one side of the device. This keeps the device from sliding in the bay, as well as from rotating, which happens when you use only one screw or one screw on each side. If the opposite side is accessible, go ahead and put at least one screw in the other side. Most devices allow for as many as four screws per side, but eight screws are not necessary in the vast majority of situations.

8. Connect the data cable from the device to the adapter card or motherboard header. Advanced technology attachment (ATA) devices, such as those that are designated as IDE drives, which include compatible hard drives and CD/DVD drives, use a 40-pin connector. Floppy drives and some tape backup drives that connect through the floppy subsystem use a 34-pin connector. They look the same except for the three rows of two pins that differentiate them. Note that if you use the master/slave and not the cable-select feature of IDE drives on the same chain, it does not matter which device connects to which connector on the cable. However, with floppy drives, drive A: must always be attached to the connector after the twist in the cable.

9. Attach a power connector from the power supply to the device, bearing in mind that there are two connector styles that are not very close in appearance. You should have no trouble telling them apart. Be sure to fully insert the connector. Watch out for the smaller connector. See the Real-World Scenario, "Do You Smell Something?"

Configuring Storage Devices

Aside from software configuration to partition and format a hard drive, there is very little to be done postinstallation with storage devices. The fact is, for non–hard drive ATA devices, such as CD-ROM and DVD-ROM drives, the only setting is the jumper or jumpers that configure them as cable select, master, slave, or stand-alone, only one of which can be chosen per drive. For floppy drives, most BIOS configuration utilities allow the swapping of the A: and B: drives for booting purposes. Other than that, there's relatively nothing you can do to alter the way a floppy drive functions, although you might find that you have to specify the capacity of the disks your drive can handle; 1.44MB is often the default.

For a hard drive, after you install the hardware, the BIOS might recognize what you have installed and put it to use. If not, you must change the status in the BIOS of the drive's installed position from *disabled* to a setting such as *auto*. You must supply the operating system and make the drive bootable, if it is so desired. Regardless, you must partition and format the drive. Today's operating systems take care of all software setup tasks in a virtually unattended fashion. Nevertheless, it doesn't hurt for you to be aware of what is happening behind the scenes, especially when troubleshooting. It's essentially the same process as the one used on the very first hard drives used with IBM's PCs in the 1980s.

The first step is to partition the drive. This can be done during setup of the operating system. The Fdisk command-line utility can be used for this purpose with older operating systems, such as Windows 98 or Windows 2000. Newer operating systems replace the Fdisk utility with DiskPart. If you are working on subsequent hard drives, Disk Management, found in Computer Management, can be used more easily. Partitioning a hard drive marks a contiguous stretch of the drive for the purpose of designating one or more drive letters. One physical drive can be made up of a single logical drive letter or many logical drives, each represented by a different letter. You can create one or more primary partitions and a single extended partition. Primary partitions can be made bootable and are represented by a single drive letter. Extended partitions are not bootable but can be further subdivided and represented by one or more drive letters.

 Real World Scenario

Do You Smell Something?

In 1990, I started a PC sales and repair business. Those were the days when you could build a computer from scratch for relatively little cost and sell it with a great markup and still come in way under the prices of the name-brand systems.

One customer was especially price conscious. In those days, a floppy drive was not the afterthought that it is today, both in use and price. You needed a floppy drive and could actually save a bit of money if you were buying quite a few units, just by opting for a cheaper model. This customer was buying 45 computers. So, one of the corners that was cut to keep the invoice amount down was floppy-drive quality. We went with a brand that I had never heard of but that my distributor listed as the cheapest. How bad could it be? How much of a difference could there be between brands and models? I found out. The customer didn't.

The cheaper drive worked just like any other, from the perspective of the user, but the difference showed while we were building the systems. The manufacturer scrimped in the production of the power connector. Where most manufacturers create a casing to receive the power supply's connector with little chance of inserting the connector upside down, this manufacturer allowed the four pins of the connector to protrude in a nondescript manner without any keying or guidance for the power supply's connector.

Unlike the well-keyed, larger Molex power connectors used on hard drives and CD/DVD drives, the Berg connector used with floppy drives can be inserted upside down rather easily if there is no well-thought-out receptacle for it. An upside-down connector causes no problems when the power cable is attached to the system. It causes no problems when the system is turned on. It does, however, "fry" the floppy's circuit board the first time the drive is accessed, which is during the bootup process, emitting the telltale aroma of burning plastic.

When one of my assistants flipped the connector on one of the floppy drives, it wasn't long before I realized someone learned a valuable lesson. The lesson was so clear you could smell it. Everyone smelled it. My assistant knew there was a right way and a wrong way to plug the connector, but it was just too easy. Out of 45 floppies, we were lucky to have lost only one. It could have been a lot worse.

The next step is to format the drive at the operating system level. Disk Management or the FORMAT command can be used for this task. This type of formatting is not to be confused with what is known as low-level formatting. IDE hard drives are low-level formatted by the manufacturer. Low-level formatting must be performed even before a drive can be partitioned. In low-level formatting, the drive controller chip and the drive meet for the very first time and learn to work together. Because IDE drives have their controllers integrated into the drive, low-level formatting is a factory process with these drives. Low-level formatting is not operating system dependent.

The formatting that is performed after partitioning lays down the logical data structures of the operating system within the boundaries of the logical drives created in the partitions. Structures such as the clusters (also known as allocation units) are created during the formatting. The root directory and the file table are created during this process. Only after formatting can a drive letter be accessed by the operating system. Only after formatting and transferring the necessary system files can a partition be used to boot the computer. In other words, formatting a hard drive creates the file system that the operating system uses to store and retrieve data. As a result, this is when you decide which file system to use. Examples are FAT, FAT32, and NTFS. Most operating systems offer the choice of one or two file systems, but not all of them.

Working with Motherboards, CPUs, Memory, and Adapter Cards

While it's true that the motherboard is a relatively low-dollar component, you have to consider that the motherboard you choose to replace your existing board might require a different processor, memory, or both. Even your adapter cards might need to be replaced with newer versions, such as replacing PCI or AGP with PCI Express. Therein lies the rub. You could start out expecting to spend one amount and more than double your expenses before you are finished. A little homework goes a long way. Catalog your existing components before heading down to the computer store or going online to purchase replacements.

Removing the Motherboard, CPU, Memory, and Adapter Cards

As noted previously, removing a component is frequently easier than installing the same part. It's generally as simple as disconnecting any cables and leads that attach to the existing board and removing or releasing any fastening hardware. The caveat is to be very cognizant of what you are removing; everything might need to be reinstalled in corresponding locations on the new motherboard. The issue that arises most often is that the case manufacturer does not mark their leads or their markings are cryptic.

It's advised that you document the removal of all external connections to your existing motherboard. In addition, try following each lead back to its source so that you can demystify similar abbreviations in your mind, reducing the amount of guesswork required when you attach them to the new motherboard.

Real World Scenario

Power Isn't Always Power

A student of mine listened intently to the lecture concerning motherboard jumpers, connectors, and headers. When lab time came, he was eager to get started installing the motherboard and connecting it to the rest of the system. At the first opportunity to power up the partially built computer, the student noticed that he had no power LED, but the power supply fan seemed to be running and there was an LED on the motherboard that illuminated. He raised his hand and called me over. Upon inspection of the lead coming from the power LED on the case, I noticed he had it plugged onto a pair of pins labeled PWR ON.

The difference between this location and the one labeled PWR LED is that the LED connection sends current through the green LED on the case whenever system power is on and the PWR ON connection supplies no such current. What it does do is allow an input from the physical power button on the front of the case to the motherboard that a compatible operating system can use to suspend and resume or completely power down, depending on how long the button is held. So, no LED illuminates by connecting in this location.

Where the student went wrong was that he not only zoned out when this was mentioned during lecture, but there was no corresponding lead from the case for the PWR ON connection, so he did not see a conflict when he plugged the LED lead into that position. No other lead appeared to belong there. The book that came with the motherboard explained the difference in pretty clear detail, but when you think you have it right, it's easy not to question yourself.

Question yourself, always.

In Exercise 13.3, you remove a motherboard, CPU, memory, and adapter cards.

EXERCISE 13.3

Removing the Motherboard, CPU, Memory, and Adapter Cards

1. With the power source removed from the system, ground yourself using an approved method, such as an antistatic wrist strap. Make sure the chassis of the computer has access to the same source of ground. This step protects you and the system from electrical hazards.

2. Remove the cover from the system, exposing the internal components. Your case might have a simple mechanical latch with a finger release mechanism, or it might have machine screws that need to be removed. Do not remove the screws that hold the power supply.

3. Detach each wiring lead and harness from the motherboard, cataloging each one as you go.

4. Remove any obstructions that might hinder motherboard removal, such as component cables attached to adapter cards.

5. Gather the appropriate antistatic packaging to plan ahead for all static-sensitive components that will be reused in the future. These include adapter cards, memory modules, and the CPU.

6. Remove all adapter cards from the motherboard, storing those to be reused in antistatic packaging. Different cases have different methods of attachment, from locking latches to machine screws.

7. If you will use the same processor, now is an excellent time to remove it from the motherboard, while the motherboard is protected from static discharge. Be sure to place it in antistatic packaging. Remove the CPU's fan and heat sink assembly from the CPU and from its power connection. Modern CPU sockets use a zero insertion force (ZIF) mechanism or a lid-and-latch mechanism (for LGAs). For ZIF sockets, release the lever on the socket to loosen the clamps that hold the CPU pins and pull the CPU straight off of the socket. For LGAs, release the latch that clamps the lid down over the CPU, raise the lid, and lift the CPU straight off the socket.

8. If you will use the same memory in the new motherboard, remove it now. Dual inline memory modules (DIMMs), such as double-data rate (DDR) and single-data rate (SDR) synchronous dynamic random access memory (SDRAM), eject the same way. Pull the release tabs away from the module, but be careful to control the force with which the module ejects, because it can hit you or become damaged.

9. Remove or release all motherboard-to-chassis retaining hardware, which includes machine screws, barbed standoffs, and the like.

10. Maneuver the motherboard off the chassis and out of the case. Depending on the combination of motherboard and case you have, this step can be as simple as lifting straight up and out. Sometimes a slight tilting of the motherboard is necessary to clear cages or other obstructions within the case.

Installing the Motherboard, CPU, Memory, and Adapter Cards

To say installation is the reverse of removal would be oversimplifying matters, because you need to be mindful of things that were not present during removal, even if you are reinstalling the same component. Furthermore, if you are building a system from scratch, there is no reverse to reference.

A new motherboard might locate connectivity for the same function in a different place from where the old motherboard did and call it something different. Installing the same motherboard can throw you a couple of curveballs as well. It's very much like traveling the same road in the other direction. The landmarks might appear different. The fact is your perspective when you install a component is different from when you remove the same component. Any documentation you already had or created for yourself will be quite useful, generally.

A word of caution: take care to observe the path between the computer's front ventilation and the power supply. Anything installed between these two extremes alters the airflow circuit. Improper routing or sloppy placement of ribbon cables and other obstructions can defeat the manufacturer's engineering design and disrupt the smooth flow of air, resulting in components overheating and possible damage to them.

Along these same lines, be sure to use a slot cover (blank bracket) on the backplane for any adapter card you remove from the system. Failure to do so can result in the creation of stagnant pockets of air that might heat up to damaging levels. Additionally, unless you are in the most controlled of lab environments, never operate the system with all or part of the cover removed. In such a state, the cooling components are unable to generate the necessary pressure to draw air across the circuitry that needs it most at an effective rate.

In Exercise 13.4, you install a motherboard, CPU, memory, and adapter cards.

EXERCISE 13.4

Installing the Motherboard, CPU, Memory, and Adapter Cards

1. With the power source removed from the system, ground yourself and make sure the chassis of the computer has access to the same source of ground.

2. Remove the cover from the system, exposing the internal components.

3. If you are reusing a chassis from which a different motherboard has been removed, take care to ensure that any leftover mounting hardware, especially metallic hardware, is necessary for the new motherboard. Any unnecessary hardware, such as brass screw-hole standoffs, must be removed or short circuits can result on the underside of the motherboard. One of the best methods of comparing the chassis's mounting holes to those of the motherboard is to pick each of the holes in the chassis in turn and determine if you can see it through a corresponding hole in the motherboard as you hold the motherboard close to the chassis exactly above the motherboard's correct placement. If you cannot see a particular mounting hole in the chassis through the corresponding hole in the motherboard, make sure you remove any mounting hardware that may have been left in that location (unless it is a flush plastic support, one that does not protrude through a motherboard hole). Additionally, you might be required to add mounting hardware. Motherboards are manufactured requiring a certain amount of support under delicate circuitry. If you leave crucial support mechanisms out, you could damage the motherboard and other components as they flex and fracture during insertion of components, such as adapter cards. As you can see, this is not a reverse step of the removal process.

EXERCISE 13.4 *(continued)*

4. If you have the most common type of modern motherboard, it is an integrated motherboard. This means most of the components that used to be added to the system afterward on adapter cards, video, network, and sound, for instance, are built into the motherboard. The connectors for these components are on the back edge of the board and must mate properly with the bezel in the backplane of the case. Visually confirm that your motherboard's connectors all have an opening in the case. If not, perhaps you have a matching interchangeable bezel that you need to swap out before mounting the motherboard.

5. Place the motherboard in position over the chassis so that any protruding mounting hardware pokes through the intended motherboard holes, paying attention to how the motherboard's connectors line up with the rear of the case.

6. Use the appropriate machine screws (there are two popular styles; one is thicker with wider or coarser threads) to secure the motherboard where screw-hole standoffs were placed in the chassis.

7. If you need to install the CPU, do so now. Make sure the lever or lid on the socket is lifted before properly orienting and inserting or positioning the CPU, and don't force the CPU to seat. Check for bent pins on the CPU or improper orientation (look for pin 1 on the chip and socket) if it doesn't drop effortlessly into place. Drop the lever (or lid and lever for LGAs) to secure the CPU. Use fresh thermal compound and install the fan and heat-sink assembly.

8. If you need to install the memory, do so now. With DIMMs, make sure the release tabs are open before inserting the module. The tabs click and lock into place when the module is inserted completely. Take care to insert the module with firm, even pressure, using equal force near the ends of the module and in the orientation that matches the module's and slot's keying.

9. If you have any expansion cards to install, do so now. These adapter cards come in a variety of slot formats, making it necessary to match the card edge to the slot in the motherboard. If you do not have a slot in the motherboard that matches your card and you require its functionality, it will be necessary to acquire an expansion card with the appropriate edge connector.

10. Using any documentation you might have—which can include the manufacturer's user guide, notes you took during removal, or silk-screened labels on the motherboard— find the proper location for each loose connection coming from the case and power supply and attach it, keeping in mind that not all connectors will be attached in all systems. It's more common to have one or more lose connectors than to have them all attached. Also reattach any obstructive cables or objects impacted by motherboard removal.

Configuring the Motherboard, CPU, Memory, and Adapter Cards

Modern motherboards automatically configure themselves for the processor and memory installed, among other things. Older motherboards allowed or required you to set jumpers or configure the BIOS to indicate the type of processor installed, its frequency, its clock multiplier, or core and I/O voltage levels. Some also required you to manually configure the amount of RAM you installed, or the full amount might not be recognized. Methods of configuring these parameters vary with the motherboard, but the newer boards detect all of this and more automatically. Nevertheless, be aware that some later BIOS implementations require that PATA and SATA positions be left as disabled until a drive is physically installed there. Setting unused positions to Auto or Enabled might result in errors during each boot.

Even newer adapter cards, on the other hand, might require configuration. However, most can be recognized automatically by a plug-and-play operating system. In other words, the installation of device drivers is handled or requested automatically. Most PCI adapters take care of requesting their own resources through the PCI bridge controller, especially simple I/O adapters, such as those that provide USB, FireWire, parallel, and serial ports.

Some adapters require more specific configuration steps during installation. For example, two or more PCIe graphics adapters that support SLI must be bridged together with special hardware that comes with the adapters. Although most sound cards tend to work with no specific configuration, advanced features will need to be implemented through the operating system or through utilities that came with the adapter. Wired network adapters tend to be easier to configure than wireless ones. Wireless adapters often require the installation of a screw-on antenna, which should be postponed until after the card is fully inserted and secured in the system. Software configuration that allows these cards to communicate with a wireless access point can be challenging for the novice. Nevertheless, even wired NICs might require static configuration of certain protocol settings, such as IP addressing, in order for them to be productive. The functions of TV- and video-capture cards are not often native to the operating system and therefore come with advanced utilities that must be learned and configured before the adapters will work as expected.

In any event, consult the documentation provided with your adapter for additional configuration requirements or options. The more specialized the adapter, the more likely it will come with specialty-configuration utilities.

Working with Power Supplies

Sometimes power supplies fail. Sometimes you grow out of your power supply and require more wattage than it can provide. Often, it is just as cost effective to buy a whole new case with the power supply included rather than dealing with the power supply alone. However, when you consider the fact that you must move everything from the old case to the new one, replacing the power supply becomes an attractive proposition. Doing so is not a difficult task.

Regardless of which path you choose, you must make sure that the power connection of the power supply matches that of the motherboard to be used. A new power supply with the single 20-pin ATX power connector is not compatible with a motherboard that has only the older P8/P9 connectors, although there are adapters that allow interconnection. The 24-pin PCI Express ATX power supply connection can also be adapted to a motherboard with the 20-pin ATX connector.

Exercise 13.5 details the process to remove an existing power supply. Use the reverse of this process to install the new power supply. Just keep in mind that you might need to procure the appropriate adapter if a power supply that matches your motherboard can no longer be found. There is no postinstallation configuration for the power supply, so there is nothing to cover along those lines. Many power supply manufacturers have utilities on their websites that allow you to perform a presale configuration, so that you are assured of obtaining the most appropriate power supply for your power requirements.

EXERCISE 13.5

Removing a Power Supply

1. With the power source removed from the system, ground yourself and the computer to the same source of ground.

2. Remove the cover from the system, exposing the internal components.

3. After locating the power supply, which can come in a variety of formats and appear on the left or right side of the case, follow all wiring harnesses from the power supply to their termini, disconnecting each one.

4. Remove any obstructions that appear as if they might hinder removal of the power supply.

5. Using the dimensions of the power supply, detectable from the inside of the case, note which machine screws on the outside of the case correspond to the power supply. There are often four such screws in a nonsquare pattern. If your case has two side panels, and you removed only one, there will likely be one or more screws holding the other panel on that appear to be for the power supply. These do not need to be removed. If all case screws have been removed, pay attention to their location and do not use these holes when securing the new power supply.

6. Remove the screws that you identified as those that hold the power supply in place. Be aware that the power supply is not lightweight, so you should support it as you remove the final couple of screws.

7. Maneuver the power supply past any obstructions that did not have to be removed, and pull the power supply out of the case.

Working with Cooling Systems

Modern cooling systems that the technician might be faced with installing or exchanging range from the classic heat sink, which is fairly straightforward to install and remove, to the newer liquid-cooled systems that have multiple components and the danger of mixing water with electricity if you are not careful. Somewhere in the middle is today's ubiquitous active heat sink, which combines the classic passive heat sink with a powered fan to force airflow onto and subsequently away from the component being cooled. In addition, the technician needs to be comfortable adding and replacing secondary cooling components, such as chassis fans that more actively bring air into and out of the case through preengineered pathways.

Removing Cooling Systems

If you have a fan that fails, the average system alerts you to this fact and, when you are not around to be alerted, shuts the system down at a configurable threshold to prevent damage. Active and passive heat sinks often clip onto the socket they are designed for or to special holes or receptacles in the motherboard, sometimes using a spring-loaded approach to remain tightly interfaced to the surface of the component they cool. As a result, the technician must be aware that there can be multiple ways to orient the heat sink over the component and still secure the heat sink. Not all orientations always provide the same coverage for the component to be cooled. Poor coverage can result in component failure or damage.

For those heat sinks that have a metal band running through the middle of them with a clip on each end, the secret to releasing the clips secured to tabs on the socket or other location is to make sure you have the right tool for the job. Some implementations allow you to use your fingers to grip the larger end and push down to clear the tab, swing the clip away from the tab, and allow the clip's spring action to maneuver the clip up and away from the tab. At that point, the other end of the clip on the other side of the heat sink comes off when you lift the heat sink from the component, angling it in the direction of the clip that's still attached.

In the case of harder-to-release clips with no finger holds, they are most often designed so that a small slotted screwdriver or, less often, a small Philips-head screwdriver can be inserted into the top portion of one end of the clip, offering you leverage to push down and pivot the clip away from the tab. You must take care to ensure that there is such a receptacle for one of these tools and that you use the right tool. Otherwise, slippage of the tool can result in a fatally wounded motherboard or other circuit board.

To remove chassis fans, you generally need to unscrew the fan from the chassis at two or more corners of the fan assembly. Better cases provide a snap-in carrier for these fans that you screw the fan into from the other side, making the simple removal of the carrier necessary in order to gain access to the screw heads. In the case of all actively powered cooling devices, you must remove the power connector from the motherboard or power-supply connector in order to remove it completely from the system. In general, you will find it easier to disconnect the power before demounting the unit.

The best liquid-cooling systems provide a mechanism that acts somewhat like the multistage airlocks between hazardous and safe areas. What this means is that during the disconnection of the fluid lines, there is a valve mechanism that causes the fluid to retreat and be cut off from the end of the connecting interface, preventing even a single drip. Still, all power should be off and removed from the system before doing anything with fluid-filled conduits. Many liquid-cooling systems have sensors that allow them to shut the system down when they detect even a minute leak in the pathway for the liquid. Follow the manufacturer's specification for removal and installation of liquid cooling systems.

Installing Cooling Systems

Exercise 13.6 steps you through the process of installing a standard heat sink on a CPU. Such a component might be active, in that it has a powered fan on top of it, but the installation process is the same, with the exception of adding power to the situation. Heat sinks for other components install more easily in general.

EXERCISE 13.6

Installing a CPU Heat Sink

To install an active or passive heat sink on a CPU, follow these steps:

1. With the power source removed from the system, ground yourself and the computer to the same source of ground.

2. Remove the cover from the system, exposing the internal components.

3. If you are replacing an existing heat sink, follow the steps in the earlier section, "Removing Cooling Systems," after removing any obstructions that might hinder removal and installation.

4. Position the heat sink over the CPU. If necessary, reorient the heat sink until the flat, smooth bottom of the heat sink fully covers the CPU's surface and the clips on the metal band running through the heat sink are in position over corresponding tabs in the socket. There are only four positions for the heat sink to square up with the CPU; two of these might appear to line up the clips with the tabs; only one of those two might also position the heat sink completely over the CPU. Pay attention to detail on this step. If, despite your best effort, you cannot seem to satisfy all of these criteria simultaneously, consider the possibility that you might have the wrong heat sink for the type of processor you have.

5. Put just a drop of thermal compound in the center of the surface of the CPU. The pressure from securing the heat sink will cause the grease to distribute thinly and evenly over the surface. There is no need to spread the compound around.

6. Using the orientation you discovered to be the best, hook the plainer clip on the end of the metal band running through the heat sink to its tab first. This clip does not have a finger or screwdriver hold on it, so it must be attached before the heat sink is in place.

7. Gently ease the mating surface of the heat sink onto the surface of the CPU, keeping your eye and possibly a finger on the attached clip, so that it does not spring free. The heat sink might have the tendency to spring back in the direction of the attached clip, so use your clip-support hand to hold the heat sink in place, once it is level with the surface of the CPU. The attached clip should be fine now.

8. Depending on the type of clip it is, use your fingers or a tool to maneuver the free clip of the metal band running through the heat sink onto its tab. Generally, you will need to guide the clip out and away from the socket as you apply downward pressure and then guide it back to catch it under the tab. Note that newer heat sinks mount to the motherboard and not the CPU socket. Because these models vary in their attachment, consult the heat sink's accompanying documentation or your removal notes for the proper installation procedure.

9. If you have an active heat sink, find the appropriate power connection and finalize the installation. Visually confirm the operation of an active heat sink before replacing the cover of the case. Because power connections vary, from onboard headers on the motherboard to harnesses coming from the power supply, you might require an adapter if your early-model motherboard does not have a header required by your active heat sink. Never operate an active heat sink without power. The CPU will quickly overheat.

Secondary fans can be installed at the front of the case, the rear of the case, or both. In any event, they generally come with a hole in each of the four corners, as well as four screws or other fastening devices. Modern case manufacturers machine the chassis to accept one or more secondary fans in the front and back each. At least two opposing fasteners should be used, but preferably all four. Because they are fans, these devices are always powered. As a result, you must find the appropriate power connection or an adapter. They are of no use if they are not powered. The front fan should be mounted to draw air in through the front vents, while the rear fan should be mounted to blow air out through the rear of the case, as does the power supply's fan. If you discover that you have a rarer power supply with an intake fan, match the rear fans to bring air into the system and the front fans to exhaust the air.

Liquid cooling systems require specialized installation. You should consult and follow the steps outlined in the manufacturer's documentation or website to install these components. One choice you might have to make is whether to mount the unit inside or outside the system unit. Some models don't give you a choice, but others fit nicely in the same space that a classic full-height 5.25-inch hard drive used to fit into. From there, all installation should follow the manufacturer's specification. However, one hurdle you might face is how much tubing to cut off during installation. Everyone likes a nice, neat installation. The temptation that arises is to slide the unit into the drive bay and cut the tubing to a length that reaches perfectly. Doing so, however, leads to disconnecting the tubing every time you need to slide the unit out for checking or refilling the water supply. Leave enough tubing so that you are able to slide the unit out enough to maintain it or even slide it out all the way.

Configuring Cooling Systems

There's no direct configuration of most cooling devices, but you might want to enter your system's BIOS management routine during startup to make your way to the environmental controls to adjust how your system responds to how well your cooling systems perform.

While such utilities differ in how you access them and where the environmental controls are, if they exist at all, every BIOS management utility that has such a set of controls places them on a page together. The name of the page might not be intuitive, so you might need to look around the utility before you find it.

You'll know you've found the right page when you see temperature references, usually in both Celsius and Fahrenheit. Some entries simply tell you the current temperatures of key components, such as the temperature of the CPU and the ambient temperature of the inside of the case. Other entries tell you the revolutions per minute (RPM) of the fans that can be monitored inside the case, for example, the CPU's cooling-fan speed. Still other entries allow you to configure the temperature and revolution thresholds that will generate audible alarms and eventually cause the system to shut itself down to prevent damage to sensitive components from excessive heat.

If the manufacturer of your specialty cooling system provides features that can be configured, they will provide documentation to guide you through the configuration process.

Identifying Tools and Diagnostics for PC Components

When you're troubleshooting hardware, there are a few common problems that any experienced technician should know about. These common issues usually have simple solutions. Knowing these problems and their solutions will make you a more efficient troubleshooter.

Most computer technicians spend a great deal of time troubleshooting and repairing systems. You should be familiar with common problems and solutions related to motherboards, hard disks, RAM, cooling, and the other major system components. However, before we talk about troubleshooting, we need to discuss the various tools you'd use.

Gathering Tools

Behind every great technician is an even greater set of tools. Your troubleshooting skills alone can get you only so far in diagnosing a problem; you also need some troubleshooting tools. And once the problem has been identified, you need a different set of tools—to fix the problem.

There are two major types of tools: hardware and software. This chapter covers only hardware troubleshooting and repair tools. Hardware tools are those tools that are "hard," meaning you can touch them, as opposed to software tools, which cannot be touched. Several different kinds of hardware tools are used in PC service today. We will discuss the most commonly used tools in this section.

Screwdrivers

The tool that can most often be found in a technician's toolkit is a set of nonmagnetic screwdrivers. Most of the larger components in today's computers are mounted in the case with screws. If these components need to be removed, you must have the correct type of screwdriver available. There are three major types: flat blade, Phillips, and Torx.

Flat-blade screwdriver The first type is often called a *flat-blade* or *flathead screwdriver*, although most people simply refer to it as a *standard screwdriver* (Figure 13.5). The type of screw that this screwdriver removes is not used much anymore (primarily because the screw head can be easily damaged).

FIGURE 13.5 A flat-blade screwdriver and screw

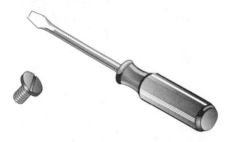

 We strongly advise against using a flathead screwdriver to *pry* anything open on a computer. Computers are usually put together very well, and if it seems that you need to pry something apart, it's probably because a screw or fastener is still holding it together somewhere.

Phillips-head screwdriver The most commonly used type of screwdriver for computers today is the *Phillips-head screwdriver* (Figure 13.6). Phillips-head screws are used because they have more surfaces to turn against, reducing the risk of damaging the head of the screw. More than 90 percent of the screws in most computers today are Phillips-head screws.

 Phillips-head screwdrivers come in various sizes, identified by numbers. The most common size is a No. 2 Phillips. It is important to have a few different-sized screwdrivers available. If you use the wrong size (for example, a Phillips-head screwdriver that is too pointed or too small), it can damage the head of the screw.

Torx screwdriver Finally, there is the type of screwdriver you use when you're working with those maddening little screws found on Compaq and Apple computers (as well as on dashboards of later-model GM cars). Of course, we're referring to the *Torx screwdriver* (Figure 13.7). The Torx type of screw has the most surfaces to turn against and therefore has the greatest resistance to screw-head damage. It is becoming more popular because people like its clean, technical look.

FIGURE 13.6 A Phillips-head screwdriver and screws

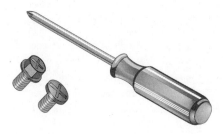

FIGURE 13.7 A Torx screwdriver and screw

The sizes of Torx drivers are given with the designation T-*xx*, where the *xx* is replaced with a number from 1 through 20. The most common sizes are T-10 and T-15, but for some notebook computers you will need to have much smaller Torx drivers on hand.

 Several screwdrivers are available with changeable tips, like bits for a drill. The advantage is that you can easily change these screwdrivers from a flat blade to a Phillips to a Torx just by changing the bits in the driver. The bits are usually stored in the handle of this type of screwdriver.

 Although it may seem convenient, don't use a multiple-bit driver that is magnetized. Magnetism and computers don't make good friends. The magnetism can induce currents in conductors and burn out components without your knowledge. It could also erase magnetic disk storage media.

Specialty Hardware/Tools

While specialty tools can include anything needed for a specific purpose, there are a few things you should always have: a parts grabber for picking up pieces that have fallen or are hard to hold on to, a chip extractor, and wire cutters/strippers/crimpers. These tools can be used to solve a number of problems.

Extension Magnet

Whenever you use screwdrivers, screws tend to get away from you and fall into some of the most precarious places, such as onto the motherboard between adapters and into the depths of a large laser printer. Although magnets must be kept away from components, such as magnetic storage media, that are sensitive to magnetic fields, extension magnets can be lifesavers when the human hand and gravity are not able to retrieve lost metallic parts.

Extension magnets, when retracted, often look similar to ballpoint pens and usually include a clip to be worn in a pocket in the same way that you would wear a pen. Be sure that no power is applied to the component before using an extension magnet, which is usually highly conductive. This shouldn't be an issue, however, unless you drop the part in a device other than the one on which you are working.

Needle-Nose Pliers

Another great tool to have in your toolkit is a pair or two of needle-nose pliers (Figure 13.8). They are great for grasping connectors or small screws when your hands are large. If a needle-nose is still too large for the job, a standard pair of tweezers will work as well.

FIGURE 13.8   A pair of needle-nose pliers

Flashlight

Another handy tool to have is a small flashlight. You'll know how especially handy it is when you're crawling around under a desk looking for a dropped screw or trying to find a particular component in a dark computer case. Many manufacturers make a powerful small flashlight that runs on two AA batteries. These devices fit well into a toolkit.

Compressed Air

When you work on a computer, typically you'll first remove the case. While the cover is off, it is a good idea to clean the computer and remove the accumulated dust bunnies. These clumps of dust and loose fibers obstruct airflow and cause the computer to run hotter, thus shortening its life. The best way to clean out the dust is with clean, dry, compressed air. If you work for a large company, it will probably have a central air compressor as a source for compressed air. If an air compressor is not available, you can use cans of compressed air, but they can be expensive—especially if several are needed. In any case, be sure to take the computer outside before blasting it with compressed air.

Soldering Iron

One tool that is used less and less in the computer service industry is the soldering iron. You might use one occasionally to splice a broken wire; otherwise, you won't have much need for it.

The soldering iron isn't used much anymore because most components have been designed to use quick-disconnect connectors to facilitate easy replacement.

Traditionally, the soldering iron was used to connect electronic components to circuit boards. The most common iron used in electronic applications has a narrow tip rated at 15 to 20 watts. Generally, the component was heated with the iron, and then rosin-core solder (*not* acid-core) was applied to the component. The solder melted and, flowing into the joint, joined the component to the circuit board.

Wire Strippers

When you're soldering, it is a good idea to have a combination wire cutter/stripper available to prepare wires for connection. Stripping a wire simply means to remove the insulation from the portion that will be involved in the connection. The tool shown in Figure 13.9 is a good example of one that does both. However, you must be careful not to cut the wire when stripping it.

FIGURE 13.9   A combination wire cutter/stripper

Loopback Plugs

Loopback plugs take the signal going out over the transmit path and wrap it back over the receive path. A standard RJ-45 Ethernet loopback plug can be made with a single pair of wires by connecting pin 1 to pin 3 and pin 2 to pin 6. Ethernet ports send out link pulses and turn on their own link LED when they receive link pulses from the other end of the physical link. This behavior allows you to exclude your NIC as the culprit if inserting the loopback plug into the NIC causes the link LED to illuminate. Using the plug with a coupler, which is a small unit with two interconnected female RJ-45 ports, enables you to test patch cords as well. You can test permanent horizontal wiring by plugging the loopback into the information outlet in the work area.

Loopback plugs and breakout boxes for parallel printer and RS-232 serial ports exist as well but usually must use special utilities to generate the appropriate traffic to test the corresponding port.

Antistatic Pads and Straps

Antistatic pads, wrist straps, ankle straps, and similar components work similarly to dissipate static electricity from the technician, protecting sensitive equipment from static damage. These components do not protect the technician—quite the opposite, they can place the technician in harm's way and should not be worn or used when performing authorized work inside AC components, such as power supplies and CRTs.

 Another option is antistatic spray. Usually applied as a mist to carpets, chairs, and so on, this reduces the amount of static electricity present and can save computers and components.

Multimeters

One of the final hardware devices we will discuss is the multimeter (see Figure 13.10). It gets its name from the fact that it is a combination of several different kinds of testing meters, including an ohmmeter, ammeter, and voltmeter. In trained hands, it can help detect the correct operation or failure of several types of components.

FIGURE 13.10 A common multimeter

The multimeter consists of a digital or analog display, two probes, and a function selector switch. This rotary switch not only selects the function being tested, it also selects the range to which the meter is set. If you're measuring a battery using an older meter, you may have to set the range selector manually (to a range close to, but greater than, 1.5 volts). Newer meters, especially digital ones, automatically set their ranges appropriately.

Never connect a non-auto-ranging meter to an AC power outlet to measure voltage. This action will almost surely result in permanent damage to the meter mechanism, the meter itself, or both.

When you're measuring circuits, it is very important to have the meter hooked up correctly so that the readings are accurate. Each type of measurement may require that the meter be connected in a different way. In the following paragraphs, we will detail the most commonly used functions of the multimeter and how to make measurements correctly with them:

Measuring resistance with a multimeter   *Resistance* is the electrical property most commonly measured in troubleshooting components. Measured in ohms, resistance is most often represented by the Greek symbol omega (Ω). A measurement of infinite resistance indicates that electricity cannot flow from one probe to the other. If you use a multimeter to measure the resistance in a segment of wire and the result is an infinite reading, there is a very good chance that the wire has a break in it somewhere between the probes.

To measure resistance, you must first set the multimeter to measure ohms. You do so either through a button on the front or through the selector dial. (Assume for the rest of this chapter that we are using newer auto-ranging multimeters.) Then you must properly connect the component to be measured between the probes (see the warning and Figure 13.11). The meter will then display the resistance value of the component being measured.

FIGURE 13.11   Connecting a multimeter to measure resistance

Selector set to
read Ohms (Ω)

Component to be tested

Do not test resistance on components while they are mounted on a circuit board! The multimeter applies a current to the component being tested. That current may also flow to other components on the board, thus damaging them.

Measuring voltage with a multimeter   You follow a similar procedure when measuring voltage, but with two major differences. First, when measuring voltage, you must be sure you connect the probes to the power source correctly: with DC voltage, the + must connect to the positive side and the – to the negative. (The position doesn't matter with AC voltage.) Second, you must change the selector to VDC (Volts DC) or VAC (Volts AC), whichever is appropriate, to tell the meter what you are measuring (see Figure 13.12). Note that these settings protect the meter from overload. If you plug a meter into a power supply while it's still set to measure resistance, you may blow the meter.

FIGURE 13.12   Connecting a multimeter to measure voltage

Selector set to read DC or AC volts

Red probe (+)   Black probe (−)

Connect directly to terminals of power source

Battery

Measuring current with a multimeter   The final measurement that is commonly made is that of current, in amperes (amps). Again, the procedure is similar to those used for the other measurements. A major difference here is that when you connect an ammeter to measure the current a circuit is drawing, you must connect the ammeter in series with the circuit being measured. Figure 13.13 illustrates the proper connection of a multimeter to measure current. Although the illustration shows the component with no connection to power, you must power the device to test the current flow.

Power Supply Testers

Power supply testers are devices that can be used in concert with or in lieu of multimeters. Some units have multiple interfaces, allowing connection of ATX motherboard connectors as well as component connectors, including Berg, Molex, and SATA power connectors. Some also include testing for the ATX12V and PCIe power connectors.

These units feature LEDs that light in multiple colors to indicate the status of the various voltage rails provided by the power supply, such as +/–12V, +/–5V, +3.3V, and +5VSB (always on and responsible for lighting the LEDs on the motherboard whenever the power supply is plugged in to the wall and hard-switched on).

FIGURE 13.13   Connecting a multimeter to measure current

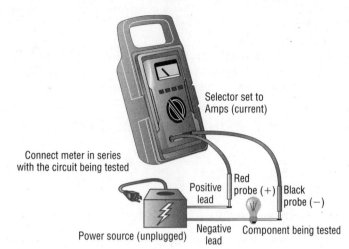

Selector set to
Amps (current)

Connect meter in series
with the circuit being tested

Positive
lead

Red
probe (+)

Black
probe (−)

Power source (unplugged)

Negative
lead

Component being tested

Cable Testers

Cable testers come in many shapes, sizes, and feature sets. You can spend less than a hundred dollars or you can spend tens of thousands. All cable testers give you the ability to detect issues with the mapping of the pins on one end of your cable to those of the other end. They will tell you if you wire the cable improperly by, for example, crossing wires when you terminate a pin on one end to the wrong pin on the other end, by leaving an open connection, or by shorting multiple wires together.

As you move up in price, these devices tend to include a headend unit and a remote unit. The headend often has a high-quality display screen and is generally more complex than the remote, which might only have a series of LEDs that alert the technician at that end to the status of the test currently being executed. The more expensive units like this can certify your cable runs to the official specifications used in structured wiring, such as ANSI/EIA/TIA-568-B. They know all the recommendations that apply to the various categories of cable, such as CAT-5e and CAT-6. They can tell you the length of the link you have created and if it is over the limit provided for by the specification.

Many of the pricier units provide a time domain reflectometer (TDR) that sends a signal onto the wire and monitors the amount of signal that returns to the headend. The tester displays a graph with a line that represents the returned signal level as a function of time, which translates directly to how far away that part of the signal was reflected back to the headend. Depending on how quickly the signal returns and in what quantity, the line spikes at the point of an open connection in the wire. You can then reliably locate the damaged portion of the cable without the extensive physical inspection required without a TDR.

Recognizing and Isolating Issues

Your value as a technician increases as you gain experience because of the reduced time it takes you to accomplish common repairs. Your ability to troubleshoot by past experiences and gut feelings will make you more efficient and more valuable, which in turn will allow you to advance and earn a better income. This section will give you some guidelines you can use to evaluate common hardware issues that you're sure to face.

Applying Basic Troubleshooting Techniques

Being able to identify and address basic troubleshooting issues is an important aspect of any PC technician's skill set. In the following sections, we discuss the basic items to check for common problems.

Identifying Motherboard and CPU Problems

Most motherboard and CPU problems manifest themselves by the system appearing completely dead. However, "completely dead" can be a symptom of a wide variety of problems, not only with the CPU or motherboard but also with the RAM or the power supply. So a POST card (described in Chapter 9) may be helpful in narrowing down the exact component that is faulty.

When a motherboard fails, it's usually because it has been damaged. Most technicians can't repair motherboard damage; the motherboard must be replaced. Motherboards can become damaged due to physical trauma, exposure to electrostatic discharge (ESD), or short-circuiting. To minimize the risk of these damages, observe the following rules:

- Handle a motherboard as little as possible, and keep it in an antistatic bag whenever it's removed from the PC case.

- Keep all liquids well away from the motherboard, because water can cause a short circuit.

- Wear an antistatic wrist strap when handling or touching a motherboard.

- When installing a motherboard in a case, make sure you use brass standoffs with paper washers to prevent any stray solder around the screw holes from causing a short circuit with the metal of the screw.

A CPU may fail because of physical trauma or short-circuiting, but the most common cause for a CPU not to work is failure to install it properly. With a PGA-style CPU, ensure that the CPU is oriented correctly in the socket. With an SECC-style CPU, make sure the CPU is completely inserted into its slot.

Identifying I/O Port and Cable Problems

I/O ports include legacy parallel and serial, USB, and FireWire ports, all of which are used to connect external peripherals to the motherboard. When a port doesn't appear to be functioning, check the following:

- The cables are snugly connected.

- The port has not been disabled in BIOS Setup.

- The port has not been disabled in Device Manager in Windows.
- No pins are broken or bent on the male end of the port or on the cable being plugged into it.

If you suspect that the cable, rather than the port, may be the problem, swap out the cable with a known good one. If you don't have an extra cable, you can test the existing cable with a multimeter by setting it to ohms and checking the resistance between one end of the cable and the other.

Use a pin-out diagram, if available, to determine which pin matches up to which at the other end. There is often—but not always—an inverse relationship between the ends. In other words, at one end pin 1 is at the left, and at the other end it's at the right on the same row of pins. You see this characteristic with D-sub connectors where one end of the cable is male and the other end is female.

Identifying Cooling Issues

A PC that works for a few minutes and then locks up is probably experiencing overheating because of a heat sink or fan not functioning properly. To troubleshoot overheating, first check all fans inside the PC to ensure they're operating, and make sure any heat sinks are firmly attached to their chips.

In a properly designed, properly assembled PC case, air flows in a specific path driven by the power supply fan and using the power supply's vent holes. Make sure you know the direction of flow and that there are limited obstructions and no dust buildup. Cases are also designed to cool by making the air flow in a certain way. Therefore, operating a PC with the cover removed can make a PC more susceptible to overheating, even though it's "getting more air."

Similarly, operating a PC with expansion-slot covers removed can inhibit a PC's ability to cool itself properly because the extra holes change the airflow pattern from what was intended by its design.

Although CPUs are the most common component to overheat, occasionally other chips on the motherboard, such as the chipset, or chips on other devices, particularly video cards, may also overheat. Extra heat sinks or fans may be installed to cool these chips.

Liquid cooling systems have their own set of issues. The pump that moves the liquid through the tubing and heat sinks can become obstructed or simply fail. If this happens, the liquid's temperature will eventually equalize with that of the CPU and other components, resulting in their damage. Dust in the heat sinks has the same effect as with nonliquid cooling systems, so keep these components clean as you would any such components. Check regularly for signs of leaks that might be starting and try to catch them before they result on damage to the system.

Identifying Case Issues

A PC case holds the drives in its bays, holds the power supply, and has lights and buttons on the front. For the first two of those functions, make sure that the drives and the power supply are tightly fastened in the case with screws.

If one of the lights or buttons on the front of the PC isn't functioning, remove the cover and check the wires that run from the back of that button/light to the motherboard. If the wire has become detached, reattach it. Refer to the motherboard manual or the writing on the motherboard itself to determine what goes where.

Identifying Hard Disk System Problems

Hard disk system problems usually stem from one of three causes:

- The adapter (that is, the IDE or SCSI interface) is bad.
- The disk is bad.
- The adapter and disk are connected incorrectly.

The first and last causes are easy to identify, because in either case the symptom will be obvious: the drive won't work. You won't be able to get the computer to communicate with the disk drive.

However, if the problem is a bad disk drive, the symptoms aren't as obvious. As long as the BIOS POST routines can communicate with the disk drive, they're usually satisfied. But the POST routines may not uncover problems related to storing information. Even with healthy POST results, you may find that you're permitted to save information to a bad disk, but when you try to read it back, you get errors. Or the computer may not boot as quickly as it used to, because the disk drive can't read the boot information successfully every time.

In some cases, reformatting the drive can solve the problems described in the preceding paragraph. In other cases, reformatting brings the drive back to life only for a short while. The bottom line is that read and write problems usually indicate that the drive is malfunctioning and should be replaced soon.

WARNING   Never low-level format IDE or SCSI drives! They're low-level formatted from the factory, and you may cause problems by using low-level utilities on these types of drives.

Identifying Floppy and Other Removable Disk Drive Problems

Most floppy-drive problems result from bad media. Your first troubleshooting technique with floppy drive issues should be to try a new disk.

One of the most common problems that develops with floppy drives is misaligned read-write heads. The symptoms are fairly easy to recognize—you can read and write to a floppy on one machine but not on any others. This is normally caused by the mechanical arm in the floppy drive becoming misaligned. When the disk was formatted, it wasn't properly positioned on the drive, thus preventing other floppy drives from reading it.

Numerous commercial tools are available to realign floppy drive read-write heads. They use a floppy drive that has been preformatted to reposition the mechanical arm. In most cases, though, this fix is temporary—the arm will move out of place again fairly soon. Given the inexpensive nature of the problem, the best solution is to spend a few dollars and replace the drive.

Another problem you may encounter is a phantom directory listing. For example, suppose you display the contents of a floppy disk, and then you swap to another floppy disk but the listing stays the same. This is almost always a result of a faulty ribbon cable; a particular wire in the ribbon cable signals when a disk swap has taken place, and when that wire breaks, this error occurs.

Identifying Keyboard and Mouse Problems

Usually, keyboard problems are environmental. Keyboards get dirty, and the keys start to stick.

If a keyboard is malfunctioning (for example, sending the wrong characters to the display), it's most cost effective to replace it rather than spend hours attempting to fix it, because keyboards are fairly inexpensive.

One way to clean a keyboard is with the keyboard cleaner sold by electronics supply stores. This cleaner foams up quickly and doesn't leave a residue behind. Spray it liberally on the keyboard and keys. Work the cleaner in between the keys with a stiff toothbrush. Blow away the excess with a strong blast of compressed air. Repeat until the keyboard functions properly. If you have to clean a keyboard that's had a soft drink spilled on it, remove the key caps before you perform the cleaning procedure; doing so makes it easier to reach the sticky plungers.

Remember that most of the dollars spent on systems are for labor. If you spend an hour cleaning a $12.00 keyboard, then you have probably just cost your company $20.00. Knowing how to fix certain things doesn't necessarily mean that you *should* fix them. Always evaluate your workload, the cost of replacement, and the estimated cost of the repair before deciding on a course of action.

Similarly, most mouse problems, such as the pointer failing to move in one direction or the other or the pointer jumping around onscreen, are due to dirt building up inside the mouse. To clean a standard mouse, remove the plate on the bottom of the mouse that holds the ball in place; then remove the ball and clean the inside chamber with an alcohol-dipped cotton swab. Clean the ball itself with mild soap and water. Don't use alcohol on the ball, because it tends to dry out the rubber.

Identifying Display Device Problems

As a general rule, there are two types of video problems: no video and bad video. If there is no video, you should first check the monitor by transferring it to another machine that you know is working and see if it works there. If it does not work, then you should replace it (remember: CompTIA recommends not working on a monitor because of the electrical charge stored within). If the display does work once transferred to another machine, then you should focus on the video card. Is it seated? Does it need to be replaced?

If there is a display, but it is bad, then you should first focus on the settings. Make certain you have the correct driver for the monitor and that you are using settings that are appropriate for that monitor. If the problem persists after you have ruled out those possibilities, then you should focus on the video card and consider replacing it if its drivers are in order and not to blame. Some physical issues with the interface to which the monitor connects, as well as the monitor's interface, are salvageable; others require replacing the adapter or monitor (maybe just its data cable). You'll know which is which when you see it.

Other graphics issues can be attributed to the memory installed on the adapter. This is the storage location of the screen or screens of information in queue to be displayed by the monitor. A problem with the memory chips or modules on the graphics adapter has a direct correlation to how well the adapter works. If that's obvious to you, then you might also realize that certain unacceptable video-quality issues can be remedied by adding additional memory to a graphics adapter. Doing so generally results in an increase in both quality and performance.

Identifying Sound Card Problems

Sound cards are traditionally one of the most problem-ridden components in a PC. They demand a lot of PC resources and are notorious for being inflexible in their configuration. The most common problems related to sound cards involve resource conflicts (IRQ, DMA, or I/O address). The problem is much less pronounced on PCI than on ISA cards.

Luckily, most sound-card vendors are aware of the problems and ship very good diagnostic utilities to help resolve them. Use your PC troubleshooting skills to determine the conflict, and then reconfigure until you find an acceptable set of resources that aren't in use.

Some sound cards aren't completely Plug and Play compatible. Windows may detect that new hardware has been installed but be unable to identify the new hardware as a working sound card. To fix this problem, run the Setup software that came with the sound card.

Identifying CD-ROM/DVD Issues

CD-ROM and DVD problems are normally media related. Although compact disc technology is much more reliable than that for floppy disks, it's not perfect. Another factor to consider is the cleanliness of the disc. On many occasions, if a disc is unreadable, cleaning it with an approved cleaner and a lint-free cleaning towel will fix the problem. The next step might be to use a commercially-available scratch-removal kit. If that fails, you always have the option to send the disc into a company that specializes in data recovery.

If the operating system doesn't see the drive, start troubleshooting by determining whether the drive is receiving power. If the tray will eject, you can assume there is power to it. Next, check BIOS Setup (for IDE drives) to make sure the drive has been detected. If not, check the master/slave jumper on the drive, and make sure the IDE adapter is set to Auto, CD-ROM, or ATAPI in BIOS Setup. Once inside the case, ensure that the ribbon cable is properly aligned with pin 1 and that both the drive and motherboard ends are securely connected.

In order to play movies, a DVD drive must have MPEG decoding capability. This is usually accomplished via an expansion board, but it may be built into the video card or sound card, or it may require a software decoder. If DVD data discs will play but not movies, suspect a problem with the MPEG decoding.

If a CD-RW or DVD drive works normally as a regular CD-ROM drive but doesn't perform its special capability (doesn't read DVD discs or doesn't write to blank CDs), perhaps you need to install software to work with it. For example, with CD-RW drives, unless you're using an operating system such as Windows XP that supports CD writing, you must install CD-writing software in order to write to CDs.

Identifying NIC Issues

In general, network interface cards (NICs) are added to a PC via an expansion slot. The most common issue that prevents network connectivity is a bad or unplugged patch cable.

Cleaning crews and the rollers on the bottoms of chairs are the most common threats to a patch cable. In most cases, wall jacks are placed 4 to 10 feet away from the desktop. The patch cables are normally lying exposed under the user's desk, and from time to time damage is done to the cable, or it's inadvertently snagged and unplugged. Tightly cinching the cable, while tying it up out of the way, is no better solution. Slack must be left in the cable to allow for some amount of equipment movement and to avoid altering the electrical characteristics of the cable. When you troubleshoot a network adapter, start with the most rudimentary explanations first. Make sure the patch cable is tightly plugged in, and then look at the card and see if any lights are on. If there are lights on, use the NIC's documentation to help troubleshoot. More often than not, shutting down the machine, unplugging the patch and power cables for a moment, and then reattaching them and rebooting the PC will fix an unresponsive NIC.

 A properly connected NIC should typically have one light illuminated (the link light). If the link light is not illuminated, it indicates a problem with the NIC, the patch cable, or the device the patch cable is connecting to (hub, switch, server, and so on) Other lights that may be illuminated include a speed light, duplex light, and/or activity light.

 Wake On LAN cards have more problems than standard network cards. In our opinion, this is because they're always on. In some cases, you'll be unable to get the card working again unless you unplug the PC's power supply and reset the card.

Identifying BIOS Issues

Computer BIOSs don't go bad; they just become out-of-date. This isn't necessarily a critical issue—they will continue to support the hardware that came with the box. It *does*, however, become an issue when the BIOS doesn't support some component that you would like to install—a larger hard drive, for instance.

Most of today's BIOSs are written to an EEPROM and can be updated through the use of software. Each manufacturer has its own method for accomplishing this. Check the documentation for complete details.

WARNING
If you make a mistake in the upgrade process, the computer can become unbootable. If this happens, your only option may be to ship the box to a manufacturer-approved service center. Be careful!

Identifying Power Supply Problems

Power supply problems can manifest themselves as a system that doesn't respond in any way when the power is turned on. When this happens, open the case, remove the power supply, and replace it with a new one. Partial failures, or intermittent power supply problems, are much less simple. A completely failed power supply gives the same symptoms as a malfunctioning wall socket, UPS or power strip, a power cord that is not securely seated, or some motherboard shorts (such as those caused by an improperly seated expansion card, memory stick, CPU, and the like), and you want to rule out those items before you replace the power supply and find you still have the same problem as when you started. Be aware that different cases have different types of on/off switches. The process of replacing a power supply is a lot easier if you purchase a replacement with the same mechanism.

WARNING
Never try to repair or disassemble a power supply. There is a high risk of electrocution, and the relatively low cost of a new power supply makes working on them something to avoid.

Removing, Installing, and Configuring Components

There are huge economies in choosing to upgrade the components of an existing computer. Think about it. You can spend hundreds, even thousands, of dollars on a nice new, shiny computer just to get the total amount of RAM you wanted. Why not spend just a fraction of that and upgrade the RAM of the computer you have? Not enough horsepower for that new RAM upgrade? Replace the processor or the entire motherboard as well. You've still saved an appreciable sum. There is little need these days to perform a forklift upgrade on computers built within the last few years. Most of what you can identify as a shortcoming in your computer's characteristics can be remedied by a component upgrade. Only if your original system still has considerable market value and can be sold outright can you justify the alternative.

Bear in mind that an upgrade not only requires that you know how to install a component but by its very nature necessitates the removal of older hardware as well. Therefore, the process presented for each component in this chapter includes removal and installation, as well as any configuration for that component after the fact.

Selecting Components

It's always important to know the components that comprise your computer system. Never is such knowledge more important than when you find yourself adding or swapping components. You must know the technology on which the available expansion slots are based. You must know the CPU, memory, and motherboard that work together to form the heart of the computer system.

Bus Types and Characteristics

When you're selecting upgrade devices, you may have a choice of bus types to which to connect the new device. It is important to understand the benefits of the various buses so you can choose wisely.

For example, you might have a choice of an ISA or PCI internal modem, or a COM port or USB external modem. Or you might need to choose between an AGP and a PCI video card.

For external ports, USB is better and faster than both COM (legacy serial) and LPT (legacy parallel), and is further advantageous because of its seamless Plug and Play integration and its hot-plugging ability.

For internal buses, AGP is the fastest and best, but it is only for video cards. PCI is the next most desirable. ISA is old technology and nearly obsolete, and you should avoid it whenever possible. One exception might be an internal modem. Because an internal modem operates at a maximum of only 56Kbps, it would be least affected by being relegated to the ISA bus. In contrast, a video card would suffer greatly on ISA.

Table 13.1 describes the speeds and characteristics of internal expansion buses.

TABLE 13.1   Comparison of ISA, PCI, PCIe, and AGP Buses

Bus	Width	Speed	Uses
ISA	8-bit or 16-bit	8MHz	Avoid if possible, or use for slow devices like modems.
PCI	32-bit	33MHz to 66MHz	Mainly nonvideo internal expansion boards
PCIe	Serial	Bidirectional 250MB/s per lane	Current and next-generation video and nonvideo cards
AGP	64-bit	66MHz to 133MHz	Current and last-generation video cards

Memory Capacity and Characteristics

When you're selecting RAM for a memory upgrade, it is important to buy the right kind. On a modern system, you must match the RAM to the motherboard's needs in the following areas:

Physical size   168-pin or 184-pin DIMMs or 184-pin RIMMs and more.

Type   SDRAM, Double Data Rate (DDR) SDRAM, or Rambus RAM.

Speed   PC100, PC133, and up, as well as the DDR-based speeds discussed in Chapter 1. Faster RAM than is required will work, but not slower.

Capacity   64MB, 128MB, 1GB, for example. The characteristics of the chips that make up memory modules lead directly to the overall capacity of the modules.

When you're shopping for RAM for a system, it's important to consult the motherboard manual to find out the type of memory you need and any special rules for installation. Without the manual, you must open the case and observe the memory slots or existing memory to determine what is needed. Some motherboards have complex charts showing the combinations and positions of the modules that they allow.

Motherboards may combine one or more RAM slots into a single logical bank. A bank must be filled completely, and all the RAM installed in that set of slots should or must be completely identical in every way. Check the motherboard documentation.

System/Firmware Limitations

One of the most common problems in upgrading to a larger hard disk is the BIOS's inability to support the larger disk size. In the original IDE specification, the size limit was 540MB. This limitation was upped to 8GB with the introduction of *Logical Block Addressing (LBA)* in 1996, which the BIOS must support. A BIOS update may be available for the motherboard to enable LBA if needed.

The 8GB limitation can be broken if the BIOS supports Enhanced BIOS Services for Disk Drives, a 1998 update. Interrupt 13h extensions to the BIOS allow for drives as large as 137GB. Large LBA is a solution for drives that exceed 137GB. Again, a BIOS update for the motherboard may enable this support if it is lacking.

If no BIOS update is available, the choices are to replace the motherboard, to use the drive at the BIOS's maximum size it can recognize, or to install a utility program (usually provided with the hard disk) that extends the BIOS to recognize the new drive. Such utilities are useful but can introduce some quirks in the system that cannot be easily undone, so their usage is not recommended except where no other alternative exists.

Power Supply Output Capacity

A power supply has a rated output capacity in watts, and when you fill a system with power-hungry devices, you must make sure that that maximum capacity is not exceeded. A simple Internet search can yield helpful yet generic tables to help you predict the power consumption of your components. Each manufacturer generally lists power requirements with their components and on the Web.

Selecting a CPU for a Motherboard

The CPU must be compatible with the motherboard in the following ways:

Physical connectivity   The CPU must be in the right kind of package to fit into the motherboard.

Speed   The motherboard's chipset dictates its frontside-bus speed; the CPU must be capable of operating externally at that speed.

Instruction set   The motherboard's chipset contains an instruction set for communicating with the CPU; the CPU must understand the commands in that set. For example, a motherboard designed for an AMD Athlon CPU cannot accept an Intel Pentium CPU, because the instruction set is different.

Voltage   The CPU requires a certain voltage of power to be supplied to it via the motherboard's interface. This can be anywhere from +5V for a very old CPU down to under +2V for a modern one. The wrong voltage can ruin the CPU.

Using Tools and Diagnostic Procedures for Personal Computer Components

The various tools that you can use to discover the available resources on a PC can make installing new hardware a lot easier. Unfortunately, the tools are of little use unless you understand the information they present. In this section, we discuss the various resources that might be used by PC components and how those resources are used. Although these topics are rarely tested today because of their automation in modern operating systems, their continued existence makes knowing about them worthwhile. As a result, this section should be treated as informational, as opposed to objectives based.

Memory address range, interrupt request lines, direct memory access channels, and input/output addresses are configurable aspects of the communication between the devices inside a PC, including the CPU.

- Memory addresses are numbers assigned to physical memory that allow software to access specific areas of memory.

- Interrupt request (IRQ) lines allow a device to signal the CPU to request its attention.

- Input/output (I/O) addresses are assigned to devices that allow the CPU to identify and signal the device.

- Direct memory access (DMA) channels allow a storage device or adapter card to communicate directly with memory without passing through the CPU, which results in a faster data transfer rate.

At some point, every computer will require the installation of a new component, whether it's a new sound card, a memory upgrade, or the replacement of a failed device. As a technician, you will be required to perform this task time and time again. Just in case the need for such knowledge arises, you should be well versed in determining and configuring the required resources.

Whenever a new component is installed into a PC, its resources must be correctly configured or the device will not function correctly. Although all but obviated today by plug-and-play technology, this was once one of the most common problems when installing new ISA-based circuit boards that could not negotiate needed resources. Today, the top trouble spot goes to missing, corrupted, or incorrect device drivers.

Understanding Computer Resources

The following sections detail the four previously mentioned main types of PC resources that you might still need to be aware of when installing a new component.

Interrupt Request Lines

IRQs are appropriately named. Interrupts are used by peripherals to interrupt, or stop, the CPU and demand attention. When the CPU receives an interrupt alert, it stops whatever it is doing as soon as feasible and handles the request. When simultaneous requests come in, special interrupt controller chips prioritize the competing requests, favoring lower interrupt numbers, making IRQ 0 the highest priority. See the sidebar "When 15 Is Less than 3."

Each device is given its own interrupt to use when alerting the CPU. (There are exceptions; PCI devices can share with one another, for example, and USB devices all use a single interrupt.) AT-based PCs have 16 interrupts defined. Given the limited number of available interrupts, this was once one of the greatest obstacles during system configuration, initially as well as during upgrades. Table 13.2 lists the standard use and other uses associated with each of the 16 AT interrupts.

TABLE 13.2 AT Interrupts

Interrupt	Most Common Use	Other Common Uses
0	System timer	None
1	Keyboard	None
2	None; this interrupt is used to cascade to the upper eight interrupts (see the sidebar "When 15 Is Less than 3")	None
3	COM2	COM4
4	COM1	COM3
5	Sound adapter	LPT2
6	Floppy-disk controller	Tape controllers

TABLE 13.2   AT Interrupts *(continued)*

Interrupt	Most Common Use	Other Common Uses
7	LPT1	Any device
8	Real-time clock	None
9	None	Any device
10	None	Any device
11	None	Any device
12	PS/2-style mouse	Any device
13	Floating-point coprocessor	None
14	Primary IDE channel	SCSI controllers
15	Secondary IDE channel	SCSI controllers and network adapters

When 15 Is Less than 3

Interrupt 2 is a special case. Earlier (XT-based) PCs had only eight interrupts because those computers used a single interrupt controller chip. The controller chip has a single output line that connects to the interrupt line of the processor (a single pin on the CPU). With the development of the AT, a second interrupt controller chip was added, providing eight more interrupts, but no mechanism was in place to treat the second controller's output separately. Rather than redesign the entire interrupt process, AT designers decided to use interrupt 2 on the original chip as a gateway to *cascade* to the second chip and interrupts 8–15. The second controller chip's output connects to interrupt 2 of the first chip. Interrupt 2, often used for early VGA adapters, was replaced by interrupt 9. As a result, you should never configure IRQ 2 for use in modern systems.

As mentioned, the CPU has a single interrupt line for the entire I/O system. Interrupt controller chips (model 8250s) interface to this single line and arbitrate among their eight interrupt inputs, with lower interrupts having higher priority. Because the entire second controller chip replaces interrupt 2, its interrupts (8–15) replace IRQ2 in the hierarchy and are at a higher priority than interrupts 3–7. The result is that you cannot simply use the numerical value of the interrupts to determine priority. Although lower IRQ values have higher priority in general, IRQ 15 is at a higher priority than IRQs 3–7, making it appear "less than 3."

Memory Usage

The CPU is capable of differentiating between *system memory*, which is what you refer to when you say that your computer has 512MB or 1GB of RAM, and *I/O memory*, which is a resource allocated to an expansion card and other components external to the CPU. A single pin on the CPU, called the IO_MEM line, allows the CPU to specify which group of memory it is referring to for read or write operations. In addition, the two blocks of memory can overlap in value, due to the fact that the CPU refers to one or the other per operation, never both, eliminating the possibility of confusion.

Memory Addresses

Many components use blocks of system memory as part of their normal functioning, often finding their data elbow to elbow with application data and code. For example, network interface cards often buffer incoming data in a block of memory until it can be processed. Doing so prevents the card from being overloaded if a burst of data is received from the network.

When the device driver loads, it lets the CPU know which block of system memory should be set aside for the exclusive use of the component. This prevents other devices and software from overwriting the information stored there. Certain system components, such as the system board and the PCI bus, also need a memory address. Memory addresses are usually expressed in a hexadecimal range with eight digits, such as 00F0000–000FFFFF. When the CPU indicates MEM with the IO_MEM line, it is referring to a memory address.

Direct Memory Access

Direct memory access (DMA) allows a device to bypass the CPU and place data directly into RAM. To accomplish this, the device must have a DMA channel devoted to its use.

All DMA transfers use a special area of memory set aside to receive data from the expansion card (or CPU, if the transfer is going the other direction) known as a *buffer*. The basic architecture of the PC DMA buffers is limited in size and memory location.

No DMA channel can be used by more than one device. If you accidentally choose a DMA channel that another card is using, the usual symptom is that no DMA transfers occur and the device is unavailable.

Certain DMA channels are assigned to standard AT devices. DMA is no longer as popular as it once was, because of advances in hardware technology, but it is still used by floppy drives and some keyboards and sound cards. The floppy disk controller typically uses DMA channel 2. A modern system is not likely to run short on DMA channels because so few devices use them anymore.

I/O Addresses

I/O (input/output) addresses are a specific area of memory that a component uses to communicate with the system. When the CPU indicates I/O with the IO_MEM line, it is referring to an I/O address. Although I/O addresses sound quite a bit like memory addresses, the major difference is that memory addresses are used to store information that will be used by the device itself. I/O addresses are used to store information that will be used by the system or to represent instructions for the device from the CPU. For instance, the I/O address range 01F0–01F7 for the primary IDE controller acts as a set of instructions, allowing the CPU to control the activities of the IDE controller.

An I/O address is typically expressed using only the last four digits of the full address, such as 03E8, because the first four digits are always zeros. All I/O addresses fall within the first 640KB, starting at 0. Although the I/O addresses for a component are technically a range, such as 03E8–03EF for COM3, you more often refer to the *base I/O address*, just 03E8 in this case. The exam asks about a few I/O addresses; Table 13.3 lists a few of the most common hexadecimal I/O address ranges.

TABLE 13.3   I/O Addresses

Port	I/O Address
COM1	0x03F8–03FF
COM2	0x02F8–02FF
COM3	0x03E8–03EF
COM4	0x02E8–02EF
LPT1	0x0378–037F
LPT2	0x0278–027F
Primary IDE	0x01F0–01F7
Secondary IDE	0x0170–0177

Determining Available Resources

The best way to determine the PC's available resources is by using hardware-configuration-discovery utilities. These software programs talk to the PC's BIOS as well as the various pieces of hardware in the computer and display which IRQ, DMA, I/O addresses, and memory addresses are being used. Most operating systems include some way of determining this information, including Device Manager in Windows 2000 and higher. Exercise 13.7 guides you through investigating your system resources.

EXERCISE 13.7

Displaying System Resources

1. Right-click My Computer and choose Properties to open the System Properties dialog box.

2. Select the Hardware tab, and then click the Device Manager button.

3. To display a device's resources, open the category by clicking the plus sign next to it and double-clicking the device name. Then, look in the Resources tab for that device.

4. In order to see the specifics about how your system allocates a certain type of resource, click the View menu in Device Manager and select Resources By Type. Resources By Connection works as well, but some categories are less intuitive.

5. Notice that the four categories correspond to the four resources presented in this section—DMA, I/O address, IRQ, and memory address. Investigate each of the four categories by clicking on the plus sign in front of them. For example, expanding the Interrupt Request category shows you all components that have IRQs assigned to them in order of IRQ number.

You can also get this same information through the System Information utility. To run it, choose Start ≻ (All) Programs ≻ Accessories ≻ System Tools ≻ System Information. Click the plus sign next to Hardware Resources, and then click one of the categories in the left pane to see the information in the right pane.

Manually Specifying a Resource Assignment

In Windows' Device Manager, you can manually specify the resources for a device to solve a problem with a *resource conflict*—that is, a situation in which two or more devices lay claim to the same resource. A resource conflict usually appears as a yellow exclamation point next to a device's name in Device Manager. Double-clicking the device opens its Properties box, and on the Resources tab you will find an explanation of the problem in the Conflicting Device list.

To change a device's resource assignments, clear the Use Automatic Settings check box and select a different configuration from the Settings Based On drop-down list. If none of the alternate configurations resolves the conflict, you can double-click a specific resource on the Resource Type list and enter a manual setting for it.

Most modern computers use a power management and configuration method called ACPI (advanced configuration and power interface), which helps prevent resource conflicts but which also limits the amount of tinkering you can do with manual resource assignments. If you get a message that a particular resource cannot be changed, or if the Use Automatic Settings check box is unavailable, it is probably because of ACPI.

If the device is not Plug and Play compatible, it may have jumpers for hard-setting the resources assigned to it. If that's the case, Windows will not be able to change these assignments; it will use the assignments the device requires, based on its jumper settings.

Summary

In this chapter, you learned how to remove, install, and configure computer components. Specifically, you explored installing and exchanging motherboards, CPUs, memory, adapter cards, storage devices, power supplies, input devices, and cooling systems. You also learned about tools and resources you need to work with and maintain various computer components.

Exam Essentials

Know how to remove, install, and configure motherboards.   Know how to choose the correct motherboard for the chassis you have. Know how to choose the correct mounting hardware to avoid shorting out electrical components. Know the various connectors and headers associated with today's motherboards. Be aware that there are various formats of BIOS routines and methods to access them.

Know how to remove, install, and configure CPUs.   Know how to choose the right CPU for the motherboard you have. Be able to remove and install a CPU in a ZIF socket.

Know how to remove, install, and configure memory.   Know the difference between various memory form factors, especially SDRAM and DDR, so you know how to choose the correct memory for your motherboard. Be aware of the fastening mechanisms that modern memory modules employ, how they affect module installation, and how to release them during module removal.

Be able to remove, install, and configure adapter cards.   Be aware that adapter cards must match available expansion slots. Know how to remove and install them and how to secure them into the computer chassis.

Know how to remove, install, and configure storage devices.   Know the difference between the data and power connectors used on storage devices. Be aware of the master/slave relationship used with ATA devices and know the strategy for setting them. Know what it means to partition and format a hard drive. Be aware of the physical differences in storage device form factors.

Know how to remove, install, and configure power supplies.   Know the difference between the modern motherboard power headers, and be aware of when an adapter might be required. Know the two most common device connectors coming from the power supply. Be familiar with how to fasten power supplies to the chassis, as well as how to unfasten them.

Understand how to remove, install, and configure input devices.   Be aware of what constitutes an input device. Know how to connect an input device to a computer and how to disconnect one. Familiarize yourself with common mouse configuration.

Be able to remove, install, and configure cooling systems.   Know that cooling systems range from passive heat sinks to liquid cooling systems. Know the specifics on removing and installing the more common devices and the general concept of dealing with the more complex devices.

Know the hardware tools mentioned.   Be able to name the hardware tools and their purpose, as discussed in this chapter.

Be aware of the need to keep systems well ventilated.   Heat can be a negative force to almost any PC component, and ventilation can help ensure there is no excessive heat buildup.

Review Questions

1. Which statement is true regarding upgrading a computer system?

   A. When upgrading RAM, you must also upgrade the CPU.

   B. When upgrading RAM, you must perform a forklift upgrade on the entire system.

   C. When upgrading RAM, it is possible that you can upgrade RAM only.

   D. RAM is the only upgrade you can perform on modern computer systems.

2. Which two of the following are today's best choices for video adapter technology?

   A. ISA

   B. PCI

   C. PCIe

   D. AGP

3. Which of the following is not a selection criterion for RAM?

   A. Physical size

   B. Solid state

   C. Speed

   D. Capacity

4. While installing a CPU, you apply gentle pressure to the surface of the CPU, but it will not seat. When you examine the pins of the CPU to see if they are straight, you find that a number of them are bent. Why are the bent pins not the original problem?

   A. The socket has a ZIF mechanism that must be released before inserting the CPU.

   B. The holes in the socket are large enough to accept pins bent up to 45 degrees from perpendicular.

   C. The bent metal protrusions around the edge of a chip are not pins. They are non-electronic tensioners to make sure the CPU maintains a tight connection.

   D. CPUs don't have pins. What you thought were pins were metallic designs in the likeness of the manufacturer's logo.

5. Which of the following statements regarding motherboard replacement is not true?

   A. As you remove any electronic components, including the motherboard and its adapters, you should place them in antistatic containers.

   B. Existing power supply connectors might not fit the new motherboard.

   C. Existing memory modules might not fit the new motherboard.

   D. When removing the motherboard, it is recommended that you not remove the expansion boards, so that you do not subject them to static.

6. For modern motherboards, which statement concerning CPU and RAM configuration is most true?

   A. Modern motherboards have intelligent BIOS routines that automatically recognize and configure themselves for the CPU and RAM.

   B. The CPU and RAM modules have DIP switches on them that must be set the same as the DIP switch on the motherboard.

   C. The motherboard is preset from the factory to work with only one CPU and only one type of RAM module.

   D. You must use an external CPU/RAM programming station to preconfigure these components for your specific motherboard.

7. Which of the following statements is true, regarding working inside a computer system?

   A. You and the chassis should be grounded to the same ground, but power should not be supplied to the system.

   B. All internal components, except the power supply, are hot-swappable. Maintaining power to the system while working ensures interruption-free service for the customer.

   C. As long as the LEDs on the motherboard are lit, you are safe to work inside the chassis.

   D. Not since the original PC has the technician been able to work inside the computer system.

8. Which of the following is not a consideration when installing an internal storage device?

   A. You should match the form factor of the drive or adapt it to an available drive bay or slot.

   B. You should secure the drive with at least two screws on one side and preferably two on each side.

   C. Due to the high revolutions at which modern hard drives spin, you must secure an external power source because the internal power supplies do not have the capacity.

   D. You need to be sure that the routing of the drive's ribbon cable, if applicable, does not obstruct the engineered flow of air across internal components.

9. Which of the following statements regarding floppy drive installation is true?

   A. Like a hard drive, the floppy drive requires no external access.

   B. Like DVD-ROM drives, floppy drives have a 5.25-inch form factor and must be installed in the larger drive bays.

   C. Because it is antiquated technology, floppy disk drives can no longer be purchased new.

   D. Although some drives might not clearly key the receptacle for the Berg power connector, you must insert the connector correctly or the drive can be damaged.

10. After manually formatting a hard drive and installing the operating system, you find that the computer does not function in the manner expected. Which of the following is a possible cause?

   A. You performed a high-level format, but neglected to perform a low-level format first.

   B. The operating system was distributed on two discs, but you only installed one.

   C. During formatting, you did not make the partition bootable.

   D. The operating system was larger than your hard drive and did not install completely.

11. What is the term for an operating system–independent operation that ties a hard drive to its controller card?

    A. High-level formatting

    B. Low-level formatting

    C. Partitioning

    D. Scrubbing

12. Which of the following is not a consideration when upgrading power supplies?

    A. You might find that you do not have a matching motherboard connector on your new power supply.

    B. You might find that your case has a nonremovable power supply.

    C. You might find that your power rating is not adequate on the new power supply.

    D. You might find that you do not have enough of the appropriate connectors coming from the power supply for the devices you have installed.

13. What does the red stripe on a ribbon cable indicate?

    A. Pin 16

    B. Pin 1

    C. The manufacturer's trademark

    D. Parity

14. What do UltraDMA/66 and higher require?

    A. Cable Select configuration

    B. An 80-wire cable

    C. Operating system support

    D. That the BIOS be set for UltraDMA instead of DMA

15. Which of the following is not an example of a standard input device connector?

    A. 1/8-inch jack

    B. Mini-DIN

    C. D-subminiature

    D. USB

16. When installing a CPU fan and heat sink, which of the following is not a consideration to keep in mind?

    A. If a tool is needed, use only the tool for which the clip to be attached was designed.

    B. Orient the fan and heat sink to be square with the CPU and to match up with the tabs that receive the clips.

    C. Match the direction that the fan blows, up or down, to the model of CPU based on heat production.

    D. Determine if you have the appropriate power connector for the fan and obtain an adapter, if necessary.

17. Which system resource allows an expansion card, for instance, to signal the CPU that it requires some of the CPU's time?

    A. I/O memory

    B. DMA channels

    C. IRQ lines

    D. Memory addresses

18. On the primary IDE channel, if a single hard disk is attached, its jumper should be set to _____.

    A. Slave

    B. Single if available, otherwise Master

    C. Master

    D. Boot

19. What are the five voltages produced by a common PC power supply? (Choose five.)

    A. +3.3VDC

    B. −3.3VDC

    C. +5VDC

    D. −5VDC

    E. +12VDC

    F. −12VDC

    G. +110VAC

    H. −110VAC

20. What is the name of the utility that allows you to check hardware resources and alter them, if allowed?

    A. Device Manager

    B. Task Manager

    C. Program Manager

    D. Control Panel

Answers to Review Questions

1. C. Very often, computer systems prove to have an upgrade path for their RAM. Also, upgrading the RAM is the least expensive upgrade compared to the increase in performance that you can observe, up to a point.

2. C, D. ISA is an antiquated computer expansion bus. PCI is liable to be replaced by its high-performance cousin, PCIe. AGP remains a popular video technology in today's market.

3. B. All RAM is solid state. The other three options are selection criteria.

4. A. You should never apply insertion pressure to a CPU. With ZIF sockets, you release the lever on the side of the socket, and the CPU should drop right in, sometimes with delicate urging but never with what could be considered pressure.

5. D. Removing the expansion boards from their slots is recommended, if not required. Any static that you discharge into the motherboard can affect the adapters while they're attached. The fact that a motherboard outside of the case is made more cumbersome with cards attached means that you are more likely to slip and discharge static with the motherboard in that state.

6. A. It's true. Sometimes you have to pat yourself on the back for being able to install the CPU and RAM, because kudos for configuring the motherboard for these components would be a bit of a stretch. The BIOS does this for you today. There are no DIP switches on these components, and there is no such thing as a CPU/RAM programming station. Manufacturers must remain more flexible than to produce motherboards for only one set of CPU and RAM modules.

7. A. You must make sure that, for electrostatic-discharge reasons, you are at the same electrical potential as the chassis and other components. The best way to do this is by using an antistatic wrist strap and ensuring it is clipped to the chassis and that the chassis is connected to ground. Alternatively, both you and the chassis can be connected in parallel to the same source of ground. Very few components on standard computer systems are hot-swappable, which is normally limited to certain drives and USB/PC Card applications. Servers are somewhat more resilient, but still not all components are hot-swappable. Motherboard LEDs light up when power is supplied to the board. This is an indication that you should not perform work inside the chassis. How many people would be out of a job if they could not work inside a computer system today?

8. C. Today's hard drives, regardless of their RPMs, have standard internal power connections. Each of the other options are valid concerns when installing an internal drive.

9. D. See the "Do You Smell Something?" Real-World Scenario in this chapter. Inserting the Berg connector upside down will damage the drive the first time the motor is activated. Floppy drives require front access for floppy disk insertion. Their form factor is only 3.5 inches, and you can still buy them new.

10. C. When manually performing a high-level format of a drive, you must make the partition bootable. Automatic operating system installation takes care of this for you, making it easy to overlook. If a low-level format is required, you are not able to partition a drive and perform a high-level format without first performing the low-level format. You do not need to install each disc for your operating system separately. Operating systems prompt you for all required distribution media during installation and do not allow you to choose partial-media installations. If you do not have enough room on your hard drive to install an operating system, the installation routine will not perform the installation.

11. B. The question describes low-level formatting, which is performed by the manufacturer for ATA (IDE) drives but must be performed by the installer for SCSI drives. Partitioning and high-level formatting are based on the operating system being used, and scrubbing is an informal term used to describe the behavior of certain integrity-checking utilities.

12. B. Personal computers do not have permanently installed power supplies. Like other electrical and electronic components, power supplies can and do fail on a regular basis. Permanently mounting a power supply to a chassis would be a disservice to the consumer. You should consider the cumulative power needs of your installed components, and you might have to obtain adapters and splitters if you do not have enough or you have the wrong types of connectors coming from the power supply.

13. B. The red stripe on the cable indicates pin 1.

14. B. UltraDMA/66 requires a special ribbon cable with extra wires to cut down on crosstalk. It does not require Cable Select to be in use, and it does not require specific operating system support because it operates at a lower level than the OS. There is no special setting in the BIOS for UltraDMA drives.

15. A. One eighth-inch jacks, or minijacks, are used for multimedia input devices, not standard input devices. Standard input devices include human interface devices, such as keyboards and mice. The other three options can be used for such devices.

16. C. The fan always blows downward to push the collected heat out through the fins of the heat sink. The other options are valid points to consider.

17. C. Interrupt request (IRQ) lines perform as stated in the question. The other three resources have nothing to do with this action.

18. B. If there is a Single setting, it should be used. Otherwise, use Master. Slave is never appropriate for a single drive. There is no such jumper setting as Boot.

19. A, C, D, E, F. With an input ranging from 110VAC to 240VAC, a PC's power supply produces +3.3VDC, +5VDC, −5VDC, +12VDC, and −12VDC.

20. A. Only Device Manager allows you access to the resources being used by the various hardware components. Task Manager and Control Panel allow you to monitor and alter certain items but not hardware resources, as Device Manager is designed to do.

Chapter

14

Installing, Configuring, and Troubleshooting Laptops

THE FOLLOWING COMPTIA A+ PRACTICAL APPLICATION EXAM OBJECTIVES ARE COVERED IN THIS CHAPTER:

✓ **1.3 Given a scenario, install, configure, detect problems, troubleshoot and repair/replace laptop components**

- Components of the LCD including inverter, screen, and video card

- Hard drive and memory

- Disassemble processes for proper re-assembly

  - Document and label cable and screw locations

  - Organize parts

  - Refer to manufacturer documentation

  - Use appropriate hand tools

- Recognize internal laptop expansion slot types

- Upgrade wireless cards and video card

- Replace keyboard, processor, plastics, pointer devices, heat sinks, fans, system board, CMOS battery, speakers

Prices on laptops have steadily dropped over the past decade or so, and for the last several years laptop sales have outpaced desktop sales. Even though they're very popular, laptop computers still aren't going to out-muscle their similarly priced desktop counterparts, and they may not for a very long time. What laptops do provide is flexibility—the flexibility to work wirelessly from anywhere and the flexibility to change peripherals in the blink of an eye.

Laptops also pose a different set of challenges to the technician than desktops because of technology differences between the platforms. Although wireless networking has become fairly commonplace with desktops, it's a fundamental technology of mobile computing. Similarly, liquid crystal display (LCD) screens are almost must-have features for desktops but are again squarely at the center of the laptop world. As you move forward in the computer industry, it's important to have a good grasp of the different technologies, especially since mobile computers make up over half of new computer sales each year. It's not inconceivable to think that the desktop computer as we know it may be a relic before too long.

This chapter takes a look at repairing laptop components. Troubleshooting laptops is an objective that finds a home in several places in the A+ exam objectives, so some of the material in this chapter may sound familiar to you. Specifically, if you want a refresher of laptop technology you may want to refer back to Chapter 4, "Understanding Laptops and Portable Devices." In addition, Chapter 9, "Troubleshooting Operating Systems, Hardware, Printers, and Laptops," spent some time reviewing laptop troubleshooting. Those chapters focused more on the "what is" behind laptops and troubleshooting. In this chapter, we'll focus on the "how to" of fixing laptops.

Disassembling and Reassembling Laptops

Desktop computers often have a lot of empty space inside their cases. This lets air circulate, and also gives the technician some room to maneuver when troubleshooting internal hardware. Space is at a premium in laptops, and rarely is any wasted. With a desktop computer, if you end up having an extra screw left over after putting it together, it's probably not a big deal. With laptops, every screw matters, and you'll sometimes find yourself trying to visually identify miniscule differences between screws to make sure you get them back into the right places.

Even though repairing a laptop poses unique issues, most of the general troubleshooting and safety tips you use when troubleshooting a desktop still apply. For example, always make sure you have a clean and well-lit work space and be cautious of ESD. For a review of general troubleshooting and safety tips, see Chapter 8, "Troubleshooting Theory and Preventive Maintenance." Here, we'll get in to specific objectives for tearing apart laptops.

> Throughout this chapter, we'll use the word "laptop" almost exclusively. The principles covered here apply to nearly all portable devices, though, such as notebooks, handhelds, and netbooks.

Using the Right Tools

It's doubtful that any technician goes into a job thinking, "Hey, I'm going to use the wrong tools just to see what happens." With laptops, though, it's especially important to ensure you have exactly the tools you need for the job. Two critical tools you need are the manufacturer's documentation and the right hand tools.

Using the Manufacturer's Documentation

Most technicians won't bat an eye at whipping out their cordless screwdriver and getting into a desktop's case. The biggest difference between most desktops is how you get inside the case. Once opened, everything inside is pretty standard fare.

Laptops are a different story. Even experienced technicians will tell you to not remove a single screw until you have the documentation handy, unless you're incredibly familiar with that particular laptop. Most laptop manufacturers give you access to repair manuals on their website; Table 14.1 lists the service and support websites for some of the top laptop manufacturers.

TABLE 14.1   Laptop Manufacturers' Service and Support Websites

Company	URL
Asus	http://support.asus.com/default.aspx
Compaq	http://www.compaq.com/country/cpq_support.html
Dell	http://support.dell.com/support/index.aspx
HP	http://www.hp.com/#Support
IBM	http://www.ibm.com/support/publications/us/library/
Sony	http://esupport.sony.com/US/perl/select-system.pl?DIRECTOR=DOCS
Toshiba	http://www.csd.toshiba.com/cgi-bin/tais/support/jsp/home.jsp

Once you are at the right website, search for the manual using the laptop's model number.

Some laptop manufacturers have a policy that if you open the case of a laptop, the warranty is voided. Be sure to understand your warranty status and implications of cracking the case before you do it.

Using the Right Hand Tools

Once you have the manual in hand or on your screen, you need to gather the right hand tools for the job. For some laptops, you only need the basics such as a small Phillips-head and straight-edge screwdriver. For others you may need a Torx driver. Gather the tools you need and prepare to open the case. A small flashlight might also come in handy.

 Real World Scenario

The Consequences of Using the Wrong Tools

It's been said once, but it's important to say it again: always use the right tool for the job when repairing laptops. If the documentation says you need a T-10 Torx driver, make sure you have a T-10 Torx driver.

Not using the right tools can result in the stripping of the screw head. If you strip a screw head in a desktop, you might have alternative methods of removing the screw. Laptops are far less forgiving. If you strip a screw head and are unable to turn the screw, you may never be able to remove it. That could result in needing to scrap the device.

Organization and Documentation

Before you crack the case of your laptop, have an organization and documentation plan in place. Know where you are going to put the parts. Have a container set aside for the screws. You can purchase small plastic containers that have several compartments in them, with lids that snap tightly shut, to place screws in. You can also use containers designed to organize prescription pills. The bottom of an egg carton works well too, provided you don't need to be mobile to fix the laptop.

For documentation, many technicians find it handy to draw a map of the computer they're getting into, such as the one shown in Figure 14.1. It can be as complex as you want it to be, as long as it makes sense to you.

The drawing in Figure 14.1 shows the locations of the screws, and also calls out where the screws should be placed once they're removed. Again, this type of documentation can be as simple or complex as you want it to be, as long as it makes sense and helps you stay organized.

FIGURE 14.1   Laptop repair "roadmap"

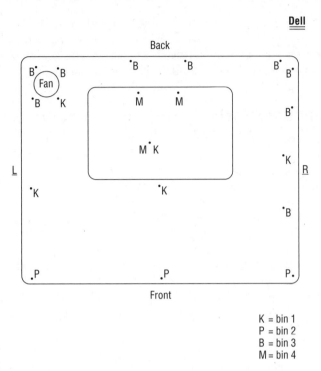

K = bin 1
P = bin 2
B = bin 3
M = bin 4

Replacing Laptop Components

You have your manual, screwdrivers, and screw container handy and are ready to go. Now you just need to figure out how to get to the defective component to replace it. It would be nice if we could just tell you one simple way to do this for all laptops, but that's not going to happen. Internal laptop structure varies widely between models as does how to get to the components.

In the following sections, we're going to assume you've figured out what's defective and needs to be replaced. We'll stay away from describing components and what they do, unless it's not been covered elsewhere in the book. The model we're going to use in the examples in the rest of this chapter is a Dell Latitude C640. This particular model is about six years old so it's a bit dated, but all of the procedures we're going to walk you through will still be similar for newer systems. For other models, please consult the manufacturer's documentation.

Understanding LCDs

Liquid crystal display (LCD) technology is one of the core reasons why laptop computers rose in popularity. Before LCD technology, displays were big and bulky and hardly mobile. Because LCD is a totally different technology than cathode-ray tube (CRT), some different components are required. This section looks at some of the components that make LCD work.

 For more details on LCD standards and concepts, please see Chapter 3, "Understanding Display Devices."

Video Card

The video card in a laptop or desktop with an LCD monitor does the same thing a video card supporting a CRT monitor would do. It's responsible for generating and managing the image sent to the screen. The big difference is that most LCD monitors are digital, meaning you need a video card that puts out a digital image. Laptop manufacturers put video cards in laptops that are compatible with the display, but with desktops it can get a bit confusing. Figure 14.2 shows an ABIT video card, with a digital video interface (DVI) port on the left and an analog (VGA) port on the right. The port in the middle is an S-video/composite video port.

FIGURE 14.2   Video card

The video card in Figure 14.2 is obviously for a desktop. Most laptop manufacturers choose to integrate the LCD circuitry on the motherboard to save space.

On the market, you can find digital-to-analog video converters, if you need to plug in an older analog monitor to a digital video card.

 Real World Scenario

Video Memory Sharing

If your video card is built into your motherboard, odds are that it doesn't have its own memory but shares system memory with the processor. Note that there is nothing wrong with this type of setup; in fact, it often brings the cost of the laptop down. It's just that instead of having 1GB of RAM and 128MB of video RAM (for example), you would only have 1GB total. So if your video card were using 128MB, the system would only be left with 896MB.

How much of a difference does all of this make? Well, it depends on what you're doing with your laptop. If you're using it for the Internet and light work, probably not much difference. If you're working with more video-intensive applications, using a computer with shared memory might slow you down some. This usually brings up two questions: One, what's the optimal balance? Two, where do I change this?

To answer question one, again, it depends on what you are doing. If you perform more video-intensive operations (or if you're gaming), then you might want to set aside more memory for the video card. If you're not as concerned with rapid pixilation, then less is fine. Which brings us to the second question: where do you set it? Shared memory is configured in the system BIOS. Each BIOS is different, so be sure to consult your owner's manual if you have any questions. Keep in mind that some BIOSs will only allow you to set aside a certain amount of memory—say, 128MB—for video memory.

How does this affect your computer when you upgrade the memory? First, keep in mind that some of your memory will be taken by the video card, so you might want to upgrade to more than you originally planned for. Second, after upgrading the memory, you will need to go into the BIOS and reconfigure how much you want allocated to the video card.

Backlight

LCD displays do not produce light, so to generate brightness, many LCD displays have a *backlight*. A backlight is a small fluorescent lamp placed behind, above, or to the side of an LCD display. The light from the lamp is diffused across the screen, producing brightness. The typical laptop display uses a *cold cathode fluorescent lamp (CCFL)* as its backlight. They're generally about eight inches long and slimmer than a pencil. Best of all, they generate little heat, which is always good thing to avoid with laptops.

Inverter

The only problem with fluorescent lighting, and LCD backlights in particular, is that they require fairly high-voltage, high-frequency energy. Another component is needed to provide the right kind of energy, and that's the *inverter*.

The inverter is a small circuit board installed behind the LCD panel that takes AC power and converts (inverts) it for the backlight. If you are having problems with flickering screens or dimness, it's more likely that the inverter is the problem and not the backlight itself.

There are two things to keep in mind if you are going to replace an inverter. One, they store and convert energy, so they have the potential to discharge that energy. To an inexperienced technician, they can be dangerous. Two, make sure that the replacement inverter was made to work with the LCD backlight you have. If they weren't made for each other, you might have problems with a dim screen or poor display quality.

> **WARNING**   Inverters can discharge energy, which can cause severe injury to you. Be careful when working with them!

LCD Screen

The screen on an LCD monitor does what you might expect—it produces the image that you see. There are two broad categories of LCD screens: active matrix and passive matrix.

> **NOTE**   For more information on active- and passive-matrix screens, see Chapter 3.

Replacing LCD Components

Many of the LCD components in a laptop can be replaced. Replacing these components often means removing the LCD display from the main chassis of the laptop. When doing so, just be careful of the video circuitry that connects the two, which is usually located in one of the laptop case hinges.

Replacing Hard Drives and Memory

Hard drives and memory are the two most common components people usually upgrade in a laptop. In this section, we'll look at how to accomplish replacing both of them.

Replacing Hard Drives

External storage devices are more popular now than they ever have been. On the small end, you can get postage-stamp-sized SD memory sticks or ultra-portable thumb drives that hold a few gigabytes each. If you need more storage, you can get external hard drives that hold in excess of one terabyte and connect to your laptop using a USB cable.

Even with all of those options, a laptop still needs an internal hard drive. Exercise 14.1 shows you how to remove and replace an internal hard drive.

We could start off each of these exercises by saying, "Check your documentation," because that is realistically what you're going to have to do for the specific model of laptop you're working on. Obviously, each of these exercises is intended to be an example of how to replace a part. Instead of telling you to check your documentation each time for the exact steps, we'll assume that it's understood.

EXERCISE 14.1

Replacing a Laptop Hard Drive

1. Turn off the computer.

2. Disconnect the computer and any peripherals from their power sources, and remove any installed batteries.

3. Locate the hard drive door and remove the screw holding it in place.

4. Lift the hard drive door until it clicks.

5. Slide the hard drive out to remove it.

6. Remove the two screws holding the hard drive to the hard drive door.

7. Attach a new hard drive to the hard drive door.

8. Slide the new hard drive back into the hard drive bay.

9. Snap the hard drive door back into place, and insert and tighten the screw to hold the door in place.

Replacing Memory

No matter how much memory your laptop has, it's probably not enough. Most laptops share their system memory with the video card, meaning that memory on a laptop might not go as far as you think.

Not long ago there weren't any standards for the physical size of laptop memory. Manufacturers weren't in a hurry to conform to each other either. After all, if they were the only ones producing memory for their systems, then they could pretty much charge what they wanted.

Fortunately two standards exist today: the 144-pin SODIMM and 172-pin MicroDIMM (for more information, see Chapter 4). Many manufacturers will use memory that conforms to one of these two standards, but others still produce proprietary memory chips only available through them. Your documentation will tell you what type of memory your system takes. Exercise 14.2 shows you how to access the memory bay so you can upgrade or replace memory chips.

EXERCISE 14.2

Replacing Laptop Memory

1. Turn off the computer.

2. Disconnect the computer and any peripherals from their power sources, and remove any installed batteries.

3. Remove the screws holding the memory door in place.

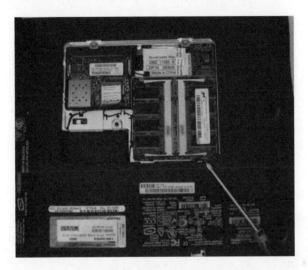

4. Use your fingers to gently separate the plastic tabs holding the memory module in place. The module should pop up so you can grab it.

5. Align the notch in the new memory module to the one in the connector.

6. Insert the new memory module into the socket at a 45-degree angle. Once full contact is made, press the module down. It should click into place.

7. Replace the memory door and fasten the screws.

Recognizing Internal Laptop Expansion Slots

As you are probably aware, laptops aren't made with internal expandability in mind. What you may not know, though, is that there are two standards for internal laptop expansion based on the PC-sized Peripheral Component Interconnect (PCI) standard. They are known as *Mini PCI* and *Mini PCIe*, and they're covered in detail in Chapter 4.

Most laptops will only come with one Mini PCI port, and common Mini PCI devices include SCSI controllers, SATA controllers, network cards, sound cards, and modems. Table 14.2 gives you the dimensions of the various Mini PCI form factors.

TABLE 14.2   Mini PCI Form Factors

Type	Connector	Size
IA	100-pin, stacking	7.5×70×45 millimeters
IB	100-pin, stacking	5.5×70×45 millimeters
IIA	100-pin, stacking	7.5×70×45 millimeters
IIB	100-pin, stacking	17.44×78×45 millimeters
IIIA	124-pin, card edge	2.4×59.6×50.95 millimeters
IIIB	124-pin, card edge	2.4×59.6×44.6 millimeters

Figure 14.3 shows you the type IIIA Mini PCI network card installed in this laptop, which happens to be in the same bay as the system memory. The connector is on the top side of the figure.

FIGURE 14.3   Mini PCI card installed in a laptop

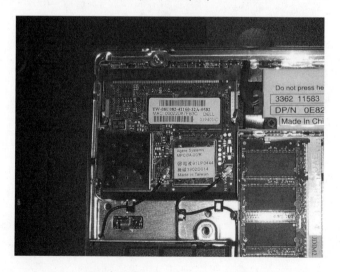

 You can tell that the card in Figure 14.3 is a type IIIA card by looking at two things. First, it has a card-edge connector, making it type III. Second, the card looks almost like a square, making it type IIIA. Type IIIB cards are about ¼″ shorter and look more rectangular.

Removing the Mini PCI card is just like removing the memory, except that this one has antenna cables you need to disconnect first. After that, spread the retaining clips just like you would for the memory, and the card will pop up. Replace it with a new card the same way you would replace a memory module.

Mini PCIe cards have a 52-pin card edge connector.

Upgrading Wireless and Video Cards

What do wireless network cards and video cards have in common in laptops? Most of the time, they're integrated into your system motherboard. If either one fails, you need to replace the entire motherboard. Some laptops have these components as separate *field-replaceable units (FRUs)*, and you can remove them as needed. The only way to know for sure is to consult your trusty service manual. This section looks at some ways you may be able to upgrade these devices.

Upgrading Wireless Network Cards

Wireless network cards and laptops are a perfect match for each other, much like peanut butter and chocolate. You can have one without the other, but what's the point, really?

Most network cards are built into the motherboard chipset of laptops. In other words, if it fails, you likely need to replace the motherboard. Network cards are special, though, in that you have many other easier ways to upgrade if you want to.

On the market you can find several external portable network cards. You can often choose from network cards that look like a thumb drive and have a USB connector to slightly bulkier PCMCIA network cards. These are even valid options if your built-in network card is still working but you want to upgrade. For example, if you have an older laptop with an 802.11b network card in it but you want to upgrade to 802.11g or 802.11n, it may be more economical to purchase an external card and use it in your system. Just be sure to disable the old card in Windows Device Manager so you don't confuse the operating system and run into device conflicts.

Upgrading Laptop Video Cards

Odds are that the laptop you're working on has an integrated video card. If the video card fails, you're likely looking at a motherboard replacement. Some laptops do have a replaceable video card. If it fails or if you choose to upgrade it, the procedure will probably resemble replacing system memory. The Dell Latitude C640 we've been using as an example has a built-in video card, so there's no way to upgrade that specific device. For an example of what it might take to replace a video card, we'll use a Dell Inspiron 6000 in Exercise 14.3.

EXERCISE 14.3

Removing a Laptop Video Card

1. Turn off the computer.

EXERCISE 14.3 *(continued)*

2. Disconnect the computer and any peripherals from their power sources, and remove any installed batteries.

3. Remove the Mini PCI card and the optical drive.

4. Remove the hard drive, the hinge cover, the keyboard, the display assembly, and the palm rest.

5. Loosen the two captive screws holding the video card/thermal cooling assembly in place.

6. Lift up on the video card/thermal cooling assembly to remove it from the motherboard.

Replacing Other Internal Components

By now you have probably gotten the idea that in order to know how to replace components inside your laptop, you need to check the laptop's manual. The upshot is, nearly every component you can think of replacing in a desktop computer is also replaceable in a laptop. It just might require a bit more work to fix the laptop than it would to fix a desktop.

The list of components included in the A+ Practical Application objectives include the keyboard, processor, plastics, pointer devices, heat sinks, fans, system board, CMOS battery, and speakers. It's impractical to list steps to remove all of these devices, as the steps we would list here will only help you if you're working on the same model of laptop we're using for an example. As a rule of thumb, you can either access components from the bottom of your laptop, such as the memory, Mini PCI card, and modem in the Latitude C640, or you're going to need to remove the keyboard to access the components from the top.

As the keyboard is often the gateway to the guts of a laptop, we will include an example of removing it. We'll also include a few other examples of components you may need to replace in your line of work. Exercise 14.4 shows you how to remove a keyboard.

EXERCISE 14.4

Removing a Laptop Keyboard

1. Turn off the computer.

2. Disconnect the computer and any peripherals from their power sources, and remove any installed batteries.

3. Remove the hard drive.

4. On the bottom of the laptop, remove the five screws marked with the letter K.

5. Turn the laptop over and open the display.

6. Remove the center control cover by inserting a small flat-edged screwdriver into the notch at the right end of the center control cover and prying it loose.

7. To release the keyboard, use a small flat-edged screwdriver to pry up on the right edge of the keyboard, near the blank key.

8. Lift the keyboard up about an inch and rotate it forward, so the keys are facing on the palm rest. Don't pull the keyboard too far or you might damage the connector cable.

EXERCISE 14.4 *(continued)*

9. Pull up on the keyboard connector to disconnect it from the keyboard interface connector on the motherboard.

10. Set the keyboard aside.

Now that the keyboard is off, you can remove several other components with relative ease. Exercise 14.5 looks at removing the processor cooling assembly and the processor.

EXERCISE 14.5

Removing the Processor Cooling Assembly and Processor

1. Turn off the computer.

2. Disconnect the computer and any peripherals from their power sources, and remove any installed batteries.

3. Remove the hard drive.

4. Remove the keyboard.

5. Loosen the four captive screws that hold the cooling assembly in place

EXERCISE 14.5 *(continued)*

6. Insert a small screwdriver into the recess in the front left side of the assembly and pry the assembly from the motherboard. If this is the first time removing the assembly, it might take some force as it's likely glued to the processor. Set the assembly aside.

7. Use a small flat-edged screwdriver to loosen the processor's ZIF socket by rotating the cam screw counterclockwise until it reaches the cam stop. (It should take about one-quarter turn.)

8. Use a microprocessor extraction tool to remove the microprocessor. If you don't have an extraction tool, you can try to use your hands. Make sure you're grounded first, and always pull straight up to avoid bending pins.

9. Set the processor aside on an antistatic mat or place in an antistatic bag.

The last internal device we'll look at removing is the CMOS battery. If the BIOS isn't maintaining system information, you will want to replace this component. Exercise 14.6 shows you how to replace the CMOS battery.

> Many laptops use the same type of round, silver watch-style batteries that desktop motherboards use. Others use packaged batteries that more closely resemble cell phone batteries, such as this laptop.

EXERCISE 14.6

Replacing the CMOS Battery

1. Turn off the computer.

2. Disconnect the computer and any peripherals from their power sources, and remove any installed batteries.

EXERCISE 14.6 *(continued)*

3.   Remove the hard drive.

4.   Remove the keyboard.

5.   Disconnect the CMOS battery from the motherboard.

6.   Pry the battery from its seat with a small straight-edged screwdriver. Note that it's adhered to the EMI shield below it, so removing it might require some force.

7.   Connect the new battery to the appropriate connector on the motherboard.

8.   Peel away the backing from the adhesive bottom of the new CMOS battery. Press the battery into the battery tray.

9.   Upgrade the BIOS using a flash BIOS CD.

Flashing the system BIOS is usually a pretty straightforward process. You can get a BIOS update from the manufacturer and burn it to a CD. Once you have the CD, you just need to boot the laptop from the CD, and the disc will automatically flash the BIOS. Exercise 14.7 shows you the steps to flash the BIOS on this model.

EXERCISE 14.7

Flashing the System BIOS

1. Turn off the computer.

2. Ensure that the computer is plugged into AC power and that the main battery is installed properly.

3. Turn on the computer and press F2 to enter the BIOS setup.

4. Reset the system boot order to ensure the system boots from the CD first.

5. Insert the flash BIOS update CD, and reboot the computer. The disc will flash the BIOS and automatically reboot.

6. Upon reboot, press F2 again to enter the BIOS setup. Verify that the settings are correct, and change the boot sequence to your preferred setting.

7. Remove the flash BIOS CD.

Removing External Hardware

In the grand scheme of things, there are two types of peripherals: internal and external. We've already discussed removing internal hardware, and compared to that, removing external components is very easy. If you have USB-type devices plugged in, removing them is as easy as disconnecting them, but other peripherals require a bit more work.

Devices that can be removed when the computer is powered on are called hot-swappable devices. If you need to turn the computer off first, then the device is not hot-swappable. There are several different hot-swappable peripherals, including mice, keyboards, some hard drives, network cards, printers, and others. Good examples of non-hot-swappable devices include motherboards and internal IDE hard drives. Odds are if it's internal to your computer case, then it's not hot-swappable. Always be sure to check your hardware documentation to see if the device is safe to plug in or disconnect with the system powered on.

Although most of the time you can just remove a USB device, make sure it's not in use when you remove it.

In Exercise 14.8, we will show you the recommended method to remove a device.

EXERCISE 14.8

Removing External Devices

1. You need to stop the device first (this is good policy even for USB devices), using the icon in the system tray that looks like a card with a green arrow over it.

2. Click on the Safely Remove Hardware icon, and you will get a screen similar to the one shown here:

3. Highlight the device you want to remove, and click Stop. Windows will then notify you that it's safe to remove the device. If it's a cabled device, just detach it. If it's PCMCIA, you can press the Eject button next to the slot in which the card is located. Other types of hardware in some laptops require you to release a latch. The following photo shows a modular front-load bay, and the right side has a CD-ROM in it:

4. Turn the computer over, and you can see the release latch. Slide it to the side, and pull on the grip on the underside of the CD-ROM. Out it comes.

Adding an external device to a laptop generally means that the computer will automatically recognize and enable the device for you, unless there's no compatible driver available. In cases like these, Windows will tell you that it detected new hardware and ask you to provide an appropriate driver.

Summary

In this chapter, we looked at repairing and replacing laptop components. We started off by quickly reviewing some general troubleshooting tips, and then looked at finding laptop documentation and tools. We also discussed organization and documentation.

Next, we covered the components of an LCD screen, which most laptops have. We discussed replacing hard drives and memory and also looked at internal expansion slot types. After that, we explored upgrading wireless, video cards, and other internal components. Finally, we explained how to safely remove an external device from your laptop.

Exam Essentials

Know where to get service manuals for laptops.   Service manuals can be found at the laptop manufacturers' websites.

Be familiar with the components of an LCD.   LCDs are made up of the video card, backlight, inverter, and screen.

Know how to recognize internal laptop expansion slot types.   Two types of internal expansion slots are Mini PCI and Mini PCIe. There are six Mini PCI form factors. Mini PCIe has a 52-pin card edge connector.

Know how to replace hardware devices from laptops.   Components are typically accessed either from the bottom of the case or by removing the keyboard and accessing them from the top. Each laptop is different, so be sure to consult your documentation.

Review Questions

1. Where can you obtain the service manual for a laptop computer?

   A. By pressing F1 while in Windows

   B. By pressing F2 while the system is booting up

   C. It comes as a paper copy with the laptop.

   D. From the manufacturer's website

2. Which of the following are components of an LCD? (Choose all that apply.)

   A. Inverter

   B. Screen

   C. CRT

   D. Backdrop

3. Which of the following are laptop memory form factor standards? (Choose two.)

   A. MiniDIMM

   B. MicroDIMM

   C. SlotDIMM

   D. SODIMM

4. Which LCD component is responsible for providing brightness?

   A. Backlight

   B. Inverter

   C. Screen

   D. Backdrop

5. What type of connector does a Mini PCIe card have?

   A. 52-pin card edge

   B. 100-pin stacking

   C. 100-pin card edge

   D. 124-pin card edge

6. How many pins does a MicroDIMM memory module have?

   A. 72

   B. 144

   C. 172

   D. 198

7. Which LCD component is responsible for providing the right kind of power to the monitor?

    A. Backlight

    B. Inverter

    C. Screen

    D. Backdrop

8. What type of connector does a Mini PCI type IA card have?

    A. 52-pin card edge

    B. 100-pin stacking

    C. 100-pin card edge

    D. 124-pin card edge

9. Which laptop component is often upgraded with an external PCMCIA device?

    A. Video card

    B. Motherboard

    C. Network card

    D. Keyboard

10. A typical backlight technology is:

    A. CRT

    B. CCFL

    C. LCD

    D. LED

11. When upgrading the system BIOS, what is one way you may be able to change the boot sequence?

    A. By inserting a boot CD

    B. By pressing F1 while in Windows

    C. By pressing F2 while the system is booting up

    D. By holding down the BIOS key as the system is booting up

12. How many pins does a SODIMM memory module have?

    A. 72

    B. 144

    C. 172

    D. 198

13. What should you do first to remove external devices from your laptop?

    A. Just remove the device.

    B. Unplug the power to the device, then remove the device.

    C. Click the Safely Remove Hardware icon.

    D. Click the Remove Hardware Now icon.

14. What type of power does the inverter provide to the backlight?

    A. Low voltage, low frequency

    B. Low voltage, high frequency

    C. High voltage, low frequency

    D. High voltage, high frequency

15. Which of the following is a digital connector for video that you may find on video card?

    A. VGA

    B. DVI

    C. LCD

    D. CRT

16. What type of connector does a Mini PCI type IIIA card have?

    A. 52-pin card edge

    B. 100-pin stacking

    C. 100-pin card edge

    D. 124-pin card edge

17. Which of the following are common types of Mini PCI card devices? (Choose all that apply.)

    A. Hard drive controller

    B. Hard drive

    C. Network card

    D. Sound card

18. Your laptop has 2GB of installed memory and uses shared video memory. If the video card is using 512MB, how much is left for the rest of the system?

    A. 2GB

    B. 1.5GB

    C. 512MB

    D. Cannot determine

19. What does FRU stand for?

    A. Field replacable unit

    B. Field recyclable unit

    C. Foreign recycled unit

    D. Failed replaced unit

20. Which two of the following are types of LCD screens?

    A. Pulsed matrix

    B. Active matrix

    C. Passive matrix

    D. Dot matrix

Answers to Review Questions

1. D. Laptop service manuals can be obtained from the manufacturer's website. It's very rare that paper service manuals are shipped with the laptop. Pressing F1 while in Windows will open Windows Help, and pressing F2 on many laptops during the system boot will take you into the BIOS.

2. A, B. The components of an LCD screen are the inverter, screen, and backlight. The video card is also a key component of the LCD system. A CRT is a different technology than LCD.

3. B, D. The two laptop memory form factor standards are the 144-pin SODIMM and 172-pin MicroDIMM.

4. A. The backlight provides light to the LCD screen. The inverter provides power to the backlight, and the screen displays the picture.

5. A. Mini PCIe cards have 52-pin card edge connectors. Mini PCI cards have either a 100-pin stacking connector or a 124-pin card edge connector.

6. C. A MicroDIMM chip has 172 pins. SODIMM memory chips have 144 pins.

7. B. The inverter provides power to the backlight. The backlight provides light to the LCD screen, and the screen displays the picture.

8. B. Mini PCI cards have either a 100-pin stacking connector or a 124-pin card edge connector. Type I cards have a 100-pin card edge connector. Mini PCIe cards have 52-pin card edge connectors.

9. C. Network cards are available in PCMCIA forms. If your network card fails or you need an upgrade, you can easily install an external PCMCIA NIC.

10. B. Many laptops use a cold cathode fluorescent lamp (CCFL) as a backlight.

11. C. Pressing F2 on many laptops during the system boot will take you into the BIOS. Pressing F1 while in Windows will open Windows Help. Inserting a boot CD will not change the boot sequence. There is no BIOS key on the laptop.

12. B. SODIMM memory chips have 144 pins. MicroDIMM chips have 172 pins.

13. C. Before removing external hardware, you should click the Safely Remove Hardware icon.

14. D. The inverter provides high voltage, high frequency power to the backlight.

15. B. A DVI connector is for digital video. A VGA connector is for analog video. LCD and CRT are monitor types.

16. D. Mini PCI cards have either a 100-pin stacking connector or a 124-pin card edge connector. Type III cards have a 124-pin card edge connector. Mini PCIe cards have 52-pin card edge connectors.

17. A, C, D. Hard drive controllers (SATA and SCSI), network cards, and sound cards can all be found in Mini PCI forms. Hard drives are not made in Mini PCI form.

18. B. If the laptop is using shared video memory, then the system memory is shared with the video card. If the video card is using 512MB (half a gigabyte), then there is 1.5GB left for the system.

19. A. The acronym FRU stands for field replaceable unit, which means that the component can be replaced by a technician while at the user's location.

20. B, C. The two types of LCD screens are active matrix and passive matrix.

Chapter 15

Resolving Printer Problems

THE FOLLOWING COMPTIA A+ PRACTICAL APPLICATION EXAM OBJECTIVES ARE COVERED IN THIS CHAPTER:

✓ **1.5 Given a scenario, detect and resolve common printer issues**

- Symptoms
    - Paper jams
    - Blank paper
    - Error codes
    - Out of memory error
    - Lines and smearing
    - Garbage printout
    - Ghosted image
    - No connectivity
- Issue resolution
    - Replace fuser
    - Replace drum
    - Clear paper jam
    - Power cycle
    - Install maintenance kit (reset page count)
    - Set IP on printer
    - Clean printer

There's definitely been a movement in modern society to avoid the use of paper when possible. Many office environments are proud to call themselves "paper-free" environments. No matter the level of your "paper-freeness," odds are you still need to print things, whether it's in the office or at home. Electronic records are great to keep, but many situations still call for a hard copy.

Printers are computer peripherals that specialize in putting ink to paper. There are several different ways that this can be accomplished, but the end result is all pretty much the same.

Different types of printers work in different ways, so you would expect that some type of problems are related to one type of printer. While this is true, there are also problems that can happen to any type of printer. This chapter will first focus on the most common types of printers and review how they physically work and discuss how to solve problems that they might be having. After we cover those areas, we'll look at performing preventive maintenance on printers to help keep things from going wrong in the first place.

Troubleshooting Printer Problems

Other than the monitor (which every computer needs), the most popular peripheral purchased for computers today is the printer. Printers are also the most complex peripheral as far as troubleshooting is concerned. In this section, we will cover the most common types of printer problems you will run into.

Printer manufacturer websites are great places to look to find troubleshooting information. They often provide descriptions of problems and detailed instructions for resolving the issue. Most printers also come with management software that you can install on your computer, which may be able to assist you in troubleshooting any issues you have.

In order to solve printer problems, you need to have a good working knowledge of how each printer type works. So in each of the printer sections, we'll do a quick review of how the printer works before we get into solving problems.

For a more detailed description of each type of printer's components and inner workings, see Chapter 5, "Installing and Configuring Printers."

Dot-Matrix Printer Problems

Dot-matrix printers are impact printers, meaning that they rely upon making a physical impact in order to print. A dot-matrix printer contains a *printhead*, which has a row of short, sturdy pins made of a hard wire. The pins in the printhead are wrapped with coils of wire to create a *solenoid* and are held in the rest position by a combination of a small magnet and a spring. To trigger a particular pin, the printer controller sends a signal to the printhead, which energizes the wires around the appropriate print wire. This turns the print wire into an electromagnet, which repels the print pin, forcing it against the ink ribbon and making a dot on the paper.

Although this might sound complex, dot-matrix printers are relatively simple devices. Therefore, only a few problems usually arise. We will cover the most common problems and their solutions here.

Low Print Quality

Problems with print quality are easy to identify. When the printed page comes out of the printer, the characters may be too light or have dots missing from them. Table 15.1 details some of the most common print quality problems, their causes, and their solutions.

TABLE 15.1   Common Dot-Matrix Print Quality Problems

Characteristics	Cause	Solution
Consistently faded or light characters	Worn-out printer ribbon	See if you can adjust the printhead to be closer to the ribbon. If not (or if it doesn't help), replace the ribbon with a new, vendor-recommended ribbon.
Print lines that go from dark to light as the printhead moves across the page	Printer ribbon-advance gear slipping	Replace the ribbon-advance gear or mechanism.
A small, blank line running through a line of print (consistently)	Printhead pin stuck inside the printhead	Replace the printhead.
A small, blank line running through a line of print (intermittently)	A broken, loose, or shorting printhead cable	Secure or replace the printhead cable.
A small, dark line running through a line of print	Printhead pin stuck in the out position	Replace the printhead. (Pushing the pin in may damage the printhead.)

TABLE 15.1   Common Dot-Matrix Print Quality Problems *(continued)*

Characteristics	Cause	Solution
Printer makes a printing noise, but no print appears on the page	Worn, missing, or improperly installed ribbon cartridge	Replace the ribbon cartridge correctly.
Printer prints garbage	Cable partially unhooked, wrong driver selected, or bad printer control board (PCB)	Hook up the cable correctly, select the correct driver, or replace the PCB (respectively).

Printout Jams inside the Printer (aka "The Printer Crinkled My Paper")

Printer jams are very frustrating because they always seem to happen more than halfway through your 50-page print job, requiring you to take time to remove the jam before the rest of your pages can print. A paper jam happens when something prevents the paper from advancing through the printer evenly. There are generally two causes of printer jams: an obstructed paper path and stripped drive gears.

Obstructed paper paths are often difficult to find. Usually it means disassembling the printer to find the bit of crumpled-up paper or other foreign substance that's blocking the paper path. A common obstruction is a piece of the *perf*—the perforated sides of tractor-feed paper—that has torn off and gotten crumpled up and then lodged in the paper path. It may be necessary to remove the platen roller and feed mechanism to get at the obstruction.

Use extra caution when printing peel-off labels in dot-matrix printers. If a label or even a whole sheet of labels becomes misaligned or jammed, *do not* roll the roller backward to realign the sheet. The small plastic paper guide that most dot-matrix printers use to control the forward movement of the paper through the printer will peel the label right off its backing if you reverse the direction of the paper. Once the label is free, it can easily get stuck under the platen, causing paper jams. A label stuck under the platen is almost impossible to remove without disassembling the paper-feed assembly. If a label is misaligned, try realigning the whole sheet of labels *slowly* using the *feed roller,* with the power off, moving it in very small increments.

Stepper Motor Problems

Printers use stepper motors to move the printhead back and forth as well as to advance the paper. The *carriage motor* is responsible for the back-and-forth motion while the *main motor* advances the paper. These motors get damaged when they are forced in any direction while the power is on. This includes moving the printhead over to install a printer ribbon as well as moving the paper-feed roller to align paper. These motors are very sensitive to stray voltages. If you are rotating one of these motors by hand, you are essentially turning it into a small generator and thus damaging it.

A damaged stepper motor is easy to detect. Damage to the stepper motor will cause it to lose precision and move farther with each step. If the main motor is damaged (which is more likely to happen) lines of print will be unevenly spaced. If the printhead motor goes bad, characters will be scrunched together. If a stepper motor is damaged badly enough, it won't move at all in any direction; it may even make high-pitched squealing noises. If any of these symptoms appear, it's time to replace one of these motors.

Stepper motors are usually expensive to replace—about half the cost of a new printer! Damage to them is easy to avoid; the biggest key is to not force them to move when the power is on.

Bubble-Jet Printer Problems

A bubble-jet printer has many of the same types of parts that a dot-matrix printer does. In this sense, it's almost as if the bubble-jet technology is simply an extension of dot-matrix printers. The parts on a bubble-jet can be divided into four categories:

- Printhead/ink cartridge
- Printhead carriage, belt, and stepper motor
- Paper-feed mechanism
- Control, interface, and power circuitry

 In this chapter, the term bubble-jet is used to refer to inkjet printers as well. In terms of operation and troubleshooting they are virtually identical.

Perhaps the most obvious difference between bubble-jet and dot-matrix printers is that dot-matrix printers often use tractor-feed paper, while bubble-jets use normal paper. The differences don't end there, though. Bubble-jet printers work by spraying ink (often in the form of a bubble, hence their name) onto a page. The pattern of the bubbles forms images on the paper.

Bubble-jet printers are the most common type of printer found in homes because they are inexpensive and produce good-quality images. For this reason, you need to understand the most common problems with these printers so your company can service them effectively. Let's take a look at some of the most common problems with bubble-jet printers and their solutions.

Print Quality

The majority of bubble-jet printer problems are quality problems. Ninety-nine percent of these can be traced to a faulty ink cartridge. With most bubble-jet printers, the ink cartridge contains the printhead and the ink. The major problem with this assembly can be described by "If you don't use it, you lose it." The ink will dry out in the small nozzles and block them if they are not used at least once a week.

An example of a quality problem is when you have thin, blank lines present in every line of text on the page. This is caused by a plugged hole in at least one of the small, pinhole ink nozzles in the print cartridge. Replacing the ink cartridge solves this problem easily.

As we warned in Chapter 5, some people try to save a buck by refilling their ink cartridge when they need to replace it. If you are one of them, *stop!* Don't refill your ink cartridges! Almost all ink cartridges are designed *not to* be refilled. They are designed to be used once and thrown away. By refilling them, you make a hole in them—ink can leak out, and the printer will need to be cleaned. The ink will probably also be of the wrong type, and print quality can suffer. Finally, using a refilled cartridge may void the printer's warranty.

If an ink cartridge becomes damaged or develops a hole, it can put too much ink on the page and the letters will smear. Again, the solution is to replace the ink cartridge. (You should be aware, however, that a very small amount of smearing is normal if the pages are laid on top of each other immediately after printing.)

One final print quality problem that does not directly involve the ink cartridge occurs when the print quickly goes from dark to light and then prints nothing. As we already mentioned, ink cartridges dry out if not used. That's why the manufacturers include a small suction pump inside the printer that primes the ink cartridge before each print cycle. If this priming pump is broken or malfunctioning, this problem will manifest itself and the pump will need to be replaced.

If the problem of the ink quickly going from dark to light and then disappearing ever happens to you, and you really need to print a couple of pages, try this trick I learned from a fellow technician. First, take the ink cartridge out of the printer. Then squirt some window cleaner on a paper towel and gently tap the printhead against the wet paper towel. The force of the tap plus the solvents in the window cleaner should dislodge any dried ink, and the ink will flow freely again. Just be careful to not rub the paper towel across the printhead as this could damage the nozzles.

After you install a new cartridge into many bubble-jet printers, the printheads in that cartridge must be aligned. *Printhead alignment* is the process by which the printhead is calibrated for use. A special utility that comes with the printer software is used to do this. You run the alignment utility, and the printer prints several vertical and horizontal lines with numbers next to them. It then shows you a screen and asks you to choose the horizontal and vertical lines that are the most "in line." Once you enter the numbers, the software understands whether the printhead(s) are out of alignment, which direction, and by how much. The software then makes slight modifications to the print driver software to tell it how much to offset when printing. Occasionally alignment must be done several times to get the images to align properly.

Most new bubble-jet printers automatically align the printhead, and no interaction is required on your part. Even if this is the case, your printer software may have an option for you to be able to manually align the printheads.

Paper Jams

Bubble-jet printers have pretty simple paper paths. Therefore, paper jams due to obstructions are less likely than they are on dot-matrix printers. They are still possible, however, so an obstruction shouldn't be overlooked as a possible cause of jamming.

Paper jams in bubble-jet printers are usually due to one of two things:

- A worn pickup roller
- The wrong type of paper

The pickup roller usually has one or two D-shaped rollers mounted on a rotating shaft. When the shaft rotates, one edge of the D rubs against the paper, pushing it into the printer. When the roller gets worn, it gets smooth and doesn't exert enough friction against the paper to push it into the printer.

If the paper used in the printer is too smooth, it can cause the same problem. Pickup rollers use friction, and smooth paper doesn't offer much friction. If the paper is too rough, on the other hand, it acts like sandpaper on the rollers, wearing them smooth. Here's a rule of thumb for paper smoothness: paper slightly smoother than a new dollar bill will work fine.

Paper-Feeding Problems

You will normally see one of two paper-feeding options on a bubble-jet printer. The first is that the paper is stored in a *paper tray* on the front of the printer. The second, which is more common on smaller and cheaper models, is for the paper to be fed in vertically from the back of the printer in a *paper feeder*.

Regardless of the feed style, the printer will have a *paper-feed mechanism*, which picks up the paper and feeds it into the printer. Inside the paper-feed mechanism are *pickup rollers*, which are small rubber rollers that rub up against the paper and feed it into the printer. They press up against small rubber or cork patches known as *separator pads*. These help keep the rest of the paper in the tray, so that only one sheet gets picked up at a time. The pickup rollers are turned by a *pickup stepper motor*.

If your printer fails to pick up paper, it could indicate that the pickup rollers are too worn. If your printer is always picking up multiple sheets of paper, it could be a couple of things, such as problems with the separator pads or your paper being too "sticky" or rough. Some printers that use vertical paper feeders have a lever with which you can adjust the amount of tension between the pickup rollers and the separator pads. If your printer is consistently pulling multiple sheets of paper, you might want to try to increase the tension using this lever.

The final component is the *paper-feed sensor*. This sensor is designed to tell the printer when it's out of paper. I have only seen this sensor fail once in my career. The printer would refuse to print because it thought it was out of paper. Cleaning the sensor didn't help, so we replaced the printer.

Stepper Motor Problems

Bubble-jet printers use stepper motors, just like dot-matrix printers do. On a bubble-jet, the *printhead carriage* is the component containing the printhead that moves back and forth. A carriage stepper motor and an attached belt (the carriage belt) are responsible for the movement. To keep the printhead carriage horizontally stable, it rests on a metal stabilizer bar. Another stepper motor is responsible for advancing the paper.

Stepper motor problems on a bubble-jet will look similar to the ones on a dot-matrix printer. That is, if the main motor is damaged, lines of print will be unevenly spaced, and if the printhead motor goes bad, characters will be scrunched together. A lot of damage may cause the stepper motor to not move at all and possibly make high-pitched squealing noises. If any of these symptoms appear, it's time to replace one of these motors. As with dot-matrix printers, stepper motors can be expensive. It may make more economical sense to replace the printer.

Power Problems

Bubble-jet printers have internal power circuits that convert the electricity from the outlet into voltages that the printer can use, typically 12V and 5V. The specific device that does this is called the *transformer.* If the transformer fails, the printer will not power up. If this happens, it's time to get a new printer.

Laser Printer Problems

The process that laser printers use to print, called the electrophotographic (EP) print process, is the most complex of all commonly used printers. You should have memorized the six-step EP process for the A+ Essentials Exam, but perhaps you've forgotten a bit. Table 15.2 gives you the six steps and a short description of what happens in each step.

> These descriptions are summaries of the process. For detailed descriptions, please see Chapter 5.

TABLE 15.2   The EP Printing Process

Step	Action
Cleaning	A rubber blade scrapes any remaining toner off of the drum and a fluorescent lamp discharges any remaining charge on the photosensitive drum.
Charging	The charging corona gets a high voltage from the high voltage power supply (HVPS). It uses the voltage to apply a strong uniform negative charge (−600VDC) to the photosensitive drum.

TABLE 15.2   The EP Printing Process *(continued)*

Step	Action
Writing	The laser scans the drum. Wherever it touches the drum, the charge is reduced from –600VDC to around –100VDC. The pattern formed on the drum will be the image that is printed.
Developing	The developing roller acquires a –600VDC charge from the HVPS and picks up toner, which gets the same –600VDC charge. As the developing toner rolls by the photosensitive drum, the toner is attracted to the lesser-charged (–100VDC) areas on the photosensitive drum and sticks to it in those areas.
Transferring	The charging corona wire or roller acquires a strong positive charge (+600VDC) and transfers it to the paper. As the photosensitive drum with ink on it rolls by, the ink is attracted to the paper.
Fusing	The 350° F fuser roller melts the toner paper and the rubberized pressure roller presses the melted toner into the paper, making the image permanent.

Looking at the steps involved in laser printing, it's pretty easy to tell that laser printers are the most complex printers that we have discussed. There is good news, though—most laser printer problems are easily identifiable and have specific fixes. Let's discuss the most common laser and page printer problems and their solutions.

Power Problems

If you turn your laser printer on and it doesn't respond normally, there could be a problem with the power it's receiving. Of course, the first thing to do is to ensure that it's plugged in!

A laser printer's DC power supply provides three different DC voltages to printer components. This can all be checked at a power interface labeled J210, which is a 20-pin female interface. Pin 1 will be in the lower-left corner, and the pins along the bottom will all be odd numbers, increasing from left to right.

 Printer voltages can be tested with a multimeter. For more information on the use of multimeters, see Chapter 13, "Installing, Maintaining, and Troubleshooting Hardware."

Using the multimeter, you should find the following voltages:

- Pin 1 +5v
- Pin 5 –5v
- Pin 9 +24v

If none of the voltages are reading properly, then you probably need to replace the fuse in the DC power supply. If one or more (but not all) of the voltages aren't reading properly, then the first thing to do is remove all optional hardware in the printer (including memory) and test again. If the readings are still bad, it's likely you need to replace the DC power supply.

No Connectivity (IP Issues)

You can connect many laser printers directly to your network by using a network cable (such as Category 5e or 6), or by using a wireless network adapter with the printer. In cases like these, the printer acts as its own print server (typically print server software is built into the printer), and it can speed up printing because you don't have a separate print server translating and then sending the directions to the printer.

For printers such as these, no connectivity can be a sign of improperly configured IP settings such as the IP address. While each printer is somewhat different, you can manually configure most laser printers' IP settings a number of ways, such as:

- Through the printer's LCD control panel. For example, on several HP LaserJet models you press Menu, navigate to the Network Config menu, select TCP/IP Config, select Manual, and then enter the IP address. You would then also configure the subnet mask and default gateway.

 For a discussion on IP addressing, please see Chapter 10.

- By using Telnet to connect to the printer's management software from your computer.
- By using the management software that came with your printer.

You can also configure most IP printers to automatically obtain an IP address from a Dynamic Host Configuration Protocol (DHCP) server. Whenever the printer is powered up, it will contact the server to get its IP configuration information just like any other client on the network. While this may be convenient, it's usually not a good idea to do this on corporate networks. Client computers will have their printer mapped to a specific IP address; if that address is changed, you will have a lot of people complaining about no connectivity.

 To see what a printer's IP address is set at, print off a configuration page from the printer's control panel. Then post the IP information near the printer so that users can easily connect to it.

Nothing Prints

You tell your computer to print, but nothing comes out of the printer. That problem is probably the most challenging to solve because it could be caused by several different things. Are you the only one affected by the problem or are others having the same issue?

Is the printer plugged in, powered on, and online? As with any troubleshooting, check your connections first.

Other times when nothing prints, you get a clue as to what the problem is. The printer may give you an "Out of Memory" error or something similar. Another possibility is that the printer will say "Processing Data" (or something similar) on its LCD display and nothing will print. It's likely that the printer has run out of memory while trying to process the print job. If your printer is exhibiting these symptoms, it's best to power the printer off and then power it back on.

Be aware that large print jobs may cause the printer to say "Processing Data" for several minutes before the print job starts. There is nothing wrong with this, although it's possible that your printer could stand a memory upgrade. But if the printer exhibits this behavior for a long time, say 20 or 30 minutes, it may be best to cycle the power.

Paper Jams

Laser printers today run at copier speeds. Because of this, their most common problem is paper jams. Paper can get jammed in a printer for several reasons. First, feed jams happen when the paper-feed rollers get worn (similar to feed jams in bubble-jet printers). The solution to this problem is easy: replace the worn rollers.

Another cause of feed jams is related to the drive gear of the pickup roller. The drive gear (or clutch) may be broken or have teeth missing. Again, the solution is to replace it. To determine if the problem is a broken gear or worn rollers, print a test page, but leave the paper tray out. Look into the paper-feed opening with a flashlight and see if the paper pickup roller(s) are turning evenly and don't skip. If they turn evenly, the problem is probably worn rollers.

If your paper-feed jams are caused by worn pickup rollers, there is something you can do to get your printer working while you're waiting for the replacement pickup rollers. Scuff the feed roller(s) with a Scotch-Brite pot-scrubber pad (or something similar) to roughen up the feed rollers. This trick works only once. After that, the rollers aren't thick enough to touch the paper.

Worn exit rollers can also cause paper jams. These rollers guide the paper out of the printer into the paper-receiving tray. If they are worn or damaged, the paper may catch on its way out of the printer. These types of jams are characterized by a paper jam that occurs just as the paper is getting to the exit rollers. If the paper jams, open the rear door and see where the paper is. If the paper is very close to the exit roller, the exit rollers are probably the problem.

The solution is to replace all the exit rollers. You must replace all of them at the same time because even one worn exit roller can cause the paper to jam. Besides, they're inexpensive. Don't be cheap and skimp on these parts if you need to have them replaced.

Real World Scenario

Printer Triage

One of the authors relates the following story. He was in the local hospital ER a while ago having his hand looked at (he had cut it pretty badly on some glass). The receptionist asked him a few questions, filled out a report in the medical database on her computer, and printed it. When the paper starting coming out of the laser printer, she grabbed it and "ripped" it from the printer as you might do if the paper were in an old typewriter! The printer's exit rollers complained bitterly and made a noise that made me cringe. She did this for every sheet of paper she printed.

The following week, that printer came in for service because it was jamming repeatedly. The problem? Worn exit rollers.

He had a word with the person in charge of computer repair at that hospital and saved them from many future repairs. The lesson? Printers don't have to be treated with kid gloves, but using them properly can prolong life and reduce need for service repairs.

Paper jams can also be the fault of the paper. If your printer consistently tries to feed multiple pages into the printer, the paper isn't dry enough. If you live in an area with high humidity, this could be a problem. I've heard some solutions that are pretty far out but that work (like keeping the paper in a Tupperware-type airtight container or microwaving it to remove moisture). The best all-around solution, however, is humidity control and keeping the paper wrapped until it's needed. Keep the humidity around *50 percent or lower* (but above 25 percent if you can, in order to avoid problems with electrostatic discharge).

Finally, a grounded metal strip called the static-eliminator strip inside the printer drains the transfer corona charge away from the paper after it has been used to transfer toner from the EP cartridge. If that strip is missing, broken, or damaged, the charge will remain on the paper and may cause it to stick to the EP cartridge, causing a jam. If the paper jams after reaching the transfer corona assembly, this may be the cause.

Blank Pages

There's nothing more annoying than printing a 10-page contract and receiving 10 pages of blank paper from the printer. Blank pages are a somewhat common occurrence in laser printers. Somehow, the toner isn't being put on the paper. There are three major causes of blank pages:

- The toner cartridge
- The transfer corona assembly
- The high-voltage power supply (HVPS)

Toner Cartridge

The toner cartridge is the source of most quality problems because it contains most of the image-formation pieces for laser printers. Let's start with the obvious. A blank page will come out of the printer if there is no toner in the toner cartridge. I know it sounds simple, but some people think these things last forever. Many laser printers give some sort of warning if the toner cartridge is low, but it's easy to check. Just open the printer, remove the toner cartridge, and shake it. You will be able to hear if there's toner inside the cartridge. If it's empty, replace it with a known, good, manufacturer-recommended toner cartridge. If it is not yet empty, shaking it redistributes the toner and may provide better printing for some time.

When shaking a toner cartridge, loose toner can fall out of the cartridge and get on your clothing. Always hold the toner cartridge away from your body when shaking it.

Another issue that crops up rather often is the problem of using refilled or reconditioned toner cartridges. During their recycling process, these cartridges may be filled with the wrong kind of toner (for example, one with an incorrect charge). This can cause toner to be repelled from the EP drum instead of attracted to it. Thus, there's no toner on the page because there was no toner on the EP drum to begin with. The solution once again is to replace the toner cartridge with the type recommended by the manufacturer.

A third problem related to toner cartridges happens when someone installs a new toner cartridge and forgets to remove the sealing tape that is present to keep the toner in the cartridge during shipping. The solution to this problem is as easy as it is obvious: remove the toner cartridge from the printer, remove the sealing tape, and reinstall the cartridge.

Transfer Corona Assembly

The second cause of the blank-page problem is a damaged or missing transfer corona wire or damaged transfer corona roller. If a wire is lost or damaged, the developed image won't transfer from the EP drum to the paper. Thus, no image appears on the printout. To determine if this is causing your problem, do the first half of the self-test (described later in this chapter in the "Self Tests" section). If there is an image on the drum but not on the paper, you know that the transfer corona assembly isn't doing its job.

To check if the transfer corona assembly is causing the problem, open the cover and examine the wire (or roller, if your printer uses one). The corona wire is hard to see, so you may need a flashlight. You will know if it's broken or missing just by looking (it will either be in pieces or just not there). If it's not broken or missing, the problem may be related to the high voltage power supply.

The transfer corona wire (or roller) is a relatively inexpensive part and can be easily replaced with the removal of two screws and some patience.

High-Voltage Power Supply (HVPS)

The HVPS supplies high-voltage, low-current power to both the charging and transfer corona assemblies in laser printers. If it's broken, neither corona will work properly. If the self-test shows an image on the drum but none on the paper, and the transfer corona assembly is present and not damaged, then the HVPS is at fault.

All-Black Pages

Only slightly more annoying than 10 blank pages are 10 black pages. This happens when the charging unit (the charging corona wire or charging corona roller) in the toner cartridge malfunctions and fails to place a charge on the EP drum. Because the drum is grounded, it has no charge. Anything with a charge (like toner) will stick to it. As the drum rotates, all the toner is transferred to the page and a black page is formed.

This problem wastes quite a bit of toner but can be fixed easily. The solution (again) is to replace the toner cartridge with a known, good, manufacturer-recommended one. If that doesn't solve the problem, then the HVPS is at fault (it's not providing the high voltage that the charging corona needs to function).

Repetitive Small Marks or Defects

Repetitive marks occur frequently in heavily used (as well as older) laser printers. The problem may be caused by toner spilled inside the printer. It can also be caused by a crack or chip in the EP drum (this mainly happens with recycled cartridges), which can accumulate toner. In both cases, some of the toner gets stuck onto one of the rollers. Once this happens, every time the roller rotates and touches a piece of paper, it leaves toner smudges spaced a roller circumference apart.

The solution is relatively simple: clean or replace the offending roller. To help you figure out which roller is causing the problem, the service manuals contain a chart like the one in Figure 15.1. To use the chart, place the printed page next to it. Align the first occurrence of the smudge with the top arrow. The next smudge will line up with one of the other arrows. The arrow it lines up with tells you which roller is causing the problem.

Remember that the chart in Figure 15.1 is only an example. Your printer may have different-sized rollers (and thus need a different chart). Check your printer's service documentation for a chart like this. It is valuable in determining which roller is causing a smudge.

Vertical White Lines on the Page

Vertical white lines running down all or part of the page are a relatively common problem on older printers, especially ones that don't see much maintenance. They are caused by foreign matter (more than likely toner) caught on the transfer corona wire. The dirty spots keep the toner from being transmitted to the paper (at those locations, that is), with the result that streaks form as the paper progresses past the transfer corona wire.

FIGURE 15.1   Laser printer roller circumference chart

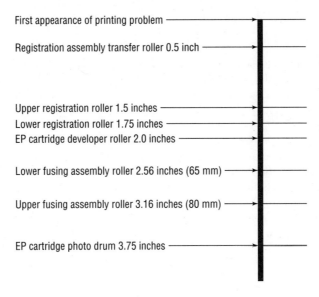

First appearance of printing problem

Registration assembly transfer roller 0.5 inch

Upper registration roller 1.5 inches
Lower registration roller 1.75 inches
EP cartridge developer roller 2.0 inches

Lower fusing assembly roller 2.56 inches (65 mm)

Upper fusing assembly roller 3.16 inches (80 mm)

EP cartridge photo drum 3.75 inches

The solution is to clean the corona wires. LaserJet Series II printers contain a small corona wire brush to help in this procedure. It's usually a small, green-handled brush located near the transfer corona wire. To use it, remove the toner cartridge and run the brush in the charging corona groove on top of the toner cartridge. Replace the cartridge and use the brush to remove any foreign deposits on the transfer corona. Be sure to put it back in its holder when you're finished.

Vertical Black Lines on the Page

A groove or scratch in the EP drum can cause the problem of vertical black lines running down all or part of the page. Because a scratch is lower than the surface, it doesn't receive as much (if any) of a charge as the other areas. The result is that toner sticks to it as though it were discharged. The groove may go around the circumference of the drum, so the line may go all the way down the page.

Another possible cause of vertical black lines is a dirty charging corona wire. A dirty charging corona wire prevents a sufficient charge from being placed on the EP drum. Because the charge on the EP drum is almost zero, toner sticks to the areas that correspond to the dirty areas on the charging corona.

The solution to the first problem is, as always, to replace the toner cartridge (or EP drum, if your printer uses a separate EP drum and toner). You can also solve the second problem with a new toner cartridge, but in this case that would be an extreme solution. It's easier to clean the charging corona with the brush supplied with the cartridge.

Image Smudging

If you can pick up a sheet from a laser printer, run your thumb across it, and have the image come off on your thumb, you have a fuser problem. The fuser isn't heating the toner and fusing it into the paper. This could be caused by a number of things—but all of them can be taken care of with a fuser replacement. For example, if the halogen light inside the heating roller has burned out, that would cause the problem. The solution is to replace the fuser. The fuser can be replaced with a rebuilt unit, if you prefer. Rebuilt fusers are almost as good as new ones, and some even come with guarantees. Plus, they cost less.

 The whole fuser may not need to be replaced. Fuser components can be ordered from parts suppliers and can be rebuilt by you. For example, if the fuser has a bad lamp, you can order a lamp and replace it in the fuser.

A similar problem occurs when small areas of smudging repeat themselves down the page. Dents or cold spots in the fuser heat roller cause this problem. The only solution is to replace either the fuser assembly or the heat roller.

Ghosting

Ghosting is what you have when you can see light images of previously printed pages on the current page. This is caused by one of two things: a broken cleaning blade or bad erasure lamps. A broken cleaning blade causes old toner to build up on the EP drum and consequently present itself in the next printed image. If the erasure lamps are bad, then the previous electrostatic discharges aren't completely wiped away. When the EP drum rotates toward the developing roller, some toner sticks to the slightly discharged areas.

Replacing the toner cartridge solves the first problem. Replacing the erasure lamps in the printer solves the second. Because the toner cartridge is the least expensive cure, you should try that first. Usually, replacing the toner cartridge will solve the problem. If it doesn't, you will have to replace the erasure lamps.

Printer Prints Pages of Garbage

This has happened to everyone at least once. You print a one-page letter, but instead of the letter you have 10 pages of what looks like garbage or many more pages with one character per page come out of the printer. This problem comes from one of two different sources: the printer driver software or the formatter board.

Printer Driver

The correct printer driver needs to be installed for the printer you have. For example, if you have an HP LaserJet III, then that is the driver you need to install. Once the driver has been installed, it must be configured for the correct page-description language: PCL or PostScript. Most HP LaserJet printers use PCL (but can be configured for PostScript). Determine what page-description language your printer has been configured for and set the printer driver to the same setting. If this is not done, you will get garbage out of the printer.

Most printers that have LCD displays will indicate that they are in Post-Script mode with a *PS* or *PostScript* somewhere in the display.

If the problem is the wrong driver setting, the garbage the printer prints will look like English. That is, the words will be readable, but they won't make any sense.

Formatter Board

The other cause of several pages of garbage being printed is a bad formatter board. This circuit board takes the information the printer receives from the computer and turns it into commands for the various components in the printer. Usually, problems with the formatter board produce wavy lines of print or random patterns of dots on the page.

It's relatively easy to replace the formatter board in a laser printer. Usually this board is installed under the printer and can be removed by loosening two screws and pulling out the board. Typically, replacing the formatter board also replaces the printer interface, which is another possible source of garbage printouts.

Example Printer Testing: HP LaserJet

Now that we've defined some of the possible sources of problems with laser printers, let's discuss a few of the testing procedures you use with them. We'll discuss HP LaserJet laser printers because they are the most popular type of laser printer, but the topics covered here apply to other types of laser printers as well.

We'll look at two ways to troubleshoot laser printers: self-tests and error codes (for laser printers with LCD displays).

Self-Tests

You can perform three tests to narrow down which assembly is causing the problem: the engine self-test, the engine half self-test, or the secret self-test. These tests, which the printer runs on its own when directed by the user, are internal diagnostics for the printers and are included with most laser printers.

Engine self-test   The engine self-test tests the print engine of the LaserJet, bypassing the formatter board. This test causes the printer to print a single page with vertical lines running its length. If an engine self-test can be performed, you know the laser print engine can print successfully. To perform an engine self-test, you must press the printer's self-test button, which is hidden behind a small cover on the side of the printer (see Figure 15.2). The location of the button varies from printer to printer, so you may have to refer to the printer manual. Using a pencil or probe, press the button, and the print engine will start printing the test page.

Half self-test   A print engine half self-test is performed the same way as the self-test, but you interrupt it halfway through the print cycle by opening the cover. This test is useful in determining which part of the print process is causing the printer to malfunction. If you stop the print process and part of a developed image is on the EP drum and part has been transferred to the paper, you know that the pickup rollers, registration rollers, laser scanner, charging roller, EP drum, and transfer roller are all working correctly. You can stop the half self-test at various points in the print process to determine the source of a malfunction.

FIGURE 15.2   Print engine self-test button location (the location may vary on different printers)

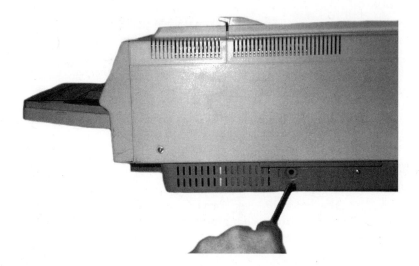

Secret self-test   To activate this test, you must first put the printer into service mode. To accomplish this, turn on the printer while simultaneously holding down the On Line, Continue, and Enter buttons (that's the first secret part, because nobody knows it unless somebody tells them). When the screen comes up blank, release the keys and press, in order, Continue and then Enter. The printer will perform an internal self-test and then display 00 READY. At this point you are ready to initiate the rest of the secret self-test. Take the printer offline, press the Test button on the front panel, and hold the button until you see the 04 Self Test message. Then release the Test button. This will cause the printer to print one self-test page. (If you want a continuous printout, instead of releasing the Test button at the 04 Self Test message, keep holding the Test button until the message 04 Self Test is displayed. The printer will print continuous self-test pages until you power off the printer or press On Line, or until the printer runs out of paper.)

Error Codes

In addition to the self-tests, you have another tool for troubleshooting HP laser printers. Error codes are a way for the LaserJet to tell the user (and a service technician) what's wrong. Table 15.3 details some of the most common codes displayed on an HP LaserJet.

TABLE 15.3   HP LaserJet Error Messages

Message	Description
00 Ready	The printer is in standby mode and ready to print.
02 Warming Up	The fuser is being warmed up before the 00 Ready state.
05 Self-Test	A full self-test has been initiated from the front panel.
11 Paper Out	The paper tray sensor is reporting that there is no paper in the paper tray. The printer will not print as long as this error exists.
13 Paper Jam	A piece of paper is caught in the paper path. To fix this problem, open the cover and clear the jam (including all pieces of the jam). Close the cover to resume printing. The printer will not print as long as this error exists.
14 No EP Cart	There is no EP cartridge (toner cartridge) installed in the printer. The printer will not print as long as this error exists.
15 Engine Test	An engine self-test is in progress.
16 Toner Low	The toner cartridge is almost out of toner. Replacement will be necessary soon.
50 Service	A fuser error has occurred. This problem is most commonly caused by fuser lamp failure. Power off the printer and replace the fuser to solve the problem. The printer will not print as long as this error exists.
51 Error	There is a laser-scanning assembly problem. Test and replace, if necessary. The printer will not print as long as this error exists.
52 Error	The scanner motor in the laser-scanning assembly is malfunctioning. Test and replace as per the service manual. The printer will not print as long as this error exists.
55 Error	There is a communication problem between the formatter and the DC controller. Test and replace as per the service manual. The printer will not print as long as this error exists.

Troubleshooting Tips for HP LaserJet Printers

Printer technicians usually use a set of troubleshooting steps to help them solve HP LaserJet printing problems. Let's detail each of them to bring our discussion of laser printer troubleshooting to a close:

1. **Is the exhaust fan operational?** This is the first component to receive power when the printer is turned on. If you can feel air coming out of the exhaust fan, this confirms

that AC voltage is present and power is turned on, that +5VDC and +24VDC are being generated by the AC power supply (ACPS), and that the DC controller is functional. If there is no power to the printer (no lights, fan not operating), the ACPS is at fault. Replacement involves removing all printer covers and removing four screws. You can purchase a new ACPS module, but it is usually cheaper to replace it with a rebuilt unit.

If you are into electronics, you can probably rebuild the ACPS yourself simply and cheaply. The main rectifier is usually the part that fails in these units; it can easily be replaced if you know what you're doing.

2. **Do the control panel LEDs work?** If so, the formatter board can communicate with the control panel. If the LEDs do not light, it could mean the formatter board is bad, the control panel is bad, or the wires connecting the two are broken or shorting out.

3. **Does the main motor rotate at power up?** Turn off the power. Remove the covers from the sides of the printer. Turn the printer back on and carefully watch and listen for main motor rotation. If you see and hear the main motor rotating, this indicates that a toner cartridge is installed, all photosensors are functional, all motors are functional, and the printer can move paper (assuming there are no obstructions).

4. **Does the fuser heat lamp light after the main motor finishes its rotation?** You will need to remove the covers to see this. The heat lamp should light after the main motor rotation and stay lit until the control panel says 00 Ready.

5. **Can the printer perform an engine test print?** A sheet of vertical lines indicates that the print engine works. This test print bypasses the formatter board and indicates whether the print problem resides in the engine. If the test print is successful, you can rule out the engine as a source of the problem. If the test print fails, you will have to further troubleshoot the printer to determine which engine component is causing the problem.

6. **Can the printer perform a control panel self-test?** This is the final test to ensure printer operation. If you can press the Test Page control panel button and receive a test printout, this means the entire printer is working properly. The only possibilities for problems are outside the printer (interfaces, cables, and software problems).

Most printers will print a test page, which contains both colors and patterns, based on your printer's capabilities. Although the exact style of pattern may vary, the idea is the same for all printers. You're checking to ensure that the printer can do what it's capable of. Many test patterns will measure gradients and resolution as well as letter qualities at various font sizes. Color printers will also print color sections, whereas black-and-white printers will often produce patterns in grayscale. If you are experiencing print-quality issues, running a test pattern is a good way to check to see what's wrong with the printer.

Performing Preventive Maintenance

Considering the amount of work they do, printers last a pretty long time. Some printers can handle over 100,000 pages per month, yet they're usually pretty reliable devices. These next sections on preventive maintenance focus on things you can do to help keep the printer running smoothly and to avoid the problems we've mentioned in this chapter. After all, going to get your print job from the printer and discovering that the printer is in the shop is a very frustrating experience!

Performing Scheduled Maintenance

When shopping for a printer, one of the characteristics you should look for is the printer's capacity, which is often quoted in monthly volume. This is particularly important if the printer will be serving in a high-load capacity. Every printer needs periodic maintenance, but printers that can handle a lot of traffic typically need it less frequently. Check the printer specifications to see how often scheduled maintenance is suggested. Never, ever fall behind on performing scheduled maintenance on a printer.

Many laser printers have LCD displays that provide useful information, such as error messages or notices that you need to replace a toner cartridge. The LCD display will also tell you when the printer needs scheduled maintenance. How does it know? Printers keep track of the number of pages they print, and when the page limit is reached, they display a message, usually something to the simple effect of *Perform user maintenance*. The printer will still print, but you should perform the maintenance.

Being the astute technician that you are, you clean the printer with the recommended cleaning kit or install the maintenance kit you purchased from the manufacturer. Now, how do you get the maintenance message to go away? Reset the page count using a menu option. For example, on many HP laser printers, you press the Menu button until you get to the Configuration menu. Once there, you press the Item key until the display shows *Service Message = ON*. Then press the plus key (+) to change the message to *Service Message = OFF*. Bring the printer back online, and you're ready to go.

Using Cleaning Solutions

With all of the ink or toner they use, printers get dirty. If printers get too dirty or if the printheads get dirty, we'll notice print problems. No one wants this to happen.

Most printers have a self-cleaning utility that is activated through a menu option or by pressing a combination of buttons on the printer itself. It's recommended that you run the cleaning sequence every time you replace the toner or ink cartridges. If you experience print-quality problems, such as lines in the output, run the cleaning routine.

Sometimes the self-cleaning routines aren't enough to clear up the problem. If you are having print-quality issues, you might want to consider purchasing a cleaning kit, which frequently comes with a cleaning solution.

Cleaning kits are often designed for one specific type of printer and should be used only on that type of printer. For example, don't apply an inkjet cleaning solution to a laser printer.

Each cleaning kit comes with its own instructions for use. Exercise 15.1 walks you through the steps of using an inkjet cleaning solution.

EXERCISE 15.1

Using an Inkjet Cleaning Solution

Use a cleaning solution if the self-cleaning routine is unsuccessful. Note that the steps for your printer might differ slightly; please consult your manual for specific instructions.

1. Power on the printer, and open the top cover to expose the area containing the print cartridges.

2. Initiate a self-cleaning cycle. When the printhead moves from its resting place, pull the AC power plug. This lets you freely move the printheads without damaging them.

3. Locate the sponge pads on which to apply the cleaning solution. They'll be in the area where the printheads normally park. Use a cotton swab or paper towel to gently soak up any excess ink in the pads.

4. Using the supplied syringe, apply the cleaning solution to the sponge pads, until they are saturated.

5. Plug the printer back into the wall outlet, and turn it on. The printheads will park themselves.

6. Turn the printer back off. Let the solution sit for at least three hours.

7. Power the printer back on, and run three printer cleaning cycles. Print a nozzle check pattern (or a test page) after each cleaning cycle to monitor the cleaning progress.

That should take care of it! If not, again, refer to your printer's manual for more instructions.

Ensuring a Suitable Environment

Printers won't complain if the weather outside is too hot or too cold, but they are susceptible to environmental issues. Here are some things to watch out for in your printer's environment:

Heat   Laser printers can generate a lot of heat. Because of this, ensure that your laser printer is in a well-ventilated area. Resist the temptation to put the laser printer in the little cubbyhole in your desk, as overheating will reduce the shelf life of your printer.

Light   The laser printer's toner cartridge contains a photosensitive drum. Exposing that drum to light will ruin the drum. While the drum is encased in plastic, it's best to avoid exposing the printer or toner cartridges to extreme light sources. Under no circumstance should you open the toner cartridge, unless you're ready to get rid of it as well as clean up a big mess.

Ozone   Laser printers that use corona wires (and many of them do) produce ozone as a by-product of the printing process. In offices, ozone can cause respiratory problems in small concentrations, and it can be seriously dangerous to people in large amounts. Ozone is also a very effective oxidizer and can cause damage to printer components.

Fortunately, laser printers don't produce large amounts of ozone, and most laser printers have an ozone filter. Ozone is another reason to ensure that your printer area has good ventilation. Also, replace the ozone filter periodically; check your printer's manual for recommendations on when to do this.

Ammonia   Ammonia isn't produced by the printer, but it is contained in many cleaning products. Ammonia can greatly reduce the printer's ability to neutralize ozone and can cause permanent damage to toner cartridges. It's best to avoid using ammonia-based cleaners near laser printers.

Using Recommended Supplies

To properly maintain a printer, you need to replace consumables such as toner or ink cartridges, assemblies, filters, and rollers on occasion. Trying to cut costs by buying cheaper supplies rarely pays off.

Whenever purchasing supplies for your printer, always get supplies from the manufacturer or from an authorized reseller. This way, you'll be sure that the parts are of high quality. Using unauthorized parts can damage your printer and possibly void your warranty.

 When it comes to printer paper, you have more flexibility. However, if your printer calls for a certain type of paper, it's best to use that paper. Not doing so can cause damage to the feed mechanism or can cause waste if the printer does not feed properly.

The area in which this is the biggest concern is ink and toner cartridges. Many businesses will recycle your toner or ink cartridges for you, refill them, and sell them back to you at a discount to new cartridges. Don't buy them. While some businesses that perform this "service" are more legitimate than others, using recycled parts is more dangerous to your hardware than using new parts. The reason for this is that refilled cartridges are more likely to break or leak than new parts, and this leakage could cause extensive damage to the inside of your printer. And again, using secondhand parts can void your warranty, so you're left with a broken printer that you have to pay for. Avoid problems like this by buying new parts. It's best to recycle your old parts—just don't buy recycled parts.

Installing Printer Upgrades

The printer market encompasses a dizzying array of products. You can find portable printers, photo printers, cheap black-and-white printers for under $30, high-end color laser printers for over $5,000, and everything in between. Most of the cheaper printers do not have upgrade options, but higher-end printers will have upgrade options, including the memory and firmware.

Installing Printer Memory

When purchasing a memory upgrade for your printer, you need to make sure of two things. First, buy only memory that is compatible with your printer model. Most printers today use a standard computer DIMM, but check your manual or the manufacturer's website to be sure. If you're not sure, purchasing the memory through the manufacturer's website (or an authorized reseller) is a good way to go. Second, be sure that your printer is capable of a memory upgrade. It's possible that the amount of memory in your printer is the maximum that it can handle.

Once you have obtained the memory, it's time to perform surgery. The specific steps required to install the memory will depend on your printer. Check with the manual or the manufacturer's website for instructions tailored to your model.

Exercise 15.2 walks you through the general steps for installing memory into a laser printer.

EXERCISE 15.2

Installing Memory into a Laser Printer

Providing additional memory to your printer can speed up the printing process, especially in heavily utilized environments. While the specific steps for your printer might be slightly different, follow these general steps for installing printer memory:

1. Turn off the printer.

2. Disconnect all cables from the printer (power and interface cables).

3. Find the area in which you need to install the memory.

4. On most HP LaserJet printers, this is in the back, on a piece of hardware called the formatter board. The formatter board is held in by tabs near the top and bottom of the board. Remove the formatter board from the printer. Other brands have different configurations. For example, on many Xerox laser printers you remove a panel on the top of the unit (underneath the paper output tray) to get to the memory.

5. If your printer requires you to remove a component (such as the formatter board) to upgrade the memory, place that component on a grounded surface, such as an anti-static work mat. Otherwise, proceed to step 6.

6. If you are replacing an existing memory module, remove the old module, being careful not to break off the latches at the end of the module that hold it in.

EXERCISE 15.2 *(continued)*

7. Insert the new memory module, making sure that any alignment notches on the memory module are lined up with the device before inserting the memory module.

8. Replace the removable component (if necessary).

9. Reconnect the power and interface cables.

10. Power on the printer.

11. Follow the printer manual's instructions on running a self-test to ensure that the memory is recognized.

Some printers require that you manually enable the added memory. Here are the steps to do that in Windows Vista/XP/2000:

1. Open the Printers and Faxes window.

2. Right-click on the printer and choose Properties.

3. On the Device Settings tab, click the Printer Memory button in the Installable Options section.

4. Select the amount of memory that is now installed.

5. Click OK.

Upgrading Printer Firmware

As with upgrading memory, methods to upgrade a printer's firmware depend on the model of printer you have. Most of the time, upgrading a printer's firmware is a matter of downloading and/or installing a free file from the manufacturer's website. Printer firmware upgrades are generally done from the print server.

Upgrading firmware is usually done for one of two reasons. One, if you are having compatibility issues, a firmware upgrade might solve them. Two, firmware upgrades can offer newer features not available on previous versions.

Summary

In this chapter, you learned about resolving printer problems. First, we reviewed the basic operation of the major printer types: dot-matrix, bubble-jet, and laser printers. Then we talked about the common problems you might see with each type.

Next, we looked at performing preventive maintenance to keep problems from happening in the first place. Items discussed include performing scheduled maintenance, using cleaning solutions, making sure the environment is suitable for the printer, using recommended supplies, and installing upgrades.

Exam Essentials

Know how to set IP addresses on a printer.   The IP address can often be obtained automatically from a DHCP server, but this is not recommended for corporate networks. Instead, you may be able to use the printer's control panel, Telnet, or printer management software to configure the IP address.

Know what could cause the printer to print garbage.   Most often this is caused by the print driver. Deleting and reinstalling it should fix the problem. Garbage printing can also be caused by a defective formatter board.

Understand what could cause print quality issues on a dot-matrix printer.   Print quality issues are generally related to either the ribbon or the printhead. The specific problem you are having will help determine the culprit.

Know what can cause unevenly spaced lines or characters on a dot-matrix or bubble-jet printer.   This is usually caused by a failing stepper motor. For line spacing problems, it's the main stepper motor. For character spacing, it will be the carriage stepper motor.

Know what causes printers to have paper jams.   In a dot-matrix printer, jams are usually caused by material getting into the rollers, such as extra perf from the tractor-feed paper. On bubble-jets and laser printers, this problem is often caused by worn pickup rollers.

Know how to use appropriate diagnostic tools including web-based utilities to troubleshoot problems.   Most printers come with management software that you can install on your computer, which may help you troubleshoot printer problems. Manufacturer's websites also have lots of information on troubleshooting common printer problems and error codes.

Understand how to upgrade printer memory and firmware.   Printer memory is upgraded by installing an additional or replacement memory chip. To do this, you must remove a panel from the printer. The specific steps depend on your printer model. Firmware is upgraded by downloading a file from the manufacturer's website and installing it.

Know what environmental hazards to watch out for around printers.   Heat, excessive light, ozone, and ammonia are all bad things for printers to be around.

Review Questions

1. You are working with a laser printer. Which of the following components offers the greatest risk to technicians?

    A. Fuser

    B. Refuser

    C. Corona wire

    D. Drum

2. You have just installed a new printer. After it is installed, it prints only garbled text. Which of the following is likely the problem?

    A. Wrong IP address

    B. Worn printhead

    C. Incorrect print drivers

    D. Unsupported printer

3. Which of the following could be the cause of paper jams on a laser printer?

    A. Defective toner cartridge

    B. Worn pickup rollers

    C. Dirty drum

    D. Broken fuser

4. What are the most common causes of crinkled paper coming out of a laser printer? (Choose all that apply.)

    A. The printer is out of toner.

    B. The printer's gears are stripped.

    C. The printer has an obstructed paper path.

    D. The printer overheated.

5. You are attempting to fix a laser printer. During printing, the toner does not seem to be placed on the paper. Which assembly is responsible for permanently pressing the toner into the paper?

    A. Transfer corona

    B. Fuser

    C. Printer controller circuitry

    D. Paper transport assembly

6. Which of the following is the most common paper feed mechanism associated with a dot-matrix printer?

   A. Gravity feed

   B. Impact feed

   C. Tractor feed

   D. Dual feed

7. What is the result of an absent or broken static-eliminator strip in a laser printer?

   A. Nothing. The printer will continue to function normally.

   B. The printer will flash a "−671 error" message.

   C. The printer will flash a "51 error" message.

   D. Paper jams may occur because the paper may curl around the photosensitive drum.

8. Which of the following most accurately describes how to obtain a firmware upgrade for your laser printer?

   A. Download the firmware upgrade for free from the manufacturer's website.

   B. Pay to download the firmware upgrade from the manufacturer's website.

   C. Have a certified laser printer technician come to your site and install a new firmware chip.

   D. Contact the manufacturer of the printer, and they will send you the firmware upgrade on a CD.

9. You have a bubble-jet printer. Recently, papers are being printed with excessive amounts of ink, and the ink is smearing. What is the most likely cause of the problem?

   A. A faulty ink cartridge

   B. A corrupted printer driver

   C. A faulty fuser

   D. Too much humidity in the air

10. When you print documents on your laser printer, you see residue from previous images on the output. What two things are the most likely causes of this problem? (Choose two.)

   A. A faulty transfer corona wire

   B. An overheating printer

   C. A bad erasure lamp

   D. A broken cleaning blade

11. Your laser printer has recently starting printing vertical black lines on documents it prints. What is the most likely cause of the problem?

   A. The printer driver is faulty.

   B. The fuser is not heating properly.

   C. There is toner on the transfer corona wire.

   D. There is a scratch on the EP drum.

12. You support an old dot-matrix printer at work. When the printer prints, there is always a blank horizontal line in the middle of each line of output. What is the most likely cause of the problem?

   A. The print ribbon is old and needs to be replaced.

   B. The print ribbon is not advancing properly.

   C. The printhead needs to be replaced.

   D. The wrong printer driver is installed.

13. You believe your laser printer has a power issue. Using a multimeter, what reading should you get from pin 9?

   A. +24V

   B. −24V

   C. +5V

   D. −5V

14. Which of the following components in a laser printer charges the drum after it has been cleaned?

   A. Transfer corona

   B. Multiplier

   C. Primary corona

   D. Conditioning wire

15. Which of the following components in a laser printer is responsible for transferring toner from the drum to the paper?

   A. Fuser

   B. Transport corona

   C. Transfer corona

   D. Development wire

16. You need to configure the IP address of your new laser printer. Which of the following are ways you may be able to do this? (Choose all that apply.)

   A. Use the printer's loopback connector.

   B. Use the printer's control panel.

   C. Telnet in to the printer's management software.

   D. Use the printer's management software that you installed on your workstation.

17. You have been using your laser printer for just over five months. Recently, you noticed that the printed characters on the left side of your documents are faint compared to the letters on the right. How can you quickly resolve this problem?

   A. Print your documents backward.

   B. Use different paper.

   C. Shake the toner cartridge.

   D. Blow the excess dust out of the cartridge.

18. The _____ in a laser printer provides voltages to the corona wires.
    A. Corona assembly
    B. HVPS
    C. ACPS
    D. DCPS

19. Which device in a bubble-jet printer contains the printhead?
    A. Ink cartridge
    B. Toner cartridge
    C. Daisy wheel
    D. Paper tray

20. What laser printer component applies −600V to the drum?
    A. Fuser
    B. Transfer roller
    C. Primary corona wire
    D. Voltage wire

Answers to Review Questions

1. **A.** When you are working with laser printers, the device most likely to cause damage is the fuser. The fuser works at high temperatures and can cause a burn.

2. **C.** If a printer is using out-of-date or incorrect printer drivers, the printer may produce pages of garbled text. The solution is to ensure that the most recent printer drivers are downloaded from the manufacturer's website.

3. **B.** The worn rollers may not be gripping and advancing the paper correctly. A defective toner cartridge could cause blotches and/or streaks on the page or not print at all. A dirty drum would cause ghost images on printed pages, and a broken fuser would result in pages that easily smudge because the toner has not been melted onto the page.

4. **B, C.** The printer's paper path is probably obstructed by something, or its gears have been stripped by paper feeding incorrectly. Obstructions are usually caused by paper from a previous jam. When cleaning out a paper jam, make sure you get all the paper.

5. **B.** The fuser assembly presses and melts the toner into the paper. The transfer corona transfers the toner from the drum to the paper. The printer controller circuitry converts signals from the PC into signals for the various printer assemblies. The paper transport assembly controls the movement of the paper through the printer.

6. **C.** Dot matrix printers often use tractor feed paper feed mechanisms. These are designed to pull or weave the paper through the printer. Some can use regular printer paper.

7. **D.** If the static-eliminator strip is absent (or broken) in a laser printer, the paper will maintain its positive charge. Should this occur, paper jams may result due to the paper curling around the photosensitive drum.

8. **A.** Firmware upgrades for laser printers are downloaded for free from the manufacturer's website. A technician does not need to install a new chip, as firmware is upgraded via software. It's unlikely that the manufacturer will send you the upgrade on a CD; they will refer you to their website to download it.

9. **A.** If an ink cartridge is faulty or develops a hole, it can release excessive amounts of ink, which will lead to smearing. A corrupted printer driver would result in printing garbage. Bubble-jet printers do not have a fuser. Excessive humidity may cause smearing, but not too much ink being disbursed.

10. **C, D.** Seeing images from previous print jobs is a phenomenon called ghosting. It's most likely due to a bad erasure lamp or a broken cleaning blade.

11. **D.** Vertical black lines are caused by a scratch or a groove in the EP drum. If the fuser was not heating properly, toner would not bond to the paper and you would have smearing. Toner on the transfer corona wire would most likely cause white streaks, not black streaks. Faulty print drivers will cause garbage to print or there will be no printing at all.

12. C. If there is a consistent blank space, it likely means that a pin is not firing properly, and the printhead needs to be replaced. If the print ribbon was old, you would have consistently faded printing. If the ribbon was not advancing properly, you would get light and dark printing. If the wrong driver is installed, you will get garbage.

13. A. Pin 9 on a laser printer should read +24V. Pin 1 is +5V, and pin 5 is −5V.

14. C. The primary corona wire applies a negative charge to the drum after it has gone through the cleaning phase.

15. C. The transfer corona in the laser printer puts a positive charge on the paper, forcing the toner on a negatively charged drum to transfer to the paper.

16. B, C, D. The IP address of your printer can be configured in several ways. You can use the printer's control panel, Telnet, or the printer management software from your workstation.

17. C. Most documents have more characters printed on the left side of the paper than on the right side. Therefore, the toner from the left side of the cartridge runs out sooner, and the print on the left side of the documents will be faint. Shaking the toner cartridge redistributes the toner evenly on both sides.

18. B. The high-voltage power supply (HVPS) provides power to the corona wires in most laser printers.

19. A. In a bubble-jet printer, the ink cartridge is the actual printhead. This is where the ink is expelled to form letters or graphics. Toner cartridges are used by laser printers to store toner. A daisy wheel is the device that impacts the letters on the paper in a daisy-wheel printer. Paper trays are the storage bins in laser printers and bubble-jet printers that allow the pickup rollers to feed the paper into the printer.

20. C. The primary corona wire applies −600V. The primary corona wire charges the drum with −600V before the image is written on it.

Chapter

16

Operating System Structures and Commands

THE FOLLOWING COMPTIA A+ PRACTICAL APPLICATION EXAM OBJECTIVES ARE COVERED IN THIS CHAPTER:

✓ **2.1 Select the appropriate commands and options to troubleshoot and resolve problems**

- MSCONFIG

- DIR

- CHKDSK (/f /r)

- EDIT

- COPY (/a /v /y)

- XCOPY

- FORMAT

- IPCONFIG (/all /release /renew)

- PING (-t –l)

- MD / CD / RD

- NET

- TRACERT

- NSLOOKUP

- [command name] /?

- SFC

✓ **2.2 Differentiate between Windows Operating System directory structures (Windows 2000, XP, and Vista)**

- User file locations

- System file locations

- Fonts

- Temporary files

- Program files

- Offline files and folders

In the simplest of contexts, the operating system is a translator between you and the hardware in your computer. Just leaving it at that level, though, means you miss out on many of the intricate details that make operating systems so complex and interesting.

Although complexity and interesting features can be fun, they can also be problematic. The more moving parts something has, the more likely it is that one of those parts will fail and need repair.

This chapter looks at the Windows Vista, Windows XP, and Windows 2000 operating systems and provides some comparisons between them. This chapter also serves as an introduction to Chapter 17, where troubleshooting and utilities are discussed in greater detail.

Using Operating Systems

One of the niceties of the Windows operating system is its flexibility. There are often several ways to accomplish one system management task. For example, you can manage your files and directories in Windows Explorer, but if you are a cagey DOS-era veteran, you can still do the same thing from the command line. In this section, you will look at various ways that you can perform system management tasks in Windows. This includes using the command line (even if you're not a cagey DOS-era veteran) as well as using graphical tools. We'll cover the following topics:

- Using command-line utilities

- Managing disks, files, and directories

- Using Windows utilities

Although we'll focus specifically on the Windows Vista, Windows XP, and Windows 2000 operating systems, many of these utilities (especially the command-line functions) are universal throughout the Windows family.

Using the Command Prompt

There are several command-line utilities that can be useful in managing a Windows-based computer. One important thing to point out, though, is that the DOS interface has gone the way of the dinosaur. Although you probably can't tell from looking at it (see Figure 16.1), the Windows command prompt is actually a 16- or 32-bit Windows program that is intentionally *designed* to have the look and feel of a DOS command line. Because it is, despite its appearance, a Windows program, the command prompt provides all the stability and configurability you expect from Windows.

FIGURE 16.1   The Windows command prompt

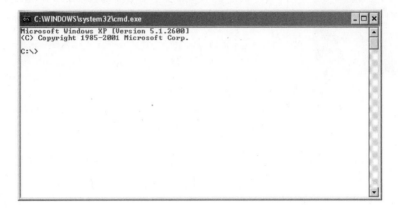

Running a Utility or Program from the Command Prompt

Windows includes several command-line utilities you can use to configure and maintain your system. Among these is the ipconfig utility, which allows you to check the TCP/IP settings of the machine. (TCP/IP is the protocol that allows networked computers to use the Internet, and as such is something you will probably see a lot of.)

You can access a command prompt by running either the 16-bit COMMAND.COM or the 32-bit CMD.EXE.

There are few actual text-based applications in newer versions of Windows. However, for a taste of the old days, check out the Edit program (see Figure 16.2), which is still provided free of charge with even the newest versions of Windows. Edit is often used to modify batch files and text configuration files. Exercise 16.1 gives you some exposure to the Edit program.

FIGURE 16.2   The Edit program in Windows Vista

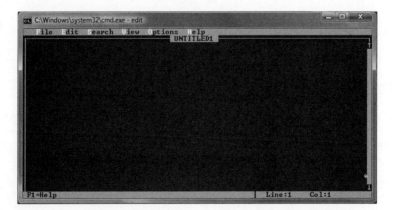

EXERCISE 16.1

Using the Edit Program

1. Open a command prompt. The quickest way to do this is to click Start ≻ Run, type **CMD** (or **COMMAND**) in the Open field, and click OK.

2. Type **EDIT** and press Enter.

3. The Edit utility opens. In the text area, type **hello**.

4. To save the file, press Alt+F. This brings up the File menu. Press A.

5. In the Save As window, type **HELLO.TXT** and click OK.

6. To exit from Edit, press Alt+F and press X (for Exit). To close the command prompt window, type **EXIT**.

Issuing Text Commands

Even though Windows is considered a graphical operating system, there are a plethora of *text-based commands* in all versions. Look for standard commands in the \Windows\System32 directory. Some commands are not listed in this directory (such as dir, CD, and CLS), but are internal to the operating system. These commands are executed by COMMAND.COM. Table 16.1 lists some of the available Windows text commands in Windows Vista, XP, and 2000.

TABLE 16.1   Windows Text Commands

Command	Purpose
ATTRIB	Allows the user to set or remove file attributes.
CD	Changes your current folder to another folder (same as CHDIR).
CHKDSK	Examines the machine's hard drives.
CLS	Clears the screen.
CONVERT	Converts a FAT file system to an NTFS file system.
COPY	Copies a file into another directory.
DEFRAG	Defragments (reorganizes) the files on your machine's hard drives, which can result in better performance.
DEL	Deletes a file from the folder.
DIR	Displays the contents of the current folder.

TABLE 16.1 Windows Text Commands *(continued)*

Command	Purpose
DISKCOPY	Duplicates floppy disks.
DISKPART	Manages partitions on the computer's hard drives.
ECHO	Repeats typed text back to the screen. Can be used to send text to a file or device by using redirection.
EDIT	Allows you to edit text files.
FIND	Searches for a text string in one file or several files.
FORMAT	Prepares a drive for use.
HELP	Displays the list of commands you can execute.
IPCONFIG	Displays the computer's IP configuration.
MD	Creates a new folder (same as MKDIR).
MEM	Provides information about how much memory is available to the system.
MOVE	Moves files from one folder to another.
PING	Establishes a connection to the specified host.
REN	Renames a file (can also use RENAME). When using it, you want to list the current name first and the new name last.
RD	Deletes a directory (same as RMDIR).
SET	Sets, displays, and removes DOS environment variables.
SETVER	Sets the version and reports the version numbers of DOS utilities.
TYPE	Displays the contents of text files.
VER	Checks the current version of the OS.
XCOPY	Duplicates files and subdirectories. An extension of the COPY command.

To issue a command from the command prompt, you need to know the structure the command uses, generally referred to as its *syntax*. You should also be familiar with the command's available switches. *Switches* enable you to further configure the command's actions. In Exercise 16.2 you will learn about a command's syntax and available switches and then run that command. The command in the exercise is ATTRIB, which is used to allow a user to set one of four attributes on a file: Read-Only, Archive, System, or Hidden.

To identify the options or switches for a DOS command, you can use the built-in Help system. Type the command followed by a forward slash and a question mark (/?). Doing so displays all the options for that command and how to use them properly, as shown in Figure 16.3.

FIGURE 16.3   Options available for ATTRIB.EXE

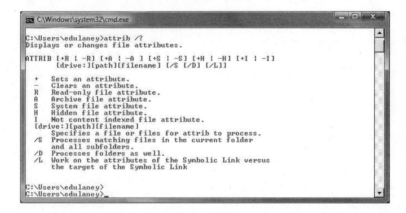

EXERCISE 16.2

Changing a File Attribute on Windows XP

1. Open a command prompt. To do this, click Start ➢ Run, type **CMD** in the Open field, and click OK.

2. In the command prompt window, type **CD /D C:** and press Enter.

3. Type **DIR** and press Enter. A list of all the files in the root of C: is shown.

4. Type **ATTRIB /?** and press Enter. Examine the available options.

5. Type **ATTRIB AUTOEXEC.BAT** and press Enter. The current attributes of the file are displayed.

6. Type **ATTRIB +R AUTOEXEC.BAT** and press Enter.

7. Repeat step 5 to view the changed attribute, and then repeat step 6 with the **–R** switch to return the file to its original attributes.

8. Type **EXIT** to close the command-prompt window.

You can use commands you've already typed at the command prompt again without having to type the same or a similar command over and over. To do so, press the up arrow on the keyboard. This steps backward one at a time through the commands you've entered and can make working with command-prompt commands much quicker. When you've found the command you're looking for, you can either press Enter to execute it again or use the left and right arrow keys to navigate through the command to make minor modifications, such as specifying a different switch.

In the next few sections, we'll look at how to use some of the more popular commands and their associated switches.

Unless otherwise specified, switches can be entered in lowercase or uppercase and have the same effect.

ATTRIB

As mentioned earlier in this chapter, the ATTRIB command is used to set file attributes, such as Read-Only or Hidden. Table 16.2 lists the switches available with ATTRIB.

TABLE 16.2   ATTRIB Switches

Switch	Purpose
+	Sets an attribute
−	Clears an attribute
R	Read-Only file attribute
A	Archive attribute
S	System attribute
H	Hidden attribute
/S	Makes the change on all matching files in the current folder (directory) and any subfolders
/D	Makes the change to the folder (directory) as well

An easy mnemonic device to remember the commonly used ATTRIB switches is the word *RASH*, for Read-Only, Archive, System, and Hidden.

For an exercise on using ATTRIB, please refer back to Exercise 16.2. But here's the proper syntax for using ATTRIB:

ATTRIB [switch] [drive:][path][filename][/S [/D]

If the file you are setting the attribute on is in the directory you're in, you don't need to specify a drive or path; you just need the filename, as in the following:

ATTRIB +R BOOT.INI

This will make the BOOT.INI file read-only, but it will work only if your current directory is the directory containing the file (usually the root of C:), or in a directory that is listed in the system's search path (the PATH environment variable).

CD/MD/RD

The CD, MD, and RD commands are used to change (or display), make, and remove directories, respectively. They're shorthand versions of the CHDIR, MKDIR, and RMDIR commands. Table 16.3 lists their usage and switches.

TABLE 16.3   CD/MD/RD Usage and Switches

Command	Purpose
CD [path]	Changes to the specified directory.
CD /D [drive:][path]	Changes to the specified directory on the drive.
CD ..	Changes to the directory that is up one level.
CD\	Changes to the root directory of the drive.
MD [drive:][path]	Makes a directory in the specified path. If you don't specify a path, the directory will be created in your current directory.
RD [drive:][path]	Removes (deletes) specified directory.
RD /S [drive:][path]	Removes all directories and files in the specified directory, including the specified directory itself.
RD /Q [drive:][path]	Quiet mode. It won't ask whether you're sure you want to delete the specified directory when you use /S.

Now that you've looked at the available switches, let's use them in Exercise 16.3.

EXERCISE 16.3

Command-Line Directory Management

1. Open a command prompt. To do this, click Start ➢ Run, type **CMD** in the Open field, and click OK.

2. Change to the root of your C: drive by typing **CD /D C:** and pressing Enter. (Note: If you are already in C:, all you have to type is **CD** and press Enter.)

3. Create a directory called C14 by typing **MD C14** and pressing Enter.

4. Change to the C14 directory by typing **CD C14** and pressing Enter.

5. Create several layers of subdirectories at once. Type **MD A1\B2\C3\D4** and press Enter.

Notice that these commands created each of the directories you specified. You now have a directory structure that looks like this: C:\C14\A1\B2\C3\D4.

6. Change back to your root directory by typing **CD**.

7. Attempt to delete the C14 directory by typing **RD C14** and pressing Enter.

Windows won't let you delete the directory, because the directory is not empty. This is a safety measure. Now let's really delete it.

8. Delete the C14 directory and all subdirectories by typing **RD /S C14** and pressing Enter. It will ask whether you're sure. If you are, type **y** and press Enter. To close the command prompt window, type **EXIT**.

Note that if you had used the /Q option in addition to /S, your system wouldn't have asked whether you were sure; it would have just deleted the directories.

CHKDSK

You can use the Windows Chkdsk utility to create and display status reports for the hard disk. Chkdsk can also correct file system problems (such as cross-linked files) and scan for and attempt to repair disk errors. You can manually start Chkdsk by right-clicking the problem disk and selecting Properties. This brings up the Properties dialog box for that disk, which shows the current status of the selected disk drive.

By clicking the Tools tab at the top of the dialog box, and then clicking the Check Now button in the Error-Checking section, you can start Chkdsk. Two CHKDSK command options to know for the exam are /F, which fixes errors on the disk that are found, and /R, which recovers readable information in bad sectors (and implies /F).

CMD

If you ever need to type in a command (for example, you want to view your environment variables the old-fashioned way or you want to test network connectivity), use the Start button. From Start, choose Run; then type **CMD** and press Enter. That will open a command prompt where you can enter your commands.

COPY

The COPY command does what it says: it makes a copy of a file in a second location. (To copy a file and remove it from its original location, use the MOVE command.) Here's the syntax for COPY:

COPY [filename] [destination]

It's pretty straightforward. There are several switches for COPY, but in practice they are rarely used. The three most used ones are /A, which indicates an ASCII text file; /V, which verifies that the files are written correctly after the copy; and /Y, which suppresses the prompt asking whether you're sure you want to overwrite files if they exist in the destination directory.

The COPY command cannot be used to copy directories. Use XCOPY for that function.

One useful tip is to use wildcards. For example, in DOS (or at the command prompt), the asterisk (*) is a wildcard that means *everything*. So you could type **COPY** *.**EXE** to copy all files that have an .EXE extension, or you could type **COPY** *.* to copy all files in your current directory.

DIR

The DIR command is short for *directory* and gives you a listing of everything in your current directory. Its usefulness is readily apparent, as it's always good to know where your files are located. There are several switches available for DIR. Table 16.4 captures some of the most commonly used ones.

TABLE 16.4　Common DIR Switches

Switch	Purpose
/A	Displays files with specified attributes.
/O	Lists the files in a sorted order. Options for sorting are N for name, E for extension, G for directories first, S by size, and D by date.
/P	Pauses after a full screen is displayed.
/Q	Displays the owner of the files and directories.
/S	Shows all files in that directory, and any subdirectories of that directory.
/W	Displays the files and directories in wide format.

If you're in the DOS world, the two most common commands you are ever going to use are CD and DIR. You need to get around and see what's there. Exercise 16.4 gives you some practice with the DIR command.

Seeing What's Out There with DIR

1. Open a command prompt. To do this, click Start ➤ Run, type **CMD** in the Open field, and click OK.

2. Obtain a directory listing by typing **DIR** and pressing Enter.

3. Switch to the root directory by typing **CD** and pressing Enter.

4. Look at the files in named order by typing **DIR /ON** and pressing Enter.

5. Check out what's on your hard drive! Type **DIR /S** and press Enter.

You'll probably have time to read the rest of this chapter before the listing stops. You can manually stop it by holding down your Ctrl key and pressing Break, or Ctrl+C.

6. Let's make it so you can actually read what's in which directories. Type **DIR /S /P** and press Enter.

This command displays one page and asks you to press any key to continue. After doing that gets tiring, you might want to press Ctrl+Break and then any key.

 If you have too much displayed on your screen, you can use the CLS command to clear your screen.

EDIT

This command, which was shown in Figure 16.2, opens the MS-DOS Editor utility, a text editor similar to Notepad. You can add a filename to open that file (if it exists) or create a new file (if it doesn't exist). Here's an example:

EDIT CONFIG.SYS

This command opens CONFIG.SYS if it's present in the current folder, or otherwise creates it and opens it.

The switches for EDIT are listed in Table 16.5.

TABLE 16.5   EDIT Switches

Switch	Purpose
/B	Forces monochrome mode
/H	Displays the maximum number of lines possible for your hardware
/R	Loads the file(s) in read-only mode
/S	Forces the use of short filenames
/<nnn>	Loads binary file(s), wrapping lines to <nnn> characters wide
[file]	Specifies an initial file to load

FORMAT

The FORMAT command is used to wipe data off disks and prepare them for new use. Before a hard disk can be formatted, it must have partitions created on it. (Partitioning was done in the DOS days with the FDISK command, but that command does not exist in Windows Vista, XP, or 2000, having been replaced with DISKPART.) The syntax for FORMAT is as follows:

FORMAT [volume] [switches]

The volume parameter describes the drive letter (for example, D:), mount point, or volume name. Table 16.6 lists some common FORMAT switches.

TABLE 16.6   FORMAT Switches

Switch	Purpose
/FS:[filesystem]	Specifies the type of file system to use (FAT, FAT32, or NTFS)
/V:[label]	Specifies the new volume label
/Q	Executes a quick format

There are other options as well to specify allocation sizes, the number of sectors per track, and the number of tracks per disk size. However, we don't recommend that you use these unless you have a very specific need. The defaults are just fine.

So, if you wanted to format your D: as NTFS, with a name of HDD2, you would type the following:

`FORMAT D: /FS:NTFS /V:HDD2`

> Before you format anything, be sure you have it backed up or are prepared to lose whatever is on that drive!

HELP

The HELP command does what it says: it gives you help. Actually, if you just type **HELP** and press Enter, your computer gives you a list of system commands you can type. To be useful, type the name of a command you want to know about after typing HELP. For example, type **HELP RD** and press Enter, and you will get information about the RD command.

As a reminder, you can also get *the same help information* by typing /? after the command, as you did in Exercise 16.2 earlier in this chapter.

> The /? switch is slightly faster and provides more information than the HELP command. The HELP command only provides information for system commands (it does not include network commands). For example, if we type **help ipconfig** at a command prompt, we get no useful information (except to try /?); however, typing **ipconfig /?** provides the help file for the ipconfig command.

IPCONFIG

In a world where it seems every computer is connected to a network, you'll do a lot of network connection troubleshooting. The IPCONFIG command is one of the first ones you should use when troubleshooting why someone can't get on the network. In fact, it's often the first one we do use. The IPCONFIG command checks your computer's IP configuration. Figure 16.4 shows a sample output.

Table 16.7 lists useful switches for IPCONFIG.

TABLE 16.7   IPCONFIG Switches

Switch	Purpose
/ALL	Shows full configuration information
/RELEASE	Releases the IP address, if you are getting addresses from a Dynamic Host Configuration Protocol (DHCP) server
/RENEW	Obtains a new IP address from a DHCP server
/FLUSHDNS	Flushes the domain name server (DNS) name resolver cache

FIGURE 16.4   IPCONFIG display

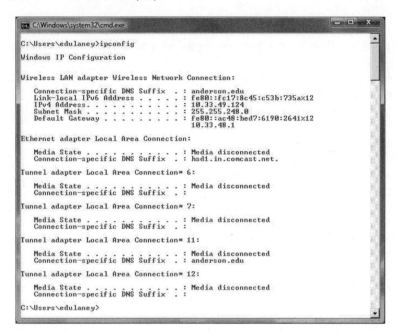

Running IPCONFIG can tell you a lot. For example, if the network cable is disconnected, it will tell you. Also, if your IP address is 0.0.0.0, you're not going to connect to any network resources.

If you get an IP address from a DHCP server but are having connectivity problems, a common troubleshooting method is to release the IP address with IPCONFIG /RELEASE and get a new one with IPCONFIG /RENEW.

More often than not, when you release and renew an IP address, you'll get the same one you had before. This in itself isn't a problem. The idea is that you basically "reset" your network card to try to get it working again.

MSCONFIG (Windows Vista and XP Only)

A new utility was introduced with Windows 98: MSCONFIG.EXE (aka the System Configuration Utility). (Even though it was introduced with Windows 98, Windows 2000 does not include it. Windows Vista and Windows XP do.) It allows users to manage their computer system's configuration. MSCONFIG.EXE lets users boot Windows in diagnostic mode, where they can select which drivers to load interactively. If you suspect a certain driver is causing problems during boot, you can use MSCONFIG.EXE to prevent that driver from loading. Additionally, each of the major configuration files (CONFIG.SYS, AUTOEXEC.BAT, WIN.INI, SYSTEM.INI) and the programs loaded at startup can be reconfigured and reordered by using a graphical interface.

NET

Depending on the version of Windows you are using, NET can be one of the most powerful commands at your disposal. While all Windows versions include a NET command, the capabilities of it differ based on whether it is server or workstation based and the version of the operating system.

While always command line based, this tool allows you to do almost anything you want with the operating system.

Table 16.8 shows common NET switches.

TABLE 16.8   NET Switches

Switch	Purpose
NET ACCOUNTS	Set account options (password age, length, etc.)
NET COMPUTER	Add and delete computer accounts
NET CONFIG	See network-related configuration
NET CONTINUE, NET PAUSE, NET START, NET STATISTICS, and NET STOP	Control services
NET FILE	Close open files
NET GROUP and NET LOCALGROUP	Create, delete, and change groups
NET HELP	See general help
NET HELPMSG	See specific message help
NET NAME	See the name of the current machine and user
NET PRINT	Interact with print queues and print jobs
NET SEND	Send a message to user(s)
NET SESSION	See session statistics
NET SHARE	Create a share
NET TIME	Set the time to that of another computer
NET USE	Connect to a share
NET USER	Add, delete, and see information about a user
NET VIEW	See available resources

These commands are invaluable troubleshooting aids when you cannot get the graphical interface to display properly. You can also use them when interacting with hidden ($) and administrative shares that do not appear within the graphical interface.

The NET command used with the SHARE parameter enables you to create shares from the command prompt, using this syntax:

NET SHARE <share_name>=<drive_letter>:<path>

To share the C:\EVAN directory as SALES, you would use the following command:

NET SHARE SALES=C:\EVAN

You can use other parameters with NET SHARE to set other options. Table 16.9 summarizes the most commonly used parameters.

TABLE 16.9   NET SHARE Parameters

Parameter	Purpose
/DELETE	Stop sharing a folder
/REMARK	Add a comment for browsers
/UNLIMITED	Set the user limit to Maximum Allowed
/USERS	Set a specific user limit

NSLOOKUP

NSLOOKUP is a command-line utility that enables you to verify entries on a DNS server. You can use NSLOOKUP in two modes: interactive and noninteractive. In interactive mode, you start a session with the DNS server, in which you can make several requests. In noninteractive mode, you specify a command that makes a single query of the DNS server. If you want to make another query, you must type another noninteractive command.

One of the key issues regarding the use of TCP/IP is the ability to resolve a hostname to an IP address—an action usually performed by a DNS server.

PING

Another useful connectivity troubleshooting command is PING, which stands for *packet Internet groper*. The PING command sends out four 32-byte packets to a destination and waits for a reply. Figure 16.5 shows a PING command.

If you cannot make a connection to the remote host, you will get back the following:

Request timed out.
Request timed out.

Request timed out.
Request timed out.

FIGURE 16.5   Pinging www.yahoo.com

Keep in mind that some Internet sites block pings as a precautionary security measure, so be sure to use a site that you know accepts them if you're using PING as a troubleshooting tool. Generally, you don't use any switches with PING. Just type **PING *IPaddress*** or **PING *hostname*** and see if it works. However, switches are available, among them **-t** (to persistently ping until we press Ctrl+C to stop the ping), **-l** (to change the buffer size), and **-n** (to change the number of packets sent).

Along with IPCONFIG and PING, another handy connectivity troubleshooting command is TRACERT, or trace route, which is discussed later. It traces the route between your computer and the destination computer and can help determine where the breakdown is if you're having connectivity problems.

SFC

The System File Checker (SFC) is a command line–based utility that checks and verifies the versions of system files on your computer. If system files are corrupted, the SFC will replace the corrupted files with correct versions.

The syntax for the SFC command is as follows:

SFC *[switch]*

Table 16.10 lists the switches available for SFC.

TABLE 16.10   SFC Switches

Switch	Purpose
/CACHESIZE=*X*	Sets the Windows File Protection cache size, in megabytes

TABLE 16.10   SFC Switches *(continued)*

Switch	Purpose
/PURGECACHE	Purges the Windows File Protection cache and scans all protected system files immediately
/REVERT	Reverts SFC to its default operation
/SCANFILE (Windows Vista only)	Scans a file that you specify and fixes problems if they are found
/SCANNOW	Immediately scans all protected system files
/SCANONCE	Scans all protected system files once
/SCANBOOT	Scans all protected system files every time the computer is rebooted
/VERIFYONLY (Windows Vista only)	Scans protected system files and does not make any repairs or changes
/VERIFYFILE (Windows Vista only)	Identifies the integrity of the file specified, and does make any repairs or changes
/OFFBOOTDIR (Windows Vista only)	Does a repair of an offline boot directory
/OFFFWINDIR (Windows Vista only)	Does a repair of an offline windows directory

To run the SFC, you must be logged in as an administrator or have administrative privileges. If the System File Checker discovers a corrupted system file, it will automatically overwrite the file by using a copy held in the *%systemroot%*\system32\dllcache directory. If you believe that the dllcache directory is corrupted, you can use SFC /SCANNOW, SFC /SCANONCE, SFC /SCANBOOT, or SFC /PURGECACHE to repair its contents.

If you attempt to run SFC from a standard command prompt in Windows Vista, you will be told that you must be an administrator running a console session in order to continue. Rather than opening a standard command prompt, choose Start ➤ All Programs ➤ Accessories, then right-click on Command Prompt and choose Run as administrator. The UAC will prompt you to continue, and then you can run SFC without a problem.

TRACERT

The TRACERT command enables you to verify the route to a remote host. Execute the command TRACERT *hostname*, where *hostname* is the computer name or IP address of the computer whose route you want to trace. TRACERT returns the various IP addresses the packet was routed through to reach the final destination. The results also include the number of hops needed to reach the destination. If you execute the TRACERT command without any options, you see a help file that describes all the TRACERT switches.

The Tracert utility determines the intermediary steps involved in communicating with another IP host. It provides a road map of all the routing an IP packet takes to get from host A to host B.

As with the PING command, TRACERT returns the amount of time required for each routing hop.

XCOPY

If you are comfortable with the COPY command, learning XCOPY shouldn't pose too many problems. It's basically an extension of COPY with one notable exception—it's designed to copy directories as well as files. The syntax is as follows:

XCOPY [source] [destination][switches]

There are 26 XCOPY switches; some of the more commonly used ones are listed in Table 16.11.

TABLE 16.11   XCOPY Switches

Switch	Purpose
/A	Copies only files that have the Archive attribute set and does not clear the attribute. (Useful for making a quick backup of files, while not disrupting a normal backup routine.)
/E	Copies directories and subdirectories, including empty directories.
/F	Displays full source and destination filenames when copying.
/G	Allows copying of encrypted files to a destination that does not support encryption.
/H	Copies hidden and system files as well.
/K	Copies attributes. (By default, XCOPY resets the Read-Only attribute.)
/O	Copies file ownership and ACL information (NTFS permissions).
/R	Overwrites read-only files.
/S	Copies directories and subdirectories but not empty directories.
/U	Copies only files that already exist in the destination.
/V	Verifies each new file.

Perhaps the most important switch is /O. If you use XCOPY to copy files from one location to another, the file system creates a new version of the file in the new location, without changing the old file. In NTFS, when a new file is created, it inherits permissions from its new parent directory. This could cause problems if you copy files. (Users who didn't have access to the file before might have access now.) If you want to retain the original permissions, use XCOPY /O.

Understanding and Navigating Directory Structures

With over several thousand files in a default installation, it is necessary to have a structure that allows you to find things. Windows provides this by allowing you to create directories, also known as folders, in which to organize files.

To navigate through directory structures, you can use the CD command from a command prompt (along with DIR to see what's there). Or you can use the graphical Windows Explorer. The ability to use drag-and-drop techniques and other graphical tools to manage directories and files makes Windows Explorer a utility that you need to be very familiar with. The program is shown in Figure 16.6 for Windows Vista and in Figure 16.7 for Windows XP.

FIGURE 16.6 The Windows Explorer program in Windows Vista

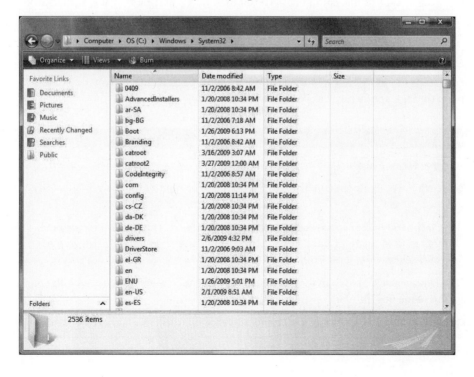

FIGURE 16.7   The Windows Explorer program in Windows XP

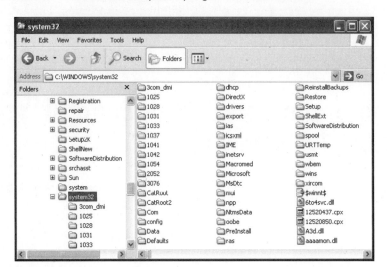

Some of the tasks you can accomplish by using Explorer include viewing files and directories, opening programs or data files, creating directories and files, copying or moving files or directories to other locations, deleting or renaming files or directories, searching for a particular file or type of file, changing file attributes, or formatting new disks (such as floppy disks). You can access many of these functions by right-clicking a file or folder and selecting the appropriate option, such as Copy or Delete, from the context menu.

To create a new file, folder, or other object, navigate to the location where you want to create the object and then right-click in the right pane (without selecting a file or directory). In the menu that appears, select New and then choose the object you want to create. Exercise 16.5 walks you through another way to complete this process.

EXERCISE 16.5

Creating a New Folder

1. Open Windows Explorer. One shortcut to do this is to hold down the Windows key and then press E.

2. In the left-hand Folders pane, click once on your C: drive. That should display the contents of C: in the right-hand pane. (If you don't have the Folders pane on the left side, click View ➢ Explorer Bar ➢ Folders.)

3. Click File ➢ New ➢ Folder. In the right-hand pane, a new folder appears with the highlighted name New Folder.

4. Type in the name of your new folder and press Enter.

While we're talking about files, let's revisit what you've learned about file attributes. File attributes determine what specific users can do to files or directories. For example, if a file or directory is flagged with the Read-Only attribute, users can read the file or directory but not make changes to it or delete it. Attributes include Read-Only, Hidden, System, and Archive, as well as Compression, Indexing, and Encryption. Not all attributes are available with all versions of Windows.

There are two ways to view and change file attributes: with the ATTRIB command-prompt command or through the properties of a file or directory. (You are limited to changes to the Read-only, Archive, System, and Hidden attributes from a command prompt.) Vista allows turning Indexing on (+i) and off (-i) at the command line.

In the Advanced Attributes dialog box, you can set archiving, indexing, compression, and encryption. See Chapter 6, "Operating System Features and Interfaces," for more information on these settings.

User File Locations

Within the Windows environment, users are required to authenticate in some way (even if it is just as Guest) before gaining access using a user account. The operating system then uses a user profile to deliver the computer settings (theme, screen saver, and so on) that are configured for them. It is important to realize that the user account authenticates the user, while the user profile holds their settings—these two entities are not the same, and one is needed before the other.

Part of the user profile involves allowing each user to have a set of files that are specific to them. Figure 16.8, for example, shows the folders automatically created for the user edulaney. The same set of folders are created automatically for each user.

While the address bar simply shows the location as edulaney, in reality the folder being viewed is beneath *%systemdrive%*\Users in Windows Vista and beneath *%systemdrive%*\ Documents and Settings in Windows XP and Windows 2000.

%systemdrive% is a variable for the system drive on your system and should be replaced with that value. By default, this is usually C:\.

When settings need to apply to everyone who uses the machine, they can be placed in All Users instead of being copied beneath each user's folder set.

FIGURE 16.8   User folders created for the user edulaney

System File Locations

In addition to knowing user file locations, you need to know where system files are located. They aren't always easy to find. Windows system files are hidden from view, by default, to protect them from accidental deletion. You can, of course, change this default setting as you did in Chapter 6 so that the files are visible. If you do so, it is safest to return to the default, hidden setting.

The essential system files for Windows are

- NTOSKRNL.EXE, the main kernel file
- HAL.DLL, the hardware abstraction layer
- WIN32K.SYS, the kernel-mode part of the Win32 subsystem
- NTDLL.DLL, which provides internal support functions and system services to the executive functions
- ADVAPI32.DLL, GDI32.DLL, KERNEL32.DLL, and USER32.DLL—the core Win32 subsystem

You'll find Windows boot files, except `NTOSKRNL.EXE`, in the root of the C: partition. Other system files are found in the system directories (e.g., `system` and `system32`). The difference between a clean install and an upgrade is the difference between files being in `C:\Windows\System32` (clean) or `C:\Winnt\System32` (upgrade).

> The term *system state data files* is used to represent key operating system files that should be included in a backup to be able to restore a system in the event of a serious failure. In each version of Windows, you can choose to back up only system state data or include/exclude it with your other backup.

Font Files

One of the subdirectories beneath *%systemdrive%*`\Windows` is the Fonts folder. This folder holds the fonts that are available for viewing and printing. A font is a collection of characters, each of which has a similar appearance (for example, the Arial font). A font family is a group of fonts that have similar characteristics. `Fontmapper` is the routine within Windows that maps an application's request for a font with particular characteristics to the available font that best matches those characteristics.

Managing Temporary Files

A *temporary file (temp file)* is just that—temporary. It is designed to store information for a short period of time and then be deleted. Almost every program of any size today uses temp files. There is one problem, however: often, the temp files become more permanent. Eventually, they begin taking up considerable disk space.

One thing you can do to improve system performance is to delete any temporary files that exist on your system. Temp files can be found in a variety of locations, including the following:

```
C:\Temp
C:\Tmp
C:\Windows\Temp
C:\Windows\Tmp
```

The way to know for sure where they're located is to determine what values the `TEMP` and `TMP` environment variables are set to. An *environment variable* is a setting that stays permanent throughout a Windows or DOS session. It is set by an entry in an `.INI` file, the Registry, or one of the MS-DOS configuration files (`CONFIG.SYS` or `AUTOEXEC.BAT`).

To find out where the temporary files are stored in your machine, start a command-line session (choose Start ➤ Run and type in either **CMD** or **COMMAND**). At the command prompt, type **SET**. This command returns all the environment variables for your system. Look for TEMP= or TMP= (or both). These variables point to directories on your hard disk; in these locations, you will find the temporary files.

In Windows Vista and XP, you can find where your temp files are going by opening the System control panel, clicking the Advanced tab, and then clicking the Environment Variables button. The temp location will be shown in the User Variables box at the top as well as the System Variables box at the bottom.

After you have found the temporary files, use Windows Explorer to delete them. You may need to reboot, and then try to delete the temp files. Otherwise, some of them may be in use, and you won't be able to delete them. Know that temporary files are written to a system on an almost nonstop basis. In addition to temporary files used for print queues, you also have cache from Internet sites and many other programs. You can manually pick files to delete, but one of the simplest solutions is to choose Properties for a drive and then click the General tab. A command button for the Disk Cleanup utility will appear, which you can use to delete most common temporary files, including the following:

- Downloaded program files
- Temporary Internet files
- Offline web pages
- Office setup files
- Recycle Bin contents
- Setup log files
- Temporary files
- WebClient/Publisher temporary files
- Temporary offline files
- Offline files
- Catalog files for the Content Indexer

Figure 16.9 shows an example of the command button in the Properties dialog box for Windows Vista.

The Recycle Bin offers an interesting anomaly: on all NTFS file systems except Windows Vista, the "deleted" files are stored in the \RECYCLER folder. With Windows Vista, the folder is called \$Recycle.Bin.

Program Files

The Program Files directory, beneath %systemroot%, holds the files needed for each of the installed applications on a machine. Windows Vista also added a Program Data directory, which is hidden by default. It contains the settings needed for applications and works similar to what the Local Settings folder did in previous operating systems.

FIGURE 16.9   The Disk Cleanup button in Windows Vista

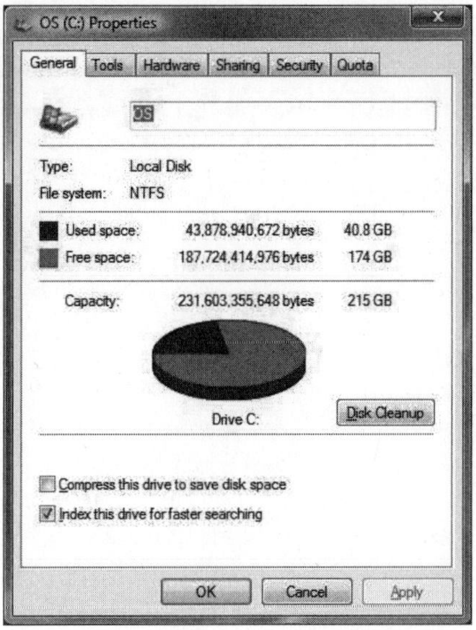

If a program doesn't have a shortcut on the Desktop or in the Programs submenu, you can start it by using the Run command and typing in the name of the program.

Offline Files

Beginning with Windows 2000, the Windows-based operating systems added the capability to work with resources that are "online" (accessed through the network or other connection) and "offline" (replicated copies of the resource stored locally). The key is to keep the files in synchronization so that multiple versions of the same file stored in different locations match each other.

Windows Vista

Windows Vista did not change what was already in place with the other operating systems; it just modified it. The two biggest modifications are the inclusion of the Sync Center and the restriction of offline file support to the Business, Enterprise, and Ultimate versions. If you do not have one of these versions, you will not have the ability to access the Offline Folders tab or do any configuration.

All versions of Vista have the Sync Center, shown in Figure 16.10. You access this by selecting Start ➢ Control Panel and clicking Network and Internet.

FIGURE 16.10   The Sync Center in Windows Vista is the primary interface for configuring synchronization.

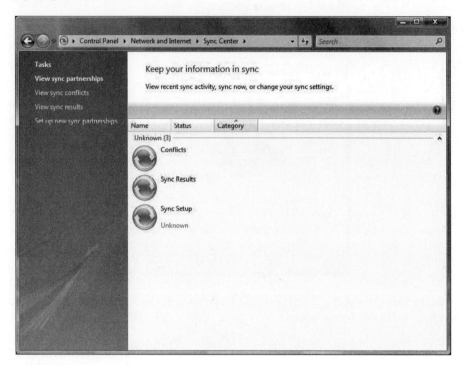

Sync partnerships can be set up with a large number of devices, ranging from a flash drive (as shown in Figure 16.11) to handheld devices. It is worth noting again that you cannot sync with network folders if you are using Windows Vista Starter, Home Basic, or Home Premium editions.

Windows XP

Offline files are accessible in Windows XP in an almost identical fashion to the way they were in Windows 2000. Before you can use this feature, though, you must turn it on. To do so, open My Computer and then choose Folder Options from the Tools menu. When the Properties dialog box appears, click the Offline Folders tab and select the Enable Offline Folders check box, shown in Figure 16.12. If Fast User Switching is turned on (the default), you have no options here. The dialog box tells you to turn off Fast User Switching.

Once you check this box, the other options become available. Select the amount of disk space you want to allow to be used for temporary storage of offline folders (10 percent is the default), whether you want to encrypt the files, and so on, and then click OK. Once you do, you can click on a network resource and then choose Make Available Offline from either the File or the right-click menu.

FIGURE 16.11 Establish a partnership with the device you want to sync with in Sync Center.

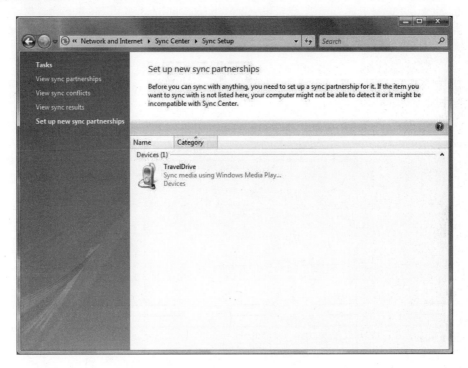

FIGURE 16.12 Offline Folders must be enabled before the feature can be used.

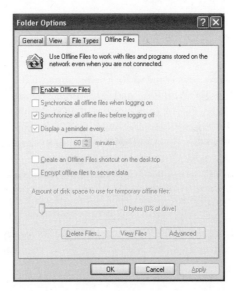

You can view the files that are stored offline by opening My Computer and then choosing Tools ➢ Folder Options. When the Properties dialog box appears, click the Offline Folders tab and click the View Files button. Synchronization is accomplished through the use of the Synchronization Manager (accessed by choosing Tools ➢ Synchronize within any Explorer window or typing **mobsync** in the Run box). Figure 16.13 shows the Synchronization Manager interface.

FIGURE 16.13 Click Setup in the Synchronization Manager to configure when synchronization should occur.

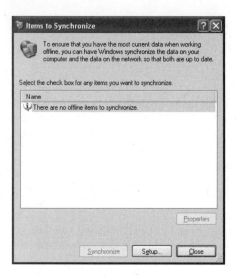

To disable offline file storage, repeat the process used to set it up, and deselect the Enable Offline Folders check box.

Windows 2000

In Windows 2000, the pop-up context menu for the resource that comes up when you right-click offers a selection called Make Available Offline. The item you choose to make available offline can be a folder, file, or even a mapped drive. When you select Make Available Offline, the Offline File Wizard starts and walks you through the steps of replicating this data locally. You can choose to do the synchronization between the copy and the original manually (you choose File ➢ Synchronize From Explorer) or automatically (you log on and log off). The last screen of the wizard offers two important check boxes:

- You can have reminders pop up regularly when you are working offline to tell you that you are not connected to the network. This is the default action.

- A shortcut can be added to the desktop for the offline material. By default, this option is not enabled; you reach the offline data the same way you would access the original data.

If the object you want to make available offline is a folder, a confirmation dialog box will ask whether you want to make available just the contents of the folder, or if you want to make available all subfolders of the original folder as well. As the files are replicated to a local location, the synchronization dialog box shows results and errors (if there are any).

 On a Windows 2000 Server, an administrator can choose to disable offline access of folders if he or she does not want to make them available for security reasons. Choosing to make a file non-cacheable prevents it from being available for offline storage. By default, however, shared resources can be made available for offline access.

When you're working offline, an icon of a computer appears in the system tray at the right end of the Taskbar. Clicking the icon will show the status of the network—whether or not you are connected to it. When you become connected to the network again, you can also click that icon in the system tray to synchronize changes you've made back to the network. Your laptop is not always able to dynamically realize when a connection to the network has been made (hot docking), so you might need to suspend (warm docking) or reboot (cold docking) before the connection is truly established.

If you reboot the system at a time when changes to the offline folders do not correspond with what is online, the icon in the system tray will have a flashing exclamation mark on it. Click the icon to bring up the dialog box.

During the synchronization process, a Setup button appears at the bottom right of the box. Choosing this option takes you to the Synchronization Manager. The Synchronization Manager offers three tabs and is worth examining for its options:

Logon/Logoff Allows you to configure whether synchronization should occur when you log on and/or log off, or whether you should always be prompted before you take any action. This can be configured independently for LAN connections, dial-up connections, VPNs, and so on. It can also be configured for web pages as well as folders.

On Idle Allows you to configure the items to be updated when the system is idle.

Scheduled Allows you to define synchronization jobs. Clicking the Add button brings up the Scheduled Synchronization Wizard, where you can schedule jobs to run every day, every week, or by some other interval.

Finally, by clicking the Settings button at the bottom of the Synchronization Manager window, you can access more options. Here, you can configure when the reminders will appear and the amount of local disk space that can be used to store offline folders. The Advanced button allows you to configure the computer so that it can never be used offline (or deviations thereof).

As a final item of note, the offline files and folders do consume hard drive space, so you need to allot for this appropriately. All offline content is stored beneath the *%systemroot%* directory in subdirectories of a hidden, system folder named CSC.

Summary

In this chapter, you learned about several aspects of using, optimizing, and troubleshooting Windows. We started with an overview of several command-line utilities you can use in Windows, including proper syntax and switches. Then we showed you how to manage disks, directories, and files, as well as several useful Windows-based utilities. We briefly reviewed the Windows system, as well as other key files you are expected to know for the exam.

Exam Essentials

Understand what each of the following commands does: CMD, HELP, DIR, ATTRIB, EDIT, COPY, XCOPY, FORMAT, MD, CD, and RD.   Many utilities that come with Windows help you navigate through or manage files and directories from a command prompt. The CMD command opens a command line, where you can type the rest of the commands. If you're not sure which utility to use, HELP will give you information. The MD, CD, and RD commands make, change, and delete (remove) directories, respectively, and the DIR command shows you what's inside the directory. To set file attributes, use ATTRIB; to modify file contents, use EDIT. The FORMAT command formats hard drives, and both COPY and XCOPY are used to copy files.

Know what the IPCONFIG **and** PING **commands are for.**   Both IPCONFIG and PING are network troubleshooting commands. You can use IPCONFIG to view your computer's IP configuration and PING to test connectivity between two network hosts.

Know where files are located.   The various versions of Windows that you need to know for this exam store files in multiple locations. You should be able to identify the location of those files mentioned in this chapter and be able to identify subtle differences—such as where the Recycle Bin files are on each operating system.

Review Questions

1. You just clicked Start ➤ Run. Which of the following can you type to open a command prompt? (Choose all that apply.)

   A. RUN

   B. CMD

   C. COMMAND

   D. OPEN

2. Which of the following commands is primarily used to modify text files?

   A. EDIT

   B. EDT

   C. NOTEPAD

   D. WORDPAD

3. Which of the following locations is common for system files?

   A. `C:\System32\Win`

   B. `C:\System\Windows32`

   C. `C:\Win\System32`

   D. `C:\Windows\System32`

4. You believe that your system files are corrupted in Windows XP. You run System File Checker. What do you do to make System File Checker automatically repair your system files if repair is needed?

   A. Run SFC /AUTOREPAIR.

   B. Run SFC /REPAIR.

   C. Run SFC /REVERT.

   D. Run SFC /SCANNOW.

5. You are at a command prompt, and your current directory is `C:\Windows\Temp\Files\Old`. Which command will get you to the root of D:?

   A. `CD..`

   B. `CD\`

   C. `CD /D D:\`

   D. `D:`

6. Which of the following commands can you use to convert a FAT partition to an NTFS partition?

    A. CONVERT

    B. CONVPART

    C. CONV

    D. You cannot convert a FAT partition to NTFS.

7. You are at a command prompt. Which command can you use to see whether you have a network connection to another computer?

    A. IPCONFIG

    B. CONNECT

    C. PING

    D. IP

8. You are at a command prompt. You want to make a file called WORK.DOC a read-only file. Which command do you use to accomplish this?

    A. ATTRIB +R WORK.DOC

    B. ATTRIB +RO WORK.DOC

    C. ATTRIB WORK.DOC

    D. READONLY WORK.DOC

9. If a program doesn't have a shortcut on the Desktop or in the Programs submenu, how can you start it?

    A. By using the Shut Down command

    B. By typing **cmd** in the Start ➤ Run box

    C. By using the Run command and typing the name of the program

    D. By typing **cmd** in the Start box followed by the program name

10. Which of the following options can be used with a command at a command prompt to see what options are available with it?

    A. /?

    B. /help

    C. /and

    D. /more

11. Which utility is shown in this graphic?

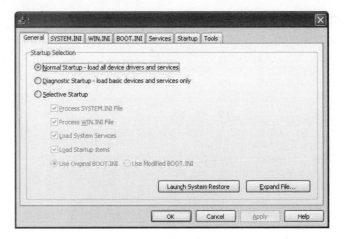

A. EDIT

B. MSCONFIG

C. FORMAT

D. IPCONFIG

12. Which of the following CHKDSK options automatically incorporates the operations that would be done with /f?

A. /e

B. /g

C. /r

D. /z

13. Which of the following options exist with COPY and not with XCOPY?

A. /a

B. /v

C. /y

D. None of the above

14. Which utility is shown in this graphic?

```
C:\WINDOWS\system32\cmd.exe                                    _ □ ×

Ethernet adapter Local Area Connection:

        Connection-specific DNS Suffix  . : anderson.edu
        IP Address. . . . . . . . . . . : 10.64.57.50
        Subnet Mask . . . . . . . . . . : 255.255.248.0
        Default Gateway . . . . . . . . : 10.64.56.1
Ethernet adapter Wireless Network Connection 2:

        Media State . . . . . . . . . . : Media disconnected
Ethernet adapter Local Area Connection 2:

        Media State . . . . . . . . . . : Media disconnected

C:\>_
```

A. Ipconfig

B. Ping

C. Tracert

D. Net

15. Which option is used with PING to continue contacting the host until stopped?

A. -t

B. -l

C. -a

D. -f

16. Which of the following commands enables you to verify entries on a DNS server?

A. sfc

B. net use

C. net lookup

D. nslookup

17. Which switch is used with SFC to purge the Windows File Protection cache and scan all protected system files immediately?

A. /purgecache

B. /revert

C. /new

D. /renew

18. Which of the following is the routine within Windows that maps an application's request for a font with particular characteristics to the available font that best matches those characteristics?

    A. PSF

    B. Font Root

    C. SliverLight

    D. Fontmapper

19. Which version of Windows Vista does *not* include offline folder capabilities?

    A. Business

    B. Enterprise

    C. Home Premium

    D. Ultimate

20. Which option is used with PING to specify a buffer size other than the default?

    A. -t

    B. -l

    C. -a

    D. -f

Answers to Review Questions

1. B, C. To open a command prompt, you can use CMD or COMMAND.

2. A. The EDIT command is a holdover from the DOS days and is used to edit text-based files. Notepad and Wordpad are both Windows-based utilities, and EDT does not exist.

3. D. The C:\Windows\System32 directory is where many of the Windows Vista, XP, and 2000 system files reside.

4. D. The SFC command will run System File Checker. The /SCANNOW option will scan files, and SFC automatically repairs files it detects as corrupted.

5. D. To change drives at the command prompt, simply type in the drive letter and a colon, and press Enter. However, if you were previously at a specific directory in D: (say, D:\TEMP), then typing D: and pressing Enter would take you to D:\TEMP.

6. A. The CONVERT command is used to convert FAT partitions to NTFS. You cannot convert NTFS to FAT, however.

7. C. The PING command tests to see whether you can reach a remote host on the network.

8. A. The ATTRIB command is used to set file attributes. To add attributes, use the plus sign (+). To remove attributes, use the minus sign (−). The Read-Only attribute is designated by R.

9. C. To run any program, select Start ➢ Run and type the name of the program in the Open field. If you don't know the exact name of the program, you can find the file by clicking the Browse button. Once you have typed the executable name, click OK to run the program.

10. A. To see the options available with a command, use /?. For example, to see what options are available with the PING command, you would enter: **ping /?**

11. B. The utility shown in the figure is Msconfig running on a Windows XP workstation.

12. C. The /r option not only locates bad sectors, but also recovers the data that is found in them (the purpose for the /f option).

13. D. XCOPY can be thought of as an expanded version of COPY. All of the options listed are available in both.

14. A. The utility shown in the figure is IPCONFIG running on a Windows XP workstation.

15. A. To continue pinging the host until stopped, use the −t option.

16. D. The NSLOOKUP utility enables you to verify DNS entries on a server.

17. A. The /purgecache option purges the Windows File Protection cache and scans all protected system files immediately.

18. D. Fontmapper is the routine within Windows that maps an application's request for a font with particular characteristics to the available font that best matches those characteristics.

19. C. The two biggest modifications to offline folders in Windows Vista are the inclusion of the Sync Center and the restriction of offline file support to the Business, Enterprise, and Ultimate versions.

20. B. To specify a buffer size to be used with PING, use the -1 option.

Chapter

17

Operating System Utilities and Troubleshooting Issues

THE FOLLOWING COMPTIA A+ PRACTICAL APPLICATION EXAM OBJECTIVES ARE COVERED IN THIS CHAPTER:

✓ **2.3 Given a scenario, select and use system utilities / tools and evaluate the results**

- Disk management tools

  - DEFRAG

  - NTBACKUP

  - Check Disk

- Disk Manager

  - Active, primary, extended and logical partitions

  - Mount points

  - Mounting a drive

  - FAT32 and NTFS

  - Drive Status

    - Foreign drive

    - Healthy

    - Formatting

    - Active unallocated

    - Failed

    - Dynamic

- Offline
- Online
- System monitor
- Administrative tools
  - Event Viewer
  - Computer Management
  - Services
  - Performance Monitor
- Devices Manager
  - Enable
  - Disable
  - Warnings
  - Indicators
- Task Manager
  - Process list
  - Resource usage
  - Process priority
  - Termination
- System Information
- System restore
- Remote Desktop Protocol (Remote Desktop / Remote Assistance)
- Task Scheduler
- Regional settings and language settings

✓ **2.4 Evaluate and resolve common issues**

- Operational Problems
  - Windows specific printing problems
    - Print spool stalled
    - Incorrect / incompatible driver form print
  - Auto-restart errors
  - Bluescreen error

- System lock-up
- Devices drivers failure (input / output devices)
- Application install, start or load failure
- Service fails to start
- Error Messages and Conditions
  - Boot
    - Invalid boot disk
    - Inaccessible boot drive
    - Missing NTLDR
  - Startup
    - Device / service failed to start
    - Device / program in registry not found
  - Event viewer (errors in the event log)
  - System Performance and Optimization
    - Aero settings
    - Indexing settings
    - UAC
    - Side bar settings
    - Startup file maintenance
    - Background processes

A quick look at the objectives for this chapter may stir a sense of déjà vu since almost every one of these topics was covered previously in the Essentials exam or in other areas of this exam. Rather than repeating all of that information, this chapter builds on what you should already know from the study of previous chapters and fills in the missing pieces.

Performing Preventive Maintenance on Operating Systems

For the most part, modern Windows operating systems are pretty resilient. There are a mind-boggling number of ways that systems could crash, but crashes don't happen often under normal circumstances. However, you do play an important role in the stability of the operating system on your computer. If you neglect to maintain it, you could be in for significant problems that would impact your productivity or someone else's.

In this section we'll take a look at some preventive steps you can take to help keep the operating system running smoothly. They include the following:

- Using hardware that's in the Windows Catalog
- Obtaining the right drivers for your hardware (those in the Windows Catalog)
- Installing Windows properly
- Shutting down properly
- Updating Windows regularly
- Creating restore points

Let's dive in.

Using Recommended Hardware

A surefire way to make sure Windows *doesn't* work right is to install hardware that Windows won't play nice with. Realistically, the vast majority of hardware on the market will work fine with Windows, considering how ubiquitous the operating system family is. However, don't just assume that the hardware will work. Always check it against the Windows Catalog to ensure that you won't have problems after it's installed.

You can find the Windows Catalog at Windows Marketplace
(http://www.windowsmarketplace.com/).

Obtaining Current Drivers

This topic goes right along with making sure that your hardware will work with Windows.
When you purchase a hardware device, odds are it's been in that box for a while. By the time
it gets made, packaged, stored, delivered to the store, stored again at the retailer, and then
purchased by you, it's entirely likely that the company that made the device has updated the
driver—even possibly a few times if there have been a lot of reported problems.

When you install a device, always go to the manufacturer's website to see if a
newer driver is available. The old driver might work fine, but the newest driver is the
one most likely to be bug-free and have all of the most current bells and whistles for
your device.

Installing Windows Properly

There are quite a few choices you make during the installation of the operating system.
Making the wrong choice isn't usually fatal, but it could have long-lasting consequences.
If you think your installation is bad, reinstall. Just be sure to choose the right options the
second time to avoid needing to install a third time. Whenever you reinstall because you
think there are problems, be sure to completely wipe out any possibility of an old problem
lingering by formatting the hard drive.

Most of the time, upgrades work well and you won't have any problems. However,
there is a bigger chance of having a problem with your operating system if you upgrade as
opposed to performing a clean installation on a freshly formatted hard drive. If there seem
to be problems as a result of an upgrade, back up everything that's critical, reformat the
hard drive, and perform a fresh installation.

Shutting Down Properly

Not shutting down properly can result in lost data from open applications or corrupted
operating system files. Neither option is good.

You would think that people are pretty aware of how to shut down, but sadly it's not
always true. When it comes to your own computers, always shut down properly by clicking
Start ➤ Turn Off Computer in Windows XP or Start ➤ Shut Down in Windows 2000. In
Windows Vista, click the Shut Down icon on the Start menu.

If you are a technician at a company, it's your responsibility to train all users on how to
properly shut down as well.

Updating Windows

Windows includes *Windows Update*, a feature designed to keep Windows current by automatically downloading updates such as patches and security fixes and installing these fixes automatically.

By default, Windows Update will run automatically when any administrator user is logged in. However, if you want to run it manually, you can do so by clicking Start ≻ All Programs ≻ Windows Update in Windows XP and Vista, or by clicking Start Windows Update (Windows XP), or by clicking Start ≻ Programs ≻ Windows Update in Windows 2000. You can also go to http://windowsupdate.microsoft.com to start the process.

Often, major updates to Windows are called *service packs*.

Here is an overview of how Windows Update works:

1. Windows Update starts (either by itself or manually).

2. Windows Update goes online to check to see what updates are available. It compares the update list to the updates that have already been applied to the computer or have been refused by the administrator.

3. If updates are available, they are downloaded automatically in the background.

4. Once the updates are downloaded, Windows Update notifies you that the download is complete and asks you if you want to install them.

If you choose not to install the updates right away, Windows will do so for you when you shut off the computer. Instead of shutting off right away, Windows Update will install the updates first and then perform a proper shutdown.

By default, Windows Update is enabled. But there might be times you want to configure it. Exercise 17.1 steps through the process of configuring Windows Update in Windows Vista, while Exercise 17.2 does the same for Windows XP.

EXERCISE 17.1

Configuring Windows Update in Windows Vista

To configure Windows Update in Windows Vista, follow these steps:

1. Click the Start button, and choose All Programs. Scroll down the list and choose Windows Update.

2. Click on the Change Settings entry on the left.

EXERCISE 17.1 *(continued)*

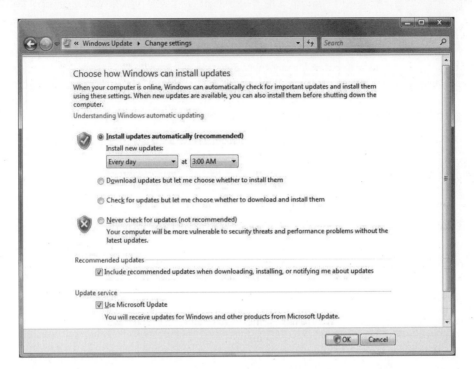

3. Choose the option that best suits your needs. You have four choices:

- Install Updates Automatically (Recommended)

- Download Updates But Let Me Choose Whether To Install Them

- Check For Updates But Let Me Choose Whether To Download And Install Them

- Never Check For Updates (Not Recommended)

4. Click OK. You will be prompted by UAC to verify that you want to make that change.

EXERCISE 17.2

Configuring Windows Update in Windows XP

To configure Windows Update in Windows XP, follow these steps:

1. Open the System Properties box (right-click My Computer and choose Properties, or double-click the System icon in Control Panel).

EXERCISE 17.2 *(continued)*

2. Select the Automatic Updates tab.

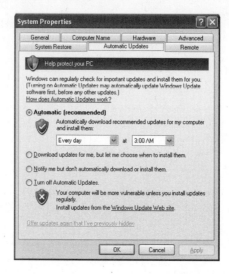

3. Choose the option that best suits your needs. You have four choices:

    -   Automatically Download Recommended Updates For My Computer And Install Them.

    -   Download Updates For Me, But Let Me Choose When To Install Them.

    -   Notify Me But Don't Automatically Download Or Install Them.

    -   Turn Off Automatic Updates.

It's not a problem if you want to choose to have control over which updates get installed and when. However, it is in your best interest to have Windows Update enabled to ensure that you have the most current patches available.

   Microsoft has an update server for large organizations that controls the update process for all hosts in the company.

Creating Restore Points

Almost everyone, no matter how hard they've tried to keep their computer running properly, will experience a computer crash at some point. Many of the ways to get your computer back up and running (such as reinstalling the operating system) take a lot of time.

In Windows XP and Vista, System Restore allows you to create restore points to make recovery of the operating system easier.

A *restore point* is a copy of your system configuration at a given point in time. Restore points are created one of three ways. One, Windows creates them automatically by default. Two, you can manually create them yourself (which is highly recommended before you make any significant changes to the system, such as installing new drivers) Three, during the installation of some programs, a restore point is created before the installation (that way, if the install fails, you can "roll back" the system to a preinstallation configuration).

Restore points are useful for when Windows fails to boot but the computer appears to be fine otherwise, or if Windows doesn't seem to be acting right and you think it was because of a recent configuration change.

To open System Restore, click Start ≻ All Programs ≻ Accessories ≻ System Tools ≻ System Restore. In Windows XP, it will open a screen like the one shown in Figure 17.1.

FIGURE 17.1   System Restore

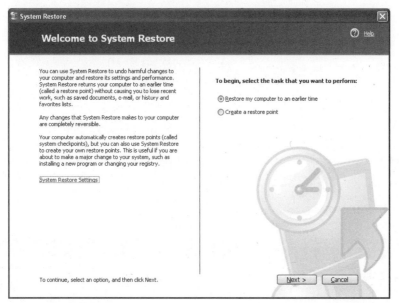

Notice in Figure 17.1 that you have two options. The first is to restore your computer to an earlier time (if you feel Windows is misbehaving), and the second is to manually create a restore point.

If you need to use a restore point and Windows won't boot, you can reboot into Safe Mode. After Safe Mode loads, you will have the option to work in Safe Mode or use System Restore. Choose System Restore and you'll be presented with restore points (if any) you can use.

One other option is a link on the left side, which takes you to System Restore settings. You can also get to the same place by opening the System control panel (right-clicking on My Computer and choosing Properties) and selecting the System Restore tab, as shown in Figure 17.2.

FIGURE 17.2 System Restore options

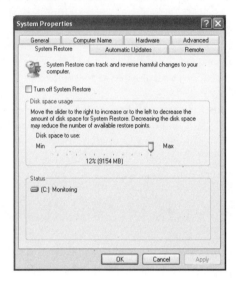

First, notice that you can turn off System Restore. Don't, unless you really don't care if your computer crashes and you can't recover it without a reinstall. The other option is to select how much disk space is available for System Restore. The less disk space you make available, the fewer restore points you will be able to have. If you have multiple hard drives, you can allocate a different amount of space per hard drive.

Exercise 17.3 demonstrates how to manually create a restore point in Windows Vista.

EXERCISE 17.3

Manually Creating a Restore Point in Windows Vista

1. Click Start ➢ Control Panel ➢ System And Maintenance ➢ System ➢ System Protection.

2. Type in the administrator password, or confirm that you want to continue.

3. Choose the System Protection tab and then click Create.

4. Fill in a description for the restore point and then click Create (you cannot click Create without putting text in for a description).

5. When the process is finished, click OK and then exit out of the Control Panel windows.

Using restore points is explained later in the Using System Restore Points in Windows Vista and XP section of this chapter.

Dealing with Boot Issues

To troubleshoot boot errors, it is useful to understand the boot sequence. The boot sequence for Windows Vista, XP, and 2000 is covered in detail in Chapters 6 and 7. Here we'll cover advanced boot options, recovery and repair options, and common issues and their solutions.

Advanced Startup Options

In most cases you will be able to just boot into your OS; however, if you have a problem that makes it difficult to get Windows up and running, the advanced options offer a number of useful tools. In Windows Vista, XP, and 2000, you access the options by pressing the F8 key when you're presented with the list of OSs installed on the computer. If you don't have the system configured to display the list of OSs (for example, if you have only one OS installed), press F8 when a message on the screen tells you that you can do so.

The options are not identical on the various versions of Windows. Let's review the advanced startup options available in Windows 2000, Windows XP, and Windows Vista:

Repair Your Computer (Windows Vista only)   Offers a list of system recovery tools that you can run to fix problems, run diagnostics, or restore the system.

Safe Mode   Starts Windows Vista, XP, and 2000 using only basic files and drivers (mouse, except serial mice; monitor; keyboard; mass storage; base video; default system services; and no network connections). Once in Safe Mode, you can restore files that are missing or fix a configuration error.

Safe Mode With Networking   Same as Safe Mode but tries to load networking components as well.

Safe Mode With Command Prompt   Similar to Safe Mode but doesn't load the Windows GUI. Presents the user with a Windows Vista, XP, or 2000 command-prompt interface.

Enable Boot Logging   Logs all boot information to a file called NTBTLOG.TXT. This file can be found in the \WINNT directory. You can then check the log for assistance in diagnosing system startup problems.

Enable VGA Mode (Windows 2000 and Windows XP only)   Starts Windows 2000/XP using the basic VGA driver but loads the rest of the system as normal. If you happen to install an incorrect video driver or a video driver corrupts, this allows you to get into the system to fix the problem.

Enable Low-Resolution Video (640 x 480) (Windows Vista only)   Starts Windows Vista using the basic VGA driver but loads the rest of the system as normal. If you happen to install an incorrect video driver or a video driver corrupts, this allows you to get into the system to fix the problem.

Last Known Good Configuration (Advanced)   Useful if you have changed a configuration setting in the Registry, which then causes the system to have serious problems and you're not able to log in. Use Last Known Good Configuration to restore the system to a prior, functional state, which will allow you to log in again. It will not save you from a corrupted file or a deleted file error.

Directory Services Restore Mode   Used only with domain controllers. If chosen, boots into a mode that doesn't load directory services. This enables you to restore directory services, such as Active Directory, to the machine. (You can't restore directory services if directory services are running.)

Debugging Mode   A sort of advanced boot logging. Requires that another machine be hooked up to the computer through a serial port. The debug information is then passed to that machine during the boot process. This option is rarely used and should not be bothered with in most cases. If it comes to this, reinstalling is far faster!

Disable Automatic Restart On System Failure (Windows Vista only)   Toggling this stops Windows from automatically rebooting when it encounters a crash.

Disable Driver Signature Enforcement (Windows Vista only)   Toggling this allows Windows to load drivers containing improper signatures.

Boot Normally (Start Windows Normally)   Continues the boot normally. It's equivalent to the Normal option in Windows 9x.

Start Windows Normally (Windows Vista only)   Continues the boot normally. It's equivalent to the Normal option in Windows 9x and the Boot Normally option in Windows XP.

Reboot (Windows XP only)   As the name implies, reboots the computer (warm boot).

Return To OS Choices Menu (Windows XP only)   Self-explanatory; returns you to the choice of installed OSs.

Using the Repair Options (Windows Vista)

The first choice that appears in Windows Vista's boot menu is Repair Your Computer. When you choose this, a stub of Windows starts with minimal video. It first asks that you choose a keyboard layout, and that you enter a username and password with administrator privileges.

At any time, you can click Cancel to return to the boot menu.

After you have provided this information, a menu of the available administrative tasks appears. This menu will differ slightly based on the vendor (for example, the bottom choice could be "Dell Factory Image Restore" if it is a Dell laptop you are working on), but will always include the following:

Startup Repair   Choose this option to fix problems with drivers or configuration settings that are preventing Windows from starting.

System Restore   Choose this option to select a restore point and revert to it.

Windows Complete PC Restore   Select this option if you want to restore the entire computer to a backup image.

Windows Memory Diagnostic Tool   Self-explanatory; used to look for memory errors.

Command Prompt   Opens a command prompt window where you can run command-line commands within a shell.

Using the Recovery Console (Windows 2000 and Windows XP)

The Recovery Console is another option you can use if Windows is not booting properly and Safe Mode and other startup options don't work. The Recovery Console is a command-line utility you can use to format drives, read data from and write data to local hard drives, stop and start services, and perform several other administrative tasks.

You can run the Recovery Console as an advanced boot option if you install it on the hard drive first. Otherwise, you need to run it from the Windows installation CD. Here's how to install the Recovery Console:

1. Put the Windows installation CD in the CD-ROM drive.

2. Click Start and then Run.

3. In the Run box, type *D:*\i386\winnt32.exe /cmdcons (where *D:*\ is your CD-ROM drive letter).

4. Follow the instructions on the screen.

To run the Recovery Console, you must be an administrator or have administrative privileges. Once you log in to the Recovery Console, you can perform activities such as changing directories or viewing files, as well as administrative duties such as trying to repair the boot sector of the hard drive. The Recovery Console is a command-line interface; much as in a Windows command prompt, you can type **help** at the Recovery Console prompt to get a list of available commands. Table 17.1 lists the available Recovery Console commands and a brief description of their functions.

TABLE 17.1   Recovery Console Commands

Command	Function
ATTRIB	Changes the attributes of a file or folder.
BATCH	Runs the commands specified in a text file so that you can perform many tasks in one step.
CD or CHDIR	Changes directories.
CLS	Clears the screen of previous output.

TABLE 17.1   Recovery Console Commands *(continued)*

Command	Function
COPY	Copies files from removable media to the system folders. (Note: With the console, you cannot use wildcards!)
DEL or DELETE	Deletes files.
DIR	Lists the contents of a directory.
DISABLE	Disables a specified service or driver.
DISKPART	Creates or deletes disk partitions.
ENABLE	Enables a specified service or driver.
EXTRACT	Extracts compressed installation files (ones with .CAB extensions) to the system partition. This command only works if you run the console from the installation CD.
FIXBOOT	Writes a new boot sector on the system partition.
FIXMBR	Writes a new Master Boot Record for the partition boot sector.
FORMAT	Formats the selected disk.
HELP	Displays a list of available Recovery Console commands.
LISTSVC	Lists all services and drivers running in Windows.
LOGON	Logs on to Windows.
MAP	Displays the drive letter mappings currently recognized. Can be helpful to use before DISKPART.
MD or MKDIR	Creates a directory.
MORE or TYPE	Displays the contents of a specified file.
RD or RMDIR	Deletes a directory.
REN or RENAME	Renames a file.
SYSTEMROOT	Makes the current directory the system root of the drive you are logged in to.

While the console can do many things, it's important to note the things that the console *can't* do. Most notably, it can't be used to back up files. Files can be copied from media to the local hard drive (specifically, to the system partition), but not the other way around. In addition, although you can change to partitions other than the system partition, you can't read files on them. So the console is handy but it's not a save-all; don't think of it as a duplicate of the command prompt.

The key functions of the Recovery Console are to be able to repair your system partition or make minor tweaks to Windows to get the operating system functional.

Creating Boot Disks or an Emergency Repair Disk

Most of the time, you won't bump into serious problems running any of the Windows versions we have been discussing. However, someday you might find yourself in a situation where the system won't boot up anymore or where you are experiencing some other type of critical error. It is extremely important to be prepared for these types of scenarios. One thing you can do when the system is running smoothly is to create startup disks or emergency repair disks (ERD) (depending on your OS). (You might also find these disks referred to as boot disks.) These disks typically enable you to at least boot the machine and access drives (and thus data) and also to troubleshoot the problem. In this section, we'll look at the different types of disks you can create in Windows.

Boot Disks and ERD in Windows 2000

To prepare for a Windows 2000 emergency, you need four OS boot disks, as well as an ERD. To create the set of four boot disks, you need the Windows 2000 Operating System CD. To create an ERD, you need to use the Emergency Repair Disk utility in the Windows Backup utility (see Figure 17.3). Let's look at this process in more detail.

To create the four Windows 2000 boot disks, insert the Windows 2000 Operating System CD into the CD-ROM drive. On the CD, browse to the Bootdisk directory and run MAKEBOOT.EXE. The program walks you through the process of creating the boot disks. Make sure you have four blank floppy disks ready. Once you have created the boot disks, you need to create an ERD.

Make sure you store these disks in a safe place. If you have an emergency, you can use the boot disks to start the Windows 2000 Setup program. At some point, you'll be asked if you want to install or repair Windows 2000. Choose Repair. Windows 2000 Setup will continue and at a later point ask you for the ERD.

Automated System Recovery in Windows XP

Windows XP introduced *Automated System Recovery (ASR*, which is integrated into the Backup utility. It first creates a backup of your system partition and then creates a recovery disk. Using these two components, you can recover from a system crash and restore the system to a functional state. Exercise 17.4 demonstrates how to use ASR to restore the system in Windows XP.

FIGURE 17.3   The Emergency Repair Disk utility in Windows 2000

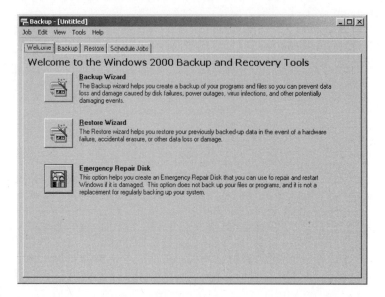

EXERCISE 17.4

Using ASR in Windows XP

1. Click Start ➤ All Programs ➤ Accessories ➤ System Tools ➤ Backup. If Backup starts in Wizard mode, deselect Always Start In Wizard Mode and click Cancel. Then start Backup again. You're taken directly to the Backup interface.

2. Click the Automated System Recovery Wizard button. In the Welcome dialog box, click Next.

3. You're prompted for the Backup Destination. By default, this is A:\BACKUP.BKF. You need to change this location, because a backup of your system partition won't fit onto a floppy disk. Use a drive other than the C: drive, because this drive will be formatted as part of the recovery process. Click Next, and then click Finish.

4. The backup procedure starts. When it's finished, you're prompted to insert a floppy disk. Do so and click OK.

5. When the disk-creation process has completed, click OK. Keep the ASR disk in a safe place.

To use ASR to recover from a system failure, run Setup from the Windows XP CD. During the text portion of the Setup program, you'll see a message to press F2; do so, and you'll be prompted to insert the ASR disk. The system then guides you through the rest of the process.

To obtain setup boot disks for Windows XP, you have to go to Microsoft's download website at www.microsoft.com/downloads and download them. These disks can be used to install XP if you can't boot from CD-ROM. You'll need six floppy disks during the download; they should be formatted and blank.

Using System Restore Points in Windows Vista and XP

Windows Vista follows the same model as Windows XP in terms of recovery, but does not include the ASR wizard. Restore points are automatically created by the operating system, but you can choose to manually create them at any time if you choose to do so.

To use restore points, open System Restore by clicking Start ➢ All Programs ➢ Accessories ➢ System Tools ➢ System Restore. It will open a screen like the one previously shown in Figure 17.1.

Notice in Figure 17.1 that you have two options. The first is to restore your computer to an earlier time (if you feel Windows is misbehaving), and the second is to manually create a restore point.

To restore your system to a previous state, choose the Restore My Computer To An Earlier Time radio button, as shown in Figure 17.1. Click Next. On the next screen, you will be shown a calendar and available restore points, as shown in Figure 17.4.

FIGURE 17.4   Available restore points

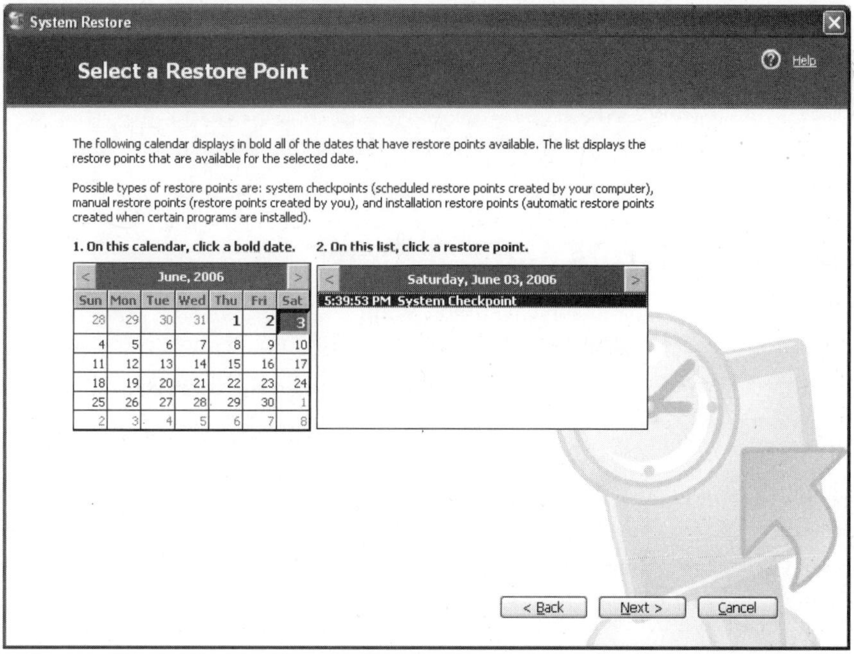

On days when restore points were created, the calendar date will be bolded. You can choose any restore point you want, and click Next. The next screen confirms the restore point you have chosen, as shown in Figure 17.5.

FIGURE 17.5 Confirming restore point selection

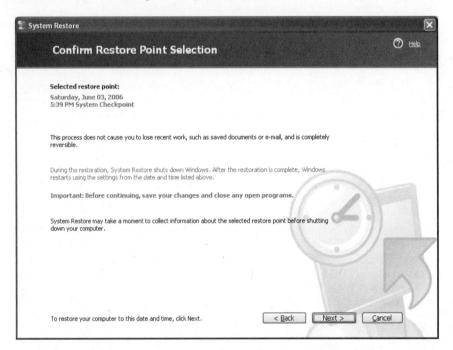

Note that at the bottom of the screen, you are told to click Next and the system will be restored to the point you selected. And, as the screen tells you, restoring the system restores only the configuration and does not cause you to lose recently saved files or documents.

Common Boot Errors and Solutions

Finally, we'll take a brief look at some common Windows Vista, XP, and 2000 boot errors. We'll explore what might be causing them and decide how to solve them.

Invalid Boot Disk You get the *Invalid Boot Disk* error when the BIOS finds a partition that could be bootable but is missing the essential system files. You can correct this problem by reinstalling the OS.

Operating System Not Found This error means exactly what it says. Essentially, the system could not find an OS, or even a valid boot partition, on any of the boot devices (floppy, hard disk, or CD-ROM). You will get this error on a brand-new computer that you have just built, until you install the OS.

Inaccessible Boot Device If, on boot-up you receive an error that states *STOP: 0x0000007B Inaccessible Boot Device*, you may have one of several problems. The most common is that Windows could not load the driver for the disk controller on the boot device. This could be because it is the wrong driver or because the disk controller is conflicting with some other hardware in the system.

This issue could also be caused by a unique installation procedure. If you are trying to run Windows Setup from a SCSI CD-ROM, Setup will not allow you to install a third-party SCSI driver when you boot from the SCSI CD-ROM. You will have to try using the boot disks to start the install.

Missing NTLDR As you've learned, NTLDR is relied on heavily during the boot process. If it is missing or corrupted, Windows NT will not be able to boot, and you'll get an error similar to *Can't find NTLDR*.

On the other hand, if you get an error such as *NTOSKRNL.EXE missing or corrupt* on boot-up, it may be an error in the BOOT.INI file. This is a common occurrence if you have improperly used the multi(0)disk(0)rdisk(0)partition(1)\WINDOWS="Microsoft Windows XP Professional" syntax for partition entries or had the partition table modified in a multi-disk setup. If these entries are correct, the NTOSKRNL.EXE file may be corrupted or missing. Boot from a startup disk and replace the file from the setup disks or CD-ROM.

The syntax shown—multi(0)disk(0)rdisk(0)partition(1)\ WINDOWS="Microsoft Windows XP Professional"—is known as the ARC (Advanced RISC Computing) naming convention, and it is used in the BOOT.INI file. More information on ARC can be found at http://support.microsoft.com/kb/102873.

Solving Windows File-Related Problems

The next set of specific Windows problems we'll discuss are those that can be traced to missing, corrupted, or misconfigured files. These issues can cause consternation to no end because they can be troublesome to fix. Thankfully, the error message usually gives an indication of which file is the problem.

In this section, you will learn about some of the various file-related problems that can occur in Windows, as well as their solutions. In addition to the boot issues you already learned about, these problems can be categorized into three main areas:

- System files not found
- Configuration file issues
- Swap file issues

Because the most easily fixed problems are related to missing system files, that's the next topic we'll cover.

System Files Not Found

Every operating system or operating environment has certain key system files that must be present in order for it to function. If these files are missing or corrupted, the OS will cease to function properly. Files can be deleted by accident rather easily, so it's important to know what these system files are, where they are located, and how to replace them.

When you boot, the presence of the system files is checked, and each file is loaded. If you remember, the computer's BIOS first checks the PC's hardware and then looks for a boot sector on one of the disks and loads the OS found in that boot sector. However, if the computer can't find a boot sector with an OS installed on any of the disks, it displays an error similar to the following:

```
No operating system found
```

This error means the computer's BIOS checked all the drives it knew about and couldn't find any disk with a bootable sector. This could be due to any number of reasons, including these:

- An operating system wasn't installed.
- The boot sector has been corrupted.
- The boot files have been corrupted.

Thankfully, there are a couple of solutions to these problems. First, if the file or files are missing, copy them from the original setup diskettes, CD-ROM, or DVD, or copy them from a backup (assuming you have one). The same holds true if you have a corrupted file, except you must delete the corrupted file first and then replace it with a new copy.

These same concepts hold true for another system file–related problem:

```
Missing NTLDR
```

This error means that the NTLDR file is either missing or corrupted. Just replace it with a fresh copy. The error should go away, and the computer will function properly. In the worst-case scenario, an OS reinstall should take care of these issues.

Configuration File Issues

In older versions of Windows, this was a common problem because users could easily edit their configuration files. Now, the Windows Registry stores nearly every configuration parameter available, but on many computers it's not secured: people can edit it. And worse yet, its structure is incredibly complex and there's no "undo" feature or Save button. Once you delete something, it's immediately gone. In addition, most software installation programs modify the Registry when a new program is installed. An error you might see is this:

```
A device referenced in the Registry can not be found
```

If you just added hardware, then it might make sense that the particular piece of hardware or its driver might be causing the problem (in which case Device Manager is the first tool you should turn to). If not, then you would have to use the Registry Editor (REGEDIT .EXE or REGEDT32.EXE) to search for corrupted or invalid entries.

Swap File Issues

Windows uses swap files (also called page files or paging files) to increase the amount of usable memory by using hard disk space as memory. However, sometimes problems can occur when a computer doesn't have enough disk space to make a proper swap file. Because Windows relies on swap files for proper operation, if a swap file isn't big enough, Windows will slow down and start running out of usable memory. All sorts of memory-related problems can stem from swap files that are incorrect or too small. Symptoms of swap-file problems include an extremely slow system and a disk that is constantly being accessed. This condition, known as hard disk *thrashing,* occurs because Windows doesn't have enough memory to contain all the programs that are running, and there isn't enough disk space for a swap file to contain them all. This situation causes Windows to swap between memory and the hard disk.

The solution to this problem is to first free up some disk space and/or add more memory. With hard drives big and cheap these days, the easiest thing to do is install a bigger hard disk. If that solution isn't practical, you must delete enough unused files that the swap file can be made large enough to be functional.

Troubleshooting Other Common Problems

Some common Windows problems don't fall into any category other than "common Windows problems." They include the following problems that you learned about in Chapter 9:

General protection faults (GPFs)   A *general protection fault (GPF)* happens in Windows when a program accesses memory that another program is using or when a program accesses a memory address that doesn't exist. Generally, GPFs are the result of sloppy programming. To fix this type of problem, a simple reboot will usually clear memory. If GPFs keep occurring, check to see which software is causing the error. Then find out if the manufacturer of the software has a patch to prevent it from GPFing.

Illegal operation   Occasionally a program will quit, apparently for no reason, and present you with a window that says *This program has performed an illegal operation and will be shut down. If the problem persists, contact the program vendor.* An *illegal operation error* usually means that a program was forced to quit because it did something Windows didn't like. Windows then displays this error window. The name of the program that quit appears at the top of the window, along with three buttons: OK, Cancel, and Details. The OK and Cancel buttons do the same thing: dismiss the window. The Details button opens the window a little farther and shows the details of the error, including which module experienced the problem, the memory location being accessed at the time, and the registers and flags of the processor at the time of the error.

System lockups   It is obvious when a system lockup occurs. The system simply stops responding to commands and stops processing completely. System lockups can occur when a computer is asked to process too many instructions at once with too little memory. Usually, the cure for a system lockup is to reboot. If the lockups are persistent, it may be a hardware-related problem instead of a software problem.

Dr. Watson/Problem Reports and Solutions   Windows 2000 and Windows XP include a special utility known as Dr. Watson. This utility intercepts all error conditions and, instead of presenting the user with a cryptic Windows error, displays a slew of information that can be used to troubleshoot the problem. This utility does not exist in Windows Vista, but was replaced with the same functionality in Problem Reports and Solutions, which can be found in Control Panel beneath System and Maintenance (see Figure 17.6).

FIGURE 17.6   The Problem Reports and Solutions in Windows Vista replaced Dr. Watson.

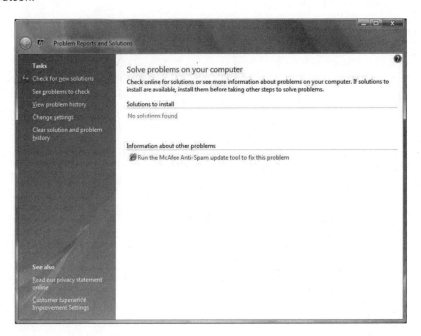

Failure to start GUI   Occasionally, the Windows GUI won't appear. The system will hang just before the GUI appears. Or, sometimes, the *Blue Screen of Death (BSOD)*—not a technical term, by the way—appears. The BSOD is another way of describing the blue-screen error condition that occurs when Windows Vista, XP, or 2000 fails to boot properly or quits unexpectedly. Because it is at this stage that the device drivers for the various pieces of hardware are installed, if your Windows GUI fails to start properly, more than likely the problem is related to a misconfigured driver or misconfigured hardware. Try booting Windows in Safe Mode to bypass this problem.

If you happen to get a BSOD with a *Fatal Exception error 0D* message, chances are that the culprit is a problem relating to the video card.

Option (sound card, modem, SCSI card, or input device) will not function   When you are using Windows, you are constantly interacting with pieces of hardware. Each piece of hardware has a Windows driver that must be loaded in order for Windows to be able to use it. In addition, the hardware must be installed and functioning properly. If the device driver is not installed properly or the hardware is misconfigured, the device won't function properly.

Cannot log on to the network (option—NIC not functioning)   If your computer is hooked up to a network (and more and more computers today are), you need to know when your computer is not functioning on the network properly and what to do about it. In most cases, the problem can be attributed to either a malfunctioning network interface card (NIC) or improperly installed network software. The biggest indicator in Windows that some component of the network software is nonfunctional is that you can't log on to the network or access any network service. To fix this problem, you must first fix the underlying hardware problem (if one exists) and then properly install or configure the network software.

Application will not install   We've all experienced this frustration. You are trying to install the coolest new program, and, for whatever reason, it just won't install properly. It may give you one of the previously mentioned errors or a cryptic installation error. If a software program won't install and it gives you any of the errors we've mentioned (such as a GPF or illegal operation), use the solutions for those errors first. If the error that occurs during install is unique to the application being installed, check the application manufacturer's website for an explanation or update. These errors generally occur when you're trying to install over an application that already exists or when you're trying to replace a file that already exists but that another application has in use. When you're installing an application, it is extremely important that you first quit all running programs so the installer can replace any files it needs to.

Application will not start   Once you have an application successfully installed, you may run into a problem getting it to start properly. This problem can come from any number of sources, including an improper installation, a software conflict, or system instability. If your application was installed incorrectly, the files required to properly run the program may not be present, and the program can't function without them. If a shared file that's used by other programs is installed, it could be a different version than should be installed that causes conflicts with other already-installed programs. Finally, if one program GPFs, it can cause memory problems that can destabilize the system and cause other programs to crash. The solution to these problems is to uninstall and reinstall the offending application, first making sure that all programs are closed.

Invalid working directory   Some Windows programs are extremely processor intensive. These programs require an area on the hard disk to store their temporary files while they work. This area is commonly known as a *working directory*, and its location is usually specified during that program's installation. However, if that directory changes after installation and the program still thinks its working directory is in the same location, the program will issue an error that says something such as *Invalid working directory*. The solution is to reinstall the program with the correct parameters for the working directory. For this reason, many programs use the Windows TEMP directory as their working directory. You will see this error only if the programmer chose to use a user-settable working directory.

Remember that there are two universal solutions to Windows problems: rebooting and obtaining an update from the software manufacturer.

Reboot First, Ask Questions Later

You just got an error message in Windows. First write down any error messages that appear. Save your work (if possible). Then reboot your computer.

Problems often occur when temporary files or information in RAM become corrupted. Rebooting clears the memory registers and most often removes problematic temporary files, thus eliminating the issue.

So if you have a software problem, reboot first. The vast majority of the time, the problem will disappear. If the problem continues, follow up with your troubleshooting process.

Understanding Windows Reporting

Error reporting is a feature in Windows XP and Windows Vista. If a program error occurs (such as Internet Explorer crashing), a window will pop up asking if you want to report the problem to Microsoft. (This works for non-Microsoft programs as well.) It only works if you have an active Internet connection. If you choose to report the problem, then technical information about the problem is gathered and sent to Microsoft. If others have reported the same problem, then additional technical information will be available to you, to help you solve the problem.

According to Microsoft, the information gathered is only used by programming groups to help solve technical problems. Your individual information is not stored or tracked in any way.

To configure (or disable) Windows reporting with Windows XP, open your System properties by right-clicking on My Computer and selecting Properties. On the Advanced tab, click the Error Reporting button at the bottom of the screen to open a window similar to the one shown in Figure 17.7.

FIGURE 17.7   Windows Error Reporting options in Windows XP

To reach this same location with Windows Vista, access Problem Reports and Solutions in Control Panel beneath System and Maintenance (refer back to Figure 17.6) and choose Change Settings, then Advanced Settings. Click Change Setting to open a window similar to the one shown in Figure 17.8.

FIGURE 17.8   Windows Error Reporting options in Windows Vista

Your two major choices are to disable or enable error reporting. If you choose to disable it, you can still be notified when errors occur. Windows Vista offers the third choice of allowing each user to choose their settings. After choosing to enable error reporting, you can choose to report Windows operating system and/or program errors. By clicking the Programs button, you can configure which programs you want to report errors on. By default, all program errors from all programs are reported, but you can configure the reporting of errors on an app-by-app basis.

Using Windows-Based Troubleshooting Utilities

In addition to learning about the many common problems and troubleshooting techniques for Windows, you should know about the different tools that Microsoft provides with Windows to troubleshoot Windows. These resources are the best to use if you have no other troubleshooting tools available. They can also be used as a starting point for troubleshooting a computer. The built-in Windows tools and commands that you should be aware of include the following:

- Disk management tools including Format, Chkdsk, Defrag, and NTBackup

- System management tools such as Device Manager, Computer Management, Task Manager, Msconfig, Regedit, Regedt32, CMD, Event Viewer, and System Restore

- File management tools, including Windows Explorer and ATTRIB

Many of these tools and commands have already been discussed in detail in this book, and were fully covered on the Essentials exam. The content that follows focuses only on those tools not already fully discussed.

Disk Management Tools

Preserving information on hard drives has never been more important than today. Not only do you want to keep your own information, you have the legal obligation to manage company records if you work for a publicly held firm. Here are some disk management utilities to be familiar with.

Chkdsk

You can use the Windows Chkdsk utility to create and display status reports for the hard disk. Chkdsk can also correct file system problems (such as cross-linked files) and scan for and attempt to repair disk errors. You can manually start Chkdsk by right-clicking the problem disk and selecting Properties. This will bring up the Properties dialog box for that disk, which shows the current status of the selected disk drive.

By clicking the Tools tab at the top of the dialog box, and then clicking the Check Now button in the Error-Checking section, you can start Chkdsk. Exercise 17.5 walks you through starting Chkdsk in the GUI, while Exercise 17.6 does the same from the command line.

EXERCISE 17.5

Running Chkdsk within Windows

1. Open Windows Explorer by holding down the Windows key and pressing E.

2. Right-click C: and choose Properties.

3. Click the Tools tab and then click the Check Now button.

4. Choose your options: you can automatically fix file system errors and/or scan for and attempt recovery of bad sectors.

5. After you have selected your options, click Start.

EXERCISE 17.6

Running Chkdsk at the Command Line

1. Open a command prompt by clicking the Start button and typing CMD in the Start Search box of Vista, or in the Run box on XP.

2. Type chkdsk /f and press Enter. The system will now scan for, and fix, file system errors.

Defrag

Defragmenting a disk involves analyzing the disk and then consolidating fragmented files and folders so they occupy a contiguous space, thus increasing performance during file retrieval. The command-line Defrag utility allows you to run a defrag from a command prompt.

In Windows XP and 2000, you can also run a defrag in Windows through the Disk Defragmenter in the Computer Management utility or by right-clicking on a hard drive in Windows Explorer, choosing Properties, selecting the Tools tab, and clicking the Defragment Now button.

In Windows Vista, choose Disk Defragmenter from the System Tools menu of the Accessories folder (beneath All Programs). This will bring up a screen similar to that shown in Figure 17.9. The difference between this and the previous operating systems is that the defragmenter, by default, automatically runs in Windows Vista at regularly scheduled intervals. When you choose to modify the schedule, you can pick whether you want it to run daily, weekly, or monthly.

FIGURE 17.9   The interface to Disk Defragmenter in Windows Vista

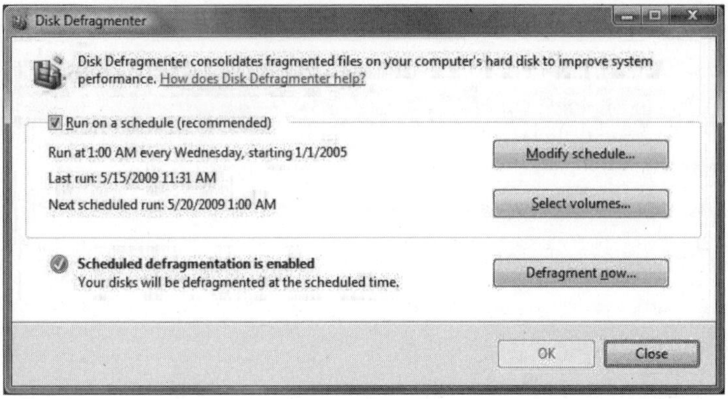

Disk Defragmenter

Disk Defragmenter consolidates fragmented files on your computer's hard disk to improve system performance. How does Disk Defragmenter help?

☑ Run on a schedule (recommended)

Run at 1:00 AM every Wednesday, starting 1/1/2005

Last run: 5/15/2009 11:31 AM

Next scheduled run: 5/20/2009 1:00 AM

Modify schedule...

Select volumes...

Scheduled defragmentation is enabled

Your disks will be defragmented at the scheduled time.

Defragment now...

OK   Close

NTBackup

If you want to back up your system, you can run the backup utility by clicking Start ➢ All Programs ➢ Accessories ➢ System Tools ➢ Backup.

Backups protect against hard drive failure, accidental deletion, and malicious deletion or attacks. They are also used to make an archive of important files for later use.

Windows 2000, XP, and Vista all allow you to schedule backups. In the earlier versions, this executable is NTBACKUP.EXE, while the primary tool in Windows Vista is SDCLT.EXE. All versions of Vista except for Starter include Automatic Backup (which, to be honest, is slimmed down in the Home Basic version), which has the ability to back up your files and data. The Business, Ultimate, and Enterprise versions of Vista include a more advanced backup utility known as Complete PC Backup that includes the operating system and applications in the backup.

Despite the importance of good backups, many users—even companies—fail to back up enough. To figure out how often to back up, consider two key questions:

- How often does your data change? (Every day? Every week? Every month?)

- How important are your files? (Can you afford to lose them? How much time or money will it cost to replace lost files? Can they be replaced?)

Your answers to these questions will give you an idea of how often you should run scheduled backups. Generally, the more important the data is and the more often it changes, the more often you want to back up.

 In addition to scheduled backups, any time you make major changes to your system, including installing new software, you should perform a backup of important files before making those changes.

Exercise 17.7 demonstrates how to schedule backups in Windows XP, while Exercise 17.8 walks through similar procedures for Windows Vista.

EXERCISE 17.7

Scheduling Backups in Windows XP

1. Open Windows Backup by choosing Start ➢ All Programs ➢ Accessories ➢ System Tools ➢ Backup. This will open the Backup Or Restore Wizard. The wizard will walk you through all of the options you can use, or you can click the Advanced Mode link to set up things manually.

2. On the Backup Or Restore Wizard screen, click Next to continue.

3. Choose Back Up Files And Settings, and click Next.

4. Choose what you want to back up (as shown in this graphic), and click Next:

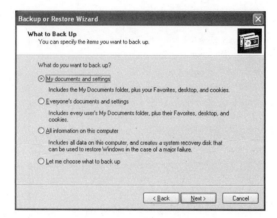

5. Confirm the backup type and the destination, and give the backup file a name (it will have a .BKF extension). For the destination, you can click the Browse button to select the right location, which might be a floppy drive, a CD or DVD burner, or a network drive. Click Next.

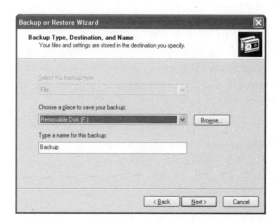

EXERCISE 17.7 (continued)

6. Specify the type of backup. If you're not sure, choose Normal. Click Next.

7. Choose your backup options: Verify Data, Hardware Compression, and Disable Volume Shadow Copy. It's a good idea to verify data, but it does take extra time. Click Next.

8. Choose to replace the current backup file (if one exists) or append the data to the end of the backup. Click Next.

9. Here is where you can schedule the backup. Choose Later, and then click the Set Schedule button. (If you don't want to schedule but want to back up the files now, click Now.)

10. In the Schedule Job window, choose how often and at what time you would like to run backups, and click OK. Then click Next.

11. You will be prompted for a username and password to run the backup. This is because only certain user accounts (such as the Administrator account) have the ability to run backups. When the process starts, Windows will log itself in as the user account you specify to perform the backup. Click Next.

12. Review the information on the confirmation page, and click Finish.

One key thing to remember is that for the backups to run properly as scheduled, the computer needs to be on when the scheduled backup is supposed to take place.

EXERCISE 17.8

Scheduling Backups in Windows Vista

1. Open Windows Backup by going to Start ➢ All Programs ➢ Accessories ➢ System Tools ➢ Backup Status And Configuration.

2. Choose Set Up Automatic File Backup. Click Continue when UAC asks if you want to.

3. Choose a destination location and click Next.

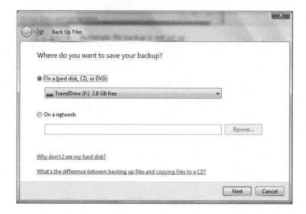

4. Choose what you want to back up and click Next.

5. Choose which file types you want to include in the backup and click Next.

6. Specify how often you want to create a backup and what which day/time to use. Click Save Settings And Start Backup.

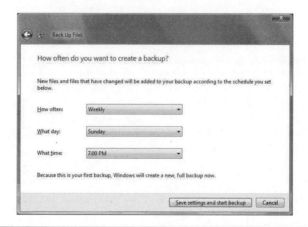

System Management Tools

Windows variants are very complicated operating systems, and it's fortunate that there are plenty of system management tools to help us in our daily computer management activities.

Device Manager

From Windows 9x forward, Microsoft has provided the Device Manager, a tool that analyzes hardware-related problems. The Device Manager displays all of the devices installed in a computer (as shown in Figure 17.10). If a device is malfunctioning, a yellow circle with an exclamation point inside it is displayed (as with the Iomega Parallel Port Interface in Figure 17.10).

FIGURE 17.10 The Windows Device Manager

With this utility, you can view the devices installed in a system and any of those devices that are failing, and you can also double-click on a device and view and set its properties (as shown in Figure 17.11). On the General tab, you will see the status of the device (whether it's working), as well as the Troubleshoot button, which can help you solve problems. The other tabs are used to configure the individual devices, add or update drivers, and verify the version of drivers installed.

In Windows Vista, XP, and 2000, you can access the Device Manager by right-clicking the My Computer icon, choosing Properties, and then clicking the Hardware tab in Windows XP or 2000 (just click on Device Manager in Windows Vista). On the XP or 2000 Hardware tab you'll see many buttons, but to access the Device Manager, click the Device Manager button.

FIGURE 17.11   Properties of a network card

Computer Management

Windows Vista, XP, and 2000 include an umbrella-like utility that can be used to manage computer settings: the Computer Management Console. In addition to including the Device Manager described earlier, the Computer Management Console can manage all the services running on that computer. It provides an Event Viewer to display any system errors and events, as well as methods to configure the software components of all the computer's hardware. Figure 17.12 shows an example of the Computer Management Console running on Windows Vista.

FIGURE 17.12   Windows Vista Computer Management Console

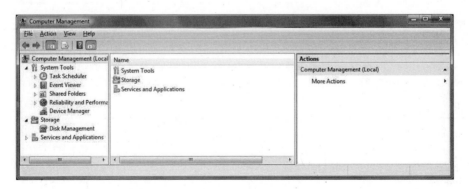

To access the Computer Management Console, choose Start ➤ Settings ➤ Control Panel ➤ Administrative Tools ➤ Computer Management. Alternatively, you can right-click My Computer and choose Manage. You will see all of the computer management tools, including the Device Manager. You can then use the Computer Management Console to manage hardware devices and software services.

> To access the Computer Management Console in Windows 2000, choose Start ➤ Settings ➤ Control Panel ➤ Administrative Tools ➤ Computer Management.

One of the primary tasks you can perform in the Computer Management Console is manage drives and their status. This is discussed later in this chapter in the "Getting Disks Ready to Store Files and Programs" section, but for now, just know that the following drive and volume status states are possible and understand their meaning:

Foreign   A disk is present that is not currently set up for this computer (in which case, you can right-click on it and choose Import Foreign Disks).

Healthy   There are no problems and the drive is working as it should.

Formatting   The disk is in the process of being formatted with whichever file system you chose.

Active Unallocated   There is space that is available for allocation to a dynamic array.

Failed   A dynamic disk is corrupted or damaged (in which case, you should right-click on it and choose Reactivate Disk to see if it corrects the problem).

Dynamic   Can contain spanned or striped volumes.

Offline   A disk that was once available is not now—it could be disconnected or damaged.

Online   The disk is working as it should and has no problems

> Anything that can be done within the Disk Management utility can also be done at the command line with the DiskPart utility.

Regional Settings

Regional settings are configured on a system through a Control Panel applet. In Windows Vista and XP, that applet is called Regional and Language Options, while in Windows 2000 it is Regional Options. From this applet, you can choose what format is used for numbers, what the layout is of the keyboard you are using, your geographic location, and the language to be used for non-Unicode programs. The ability to support so many languages is provided through the use of the Unicode standard. In Unicode, and the Unicode Character Set (UCS), each character has a 16-bit value. This allows the same character to be interpreted/represented by 65,536 different entities

System Information

System Information exists as a stand-alone utility in Windows Vista and XP (Start ➤ All Programs ➤ Accessories ➤ System Tools ➤ System Information, or simply `msinfo32.exe`), and as a Computer Management add-in in Windows 2000. Offering no ability to change any values, this tool shows information about the system and is divided into System Summary, Hardware Resources, Components, and Software Environment, by default. Other top-level divisions, such as Office Applications and Internet Settings, can also appear here (there will be slight differences based on the OS.)

You can choose any of the options to quickly see what is in use. For example, you can choose IRQs to generate a two-column display of IRQ Number and Device. Choosing I/O, DMA, or Memory shows three columns: Address Range, Device, and Status. Conflicts/Sharing should (ideally) contain a single line: No Conflicted/Shared Resource. Forced Hardware should likewise display a single line: No Forced Hardware.

System Monitor/Performance Monitor

CompTIA's objectives include "System Monitor." Over the years, and with varying versions of Windows, System Monitor and Performance Monitor have been combined into one entity. That entity in Windows Vista is known as Reliability and Performance Monitor, and is shown in Figure 17.13. Using the Performance Monitor tool, you are able to monitor desired information about the system.

FIGURE 17.13   The Performance Monitor in Windows Vista

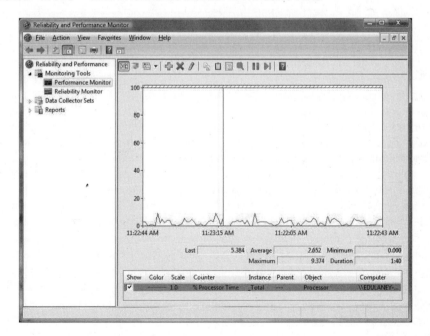

This differs from Windows XP and Windows 2000, in which you reach the same location by opening Performance (`perfmon.msc`), and then selecting System Monitor (shown in Figure 17.14).

FIGURE 17.14 The System Monitor in Windows XP

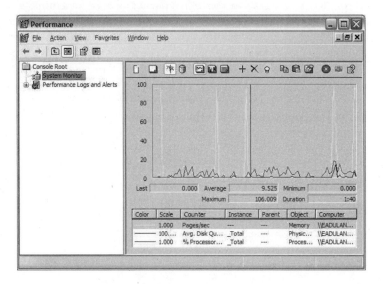

Regardless of the name used, the monitor allows you to gather real-time statistics about what the system is doing right now in chart format (the default), histogram format (similar to a bar chart), or report format. You can also choose to record data to create and compare with a baseline (to get a long-term look at how the system is operating) or send administrative alerts when thresholds are reached.

Within this tool, the system is divided into a number of different objects. The number of objects depends on how the system workstation is configured: as more items are added to the workstation, more objects become available. For each object, there are one or more counters—subsets of the overall object. Those counters may be one of two types: actual (a true number or an average) or a percentage (from 0 to 100). When looking at disk operations, for example, you can see how many reads are performed per second, which might be either a real number or the percent of time the disk is busy performing reads.

When selecting counters, you want to avoid mixing and matching actual numbers and percentages in the same report or chart. Because the highest number a percentage counter can obtain is 100, and the highest number an actual counter can obtain is unlimited, the scale will be confusing, and you may not be able to interpret what you are seeing without confusion.

If the workstation has more than one like item, the multiples are known as instances. For example, if you want to look at disk activity, you would view the object called PhysicalDisk. A good counter to choose would be %Disk Read Time. If you have more than one physical disk in the system, choose the instance (disk) that you want to monitor. One of the instances that will always appear when there are multiples is _Total. The _Total instance provides an aggregate measurement of all instances for a full system view.

Task Manager

Another tool you can use to check on and control your Windows Vista, XP, or 2000 environment is the Task Manager. Any time you run a program, it displays as a button on the Taskbar. Sometimes, however, you may run into problems with running tasks. For example, a task (program) may hang. You'll know this has happened because you won't be able to use any of the program's functions—the program will be unresponsive. To deal with this situation, as well as for other reasons, you can use the Task Manager (see Figure 17.15).

FIGURE 17.15   The Task Manager in Windows Vista

Image Name	User Name	CPU	Memory (...	Description
ApMsgFwd.exe	edulaney	00	584 K	ApMsgFwd
ApntEx.exe	edulaney	00	984 K	Alps Point...
Apoint.exe	edulaney	00	1,556 K	Alps Point...
csrss.exe		00	1,416 K	
DataSafeOnli...	edulaney	00	11,732 K	DataSafe...
DellDock.exe	edulaney	00	8,704 K	Dell Dock
DLG.exe	edulaney	00	1,100 K	Digital Lin...
dwm.exe	edulaney	00	22,156 K	Desktop ...
ehmsas.exe	edulaney	00	808 K	Media Ce...
ehtray.exe	edulaney	00	596 K	Media Ce...
explorer.exe	edulaney	00	40,772 K	Windows ...
ezi_ra.exe	edulaney	00	2,508 K	Remote A...
GoogleDeskto...	edulaney	00	9,648 K	Google D...
GoogleToolba...	edulaney	00	560 K	GoogleTo...
HelpPane.exe	edulaney	00	10,860 K	Microsoft...

Processes: 82   CPU Usage: 3%   Physical Memory: 39%

To access the Task Manager, press Ctrl+Alt+Del. In Windows 2000, you then have to click Task Manager on the Windows Security screen. By default, Windows Vista and XP do not display the Windows Security screen if you press Ctrl+Alt+Del; instead, Task Manager opens right away. You can change this by opening User Accounts in Control Panel and clicking Change The Way Users Log On Or Off.

To get to the Task Manager directly in any of the Windows versions that include it, you can press Ctrl+Shift+Esc.

In Windows 2000, the Task Manager has three tabs: Applications, Processes, and Performance. In Windows XP, the Task Manager can have two additional tabs: Networking and Users. Windows Vista adds yet another—Services. Let's look at the tabs in more detail:

Applications   The Applications tab lets you see what tasks are open on the machine. You also see the status of each task, which can be either Running or Not Responding. If a task or application has stopped responding (that is, it's hung), you can select the task in the list and click End Task. Doing so closes the program, and you can try to open it again. Often, although certainly not always, if an application hangs, you'll have to reboot the computer to prevent the same thing from happening again shortly after you restart the application. You can also use the Applications tab to switch to a different task or create new tasks.

Processes   The Processes tab lets you see the names of all the processes running on the machine. You also see the user account that's running the process, as well as how much CPU and RAM resources each process is using. To end a process, select the process in the list and click End Process.

When you access the Processes tab, you'll likely see dozens of files that you don't recognize. In most cases, these represent the background processes that are running on the system; while some are associated with the operating system, others are associated with applications that need to always keep running in the background (such as antivirus software). If you regularly see a background process listed that you do not want there, you need to identify how it is starting (from the Startup folder, a Registry entry, etc.) and remove it from there; ending it in Task Manager only ends this one instance of it.

You can also change the priority of a process in Task Manager's Processes display by right-clicking on the name of the process and choosing Set Priority. The six priorities, from lowest to highest, are as follows:

Low   For applications that need to complete sometime but that you don't want interfering with other applications. On a numerical scale from 0 to 31, this equates to a base priority of 4.

Below Normal   For applications that don't need to drop all the way down to Low. This equates to a base priority of 6.

Normal   The default priority for most applications. This equates to a base priority of 8.

Above Normal   For applications that don't need to boost all the way to High. This equates to a base priority of 10.

High   For applications that must complete soon, when you don't want other applications to interfere with the applications' performance. This equates to a base priority of 13.

Realtime   For applications that must have the processor's attention to handle time-critical tasks. Applications can be run at this priority only by a member of the Administrators group. This equates to a base priority of 24.

If you decide to change the priority of an application, you'll be warned that changing the priority of an application may make it unstable. You can generally ignore this option when changing the priority to Low, Below Normal, Above Normal, or High, but you should heed this warning when changing applications to the Realtime priority. Realtime means that the processor gives precedence to this process over all others—over security processes, over spooling, over everything—and is sure to make the system unstable.

Task Manager changes the priority only for that instance of the running application. The next time the process is started, priorities revert back to that of the base (typically Normal).

Services (Windows Vista only)   The Services tab lists the name of each running service as well as the process ID associated with it, its description, status, and group. A button labeled Services appears on this tab, and clicking it will open the MMC console for Services, where you can configure each service. Within Task Manager, right-clicking on a service will open a context menu listing three choices: Start Service, Stop Service, and Go To Process (this takes you to the Processes tab). You'll learn more about services in the "Windows Services" section, later in this chapter.

Performance   The Performance tab contains a variety of information, including overall CPU usage percentage, a graphical display of CPU usage history, page-file usage in MB, and a graphical display of page-file usage. This tab provides you with additional memory-related information, such as physical and kernel memory usage, as well as the total number of handles, threads, and processes. Total, limit, and peak commit-charge information also displays. Some of the items are beyond the scope of this book, but it's good to know that you can use the Performance tab to keep track of system performance. Note that the number of processes, CPU usage percentage, and commit changes always display at the bottom of the Task Manager window, regardless of which tab you have currently selected. With Windows Vista, a Resource Monitor button appears at the bottom of this tab. Clicking this button opens the Resource Monitor, shown in Figure 17.16.

FIGURE 17.16   The Resource Monitor in Windows Vista

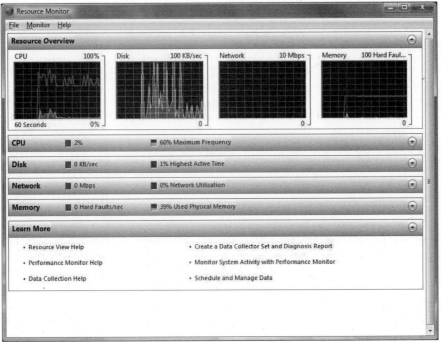

Networking (Windows XP and Vista only)   This tab only appears if you are connected to a network. The Networking tab provides you with a graphical display of the performance of your network connection. It also tells you the network adapter name, link speed, and state. If you have more than one network adapter installed in the machine, you can select the appropriate adapter to see graphical usage data for that adapter.

Users (Windows XP and Vista only)   The Users tab, which is available if you have more than one user account on your computer, provides you with information about the users connected to the local machine. You'll see the username, ID, status, client name, and session type. You can right-click on any connected user to perform a variety of functions, including sending the user a message, disconnecting the user, logging off the user, and initiating a remote control session to the user's machine.

Task Scheduler

Accessible either beneath Computer Management, or Start ➤ All Programs ➤ Accessories ➤ System Tools, the Task Scheduler allows you to configure an application to run automatically or at any regular interval (see Figure 17.17).There are a number of terms used to configure tasks: Action (what the task actually does), Condition (an optional requirement that must be met before task runs), Setting (any property that affects the behavior of a task), and Trigger (the required condition for the task to run).

FIGURE 17.17   Windows Task Scheduler in Windows Vista

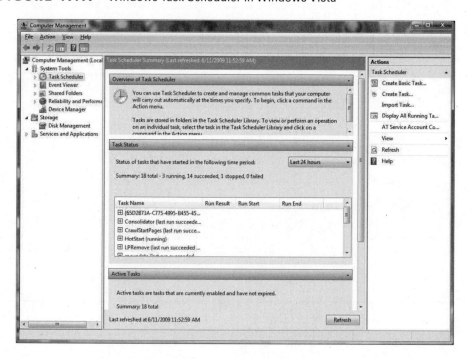

For example, you could configure a report to automatically run (action) every Tuesday (trigger) when the system has been idle for ten minutes (condition), and only when requested (setting). Figure 17.18 shows the dialog boxes used to configure the task.

FIGURE 17.18   Task configuration dialog boxes in Windows Vista

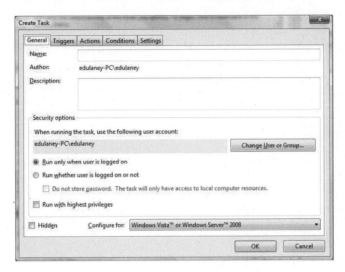

Windows Services

To configure Windows services, open Administrative Tools in Control Panel and choose Services (or right-click My Computer, choose Manage, and then click Services under Services and Applications). You'll see a window similar to the one in Figure 17.19.

FIGURE 17.19   Windows services

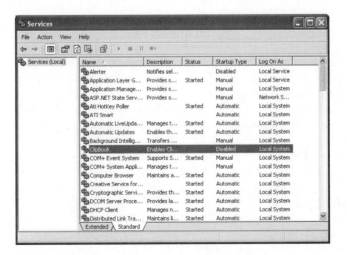

The services are listed in alphabetical order by default. You can also see which services are started, and if they start automatically when Windows boots or if they need to be started manually. If you're not sure what the service does, double-clicking it will give you more details. If a service is running but it's not needed, you can stop it in this applet. Also, the various tabs of the service's properties allow you to configure how it operates.

The General tab gives you a description of the service, lets you configure its startup options, and start, stop, or pause the service. Under the Logon tab, you can set the account the computer will use to run the service. Unless you have a specific need, there's no need to change this. Recovery lets you specify actions to take if the service fails, and the Dependencies tab lets you see what services are dependent on this service, as well as what services this one is dependent on. If this service has dependents, disabling it will affect those dependents as well.

Event Viewer

Windows Vista, XP, and 2000 employs comprehensive error and informational logging routines. Every program and process theoretically could have its own logging utility, but Microsoft has come up with a rather slick utility, the Event Viewer, which, through log files, tracks all events on a particular Windows computer. Normally, though, you must be an administrator or a member of the Administrators group to have access to the Event Viewer.

To start the Event Viewer, log in as an administrator (or equivalent) and choose Start ➢ Programs ➢ Administrative Tools ➢ Event Viewer. From here, you can view the System, Application, and Security log files:

- The System log file displays alerts that pertain to the general operation of Windows.

- The Application log file logs server application errors.

- The Security log file logs security events such as login successes and failures.

These log files can give a general indication of a Windows computer's health. Other log files can be created by the programs you install, and Windows Vista includes two additional ones: Setup and Forwarded Events, as shown in Figure 17.20.

One situation that does occur with the Event Viewer is that the log files get full. Although this isn't really a problem, it can make viewing log files confusing because there are many entries. Even though each event is time- and date-stamped, you should clear the Event Viewer every so often. To do this, open the Event Viewer and choose Clear All Events from the Log menu (before you do so, consider saving them to a file using the Action menu in case you need to refer back to them at any time). Doing so erases all events in the current log file, allowing you to see new events more easily when they occur.

The Event Viewer is the first tool to turn to if you have a device or service that fails to start. You want to check the log files and see if they are recording information about that failure that you can use to diagnose the problem.

Disk and Remote Management

Where there are files, there are disks. That is to say, all the files and programs we've talked about so far reside on *disks*. Disks are physical storage devices, and these disks also need to be managed. There are several aspects to disk management. One is concerned with getting disks ready to be able to store files and programs. Another deals with backing up your data. Yet another involves checking the health of disks and optimizing their performance. We'll look at these aspects in more detail.

Getting Disks Ready to Store Files and Programs

For a hard disk to be able to hold files and programs, it has to be partitioned and formatted. *Partitioning* is the process of creating logical divisions on a hard drive. A hard drive can have one or more partitions. *Formatting* is the process of creating and configuring a file allocation table (FAT) and creating the root directory. Several file system types are supported by the various versions of Windows, such as FAT16, FAT32, and NTFS. Windows *9x*, Me, and newer use FAT32, but they recognize and support FAT16. Windows Vista, XP, 2000, and Vista also support a newer, more robust file system type called NTFS (New Technology Filesystem) and recognize and support FAT16 and FAT32. The file table for the NTFS is called the Master File Table (MFT).

The following is a list of the major file systems that are used with Windows and the differences among them:

File Allocation Table (FAT)   An acronym for the file on this file system used to keep track of where files are. It's also the name given to this type of file system, introduced in 1981. Many OSs have built their file system on the design of FAT, but without its limitations. A FAT file system uses the *8.3 naming convention* (eight letters for the name, a period, and then a three-letter file identifier). This later became known as *FAT16* (to differentiate it from FAT32) because it used a 16-bit binary number to hold cluster-numbering information. Because of that number, the largest FAT disk partition that could be created was approximately 2GB.

Virtual FAT (VFAT)   An extension of the FAT file system that was introduced with Windows 95. It augmented the 8.3 file-naming convention and allowed filenames with up to 255 characters. It created two names for each file: a *long name* and an 8.3-compatible name so that older programs could still access files. When VFAT was incorporated into Windows 95, it used 32-bit code for improved disk access while keeping the 16-bit naming system for backward compatibility with FAT. It also had the 2GB disk partition limitation.

FAT32   Introduced along with Windows 95 OEM Service Release 2. As disk sizes grew, so did the need to be able to format a partition larger than 2GB. FAT32 was based more on VFAT than on FAT16. It allowed for 32-bit cluster addressing, which in turn provided for a maximum partition size of 2 terabytes (2048GB). It also included smaller cluster sizes to avoid wasted space (discussed later). FAT32 support is included in Windows 98, Me, 2000, XP, and Vista.

NT File System (NTFS)   Introduced along with Windows and available on 2000, XP, and Vista. NTFS is a much more advanced file system in almost every way than all versions of the FAT file system. It includes such features as individual file security and compression, RAID support, as well as support for extremely large file and partition sizes and disk transaction monitoring. It is the file system of choice for higher-performance computing. NTFS5 is the version shipping with 2000 and above with improvements over the original NTFS.

When you're installing any Windows OS, you will be asked first to format the drive using one of these disk technologies. Choose the disk technology based on what the computer will be doing and which OS you are installing.

To create a FAT16 or FAT32 partition, you can use the FDISK command. To format a partition, you can use the FORMAT command. FORMAT.EXE is available with all versions of Windows. You can run FORMAT from a command prompt or by right-clicking a drive in Windows Explorer and selecting Format. However, when you install Windows it performs the process of partitioning and formatting for you if a partitioned and formatted drive does not already exist.

 Be extremely careful with the FORMAT command! When you format a drive, all data on the drive is erased.

In Windows Vista, XP, and 2000, you can manage your hard drives through the Disk Management component. To access Disk Management, access Control Panel and double-click Administrative Tools. Then, double-click Computer Management. Finally, double-click Disk Management. The Disk Management screen looks similar to the one shown in Figure 17.21.

FIGURE 17.21   The Disk Management screen

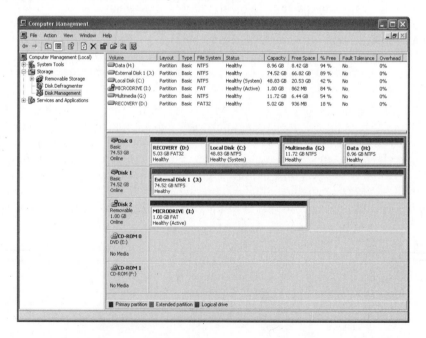

The Disk Management screen lets you view a host of information regarding all the drives installed in your system, including CD-ROM and DVD drives. In Figure 17.21, you can see that this computer has three disks (Disk 0, Disk 1, and Disk 2), one DVD (CD-ROM 0), and one CD-ROM (CD-ROM 1) drive installed. In this example, you can see that Disk 0 has four partitions. A different drive letter is assigned to each partition on Disk 0 (C:, D:, G:, and H:). The list of devices in the top portion of the screen shows you additional information for each partition on each drive, such as the file system used, status, free space, and so on. If you right-click a partition in either area, you can perform a variety of functions, such as formatting the partition and changing the name and drive-letter assignment. For additional options and information, you can also access the properties of a partition by right-clicking it and selecting Properties.

Windows Vista, XP, and 2000 support both basic and dynamic storage. Basic supports only one partition, while dynamic can be simple, spanned, or striped. Spanning allows for space from multiple disks to be combined into a single volume but does not include any redundancy. Striping is similar in that it combines spaces from two or more drives, but it also incorporates some redundancy. The partition that the operating system boots from must be designated as *active*. Only one partition on a disk may be marked active. With basic storage, Windows drives can be partitioned with *primary* or *extended* partitions. The difference is that extended partitions can be divided into one or more logical drives and primary partitions cannot be further subdivided. Each Vista, XP, and 2000 hard disk can be divided into a total of four partitions, either four primary partitions or three primary and one extended partition.

Finally, there is the concept of a *logical partition*. In reality, all partitions are logical in the sense that they don't necessarily correspond to one physical disk. One disk can have several logical divisions (partitions). A logical partition is any partition that has a drive letter.

Sometimes, you will also hear of a logical partition as one that spans multiple physical disks. For example, a network drive that you know as drive H: might actually be located on several physical disks on a server. To the user, all that is seen is one drive, or H:.

Just as you can convert FAT volumes to NTFS without losing data (but there is no way back), you can similarly convert a disk's type from basic to dynamic, but there is no easy means of converting it back. Should you need to convert back for some reason, you must first delete the volumes and then use the Revert To Basic Disk command that becomes available.

The following are advantages of converting to dynamic disks:

- Existing partitions become simple volumes.
- All fault-tolerant volumes become dynamic volumes.

Of course, conversion also has its disadvantages and limitations:

- The disk cannot contain partitions or logical drives.

To perform the upgrade, close all applications that could be accessing the disks and verify that there is a minimum of 1MB unallocated space on the disk. Although no data is actually affected, you should always make a backup before undertaking any major system change.

Make the appropriate selection from the pop-up menu and move past several warnings that attempt to make certain you understand the ramifications of what you are doing. A reboot is required.

After the reboot, each of the drives will be converted individually, and a second reboot will be needed. Before each reboot, you are prompted to confirm the action. When the system comes back up, the view will have changed from Primary and Logical partitions to one of Simple Volumes and unallocated space.

Remote Desktop Connection and Assistance

Windows contains two remote connectivity applications, called Remote Desktop Connection and Remote Assistance. The following sections describe each in more detail.

Remote Desktop Connection

The *Remote Desktop* feature of Windows would probably be more accurately named remote control. Remote Desktop allows you to connect to another computer and take control over that computer as if you were sitting in front of it. This utility allows you to connect to your work computer from home, for example, and it can also work as a great troubleshooting tool. On the flip side, it can also be a huge security risk.

Remote Desktop classifies computers into two categories: home computer and remote computer. The *home computer* is the one that you are sitting at. For it to use Remote Desktop, it needs to have *Remote Desktop Connection* installed (which it is by default in Windows Vista and XP). The *remote computer* is the one you are connecting to. It needs to have Remote Desktop installed, which is separate from Remote Desktop Connection.

Windows XP Home does not have Remote Desktop, only Remote Desktop Connection. Therefore, Windows XP Home computers can be only home computers, not remote computers. With Vista, you cannot use Remote Desktop Connection to connect to remote computers running Starter, Home Basic, or Home Premium versions.

When using Remote Desktop, keystrokes and mouse movements are transmitted from the home computer to the remote computer. Programs that you open on the remote computer (from the home computer) run normally on the remote computer. You (from the home computer) can see the Desktop of the remote computer, just as if you were sitting there. Finally, sound can be passed from the remote computer to the home computer. This is enabled by default, but it consumes a lot of bandwidth so you might not want to use it.

You can connect to more than one remote computer at a time, but if you do, the connections will likely be very slow because this application is bandwidth-intensive.

By default, users are not allowed to remotely connect to your computer. To change this, you need to open System Properties (right-click My Computer and select Properties) and click the Remote tab, as shown in Figure 17.22.

FIGURE 17.22   System Properties Remote tab

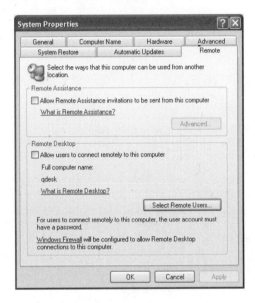

Check the Allow Users To Connect Remotely To This Computer check box to enable access. Then to choose which users can connect remotely, click the Select Remote Users button. For users to be able to access your computer, they must have a user account and password on your computer.

To configure Remote Desktop Connection options, open Remote Desktop Connection by clicking Start ➤ All Programs ➤ Accessories ➤ Communications ➤ Remote Desktop Connection. This opens a window like the one in Figure 17.23.

FIGURE 17.23   Remote Desktop Connection

This is the window you would use to connect to another computer. By clicking the Options button, you can configure desired settings. Looking at Figure 17.24, you can see that there are five tabs of configuration options.

FIGURE 17.24 Remote Desktop Connection options

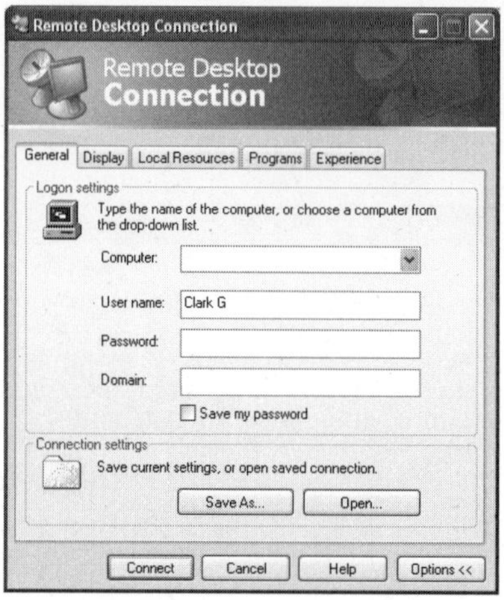

On the bottom of the General tab, you'll notice that you can save these settings into different profiles. This might be handy if you connect to different computers.

The Display tab lets you set the size of your Remote Desktop window, up to full screen. It also allows you to configure the depth of color used, much like when you configure your own Desktop.

The Local Resources tab (shown in Figure 17.25) lets you configure sound (good to leave off unless absolutely necessary), keyboard settings, and connectivity to local devices.

FIGURE 17.25 Local Resources Tab

On the Programs tab, you can choose to start applications when the remote connection is made.

Finally, the Experience tab lets you choose your connection speed as well as a few graphical options (such as allowing themes or the Desktop background) designed to help optimize your connection.

Remote Assistance

Have you ever tried explaining a computer problem you're having to someone else, and it just isn't sinking in? Or how about being on the other end, and having a user trying in vain to explain a problem to you but they just don't have the right words to get their point across?

The Remote Assistance feature of Windows allows you to access someone else's computer in an effort to repair it.

Looking back at Figure 17.22, you will see a check box marked Allow Remote Assistance Invitations To Be Sent From This Computer. By checking that box, you can send an invitation to a person on another computer to connect to yours, with the intention of letting them fix a problem. By clicking the Advanced button, you can choose whether or not to allow remote users to be able to take control over your machine. If you want them to fix the problem, then let them take control. Otherwise, you can just give them a guided tour once they're connected.

 For Remote Assistance to work, you should be running either Windows Messenger or a MAPI-compliant e-mail system such as Outlook or Outlook Express.

Once you have enabled Remote Assistance on the Remote tab of your system properties, you can send an invitation to others to connect to your computer. Here's how:

1. Click Start ➤ Help and Support

2. Click the link that says Invite A Friend To Connect To Your Computer With Remote Assistance. That will take you to another Help and Support menu.

3. Click Invite Someone To Help You.

4. If you use Windows Messenger (or MSN Messenger), highlight the person on your contacts list and click Invite This Person. If you do not use Messenger, type their e-mail address in the Type An E-mail Address box, and click Invite This Person.

Upon receiving the invitation, the user will be given the opportunity to accept. After they accept, you will be notified that they have accepted, and the session is started.

To end a Remote Assistance session, click the Disconnect or Close button in the Remote Assistance window.

Differences Between Remote Desktop and Remote Assistance

Both remote programs use the same base technology, but there are differences. Remote Desktop was designed to give you remote access to a Windows session running on your computer, even if you're not there. For example, you can be at home and log in to your work computer to access files or applications.

Remote Assistance allows a friend or a technician to use an Internet connection to access your computer to provide help. By default, the friend sees your Desktop and communicates with you through a messenger window. If you choose, you can allow that friend to have control over your computer.

System Performance and Optimization

Windows Vista introduced a number of features that an administrator should be aware of in order to understand how to better optimize a system. These include the Aero interface, the User Account Control feature, indexing, and Sidebar.

The first of these is the Aero interface. Microsoft maintains a list of common issues with Aero—and solutions—at

```
http://windowshelp.microsoft.com/Windows/en-us/help/c33fe91a-9e6f-41f4-ae82-
3ed2d5fa2fbf1033.mspx
```

and you are strongly encouraged to visit that site. An acronym for Authentic, Energetic, Reflective, and Open, Acro differs from previous GUIs in that its windows are translucent and it allows the ability to create a 3D stack of open windows and cycle through them (known as *Flip 3D*). To configure Aero, right-click on the desktop and choose Personalize from the context menu, then choose Window Color And Appearance, as shown in Figure 17.26.

FIGURE 17.26 Configuring Aero

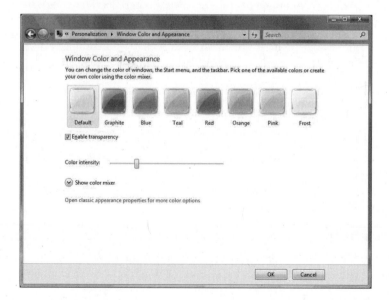

Here, you can turn off the transparency, as well as change the colors used for windows. Aero can be turned off altogether by clicking Open Classic Appearance Properties For More Color Options. This brings up the Appearance Settings dialog box shown in Figure 17.27, from which you can choose to use Windows Standard, Windows Classic, or another interface (choosing anything but the default of Windows Aero turns Aero off).

FIGURE 17.27   Choosing an interface besides Aero

The User Account Control (UAC) feature was discussed in Chapter 6, "Operating System Features and Interfaces," and has the sole purpose of keeping the user from running programs that could pose a potential threat by escalating privileges to that of administrator. While turning UAC off is an option, it is not a recommended option. If you have a program you regularly run and do not want to be prompted each time, you can right-click the icon for that program and then click Properties. Choose the Compatibility tab and then select the Run This Program As An Administrator check box. This will prevent the prompt from occurring each time you use the program.

 Operating system programs are typically not able to have this feature set and the Privileges will stayed grayed out on the Compatibility tab.

Indexing services have existed since early versions of Windows and allow the operating system to quickly find files by looking through a database of entries rather than having to start from scratch each time. The primary interface for configuring indexing is the Indexing Options applet in Control Panel. Figure 17.28 shows this interface for Windows Vista, and it differs from previous OS versions simply in the addition of the Pause button.

FIGURE 17.28 Configuring Indexing

The Advanced button takes you to the heart of the configuration. From here, you can choose whether to include encrypted files, and what types of files to include in the index. Most meaningful is the ability to choose whether the index should index properties only (the default) or also include file contents. While choosing to include contents in the index greatly decreases search time, it can also slow the system down on a regular basis as it builds the index.

The Sidebar is a new feature allowing easy access to gadgets. To configure the Sidebar, right-click on an area of it and choose Properties (if the Sidebar is not visible, click Start ➤ All Programs ➤ Accessories ➤ Windows Sidebar). This will bring up the dialog box shown in Figure 17.29.

FIGURE 17.29 Configuring the Sidebar

In addition to choosing Properties from the context menu, you can choose Close Sidebar, Bring Gadgets To Front, and Add Gadgets. When you select Add Gadgets, a list of common ones appears, as shown in Figure 17.30. Double-click on any gadget to add it, or choose Get More Gadgets Online to see many more.

FIGURE 17.30   Standard gadgets that can be added to the Sidebar

To remove a gadget, right-click on it and choose Close Gadget. You can also drag any gadget from the Sidebar directly onto the Desktop and drag them from the Desktop into the Sidebar as you wish.

> The CompTIA objectives for this exam list Startup File Maintenance and Background Processes as well beneath the System Performance and Optimization category. Both have been adequately addressed previously.

Common Operational Problems

CompTIA wants you to be aware of seven somewhat common operational problems that can occur with Windows. All seven are discussed in this section.

Printing Problems

Most printing problems today are due to either improper configuration or actual physical problems with the printer. Physical printer problems are addressed in two other chapters in this book, and so configuration is the focus here.

The Windows architecture is such that when a client wants to print to a network printer, a check is first done to see if the client has the latest printer driver. If it doesn't—as judged by the print server—the new driver is sent from the server to the client, and then the print job is accepted. This is an enormous help to the administrator, for when a new driver comes out, all the administrator must do is install it on the server, and the distribution to the clients becomes automatic.

Errors occur when a client is configured with a printer different from the one in use. For example, suppose the network has an ABC 6200 printer, but you don't see that among the list of choices when you install the printer. Rather than taking the time to get the correct driver, you choose the ABC 6000, because you've been told that it's compatible. All will work well in this scenario until a new driver is released and loaded on the server. This client won't update (while all others configured with 6200 will), and thus there is the potential for printing problems to occur.

You can solve most other problems using the Printing Troubleshooter (go to Start ➤ Help and Support, and type **Printing Troubleshooter**). It will walk you through solving individual printing problems.

Auto-Restart Errors

If the system is automatically restarting, there is the possibility that it has a virus or is unable to continue current operations (has become unstable). To solve issues with viruses, Trojans, and the like, install virus detection software on every client (as well as on the server), keep the definitions current, and run them often.

If the problem is with the system being unstable, examine the log files and try to isolate the problem. Reboot in Safe Mode, and correct any incompatibility issues. You can also deselect the Automatically Restart On Startup And Recovery option of the System applet (Advanced tab) in Control Panel to prevent the system from rebooting

Occasionally, systems reboot when they have been updated. This is a necessary process, and users are always given warning before the reboot is to occur. If no one is present to choose to reboot later (it's the middle of the night, for example) the reboot will take place.

Blue Screens

Once a regular occurrence when working with Windows, blue screens (also known as the Blue Screen of Death) have become less common. Occasionally, systems will lock up; you can usually examine the log files to discover what was happening when this occurred and take steps to correct it.

System Lockup

The difference between a blue screen and a system lockup is whether the dump message that accompanies a blue screen is present. With a regular lockup, things just stop working. As with blue screens, these are mostly a thing of the past (the exception may be laptops, which go to Hibernate mode). If they occur, you can examine the log files to discover what was happening and take steps to correct it.

Driver Failure

Drivers are associated with devices, and you can access them by looking at the properties for the device. The following, for example, are the three tabs of an adapter's Properties dialog box:

General   This tab displays the device type, manufacturer, and location. It also includes text regarding whether the device is currently working properly and a Troubleshooter command button to walk you through diagnostics.

Driver   Access this tab to view information on the current driver and digital signer. Three command buttons allow you to see driver details and uninstall or update the driver.

Resources   This tab shows the system resources in use (I/O, IRQ, and so on) and whether there are conflicts.

In Device Manager, you can also expand the Monitors tree, right-click Shown Monitors, and choose Properties from the context menu. Doing so shows the General and Driver tabs discussed in the preceding list, but not Resources.

Application Failures

If applications fail to install, start, or load, you should examine the log files associated with them to try to isolate the problem. Many applications write logs that can be viewed with the Event Viewer (choose Application Logs), and others (mostly legacy) write to text files that you can find in their own directories.

Common steps to try include closing all other applications and beginning this one, reinstalling fresh, and checking to see whether the application works properly on another machine.

Services Fail to Start

Just as with applications, if services fail to start, you should examine the log files associated with them to try to isolate the problem. Most services write logs that can be viewed with the Event Viewer. Common steps to try include closing other services and beginning this one, reinstalling fresh, and checking to see whether the service runs works properly on another machine.

Summary

In this chapter, you learned about preventive maintenance for operating systems. Keeping your computer healthy will save you a lot of stress. Examples we discussed included using approved hardware and making sure you have the right driver, installing and shutting down Windows properly, updating Windows, performing backups, and creating restore points.

Then we talked about options for dealing with boot issues, including advanced startup options, using repair options or the Recovery Console, and creating emergency boot disks or repair disks. We also identified some common boot errors and their options.

Next we gave you some tips for troubleshooting the Windows environment. Just as with troubleshooting hardware, it is important that you know how to troubleshoot software problems. However, troubleshooting software is actually more difficult because the problems can appear to be more phantom-like. You then learned how to use the various built-in Windows troubleshooting utilities. You learned what each utility is for and how to use it. We also discussed when to apply a particular utility to a problem.

We then looked at disk and remote management. Finally we covered system optimization.

Exam Essentials

Know the main administrative tools.   You should know the primary graphical tools for troubleshooting Windows and working with the operating system. These include the disk management tools, Disk Manager and drive basics, System Monitor, administrative tools, Device Manager, Task Manager, System Information, System Restore, Remote Desktop, Task Scheduler, and Regional Settings

Know how to create an emergency repair disk (ERD) or enable Automated System Recovery (ASR).   Both the ERD (Windows 2000) and ASR (Windows XP) can help you recover a system that has crashed because of Windows problems. However, before either option is available, you must first go to Windows Backup and create the appropriate disk.

Understand how to fix software-related problems.   Most software problems boil down to a missing or corrupted file. If this is the case, then reinstalling that file (or the application) can often fix the problem. Try rebooting first, and if the problem doesn't go away, you might need to reinstall.

Review Questions

1. What do you use in Windows XP to create a recovery disk?

    A. Automated System Recovery (ASR)

    B. `RDISK.EXE`

    C. Enhanced Startup Disk (ESD)

    D. Emergency Recovery System (ERS)

2. What is the default interface used by Windows Vista?

    A. Translucent

    B. Sidebar

    C. UAC

    D. Aero

3. What does Safe Mode allow you to do?

    A. Run Windows without processing `AUTOEXEC.BAT` and `CONFIG.SYS`.

    B. Boot the system without scanning drives.

    C. Start Windows using only basic files and drivers.

    D. Skip loading the Registry.

4. Which of the following are not tabs found, by default, on the Windows Vista Task Manager?

    A. Services

    B. System

    C. Processes

    D. Applications

5. In order to delete and/or replace system files, which command do you use to remove the Hidden, System, and Read-Only attributes on the file before you replace the file?

    A. `UNDELETE`

    B. `ERASE`

    C. `ATTRIB`

    D. `DELETE`

6. All of the following are common problems faced in troubleshooting Windows and applications except _____.

    A. General protection faults

    B. Valid working directory

    C. System lockup

    D. Application will not start or load

7. Which Control Panel applet is used to set the keyboard language layout in Windows Vista?

A. Regional and Language Options

B. Regional Options

C. Locale

D. Administrative

8. All of the following are Windows file-related problems except _____.

A. System files not found

B. Configuration file issues

C. AUTOEXEC.BAT issues

D. Swap file issues

E. Boot file issues

9. Symptoms of swap file problems include extremely slow system speed and a disk that is constantly being accessed, which is referred to as _____.

A. Clocking

B. Thrashing

C. Booting

D. Filtering

10. What is the quickest solution to fixing a corrupted NTOSKRNL.EXE file?

A. Reinstall Windows.

B. Replace the corrupted file with a new one.

C. Modify the BOOT.INI file to point to the backup NTOSKRNL.EXE file.

D. Boot from a startup disk and replace the file from the setup disks or CD-ROM.

11. Which of the following is the most common error in Windows, and it happens when a program accesses memory another program is using or when a program accesses a memory address that doesn't exist?

A. General protection fault

B. Windows protection error

C. Illegal operation

D. System lockup

12. Which Windows error message is displayed when a program is forced to quit because it did something Windows didn't like?

A. General protection fault

B. Windows protection error

C. Illegal operation

D. System lockup

13. Which of the following Control Panel applets is used to configure how Windows files are searched?

   A. Indexing Options

   B. Bing

   C. Search options

   D. Folder Options

14. In Windows XP, how do you access advanced startup options?

   A. By pressing the spacebar when prompted to do so

   B. By holding down Ctrl+Alt+Del after the Windows logo displays for the first time

   C. By pressing Esc after the OS menu displays

   D. By pressing F8 during the first phase of the boot process

15. Which advanced startup option in Windows 2000 would you use to be able to return to a previously functioning environment?

   A. Command Prompt Only

   B. Safe Mode

   C. Step-By-Step Configuration

   D. Debugging Mode

   E. Last Known Good Configuration

16. In Windows 2000, which utility do you use to create an ERD?

   A. Disk Management

   B. Backup

   C. SYSEDIT

   D. Windows 2000 doesn't support making an ERD.

17. In Windows XP, which of the following utilities is responsible for finding, downloading, and installing Windows service packs?

   A. Update Manager

   B. Service Pack Manager

   C. Windows Update

   D. Download Manager

18. Windows XP includes a feature called a _____, which is a copy of your system configuration that can be used to roll back the system to a previous state if a configuration error occurs.

   A. Restore point

   B. Repair point

   C. Roll back point

   D. Registry

19. Which of the following items are used to populate the Sidebar in Windows Vista?

   A. Implements

   B. Applets

   C. Widgets

   D. Gadgets

20. You have an application open in Windows 2000 that is not responding. Which of the following utilities can you use to forcibly close the nonresponsive application?

   A. Application Manager

   B. Task Manager

   C. Windows Explorer

   D. Device Manager

Answers to Review Questions

1. A. Windows XP introduced a new feature for system recovery, Automated System Recovery (ASR). Included with XP, it makes a backup of your system partition and creates a recovery disk.

2. D. The default interface used with Windows Vista is Aero. You can, however, choose to use the Classic Windows interface in its place.

3. C. Safe Mode is a good option to choose to restore files that are missing or to fix a configuration error. With only basic files and drivers loaded, you can more easily identify the source of the problem.

4. B. System is not a standard Task Manager tab in any version of Windows. All other choices are standard tabs that appear by default.

5. C. In order to delete and/or replace system files, you must use the ATTRIB command to remove the Hidden, System, and Read-Only attributes on the file.

6. B. A valid working directory is not a common problem faced in troubleshooting Windows and applications.

7. A. The Regional and Language Options is used in Windows Vista (and XP). In Windows 2000, the applet was Regional Options.

8. C. Windows file-related problems do not include AUTOEXEC.BAT issues. AUTOEXEC.BAT is a DOS batch file that is automatically executed during boot-up if the file is present.

9. B. Thrashing means an extremely slow system speed and a disk that is constantly being accessed. This condition occurs because Windows doesn't have enough memory to contain all the programs that are running.

10. D. The solution to a corrupt NTOSKRNL.EXE file is to boot from a startup disk and replace the file from the setup disks or CD-ROM. Replacing the corrupted NTOSKRNL.EXE file might also be the solution, but the quickest fix (provided it's the problem) is to look at the BOOT.INI file.

11. A. A general protection fault is the most common error in Windows. It happens when a program accesses memory that another program is using or when a program accesses a memory address that doesn't exist. Generally, GPFs are the result of sloppy programming; they can often be fixed by clearing the memory with a reboot.

12. C. *Illegal operation* is the Windows error message displayed when a program is forced to quit because it did something Windows didn't like. The error's details include which module experienced the problem, the memory location being accessed at the time, and the registers and flags of the processor at the time of the error.

13. A. The Indexing Options applet is used to configure how Windows files are searched.

14. D. Pressing F8 during the first phase of the boot process brings up the Advanced Startup Options menu in Windows 2000, XP, and Vista.

15. E. Last Known Good Configuration enables you to restore the system to a prior, functional state if a change was made to the Registry that turned out to be problematic.

16. B. The Backup utility lets you create an ERD in Windows 2000.

17. C. Windows Update is responsible for finding updates, patches, and service packs, downloading them, and installing them on your computer.

18. A. Windows XP automatically creates restore points, which are copies of your system configuration. You can also create them manually through the System Restore utility.

19. D. The Sidebar is populated with gadgets.

20. B. Task Manager will show you a list of running processes and applications and allow you to close applications that are not responsive (or even ones that are running normally).

Chapter

18

Installing and Troubleshooting Networks

THE FOLLOWING COMPTIA A+ PRACTICAL APPLICATION EXAM OBJECTIVES ARE COVERED IN THIS CHAPTER:

✓ **3.1 Troubleshoot client-side connectivity issues using appropriate tools**

- TCP/IP settings
  - Gateway
  - Subnet mask
  - DNS
  - DHCP (dynamic vs. static)
  - NAT (private and public)
- Characteristics of TCP/IP
  - Loopback addresses
  - Automatic IP addressing
- Mail protocol settings
  - SMTP
  - IMAP
  - POP
- FTP settings
  - Ports
  - IP addresses
  - Exceptions
  - Programs

- Proxy settings
  - Ports
  - IP addresses
  - Exceptions
  - Programs
- Tools (use and interpret results)
  - Ping
  - Tracert
  - Nslookup
  - Netstat
  - Net use
  - Net /?
  - Ipconfig
  - Telnet
  - SSH
- Secure connection protocols
  - SSH
  - HTTPS
- Firewall settings
  - Open and closed ports
  - Program filters

✓ **3.2 Install and configure a small office home office (SOHO) network**

- Connection types
  - Dial-up
  - Broadband
    - DSL
    - Cable
    - Satellite
    - ISDN

- Wireless
  - All 802.11
  - WEP
  - WPA
  - SSID
  - MAC filtering
  - DHCP settings
- Routers/Access points
  - Disable DHCP
  - Use static IP
  - Change SSID from default
  - Disable SSID broadcast
  - MAC filtering
  - Change default username and password
  - Update firmware
  - Firewall
- LAN (10/100/1000BaseT, Speeds)
- Bluetooth (1.0 vs. 2.0)
- Cellular
- Basic VoIP (consumer applications)
- Basics of hardware and software firewall configuration
  - Port assignment/setting up rules (exceptions)
  - Port forwarding/port triggering
- Physical installation
  - Wireless router placement
  - Cable length

As a technician, you will find the world is one where everything is now connected. Rare is the PC that does not communicate with a network or the Internet, and rarer still is the user who does not expect this as a seamless part of their computing experience. You must know far more than just how PCs operate—you must know how they communicate with each other.

It's important that you are familiar with the materials in Chapter 10, "Understanding Networking," in addition to the material in this chapter, as you prepare for your technician exam. You are expected to have the essentials down before preparing for the elective.

While Chapter 10 covered a lot of networking material, it was more of the "what is" variety. Think of this chapter as the "How-to" for networking. In this chapter, we'll focus on real-world applications. This includes installing and configuring small office or home office networks, as well as troubleshooting some common network client-side issues you may run into.

Installing and Configuring SOHO Networks

Nearly every small office has a network, and it seems like most homes these days have one or more computers that need access to the Internet. As a technician, you may be asked to set up or troubleshoot any number of these types of networks. This section will give you the background you need to feel comfortable that you can get the job done. Most of the principles we talk about here also apply to larger networks as well, so they're helpful if you're in a corporate environment too.

Before we get into the different installation and configuration sections, though, it's critical to introduce a topic that permeates this whole section: *planning*. Before installing a network or making changes to it, *always* plan ahead. We'll talk specifically about how to do that as we move throughout this chapter, but always keep planning in the back of your mind. Planning ahead of time will help you avoid many problems you could potentially run into, which will save you time in the long run.

In this section, we'll look at choosing connection types, network installation, and basics of hardware and software firewalls.

Choosing Connection Types

You already know that for computers to talk to each other, they need to be connected in some way. This can be with physical wires or through the air with one of several wireless technologies. The type of connection you choose depends on the purpose of the connection and the needs of the user or users.

You also need to think about the future. Remember that planning concept? When choosing a connection type, think about not only what the needs are today, but what the needs of the individual or organization could be. There is no sense in going overboard and recommending a top-of-the-line expensive solution if it's not needed, but you do want to plan for expansion if that's a possibility.

For our purposes here, we'll break the connection types into two categories. First we'll look at connections designed to facilitate Internet access, and then we'll look at internal network connections. After that, we will talk about another consumer option that is growing in popularity, voice-over IP (VoIP).

Choosing an Internet Connection

If you'll recall from Chapter 10, we broke Internet connections into two categories: dial-up and broadband. Here we will focus more on why you might or might not recommend a specific connection type based on the situation.

Your Internet connection will give you online service through an *Internet service provider (ISP)*. The type of service you want will often determine who your ISP choices are. For example, if you want cable Internet your choices are limited to your local cable companies and a few national providers. But if you want dial-up, you will likely have several local and national ISPs to choose from.

Dial-Up/POTS

Dial-up used to be the most common Internet access in the United States. While its popularity has waned in favor of broadband access, it's still pretty common. In a *dial-up* Internet connection, the computer connecting to the Internet uses a modem to connect to the ISP over a standard telephone line. The telephone company technicians usually call the phone line that goes into your house a *POTS line* (short for *plain old telephone service*). However, the proper, more formal acronym is *public switched telephone network (PSTN)*.

Dial-up Internet connections are pretty slow when compared to the other methods listed here. At the most, dial-up connections are theoretically limited to 56Kbps, but in the real world you are most likely to get speeds around 40Kbps for downloads. The maximum upload speed (from your computer to the Internet) for this connection is around 33.6Kbps.

To make a connection with POTS, you must have a modem installed on or connected to your computer. You also must connect your home phone line to the line port on your modem. Then you must configure some software on your computer known as a dialer. A *dialer* is a special program that initiates the connection with the ISP by accessing the phone line, dialing the ISP's access number, and establishing the connection. Most versions of Windows have a built-in dialer known as *Dial-Up Networking*. Some ISPs may have their own dialer program that they give you on disc when you sign up for their service. ISPs such as AOL, NetZero, and Earthlink have their own dialer software; AOL has its own program, which encompasses dialer, browser, and other functions in one software package but can also function as an Internet dialer.

It seems that dial-up is considered to be a relic from the Stone Age of Internet access. But there are some reasons why it might be the right solution:

- The only hardware it requires is a modem and a phone cord.

- It's relatively easy to set up and configure.

- It's the cheapest online solution (usually $10–20 per month).

- You can use it wherever there is phone service, which is just about everywhere.

Of course, there are reasons why a dial-up connection might not be appropriate. The big one is speed. If your client needs to download any files or has any substantial data requirements, dial-up is probably too slow. Another reason is that with limited bandwidth, it's really only good for one computer. It *is* possible to share a dial-up Internet connection by using software tools, but it's also possible to push a stalled car up a muddy hill. Neither option sounds like much fun.

Digital Subscriber Line (DSL)

One of the first methods of broadband Internet access to become popular was a technology called *digital subscriber line (DSL)*. DSL uses the existing phone line from your home to the phone company to carry digital signals at higher speeds. Essentially, DSL piggybacks a digital signal on the line used for analog communication (your voice). So, with DSL it is possible to have high-speed Internet access and use your phone at the same time.

DSL can provide very quick download speeds; some providers offer packages that promise 12–15Mbps downloads. Uploads are still going to be slower, perhaps about 1Mbps. Considering that most Internet traffic is downloaded to the end user, this isn't normally a problem.

To connect using DSL you need a special device, most often called a DSL modem. This is actually a misnomer, because modems change digital to analog and back again (they *mo*dulate and *demo*dulate, hence their name). Because DSL is digital, the signals are never changed into analog. The correct term for the device used to access DSL is a *DSL endpoint*. Endpoints often have the functions of network bridges or routers. Endpoints can be either internal or external. Internal endpoints go inside a computer as an expansion card, but that means only that a computer can access the Internet directly. Internal DSL endpoints are rare. External endpoints can be hooked to a switch, router, or wireless router, which can share the Internet connection with multiple computers.

Here are some advantages to using DSL:

- It's *much* faster than dial-up.

- Your bandwidth is not shared with other users.

- It's generally very reliable (depending on your ISP).

There are some potential disadvantages as well:

- DSL may not be available in your area. There are distance limitations as to how far away from the phone company's central office you can be to get DSL. Usually this isn't a problem in metro areas, but it could be a problem in rural areas.

- DSL requires more hardware than dial-up: a network card, network cable, a DSL modem, a phone cord, and a noise filter. The noise filter is so when you're on the phone, you don't hear any extra static from the DSL connection. A DSL modem package usually comes with a network cable and noise filters, but many ISPs will make you pay for that package.

- The cost is higher. Lower-speed packages often start off at around $20–30 per month, but the ones they advertise with the great data rates can easily run you $150 a month or more.

- If you are in a house or building with older wiring, the older phone lines may not be able to support the full speed you pay for.

That said, DSL is a popular choice for both small businesses and residential offices. If it's available, it's easy to get the phone company to bundle your service with your land line and bill you at the same time. Often you'll also get a package discount for having multiple services. Most important, you can hook the DSL modem up to your router or wireless router and share the Internet connection among several computers. The phone companies don't like the fact that you can do this (they want you to pay for more access), but as of now there's not a lot they can do about it.

To see if DSL is available in your area, go to www.dslreports.com. You can also talk to your local telephone provider.

With many people using their cell phones as their home phones, and land lines slowly fading into history, you may wonder if this causes a problem if you want DSL. Not really. Many phone providers will provide you DSL without a land line (called *naked DSL*). Of course, you are going to have to pay a surcharge for the use of the phone lines if you don't already use one.

Cable

The other popular broadband Internet access method these days is *cable Internet*. Cable Internet provides broadband Internet access via the television cable that runs to your home via a specification known as *Data Over Cable Service Internet Specification (DOCSIS)*. It is theoretically available to anyone with a cable TV connection and a cable provider that provides the service.

Cable Internet providers offer packages similar to those offered by DSL providers. Some cable ISPs do claim that they can offer speeds much faster than DSL, promising up to 50Mbps downloads. Reading the fine print, however, shows that they will offer to boost your speed for the first 10-20MB of a file download, and then you're throttled back to your normal speed.

Here are the advantages to using cable:

- It's *much* faster than dial-up, and it can be faster than DSL (particularly for uploads).
- You're not required to have or use a telephone land line.
- It's generally very reliable (depending on your ISP).

As with anything else, there are possible disadvantages:

- Cable may not be available in your area. In metro areas this normally isn't a problem, but it could be one in rural areas.
- Cable requires more hardware than dial-up: a network card, network cable, and a cable modem. Most ISPs will charge you a one-time fee or a monthly lease fee for the cable modem.
- Your bandwidth is shared with everyone on your network segment, usually a neighborhood-sized group of homes. Everyone shares the available bandwidth. During peak times, your access speed may slow down.
- Security could be an issue. Essentially you are on a LAN with all the neighbors in your cable segment. Thus, if you (or your cable company) don't protect your connection, theoretically you could see your neighbors' computers and they could see yours. This usually isn't a problem any more, but know that it is a possibility.
- The cost is higher. Lower-speed packages often start off at around $20–30 per month, but the ones they advertise with the great data rates can easily run you $150 a month or more.

Cable modems can be connected directly to a computer, but can also be connected to a router or wireless router just as a DSL modem. Therefore, you can share an Internet connection over a cable modem.

The choice between cable and DSL is a common one that people have to make if both are available in their area. In the end, both are going to cost about the same, and both provide similar levels of service. The decision may come down to which one you can get a better deal on or which one you feel more comfortable with.

For detailed information about cable Internet availability and performance, check out www.cablemodemhelp.com.

Integrated Services Digital Network (ISDN)

Integrated Services Digital Network (ISDN) is a digital, point-to-point network capable of maximum transmission speeds of about 2Mbps, although speeds of 128Kbps are more common. ISDN uses the same two-pair UTP wiring as POTS, but it can transmit data at much higher speeds. That's where the similarity ends. What makes ISDN different from a regular POTS line is how it uses the copper wiring. Instead of carrying an analog (voice) signal, it carries digital signals. While not nearly as fast as other broadband services, it still is considered a broadband type of access.

A computer connects to an ISDN line via an *ISDN terminal adapter* (often referred to as an *ISDN TA* or an *ISDN modem*). An ISDN terminal adapter is not an actual modem because it does not convert a digital signal to an analog signal; ISDN signals are digital. Computers also need a *network terminator* to connect to the ISDN TA, but most TAs have them built in. If you have multiple users on the network who need Internet access through the ISDN line, you need an ISDN router.

An ISDN line has two types of channels. The data is carried on a channel called a *Bearer*, or *B channel*, which can carry 64Kbps of data. The second type of channel is used for call setup and link management and is known as the *signal*, or *D channel*. This channel has only 16Kbps of bandwidth. A typical 144Kbps *basic rate interface (BRI)* ISDN line has two B channels and one D channel. One B channel can be used for a voice call while the other is being used for data transmissions, or both can be used for data. When the B channels are combined to maximize data throughput (which is common), the process is called *bonding* or *inverse multiplexing*. Multiple BRI ISDN lines can also be bonded together to form higher throughput channels.

BRI ISDN is also known as 2B+D because of the number and type of channels used. BRI ISDN is more common in Europe than it is in the United States.

You can also obtain a *Primary Rate Interface (PRI)*, also known as 23B+D, which means it has 23 B channels and one D channel. The total bandwidth of a 23B+D ISDN line is 1536Kbps (23 B channels × 64Kbps per channel + 64Kbps for the D channel). This is typically carried on a dedicated T1 connection and is fairly popular in the United States.

The main advantages of ISDN are:

- Faster connection than dial-up

- Runs over phone lines

- Flexibility. Each B channel can support voice or data. If you have a BRI ISDN connection, you can have two separate voice conversations happening at once, two datastreams, one of each, or both channels can be bridged into one.

- Easy support for video teleconferencing

- No conversion from digital to analog

However, ISDN does have a few disadvantages:

- It's more expensive than POTS.

- You need an ISDN modem and perhaps an ISDN router.

- ISDN is a type of dial-up connection and therefore the connection must be initiated. Even though it's technically dial-up, the connection is typically maintained at all times.

BRI ISDN connections were starting to become popular in home applications in the mid-to-late 1990s as an alternative to dial-up before broadband really took off. Today you'll rarely see it used in a home, but occasionally used in an office. You will find PRI ISDN to be more common in office environments. BRI rates start at about $20–40 per month, while PRI solutions typically start in the $300-per-month range.

If you need a dedicated Internet connection, which will serve as Internet-only, then one of the other broadband services is likely a better choice. If you want a line that can support both Internet and voice, and provide flexibility to go between the two, then ISDN could be the right solution (although VoIP could be as well—VoIP is discussed later in this chapter in the "Using Your Network Connections" section).

Satellite

One type of broadband Internet connection that does not get much fanfare is satellite Internet. *Satellite Internet* is not much like any other type of broadband connection. Instead of a cabled connection, it uses a satellite dish to receive data from an orbiting satellite and relay station that is connected to the Internet. Satellite connections are typically a lot slower than wired broadband connections, often maxing out at around 1Mbps.

The need for a satellite dish and the reliance upon its technology is one of the major drawbacks to satellite Internet. People who own satellite dishes will tell you that there are occasional problems due to weather and satellite alignment. You must keep the satellite dish aimed precisely at the satellite, or your signal strength (and thus your connection reliability and speed) will suffer. Plus, cloudy or stormy days can cause interference with the signal, especially if there are high winds that could blow the satellite dish out of alignment.

Another drawback to satellite technology is the delay (also called *propagation delay*), or *latency*. The delay occurs because of the length of time required to transmit the data and receive a response via the satellite. This delay (between 250 and 350 milliseconds) comes from the time it takes to transmit data the approximately 35,000 kilometers into space and return. To compare it with other types of broadband signals, cable and DSL have a delay between customer and ISP of 10 to 30 milliseconds. With standard web and e-mail traffic, this delay, while slightly annoying, is acceptable. However, with technologies like VoIP and live Internet gaming, this delay is intolerable.

Online gamers are especially sensitive to propagation delay. They often refer to it as *ping time*. The higher the ping time (in milliseconds), the worse the response time in the game is. It sometimes means the difference between winning and losing an online game.

Satellite connections are most useful when you are in an area where you can't get a wired connection, or if your Internet access needs are mobile and cellular data rates just don't cut it.

Table 18.1 summarizes the connection types we have just discussed.

TABLE 18.1   Common Internet Connection Types and Speeds

Designation	Download Speed Range	Description
POTS	2400bps to 56Kbps	Plain old telephone service. A regular analog phone line
DSL	256Kbps to 12Mbps	Digital subscriber line. Shares existing phone wires with voice service
Cable	128Kbps to 50Mbps	Inexpensive broadband Internet access method with wide availability

TABLE 18.1   Common Internet Connection Types and Speeds *(continued)*

Designation	Download Speed Range	Description
ISDN	64Kbps to 1.5Mbps	Integrated Services Digital Network. Once popular for home office Internet connections
Satellite	128Kbps to 1.5Mbps	Great for rural areas without cabled broadband methods

Choosing Internal Network Connections

Along with deciding how your computers will get to the outside world, you need to think about how your computers will communicate with each other on your internal network. The choices you make will depend on the speed you need, distance and security requirements, and cost involved with installation and maintenance. It may also depend some on the abilities of the installer or administrative staff. You may have someone who is quite capable of making replacement Category 6 cables, but making replacement fiber-optic cables is a much more daunting task. Your choices for internal connections can be lumped into two groups: wired and wireless.

Many networks today are a hybrid of wired and wireless connections. Understand the fundamentals of how each works separately; then you can understand how they work together. Every wireless connection eventually connects back to a wired network point somehow.

Wired Network Connections

Wired connections form the backbone of nearly every network in existence. Even as wireless becomes more popular, the importance of wired connections still remains strong. In general, wired networks are faster and more secure than their wireless counterparts.

When it comes to choosing a wired network connection type, you need to think about speed, distance, and cost. You learned about several types of wired connections in Chapter 10, such as coaxial, UTP, STP, and fiber-optic, but the only two you'll want to go with today are UTP and fiber. You'll run one of the two (or maybe a combination of the two) as an Ethernet star network. Table 18.2 shows a summary of the more common Ethernet standards along with the cable used, speed, and maximum distance.

TABLE 18.2   Common Ethernet Standards

Types	Cables Used	Maximum Speed	Maximum Distance
10BaseT	UTP CAT-3 and above	10Mbps	100m (~300 feet)

TABLE 18.2   Common Ethernet Standards *(continued)*

Types	Cables Used	Maximum Speed	Maximum Distance
100BaseTX	UTP CAT-5 and above	100Mbps	100m
100BaseFX	Multi-mode fiber	100Mbps	400m (~1200 feet)
1000BaseT	UTP CAT-5e and above	1Gbps	100m
10GBaseSR	Multi-mode fiber	10Gbps	26m (~80 feet)
10GBaseLR	Single mode fiber	10Gbps	25km (~16 miles)
10GBaseER	Single mode fiber	10Gbps	40km (~25 miles)
10GBaseLW	Single-mode fiber	10Gbps	10km
10GBaseT	UTP CAT-6	10Gbps	100m

The first question you need to ask yourself is, "How fast does this network need to be?" There really is no point installing a 10BaseT network these days, as even the slowest wireless LAN speeds can deliver that. For most networks, 100Mbps is probably sufficient. If the company has higher throughput requirements, then you can start looking into Gigabit Ethernet (1Gbps) or faster (up to 10Gbps).

The second question is then, "What is the maximum distance I'll need to run any one cable?" In most office environments, you can configure your network in such a way that 100 meters will get you from any connectivity device to the end user. If you need to go longer than that, you'll definitely need fiber for that connection.

As you're thinking about what type of cable you will go with, also consider the hardware you'll need too. If you are going to run fiber to the desktop, you'll need fiber network cards, routers, and switches. If you are running UTP, you need UTP network cards, routers, and switches. If you're going to run Gigabit, all of your devices need to support it.

The third question to ask yourself is, "How big of a deal is security?" Most of the time, the answer lies somewhere between "very" and "extremely!" Copper cable is pretty secure, but it does emit a signal which can be intercepted, meaning people can tap into your transmissions (hence the term *wiretap*). Fiber-optic cables are immune to wiretapping. Normally this isn't a big deal, as copper cables don't exactly broadcast your data all over like a wireless connection does. But if security is of the utmost concern, then fiber is the way to go.

Finally, ask yourself about cost. Fiber cables and hardware are more expensive than their copper counterparts. Table 18.3 summarizes your cable choices and provides characteristics of each.

Real World Scenario

Always Choose a Switch Over a Hub

The terms *hub* and *switch* are often used interchangeably, as they both provide similar types of connectivity. For most usage, not differentiating between the terms is no big deal. When it comes to the service that each provides, it can be a huge deal.

A hub is essentially a multiport repeater with no built-in intelligence. It gets a signal, it passes a signal. One of the downsides to using a hub is that if one connection on the network is slower than the others, all traffic on the network is slowed down. As an example, if you have a 10/100 hub, and all computers attached to the hub have 100Mbps-capable NICs (and CAT-5 or better cables), then the network will run at 100Mbps. But connect one NIC that only runs at 10Mbps to that hub and all traffic will slow down to that pace. You've essentially wasted money on more expensive NICs and the hub because you're not getting the speed you paid for. A second major downside to hubs is that they share bandwidth between each device, whereas switches provide the full bandwidth to each device connected to it.

A switch has the intelligence to sense the speed of each connection, and treat each connection separately. In our example, if you use a switch instead of a hub, the computers with 100Mbps capability will still run at 100Mbps, and the one computer with the slower NIC will run at 10Mbps. If given a choice, always go with a switch over a hub.

TABLE 18.3   Cable Types and Characteristics

Characteristics	Twisted-Pair	Fiber-Optic
Transmission rate	CAT-5: 100Mbps CAT-5e: 1Gbps CAT-6: 10Gbps	100Mbps or more
Maximum length	100 meters (328 feet)	>10 miles
Flexibility	Very flexible	Fair
Ease of installation	Very easy	Difficult
Connector	RJ-45	Special (SC, ST, and others)
Interference (security)	Susceptible	Not susceptible

TABLE 18.3   Cable Types and Characteristics *(continued)*

Characteristics	Twisted-Pair	Fiber-Optic
Overall cost	Inexpensive	Expensive
NIC cost	100Mbps, $15–$40 1Gbps, $30 and up	$100–$150; Server NICs can easily run $600–$800
10m cable cost	CAT-6, $12–$15 CAT-5/5e, $8–$12	Depends on mode and connector type, but generally $20–$40
8-port Switch Cost	100Mbps, $30–$100 1Gbps, $70–$400	$350 and up

Understand that the costs shown in Table 18.3 are approximate and are for illustrative purposes only. The cost for this equipment in your area may differ. Fiber has gotten considerably cheaper in the last five to ten years, but is still far more expensive than copper.

Fiber-optic cabling has some obvious advantages over copper, but as you can see it may be prohibitively expensive to run fiber to the desktop. What a lot of organizations will do is use fiber sparingly, where it is needed the most, and then run copper to the desktop. Fiber will be used in the server room and perhaps between floors of a building, as well as any place where a very long cable run is needed.

Wireless Network Connections

People love wireless networks for one major reason: convenience. Wireless connections enable a sense of freedom in users. They're not stuck to their desk, but they can work from anywhere! (I'm not sure if this is actually a good thing or not.) Wireless isn't as fast and it tends to be a bit more expensive than wired copper networks, but the convenience factor far outweighs the others.

WIRELESS LAN (WLAN)

When thinking about using wireless for network communications, the only real technology option available today is IEEE 802.11. Bluetooth and cellular (which we'll cover in just a bit) can help mobile devices communicate, but they aren't designed for full Wireless LAN (WLAN) use. Your choice becomes which 802.11 standard you want to use. Table 18.4 summarizes your options.

TABLE 18.4   802.11x Standards

Type	Frequency	Maximum Data Rate	Indoor Range	Outdoor Range
a	5GHz	54Mbps	35m	120m
b	2.4GHz	11Mbps	40m	140m
g	2.4GHz	54Mbps	40m	140m
n	2.4/5GHz	300Mbps	70m	250m

So how do you choose which one is right for your situation? You can apply the same thinking you would for a wired network, in that you need to consider speed, distance, security, and cost.

Security concerns on wireless networks are similar regardless of your choice, although n promises to have better security than its predecessors. You're broadcasting network signals through air; there will be some security concerns. The maximum range for all three established standards (a, b, and g) is about the same, so that's not likely going to sway you one way or another. It comes down to speed and cost.

The slowest and cheapest option is 802.11b. Deciding that you are going to install an 802.11b network from the ground up at this point is a bit like saying you are going to use 10BaseT. You could, but why? In fact, it might even be a challenge to find 802.11b-only devices for your network. Most devices that support 802.11b are branded as 802.11b/g (or 802.11g/b), meaning they support both network types.

Shortly after 802.11b came along, the 802.11a standard was released. Its hardware was more expensive and the technology never developed critical mass like 802.11b did. With 802.11g out there, 802.11a installations are all but dead.

That brings us to your most likely choice: 802.11g. Devices are plentiful, and all 802.11g devices are backward compatible with 802.11b ones. So if you have older wireless-B devices on your network, the new 802.11g ones will still be able to communicate with them. Network cards will run you anywhere between $20–$100, and you can get wireless access points and wireless routers for as little as around $40.

Our newest WLAN entrant is 802.11n. At the time of this writing, this standard was still under development; it is expected to be made official in early 2010. That hasn't stopped hardware manufacturers from selling 802.11n devices, though: 802.11n offers a speed upgrade over 802.11g, and it is backward compatible. Right now, 802.11n devices are more expensive than their 802.11g counterparts. In addition, there have been some cases of hardware from competing manufacturers not playing nice with each other. If you decide to go with 802.11n, it would be best to buy hardware all from the same vendor, at least until the standard is finalized.

BLUETOOTH

Bluetooth is not designed to be a WLAN, but rather a wireless personal area network (WPAN). In other words, it's not the right technology to use if you want to set up a wireless network for your office. It is, however, a great technology to use if you have wireless devices that you want your computer to be able to communicate with. Examples include the BlackBerry, mice, keyboards, headsets, and printers.

While most laptop computers now come with built-in WiFi capabilities, they don't necessarily come Bluetooth enabled. To use Bluetooth devices, you will need to add an adapter, such as the one shown in Figure 18.1.

FIGURE 18.1 Bluetooth USB adapter

There are two Bluetooth standards you might run across. Version 1.2 was adopted in 2003, and supports data rates of up to 1Mbps. Version 2.1+EDR, adopted in 2007, supports data rates of up to 3Mbps. Version 2.1+EDR is backward-compatible with older Bluetooth standards. Most mobile Bluetooth devices are Class 2 devices, which have a maximum range of 10 meters.

CELLULAR

You're probably pretty familiar with what a cell phone is, so there isn't a lot of point in discussing them here. And of course, cell phones work as a wireless network, with cell towers playing the role of the wireless hub. What you have probably noticed too is that cell phones offer much more than they used to. Instead of just offering voice communications, you can now get e-mail and Internet, and download files and applications to handheld devices. The lines between voice and data communications continue to blur, and part of the reason for that is advancement in cellular WAN technology.

To be clear, you're probably not going to set up your own cellular network unless you work for a major phone company. Cellular WAN isn't just limited to cell phones and Black-Berrys, though, you can purchase cellular WAN cards for laptops as well, usually referred to as a *cellular modem*.

The two major global standards for cellular communications in use today are *Global System for Mobile Communications (GSM)*, which is the most popular, and *Code Division Multiple Access (CDMA)*. GSM is available globally, and CDMA is available only in the United States. GSM and CDMA are not compatible with each other. Table 18.5 shows some of their key features.

TABLE 18.5 Cellular Standards

Standard	Maximum Data Rate	Range	Availability
GSM	171Kbps	35 kilometers (22 miles)	Worldwide
CDMA	3Mbps	100 kilometers (62 miles)	United States

When you choose a cellular provider, you automatically choose a standard too. If you or the people on your network are going to do a lot of worldwide travel and need mobile access, a carrier that uses GSM is the best choice. Otherwise, you'll get higher throughput rates from a carrier using CDMA.

Using Your Network Connections

People generally use their Internet connections for what you would think they use them for—to get on the Internet. Over the last 15 to 20 years, though, there has been an almost complete juxtaposition of communication lines (such as the phone line) and data, and how we utilize them.

First we had phone lines, which were great at carrying the human voice (as an analog signal) but not as efficient at dealing with data. When modems were invented, the goal was to deliver digital data over analog phone lines by modulating and demodulating the signal. Now we have no shortage of dedicated data connections, and people have been working on how to get voice communications to work across those lines. One option that we mentioned earlier is ISDN, but its limitations on data speed make those types of connections rare for home use today. Another option is VoIP, which utilizes your existing digital connection (such as a cable or DSL modem) to transmit voice.

Voice over IP, or VoIP, is a technology that is rapidly gaining acceptance. VoIP breaks up telephone conversations into data packets that are then sent over a TCP/IP network (such as the Internet). This means that the average person can make free long-distance phone calls via the Internet. A great example of this technology is the service known as Vonage. It works by connecting a telephone to a special black box that is, in turn, connected to the Internet through your home's broadband Internet connection. The box samples the voice coming in from the telephone and converts the samples into the packets that travel over the Internet to the VoIP service provider, where they are then routed to either the traditional telephone network or to another subscriber.

Installing the Network

Before you run your first cable or place your first wireless router, know exactly where everything is supposed to go on the network. The only way you'll be able to do this is to plan ahead. If you have planned the installation before you begin, the actual physical work of installing the network will be much easier.

Keys to Planning a Network

Every network is going to be somewhat different, but there are some general things to keep in mind as you go through your planning.

Get a map.   Understand the layout of the space you're installing the network in. Get a map of the office or draw one yourself. Add distances or a scale if possible so you can determine how far you'll need to run cables or how many wireless access points you'll need. Mark any potential obstacles or hazards that you may run into when you try to run cable, such as your fluorescent lights, water pipes, or cinder block walls.

Locate your server(s).   If you are installing a small network, you may not have to worry about this. But if you have a network with one or more dedicated servers, decide where they will be located. They need to be in a secured location where only authorized people have access to them. This can be anything from a small closet or an elaborate server room with raised, antistatic floors. Just make sure it's temperature controlled as server closets tend to get very hot, and we know that heat and computers don't mix well.

Identify where client computers will be.   If you are setting up an office in a cubicle farm, just assume one computer (or more, depending on the cubicle type) per cube. This will help you determine where you need shared network resources as well as cable placement.

Locate network resources.   If your network users are going to share resources such as printers, where will they be located? If there are dozens or even hundreds of users, you may need multiple printer locations or "printer banks." Locate these and other shared resources in enough places so that users don't have to walk from one end of the office to the other just to pick up printouts.

Determine how you are going to connect.   If you are going to go all wireless, you can start figuring out how many wireless routers or access points you'll need. If you are going to have wired connections, start determining how long the cable runs will be. Table 18.6 recaps some of the distances you may need to be aware of for the exam. If you need a refresher, these standards are covered in more depth in Chapter 10.

TABLE 18.6   Common Connectivity Types and Maximum Distances

Connectivity Type	Maximum Distance
Thinnet coaxial (10Base2)	185m
Thicknet coaxial (10Base5)	500m
UTP (*x*BaseT)	100m
Multi-mode fiber	Up to 400m depending on the standard
Single-mode fiber	Up to 40km depending on the standard
802.11a	35m indoors, 120m outdoors
802.11b/g	40m indoors, 140m outdoors
802.11n	70m indoors, 250m outdoors

The wireless distances are approximate, and may be lessened by obstructions such as steel beams and thick walls.

Designate additional connectivity areas if needed.   If you are running cables and some systems are outside of your maximum cable length, you will need to install a repeater of some sort. The best choice is probably a switch, which repeats signals. If you have several hundred computers, though, and you want to separate out networks, then a router is the best choice. These connectivity locations can be just a small closet. Other times, if no space is available, some administrators will put the switch in the drop ceiling. Although there is nothing wrong with this (as long as it's secured), it can be challenging to find power up there and it does make it more difficult to add to that switch.

Physical Installation

You shouldn't begin to physically install the network until all of your plans are complete and you've double-checked them. There are few things more annoying than getting halfway through an installation and determining that your plans need to change drastically. Here we'll look at installation of three groups of items: network cards, cables, and connectivity devices.

Installing and Configuring Network Interface Cards

In the old days (1980s) of personal computers, NICs were a pain to install. Not only did you have to configure the hardware manually, but you had to configure the network protocol stack manually. This usually involved a configuration program of some kind and was very cumbersome. With Windows and Plug and Play, it's much simpler.

> The CompTIA A+ exam tests your ability to install a NIC. For the exam, you must understand how to both install and configure a NIC.

INSTALLING A NIC

Before you can begin communicating on your network, you must have a NIC installed in the machine. Installing a NIC is a fairly simple task if you have installed any expansion card before; a NIC is just a special type of expansion card. In Exercise 18.1, you will learn how to install a NIC.

EXERCISE 18.1

Installing a NIC in Windows Vista and Windows XP

Follow these steps to install a NIC:

1. Power off the PC, remove the case and the metal or plastic blank covering the expansion slot opening, and insert the expansion card into an open slot.

2. Secure the expansion card with the screw provided.

Note: These first two steps may not be necessary if you have an onboard NIC.

3. Put the case back on the computer and power it up (you can run software configuration at this step, if necessary). If there are conflicts, change any parameters so that the NIC doesn't conflict with any existing hardware.

4. Install a driver for the NIC for the type of operating system that you have. Windows should autodetect the NIC and install the driver automatically. It may also ask you to provide a copy of the necessary driver if it does not recognize the type of NIC you have installed. If the card is not detected at all, run the Add New Hardware Wizard by double-clicking the Add Hardware icon in Control Panel.

5. After installing a NIC, you must hook the card to the network using the appropriate cable (if using wired connections). Attach this patch cable to the connector on the NIC and to a port in the wall (or connectivity device), thus connecting your PC to the rest of the network.

CONFIGURING A NIC

Configuring a NIC used to mean setting up an IRQ, I/O port, and base memory address. Fortunately Windows Plug and Play takes care of all of that for you now. So today, configuring a NIC generally means setting it up with the right IP address and TCP/IP configuration information.

There are two ways to do this. The first is to automatically obtain IP configuration information from a Dynamic Host Configuration Protocol (DHCP) server, if one is available on the network. The other way is to manually enter in the configuration information yourself.

If you have a small network of 10 computers or less and do not have a DHCP server, but want your computers to configure themselves automatically, set the NIC up to get its IP information from the DHCP server anyway. Microsoft Windows operating systems will automatically configure themselves with an APIPA address if they are unable to locate a DHCP server, and with the APIPA address the computers on a local network will be able to communicate with one another.

To configure your NIC, you need to open Network Connections in Control Panel. You'll see the name of a connection, such as "Local Area Connection." Right-click on that, and click Properties. Figure 18.2 shows you what this screen will look like.

On that screen, highlight Internet Protocol (TCP/IP) and click Properties. This will take you to a screen similar to the one in Figure 18.3.

As you can see in Figure 18.3, this computer is configured to obtain its information from a DHCP server. (If you have a wireless router, as many people do on their home networks, it can function as a DHCP server. We'll talk more about that in a few sections.) If you wanted to configure the client manually, you would click Use The Following IP Address and enter in the correct information. To supply the client with a DNS server address automatically, click Use The Following DNS Server Address.

FIGURE 18.2   Local Area Connection properties

FIGURE 18.3   TCP/IP properties

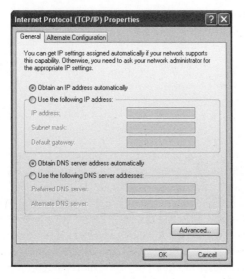

If you manually configure the IP address, you must also configure the DNS server address manually. Otherwise, the client will not have access to a DNS server. Client computers can broadcast to find a DHCP server, but they cannot broadcast to find a DNS server.

WIRELESS CARD INSTALLATION

Installing a wireless NIC is just like installing a normal, wired NIC. The only difference is in the configuration of the NIC. You must configure the NIC to connect to your preferred wireless network (by its SSID) and configure any security settings (such as wireless encryption keys).

To configure a wireless card under Windows XP or Vista, you must first install the wireless card. For a desktop, this means powering off the computer, removing the case cover, and inserting the card into an open slot (assuming the wireless card expansion card type and bus slot type match). Then you can power the computer back up, and the computer should recognize that a new card was installed and prompt you to install the driver.

On a laptop, simply insert the wireless PC Card into any open PC Card slot with the laptop powered up. Once you have done this, Windows will recognize the card and ask you to install the driver. With the Intel Centrino (or any laptop with integrated wireless), no external adapter needs to be added, but you might need to use a key combination to enable the antenna. USB-attached NICs are an option for modern computers of all types.

For both a desktop and a laptop, once Windows recognizes the card, it will prompt you to search for the card's driver, as it does with the installation of other hardware, or it will use a distribution driver for the card. This is common for devices that Microsoft knew about before publishing the operating system. You can then proceed as with other expansion cards that have more complex installation methods. If prompted, insert the driver disc and let Windows finish installing the driver.

Once the driver is installed, you may have to reboot (but only in very unique cases). Then the wireless card should be ready to use.

Bear in mind that these are general steps. Always consult the documentation that comes with the hardware to ensure that there isn't a special step that is unique to that card.

WIRELESS CONNECTION CONFIGURATION

Now that your wireless card is installed in your computer, you can configure the connection so you can use it. Windows XP and Vista are beautiful for wireless use because they have utilities for connecting to wireless networks built into the operating system. Windows uses the Wireless Zero Configuration Service to automatically connect to wireless access points using IEEE 802.11 protocols (WiFi).

To configure a wireless connection, you can simply bring a Windows XP or Vista laptop or computer within range of a wireless access point, and Windows will detect the presence of an access point and alert you to its presence. Alternatively, if you would like control over the connection, you can open the network control panel (Start ➢ Control Panel ➢ Network Connections), right-click on the wireless card, and choose View Available Wireless Connections. This will bring up the screen shown in Figure 18.4.

From this screen you can view the SSIDs of the available wireless networks, including the one to which you are connected (the one that says "Connected" next to it). The bars in the far-right column indicate the relative signal strength of each connection. The more green bars showing, the stronger the signal, and the better (and faster) the connection.

FIGURE 18.4   Available wireless connections

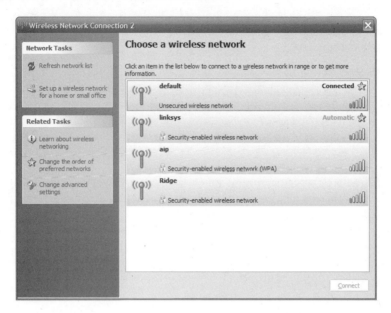

 If the connection shows a lock icon underneath it, it is a secured wireless network and you will need to enter some sort of password to gain access to that network.

To connect to any network, double-click on it, and Windows will try to connect to that network. You'll see a window similar to the one in Figure 18.5 that shows you the connection is in process. Once you are connected, Windows will display "Connected" next to that connection.

FIGURE 18.5   Connecting to a wireless network

 The weaker the signal, the longer the connection will take.

Installing Network Cables

Network cables are not the most fun thing to install. Proper installation of network cables generally means running cables through ceilings and walls and making a mess of the office. Thank goodness for wireless!

WARNING Be sure to use plenum cable if you are running cables through spaces where there is air ventilation, such as drop ceilings. PVC-coated cables will produce poisonous gas when burned. Also be sure that you have the proper permission to run the cables, and that you aren't violating any building codes.

If you are installing a wired network in an existing office space, you may want to look into hiring out the cable installation to a third party. You'll find many companies that have the tools needed to properly install a wired network.

When installing a wired network yourself, always be aware of the maximum cable lengths, as outlined in Table 18.6. In addition, utilize cable troughs in ceilings and walls, or other conduit in walls to keep your cables organized. Figure 18.6 shows a cable trough; they come in a variety of lengths and quality.

FIGURE 18.6 Cable trough

Finally, if you must run cables across the floor in a walkway (which isn't recommended), use a floor cable guard to avoid creating a trip hazard and to protect your cables. A floor cable guard is shown in Figure 18.7.

FIGURE 18.7 Floor cable guard

When running cables through a ceiling, never run the cables directly across fluorescent lights. These lights emit electromagnetic radiation (EMI) that can interfere with network communications. Utilize your cable troughs to keep cables in one place and away from lights.

Installing and Configuring Wireless Access Points and Wireless Routers

Instead of using switches and hubs, wireless networks use either a *wireless access point (WAP)* or a *wireless router* to provide central connectivity. A WAP functions essentially like a wireless hub, whereas wireless routers provide more functionality, similar to that of a wired router. Based on looks alone, they are pretty much identical and physically installing them is similar. The differences come in configuring them, as they will have different options.

In this section, we're going to talk about installing and configuring WAPs and wireless routers interchangeably; just remember that a lot of the features available in a wireless router may not be available in a WAP.

PHYSICALLY INSTALLING A WIRELESS ACCESS POINT OR ROUTER

After unwrapping the device from its packaging (and reading the instructions, of course), you must choose a place for the unit. If it is supplying wireless access to your home network and the Internet, locate it where you can receive access in the most places. Keep in mind that the more walls the signal has to travel through, the lower the signal strength.

In addition, you may choose to have some computers plug directly into the device using a CAT-5 or other UTP cable. If so, it makes sense to locate the device near the computer or computers you will want to physically connect.

Place the WAP in the center of your home, close to a network connection. Or if you have only one computer, place it close to the broadband Internet connection you are using (i.e., the cable modem or DSL line).

In many offices, WAPs and wireless routers are often placed in the ceiling, with the antennae pointed downward through holes in the ceiling tiles. You can purchase metal plates designed to replace ceiling tiles to hold these devices. The plates have holes precut in them for the antennae to stick through, are designed to securely hold the device, easily open for maintenance, and often lock for physical security.

For wireless connectivity devices placed in a ceiling (or other places with no easy access to an electrical outlet), *Power over Ethernet (PoE)* is a very handy technology to supply both power and an Ethernet connection.

Once you have chosen the location, plug the unit into a wall outlet and connect the two antennae that come with the unit (as needed). They will screw onto two bungs on the back of the unit. Once the unit is plugged in, you need to connect it to the rest of your network.

If you are connecting directly to the Internet through a cable modem or DSL or to a wired hub or router, you will most likely plug the cable into the Internet socket of the device, provided it has one. If not, you can use any of the other wired ports on the back of the device to connect to the rest of your network. Make sure that you get a link light on that connection.

At this point, the device is configured for a home network, with a few basic caveats. First, the default SSID (for example, Linksys) will be used, along with the default administrative password and the default IP addressing scheme. Also, there will be no encryption on the connection, but if you have nothing to protect, except for the Internet connection, you can leave that off. This is known as an *open access point*. Many wireless manufacturers have made their devices so easy to configure that for most networks it is Plug and Play.

WARNING   If you have personal data on your home network and more than one computer, you should never keep the default settings. Anyone could snoop your access point from the road in front of or behind your house and possibly get on your home network. It's too easy for identity theft!

From a computer on the home network, insert the device's setup CD into the computer's CD-ROM drive. It will automatically start and present you with a wizard that will walk you through setting the name of the SSID of this new access point, as well as changing the default setup password, setting any security keys (encryption keys, or WEP keys) for this connection, and generally configuring the unit for your network's specific configuration. Then you're done!

CONFIGURING A WIRELESS ACCESS POINT OR ROUTER

Each access point manufacturer uses different software, but you can usually configure their parameters with the built-in, web-based configuration utility that's included with the product. If not, your manual will instruct you on how to configure the device. The items that require configuration depend on the choices you make about your wireless network. The parameter that needs immediate attention is the *service-set identifier (SSID)*.

An SSID is a unique name given to the wireless network. All hardware that is to participate on the network must be configured to use the same SSID. Essentially, the SSID is the network name. When you are using Windows to connect to a wireless network, all available wireless networks will be listed by their SSID when you select View Available Wireless Networks.

When you first install the wireless network, the default SSID is used, and there is no security enabled. In other words, it's pretty easy to find your network (Linksys) and anyone within distance of your signal can get on your network with no password required. This is obviously a security risk. Let's look at how to change that and other parameters you'll want to modify.

For the rest of this example, we'll use a Linksys WRT54G wireless router. First, you need to log in to your device. The default internal address of the router is 192.168.1.1, so to log in, open Internet Explorer (or your preferred Internet browser) and type **192.168.1.1** into the address bar. You'll get a screen similar to the one in Figure 18.8.

You should have already set up the username and password using the CD provided with the device. If not, look in the manual for the default username and password. You'll definitely want to change these as soon as possible. Once you're logged in, the first screen you'll see is similar to the one in Figure 18.9. On this screen, you can see two basic sections along the left-hand side: Internet Setup and Network Setup. The Internet Setup portion identifies how you configure your incoming connection from the ISP. In most cases, your cable or DSL provider will just have you use DHCP to get an external IP address from their DHCP server, but there are options to configure this manually as well. The hostname is the name of your device, and some ISPs require you put in a domain name as well. If it's needed, they will tell you what to put in.

FIGURE 18.8   Logging in to the wireless router

FIGURE 18.9   Basic setup screen

The Network Setup portion lets you configure your router's internal IP address, in this case 192.168.1.1, and subnet mask. On this router, DHCP is also configured on this screen. If you want the device to act as a DHCP server for internal clients, enable it here, specify the starting IP address, and specify the maximum number of DHCP users. (Author's note: I just realized that I have my router set up to allow 50 DHCP leases at once. In my home, I have three computers that connect to my network and need a DHCP lease, so having it set to 50 is overkill. I should probably change that!) Disabling DHCP makes your network a bit more secure, as random clients can't obtain an IP address automatically. Disabling DHCP means that clients will have to use a static IP address.

Most wireless routers (like the one used in this example) describe the settings on the configuration pages to the right of the setting. So if you're not totally sure what the setting does, you may get some help from the information on the right. If not, there's always the manual or online help!

By clicking on the Wireless tab, you'll be taken to the Basic Wireless Settings screen, as shown in Figure 18.10.

FIGURE 18.10   Basic Wireless Settings screen

There are a couple of critical settings here. The first is your SSID. Always change it from the default to something else. The second is the Wireless SSID Broadcast. By default this is enabled, which means that anyone within range can detect your signal and see your SSID. By disabling this, your router no longer broadcasts the SSID. This is highly recommended as it increases security.

Disabling your SSID broadcast makes you far less susceptible to "wardriving," which is when someone drives through your neighborhood looking for a wireless signal. If you're not broadcasting, you're not as likely to be found.

Still on the Wireless tab, under the Wireless Security section, you'll find more key configuration options. The first is the security mode. In Figure 18.11, this router is configured to use WEP at 64-bit encryption. You can see the four WEP keys the system generated.

FIGURE 18.11   Wireless Security section

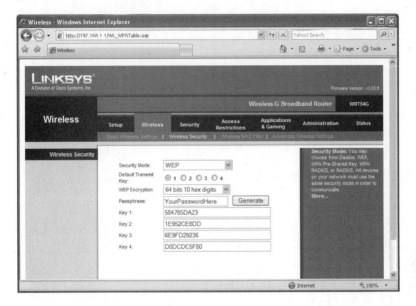

If security is enabled, and you are using WEP, the client will be required to know the passphrase as well as the WEP key to connect to the wireless router. As we discussed in Chapter 10, though, WEP is not very secure (again, something I should change!). Changing from WEP 64-bit to WEP 128-bit will help, but WEP is still a problem. Many routers will also let you choose other security methods, such as WPA, which is more secure. Another option may be for you to use a RADIUS server for security purposes.

Remote Authentication Dial-In User Service (RADIUS) is a service that provides centralized authentication on a network. For your wireless router to use RADIUS, you need to have a RADIUS server on your network. The A+ exam won't test you on RADIUS, but other exams such as Network+ will.

The last section we'll look at on the Security tab is Wireless MAC Filter, shown in Figure 18.12. Enabling the wireless MAC filter is another great option to improve the security of your wireless network. By doing so, and choosing the Permit Only option, you can configure the MAC addresses that are allowed to obtain a wireless connection with your router.

If you choose to enable this, you will also need to specify the MAC addresses allowed to use the router (or not use the router, if you chose Prevent PCs). To do so, click the Edit MAC Filter List button.

Most wireless routers also provide you with some level of firewall protection. On this router, the firewall options are on the Security tab, as shown in Figure 18.13.

FIGURE 18.12 Wireless MAC Filter section

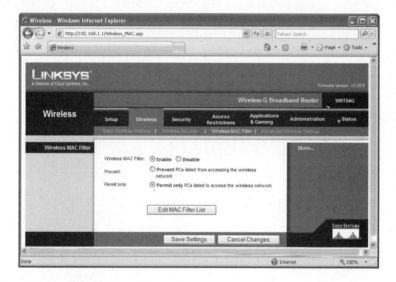

FIGURE 18.13 Firewall options

Changing the password periodically, just as with changing your network login password or email password, is a good idea to improve security. On this router, changing your password is done on the Administration tab, in the Management section, as shown in Figure 18.14.

Finally, Figure 18.15 shows you how to upgrade the router's firmware. You will first have to download the updated firmware from the manufacturer's website and save it to a local computer. Then you can update the firmware from this screen.

FIGURE 18.14 Setting the router password

FIGURE 18.15 Updating the firmware

Real World Scenario

Sharing an Internet Connection

Wireless routers have many advantages over wireless access points. One of the biggest advantages is the ability to share an Internet connection. By doing this you pay for only one connection, but you can connect as many computers as you would like (or is reasonable) to your wireless router. Here is how to do that.

First, ensure your DSL modem or cable modem is connected properly. Then, connect your wireless router to your cable modem or DSL modem using a UTP cable (CAT-5 or better). In most cases, the wireless router will have a wired Internet port on the back of it. Connect the cable here and plug it into your broadband modem. Finally, you can connect computers to your wireless router.

Many ISPs, in an attempt to prohibit this sort of behavior, will restrict access through the modem to one MAC address. This isn't a problem. You can do one of two things. The first option is, when you first make your connection to the ISP, just make sure that your computer is already connected through your router. The ISP will see the MAC address of the router and assume that is your computer. The second option is that most wireless routers will allow you to clone your computer's MAC address (see the following graphic). Your router will simply tell the ISP that it has the same MAC address as your computer, which was previously connected directly to the cable or DSL modem. ISPs may not like it, but sharing a wireless Internet connection is very economical option for a small office or home network.

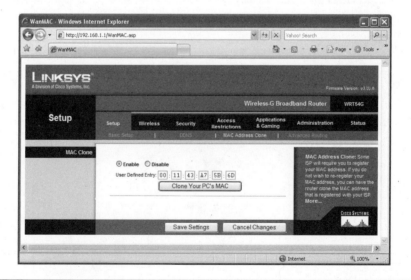

Understanding Firewall Basics

A *firewall* is a hardware or software solution that serves as your network's security guard. For networks that are connected to the Internet, they're probably the most important device on the network. Firewalls can protect you in two ways. They protect your network resources from hackers lurking in the dark corners of the Internet, and they can simultaneously prevent computers on your network from accessing undesirable content on the Internet. At a basic level, firewalls filter packets based on rules defined by the network administrator.

Firewalls can be stand-alone "black boxes," software installed on a server or router, or some combination of hardware and software. Most firewalls will have at least two network connections: one to the Internet, or *public side*, and one to the internal network, or *private side*. Some firewalls have a third network port for a second semi internal network. This port is used to connect servers that can be considered both public and private, such as web and e-mail servers. This intermediary network is known as a *demilitarized zone (DMZ)*. Personal software-based firewalls will run on computers with only one NIC.

Types of Firewalls

We've already stated that firewalls can be software or hardware based, or a combination of both. Keeping that in mind, there are two general categories of firewalls: network based and host based.

Network-Based Firewalls

A *network-based firewall* is what companies use to protect their private network from public networks. The defining characteristic of this type of firewall is that it's designed to protect an entire network of computers instead of just one system. It's generally a stand-alone hardware device with specialized software installed on it to protect your network.

Host-Based Firewalls

In contrast to network-based firewalls, a *host-based firewall* is implemented on a single machine so it only protects that one machine. This type of firewall is usually a software implementation because you don't need any additional hardware in your personal computer to run it. All current Windows client operating systems come with Windows Firewall, which is a great example of a host-based solution. Host-based firewalls are generally not as secure as network firewalls, but for small businesses or home use they're an adequate, cheap solution.

How Firewalls Work

Firewalls are configured to allow only packets that pass specific security restrictions to get through them. They can also permit, deny, encrypt, decrypt, and proxy all traffic that flows through them, most commonly between the public and private parts of a network. The network administrator decides on and sets up the rules a firewall follows when deciding to forward data packets or reject them.

The default configuration of a firewall is generally *default deny*, which means that all traffic is blocked unless specifically authorized by the administrator. While this is very secure, it's also time consuming to configure the device to allow legitimate traffic to flow through it. The other option is *default allow*, which means all traffic is allowed through unless the administrator denies it. If you have a default allow firewall and don't configure it, you might as well not have a firewall at all.

The basic method of configuring firewalls is to use an *access control list (ACL)*. The ACL is the set of rules that determines which traffic gets through the firewall and which traffic is blocked. ACLs are typically configured to block traffic by IP address, port number, domain name, or some combination of all three. How you configure your ACLs is sometimes referred to as *port assignment* or setting up rules.

Packets that meet the criteria in the ACL are passed through the firewall to their destination. This is known as *port forwarding*. For example, let's say you have a computer on your internal network that is set up as a web server. To allow Internet clients to access the system, you need to allow data on port 80 (HTTP) to get to that computer.

The final concept you may be tested on in the A+ exam is *port triggering*. Port triggering is essentially an automated form of port forwarding. It allows traffic to enter the network on a specific port after a computer makes an outbound request on that specific port. For example, if a computer on your internal network makes an outbound Telnet request (port 23), subsequent inbound traffic destined for the originating computer on port 23 would be allowed through.

Troubleshooting Client-Side Connectivity Issues

As a technician you are going to be called on to solve a variety of issues, including hardware, software, and networking problems. Networking problems can sometimes be the most tricky to solve, considering that it could be either a software or a hardware problem or a combination of the two causing your connectivity issue.

The first adage for troubleshooting any hardware problem is to check your connections. That holds true for networking as well, but then your troubleshooting will need to go far deeper than that in a hurry. As with troubleshooting anything else, follow a logical procedure when troubleshooting and be sure to document your work. For a refresher of the troubleshooting process, see Chapter 8.

Connectivity issues, when not caused by hardware, are generally the result of a messed-up configuration. And since the most common protocol in use today, TCP/IP, has a lot of configuration options, you can see how easy it is to configure something incorrectly. In this section, we'll look at troubleshooting TCP/IP settings and protocols, using some client-side connectivity troubleshooting tools, and troubleshooting proxy and firewall settings.

Troubleshooting TCP/IP Settings

TCP/IP is something most of us use every day. In fact, some of us have a hard time living without it, being deprived of our online oxygen. When it's working like it's supposed to,

TCP/IP is a reliable and flexible protocol that satisfies most of our networking needs. When it doesn't work, though, it can be challenging to troubleshoot because of its complexity. The key is to understand what is working and what isn't to narrow down the problem, and then look for the right solution. To help you with that, we'll break down TCP/IP into some smaller components to understand how each one works and what you may need to keep in mind when solving problems.

Basic TCP/IP Settings

Each computer or device that wants to participate on a TCP/IP network needs a unique *IP address* on that network. If two or more devices have the same IP address, you will run into communication problems. These problems can be challenging to track down, as they usually manifest themselves as intermittent connectivity problems. The good news is, Windows and most other operating systems will give you a pop-up warning if it detects another system on the same network with the same IP address.

The second piece of required information to communicate on a TCP/IP network is the *subnet mask*. As you learned in Chapter 10, the subnet mask defines the network address for the computer. For example, a computer using the address 172.16.10.1 with a mask of 255.255.0.0 will have a network address of 172.16.0.0. If it sends a message to any other computer with a 172.16.*x*.*x* address, it will assume that computer is on the same local network. If the computer it's sending the message to is on another network, the packets get sent to the default gateway.

That brings us to our third standard (but not required) component: the *default gateway*. The default gateway is the door out of your local network and onto another network, perhaps the Internet. In physical terms, the default gateway is generally a router that takes you off your local network segment. If all you have is one network segment with no connectivity to any other networks, you do not need to configure a default gateway.

Using these three settings, let's look at a few common troubleshooting scenarios. Your computer is using the address 172.16.10.1 with a mask of 255.255.0.0. It is sending to computer 172.16.100.2. Looking at these addresses, you can see that both of them are supposed to be on the 172.16.0.0 network. But what if the 100.2 host is configured with a subnet mask of 255.255.255.0? Because of the incorrect mask, the 100.2 host will believe that the network address is *really* 172.16.100.0, meaning that it thinks it's on a different network than your computer. Your computer will send messages to that computer without a problem, but you will not receive messages back, as the 100.2 host will be sending messages to the default gateway bound for an external network.

 Really, anything other than 255.255.0.0 will cause a problem in the example here, but using 255.255.255.0 made the case easy to describe.

Here's another scenario. Let's say that again, your computer is using the address 172.16.10.1 with a mask of 255.255.0.0, and the internal IP address of your router is 172.16.1.1. For some reason your default gateway gets set at 172.16.1.100. When you send messages to computers on your local network, such as 176.16.10.2, you're fine. But when you try to get on the Internet, or send messages to a computer on another subnet, your communication times out. This is because your default gateway is wrong and messages aren't being sent to the router. Local subnet communications will be fine, but you won't be able to talk to any computers outside your network.

The bottom line? Always make sure that the IP address, subnet mask, and default gateway are configured properly.

DNS

Domain Name System (DNS) provides great utility on networks, especially the Internet. Running on a DNS server, DNS resolves hostnames to IP addresses to facilitate communication. When you type **www.google.com** into your browser, DNS translates that into an IP address so the computers can talk to each other.

If you want to use DNS, your computer needs to be configured with the address of one or more DNS servers. Two is recommended, just in case the first one fails or is overloaded. If your clients get TCP/IP configuration information from a DHCP server, the DHCP server can also provide this address. If your clients are configured manually, then you need to enter this address too.

If your client is unable to get to a website, there are a few ways to see what the problem is. First, check to see if they can get to a different website. Google not responding? Check Microsoft.com or another harmless site to see if it responds. If it does, odds are that the first site is having temporary problems. If not, use the ping utility (which we'll talk about in a bit) to ping the website name. It will give you one of three responses: a valid reply indicating that the site is up; a request time-out, which may indicate that the site is down; or a message saying it was unable to resolve the hostname. If you get the third one, it could be a DNS problem. Double-check the configuration on the client to ensure it has the right IP address.

DHCP

Dynamic Host Configuration Protocol (DHCP) is another wonderful invention that makes network administration much easier. DHCP is a server-based utility that sends out TCP/IP configuration information to client computers. You can use a DHCP server to provide clients with an IP address, subnet mask, default gateway, DNS server, and a plethora of other information. This is referred to as *dynamic addressing*. If you instead type all of that information into a client manually, that is called *static addressing*.

From the client side, the first thing to check is to see if the system is enabled as a DHCP client. On your TCP/IP properties screen, you will see something like the setting in Figure 18.16.

Properly configured DHCP clients will be set to obtain an IP address automatically. When the system boots up, it will broadcast for a DHCP server to provide it with IP configuration information. If the DHCP server is available, it will respond. If no DHCP server is available, the client computer may configure itself with an automatic address.

Because DHCP requests are broadcasts, they do not get passed through routers. This can cause problems if your DHCP server is on one side of a router and the client is on the other side. A fix for this is to have a *DHCP proxy* or *DHCP relay* available, which is a service that can be installed on the router or on a server on the non-DHCP server side. The DHCP proxy will intercept DHCP broadcast requests and forward them directly to the DHCP server.

FIGURE 18.16   A DHCP-enabled client

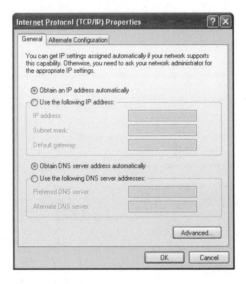

Automatic Private IP Addressing

Automatic Private IP Addressing (APIPA) is a TCP/IP standard used to automatically configure IP-based hosts that are unable to reach a DHCP server. APIPA addresses are in the 169.254.0.0 range with a subnet mask of 255.255.0.0. If you see a computer that has an IP address beginning with 169.254, you know that it has configured itself.

Typically the only time you will see this is when a computer is supposed to receive configuration information from a DHCP server, but for some reason that server is unavailable. Even while configured with this address, the client will continue to broadcast for a DHCP server, so it can be given a real address once the server becomes available.

APIPA is also sometimes known as *zero configuration networking*, or *address auto-configuration*. If you are setting up a small local area network that had no need to communicate with any networks outside of itself, you can use APIPA to your advantage. Set the client computers to automatically receive DHCP addresses, but don't set up a DHCP server. The clients will configure themselves and be able to communicate with each other using TCP/IP. In Microsoft implementations, this is limited to 10 addresses.

NAT

Network Address Translation (NAT) is the process of translating private, nonroutable IP addresses into public IP addresses. There are three ranges of private, nonroutable IP addresses, as shown in Table 18.7.

TABLE 18.7 Private IP Address Ranges

Class	IP Address Range	Subnet Mask	Number of Hosts
A	10.0.0.0–10.255.255.255	255.0.0.0	16.7 million
B	172.16.0.0–172.31.255.255	255.255.0.0	1 million
C	192.168.0.0–192.168.255.255	255.255.255.0	65,536

These private addresses are not allowed to be used on the Internet and cannot be routed. The fact that they are nonroutable is actually an advantage, as a network administrator can use these addresses to essentially hide an entire network from the Internet.

This is how it works. The network administrator sets up a NAT-enabled router, which functions as the default gateway to the Internet. The external interface of the router has a live, public IP address provided by the ISP, such as 155.120.100.1. The internal interface will have an administrator-assigned address within one of these ranges, such as 192.168.1.1. All computers on the internal network will then also need to be on the 192.168.1.0 network. To the outside world, any request coming from the internal network will appear to come from 155.120.100.1. The NAT router translates all incoming packets and sends them to the appropriate client. This type of setup is very common today.

You may look at your own computer, which has an address in a private range, and wonder, "If it's nonroutable, then how am I on the Internet?" Remember, the NAT router technically makes the Internet request on your computer's behalf, and the NAT router is using a live IP address.

 Don't make the mistake of thinking that if your internal network is using private addresses through NAT that it can't be hacked. It can. Hackers just have to use more tools and try a little harder to uncover your internal structure. Even if you're using NAT, you still need protective features such as firewalls and anti-malware software.

Loopback Address

The IP address of 127.0.0.1 is reserved as the *loopback address*. It's used to test basic TCP/IP functionality for your network card. If you're having trouble connecting to any other computer using TCP/IP, you can type **ping 127.0.0.1** to test your network card. If you get an error message back, it could indicate a bad network card or a bad TCP/IP installation.

In hindsight, it is probably pretty silly that the designers of TCP/IP wasted an entire Class A address space for just one IP address. In fairness to them, though, how could they have envisioned how widespread the use of TCP/IP would become? Still, this is an address you need to memorize, and know that you can't use the 127 network address space for computers on your network.

Specific TCP/IP Protocols

Each TCP/IP-related protocol at the Process/Application layer of the DOD model uses a unique port number to communicate. In addition, many protocols require special configuration. In this section we'll look at some protocols that are tested on the A+ exam, including three e-mail protocols, one file transfer protocol, and two secure connection protocols.

SMTP

The first e-mail protocol we'll look at is *Simple Mail Transfer Protocol (SMTP)*. It operates on TCP port 25, and is used to send e-mail to an e-mail server. As it's designed to send only, it's referred to as a *push protocol*. An e-mail client locates its e-mail server by querying the DNS server for an MX (mail exchange) record. After locating the server, SMTP is used to push the message to the e-mail server.

You probably won't run into a lot of problems using SMTP. One of the most common issues is if you're using a firewall but the administrator has closed TCP port 25. In addition, if the DNS server is unavailable or doesn't have a correct MX entry, sending e-mail will fail.

POP

The first protocol commonly used to retrieve e-mail from e-mail servers is *Post Office Protocol (POP)*. The most current version of POP is POP3, which operates on TCP port 110. While popular, many e-mail clients choose to use IMAP instead as it supports more features than POP3.

IMAP

The second protocol commonly used to retrieve e-mail from e-mail servers is *Internet Message Access Protocol (IMAP)*. The e-mail client chooses which protocol to use in order to retrieve e-mail. Most current e-mail clients, such as Microsoft Outlook and Gmail, are configured to be able to use either IMAP or POP3.

The current version of IMAP is IMAP4, and it operates on TCP port 143. IMAP has some advantages over POP3. One of them is that IMAP works in connected and disconnected modes. With POP3, the client makes a connection to the e-mail server, downloads the e-mail, and then terminates the connection. IMAP allows the client to remain connected to the e-mail server after the download, meaning that as soon as another e-mail enters the inbox IMAP notifies the e-mail client and is ready to download it. Another advantage is that IMAP allows multiple clients to be simultaneously connected to the same inbox. This can be useful for BlackBerry users who have both Outlook and their BlackBerry operational at the same time, or for cases where multiple users monitor the same mailbox, such as on a customer service account. IMAP allows each connected user or client to see changes made to messages on the server in real time.

FTP

A protocol optimized for sending and managing files over an Internet connection is the *File Transfer Protocol (FTP)*. If you have ever downloaded a file from the Internet, odds are you've used FTP whether or not you realized it. FTP servers listen for incoming requests on TCP port 21. In addition, most FTP connections require the use of TCP port 20 for sending data. If on the test you're asked for one port that FTP uses, go with 21, but realize that in the real world you need to make sure TCP port 20 is open too.

Users typically log in to an FTP server in order to download files. In cases where the FTP server is secured, this means entering a correct username and password. If you are using a third-party FTP tool, it will prompt you for credentials. If you are using a browser such as Internet Explorer to connect via FTP, the correct syntax in the address window is `ftp://username:password@ftp.ftpsite.com`.

> In Windows Vista and XP, you can type a URL such as the one in the ftp example into the Run box to connect as well.

Many public FTP servers are set up to allow anonymous access. In order to log in, use the username of **anonymous** and provide an e-mail address as the password. Of course, there is no rule stating that you have to use your real e-mail address, but the FTP site administrators would prefer that you do.

FTP can be a little tricky to use through firewalls. Not only does FTP require two ports (20 and 21) to establish the connection and send data, but most FTP requests result in FTP opening an arbitrary higher-numbered port (such as 13426) to transfer the data. Most current firewalls are capable of dealing with this, as they are what is known as *stateful firewalls*. A stateful firewall (as opposed to a *stateless firewall*) keeps track of all data associated with one specific connection. In other words, when FTP decides to open the arbitrary port, the stateful firewall responds by allowing data to go through that arbitrary port because it's associated with the connection established on port 21. A stateless firewall doesn't have this intelligence, and the data transfer will most likely fail.

One other interesting dilemma with FTP and firewalls has to do with large file transfers. During the file transfer, the control port (21) will remain idle as data is transferred. If the file transfer lasts too long, the firewall may determine that the connection has timed out and terminate the session on port 21. This could cause the transfer to fail and the client to receive an error message. Again, data transfers through a stateful firewall shouldn't run into this problem, but be aware that it could exist.

SSH

The *Secure Shell (SSH)* protocol was developed to allow encrypted data exchange between two computers. It was originally designed to be a replacement for the insecure Telnet command,

and it operates on TCP port 22. A common client interface using SSH is called OpenSSH (www.openssh.com).

The problem with Telnet and other insecure remote management comments (such as rcp and ftp) is that the data they transmit, including passwords, is sent in plain text. Anyone eavesdropping on the line can intercept the packets and thus obtain usernames and passwords. SSH overcomes this by encrypting the traffic, including usernames and passwords.

HTTPS

The protocol used for most Internet traffic, *Hypertext Transfer Protocol (HTTP)*, is not secure. An alternative is *Hypertext Transfer Protocol Secure (HTTPS)*, which is secure. HTTP uses port 80, and HTTPS uses port 443 by default. Network administrators can specify an alternate port for HTTPS use if they so choose. HTTPS connections are secured using either *Secure Sockets Layer (SSL)* or *Transport Layer Security (TLS)*.

From the client side, the most common error you will encounter is users not knowing what the proper context is. To access most websites, we use **http://** in the address bar. To get to a site using HTTPS, you need to use **https://** instead.

Do not enter any sensitive personal information into a website if the address begins with just http://. You're just asking for someone to steal the information. Sites using HTTPS are much more secure.

Using Client-Side Tools

You should have a good knowledge of diagnostic procedures and the ability to recognize the right tool to use for a particular situation. In addition to knowing the purpose of each of the utilities discussed here, you should be able to recognize the output that they provide and be able to identify the tool used just by looking at that output.

In this section, we will look at common tools, followed by a list of some of the symptoms of common problems you are likely to encounter during your days as a technician.

CompTIA also expects you to be familiar with cable-testing devices. This is a broad category of any type of device that can isolate a break or problem with a cable or termination.

PING **Command**

The PING command is one of the most useful commands in the TCP/IP protocol. It sends a series of packets to another system, which in turn sends back a response. This utility can be extremely useful for troubleshooting problems with remote hosts. Pings are also called ICMP echo requests/replies, as they use the ICMP protocol.

The PING command indicates whether the host can be reached and how long it took for the host to send a return packet. Across wide area network links, the time value will be much larger than across healthy LAN links.

The syntax for PING is **ping *hostname*** or **ping *IP address***. Figure 18.17 shows what a ping should look like.

FIGURE 18.17   A successful ping

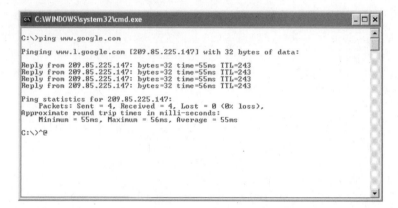

As you can see, by pinging with the hostname, we found the host's IP address thanks to DNS. The time is how long in milliseconds it took to receive the response. On a LAN you want this to be 10ms or less, but 55ms for an Internet ping isn't too bad.

There are several options for the PING command, and you can see them all by typing **ping /?** at the command prompt. Table 18.8 lists some of the more useful ones.

TABLE 18.8   PING Options

Option	Function
-t	Persistent ping. Will ping the remote host until stopped by the client (by using Ctrl+C)
-n *count*	Specifies the number of echo requests to send
-l *size*	Specifies the packet size to send

Some webmasters have configured their routers to block pings in order to avoid problems such as someone trying to eat up bandwidth with a *ping of death* (sending a persistent ping with a huge buffer to overwhelm the recipient). For example, if you ping www.microsoft.com you won't get a response, even though the site is functional.

TRACERT Command

Tracert (trace route) is a command-line utility that enables you to verify the route to a remote host. Execute the command TRACERT *hostname*, where *hostname* is the computer name or IP address of the computer whose route you want to trace. Tracert returns the different IP addresses the packet was routed through to reach the final destination. The results also include the number of hops needed to reach the destination. If you execute the TRACERT command without any options, you see a help file that describes all the TRACERT switches.

This utility determines the intermediary steps involved in communicating with another IP host. It provides a road map of all the routing an IP packet takes to get from host A to host B.

Timing information from TRACERT can be useful for detecting a malfunctioning or overloaded router. Figure 18.18 shows what a TRACERT output looks like.

FIGURE 18.18   TRACERT output

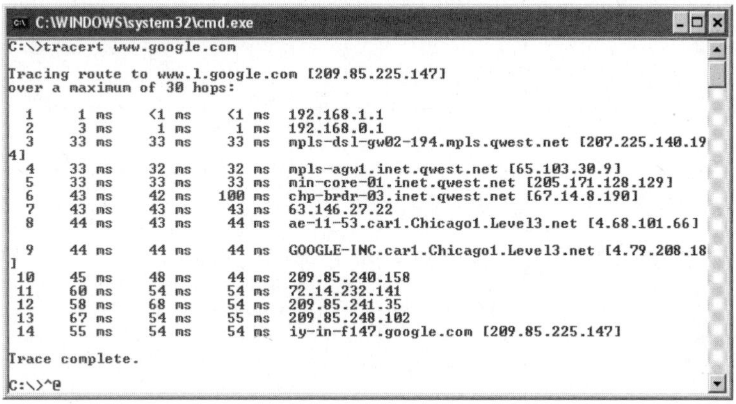

```
C:\WINDOWS\system32\cmd.exe

C:\>tracert www.google.com

Tracing route to www.l.google.com [209.85.225.147]
over a maximum of 30 hops:

  1     1 ms    <1 ms    <1 ms  192.168.1.1
  2     3 ms     1 ms     1 ms  192.168.0.1
  3    33 ms    33 ms    33 ms  mpls-dsl-gw02-194.mpls.qwest.net [207.225.140.19
4]
  4    33 ms    32 ms    32 ms  mpls-agw1.inet.qwest.net [65.103.30.9]
  5    33 ms    33 ms    33 ms  min-core-01.inet.qwest.net [205.171.128.129]
  6    43 ms    42 ms   100 ms  chp-brdr-03.inet.qwest.net [67.14.8.190]
  7    43 ms    43 ms    43 ms  63.146.27.22
  8    44 ms    43 ms    44 ms  ae-11-53.car1.Chicago1.Level3.net [4.68.101.66]

  9    44 ms    44 ms    44 ms  GOOGLE-INC.car1.Chicago1.Level3.net [4.79.208.18
]
 10    45 ms    48 ms    44 ms  209.85.240.158
 11    60 ms    54 ms    54 ms  72.14.232.141
 12    58 ms    68 ms    54 ms  209.85.241.35
 13    67 ms    54 ms    55 ms  209.85.248.102
 14    55 ms    54 ms    54 ms  iy-in-f147.google.com [209.85.225.147]

Trace complete.

C:\>^@
```

NSLOOKUP Command

Nslookup is a command-line utility that enables you to verify entries on a DNS server. You can use nslookup in two modes: interactive and noninteractive. In interactive mode, you start a session with the DNS server, in which you can make several requests. In noninteractive mode, you specify a command that makes a single query of the DNS server. If you want to make another query, you must type another noninteractive command.

One of the key issues regarding the use of TCP/IP is the ability to resolve a hostname to an IP address—an action usually performed by a DNS server.

NETSTAT Command

The netstat utility is used to check out the inbound and outbound TCP/IP connections on your machine. It can also be used to view packet statistics, such as how many packets have been sent and received and the number of errors.

When used without any options, the NETSTAT command produces output similar to what you see in Figure 18.19, which shows all the outbound TCP/IP connections.

FIGURE 18.19 NETSTAT output

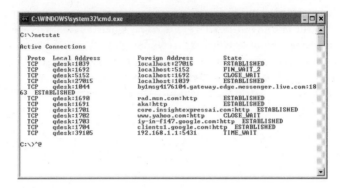

There are several useful command-line options for NETSTAT, as shown in Table 18.9.

TABLE 18.9 NETSTAT Options

Option	Function
-a	Displays all connections and listening ports.
-b	Displays the executable involved in creating each connection or listening port. In some cases, well-known executables host multiple independent components, and in these cases the sequence of components involved in creating the connection or listening port is displayed. In this case, the executable name is in brackets, [ ], at the bottom; at the top is the component it called; and so forth until TCP/IP was reached. Note that this option can be time consuming and will fail unless you have sufficient permissions.
-e	Displays Ethernet statistics. This may be combined with the -s option.
-f	Displays fully qualified domain names (FQDN) for foreign addresses
-n	Displays addresses and port numbers in numerical form
-o	Displays the owning process ID associated with each connection
-p proto	Shows connections for the protocol specified by proto; proto may be any of the following: TCP, UDP, TCPv6, or UDPv6. If used with the -s option to display per-protocol statistics, proto may be any of IP, IPv6, ICMP, ICMPv6, TCP, TCPv6, UDP, or UDPv6.
-r	Displays the routing table
-s	Displays per-protocol statistics. By default, statistics are shown for IP, IPv6, ICMP, ICMPv6, TCP, TCPv6, UDP, and UDPv6; the -p option may be used to specify a subset of the default.

NET USE Command

The NET USE command is used to establish network connections via a command prompt. For example, to connect to a shared network drive and make it your M: drive, you would use the syntax **net use m: *server**share*.**

NET USE can also be used to connect to a shared printer: **net use lpt1: *printername*.** For more information, type **net use /?** at a command prompt.

NET /? Command

The NET /? command is basically a catch-all help request. It will instruct you to use the NET command you are interested in for more information. Sample output from this command is shown in Figure 18.20.

FIGURE 18.20   NET /? output

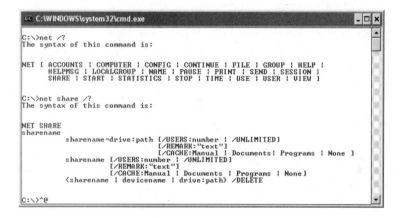

IPCONFIG Command

With Windows-based operating systems, you can determine the network settings on the client's network interface cards, as well as any that a DHCP server has leased to your computer, by typing the following at a command prompt: **ipconfig /all.**

IPCONFIG /ALL also gives you full details on the duration of your current lease. You can verify whether a DHCP client has connectivity to a DHCP server by releasing the client's IP address and then attempting to lease an IP address. You can conduct this test by typing the following sequence of commands from the DHCP client at a command prompt:

```
ipconfig /renew
ipconfig /release
```

Ipconfig is one of the first tools to use when experiencing problems accessing resources, as it will show you whether an address has been issued to the machine. If the address displayed falls within the 169.254.*x.x* category, this means the client was unable to reach the DHCP server and has defaulted to Automatic Private IP Addressing (APIPA), which will prevent the card from communicating outside its subnet, if not altogether.

In the Linux world, a utility similar to ipconfig is ifconfig.

Figure 18.21 shows output from IPCONFIG, and Figure 18.22 shows you the output from IPCONFIG /ALL.

FIGURE 18.21 IPCONFIG output

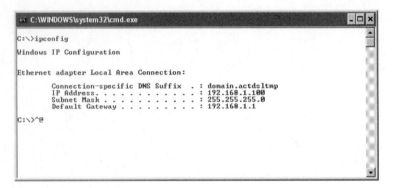

```
C:\WINDOWS\system32\cmd.exe                                    _ □ x

C:\>ipconfig

Windows IP Configuration

Ethernet adapter Local Area Connection:

        Connection-specific DNS Suffix  . : domain.actdsltmp
        IP Address. . . . . . . . . . . . : 192.168.1.100
        Subnet Mask . . . . . . . . . . . : 255.255.255.0
        Default Gateway . . . . . . . . . : 192.168.1.1

C:\>^@
```

FIGURE 18.22 IPCONFIG /ALL output

```
C:\WINDOWS\system32\cmd.exe                                    _ □ x

C:\>ipconfig /all

Windows IP Configuration

        Host Name . . . . . . . . . . . . : qdesk
        Primary Dns Suffix  . . . . . . . :
        Node Type . . . . . . . . . . . . : Unknown
        IP Routing Enabled. . . . . . . . : No
        WINS Proxy Enabled. . . . . . . . : No
        DNS Suffix Search List. . . . . . : domain.actdsltmp

Ethernet adapter Local Area Connection:

        Connection-specific DNS Suffix  . : domain.actdsltmp
        Description . . . . . . . . . . . : Broadcom NetXtreme 57xx Gigabit Cont
roller
        Physical Address. . . . . . . . . : 00-11-43-A7-5B-6D
        Dhcp Enabled. . . . . . . . . . . : Yes
        Autoconfiguration Enabled . . . . : Yes
        IP Address. . . . . . . . . . . . : 192.168.1.100
        Subnet Mask . . . . . . . . . . . : 255.255.255.0
        Default Gateway . . . . . . . . . : 192.168.1.1
        DHCP Server . . . . . . . . . . . : 192.168.1.1
        DNS Servers . . . . . . . . . . . : 192.168.0.1
                                            205.171.3.25
        Lease Obtained. . . . . . . . . . : Sunday, April 05, 2009 8:25:24 AM
        Lease Expires . . . . . . . . . . : Monday, April 06, 2009 8:25:24 AM

C:\>^@
```

In Exercise 18.2, you will renew an IP address on a Windows XP system within the graphical interface. In Exercise 18.3, you will perform this same operation in Windows Vista, and Exercise 18.4 shows you how to renew your lease from the command line.

EXERCISE 18.2

Renew an IP Address on a Windows XP System

This exercise assumes you are using Windows XP and dynamic IP assignments from a DHCP server:

1. Choose Start ➢ Control Panel and then click the Network Connections icon. A list of the LAN or high-speed Internet connections presently known appears.

2. Right-click on your connection and choose Status. In the connection status box, the first tab that appears is General, and it displays information such as whether you are connected, the speed of the connection, and how long the connection has been there.

3. Click the Support tab. Here, you can see whether the address is static or assigned by DHCP, the present address, the subnet mask, and the default gateway values.

4. Click the Details button. This expands the information by also showing you the physical (MAC) address and lease information, among other things. Note the date and time of the Lease Obtained values. Click Close.

5. Back at the Support tab, click the Repair button. This will attempt to establish or renew the connection. If the network (DHCP) is functioning properly, a notification that it finished will appear in a short time. Click the Details button again. The Lease Obtained values should reflect the current date and time.

The interface in Windows XP provides a convenient way to interact with the network components. The next exercise shows how to perform a similar action in Windows Vista.

EXERCISE 18.3

Renew an IP Address in Windows Vista

This exercise assumes the use of Windows Vista and dynamic IP assignments from a DHCP server:

1. From the Start menu, right-click on Network to open the Network and Sharing Center.

2. In the left-hand pane, click Manage Network Connections. This will open a new window displaying your network connections.

3. Right-click on your connection and choose Status. On the General tab of the network connection's status you will see information such as whether you are connected, the speed of the connection, and how long the connection has been active.

EXERCISE 18.3 *(continued)*

4. Click the Details button. This expands the information by also showing you the physical (MAC) address and lease information, among other things.

5. Back at the General tab, click the Diagnose button. This will diagnose any network problems and attempt to establish or renew the connection. If the network (DHCP) is functioning properly, a notification that it finished will appear in a short time. If not, Windows Vista will attempt to repair the connection.

While Windows Vista provides this interface to troubleshoot connection problems, some administrators still prefer the reliability of a command-line interface. The next exercise shows how to perform a similar action, using the command line to do so.

EXERCISE 18.4

Renew an IP Address from the Command Line

This exercise assumes you are using Windows XP or Vista and dynamic IP assignments from a DHCP server:

1. Open a command prompt (choose Start ≻ Run, and then type **CMD**).

2. Type **IPCONFIG** and view the abbreviated list of information.

3. Type **IPCONFIG /ALL** to see the full list. Notice the date and time on the lease for the IP address.

4. Type **IPCONFIG /RENEW** followed by **IPCONFIG /ALL**. The date and time on the lease for the IP address should be the current date and time.

5. Close the command-prompt window by typing **EXIT**.

Telnet and SSH

Telnet is a command-line utility used to establish a connection with a remote computer. Its use has fallen out of favor due to its lack of security. Many users prefer to use SSH in its place.

Troubleshooting Proxies and Firewalls

A *proxy server* (or proxy) makes requests of a computer for another computer. Said another way, it can act on behalf of the whole network to completely separate packets from internal hosts and external hosts. For example, if an internal host sends a request to a host on the Internet, the proxy would get the request first, where it would be examined, broken down, and handled by an application that would create a new packet requesting information from the external server.

Most firewalls can also implement proxy services, which makes them act as proxies. Proxies make good firewalls because they dissect the entire packet so that each section of it can be scrutinized for invalid data at each layer of the OSI model and then look at everything from information in the packet header to the actual contents of the message. This includes examining attachments for viruses, which has obvious benefits.

There are many types of proxy servers, such as IP proxies, Web proxies, FTP proxies, and SMTP proxies.

In regard to troubleshooting proxies and firewalls, they are pretty much one and the same when it comes to the A+ exam (even though they can be different in the real world). The key is to ensure that the ports you need to use are open, while at the same time securing the rest of your network. This can mean allowing only certain computers (based on their IP address) to use certain ports, or limiting which computers can access certain websites.

Summary

In this chapter, you learned about installing and configuring a small office or home office network and troubleshooting client-side connectivity.

The chapter started off by discussing connection types you would likely encounter when setting up a small network, such as dial-up, DSL, cable, and ISDN. Then we looked at internal network connections such as LAN (10/100/1000BaseT), wireless, Bluetooth, and cellular. Then we spent some time discussing physical installation, including how to configure wireless routers and access points.

The next major section was on troubleshooting client-side connectivity issues. We examined TCP/IP settings in detail, and looked at characteristics of some common TCP/IP protocols. Next, we covered some client-side tools that you need to be familiar with. Finally, we closed by taking a look at proxies and firewalls.

Exam Essentials

Understand the advantages of using a dial-up connection.   Dial-up connections are generally cheaper and easier to configure than broadband connections. They are also available in more locations than broadband.

Know the speed of a BRI ISDN connection.   A BRI ISDN connection has two 64kbps B channels and one 16kbps D channel, for a total of 144kbps.

Know the maximum distance for several cable types.   UTP can go up to 100 meters. Thinnet coax can reach 185 meters. Multimode fiber generally is good for up to 400 meters, and single-mode fiber can run as long as 40 kilometers.

Know the maximum data rate and range of 802.11b and 802.11g.   Both have a maximum indoor range of about 40 meters and an outdoor range of about 140 meters. 802.11b runs at 11Mbps and 802.11g runs at 54Mbps.

Be able to install a network interface card.   To install a NIC in a desktop PC, with the power off remove the case cover, locate an unused slot that matches the NIC's expansion slot type, insert the NIC into the available slot, and secure it with a screw or other retainer. Finally, reinstall the case cover, power up the computer, and install the driver software.

Be able to set up a wireless connection.   Windows uses the Wireless Zero Configuration Service to automatically connect to wireless access points using IEEE 802.11 protocols (WiFi). Simply locate the wireless access point you wish to connect to and double-click on it. Windows will connect you automatically.

Know the basics of how firewalls work.   Firewalls limit traffic based on a set of rules. These rules are usually configured as access control lists (ACLs).

Know which components of TCP/IP configuration are required.   To communicate using TCP/IP. your computer needs to have a unique IP address and a subnet mask. A default gateway address and DNS server address are optional.

Know what IP addresses APIPA uses.   Automatic Private IP Addressing uses IP addresses in the 169.254.*x.x* range with a subnet mask of 255.255.0.0.

Know what the IP loopback address is.   The IP loopback address is 127.0.0.1.

Know the private IP address ranges.   The private Class A addresses are 10.0.0.0-10.255.255.255. Class B is 172.16.0.0-172.31.255.255. Class C is 192.168.0.0-192.168.255.255.

List the utilities that can be used for troubleshooting.   Be familiar with the following utilities: ping, tracert, nslookup, netstat, net use, net /?, ipconfig, Telnet, and SSH.

Review Questions

1. To increase security, you decide to use your firewall to block the Telnet protocol. Which port will you need to block to prevent Telnet from being used?

    A. 21

    B. 22

    C. 23

    D. 24

2. When SSL and HTTP are used together, what does the beginning of a site address become?

    A. `https://`

    B. `ssl://`

    C. `asp://`

    D. `tcp://`

3. Which troubleshooting tool can be used at the command line to see the IP configuration data given by a DHCP server to a Windows XP workstation?

    A. `Ifconfig`

    B. `Ipconfig`

    C. `Winipcfg`

    D. `Hijack`

4. You are administering a system that has been locked down for security reasons. You notice that among all of the other ports, port 443 and port 80 have been disabled. What services are associated with these ports? (Choose two.)

    A. Telnet

    B. FTP

    C. HTTP

    D. HTTPS

5. Which of the following protocols can be used by a client to access e-mail on a server?

    A. DNS

    B. FTP

    C. POP3

    D. SMTP

6. Which tool can be used to test connectivity and see the path taken to reach another host?

    A. `Ping`

    B. `Ipconfig`

    C. `Tracert`

    D. `Nslookup`

7. Which of the following is a command-line utility that enables you to verify entries on a DNS server?

   A. Ping

   B. Ipconfig

   C. Tracert

   D. Nslookup

8. Which of the following technologies is limited to 10 meters?

   A. 802.11

   B. 802.1x

   C. Bluetooth

   D. UTP

9. Which elements are required to communicate on a TCP/IP network? (Choose all that apply.)

   A. IP address

   B. Subnet mask

   C. Default gateway

   D. DNS server

10. What is the lowest grade of cable required to run 1000BaseT?

    A. UTP CAT-5

    B. UTP CAT-5e

    C. UTP CAT-6

    D. Multimode fiber

11. You are installing a network and will use wired connections. You have a distance of 80 meters between nodes in some cases. What is the maximum distance you can run UTP cable?

    A. 10 meters

    B. 100 meters

    C. 185 meters

    D. 400 meters

12. You need to recommend a wireless cellular service to a client who travels globally. Which type of service should you recommend?

    A. WiFi

    B. Bluetooth

    C. GSM

    D. CDMA

13. Which of the following 802.11x standards provides data transmission speeds up to 54Mbps? (Choose all that apply.)

    A. 802.11a

    B. 802.11b

    C. 802.11g

    D. 802.11i

14. Firewalls use a set of rules to make determinations on which traffic to block. What are those rules called?

    A. NAT

    B. SSID

    C. WPA

    D. ACL

15. Which of the following addresses is a nonroutable IP address?

    A. 172.18.32.1

    B. 192.169.32.1

    C. 168.192.32.1

    D. 18.172.32.1

16. APIPA addresses are in which address range?

    A. 192.168.0.0

    B. 172.16.0.0

    C. 169.254.0.0

    D. 10.0.0.0

17. Which utility is used to view the inbound and outbound TCP/IP connections on your machine?

    A. Netstat

    B. Nbtstat

    C. Ipconfig

    D. Nslookup

18. Which command is used to determine if another computer is reachable via TCP/IP?

    A. IPCONFIG

    B. NBTSTAT

    C. NET USE

    D. PING

19. Which of the following acronyms describes the "name" of a wireless network? What is the name of a wireless network called?

    A. WEP

    B. WPA

    C. SSID

    D. MAC

20. Which of the following are examples of ways you can increase the security of your wireless network? (Choose all that apply.)

    A. Enable MAC filtering

    B. Enable SSID broadcasts

    C. Change the SSID from the default

    D. Use WPA

Answers to Review Questions

1. C. The Telnet protocol uses port 23. If this port is blocked, Telnet cannot be used.

2. A. When SSL and HTTP are used together, the beginning of the site address becomes `https://`.

3. B. The ipconfig utility can be used at the command line with Windows XP to see the networking configuration values. Ifconfig is a Unix-based utility; winipcfg is a Windows-based utility similar to ipconfig, and there is no Windows hijack utility.

4. C, D. Each TCP/IP protocol uses a particular port number. In this case, the HTTP protocol uses port 80 and HTTPS uses port 443. Telnet uses port 23. FTP requires two ports (21 and 20) to establish the connection and send data; most FTP requests result in FTP opening an arbitrary higher-numbered port (such as 13426) to transfer the data.

5. C. The IMAP and POP3 protocols can be used to retrieve e-mail from mail servers. DNS resolves hostnames to IP addresses. FTP is for file downloads. SMTP is for sending e-mail to an e-mail server.

6. C. The tracert (trace route) utility can be used to test connectivity and see the path taken to reach another host. Ping is used to see if another system is active and reachable. Ipconfig shows your IP configuration information, and nslookup allows you to verify entries on a DNS server.

7. D. Nslookup is a command-line utility that enables you to verify entries on a DNS server. Ping is used to see if another system is active and reachable. The tracert (trace route) utility can be used to test connectivity and see the path taken to reach another host. Ipconfig shows your IP configuration information.

8. C. Bluetooth is a wireless standard; Class 2 devices are limited in range to about 10 meters.

9. A, B. To communicate on a TCP/IP network, you need to have a unique IP address and a valid subnet mask. The default gateway and DNS server are optional.

10. B. In order to run 1000BaseT, you need CAT-5e or better. The T in 1000BaseT indicates twisted pair, and not fiber-optic cable.

11. B. UTP cable can run for a maximum distance of 100 meters. Thinnet coaxial can run up to 185 meters, and multimode fiber can run up to 400 meters.

12. C. WiFi and Bluetooth are not cellular standards. Of the two cellular standards, GSM is used worldwide and CDMA is used only in the United States.

13. A, C. Both 802.11a and 802.11g provide data transmission speeds of up to 54Mbps. 802.11b only goes up to 11Mbps. 802.11i is a security standard.

14. D. Firewalls use an access control list (ACL) to determine which packets are allowed through it.

15. A. Private, nonroutable addresses are 10.0.0.0-10.255.255.255, 172.16.0.0-172.31.255.255, and 192.168.0.0-192.168.255.255.

16. C. Automatic Private IP Addressing addresses are in the 169.254.0.0 network. The other network addresses listed are private nonroutable IP addresses.

17. A. The netstat utility is used to view TCP/IP connections on your computer. Nbtstat shows NetBIOS over TCP/IP information. Ipconfig shows your IP configuration information. Nslookup is a command-line utility that enables you to verify entries on a DNS server.

18. D. To see if another computer is online and available, you can use the PING command. IPCONFIG shows your IP configuration information. NBTSTAT shows NetBIOS over TCP/IP information. NET USE allows you to make a connection to a shared network resource such as a printer or a hard drive.

19. C. The Service Set Identifier (SSID) is the name of the wireless network. You should always change the SSID from the default! WEP and WPA are wireless security standards. MAC is the hardware address built into network cards.

20. A, C, D. Enabling MAC filtering only allows specific computers to use the wireless router. You should disable SSID broadcasts, not enable them, to increase security. Changing the SSID from the default is always a good idea, and you should use some sort of wireless security such as WPA or WEP.

Chapter

19

System Security

THE FOLLOWING COMPTIA A+ PRACTICAL APPLICATION EXAM OBJECTIVES ARE COVERED IN THIS CHAPTER:

✓ **4.1 Given a scenario, prevent, troubleshoot, and remove viruses and malware**

- Use antivirus software

- Identify malware symptoms

- Quarantine infected systems

- Research malware types, symptom, and solutions (virus encyclopedia)

- Remediate infected systems

- Update antivirus software

  - Signature and engine updates

  - Automatic vs. manual

- Schedule scans

- Repair boot blocks

- Scan and removal techniques

  - Safe mode

  - Boot environment

- Educate end user

✓ **4.2 Implement security and troubleshoot common issues**

- Operating systems

  - Local users and groups: Administrator, Power Users, Guest, Users

  - Vista User Access Control (UAC)

  - NTFS vs. Share permissions

    - Allow vs. deny

- Difference between moving and copying folders and files
- File attributes
- Shared files and folders
  - Administrative shares vs. local shares
  - Permission propagation
  - Inheritance
- System files and folders
- Encryption (Bitlocker, EFS)
- User authentication
- System
  - BIOS security
    - Drive lock
    - Passwords
    - Intrusion detection
    - TPM

In this chapter, we will look at security from a slightly different viewpoint than we did in Chapter 11. Not only is the topic important enough that CompTIA has added it to the Practical Application exam, but it is also weighted higher here than on the Essentials exam.

It is highly recommended that you read Chapter 11 in addition to this chapter as you study for the elective exam. Some of the topics are identical between the two exams and attempts have been made to limit replication and focus more in this chapter on topics not discussed there.

This chapter will look at methods of hardening and updating the operating system. We'll then explore some of the Microsoft file systems. We'll also look at access control, viruses and malware, and the ways of recognizing common attacks. Additionally, this chapter includes a discussion of various methods for recovering the operating system in the event something goes awry.

Security Basics

One of the first steps in developing a secure environment is to develop a baseline of the minimum security needs of your organization. A *security baseline* defines the level of security that will be implemented and maintained. You can choose to set a low baseline by implementing next to no security, or a high baseline that doesn't allow users to make any changes at all to the network or to their systems. In practicality, most implementations fall between the two extremes; you must determine what is best for your organization.

Microsoft provides a tool, the Microsoft Security Baseline Analyzer, for establishing a security baseline and for subsequent evaluations of security on Windows 2000 and higher OSs.

The baseline provides the input needed to design, implement, and support a secure network. Developing the baseline includes gathering data on the specific security implementation of the systems with which you'll be working.

You can find the Microsoft TechNet website at `http://technet.microsoft.com/default.aspx` and the Microsoft security website at `http://www.microsoft.com/security/`. These two sites provide a lot of valuable information on current security issues.

Viruses and Malware

A *virus* is a piece of software designed to infect a computer system. The virus may do nothing more than reside on the computer. A virus may also damage the data on your hard disk, destroy your operating system, and possibly spread to other systems. Viruses get into your computer in several ways, including: on contaminated media (floppy, USB drive, or CD), through e-mail and peer-to-peer sites, or as part of another program.

You want to make certain that your systems, and the data within them, are kept as secure as possible. The security prevents others from changing the data, destroying it, or inadvertently harming it.

Viruses can be classified as polymorphic, stealth, retroviruses, multipartite, armored, companion, phage, and macro viruses. Each type of virus has a different attack strategy and different consequences.

Estimates for losses due to viruses are in the billions of dollars. These losses include financial loss as well as lost productivity.

The Windows Security Center continues to expand and improve with each release of Windows. Figure 19.1 shows this interface as it appears in Windows Vista. All of the options shown on this interface can be accessed individually, but this provides a one-stop location for viewing the status of each at the same time.

The following sections will introduce the symptoms of a virus infection, explain how a virus works, and describe the types of viruses you can expect to encounter and how they generally behave. I'll also discuss how a virus is transmitted through a network and look at a few hoaxes.

Symptoms of a Virus/Malware Infection

Many viruses will announce that you're infected as soon as they gain access to your system. They may take control of your system and flash annoying messages on your screen or destroy your hard disk. When this occurs, you'll know that you're a victim. Other viruses will cause your system to slow down, cause files to disappear from your computer, or take over your disk space.

FIGURE 19.1 The Windows Security Center offers a quick glimpse of current protection settings.

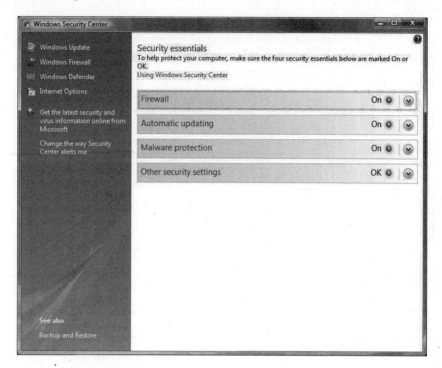

 Viruses are the most common type of malware. In this section, we use the term *virus* to refer to all types of malware.

You should look for some of the following symptoms when determining if a virus infection has occurred:

- The programs on your system start to load more slowly. This happens because the virus is spreading to other files in your system or is taking over system resources.

- Unusual files appear on your hard drive, or files start to disappear from your system. Many viruses delete key files in your system to render it inoperable.

- Program sizes change from the installed versions. This occurs because the virus is attaching itself to these programs on your disk.

- Your browser, word processing application, or other software begins to exhibit unusual operating characteristics. Screens or menus may change.

- The system mysteriously shuts itself down or starts itself up and does a great deal of unanticipated disk activity.

- You mysteriously lose access to a disk drive or other system resources. The virus has changed the settings on a device to make it unusable.

- Your system suddenly doesn't reboot or gives unexpected error messages during startup.

- You notice an X in the system tray over the icon for your virus scanner, or the icon for the scanner disappears from the system tray altogether.

This list is by no means comprehensive. What is an absolute, however, is the fact that you should immediately quarantine the infected system. It is imperative that you do all you can to contain the virus and keep it from spreading to other systems within your network, or beyond.

How Viruses Work

A virus, in most cases, tries to accomplish one of two things: render your system inoperable or spread to other systems. Many viruses will spread to other systems given the chance and then render your system unusable. This is common with many of the newer viruses.

If your system is infected, the virus may try to attach itself to every file in your system and spread each time you send a file or document to other users. Figure 19.2 shows a virus spreading from an infected system either through a network or by removable media. When you give removable media to another user or put it into another system, you then infect that system with the virus.

FIGURE 19.2   Virus spreading from an infected system using the network or removable media

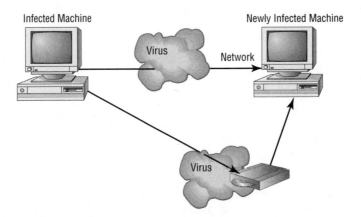

Many newer viruses spread using e-mail. The infected system attaches a file to any e-mail that you send to another user. The recipient opens this file, thinking it's something you legitimately sent them. When they open the file, the virus infects the target system. The virus might then attach itself to all the e-mails the newly infected system sends, which in turn infects the recipients of the e-mails. Figure 19.3 shows how a virus can spread from a single user to literally thousands of users in a very short time using e-mail.

FIGURE 19.3   An e-mail virus spreading geometrically to other users

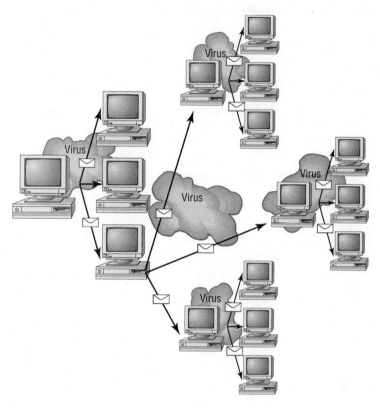

Types of Viruses

Viruses take many different forms. The following sections briefly introduce these forms and explain how they work. These are the most common types, but this isn't a comprehensive list.

 The best defense against a virus attack is up-to-date antivirus software installed and running. The software should be on all workstations as well as on the server. Special e-mail virus scanners should be installed on e-mail servers as well.

Armored Virus

An *armored virus* is designed to make itself difficult to detect or analyze. Armored viruses cover themselves with protective code that stops debuggers or disassemblers from examining critical elements of the virus. The virus may be written in such a way that some aspects of the programming act as a decoy to distract analysis while the actual code hides in other areas in the program.

From the perspective of the creator, the more time it takes to deconstruct the virus, the longer it can live. The longer it can live, the more time it has to replicate and spread to as many machines as possible. The key to stopping most viruses is to identify them quickly and educate administrators about them—the very things that the armor intensifies the difficulty of accomplishing.

Companion Virus

A *companion virus* attaches itself to legitimate programs and then creates a program with a different filename extension. This file may reside in your system's temporary directory. When a user types the name of the legitimate program, the companion virus executes instead of the real program. This effectively hides the virus from the user. Many of the viruses that are used to attack Windows systems make changes to program pointers in the Registry so that they point to the infected program. The infected program may perform its dirty deed and then start the real program.

Macro Virus

A *macro virus* exploits the enhancements made to many application programs. Programmers can expand the capability of applications such as Word and Excel. Word, for example, supports a mini-BASIC programming language that allows files to be manipulated automatically. These programs in the document are called *macros*. For example, a macro can tell your word processor to spell-check your document automatically when it opens. Macro viruses can infect all the documents on your system and spread to other systems via e-mail or other methods. Macro viruses are the fastest-growing exploitation today.

Multipartite Virus

A *multipartite virus* attacks your system in multiple ways. It may attempt to infect your boot sector, infect all of your executable files, and destroy your application files. The hope here is that you won't be able to correct all the problems and will allow the infestation to continue. The multipartite virus in Figure 19.4 attacks your boot sector, infects application files, and attacks your Microsoft Word documents.

Phage Virus

A *phage virus* modifies and alters other programs and databases. The virus infects all of these files. The only way to remove this virus is to reinstall the programs that are infected. If you miss even a single incident of this virus on the victim system, the process will start again and infect the system once more.

Polymorphic Virus

Polymorphic viruses change form in order to avoid detection. These types of viruses attack your system, display a message on your computer, and delete files on your system. The virus will attempt to hide from your antivirus software. Frequently, the virus will encrypt parts of itself to avoid detection. When the virus does this, it's referred to as *mutation*. The mutation process makes it hard for antivirus software to detect common characteristics of the virus. Figure 19.5 shows a polymorphic virus changing its characteristics to avoid detection. In this example, the virus changes a signature to fool antivirus software.

FIGURE 19.4   A multipartite virus commencing an attack on a system

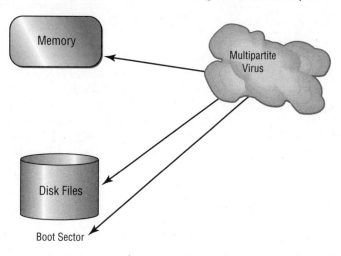

FIGURE 19.5   The polymorphic virus changing its characteristics

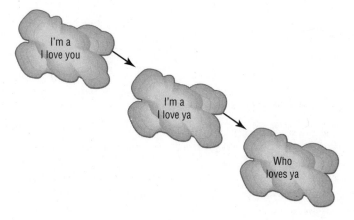

  A *signature* is an algorithm or other element of a virus that uniquely identifies it. Because some viruses have the ability to alter their signature, it is crucial that you keep signature files current, whether you choose to manually download them or configure the antivirus engine to do so automatically.

Retrovirus

A *retrovirus* attacks or bypasses the antivirus software installed on a computer. You can consider a retrovirus to be an anti-antivirus. Retroviruses can directly attack your antivirus software and potentially destroy the virus definition database file. Destroying this information without your knowledge would leave you with a false sense of security. The virus may also directly attack an antivirus program to create bypasses for itself.

Stealth Virus

A *stealth virus* attempts to avoid detection by masking itself from applications. It may attach itself to the boot sector of the hard drive. When a system utility or program runs, the stealth virus redirects commands around itself in order to avoid detection. An infected file may report a file size different from what is actually present in order to avoid detection. Figure 19.6 shows a stealth virus attaching itself to the boot sector to avoid detection. Stealth viruses may also move themselves from fileA to fileB during a virus scan for the same reason.

FIGURE 19.6   A stealth virus hiding in a disk boot sector

This is a disk

Boot Record | Virus

An updated list of the most active viruses and spyware is on the Panda Security site at www.pandasecurity.com/homeusers/security-info/.

Virus Transmission in a Network

Upon infection, some viruses destroy the target system immediately. The saving grace is that the infection can be detected and corrected. Some viruses won't destroy or otherwise tamper with a system; they use the victim system as a carrier. The victim system then infects servers, file shares, and other resources with the virus. The carrier then infects the target system again. Until the carrier is identified and cleaned, the virus continues to harass systems in this network and spread.

Antivirus Software

The primary method of preventing the propagation of malicious code involves the use of *antivirus software*. Antivirus software is an application that is installed on a system to protect it and to scan for viruses as well as worms and Trojan horses. Figure 19.7 shows an example of an antivirus program—Sophos, in this case—and the statistics it offers as to the last update, number of quarantined files, and so on.

Present Virus Activity

New viruses and threats are released on a regular basis to join the cadre of those already in existence. From an exam perspective, you need only be familiar with the world as it existed at the time the questions were written. From an administration standpoint, however, you need to know what is happening today.

To find this information, visit the CERT/CC Current Activity web page at `http://www.us-cert.gov/current/current_activity.html`. Here you'll find a detailed description of the most current viruses as well as links to pages on older threats.

FIGURE 19.7   An example of antivirus software

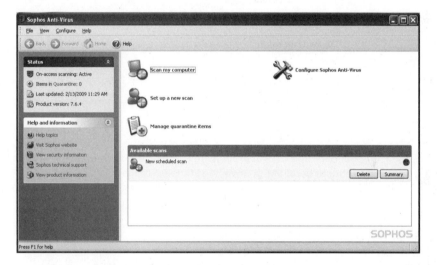

As a comparison, Figure 19.8 shows another antivirus—McAfee in this case—that is not properly configured on the workstation. The prompt to fix is present, as is information that the signature file is too old to be reliable.

Most viruses have characteristics that are common to families of virus. Antivirus software looks for these characteristics, or fingerprints, to identify and neutralize viruses before they impact you.

More than 60,000 known viruses, worms, bombs, and other malware have been defined. New ones are added all the time. Your antivirus software manufacturer will usually work very hard to keep the definition database files current. The definition database file contains all of the known viruses and countermeasures for a particular antivirus software product. You probably won't receive a virus that hasn't been seen by one of these companies. If you keep the virus definition database files in your software up-to-date, you probably won't be overly vulnerable to attacks.

FIGURE 19.8   An example of an antivirus program in need of configuration and updating

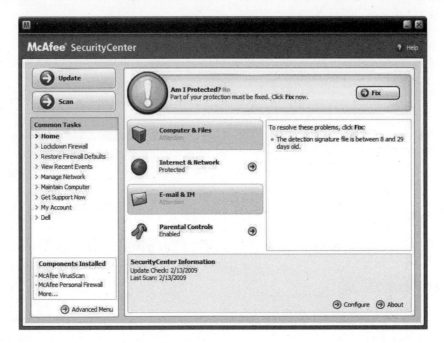

 The best method of protection is to use a layered approach. Antivirus software should be at the gateways, at the servers, and at the desktop. If you want to go one step further, you can use software at each location from different vendors to make sure you're covered from all angles.

The second method of preventing viruses is education. Teach your users not to open suspicious files and to open only those files that they're reasonably sure are virus free. They need to scan every disk, e-mail, and document they receive before they open them.

You should also have all workstations scheduled to be automatically scanned on a regular basis. Every antivirus program we are aware of includes the ability to configure automatic scanning on a regular basis. Should that feature be missing from one, you can always use the Task Scheduler included with the operating system. Figure 19.9 shows the interface for the Task Scheduler in Windows Vista, obtainable from Start ➢ All Programs ➢ Accessories ➢ System Tools ➢ Task Scheduler.

 You can educate yourself and stay current on malware types, symptoms, and solutions by consulting the virus encyclopedia at http://www.viruslist .com/en/viruslist.html.

FIGURE 19.9 The Task Scheduler could be used to configure running of an antivirus program if the program lacked such a feature.

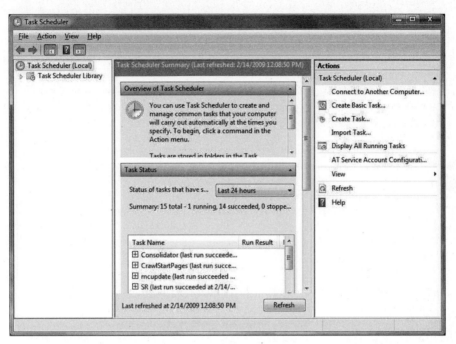

Recognizing Common Attacks

Most attacks are designed to exploit potential weaknesses. Those weaknesses can be in the implementation of programs or in the protocols used in networks. Many types of attacks require a high level of sophistication and are rare. You need to know about them so that you can identify what has happened in your network.

In this section, we'll look at these attacks more closely.

Back Door Attacks

The term *back door attack* can have two meanings. The original term *back door* referred to troubleshooting and developer hooks into systems. During the development of a complicated operating system or application, programmers add back doors or maintenance hooks. These back doors allow them to examine operations inside the code while the code is running. The back doors are stripped out of the code when it's moved to production. When a software manufacturer discovers a hook that hasn't been removed, it releases a maintenance upgrade or patch to close the back door. These patches are common when a new product is initially released.

The second type of back door refers to gaining access to a network and inserting a program or utility that creates an entrance for an attacker. The program may allow a certain user ID to log on without a password or to gain administrative privileges.

Such an attack is usually used as either an access or a modification attack. A number of tools exist to create back door attacks on systems. One of the more popular tools is Back Orifice, which has been updated to work with Windows Server 2008 as well as earlier versions. Another popular back door program is NetBus. Fortunately, most conventional antivirus software will detect and block these types of attacks.

Back Orifice and NetBus are remote administration tools used by attackers to take control of Windows-based systems. These packages are typically installed by using a Trojan horse program. Back Orifice and NetBus allow a remote user to take full control of systems that have these applications installed. Back Orifice and NetBus run on all of the current Windows operating systems.

Spoofing Attacks

A *spoofing attack* is an attempt by someone or something to masquerade as someone else. This type of attack is usually considered an access attack. A common spoofing attack that was popular for many years on early Unix and other time-sharing systems involved a programmer writing a fake logon program. This program would prompt the user for a user ID and password. No matter what the user typed, the program would indicate an invalid logon attempt and then transfer control to the real logon program. The spoofing program would write the logon and password into a disk file, which was retrieved later.

The most popular spoofing attacks today are IP spoofing and DNS spoofing. With *IP spoofing*, the goal is to make the data look as if it came from a trusted host when it didn't (thus spoofing the IP address of the sending host). With *DNS spoofing*, the DNS server is given information about a name server that it thinks is legitimate when it isn't. This can send users to a website other than the one they wanted to go to, reroute mail, or do any other type of redirection wherein data from a DNS server is used to determine a destination.

Always think of spoofing as fooling. Attackers are trying to fool the user, system, and/or host into believing that they're something they aren't. Since the word *spoof* can describe any false information at any level, spoofing can occur at any level of a network.

The important point to remember is that a spoofing attack tricks something or someone into thinking something legitimate is occurring.

Man-in-the-Middle Attacks

Man-in-the-middle attacks tend to be fairly sophisticated. This type of attack is also an access attack, but it can be used as the starting point for a modification attack. The method used in these attacks clandestinely places a piece of software between a server and the user that neither the server administrators nor the user is aware of. This software intercepts data and then sends the information to the server as if nothing were wrong. The server responds back to the software, thinking it's communicating with the legitimate client. The attacking software continues sending information on to the server, and so forth.

If communication between the server and user continues, what's the harm of the software? The answer lies in whatever else the software is doing. The man-in-the-middle software may be recording information for someone to view later or altering it, or in some other way compromising the security of your system and session.

A man-in-the-middle attack is an active attack. Something is actively intercepting the data and may or may not be altering it. If it's altering the data, the altered data masquerades as legitimate data traveling between the two hosts.

In recent years, the threat of man-in-the-middle attacks on wireless networks has increased. Because it's no longer necessary to connect to the wire, a malicious rogue can be outside the building intercepting packets, altering them, and sending them on. A common solution to this problem is to enforce Wired Equivalent Privacy (WEP) or WPA (Wi-Fi Protected Access) across the wireless network.

Replay Attacks

Replay attacks are becoming quite common. These attacks occur when information is captured over a network. Replay attacks are used for access or modification attacks. In a distributed environment, logon and password information is sent between the client and the authentication system. The attacker can capture this information and replay it again later. This can also occur with security certificates from systems such as Kerberos: the attacker resubmits the certificate, hoping to be validated by the authentication system and circumvent any time sensitivity.

If this attack is successful, the attacker will have all the rights and privileges from the original certificate. This is the primary reason that most certificates contain a unique session identifier and a time stamp: if the certificate has expired, it will be rejected, and an entry should be made in a security log to notify system administrators.

Password-Guessing Attacks

Password-guessing attacks occur when an account is attacked repeatedly. This is accomplished by sending possible passwords to the account in a systematic manner. These attacks are initially carried out to gain passwords for an access or modification attack. There are two types of password-guessing attacks:

Brute-force attack   A *brute-force attack* is an attempt to guess passwords until a successful guess occurs. This type of attack usually occurs over a long period. To make passwords more difficult to guess, make them complex and much longer than two or three characters (six should be the bare minimum), and use password lockout policies.

Dictionary Attack   A *dictionary attack* uses a dictionary of common words to attempt to find the user's password. Dictionary attacks can be automated, and several tools exist in the public domain to execute them.

Some systems will identify whether an account ID is valid and whether the password is wrong. Giving the attacker a clue as to a valid account name isn't a good practice. If you can enable your authentication to either accept a valid ID/password group or require the entire logon process again, you should.

Denial-of-Service (DoS) and Distributed DoS (DDoS) Attacks

Denial-of-service (DoS) attacks prevent access to resources by users authorized to use those resources. An attacker may attempt to bring down an e-commerce website to prevent or deny usage by legitimate customers. DoS attacks are common on the Internet, where they have hit large companies such as Amazon.com, Microsoft, and AT&T. These attacks are often widely publicized in the media. Most simple DoS attacks occur from a single system, and a specific server or organization is the target.

There isn't a single type of DoS attack, but there are a variety of similar methods that have the same purpose. It's easiest to think of a DoS attack by imagining that your servers are so busy responding to false requests that they don't have time to service legitimate requests. Not only can the servers be physically busy, but the same result can occur if the attack consumes all the available bandwidth.

 Real World Scenario

Responding to an Attack

As a security administrator, you know all about the different types of attacks that can occur, and you're familiar with the value assigned to the data on your system. Now imagine that the log files indicate that an intruder entered your system for a lengthy period last week while you were away on vacation.

The first thing you should do is to make a list of questions you should begin asking to deal with the situation, using your network as a frame of reference. Some of the questions you should be thinking of include the following:

1. How can you show that a break-in really occurred?

2. How can you determine the extent of what was done during the entry?

3. How can you prevent further entry?

4. Whom should you inform in your organization?

5. What should you do next?

The most important question on the list, though, is whom you should inform in your organization. It's important to know the escalation procedures without hesitation and to be able to act quickly.

Several types of attacks can occur in this category. These attacks can deny access to information, applications, systems, or communications. In a DoS attack on an application, the attack may bring down a website while the communications and systems continue to operate. A DoS attack on a system crashes the operating system (a simple reboot may restore the server to normal operation). A DoS attack against a network is designed to fill the communications channel and prevent authorized users access. A common DoS attack involves opening as many TCP sessions as possible; this type of attack is called a TCP SYN flood DoS attack.

Two of the most common types of DoS attacks are the ping of death and the buffer overflow attack. The *ping of death* crashes a system by sending *Internet Control Message Protocol* (ICMP) packets (think echoes) that are larger than the system can handle. *Buffer overflow attacks*, as the name indicates, attempt to put more data (usually long input strings) into the buffer than it can hold. Code Red, Slapper, and Slammer are all attacks that take advantage of buffer overflows, and sPing is an example of a ping of death.

A *distributed denial-of-service (DDoS)* attack is similar to a DoS attack. This type of attack amplifies the concepts of a DoS by using multiple computer systems to conduct the attack against a single organization. These attacks exploit the inherent weaknesses of dedicated networks such as DSL and cable. These permanently attached systems usually have little, if any, protection. An attacker can load an attack program onto dozens or even hundreds of computer systems that use DSL or cable modems. The attack program lies dormant on these computers until they get an attack signal from a master computer. This signal triggers these systems, which launch an attack simultaneously on the target network or system.

The master controller may be another unsuspecting user. The systems taking direction from the master control computer are referred to as *zombies*. These systems merely carry out the instruction they've been given by the master computer.

Remember that the difference between a DoS attack and a DDoS attack is that the latter uses multiple computers—all focused on one target.

The nasty part of this type of attack is that the machines used to carry out the attack belong to normal computer users. The attack gives no special warning to those users. When the attack is complete, the attack program may remove itself from the system or infect the unsuspecting user's computer with a virus that destroys the hard drive, thereby wiping out the evidence.

Can You Prevent Denial Attacks?

In general, there is little you can do to fully prevent DoS or DDoS attacks. Your best method of dealing with these types of attacks involves countermeasures and prevention. Many operating systems are particularly susceptible to these types of attacks. Fortunately, most operating system manufacturers have implemented updates to minimize their effects. Make sure your operating system and the applications you use are up-to-date.

TCP Attacks

TCP operates by using synchronized connections. The synchronization is vulnerable to attack; this is probably the most common attack used today. As you may recall, the synchronization, or handshake, process initiates a TCP connection. This handshake is particularly vulnerable to a DoS attack referred to as a *TCP SYN flood attack*. The protocol is also susceptible to access and modification attacks, which are briefly explained in the following sections.

TCP SYN or TCP ACK Flood Attack

The *TCP SYN flood*, also referred to as the *TCP ACK attack*, is very common. The purpose of this attack is to deny service. The attack begins as a normal TCP connection: the client and server exchange information in TCP packets.

In this attack, the client continually sends and receives the ACK packets but doesn't open the session. The server holds these sessions open, awaiting the final packet in the sequence. This causes the server to fill up the available sessions and denies other clients the ability to access the resources.

This attack is virtually unstoppable in most environments without working with upstream providers. This type of attack can also be undetectable. An attacker can use an invalid IP address, and TCP won't care, because TCP will respond to any valid request presented from the IP layer. Two methods for mitigating are to configure time-outs for sessions on a server and/or to increase the buffer size on the server to accept more connections.

TCP Sequence Number Attack

TCP sequence number attacks occur when an attacker takes control of one end of a TCP session. This attack is successful when the attacker kicks the attacked end off the network for the duration of the session. Each time a TCP message is sent, both the client and the server generate a sequence number. In a TCP sequence number attack, the attacker intercepts and then responds with a *sequence number* similar to the one used in the original session. This attack can either disrupt or hijack a valid session. If a valid sequence number is guessed, the attacker can place himself between the client and the server.

In this case, the attacker effectively hijacks the session and gains access to the session privileges of the victim's system. The victim's system may get an error message indicating that it has been disconnected, or it may reestablish a new session. In this case, the attacker gains the connection and access to the data from the legitimate system. The attacker then has access to the privileges established by the session when it was created.

This weakness is again inherent in the TCP protocol, and little can be done to prevent it. Your major defense against this type of attack is knowing that it's occurring. Such an attack is also frequently a precursor to a targeted attack on a server or a network.

TCP/IP Hijacking

TCP/IP hijacking, also called *active sniffing*, involves the attacker gaining access to a host in the network and logically disconnecting it from the network. The attacker then inserts another machine with the same IP address. This happens quickly and gives the attacker access to the session and to all the information on the original system. The server won't know that this has occurred and will respond as if the client were trusted.

TCP/IP hijacking presents the greatest danger to a network because the hijacker will probably acquire privileges and access to all the information on the server. As with a sequence number attack, there is little you can do to counter the threat. Fortunately, these attacks require fairly sophisticated software and are harder to engineer than a DoS attack; an example might be a TCP SYN attack.

UDP Attacks

A *UDP attack* attacks either a maintenance protocol or a UDP service in order to overload services and initiate a DoS situation. UDP attacks can also exploit UDP protocols.

UDP packets aren't connection oriented and don't require the synchronization process described in the previous section. UDP packets, however, are susceptible to interception, and UDP can be attacked. UDP, like TCP, doesn't check the validity of IP addresses. The nature of this layer is to trust the layer below it, the IP layer.

The most common UDP attacks use *UDP flooding*. UDP flooding overloads services, networks, and servers. Large streams of UDP packets are focused at a target, causing the UDP services on that host to shut down. UDP floods also overload the network bandwidth and cause a DoS situation to occur.

ICMP Attacks

ICMP attacks occur by triggering a response from the ICMP protocol when it responds to a seemingly legitimate maintenance request. From earlier discussions, you'll recall that ICMP is often associated with echoing.

ICMP supports maintenance and reporting in a TCP/IP network. It's part of the IP level of the protocol suite. Several tools, including ping, use the ICMP protocol. Until fairly recently, ICMP was regarded as a benign protocol that was incapable of much damage. However, it has now joined the ranks of common methods used in DoS attacks. Two primary methods use ICMP to disrupt systems: smurf attacks and ICMP tunneling.

Smurf Attacks

Smurf attacks are becoming common and can create havoc in a network. A smurf attack uses IP spoofing and broadcasting to send a ping to a group of hosts in a network. When a host is pinged, it sends back ICMP message traffic information indicating status to the originator. If a broadcast is sent to a network, all of the hosts will answer back to the ping. The result is an overload of the network and the target system.

The attacker sends a broadcast message with a legal IP address. In this case, the attacking system sends a ping request to the broadcast address of the network. This request is sent to all the machines in a large network. The reply is then sent to the machine identified with the ICMP request (the spoof is complete). The result is a DoS attack that consumes the network bandwidth of the replying system, while the victim system deals with the flood of ICMP traffic it receives.

Smurf attacks are very popular. The primary method of eliminating them involves prohibiting ICMP traffic through a router. If the router blocks ICMP traffic, smurf attacks from an external attacker aren't possible.

ICMP Tunneling

ICMP messages can contain data about timing and routes. A packet can be used to hold information that is different from the intended information. This allows an ICMP packet to be used as a communications channel between two systems. The channel can be used to send a Trojan horse or other malicious packet.

The countermeasure for ICMP attacks is to deny ICMP traffic through your network. You can disable ICMP traffic in most routers, and you should consider doing so in your network.

New Attacks on the Way

The attacks described in this section aren't comprehensive. New methods are being developed as you read this book. Your first challenge in these situations is to recognize that you're fighting the battle on two fronts.

The first front involves the inherently open nature of TCP/IP and its protocol suite. TCP/IP is a robust and rich environment. This richness allows many opportunities to exploit the vulnerabilities of the protocol suite.

The second front of this battle involves the implementation of TCP/IP by various vendors. A weak TCP/IP implementation will be susceptible to all forms of attacks, and there is little you'll be able to do about it except to complain to the software manufacturer. Fortunately, most of the credible manufacturers are now taking these complaints seriously and doing what they can to close the holes they have created in your systems. Keep your updates current, because this is where most of the corrections for security problems are implemented.

IPv6 addresses many of the security issues present in the IPv4 protocol that is used today.

Recovering Operating Systems

Windows includes a number of tools to simplify recovering an operating system after a serious problem has occurred. System Restore is one such tool, as discussed in a later section. Others we'll look at here are the Recovery Console, Recovery CD, Automated System Recovery (ASR), and emergency repair disks (ERDs).

Recovery Console

The Recovery Console is a command-line utility used for troubleshooting. From it, you can format drives, stop and start services, and interact with files. The latter is extremely important because many boot/command-line utilities bring you into a position where you can interact with files stored on FAT or FAT32, but not NTFS. The Recovery Console can work with files stored on all three file systems.

The Recovery Console isn't installed on a system by default. To install it, use the following steps:

1. Place the Windows CD in the system.
2. From a command prompt, change to the i386 directory of the CD.
3. Type **winnt32 /cmdcons**.
4. A prompt appears, alerting you to the fact that 7MB of hard drive space is required and asking if you want to continue. Click Yes.

Upon successful completion of the installation, the Recovery Console (Microsoft Windows 2000 Recovery Console, for example) is added as a menu choice at the bottom of the startup menu. To access it, you must choose it from the list at startup. If more than one installation of Windows 2000 or Windows NT exists on the system, another boot menu will appear, asking which you want to boot into, and you must make a selection to continue.

To perform this task, you must give the administrator password. You'll then arrive at a command prompt. You can give a number of commands from this prompt, two of which are worth special attention: EXIT restarts the computer, and HELP lists the commands you can give. Table 19.1 lists the other commands available, most of which will be familiar to administrators who have worked with MS-DOS.

TABLE 19.1   Recovery Console Commands

Command	Purpose
ATTRIB	Shows the current attributes of a file or folder, and lets you change them
BATCH	Runs the commands within an ASCII text file
CD	Used without parameters, it shows the current directory. Used with parameters, it changes to the directory specified.
CHDIR	Works the same as CD
CHKDSK	Checks the disk for errors
CLS	Clears the screen
COPY	Allows you to copy a file (or files, if used with wildcards) from one location to another
DEL	Deletes a file
DELTREE	Recursively deletes files and directories
DIR	Shows the contents of the current directory.
DISABLE	Allows you to stop a service/driver
DISKPART	Shows the partitions on the drive, and lets you manage them
EXPAND	Extracts compressed files
ENABLE	Allows you to start a service/driver
FIXBOOT	Writes a new boot sector
FIXMBR	Checks and fixes (if possible) the master boot record
FORMAT	Allows you to format a floppy or partition

TABLE 19.1   Recovery Console Commands *(continued)*

Command	Purpose
LISTSVC	Shows the services/drivers on the system
LOGON	Lets you log on to Windows 2000
MAP	Shows the maps currently created
MD	Makes a new folder/directory
MKDIR	Works the same as MD
MORE	Shows only one screen of a text file at a time
RD	Removes a directory or folder
REN	Renames a file or folder
RENAME	Works the same as REN
RMDIR	Works the same as RD
SYSTEMROOT	Works like CD but takes you to the system root of whichever OS installation you're logged on to
TYPE	Displays the contents of an ASCII text file

During the installation of the Recovery Console, a folder named Cmdcons is created in the root directory to hold the executable files and drivers it needs. A file named Cmldr, with attributes of System, Hidden, and Read-Only, is also placed in the root directory.

If you want to delete the Recovery Console (to prevent users from playing around, for example), you can do so by deleting the Cmldr file and the Cmdcons folder, and removing the entry from the Boot.ini file.

Recovery CD/DVD

If you want to recover your computer and bring it back to the point where it was when it was new (minus any files you added since purchasing the machine), you can use the Recovery CD set or DVD. With Dell computers, for example, this is known as the Reinstallation DVD and accompanies each machine shipped; it can be used only to reinstall the operating system on the machine. After the Reinstallation DVD finishes, you must then use a similar DVD to reinstall the applications that were on the machine when it shipped.

WARNING   Use the Recovery sets only when nothing else seems to work and you are ready to start from scratch.

Automated System Recovery

It's possible to automate the process of creating a system recovery set by choosing the ASR Wizard on the Tools menu of the Backup utility (Start ➢ All Programs ➢ Accessories ➢ System Tools ➢ Backup).

NOTE   In Windows Vista, Backup appears as Backup Status and Configuration.

This wizard walks you through the process of creating a disk that can be used to restore parts of the system in the event of a major system failure.

The default name of this file is BACKUP.BKF; it requires a floppy disk. The backup set contains all the files necessary for starting the system, whereas the floppy becomes a bootable pointer to that backup set and can access and decompress it.

Emergency Repair Disk

The Windows Backup and Recovery Tool/Wizard allows you to create an emergency repair disk (ERD). As the name implies, this is a disk you can use to repair a portion of the system in the event of a failure.

When you choose this option, the tab changes to the Backup tab, and a prompt tells you to install a blank, formatted floppy disk. A check box inquires whether you want to save the Registry as well. (The default is no.) If you don't choose to save the Registry, the following files are placed on the floppy disk:

- SETUP.LOG
- CONFIG.NT
- AUTOEXEC.NT

This doesn't leave you much to work with. The disk isn't bootable and contains only three minor configuration utilities.

If you check the box to include the Registry in the backup, the floppy disk contains the preceding files plus the following:

- SECURITY._
- SOFTWARE._
- SYSTEM._
- DEFAULT._

- SAM._
- NTUSER.DAT
- USRCLASS.DAT

The user profile (NTUSER.DAT) is for the default user; the files with the ._ extension are compressed files from the Registry. The compression utility used is EXPAND.EXE, which offers you the flexibility of restoring any or all files from any Microsoft operating system, including this utility (Windows 95/98, Windows NT, and so on). Because this floppy contains key Registry files, it's important that you label it appropriately and store it in a safe location, away from users who should not have access to it.

> During the process of creating the backup, the Registry files are also backed up (in uncompressed state) to %systemroot%\repair\RegBack.

As before, the floppy isn't bootable, and you must bring the system up to a point (booted) where the floppy can be accessed before it's of any use.

Diagnostic Tools

Most of the tools that fall into this section have already been covered elsewhere in this chapter. Those that have not already been addressed are the boot menu and System File Checker.

Safe Mode

If, when you boot, Windows won't come all the way up (it hangs or is otherwise corrupted), you can often solve the problem by booting into Safe Mode. Safe Mode is a concept borrowed from Windows 95 wherein you can bring up part of the operating system by bypassing the settings, drivers, or parameters that may be causing it trouble during a normal boot. The goal of Safe Mode is to provide an interface with which you're able to fix the problems that occur during a normal boot and then reboot in normal mode.

To access Safe Mode, you must press F8 when the operating system menu is displayed during the boot process. A menu of Safe Mode choices will then appear, as listed in Table 19.2. Select the mode you want to boot into.

TABLE 19.2   Safe Mode Startup Menu

Choice	Loaded
Safe Mode	Provides the VGA monitor, Microsoft mouse drivers, and basic drivers for the keyboard (storage system services, no networking)
Safe Mode With Networking	Same as Safe Mode, but with networking

TABLE 19.2   Safe Mode Startup Menu *(continued)*

Choice	Loaded
Safe Mode With Command Prompt	Same as Safe Mode, but without the interface and drivers/services associated with it
Enable Boot Logging	Creates `ntbtlog.txt` in the root directory during any boot—normal attempted
Enable VGA Mode	Normal boot with only basic video drivers
Last Known Good Configuration	Uses the last backup of the Registry to bypass corruption caused during the previous session
Debugging Mode	Sends information through the serial port for interpretation/troubleshooting at another computer
Boot Normally	Bypasses any of the options here
Return To OS Choices Menu	Gives you an out in case you pressed F8 by accident

You need to keep a few rules in mind when booting in different modes:

- If problems don't exist when you boot to Safe Mode but do exist when you boot to normal mode, the problem isn't with basic services/drivers.

- If the system hangs when you load drivers, the log file can show you the last driver it attempted to load, which is usually the cause of the problem.

- If you can't solve the problem with Safe Mode, restore the Registry from the ERD to a state known to be good. Bear in mind that doing so will lose all changes that have occurred since the last ERD was made.

System File Checker

The purpose of this utility is to keep the operating system alive and well. SFC.EXE automatically verifies system files after a reboot to see if they were changed to unprotected copies. If an unprotected file is found, it's overwritten by a stored copy of the system file from `%systemroot%\system32\dllcache`. (`%systemroot%` is the folder into which the operating system was installed.)

Storing system files (some of which can be quite large) in two locations consumes a large amount of disk space. When you install an operating system, make sure you leave ample hard drive space on the `%systemroot%` drive for growth.

Only users with the Administrator group permissions can run SFC. It also requires the use of a parameter. The valid parameters are as follows:

Parameter	Function
/CACHSIZE=	Sets the size of the file cache
/CANCEL	Stops all checks
/ENABLE	Returns to normal mode
/PURGECACHE	Clears the cache
/QUIET	Replaces files without prompting
/SCANBOOT	Checks system files on every boot
/SCANNOW	Checks system files now
/SCANONCE	Checks system files at the next boot

Security and Troubleshooting

Hardening is the process of reducing or eliminating weaknesses, securing services, and attempting to make your environment immune to attacks. Typically, when you install operating systems, applications, and network products, the defaults from the manufacturer are to make the product as simple to use as possible and allow it to work with your existing environment as effortlessly as possible. That isn't always the best scenario when it comes to security.

You want to make certain that your systems, and the data within them, are kept as secure as possible. The security prevents others from changing the data, destroying it, or inadvertently harming it. This can be done by assigning users the least privileges possible in the Administrator/Power Users/Users/Guest hierarchy and hardening as much of the environment as possible.

Hardening the OS

Any network is only as strong as its weakest component. Sometimes, the most obvious components are overlooked, and it's your job as a security administrator to make certain that doesn't happen. You must make sure the operating systems running on the workstations and on the network servers are as secure as they can be.

Hardening an operating system (OS) refers to the process of making the environment more secure from attacks and intruders. This section discusses hardening an OS and the methods of keeping it hardened as new threats emerge. This section will also discuss some of the vulnerabilities of the more popular operating systems and what can be done to harden those OSs.

Hardening Windows Vista

The update for Microsoft's Windows XP line of products is Windows Vista, which is available in a number of editions. This product added or enhanced a number of security features, such as:

- Internet Connection Firewall (now called the Windows Firewall)

- Wireless connections

- Software restriction policies

- Encryption and cryptography enhancements

The best method of hardening the operating system, however, is to keep each implementation of it current. As of this writing, one service pack has been released. That service pack should be installed in every installation, and as an administrator, you should routinely monitor any security patches or updates released by Microsoft at the Windows Security Blog (http://windowsteamblog.com/blogs/windowssecurity/default.aspx).

> You can find the Windows Vista Security Guide at http://technet
> .microsoft.com/en-us/library/bb629420.aspx.

One new feature worth being aware of for the exam is the Vista User Account Control (UAC). (Don't be confused: currently, the CompTIA objectives mistakenly refer to the User *Access* Control, but they mean Account). UAC is an attempt at taking security to the application level by allowing software to run only as a regular user (and not administrator) by default. This is an attempt to limit privilege escalation and will bring up a prompt if an application attempts to escalate its privileges. Some applications—such as administrative tools within the operating system—naturally must escalate their privileges to run properly, and they will appear in listings with a Windows security shield beside them, similar to the one shown in Figure 19.10.

FIGURE 19.10 The Windows security shield indicates that the application must run with administrator privileges.

You can toggle UAC on and off by going to the user account and choosing the toggle option listed as the last item (as shown in Figure 19.11). When you choose to turn it off, naturally UAC will kick in and ask you to verify that you really want to do so. Once you choose Continue, UAC will not prompt you further when permissions need to be elevated.

FIGURE 19.11   Toggle the UAC settings on or off in Windows Vista.

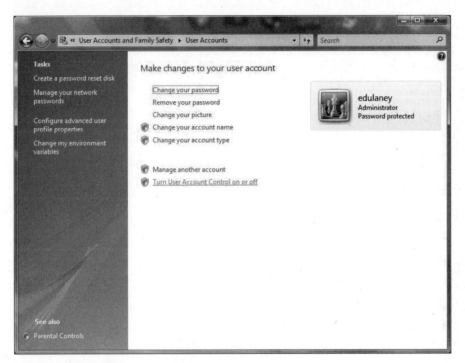

Hardening Microsoft Windows XP

Windows XP functions as a replacement for both the Windows $9x$ family and Windows 2000 Professional. There are multiple versions of Windows XP, including the Home, Media Center, and Professional editions.

The Windows XP Home edition was intended specifically to replace Windows $9x$ clients and could be installed either as an upgrade from Windows $9x$ or as a fresh installation on new systems. Media Center adds entertainment options (such as a remote control for TV), and Windows XP Professional is designed for the corporate environment. Windows XP Professional has the ability to take advantage of the security possible from Windows $200x$ servers running Active Directory.

With Microsoft's increased emphasis on security, it's reasonable to expect that the company will be working hard to make this product secure. At the time of this writing, the third service pack for XP is available. The service packs fix all known security openings within the operating system.

Hardening Microsoft Windows 2000

Windows 2000 entered the market at the millennium. It includes workstation and several server versions. The market has embraced these products, and they offer reasonable security when updated. Windows 2000 provides a Windows Update icon on the Start menu; this icon allows you to connect to the Microsoft website and automatically download and install updates. A large number of security updates are available for Windows 2000—make sure they're applied.

> In the Windows environment, the Services manager or applet is one of the primary methods (along with policies) used to disable a service.

The server and workstation products operate in a manner similar to Windows NT 4. These products run into the most security-related problems when they're bundled with products that Microsoft has included with them. Some of the more attack-prone products include Internet Information Server (IIS), FTP, and other common web technologies. Make sure these products are disabled if they aren't needed, and keep them up-to-date with the most recent security and service packs.

Many security updates have been issued for Windows 2000. The Microsoft TechNet and Security websites provide tools, whitepapers, and materials to help secure Windows 2000 systems.

> You can find the Microsoft TechNet website at http://technet.microsoft.com/default.aspx. The Microsoft security website is at www.microsoft.com/security/.

Windows 2000 includes extensive system logging, reporting, and monitoring tools. These tools help make the job of monitoring security fairly easy. In addition, Windows 2000 provides a great deal of flexibility in managing groups of users, security attributes, and access control to the environment.

The Event Viewer is the major tool for reviewing logs in Windows 2000. Figure 19.12 shows a sample Event Viewer log. A number of different types of events can be logged using the Event Viewer, and administrators can configure the level of events that are logged.

Another important security tool is Performance Monitor. As an administrator of a Windows 2000 network, you must know how to use Performance Monitor. This tool can be a lifesaver when you're troubleshooting problems and looking for resource-related issues.

Windows 2000 servers can run a technology called *Active Directory (AD)*, which lets you control security configuration options of Windows 2000 systems in a network. Unfortunately, you won't be able to access the full power of AD unless all the systems in your network are running Windows 2000 or higher.

FIGURE 19.12   Event Viewer log of a Windows 2000 system

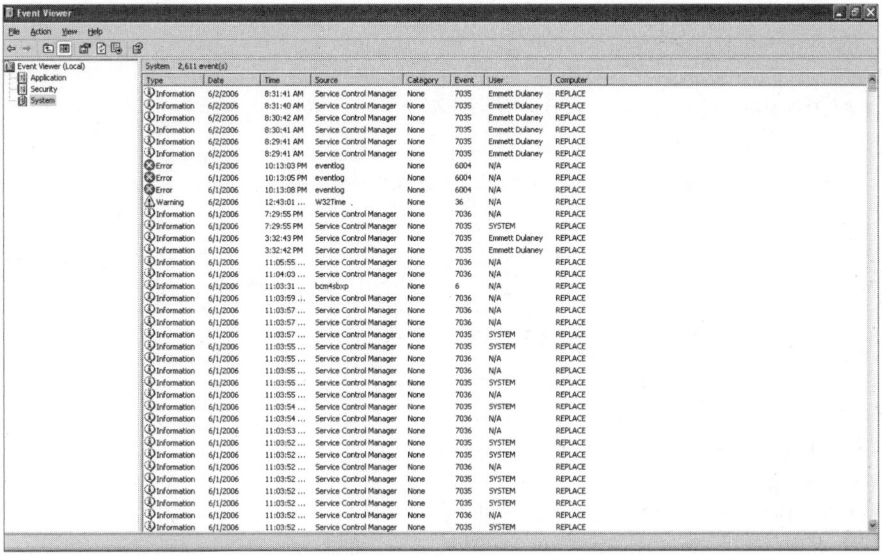

Updating Your Operating System

OS manufacturers typically provide product updates. For example, Microsoft provides a series of regular updates for their operating systems (proprietary systems) and other applications. However, in the case of public source systems (such as Linux), the updates may come from a newsgroup, the manufacturer of the version you're using, or a user community.

In both cases, public and private, updates help keep OSs up to the most current revision level. Researching updates is important; when possible, feedback is also recommended from other users before you. In a number of cases, a service pack or update has rendered a system unusable. Make sure your system is backed up before you install updates.

> **NOTE**
>
> Make sure you test updates on test systems before you implement them on production systems.

Three different types of updates are discussed here: hotfixes, service packs, and patches.

Hotfixes

Hotfixes are used to make repairs to a system during normal operation, even though they may require a reboot. A hotfix may entail moving data from a bad spot on the disk and remapping the data to a new sector. Doing so prevents data loss and loss of service. This type of repair may also involve reallocating a block of memory if, for example, a memory problem occurred. This allows the system to continue normal operations until a permanent repair can be made. Microsoft refers to a bug fix as a *hotfix*. This involves the replacement of files with an updated version.

Service Packs

A *service pack* is a comprehensive set of fixes consolidated into a single product. A service pack may be used to address a large number of bugs or to introduce new capabilities in an OS. When installed, a service pack usually contains a number of file replacements.

Make sure you check related websites to verify that the service pack works properly. Sometimes a manufacturer releases a service pack before it has been thoroughly tested. An untested service pack can cause extreme instability in an OS or, even worse, render it inoperable.

Patches

A *patch* is a temporary or quick fix to a program. Patches may be used to temporarily bypass a set of instructions that have malfunctioned. Several OS manufacturers issue patches that can be either manually applied or applied using a disk file to fix a program.

When you're working with customer support on a technical problem with an OS or an applications product, customer service may have you go into the code and make alterations to the binary files that run on your system. Double-check each change to prevent catastrophic failures due to improperly entered code.

When more data is known about the problem, a service pack or hotfix may be issued to fix the problem on a larger scale. Patching is becoming less common, because most OS manufacturers would rather release a new version of the code than patch it.

Other

In addition to keeping what you want current, you also want to remove what you don't want. Windows Defender (choose Start ➢ Control Panel ➢ Security ➢ Windows Defender) can identify spyware and unwanted software. Figure 19.13 shows the interface for this utility in Windows Vista. Defender is native to all versions of Vista but must be downloaded and installed for XP Service Pack 2 or later.

As with similar programs, in order for Windows Defender to function properly, you need to keep the definitions current and scan on a regular basis. In Exercise 19.1, you'll run Windows Defender in Windows Vista; Exercise 19.2 mirrors these actions using Windows XP.

FIGURE 19.13   Windows Defender can identify security threats.

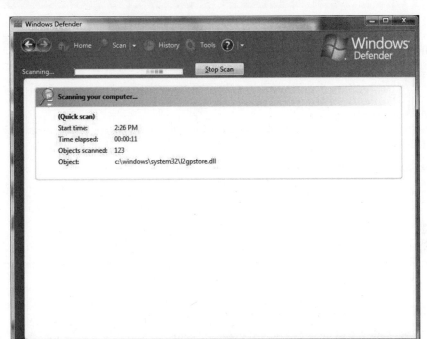

EXERCISE 19.1

Run Windows Defender in Windows Vista

The following steps are necessary to run a scan of your system using Windows Defender within Windows Vista:

1. Choose Start ➢ Control Panel ➢ Security ➢ Windows Defender.

2. If you are prompted that Defender is not configured, choose to turn it on (this will bring up a UAC prompt to continue if UAC is toggled on).

3. From the drop-down list next to help (a question mark in a blue circle), choose Check For Updates (again, if UAC is toggled on, you will be prompted to continue).

4. Click Scan.

5. Upon completion, the message "Your computer is running normally" should appear within the frame "No unwanted or harmful software detected." If anything else appears, resolve those issues.

6. Exit Windows Defender.

EXERCISE 19.2

Run Windows Defender in Windows XP

The following steps are necessary to run a scan of your system using Windows Defender within Windows XP:

1. Choose Start ➤ Control Panel ➤ Security ➤ Software Explorers. Windows Defender will appear.

2. From the drop-down list next to help (a question mark in a blue circle), choose Check For Updates.

3. Click Scan.

4. Upon completion, the message "Your computer is running normally" should appear within the frame "No unwanted or harmful software detected." If anything else appears, resolve those issues.

5. Exit Windows Defender.

Working with Filesystems

Several file systems are involved in the OSs we've discussed, and they have a high level of interoperability between them—from a network perspective, that is. Through the years, the different vendors have implemented their own sets of file standards. Some of the more common file systems include the following:

Microsoft FAT   Microsoft's earliest file system was referred to as File Allocation Table (FAT). FAT is designed for relatively small disk drives. It was upgraded first to FAT16 and finally to FAT32. FAT32 allows large disk systems to be used on Windows systems. FAT allows only two types of protection: share-level and user-level access privileges. If users have write or change access to a drive or directory, they have access to any file in that directory. This is very unsecure in an Internet environment.

Microsoft NTFS   The New Technology File System (NTFS) was introduced with Windows NT to address security problems. Before Windows NT was released, it had become apparent to Microsoft that a new file system was needed to handle growing disk sizes, security concerns, and the need for more stability. NTFS was created to address those issues.

Although FAT was relatively stable if the systems that were controlling it kept running, it didn't do well when the power went out or the system crashed unexpectedly. One of the benefits of NTFS was a transaction-tracking system, which made it possible for Windows NT to back out of any disk operations that were in progress when Windows NT crashed or lost power.

With NTFS, files, directories, and volumes can each have their own security. NTFS's security is flexible and built in. Not only does NTFS track security in ACLs, which can hold permissions for local users and groups, but each entry in the ACL can specify what type of access is given. This allows for a great deal of flexibility in setting up a network. In addition, special file-encryption programs were developed to encrypt data while it was stored on the hard disk.

Full Control, Change, and Read are permissions available in FAT32. NTFS offers six permissions (Full Control, Modify, Read & Execute, List Folder Contents, Read, and Write) that are preconfigured from a list of 14 granular permissions (Advanced Permissions).

Microsoft strongly recommends that all network shares be established using NTFS. Several current OSs from Microsoft support both FAT32 and NTFS. It's possible to convert from FAT32 to NTFS without losing data, but you can't do the operation in reverse (you would need to reformat the drive and install the data again from a backup tape).

If you're using FAT32 and want to change to NTFS, the convert utility will allow you to do so. For example, to change the E: drive to NTFS, the command is convert e: /FS:NTFS.

Converting to NTFS cannot be undone or reversed.

Share permissions apply only when a user is accessing a file or folder through the network. Local permissions and attributes are used to protect the file when the user is local. With FAT and FAT32, you do not have the ability to assign "extended" or "extensible" permissions, and the user sitting at the console effectively is the owner of all resources on the system. As such, they can add, change, and delete any data or file that they want.

With NTFS as the file system, however, you are allowed to assign more comprehensive security to your computer system. NTFS permissions are able to protect you at the file level. Share permissions can be applied to the directory level only. NTFS permissions can affect users logged on locally or across the network to the system where the NTFS permissions are applied. Share permissions are in effect only when the user connects to the resource via the network.

Permissions can be allowed or denied individually on a per-folder basis. You can assign any combination of the values shown in Table 19.3.

TABLE 19.3   NTFS Folder Permissions

NTFS Permission	Meaning
Full Control	Gives the user all the other choices and the ability to Change Permission. The user also can take ownership of the directory or any of its contents.
Modify	Combines the Read & Execute permission with the Write permission and further allows the user to delete everything, including the folder
Read & Execute	Combines the permissions of Read with those of List Folder Contents and adds the ability to run executables
List Folder Contents	The List Folder Contents permission (known simply as List in previous versions) allows the user to view the contents of a directory and to navigate to its subdirectories. It does not grant the user access to the files in these directories unless that is specified in file permissions.
Read	Allows the user to navigate the entire directory structure, view the contents of the directory, view the contents of any files in the directory, and see ownership and attributes
Write	Allows the user to create new entities within the folder, as well as to change ownership, permissions, and attributes

Clicking the Advanced command button allows you to configure auditing and ownership properties. You can also apply NTFS permissions to individual files. This is done from the Security tab for the file, and Table 19.4 lists the NTFS file permissions.

TABLE 19.4   NTFS File Permissions

NTFS Permission	Meaning
Full Control	Gives the user all the other permissions as well as permission to take ownership and change permission
Modify	Combines the Read & Execute permission with the Write permission and further allows the user to delete the file
Read & Execute	Combines the Read permission with the ability to execute

TABLE 19.4   NTFS File Permissions *(continued)*

NTFS Permission	Meaning
Read	Allows the user to view the contents of the file and to see ownership and attributes
Write	Allows the user to overwrite the file, as well as to change attributes and see ownership and permissions

By default, the determination of NTFS permissions is based on the *cumulative* NTFS permissions for a user. Rights can be assigned to users based on group membership and individually; the only time permissions do not accumulate is when the Deny permission is invoked. Be careful; Deny can be dangerous since it overrides Allow. Be cautious when adding Deny to a group as doing so may have unexpected results.

General Rules for Security and Troubleshooting

As with most objectives, there are a number of general rules to adhere to, regardless of which OSs are employed on your servers and clients. Among those rules, as they relate to topics discussed here, are the following:

- Know the authentication possibilities for the OSs you use, and know what each allows. In addition to those that come standard with the OS, you can also employ add-on devices such as biometric scanners to increase the security of the authentication process (authentication is discussed in Chapter 11, while add-on devices are discussed later in this chapter).

- Understand that firewalls can be software- or hardware-based, and are usually some combination of the two. Software-only firewalls are usually limited to home use and provide the line of defense preventing outside users from gaining access to the home computer.

- Event logging is used to record events and provide a trail that can be followed to determine what was done. Auditing involves looking at the logs and finding problems (this is explained in a later section in this chapter).

- Wireless clients can be configured to access the network the same as wired clients, but wireless security is a touchy issue. There are protocols that you can use to add security, but it's still difficult to secure a wireless network the same way you can secure a wired one. Having an unsecured wireless connection is the same as leaving a security door open.

- Data access can be limited a number of different ways—permissions to the data and basic local security policies are two universal methods that should be used regardless of the OS you're employing (this is covered later in this chapter).

- The file system you're using can determine what permissions you have available to assign to resources. NTFS offers a great deal of granularity in terms of permissions, whereas FAT32 offers few choices. You can convert from FAT32 to NTFS without data loss by using the convert utility.

- To increase the level of authentication, you can employ biometrics, key fobs, and smart cards. Smart-card readers may be contact-based (you have to insert the card) or contactless (the card is read when it's in proximity to the reader). Key fobs are often used to provide a randomly generated number that you can enter for authentication, and biometric devices identify the user by some physical aspect (such as a thumbprint), a topic covered later in this chapter.

While key fobs are often thought of as devices that generate random numbers, the term is also used for many small devices that allow for keyless entry into buildings or vehicles. While those only require proximity and a clear line of sight, when it comes to true security, you want something that also incorporates a challenge/response to authenticate the user.

Access Control

Access control lists (ACLs) enable devices in your network to ignore requests from specified users or systems, or to grant them certain network capabilities. You may find that a certain IP address is constantly scanning your network, and thus you can block this IP address from your network. If you block it at the router, the IP address will automatically be rejected any time it attempts to utilize your network.

ACLs allow a stronger set of access controls to be established in your network. The basic process of ACL control lets the administrator design and adapt the network to deal with specific security threats.

Working with Policies

One of the most wide-sweeping administrative features that Windows 200*x* offered over its predecessors and other OSs is that of *Group Policy*. A part of IntelliMirror, the Group Policy feature enables administrators to control desktop settings, utilize scripts, perform Internet Explorer maintenance, roll out software, redirect folders, and so forth. All of these features can be an administrator's dream in supporting LAN users.

Consider this analogy: when you connect a television set to the subscription cable coming through the living-room wall, you get all the channels to which you subscribe. If you pay an extra $50 per month (depending on where you live), you can get close to 100 channels, including a handful of premium channels.

When you turn on the television, you're free to watch any of the channels—regardless of whether the content is questionable or racy. And when you're gone, your children are free to do the same. Enter the V-chip. Before leaving your children alone with the television, you enable the V-chip. The V-chip lets you (the "administrator") restrict access to stations that air questionable or racy programming.

How is this example analogous to an OS? On Windows 2000 Professional, for example, users can do just about anything they want. They can delete programs and never be able to run them again; they can send huge graphics files to a tiny printer that can print only one page every 30 minutes; they can delete the Registry and never be able to use the system again; and so forth. Enter Group Policy.

Group Policy places restrictions on what a user/computer is allowed to do. It takes away liberties that were otherwise there; therefore, they are never implemented for the benefit of the user (restrictions don't equal benefits) but are always there to simplify administration for the administrator.

From an administrator's standpoint, if you take away the ability to add new software, then you don't have to worry about supporting untested applications. If you remove the ability to delete installed printers (accidentally, of course), then you don't have to waste an hour reinstalling the printer. By reducing what users can do, you reduce what you must support, and you also reduce the overall administrative cost of supporting the network/computer/user.

Group Policies work well for users who connect to the LAN, including roaming users, but not for users who don't connect to the LAN, such as mobile users. Let's clarify the difference. As the name implies, *roaming users* are users who roam throughout the LAN using different computers. One example is a secretary in a secretarial pool. On Monday, the secretary may be working in Accounting, on Tuesday in Human Resources, and for the remainder of the week in Marketing. Within each department, the secretary uses a different computer but is still on the same LAN. By placing the secretary's profile on the network and configuring them as a roaming user, you give them the same desktop and access to all resources regardless of where they work on any given day. Not only that, but the same Group Policy applies (and is routinely refreshed), to prevent the secretary from permanently deleting software that has been assigned, changing the desktop, and so on.

An example of a *mobile user*, on the other hand, is a salesperson who is in the field calling on customers. In their possession is a $6,000 laptop capable of doing everything shy of changing the oil of the company car. Whenever the salesperson has a problem with the computer, they call from 3,000 miles away and begin the conversation with, "It did it again." You not only have no idea to whom you're talking, you have no idea what "it" refers to.

In short, roaming users use different computers within the same LAN, whereas mobile users use the same workstation but don't connect to the LAN. Because you can't force mobile users to connect to a server on your LAN each time they boot (and when they do, it's over slow connections), you're less able to enforce administrative restrictions—such as Group Policies. However, it isn't impossible to apply administrative restrictions to mobile users. System Policies (used in Windows 9x) are the predecessors of Group Policies. They're restricted to governing Registry settings only, whereas Group Policies exceed that functionality.

In the absence of a regular connection to the LAN (and, therefore, to Active Directory), there are a number of Group Policy restrictions that you can't enforce or utilize. Therefore, it's always in the best interest of the administrators to have the systems connect to the network (and require them to do so) whenever possible. The following is a list of restrictions that can't be enforced without such a connection:

Assigning and publishing software   The Software Installation extension enables you to centrally manage software. You can publish software to users and assign software to computers.

Folder redirection   The Folder Redirection extension lets you reroute special Windows folders—including My Documents, Application Data, Desktop, and the Start Menu—from the user profile location to elsewhere on the network.

Remote installation   The Remote Installation Services (RIS) extension enables you to control the Remote Operating System Installation component, as displayed to the client computers.

Roaming profiles   By placing the user's profile on the server, they can have the same desktop regardless of which computer they use on a given day. That profile is the collection of all the computer settings specific to them. By placing these in one location accessible from anywhere (on the server), it is possible for those settings to "roam" with them to any machine they may use.

In addition to these, you can place all the other settings directly on the mobile computer—making them local policies. Local policies can apply to the following:

Administrative templates   The administrative templates consist mostly of the Registry restrictions that existed in System Policies. They let you manage the Registry settings that control the desktop, including applications and OS components.

Scripts   Scripts enable you to automate user logon and logoff.

Security settings   The Security Settings extension lets you define security options (local, domain, and network) for users within the scope of a Group Policy object, including Account Policy, encryption, and so forth.

Creating the Local Policy

You can create a local policy on a computer by using the Group Policy Editor. You can start the Group Policy Editor in one of the following two ways:

- Choose Start ➤ Run, and then enter **gpedit.msc**.

- Choose Start ➤ Run, and then enter **MMC**. In the MMC console, choose Console ➤ Open, and then select GPEDIT.MSC from the System32 directory of the %systemroot% folder.

When opened, a local policy has two primary divisions: Computer Configuration and User Configuration. The settings you configure beneath Computer Configuration apply to the computer, regardless of who is using it. Conversely, the settings you configure beneath User Configuration apply only if the specified user is logged on. Each of the primary divisions can be useful for certain circumstances. Note that the Computer Configuration settings are applied whenever the computer is on, whereas the User Configuration settings are applied only when the user logs on.

The following options are available under the Computer Configuration setting:

Software Settings   These settings typically are empty on a new system.

Administrative Templates   These settings are those administrators commonly want to apply.

Windows Settings   The Windows Settings are further divided:

> **Scripts**   Scripts are divided into Startup and Shutdown, both of which enable you to configure items (.EXE, .CMD, .BAT, and other files) to run when a computer starts and stops. Although your implementation may differ, for the most part, little here is pertinent to the mobile user.

> **Security Settings**   Security Settings are divided into Account Policies, Local Policies, Public Key Policies, and IP Security Policies on the local machine.

> The following sections examine some of the Security Settings choices.

Account Policies

Account Policies further divides into Password Policy and Account Lockout Policy. The following seven choices are available under Password Policy, and the majority of them were previously in the Account Policy menu of User Manager on Windows NT Workstation:

Enforce Password History   This allows you to require unique passwords for a certain number of iterations. The default number is 0, but it can go as high as 24.

Maximum Password Age   The default is 42 days, but values range from 0 to 999.

Minimum Password Age   The default is 0 days, but values range from 0 to 999.

Minimum Password Length   The default is 0 characters (meaning no passwords are required), but you can specify a number up to 14.

Passwords Must Meet Complexity Requirements Of The Installed Password Filter   The default is disabled.

Store Password Using Reversible Encryption For All Users In The Domain   The default is disabled.

User Must Logon To Change The Password   The default is disabled, thus allowing a user with an expired password to specify a new password during the logon process.

Because the likelihood of laptops being stolen always exists, it's strongly encouraged that you use good password policies for this audience. Here's an example:

- Enforce Password History: 8 passwords remembered
- Maximum Password Age: 42 days
- Minimum Password Age: 3 days
- Minimum Password Length: 6 to 8 characters

Leave the other three settings disabled.

Account Lockout Policy

The Account Lockout Policy setting divides into the following three values:

Account Lockout Counter   This is the number of invalid attempts before lockout occurs. The default is 0 (meaning the feature is turned off). Invalid attempt numbers range from 1 to 999. A number greater than 0 changes the values of the following two options to 30 minutes; otherwise, they are "not defined."

Account Lockout Duration   This is a number of minutes ranging from 1 to 99999. A value of 0 is also allowed here and signifies that the account never unlocks itself—administrator interaction is always required.

Reset Account Lockout Counter After   This is a number of minutes, ranging from 1 to 99999.

When you're working with a mobile workforce, you must weigh the choice of users calling you in the middle of the night when they've forgotten their password against keeping the system from being entered if the wrong user picks up the laptop. A good recommendation is to use a lockout after five attempts for a period of time between 30 and 60 minutes.

Local Policy Settings

The Local Policies section divides into three subsections: Audit Policy, User Rights Assignment, and Security Options. The Audit Policy section contains nine settings; the default value for each is No Auditing. Valid options are Success and/or Failure. The Audit Account Logon Events entry is the one you should consider turning on for mobile users to see how often they log in and out of their machines.

When auditing is turned on for an event, the entries are logged in the Security log file.

The User Rights Assignment subsection of Local Policies is where the meat of the old System Policies comes into play. User Rights Assignment has many options, most of which are self-explanatory. Also shown in the list that follows are the defaults for who can perform these actions; Not Defined indicates that no one is specified for this operation. You can add groups and users, but you can't remove them. (This functionality isn't needed.) If you want to "remove" users or groups from the list, uncheck the box granting them access. If your mobile users need to be able to install, delete, and modify their environment, make them a member of the Power Users group.

The Security Options section includes a great many options, which, for the most part, are Registry keys. The default for each is Not Defined; the two definitions that can be assigned are Enabled and Disabled, or a physical number (as with the number of previous logons to cache).

Working with Disks and Directories

The basic building block of storage is the disk. Disks are partitioned (primary, logical, extended) and then formatted for use. With the Windows operating systems this exam focuses on, you can choose to use either FAT32 or NTFS. The advantage of NTFS is that it offers security and many other features that FAT32 can't handle.

If you're using FAT32 and want to change to NTFS, the convert utility will allow you to do so. For example, to change the E: drive to NTFS, the command is convert e: /FS:NTFS.

Once the disk is formatted, the next building block is the directory structure, in which you divide the partition into logical locations for storing data. Whether these storage units are called directories or folders is a matter of semantics—they tend to be called *folders* when viewed in the graphical user interface (GUI) and *directories* when viewed from the command line.

You can create directories from the command line using the MD command and from within the GUI by right-clicking in a Windows Explorer window and choosing New ➤ Folder. Once the folder exists, you can view or change its properties, as shown in Figure 19.14, by right-clicking the icon of its folder and choosing Properties.

FIGURE 19.14 Changing the attributes associated with a directory

In the Attributes section, you can choose to make the directory read-only or hidden. By clicking the Advanced button, you can configure indexing, archiving, encryption, and compression settings.

Even though encryption and compression settings appear in the same frame on the dialog box, the two features are mutually exclusive.

The building blocks of directories are files. You can create a file either from within an application or by right-clicking, choosing New, and then selecting the type of item you want to create, as shown in Figure 19.15.

FIGURE 19.15 You can create files of various types with a right-click.

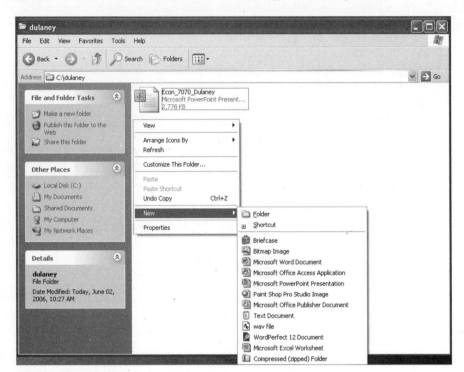

Once the file has been created, you can right-click the file's icon and change properties and permissions associated with the file by choosing Properties from the context menu. Know that when users copy or move a file, they may get results different than what they expected when it comes to permissions. In most operating systems, a file copied into a folder will, by default, inherit the rights of the folder. This will be the same with encryption as well—if a user copies an unencrypted file into an encrypted folder, the file will become encrypted. Conversely, if the user copies an encrypted file into an unencrypted folder, the file becomes unencrypted.

If a user moves a file from one folder to another, the file system will keep the permissions that existed as long as the new folder can support them. This is an important caveat, for if an NTFS file is moved to a FAT-based flash drive, the permissions existing only in NTFS will be gone.

Administrative Tools for Disks and Directories

The administrative tools that fall into this section are the primary tools used on a regular basis. Most of them relate to data and drives, but that isn't true of all of them. The tools that CompTIA wants you to know are as follows:

CHKDSK   CHKDSK is an old MS-DOS command that is used to correct logical errors in the FAT. The most common switch for CHKDSK is /F, which fixes the errors that it finds. Without /F, CHKDSK is an information-only command.

DEFRAG   This command runs the Disk Defragmenter utility. It works only under MS-DOS or from startup disks. Disk Defragmenter reorganizes the file storage on a disk to reduce the number of files that are stored noncontiguously. This makes file retrieval faster, because the read/write heads on the disk have to move less.

There are two versions of Disk Defragmenter: command-line version, and a Windows version that runs from within Windows. The Windows version is located on the System Tools submenu on the Start menu (Start ➤ All Programs ➤ Accessories ➤ System Tools ➤ Disk Defragmenter). In Exercise 19.3, you will run the Disk Defragmenter in Windows Vista; Exercise 19.4 mirrors these actions in Windows XP.

EXERCISE 19.3

Run Disk Defragmenter in Windows Vista

The following steps are necessary to run a disk defragmentation operation of your system using Disk Defragmenter within Windows Vista:

1. Choose Start ➤ All Programs ➤ Accessories ➤ System Tools ➤ Disk Defragmenter.

2. If you are prompted by UAC to continue, choose to do so. The Disk Defragmenter utility will appear.

3. Click the Defragment Now button.

4. Choose the disks to defragment and click OK.

5. Exit Disk Defragmenter.

EXERCISE 19.4

Run Disk Defragmenter in Windows XP

The following steps are necessary to run a disk defragmentation operation of your system using Disk Defragmenter in Windows XP:

1. Choose Start ➤ All Programs ➤ Accessories ➤ System Tools ➤ Disk Defragmenter. The Disk Defragmenter utility will appear.

2. Choose the disks to defragment and click Analyze. The results will tell you if the possible changes are worth doing.

3. If the analysis suggests that you should defragment, click the Defragment button.

4. Upon completion, exit Disk Defragmenter.

The available switches for the command-line version (`defrag.exe`) include the following:

-a	Analyze only
-f	Force defragmentation even if disk space is low
-v	Verbose output

Device Manager   Device Manager shows a list of all installed hardware and lets you add items, remove items, update drivers, and more. This is a Windows-only utility. In Windows 2000/XP/Vista, you display the System Properties, click the Hardware tab, and then click the Device Manager button to display it. Figure 19.16 shows the Device Manager in Windows XP.

FIGURE 19.16   The Device Manager in Windows XP

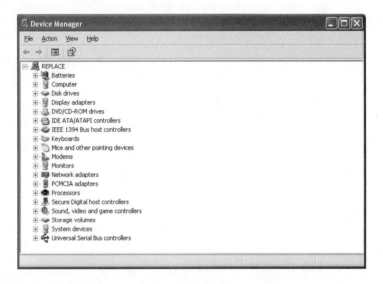

Event Viewer   This utility provides information about what's been going on system-wise, to help you troubleshoot problems. The Event Viewer shows warnings, error messages, and records of things happening successfully. It's found in NT-based versions of Windows only (which include Windows 2000, Windows XP, and Windows Vista). You can access it through Computer Management, or you can access it directly from the Administrative Tools in Control Panel.

MSCONFIG (System Configuration Utility)   This utility helps troubleshoot startup problems by allowing you to selectively disable individual items that normally are executed at startup. There is no menu command for this utility; you must run it with the Run command (on the Start menu). Choose Start ➤ Run, and type MSCONFIG. It works in most versions of Windows, although the interface window is slightly different among versions.

NTBackup   With Windows 2000 and XP, you can access this utility from the System Tools menu, or from the Tools tab in a hard disk's Properties box. Its purpose is to back up files in a compressed format, so the backups take up less space than the original files would if they were copied. To restore the backup, you must use the same utility again, but in Restore mode. The best insurance policy you have against devastating loss when a failure occurs is a backup of the data that you can turn to when the system is rebuilt.

When you start the program, by default it begins the Backup Or Restore Wizard (you can disable this default action by deselecting Always Start In Wizard Mode in the first dialog box). The wizard will walk you through any backup/restore operation you want to do, or you can click Advanced Mode to get to the interface shown in Figure 19.17.

FIGURE 19.17   The Backup utility in Windows XP

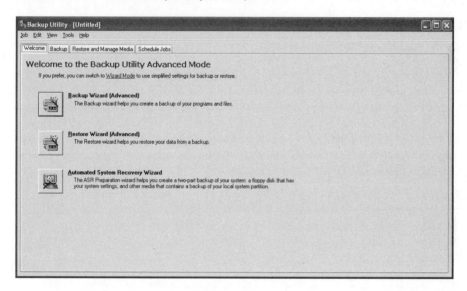

Five backup type choices are available:

Normal   A full backup of all files, regardless of the state of the archive bit (the default). After the files are backed up, the archive bit is turned off.

Copy   A full backup of all files, regardless of the state of the archive bit. The archive bit is left in its current state.

Incremental   Backs up only files for which the archive bit is currently turned on. After the files are backed up, the archive bit is turned off.

Differential   Backs up only files for which the archive bit is currently turned on. The archive bit is left in its current state.

Daily   Backs up only those files with today's date, regardless of archive bit status.

You can also perform backups from the command line by using the `ntbackup.exe` executable. You can't restore files from the command line with this utility, however. Options include the following:

/A   Performs an append

/F   Identifies the disk path and filename

/HC:{on|off}   Toggles hardware compression on or off

/J   Signifies the job name

/M   Must be followed by a backup type name: `copy`, `daily`, `differential`, `incremental`, or `normal`

/N   Signifies a new tape name; can't be used in conjunction with /A

/P   Signifies the media pool name

/T   Followed by the tape name

/V:{yes|no}   Toggles whether to do verification after the completion of the backup

Regedit and Regedt32 (Registry Editor)   The Registry Editor is used to change values and variables stored in a configuration database known as the Registry. This centralized database contains environmental settings for various Windows programs along with registration information, which details the types of file extensions associated with applications. So, when you double-click a file in Windows Explorer, the associated application runs and opens the file you double-clicked.

The Registry Editor, shown in Figure 19.18, enables you to make changes to the large hierarchical database that contains all of Windows' settings. These changes can potentially disable the entire system, so they should not be made lightly.

FIGURE 19.18   The Registry Editor in Windows XP

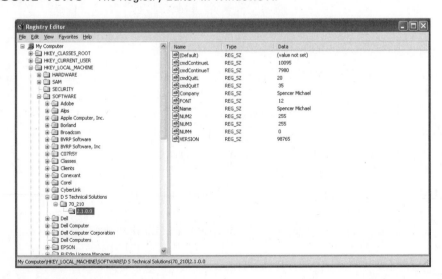

There is no menu command for the Registry Editor. You must run it with the Run command. Regedit is the name of the program. Windows 2000 includes a second Registry Editor program called Regedt32. This alternative program accesses the same Registry but does so in a slightly different way; it shows each of the major key areas in a separate window. In Windows XP and Vista, the command REGEDT32 is present, but running it launches Regedit; they have been rolled into a single utility.

The Registry holds great power but can also cause great harm. Never edit the Registry without being completely sure what you're doing.

Remote Desktop   The Remote Desktop feature of Windows XP and Vista allows you to remotely connect to your workstation and use it for a variety of purposes—work from home, teach a user how to do a task, and so on. Two elements are involved:

Turning on the ability to access remotely

Accessing remotely

To do the first, access the System Properties, click the Remote tab, and select the Allow Users To Connect Remotely To This Computer Under Remote Desktop check box. Click Apply, and then click OK to exit.

To access the computer from another XP workstation, choose Start ➤ All Programs ➤ Accessories, and choose Remote Desktop Connection. If you click the Options button, you'll see choices similar to those in Figure 19.19.

FIGURE 19.19   The Remote Desktop Connection dialog box in Windows XP

One of the simplest ways to connect is to enter the IP address of the host. Once you give a valid username and password, you're connected to the host and able to work remotely.

System Restore   System Restore is arguably the most powerful tool in Windows XP and Windows Vista. It can allow you to restore the system to a previous point in time. You can access it from Start ➢ All Programs ➢ Accessories ➢ System Tools ➢ System Restore and use it to roll back as well as to create a restore point, as shown in Figure 19.20.

FIGURE 19.20   Create a restore point or return to one with System Restore.

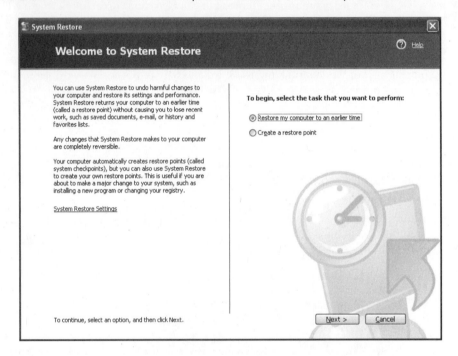

In addition to letting you manually create a restore point, Windows XP and Vista create a restore point automatically every 24 hours, as well as when you install unsigned device drivers or install (or uninstall) a program with Windows Installer or InstallShield. By default, restore points are kept for 90 days and then deleted in order to conserve space.

 You must be a member of Computer Administrators to run System Restore.

Task Manager   Task Manager shows running programs and the system resources they're consuming. It can be used for informational purposes, but it's most often used to shut down a nonresponsive application.

There are many ways to display the Task Manager; we show three here. The first is to press Ctrl+Alt+Delete and click the Task Manager button (if required). The second is to right-click in an empty location on the Taskbar and choose Task Manager from the context menu. The third method is to hold down Ctrl+Shift and press Esc.

A list of running tasks appears under the Applications tab; you can click one of them and then click End Task to shut it down. Because this shutdown method fails to close files gracefully, you should use it only as a last resort, not as a normal method of shutting down an application. You can also choose the Processes tab to see all processes—not just applications—running, or choose Performance to see CPU, paging, memory, and other parameters. The Networking tab shows usage for all found connections, and the Users tab shows the current users and lets you disconnect them, log them off, or send them a message.

Windows Explorer   Windows Explorer is the primary file-management interface in Windows. It displays the list of files in the current location at the right and a folder tree of other locations at the left. It starts with the My Documents folder as its default location when opened. Windows Explorer is available in all Windows versions and works approximately the same way in each.

Auditing and Logging

Most systems generate *security logs* and *audit files* of activity on the system. These files do absolutely no good if they aren't periodically reviewed for unusual events. Many web servers provide message auditing, as do logon, system, and application servers.

The amount of information these files contain can be overwhelming. You should establish a procedure to review them on a regular basis. A rule of thumb is never to start auditing by trying to record everything, because the sheer volume of the entries will make the data unusable. Approach auditing from the opposite perspective, and begin auditing only a few key things; then, expand the audits as you find you need more data.

These files may also be susceptible to access or modification attacks. The files often contain critical systems information, including resource sharing and security status. An attacker may be able to use this information to gather more detailed data about your network.

In an access attack, these files can be deleted, modified, and scrambled to prevent systems administrators from knowing what happened in the system. A logic bomb could, for example, delete these files when it completes. Administrators might know that something happened, but they would get no clues or assistance from the log and audit files.

In addition to checking logs and audit files, you should consider periodically inspecting systems to see what software is installed and whether passwords are posted on sticky notes on monitors or keyboards. A good way to do this without attracting attention is to clean all the monitor faces. While you're cleaning the monitors, you can also verify that physical security is being upheld. If you notice a password on a sticky note, you can "accidentally" forget to put it back. You should also notify that user that this is an unsafe practice and not to continue it.

You should also consider obtaining a vulnerability scanner and running it across your network. A *vulnerability scanner* is a software application that checks your network for any known security holes; it's better to run one on your own network before someone outside the organization runs it against you.

You should always work within the guidelines established by your company. Before trying to hack your system to check for vulnerabilities, make sure company policy allows it.

BIOS Security

We discussed BIOS security, and all the objectives related to it, in Chapter 11. The material that follows reviews information located there. The system Basic Input/Output System (BIOS) is used to power up the system and can also allow you to assign a password. Actually, most BIOS implementations allow for both user and supervisor passwords to be set. The supervisor's password allows access to the BIOS setup program. Once enabled/activated, passwords are stored in CMOS and must be given before the system will fully boot.

This provides a simple security solution as users must supply a password in order to be able to access the system; if they cannot give the correct value, the drives are essentially locked. The supervisor password is only needed when the user attempts to access the setup program. Passwords used for BIOS-level security should follow the same rules as passwords for any account.

One other feature to be aware of in the BIOS setup from most vendors is the ability to toggle chassis intrusion detection. If enabled, this will notify you (via a pop-up) if someone has opened the case.

There are two common ways to work around the password requirements. Casual hackers will most likely remove the battery (thus erasing the CMOS). Others will use a backdoor password, which many BIOS manufacturers allow to bypass the one set by the user. Many of these values can be found on the Internet and are known by more professional hackers.

Another method for getting around the password is to change the jumper for resetting CMOS settings to defaults.

Within the advanced settings on some BIOS configuration menus, you can choose to enable or disable TPM. A *Trusted Platform Module (TPM)* can be used to assist with hash key generation. BitLocker can be used with or without TPM. It is much more secure when coupled with TPM (and is preferable), but does not require it.

The security that you can implement is greatly influenced by, and dependent on, your hardware and software choices. To illustrate, support for BitLocker is only included in the Ultimate and Enterprise versions of Windows Vista.

Encrypting File System

BitLocker is far from the only way to encrypt data. Versions of Windows since Windows 2000 have included the Encrypting File System (EFS). EFS allows you to toggle an attribute for a file or folder just as you would any other, and it protects the contents. If the object you select is a folder, all contents of the folder—files, subfolders and so on—also become encrypted. Files that are pasted into an encrypted folder become encrypted as well, but files that are placed in the folder with drag-and-drop do not become encrypted automatically.

In order for you to use EFS, the file system must be NTFS, and the files must not be compressed. Some files (system files in particular) cannot be compressed. If you move or copy an encrypted file to one of these partitions, it becomes unencrypted automatically.

From the time a file is encrypted, a digital code associated with the user (encryption certificate) is assigned to it. This allows the encrypting user to open and work with the file exactly as if it were unencrypted, but prevents anyone else from doing so. Because only the encrypting user can open the file, EFS is perfect for personal data but unusable for any data you want to share.

You can use the Export command in the Certificates snap-in to copy your file encryption certificates to another location—such as to removable media. Doing so will allow you to unencrypt your files should a restore operation be necessary after a media failure (at which time you can use the Import command to bring them back from the removable media).

EFS is an integrated component of the NT kernel. To encrypt an entity, simply choose its properties and click the Advanced button to open the Advanced Attributes dialog box. Check the box Encrypt Contents To Secure Data and click OK. Each encrypted file is given a unique encryption key. All keys are stored in nonpaged memory for security purposes.

When you choose to encrypt a file, a dialog box appears asking if you want to encrypt only the one file or the file and its parent folder (the default action). A check box gives you the option of choosing to always encrypt only the file, preventing the dialog box from reappearing in the future.

In some operating system versions—including Windows Vista Starter, Home Basic, and Home Premium—EFS is not fully supported (there is the ability to decrypt) and the choice will appear grayed out on the advanced property options, as shown in Figure 19.21.

General Rules for the Exam on Access Control

There are a number of general rules to adhere to, regardless of which operating systems are employed on your servers and clients. Most of these are common sense. You can look at these rules in various ways, but one way is to make sure that you understand each of them and would be able to justify them should you see a test question on them.

- Limit access to the operating system to only those who need it. As silly as it may sound, every user should be a user who has to access the system. This means that every user has a unique username and password and it is shared with no one else. You do not allow users to use guest accounts or admin accounts. In Windows, this is the administrator account (the same functionality exists, however, in every other operating system, but has a different name: root in Unix, supervisor in NetWare, and so forth). The default Systems Administrator (SA) account on Microsoft's SQL Server is often targeted by hackers because it's well documented and known to them.

FIGURE 19.21   In Windows Vista Home Premium, the EFS option cannot be chosen.

 The Guest account is used when someone must access a system but lacks a user account on that system. The Guest account leaves a security risk at the workstation and should be disabled. To turn the Guest account off, follow these steps:

1. Choose Start ➢ Control Panel ➢ User Accounts.

2. Click Guest. Click Turn Off The Guest Account.

3. Exit the User Accounts dialog box. Exit Control Panel.

- Limit access to only what users need access to. In other words, you start out assuming that they need access to nothing, and then back slowly off that. It is always better to tweak settings for a user who has too little permission than to recover important files that a user with too much permission "accidentally" deletes.

- Encourage users to use passwords that are difficult to guess. A long password composed of both uppercase and lowercase letters, numbers, and symbols is the most resistant to being broken.

- Manage as much as possible by groups. Trying to manage individual users becomes more of a nightmare as the size of the systems increases. Make it easier by creating groups. Users with similar traits, job duties, and so forth are added to groups, and the groups are assigned the permissions that the users need. If a user needs access to more than what a specific group offers, you make them a member of multiple groups— you do not try to tweak their settings individually.

- Guard all administrative tools, utilities, and so forth behind secure rights and permissions. You should regularly check to see who has used such tools (see the auditing topic later in this list) and make sure they are not being used by users who should not be able to do so.

- Control permissions to resources as granularly as possible. Know the ones that exist in your environment and how to use them effectively.

 If at all possible, don't share the root directories of a disk drive. Doing so allows access to system files, passwords, and other sensitive information. Establish shares off hard drives that don't contain system files.

- Know the authentication possibilities for the operating systems you use and know what each allows. In addition to those that come standard with the operating system, you can also employ add-on devices such as biometric scanners to increase the security of the authentication process.

- Understand that firewalls can be software or hardware based, and are usually some combination of the two. Software-only firewalls are usually limited to home use and provide the first line of defense, preventing outside users from gaining access to the home computer.

- Block as much as possible from coming into your network. This includes traffic (turn off protocols/services that you do not need) and data (do not allow in e-mail with attachments containing .SCR, .PIF, and other red-flag files).

- Audit event logs. Event logging is used to record events and provide a trail that can be followed to determine what was done. Auditing involves looking at the logs and finding problems.

- Take wireless security seriously. Wireless clients can be configured to access the network in the same way as wired clients, but wireless security is a touchy issue. There are protocols that can be used to add security, but it is still difficult to secure a wireless network in the same way that you can secure a wired one. Unused wireless connections are the same as leaving a security door open.

- Limit data access. There are many ways to do this. Permissions to the data and basic local security policies are two universal ways that should be used regardless of the operating system you are employing.

- Assign appropriate permissions. The file system you are using can determine what permissions you have available to assign to resources. NTFS offers a great deal of granularity in terms of permissions, whereas FAT32 offers very few choices. You can convert from FAT32 to NTFS, without data loss, by using the convert utility.

- Use various tools to increase the level of authentication. You can employ biometrics, key fobs, and smart cards. Smart card readers may be contact based (you have to insert the card) or contactless (the card is read when it is in proximity to the reader). Key fobs are used to provide access to a resource, and may incorporate a randomly generated number that you can enter for authentication. Biometric devices identify the user by some physical aspect (such as a thumbprint).

Summary

In this chapter, we covered the key elements that an information technology specialist should be familiar with as related to security. Security is a set of processes and products. In order for a security program to be effective, all of its parts must work and be coordinated by the organization.

Typically, your network will run many protocols and services. These protocols allow connections to other networks and products. However, they also create potential vulnerabilities that must be understood. You must work to find ways to minimize the vulnerabilities. Many protocols and services offered by modern operating systems are highly vulnerable to attack. New methods of attacking these systems are developed every day.

Exam Essentials

Know the concepts of data security.   You should know that it's imperative to keep the system up-to-date and to install all relevant upgrades as they become available. You should also understand the importance of using a secure file system.

Know the purpose and characteristics of access control.   The purpose of access control is to limit who can access what resources on a system. The characteristics depend on the type of implementation utilized. You should always harden your systems to make them as secure as possible.

Know the purpose and characteristics of auditing and logging.   Log files are created to hold entries about the operations that take place on the system. Auditing is merely viewing those log files. There is often a fair amount of granularity in choosing what you want to allow into a log—the danger in recording too much information is that it can overwhelm you when you examine it.

Diagnose and troubleshoot software and data security issues.   It is important to know why policies exist and the types of possibilities they offer to an administrator. What were once called System Policies have now become Group Policies in the Microsoft world, and they can allow you to lock down workstations and prevent users from making changes that you do not want them to be able to make.

Know the recovery options.   Be familiar with the recovery console, ASR, and ERD.

Know the common operational problems.   Blue screens and lockups are far less common that they used to be, but they do occasionally occur. Know how to deal with them and the other issues listed.

Know the common errors.   Be able to identify how to get to error logs, and know the logs created during installation.

Know the boot menu options.   Know how to access the boot menu and what options appear there.

Know the characteristics and types of viruses used to disrupt systems and networks.   Several different types of viruses are floating around today. The most common ones are polymorphic viruses, stealth viruses, retroviruses, multipartite viruses, and macro viruses.

Be able to describe how antivirus software operates.   Antivirus software looks for a signature in the virus to determine what type of virus it is. The software then takes action to neutralize the virus based on a virus definition database. Virus definition database files are regularly made available on vendor sites.

Review Questions

1. Which of the following terms refers to the prevention of unauthorized disclosure of keys?

    A. Authentication

    B. Integrity

    C. Access control

    D. Nonrepudiation

2. Which of the following is a hacker's favorite target account on Microsoft's SQL Server?

    A. Ordinary user account

    B. Default systems administrator account

    C. Temporary user account

    D. Print operators

3. You're in the process of securing the IT infrastructure by adding fingerprint scanners to your existing authentication methods. This type of security is an example of which of the following?

    A. Access control

    B. Physical barriers

    C. Biometrics

    D. Softening

4. Which file extension should *not* be allowed with an e-mail attachment?

    A. .DOC

    B. .SCR

    C. .TXT

    D. .XLS

5. Which type of attack denies authorized users access to network resources?

    A. DoS

    B. Worm

    C. Logic bomb

    D. Social engineering

6. As the security administrator for your organization, you must be aware of all types of attacks that can occur and plan for them. Which type of attack uses more than one computer to attack the victim?

    A. DoS

    B. DDoS

    C. Worm

    D. UDP attack

7. A server in your network has a program running on it that bypasses authentication. Which type of attack has occurred?

    A. DoS

    B. DDoS

    C. Back door

    D. Social engineering

8. You've discovered that an expired certificate is being used repeatedly to gain logon privileges. Which type of attack is this most likely to be?

    A. Man-in-the-middle attack

    B. Back door attack

    C. Replay attack

    D. TCP/IP hijacking

9. A junior administrator comes to you in a panic. After looking at the log files, he has become convinced that an attacker is attempting to use an IP address to replace another system in the network to gain access. Which type of attack is this?

    A. Man-in-the-middle attack

    B. Back door attack

    C. Worm

    D. TCP/IP hijacking

10. A server on your network will no longer accept connections using the TCP protocol. The server indicates that it has exceeded its session limit. Which type of attack is probably occurring?

    A. TCP ACK attack

    B. Smurf attack

    C. Virus attack

    D. TCP/IP hijacking

11. A smurf attack attempts to use a broadcast ping on a network; the return address of the ping may be a valid system in your network. Which protocol does a smurf attack use to conduct the attack?

    A. TCP

    B. IP

    C. UDP

    D. ICMP

12. Your system log files report an ongoing attempt to gain access to a single account. This attempt has been unsuccessful to this point. What type of attack are you most likely experiencing?

   A. Password-guessing attack

   B. Back door attack

   C. Worm attack

   D. TCP/IP hijacking

13. A user reports that she is receiving an error indicating that her TCP/IP address is already in use when she turns on her computer. A static IP address has been assigned to this user's computer, and you're certain this address was not inadvertently assigned to another computer. Which type of attack is most likely under way?

   A. Man-in-the-middle attack

   B. Back door attack

   C. Worm

   D. TCP/IP hijacking

14. Which of the following programs can identify spyware and unwanted software on a Windows Vista machine?

   A. Windows Defender

   B. System Integrity Checker

   C. NetBus

   D. Recovery Console

15. Which of the following combines many stand-alone utilities into a simple interface where you can get a quick glimpse of security settings on a machine?

   A. QuickStat

   B. Windows Security Center

   C. Cipher

   D. Windows Defender

16. Which of the following types of viruses modifies and alters other programs and databases?

   A. Talkabout

   B. Backdoor

   C. Phage

   D. Hijack

17. What could be used with Windows to configure running an antivirus program if the program itself lacked such a feature?

   A. Cron

   B. At

   C. Later

   D. Task Scheduler

18. In which of the following operating systems is EFS fully supported (choose all that apply)?

    A. Windows XP Professional

    B. Windows Vista Home Basic

    C. Windows Vista Home Premium

    D. Windows Vista Starter

19. Which of the following is a software application that checks your network for any known security holes?

    A. Man-in-the-middle

    B. Vulnerability scanner

    C. Worm

    D. Port check

20. Which of the following is the Group Policy Editor?

    A. gpedit.msc

    B. regedit.exe

    C. poledit.com

    D. group.sh

Answers to Review Questions

1. C. Access control refers to the process of ensuring that sensitive keys aren't divulged to unauthorized personnel.

2. B. The default administrator account is a favorite target of hackers on Microsoft's SQL Server.

3. C. Adding a fingerprint scanner, or any device that identifies a person by a physical trait, is considered biometric.

4. B. The .SCR extension is used for screen savers. Screen savers, as executables, actually have the ability to do nasty things, such as lock the screen, and can wreak havoc.

5. A. Although the end result of any of these attacks may result in denying authorized users access to network resources, a DoS attack is specifically intended to prevent access to network resources by overwhelming or flooding a service or network.

6. B. A DDoS attack uses multiple computer systems to attack a server or host in the network.

7. C. In a back door attack, a program or service is placed on a server to bypass normal security procedures.

8. C. A replay attack attempts to replay the results of a previously successful session to gain access.

9. D. TCP/IP hijacking is an attempt to steal a valid IP address and use it to gain authorization or information from a network.

10. A. A TCP ACK attack creates multiple incomplete sessions. Eventually, the TCP protocol hits a limit and refuses additional connections.

11. D. A smurf attack attempts to use a broadcast ping (ICMP) on a network. The return address of the ping may be a valid system in your network. This system will be flooded with responses in a large network.

12. A. A password-guessing attack occurs when a user account is repeatedly attacked using a variety of passwords.

13. D. One of the symptoms of a TCP/IP hijacking attack may be the unavailability of a TCP/IP address when the system is started.

14. A. Windows Defender can identify spyware and unwanted software running on a Windows Vista machine.

15. B. Windows Security Center combines many stand-alone utilities into a simple interface where you can get a quick glimpse of security settings on a machine.

16. C. A phage virus modifies and alters other programs and databases. The only way to remove this virus is to reinstall the programs that are infected.

17. D. The Task Scheduler could be used to configure running an antivirus program if the program lacked such a feature.

18. A. In some operating system versions—including Windows Vista Starter, Home Basic, and Home Premium—EFS is not fully supported (there is the ability to decrypt) and the choice will appear grayed out on the advanced property options.

19. B. A vulnerability scanner is a software application that checks your network for any known security holes; it's better to run one on your own network before someone outside the organization runs it against you.

20. A. Group Policy Editor can be started with `gpedit.msc` at the Run prompt, or within the Microsoft Management Console.

Appendix

About the Companion CD

IN THIS APPENDIX:

✓ What you'll find on the CD

✓ System requirements

✓ Using the CD

✓ Troubleshooting

What You'll Find on the CD

The following sections are arranged by category and summarize the software and other goodies you'll find on the CD. If you need help with installing the items provided on the CD, refer to the installation instructions in the "Using the CD" section of this appendix.

Some programs on the CD might fall into one of these categories:

Shareware programs are fully functional, free, trial versions of copyrighted programs. If you like particular programs, register with their authors for a nominal fee and receive licenses, enhanced versions, and technical support.

Freeware programs are free, copyrighted games, applications, and utilities. You can copy them to as many computers as you like—for free—but they offer no technical support.

GNU software is governed by its own license, which is included inside the folder of the GNU software. There are no restrictions on distribution of GNU software. See the GNU license at the root of the CD for more details.

Trial, *demo*, or *evaluation* versions of software are usually limited either by time or by functionality (such as not letting you save a project after you create it).

Sybex Test Engine

For Windows

The CD contains the Sybex test engine, which includes all of the assessment test and chapter review questions in electronic format, as well as bonus exams located only on the CD.

PDF of the Book

For Windows

We have included an electronic version of the text in `.pdf` format. You can view the electronic version of the book with Adobe Reader.

Adobe Reader

For Windows

We've also included a copy of Adobe Reader so you can view PDF files that accompany the book's content. For more information on Adobe Reader or to check for a newer version, visit Adobe's website at www.adobe.com/products/reader/.

Electronic Flashcards

For PC, Pocket PC, and Palm

These handy electronic flashcards are just what they sound like. One side contains a question or fill-in-the-blank question, and the other side shows the answer.

System Requirements

Make sure your computer meets the minimum system requirements shown in the following list. If your computer doesn't match up to most of these requirements, you may have problems using the software and files on the companion CD. For the latest and greatest information, please refer to the ReadMe file located at the root of the CD-ROM.

- A PC running Microsoft Windows 98, Windows 2000, Windows NT4 (with SP4 or later), Windows Me, Windows XP, or Windows Vista
- An Internet connection
- A CD-ROM drive

Using the CD

To install the items from the CD to your hard drive, follow these steps:

1. Insert the CD into your computer's CD-ROM drive. The license agreement appears.

Windows users: The interface won't launch if you have Autorun disabled. In that case, click Start ➤ Run (for Windows Vista, Start ➤ All Programs ➤ Accessories ➤ Run). In the dialog box that appears, type D:\Start.exe. (Replace *D* with the proper letter if your CD drive uses a different letter. If you don't know the letter, see how your CD drive is listed under My Computer.) Click OK.

2. Read the license agreement, and then click the Accept button if you want to use the CD.

The CD interface appears. The interface allows you to access the content with just one or two clicks.

Troubleshooting

Wiley has attempted to provide programs that work on most computers with the minimum system requirements. Alas, your computer may differ, and some programs may not work properly for some reason.

The two likeliest problems are that you don't have enough memory (RAM) for the programs you want to use or you have other programs running that are affecting installation or running of a program. If you get an error message such as "Not enough memory" or "Setup cannot continue," try one or more of the following suggestions and then try using the software again:

Turn off any antivirus software running on your computer. Installation programs sometimes mimic virus activity and may make your computer incorrectly believe that it's being infected by a virus.

Close all running programs. The more programs you have running, the less memory is available to other programs. Installation programs typically update files and programs; so if you keep other programs running, installation may not work properly.

Have your local computer store add more RAM to your computer. This is, admittedly, a drastic and somewhat expensive step. However, adding more memory can really help the speed of your computer and allow more programs to run at the same time.

Customer Care

If you have trouble with the book's companion CD-ROM, please call the Wiley Product Technical Support phone number at (800) 762-2974. Outside the United States, call +1(317) 572-3994. You can also contact Wiley Product Technical Support at http://sybex .custhelp.com. John Wiley & Sons will provide technical support only for installation and other general quality-control items. For technical support on the applications themselves, consult the program's vendor or author.

To place additional orders or to request information about other Wiley products, please call (877) 762-2974.

Glossary

Numbers

802.11a   A wireless standard that operates at 5GHz and provides wireless speeds up to 54Mbps.

802.11b   A wireless standard that operates at 2.4GHz and provides wireless speeds up to 11Mbps.

802.11g   A wireless standard that operates at 2.4GHz, is backward compatible with 802.11b, and provides data transmission of up to 54Mbps.

802.3   An IEEE standard that defines a physical bus topology network that uses a 50-ohm coaxial baseband cable and carries transmissions at a minimum of 10Mbps. (The current standard supports speeds up to 10Gbps.) This standard groups data bits into frames and uses the Carrier Sense Multiple Access with Collision Detection (CSMA/CD) cable access method to put data on the cable. Ethernet is a common implementation of IEEE 802.3.

802.5   An IEEE standard that specifies a physical star, logical ring topology that uses a token-passing technology to put the data on a network cable. IBM's Token Ring is the most common implementation of IEEE 802.5.

A

access control list (ACL)   The set of rules that determines which traffic gets through a firewall and which traffic is blocked.

access point (AP)   The device that allows wireless devices to talk to each other and the network. It provides the functions of network access as well as security monitoring.

Active Directory   The replacement for NT Directory Service (NTDS) that was first included with Windows 2000 and is now a core part of Windows. It acts similarly to Novell Directory Services (NDS), which is now known as eDirectory because it's a true X.500-based directory service.

active hub   A type of hub that uses electronics to amplify and clean up the signal before it is retransmitted to the other ports.

active sniffing   Involves an attacker gaining access to a host in the network by injecting traffic onto the network in order to obtain data that would otherwise be unavailable.

adapter card   *See* expansion card.

Address Resolution Protocol (ARP)   A TCP/IP protocol used to resolve IP addresses to MAC addresses.

allocation unit   *See* cluster.

answer file   In an unattended installation, this file contains all of the correct parameters (time zone, regional settings, administrator username, and so on) needed for installation.

antivirus (or antivirus software)   A category of software that uses various methods to identify the presence of a virus and remove or quarantine the virus on a computer. It typically also protects against future infection. *See also* virus.

AppleTalk   A proprietary network protocol for Macintosh computers.

archive   Any collection of data that is removed from the system because it's no longer needed on a regular basis.

archive bit   An attribute of the file that is cleared during backup. Windows Backup works by looking at the archive bit.

armored virus   A virus that is protected in a way that makes disassembling it difficult. The difficulty makes it "armored" against antivirus programs that have trouble getting to and understanding its code.

AT system connector   The 12-pin power connector found on older motherboards that receives the P8/P9 pair of 6-conductor connectors from the power supply.

attack   Any unauthorized intrusion into the normal operations of a computer or computer network. The attack can be carried out to gain access to the system or any of its resources.

attended installation   An installation where a user is required to provide answers to options during the installation process.

ATX system connector   The 20-pin power connector found on ATX motherboards to which ATX power supplies connect. These connectors have been replaced by the 24-pin ATX12V connector.

audit files   Files that hold information about a resource's access by users.

authentication   A process that proves that a user or system is actually who they say they are.

Automatic Private IP Addressing (APIPA)   A TCP/IP standard used to automatically configure IP-based hosts that are unable to reach a DHCP server.

Automated System Recovery (ASR)   ASR first creates a backup of your system partition and then creates a recovery disk. Using these two components, you can recover from a system crash and restore the system to a functional state.

B

B channel   The ISDN channel that carries 64Kbps of data; also known as a bearer channel.

back door (backdoor)   An opening left in a program application (usually by the developer) that allows additional access to data. Typically, these are created for debugging purposes and aren't documented. Before the product ships, the back doors are closed; when they aren't closed, security loopholes exist.

backlight   A small fluorescent lamp placed behind or below an LCD display to provide light.

backup   A copy of files stored in a location other than where they originally came from.

backup policy   Rules that dictate what information should be backed up and how it should be backed up.

bandwidth   In communications, the difference between the highest and the lowest frequencies available for transmission in any given range. In networking, the transmission capacity of a computer or a communications channel stated in megabits or megabytes per second; the higher the number, the faster the data transmission takes place.

barcode reader   An often handheld unit that scans barcodes into a computer, replacing the need for a user to type the data in by hand.

barcode scanner   *See* barcode reader.

basic rate interface (BRI)   An ISDN line with two B channels. Each channel can be used separately for voice and/or data transmissions.

basis weight   A measurement of the "heaviness" of paper. The number is the weight, in pounds, of 500 17″ × 22″ sheets of that type of paper.

beep code   A series of beeps from the computer's speaker that indicate a problem. The number, duration, and pattern of the beeps can sometimes tell you what component is causing the problem.

Bell-La Padula model   A model designed for the military to address the storage and protection of classified information. This model is specifically designed to prevent unauthorized access to classified information. The model prevents the user from accessing information that has a higher security rating than they are authorized to access. It also prevents information from being written to a lower level of security.

Berg connector   The smaller power connector that most often provides power to floppy diskette drives and other small devices that require less current to power their motors than provided by a Molex connector.

Biba model   A model similar in concept to the Bell-La Padula model but more concerned with information integrity (an area the Bell-La Padula model doesn't address). In this model, there is no write up or read down. If you're assigned access to top-secret information, you can't read secret information or write to any level higher than the level to which you're authorized. This model keeps higher-level information pure by preventing less-reliable information from being intermixed with it.

biometric device   Any device that scans a unique human trait, such as fingerprints or voice, in order to authenticate the identity of the user.

biometrics   The science of identifying a person by using one or more of their features. The feature can be a thumbprint, a retina scan, or any other biological trait.

BIOS   The firmware embedded in a ROM chip that is responsible for running POST, booting the system, and presenting an interface for its own configuration.

blanks   Pieces of metal or plastic that come with the case and cover the expansion slot openings to help keep dust and other matter from the inside of the computer.

blue screen of death (BSOD)   A condition that occurs when Windows encounters a critical error from which it cannot recover and is followed by a dump of physical memory. The name comes from the fact that the error screen is blue and you have no choice but to attempt to reboot the computer.

Bluetooth   A popular standard for wireless communication that operates in the 2.4GHz range. The current Bluetooth standard is Version 2.1, which can support data transmissions of up to 3Mbps. The most common type of Bluetooth device (Class 2) has a transmission range of 10 meters (30 feet) and consumes 2.5 mW of power.

Bluetooth Special Interest Group (SIG)   The consortium of companies that developed the Bluetooth technology.

Blu-ray disc (BD)   A newer optical disc format that holds more information than a standard DVD.

BNC connector   A type of connector used to attach stations to a Thinnet network.

bonding   Combining two bearer channels into one 128Kbps data or voice connection to maximize throughput.

boot logging   Logs all boot information to a file called NTBTLOG.TXT. You can then check the log for assistance in diagnosing system startup problems.

bridge   A type of connectivity device that operates in the Data Link layer of the OSI model. Similar to a switch.

broadband   The general designation for higher-speed Internet connections.

broadcast   To send a signal to all entities that can listen to it. In networking, it refers to sending a signal to all entities connected to that network.

brute-force attack   A type of attack that relies purely on trial and error.

BSB (backside bus)   When present, the bus between the Northbridge and the cache controller. Often implemented in SECCs and multicavity modules (MCMs), where the CPU and L2 cache are collocated.

bubble-jet printer   A type of sprayed-ink printer. It uses an electric signal that energizes a heating or vibrating element, causing ink to vaporize and be pushed out of the pinhole and onto the paper. *Also see* inkjet printer.

bus   A parallel set of communications lines that act as a cohesive unit and optionally have multiple arbitrary insertion points.

C

cable Internet   Internet access across a common cable television service.

cable modem   A device used to obtain broadband Internet access through a cable television provider.

cache memory   One of two or three levels of fast silicon memory of limited size most often forged from static RAM and positioned between the CPU and RAM.

calibration   The process by which a device such as a printer (or a scanner) is brought within functional specifications.

caliper   The thickness measurement of a given sheet of paper, which can affect a printer's feed mechanism.

carriage belt   The printer belt placed around two small wheels or pulleys and attached to the printhead carriage. The carriage belt is driven by the carriage motor and moves the printhead back and forth across the page during printing.

carriage motor   A stepper motor used to move the printhead back and forth on a dot-matrix printer.

carriage stepper motor   The printer motor that makes the printhead carriage move.

CD-recordable   Also known as CD-R, a CD that can be written to one time.

CD-rewritable   Also known as CD-RW, a CD that can be written to, erased, and rewritten to multiple times.

cell   A shorthand term for a cellular phone network.

centralized processing   A network processing scheme in which all "intelligence" is found in one computer and all other computers send requests to the central computer to be processed. Mainframe networks use centralized processing.

certificates   A common form of authentication.

Challenge Handshake Authentication Protocol (CHAP)   An authentication protocol that challenges a system to verify identity.

characters per second (cps)   A rating of how fast dot-matrix printers can produce output.

charging corona   The wire or roller that is used to put a uniform charge on the EP drum inside a toner cartridge.

charging step   The second step in EP printing, at which a special wire or roller in the toner cartridge gets a high voltage from the high voltage power supply (HVPS). It uses this high voltage to apply a strong, uniform negative charge (around −600VDC) to the surface of the photosensitive drum.

chip creep   Movement of components, such as Integrated Circuits, RAM chips, and expansion cards, out of their sockets.

chipset   Commonly one or two integrated circuits comprising Northbridge and Southbridge functionality, allowing the CPU to communicate with I/O components of various speeds and capabilities.

Clark-Wilson model   An integrity model for creating a secure architecture.

cleaning cycle   A set of steps the bubble-jet or inkjet printer goes through in order to purge the printheads of any dried ink.

cleaning step   The first step in the EP print process, at which excess toner is scraped from the EP drum with a rubber blade.

client computers   A computer that requests resources from a network, often referred to as a workstation.

client software   Software that allows a device to request resources from a network.

cluster   Also known as allocation unit, the collection of sectors that is treated as a single unit by the operating system. Only one file can occupy a cluster at a time.

CMOS memory   The extremely small storage space that holds user settings and dynamically discovered parameters for the BIOS.

CMYK (cyan, magenta, yellow, and black)   The four standard colors used in printers. Some printers will have all colors on the same cartridge. Others will have separate black and CMY cartridges, while higher-end (mostly laser) printers will have separate cartridges for each color.

coaxial cable   A medium for connecting computer components that contains a center conductor, made of copper, surrounded by a plastic jacket, with a braided shield over the jacket.

Code Division Multiple Access (CDMA)   A cellular standard of Qualcomm. It allows for multiple transmissions to occur at the same time without interference.

cold cathode fluorescent lamp (CCFL)   A common type of backlight used in laptop computers.

collision   When two or more stations transmit onto a shared medium simultaneously, invalidating the data sent from each station.

companion virus   A virus that creates a new program that runs in place of an expected program of the same name.

compression   A feature that gives you the option of compressing existing files in a particular folder. If the feature is turned on, Windows automatically compresses the subfolders and files. If not, only new files created in the directory are compressed.

computer vacuum   A small handheld device designed for sucking up dust and other little particles without causing ESD problems.

computer virus   See *virus*.

confidentiality   Keeping data secret.

connectivity device   Any device that facilitates connections between network devices. Some examples include hubs, routers, switches, and bridges.

contention   Competition between two or more network devices for the same bandwidth.

corona roller   A type of transfer corona assembly that uses a charged roller to apply charge to the paper.

corona wire   A type of transfer corona assembly. Also, the wire in that assembly that is charged by the high-voltage power supply. It is narrow in diameter and located in a special notch under the EP print cartridge.

CPU   The main integrated circuit of a computer system that interfaces with almost all other components and runs application and system processes. Intel and AMD are the most common CPU manufacturers for PC-compatible computers.

cylinder   The collection of similarly numbered tracks across all writable surfaces of a hard disk assembly.

D

daisy-wheel printer   An impact printer that uses a plastic or metal print mechanism with a different character on the end of each spoke of the wheel. As the print mechanism rotates to the correct letter, a small hammer strikes the character against the ribbon, transferring the image onto the paper.

Data Over Cable Service Internet Specification (DOCSIS)   The standard used by most cable systems for transmitting Internet traffic to a subscriber via television cable.

D channel   The signaling channel of an ISDN circuit; also referred to as the Delta channel.

DDR   A type of SDRAM that doubles the data rate of standard SDRAM by transmitting a single bit on both edges of each FSB clock cycle.

DDR2   A type of SDRAM that uses both edges of each cycle, transferring two bits per edge.

DDR2-667   A form of DDR2 memory that populates a PC2-5300 module and is made for a 667MHz FSB.

DDR3   A type of SDRAM that uses both edges of each FSB clock cycle, transferring four bits per edge.

DDR3-1600 A form of DDR3 memory that populates a PC3-12800 module and is made for a 1600MHz FSB.

dedicated server The server that is assigned to perform a specific application or service.

de facto Latin translation for "by fact." Any standard that is a standard because everyone is using it.

de jure Latin translation for "by law." Any standard that is a standard because a standards body decided it should be so.

demineralized water Water that has had minerals and impurities removed; it does not leave residue and is recommended for cleaning keyboards and other non-metal computer parts.

denatured isopropyl alcohol Also known as electronics cleaner, it is found in electronics stores and used to clean contacts.

denial-of-service (DoS) attacks Attacks that prevent access to resources by users authorized to use those resources.

Department of Defense (DOD) model A four-layer networking model loosely corresponding to the OSI model, upon which the basis for the TCP/IP protocol suite was developed.

developing roller The roller inside a toner cartridge that presents a uniform line of toner to help apply the toner to the image written on the EP drum.

developing step The fourth step in the EP print process, at which the image written on the EP drum by the laser is developed—that is, it has toner stuck to it.

device driver A software file that allows an operating system to communicate with a hardware device. Also called a driver.

dialer A special program for dial-up networking that initiates the connection with the ISP, takes the phone off hook, dials the ISP's access number, and establishes the connection.

dial-up An Internet connection wherein the computer connecting to the Internet uses a modem to connect to the ISP over a standard telephone line.

dictionary attack The act of attempting to crack passwords by testing them against a list of dictionary words. With today's powerful computers, an attacker can combine one of many available automated password cracking utilities with several large dictionaries or "wordlists" and crack huge numbers of passwords in a matter of minutes. Any password based on any dictionary word is vulnerable to such an attack.

Digital Subscriber Line (DSL) A broadband Internet access technology that uses the existing phone line from your home to the phone company to carry digital signals at higher speeds.

DIMM A memory module packaging style that features a circuit board with independent pins on both sides of the module's card edge.

directories   Another term for folders that can contain files on your storage devices.

distributed denial of service (DDoS) attack   A derivative of a DoS attack in which multiple hosts in multiple locations all focus on one target to reduce its availability to the public. *See* denial of service (DoS) attack.

distributed processing   A computer system in which processing is performed by several separate computers linked by a communications network. The term often refers to any computer system supported by a network, but more properly refers to a system in which each computer is chosen to handle a specific workload and the network supports the system as a whole.

Domain Name System (DNS)   A system which resolves computer hostnames to IP addresses.

domains   Also referred to as a client-server networking model, a domain is a network where security is managed by a centralized server, often known as a domain controller.

DoS attack   *See* denial-of-service (DoS) attack.

dot-matrix printer   An impact printer that has a printhead containing a row of pins (short, sturdy stalks of hard wire) that are used to strike the ink ribbon to create an image.

double-sided memory   A memory module that comprises two modules in one.

draft quality   The poorest quality standard of output from a dot-matrix printer, suitable only for early document review.

DRAM   A pervasive type of volatile memory that requires a periodic refresh signal to keep its contents.

DRDRAM   A type of SDRAM from Rambus implemented on RIMMs.

drive interface   An interface and related circuitry designed to connect one of a few possible drive types to a motherboard or adapter card; often manifests as a header on the motherboard.

driver   A software file that allows an operating system to communicate with a hardware device. Also called a device driver.

DSL endpoint   The device used to access DSL, commonly referred to mistakenly as a DSL modem.

D-subminiature   Also known as D-sub, a trapezoidal connector and port pairing that features an interface that is broader on one edge than the other with angled sides connecting the edges; commonly found on classic I/O ports, such as RS-232 serial and parallel.

dual-channel memory   A RAM implementation scheme in which the memory controller requires two paired standard memory modules to read from or write to simultaneously. RIMM offers a single module that alone satisfies both channels on compatible motherboards.

dye-sublimation printer   A printer that uses heat to diffuse solid dyes onto the printing surface as a gas that resolidifies without ever going through a liquid state.

Dynamic Host Configuration Protocol (DHCP)   A protocol (and service) in the TCP/IP protocol suite that automatically configures network clients with IP configuration information when they join the network.

E

ECC   An error-checking scheme that is able to discover one or two bits in a byte that contain errors, and correct single-bit errors.

electromagnetic interference (EMI)   Any electromagnetic radiation released by an electronic device that disrupts the operation or performance of any other device.

electronic stepper motor   A special electric motor in a printer that can accurately move in very small increments. It powers all of the paper transport rollers as well as the fuser rollers.

electrostatic discharge (ESD)   Occurs when two objects of dissimilar electrical charge come in contact with each other; the charge can damage electronic components.

emergency repair disk (ERD)   A disk that contains backup copies of portions of your Registry. It can be used to recover the system in the event of an operating system failure.

envelope feeder   A special device for feeding envelopes into a printer.

environment variable   A variable used by the operating system that holds a value defining the computing environment.

EP print process   The process by which an EP laser printer forms images on paper.

eSATA   An external interface for the attachment of SATA devices that requires a shielded cable and different connector from the one used with internal SATA attachment.

Ethernet   A network technology based on the IEEE 802.3 CSMA/CD standard. The original Ethernet implementation specified 10MBps, baseband signaling, coaxial cable, and CSMA/CD media access. Ethernet standards now support data transmissions of up to 10Gbps.

expansion card   A daughter card that is inserted into a bus slot in the motherboard to expand the native capabilities of a computer system.

expansion slot   One of the arbitrary insertion points in an expansion bus, based on a specific technology—PCI, for example.

F

feeder   A device that feeds paper or other media into a printer.

feed roller   The rubber roller in a laser printer that feeds the paper into the printer.

field-replaceable units (FRUs)   Parts that are designed to be able to be replaced by a technician working in the field.

file locking   A feature of many network operating systems that "locks" a file to prevent more than one person from updating the file at the same time.

file permissions   These serve the purpose of controlling who has access and what type of access to what files or objects they have.

file servers   Servers on a network designed to hold and store files for clients.

File Transfer Protocol (FTP)   A protocol in the TCP/IP protocol suite that is optimized for file transfers. It uses ports 20 and 21.

finisher   A device on a printer that performs such final functions as folding, stapling, hole punching, sorting, or collating the documents being printed.

firewall   Software or hardware used to limit traffic based on a set of rules, usually an access control list.

FireWire   Apple's original implementation of IEEE 1394b, a high-speed serial I/O interface, ideal for video applications between a computer and an external video source or destination. FireWire is a competing standard of USB.

firmware   Systems programming software embedded in a hardware device, such as a ROM chip; often used to control the low-level functionality of the system in which it is installed.

flash memory   A nonvolatile form of solid-state memory similar in makeup to primary RAM but used for semipermanent storage, similar to writable disks.

floppy disk   Also known as floppy diskette, an older removable magnetic secondary-storage medium that requires a floppy diskette drive for access. *See* also minifloppy diskette and microfloppy diskette.

floppy diskette drive (FDD)   A disk drive that reads from and writes to floppy diskettes.

font   The typestyle used for printing a document. The font can be loaded onto the hard drive of the computer or the onboard memory of the printer.

format   To prepare a volume (such as a hard drive) to receive files and folders by defining the file structure.

formatting   The process of preparing the partition on a storage device such as a hard drive or flash memory to store data in a particular fashion.

frame   The Data Link layer product that includes a portion of the original user data, upper-layer headers, and the Data Link header and trailer.

frontside bus   The high-speed bus controlled by the Northbridge on which RAM, cache (in the absence of the backside bus [BSB]), PCIe slots, AGP slots, and other local-bus components are interconnected with the CPU and, in some cases, each other.

full-duplex communication   Communications where both entities can send and receive simultaneously.

function key   Key marked with the letters F*n* that produces particular functions when pressed and held while pressing one of the function keys.

fuser   A device on an EP printer that uses two rollers to heat the toner particles and melt them to the paper. The fuser is made up of a halogen heating lamp, a Teflon-coated aluminum fusing roller, and a rubberized pressure roller. The lamp heats the aluminum roller. As the paper passes between the two rollers, the rubber roller presses the paper against the heated roller. This causes the toner to melt and become a permanent image on the paper.

fusing step   The sixth and final step in the EP printing process, when the toner image on the paper is fused to the paper using heat and pressure. The heat melts the toner, and the pressure helps fuse the image permanently to the paper.

G

general protection fault (GPF)   A general protection fault (GPF) happens in Windows when a program accesses memory that another program is using or when a program accesses a memory address that doesn't exist.

Global System for Mobile Communications (GSM)   The most popular cellular standard. It uses a variety of bands to transmit. The most popular are 900MHz and 1800MHz, but 400, 450, and 850MHz are also used.

H

half-duplex communication   Communications that occur when only one entity can transmit or receive at any one instant.

hard disk drive   A disk drive that contains magnetically coated platters in a sealed case and is often used as the main secondary-storage medium.

hardening   The process of reducing or eliminating weaknesses, securing services, and attempting to make your environment immune to attacks.

header   In hardware, a technology-specific connector on a circuit board for cabling an internal peripheral device to the board. In software, protocol-specific control information added to the original data or to the protocol data unit from the next-higher protocol in the stack. Information attached to the beginning of a network data frame.

heat sink   A block of aluminum or other metal, with veins throughout or fins, that sits on top of a heat-producing component, drawing its heat away.

heat spreader   A flat heat sink of sorts that adds surface area to a heat-producing component, allowing better heat transfer to the surrounding air; often coupled with a fan for devices that run at a higher temperature.

hermaphroditic data connector   A connector that is both male and female.

high-voltage probe   A tool with a very large needle, a gauge that indicates volts, and a wire with an alligator clip used to discharge electricity from electronic devices.

hop   In networking, an intermediate device and cabling between two other devices.

host   Any computer or device on a TCP/IP network that has an IP address.

host-based firewall   A firewall implemented on a single machine. It is usually a software implementation. Contrast with *network-based firewall*.

hot fix/hotfix   Another word for a patch. When Microsoft rolls a bunch of hotfixes together, they become known as a service pack.

hot-swappable   A device that can be inserted and removed without removing power from the host component.

hub   A basic connectivity device used to link several computers together into a physical star topology. A hub repeats any signal that comes in on one port and copies it to the other ports.

Hypertext Transfer Protocol (HTTP)   A protocol in the TCP/IP protocol suite that is the backbone for Internet (web) traffic. It uses port 80.

Hypertext Transfer Protocol Secure (HTTPS)   Secure protocol for most Internet traffic; it uses port 443 by default.

I

IBM data connector (IDC)   A unique, hermaphroditic connector commonly used with IBM's Token Ring technology and Type 1 or 2 STP cable.

ICMP   *See* Internet Control Message Protocol (ICMP).

ICMP attack   An attack that occurs by triggering a response from the Internet Control Message Protocol (ICMP) when it responds to a seemingly legitimate maintenance request. *See also* Internet Control Message Protocol (ICMP).

illegal operation error   An illegal operation error usually means that a program was forced to quit because it did something Windows didn't like.

impact printers   Any printer that forms an image on paper by forcing a character image against an inked ribbon. Dot-matrix, daisy-wheel, and line printers are all impact printers, whereas laser printers are not.

incident   An attempt to violate a security policy, a successful penetration, a compromise of a system, or unauthorized access to information.

Information Flow model   A model concerned with all the properties of information flow, not only the direction of the flow.

infrared   A type of wireless transmission between devices that use radiation in the infrared range of the electromagnetic spectrum.

Infrared Data Association (IrDA)   The association that creates and maintains infrared standards.

infrared transmissions   Wireless transmission between devices that use radiation in the infrared range of the electromagnetic spectrum.

ink cartridge   A reservoir of ink and a printhead, in a removable package.

inkjet printers   A type of sprayed-ink printer. Often called a bubble-jet.

inoculating   Making the computer resistant to computer viruses.

input device   A device, such as a keyboard or mouse, that allows information outside the computer system to be read into the system.

Integrated Services Digital Network (ISDN)   A worldwide digital communications network emerging from existing telephone services, intended to replace all analog systems with a completely digital transmission system.

integrated system board   A motherboard that has I/O interfaces and their circuitry built in.

interface   The point of connectivity between a port in the system unit and a cable with an opposite-gender compatible connector. The port or connection through which a device attaches to an external component, such as a printer's parallel or USB port for connection to a computer, as well as the software that enables the port to communicate with the external component, such as a Windows XP driver for an HP LaserJet.

interface software   The operating system-specific driver that enables communication between the computer and a peripheral.

Internet Control Message Protocol (ICMP)
A message and management protocol for TCP/IP that transmits error messages and network statistics. The ping utility uses ICMP.

Internet Message Access Protocol (IMAP)   A protocol commonly used to retrieve e-mail from e-mail servers.

Internet Protocol (IP)   The underlying communications protocol on which the Internet is based. IP provides addressing on a TCP/IP network and allows a data packet to travel across many networks before reaching its final destination.

Internet service provider (ISP)   A company that provides Internet access and e-mail addresses for users.

Internetwork Packet Exchange/Sequenced Packet Exchange (IPX/SPX)   The default communication protocol for versions of the Novell NetWare operating system before Net-Ware 5. IPX and SPX correspond loosely to IP and TCP, respectively, in the TCP/IP protocol suite.

inverse multiplexing   *See* bonding.

inverter   A small circuit board installed behind the LCD panel that takes AC power and converts (inverts) it for the backlight.

IP spoofing   An attack during which a hacker tries to gain access to a network by pretending their interface has the same network address as the internal network.

ISDN terminal adapter   The device that connects a computer to an ISDN line.

K

Kerberos   An authentication scheme that uses tickets (unique keys) embedded within messages. Named after the three-headed guard dog that stood at the gates of Hades in Greek mythology.

KVM switch   A device that switches a single keyboard/video/mouse set among multiple computer systems.

L

L1 cache   Cache memory that is built into the processor die (the CPU's silicon wafer).

L2 cache   Cache memory that can be collocated with the CPU in the same packaging or placed on the motherboard, external to the CPU packaging. L2 cache is not built into the processor die.

L3 cache   Cache memory on the motherboard that is named as such only when L2 cache is in the CPU packaging. L3 cache is the new name, in such a situation, for what used to be termed L2 cache.

lane   In PCIe, a switched point-to-point signal path between any two PCIe components. The designation x16, for example, in PCIe represents a component's ability to communicate over 16 lanes simultaneously.

laser printer   A generic name for a printer that uses the electrophotographic (EP) print process.

Last Known Good Configuration   An advanced boot option that lets you restore the system to a prior, functional state, which will allow you to log in again.

latency   The amount of delay between sending a network data request and receiving a response.

LCD cutoff switch   Switch for changing the display state on a laptop accessed by pressing the function key and another key, often F8 or F4.

letter quality (LQ)   A category of dot-matrix printer that can print characters that look very close to the quality a laser printer might produce.

link   In PCIe, the single lane or combined collection of lanes that the PCIe switch interconnects between devices. Two PCIe devices can only request links as wide as the narrowest lane rating between the two, such as four lanes between an x4 component and an x16 component.

liquid cooling   A cooling method used to keep CPUs and other hot-running components from overheating by pumping a liquid from outside the system through tubing that leads to blocks that mount to the components like heat sinks.

local area network (LAN)   A group of computers and associated peripherals connected by a communications channel, capable of sharing files and other resources among several users.

logical topologies   The topology that defines how the data flows in a network.

loopback address   Used to test basic TCP/IP functionality for your network card. The IP address 127.0.0.1 is reserved as the loopback address.

M

MAC address   The unique physical address for each NIC.

macro virus   A software exploitation virus that works by using the macro feature included in many applications.

main motor   A printer stepper motor that is used to advance the paper.

maintenance station   Provides a zero position for an ink- or bubble-jet printhead and keeps the print nozzles clear between print jobs.

man-in-the-middle attack   An attack that occurs when someone/-thing that is trusted intercepts packets and retransmits them to another party. Man-in-the-middle attacks have also been called TCP/IP hijacking in the past.

Material Safety Data Sheet (MSDS)   A document that contains safety information about a given product. Information provided includes safe handling procedures, what to do in case of an accident, and disposal information.

Media Access Control (MAC)   One of two layers of the Data Link layer in the OSI model.

memory bank   A requirement of a CPU and memory controller, based on system-bus width and single/dual-channel support, that reflects on the minimum number of memory chips or modules required to satisfy a single read or write cycle. Leads to physical constraints that must be observed during initial installation or upgrading of the system's RAM, such as the ability to install single modules or a minimum of a pair, quad, and so forth.

mesh topology   A type of logical topology in which each device on a network is connected to every other device on the network. This topology uses routers to search multiple paths and determine the best path.

microfloppy diskette   A floppy diskette that has a 3½″ form factor.

microSD   A solid-state, or flash, memory card format related to SD cards.

minifloppy diskette   A floppy diskette that has a 5¼″ form factor.

miniSD   A solid-state, or flash, memory card format related to SD cards.

modem   A contraction of the term *modulator/demodulator*. Modems connect digital devices over analog connections. The term has been adapted for any device that connects personal computers and personal networks to a service provider's network, such as DSL modems and cable modems, for instance.

Molex connector   The larger power connector that most often provides power to hard disk drives and other devices that require more current to power their motors than offered by a Berg connector.

mopiers   A laser printer that includes copier-like functions (coalition, stapling, and so on), so each "copy" is essentially an original.

motherboard   The main system board on which the primary components of the computer, such as the CPU and RAM, are manufactured or installed.

mouse pad   A cushioned pad used to provide a proper tracking surface for mouse usage, large enough for the mouse to control the cursor's motion across the entire screen.

multicore   The CPU technology that places multiple processor dies in the same packaging, or the equivalent thereof.

multifactor   The term employed anytime more than one factor must be considered.

multifunction printers   A peripheral that is essentially a printer, copier, scanner, and fax machine all in one.

MultiMediaCard (MMC)   A solid-state, or flash, memory card format.

multipartite virus   A virus that attacks a system in more than one way.

multipurpose server   A server that has more than one use. For example, a multipurpose server can be both a file server and a print server.

multistation access unit (MAU)   The central device in a Token Ring network that provides both the physical and logical connections to the stations.

Musical Instrument Digital Interface (MIDI)   A technology that daisy-chains components to one another with a 5-pin standard DIN connector and uses special packets to communicate with other MIDI devices and the computer's audio subsystem.

N

near-letter quality (NLQ)   A category of dot-matrix printer that can come close to the quality of a laser printer, but still is lacking somewhat in print quality.

NetBEUI (NetBIOS Extended User Interface)   A network device driver for the transport layer supplied with Microsoft's LAN Manager.

NetBIOS (network basic input/output system)   In networking, a layer of software, originally developed in 1984 by IBM and Sytek, that links a network operating system with specific network hardware. NetBIOS provides an application program interface (API) with a consistent set of commands for requesting lower-level network services to transmit information from node to node.

network   A group of computers and associated peripherals connected by a communications channel capable of sharing files and other resources between several users.

Network Address Translation (NAT)   The process of translating private, nonroutable IP addresses into public IP addresses.

network-based firewall   A firewall designed to protect an entire network of computers instead of just one system. It's generally a stand-alone hardware device with specialized software installed on it to protect your network.

network interface card (NIC)   In networking, the PC expansion board that plugs into a personal computer or server and works with the network operating system to control the flow of information over the network. The network interface card is connected to the network media (twisted-pair, coaxial, or fiber optic cable, or wireless), which in turn connects all the network interface cards in the network.

nondedicated server   A computer that can be both a server and a workstation. In practice, by performing the functions of both server and workstation, this type of server does neither function very well. Nondedicated servers are typically used in peer-to-peer networks.

nonintegrated system board   A motherboard that has no I/O interfaces built in, except for a keyboard and possibly mouse interfaces.

noninterference model   A model intended to ensure that higher-level security functions don't interfere with lower-level functions.

nonparity memory   A memory subsystem that does not support parity checking, possibly resulting in fewer chips populating the memory module.

Northbridge   The functional part of the chipset that controls local-bus communication among components connected to the frontside bus, such as the CPU and memory.

NWLINK   The Microsoft implementation of Novell's IPX/SPX protocol.

O

Occupational Safety and Health Administration (OSHA)   A United States federal agency in charge of administering the Occupational Safety and Health Act. OSHA is responsible for ensuring that employees have a safe work environment.

open access point   A wireless access point that employs no encryption or authentication, allowing any device that receives the signal potential access to the connected network.

Open Systems Interconnection (OSI) model   A seven-layer theoretical networking model developed by the International Organization of Standardization (ISO).

P

packet   A group of bits ready for transmission over a network. It includes a header, data, and a trailer.

page-description language   Describes the whole page being printed. The controller in the printer interprets these commands and turns them into laser pulses or firing print wires.

page printer   A printer that gets its instructions one page at a time, such as a laser printer.

paper feeder   *See* feeder.

paper feed mechanism   The portion of the printer that picks up paper from the paper drawer and feeds it into the printer.

paper feed sensors   The sensors on the paper feed mechanism that detect when the printer has paper or is out of paper.

paper pickup roller   A D-shaped roller that rotates against the paper and pushes one sheet into a printer.

paper tray   The tray that holds paper until it is fed into a printer.

parallel interface   A legacy port and cable-connector pairing based on a DB25 interface most commonly used for attaching a printer to a computer.

parity checking   Storing an extra bit with and based on each byte in memory. When a byte is accessed, the validity of the parity bit is checked. If the check shows an error, the byte is rejected because there is no way to determine the nature of the error.

parked   When the printhead is in the locked, resting position.

partition   A logical grouping of data organized to fall under a single drive letter for primary partitions and multiple drives for extended partitions.

partitioning   The process of assigning part or all of a hard drive for use by the computer.

passive hub   A type of hub that electrically connects all network ports together. This type of hub is not powered.

Password Authentication Protocol (PAP)   An authentication protocol that offers no true security, but it's one of the simplest forms of authentication. The username and password values are both sent to the server as clear text and checked for a match.

password guessing   Attempting to enter a password by guessing its value.

patch   A fix for a known software problem.

path   The location to a file or folder.

PC100   An SDR SDRAM module based on a 100MHz FSB.

PC2-3200   A DDR2 SDRAM module capable of 3200MBps of throughput and populated with DDR2-400 memory chips and based on a 400MHz FSB.

PC2700   A DDR SDRAM module capable of 2700MBps of throughput and populated with DDR333 memory chips and based on a 333MHz FSB.

PC3200   A DDR SDRAM module capable of 3200MBps of throughput and populated with DDR333 memory chips and based on a 333MHz FSB.

phage virus   A virus that modifies and alters other programs and databases.

physical topology   A description that identifies how the cables on a network are physically arranged.

pickup rollers   *See* paper pickup roller.

pickup stepper motor   The motor that turns the pickup roller in a printer.

piconet   A Bluetooth network. A Bluetooth-enabled device can communicate with up to seven other devices in a single piconet. Devices can also be members of multiple piconets.

platters   The physical discs on which magnetic or optical data is stored. Hard drive platters, for example, are on a spindle inside a sealed encasement.

plenum-rated   When referring to coaxial covering, a designation that means the coating does not produce toxic gas when burned (as PVC does) and is rated for use in air plenums that carry breathable air.

Plug and Play (PnP)   A standard set of specifications that was developed by Intel to enable a computer to detect a new device automatically and install the appropriate driver.

polymorphic   An attribute of some viruses that allows them to mutate and appear differently each time they crop up. The mutations make it harder for virus scanners to detect (and react) to the viruses.

port   The part of an interface found on the computer side to which an opposite-gendered connector from a cable attaches.

port assignment   Configuring an ACL, or setting up rules that determine what gets through a firewall.

port forwarding   Allowing packets that meet the criteria in the ACL to pass through the firewall to their destination.

port number   The logical channel that TCP/IP-based protocols use to communicate.

port triggering   An automated form of port forwarding. It allows traffic to enter the network on a specific port after a computer makes an outbound request on that specific port.

POST card   A circuit board that fits into an ISA or PCI expansion slot in the motherboard and reports numeric codes as the boot process progresses. By looking up the number where the card stops, you can identify the source of problems.

Post Office Protocol (POP)   A TCP/IP protocol optimized for the receiving of e-mail. The current standard is POP3, which uses port 100.

POTS line   A Plain Old Telephone Service line, the original analog technology for phone lines still in use today for standard phone service.

power circuits   The set of conductive pathways that converts 110V or 220V house current into the voltages a bubble-jet printer uses (usually 12V and 5V) and distributes those voltages to the other printer circuits and devices that need it.

power-on self-test (POST)   Part of the boot process controlled by the BIOS that verifies the working condition of the hardware the BIOS knows about.

power supply   A component that converts an external power source to the power required by the other components of the system it powers.

primary partition   The first partition created in an operating system.

Primary Rate Interface (PRI)   A form of ISDN that contains 23 64-bit B channels and 1 64-bit D channel for a total combined speed of 1536Kbps.

print buffer   A small amount of memory located on the printer used to hold print jobs.

print consumables   Products a printer uses in the print process that must be replaced occasionally. Examples include toner, ink, ribbons, and paper.

printer control circuits   Runs a printer's stepper motors, loads paper, and so on. Monitors the health of the printer and reports that information back to the computer.

printer controller assembly   A large circuit board in a laser printer that converts signals from the computer into signals for the various parts in a printer.

printer-resident fonts   Fonts that are installed into the onboard memory of the printer.

printer ribbon   A fabric strip that is impregnated with ink and wrapped around two spools encased in a cartridge. This cartridge is used in dot-matrix printers to provide the ink for the print process.

printers   Electromechanical output devices that are used to put information from the computer onto paper.

printhead   The part of a printer that creates the printed image. In a dot-matrix printer, the printhead contains the small pins that strike the ribbon to create the image, and in an inkjet printer, the printhead contains the jets used to create the ink droplets as well as the ink reservoirs. A laser printer creates images using an electrophotographic method similar to that found in photocopiers and does not have a printhead.

printhead alignment   The process by which the printhead is calibrated for use. A special utility that comes with the printer software is used to do this.

printhead carriage   The component of a bubble-jet printer that moves back and forth during printing. It contains the physical as well as electronic connections for the printhead and (in some cases) the ink reservoir.

print media   Another name for the media being printed on. Examples include paper, transparencies, and labels.

print queue   The line of all print jobs.

print server   A network server that hosts one or more printers for clients to use.

print spooler   A service that formats print jobs in the language that the printer needs.

propagation delay   In satellite Internet, the delay caused by the length of time required to transmit data and receive a response via satellite.

protocol   In networking and communications, the specification that defines the procedures to follow when transmitting and receiving data. Protocols define the format, timing, sequence, and error-checking systems used.

proxy server   Also called a proxie, it makes requests of a computer for another computer.

PS/2 port   A 6-pin mini-DIN connector named after the second generation of IBM personal computers and still a choice today, trailing behind USB in popularity, for mouse and keyboard attachment.

public switched telephone network (PSTN)   The network that carries standard, non-packetized voice and data traffic from subscribers. Traffic can originate from POTS, ISDN, and DSL lines but does not include DSL's data-band traffic.

R

radio frequency interference (RFI)   Another term for *electromagnetic interference (EMI)*.

Rambus   *See* DRDRAM.

rasterizing   The process of converting signals from the computer into signals for the various assemblies in a laser printer.

recovery CD/DVD   A CD-ROM set or DVD that comes with a particular model and brand of computer and usually contains an image of the entire Windows installation, along with applications, utilities, and drivers specifically for that computer. Also called by other names, such as restoration CD or reinstallation DVD.

remote computer   In Remote Desktop, the remote computer is the one that you are not sitting at; it's the one you make a connection to while sitting at the home computer.

Remote Desktop   A feature of Windows that allows you to connect to another computer and take control over that computer as if you were sitting in front of it. Also the name of the software that lets your computer be a remote computer in a remote desktop connection.

Remote Desktop Connection   The software that lets a computer act as a home computer in the Remote Desktop application.

replay attack   Any attack where the data is retransmitted repeatedly (often fraudulently or maliciously). In one such possibility, a user can replay a web session and visit sites intended only for the original user.

resource   On a network, any device that clients can access, such as printers or shared drives.

restore point   A copy of your system configuration at a given point in time.

retrovirus   A virus that attacks or bypasses the antivirus software installed on a computer.

ribbon cartridge   The container that holds the printer ribbon.

riser card   A daughter card with expansion slots that inserts into a motherboard; used in low-profile cases.

root directory   The first directory on a logical file system, such as C:\.

router   In networking, an intelligent connecting device that can send packets to the correct local area network segment to take them to their destination. Routers link LAN segments at the Network layer of the OSI model for computer-to-computer communications.

S

Safe Mode   Starts Windows using only basic files and drivers, such as mouse (except serial mice), monitor, keyboard, mass storage, base video, and default system services.

Satellite Internet   A type of Internet connection that uses a satellite dish to receive data from a satellite and a relay station that is connected to the Internet.

scanner   An optical device used to digitize images such as line art or photographs, so that they can be merged with text by a page-layout or desktop publishing program or incorporated into a CAD drawing.

scatternet   A network of two or more piconets.

SDRAM   A form of DRAM that is synchronized to the system clock. Varieties include SDR, DDR, DDR2, DDR3, and DRDRAM.

sector   A portion of a track that most often stores 512 bytes (½KB).

Secure and Fast Encryption Routine (SAFER+)   The encryption protocol used by Bluetooth devices.

Secure Digital (SD)   A solid-state, or flash, memory card format.

Secure Shell (SSH)   A protocol developed to allow encrypted data exchange between two computers.

security log   A log file used in Windows to keep track of security events specified by the domain's audit policy.

separator pads   Rubber patches that help keep the paper in place so that only one sheet goes into a printer.

service packs   Major patches or upgrades to the Windows operating system are released in groups known as service packs.

service-set identifier (SSID)   The identifier (name) of a wireless router or wireless access point. The unique name of a wireless network that differentiates it from other wireless networks that are also in range of a wireless client.

shielded twisted-pair (STP)   Copper network cable which has two or four pairs of twisted wires, shielded by a braided mesh and covered with an outside coating.

SIMM   A memory module packaging style that features a circuit board with identical pin functions on both sides of the module's card edge.

Simple Mail Transfer Protocol (SMTP)   A TCP/IP protocol optimized for sending e-mail. It uses port 25.

single-channel memory   A RAM implementation scheme in which the memory controller allows standard memory modules to be installed one per bank.

single-purpose server   A server that is dedicated to one purpose (for example, a file server or a printer server).

single-sided memory   A memory module that has chips and pin functions that match the specification for a single module.

site license   A software license that is valid for all installations at a single site.

smurf attack   An attack in which large volumes of ICMP echo requests (pings) are broadcast to all other machines on the network and in which the source address of the broadcast system has been spoofed to appear as though they came from the target computer. When all the machines that received the broadcast respond, they flood the target with more data than it can handle.

social engineering   An attack where an attacker obtains information from people by deceiving them.

SODIMM   A small-form factor memory module based on DIMM principles and designed for the mobile computing sector.

solenoid   In daisy-wheel printers, the small electromechanical hammer that strikes the back of the petal containing the character.

solid-ink printers   A printer that uses ink in a waxy solid form, rather than in liquid form. This allows the ink to stay fresh and eliminates problems like spillage.

solid-state drives (SSD)   A newer-style drive that has no moving parts, but uses flash memory to emulate a conventional hard disk drive.

Sony/Philips Digital Interface (S/PDIF)   A digital audio technology that attaches by coaxial or fiber-optic cable.

Southbridge   The functional part of the chipset that controls non-local bus communication among components connected to the various I/O buses, including PCI, IDE, USB, RS-232, and parallel.

spam   Unwanted, unsolicited e-mail sent in bulk.

special permissions   Permissions in Windows operating systems, including Read, Write, Execute, Delete, Change Permissions, Take Ownership, and Full Control.

spoofing An attempt by someone or something to masquerade as someone else.

SRAM A faster type of volatile memory that does not require a periodic refresh and is commonly used for cache memory.

stabilizer bar A small metal bar on a printer that holds the printer carriage as it crosses the page.

standard permissions Collection of special permissions, including Full Control, Modify, Read & Execute, Read, and Write. Each of these standard permissions automatically assigns multiple special permissions at once.

star topology A networking topology characterized by endpoints wiring directly to a central concentrating device, thus not affecting other endpoints when they have connectivity issues.

static-charge eliminator strip The device in EP process printers that drains the static charge from the paper after the toner has been transferred to the paper.

stealth virus A virus that attempts to avoid detection by masking itself from applications.

stepper motor A very precise motor that can move in very small increments. Often used in printers.

straight tip (ST) One of the most common fiber-optic connectors similar in style to the BNC connector used in 10Base2 Ethernet.

sublimate To go from a solid state to a gaseous state without passing through a liquid state.

subnet mask A required part of any TCP/IP configuration, used to define which addresses are local and which are on remote networks.

subscriber connector (SC) A type of fiber-optic cable connector.

surge protectors Surge protectors attempt to keep power surges at bay. They often look like a power strip, but they have a fuse inside them which is designed to blow if it receives too much current, and not transfer the current to the devices plugged into it. Surge protectors may have plug-ins for RJ-11 (phone), RJ-45 (Ethernet), and BNC (coaxial cable) connectors.

swap file Also called the page file, the swap file is the virtual memory in Windows.

switch 1) A Layer 2 device similar to a hub in its port count but more advanced with the ability to filter traffic based on the destination MAC address of each frame. 2) Option used with commands to specify operations that command should perform.

syntax The correct format for interacting with a command.

system tray Located on the Windows Taskbar, contains a clock by default, but other Windows utilities (for example, screensavers or virus-protection utilities) may put their icons here when running to indicate that they are running and to provide the user with a quick way to access their features.

T

TCP ACK attack   An attack that begins as a normal TCP connection and whose purpose is to deny service. It's also known as a TCP SYN flood.

TCP/IP hijacking   An attack in which the attacker commandeers a TCP session from a legitimate user after the legitimate user has achieved authentication, thereby removing the need for the attacker to authenticate himself.

TCP sequence attack   An attack wherein the attacker intercepts and then responds with a sequence number similar to the one used in the original session. The attack can either disrupt a session or hijack a valid session.

TCP SYN flood   *See* TCP ACK attack.

temporary file (temp file)   A file designed to store information for a short period of time and then be deleted.

thumb drive   A solid-state device with USB attachment that takes the place of older floppy diskettes and holds much more data than floppies ever did.

token passing   A media-access method that gives every NIC equal access to the cable. The token is a special packet of data that is passed from computer to computer. Any computer that wants to transmit has to wait until it has the token, at which point it can add its own data to the token and send it on.

Token Ring   A local area network with a logical ring structure that uses token passing to regulate traffic on the network and avoid collisions.

toner   A carbon substance mixed with polyester resins and iron oxide particles. During the EP printing process, toner is first attracted to areas that have been exposed to the laser in laser printers and is later deposited and melted onto the print medium.

topology   The layout of a network. Basic LAN topologies are bus, ring, and star. WAN topologies include full and partial meshes. *Topology* can describe either the logical or physical layout. See Chapter 10 for more information.

tracks   The concentric rings on a platter where data is stored. Tracks are subdivided into sectors.

transfer corona assembly   The part of an EP process printer that is responsible for transferring the developed image from the EP drum to the paper.

transferring step   The fifth step in the EP print process, when the developed toner image on the EP drum is transferred to the print medium using the transfer corona.

transformer   A device that takes one type of electrical current and turns it into a different type of electrical current.

Transmission Control Protocol (TCP)   A core protocol in the TCP/IP protocol suite that establishes connections and guarantees packet delivery.

Transmission Control Protocol/Internet Protocol (TCP/IP) suite   A set of computer-to-computer communications protocols that encompasses media access, packet transport, session communications, file transfer, e-mail, and terminal emulation. TCP/IP is supported by a very large number of hardware and software vendors and is available on many different computers from PCs to mainframes. It is the protocol of the Internet and the most widely-used communications protocol in existence today.

tree   A modified networking topology that interconnects the concentrators of a star topology to form tiers of connectivity for endpoints to reduce the number of concentrators between any two endpoints.

Trojan horse   Any application that masquerades as one thing in order to get past scrutiny and then does something malicious. One of the major differences between Trojan horses and viruses is that Trojan horses tend not to replicate themselves.

TV tuner card   A class of internal and external devices that allows you to connect a broadcast signal, such as home cable television, to your computer and display it.

U

unattended installation   An installation method that does not require human intervention once started and is frequently used when installing over the network. Unattended installations use answer files to supply the necessary parameters to Windows Setup.

uninterruptible power supply (UPS)   A UPS is designed to protect everything that's plugged into it from power surges, power sags, and even power outages. The device contains one or more batteries and fuses. Energy is stored in the batteries, and if the power fails, the batteries can power the computer for a period of time so the administrator can then safely power it down.

universal data connector (UDC)   Another name for an IBM data connector.

unshielded twisted-pair (UTP)   Networking cable that has four twisted pairs of copper wire and a flexible outer coating.

User Datagram Protocol (UDP)   Part of the TCP/IP suite that performs a similar function to TCP, with less overhead and more speed but with lower reliability. It is a connectionless protocol, meaning that it does not guarantee packet delivery.

V

video capture card   A stand-alone device that is often used to save a video stream to the computer for later manipulation or sharing.

virtual memory   A general term for a type of computer technology where hard disk space is used to supplement a computer's physical memory. The memory controller uses a swap file on the hard drive to offload the least recently used contents of RAM to make room for additional applications and data.

Virtual Private Network (VPN)   A secure network where computers that are not local to the network appear to be local. Used frequently to securely connect LANs together across a WAN or for network users to remotely access the network.

virus   A small, deviously genius program that replicates itself to other computers, generally causing those computers to behave abnormally.

voice-over IP (VoIP)   The technology that encapsulates voice traffic into IP packets and transmits it across a TCP/IP network.

voltage selector switch   The switch on a power supply that allows you to manually change the input voltage between 60Hz, 110VAC to 50Hz, 220VAC.

vulnerability scanner   A software application that checks your network for any known security holes.

W

watt   The unit of measure for power, equal to the number of volts in a circuit times the number of amps.

webcams   A video-only camera that connects to a computer so that the video it captures can be sent across the Internet in real time.

wide area networks (WAN)   A network that expands LANs to include networks outside of the local environment and also to distribute resources across distances.

WiFi   A collection of IEEE 802.11x standards.

WiFi Protected Access (WPA)   An enhancement of 802.11 encryption that secures WiFi communications. The current standard is WPA2.

Windows Catalog   A list of all the hardware that works with Windows that also details which versions of Windows the hardware works with. The new name for the Hardware Compatibility List.

Windows Update   A feature designed to keep Windows current by automatically down-loading updates such as patches and security fixes and installing these fixes automatically.

Wired Equivalency Protocol (WEP)   An old security protocol developed for WiFi. It has security flaws and is easily compromised.

wireless access point (WAP)   A central hub that looks nearly identical to wireless rout-ers and provides central connectivity like wireless routers, but doesn't have nearly as many features.

Wireless Personal Area Network (WPAN)   Another name for a Bluetooth network.

workgroups   A collection of peer-to-peer computers with no dedicated server or central-ized security.

working directory   An area on the hard disk where programs store their temporary files while they work.

workstation   1) In networking, any personal computer (other than the file server) attached to the network. 2) A high-performance computer optimized for graphics applications such as computer-aided design, computer-aided engineering, and scientific applications.

worm   A program similar to a virus. Worms, however, propagate themselves over a network. *See also* virus.

writing step   The third step in the EP print process, during which the items being printed are written to the EP drum. In this step, the laser is flashed on and off as it scans across the surface of the drum. The area on which the laser shines is discharged to almost ground (–100V).

Z

zero insertion force (ZIF)   A mechanism on which chip sockets are mounted that allows insertion of the chip with no downward force except gravity.

Index

Note to the Reader: Throughout this index **boldfaced** page numbers indicate primary discussions of a topic. *Italicized* page numbers indicate illustrations.

O

S

Wiley Publishing, Inc.
End-User License Agreement